MAZDA MIATA MX-5 EUNOS ROADSTER 1.8

ENTHUSIAST'S SHOP MANUAL

By Rod Grainger & Pete Shoemark

VELOCE PUBLISHING
THE PUBLISHER OF FINE AUTOMOTIVE BOOKS

Also from Veloce –

SpeedPro Series
4-Cylinder Engine Short Block High-Performance Manual – New Updated & Revised Edition (Hammill)
Aerodynamics of Your Road Car, Modifying the (Edgar and Barnard)
Alfa Romeo DOHC High-performance Manual (Kartalamakis)
Alfa Romeo V6 Engine High-performance Manual (Kartalamakis)
BMC 998cc A-series Engine, How to Power Tune (Hammill)
1275cc A-series High-performance Manual (Hammill)
Camshafts – How to Choose & Time Them For Maximum Power (Hammill)
Competition Car Datalogging Manual, The (Templeman)
Custom Air Suspension – How to install air suspension in your road car – on a budget! (Edgar)
Cylinder Heads, How to Build, Modify & Power Tune – Updated & Revised Edition (Burgess & Gollan)
Distributor-type Ignition Systems, How to Build & Power Tune – New 3rd Edition (Hammill)
Fast Road Car, How to Plan and Build – Revised & Updated Colour New Edition (Stapleton)
Ford SOHC 'Pinto' & Sierra Cosworth DOHC Engines, How to Power Tune – Updated & Enlarged Edition (Hammill)
Ford V8, How to Power Tune Small Block Engines (Hammill)
Harley-Davidson Evolution Engines, How to Build & Power Tune (Hammill)
Holley Carburetors, How to Build & Power Tune – Revised & Updated Edition (Hammill)
Honda Civic Type R High-Performance Manual, The (Cowland & Clifford)
Jaguar XK Engines, How to Power Tune – Revised & Updated Colour Edition (Hammill)
Land Rover Discovery, Defender & Range Rover – How to Modify Coil Sprung Models for High Performance & Off-Road Action (Hosier)
MG Midget & Austin-Healey Sprite, How to Power Tune – Enlarged & updated 4th Edition (Stapleton)
MGB 4-cylinder Engine, How to Power Tune (Burgess)
MGB V8 Power, How to Give Your – Third Colour Edition (Williams)
MGB, MGC & MGB V8, How to Improve – New 2nd Edition (Williams)
Mini Engines, How to Power Tune On a Small Budget – Colour Edition (Hammill)
Motorcycle-engined Racing Cars, How to Build (Pashley)
Motorsport, Getting Started in (Collins)
Nissan GT-R High-performance Manual, The (Gorodji)
Nitrous Oxide High-performance Manual, The (Langfield)
Optimising Car Performance Modifications (Edgar)
Race & Trackday Driving Techniques (Hornsey)
Retro or classic car for high performance, How to modify your (Stapleton)
Rover V8 Engines, How to Power Tune (Hammill)
Secrets of Speed – Today's techniques for 4-stroke engine blueprinting & tuning (Swager)
Sportscar & Kitcar Suspension & Brakes, How to Build & Modify – Revised 3rd Edition (Hammill)
SU Carburettor High-performance Manual (Hammill)
Successful Low-Cost Rally Car, How to Build a (Young)
Suzuki 4x4, How to Modify For Serious Off-road Action (Richardson)
Tiger Avon Sportscar, How to Build Your Own – Updated & Revised 2nd Edition (Dudley)
Triumph TR2, 3 & TR4, How to Improve (Williams)
Triumph TR5, 250 & TR6, How to Improve (Williams)
Triumph TR7 & TR8, How to Improve (Williams)
V8 Engine, How to Build a Short Block For High Performance (Hammill)
Volkswagen Beetle Suspension, Brakes & Chassis, How to Modify For High Performance (Hale)
Volkswagen Bus Suspension, Brakes & Chassis for High Performance, How to Modify – Updated & Enlarged New Edition (Hale)
Weber DCOE, & Dellorto DHLA Carburetors, How to Build & Power Tune – 3rd Edition (Hammill)

Workshop Pro Series
Car electrical and electronic systems (Edgar)
Setting up a home car workshop (Edgar)

RAC Handbooks
Caring for your car – How to maintain & service your car (Fry)
Caring for your car's bodywork and interior (Nixon)
Efficient Driver's Handbook, The (Moss)
Electric Cars – The Future is Now! (Linde)
First aid for your car – Your expert guide to common problems & how to fix them (Collins)
How your car works (Linde)
Pass the MoT test! – How to check & prepare your car for the annual MoT test (Paxton)
Selling your car – How to make your car look great and how to sell it fast (Knight)
Simple fixes for your car – How to do small jobs for yourself and save money (Collins)

Enthusiast's Restoration Manual Series
Citroën 2CV Restore (Porter)
Classic Car Bodywork, How to Restore (Thaddeus)
Classic British Car Electrical Systems (Astley)
Classic Car Electrics (Thaddeus)
Classic Car Suspension, Steering & Wheels, How to Restore & Improve (Parish – translator)
Classic Cars, How to Paint (Thaddeus)
Jaguar E-type (Crespin)
Reliant Regal, How to Restore (Payne)
Triumph TR2, 3, 3A, 4 & 4A, How to Restore (Williams)
Triumph TR5/250 & 6, How to Restore (Williams)
Triumph TR7/8, How to Restore (Williams)
Ultimate Mini Restoration Manual, The (Ayre & Webber)
Volkswagen Beetle, How to Restore (Tyler)
VW Bay Window Bus (Paxton)

Expert Guides
Land Rover Series I-III – Your expert guide to common problems & how to fix them (Thurman)
MG Midget & A-H Sprite – Your expert guide to common problems & how to fix them (Horler)

General
Mazda MX-5/Miata 1.6 Enthusiast's Workshop Manual (Grainger & Shoemark)
Mazda MX-5/Miata 1.8 Enthusiast's Workshop Manual (Grainger & Shoemark)
Mazda MX-5 Miata, The book of the – The 'Mk1' NA-series 1988 to 1997 (Long)
Mazda MX-5 Miata, The book of the – The 'Mk2' NB-series 1997 to 2004 (Long)
Mazda MX-5 Miata Roadster (Long)
Mazda Rotary-engined Cars (Cranswick)

www.veloce.co.uk

First published in 2000. Reprinted 2001, 2003, 2004, 2006, 2008, 2010, 2011, 2013, 2015, 2017 and September 2018 by Veloce Publishing Limited, Veloce House, Parkway Farm Business Park, Middle Farm Way, Poundbury, Dorchester, Dorset, DT1 3AR, England.
Fax 01305 250479/e-mail info@veloce.co.uk/web www.veloce.co.uk or www.velocebooks.com.

ISBN: 978-1-787114-20-3 UPC: 6-36847-01420-9

© Rod Grainger and Veloce Publishing Ltd 2000, 2001, 2003, 2004, 2006, 2008, 2010, 2011, 2013, 2015, 2017 & 2018. All rights reserved. With the exception of quoting brief passages for the purpose of review, no part of this publication may be recorded, reproduced or transmitted by any means, including photocopying, without the written permission of Veloce Publishing Ltd. Throughout this book logos, model names and designations, etc, have been used for the purposes of identification, illustration and decoration. Such names are the property of the trademark holder as this is not an official publication. Readers with ideas for automotive books, or books on other transport or related hobby subjects, are invited to write to the editorial director of Veloce Publishing at the above address. British Library Cataloguing in Publication Data - A catalogue record for this book is available from the British Library.
Typesetting, design and page make-up all by Veloce Publishing Ltd on Apple Mac. Printed and bound by CPI Group (UK) Ltd, Croydon, CR0 4YY.

Contents

CHAPTER 1: GENERAL ADVICE & USING THIS MANUAL

1. Using this manual _____ 1:1
   - Conventions _____ 1:1
   - Symbols & cross-references _____ 1:1
   - Hey! Watch out! _____ 1:2
2. Working procedures _____ 1:2
   - General _____ 1:2
   - Work area & storage facilities _____ 1:2
   - Hose connections _____ 1:2
   - Gaskets & seals _____ 1:3
   - Screws, bolts & nuts _____ 1:4
   - Torque tightening by feel _____ 1:4
   - Electrical connections & wire color coding _____ 1:4
   - Wrestling with two-piece plastic panel fasteners _____ 1:5
3. Jacking & supporting the car _____ 1:5
4. Cleaning components _____ 1:6
5. Buying new parts _____ 1:7
6. Tools & equipment _____ 1:7
7. Dealing with breakdowns _____ 1:8
8. Technical specifications _____ 1:9
   - General _____ 1:9
   - Dimensions _____ 1:9
   - Transmission _____ 1:9
   - Chassis _____ 1:9
   - Engine - detail _____ 1:9
   - Lubrication system (engine) _____ 1:12
   - Cooling system _____ 1:12
   - Fuel & emission control systems _____ 1:13
   - Electrical system (engine) _____ 1:13
   - Clutch _____ 1:14
   - Transmission (gearbox), manual _____ 1:14
   - Transmission, automatic _____ 1:15
   - Driveshaft (propshaft) _____ 1:15
   - Front axle _____ 1:16
   - Rear axle _____ 1:16
   - Differential _____ 1:16
   - Steering _____ 1:16
   - Braking system _____ 1:16
   - Wheels & tires _____ 1:17
   - Suspension _____ 1:17
   - Wheel alignment _____ 1:18
   - Electrical system (body) _____ 1:18

CHAPTER 2: TUNE-UP & MAINTENANCE

1. Introduction _____ 2:1
2A. Maintenance schedule: USA _____ 2:2
2B. Maintenance schedule: USA (abnormal operating conditions) ___ 2:3
2C. Maintenance schedule: Canada _____ 2:4
2D. Maintenance schedule: UK & rest of world _____ 2:6
3. Engine oil & oil filter - changing _____ 2:7
4. Drivebelts (external) - inspection, replacement & adjustment ___ 2:8
5. Air cleaner (filter) element - replacement _____ 2:9
6. Sparkplugs - checking, cleaning & adjusting _____ 2:9
7. Idle speed - checking & adjustment _____ 2:10
8. Transmission (manual) oil - checking level & changing _____ 2:10
9. Transmission (auto) fluid - checking level & changing _____ 2:11
10. Differential oil - checking level & changing _____ 2:11
11. Battery - checking charge, specific gravity & electrolyte level ___ 2:12
12. Ignition timing - checking & adjusting _____ 2:13
13. Driveaxles (halfshafts), rear - checking _____ 2:13
14. Engine coolant - topping-up & changing _____ 2:14
15. Lights, horn, wipers & washers - checking _____ 2:15
16. Tires - checking pressures & condition _____ 2:15
17. Body - general maintenance _____ 2:16
18. Steering & suspension - checking _____ 2:17
19. Exhaust system - checking _____ 2:18
20. Brake & clutch fluid - checking level & replacing _____ 2:18

CHAPTER 3: ENGINE & CLUTCH

1. Major work possible with engine in car _____ 3:1
2. Major work requiring engine removal _____ 3:1
3. Engine removal methods & preparation _____ 3:1
4. Engine - removal (with transmission) _____ 3:1
5. Engine - removal (without transmission) _____ 3:12
6. Engine dismantling - general advice _____ 3:12
7. Engine dismantling _____ 3:13
   - Intake manifold & wiring removal _____ 3:13
   - Fuel rail removal _____ 3:14
   - Starter motor removal _____ 3:14
   - Engine mounting removal _____ 3:14
   - Oil filter & oil cooler removal _____ 3:14
   - Alternator removal _____ 3:14
   - Exhaust manifold removal _____ 3:15
   - Clutch removal _____ 3:16
   - Sparkplug wires & coils removal _____ 3:16
   - Thermostat removal _____ 3:16
   - Cambox cover removal _____ 3:17
   - Camshaft drivebelt removal _____ 3:17
   - Camshaft drivebelt tensioner wheel & tensioner spring removal __ 3:18
   - Camshaft pulleys removal _____ 3:18
   - Cylinder head front sealing plate removal _____ 3:19
   - Thermostat housing removal _____ 3:19
   - Water pump removal _____ 3:19
   - Crankshaft inner pulley removal _____ 3:19
   - Camshaft removal _____ 3:20
   - Cam followers removal _____ 3:20
   - Cylinder head removal _____ 3:20
   - Valves removal _____ 3:21
   - Valve guides removal & installation _____ 3:21
   - Oil pan removal _____ 3:22
   - Oil pump, pickup pipe & oil pan baffle removal _____ 3:22
   - Oil pump & oil pressure relief valve teardown _____ 3:23
   - Flywheel (driveplate - auto trans) removal _____ 3:23
   - Engine backplate removal _____ 3:23
   - Crankshaft rear oil seal housing removal _____ 3:23
   - Connecting rod (big end) caps, con rods & pistons removal __ 3:24
   - Main bearing caps & crankshaft removal _____ 3:24
   - Piston oil jets removal _____ 3:25
   - Pistons removal from connecting rods _____ 3:25
   - Piston rings removal _____ 3:25
   - Engine teardown conclusion _____ 3:26
8. Engine components - checking & repair _____ 3:26
   - Checking & repair general _____ 3:26
   - Cylinder head & valves removing carbon _____ 3:26
   - Cylinder head checking & repair _____ 3:26
   - Valves, guides & valve seats checking, repair & valve lapping __ 3:26
   - Valve springs checking & repair _____ 3:27
   - Camshafts & camshaft bearings checking & repair _____ 3:28
   - Cam followers checking & repair _____ 3:28
   - Cylinder block checking & repair: core plug renewal _____ 3:29
   - Pistons: removing carbon _____ 3:29
   - Pistons, piston rings & piston pins checking & repair _____ 3:29
   - Connecting rods checking & repair _____ 3:30
   - Crankshaft & crankshaft bearings checking & repair _____ 3:30
   - Cam drivebelt, tensioner, idler & pulleys checking & repair __ 3:31
   - Oil pump checking & repair _____ 3:31
   - Oil jets checking & repair _____ 3:31
   - Flywheel, pilot bearing & starter ring gear checking & repair __ 3:31
   - Driveplate (auto-trans) & starter ring gear checking & repair __ 3:32
   - Clutch cover, disc, release bearing & fork checking & repair __ 3:32
9. Engine rebuild _____ 3:32
   - Engine rebuild general _____ 3:32
   - Piston rings installation _____ 3:32
   - Pistons & connecting rods rebuild & installation _____ 3:33
   - Oil jets rebuild & installation _____ 3:33
   - Crankshaft & bearing shells installation _____ 3:33
   - Connecting rods & caps fitting to crankshaft _____ 3:34
   - Crankshaft rear cover: oil seal installation _____ 3:34
   - Crankshaft rear cover installation _____ 3:34
   - Oil pump rebuild & fitting new oil seal _____ 3:35
   - Oil pump installation _____ 3:35
   - Oil pan baffle, oil pump pickup pipe & oil pan installation ___ 3:35
   - Engine backplate installation _____ 3:36
   - Flywheel (driveplate - auto trans) installation _____ 3:36
   - Water pump installation _____ 3:36
   - Valves, springs & valve stem oil seals installation _____ 3:36
   - Cylinder head installation _____ 3:37

0:3

Mazda Miata, MX-5, Eunos & Roadster

Thermostat housing installation	3:37
Cylinder head seal plate installation	3:38
Cam followers installation	3:38
Camshafts installation	3:38
Camshaft oil seals installation	3:38
Camshaft pulleys installation	3:38
Cam drivebelt idler & tensioner wheels & spring installation	3:39
Crankshaft inner (cam drivebelt) pulley installation	3:39
Camshaft drivebelt installation & valve timing	3:39
Cam drivebelt covers, w/pump & crankshaft pulley installation	3:40
Cambox cover installation	3:41
Thermostat & thermostat housing cover installation	3:41
Engine mounting bracket (right-hand) installation	3:41
Oil pressure gauge sender unit installation	3:41
Alternator installation	3:42
Oil cooler & oil filter installation	3:42
Starter motor installation	3:42
Heater outlet cover installation	3:43
Ignition coils & sparkplug wires installation	3:43
Clutch cover & disc installation	3:43
Engine mounting bracket (left-hand) installation	3:43
Power steering pump bracket installation	3:43
Coolant inlet casting installation	3:44
Dipstick tube installation	3:44
Engine lifting eyes installation	3:44
Camshaft position sensor installation	3:44
Manifolds installation special note	3:44
10. Transmission (gearbox) - installation (engine out of car)	3:45
11. Engine & transmission - installation as a unit	3:45
12. Engine - installation (without transmission)	3:55
13. Camshaft drivebelt (timing belt) - replacement (engine in car)	3:56
14. Camshafts & followers - removal & installation (engine in car)	3:57
15. Cylinder head - removal & installation (engine in car)	3:57
Cylinder head checking	3:58
16. Crankshaft front oil seal - replacement (engine in car)	3:58
17. Crankshaft rear oil seal - replacement (engine in car)	3:59
18. Camshaft oil seal - replacement (engine in car)	3:59
19. Starter ring gear - replacement (engine in car)	3:60
20. Engine mountings - replacement (engine in car)	3:60
21. Clutch & release bearing - removal & installation (engine in car)	3:60
22. Clutch master cylinder - removal & installation	3:60
23. Clutch master cylinder - overhaul	3:61
24. Clutch release (slave) cylinder - removal & installation	3:62
25. Clutch release (slave) cylinder - overhaul	3:62
Dismantling & checking	3:62
Rebuild	3:63
26. Clutch hydraulic system - bleeding	3:63
27. Clutch hydraulic lines/hoses - replacement	3:63
28. Clutch pedal height & free play - checking & adjustment	3:64
29. Clutch pedal removal & installation	3:65

CHAPTER 4: TRANSMISSION & DRIVELINE

1. Transmission (gearbox) - preparation for removal	4:1
2. Transmission (gearbox), manual - removal	4:1
3. Transmission (gearbox), automatic - removal	4:4
4. Transmission (gearbox), manual - dismantling & rebuild general	4:5
5. Transmission (gearbox), manual - teardown	4:6
6. Transmission (gearbox), manual - components checking & repair	4:13
Mainshaft gear pinions	4:13
Mainshaft	4:14
Input shaft & countershaft	4:14
Clutch/selector hubs & forks	4:14
Synchro rings	4:14
Bearings	4:14
Springs	4:14
Casings	4:15
7. Transmission (gearbox), manual - rebuild	4:15
8. Transmission (gearbox), manual - installation	4:24
9. Transmission (gearbox), automatic - installation	4:24
10. Driveshaft (propshaft) - removal, checking, repair & installation	4:25
11. Transmission (gearbox) rear oil seal - replacement	4:26
12. PPF (Power Plant Frame) - removal & installation	4:26
13. Driveaxles - removal, checking, repair & installation	4:26
14. Driveaxle - dismantling, rebuild & new boots	4:27
15. Differential unit & carrier - removal & installation	4:27
16. Differential side (driveaxle) oil seals - replacement	4:28
17. Differential nose (pinion) oil seal - replacement	4:28
18. Differential unit carrier mountings - replacement	4:28
19. Differential unit - teardown & rebuild	4:28
20 Transmission (gearbox), automatic - troubleshooting	4:28

CHAPTER 5: ENGINE MANAGEMENT. FUEL. IGNITION & EXHAUST SYSTEMS

1. Introduction	5:1
2. PCM system - component summary	5:1
Air cleaner (ACL)	5:1
Air valve (BAC valve)	5:2
Camshaft position sensor (CMP)	5:2
Catalytic converter	5:2
Charcoal canister	5:2
Clutch switch	5:2
Coolant temperature sensor	5:2
Crankshaft position sensor (CKP)	5:2
Data link connector (DLC)	5:2
Exhaust gas recirculation (EGR) system	5:2
Fuel pump relay (FPR)	5:2
Fuel filter	5:2
Fuel pump	5:2
Fuel vapor valve	5:2
Heated oxygen sensor	5:2
Idle air control (IAC) valve	5:2
Ignition coil	5:2
Ignition control module	5:2
Ignition switch	5:2
Injector	5:2
Intake air temperature (IAT) sensor	5:2
Main relay	5:2
Malfunction indicator lamp	5:2
Mass airflow sensor (MAF)	5:2
Neutral switch	5:2
On board diagnostic (OBD) system	5:2
Positive crankcase ventilation (PCV) valve	5:3
Power steering pressure (PSP) switch	5:3
Powertrain control module (PCM)	5:3
Pressure regulator	5:3
Pressure regulator control (PRC) solenoid valve	5:3
Purge solenoid valve	5:3
Resonance chamber	5:3
Stoplight switch	5:3
Throttle body	5:3
Throttle sensor	5:3
Two port check valve (three port, automatic trans)	5:3
3. PCM system - overview	5:3
Fuel system	5:4
Air intake system	5:4
Emission control system	5:4
4. Powertrain control system - troubleshooting tips	5:5
Fault codes	5:5
5. Engine compression check	5:6
6. Air intake system checks	5:6
7. Throttle body - removal, inspection & installation	5:6
8. Accelerator cable & pedal - adjustment & cable replacement	5:7
9. Intake manifold - removal, checking & installation	5:9
10. Air intake control (IAC) valve - checking	5:11
11. Air (BAC) valve - removal, checking & installation	5:11
12 Fuel system - description	5:11
13. Fuel system - safety, depressurizing & repressurizing	5:11
Releasing fuel system pressure	5:11
Disconnecting fuel lines	5:11
Priming fuel system	5:12
14. Fuel system - checking	5:12
Fuel pump relay checking	5:12
Fuel pump checking	5:12
Fuel pressure checking	5:12
Fuel pressure hold checking	5:12
Fuel maximum pressure checking	5:13
Fuel line pressure checking	5:13
Pressure regulator control (PRC) valve checking	5:13

Contents

Injector operation checking	5:13
Fault not located?	5:13
15. Fuel tank - removal, checking & installation	5:13
Draining the fuel tank	5:14
Inspection & repair	5:16
16. Fuel pump/fuel gauge sender - removal & installation	5:18
17. Fuel pump relay - removal & installation	5:20
18. Fuel pressure regulator - removal & installation	5:20
19. Fuel injectors & rail - removal, leak testing & installation	5:20
20. Fuel filter - removal & installation	5:21
21. Emissions control system - introduction	5:22
22. PCV valve - checking & replacement	5:22
23. EVAP/EGR systems - component checking & replacement	5:22
Fuel vapor valve	5:23
Two-way check valve (three-way check valve, auto trans)	5:23
EVAP system hoses	5:24
Charcoal canister	5:24
Purge solenoid valve	5:24
EGR valve	5:24
EGR solenoid valves	5:24
EGR boost sensor	5:25
EGR valve position sensor	5:25
24. Dechoke control system - description	5:25
25. Ignition system - introduction	5:25
26. Ignition timing - checking & adjusting	5:25
27a. Ignition system checks	5:26
Self-diagnosis (OBD system) checks	5:26
Sparkplugs	5:26
Sparkplug leads	5:27
Ignition coils	5:27
27b. Ignition coils - removal & installation	5:27
28. PCM (powertrain control module)	5:28
29a. Camshaft position sensor - removal, checking & installation	5:29
29b. Crankshaft position sensor - adjustment, removal & installation	5:29
30. Mass airflow (MAF) sensor - removal, checking & installation	5:30
31. Engine coolant temp. sensor - removal, checking & installation	5:30
32. TPS unit - checking, adjustment, removal & installation	5:31
33. Heated oxygen sensor - checking, removal & replacement	5:31
34. Power steering pressure switch - checking, removal & installation	5:32
35. Main (fuel injection) relay - checking & replacement	5:32
36. Clutch switch - checking, removal & installation	5:33
37. Neutral switch - checking, removal & installation	5:33
38. Exhaust system - checking, removal & replacement	5:34
39. Exhaust manifold removal & installation	5:36

CHAPTER 6: COOLING, HEATING & AIR CONDITIONING SYSTEMS

1. Introduction	6:1
2. Engine coolant - topping-up & changing	6:1
Mixing engine coolant	6:2
Topping up the cooling system	6:2
Changing the coolant	6:2
3. Cooling system - checking	6:2
4. Cooling system - hose replacement	6:3
Top hose	6:3
Bottom hose	6:3
Coolant inlet casting & hose connections	6:4
Heater hose connections	6:4
Intake manifold hose connections	6:4
After fitting new hoses	6:4
5. Radiator - removal & installation	6:4
6. Thermostat - removal, testing & installation	6:5
7. Water pump - removal & installation	6:6
8. Radiator fan/s - testing, removal & installation	6:6
Checking coolant temperature sensor	6:7
Fan motor testing	6:7
Fan motor removal & installation	6:7
Fan relay testing	6:7
9. Heating & ventilation system - how it works	6:8
10. Blower unit - checking	6:8
Checking the circuit breaker or fuse	6:8
Checking the blower motor voltage	6:8
Checking the blower resistor	6:8
11. Blower unit - resistor removal & installation	6:8
12. Blower motor - removal & installation	6:9
13. Blower unit - removal & installation	6:9
14. Heater unit - removal, inspection & installation	6:9
15. Heater/air con control assy - removal, inspection & installation	6:11
Checking the blower & air conditioning switch	6:11
16. Air conditioning system - checking	6:12
Precautions	6:12
Visual check of refrigerant charge	6:13
Checking thermoswitch operation	6:13
Checking system fittings & refrigerant lines	6:13
Checking the condenser cooling fan	6:13
Checking the air conditioning relay	6:13
Magnetic clutch checks	6:13

CHAPTER 7: ELECTRICAL SYSTEM

1. Introduction	7:1
2. Electrical system - procedures, precautions & jump starting	7:1
Isolating & reconnecting battery	7:1
Electrical test equipment	7:1
Wiring connectors	7:2
Wiring & color coding	7:2
Fuses & relays	7:3
Power point	7:3
Booster (Jump) starting	7:3
3. Fuses & relays - location, removal & replacement	7:4
4. Charging system - general	7:6
5. Battery - removal, checking, charging & installation	7:6
Removal & cleaning	7:7
Battery voltage check	7:7
Battery charging	7:7
Battery installation	7:8
Installing a new battery	7:8
6. Charging system - troubleshooting	7:8
7. Alternator - checking	7:8
Checking the terminal voltages	7:8
Checking alternator operation	7:8
Checking the dark current	7:8
8. Alternator - removal, overhaul & installation	7:8
9. Starter system - description & troubleshooting	7:10
Initial checks	7:10
Interlock switch - checking (manual trans)	7:11
Range switch checking & adjustment (auto trans)	7:11
10. Starter motor - removal, overhaul & installation	7:12
Testing	7:12
11a. Ignition switch - t/shooting, removal & installation	7:14
11b. Key (ignition) reminder switch - troubleshooting	7:14
12. Combination switch - t/shooting, removal & installation	7:14
13. H/light retract & haz. warn. switch - removal, t/shooting & install.	7:15
14. Instrument panel - removal, t/shooting & installation	7:16
Removal	7:16
Bulb replacement	7:17
Speedometer	7:17
Tachometer (rev counter)	7:18
Engine temperature sender unit & gauge	7:18
Fuel gauge sender & fuel gauge	7:18
Oil pressure gauge	7:18
General checks	7:18
Installation	7:18
15. Warning lamps, switches & sensors - location & t/shooting	7:19
Brake warning circuit	7:19
Hazard warning indicator light circuit (not fitted on all models)	7:19
"Hold" circuit (auto transmission models)	7:19
Seatbelt warning circuit (where fitted)	7:19
Windshield washer fluid level sensor circuit (where fitted)	7:20
16. Lighting system - initial troubleshooting	7:20
17. Headlight circuit - troubleshooting	7:20
18. Headlight raise/retract system - troubleshooting	7:21
19. Headlight dim-dip system (if fitted) - troubleshooting	7:22
20. Headlight passing light (flasher) system - troubleshooting	7:22
21. Headlight beam - adjustment	7:22
22. Headlamp deck height - adjustment	7:23
23. Headlight retractor motor - t/shooting, removal & installation	7:23
24. Headlight unit - removal, installation & bulb replacement	7:25
25. Parking light (sidelight) circuit -troubleshooting	7:26
Parking front & rear, side marker & license plate lights.	7:26

Mazda Miata, MX-5, Eunos & Roadster

26. Daytime running lights (DRL) circuit - troubleshooting _____ 7:26
27. Stop (brake) light circuit - troubleshooting _____ 7:28
28. Turn signal & hazard warning circuit - troubleshooting _____ 7:28
29. Backup (reversing) light circuit - troubleshooting _____ 7:30
30. Tail light unit - bulb & lens replacement _____ 7:32
31. Front combination light unit - bulb replacement _____ 7:32
32. Side marker lights (where fitted) - bulb replacement _____ 7:33
33. Turn signal side repeater lights (where fitted) - bulb replacement _____ 7:33
34. License plate light - bulb replacement _____ 7:33
35. Foglight, rear (where fitted) - bulb replacement _____ 7:33
36. Driving/foglights, front (where fitted) - bulb replacement _____ 7:33
37. Interior lights - troubleshooting & bulb replacement _____ 7:34
38. Trunk (boot) light - troubleshooting & bulb replacement _____ 7:35
39. Panel light control switch (where fitted) - testing _____ 7:35
40. Horn circuit - troubleshooting & horn replacement _____ 7:35
41. Rear window defogger (where fitted) - troubleshooting & repair _____ 7:36
42. Cruise control system - self-diagnosis function _____ 7:37
43. Cruise control system - troubleshooting _____ 7:38
44. Airbag system - working procedures, disarming & re-arming _____ 7:40
  Description _____ 7:40
  Working procedures _____ 7:40
  Disarming/re-arming airbag system _____ 7:41
45. Airbag system - troubleshooting _____ 7:41
46. Airbag module (driver's) - removal & installation _____ 7:41
47. Airbag module (passenger's) - removal & installation _____ 7:42
48. Windshield wiper & washer system - troubleshooting _____ 7:43
49. Wiper motor - t/shooting, removal, o/haul & installation _____ 7:43
50. Wiper mechanism - removal, installation & adjustment _____ 7:46
51. Windshield washer pump motor - testing & replacement _____ 7:47
52. Headlight washer system (if fitted) - troubleshooting _____ 7:47
53. Cigarette lighter - removal & installation _____ 7:48
54. Audio unit _____ 7:49
  Removal & installation _____ 7:49
  Security _____ 7:49
  Audio system troubleshooting _____ 7:49
  Nothing works _____ 7:49
  System works on one stereo channel only _____ 7:49
  System won't play cassette tapes _____ 7:49
  Radio inoperative (cassette tape player OK) _____ 7:49
  CD player inoperative - disc will not load _____ 7:50
  CD skips during play _____ 7:50
55. Antenna (manual) - removal & installation _____ 7:50
56. Antenna (power) - removal & installation _____ 7:50
57. Alarms & immobilisers - general _____ 7:51
58. Wiring diagrams - general _____ 7:51

CHAPTER 8: SUSPENSION & STEERING

1. Introduction _____ 8:1
2. Wheel alignment - general _____ 8:1
3. Wheel alignment - checking & adjustment _____ 8:3
  Toe-in (front wheels) - adjustment _____ 8:3
  Caster angle (front wheels) - adjustment _____ 8:3
  Camber angle (front wheels) - adjustment _____ 8:4
  Toe-in (rear wheels) adjustment _____ 8:4
  Camber angle (rear wheels) adjustment _____ 8:4
4. Shock absorber & spring (front) - removal, o/haul & installation _____ 8:5
  Checking _____ 8:6
5. Wishbone, lower front - removal, o/haul & installation _____ 8:7
6. Wishbone, upper front - removal, o/haul & installation _____ 8:9
7. Stabilizer bar (front) - removal, checking & installation _____ 8:11
8. Crossmember (front) - removal & installation _____ 8:11
9. Steering (manual) - description _____ 8:12
10. Steering (manual) - checking _____ 8:13
11. Steering wheel & column - removal, checking & installation _____ 8:13
12. Tie rod ball joint & rack dust boot - removal & installation _____ 8:16
13. Steering (manual) rack - removal, o/haul & installation _____ 8:17
14. Steering (power) - description _____ 8:18
15. Steering (power) - fluid level check & air bleeding _____ 8:18
16. Steering (power) - checking for leaks _____ 8:18
17. Steering (power) - pressure check _____ 8:19
18. Steering (power) - checking _____ 8:19
19. Steering (power) rack - removal, o/haul & installation _____ 8:19
20. Steering (power) pump - removal & installation _____ 8:21
21. Steering (power) pump - dismantling, o/haul & reassembly _____ 8:21

22. Shock absorber & spring (rear) - removal, o/haul & installation _____ 8:22
23. Wishbone, lower rear - removal, o/haul & installation _____ 8:23
24. Wishbone, upper rear - removal, o/haul & installation _____ 8:24
25. Stabilizer bar (rear) - removal, checking & installation _____ 8:24
26. Crossmember (rear) - removal, checking & installation _____ 8:25

CHAPTER 9: BRAKES, WHEELS & TIRES

1. Brake system - Introduction & on-vehicle checks _____ 9:1
2. Brake hydraulic system - topping-up fluid & bleeding _____ 9:1
3. Brake system hydraulic fluid - replacement _____ 9:2
4. Brake lines & hoses - checking & replacement _____ 9:2
  Rigid line replacement _____ 9:2
  Flexible hose replacement _____ 9:3
5. Brake pedal - removal, installation & adjustment _____ 9:3
6. Brake master cylinder & servo - removal, installation & adjustment _____ 9:4
  Master cylinder removal _____ 9:4
  Vacuum servo (power brake) unit removal _____ 9:4
  Vacuum servo (power brake) unit installation _____ 9:4
  Master cylinder installation _____ 9:5
  Special notes: ABS equipped cars _____ 9:5
7. Brake master cylinder - overhaul _____ 9:6
8. Brake servo - checking (in-situ) _____ 9:7
9. Brake proportioning bypass valve - checking (in-situ) _____ 9:7
10. Brake pads (front) - wear check _____ 9:7
11. Brake pads (front) - removal & installation _____ 9:8
12. Brake disc (front) - checking, removal & installation _____ 9:9
13. Brake caliper (front) - removal & installation _____ 9:10
14. Brake caliper (front) - overhaul _____ 9:10
15. Brake pads (rear) - wear check _____ 9:11
16. Brake pads (rear) - removal & installation _____ 9:12
17. Brake disc (rear) - checking, removal & installation _____ 9:14
18. Brake caliper (rear) - removal & installation _____ 9:14
19. Brake caliper (rear) - overhaul _____ 9:15
20. Parking brake - checking & adjustment _____ 9:16
21. Parking brake lever - removal, checking & installation _____ 9:16
22. Parking brake cable - removal, checking & installation _____ 9:17
  Lever to compensator cable - replacement _____ 9:17
  Compensator to brake cables - replacement _____ 9:17
23. ABS (anti-lock brake system) - checking _____ 9:18
24. Tires - checking _____ 9:18
  Tread wear _____ 9:18
  Tire damage _____ 9:18
  Matching tires _____ 9:19
  Tire size & ratings _____ 9:19
25. Wheel changing (with car's toolkit) _____ 9:19
26. Tires - rotation _____ 9:20
27. Tire pressures - checking & adjusting _____ 9:20
28. Tire fitting & wheel balancing _____ 9:20
29. Wheels - checking & maintenance _____ 9:20
30. Wheel hubs & bearings - checking & overhaul _____ 9:20
31. Wheel studs - removal & installation _____ 9:23

CHAPTER 10: INTERIOR

1. Introduction _____ 10:1
2. Console, rear (between seats) - removal & installation _____ 10:1
3. Dash center panel - removal & installation _____ 10:2
4. Dash panel - removal, checking & installation _____ 10:3
5. Interior trim - removal & installation _____ 10:7
  Front header rail trim & sun visors _____ 10:7
  A-pillar trim _____ 10:7
  Front side (footwell) trim _____ 10:7
  Scuff plate _____ 10:8
  Quarter trim _____ 10:8
  Door speaker & grille _____ 10:9
  Door trim _____ 10:9
6. Door glass & lifter mechanism - removal & installation _____ 10:11
7. Window lift system (power) - checking & overhaul _____ 10:13
8. Window lift system (manual) - checking & overhaul _____ 10:15
9. Door glass alignment - checking & adjustment _____ 10:15
  Height adjustment _____ 10:15
  Inward/outward adjustment _____ 10:15
  Fore/aft adjustment _____ 10:16
  Adjustment checks _____ 10:16

Contents

10. Door latch & lock assembly - removal, overhaul & installation __ 10:16
    Aftermarket central locking _____ 10:17
11. Seats - removal, checking, overhaul & installation _____ 10:17
12. Carpets - removal & installation _____ 10:19
13. Trunk (boot) carpet & trim - removal & installation _____ 10:20
14. Seatbelts - removal, checking & installation _____ 10:21
15. Brace bar - removal & installation _____ 10:21
    Removal _____ 10:21
    Installation _____ 10:21

CHAPTER 11: BODY

1. Introduction _____ 11:1
2. Body - maintenance & cosmetic care _____ 11:1
    Why maintenance matters _____ 11:1
    Washing _____ 11:1
    Polishing _____ 11:2
    Vinyl trim cleaners & polishes _____ 11:2
    Tar spots _____ 11:2
    Color restorers _____ 11:2
3. Paintwork - damage repair _____ 11:2
4. Body - damage repair & painting _____ 11:2
    Assessing the damage _____ 11:3
    Pulling out a dent _____ 11:3
    Repairing holed or gashed areas _____ 11:3
    Filling _____ 11:4
    Sanding _____ 11:4
    Painting _____ 11:4
    Finishing _____ 11:5
5. Hood (bonnet) - removal & installation _____ 11:6
6. Trunk (boot) lid, fittings & rear panel - removal & installation ___ 11:6
    Trunk lid removal & installation _____ 11:7
    Trunk latch - removal, installation & adjustment _____ 11:7
    Rear finisher (license plate) panel & trunk lock barrel - removal __ 11:8
    Trunk lid balance springs - removal, installation & adjustment __ 11:9
    Trunk lid hinges - removal & installation _____ 11:10
7. Fuel filler cable & lid - removal, installation & emergency opening 11:10
8A. Door mirror - removal & installation _____ 11:11
8B. Door mirror (power) - checking _____ 11:11
9. Door - removal, installation & adjustment _____ 11:12
10. Bumper (rear) - removal & installation _____ 11:13
11. Bumper (front) - removal & installation _____ 11:15
12. Fender (wing), front - removal & installation _____ 11:17
13. Windshield - removal & installation _____ 11:18
14. Hard top - installation & adjustment _____ 11:19
15. Convertible top - removal, installation & adjustment _____ 11:19
16. Convertible top rear window & rain rail - removal & installation 11:21
17. Convertible top fabric - removal & installation _____ 11:22
18. Convertible top - fabric repairs _____ 11:25

CHAPTER 12: UNDERBODY & RUSTPROOFING

1. Introduction _____ 12:1
2. Rustproofing - why it's a good idea _____ 12:1
3. Rustproofing procedure _____ 12:1

CHAPTER 13: TROUBLESHOOTING

Introduction _____ 13:1
Engine problems _____ 13:1
    Won't start/stops suddenly _____ 13:1
    Does not crank when starter operated _____ 13:1
    Cranks very slowly when starter operated _____ 13:1
    Cranks normally, but does not start _____ 13:2
    Difficult to start when cold _____ 13:2
    Difficult to start when warm _____ 13:2
    Starts, but doesn't run normally _____ 13:2
    Idle (tickover) erratic or rough _____ 13:2
    Stalls _____ 13:2
    Hesitates or stumbles during acceleration _____ 13:2
    Power surges/losses when gas pedal held steady _____ 13:2
    Lacks power _____ 13:3
    Engine runs roughly during deceleration _____ 13:3
    Abnormal fuel consumption _____ 13:3
    Low oil pressure _____ 13:3
    Excessive oil consumption _____ 13:3
Clutch problems _____ 13:3
    Clutch does not release when pedal depressed _____ 13:3
    Clutch slipping _____ 13:3
    Clutch judder _____ 13:3
    Unusual noise _____ 13:3
Transmission (manual) problems _____ 13:3
    Gear engagement difficult or noisy _____ 13:3
    Transmission jumps out of gear _____ 13:4
    Unusual noises _____ 13:4
    Abnormal vibration _____ 13:4
Transmission (automatic) problems _____ 13:4
    General _____ 13:4
Final drive problems _____ 13:4
    Engine runs normally, & gears engage, but car does not move __ 13:4
    Abnormal noise or vibration _____ 13:4
Cooling system problems _____ 13:4
    Overheating indicated &/or steam from under hood (bonnet) __ 13:4
    Coolant ejected from overflow pipe/oil in coolant _____ 13:4
    Temperature gauge needle does not reach 'normal' sector _____ 13:4
    Coolant loss _____ 13:4
Steering & suspension problems _____ 13:4
    Car wanders off line _____ 13:4
    Excessive steering free play _____ 13:4
    Steering excessively stiff or heavy (manual steering) _____ 13:4
    Steering excessively stiff or heavy (power steering) _____ 13:4
    Wheel (front) wobble or vibration _____ 13:4
    Wheel (rear) wobble or vibration _____ 13:5
    Car rolls excessively or wallows in corners _____ 13:5
    Abnormal tire wear _____ 13:5
Abnormal smells, noises or vibration _____ 13:5
    Fuel smells in or around car _____ 13:5
    Smell of burning _____ 13:5
    Sulfur (sulphur) smell from exhaust _____ 13:5
Unusual noises _____ 13:5
    Pinging or knocking sound when engine under load _____ 13:5
    Light tapping or rattling noise from engine _____ 13:5
    Rumbling or knocking noises from engine _____ 13:5
    Squealing or screeching from under hood (bonnet) _____ 13:5
    Whistling noises from under hood (bonnet) _____ 13:5
    Exhaust system noises _____ 13:5
    Droning or rumbling from wheel area _____ 13:5
    Clutch noises _____ 13:5
    Suspension noises _____ 13:5
Brake system problems _____ 13:5
    Poor brake performance _____ 13:5
    Brakes pull to one side _____ 13:6
    Brakes dragging _____ 13:6
    Excessive pedal movement _____ 13:6
    Brake noise or vibration _____ 13:6
    Anti-lock braking system (ABS) malfunction _____ 13:6
    Parking brake ineffective _____ 13:6
Electrical problems _____ 13:6
    Battery becomes discharged frequently _____ 13:6
    Headlights dim or inoperative _____ 13:6
    Turn signals inoperative on one side only _____ 13:6
    Turn signals inoperative on both sides of car _____ 13:6
    Burned out fuses or circuit breaker open _____ 13:6

INDEX

Index _____ 14:1

Visit Veloce on the Web - www.veloce.co.uk

Introduction & thanks

It's been six years - and I'm pleased to say several reprints - since the original Enthusiast's Manual for the 1.6 liter Miata/MX-5/Eunos was published. This new manual for 1.8 liter models has been over two years in the making and I'd like to extend my sincere thanks to all those enthusiasts who've waited so patiently for this book: I hope you'll all think it was worth the long, long wait ...

After more than ten years of production, the basic 'rightness' of Mazda's groundbreaking design has been proven by the simple fact that it has now become the most successful traditional sportscar ever, having passed the MGB's sales figures some time ago. However, the ultimate flattery must really be the whole plethora of 'me-too' designs from many manufacturers all clamouring to enter the market which Mazda single-handedly recreated at the beginning of the 1990s.

When Mazda launched the Miata & Eunos, followed by the MX-5, the motoring world was astonished to see something that had been presumed extinct: the traditional sports roadster was back, and back with a bang! Mazda's modern roadster was hailed as a future classic as soon as it hit the streets. Mazda had thrown away the conventional car maker's shackles and produced a true sportscar designed by enthusiasts for enthusiasts: therefore, in producing this book, we have endeavored to use the same ethos to provide a true enthusiast's manual.

Our working environment was an ordinary domestic garage equipped with ordinary tools. Because of this, you can be sure we encountered the same problems you will and, more importantly, that our workarounds will work for you too. All of the strip and rebuild work and photography for this edition was carried out by Nick, 'Wally' and myself (Rod). Wally is a fictional technical adviser of dubious ability, so we allowed him to make all the mistakes: we figured this would make the rest of us look better and allow us to tell you how to avoid potential mistakes in your own work.

We've gone to great lengths to make this the most friendly, easy to use and detailed workshop manual for owners that's ever existed. If you think we've succeeded, like our work and want to show your appreciation, send us an old (non-British) license plate for our garage wall (we've got quite a few already from readers of the original 1.6 manual). Of course, you can just write and tell us what you think of the manual and how we can make future editions better - we'll always be pleased to hear from you.

Thanks

Like the original, this project has taken well over two years to complete and really would not have been possible without the help and support of many people. Judith Brooks, Nick Barwis and Kevin Quinn have all had to cover for me at the Veloce offices while I've spent several months at home writing this manual on my portable AppleMac: there were just too many distractions in the office to allow good progress. Nick Barwis also took the photographs during the strip and rebuild of the 1.8 liter project car.

Although this is a completely new manual, some of it is based on the original 1.6 liter manual so, once again, I'd like to thank Pete Shoemark, co-writer of the original book. Thanks, too, to my Dad who kindly loaned me the camera and lenses which produced the photographs in this book and the original. Tim Parker 'our man in America' and his team at Motorbooks International helped out by obtaining Mazda's US model literature. Norman Garrett of the Miata Club of America and a concept engineer during the car's creation, was very enthusiastic and helpful to me when I was creating the original manual. Mazda very kindly allowed the reproduction of their line drawings. Last, but as they say not least, the thousands of enthusiasts who bought my original manual provided the impetus for this one and helped my company, Veloce Publishing to grow successfully. My thanks and best wishes to all of you.

Rod Grainger

Above - Let's just say that as a mechanic, Nick Barwis makes a great photographer!
Left - The original crew. From left to right, Rod, Judith and Pete. Wally's just tinkering under there ... Bottom left is puppy Hubble (who's now fully grown).

1

General advice & technical specifications

1. USING THIS MANUAL

Sorry about this, but we're not a huge, Intergalactic Corporation. We're just a bunch of enthusiasts with the ability to publish this manual so, in today's litigation crazy world, we need to draw your attention to the following -

IMPORTANT NOTE. While we have prepared this manual with great diligence and care, it's possible that it contains errors or that information is omitted. Also be aware that we cannot foresee every possible area of personal danger or possibility of mechanical damage, and warn our readers accordingly. The authors, publishers and retailers therefore accept no responsibility for personal injury or mechanical damage which is in any way related to the use of this publication. If you use the information contained within this manual, you accept full personal responsibility for the consequences: if this is not acceptable to you, return the pristine book to your supplier for a refund.

As the majority of these cars are in the USA, we've written this manual in American English. We don't think different spellings will lead to any problems for other English speakers, but different terminology might: we've therefore tried to include the English English equivalent word in brackets where we feel there is a possibility of misunderstanding.

In chapter 2, we cover the basic maintenance operations necessary to keep your car in peak condition. Most of these tasks are relatively simple to do, and if they're not, we'll tell you. In chapters 3 onward we look, in detail, at the various major assemblies and systems which together make up your car.

We reasoned that a car like this would appeal to a broad spectrum of individuals who would approach the maintenance and repair of their car in a variety of ways. Some of you may have no intention of ever lifting the hood (bonnet), while others may want to become familiar with the innermost secrets of the car. We hope that we have provided a manual with something of real value to *all* owners.

Wherever possible, we have placed emphasis on diagnosing suspected faults before giving detailed information on how to track down and resolve specific problems. With complex electronic sensing and control systems, it is often difficult to locate problems using traditional methods, and unless you work methodically and logically, you can easily waste hours without result, or, worse still, introduce further problems by altering settings that are, in fact, correct.

We have concentrated on descriptive and diagnostic information because we feel strongly that you need to understand your car before you attempt to work on it. This gives you the opportunity to understand what is likely to have caused any particular breakdown or difficulty, and with this information, make your decision about how best to deal with the situation. Despite its obvious affinity with European sports roadsters of the 1950s and 1960s, make no mistake, this is very much a car of today with all that this implies; crammed into that little bodyshell is all the technical sophistication of its era.

In some respects, Mazda's roadster can seem a daunting prospect for home maintenance and repair. It has a sophisticated engine management system, which, when hooked up to the equally sophisticated diagnostic equipment available to Mazda dealers, offers fast identification of many system faults. When we researched and wrote this book, it would have been easy just to relate the official test procedures, but we were determined to base the book on normal home workshop tools and working methods.

This might seem to suggest that home diagnosis is not possible, but in many cases you can use alternative methods to avoid the need for expensive test equipment, and we made strenuous efforts to pack in as much of this type of information as we could. Where home testing and diagnosis really is out of the question, we indicate this in the text. Equally, where many hours of painstaking work could easily be avoided with a few minutes of dealer attention, we say so; after all, you bought your Mazda for the fun and exhilaration that comes from driving it.

CONVENTIONS

The various chapter headings should be reasonably self-explanatory - we grouped together related assemblies and systems in what seemed a logical way. You may realize, however, that linking the disparate aspects of the car to a surprising degree is the Power Train Control module (*nee* Engine Control Unit). The role of this computer (the PCM) is fundamental: it reads data sent to it from all over the vehicle, processes the data and then sends control data to many components. In this sense, *Chapter 5, Fuel, Ignition & Exhaust Systems*, forms the core of the book, and it is here that you'll find much about how various systems, and sub-systems, inter-relate, giving you a real insight to diagnosing problems in a logical manner.

Within each chapter, you'll find the text sub-divided into sections, these being further sub-divided into numbered paragraphs, sometimes with subsection headings to tell you which part of a procedure you're dealing with.

Right and left. All references to right and left are from the point of view of someone standing behind the car and looking forward.

SYMBOLS & CROSS-REFERENCES

While we have tried to avoid the irritation of cross-references as far as possible, in some cases this was unavoidable if the book was to be kept to a reasonable size and price. We have adopted a number of conventions to help you find your way around: where a particular procedure requires you to carry out operations described in detail elsewhere in the book, you will find a symbol like this appearing in the text -

☞ 3/4/1-51.

This tells you that, at this point in the current procedure, you should carry out work

Mazda Miata, MX-5, Eunos & Roadster

described in chapter 3, section 4, paragraphs 1 to 51. You should move to the part of the book indicated, carry out the operations detailed there, and then resume the current task where you left off. Please note that the first number is always the chapter number, even when the cross-reference is in the same chapter.

Drawings are numbered in relation to the appropriate text. For example, D22/1 relates to section 22, paragraph 1 of the chapter in which the drawing appears. To help you, we have included a symbol in any text where reference to a particular drawing will be helpful: if the symbol's followed by a + sign, there's more than one drawing. The symbol looks like this -

Photographs will be found close to the text to which they relate, and illustrate part or all of the specific procedure being described. Each photograph is numbered in relation to the appropriate text. For example, a photo caption beginning 7/47 indicates that the photo relates to section 7, paragraph 47 of the chapter in which it appears. We have created a photo symbol for the text to tell you when reference to a particular photo will be helpful: if the symbol's followed by a + sign, there's more than one photo. Here's the photo symbol -

HEY! WATCH OUT!

We have assumed that you will be working responsibly at all times, and taking appropriate precautions to avoid damage or personal injury. On occasions where a particular procedure may carry a special risk to the operator's safety, we have drawn attention to this by placing a **Warning!** in the text. If you see this, be aware that it is there to draw attention to a serious risk of *personal* injury if special care or precautions are not observed. Don't ignore these warnings - we put them in because there is a **real** risk of injury. **Don't assume that tasks which don't carry this warning are safe; we cannot possibly foresee every potential danger in every situation.** Try to be aware of potential dangers whenever working on or around your car. Don't think just in terms of the obvious, go a little deeper. Here are just five examples of the level of awareness you should maintain. 1) Remember that most fluids used by the car or for maintenance/cleaning are in some way dangerous: read the maker's instructions and don't make assumptions. 2) Old engine oil has been proved to cause skin cancer in mice - so protect your skin with gloves or barrier cream and wash contaminated areas quickly. 3) If you're working on the car's fuel system in your garage, remember that if the garage contains a house heating boiler, the ignition sequence may occur while there are gas (petrol) fumes in the air - it's also possible the boiler has a constant pilot flame. 4) Slipping on spilled oil, or other fluids, could put you in hospital for a long time. 5) A metal watch strap, bracelet or even a ring could cause a short between a live terminal and ground (earth).

In other cases, there may be some risk of serious damage to the car if special care is not taken. We have identified such instances by placing **Caution!** in the text. What we mean here is that you need to take even more care than usual if you are to avoid accidentally damaging some component of the car or, perhaps, your tools. These messages mean business, so please don't just skip past them. **Don't assume that tasks which don't carry this warning are safe; we cannot possibly foresee every potential danger in every situation.**

Other specific information of special note, but which does not pose a serious risk of personal injury or damage to the car, will be highlighted by the less dramatic 'Note:' You should take note of the information which follows - it could save you making mistakes in a procedure.

2. WORKING PROCEDURES

GENERAL

1   Before you start **any** operation on your car, read through the details carefully. Check any drawings or photographs relating to the task, and compare this information with your own car. If necessary re-read the section until you are confident that you know what you will be doing. Not only does this minimize mistakes, it will actually save you time when you do the job for real - you won't need to constantly refer back to the manual for procedural details.

2   You should remember that the project car for this book was a right-hand drive model. There are instances where this affects the procedure described to some degree. For example, the power steering pipe routing is the same on all cars, except where it connects into the steering rack - there are extra-long pipes on the RHD version. We have tried to cover these differences throughout the book, and, where necessary, we have shown a drawing of the LHD version for comparison with the photographs, but there may be further minor variations which were not apparent during the photographic project work.

THE WORK AREA AND STORAGE FACILITIES

3   On occasions, you may need to work on your car on the roadside in the event of a breakdown, or if you do not have access to a garage. For simple procedures this may be acceptable, but if a major repair or overhaul is envisaged, you should make strenuous efforts to find somewhere under cover. If absolutely unavoidable, you could remove major assemblies outside, but any dismantling work should take place under some sort of roof.

4   Most of us will be working inside a normal domestic garage with restricted floor area and ceiling/rafter height. Before you start work, make sure that you have sufficient room to work comfortably. If you have the same kind of garage that most of us have to use, clear out as much junk as you can (especially on or around the bench area), and arrange your garden tools, bicycles, ski equipment, or whatever, neatly, and well away from your work area. Try to keep at least one side of the garage clear of domestic items.

5   You'll need plenty of light as well. Make sure you have adequate general lighting, with extra lighting over the workbench, plus one or two inspection lights for use around and under the car and a flashlight for use in confined spaces.

6   Don't forget that you'll need somewhere to store removed parts safely, and this requirement will vary according to what you intend to do. In most cases, you can lay out the parts on shelves or in boxes, though some of the bigger assemblies, especially things like the dash panel, seats or the hood, will obviously require much more space.

7   If you're going to undertake a major overhaul which entails removal of the engine and transmission, you'll need around twice the area required to park the car, plus adequate access to allow the engine/transmission assembly to be removed. You'll need to assess the likely space requirement and make suitable arrangements *before* you start work.

8   Set aside an area where you can safely leave major parts or assemblies, with no risk of accidental damage. You'll know best how you can arrange this according to your own circumstances. You may be planning to carry out major work over an extended period, maybe over the winter months. If so, plan some kind of long-term storage for removed parts, with dustsheets to cover removed major assemblies or body parts until they are needed again. We won't bother describing some utopian home workshop - just try to give it a little thought before you start.

9   The seasoned home mechanic will instinctively collect handy containers - plastic tubs and resealable plastic bags are great for tiny, easily lost parts, and cardboard cartons are good for bigger parts. If money is no object, get some stackable plastic bins.

10   Use PVC electrical tape or masking tape to identify parts, hose and wiring connections, etc, as parts are removed/disconnected - you can write on the tape or on the part itself with a fine-point indelible marker pen. You can also use card or paper labels for this. Have a notepad handy for making simple sketches of how specific parts fit together, or how wiring or hoses are routed. Avoid pens that use water-based inks which will rub off easily.

11   If you are unfamiliar with car repair work, the value of marking things cannot be overstressed - you'll be surprised how easy it is to get confused about which wire or bolt goes where, even just a few hours after you disconnected them. In many cases you can make life easier for yourself by refitting bolts and screws as you remove them, either screwing them loosely back into position after removing the component they retain, or, in the case of covers, pushing the screw back through the cover and through a piece of card. When you get round to installing the part, the fasteners will be in the correct relative positions - this is especially important where you have similar screws or bolts of varying length.

HOSE CONNECTIONS

12   You will encounter hose connections dur-

1: General advice & technical specifications

ing many procedures on the car, and the way you deal with them will depend to some extent on the function of the hose.

Cooling system hoses

13   **Warning!** If the engine has been run within the last hour or so, the engine coolant will be hot and under pressure. Removing the radiator filler or coolant reservoir caps, or disconnecting any hose, can result in the water boiling as pressure is released, resulting in scalding steam being ejected. Always allow the engine to cool before removing either cap. Wear eye protection, gloves and overalls for safety if there is any doubt. Place some thick rag over the radiator cap and turn it slowly counter-clockwise until it reaches the first stop position. Wait until pressure has vented before removing the cap completely.

14   **Caution!** Before you disconnect any hose, you'll need to drain the cooling system partially or fully ☞ 6/2.

15   The coolant hoses are generally secured by spring clamps (clips), and these should be moved clear of the stub over which the hose is fitted *before* you attempt to remove the hose itself. Use pliers to grasp the clip ends, squeezing them together to release the clamp's grip on the hose. Slide the clamp an inch or so along the hose until it lies clear of the stub, then release it.

16   To free the hose from its stub, always try to *push* it off, using a screwdriver blade to lever it. If you try pulling on the hose you'll only tighten the grip on the stub, and hoses rarely come off this way. If it has been in place a long time, the hose may be stuck on the stub. If necessary, try working a small screwdriver blade under the hose end if access permits.

17   As a last resort, cut off the old hose by slitting it lengthways through the stub area with a craft knife (**Warning!** Watch your fingers!) being careful not to score the stub. Of course, if you have to do this the hose will be destroyed, so make sure that you have a new hose of the correct type before you take such drastic action ☞ 6/4.

18   ☞ When re-installing used hoses, always try to get the clamps positioned in their original indentations; this will provide the best seal.

Fuel system hoses

19   The fuel system hoses can be approached

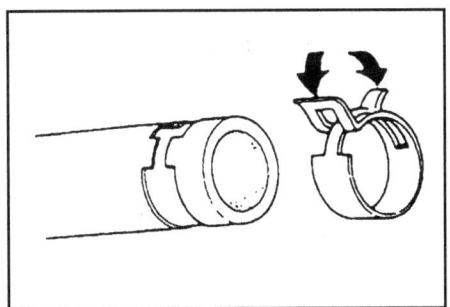

D2/18 TYPICAL HOSE CLAMP (CLIP).
Squeeze ears together to release clamp tension. When re-installing clamps, refit them in existing hose indentations.

in much the same way as described above for the cooling system hoses, though, of course, they are considerably smaller in size. **Warning!** Although the hose content is not hot, it is normally under a lot of pressure, and you must always depressurize the fuel system before you start disconnecting fuel hoses and pipes.

20   **Warning!** Whenever the fuel system is disconnected, fuel vapor will be present. Be aware of the potential fire hazard. Have available a fire extinguisher of the type approved for automotive fires. Make sure that the working area is well ventilated - working in a poorly ventilated building will increase the risk of a dangerous build-up of fuel vapor. We do not recommend that you carry out fuel system work with the vehicle over an access pit - fuel vapor is heavier than air and will collect in the access pit where it will persist for some time, presenting a significant fire hazard.

21   For full details of fuel system working procedures ☞ 5/13.

Brake hoses

22   Before disconnecting any part of the brake system, make sure that you have any necessary replacement parts ready, or the car will be immobilized until you can obtain them. You will also need a supply of fresh hydraulic fluid of the correct specification, and be prepared to bleed air from the brake system after any disconnection.

23   **Warning!** Hydraulic fluid is harmful if swallowed or if it gets into the eyes or bloodstream. If any of these things happen, get prompt medical attention. Avoid skin contact with the fluid and wash contaminated skin promptly. Wear protective gloves when working with brake fluid - particularly if you have open cuts.

24   **Caution!** Hydraulic fluid may damage any painted finish or plastic parts it contacts. Take care to avoid contact, and wash off any accidental spills immediately using detergent or denatured alcohol (meths).

25   If you need to disconnect any of the metal brake pipes, be aware of the possibility of corrosion at the union. In cases of severe corrosion it's not uncommon for the pipe to be frozen (seized) inside the union, in which case it is likely that the pipe will twist and fracture as the union is unscrewed - this is no real problem if you were intending to fit a new pipe anyway, but beware of the possibility of this problem if you don't have a new pipe ready to fit. As the union is freed, there will be a little fluid leakage. Don't worry too much about this, but use some rag to catch the spills to avoid damage to paintwork or plastic parts in the vicinity.

26   Where a flexible brake hose is to be removed, slacken the flare nut which secures it to the body bracket, then withdraw the retaining clip to release the bracket end of the hose. Once this is free, unscrew the hose union bolt at the caliper end and remove the hose.

27   Install the hose using new copper washers at the unions. **Warning!** Make sure the union locating peg engages correctly otherwise the hose will take up the wrong attitude and might come into contact with moving items, or rub on bodywork.

28   Tighten the union bolt to the specified torque figure. Be sure that suspension or steering movement will not cause damage to the hose. Bleed air from the system.

29   For detailed information on the brake hydraulic system ☞ 9.

GASKETS AND SEALS

30   You'll normally need to fit new gaskets and seals whenever you disturb the old ones, unless advised differently in the text. With this in mind, make sure that you get the appropriate parts ready *before* you start.

31   You need to remove all traces of old gaskets before you fit new ones. You can use a gasket remover for this (available from auto parts stores), or you can carefully scrape off any residue using a soft metal scraper. Beware of using an old screwdriver to remove gaskets - this often causes scoring of the joint surfaces which can cause leaks.

32   Unless advised to the contrary, fit the new gasket dry. Gasket cement or jointing compound is rarely required, though we like to keep a tube of silicone-based sealant handy (the type that is squeezed from a tube in a semi-liquid state and which then sets to a rubbery consistency). This sealant can be used to seal a joint where a new gasket or O-ring is not available, or in cases where light damage to a sealing face is discovered, but must be used with care; it will not withstand direct combustion heat and is dissolved by fuel.

33   Note also that, if silicone-type sealant gets into the engine, it can obstruct oil passages with catastrophic results; never apply more than a thin film, and wipe excess away from the inside edge of the joint face before assembly. You should also leave the sealant to harden slightly for around ten minutes before you assemble the parts (unless its manufacturer says otherwise).

34   O-rings are used extensively to seal passages and small components, and should be replaced by new items if disturbed. Even if old rings seem to be in good condition, the rubber will have compressed and hardened, and it is very likely that they'll leak if reused. It is well worth having a selection of O-rings in the workshop; these can be purchased from auto parts stores and are inexpensive.

35   You can also buy O-ring kits which allow you to make up your own O-rings of any diameter. The material is cut to size with a craft knife or scalpel blade, and then joined using an isocyanate adhesive. This system is reputed to work very well, though we would have some reservations where the seal is of vital importance.

36   Oil seals lead a particularly hard life, and should always be replaced by new items during an overhaul. As with O-rings, the rubber material hardens with age and the effects of heat; in addition, the fine seal lip will wear down and so will grip the shaft less securely. If the old seal is badly damaged, rather than just worn down, check the shaft or component on which it was fitted for damage. If necessary, replace the damaged part before you fit a new seal, or you'll find yourself repeating the overhaul in a short while.

Mazda Miata, MX-5, Eunos & Roadster

37   Make a note of the fitted direction of the seal during removal, and ensure you fit the new one in the same orientation. In most cases, the seal case is located by a shoulder or rib in the outer bore, but, if this is not present, normal practice is to fit the seal flush with or fractionally below the outer face of the casting or component which carries it. Before you refit the shaft through the seal, lubricate it and the seal lip to prevent damage during installation and to provide lubrication in use.

38   A seal should be pressed home carefully, making sure that it enters its bore squarely. If you force the seal in at an angle, the usual result is damage to the seal's metal casing, and this will often result in leakage. Use a blunt, tubular drift to press the seal home - sockets of the appropriate diameter are very useful for this.

SCREWS, BOLTS & NUTS

39   All threaded fasteners should be checked carefully before they are re-used: reject any which show signs of wear or damage to the threads. If you need to fit new bolts, it's preferable to obtain these through a Mazda dealer; this way you know that not only is the bolt of the right size, it is also of the correct material - something not readily apparent from casual examination. If you purchase new bolts or nuts elsewhere, a reputable supplier will be able to check that the replacement is of the correct material if you take along the old one when ordering.

40   Where the bolt or screw fits directly into a casting or captive nut, clean out any dirt or oil from the threads with degreasing solvent, then blow the threads clear with compressed air. Failure to do so can prevent the bolt or screw seating fully, or can damage the bolt/screw or casting threads. Even a small amount of dirt on the threads can prevent the correct torque setting being applied. In some instances, the bolt threads should be given a light coating of copper-based or other anti-sieze grease during installation. This is especially important where they are subject to high temperatures, as is the case with exhaust system fasteners.

41   Plain nuts can be re-used if they are in good condition, but special nuts should be replaced by new items. This includes Nyloc and other self-locking nuts, which rely on the grip of the plastic ring insert to prevent them loosening in service; once used, the insert's grip is much diminished.

42   In most cases, you'll find specific torque wrench settings in the text, and these should be adhered to closely. The settings assume clean, dry and undamaged threads; you cannot accurately torque-tighten where there is any sort of damage or obstruction. If you accidentally overtighten a fastener, or in cases where you need to check torque after an earlier overhaul, back the fastener off by a quarter turn, then tighten to the specified setting.

43   Where castellated nuts are fitted, always tighten to the lower end of the specified torque range and check whether the cotter (split) pin can be fitted. If necessary, tighten a little more until the pin can be slid home; never back the nut off to allow the pin to fit unless instructed to do so.

44   Mechanical locking methods, like locking tabs, or the cotter pins used to secure castellated nuts should always be replaced by new items. Use a locking tab or cotter pin of the correct size or diameter, and always bend it over correctly to ensure security. With cotter pins, use pliers to bend over the pin ends, and cut off any excess with side cutters. In the case of locking tabs, bend the tab up against the side of the bolt or nut hexagon, then tap it firmly into position with a small hammer.

TORQUE TIGHTENING BY FEEL

45   There are many occasions when working on your car that you'll run into problems when attempting to tighten fasteners to a specified torque setting. Usually, this is because you are unable to reach the fastener in question using a torque wrench.

46   Once upon a time, professional mechanics took pride in being able to tighten even vital fasteners like head nuts or bearing cap bolts by feel, with no ill effects. These guys were good. Because they did this day in, day out, for years, they got to be pretty accurate with this approach. They may have wrecked a few threads as apprentices, but the machinery they worked on was so tough and forgiving that a bit of practice usually meant they could tighten down reliably and without damage, ninety nine times out of a hundred.

47   However, times and technology change, and modern vehicles are designed and built to much finer tolerances. The use of light alloy castings in place of cast iron allows little room for making mistakes; the old approach of over-engineering, with the resulting latitude in torque ranges, is long gone. If you try to tighten a bolt until it 'feels about right' you stand a good chance of stripping threads, or worse.

48   If you've ever sheared off a bolt by over-tightening, you'll have a good idea of how much time wasting and hassle results from a simple mistake. Here are a few tips (we know what we're talking about here - we've seen Wally shear off those bolts and strip those threads!) -

* **Rule 1: Use the torque wrench.** *Always make the effort to use the torque wrench where a tightening torque is specified.*
* **Rule 2: Are you sure you can't reach the bolt?** *Try a shorter or longer extension and try again. You may need to play around with your socket accessories a little. Try using flexible joints. You may find that special ball-end sockets and accessories would give that little bit of movement you need, or you could try using a $^3/_8$in drive socket set instead of $^1/_2$in drive set.*
* **Rule 3: OK, you can't use the torque wrench.** *So make one that you can use. If you can't get in there with a conventional torque wrench, improvise. We have made our own 'torque crescent wrench' before - here's how:*

Get a strip of steel and drill a hole in one end so that you can hook a spring balance into it. Fix it onto a crescent wrench/open-ended spanner/combination wrench, or whatever you can fit on the bolt head, using a couple of worm-drive hose clips. Position the strip so that the hole for the spring balance is 12 inches from the center of the jaws. Fit the tool to the bolt head and hook up the spring balance.

Now, if you need to apply 24lbf ft, remember a foot-pound is a force of one pound applied to a lever one foot in length: pull on the spring balance until you see 24lb on the scale, and you've done it.

* **Rule 4: Use your brain.** *The human brain is pretty good at remembering things, especially short-term. If you really can't get to that bolt head with anything but a wrench, find a nut and bolt of the same size and clamp the nut in a vise. Screw in the bolt and torque tighten it to the specified pressure. Hold the torque wrench in a position that corresponds with the length of the wrench you intend to use on the real thing, and try to gauge how hard you need to pull it.*

Do this a few times with the torque wrench, then try it using the plain wrench. Use the torque wrench to check how much torque you applied. Repeat until you get good at attaining the correct pressure every time. Now rush over to the car before you forget, and apply precisely the right torque to your inaccessible fastener.

ELECTRICAL CONNECTIONS AND WIRE COLOR CODING

49   The Mazda's wiring is color coded to make tracing and troubleshooting easier, and to assist identification (see accompanying panel). We have used Mazda's own abbreviations for wire colors throughout this book.

Note that where more than one color is

CODE	COLOR	CODE	COLOR
B	Black	O	Orange
BR	Brown	P	Pink
G	Green	R	Red
GY	Gray	V	Violet
L	Blue	W	White
LB	Light Blue	Y	Yellow
LG	Light Green	—	—

D2/49 STANDARD MAZDA WIRE COLOR CODING.

indicated, for example LB/Y, the main wire color (light blue) is shown first and the second, or tracer, color (yellow) is shown after the slash.

Physical tracing of an individual wire from harness to harness is next to impossible on a modular wiring system of this complexity (we reckon that some of the main harness sections we encountered must have held a hundred or more individual wires, all tightly bound into a harness, but spurring off here and there). To compound the problem, more than twenty separate harnesses make up the car's wiring system.

50   In reality, modern wiring is of such high

1: General advice & technical specifications

quality that you would be unlucky to experience problems in the life of the car. In most cases any fault will be found at the wire ends - usually at the connector terminal, or will turn out to be a component failure. If you do find an internally broken or intermittent wire, try to trace the route of that part of the harness, and tape a new wire of the same size and, preferably, of the same color as the original to the outside of the harness with PVC electrical tape.

51 If you want to add electrical accessories to the car, try to do so intelligently. When fitting accessory items it is tempting to do the minimum of dismantling to get access, and this invariably means that later access to some part of the car will be difficult because of straggling wires. Try to use connectors of the type already used on the car, so that panels or assemblies can still be removed for servicing.

52 Be aware that if you patch into existing wiring using Scotchloks or similar snap-together wire connectors, you may be imposing too much load on that circuit or fuse. Patching in like this is just about unavoidable, but think about what you are doing - for example, if you hook into the instrument panel lighting circuit to run the rear window demister on your new hardtop, you'll be drawing too much power through a 10A fuse, so don't be surprised when it blows.

53 If you need to cut an accessory wire in the course of removing other components, you should reconnect it in a way that allows for subsequent dismantling. We prefer to use screw-type connectors - they seem to work more reliably than other types. Cut the wire and bare the ends using an insulation stripping tool. Fit the bared ends into the connector and tighten the screws to secure the bared wires. If you use Scotchloks, or similar, make sure that you use the correct size - if too small you'll cut through some of the conductor strands and restrict the carrying capacity of the circuit. Conversely, if the connector is too big it will be a loose fit on the conductor, and may have only intermittent contact.

WRESTLING WITH PLASTIC TWO-PIECE PANEL FASTENERS

Crosshead type

54 When you work on some areas of the car, it seems as if it is held together with these fasteners. They look for all the world like crosshead screws through cup washers, but once you look closely, they are actually two parts of a widely-used fastener arrangement for holding access covers and the like. The idea is that during assembly, the crossheaded center pin pushes into a split outer part, which is wedge-shaped internally. As the pin is pushed home it forces the outer part to expand in its hole and lock the panel (or whatever) in position. The crossheaded pin actually has a thread of sorts, presumably intended to unscrew to allow removal. Great idea, except that it doesn't really work!

55 What actually happens is that the screw part just turns in the outer section, and that means that you can't shift either of them without destroying them. We came across so many of these little devils that we took the trouble to work out a surefire method of shifting them. We figured that the outer, wedge-shaped piece was failing to grip the screw thread because it was a slack fit in the panel hole. What you need to do is work a flat screwdriver blade under the 'washer' part. This distorts it and makes it grip the screw, which can then be (very carefully) removed.

56 Don't push on the screwdriver when turning the crosshead pin, or you will just force it back into the outer part. You have to be careful, though; the screw slot is very soft and easily damaged.

Plain head type

57 This type of fastener is similar to the crosshead type described above, but it has no thread on the pin and a plain head. To remove the fastener, you need to pry out the center pin, using a small screwdriver under the head. Take care not to damage the pin head or surround when you do this, especially where the fastener is in a prominent position.

58 Once the center pin has been popped out, the grip of the surround is released and you will find that it can be lifted out easily. When installing this type of fastener, grip the top of the pin so that it can be pushed back into place, then depress the pin head to lock it there.

General purpose trim fasteners

59 These are low tech, low cost versions of the types described above, and are widely used to secure odd bits of trim and the carpet sections. They have broad circular heads and are a simple push-fit in the associated panel. The only thing to remember with this type of fastener is that you need to lever them out from near the shank of the pin; if you lever near the outside of the head you'll probably find that it breaks off.

60 You can use a pair of screwdriver blades to lever them out, or if you have a pair of snipe (needle)-nose pliers with cranked ends, these work very well instead. Where the fasteners are used to hold carpets, do not attempt to get them out by pulling on the carpet; this usually just pulls the carpet over the head of the pin, and you'll then have to remove it by levering anyway.

Other plastic clips

61 There are many examples of plastic clips and stops which are pushed through holes in the bodywork. In most cases we note how they are best removed but, as a general rule, they'll be found to have small tabs which spring out to lock them in place. Always check around the back of the pin for these tabs: squeeze them together to free the clip.

Screw covers and blanking pieces

62 Where a visible screw head would be considered unsightly, you will probably find a small blanking cover fitted into the trim panel secured by the screw underneath. Again, we have generally described how these fit and how you need to remove them - the exact method varies a little.

63 Mostly, you can pry them out with a fine screwdriver blade, but be very careful not to lose them as they fly off - keep your hand or a finger over them to prevent this.

64 In some cases, these covers should only be fitted in one direction, and need to be removed at a specific point. In one or two examples, they are locked in position and need to be freed by depressing a locking pin or tab. It's not always obvious exactly where, or how, to do this.

65 We think that we have found and described all such fittings, but if we missed one or two types and there are no specific instructions in the text, do as we did, and work around the clip or cover to establish where it is held, and from this deduce how to go about freeing it. Usually, if you can't reach behind to free a locking tab, you need to lift the edge of a panel and free a hidden tab below it.

3. JACKING AND SUPPORTING THE CAR

1 There are a number of operations described in this manual which will require you to work under the car, so you need to make some provision for this. In an ideal world, we would all have vehicle lifts, but most of us must make do with less exotic equipment. When we worked on our project vehicle, we deliberately restricted ourselves to the use of equipment available to the average enthusiast owner, even though this made photographic access more difficult.

2 Unless you happen to have an access pit in the floor of your garage, you'll need to raise the car high enough to permit good working access below the body, while preserving complete personal safety. **Warning! Don't forget that a car is very heavy - if it collapses while you're under it, you'll be killed or badly injured: don't take any chances. Always make sure the car is absolutely safely supported on jack (axle) stands or metal ramps, and that wheels remaining on the ground are securely chocked. Do not go beneath a car supported by a jack or jacks alone.**

3 We used a small hydraulic jack with wheels and four large jack stands (axle stands/safety stands) to achieve good access during the work on our project car. You can purchase a suitable jack from tool or auto parts stores, or from mail order sources. We recommend that you avoid the small jacks which have a lifting capacity of 1500Kg/ 1.5 tons, which is adequate, but these small jacks have a restrictive lift range of only around 200mm/8 inches. The type of jack we used had a capacity of 2000Kg/ 2 tons and a lift range of just under 300mm/12 inches.

4 You'll find that the lift range is significant when you need to raise the car enough to work underneath. The further the jack can lift, the less need there will be to jack in stages, saving you a lot of time. As rule of thumb, buy the biggest lift capacity you can afford.

5 Jack stands (axle stands) come in various sizes too, and again, the rule is the bigger the better. Bigger versions are not only stronger than the smaller types, they allow you to raise the vehicle much higher, too, and every extra inch helps. There are a few operations on the car which will

Mazda Miata, MX-5, Eunos & Roadster

require at least 460mm/18 inches clearance underneath, and in all cases, more space means more comfortable working conditions. Remember that if you use a crawler board, you lose a little clearance.

6 ◻+ Jacking the vehicle to any height takes time because it often needs to be done in stages. We jacked each end of the vehicle in turn, supporting it on a pair of stands placed under the vehicle jacking points on the rockers (sills) with small wood blocks inserted to protect the paint/metalwork. Once we had raised one end part way, we positioned the first pair of stands, lowered the jack so that the vehicle was supported on the

3/6a Use wood strips to protect paint.

3/6b Chock wheels.

stands, and then moved to the other end of the car. **Warning!** If you are only jacking one end or side of the car, remember to chock those wheels which remain on the ground.

7 Next, we repeated the jacking operation and fitted a second pair of stands. Then we moved back to the other end and repeated the process until we had the car high enough to be able to work underneath. **Warning!** Don't be tempted to jack too much at each stage, because the vehicle will become unstable, and you may run out of jacking range.

8 ◻+ On one or two occasions we had to

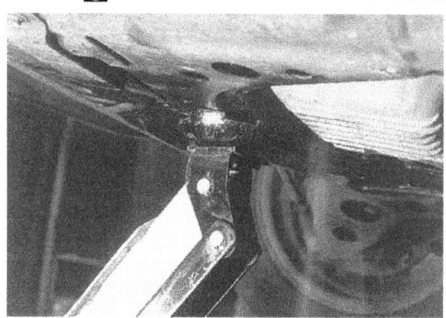
3/8a Jack pad at center of crossmember.

3/8b Jack pad at center of diff. casing.

use large pieces of lumber positioned under the jack wheels to get enough lift to raise the vehicle fully, because the hydraulic jack we had could only lift around a foot at a time. This is safe enough if you take great care to position the blocks accurately, and make sure that the jack is kept at the exact center of the car. At the front of the car we positioned the jack pad under the crossmember to the rear of the engine. At the back we used the differential casing as a lifting point. As luck would have it, the heavy finning at the bottom of the casing fitted neatly into the jack pad, locating it very securely.

9 If you decide to use our method, work carefully and methodically, checking that the supports are absolutely secure at each stage. Also, be sure to place wooden chocks on each side of the road wheels before starting, and remember that, once all four wheels have been raised clear of the ground, excessive jacking at either end might topple the car off its stands.

10 ◻ We suggest that you proceed cautiously, raising each end in turn by a few inches so that the car stays more or less level and minimizes this risk. It may be tempting to go for the maximum lift each time, but you increase the risk of toppling

3/10 Car safely supported.

if you do so. **Warning!** Finally, *before* you venture underneath, give the car a really good shake to check that there is absolutely no danger of it collapsing on top of you.

11 The car has four reinforced jacking points located near the ends of each sill. These are mostly intended for wheel changing, and the small scissor jack supplied with the car has a slotted pad which fits over the reinforced seam sections. Don't use these points for other types of jack. They do provide ideal locations for jack stands.

12 You may have noted the longitudinal box sections just inboard of the jacking points. These are strengthening sections which give rigidity to the floor. **Caution!** These box sections are definitely not suitable for jacking, and any attempt to raise the car at these points will simply collapse the box section.

13 There are a few operations which will require you to have the car raised enough for access underneath, but with the car supported on its wheels. An example of this is where work is carried out on the suspension. After completing an overhaul you'll need to have the car resting on its wheels while the suspension pivots are tightened. For this you need to use fabricated steel wheel ramps. You will need to fit the wheels, position the ramps below them and then lower the car onto the ramps.

14 ◻ For other tasks where temporary access is required and access to the suspension is not necessary, you can, in theory, drive the car up onto the ramps. In practice, however, the ramps usually skid across the floor as you attempt to do this, and we would advise jacking the car and then lowering it onto the stands. When doing this, position the ramp end nearest the garage door. That way you can drive the car off when work is finished.

3/14 Ramps allow good access.

4. CLEANING COMPONENTS

1 With just about any overhaul procedure on the car it is advisable to clean the area concerned before you start. Not only will this make the work easier, it will minimize the risk of dirt getting into the assembly in question.

2 For large areas, such as the underside of the car or engine compartment, a hot pressure wash is a good starting point. You might find this type of facility at a local carwash, or you could use a domestic pressure wash instead. Take care to protect vulnerable areas like electrical components or connectors from the ingress of water. Exposed connectors are usually splashproof, but will not withstand direct high pressure jets.

3 Tape up or cover vulnerable components with plastic bags before you start pressure washing. **Caution!** Remember that if you saturate connectors under the hood you stand a good chance of damaging electronic components if power is applied while they are wet. If you think connectors may have water inside them, disconnect and dry out before attempting to start the engine.

4 If you pressure wash the suspension, try to

1: General advice & technical specifications

keep the water away from the brake components, or you may find that the brakes will not work until they have dried out. If you think that you have soaked the brakes, drive very slowly with the brake pedal depressed lightly. The heat generated will quickly dry off the disc and pads.

5 During dismantling, use a proprietary degreasing solvent to clean parts as you work. **Warning!** Follow the maker's directions when using these cleaning products, and never use gasoline for cleaning purposes. When disposing of used solvents, do so responsibly with regard to the environment. In most areas, your local authority will be happy to advise about disposal methods and may provide such facilities.

6 **Warning!** When working on brake parts, use only brake cleaner or denatured alcohol (methylated spirit). Use of any other type of solvent may cause damage or deterioration of the seals, with a consequent risk of brake failure.

7 **Warning!** Brake friction materials may contain asbestos, which is hazardous if inhaled as dust. Wear gloves when handling dirty brake parts, and clean only with brake cleaner, disposing of contaminated rags or wipes safely. Never use compressed air to clean any brake part.

5. BUYING NEW PARTS

1 When buying parts you'll need to make a few decisions about where you source them. In the main, you'll probably want to obtain parts through your Mazda dealer, and this is certainly the safest option; you know that the parts you buy will fit correctly and be of good quality. If the car is still under warranty, use of non-genuine parts may invalidate it, so bear this in mind, too.

2 📷 🔍+ Major parts and assemblies will

5/2 Vehicle data on these firewall plates.

probably have to be obtained through a Mazda dealer. To save time when ordering parts, and to make sure that you get the correct part for your particular car, have ready as much information as possible. The main things to note are the VIN (Vehicle Identification Number) and the engine model and number. On automatic transmission cars, you should also note the model and number of the transmission. You will find this information in the locations pictured.

3 Your Mazda dealer can tell a lot about your car from these numbers. For example, they'll

D5/2A VIN (VEHICLE IDENTIFICATION NUMBER) STAMPED INTO FIREWALL HERE.

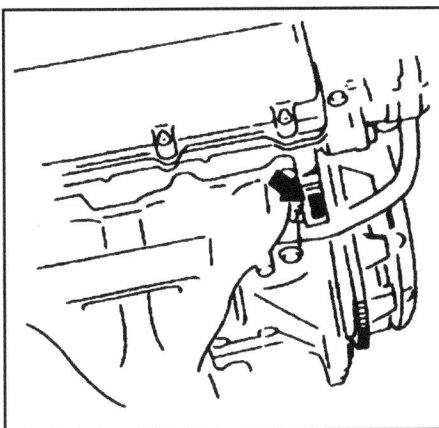

D5/2B ENGINE MODEL & NUMBER ARE HERE.

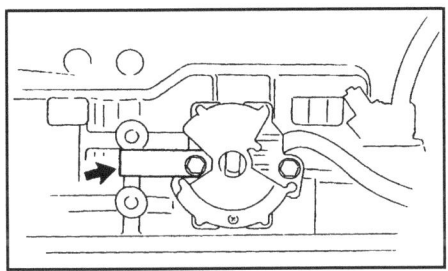

D5/2C AUTO. TRANS. MODEL & NUMBER HERE.

indicate any instances where a modification is required to rectify minor defects found after the car was built (major defects will have been covered by the normal recall procedures operating in most countries). If you order a part and a revised fitment is available, your dealer will be able to advise on this. This type of information is not generally available from other suppliers, and this alone helps offset the slightly higher prices charged by Mazda dealers.

4 You can purchase consumable items needed for maintenance procedures from other sources. Items such as sparkplugs, oil, brake pads and light bulbs can be found in most auto parts stores and some gas stations, and this may be more convenient and less expensive than a visit to your dealer. Remember that you'll need to check that any parts or materials obtained from such sources are suitable for use on your Mazda.

5 Auto parts stores will carry application charts and lists for many of the products they stock, and these will provide some guidance about suitability. Don't forget, though, that these lists are compiled by third-party manufacturers, and may not be 100 per cent reliable in all cases. The store is unlikely to be able to make too much sense of the vehicle details, but you should take these with you anyway - they may help. If at all possible, take with you the old part and check that the new component is identical.

6 The bigger auto parts stores may also carry things like clutches, brake parts, pistons and valves, though they tend to concentrate more on parts for mainstream family cars rather than sportscars. Prices are often lower than they would be from a franchised dealer, and the quality of the parts is generally good. The down side is that you can never be sure if non-original parts will perform or last as well as genuine parts. If you fit a non-original clutch disc, it may wear out more quickly than the original, and this will mean you need to fit another one sooner.

7 With items like brake pads, you can rarely tell by looking at them if the pad material is of the correct grade, and in extreme cases this has been known to be downright dangerous. We are not saying that non-original parts are no good; many are fine, and reputable stores will not sell you substandard parts. Do use your discretion, however, and don't be tempted to spoil a finely balanced car by using poor quality parts just to save a little money.

8 Finally, don't forget specialist suppliers like auto-electrical specialists, tire specialists and performance car and tuning specialists. The range of services offered by these companies is very wide and very variable, but often they may be able to supply parts or services that even franchised dealers have trouble with. We cannot give specific recommendations here - the best policy is to use tried and trusted local companies. In this respect, personal recommendation counts for far more than impressive trading premises.

6. TOOLS & EQUIPMENT

1 We've tried to base this manual on the type of tools that most enthusiasts will already have, and this is a difficult thing to define. You will not get very far using the tools which came with the car - they are intended for the most simple roadside repairs only, and few enthusiast owners will wish to travel far without a better selection in the trunk. On the other hand, only the most dedicated owner will have a fully equipped professional workshop at their disposal.

2 If you are experienced in car repairs and maintenance, you will already have the basic hand tools you need for almost any job on these cars (we assume that you will have metric sized tools). Where you need more specialized tools, this is indicated in the text.

3 If you are a newcomer to the delights of home maintenance and repair, we suggest that you begin building your tool set slowly. Don't be tempted by offers of hundreds of tools for next to nothing - the tools are badly made from inferior materials,

Mazda Miata, MX-5, Eunos & Roadster

and are usually worse than useless. Buy only quality tools as and when you can afford and need them, sticking to known, quality brands - in the long term you won't regret it.

4   Wrenches should cover the range 8mm to around 19mm - you will rarely need larger or smaller sizes than this. You will need both crescent (open-ended) and box-end (ring) wrenches (spanners) and, if money is tight, you can get both in the form of combination wrenches, with a box-end and crescent wrench combined in the same tool.

5   You will also need a $1/2$in drive socket set covering the range 8mm to around 30mm. The set will come with a range of extensions, T-bars and a ratchet, and you can expand on this as the need arises. Again, go for quality in preference to quantity. Just about every fastener will require torque tightening, so you will need a torque wrench. The preset type is best, but if money is tight, the simple bending beam type will suffice.

6   A range of screwdrivers with both slotted and crosshead tips will be required. Be especially careful with crosshead screwdrivers; these come in a variety of tip profiles, and you need to be careful that the type you choose fits snugly in the Japanese pattern screws. Many cheap brands will be a sloppy fit and will tear out the screw heads. You'll need several sizes in each type and, on occasions, you may also need specialized screwdrivers to reach awkward or inaccessible screws.

7   In addition to the above, you'll require pliers, needle-nosed pliers and a pair of electrical side cutters, plus self-grip pliers (Vise Grip, Mole Grip, or similar). Occasionally, you'll need snap ring (circlip) pliers, and this is one area where a cheap set with interchangeable tips will usually be adequate. You will also need items like Allen (socket) screw wrenches, feeler gauges and a sparkplug gapping/adjusting tool.

8   To supplement the basic list of hand tools described above, there are other pieces of equipment that you'll find essential for all but the most simple dismantling and installation work. We suggest that you acquire these as and when you need them to spread the cost a little. In most instances, we have indicated where these tools will be required.

General workshop tools
Wheeled hydraulic jack
Jack (axle) stands
Fabricated steel wheel ramps
Bench (with engineer's vise)
Large and small hammers (ball pein type)
$1/2$in cold chisel
Assorted drifts and punches (as required)
Plastic or rubber faced hammer
Steel straight edge and scribing tool
Hacksaw and blades
Assorted files and abrasive papers
Inspection light

Specialized tools
Multi-purpose puller
Valve spring compressor
Piston ring compressor
Impact driver
Balljoint separator
Engine hoist

Measuring equipment
Vernier caliper
Internal and external micrometer
Dial indicator gauge and stand, with clamp or magnetic base
Steel tape rule

Test equipment
Ohmmeter, voltmeter and ammeter (or a multimeter, which will cover ohms, volts amps and more besides)
Booster (jumper) leads
Continuity tester
Timing light (strobe type)
Engine compression tester
Thermometer
Spring scale

7. DEALING WITH BREAKDOWNS

INITIAL SAFETY

1   **Warning!** If your car suffers a roadside breakdown, the first consideration is safety - yours, your passenger's and that of other road users. If you can, get the car off the road, or at least try to stop where visibility is good. Don't forget that what might appear to be a clear view for a good distance while you are stationary, may seem a lot different to another vehicle approaching at speed. If your car has hazard warning lights, use them, even in daylight. In many European countries, all cars have to carry reflective warning triangles by law. These should be placed well in advance of your car. Anything which catches the attention of approaching drivers is a good thing.

WHAT'S THE PROBLEM?

2   Try to work out why the car has stopped. In some cases, this will be pretty obvious, but if there has been some mechanical failure it will help you or the repair/recovery service if you can give some indication of what went wrong. Perhaps you heard unusual noises, felt vibration or smelled or saw smoke just before the car broke down? Perhaps a warning light was on? If so, this information is likely to be significant and helpful in reaching a quicker diagnosis. For detailed troubleshooting information ☞ 15.

TOWING THE CAR

3   This may not be your problem, and a professional recovery driver should know how to deal with your car, but be aware of a couple of important points about your Mazda which affect towing procedures. We assume that you will comply with any local laws regarding safe towing practice.

Automatic transmission models
4   **Caution!** You should get the car recovered on a breakdown truck if possible. If it has to be towed, you should arrange to have a suspended tow with the **rear** wheels clear of the road. If the car has to be towed from the front, a towing dolly must be fitted under the rear wheels.

5   **Caution!** If you have no option but to tow with all four wheels on the ground, do not tow at more than 35mph/56kph or for more than 35 miles/56km or you'll damage the transmission. **Warning!** Release the parking brake, shift into **N** (neutral) and set the ignition switch to **ACC** before towing commences. If you need to tow for longer distances without a towing dolly, you'll have to remove the propshaft to isolate the transmission and prevent damage.

Manual transmission models
6   Generally less of a problem than towing an auto transmission car - you won't damage the transmission by towing. **Warning!** Release the parking brake, shift into neutral and set the ignition switch to **ACC** *before* towing commences.

All models
7   **Caution!** Mazda cautions that the hooks at the front and rear of the car are for tie-down purposes only and are not designed for towing. Mazda states that damage to the car bodywork may result if these points are used for towing, and this may well be right. The front tie-down hooks lie inside the air intake, and there is every chance that a jerking tow rope would damage the surrounding bodywork. Unfortunately, there is no better towing point that we could find. Mazda acknowledges the problem, but does not suggest any alternative to the tie-down hooks. We can only suggest that you exercise great caution if you do tow from these hooks.

8   **Warning!** If you are steering your car while being towed by another vehicle (check that it is legal to do this in your area first), remember that, without the engine running, there will be no electrical power apart from that provided by the battery. You'll need to operate brake and turn signal lights, but the Mazda's reserve battery capacity is limited, so try not to use the headlights which will rapidly discharge the battery: where possible, avoid towing at night altogether.

9   **Warning!** Without the engine running, the power brake system and the power steering (where fitted) will be inoperative. The steering and brakes will still work, but will require much more effort: be prepared for this.

10   **Warning!** Being towed by another car requires a little skill and, unless you trust the driver of the tow car completely, can be a frightening experience. Before you start out, agree your route and speed, and arrange some sort of signal (such as flashing the towed car's headlights) to indicate to the tow car that you wish to stop.

11   When you move off, the tow car should creep forward until the slack in the tow rope is taken up. The driver of the car being towed should use the brakes to make sure that the rope stays taut at all times, and this means that he will have to anticipate when the driver of the tow car is likely to start slowing. To some extent, the car being towed

1: General advice & technical specifications

should be braking for both cars. If you can get this to work smoothly, you are unlikely to suffer from the rope breaking, but get it wrong and you will break the rope. Note also the comments about the risk of damage to the bodywork if you tow from the tie-down hooks - you'll minimize this risk if you keep the rope taut.

8. TECHNICAL SPECIFICATIONS

GENERAL

Dimensions
Overall length	3948mm/155.4in
Overall width	1676mm/65.9in
Overall height	1230mm/48.4in
Wheelbase	2265mm/89.2in
Tread (Track):	
Front	1410mm/55.5in
Rear	1428mm/56.2in

Transmission
Type	
Standard	5-speed manual
Optional	4-speed automatic

Chassis
Type	Unitary steel body, steel and plastic panels
Suspension	Fully independent front and rear. Adjustable double-wishbone Coils springs, gas-filled shock absorbers. Front & rear stabilizer bars
Steering	Rack-and-pinion, optional engine speed-sensing power steering
Brakes	Power-assisted disc, dual circuit hydraulics
Tires	185/60R 14 82H (14 inch wheels)
	195/50R15 81V (15 inch wheels)
	Other sizes may be found as original equipment.

ENGINE - DETAIL

Type	In-line 4-cylinder, dohc, 4-stroke
Combustion chamber type	Pentroof
Displacement	1840cc/112cu in
Bore	83mm/3.27in
Stroke	85mm/3.35in
Compression ratio	9.0:1
Compression pressure	1255kPa/12.8kgf cm2/182psi at 300rpm
Valve system	Belt-driven, dohc 16 valve
Valve timing	
Intake opens at	5° BTDC
Intake closes at	48° ABDC
Exhaust opens at	56° BBDC
Exhaust closes at	14° ATDC
Valve clearances	0 (hydraulic lifters)

Cylinder head
Material	Aluminum alloy
Height	133.8-134.0mm/5.268-5.276in
Maximum distortion	0.10mm/0.004in
Grinding limit	0.20mm/0.008in
Cylinder head to HLA clearance	
Standard	0.025-0.066mm/0.0099-0.00259in
Maximum	0.18mm/0.0071in

Valves and guides
Valve head margin width	
Intake	0.9mm/0.035in
Exhaust	1.0mm/0.039in
Valve face angle	45°
Valve length - standard	
Intake	101.89mm/4.0114in
Exhaust	101.99mm/4.0153in

Mazda Miata, MX-5, Eunos & Roadster

Valve length - minimum
    Intake 100.39mm/3.9524in
    Exhaust 100.49mm/3.9563in
Valve stem diameter
    Intake 5.970-5.985mm/0.2351-0.2356in
    Exhaust 5.965-5.980mm/0.2349-0.2354in
Valve stem diameter - minimum
    Intake 5.920mm/0.2331in
    Exhaust 5.915mm/0.2329in
Valve guide bore diameter
    Intake & exhaust 6.01-6.03mm/0.2367-0.2374in
Valve stem to guide clearance
    Intake 0.025-0.060mm/0.0010-0.0023in
    Exhaust 0.030-0.065mm/0.0012-0.0025in
    Service limit 0.020mm/0.008in
Valve guide projection above head surface
    Intake & exhaust 18.3-18.9mm/0.721-0.744in

Valve seats
Valve seat angle .... 45°
Contact width 0.8-1.4mm/0.032-0.055in
Rebate in head
    Standard 43.5mm/1.713in
    Maximum 45.0mm/1.772in

Valve springs
Free length (standard)
    Intake & exhaust 46.26mm/1.821in
Free length - minimum
    Intake & exhaust .... 39.5mm/1.560in (at set load of 224-253N/22.8-25.8kg/50.2-56.7lb)
Out-of-square limit
    Intake & exhaust 1.62mm/0.0638in

Camshafts
Cam lobe height
    Intake 44.094mm/1.7360in
    Service limit 43.894mm/1.7281in
    Exhaust 44.600mm/1.7559in
    Service limit 44.400mm/1.7480in
Camshaft journal diameter
    Standard 25.940-25.965mm/1.0213-1.0222in
    Out-of-round limit 0.03mm/0.0012in
Camshaft bearing oil clearance
    Standard 0.035-0.081mm/0.0014-0.0031in
    Service limit 0.15mm/0.006in
Camshaft runout (maximum) 0.03mm/0.0012in
Camshaft endfloat/endplay/lash
    Standard 0.07-0.19mm/0.0028-0.0074in
    Service limit 0.20mm/0.008in

Cylinder block
Height 221.5mm/8.720in
Maximum distortion 0.15mm/0.006in
Grinding limit 0.20mm/0.008in
Cylinder bore diameter
    Standard 83.000-83.019mm/3.2678-3.2684in
    +0.25mm/0.010in oversize 83.256-83.263mm/3.2778-3.2780in
    +0.50mm/0.020in oversize 83.506-83.513mm/3.2877-3.2879in
Maximum bore taper/ovality 0.019mm/0.0007in

Pistons
Piston diameter (90 degrees to pin bore, 16.5mm below oil ring groove base)
    Standard 82.954-82.974mm/3.2660-3.2666in
    +0.25mm/0.010in oversize 83.211-83.217mm/3.2761-3.2762in
    +0.50mm/0.020in oversize 83.461-83.467mm/3.2859-3.2861in
Piston to cylinder bore clearance

1: General advice & technical specifications

    Standard 0.032-0.059mm/0.0013-0.0023in
    Service limit 0.15mm/0.006in

Piston rings
End gap (ring installed in bore)
    Top 0.15-0.30mm/0.006-0.011in
    2nd 0.15-0.30mm/0.006-0.011in
    Oil (rail) 0.20-0.70mm/0.008-0.027in
    Service limit (all rings) 1.0mm/0.039in
Piston ring to groove clearance
    Top 0.03-0.065mm/0.0012-0.0025in
    2nd 0.03-0.07mm/0.0012-0.0027in
    Service limit 0.15mm/0.006in

Piston (gudgeon/wrist) pins
Diameter 19.987-19.993mm/0.7869-0.7871in
Pin to piston clearance .... -0.005-0.013mm/-0.0002-0.0005in

Connecting rods
Connecting rod (small end) bush inner diameter 20.003-20.014mm/0.7876-0.7879in
Connecting rod (small end) bush to piston pin clearance 0.010-0.027mm/0.0004-0.0010in
Length between centers 132.85-132.95mm/5.231-5.234in
Bend limit .... 0.050mm/0.0020in per 50mm/1.97in
Side clearance (at crankpin)
    Standard 0.110-0.262mm/0.0044-0.0103in
    Service limit 0.30mm/0.012in

Crankshaft
Runout (maximum) 0.04mm/0.0016in
Main bearing journal diameter
    Standard 49.938-49.956mm/1.9661-1.9667in
    -0.25mm/-0.010in 49.704-49.708mm/1.9569-1.9570in
    -0.50mm/-0.020in 49.454-49.458mm/1.9470-1.9471in
    -0.75mm/-0.30in 49.204-49.208mm/1.9372-1.9373in
Main bearing journal taper & ovality limit 0.05mm/0.0020in
Crankpin diameter
    Standard 44.940-49.956mm/1.7693-1.7699in
    -0.25mm/-0.010in 44.690-44.706mm/1.7595-1.7600in
    -0.50mm/-0.020in 44.440-44.456mm/1.7497-1.7502in
    -0.75mm/-0.30in 44.190-44.206mm/1.7398-1.7403in
Crankpin taper & ovality limit 0.05mm/0.0020in

Main bearings
Oil clearance
    Standard 0.018-0.036mm/0.0008-0.0014in
    Service limit 0.10mm/0.004in
Available undersizes .... -0.25, -0.50 & -0.75mm/-0.010, -0.020 & -0.030in

Connecting rod (big end/crankpin) bearings
Oil clearance
    Standard 0.022-0.044mm/0.0009-0.0017in
    Service limit 0.10mm/0.004in
Available undersizes .... -0.25, -0.50 & -0.75mm/-0.010, -0.020 & -0.030in

Crankshaft thrust bearings
Crankshaft endfloat (endplay/lash)
    Standard 0.080-0.282mm/0.0032-0.0111in
    Service limit 0.30mm/0.012in
Thrust bearing width
    Standard 2.500-2.550mm/0.0985-0.1003in
    +0.25mm/+0.010in 2.625-2.675mm/0.1034-0.1053in
    +0.50mm/+0.020in 2.750-2.800mm/0.1083-0.1102in
    +075mm/+0.030in 2.875-2.925mm/0.1132-0.1151in

Camshaft drivebelt (timing belt)
Deflection (between cam pulleys) at 98N/10kg/22lb 9.0-11.5mm/0.36-0.45in

Mazda Miata, MX-5, Eunos & Roadster

LUBRICATION SYSTEM (ENGINE)

Oil pump
Type .... Trochoid gear
Relief pressure 344-441kPa/3.5-4.5kg cm2/50-63psi)
Oil pressure
    At 1000 rpm 98-196kPa/1.0-2.0kgf cm2/15-28psi
    At 3000 rpm 295-392kPa/3.0-4.0kgf cm2/43-56psi
Inner rotor tip to outer rotor clearance
    Standard 0.02-0.18mm/0.0008-0.0070in
    Service limit 0.20mm/0.0079in
Outer rotor to pump body clearance
    Standard 0.09-0.18mm/0.0036-0.0070in
    Service limit 0.20mm/0.0079in
Side clearance
    Standard 0.03-0.12mm/0.0012-0.0047in
    Service limit 0.14mm/0.0055in

Oil filter
Type .... Full-flow, paper element, canister
Relief pressure 79-117kPa/0.8-1.2kgf cm2/12-17psi

Engine oil
Capacity
    Dry engine .... 4 liters/4.2 US qt/3.5 Imp qt
    Refill only .... 3.6liters/3.8 US qt/3.2 Imp qt
    Refill & new oil filter .... 3.75 liters/4.0 US qt/3.3 Imp qt
Grade .... API SG, SH or higher (ECII)
Viscosity
    Above -25 degrees C (-13F) .... SAE 10W-30
    Below 0 degrees C (32F) .... SAE 5W-30

COOLING SYSTEM

General
Type .... Pump assisted thermosyphon, electric cooling fan
Coolant capacity .... 6.0 liters/6.3 US qt/5.3 Imp qt
Coolant mixture percentages & specific gravity
    Above -16 degrees C (3F) .... 65 per cent water, 35 per cent antifreeze (SG 1.054)
    Above -26 degrees C (-15F) .... 55 per cent water, 45 per cent antifreeze (SG 1.066)
    Above -40 degrees C (-40F) .... 45 per cent water, 55 per cent antifreeze (SG 1.078)

Water pump
Pump type .... Belt-driven, centrifugal
Pump seal .... Unified mechanical

Thermostat
Type .... Wax, two stage
Opening temperature
    Sub .... 83.5-86.5 degrees C (183-187F)
    Main .... 86.5-89.5 degrees C (188-193F)
Full-open temperature .... 100 degrees C (212F)
Full-open lift
    Sub .... 1.5mm/0.06in minimum
    Main .... 8.0mm/0.31in minimum

Radiator
Type .... Corrugated fin
Cap opening pressure 73.6-102kPa/0.75-1.05kg cm2/10.7-14.9psi
Cooling system checking pressure 103kPa/1.05kg cm2/14.9psi
Fan type .... Electric
Number of blades 5
Fan diameter 320mm/12.6in
Fan motor rating .... 12 volt, 70W (man. trans.)/80W (auto. trans.)
Fan motor current .... 5.9 amps (man. trans.)/6.7 amps (auto. trans.)

1: General advice & technical specifications

FUEL AND EMISSION CONTROL SYSTEMS

General
Ignition timing .... 9-11 degrees BTDC

Throttle body
Throat diameter 55mm/2.2in

Fuel pump
Type .... Impeller (immersed in fuel tank)
Output pressure 480-657kPa/4.9-6.7kg cm2/69-95psi

Fuel filter
Type
    Low pressure .... Nylon strainer
    High pressure .... Paper element

Fuel pressure regulator
Type .... Diaphragm
Regulating pressure .... 265-314kPa/2.7-3.2 kg cm2/38-46psi

Injectors
Type .... High ohmic
Drive type .... Voltage
Resistance .... 12-16 ohms at 20 degrees C (68F)

Idle air control (IAC) valve
Resistance .... 10.7-12.3 ohms at 20 degrees C (68F)

Air valve
Opening temperature .... Below 40 degrees C (104F)

Purge solenoid valve
Resistance .... 23-27 ohms at 20 degrees C (68F)

Camshaft position sensor
Type .... Hall element

Engine coolant temperature sensor
Resistances
    20 degrees C (68F) .... 2.21-2.69 kilo ohms
    80 degrees C (179F) .... 0.287-0.349 kilo ohms

Fuel tank
Capacity .... 48 liters/12.7 US gal/10,5 Imp gal

Air cleaner
Type .... Disposable paper element

Accelerator cable
Lash (freeplay) 1-3mm/0.039-0.118in

Fuel
Specified grade
    (R+M)/2 method .... 87 octane or higher, unleaded
    RON (Research Octane Number) method .... 90 or higher, unleaded
    Warning! Do not use leaded fuel.

ELECTRICAL SYSTEM (ENGINE)

Battery
Type .... S46A24L(S), maintenance-free, gel electrolyte
Capacity .... 32 amp hours
Voltage & polarity .... 12 volt, negative (-) ground (earth)
Dark current .... 20.0 mA (ignition switch OFF)

Mazda Miata, MX-5, Eunos & Roadster

Alternator
Type .... AC
Output
    Manual transmission .... 12 volt, 60 amps
    Automatic transmission .... 12 volt, 70 amps
Regulator type .... Built-in IC regulator
Regulated voltage .... 14.3-14.9 volts
Brush length
    Standard 21.5mm/0.85in
    Service limit 8mm/0.32in
Drivebelt deflection
    New 5.5-7mm/0.22-0.27in
    Used 6-7.5mm/0.4-0.29in

Starter motor
Type .... Direct (man. trans.); coaxial reduction (auto. trans.)
Output .... 12.0 volts, 0.95kW (man. trans.); 12 volts, 1.4kW (auto. trans.)
Brush length
    Standard .... 17.0mm/0.67in (man. trans.); 17.5mm/0.69in (auto. trans.)
    Service limit .... 11.5mm/0.45in (man. trans.); 12.0mm/0.47in (auto. trans.)

Ignition system
Type .... Electronic, electronic spark (ignition) advance (ESA)
Advance control .... By PCM (Powertrain Control Module)/ECU
Ignition timing (with data link TEN terminals grounded)
    Manual transmission .... 10 degrees BTDC at 850rpm
    Automatic transmission .... 10 degrees BTDC at 800rpm
Ignition coil .... Molded, incorporating ignition control mudule
Ignition coil primary winding resistance .... Not applicable
Ignition coil secondary winding resistance .... 8.7-12.9 kilo ohms
Sparkplugs - standard fitment
    NGK BKR5E-11
    NipponDenso K16PR-U11
Sparkplugs - alternative fitments
    NGK BKR6E-11
    NipponDenso K20PR-U11
Plug gap 1.0-1.1mm/0.040-0.043in
Firing order .... 1-3-4-2 (number one cylinder nearest radiator)

CLUTCH

Type .... Single dry plate
Control type .... Hydraulic
Pedal type .... Pendant
Pedal ratio 6.13
Pedal stroke 120mm/4.72in
Pedal height (from carpet) 175-185mm/6.89-7.28in
Flywheel runout limit 0.2mm/0.008in
Clutch disc runout limit 0.7mm/0.028in
Clutch disc outer diameter 215mm/8.46in
Clutch disc inner diameter 150mm/5.91in
Friction material thickness
    Flywheel side 3.5mm/0.14in
    Clutch cover side 3.8mm/0.15in
Clutch disc minimum thickness .... 0.3mm/0.012in above rivet heads
Clutch cover type .... Diaphragm spring
Installed pressure 4.310N/440kg/968lb

TRANSMISSION (GEARBOX), MANUAL

Type .... 5-speed, synchromesh, floor shift
Oil capacity .... 2.0 liters/2.1 US qt/1.8 Imp qt
Oil grade
    Above 10 degrees C (50F) .... API GL-4 , GL-5 or higher SAE 80W-90
    All seasons .... API Service GL-4, GL-5 or higher SAE 75W-90
    Synthetic oils work well with this transmission

1: General advice & technical specifications

Gear ratios
    1st 3.136:1
    2nd 1.888:1
    3rd 1.330:1
    4th 1.000:1
    5th 0.814:1
    Reverse 3.758:1
Mainshaft
    Max. runout 0.03mm/0.0012in
    Shaft to gear/bush clearance .... 0.15mm/0.006in max
Reverse idler gear
    Bush to shaft clearance 0.02-0.05mm/0.0008-0.0020in
    Bush to shaft clearance (max) 0.15mm/0.006in
Shift fork & rod
    Fork to clutch sleeve clearance 0.2-0.3mm/0.008-0.012in
    Fork to clutch sleeve clearance (max) 0.5mm/0.020in
    Shift rod gate to control lever clearance .... 0.8mm/0.032in max
Synchronizer ring to gear face clearance (installed)
    Standard 1.5mm/0.059in
    Service limit 0.8mm/0.031in
Shift rod 5th/reverse spring
    Free length 76.5mm/3.012in
1st/2nd detent ball spring
    Free length 22.5mm/0.886in
3rd/4th detent ball spring
    Free length 22.5mm/0.886in
5th/reverse detent ball spring
    Free length 17.0mm/0.669in

TRANSMISSION, AUTOMATIC

ATF capacity
    Total .... 6.7 liters/7.1 US qt/5.9 Imp qt
    Oil pan .... 4.0 liters/4.2 US qt/3.5 Imp qt
ATF grade .... Dexron II or M-III
Gear ratios
    1st 2.841:1
    2nd 1.458:1
    3rd 1.000:1
    OD (4th) 0.720:1
    Reverse 2.182:1
Torque converter stall torque ratio 1.900:1
Engine stall speed
    R, D, S, L ranges 2750-3150rpm
Time lag
    N to D range .... 0.5-1.5 seconds
    N to R range .... 0.7-1.7 seconds
Line pressure at idle
    D range 314-372kPa/3.2-3.8kg cm2/43-54psi
    S range 785-921kPa/8.0-9.4kg cm2/114-133psi
    L range 314-372kPa/3.2-3.8kg cm2/43-54psi
    R range 392-490kPa/4.0-5.0kg cm2/57-71psi
Line pressure at stall
    D range 804-922kPa/8.2-9.4kg cm2/117-133psi
    S range 785-921kPa/8.0-9.4kg cm2/114-133psi
    L range 804-922kPa/8.2-9.4kg cm2/117-133psi
    R range 392-490kPa/19.2-21.1kg cm2/273-300psi
Specified line pressure
    Barometric 1884-2069kPa/19.2-21.1kg cm2/273-300psi
    200mm Hg/7.87in Hg 1226-1324kPa/12.5-13.5kg cm2/178-192psi
    400mm Hg/15.7in Hg 390-490kPa/4.0-5.0kg cm2/57-71psi

DRIVESHAFT (PROPSHAFT)

Maximum runout 0.4mm/0.016in

Mazda Miata, MX-5, Eunos & Roadster

FRONT AXLE

Wheel bearing type .... Angular ball, integral with hub
Wheel bearing play (max) 0.05mm/0.002in

REAR AXLE

Wheel bearing type .... Angular ball, integral with hub
Wheel bearing play (max) 0.05mm/0.002in
Axleshafts (driveshafts/halfshafts) .... Constant velocity with two joints

DIFFERENTIAL

Type .... Standard or Torsen type B limited slip
Reduction gear type .... Hypoid gear
Reduction ratio .... 4.100:1 (man. trans.); 4.300:1 (auto.trans)
Differential gear type .... Straight-cut bevel
Ring gear size 182.88mm/7.20in
Drive pinion preload (oil seal removed) .... 0.9-1.3Nm/9-14kgf cm/7.9-12.1 lbf in
Backlash
    Side and pinion gears 0-0.1mm/0-0.0039in
    Ring gear 0.09-0.11mm/0.0035-0.0043in
Oil
    Grade .... API GL-5 or higher
    Above -18 degrees C/0F .... Viscosity SAE 90W
    Below -18 degrees C/0F .... Viscosity SAE 80W
    Capacity .... 1.00 liter/1.06 US qt/0.88 Imp qt

STEERING

Steering wheel
Outer diameter 370mm/14.6in
Free play 0-30mm/0-1.18in
Turns, lock-to-lock
    Manual 3.36
    Power 2.80

Steering column assembly
Type .... Collapsible
Joint type .... 2-cross joints

Steering system
Mechanism .... Rack-and-pinion, manual or power assisted (engine speed sensing)
Rack stroke 121mm/4.76in
Fluid type (power steering) .... ATF Dexron II or M-III
Fluid capacity (power steering) .... 0.8 liter/0.85 US qt/0.70 Imp qt

BRAKING SYSTEM

Hydraulic fluid
Fluid type .... SAE J1703 or FMVSS116 DOT-3 or DOT-4

Brake pedal
Type .... Pendant
Height (carpet installed) 171-181mm/6.73-7.13in
Freeplay (lash) 4-7mm/0.16-0.28in
Reserve travel* 95mm/3.74in
(*Carpet removed, clearance with pedal depressed with force of 589N/60kg/132Ib)
Lever ratio 4.1:1

Master cylinder
Type .... Tandem
Bore 22.22mm/0.875in

Front brakes
Type .... Disc, ventilated

1: General advice & technical specifications

Pad area x thickness
    Standard .... 1849mm2 x 8mm/2.76in2 x 0.31in
    Service limit 1.0mm/0.04in
Disc area (effective diameter) x thickness
    Standard .... 255.0mm x 20mm/10.04in x 0.79in
    Service limit 18.0mm/0.71in
Disc maximum runout 0.05mm/0.002in
Caliper bore diameter 51.1mm/2.01in

Rear brakes
Type .... Disc, solid
Pad area x thickness
    Standard .... 2704mm2 x 8.0mm/4.19in x 0.31in
    Service limit thickness 1.0mm/0.04in
Disc area (effective diameter) x thickness
    Standard .... 251.0mm x 9.0mm/9.88in x 0.35in
    Service limit thickness 8.0mm/0.31in
Disc maximum runout 0.05mm/0.002in
Caliper bore diameter 31.75mm/1.25in

Parking brake (handbrake)
Type .... Rear wheels only, mechanical via cables
Adjustment .... 7-9 notches with 196N/20kg/44lb pull

Power brake (servo) unit
Type .... Single diaphragm
Diameter 214mm/8.0in

WHEELS AND TIRES

Wheels
Size
    Standard .... 14 x 5 1/2-JJ or 15 x 6-JJ
                                                   Other sizes, too, may be found as original equipment
    Temporary spare .... 14 X 4T
Offset 45mm/1.77in
Pitch circle diameter 100mm/3.94in
Material
    Standard .... Aluminum alloy or steel
    Temporary spare .... Steel

Tires
Size
    Standard .... P185/60R14 82H or 195/50R15
                                                   Other sizes, too, may be found as original equipment
    Temporary spare T115/70D14
Air pressure (US and Canada)
    Standard 177kPa/1.8kg cm2/26psi
    Temporary spare .... 412kPa/4.2kg cm2/60 psi

Wheel & tire
Wheel runout limit (at rim)
    Horizontal 1.5mm/0.0591in
    Vertical 2.0mm/0.0787in
Maximum imbalance (at rim edge) 10g/0.35oz

SUSPENSION

Front
Type .... Double wishbone, coil spring & telescopic shock absorber
Stabilizer bar (anti-roll bar) diameter 19mm/0.75in
    Other markets .... Check with dealer
Shock absorber type .... Double-acting, low-pressure gas-charged

Rear
Type .... Double wishbone, coil spring & telescopic shock absorber

Mazda Miata, MX-5, Eunos & Roadster

Stabilizer bar (anti-roll bar) diameter 11mm/0.43in
Shock absorber type .... Double-acting, low-pressure gas-charged

Wheel alignment - front
(Alignment measured with full fuel tank, correct coolant and engine oil levels, spare tire, jack and tools in correct position in trunk, but no driver/passenger or other load in car.)
Total toe-in
    Dimension .... 3mm (plus or minus 4mm)/0.12in (plus or minus 0.15in)
    Degrees .... 0 degrees 18 minutes (plus or minus18 minutes)
Maximum steering angle
    Inner .... 37 degrees 23 minutes (plus or minus 2 degrees)
    Outer .... 3 degrees 32 minutes (plus or minus 2 degrees)
Camber angle .... 0 degrees 24 minutes (plus or minus 1 degree)
Camber angle (max difference left to right) .... 1 degrees 30 minutes
Caster angle .... 4 degrees 30 minutes (plus or minus 1 degree)
King pin inclination (kpi) .... 11 degrees 20 minutes

Wheel alignment - rear
(Alignment measured with full fuel tank, correct coolant and engine oil levels, spare tire, jack and tools in correct position in trunk, but no driver/passenger or other load in car.)
Total toe-in
    Dimension .... 3mm (plus or minus 4mm)/0.12in (plus or minus 0.15in)
    Degrees .... 0 degrees 18 minutes (plus or minus18 minutes)
Camber angle .... 0 degrees 43 minutes (plus or minus 1 degree)
Camber angle (max difference left to right) .... 1 degrees 30 minutes

ELECTRICAL SYSTEM (BODY)

Instrument panel lamps (all 12 volt)
High beam warning 3.4W
Turn signal 3.4W
Illumination 3.4W
Engine check 1.4W
Brake 1.4W
Charge 1.4W
Seatbelts 1.4W
Air bag 1.4W
Headlight retractor 1.4W
O/D off 1.4W
ABS system 1.4W
Washer low 1.4W
Rear window defrost 1.4W

Exterior lights
Note: for markets other than US, Canada and UK check official "Owners Manual" (handbook) that came with car for bulb specification.
Headlights
    US and Canada 60/40W
    UK 60/55W
Front turn signal/parking (US and Canada) 27/8W
Front turn signal (UK) 21W
Front side marker (US and Canada) 3.8W
Side turn signal (UK) 5W
License plate
    US and Canada 7.5W
    UK 5W
Rear turn signal
    US and Canada 27W
    UK 21W
Rear side marker 3.8W
Brake/tail
    US and Canada 27/8W
    UK 21/5W
Backup (reversing) lights
    US and Canada 27W
    UK 21W
Hi-mount brakelight

1: General advice & technical specifications

US and Canada	21W
UK	18.4W
Parking lights (UK)	5W
Fog light, rear (UK)	21

Interior lights

Interior light	8W
Ashtray	3.4W
Heater control panel	1.4
A/C switch	1.4W
Hazard switch	1.4W
Cruise control switch	1.4W
Trunk light	3.8

AIR CONDITIONING SYSTEM

Refrigerant type	R-134a

Veloce SpeedPro books –

978-1-903706-59-6   978-1-903706-75-6   978-1-903706-76-3   978-1-903706-99-2   978-1-845840-21-1   978-1-787111-68-4

978-1-787111-69-1   978-1-787111-73-8   978-1-845841-87-4   978-1-845842-07-9   978-1-845842-08-6   978-1-845842-62-8

978-1-845842-89-5   978-1-845842-97-0   978-1-845843-15-1   978-1-845843-55-7   978-1-845844-33-2   978-1-845844-38-7

978-1-845844-83-7   978-1-845846-15-2   978-1-845848-33-0   978-1-787111-76-9   978-1-845848-69-9   978-1-845849-60-3

978-1-845840-19-8   978-1-787110-92-2   978-1-787110-47-2   978-1-903706-94-7   978-1-787110-87-8   978-1-787110-90-8

978-1-787110-01-4   978-1-901295-26-9   978-1-845841-62-1   978-1-787110-91-5   978-1-787110-88-5   978-1-903706-78-7

2
Tune-up & maintenance

1. INTRODUCTION

Regular maintenance is *vitally* important for the long term health of your car. Ignoring the recommended maintenance procedures will invariably lead to a general deterioration as many areas of minor wear or incorrect adjustment mount up. In the longer term, high repair bills become inevitable. More significantly, the inexorable decline of any neglected car means that driving enjoyment and fuel economy are impaired, resale value is adversely affected and, eventually, the safety of the driver and other road users is compromised.

By definition, most owners of Mazda's popular roadster are enthusiasts and, as such, will want to ensure that their car is kept in top condition. We suggest that you add cleaning and polishing to regular mechanical maintenance procedures: as you wash the vehicle, you automatically give it a close visual inspection, and this is fundamental to the maintenance of body and external fittings.

Once you start to get into regular maintenance checks, you will find that you'll begin to spot potential trouble before serious problems develop. Very often these will be outside conventional maintenance procedures, but the fact that general scrutiny is required during maintenance tasks ensures that incidental items, like burned out bulbs, cracked lenses or damaged wiring, get spotted along the way.

In most cases, the procedures required to carry out maintenance work are straightforward and require no special tools or skills; even where this is not the case, or if you decide to let a professional mechanic take care of the work for you, be aware of what is required at each service interval. That way you can be sure that the necessary work has been carried out correctly.

Please note that the initial check/service of a new car should be carried out by a Mazda dealer in order to preserve the car's warranty. For this reason we have not included details of the initial check/service.

In the maintenance schedules which follow, we have adhered closely to Mazda's recommendations, which means that you will be able to maintain your car as its maker intended. We've also added a few extra items of our own which we believe will prove worthwhile. Each maintenance item is marked to indicate whether it is an official Mazda procedure or one recommended by us.

○ Denotes an official Mazda maintenance operation.
❏ Denotes a Veloce-recommended maintenance operation, additional to the official schedule.

Where necessary, maintenance operations are referenced to a procedure described in this chapter or elsewhere in the manual. If you want more information on a particular component, system or procedure, you'll usually find more to read in the related chapter.

THE BASIS OF MAINTENANCE INTERVALS

Mazda's official maintenance schedules are based on an anticipated average monthly mileage for the market area in which the car was originally sold. In addition to this factor, there is a minimum time interval at which each maintenance operation must be undertaken. Also taken into consideration are other factors, such as prevailing operating conditions, plus local conventions/legislation about maintenance intervals in each market.

ABNORMAL OPERATING CONDITIONS - US MARKET CARS

Owners of US market cars should follow the maintenance schedule laid out in section 2A below wherever normal operating conditions apply. In areas where unusually harsh environmental conditions apply, or where the type of usage might cause accelerated wear, Mazda has prescribed a revised set of mileage/time intervals and operations. These appear within the maintenance schedule described in section 2B. Mazda's list of criteria for abnormal operating conditions follows. If your car is subject to any of these criteria, use the schedule in section 2B to maintain your car.

Repeated short distance driving
Driving in dusty conditions
Driving in areas where road salt or other corrosive materials are used
Driving on rough or muddy roads
Extended periods of idling and/or low-speed operation
Driving for prolonged periods in cold temperatures and/or extremely humid conditions

HOW TO INTERPRET MAINTENANCE SCHEDULES

Whichever schedule is applicable to your car and market, each interval heading comprises both a time and distance factor. It is important that you carry out the prescribed maintenance operation at **whichever** of these points is reached **first.**

Apart from the weekly checks, all maintenance operations are based around the time/mileage intervals. As soon as you reach either one of these points, you need to carry out all the operations listed under that heading. This means, for example, that if your car does a lot of miles, you may end up doing the 6 month or 7500 mile or 12,000km maintenance sequence every four or five months. Conversely, if you do lots of short journeys, you may need to carry out these tasks after only 4000 miles, if the six month time interval has been reached.

Depending on market, once the car reaches an age of 60-72 months or a mileage of 54,000-60,000 miles/90,000-96,000km, the maintenance cycle starts again from the original threshold. When this happens, remember that you'll need to be increasingly vigilant when it comes to inspecting components and checking systems; age and use will begin to have a more marked effect, particularly upon things like hoses, sparkplug wires, wheel bearings and brake internal parts, etc. You should

Mazda Miata, MX-5, Eunos & Roadster

also pay ever closer attention to the main body structure, watching out for signs of corrosion and ageing.

2A. MAINTENANCE SCHEDULE: USA

Note: This schedule relates to US market cars used under normal driving conditions. If you use your car in harsh conditions (see earlier description) follow the schedule described in section 2B.

☞ 1/1,2 & 2/1.

WEEKLY

ENGINE
❏ Check the engine oil level ☞ 2/3
❏ Check the engine coolant level ☞ 2/14

ELECTRICAL
❏ Check the operation of the electrical components, particularly lights ☞ 2/15
❏ Raise and clean the headlights ☞ 2/15
❏ If you suspect a problem, remove and check the battery ☞ 2/11

BODY
❏ Wash the bodywork and wheels, checking and rectifying any paint or trim defects noted ☞ 2/17
❏ Clean the windshield, other windows and mirrors ☞ 2/15
❏ Check wiper blades ☞ 2/15/6-11
❏ Check and top-up the windshield washer reservoir ☞ 2/15
❏ Check and top-up the headlight washer reservoir (if applicable) ☞ 2/15

TIRES
❏ Check the tires and tire pressures ☞ 2/16

6 MONTHS OR 7500 MILES OR 12,000KM

ENGINE
○ Change the engine oil and filter ☞ 2/3
❏ Check power steering fluid level ☞ 2/18/18

AUTOMATIC TRANSMISSION
❏ Check the automatic transmission fluid (ATF) level

BRAKES
❏ Check brake fluid level in master cylinder ☞ 2/20
❏ Inspect the brake lines, hoses and connections ☞ 9/4
❏ Inspect/replace the brake pads ☞ 9/10 & 9/15
❏ Check the brake discs for wear or damage ☞ 9/12 & 9/17
❏ Check the operation and adjustment of the parking brake ☞ 9/20

BODY
○ Check and lubricate locks and hinges ☞ 2/17
❏ Check the condition of the convertible top ☞ 2/17
❏ Check that rear window zipper operates smoothly ☞ 2/17
❏ Wash the exterior of the car thoroughly ☞ 2/17
❏ Pressure-wash the underbody ☞ 2/17

12 MONTHS OR 15,000 MILES OR 24,000KM

ENGINE
○ Change the engine oil and filter ☞ 2/3
❏ Check power steering fluid level ☞ 2/18/18

AUTOMATIC TRANSMISSION
❏ Check the automatic transmission fluid (ATF) level

BRAKES
❏ Check brake fluid level in master cylinder ☞ 2/20
❏ Inspect the brake lines, hoses and connections ☞ 9/4
❏ Inspect/replace the brake pads ☞ 9/10 & 9/15
❏ Check the brake discs for wear or damage ☞ 9/12 & 9/17
❏ Check the operation and adjustment of the parking brake ☞ 9/20

BODY
○ Check and lubricate locks and hinges ☞ 2/17
❏ Check the condition of the convertible top ☞ 2/17
❏ Check that rear window zipper operates smoothly ☞ 2/17
❏ Wash the exterior of the car thoroughly ☞ 2/17
❏ Pressure-wash the underbody ☞ 2/17

AIR CONDITIONING SYSTEM
○ Have the air conditioning system checked by a Mazda dealer or air conditioning specialist ☞ 6/16
❏ Check that seatbelts and fasteners are in good, undamaged condition, and that the inertia lock system operates correctly.

18 MONTHS OR 22,500 MILES OR 36,000KM

ENGINE
○ Change the engine oil and filter ☞ 2/3
❏ Check power steering fluid level ☞ 2/18/18

TRANSMISSION
❏ Check automatic transmission fluid (ATF) level

BRAKES
❏ Check brake fluid level in master cylinder ☞ 2/20
❏ Inspect the brake lines, hoses and connections ☞ 9/4
❏ Inspect/replace the brake pads ☞ 9/10 & 9/15
❏ Check the brake discs for wear or damage ☞ 9/12 & 9/17
❏ Check the operation and adjustment of the parking brake ☞ 9/20

BODY
○ Check and lubricate locks and hinges ☞ 2/17
❏ Check the condition of the convertible top ☞ 2/17
❏ Check that rear window zipper operates smoothly ☞ 2/17
❏ Wash the exterior of the car thoroughly ☞ 2/17
❏ Pressure-wash the underbody ☞ 2/17

24 MONTHS OR 30,000 MILES OR 48,000KM

ENGINE
○ Change the engine oil and filter ☞ 2/3
○ Inspect and replace or adjust external drivebelts ☞ 2/4
○ Replace the air cleaner (filter) element ☞ 2/5
❏ Check power steering fluid level ☞ 2/18/18
○ Replace engine coolant (☞ 2/14) every 24 months or 30,000 miles or 48,000km *after* initial replacement at 36 months or 45,000 miles or 72,000km.

IGNITION SYSTEM
○ Replace the sparkplugs ☞ 2/6

FUEL SYSTEM
○ Check and adjust engine idle speed*2 ☞ 2/7
○ Check fuel lines and connections for leaks*2 ☞ 5/13 and 5/14

COOLING SYSTEM
○ Check cooling system ☞ 6/2 & 6/3
○ Check hose condition ☞ 6/4

TRANSMISSION
❏ Check manual transmission oil level ☞ 2/8
❏ Check the automatic transmission fluid (ATF) level ☞ 2/9

BRAKING SYSTEM
❏ Replace brake fluid 9/2
○ Inspect the brake lines, hoses and connections ☞ 9/4
○ Inspect/replace the brake pads ☞ 9/10 & 9/15
○ Check the brake discs for wear or damage ☞ 9/12 & 9/17
❏ Check the operation and adjustment of the parking brake ☞ 9/20

STEERING & SUSPENSION
○ Check manual steering system ☞ 2/18
○ Check power steering system ☞ 2/18
○ Check power steering for leaks ☞ 2/16
○ Check the front suspension balljoints and dust boots for wear or damage ☞ 2/18

TRANSMISSION
○ Check the rear driveaxles (halfshaft) and their dust boots for wear or damage ☞ 2/13

CHASSIS & BODY
○ Check and, if necessary, tighten loose fittings and fasteners
○ Check and lubricate locks and hinges ☞ 2/17
❏ Check the condition of the convertible top ☞ 2/17
❏ Check that rear window zipper operates smoothly ☞ 2/17
❏ Wash the exterior of the car thoroughly ☞ 2/17
❏ Pressure-wash the underbody ☞ 2/17

2: Tune-up & maintenance

SEATBELTS
❏ Check that seatbelts and their fasteners are in good, undamaged condition, and that the inertia lock system operates correctly.

EXHAUST SYSTEM
❏ Inspect the exhaust system, heatshields and catalytic converter ☞ 2/19

AIR CONDITIONING SYSTEM
❏ Have the air conditioning system checked by a Mazda dealer or air conditioning specialist ☞ 6/16

30 MONTHS OR 37,500 MILES OR 60,000KM

As per 6 month or 7500 miles or 12,000km schedule.

36 MONTHS OR 45,000 MILES OR 72,000KM

As per 12 month or 15,000 miles or 24,000km schedule, plus -

ENGINE
❏ After **first** 36 months or 45,000 miles or 72,000km replace engine coolant ☞ 2/14, thereafter every 24 months or 30,000 miles or 48,000km.

42 MONTHS OR 52,500 MILES OR 84,000KM

As per 6 month or 7500 miles or 12,000km schedule.

48 MONTHS OR 60,000 MILES OR 96,000KM

As per 24 month or 30,000 miles or 48,000km schedule, plus -

ENGINE
❏ Replace the camshaft drivebelt (timing belt) ☞ 3/13
Note: this operation is required for all states except California and Massachusetts market cars, for which Mazda recommends inspection of the drivebelt at this interval*². Regardless of where you live, we would strongly advise you to replace the drivebelt at this age/mileage.

FUEL SYSTEM
❏ Check emission system hoses/tubes and connections for leaks*² ☞ 5/23
❏ Check and adjust engine idle speed*¹ ☞ 2/7
❏ Replace the fuel filter ☞ 5/20
Note: Mazda specifies this operation for all states except California and Massachusetts, but recommends that it is carried out on California and Massachusetts market cars too.
❏ Check fuel lines and connections for leaks*¹ ☞ 5/13 and 5/14

TRANSMISSION
❏ Replace the manual transmission oil ☞ 2/8
❏ Replace the differential oil ☞ 2/10

54 MONTHS OR 67,500 MILES OR 108,000KM

Repeat maintenance cycle, starting at 6 months or 7500 miles or 12,000km schedule. **Caution!** Observe 90,000 miles or 144,000km and 105,000 miles or 168,000km schedules on a cumulative basis.

90,000 MILES OR 144,000KM

ENGINE
California & Massachusetts market cars only. Mazda recommend inspection of the camshaft drivebelt (timing belt) at this interval*²

105,000 MILES OR 168,000 KM

ENGINE
❏ California and Massachusetts market cars only (if not already done at and earlier interval). Replace the camshaft drivebelt (timing belt) ☞ 3/13

FUEL SYSTEM
❏ California and Massachusetts market cars only. Check fuel lines and connections for leaks ☞ 5/13 and 5/14

Notes (see text references) -
*¹ Applies to all USA states except California and Massachusetts; however it is advisable to carry out this maintenance at this interval regardless of where you live.
*² This operation is recommended by Mazda, but is not necessary for emission warranty coverage or manufacturer recall liability.
*³ This operation is required in all states except California and Massachusetts.

2B. MAINTENANCE SCHEDULE: USA (ABNORMAL OPERATING CONDITIONS)

Note: This schedule relates to all US market cars used under "abnormal driving conditions" defined by Mazda as -
• "Repeated short distance driving."
• "Driving in dusty conditions."
• "Driving with extensive use of brakes."
• "Driving in areas where salt or other corrosive materials are used."
• "Driving on rough or muddy roads."
• "Extended periods of idling or low speed operation."
• "Driving for long periods in cold temperatures or extremely humid climates."
This schedule could be used for other territories where similar operating conditions apply.

☞ 1/1,2 & 2/1.

WEEKLY

ENGINE
❏ Check the engine oil level ☞ 2/3
❏ Check the coolant level ☞ 2/14

ELECTRICAL
❏ Check the operation of the electrical components ☞ 2/15
❏ Raise and clean the headlights ☞ 2/15
❏ If you suspect a problem, remove and check the battery ☞ 2/11

BODY
❏ Wash the bodywork and wheels, checking and rectifying any paint or trim defects ☞ 2/17
❏ Clean the windshield, other windows and mirrors ☞ 2/15
❏ Check and top-up the windshield washer reservoir ☞ 2/15
❏ Check wipers ☞ 2/15.6
❏ Check and top-up the headlight washer reservoir (if applicable) ☞ 2/15

TIRES
❏ Check the tires and tire pressures ☞ 2/16

3 MONTHS OR 3000 MILES OR 4800KM

ENGINE
❏ Puerto Rico only. Change the engine oil ☞ 2/3
Note: Although this interval is specified by Mazda only for cars sold in Puerto Rico, other owners operating their cars in similarly tough conditions may wish to include it in their schedule.

4 MONTHS OR 5000 MILES OR 8000KM

ENGINE
❏ Change the engine oil and filter ☞ 2/3
❏ Check power steering fluid level ☞ 2/18/18

TRANSMISSION
❏ Check automatic transmission fluid (ATF) level

BRAKES
❏ Check brake fluid level in master cylinder ☞ 2/20
❏ Inspect the brake lines, hoses and connections ☞ 9/4
❏ Inspect/replace the brake pads ☞ 9/10 & 9/15
❏ Check the brake discs for wear or damage ☞ 9/12 & 9/17
❏ Check the operation and adjustment of the parking brake ☞ 9/20

BODY
❏ Check and lubricate locks and hinges ☞ 2/17
❏ Check the condition of the convertible top ☞ 2/17
❏ Check that rear window zipper operates smoothly ☞ 2/17
❏ Wash the exterior of the car thoroughly ☞ 2/17
❏ Pressure-wash the underbody ☞ 2/17

8 MONTHS OR 10,000 MILES OR 16,000KM

As 4 months or 5000 miles or 8000km schedule.

12 MONTHS OR 15,000 MILES OR 24,000KM

As 4 months or 5000 miles or 8000km schedule, plus -

FUEL SYSTEM
❏ Inspect air cleaner (filter) element ☞ 2/5

BRAKES
❏ Check brake fluid level in master cylinder ☞ 2/20
❏ Inspect the brake lines, hoses and connections ☞ 9/4

Mazda Miata, MX-5, Eunos & Roadster

○ Inspect/replace the brake pads ☞ 9/10 & 9/15
○ Check the brake discs for wear or damage ☞ 9/12 & 9/17
❏ Check the operation and adjustment of the parking brake ☞ 9/20

CHASSIS & BODY

○ Check and, if necessary, tighten loose fittings and fasteners

AIR CONDITIONING SYSTEM

○ Have the air conditioning system checked by a Mazda dealer or air conditioning specialist ☞ 6/16.

16 MONTHS OR 20,000 MILES OR 32,000KM

As 4 months or 5000 miles or 8000km schedule.

20 MONTHS OR 25,000 MILES OR 40,000KM

As 4 months or 5000 miles or 8000km schedule.

24 MONTHS OR 30,000 MILES OR 48,000KM

ENGINE

○ Change the engine oil and filter ☞ 2/3
○ Inspect and replace or adjust external drivebelts ☞ 2/4

IGNITION SYSTEM

○ Replace the sparkplugs ☞ 2/6

FUEL SYSTEM

○ Replace the air cleaner (filter) element ☞ 2/5
○ Check and adjust engine idle speed*² ☞ 2/7
○ Check fuel lines and connections for leaks*² ☞ 5/13 and 5/14

COOLING SYSTEM

○ Check cooling system ☞ 6/2 & 6/3
○ Check hose condition ☞ 6/4
○ Replace engine coolant (☞ 2/14) every 24 months or 30,000 miles or 48,000km *after* initial replacement at 36 months or 45,000 miles or 72,000km.

TRANSMISSION

○ Replace manual transmission oil ☞ 2/8
○ Replace differential oil ☞ 2/10
❏ Check automatic transmission fluid (ATF) level ☞ 2/9
○ Check the rear driveaxles (halfshaft) and their dust boots for wear or damage ☞ 2/13

BRAKING SYSTEM

❏ Replace brake fluid 9/2
○ Inspect the brake lines, hoses and connections ☞ 9/4
○ Inspect/replace the brake pads ☞ 9/10 & 9/15
○ Check the brake discs for wear or damage ☞ 9/12 & 9/17
❏ Check the operation and adjustment of the parking brake ☞ 9/20

STEERING & SUSPENSION

○ Check manual steering system ☞ 2/18
○ Check power steering system ☞ 2/18
○ Check power steering for leaks ☞ 2/16
○ Check power steering fluid level ☞ 2/18/18
○ Check the front suspension balljoints and dust boots for wear or damage ☞ 2/18

CHASSIS & BODY

○ Check and, if necessary, tighten loose fittings and fasteners
○ Check and lubricate locks and hinges ☞ 2/17
❏ Check the condition of the convertible top ☞ 2/17
❏ Check that rear window zipper operates smoothly ☞ 2/17
❏ Wash the exterior of the car thoroughly ☞ 2/17
❏ Pressure-wash the underbody ☞ 2/17

SEATBELTS

❏ Check that seatbelts and their fasteners are in good, undamaged condition, and that the inertia lock system operates correctly.

EXHAUST SYSTEM

○ Inspect the exhaust system, heatshields and catalytic converter ☞ 2/19

AIR CONDITIONING SYSTEM

○ Have the air conditioning system checked by a Mazda dealer or air conditioning specialist ☞ 6/16

28 MONTHS OR 35,000 MILES OR 56,000KM

As 4 months or 5000 miles or 8000km schedule.

32 MONTHS OR 40,000 MILES OR 64,000KM

As 4 months or 5000 miles or 8000km schedule.

36 MONTHS OR 45,000 MILES OR 72,000KM

As 12 months or 15,000 miles or 24,000km schedule, plus -

ENGINE

○ After *first* 36 months or 45,000 miles or 72,000km replace engine coolant ☞ 2/14, thereafter every 24 months or 30,000 miles or 48,000km.

40 MONTHS OR 50,000 MILES OR 80,000KM

As 4 months or 5000 miles or 8000km schedule.

44 MONTHS OR 55,000 MILES OR 88,000KM

As 4 months or 5000 miles or 8000km schedule.

48 MONTHS OR 60,000 MILES OR 96,000KM

As 24 month or 30,000 miles or 48,000km schedule, plus -

ENGINE

○ Replace the camshaft drivebelt (timing belt) ☞ 3/13

Note: This operation is required for all states except California and Massachusetts market cars, for which Mazda recommends inspection of the drivebelt at this interval*². Regardless of where you live, we would strongly advise you to replace the drivebelt at this age/mileage.

FUEL SYSTEM

○ Check emission system hoses/tubes and connections for leaks*² ☞ 5/23
○ Check and adjust engine idle speed*¹ ☞ 2/7
○ Replace the fuel filter ☞ 5/20

Note: Mazda specifies this operation for all states except California and Massachusetts, but recommends that it is carried out on California and Massachusetts market cars, too.

○ Check fuel lines and connections for leaks*¹ ☞ 5/13 and 5/14

52 MONTHS OR 65,000 MILES OR 104,000KM

Repeat maintenance cycle, starting at 4 months or 5000 miles or 8000km schedule. **Caution!** Observe 90,000 miles or 144,000km and 105,000 miles or 168,000km schedules on a cumulative basis.

90,000 MILES OR 144,000KM

ENGINE

California and Massachusetts market cars only. Mazda recommends inspection of the camshaft drivebelt (timing belt) at this interval*²

105,000 MILES OR 168,000KM

ENGINE

○ California and Massachusetts market cars only. Replace the camshaft drivebelt (timing belt) if not already done at an earlier interval ☞ 3/13

FUEL SYSTEM

○ California and Massachusetts market cars only. Check fuel lines and connections for leaks ☞ 5/13 and 5/14

Notes (see text references) -

*¹ Applies to all USA states except California and Massachusetts; however it is advisable to carry out this maintenance at this interval regardless of where you live.

*² This operation is recommended by Mazda, but is not necessary for emission warranty coverage or manufacturer recall liability.

*³ This operation is required in all states except California and Massachusetts.

2C. MAINTENANCE SCHEDULE: CANADA

Note: This schedule can also be used for other countries with similar climate/topography.
☞ 1/1,2 & 2/1.

WEEKLY

ENGINE

❏ Check the engine oil level ☞ 2/3
❏ Check the coolant level ☞ 2/14

ELECTRICAL

❏ Check the operation of the electrical components, especially lights ☞ 2/15
❏ Raise and clean the headlights ☞ 2/15
❏ If you suspect a problem, remove and check the battery ☞ 2/11

2: Tune-up & maintenance

BODY
❏ Wash the bodywork and wheels, checking and rectifying any paint or trim defects ☞ 2/17
❏ Clean the windshield, other windows and mirrors ☞ 2/15
❏ Check and top-up the windshield washer reservoir ☞ 2/15
❏ Check wipers ☞ 2/15.6
❏ Check and top-up the headlight washer reservoir (if applicable) ☞ 2/15

TIRES
❏ Check the tires and tire pressures ☞ 2/16

5 MONTHS OR 5000 MILES OR 8000KM

ENGINE
○ Change the engine oil and filter ☞ 2/3
○ Inspect and replace or adjust external drivebelts ☞ 2/4
○ Check power steering fluid level ☞ 2/18/18

COOLING SYSTEM
○ Check cooling system and coolant strength ☞ 6/2 & 6/3

TRANSMISSION
○ Check automatic transmission fluid (ATF) level ☞ 2/9
○ Check differential oil level ☞ 2/10

BRAKES
○ Check brake fluid level in master cylinder ☞ 2/20
❏ Inspect the brake lines, hoses and connections ☞ 9/4
❏ Inspect/replace the brake pads ☞ 9/10 & 9/15
❏ Check the brake discs for wear or damage ☞ 9/12 & 9/17
❏ Check the operation and adjustment of the parking brake ☞ 9/20

STEERING
○ Check level of power steering fluid (if applicable) ☞ 2/18/18

BODY
○ Check and lubricate locks and hinges ☞ 2/17
○ Check and top-up the windshield washer reservoir ☞ 2/15
❏ Check the condition of the convertible top ☞ 2/17
❏ Check that rear window zipper operates smoothly ☞ 2/17
❏ Wash the exterior of the car thoroughly ☞ 2/17
❏ Pressure-wash the underbody ☞ 2/17

ELECTRICAL
○ Check the operation of the electrical components, especially lights ☞ 2/15

10 MONTHS OR 10,000 MILES OR 16,000KM

As 5 months or 5000 miles or 8000km schedule, plus -

AIR CONDITIONING SYSTEM
○ Have the air conditioning system checked by a Mazda dealer or air conditioning specialist ☞ 6/16

15 MONTHS OR 15,000 MILES OR 24,000KM

As 5 months or 5000 miles or 8000km schedule, plus -

COOLING SYSTEM
○ Check cooling system ☞ 6/2 & 6/3
○ Check hose condition ☞ 6/4

FUEL SYSTEM
○ Check and adjust engine idle speed ☞ 2/7
○ Inspect air filter element ☞ 2/5

BRAKING SYSTEM
○ Inspect/replace the brake pads ☞ 9/10 & 9/15
○ Check the brake discs for wear or damage ☞ 9/12 & 9/17

TIRES
○ Rotate tires to even wear ☞ 2/16/11

CHASSIS & BODY
○ Check and, if necessary, tighten loose fittings and fasteners

20 MONTHS OR 20,000 MILES OR 32,000KM

As 10 months or 10,000 miles or 16,000km schedule.

25 MONTHS OR 25,000 MILES OR 40,000KM

As 5 months or 5000 miles or 8000km schedule.

30 MONTHS OR 30,000 MILES OR 48,000KM

ENGINE
○ Change the engine oil and filter ☞ 2/3
○ Inspect and replace or adjust external drivebelts ☞ 2/4

COOLING SYSTEM
○ Check cooling system and coolant strength ☞ 6/2 & 6/3
○ Check hose condition ☞ 6/4
○ Replace engine coolant (☞ 2/14) every 30 months or 30,000 miles or 48,000km *after* initial replacement at 45 months or 45,000 miles or 72,000km.

FUEL SYSTEM
○ Check and adjust engine idle speed ☞ 2/7
○ Replace air cleaner (filter) element ☞ 2/5
○ Check fuel lines and connections for leaks*2 ☞ 5/13 and 5/14
○ Replace the fuel filter ☞ 5/20

IGNITION SYSTEM
○ Replace the sparkplugs ☞ 2/6

TRANSMISSION
○ Replace manual transmission oil ☞ 2/8
○ Replace automatic transmission fluid (ATF) level ☞ 2/9
○ Replace differential oil ☞ 2/10

○ Check the rear driveaxles (halfshaft) and their dust boots for wear or damage ☞ 2/13

BRAKING SYSTEM
○ Replace brake fluid 9/2
○ Inspect/replace the brake pads ☞ 9/10 & 9/15
○ Check the brake discs for wear or damage ☞ 9/12 & 9/17
○ Check brake fluid level in master cylinder ☞ 2/20
○ Inspect the brake lines, hoses and connections ☞ 9/4
○ Check the operation and adjustment of the parking brake ☞ 9/20

STEERING & SUSPENSION
○ Check steering geometry ☞ 8/3
○ Check level of power steering fluid (if applicable) ☞ 2/18/18
○ Check power steering for leaks ☞ 2/16
○ Check manual steering system ☞ 2/18
○ Check power steering system ☞ 2/18
○ Check suspension components for serviceability/damage ☞ 8
○ Check the front suspension balljoints and dust boots for wear or damage ☞ 2/18

CHASSIS & BODY
○ Check and, if necessary, tighten loose fittings and fasteners
○ Check and lubricate locks and hinges ☞ 2/17
○ Check and top-up the windshield washer reservoir ☞ 2/15
❏ Check the condition of the convertible top ☞ 2/17
❏ Check that rear window zipper operates smoothly ☞ 2/17
❏ Wash the exterior of the car thoroughly ☞ 2/17
❏ Pressure-wash the underbody ☞ 2/17

ELECTRICAL
○ Check the operation of the electrical components, especially lights ☞ 2/15

TIRES
○ Rotate tires to even wear ☞ 2/16/11

EXHAUST SYSTEM
○ Inspect the exhaust system, heatshields and catalytic converter ☞ 2/19

35 MONTHS OR 35,000 MILES OR 56,000KM

As 5 months or 5000 miles or 8000km.

40 MONTHS OR 40,000 MILES OR 64,000KM

As 10 months or 10,000 miles or 16,000km.

45 MONTHS OR 45,000 MILES OR 72,000KM

As 15 months or 15,000 miles or 24,000km, plus

ENGINE
○ After *first* 45 months or 45,000 miles or 72,000km replace engine coolant ☞ 2/14,

Mazda Miata, MX-5, Eunos & Roadster

thereafter every 30 months or 30,000 miles or 48,000km.

50 MONTHS OR 50,000 MILES OR 80,000KM

As 10 months or 10,000 miles or 16,000km.

55 MONTHS OR 55,000 MILES OR 88,000KM

As 5 months or 5000 miles or 8000km schedule.

60 MONTHS OR 60,000 MILES OR 96,000KM

As 30 months or 30,000 miles or 48,000km schedule, plus -

ENGINE
❍ Replace the camshaft drivebelt (timing belt) ☞ 3/13

FUEL SYSTEM
❍ Check fuel lines and connections for leaks ☞ 5/13 and 5/14
❍ Check PCV valve ☞ 5/22
❍ Check emission system hoses/tubes and connections for leaks ☞ 5/23

65 MONTHS OR 65,000 MILES OR 104,000KM

Repeat maintenance cycle, starting at 5 months or 5000 miles or 8000km schedule.

Notes (see text references) -

*¹ Applies to all USA states except California and Massachusetts; however it is advisable to carry out this maintenance at this interval regardless of where you live.

*² This operation is recommended by Mazda, but is not necessary for emission warranty coverage or manufacturer recall liability.

*³ This operation is required in all states except California and Massachusetts.

2D. MAINTENANCE SCHEDULE: UK AND REST OF WORLD

Note: If you have reason to believe that the USA, USA abnormal driving conditions or Canadian maintenance schedules would better suit your territory/model, consult an owner's manual (handbook) for your market to see which schedule should be applied.
☞ 1/1, 2 & 2/1.

WEEKLY

ENGINE
❑ Check the engine oil level ☞ 2/3
❑ Check the engine coolant level ☞ 2/14

ELECTRICAL
❑ Check the operation of the electrical components, particularly lights ☞ 2/15
❑ Raise and clean the headlights ☞ 2/15
❑ If you suspect a problem, remove and check the battery ☞ 2/11

BODY
❑ Wash the bodywork and wheels, checking and rectifying any paint or trim defects noted ☞ 2/17
❑ Clean the windshield, other windows and mirrors ☞ 2/15
❑ Check wiper blades ☞ 2/15/6-11
❑ Check and top-up the windshield washer reservoir ☞ 2/15
❑ Check and top-up the headlight washer reservoir (if applicable) ☞ 2/15

TIRES
❑ Check the tires and tire pressures ☞ 2/16

6000 MILES OR 10,000KM

ENGINE
❍ Change the engine oil and filter (☞ 2/3) if the car is often used in dusty conditions/for extended periods at idling speed or low speed operation/driving for long periods in cold temperatures/used regularly for trips of less than 5 miles/8km.

FUEL SYSTEM
❍ Inspect air filter element ☞ 2/5 if vehicle is used in sandy areas or unusually dusty conditions.

12 MONTHS OR 9000 MILES OR 15,000KM

ENGINE
❍ Inspect and replace or adjust external drivebelts ☞ 2/4
❍ Change the engine oil and filter ☞ 2/3

FUEL SYSTEM
❍ Inspect air filter element ☞ 2/5

ELECTRICAL SYSTEM
❍ Check the battery ☞ 2/11
❍ Check the operation of all electrical components but particularly lights ☞ 2/15

BRAKES
❍ Check brake pedal operation and adjustment ☞ 9/5
❍ Inspect the brake lines, hoses and connections ☞ 9/4
❍ Check brake fluid level in master cylinder (☞ 2/20) or if the brakes are used very extensively (eg: mountainous area), or the car is used in a very moist climate, replace the brake fluid ☞ 2/20.
❍ Check the operation and adjustment of the parking (hand) brake ☞ 9/20
❍ Inspect/replace the brake pads ☞ 9/10 & 9/15
❍ Check the brake discs for wear or damage ☞ 9/12 & 9/17
❍ Inspect brake booster (servo) unit and its hoses/pipes.

CLUTCH
❍ Check clutch pedal operation and adjustment ☞ 3/28
❍ Check clutch fluid level in master cylinder ☞ 2/20

SUSPENSION & STEERING SYSTEMS
❍ Check power steering fluid level ☞ 2/18/18
❍ Check manual steering system ☞ 2/18
❍ Check power steering system ☞ 2/18
❍ Check power steering for leaks ☞ 2/16
❍ Check suspension components for serviceability/damage ☞ 8
❍ Check the front suspension balljoints and dust boots for wear or damage ☞ 2/18
❍ Check steering geometry ☞ 8/3

TRANSMISSION
❑ Check automatic transmission fluid (ATF) level ☞ 2/9

BODY
❍ Check and, if necessary, tighten loose fittings and fasteners
❍ Check body for rust/perforation: repair as necessary
❍ Check and lubricate locks and hinges ☞ 2/17
❍ Pressure-wash the underbody and inspect ☞ 2/17
❑ Check the condition of the convertible top ☞ 2/17
❑ Check that rear window zipper operates smoothly ☞ 2/17
❑ Wash the exterior of the car thoroughly ☞ 2/17

TIRES
❍ Check the tires and tire pressures ☞ 2/16

AIR CONDITIONING SYSTEM
❍ Have the air conditioning system checked by a Mazda dealer or air conditioning specialist ☞ 6/16

24 MONTHS OR 18,000 MILES OR 30,000KM

ENGINE
❍ Inspect and replace or adjust external drivebelts ☞ 2/4
❍ Change the engine oil and filter ☞ 2/3

COOLING SYSTEM
❍ Check cooling system ☞ 6/3
❍ Check hose condition ☞ 6/4
❍ Replace coolant ☞ 6/2

FUEL SYSTEM
❍ Check and adjust engine idle speed ☞ 2/7
❍ Inspect air filter element ☞ 2/5
❍ Check fuel lines and connections for leaks ☞ 5/13 & 5/14

IGNITION SYSTEM
❍ Check ignition timing ☞ 5/26
❍ Check sparkplug gaps and condition ☞ 2/6
Note: We recommend that you renew sparkplugs at this interval.

EMISSION CONTROL SYSTEM
❍ Inspect EVAP & EGR systems ☞ 5/23

ELECTRICAL SYSTEM
❍ Check the battery ☞ 2/11
❍ Check the operation of all electrical components but particularly lights ☞ 2/15
❍ Check headlight beam adjustment ☞ 7/27

BRAKES
❍ Check brake pedal operation and adjustment ☞ 9/5

2: Tune-up & maintenance

○ Inspect the brake lines, hoses and connections ☞ 9/4
○ Replace brake fluid ☞ 2/20
○ Check the operation and adjustment of the parking (hand) brake ☞ 9/20
○ Inspect/replace the brake pads ☞ 9/10 & 9/15
○ Check the brake discs for wear or damage ☞ 9/12 & 9/17
○ Inspect brake booster (servo) unit and its hoses/pipes.

CLUTCH
○ Check clutch pedal operation and adjustment ☞ 3/28
○ Check clutch fluid level in master cylinder ☞ 2/20

SUSPENSION & STEERING SYSTEMS
○ Check power steering fluid level ☞ 2/18/18
○ Check manual steering system ☞ 2/18
○ Check power steering system ☞ 2/18
○ Check power steering for leaks ☞ 2/16
○ Check suspension components for serviceability/damage ☞ 8
○ Check the front suspension balljoints and dust boots for wear or damage ☞ 2/18
○ Check steering geometry ☞ 8/3

TRANSMISSION
❏ Replace automatic transmission fluid (ATF) ☞ 2/9
○ Check manual transmission oil level ☞ 2/8
○ Check differential oil level ☞ 2/10
○ Check the rear driveaxles (halfshaft) and their dust boots for wear or damage ☞ 2/13

BODY
○ Check and, if necessary, tighten loose fittings and fasteners
○ Check body for rust/perforation: repair as necessary
○ Check and lubricate locks and hinges ☞ 2/17
○ Pressure-wash the underbody and inspect ☞ 2/17
❏ Check the condition of the convertible top ☞ 2/17
❏ Check that rear window zipper operates smoothly ☞ 2/17
❏ Wash the exterior of the car thoroughly ☞ 2/17

EXHAUST SYSTEM
○ Inspect the exhaust system, heatshields and catalytic converter ☞ 2/19

TIRES
○ Check the tires and tire pressures ☞ 2/16

SEATBELTS
○ Check that seatbelts and fasteners are in good, undamaged condition, and that the inertia lock system operates correctly.

AIR CONDITIONING SYSTEM
○ Have the air conditioning system checked by a Mazda dealer or air conditioning specialist ☞ 6/16.

36 MONTHS OR 27,000 MILES OR 45,000KM
As per 12 month or 9000 miles or 15,000km schedule, except -
FUEL SYSTEM
○ Replace air cleaner (filter) element ☞ 2/5

48 MONTHS OR 36,000 MILES OR 60,000KM
As per 24 month or 18,000 miles or 30,000km schedule, plus -
FUEL SYSTEM
○ Replace fuel filter ☞ 5/20

60 MONTHS OR 45,000 MILES OR 75,000KM
As per 12 month or 9000 miles or 15,000km schedule.

72 MONTHS OR 54,000 MILES OR 90,000KM
As per 24 month or 18,000 miles or 30,000km schedule, plus/except -
ENGINE
○ Replace the camshaft drivebelt (timing belt) ☞ 3/13
FUEL SYSTEM
○ Replace air cleaner (filter) element ☞ 2/5
TRANSMISSION
○ Replace manual transmission oil ☞ 2/8
○ Replace the differential oil ☞ 2/10

84 MONTHS OR 63,000 MILES OR 105,000KM
Repeat maintenance cycle, starting at 12 months or 9000 miles or 15,000km schedule.

3. ENGINE OIL & OIL FILTER - CHANGING

☞ 1/1, 2 & 2/1.

1   The engine oil should be changed with the engine at normal operating temperature, preferably after a journey of several miles. This ensures that the oil drains easily and that any contaminants are held in suspension in the oil and are flushed out. You'll need a drain tray or similar container able to take at least 4 liters/4.2 US or 3.5 Imp quarts of oil. You'll also need fresh oil and a replacement oil filter, of course. The oil pan will take around 3.6 liters/3.8 US or 3.2 Imp quarts and the filter a further 0.4 liters/0.2 US or 0.1 Imp quarts.

2   The type of oil specified by Mazda varies to some extent according to operating conditions, and you'll find details of any special requirements for your territory in the official owners manual (handbook) for the relevant market. Oil quality is always defined on the can or bottle. Buy oil carrying a major brand name from a reputable outlet; that way you can be sure the oil is appropriate for the local climate. For most areas, any engine oil that meets or exceeds API (American Petroleum Institute) SG, SH or SJ standard, and has a viscosity of SAE 5W-30, SAE 10W-30 or SAE 10W-40, will

3/3a Remove engine oil filler cap ...

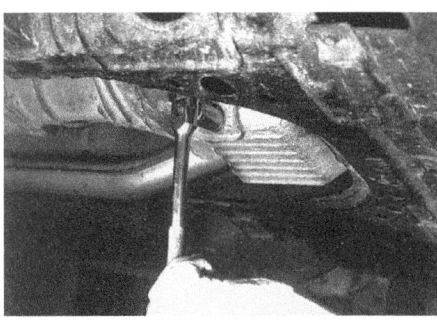
3/3b ... loosen the oil pan drain plug ...

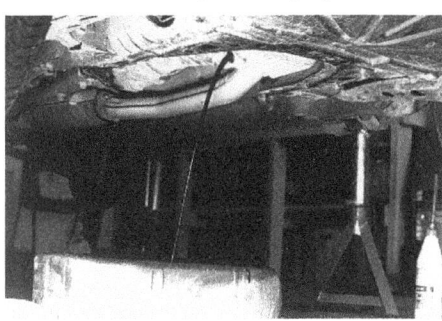
3/3c ... and allow the oil to drain.

be fine. For unusually cold or hot climates, consult the official owners manual (handbook), or seek advice from a local Mazda dealer. Whether you use mineral oil, semi-synthetic or fully synthetic oil is up to you: generally, the more you pay, the better the oil's lubricating performance, which means greater longevity for your engine and more efficient performance (less power loss through friction).

3   ◻+ Remove the oil filler cap from the cambox cover. Place the drain tray below the drain plug - taking into account that the oil will initially flow in an arc - and carefully unscrew the 19mm drain plug. Once you've loosened the plug with a wrench or socket, continue unscrewing it by hand, holding the plug against the oil pan as you come to the end of the thread. Once the last thread has come free, remove the plug quickly to avoid having used oil running down your arm. **Warning!** The oil will be quite hot.

4   ◻ Leave the oil to drain. Meanwhile, remove the oil filter using a commercially available oil filter wrench, of which there are numerous types available, including versions for use with socket set drive bars. The filter is located on the side of the block, just to the rear of the alternator. Access is not too easy - you'll have to work around the alternator

Mazda Miata, MX-5, Eunos & Roadster

3/4 Use a strap wrench to loosen filter ...

and the engine mounting, so it's important that the wrench you use will work in the confined space available. If you need to buy a wrench, we suggest you purchase it from your Mazda dealer, or at least ask where they got theirs - that way you'll get one that works.

5 Place some rag below the filter to catch any oil spillage, then loosen the filter with the wrench and remove it by hand - **Warning!** The oil may be hot. Carefully clean around the mounting face with clean rag, and, while you're doing this, remove the oil dipstick and wipe it clean, too. Once the old oil has drained fully, clean the drain plug and oil pan threads, fit a new sealing ring to the drain plug and initially screw the plug in by hand to make sure it does not become crossthreaded. Next, tighten the plug to 30-41Nm/3.0-4.2kgf m/ 22-30Ibf ft. Smear some oil on the sealing ring of the new oil filter, then screw it into place and hand tighten only. (Never use a wrench to tighten a filter - you will either damage the threads or find it impossible to remove when the next filter change is due.)

6 Add the fresh oil slowly through the cambox opening. After about 3 liters have been added, start checking the level using the dipstick. Take care not to overfill the engine - if you do you will have to drain off the excess. Refit the dipstick and filler cap, start the engine and let it idle for a few minutes, then switch it off and allow it to stand for a further minute or two. Recheck the oil level and top-up if required - the oil level will have dropped slightly as the oil filter filled under system pressure.

4. DRIVEBELTS (EXTERNAL) - INSPECTION, REPLACEMENT & ADJUSTMENT

☞ 1/1, 2 & 2/1.

INSPECTION

1 In the context of maintenance, "external drivebelts" are those which transfer drive from the crankshaft to the alternator, water pump, power steering pump (if fitted) and air conditioning system compressor (if fitted). The drivebelt arrangement varies, depending on whether power steering and/ or air conditioning are part of the car's specification. Checking and adjustment of these belts is similar for all configurations.

2 Start by carefully examining the belt or belts for signs of wear or damage. Excessive wear is often due to incorrect adjustment, but eventually all belts wear out and must be replaced. Indications of serious wear are obvious scuffing, cracking or fraying of the belt structure, or glazing of the friction faces. In time, the belt material will begin to break down, and cracking will begin to form on the working area of the belt.

3 Traditional V-belts work by being pinched between the pulley faces, and must be tensioned correctly to achieve sufficient grip. Eventually, wear on the working faces of the belt may allow the belt to bottom out in the pulley groove: any belt that gets this worn can never be made to work properly

3/5 ... then unscrew and remove by hand.

and will slip even if excessive tension is applied.

4 V-ribbed belts are shallower in depth but wider in section, and use a number of small V-sections working in corresponding grooves on the pulley faces. These belts rely on their greater surface area to achieve grip, and are generally more flexible and less prone to cracking. However, always make sure that they sit on the pulleys correctly - it's all too easy to fit them so that they are displaced by one rib either way, which means the belt will have less grip than it should.

REPLACEMENT

5 Regardless of the type of belt used, if you find signs of wear or damage, fit a new belt right away - don't wait until the belt breaks in service. The most basic configuration of drivebelt you'll find is a single belt driven from the crankshaft, and running around the alternator and water pump pulleys. If power steering, air conditioning, or both, are fitted, your car will feature a second drivebelt which you'll need to remove to access the alternator/ water pump drivebelt.

6 Where power steering is fitted, but no

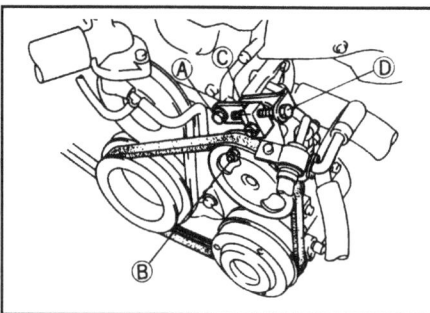

D4/6-7 DRIVEBELT ARRANGEMENT (POWER STEERING & AIR CONDITIONING).
(See text).

air conditioning, a second, outer belt runs from the crankshaft pulley up around the power steering pump. Refer to the accompanying diagram (ignore the fact that it shows an air conditioning compressor). Slacken bolt **A** and nuts **B** (accessed thru pulley) and **C**. Back off the adjuster bolt **D** and remove the belt.

7 If the car has power steering and air conditioning, a longer outer belt is used to accommodate the extra pulley, but the removal procedure is essentially the same as just described.

8   If the car has air conditioning but no power steering, the belt runs around an idler pul-

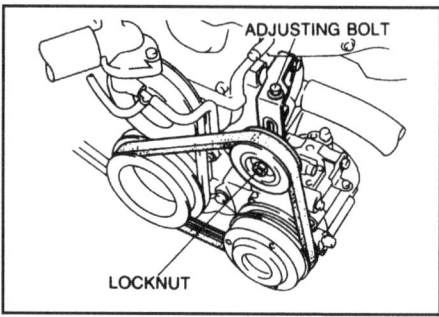

D4/8 DRIVEBELT ARRANGEMENT (AIR CON ONLY).

ley, occupying the position normally used for the power steering compressor, and then around the air conditioning pump. On these cars, slacken the locknut at the centre of the idler pulley, then back off the adjuster bolt and remove the belt.

9   Once the outer belt, where fitted, has been removed, you can remove the inner alternator belt. Slacken the alternator pivot bolt **B** below the alternator body and then the clamp bolt **A**. Back off the alternator adjuster bolt **C** to release belt tension and remove the belt.

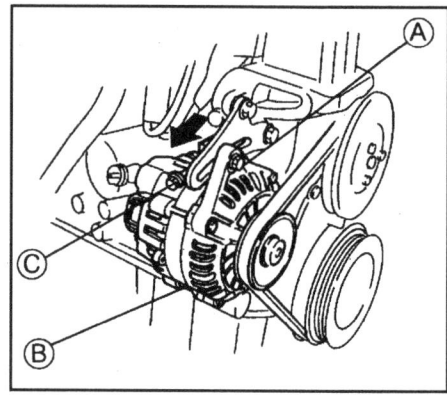

D4/9 ADJUSTING ALTERNATOR DRIVEBELT.
(See text)

10 Clean the pulleys. Place the new belt in position over the pulley. Make sure that V-ribbed type belts are fitted so that all the grooves of the pulley are filled by the belt.

ADJUSTMENT

11   To check the deflection of the alternator/water pump belt, with your thumb press the belt inward midway between the crankshaft and alter-

2: Tune-up & maintenance

4/11 Use thumb to check belt tension.

nator pulleys. You need to apply moderate pressure - specifically 98N/10kg/22lb - though absolute accuracy is not vital. A new belt should be set to allow 8-9mm/0.32-0.35in (0.22-0.27in 1995 on) deflection, while a used belt (one that's run for more than 5 minutes) is set to give 9-10mm/0.36-0.39in (0.24-0.29in 1995 on). Refer to diagram 4/9 and set the belt tension using bolt **C**, then tighten the remaining bolts as follows: **A** 19-25Nm/1.9-2.6kgf m/14-18lbf ft), **B** 38-51Nm/3.8-5.3kgf m/28-38lbf ft.

12   If your car has a secondary belt driving power steering or air conditioning, or both, check its tension midway between the crankshaft pulley and the power steering pump or idler pulley. Press the belt inward with your thumb midway between the two pulleys. You need to apply moderate pressure - actually 98N/10kg/22lb - though absolute accuracy is not vital. A new belt should be set to allow 8-9mm/0.32-0.35in deflection, while a used belt (one that's run for more than 5 minutes), is set to give 9-10mm/0.36-0.39in.

13   (D4/6-7) To adjust the belt tension, make sure that you slacken off the pivot bolt(s) or nut(s) before setting the tension using the adjuster bolt. If you omit to do this you'll almost certainly cause damage. On cars with power steering, slacken **A**, **B** and **C** and set the belt tension with the adjuster bolt **D**. Once the correct tension has been set, tighten the various fasteners shown in the accompanying line drawing to the following torque figures: **A** 32-46Nm/3.2-4.7kgf m/24-33lbf ft, **B** 38-51Nm/3.7-5.5kgf m/27-39 lbf ft, **C** 19-25Nm (1.9-2.6kgf m/14-18 lbf ft.

14   (D4/8) If your car has air conditioning with manual steering, there is an idler pulley in place of the power steering pump. On these cars, slacken the idler pulley locknut, and turn the adjusting bolt to set belt tension (as above). Once set correctly, tighten the pulley locknut to 38-51Nm/3.8-5.3kgf m/28-38lbf ft.

5. AIR CLEANER (FILTER) ELEMENT - REPLACEMENT

☞ 1/1, 2 & 2/1.

1   The air cleaner element will require replacement at regular intervals and, if the car is used in unusually dusty areas, will require more frequent replacement. Also, any time the element gets contaminated with oil or water, it must be replaced. Note that it is not possible to clean the element - even blowing through it with compressed air will not make it adequately seviceable.

2   ✚ You can gain access to the element after removing the cover (incorporating the MAF unit) of the air cleaner casing. Start by disconnecting the hose clamp which secures the trunking to the MAF unit, and pull the trunking clear. Unplug the electrical connector from the MAF unit. On some cars you may need to release wiring from a clip at the back of the air cleaner unit. Remove the 10mm screws securing the cover and lift the cover away. The air cleaner element can now be lifted out.

3   Fit the new element into the casing, refit

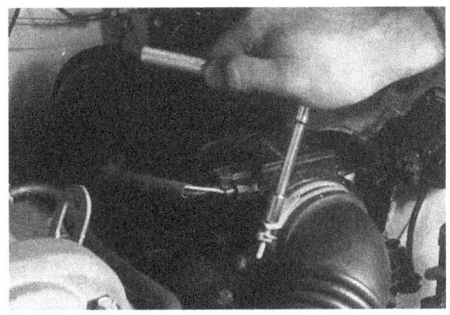

5/2a Release clamp & detach hose ...

5/2b ... release MAF unit electrical connector ...

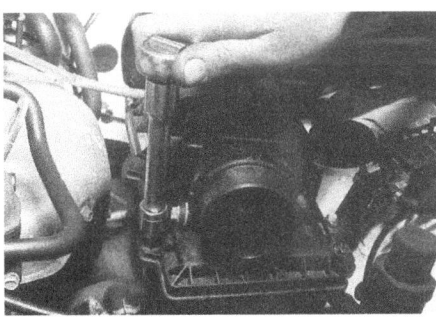

5/2c ... remove cover retaining screws...

5/2d ... lift out air cleaner element.

the cover and tighten the securing screws to 7.9-10.7Nm/80-110kgf cm/70-95.4lbf in. Reconnect the MAF unit electrical connector. Reconnect the air intake trunking and tighten the hose clamp which secures it.

6. SPARKPLUGS - CHECKING, CLEANING & ADJUSTING

☞ 1/1, 2 & 2/1.

1   The sparkplugs should be replaced at the prescribed service intervals. Between these intervals it is permissible to clean and re-gap the plugs, though you may feel, as we do, that so much depends on the correct operation of these relatively inexpensive consumable items, that it's preferable to fit new plugs whenever their operation is suspect. If you need to check, clean and re-gap the plugs between changes; the procedure is outlined below. Even if you intend to fit new plugs, read through this section; you can assess engine condition from the appearance of the used plugs.

2   Carefully disconnect the sparkplug wire caps from each sparkplug, then remove the sparkplugs and examine their electrodes for signs of erosion. Check the ceramic insulator nose and the ribbed external insulator between the plug body and terminal for cracks or tracking lines. If wear of electrodes is clearly visible, or damage is noted to ceramic insulators, replace the sparkplug.

3   You can tell quite a lot about engine condition by examining the business end of sparkplugs, but only if the car has been driven several miles, and then not allowed to idle for more than a few seconds before the plugs are removed. Normal operation will produce an even, grey/brown deposit on the electrodes and on the porcelain insulator around the center electrode. A sooty, black deposit is indicative of an excessively rich fuel/air mixture, and an oily, black appearance indicates oil fouling (often discovered in a worn engine where a significant amount of engine oil is getting burnt as it works past worn rings or valve guides).

4   At the other extreme, very light deposits and a glazed appearance on the electrodes is indicative of overheating - if the correct plug grade is in use, this could be due to a weak fuel/air mixture, the wrong grade of fuel or incorrect ignition timing. For details of the recommended plug types see the specifications in chapter 1. Note that optional plug grades are included which are primarily for use in abnormal operating conditions: as a rule you should stick to the standard types listed. If you use the car in unusual climatic conditions, or intend to go racing in it, consult a Mazda dealer or a recognized tuning specialist for specific advice on plug grades. Note that you may need to change the plug grade if you have modified the engine or fitted high performance parts.

5   It's permissible to remove light deposits from the plug electrodes using fine abrasive paper - hold the plug with the electrode end downwards so that any debris drops away and not into the recess around the insulator. Use a wire brush to clean the plug threads.

Mazda Miata, MX-5, Eunos & Roadster

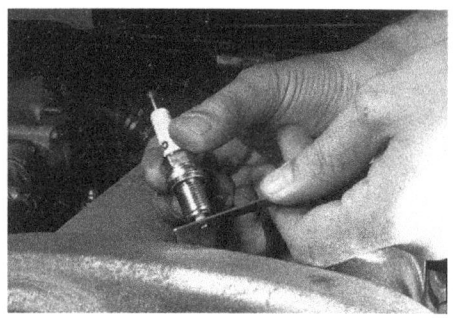

6/6 Measuring sparkplug electrode gap.

6/7 Correct connection of sparkplug wires.

6　　Once you've checked and cleaned the plug electrodes, or before new plugs are installed, check the electrode gap. It is worth buying a plug gapping tool for this task; these have wire-type feeler gauges and special tools for setting the gap by bending the ground (earth) electrode. Note that you should never attempt to bend the center electrode; if you do, you're likely to break the insulator nose. Set the electrode gap to 1.0-1.1mm/0.040-0.043in.

7　　Before installing the new or cleaned plugs, apply a small trace of copper-based, antiseize compound or molybdenum disulfide grease to the plug threads; this will make removal easier next time, and lessens the risk of a frozen (seized) plug tearing out the plug threads in the cylinder head. **Caution!** Do not overtighten the sparkplugs, the correct torque is 15-22Nm/1.5-2.3kgf m/11-16lbf ft. Reconnect the sparkplug wires (HT leads).

7. IDLE SPEED - CHECKING & ADJUSTMENT

☞ 1/1, 2 & 2/1.

1　　The correct idle speed for an engine at normal temperature with the transmission in neutral (manual trans) or **P** (auto trans) is 800-900rpm (MT) or 750-850 (AT). With air conditioning on, idle should increase to 1000rpm (MT only).

2　　The onboard rev counter (tachometer) is not very accurate at measuring these sort of engine speeds, so you should assume that the idle speed is OK if the engine does not seem to be running excessively fast at idle, nor so slowly that it stalls at the least provocation.

3　　Idle speed can be altered by small adjustments of the air adjusting screw (see diagram). However, as this action may be illegal in some territories, we advise you to leave it to your Mazda dealer to set idle speed using the appropriate SSTs (special service tools). **Do not** attempt to adjust the throttle adjusting screw, which is factory set and should never be disturbed.

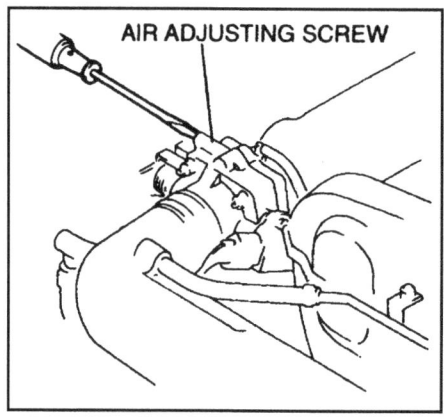

D7/3 USING AIR ADJUSTING SCREW TO ADJUST IDLE SPEED.
(See text.)

7/3 Air adjusting screw (see text).

8. TRANSMISSION (MANUAL) OIL - CHECKING LEVEL & CHANGING

☞ 1/1, 2 & 2/1.

1　　Checking or changing the transmission oil requires the car to be raised so you can get access to the filler and drain plugs. Place the car on jack (axle) stands, or on fabricated steel wheel ramps. **Caution!** The car must be raised to a *level* position to ensure the oil level reading is correct. If you have access to a vehicle lift, or can get the oil changed by a Mazda dealer or service station, we suggest that you do so. Unless you need to do other work under the car, you need to do a lot of preparatory work to gain access. For details of jacking and supporting the car ☞ 1/3.

CHECKING LEVEL

2　　With the car safely supported, unscrew and remove the transmission oil level/filler plug **A**, which is situated halfway up the transmission casing on the left-hand side.

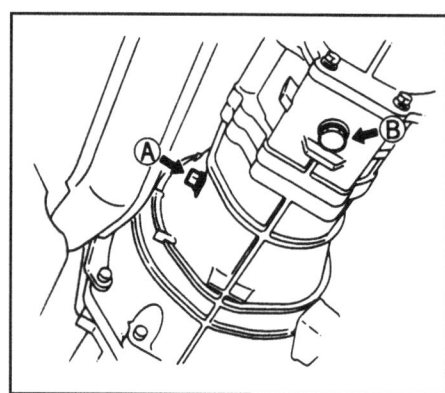

D8/2 LOCATION OF MANUAL TRANSMISSION DRAIN AND LEVEL/FILLER PLUGS.

3　　You'll need a syringe, or transmission oil in a pack with a built-in tube. Add fresh oil through the filler/level plug hole until the oil is level with the hole - allow any excess to drain out for at least ten minutes. The correct oil grade, which will be marked on the container, is most commonly API Service GL-4 or GL-5 SAE 75W-90. Where temperatures are constantly above 10 degrees C/50 degrees F, you can use API Service GL-4 or GL-5 SAE 80W-90. These gearboxes respond well to synthetic oils of the appropriate grade, particularly if you feel the gearchange is too notchy.

4　　Once the oil level is correct, install the filler/level plug (**A**) and tighten it to 25-39Nm/2.5-4.0kgf m/18-28lbf ft.

CHANGING TRANSMISSION OIL

5　　With the car safely supported, position a drain tray under the transmission drain plug, then remove the filler plug **A** (diagram D8/2), followed by the drain plug **B**. The transmission holds 2.0 liters/2.1 US or 1.8 Imp quarts of oil, so have ready a container of at least this capacity. The transmission

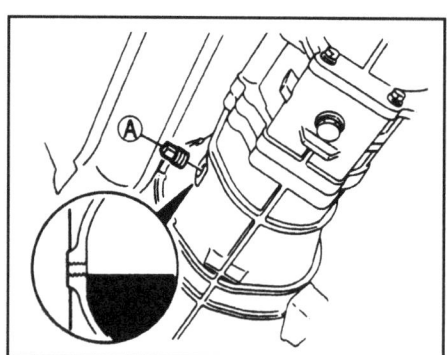

D8/4 CORRECT OIL LEVEL FOR MANUAL TRANSMISSION.
A = Filler/level plug.

2: Tune-up & maintenance

8/3 Topping-up transmission oil.

oil is viscous and will take a while to drain completely. It will drain quicker, and more contaminants will be flushed out, if the car has been driven and the transmission is warm. **Warning!** Take care to avoid burns from the hot oil and/or the exhaust system.

6 When the oil has finished draining, clean the drain plug and drain hole threads, and then install the plug using a new sealing washer. Tighten the plug to 40-58Nm/4.0-6.0kgf m/29-43lbf ft.

7 Add fresh oil (see specification in step 3) through the filler/level plug hole until the oil is level with the hole - allow any excess to drain out for at ten minutes.

8 Once the oil level is correct, install the filler plug and tighten it to 25-39Nm/2.5-4.0kgf m/18-28lbf ft.

9. TRANSMISSION (AUTO) FLUID - CHECKING LEVEL & CHANGING

☞ 1/1, 2 & 2/1.

1 The automatic transmission fluid (ATF) should be checked and changed at the specified intervals or transmission performance will deteriorate and wear or damage may result.

CHECKING

2 Position the car on a flat, level surface. **Warning!** Make sure that the parking (hand) brake is applied and that the rear wheels are secured by chocks; the car must be unable to move during the checking procedure.

3 Start the engine and wait until it's at normal temperature before commencing the test. The transmission fluid must be at 60-70°C (140-158°F) during the test, and the best way to ensure this is to carry out the check after a run of several miles.

4 Apply the footbrake, holding the pedal down firmly while shifting into each range in turn, leaving the shift lever in each position for several seconds. This distributes the oil around the transmission, leaving the level as it would normally be during driving. Shift back to **P** (Park) and leave the engine idling.

5 Withdraw the transmission dipstick, wipe it clean, then reinsert it, pushing it fully home. Withdraw the dipstick again and note the level indicated. This must lie between the **F** (Full) and **L** (Low) marks. Examine the oil on the dipstick for discoloration or abnormal smells.

6 Heavy discoloration, or a muddy appearance, may indicate burning of the drive plates, while an abnormal smell can suggest general overheating of the transmission (or fluid in bad need of changing). In either case, try changing the fluid as described below and see if the condition improves, before having the transmission checked professionally.

7 Top-up the transmission if required by adding fresh fluid through the dipstick guide tube. The oil is usually supplied in plastic packs with flexible filler tubes to facilitate this. The correct fluid grade is ATF (Automatic Transmission Fluid), Dexron II or M-III.

CHANGING

8 During the oil change procedure the car must be level, but raised clear of the ground to allow access to the underside of the transmission. You will need to jack the car and support it on jack (axle) stands. **Warning!** Ensure that the car is secure before venturing underneath ☞ 1/3.

9 Note that the oil change should be carried out after a run, while the oil in the transmission is hot. This will ensure that it drains quickly and completely, and that any contaminants are in suspension and thus flushed out. You will need a drain tray with a capacity of around 4 litres/1 gallon to catch the used oil.

10 Position the drain tray under the transmission oil pan, then loosen the oil pan bolts by around one turn each. Leave one bolt loosely in place at each corner and remove the rest. **Warning!** You'll need to be careful during the next stage - the oil in the transmission is hot and could burn if you get it on your skin.

11 Support the oil pan with one arm and remove the remaining bolts, then quickly lower one end of the oil pan so that the oil drains into the drain tray. Leave any residual oil to drain off and then remove the oil pan for cleaning.

12 Carefully clean out the oil pan, removing all traces of old oil and contaminants from it and its magnet. Clean the transmission case gasket face, then install the oil pan using a new gasket. Tighten the oil pan bolts evenly and progressively to 5.9-7.8Nm/60-80kgf cm/53-69lbf in.

13 Through the dipstick guide tube, add just under 4.0 liters/4.2 US or 3.5Imp quarts of ATF.

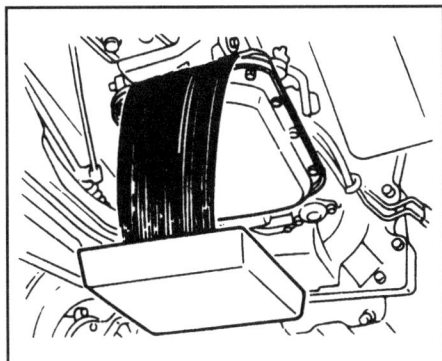

D9/11 DRAINING THE AUTOMATIC TRANSMISSION UNIT.

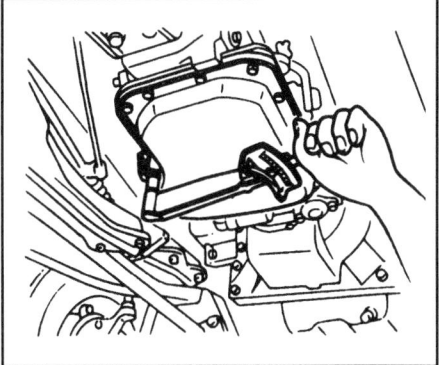

D9/12 TORQUE TIGHTEN OIL PAN BOLTS.

After lowering the car to the ground and chocking the rear wheels, apply the parking brake and go through the oil level check described earlier in this section. If necessary, add a little extra oil to bring the level to within the prescribed range on the dipstick.

14 **Caution!** Take care not to overfill the transmission. If you do, you'll need to remove the excess, using a hand operated pump or syringe and a long tube introduced down the dipstick guide tube. Failing this, you will have to remove the oil pan again to drain off the excess oil.

10. DIFFERENTIAL OIL - CHECKING LEVEL & CHANGING

☞ 1/1, 2 & 2/1.

CHECKING

1 The way you go about tackling this operation will depend on your agility and facilities. The car needs to be resting on a level surface during the check, either on its wheels, or raised and supported on jack (axle) stands. If you can reach the filler/level plug on the back of the differential housing without having to jack and support the car, so much the better, but if you cannot reach the plug this way ☞ 1/3.

2 Unscrew and remove the combined 23mm filler/level plug - this is the higher of the two plugs on the back of the differential housing. Verify that the oil level is level with the bottom edge of the hole. If necessary, add oil until it is at the correct level, but do not overfill; leave any excess to drain out for at least ten minutes before installing the plug. The correct grade of oil (you'll find appropriate markings on the container) is API GL-5. If ambient

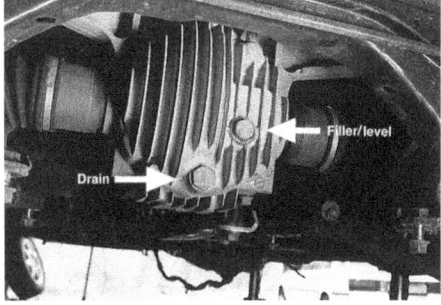

10/2 Differential drain & filler/level plugs.

temperature will not be above 18 degrees C (0 degrees F) use oil of viscosity SAE 80W and SAE 90W for ambient temperatures above this level.

3   Clean the plug and threads in the filler hole, then install the plug using a new sealing washer, tightening it to 39-53Nm/4.0-5.5kgf m/29-39lbf ft. Wipe off any residual oil from the outside of the differential housing.

CHANGING

4   It's best if the oil is hot when drained because it will flow more freely, and it's more likely that contaminants will remain in suspension and get flushed out with the old oil. If you can, run the car for a few of miles before draining the oil.

5   Place a drain tray of at least 1.2 liters/1.27 US or 1 Imp quart capacity below the differential housing, and remove the combined 23mm filler/level (upper) plug and the 24mm drain (lower) plug. **Warning!** The oil could be hot. Leave the oil to drain. This may take a while due to the viscosity of the oil, and will be speeded up a little if the car has been used recently and the oil is still warm.

6   When the old oil has finished draining, clean the drain plug, filler/level plug and the casing hole threads, then install the drain plug using a new sealing washer. Tighten it to 39-53Nm/4.0-5.5kgf m/29-39lbf ft.

7   Add oil through the filler/level hole until it is just level with the bottom of the hole; do not overfill. Leave any excess oil to drain out for at least ten minutes before installing the plug. The oil capacity is 1.0 liter/1.06 US or 0.88 Imp quarts.

8   Install the filler/level plug using a new sealing washer, tightening it to 39-53Nm/4.0-5.5kgf m/29-39lbf ft. Wipe away any spilled oil from the outside of the differential housing.

11. BATTERY - CHECKING CHARGE, SPECIFIC GRAVITY & ELECTROLYTE LEVEL

☞ 1/1, 2 & 2/1.

Warning! Battery electrolyte is extremely corrosive. Take care not to drop the battery or damage its casing. Take care to avoid eye or skin contact during handling (use disposable plastic gloves and eye protection). If electrolyte splashes on the skin, wash immediately with copious amounts of water and get medical assistance if burning is noted. If splashes enter the eyes, wash immediately with copious amounts of water and summon immediate medical assistance. Contact between electrolyte and clothing will quickly cause damage - wash immediately in water to minimize damage.

1   Note that specific gravity testing and topping-up of electrolyte can only be applied where a conventional replacement battery with removable cell caps has been fitted. The original, maintenance-free battery supplied with the car contains a gel-type electrolyte and does not have removable cell caps: it should not be tampered with. Most replacement batteries are also of the maintenance-free type. For information on checking and charging the original battery ☞ 7/5.

11/2 Battery access with cover removed.

REMOVAL AND CHECKING

2   📷 Disarm any security alarms (vehicle or audio). Remove the spare wheel after releasing the wing nut which secures it. If applicable, undo the 13mm plastic nut holding the battery cover to the bodyshell near the rear lamp lens: this can usually be done with your fingers. Lift the battery cover off the poppers beneath its base and remove it.

3   Use a 10mm wrench or socket to loosen the negative (-) terminal clamp. **Warning/Caution!** Take great care not to short the tool against the positive (+) terminal (which should be fully covered by a plastic protector). Lift the negative terminal clamp from its post and tie it back out of harm's way. Lift the protector, then loosen and remove the positive (+) terminal clamp.

4   If your battery fixing arrangement features a tall end bracket, release the bracket after releasing the two 10mm bolts which secure it. Loosen the single 10mm clamp nut until the hook of the threaded rod can be released from the base bracket. Lift the clamp away. **Warning/Caution!** Take great care not to short the two battery terminals with the clamp as it is removed.

5   📷 Pull off the two vent hoses from the battery vent manifold (replacement batteries may have a different vent hose arrangement). Lift the battery out of the trunk and place it on the bench for examination and charging.

6   If you detect signs of electrolyte on the exterior of the battery, it may be that the casing has been damaged, in which case a new battery must be fitted. If electrolyte has leaked into the trunk, you must remove and neutralize any traces, or serious corrosion will result. With luck, any leakage will be confined to the plastic tray in which the battery sits. Given the battery's location in the trunk, if you have any reason to suspect casing

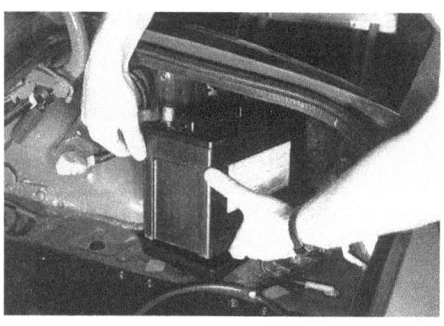

11/5 Carefully lift the battery from the trunk.

damage, fit a new battery immediately.

7   You'll need to wash the area affected by an electrolyte leak with an alkaline solution to neutralize the acid. Make up a solution of warm water to which a couple of tablespoons of sodium bicarbonate have been added and dissolved. You can get sodium bicarbonate from pharmacies and general stores, where it is sold as a raising agent for home baking (baking soda). The solution will fizz as it contacts the electrolyte. Don't breathe the fumes produced, and wear eye and skin protection throughout the operation.

8   If the battery is undamaged, wipe over its casing with a rag or paper wipe dampened with the sodium bicarbonate solution. This will clean the casing and remove any acid residue. The terminal posts can be cleaned using abrasive paper or a small wire brush (or you can buy special cleaning tools from auto parts stores). Once clean, coat the terminals with petroleum jelly (Vaseline) or battery terminal grease to prevent corrosion - don't use regular grease for this.

BATTERY VOLTAGE CHECK

9   You can check battery condition by using a voltmeter (or a multimeter set to volts). Connect the meter negative (-) probe to the battery negative terminal, and the positive (+) probe to the battery positive terminal.

10   A reading of 12.4 volts or more shows that the battery is in good condition.

11   If you get a reading of below 12.4 volts, go through the normal recharging procedure. If the battery voltage remains below 12 volts after recharging, you need to fit a new battery. If, after charging, battery voltage is above 12.4 volts, but you still experience repeated battery discharge, check the charging system ☞ 7/6.

ELECTROLYTE SPECIFIC GRAVITY CHECK

12   **Caution!** This sub-section applies only to a conventional battery fitted as a replacement for the original maintenance-free, gel-type battery. Remove each cell cap in turn and use a battery hydrometer to measure the specific gravity of the electrolyte in each cell. The specific gravity readings found should be compared with the following:

Electrolyte specific gravity at 20 degrees C (68 F)
Fully charged: 1.270-1.290
Half charged: 1.190-1.210
Discharged: 1.110-1.130

13   It will be noted that the specific gravity varies according to the state of charge of the battery, and will also be affected by variations in ambient temperature. A low reading on all cells is indicative of a low state of charge. More significantly, a low reading on only one cell indicates that the cell may be defective, and if you have experienced starting problems it may be preferable to fit a new battery, or at least to have it checked out professionally.

14   If the battery requires charging, do so, then recheck the specific gravity of each cell before

2: Tune-up & maintenance

installing it in the trunk. **Warning!** Excessively high charging rates could explode the battery due to gas build-up. Any form of charging releases hydrogen and oxygen from the battery. This is a potentially explosive mixture - keep well away from any potential source of ignition, and make sure the charging area is well ventilated. When handling the battery, take care to avoid short circuits - they can be dramatic and dangerous.

TOPPING-UP

15 **Caution!** This sub-section applies only to a conventional battery fitted as a replacement for the original maintenance-free, gel-type battery. If the battery electrolyte level is low, top-up the cell or cells using distilled or demineralized water only. **Caution!** Do not overfill the cells or excess electrolyte may be expelled in service - the correct electrolyte level is around 5mm/0.25in above the top edge of the plates. Always top-up the battery just before a run to ensure that the extra liquid mixes thoroughly with the electrolyte - this is especially important in winter, and will reduce the risk of the battery freezing and splitting while the car is parked.

BATTERY CHARGING

16 **Warning!** Excessively high charging rates could explode the battery due to overheating and gas build-up. Any form of charging releases hydrogen from the battery. This is a potentially explosive gas - keep well away from any potential source of ignition, and make sure the charging area is well ventilated. When handling the battery, take care to avoid short circuits - they can be dramatic and dangerous. Mazda recommends that the battery be stood in a tray of water with the water level at half the battery's height during recharging.

17 The standard S46A24L(S) battery fitted to these cars when new should normally be re-charged at 3A or less. This slow (trickle) charging procedure is always preferable where time allows. **Caution!** If you need to fast charge the battery, never exceed 20A, and don't fast charge for more than 30 minutes: be aware that repeated fast charging shortens battery life. If the battery becomes hot to the touch during charging, discontinue charging and allow it to cool down, or reduce the charge rate.

18 Depending on how discharged the battery is, trickle charging at 2-3 amps could take 12 to 16 hours to restore it fully. It's always preferable to use a current-controlled charger, so if you intend to buy a charger, try to get one of these units if you can. A current-controlled charger allows you to set the charge rate. Cheaper, voltage-controlled units find their own charging current - the current starts out high, then slowly falls back to zero as the battery reaches full charge. With this type of charger it is harder to gauge how long you need to perform the charging operation and there is a real possibility of battery damage.

19 Noting the precautions outlined earlier, check that the battery terminals are clean, then connect the charger clamps to the battery terminal posts, negative (-) to negative, and positive (+) to positive. Switch on the charger at the selected rate and charge for the prescribed amount of time. On cheaper units watch the charger meter to ensure it does not charge the battery at over 3 amps for more than half an hour before falling below 3 amps and then to zero. Disconnect the charger and check the battery voltage. Resume charging for a while if required.

20 If you are unable to get the battery up to 12 volts, this indicates that it's at or near the end of its useful life.

BATTERY INSTALLATION

21 With the battery clean and fully charged, place it in its tray in the trunk, remembering to install the vent hoses. Reassemble and secure the clamp (do not overtighten it). Install the end bracket (if applicable), then connect the battery leads, positive (+) wire clamp and protector first, negative (-) wire clamp last. **Warning!** Take care not to short the battery terminals with the wrench or battery clamp during installation. Install the battery cover, followed by the spare wheel.

INSTALLING A NEW BATTERY

22 Any purpose designed replacement battery you purchase is likely to require some modification to securing brackets/clamps, and to the battery cover. The battery will come with instructions and, maybe, a fitting kit. **Caution!** We strongly advise that you do not try to fit anything but a sealed battery in place of the original type.

12. IGNITION TIMING - CHECKING & ADJUSTING

☞ 1/1, 2.

4 To carry out this check, you'll need a 12 volt stroboscopic timing light ("Strobe") of the sort that has crocodile clip connectors, and an inductive sensor which clips on the outside of a high tension ignition wire. You should also check the timing marks on the lower (crankshaft) pulley and the nearby scale. Clean the marks and, if necessary, use typist's correction fluid/white paint to make them more visible. Note that each mark equates to two degrees of crankshaft rotation. The test should be conducted at normal operating temperature, so run the engine for a while before starting the test, or do it after a run. Switch off the engine.

5 Open the data link connector cover and bridge the **TEN** (test engine) and **GND** (ground) terminals with a piece of stiff copper wire. Terminal positions are marked inside the cover.

6 There is a purpose-supplied 12 volt power source in the engine compartment in the form of a blue connector block with a single brass male terminal; it's located just behind the left-hand headlamp. Clip the power lead of your timing light to this terminal and clip the ground cable to any bare metal item on the engine block. Attach the timing light inductor clip to the ignition wire feeding the sparkplug nearest the radiator (number one cylinder). **Warning!** Ensure all timing light leads are tied back well away from the fans and moving pulleys. **Warning!** Make sure you are not wearing loose clothing that could get caught in moving parts (no, we're not suggesting you work in the buff - but wearing a tie would be a very bad idea ...).

7 ◻ Start the engine, and, if necessary, adjust the idle speed (☞ 2/7) to the specified setting. Aim the light at the timing marks near the crankshaft pulley at the front of the engine. The mark on the pulley should appear frozen at against the scale at 10 degrees btdc (plus or minus 1 degree). If adjustment is needed, slacken the camshaft position sensor 12mm lock bolt just enough to allow the sensor body to be rotated.

12/7 Strobe 'freezes' pulley timing mark.

Note this lock bolt has a tall head to make it more accessible, but it is still not easy to access: a flat, box-end wrench (ring spanner) is the best tool for the job. Rotate the sensor body gently (anti-clockwise = advance) until the timing is correct, then tighten the lock bolt securely.

8 Recheck the timing setting, then gradually increase engine speed and confirm that the ignition timing mark advances in relation to the scale. If it fails to do so, you'll need to check the ignition system. Finally, disconnect the timing light, remove the jumper wire and close the data link connector cover.

9 Note that if you had to adjust the ignition timing, it will almost certainly have affected idling speed, which should be checked and reset as necessary.

13. DRIVEAXLES (HALFSHAFTS), REAR - CHECKING

☞ 1/1, 2 & 2/1.

1 Chock the front wheels and support the rear of the car on jack (axle) stands or metal wheel ramps. **Warning!** Do not go beneath the car unless

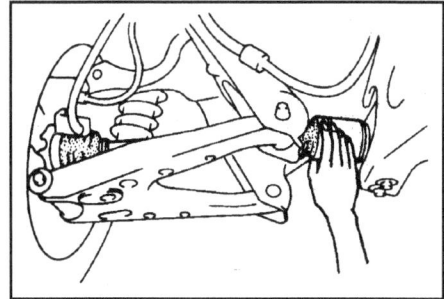

D13/2 CHECKING DRIVEAXLE BOOTS.

Mazda Miata, MX-5, Eunos & Roadster

it is absolutely securely supported.

2   With your fingers, open up the 'concertina' sections of the dust boots at both ends of the shafts, and check carefully for tears or fatigue cracks. Damaged boots must be replaced quickly, otherwise damage to the shaft joints will quickly occur. Also check that the boot retaining clamps are secure.

3   If the inboard joint casing (adjacent to the differential unit) is wet with oil, failure of the shaft seal within the differential casing is indicated. Check the oil level within the differential unit: if the oil loss is serious, renew the seal as quickly as possible.

4   Grasp each shaft firmly and make sure that you cannot twist it back and forth sufficiently to cause a loud clunk, which would indicate severe wear of the splines or joints.

14. ENGINE COOLANT - TOPPING-UP & CHANGING

☞ 1/1, 2 & 2/1.

Warning! If the engine has been run within the last hour or so, the engine coolant will be hot and under pressure. Removing the radiator cap or coolant reservoir cap can result in the coolant suddenly boiling as pressure is released, resulting in scalding steam being ejected. Always allow the engine to cool before removing either cap. Wear eye protection, gloves and overalls for safety. Place rag over the radiator cap, then turn the cap slowly counter-clockwise until it reaches the first stop position. Wait until pressure has vented before removing the cap completely.

Warning! Antifreeze is very toxic, and yet its sweet smell can be attractive to children and animals: mop up spills quickly, and keep containers tightly sealed out of the reach of youngsters. Antifreeze can cause skin damage and will damage paintwork, too.

1   The engine coolant level should be checked regularly and topped-up as required - we suggest that you give the level a quick visual check on a weekly basis. The check should be carried out on fairly level ground, and with the engine cold to avoid any risk of scalding (see warning above).

2   Remove the radiator cap and check that the coolant level is just below the filler neck. Also check that the coolant level in the reservoir is between the **FULL** and **LOW** level marks. Add only pre-mixed coolant to adjust the levels as necessary.

MIXING ENGINE COOLANT

3   It is important to use coolant made up in the correct proportions from distilled or demineralized water and ethylene glycol-based antifreeze. Never use water direct from a faucet (tap) or you risk corrosion and scale deposits in the cooling system. Never use alcohol or methanol-based antifreeze.

4   To check the existing coolant mixture you'll need a thermometer and a coolant hydrometer. The specific gravity of the coolant mixture varies according to ambient temperature and the water/

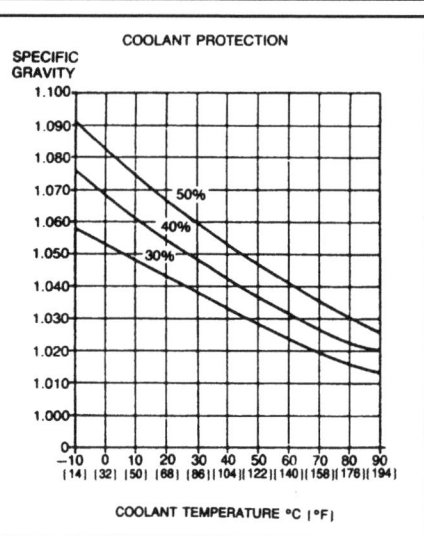

D14/5 COOLANT PROTECTION GRAPH.

antifreeze ratio. The recommended proportions for frost protection at various air temperatures are as follows -

Protection down to (degrees)	Water /Antifreeze (%)	Specific gravity at 20C/68F
- 16C/3F	65/35	1.054
- 26C/-15F	55/45	1.066
- 40C/-40F	45/55	1.078

5   ◐ Note the point made above about how ambient temperature will affect the specific gravity of the coolant. The accompanying graph illustrates this relationship.

6   Having checked the specific gravity required for operation in your temperature zone, mix the appropriate proportions of antifreeze and distilled/demineralized water in a clean container. Store the mixture in a sealed plastic drum or similar for use when topping-up the cooling system.

TOPPING-UP THE COOLING SYSTEM

7   Before adding fresh coolant, check the general condition of the existing coolant. Look for signs of scale build-up around the filler neck, and also for signs of oil contamination. If the coolant is dirty or contaminated, you should drain the system, flush it out, and then add fresh coolant. Note that if oil contamination is present, this may indicate a failed seal or gasket in the engine, especially if there has been a significant coolant loss recently. If, for example, the head gasket blows between a cooling system passage and a combustion chamber, combustion pressure may well force coolant out of the system and cause oil contamination of the remainder. Always investigate and monitor such incidents closely - you could avoid expensive repair bills if you act quickly.

CHANGING THE COOLANT

8   The engine coolant should be changed at the specified intervals, or more frequently if there have been signs of contamination or deterioration

of the existing coolant (see above). This task should be undertaken with the engine cold. The cooling system capacity is 6.0 liters (6.3 US qt/5.3 Imp qt), so you'll need a container of sufficient size to hold this amount of liquid comfortably.

9   ◐+ Remove the radiator filler cap. Position the drain container below the radiator drain plug (there's an access opening in the engine undertray). Loosen the drain plug using a screwdriver and allow the coolant to drain.

10   Place a hose in the radiator filler neck and allow the system to flush through for a while, until the emerging water is completely clear, then allow

14/9a Radiator drain plug.

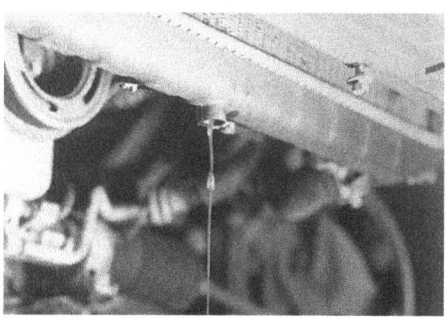

14/9b Let coolant drain into receptacle.

the system to drain completely. While this is taking place, remove, empty, wash out and refit the coolant reservoir. Tighten the radiator drain plug and tighten it securely.

11   ◐+ Slowly add fresh coolant to the radiator - no faster than 1 liter (1.1 US qt/0.9 Imp qt) per minute - until the level is just below the filler neck. Run the engine at idle for a while with the radiator cap removed. When the top radiator hose feels hot to the touch, top-up the coolant to bring its level back to just below the filler neck. Switch off the engine, fit the radiator cap and top-up the coolant reservoir to between the **FULL** and **LOW** marks.

14/11a Refilling radiator.

2: Tune-up & maintenance

14/11b Topping-up coolant reservoir.

15. LIGHTS, HORN, WIPERS & WASHERS - CHECKING

☞ 1/1, 2 & 2/1.

1   Periodically, you should check that the main electrical sub-systems are functioning normally. We recommend a weekly general inspection. You should also check around the car before undertaking a long journey.

LIGHTS CHECK

2   In some countries it's compulsory to carry a set of replacement bulbs in the car, a practice we would recommend. Although storage space is at a premium in these cars, you'll find that there are a few small recesses in the trunk which would be suitable for this purpose. You may be able to obtain a boxed set of bulbs from an auto parts store. Alternatively, have a set made up by your Mazda dealer, parts store or auto-electrical shop. We further suggest that you purchase a replacement fuse of each type used on the car (you only need one of each rating) and keep these with your spare bulbs.

3   It is pretty easy to monitor the condition of all external lights on your car with minimum effort. If you position an old mirror on the back wall of your garage, you can check the operation of the tail, brake and rear turn signal lights as you park the car. Alternatively, if you regularly park in front of a large window, such as a shop front, you can use this in the same way. It is usually pretty obvious if a headlight bulb has failed, and you can also check these and the other lights while driving, as you approach buildings with lots of glass in the frontage. If you live miles from civilisation and there is nothing more reflective than a tree around, you'll need to walk around the car and check each light in turn. An assistant will be needed in the case of brake lights.

4   Of special importance is a regular check on the headlight lenses. Because these are normally retracted while the car is parked, it's easy for dirt build-up or damage to go unnoticed. Use the manual control to raise the lights for checking and cleaning. While water works fine for cleaning, a silicone-based polish will help prevent dirt sticking to the lens surface.

HORN

5   This is easy enough to check while driving (if you're a bad-tempered driver you might get to check this most days!) Note that it is illegal to have a non-functioning horn in many countries/states.

WIPERS AND WASHERS

6   Check that the wiper and washer systems function normally. Have you ever noticed how washer reservoirs run out only on days when you really need them and there's no water around? Check that the reservoir is full, and remember to add a screenwash additive for better dirt, grease and bug removal.

7   ◘+ On most cars, the windshield washer reservoir is mounted on the firewall inside the engine compartment, the exact location and design varying according to market. On ABS-equipped cars the washer filler will be found in the closing panel ahead of the radiator.

8   Cars for some markets also have headlight washer systems. The reservoir will be found in the nose of the car, with a remote filler point accessible under the hood (bonnet).

9   If the washer system does not operate normally, check that the reservoir is full and that the washer motor can be heard running when the system is operated. If this does not resolve the

15/7a Windshield washer reservoir (location varies).

15/7b Washer filler location (cars with ABS).

problem, check that the washer jet(s) are clear. Blockages can usually be cleared using a pin or fine wire. You can also adjust the jet angle using a pin - locate the pin in the jet and swivel it to the desired angle. Check the adjustment while driving the car - note that the airflow over the car will affect the way the water hits the windshield, and you may need to compensate a little for this.

10   If the wipers leave streaks across the windshield, check for an oil film on the glass. This is often caused by diesel fumes, and can be removed by washing with a detergent solution. Once the dirt is removed, dry the windshield with a handful of newspaper - this will leave the surface really clean and grease-free.

11   If cleaning the windshield fails to improve the operation of the wipers, check the blade condition, and fit new blades if the wiping edge is worn or damaged. Note that the blades will last a lot longer if you clean the screen regularly - dirt and bug remains are abrasive and will soon damage the fine blade edge.

16. TIRES - CHECKING PRESSURES & CONDITION

☞ 1/1, 2 & 2/1.

PRESSURE CHECKS AND ADJUSTMENT

1   Tire pressures need to be maintained regularly, and should be checked when the tires are cold. These cars are known to be especially sensitive to pressure settings and, if they're not correct the car's handling characteristics will be adversely affected. **Warning!** Incorrect tire pressures can put your life and that of other road users at risk.

2   It is preferable to check tire pressures after the car has been standing for some hours. An accurate pressure reading can only be made while the tires are at ambient temperature. When you drive the car, the tire temperature rises, and this means that a pressure reading taken at a gas station will be misleading. Also, gas station gauges can be very inaccurate.

3   ◘ We recommend that you use a simple pressure gauge which can be carried in the car. You can buy inexpensive pocket pressure gauges at auto parts stores, and if you don't have compressed air in your garage, you can use a footpump or a small electric compressor to inflate the tires.

16/3 Checking tire pressure.

4   The specified tire pressure (front and rear) for standard tires is 179kPa/1.8kgf cm2/26psi. Snow tires (175/65R 14-M+S) should be inflated to 119kPa/1.8kgf cm2/26psi (front) and 200kPa/2.0kgf cm2/29psi (rear). In the case of the temporary 'spacesaver' spare tire, inflate to 41kPa/4.2kgf cm2/60psi. The temporary spare is of much smaller section than the normal tire, and this is why it needs the extra pressure. **Warning!** If you ever need to use the temporary spare, note the speed restriction label and get the normal wheel installed again as soon as you can.

Mazda Miata, MX-5, Eunos & Roadster

TIRE CONDITION CHECKS

5 As mentioned above, the tires and wheels have a profound effect on the car's handling and roadholding, and should be checked regularly. Note also that if you have reason to suspect possible damage, as might be caused by running over an object in the road, or accidentally kerbing the wheels, make a point of checking for damage as soon as you can stop the car.

6 Once each week check each wheel and tire. Inspect the tire generally for wear, splits or other damage, and for foreign objects like stones or nails embedded in the treads. Tire condition and tread wear limit laws vary from one country to another, and you should be aware of and conform with local laws applicable to your car. In addition to these requirements, the tires must be replaced when the tread depth falls to 1.6mm/0.063in or less, or whenever the tread has worn down enough to reach the wear indicator bars built into the tire tread pattern. The wear indicators on snow tires will be exposed when tread depth has been reduced by 50 per cent.

7 You should also take into consideration seasonal factors. A part-worn tire with around 2mm, or so, tread remaining might be acceptable during dry summer weather, but the same tire should be discarded if noted during late fall (autumn) - at this time of year, much more reliance is placed on the tire's ability to deal with water and mud, and, with the approach of winter, snow and ice may be a problem in some areas. As with pressures, these cars are especially sensitive to tire condition, and you will notice a significant improvement in the way the car steers and handles after new tires have been installed.

8 While checking the tread, take note of *how* the tread is wearing - this can tell you a lot about potential tire and suspension problems. This topic is covered in detail later in this manual ☞ 9/24.

9 During the tire check, look out for stones, nails or other items embedded in the tire. If found, pry out the object with an old screwdriver or similar tool. Modern tire construction methods give us tires which are pretty resistant to punctures, but if an object has penetrated the tire sufficiently for it to be punctured (you should hear the leak hissing as the object is pulled out), mark the site of the puncture, then fit the emergency spare wheel and get the damaged tire repaired or replaced.

10 Examine the tire tread and both sidewalls (don't forget the inner wall!) for splits, cuts or bulges. Splits or cuts are usually caused by running over road debris - steel strapping from packing cases is a common culprit. Bulges in either the tread or sidewall denote a structural failure of the tire casing, and in extreme cases you may find the casing plies, fine steel strands, sticking out of the tire. If you find damage of this type, again, install the temporary spare and get a new tire fitted.

TIRE ROTATION

11 To maximize tire life, the tires (and wheels) should be rotated at the intervals specified in the relevant maintenance schedule. Even if the schedule for your car doesn't list tire rotation as an operation, you can carry this out on an annual basis.

12 The purpose of tire rotation is to get better tire mileage by evening out wear. Front and rear tires wear differently; the front ones tend to scrub out on the edges, while the rear ones wear out more evenly. By interchanging the tires front to rear, you even out this wear and get better mileage overall.

13 Jack the car on one side (☞ 1/3), having loosened the lug nuts (wheel nuts) by a turn each on both wheels. Move the front wheel to the back and install the rear wheel at the front, then tighten the lug nuts provisionally. Lower the car to the ground, tighten the lug nuts fully, then check the tire pressures. Repeat the process on the other side of the car. **Warning!** After this procedure, the steering will have a different 'feel' which you'll quickly get used to.

17. BODY - GENERAL MAINTENANCE

☞ 1/1, 2 & 2/1.

LOCKS AND HINGES

1 The various locks, catches and hinges around the body require occasional maintenance to ensure smooth operation and to minimize wear. This maintenance applies to the door hinges and locks, the hood (bonnet) and trunk (boot) hinges and catches, and minor mechanical parts like the seat hinges and runners. It also applies to the moving parts of the convertible top. In predominantly hot, dry areas, it's likely that the car will be used with the top down for much of the time. Conversely, in colder or wetter areas, the top may remain up a lot of the time. Either way, the moving parts will be static for long periods, and this can lead to them freezing (seizing) in one position.

2 Operate the catch or hinge concerned and check that it moves smoothly and easily. If dirt has built up, this should be cleaned off. Electrical switch cleaner is often effective for this purpose, but care should be taken that this does not cause discoloration of nearby paint or upholstery.

3 Lubrication can be carried out with a number of products. General purpose lubricating oil is fine if used carefully, though most areas where this would have been used traditionally can usually be treated with a more modern silicone-based lubricant like WD40. On the heavier pivots, grease is preferable: either plain grease from a can or an aerosol grease.

4 If using the latter, beware of overspray on adjacent trim or upholstery. We have found motorcycle chain lube to be good on heavier items like door hinges. This product is formulated to penetrate into the mechanism. Its solvent then evaporates, leaving a specially sticky grease coating which lasts well and resists the effects of weather.

5 After lubrication, operate the catch or pivot repeatedly to distribute the grease or oil evenly, then wipe away any excess. This is especially important in areas like the door catches and strikers, where any excess is likely to get on your clothing.

CLEANING THE BODYWORK

6 Wash the car using plenty of water - a hose or domestic pressure wash is ideal for this. Alternatively, use water from a bucket, but remember to change the water regularly before the dirt turns it into an abrasive. To avoid any risk of damage to the paint finish, soak the bodywork thoroughly to soften the film of dirt, then gently hose it away, using a soft brush to agitate the dirt and loosen it. Don't scrub at the paintwork during this stage, or you'll cause tiny scratches to form, dulling the finish.

7 By all means use a detergent additive in moderation - this will help shift the greasy road dirt which builds up where the car is used in areas of high traffic density (in other words, just about everywhere). Beware of using too much detergent or you'll remove any body wax as well as the dirt. Whatever method and solution you use for the job, always wash the car on an overcast day if possible, or park it in the shade while you work; if the sun is shining on the car and the paintwork heats up, you'll find that you will have problems with spotting as the water keeps drying out too fast.

8 All external parts of the car should be cleaned in this way, including the plastic body parts, the hard or soft top and the wheels. Follow up by rinsing thoroughly with clean water. When rinsing, check how the water lies on the hood or trunk lid - if it forms small beads, the coating of polish is still good, while a continuous film tells you that it's time to wax the car. The paintwork can be dried off using an old (but clean) towel to prevent marking from the water droplets - some owners may prefer to use a traditional chamois leather; expensive, but effective. You may wish to try out some of the newer synthetic chamois leathers.

9 In the case of the wheels, note that they are lacquer-coated; don't use abrasive cleaners or you'll damage the lacquer film and then rapid corrosion will set in. Never, ever, use a wire brush to clean them. If your car has signs of peeling lacquer, or damage has resulted from stone chips, have the wheels blasted and re-lacquered professionally before the alloy surface gets pitted by corrosion. If you encounter stubborn staining or marking of the wheels, you could try one of the specialist products formulated for use on alloy wheels. Check with the store that it will not damage your lacquer coating before use.

10 Don't forget the wheel wells (wheelarches) or the lower edges of the rockers (sills) during regular washes. These areas are easily overlooked, and this explains why they are often the first areas to suffer corrosion problems - don't just deal with the easy-to-reach parts, or you'll get a nasty surprise when you do get round to the difficult ones. Pay special attention to the lip which lies inside the edge of many panels. These lips give strength and rigidity but, unfortunately, also provide tiny ledges where dirt can often build up unnoticed until the paint begins to blister.

11 Inside each wheel well you'll notice plastic liners attached with 10mm bolts. Be aware that road dirt can get behind these and build up - this can lead to corrosion if left too long. It is

2: Tune-up & maintenance

a good idea to remove the liners each spring and fall and clean out any build-up of dirt, especially to the rear of the wheels where most of it gets thrown by the tires. You can guard against corrosion here (and elsewhere) by applying a wax-based underbody coating before the liners are reinstalled.

12 Don't forget that road dirt contains all kinds of pollutants, many of which are corrosive. In northern areas where the winter roads are salted to clear snow, salt corrosion is a real problem. If you drive your car all year and live in such an area, you need to wash the bodywork at least as often as during the summer.

POLISHING THE BODY

13 We recommend that you polish your car at least twice a year, or whenever water stops beading on the paint. Spring and fall are the best times - that way you get protection from summer sun and winter rain and snow. Polishing takes a little time to do, especially if you use a traditional, quality wax. On the other hand, we are talking about a small car here, so you can afford to lavish attention on the body.

14 The choice of polish is up to you. There are hi-tech, wax-in-30-seconds products, and wax-as-you-wash additives. We've used them, and don't rate them highly. The way we figure it, if the instant shine products work, why are there still expensive, labor-intensive traditional waxes on sale? Take our advice and use a traditional, non-abrasive paste or cream body wax - you'll work hard a couple of times a year, but the rest of the time you can rest easy about your paint.

15 As with washing, polishing should be carried out on a dull day, or under shade, **never** in full sun or while the bodywork is still hot. Be sure to use really soft, clean rag for polishing and buffing the paint. Work on a small area at a time (we like to complete one panel at a time and then move to the next - that way, nothing gets missed). Apply the polish sparingly with a light circular action - if the paint has not been waxed for a long time and it soaks in, apply a little more. When it has dried to a white color, use a clean rag to buff to a good finish. Don't skip seams and crevices - they need waxing more than the flat areas. Finally, hand buffing is always preferable to using a power polisher.

TAR SPOTS

16 Road tar spotting on your paint can be removed using a proprietary solvent. Always follow the maker's directions, and we further suggest you try out the product on an unobtrusive area first to check for paint discoloration. Note that tar spots are much easier to remove from polished paintwork than from neglected and faded paint.

COLOR RESTORERS

17 Most of these products are nothing less than fine abrasives, and are designed to remove the surface layer of the paint to expose the unoxidized layer below. If you need to use them, do so sparingly, or you could cut through to the primer or bare metal - and the paint finish is none too thick. On the whole, steer clear. That said, if you've just bought a used Miata with dull paint at a bargain price - try a color restorer before booking a paint job - you might be pleasantly surprised. You might also like to try one of the color-impregnated polishes - these are designed to cover minor scratches and blemishes in the paint finish. In either case, follow the maker's directions for use, and with any abrasive restorer or wax, don't rub too hard, especially near edges.

CLEANING AND RESTORING THE CONVERTIBLE TOP AND TRIM

18 You can purchase a wide range of products which are specifically designed for cleaning items like the convertible top, dash panel, interior trim and the various body seals, and the like. They make these parts look like new and offer a degree of protection from sun damage and chemical attack. This type of cleaner also works well on tire sidewalls.

19 When dealing with the convertible top, remember it is an expensive part to replace - regular maintenance will get the best out of it. Mechanical maintenance of the frame and catch parts is described earlier in this section. You should also check the fabric regularly, especially if your car is normally used with the top permanently raised or lowered. If the top is kept stowed over long periods, it's a good idea to raise it once in a while, and then re-stow it, checking that the window is laid flat and the top fabric is folded carefully to avoid puckers and creases.

20 There are a number of proprietary products around which will keep the 'plastic' window of the soft top in good condition and stop it becoming opaque.

PRESSURE WASHING THE UNDERBODY

21 At least once each year you should pressure wash the underside of the car to remove accumulated road dirt, and chemical pollutants such as road salt. It helps if you can raise the car on jack (axle) stands (☞ 1/3) and remove the wheels to improve access. Where the underbody has a wax-type coating for corrosion protection, careful pressure washing will do no damage, though you should be aware that hot pressure washing or steam cleaning may damage or remove this coating, which will then need to be re-applied.

22 Inspect the underbody after pressure washing. **Warning!** Make certain that the car is supported safely, and **never** get under a car supported only by a jack. Check for signs of damage to the underbody coating, or of developing corrosion. **Caution!** Repair any such damage promptly to prevent it from getting worse.

18. STEERING & SUSPENSION - CHECKING

☞ 1/1, 2 & 2/1.

1 The steering and suspension components should be checked at regular intervals, preferably after the underside of the car has been pressure washed to remove road dirt. It should be noted that these cars are very sensitive to incorrect steering or suspension adjustment, and such misalignment will impair handling and may also result in rapid or uneven tire wear.

2 If you note such symptoms, carry out a check right away, even if this is not due on the maintenance schedule for some time. This could improve the car's driveability, reduce tire wear, and maybe even save your life. Preliminary checks can be carried out with the car sat on its wheels, but for a full check you will need to jack the car and support it on safety stands.

CHECKS WITH THE CAR ON THE GROUND

3 Preliminary checks on the steering can be carried out without dismantling. Sit in the driver's seat with the front wheel in the straight ahead position, and gently turn the wheel to and fro to gauge the amount of freeplay (lash) before any slack in the steering mechanism is taken up. You can gauge this better by leaning out of the car and noting when the road wheels begin to move.

4 Allowable freeplay at the steering wheel rim is 0-30mm/0-1.18in before the road wheels begin to move. Excessive play normally indicates wear in the steering balljoints, steering column universal joints or in the rack itself. Less likely causes are loose steering column clamps or rack mountings.

5 Next, try pulling the steering wheel left and right, then up and down, all at right angles in relation to the steering column. There should be no play felt here. If there is, check for wear in the steering column and joints, and check the security of the steering wheel and the clamps at the upper and lower ends of the intermediate shaft.

6 Relatively little can be determined about suspension condition while the car is resting on its wheels - the weight of the car will tend to disguise wear or stiffness in the suspension joints and pivots. You can, however, perform a quick check of shock absorber condition as follows.

7 Press down firmly on each corner of the car in turn and release it. The car should return to its normal height quickly and stop - if it continues to bounce like a 20 year old Oldsmobile, the shocker at that corner is shot. The chances are that the shock absorber seals have failed. If you discover this problem, note that shock absorbers must be replaced as an axle set: you might like to take the opportunity to upgrade all four units.

CHECKS WITH THE CAR RAISED

8 Park the car on a smooth, level surface, then jack it so that all four wheels are raised clear of the ground. **Warning!** Support the car securely on jack (axle) stands before proceeding further ☞ 1/3.

9 On manual steering cars, turn the steering from lock-to-lock at least five times to settle the steering components. While doing so, note any unusually slack or tight spots which might indicate wear or damage in the intermediate shaft joints or the rack mechanism, possibly as a result of impact damage. If noted, these faults should be investigated and rectified.

10 In the case of cars with power steering, the

Mazda Miata, MX-5, Eunos & Roadster

engine should be running during the check (ensure adequate ventilation of the working area), and you will need a thermometer to measure the power steering fluid temperature. Before you check the steering resistance, check and top-up the power steering fluid, and make sure there's no air in the system, as described below.

11   With the engine running on power steering cars, turn the steering wheel from lock-to-lock until the fluid temperature in the reservoir reaches 50-60 degrees C (122-140 F) - you can check this using the thermometer inserted into the fluid reservoir.

12   If the steering feels abnormally stiff with the wheels clear of the ground, the rack mechanism may be at fault, or the steering balljoints may be badly worn or damaged. Hook a pull scale (spring balance) to the outer edge of one of the steering wheel spokes and check the effort needed to turn the wheel during one complete revolution.

13   On manual steering cars this should be in the range 5-29.4N/0.5-3.0kg/1.1-6.6lb, whilst, for power steering cars, the normal resistance should be in the range 24-35N/2.4-3.6kg/5.3-7.9lb. If the effort's outside these limits a problem is indicated. For more information on manual steering systems ☞ 8/10, 8/12 & 8/13. In the case of power steering systems, refer to the fluid level checks described below. If this fails to resolve the fault ☞ 8/17 to 8/20.

14   While you've got the car raised on safety stands, visually check the steering and suspension parts. Obvious signs of wear or damage, like torn dust boots, should be investigated and repaired immediately, or further deterioration will result.

15   Push and pull on the steering balljoints and steering/suspension knuckles and feel for freeplay. You can determine minute amounts of wear this way, though you will probably not be able to *see* any movement. Try to establish which component is responsible for any movement, then turn to chapter 8 for a more detailed account of repair procedures.

16   It is not easy to detect wear or incorrect adjustment in the suspension wishbones with the suspension fully assembled; the assembly rides on rubber bushes and this tends to mask wear a little. If you suspect that there may be wear, or if you know that a wheel has been 'kerbed', we suggest that you check this more thoroughly, or have a Mazda dealer check and set up the suspension for you. Refer to chapter 8 for detailed checking and overhaul procedures.

17   You should also check the wheel bearings for play while you're in the neighborhood. Grab hold of the top and bottom of the wheel and rock it to and fro. Now grasp the front and back of the wheel and do the same. Even a minute amount of freeplay in the wheel bearings will be magnified at the wheel rim, but 2mm/0.08in, or more, at the wheel rim usually means trouble.

POWER STEERING - CHECKING FLUID LEVEL AND AIR BLEEDING

18   ◻ Fluid level in the power steering fluid reservoir should be checked periodically according to the maintenance schedule, and whenever abnormal steering operation is suspected. Note that low fluid level or air in the hydraulic system can result in excessive steering effort being required, or abnormal noise from the steering system. Pull out the combined filler plug and dipstick, and check that the fluid level lies between the high and low marks. **Caution!** If you need to add fluid, use only ATF (automatic transmission fluid), Dexron II or M-III.

19   To bleed air from the hydraulic system, jack the front of the car so the wheels are just clear of the ground, supporting the car on jack (axle) stands placed under the front jacking points - we suggest that you place small wood blocks between the rockers and the stands to prevent damage to the paint finish ☞ 1/3.

20   With the engine off, turn the steering fully to the left and then back to the right several times, and check whether the fluid level in the power steering fluid reservoir drops. If it does, top-up the fluid in the reservoir and repeat this procedure until the level remains stable.

21   Next, start the engine and allow it to idle. Turn the steering wheel fully to the left and then back to the right several times, and check whether the fluid level in the power steering fluid reservoir drops or becomes foamy. If it does, top-up the fluid in the reservoir as necessary, then repeat the procedure until the level remains stable, indicating that any air has been expelled.

CHECKING FOR POWER STEERING SYSTEM LEAKS

22   In the event of power steering problems, it's a good idea to check the system for possible fluid leakage between the steering rack and pump. Start by jacking the front of the car and supporting it on safety stands as described above.

23   Start the engine and let it idle. Turn the steering from lock-to-lock a few times, then hold it at full lock in each direction to place the system under pressure. **Caution!** Do not keep the steering fully turned for more than 15 seconds or damage may result. Check for signs of leakage along both pipes and at their unions. If leakage is found, check and tighten the affected union, or replace worn or damaged hoses as required.

19. EXHAUST SYSTEM - CHECKING

☞ 1/1, 2 & 2/1.

1   The exhaust system should be checked regularly, and whenever unusual exhaust noise or rattles from underneath the car indicate a potential problem. **Warning!** You should only carry out the check when the exhaust system is completely cold, and the car needs to be raised clear of the ground and supported on jack (axle) stands before you start ☞ 1/3.

2   Lying under the car (and wearing safety glasses to protect your eyes), check the system from front to back, remembering to check the top surface nearest the body underside - a mirror helps here.

3   Look for signs of corrosion. This may not be readily apparent - the metal-sprayed exhaust components tend to look nice and shiny right up to the time they perforate through from the inside.

4   Check the exhaust and body-mounted heatshields. If these are loose or damaged, they should be repaired or replaced as necessary. The exhaust manifold heatshield can be checked from under the hood (bonnet). Check also the exhaust system hangers, and fit new ones if they are torn or perished.

5   For more information on checking the exhaust system ☞ 5.

20. BRAKE & CLUTCH FLUID - CHECKING LEVEL & REPLACING

☞ 1/1, 2 & 2/1.

CHECKING

1   The level and condition of the hydraulic fluid in the brake and clutch reservoirs should be checked regularly, and whenever there is concern over the operation of the hydraulic system concerned.

2   ◻+ Remove the reservoir top, taking care to avoid spilling the fluid. Note that the reservoirs

18/18 Checking power steering fluid level.

20/2a Ready to top-up brake fluid (rhd car).

20/2b Fluid level close to "MAX."

2: Tune-up & maintenance

20/2c Clutch master cylinder reservoir (rhd car).

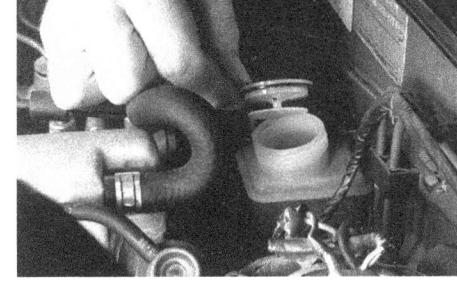
20/2d Don't forget secondary cap (rhd car).

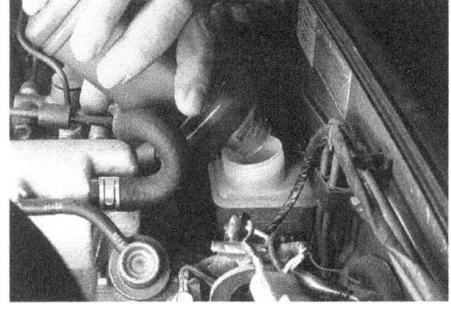
20/7 Topping-up clutch fluid reservoir (rhd car).

may have secondary caps. **Caution!** Hydraulic fluid will discolor and damage painted and plastic parts. In the event of spillage, wash off all traces immediately.

3 Check visually for signs of contamination of the fluid. If it looks dirty and discolored, you should change the fluid as a precaution. If you note bubbles in the fluid, or the operation of the brake or clutch seems spongy and imprecise, there may be air in the system, possibly as a result of seal failure.

4 For details of bleeding air from the clutch hydraulic system ☞ 3.

5 For information on bleeding air from the brake hydraulic system ☞ 9.

6 If repair of either the brake or clutch hydraulic system components is required, you'll find details of overhaul procedures for the brake and clutch assemblies in the relevant chapters.

7 📷 Top-up to the **MAX** level line using only fresh hydraulic fluid conforming to SAE J1703 or FMVSS116: DOT-3 or DOT-4. After topping-up, refit the reservoir top securely and wipe any traces of fluid off the reservoir body.

REPLACING HYDRAULIC FLUID

8 If you need to replace the hydraulic fluid, this can be done as an extension of the air bleeding procedure.

9 Clutch hydraulic system ☞ 3 and brake hydraulic system ☞ 9.

Notes

3

Engine & clutch

1. MAJOR WORK POSSIBLE WITH ENGINE IN CAR

1   You can undertake the following tasks without removing the engine from the car -
*Camshaft drivebelt: renewal
Camshafts, camshaft pulleys and camshaft followers: removal and installation
Cylinder head and gasket: removal and fitting
Crankshaft/oil pump oil seal (front): renewal
*Crankshaft oil seal (rear): renewal
*Starter ring gear: removal and installation
*Clutch and clutch release bearing: removal and installation
Water (coolant) pump: removal and installation*
*These tasks require removal of transmission.

2. MAJOR WORK REQUIRING ENGINE REMOVAL

1   The following tasks are best accomplished by removing the engine from the car -
*Oil pan (sump) and baffle plate: removal and installation
Connecting rod (big-end) bearings: renewal
Main bearings and crankshaft thrust washers: renewal
Crankshaft: removal and installation
Pistons and connecting rods: removal and installation
Oil pump: removal and installation*

3. ENGINE REMOVAL METHODS AND PREPARATION

1   The engine can be removed by itself or as a unit with the transmission. The latter is probably easier as the procedure is more straightforward, particularly when it comes to installation. However, the weight of engine and transmission combined is considerable and this should be borne in mind. We didn't have a means of weighing the engine and transmission but would estimate that, together, they weigh between 136 and 181kg (300 and 400lb), with the transmission alone accounting for between a quarter and a third of the total.
2   You'll need a hoist capable of lifting double this weight - as a safety margin - and capable of a vertical lift of not less than 650mm (25.6in) from a starting point of 810mm (32in) above the ground, plus whatever height you have the car raised above the ground. The hoist also needs to be mounted on wheels or castors so that it can be easily moved back and forth - even when carrying the weight of the engine or engine and transmission. We hired a hoist from a tool/machinery hire company of the kind you find in every small town. The hire charge was small and the whole hoist could be quickly dismantled to fit into the trunk of an ordinary family car. These hire companies usually deliver, too, if it's more convenient. Don't forget to hire a suitable rope or chain at the same time to sling the engine.

3   Before you remove the engine, think about where and how you're going to work on it once it's out. Bear in mind not only the weight of the engine, but also its height of around 610mm (24in). It's no use putting it on the workbench only to find that you can't comfortably reach the top of the engine to work on the cams and head! With manifolds in place the engine's overall size is 610mm long, 610mm high and 560mm wide (24in x 24in x 22in). In addition, the transmission is 1020mm (40in) long. A good plan of action might be to place the engine on top of a couple of securely stacked pallets for major dismantling, moving individual components to the workbench for further work. You'll need a block of hardwood 305mm (12in) long by 100 x 100mm (4 x 4in) or 125 x 125mm (5 x 5in) to place under the shallow end of the engine's oil pan to make it stable on your work surface. Of course, if you have the luxury of an engine stand you can bolt the engine to that before releasing it from the engine crane.
4   If the engine/engine and transmission unit is dirty you'll be well advised to clean its exterior before dismantling starts: you could even get it steam cleaned before the car's immobilized. Make sure you've got solvents, brushes, scrapers, rags and old newspapers ready. **Warning!** Do not use gasoline/petrol as a cleaning solvent.
5   Read through the *whole* procedure *before* starting the job.
6   The specific tool requirements are detailed in the relevant text, but you'll find the following useful: plastic bags and twist wire (the sort you use for gardening) for keeping, identifying and tying back components; adhesive tape (duct tape is fine) to wrap over the end of open pipes, etc; a magnet and stiff wire for picking up dropped small components; a torch for looking into nooks and crannies; portable mains lighting and containers for the oil and coolant which will be drained.
7   Don't forget that when the engine is out you'll have great access to the engine compartment. Plan to fix that chipped paint, weeping hydraulic joint, etc., whilst you have the opportunity ...

4. ENGINE - REMOVAL (WITH TRANSMISSION)

☞ First read 1/1, 2.

1   📷 If you don't have access to a workshop pit or a car lift, raise the whole car high enough to

4/1 You'll need good access to car's underside.

3:1

Mazda Miata, MX-5, Eunos & Roadster

give yourself comfortable access to the underside and support on axle stands☞ 1/3. (**Warning!** The car must be absolutely secure and stable.)

2   Depressurise fuel system☞ 5/13.
3   Disconnect the battery☞ 7/2.
4   📷Owners of cars with automatic transmission can skip to☞ 3/4/11. Drop the car's soft top to make working inside easier. Start by lifting the ashtray out of its recess in the between-seats console.
5   📷 Unscrew the shiftlever knob; it can be quite tight.
6   📷+ Unscrew and remove the crosshead

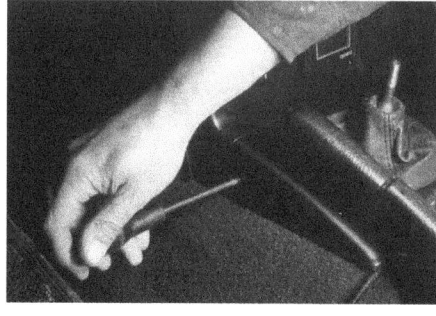
4/6b ... and one each side at front.

4/9 Four bolts secure boot baseplate.

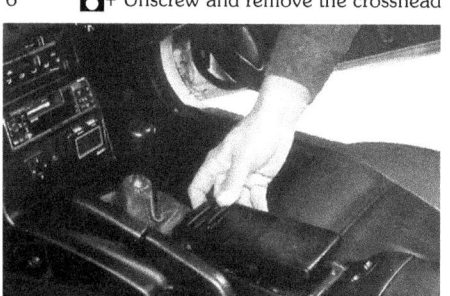
4/4 Lift ashtray from recess.

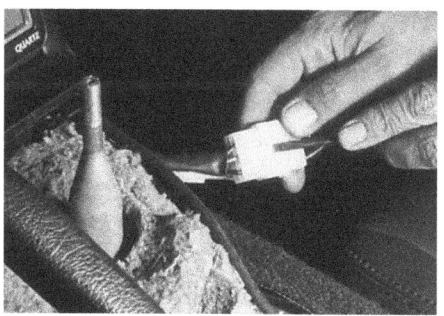
4/7a Press tab to release connector ...

4/10a Lift boot and unscrew three bolts ...

4/5 Unscrew gearlever knob.

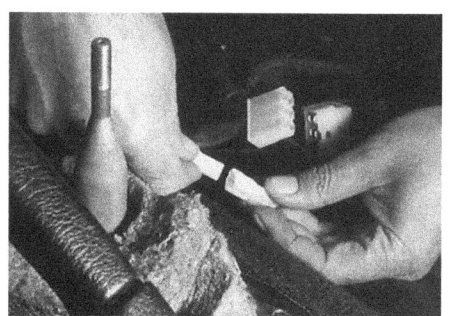
4/7b ... and ditto for smaller connector.

4/10b ... then lift gearlever out of turret.

(Philips) screws which secure the centre console: there are two in the storage compartment; one in the space beneath the ashtray and one each side at the front end. Lift the front of the console and pull it forward until it clears the trunk (boot) and fuel filler cap release levers, but note that it's still connected to several wires.

7   📷+ Disconnect the two white connector blocks which connect the wiring for the ashtray light and the power windows (if applicable). Both connectors have tabs which need to be pushed down to release them. Remove the console.

8   📷 Lift away the two wads of soundproofing material from the shiftlever base.
9   📷 Next, unscrew and remove the four 10mm bolts which secure the shiftlever boot base to the transmission tunnel.
10   📷+ Lift the gaiter assembly up over the shiftlever. If it's stuck and will not slide up the shiftlever, simply lift the gaiter high enough to give access to the gearlever's three retaining bolts. Remove the three 10mm bolts securing the shiftlever to the transmission turret. Lift the shiftlever out of the turret.

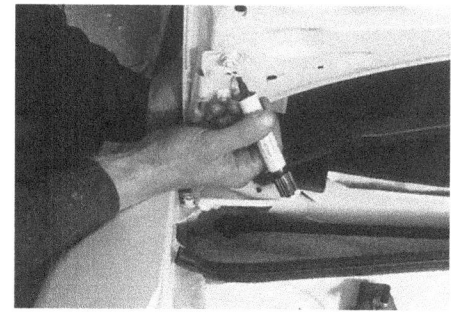
4/11 Mark relative position hinge and hood.

11   📷 Moving to the engine compartment, mark engine hood (bonnet) hinge positions so that the hood will be correctly aligned when refitted.
12   📷 Disconnect windscreen washer hose at the first connector on the underside of the hood.
13   📷 Slacken and remove the four 14mm nuts holding the hood to its hinges (you'll need someone to support the hood while this is done). Lift the hood away and store it safely.
14   📷 Remove the front wheels.
15   📷+ Remove the 10mm bolts retaining the engine undertray, starting in the wheelarches

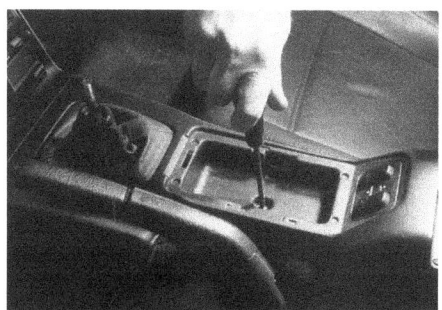
4/6a One screw here, two in rear compartment ...

4/8 Remove sound deadening material.

3: Engine & clutch

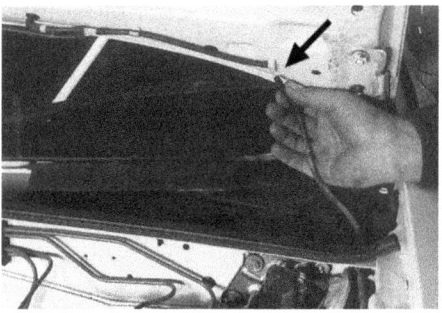
4/12 Disconnect washer hose.

4/13 Remove four hinge bolts.

4/14 Remove front wheels.

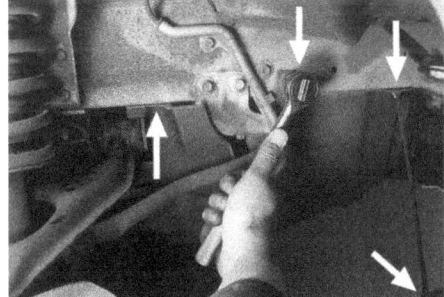
4/15a Three bolts each side ...

4/15b ... one of which secures stay ...

4/15c ... some cars have this front left fixing ...

4/15d ... two bolts at rear ...

4/15e ... and three at front secure undertray.

4/15f Lift away undertray.

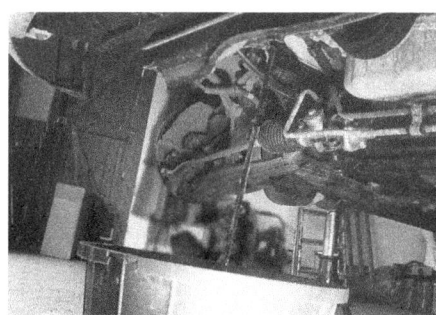
4/16 Drain coolant into suitable receptacle.

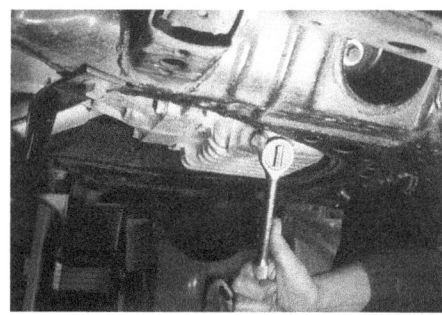
4/17a Remove drain plug and ...

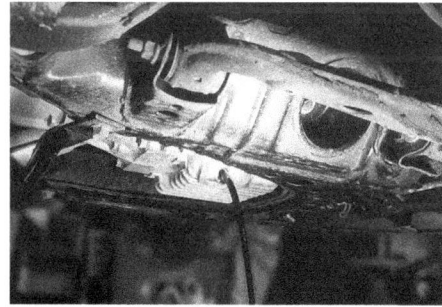
4/17b ... drain the engine oil.

4/18a Remove drain plug and ...

where there are three fixings on each side. You'll also have to remove the 10mm nut that holds the stay (or stays) to the lower part of the front wing (or wings). Note that on some right-hand drive cars the windscreen washer reservoir is mounted forward of the left-hand wheelarch, in which case one of the undertray fixings will be a deeply recessed 10mm nut near the reservoir body. Remove the two 10mm bolts at the rear of the undertray and three at the front; then lift the undertray out from beneath the car.

16   📷 The next step is to drain the radiator. Unscrew and remove the crosshead drain screw from the bottom of the radiator, having first placed a suitable receptacle underneath. If you use a clean receptacle you can retain the coolant for re-use.

17   📷+ Place a drainer can under the sump and then, using a 19mm socket, loosen and remove the sump drain plug.

18   📷+ Manual transmission cars only: loosen and remove the 24mm transmission drain plug once a suitable receptacle is in place to catch the oil.

19   Working from above the engine compartment and starting at the right-hand side of the engine proceed as follows -

20   📷 First, disconnect the hose from the

3:3

Mazda Miata, MX-5, Eunos & Roadster

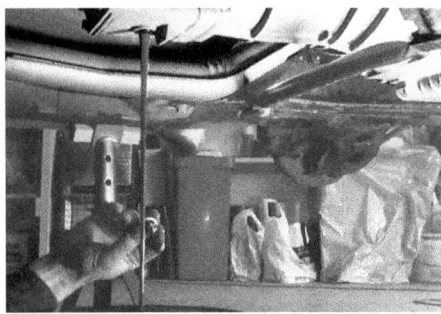

4/18b ... drain the transmission oil.

4/23 Release wiring clamp (clip).

27   Next, press in the tabs to release the clip holding the cable harness to the rear of the cambox cover.

28   Release the tie retaining the wiring harness to a bracket on the intake manifold. Pull the wiring harness over to the right and tie it out of harm's way.

29   Use a screwdriver to push the vacuum tube with blue dashes from the stub on the plenum chamber, and the vacuum tube with red dashes from the EGR valve at the rear of the intake manifold.

30   Disconnect the throttle cable as

brake servo at its stub on the intake manifold. Using pliers slide the clamp (clip) back on the hose until it's past the stub, and then work the hose off of the stub. Use a screwdriver to push the hose off rather than trying to pull it, which just makes it tighter.

21   Press the release tab on the outside and then separate the two halves of the fuel injection wiring harness connector.

22   Push down the release tab and pull the electrical connector from the EGR valve at the rear of the manifold.

23   Use a screwdriver to release the clamp

holding together the various electrical wires for the fuel injection system.

24   Use a cranked screwdriver to depress the release tangs of the connector next to the coils at the back of the block, and separate the two halves of the connector.

25   Press the tab to release the black connector of the heated oxygen sensor at the rear of the exhaust side cambox cover.

26   Press the tab and remove the electrical connector of the camshaft position sensor at the very rear of the exhaust side cambox cover.

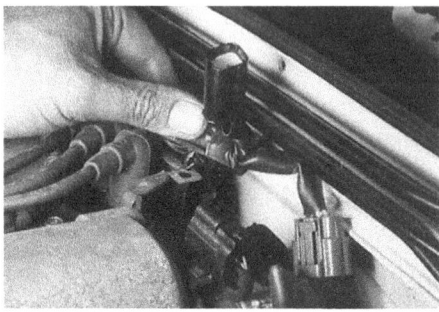

4/27 Tabs secure loom to coil bracket.

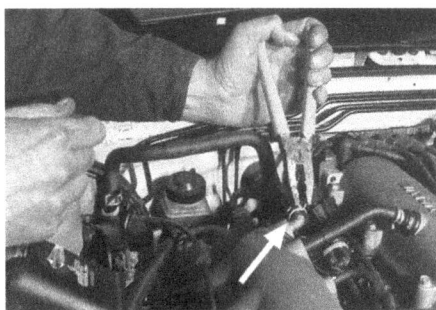

4/20 Disconnect brake servo vacuum hose.

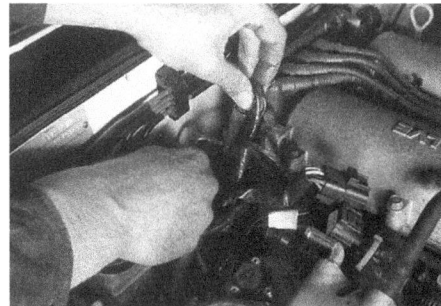

4/24 Cranked screwdriver will release tab.

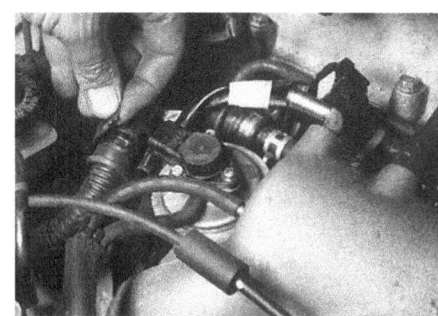

4/28a Release tie holding loom ...

4/21 Release fuel injection loom connector.

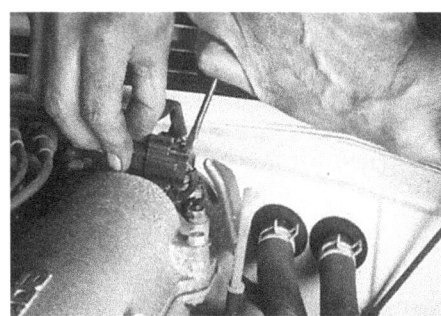

4/25 Release oxygen sensor connector.

4/28b ... pull loom to side and secure.

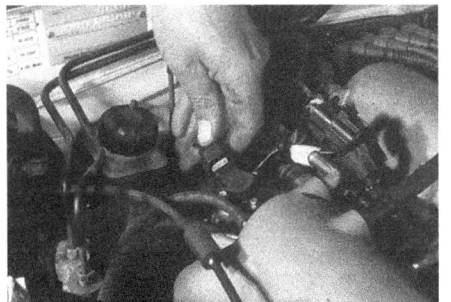

4/22 Release EGR electrical connector.

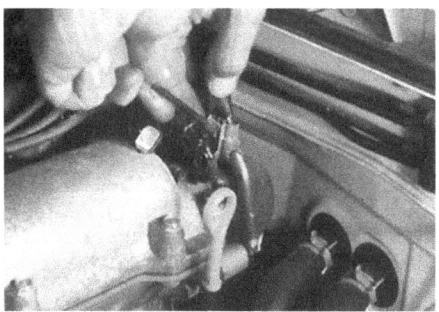

4/26 Release cam position sensor connector.

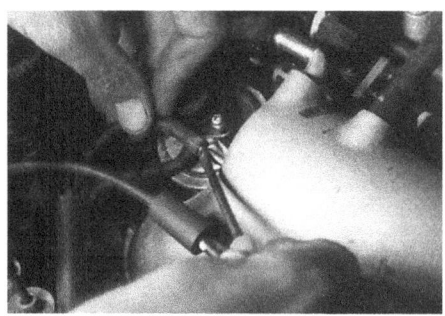

4/29a Push first EGR hose off stub ...

3: Engine & clutch

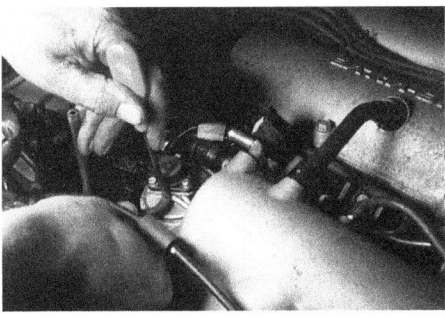
4/29b ... followed by second hose.

4/31 Disconnect EVAP hose.

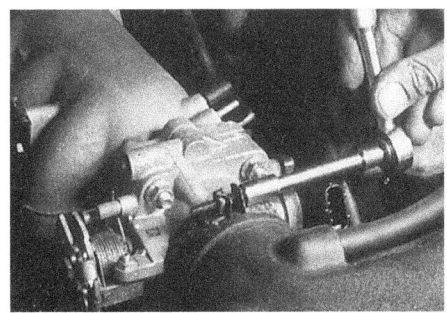
4/34b ... and clamp at throttle body ...

follows. Slacken the adjuster nut behind the bracket and then pull the cable out of the slot in the bracket. You'll now have enough slack to release the cable from the lower arc of the throttle spindle quadrant, and slide the nipple out. Tie the cable out of harm's way.

31   At the front of the manifold, just behind the throttle body, push off the vacuum hose connecting with the EVAP solenoid mounted on the right-hand inner fender (wing), and pull the hose out of the way.

32   Next stage is to start releasing the wiring harness that goes to the engine from just beneath the charcoal canister. First, disconnect the black electrical connector of the fuel pressure regulator solenoid in the valley of the intake manifold.

33   Do the same with the black electrical connector of the TPS unit on the inside of the throttle body.

34   + Next, to make access easier, remove the rigid air hose from the front of the engine. Using an 8mm socket or spanner, release the worm drive clamps (clips) holding the hose to the MAF (mass airflow sensor) of the top of the air filter box and at

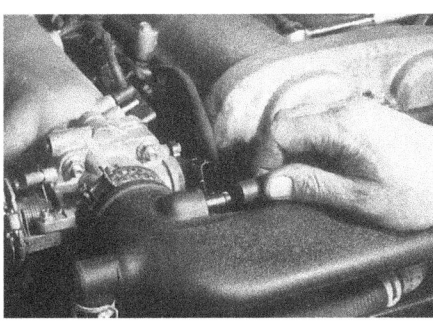
4/34c ... then cambox vent hose ...

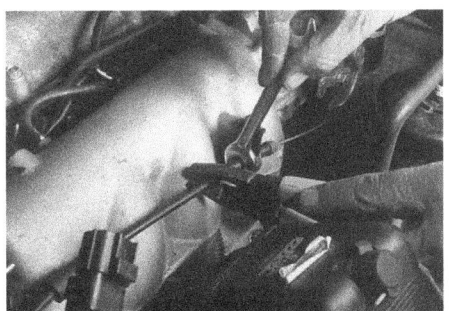
4/30a Slacken outer cable adjuster nut ...

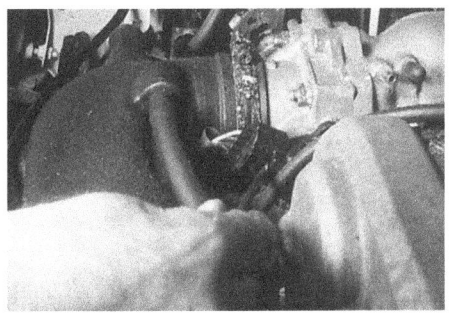
4/33 Release TPS electrical connector.

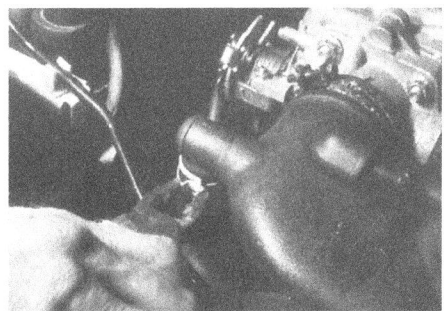
4/34d ... and bypass hose.

the other end to the throttle body on the intake manifold. Pull the cambox cover's ventilation hose off of the air intake trunking near the throttle body. Using pliers release the clamp (clip) retaining the short air bypass hose to the rigid air intake hose on the right-hand side. Pull the rigid air hose off of the throttle body and the MAF sensor, and remove it from the engine compartment.

35   Remove the 10mm nut retaining the ground (earth) strap to the bracket by the side of the throttle body.

36   Lift the bracket holding the wiring harness off the same stud.

4/30b ... and pull outer cable from bracket ...

4/34e Lift rigid air hose away.

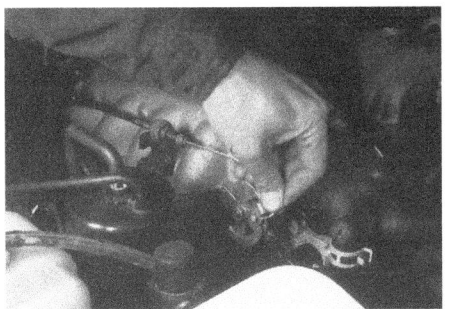
4/30c ... then release inner cable nipple.

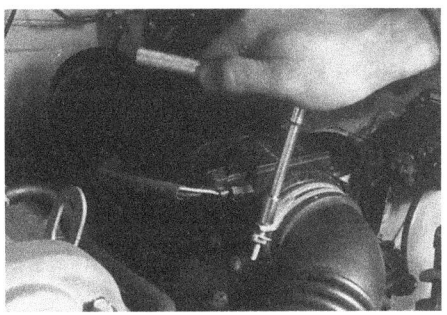
4/34a Release clamp at MAF sensor ...

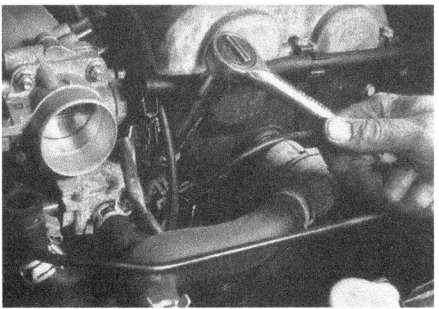
4/35 Release ground (earth) strap.

3:5

Mazda Miata, MX-5, Eunos & Roadster

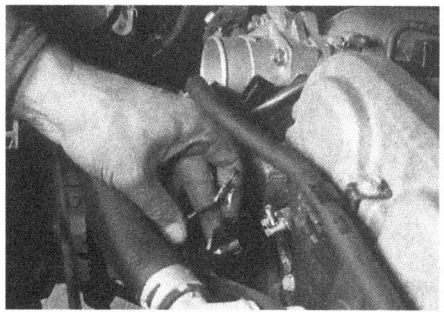

4/36 Release loom from alternator bracket.

37 ⊙ Press in the retaining tab and pull the green plastic connector from the IAC valve beneath the throttle body.

38 ⊙ Removing the aluminium manifold support will give better access to the electrical connections of several components. The support is held at its base by a 17mm bolt which can be accessed with a socket wrench, and at the top by two 17mm bolts which, again, can be accessed with sockets. Once the bolts are removed the support can be pulled away.

39 ⊙ At the alternator the grey electrical

4/37 Release IAC valve electrical connector.

4/38 Bolts securing manifold support.

connector block is released by pushing the spring clip on the left-hand side of its body inwards as the plug is pulled.

40 To remove the alternator's live connection, pull the rubber boot off and slide it down the lead, then undo the 12mm nut.

41 ⊙ There are two electrical connections to the starter motor. One is a conventional plug type and the other, the live connection of the starter motor, is held by a 12mm nut accessible by lifting the rubber covering boot.

42 The electrical connector to the oil pressure

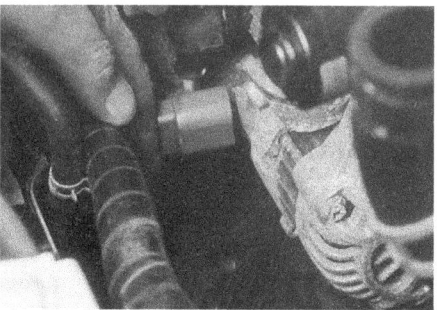

4/39 Release alternator connector.

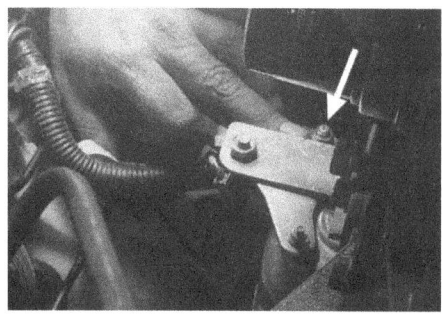

4/41 Starter live connection (arrowed).

switch above the oil filter needs to be detached after pressing its tang.

43 Release the harness from the two plastic clips holding it to the oil cooler hose running along the right-hand side of the engine beneath the manifold; the harness can then be pulled through the manifold area and tied out of harm's way.

44 ⊙ Pull the wire connector from the top of the power steering pump and release its wire from the clip on the timing cover.

45 Pull the wiring harness to the side and tie out of harm's way.

4/44 P/S pump electrical connector.

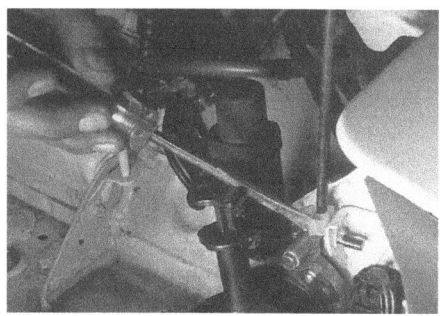

4/46 Release bonnet stay from clip.

46 ⊙ Release the bonnet stay from its clip on the left-hand headlamp housing using a screwdriver to release the clip's locking pawl.

47 ⊙+ After marking one of them to ensure correct reconnection, using pliers, release the clamps securing the rubber fuel hoses from the fuel injector rail to the metal fuel feed and return pipes on the right-hand inner fender (wing). Slide the clamps back until they're off the pipe stubs and then, using a screwdriver, push the rubber hoses off the stubs: they'll be very tight. Use tape to protect the open ends of the two rigid fuel lines.

48 ⊙+ Using pliers, release the clamp, slide

4/47a Release fuel hose clamps and ...

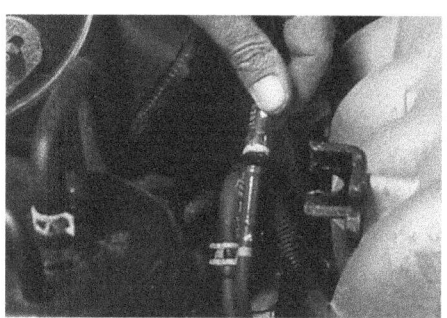

4/47b ... release hoses from rigid fuel lines.

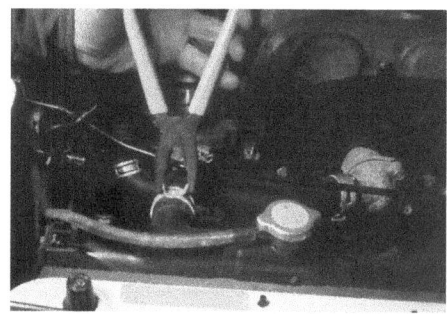

4/48a Release clamp, slide it back then ...

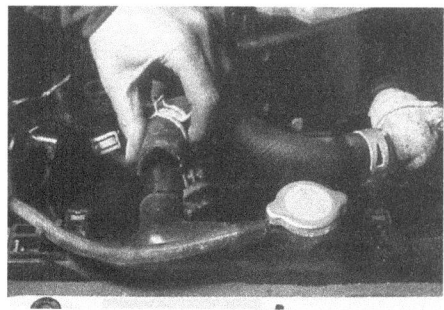

4/48b ... release top hose from rad stub.

3: Engine & clutch

it back and then push the radiator top hose from the stub at the top of the radiator.

49 Press the locking tang and release the black electrical connector plug from the MAF sensor on top of the air filter unit.

50 Using a 10mm socket, remove the bolts securing the air intake to the left-hand front wing. Using a 10mm socket, slacken the clamp holding the air intake hose to the air filter body. Pull the hose off the stub on the filter body and remove the intake.

51 Using a screwdriver, release the cable tie securing the wiring harness to the air filter cover. Tie the harness out of harm's way on the inner wing.

52 Using a 10mm socket, remove the four bolts securing the air filter cover and then lift the air filter cover off.

53 Lift the air filter element out of the air filter body.

54 Remove the 10mm bolt securing the headlamp dimmer diode to the left-hand inner fender and lift the unit from the filter body location stud. Note that this device is not fitted in all markets.

55 Next, using a 12mm socket, remove bolts and one nut securing the air filter lower body to the left-hand inner wing. Lift out the air filter lower body.

56 Next, the power steering pump will have to be detached from the crankcase *without* disconnecting its hoses. The power steering pump swivel pin retaining nut is accessed through holes in the pump pulley, so, if necessary, rotate the crank using a 21mm socket on the pulley bolt, until the holes in the pulley allow access to the 14mm nut which needs to be slackened.

57 Using a 12mm socket slacken the lower bolt on the adjustment strap, followed by the

4/49 Release MAF sensor connector.

4/50a Undo single bolt, followed by ...

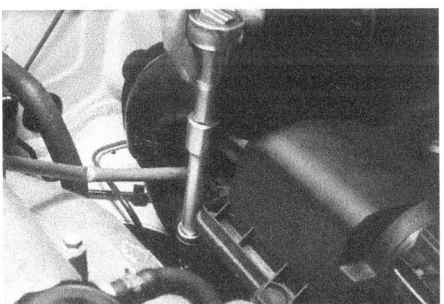
4/50b ... slackening the clamp at airbox end ...

4/50c ... and lift intake away.

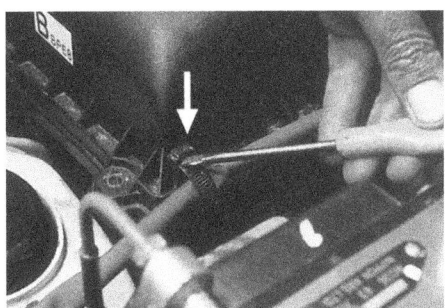
4/51 Release loom from back of airbox.

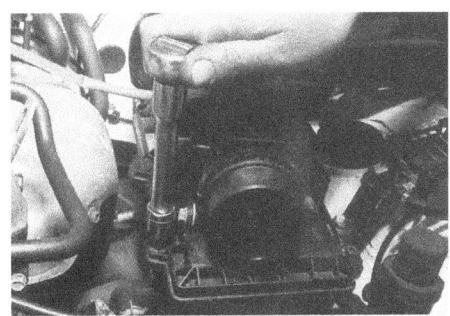
4/52 Four bolts secure cover.

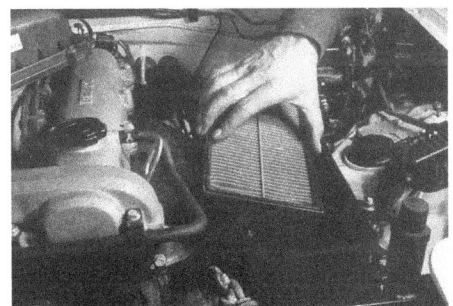
4/53 Lift out air filter element.

4/55a Remove bolts and nut securing body ...

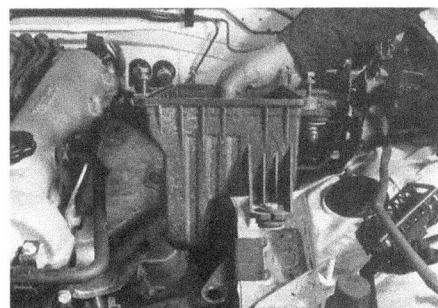
4/55b ... and lift air filter body out.

4/56 Pivot pin nut accessed through pulley.

4/57a Slacken lower bolt on strap ...

4/57b ... followed by bolt in threaded block.

Mazda Miata, MX-5, Eunos & Roadster

nut and bolt securing the threaded block to the other end of the strap.

58 Unscrew and remove the power steering pump drivebelt tension adjuster screw (12mm).

59 Remove the 12mm nut and bolt securing the adjustment strap threaded block to the pump body bracket.

60 Push the pump inwards until the drivebelt is slack enough to remove. Take the belt off the two pulleys.

61 + Remove the nut from the power steering pump pivot pin and pull the pin out towards the back of the engine. The pin may need

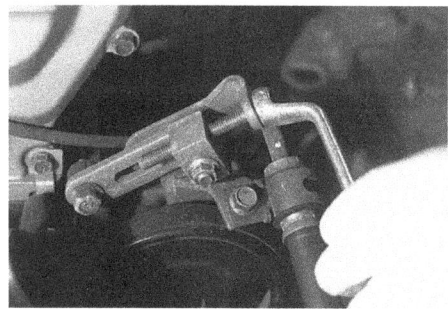
4/58 Unscrew and remove adjuster screw.

4/60 Push pump inward and release drivebelt.

4/61a Remove nut, pull out pivot pin ...

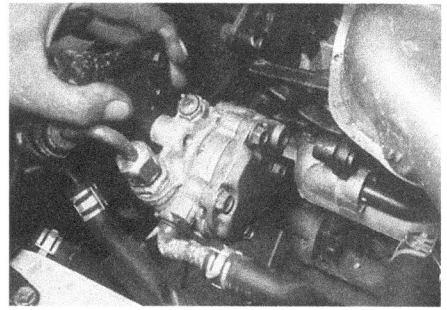
4/61b ... and pull pump to one side.

to be driven out with a soft drift. Pull the power steering pump off of its bracket on the block and push it down close to the anti-roll bar, to which it should be tied so that it's out of harm's way.

62 If an air conditioning compressor is fitted, it should be removed from its mounting on the lower left-hand side of the cylinder block, **without** disconnecting its hoses, and tied safely away from the engine. Our car did not have a compressor so we cannot give full details of fixings, but believe four bolts secure the unit to its cradle. There is also an electrical connector. Note: if your car has air conditioning but does not have power steering, you'll have to slacken the belt adjuster mechanism above the compressor to release the drivebelt. **Warning!** Do not, under any circumstances, try to slacken or disconnect air conditioning pipe unions and take great care not to damage the pipes with sharp tools - the refrigerant in the system can be extremely dangerous.

63 + Using pliers, release the clip securing the hose to the water inlet aluminium casting on the left-hand side of the cylinder block. Lever the hose off of its stub. At the other end of the same hose, repeat the procedure, and then remove the hose completely.

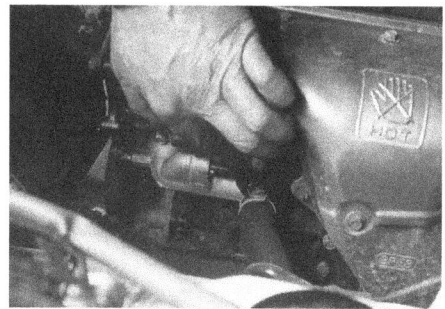
4/63a Release clamp and slide it back ...

4/63b ... repeat process at other end.

64 We didn't remove the radiator and its attached fans during the engine and transmission removal sequence, and found that we still had enough clearance (just) to pull the engine/transmission assembly forward and lift it out of the engine compartment. However, on reflection, we think that for the small amount of extra work involved it is a good idea to remove the radiator (with fan or fans attached) at this point because it is easily damaged during the engine lift. You'll need to release the electrical connections to the fans, pipework for the auto transmission oil cooler (if

applicable), bottom hose, reservoir hose and, finally, the two bolts securing the radiator before lifting it out of its bottom brackets. More info ☞ 6.

65 Release the two clamps securing the two heater hoses to their bulkhead stubs and release the hoses. These connections can be very stubborn and you'll probably need to use a screwdriver and block of wood against the bulkhead to lever them off.

66 Unscrew and remove the 10mm bolt securing the engine earth strap to the left-hand firewall/inner fender area.

67 Next, moving beneath the car, it will be

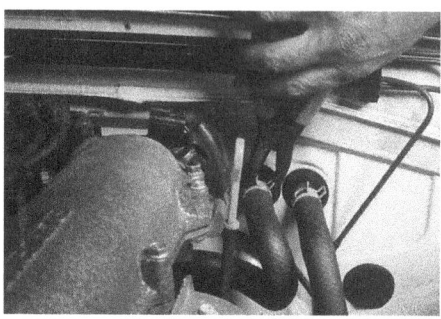
4/65 Release heater hose clamps.

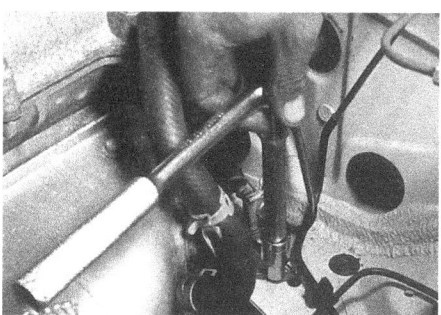
4/66 Release ground (earth) strap.

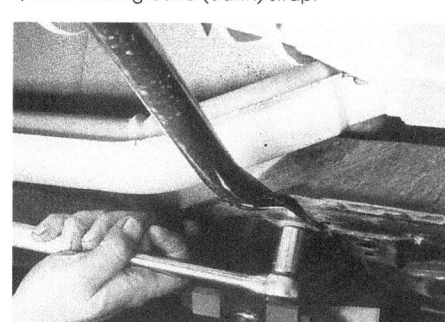
4/68 Front brace secured by two bolts.

necessary to remove/release the exhaust system, clutch slave cylinder pipework (if applicable) and the bracket securing the right-hand rear engine compartment harness to the rear of the crankcase/bellhousing.

68 Using a 17mm socket, remove the two bolts securing the cross brace beneath the transmission. This will improve access.

69 + At the rear of the car, remove the six 17mm bolts which secure the brace bar assembly to the underframe of the car and the suspension subframe. Lift the bar away, noting that the rear

3: Engine & clutch

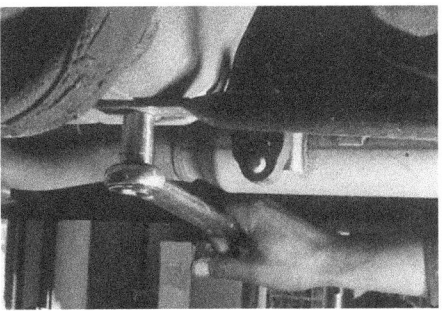

4/69a Rear brace ('performance bar') ...

4/74a Release cylinder and pipe bracket bolts.

4/75b ... knurled nut, remove speedo cable.

4/69b ... is secured by three bolts ...

4/74b Tie release cylinder to one side.

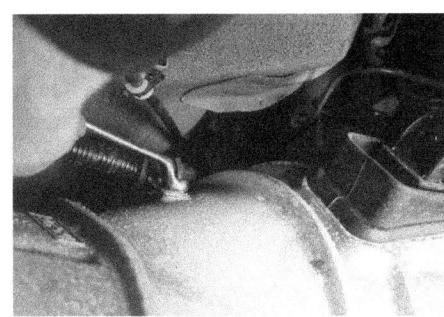

4/76 Release loom from bellhousing.

4/69c ... each side.

4/72 Release clutch pipe bracket.

right-hand corner carries a clip.

70   Remove the heated oxygen sensor from the exhaust downpipe ☞ 5/33.

71   Remove the exhaust system ☞ 5/38.

72   ◪ Manual transmission cars only. From beneath the car, using extensions and a universal joint, remove the 12mm bolt securing the clutch pipe bracket to the bellhousing.

73   If you are unable to release the 10mm bolt holding the wiring harness to a bracket on the right-hand side of the bellhousing, then remove the 12mm bellhousing bolt that holds the loom's bracket.

74   ◪+ Manual transmission cars only. Using a 12mm socket with extension bar and, if necessary, universal joint, undo and remove the two 12mm bolts securing the clutch release (slave) cylinder to the side of the bellhousing. The upper bolt can be accessed via the space between the subframe and right-hand wheelarch and the lower bolt from beneath the subframe (using a crescent or box wrench/open-ended or ring spanner). Just above the release cylinder there is a bracket securing the release cylinder's hydraulic pipework to the bellhousing. This is retained by a 10mm bolt. Remove the bolt. Pull the clutch release cylinder and its pipework some way through the gap between the subframe and inner wing, and tie out of harm's way.

75   ◪+ Using vise grip pliers or a pipe wrench, unscrew the knurled collar securing the speedometer cable to the speedometer drive in the transmission. Pull the speedometer cable out through the PPF frame and tie it to the pipework underneath the right-hand side of the car out of harm's way.

76   ◪ If applicable, unscrew and remove the 10mm bolt securing the wiring bracket to the left-hand side of the transmission bellhousing.

4/75a Use vise grip pliers to release ...

4/77a Four connectors above transmission.

77   ◪+ Manual transmission. Reach above the transmission to release the wiring clipped above it by bending open the clips with your fingers. This should allow you to access the four electrical connectors (two each) for the neutral and reversing light switches. If you can't release the bullet connectors then it's possible just to unscrew the reversing light switch and free the wiring that way.

78   ◪+ If applicable, unscrew and remove the one 17mm bolt and two 14mm bolts securing the bracket between the PPF and the transmission

4/77b You can unscrew switches to free wiring.

3:9

Mazda Miata, MX-5, Eunos & Roadster

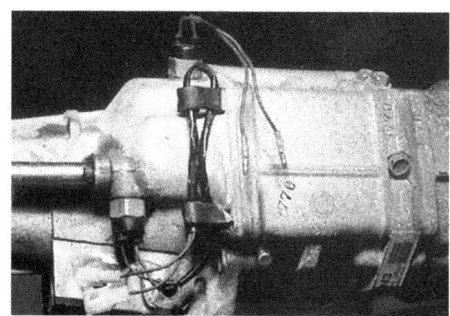

4/77c You can't see this layout from below.

4/78a Remove this bolt ...

4/78b ... these two bolts and then ...

4/78c ... remove transmission support bracket.

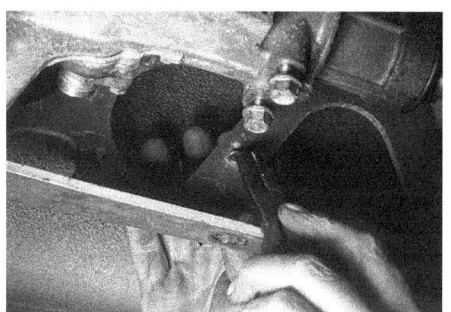

4/79 Squeeze ears and pull loom clip free.

extension. Remove the bracket.

79 ◯ Detach the wiring harness from the side of the PPF by squeezing together the ears of the plastic fixings behind the PPF and pulling the fixings through.

80 ◯ Using a 10mm ring spanner or socket, remove the bolt securing the ground (earth) connection at the rear of the PPF.

81 Once free, tie the wiring harness to the pipework on the right-hand side of the car's underbody to keep it out of harm's way.

82 Auto transmission only. Disconnect the shift rod, electrical and hydraulic connections to

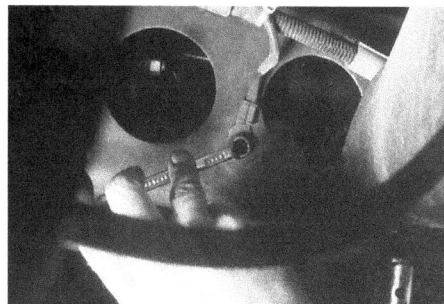

4/80 Release ground (earth) strap.

4/84 Dab of paint on collar and PPF

the transmission. For more information ☞ 4/3.

83 Using a 17mm socket, unscrew and remove the rearmost long bolt securing the PPF to the rear axle casing.

84 ◯ The second bolt (nearest front of car) is the so-called 'reamer bolt' because it is a precise fit in its shaped housing and this ensures that the PPF is correctly aligned. Mark the bolt collar position relative to the PPF with a dab of paint to ensure everything goes back together exactly as it was on reassembly, then undo and remove the second 17mm bolt. Note that even on our two-year-old, 9000 mile (14,500km) car, the two bolts at the rear

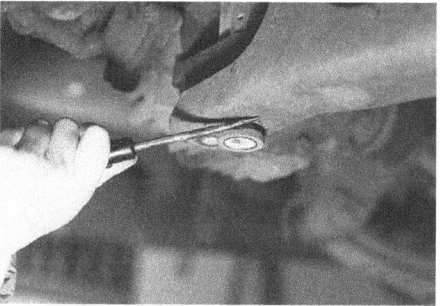

4/85 Lever out the reamer bolt collar.

of the PPF were heavily corroded and therefore may be difficult to remove on older cars: use plenty of penetrating oil.

85 ◯ Using a chisel or pry bar (jemmy) in the cutouts, lever the reamer bolt collar out of the PPF.

86 ◯+ At the front of the PPF two bolts secure the PPF to the transmission. Note the holes in the PPF are elongated; therefore, it's a good idea to mark the relative position of the PPF and the transmission casing with a dab of paint to ensure perfect reassembly when the time comes. Unscrew and remove the two 17mm bolts (they're 198mm/ 8in long!).

4/86a Paint on transmission and PPF ...

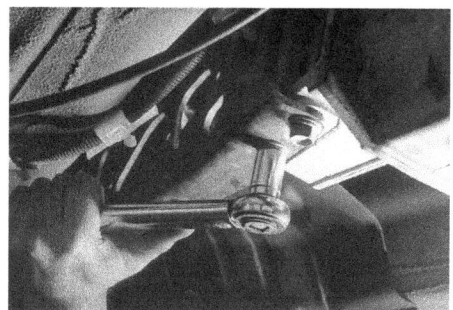

4/86b ... then unscrew PPF securing bolts.

87 ◯+ **Caution!/Warning!** Do not try to remove the PPF at this stage without first supporting the transmission. The transmission must not be allowed to drop sufficiently for the camshaft position sensor or the coils to come into contact with the firewall which would cause substantial damage. For the same reason the transmission must not be allowed to move excessively side-to-side. Lift the transmission a little to take the strain off the PPF, then pass some strong rope around the transmission and through the shiftlever opening in the floor. Tie it to a metal bar above the transmission tunnel to

4/87a Transmission and propshaft supported ...

3: Engine & clutch

4/87b ... by rope slings.

4/89b Remove right-hand engine mount.

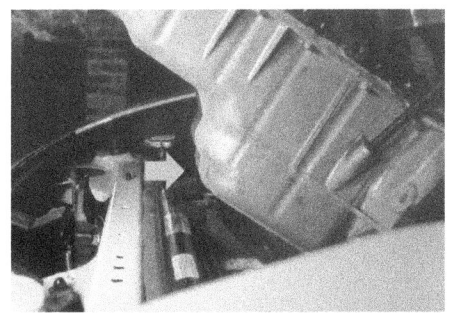
4/91d ... watch this space ...

stop the transmission dropping when the PPF frame is removed. It's a good idea, too, to pass a piece of rope through the propeller shaft universal joint at the transmission end and up through the transmission tunnel, and tie it to a rod or bar to stop the driveshaft dropping to the ground when the transmission is pulled off of it. Those with auto transmissions will have to support the transmission on a floor jack and make sure there is something soft beneath the driveshaft nose.

88   At this point the PPF frame can be removed completely by manoeuvring it off the transmission and differential casings. **Caution!** Do not remove the upper spacers from the rear of the PPF: if they are removed, the PPF will have to be replaced as vehicle handling will be severely impaired.

89   Next, using a 12mm socket and extension bar, remove the nuts and washers from the engine mountings on both sides of the car. Note: we found that removing the left-hand engine mounting bracket from the engine made engine removal much easier; it's secured by three 14mm bolts.

90   **Caution! Before** commencing the engine lift procedure, do a last check around the whole engine and transmission to ensure that **all** pipes, hoses, cables and wires are disconnected and clear of the engine and transmission.

91   Position the engine crane so that its lifting hook/eye is at the mid-point between the engine's two lifting eyes and as close to the cambox cover as possible. Using rope or chain (strong enough to take twice the weight of the engine and transmission) passed through the lifting eyes of the cylinder head, and connected to the engine crane hook/eye, begin lifting the engine. The whole unit

4/88 Remove PPF frame.

4/91a Crane eye close to cambox cover ...

4/91e ... this one too...

4/91b ... increase angle as engine lifts ...

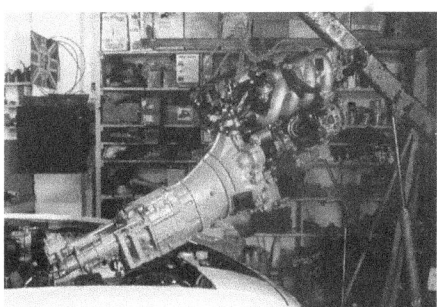
4/91f ... all clear!

4/89a Unscrew engine mount nuts.

4/91c ... wood block protects body ...

needs to be lifted until the engine mounting studs spring free and then gradually inched forward until it assumes an angle which allows you to lift it higher and higher as you pull it further forward. **Caution!** Throughout this process, watch the radiator and fan (if still fitted) area very carefully in case the engine comes into contact, ditto the space between the camshaft position sensor and coils and the firewall (bulkhead). It's a good idea to place a thin block of wood between the top of the transmission and the bulkhead/transmission tunnel joint to prevent damage to the area as the transmission slides past it. At all times check very carefully that nothing is straining, such as a wire or a piece of pipework you've forgotten to disconnect. **Warning!** When lifting the engine/transmission unit, do not go beneath the car and keep your hands out of the engine compartment.

92   If required, the transmission can now be separated from the engine while the latter is still attached to the sling.

93   Auto transmission. Remove the dipstick tube. Remove the two bolts securing the torque converter cover at the base of the bellhousing. **Caution!** Do not roll the transmission onto its side, otherwise contaminants in the unit's oil pan will

3:11

wash into the transmission mechanism. Mark the relative positions of the driveplate and torque converter with paint, then remove the nuts or bolts, as applicable, securing the torque converter to the driveplate. Access to each fixing is achieved by rotating the crankshaft.

94   All cars. The bellhousing is fixed to the engine by a ring of 17mm headed bolts, and one 14mm headed nut with a 12mm headed bolt passing through the starter motor flange with a nut on the bellhousing side. Once the fixings have been removed, pull the transmission backwards until it is completely disengaged from the engine. **Caution!**

4/95 Lower engine onto workbench.

Auto transmission only: make sure the torque converter stays in the transmission bellhousing during this process.

95   The engine can now be gently lowered onto the bench or engine stand. If using a bench or flat surface, make sure that you have pieces of wood of the correct size to place under the front of the sump so that the whole unit is level and stable.

5. ENGINE - REMOVAL (WITHOUT TRANSMISSION)

First read 1/1, 2.

1   3/4/1-3, 11-17 and 19-74 (including radiator removal).

2   Position the engine crane so that its lifting hook/eye is at the mid-point between the engine's two lifting eyes and as close to the cambox cover as possible. Using rope or chain (strong enough to take twice the weight of the engine and transmission) passed through the lifting eyes of the cylinder head, and the hook/eye of the crane, operate the crane so that it just begins to take the weight of the engine (ie: all slack is taken out of the rope or chain).

5/2 Crane lifting eye close to cambox.

3   From beneath the car you can gain access to the 14mm nuts securing the engine mountings to the subframe. The nuts are located in recesses each side of the subframe between the pivots of the lower swinging arm. Undo and remove the nuts and keep together with their washers.

4   Note: we found that removing the left-hand engine mounting bracket from the engine made engine removal much easier; it's secured by three 14mm bolts. (This is because instead of having to lift the engine substantially to free the mountings, the engine can be lifted a little and then

5/3 Release engine mounting nuts.

pulled toward the left-hand side of the compartment to free it from the right-hand mount.)

5   Auto transmission cars. Remove the auto trans dipstick tube. Remove the two bolts securing the torque converter cover at the base of the bellhousing. Mark the relative positions of the driveplate and torque converter with paint, then remove the nuts or bolts, as applicable, securing the torque converter to the driveplate. Access to each fixing is achieved by rotating the crankshaft.

6   You'll need 14mm and 17mm sockets, a universal joint and extension(s) of around 450mm (18in) to reach all the bellhousing bolts and nuts, which are also very tight!

7   Start by removing the nut and bolt holding the starter motor. Both nut and bolt are 14mm (smaller than the rest of the bellhousing bolts) and are situated about halfway up the right-hand side of the bellhousing. The head of the lower bolt holding the starter motor will have to be held by a second person, and can be accessed via the space above the front subframe in the right-hand front wheelarch. Once a helper is holding the bolt head, the nut can be released from the transmission side. There are no nuts for the top starter motor bolts, so these can be unscrewed and removed from the transmission side. Note: both of these bolts also secure brackets fixing wiring and (manual cars) hydraulic pipe. Once free, tie these brackets and their wiring/pipework to one side away from the bellhousing.

8   You are now left with seven 17mm bolts and one 17mm nut and bolt holding the transmission bellhousing to the engine. Using a diagonal sequence, first of all loosen each of these bolts and one nut by half a turn. Then remove all of the bolts and the nut.

9   Place a jack beneath the forward end of the transmission and raise its pad until it just takes the weight of the unit. Use a block of wood between the pad and transmission underside.

10   **Caution!** Make one final careful check using a lead light or torch to check all around the engine that everything is disconnected from the unit and it really is ready to lift.

11   Lift the engine vertically, jacking the transmission simultaneously, until the engine mountings spring clear of their seats. **Caution!** Make sure nothing above the transmission gets crushed in the process. You can then move the engine crane backwards so that the engine moves forward in its bay until the crankshaft pulley is just touching the suspension stabilizer bar and the clutch has disengaged from the transmission input shaft (or driveplate from torque converter). Hold the engine steady and lift vertically until it is clear of the engine compartment. The engine crane can then be moved backward, drawing the engine clear of the car, and the engine placed wherever it is to be first worked upon.

12   Lower the transmission to its normal position, but still supported by a floor jack.

6. ENGINE DISMANTLING - GENERAL ADVICE

First read 1/1, 2.

1   You'll find the teardown of the engine is made much easier if all external oil and dirt is cleaned off first. There will also be less risk of contaminating and damaging components with bearings or fine operating clearances.

2   Place the engine on a bed of several thicknesses of newspaper or cardboard which will absorb solvents and oil.

3   Use a combination of proprietary solvent or kerosene (paraffin) and brushes and scrapers to remove congealed oil and dirt. Wipe off excess cleaning fluid with a rag once the exterior of the engine and its fittings are clean. **Warning!** Do not use gasoline/petrol as a cleaning solvent. Take care not to let cleaning fluid run into the alternator through its cooling slots, nor to contaminate the clutch. Don't forget you have the opportunity to clean up the engine bay while the engine's out.

4   Obtain a complete set of engine gaskets before beginning the engine teardown (see the advice on ordering parts in Chapter 1).

5   Don't throw away any of the old gaskets or seals removed during the engine teardown; they might be useful as patterns or reference if there are any shortcomings in your new gasket/seal kit.

6   Have plenty of plastic bags or other transparent containers for storing bits and pieces as they are removed. Identify the components and where they've come from. Adhesive tape and gardening wire will also be useful.

7   Make it a habit to re-install bolts, screws and nuts (with attendant washers, spacers and brackets) finger-tight after components are dismantled. You'll be surprised how much head scratching and confusion this will prevent when it comes to the rebuild.

3: Engine & clutch

7. ENGINE DISMANTLING

☞ First read 1/1, 2.

Warning! The engine unit should be at a comfortable working height and supported by wooden blocks to make it stable. If you have access to one, an engine dismantling stand will make life easier. We managed without and didn't hit any big problems.

1 ◻ Start on the right-hand side of the engine -

INTAKE MANIFOLD AND WIRING REMOVAL

2 ◻+ Undo and remove the two 10mm nuts securing the metal EGR pipe connection to the intake manifold. Undo the single 12mm nut holding the EGR pipe to the heater hose outlet casting.

3 ◻ Unscrew the single 10mm nut holding the fuel injection wiring ground (earth) strap to the intake manifold.

4 ◻ Next, using pliers, release the clamps (clips) of the two hoses at the BAC valve stubs below the throttle body on the inlet manifold. Pull the hoses off the stubs, or push them off with a screwdriver.

7/1 Right-hand side of engine.

7/2a Two nuts secure EGR pipe to manifold.

7/2b Release EGR pipe bracket.

7/3 Release ground (earth) strap.

7/4 Release hose clamps at BAC valve.

7/5 Pull PCV valve from grommet.

7/6 Free hose from PRC valve solenoid.

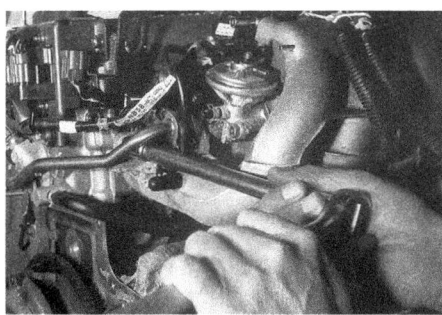
7/7a Remove nine securing nuts and ...

7/7b ... lift away intake manifold.

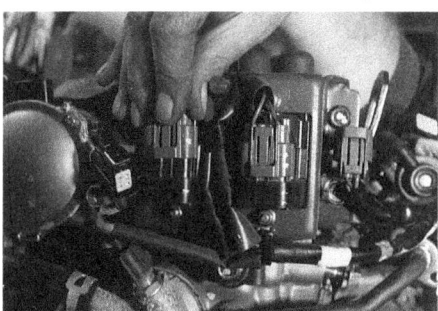
7/8 Coil electrical connectors marked.

7/9 Coolant temperature sensor connector.

5 ◻ Pull the non-return valve of the positive crankcase ventilation system from its grommet in the right-hand cambox cover.

6 ◻ At the front of the manifold, between the plenum chamber and the cylinder head, just behind the throttle body, is the PRC (fuel pressure control) valve solenoid. Disconnect the hose from the pressure regulator at the solenoid.

7 ◻+ Using a 12mm socket and extension bar, undo and remove the nine nuts securing the intake manifold to the cylinder head (starting from the outermost nuts and working inward in a spiral).

Lift away the intake manifold.

8 ◻ Depress its locking tab and pull the electrical connector from the back of the left-hand coil unit. Repeat the process for the right-hand coil unit. Note how both connectors have been marked with paint spots to identify their positions.

9 ◻ Depress the tab and pull off the electrical connector from the engine coolant temperature sensor.

10 Release the harness from the small clip beneath the right-hand coil unit.

11 ◻ The wiring harness for the fuel injectors

3:13

Mazda Miata, MX-5, Eunos & Roadster

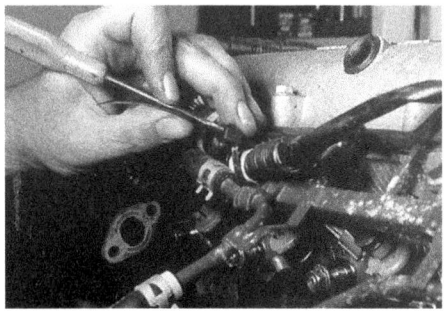

7/11 Release wiring tie.

7/14b ... and lift away starter motor.

OIL FILTER AND OIL COOLER REMOVAL

16   Unscrew and remove the oil filter canister (you may need to use an oil filter wrench).

17   Behind the oil filter is an oil cooler still connected by a hose to a stub at the rear of the cylinder head. Release the hose clamp and then push the hose off its stub with a screwdriver.

18   Unscrew the 29mm nut and pull the oil cooler unit off of the central threaded stub. Quite a lot of oil is likely to run out.

ALTERNATOR REMOVAL

19   First of all, slacken the alternator

7/12 Release engine lifting eye.

is tied to the rail by a plastic tie at about the mid-point. Lift the locking tang of the tie and open it to release the harness.

12   Using a 14mm socket, unscrew and remove the bolt securing the rear engine lifting eye and grey connector block to the cylinder head.

FUEL RAIL REMOVAL

13   Using a 12mm socket, remove the three bolts securing the fuel injection system fuel rail to the cylinder head. Don't lose the three collars which will be freed as the bolts are withdrawn.

STARTER MOTOR REMOVAL

14   The starter is now fixed by a single 14mm bolt. Remove the bolt from the starter motor mounting bracket and then remove the starter motor.

ENGINE MOUNTING REMOVAL

15   Unscrew the three 14mm bolts securing the right-hand engine mounting bracket to the crankcase. Note that the upper of the three bolts is longer.

7/15 Three bolts secure engine mounting.

7/18a Undo securing nut and ...

7/18b ... lift away oil cooler unit.

7/13 Fuel rail secured by three bolts.

7/16 Remove oil filter canister.

7/19a Slacken alternator pivot bolt ...

7/14a Remove single remaining bolt ...

7/17 Release oil cooler hose clamp.

7/19b ... then top strap inner bolt ...

3: Engine & clutch

7/19c ... then adjuster locking bolt.

7/21 Single bolt secures bracket.

7/25b ... then lift away heatshield.

pivot bolt using a 14mm socket. Slacken the alternator top strap inner bolt using a 14mm socket. Slacken the 12mm adjuster lock bolt with a socket.

20   + Using a 12mm socket, turn the adjusting screw anti-clockwise to slacken the drivebelt until there's enough slack to allow belt removal. Unscrew and remove the pivot bolt completely and lift away the alternator.

21   Using a 17mm socket, unscrew the bolt securing the bracket at the top right-hand front of the cylinder block.

22   Press the tab and pull the electrical

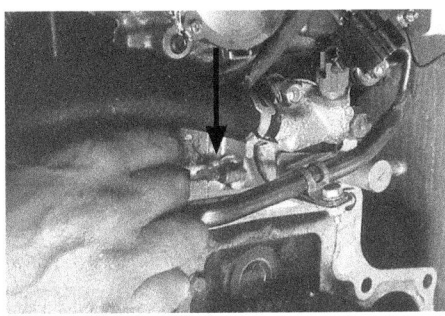

7/22 Temp. gauge sender connection.

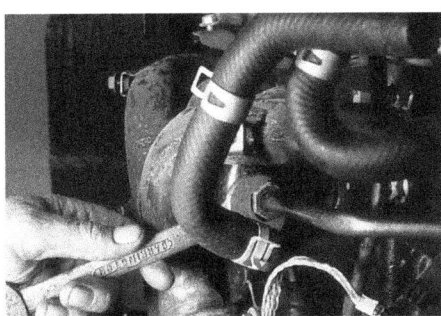

7/26 Undo EGR pipe union.

7/20a Turn adjuster bolt to slacken belt ...

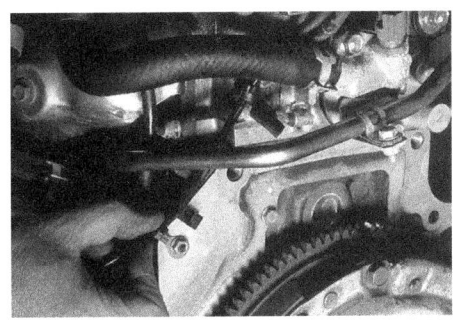

7/23 Release oxygen sensor wire from clip.

7/27a Undo securing nuts and ...

connector from the temperature gauge sender unit in the outlet casting at the rear of the cylinder head.

23   Release the heated oxygen sensor wire from the clip on the engine backplate.

24   Move to the left-hand side of the engine.

EXHAUST MANIFOLD REMOVAL

25   + Using a 10mm socket, remove the fixings that secure the exhaust manifold heatshield to the manifold; there are six bolts and three nuts. Lift away the heatshield.

26   Using a crescent wrench (open-ended

7/20b ... then remove belt and pivot bolt ...

7/27b ... lift away exhaust manifold.

spanner), unscrew the 22mm union nut securing the EGR pipe to the exhaust manifold.

27   + Using a 14mm socket and extension, unscrew the nine exhaust manifold retaining nuts (the threaded studs will normally be corroded and this can make it very difficult to get the nuts off without damaging them - penetrating oil may help). Lift away manifold and gasket.

28   Next, using pliers, release the clamp on the small bore water hose at the front of the water pump outlet and, using a screwdriver, push the hose off its stub.

7/20c ... and lift away alternator.

7/25a Remove securing bolts and nuts ...

3:15

Mazda Miata, MX-5, Eunos & Roadster

7/28 Release clamp and hose from stub.

7/30b ... lift dipstick tube from oil pan.

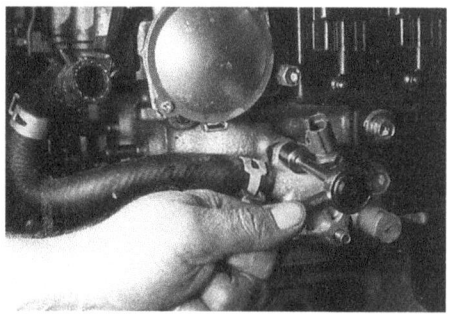
7/34 Remove heater hose outlet casting.

7/29a Undo two outlet casting bolts ...

7/31a Temporarily replaced bolt + paint mark.

7/29b ... and lift casting away.

7/31b Undo pressure plate bolts progressively.

29   📷+ Using a 12mm socket, unscrew and remove the two bolts securing the water pump outlet casting to the cylinder block. Pull the casting off of its gasket - be careful, as it may come away suddenly.

30   📷+ Next, using a 10mm socket, undo the nut which secures the dipstick tube and the engine ground (earth) strap. Pull the dipstick tube bracket bolt through the backplate and then lift the dipstick tube up out of its recess in the sump.

CLUTCH REMOVAL

31   📷+ If the clutch cover (pressure plate) is to be re-used, mark its position relative to the flywheel with a dab of paint. Replace one of the bellhousing bolts as shown in the photograph and use a screwdriver wedged into the flywheel teeth to prevent the flywheel from turning as the clutch cover retaining bolts are undone.

32   Initially, in a progressive diagonal sequence, slacken each 14mm bolt by half a turn. Then, gradually slacken off all of the bolts until the pressure plate is loose.

33   📷 When all the bolts are no longer under tension, remove them completely and lift the clutch pressure plate away from the flywheel. Mark the outward side of the driven plate (it's the side from which the boss protrudes the furthest).

34   📷 Using a narrow 12mm socket, remove the securing bolt from the heater hose outlet casting and then pull the cover away.

SPARKPLUG WIRES AND COILS REMOVAL

35   Using your fingers pull the sparkplug wires (HT leads) connectors from the sparkplug recesses, As you do so, release the wires from the clips in the valley between the cambox covers.

36   📷 Unscrew and remove the three 12mm bolts which secure the coil assembly bracket to the rear of the cylinder head and lift it away.

37   Move to the front of the engine.

THERMOSTAT REMOVAL

38   📷 Undo and remove the 12mm bolt and 12mm nut that secure the thermostat housing cover.

39   📷 The thermostat can now be pulled from the housing. Note that, in our particular car, the thermostat was installed with its two valves in line with the stud and bolt hole (the small brass valve being the higher of the two).

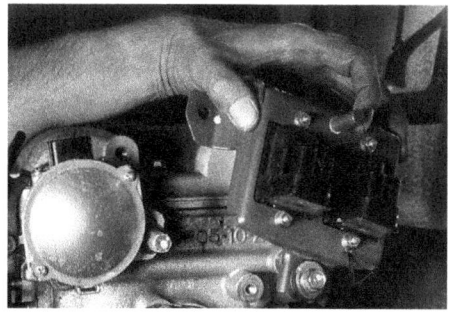
7/36 Three bolts secure coil bracket.

7/30a Release support bracket then ...

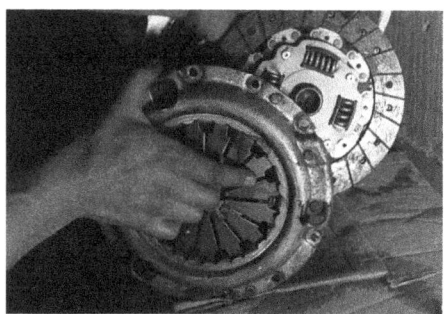
7/33 Remove clutch pressure and driven plates.

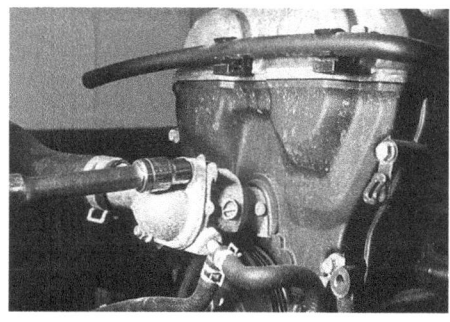
7/38 Nut and bolt secure thermostat housing.

3: Engine & clutch

7/39 Lift out thermostat.

7/42 Thirteen bolts secure cambox cover.

7/44a Four more bolts retain middle ...

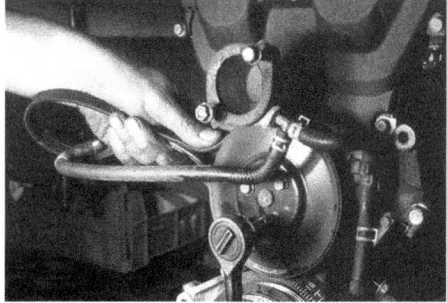

7/40 Grip pulley with belt.

10mm chrome dome-headed bolts which hold the cambox cover to the cylinder head. Unscrew the bolts progressively in a diagonal sequence until they are all loose enough to unscrew with your fingers. Note: a short 75mm/3 inch extension is also needed. There are four cambox cover bolts down each side of the cambox; three down in the center valley and two at the front. Note that the two front bolts, which also secure the vent hose clips, are shorter than the others. Once the bolts have been removed the cambox cover can be lifted clear of the cylinder head.

7/44b ... and lower covers.

40   Using a 10mm socket, and gripping the pulley with the drivebelt as shown in the photograph, slacken and remove the three bolts securing the water pump pulley to the pump spindle boss.

41   Unscrew the four 10mm bolts that secure the crankshaft pulley to the crankshaft nose. Rock the pulley gently side-to-side to work it off the boss on the crankshaft nose.

CAMBOX COVER REMOVAL

42   Unscrew and remove the thirteen

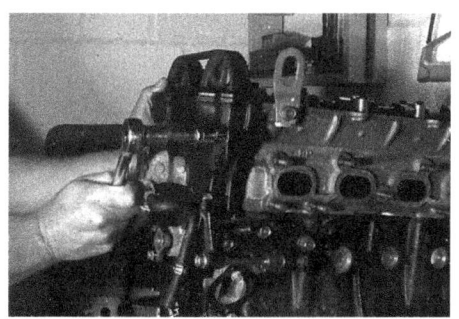

7/43a Remove four securing bolts ...

CAMSHAFT DRIVEBELT REMOVAL

45   **Caution!** Mazda has provided various markings to assist in making sure that the two camshafts and crankshaft are correctly positioned relative to each other when fitting a camshaft drivebelt, and thus critical valve timing is preserved. Frankly, we found the manufacturer's markings hard to use and open to error. Therefore, while we do describe use of the manufacturer's markings, we strongly recommend you use the following backup procedure before removing the existing camshaft drivebelt.

46   Remove the sparkplugs. Using a 21mm socket on the crankshaft nose bolt, rotate the crankshaft clockwise (viewed from the front) until the cutout in the rear flange of the crankshaft drivebelt pulley is vertical and aligns with the arrow-shaped boss in the oil pump body. Simultaneously, the letter "E" on the exhaust (left-hand) cam pulley and the letter "I" on the intake cam pulley should both be more-or-less vertical. Note: this coincidence of relative positions will occur only once in every two revolutions of the crankshaft.

47   When all is correctly positioned, use a straight edge running from the center of the

7/41a Four bolts secure ...

7/43b ... and lift away upper cover.

43   Undo and remove the four 10mm bolts securing the upper section of the timing cover. Pull the cover forward slightly at the top, and then lift away from the lower section.

44   There are four 10mm bolts retaining the middle and lower drivebelt covers. One of these is adjacent to the water pump center boss and is longer than the other three. Once the bolts retaining the drivebelt covers have been removed, the covers can be withdrawn, the lower one having to be maneuverd around the power steering pump bracket if that is still in place.

7/41b ... crankshaft outer pulley.

7/46 Notch and pointer aligned.

Mazda Miata, MX-5, Eunos & Roadster

7/47 Straightedge thru pulley centers, mark pulleys.

crankshaft pulley and across the center of each camshaft pulley in turn, to make alignment marks with a scriber or indelible pen at the two points where the straight edge crosses the rim of each camshaft pulley - don't allow the pulleys to move at all until all alignment marks have been made. Identify the exhaust cam pulley with the letter "E" written in indelible ink.

48 If the camshaft drivebelt is to be re-used - a false economy unless the belt has been in place for less than 50,000km/30,000 miles and is completely damage-free - mark the outward edge of the belt with a white dot (typist's correction fluid is good for this) so that the belt can be installed to run in the same direction.

49 ◉+ Slacken the central locking bolt on

7/49a Slacken locking bolt then pull ...

7/49b ... tensioner wheel sideways to slacken belt.

7/51a Unscrew crankshaft nosebolt.

7/51b Pull off cambelt guide plate.

the tensioner jockey wheel and pull the wheel backwards as far as possible to relieve the tension on the drivebelt. Whilst holding the wheel back, retighten the central screw. The drivebelt will now be loose.

50 **Caution!** Avoid rotating the crankshaft whilst the drivebelt is loose or removed. If you must turn the crankshaft, do it very slowly and carefully, stopping at the least sign of contact between valve heads and pistons - which could result in bent valve stems. In fact, our engine showed no signs of such contact when we checked by turning the crank with the cams in various different positions, but it's possible tolerances will vary from engine to engine, particularly if high-performance camshafts are fitted.

51 ◉+ Unscrew the 21mm crankshaft pulley bolt whilst holding the flywheel locked with a screwdriver wedged against a bellhousing bolt. The camshaft belt guide plate then simply pulls forward over the square key in the crankshaft nose.

52 The camshaft drivebelt can now be slid off the three pulleys.

CAMSHAFT DRIVEBELT TENSIONER WHEEL AND TENSIONER SPRING REMOVAL

53 ◉+ Slacken and remove the tensioner wheel 14mm lockbolt whilst holding the wheel against spring tension sufficient to prevent the bolt binding. Unclip the tensioner spring from the tensioner wheel bracket and from its anchor pin (noting that the longer eye faces the tensioner with its open end downward), then lift away the tensioner wheel assembly and the spring. **Caution!** Note that on our 9000 mile (14,500km) two-year-old engine, the camshaft belt tensioner pulley pivot pin was quite severely corroded. This could lead to seizure and loss of correct belt tension. On reassembly, ensure the pivot pin is thoroughly cleaned and coated with copper grease or similar.

7/53a Relieve spring tension, undo bolt ...

7/53b ... unclip spring eye then lift ...

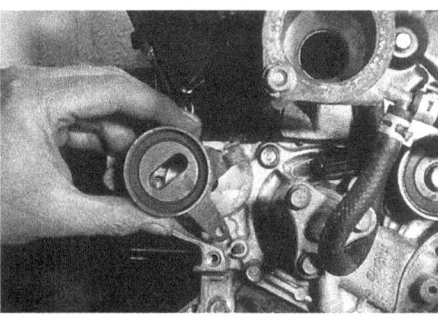

7/53c ... tensioner wheel off its pivot pin.

CAMSHAFT PULLEYS REMOVAL

54 ◉ There is a hex-shaped section on each of the two camshafts between bearings two and three (counting from the front of the engine). Use a 24mm crescent wrench to hold each cam in a locked position (**Caution!** Do not wedge the wrench against the side of the cambox - it's a fragile casting which could easily be broken) while the 14mm bolt retaining each drive pulley is slackened and removed together with the large washer.

55 ◉+ Note that each drive pulley is located on a spigot which can engage with any of three

7/54 Lock cam with a crescent wrench.

3:18

3: Engine & clutch

slots. To ensure correct orientation on rebuild, place a paint mark across the top of the spigot and onto the adjoining area of the pulley (see photo). Also mark the pulley with an "I" (intake) or "E" (exhaust) as appropriate. Each drive pulley can now be pulled forward off of its locating spigot.

CYLINDER HEAD FRONT SEALING PLATE REMOVAL

56   ◘+ After undoing the six 10mm retaining bolts, the seal plate can be lifted away from the front of the cylinder head. Note: there is a rubber seal which fits around the thermostat housing casting and which should not be lost.

THERMOSTAT HOUSING REMOVAL

57   ◘+ Unscrew and remove the two 12mm bolts holding the thermostat housing to the front of the cylinder head. This will be difficult with sockets as there is little room, so use a box end wrench (ring spanner). Once the two bolts have been removed the housing can be pulled forward off of the cylinder head. **Warning!** It will probably come free rather suddenly. Note: the thermostat housing connection is sealed by an O-ring which should be replaced. Note the position of the rubber seal on the top of

7/55a Paint mark on spigot and pulley.

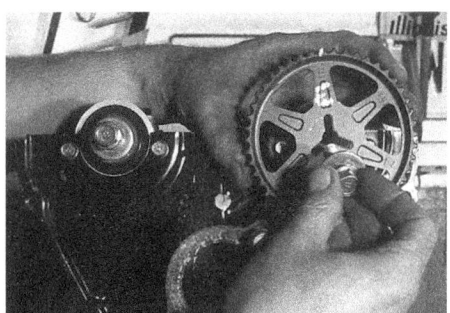
7/55b Remove pulley. Note "E" mark.

7/56a Remove six bolts then ...

7/56b ... lift away seal plate.

7/57a Remove two bolts and ...

7/57b ... lift away thermostat housing.

the water pump housing.

WATER PUMP REMOVAL

58   ◘ Unscrew and remove the 14mm bolt securing the camshaft drivebelt idler wheel and lift the wheel away.

59   ◘+ Slacken and then unscrew - in a diagonal sequence - the four 12mm bolts holding the water pump body to the front of the cylinder block. Once the bolts are out, the pump body can be pulled away. **Warning!** It will come free suddenly as the gasket seal breaks. **Caution!** You can tap the back of the casting with a wooden hammer handle

7/58 One bolt secures idler wheel.

7/59a Remove four bolts ...

7/59b ... and remove water pump.

or soft-faced mallet to help break the joint's adhesion, but don't use a sharp implement to lever the casting away from the cylinder block.

CRANKSHAFT INNER PULLEY REMOVAL

60   ◘+ Using your fingers or, if necessary, pliers, remove the square key protruding from the crankshaft nose. Find some small screws which will fit into the threaded holes in the face of the cam belt drive pulley. The screws we found were approximately 3mm in diameter. Once the screws are in place, use a pair of vise grip (mole grip) pliers

7/60a Remove key from crankshaft nose.

7/60b Insert small screws into pulley.

3:19

Mazda Miata, MX-5, Eunos & Roadster

7/60c Use vise grips to pull pulley off.

7/64b ... then lift off caps.

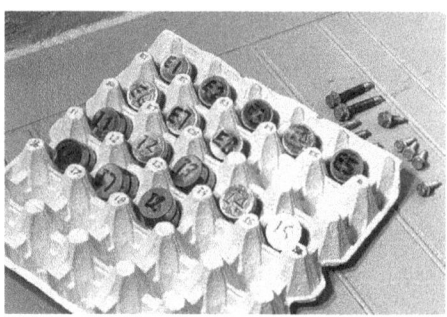

7/66b ... store them safely (eggbox ideal).

to pull the pulley forward off the crankshaft nose.

CAMSHAFT REMOVAL

61 Note that it is not necessary to remove the camshafts to facilitate cylinder head removal.

62 If you intend to remove the exhaust camshaft, remove the camshaft position sensor at this point.

63 Each camshaft is retained by five bearing caps and each cap is numbered (very faintly on our project engine) from the front of the engine backwards. The first cap is simply marked with an "E" for the exhaust camshaft and an "I" for the intake camshaft; each subsequent cap is marked "E2," "E3," etc. If the markings on your engine's caps are very faint, it's best to dot punch the caps to mark their correct positions for reassembly. Each cap is also marked with an arrow shape pointing toward the front of the engine to ensure correct orientation.

64 Undo and remove the ten 10mm bolts retaining the bearing caps for each camshaft. **Caution!** The bolts must be undone progressively and in sequence to prevent camshaft distortion and bearing damage: they must be undone by half a turn on the first pass, followed by a full turn on the second pass and then removed completely on the third pass. The sequence is simply a spiral that works inward from the outermost caps of each cam (see diagram). Once all of the cap bolts have been removed for a complete camshaft, the individual caps can be lifted. They will be a little tight as they are located on close-fitting spigots. The front cap of each cam really is rather difficult to remove: not only is it mounted on spigots, there is sealing compound around its edges and the cap also tends to get held by the oil seal. Very gently tapping the caps backwards and forwards with a nylon or leather-faced mallet will eventually loosen them. Discard the old oil seals and fit new ones during the rebuild. **Caution!** Do not insert sharp implements between the base casting and the cap.

65 Once all the caps are removed, each camshaft can be lifted away from the cylinder head. **Caution!** Take great care not to scratch the bearing surfaces with the sharp edges of the cam lobes.

CAM FOLLOWERS REMOVAL

66 Once the camshafts are removed the hydraulic cam followers should be wiped clean, numbered with indelible ink and removed. **Caution!** It is essential, when the engine is reassembled, that each cam follower is replaced in the bore from which it was taken. If there is any danger at all that the numbers will be erased during cleaning or storage - and a good idea anyway - place the cam followers in an egg tray or similar with numbered compartments. If you find the followers difficult to remove with your fingers you can use a valve grinding suction tool to remove them, but make sure it's clean.

CYLINDER HEAD REMOVAL

67 There are ten 12mm bolts holding the cylinder head to the cylinder block. **Caution!**

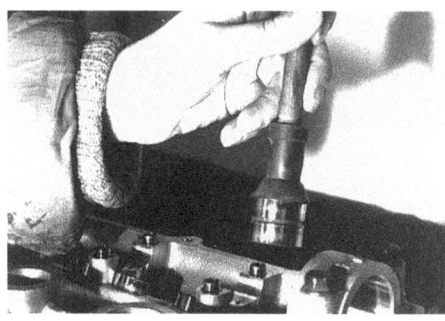

7/66c Valve grinder can be useful tool.

The bolts must be loosened in a sequence which spirals inward from the outer bolts of the head - this minimizes distortion. Initially loosen each bolt half a turn, then a whole turn, followed by full removal. A 125mm/5 inch socket extension will be needed as the bolts are quite deeply recessed in the cambox. Note: it doesn't matter that the bolts have splined heads - your ordinary socket will still work. Once the ten bolts have been loosened and removed, the cylinder head can be lifted. It may be necessary to use a leather or other soft-faced mallet just to tap the head gently upwards to loosen it. Alternatively, you can use a hammer and a block of wood (see

D7/64 CAMSHAFT BEARING CAPS BOLT LOOSENING SEQUENCE.

D7/67 CYLINDER HEAD BOLT LOOSENING SEQUENCE.

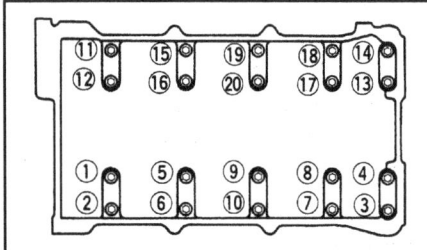

7/64a Remove camshaft cap bolts and ...

7/66a Lift out numbered cam followers ...

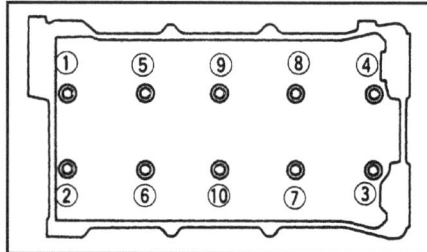

7/67a Remove ten securing bolts and ...

3: Engine & clutch

7/67b ... jar head free from block.

7/68 Cover oilway with adhesive tape.

compressing tool. Unfortunately, like us, you're likely to find that the tool won't operate properly on the head because the valve springs and stems are so deeply recessed in the cambox.

70 📷+ To get around the problem of valve spring compressor reach we made a spacer out of an old tube (box) spanner. To give better access to the valve keepers we cut triangular 'windows' in each side of the tube using a hacksaw; cleaning up the rough edges with a file. The original tube spanner had an external diameter of 25mm/1 inch and a length of 60mm/2.4 in - in fact, another 12.5mm/0.5 inch in length would have been better.

71 Mount the cylinder head horizontally in a vise (fitted with jaw protectors) so that you have access to all of the valves on one side of the head. **Caution!** Don't overtighten the vice; it should be just tight enough to grip the head.

72 📷+ Place the spacer tube on the valve spring cap and then locate the spring compressor in position so that it is bearing centrally on both spacer rim and valve head. Tighten the compressor until you see that the spring cap has been pushed far enough down the valve stem to free the valve keepers. Remove the keepers with needle-nosed pliers, a screwdriver with a magnetic tip or a

screwdriver with a small blob of sticky grease on the tip.

73 📷 Carefully release the compressor until the spring has reached its full free length. **Warning!** Whilst releasing the compressor, make sure it stays squarely seated on both spacer and valve head; if it slips off after the keepers have been removed, the spring and cap are free to fly off the valve stem with very considerable force. With the compressor removed, the spring cap, spring and spring seat can be withdrawn over the valve stem. Thread a length of gardening wire through these components to keep them together and correctly orientated. Withdraw the valve from the combustion chamber side of the head.

74 **Caution!** It's essential that not only is each valve and spring set kept together - assuming the components will be re-used - but also that you know exactly where each valve came from so that it can be installed in original position. It's suggested that the stem of each valve is pushed through a piece of cardboard and that the cardboard is marked "E1" (exhaust 1) - counting from the front of the head - until you have a row of valves in the card sheet, each with a position ID. Of course, the spring sets should be tagged using the same ID system.

75 📷 Lever the valve stem oil seal from the top of the valve guide using a screwdriver. You should have new seals in your new gasket set.

76 📷 Use the same process to remove the other valves from the head.

VALVE GUIDES REMOVAL AND INSTALLATION

77 Don't remove the valve guides unless inspection shows that they need to be renewed ☞ 3/8.

78 Mazda dealers have SSTs (special service tools) designed specifically for the safe and easy

VALVES REMOVAL

69 In order to remove a valve, its valve spring must be compressed sufficiently to free the two valve keepers (split collets) around the upper part of its stem. If you don't have one already, you'll be able to buy, borrow or hire a universal valve spring

7/72a Position keeper removal tool ...

7/70a Making valve keeper removal tool.

7/72b ... and use valve spring compressor.

7/75 Remove valve stem seals.

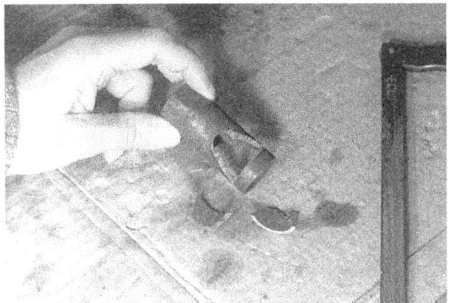

7/70b The finished tool.

7/73 Remove valve.

7/76 Valve and spring components.

Mazda Miata, MX-5, Eunos & Roadster

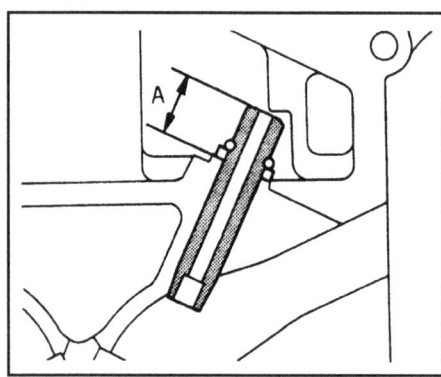

D7/79 CORRECT VALVE GUIDE POSITION. (See text).

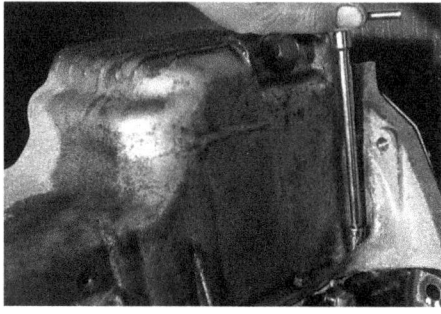

7/80a Limited access to this bolt.

7/80b Eighteen bolts secure oil pan ...

7/80c ... two are very long.

removal and installation of valve guides: borrow the set if you can. Otherwise you'll have to get your local small machine shop to machine a drift. It will need to be 150mm/6in long (or longer) and initially of 12.5mm/0.5 inch diameter. The first 51mm/2in of the drift should be machined to a diameter of 5.980mm/0.2354 inch, the next 51mm/2in should be machined to a diameter of 9mm/0.3543in with only a small radius in the corner of the shoulder. Using the drift inserted narrowest end first into the guide from the combustion chamber end, drive the guide out into the cambox. Repeat the process for the other guides.

79   The new guides can be driven in from the cambox side using the same tool, but check the guide height frequently as dimension "A" (see picture) must be between 18.3-18.9mm /0.721-0.744in. Note that the replacement valve guides will all be of the exhaust type but they can also be used for intake valves.

OIL PAN REMOVAL

80   + Turn the engine upside-down. There are nine 10mm bolts on each side of the oil pan securing it to the bottom of the cylinder block; two of these are long bolts situated close to the flywheel. Access to the bolt on the oil pan flange closest to the starter motor mounting is difficult with standard ½ inch drive sockets. The bolt can be undone using a socket system with a smaller drive or progressively with a box end wrench.

81   + Once all of the bolts have been removed, you'll need to break the seal between the flanges of the oil pan baffle and the oil pan itself. **Caution!** The oil pan cannot be removed until the seal with the baffle has been broken. You'll see that there is a small cutout on each side of the oil pan flange where you should just be able to see the bright metal of the baffle. Use a sharp woodworking chisel to break the seal between baffle and oil pan flange on both sides of the oil pan. When the seal is broken, lift the oil pan off the cylinder block.

OIL PUMP, PICKUP PIPE AND OIL PAN BAFFLE REMOVAL

82   + The oil pump pickup is retained by

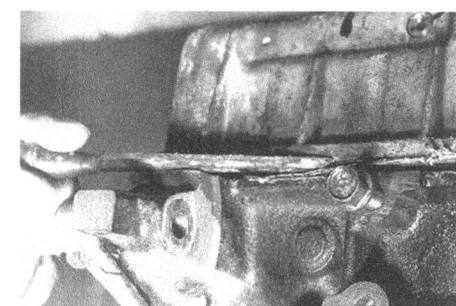

7/81a Chisel will separate baffle and oil pan.

7/81b Once free, remove oil pan.

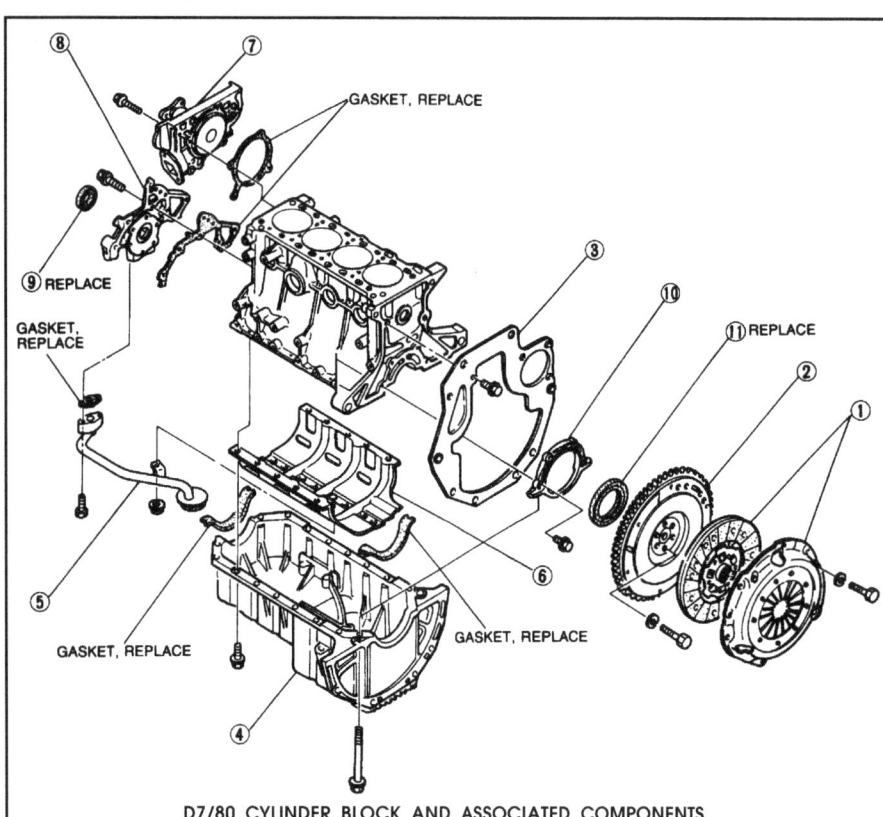

D7/80 CYLINDER BLOCK AND ASSOCIATED COMPONENTS.
1 Clutch disc (driven plate) and cover (pressure plate). 2 Flywheel. 3 Backplate. 4 Oil pan (sump). 5 Oil pump pickup. 6 Baffle. 7 Water pump. 8 Oil pump. 9 Crankshaft front seal. 10 Crankshaft rear seal housing. 11 Crankshaft rear seal.

3: Engine & clutch

7/82a Remove three securing bolts ...

7/82b ... and lift away oil pump pickup.

7/83 Break seal and lift away baffle.

two 10mm bolts at the oil pump end and a 10mm nut near the pickup end. Unscrew the fixings, lift away the oil pump pickup.

83   Using a sharp woodworking chisel, break the seal between the baffle and the cylinder block. Lift off the baffle.

84   + Remove the six 12mm bolts securing the oil pump. The oil pump body can now be pulled away from the front of the cylinder block and off over the nose of the crankshaft. If you have trouble breaking the gasket seal, use light blows from a soft-faced mallet to start the pump moving.

7/84a remove six securing bolts ...

7/84b ... and lift away oil pump.

Caution! Do not force a sharp tool into the joint as a wedge or lever.

OIL PUMP AND OIL PRESSURE RELIEF VALVE TEARDOWN

85   Place the oil pump on the bench with the backplate upward. You'll see that the backplate is held to the oil pump body by six countersunk crosshead screws. You'll need an ordinary impact screwdriver to loosen them. Select the crosshead bit which fits the screws best (**Caution!** Don't use an undersize bit.)

86   Slacken and remove the screws in a diagonal sequence. Once the cover is off the pump, the rotors can be removed.

87   The oil pressure relief valve can be dismantled by pushing the spring cap down with a screwdriver whilst withdrawing the straightened split pin, then removing the spring retaining cap spring and domed top from the pressure relief valve bore.

FLYWHEEL (DRIVEPLATE - AUTO TRANS) REMOVAL

88   Lock the crankshaft by wedging a

7/85 Use impact driver to loosen screws.

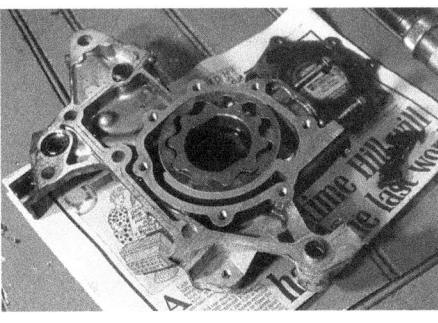

7/86 The oil pump rotors.

7/88 Remove flywheel securing bolts.

hammer handle between a crank web and the side of the cylinder block. Undo and remove the six 19mm bolts holding the flywheel to the crankshaft flange. Note: the bolts should be loosened half a turn each initially and in a diagonal sequence.
Caution! It's a good idea to make sure that the same relationship between crankshaft and flywheel position is kept on reassembly to maintain balance. Mark the top of the flywheel and mark the top of the crankshaft (once the flywheel has been removed) using indelible ink so that the flywheel can be installed in exactly the same position. Once the bolts have been removed the flywheel can be lifted away - it's heavy!

89   The procedure for automatic transmission cars, which will be fitted with a torque converter driveplate, is the same as the flywheel removal procedure, except that the driveplate will be lighter and there will be a backing plate between the bolt heads and the face of the driveplate and an adaptor between the crank and driveplate.

ENGINE BACKPLATE REMOVAL

90   With the flywheel out of the way, the single 10mm bolt now holding the backplate to the cylinder block can be unscrewed and the backplate removed.

CRANKSHAFT REAR OIL SEAL HOUSING REMOVAL

91   + The housing is fixed to the cylinder block by four 10mm headed bolts. Unscrew and remove the four bolts. Note that the two lower bolts (closest to the oil pan flange) are slightly longer. Once the four bolts have been removed, the housing

D7/89 DRIVEPLATE REMOVAL (AUTOMATIC TRANSMISSION MODELS).

Mazda Miata, MX-5, Eunos & Roadster

7/91a Unscrew four bolts and ...

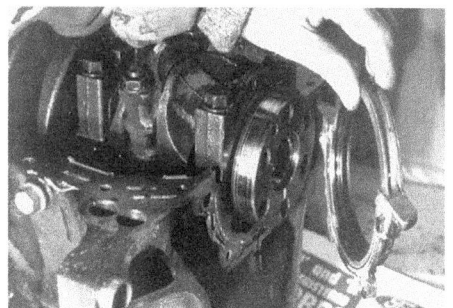

7/91b ... lift away seal housing.

can be pulled away from the cylinder block. If necessary, gentle leverage can be applied by inserting a screwdriver between the rearmost main bearing cap and the back of the seal housing.

CONNECTING ROD (BIG END) CAPS, CONNECTING RODS AND PISTONS REMOVAL

92　　The connecting rod caps are marked across their joints with the con-rods by Mazda - our engine had diagonal stamp marks across the joints. This is fine to tell you which cap goes with which rod, but won't tell you which rod and cap come from which bore. We recommend that you use a center punch to mark each connecting rod and cap with an appropriate number of dots to ensure that they remain a pair and are installed on the correct crank web. Note: before removing the connecting rod caps, it's a good idea to check con-rod bearing side clearance 3/8.

93　　+ Each connecting rod cap is retained by two 14mm nuts which should be slackened alternately and progressively. Once the nuts have been removed, each cap can be lifted off of the con-rod studs: if the bearing shell sticks to the crankshaft, gently lift the shell off and keep it with

7/92a Mazda's own con-rod joint mark.

7/92b Center punched ID marks.

the correct cap. **Caution!** It's a good idea to place a length of soft fuel hose over each con-rod stud so that they don't scratch the crankshaft journals as it is rotated and during con-rod/piston removal. Note: there are plenty of protuberances on the flywheel which, if necessary, will allow it to be turned with the leverage of a screwdriver or similar.

94　　**Caution!** If there's a ring of carbon around the top of the bore, above the piston's travel, scrape it away with a sharp-edged tool - this will make piston removal easier. If, after carbon removal, there is still a very distinct ridge remaining

7/93a Remove securing nuts and ...

7/93b ... lift cap from con-rod.

7/94 Carbon build-up at bore top.

(caused by bore wear), it must be removed before attempting to remove the piston, otherwise piston ring damage could occur (this does not matter if the cylinders are going to be rebored and new pistons/rings fitted). You can buy/hire a tool called a ridge reamer to remove this ridge and you'll need to follow the tool manufacturer's instructions.

95　　Once the carbon/wear ridge has been removed, each piston and con-rod assembly can be pushed out through the top of the cylinder block using the wooden or rubber-covered handle of a hammer. **Caution!** Be careful that the piston doesn't come out of the bore suddenly and drop to the

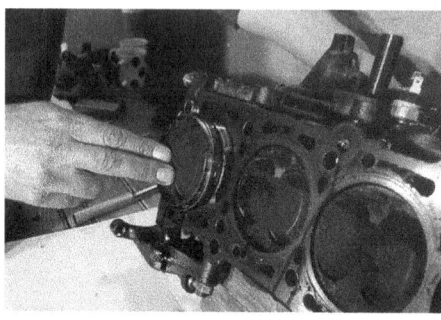

7/95 Push piston/rod out from beneath.

floor.

96　　Remove the shell bearings from con-rods and caps and, if they are to be re-used, wipe clean and number their backs with indelible ink so that they can be reinstalled in original positions. **Caution!** It's essential that shells are not mixed up if they're to be re-used, but if the shells have done more than 48,000km/30,000 miles they should be replaced, even if they look fine. Temporarily install bearing caps to con-rods and retain with finger-tightened nuts.

MAIN BEARING CAPS AND CRANKSHAFT REMOVAL

97　　There are five main bearing caps which may, or may not, be marked to indicate position; however, each bearing cap does have an arrow cast into its bottom which points towards the front of the engine. It's a good idea to center punch an appropriate number of dots into the side of each main bearing cap so that they can be installed in exactly the positions they were taken from. Note: before removing the caps, it would be a good idea to check crankshaft lash (endfloat) 3/8.

98　　Each main bearing cap is held by

7/97 Center punched ID marks.

3: Engine & clutch

7/98 Use correct sequence to undo bolts.

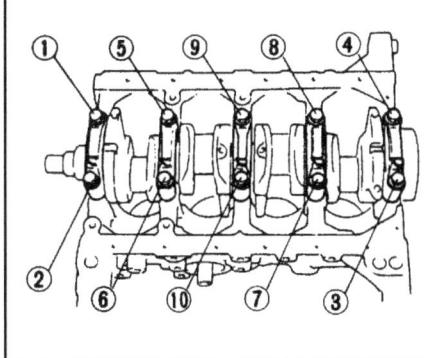

D7/98 MAIN BEARING CAP BOLTS LOOSENING SEQUENCE.

two 14mm headed bolts. The ten main bearing cap bolts must be undone in a sequence that spirals inward starting front left, front right, rear right, rear left, cap 2 left, etc. Undo each bolt half a turn initially, followed by a full turn on the next sequence, after which they can be loosened completely. It's suggested you leave the loose bolts in place as they can be used to lever the caps backwards and forwards to loosen them: then each cap and its pair of bolts can be lifted off together. If a bearing shell sticks to the crankshaft journal, remove it and keep it with its original main bearing cap. **Caution!** It's essential that shells are not mixed up if they are to be re-used but, if the shells have done more than 50,000km/30,000 miles, it's our advice that they should be replaced even if they look fine.

99 ◘ When the five main bearing caps have been removed the crankshaft can be lifted clear of the cylinder block. Once again, if bearing shells adhere to the crank journals, lift them off carefully, noting which journal they belong to. Two semi-circular thrust washers should be stuck, one each

7/99 Lift crankshaft from cylinder block.

side, of main bearing number 4: these can be lifted from their recesses and kept with the bearing shells.
100 The bearing shells can be removed one at a time, wiped clean and then their position number marked on their backs with an indelible pen. **Caution!** Do not attempt to stamp numbers or punch dots into bearing shells.

PISTON OIL JETS REMOVAL

101 The piston oil jet at the base of each cylinder bore can be removed with a 14mm socket and 125 mm/5 inch extension. Lift away the jet complete with banjo bolt and two copper washers.

PISTONS REMOVAL FROM CONNECTING RODS

102 ◘ The skirt of each piston is asymmetrical, having a section cutaway on one side to clear the oil jet in the base of each cylinder bore. To make sure that the piston will be installed, or a new piston fitted, with the same orientation, mark the side of each con-rod which is adjacent to the piston skirt cutaway. If the old pistons are to be re-used, mark the skirt of each in indelible ink to indicate which cylinder the piston came from.
103 ◘ Using a pair of needle-nosed pliers,

7/102 Mark con-rods.

grasp the wire spring clips which will be found on each side of the piston retaining the piston pin (wrist/gudgeon pin). Discard the clips as new ones should be used on rebuild.
104 ◘+ The piston pin is an interference fit in the piston and, therefore, warming the piston to expand the aluminum will make it easier to push the slower expanding steel piston pin out. Mount the connecting rod in a vise with jaw protectors. Using a normal domestic butane torch, heat the piston evenly and quickly: it doesn't need to be seriously hot and you should avoid heating the piston pin itself. As soon as the piston is hot enough

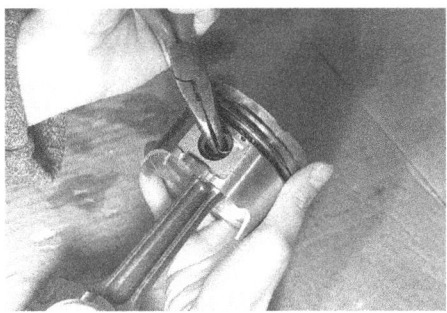

7/103 Remove piston pin clips.

7/104a Heat piston ...

7/104b ... then push out piston pin.

to make a drop of water sizzle, use a metal drift - it can be a solid rod or, say, a tube (box) spanner - of 15-16mm/0.6 inches outside diameter and at least 100mm/4 inches in length, to push the pin through the piston and connecting rod until it emerges from the other side of the piston. You'll need a rag to catch it as it may well be fairly hot by now. You'll find that using this method will allow you to push out the piston pin without using any more than hand pressure. The piston can now be removed from the connecting rod.

PISTON RINGS REMOVAL

105 **Caution!** It's important that the rings are removed carefully; if they are twisted too much or opened too far they will snap. Remove the topmost ring first and work your way down. If the rings are likely to be re-used, place each set in a bag marked with the number of the piston from which they were removed.
106 ◘ You can buy a piston ring removal tool from your local tool shop and it will make life easier, or you can use the following method as we did. Use three old feeler gauge blades or three pieces of hacksaw blade as groove bridges to remove the rings without twisting them. Take care not to scrape/score the piston here, especially if using the latter method. The trick is to pull the ring out far enough with your fingers to insert two strips between the piston ring and the piston on the opposite side to the piston ring gap. Then, hold one of the strips in that position and slide the other around until it is supporting one end of the ring. Slide a third strip between the ring and piston on the opposite side of the piston to the ring gap and then slide that strip around until it supports the other end of the ring. With the ring held clear of its ring groove by the three strips, it can be slid evenly upwards to remove it from the piston. You don't need to use this

Mazda Miata, MX-5, Eunos & Roadster

7/106 Metal strips support rings.

procedure for the three-piece oil scraper ring as the thin rings above and below the corrugated spacer are so thin that they can be opened with your fingers and carefully slid off of the piston. Again, be careful not to twist the rings as they could snap. The corrugated spacer is easily removed by fingers.

ENGINE TEARDOWN CONCLUSION
107   Phew, that's it - the engine is now completely disassembled! Individual components need to be thoroughly cleaned and then inspected as described in the following sections of this chapter. If the engine is to be left in a dismantled state for longer than a few days, double-check that you've ID'd components which have to go back in original positions and spray all components with silicone-based lubricant to keep corrosion at bay. Wrap the block in plastic sheeting and place other cleaned components in plastic bags to keep them clean.

8 ENGINE COMPONENTS - CHECKING AND REPAIR

☞ First read 1/1, 2.

CHECKING AND REPAIR GENERAL
1   **Caution!** It's important that **all** the items mentioned in this section are checked thoroughly for excessive wear or damage. One small fault is all it takes to destroy the value of an otherwise good engine rebuild. Don't believe it? Wally once rebuilt an engine with a reground crankshaft and forgot to check that the crank's oilways were clear. They weren't, they contained swarf from the machining: the engine ran for just 200 miles (320km) before the bearings started to knock and the whole job had to be done again ... Also bear in mind that components which are within tolerance, but getting close to wear limits, will have a relatively short service life remaining: is it really worth using them in your rebuild?
2   All components must be thoroughly clean before inspection occurs.
3   Micrometers. Some components simply have to be measured with a micrometer to establish whether or not they are serviceable. A set of micrometers is not hugely expensive and will prove a worthwhile investment if you intend to do a lot of mechanical work. If you can't use a micrometer, you're bound to know an engineer or mechanic who can and who you can invite to help you: it won't take long if you have all the components cleaned, together and ready to be measured.

CYLINDER HEAD AND VALVES REMOVING CARBON
4   📷 Place the cylinder head cambox side down on your workbench. Cover the oilway with tape as shown. Using a small diameter - around 25mm/1 inch - wire brush mounted in an electric drill, brush away all traces of carbon build-up. **Caution!** This process should not remove any metal from the combustion chambers; take care not to scratch the gasket surface of the head or the

8/4 Clean the combustion chambers.

valve seats if the valves are not in place.
5   Mount each valve, by its stem, in a vise fitted with jaw protectors. The same combination of wire brush and electric drill can be used to remove all traces of carbon from the valve head and lower part of stem. **Caution!** Take care not to scratch the valve seat with the wire brush.

CYLINDER HEAD CHECKING AND REPAIR
6   Visually check the combustion chambers for cracking between valve openings and the percussive damage which can result from bits of broken ring, valve or piston entering the combustion chamber. Also check the machined face between each combustion chamber for erosion or burning. If your car's head is suffering from any of these problems, you'll need to consult a machine shop which will advise on the possibility of repair. Maximum head machining tolerance is given in the next step.
7   📐 Using a straight edge longer than the cylinder head and a set of feeler gauges, check the machined (gasket) face of the head for distortion. Check in straight and diagonal planes and also crosswise at each end (see diagram). If you find a gap of more than 0.10mm/0.004in the head will have to be machined flat by your local machine shop. No more than 0.10mm/0.004in should be removed and the minimum total head (deck) height is 133.8mm/5.268in. If the head can't be brought back within tolerance before you run out of metal, you'll have to buy another.
8   📐 Use the same measuring method (see diagram) to check for longitudinal and twisting distortion in the head flanges of intake and exhaust manifolds. 0.15mm/0.006in is the maximum allowable distortion. These faces can be reground, but only to a maximum of 0.20mm/0.008in.
9   Before having a distorted head machined,

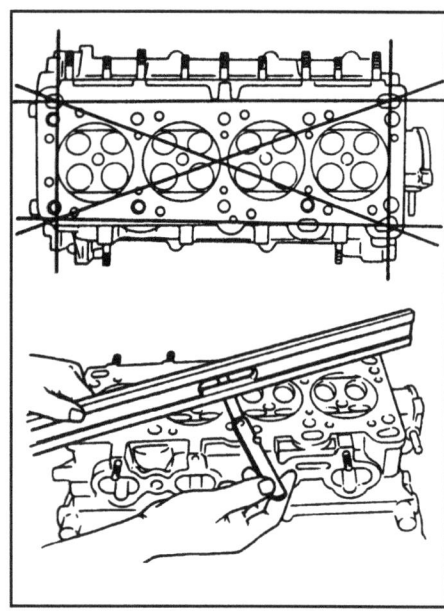

D8/7 CHECK FOR CYLINDER HEAD DISTORTION.

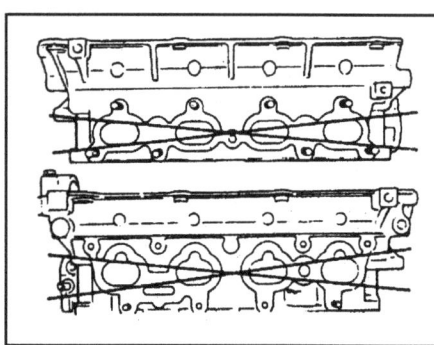

D8/8 CHECK FOR MANIFOLD FACE DISTORTION.

check that other wear areas like camshaft bearings and valve seats are within tolerance, otherwise you may have the work done for nothing ...

VALVES, GUIDES AND VALVE SEATS CHECKING, REPAIR AND VALVE LAPPING
10   Inspect each valve for obvious signs of damage such as a chipped, cracked or burned seat or a bent stem. Also check the stem tip, where the follower bears, for chipping or uneven wear. Any of these faults will mean a new valve is needed.
11   📷 Check the section of the valve stem which slides back and forth in the guide: you should not be able to see or feel (with a fingernail) a lip at either end of the wearing section. If you have access to a micrometer, check the thicker portion of the valve stem at top, bottom and center to ensure that it's in tolerance at between 5.970-5.985mm/0.2351-0.2356 inch for intake valves and 5.965-5.980mm/0.2349-0.2354 inch for exhaust valves. If a valve's out of tolerance or shows visible wear, replace it.
12   Check that the overall length of each valve is not less than 100.39mm/3.9524in for intake valves and 100.49mm/3.9563in for exhaust valves. Too short? Throw it away!

3: Engine & clutch

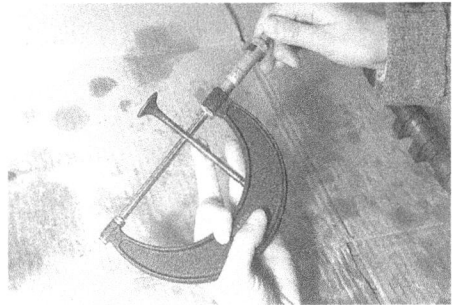

8/11 Check for valve stem wear.

8/15b ... valve seat using to-and-fro action.

13 Check the margin of the valve head; it's the bit between the face and the beginning of the seat on the back of the head. The margin must not be less than 0.9mm/0.035in for intake valves or 1mm/0.039 inch for exhaust valves. Less margin than this means that the valve has been ground too much or has worn excessively and must be renewed.

14 If you have access to an internal micrometer small enough, measure the internal bore of the valve guides at top, bottom and center, then deduct the diameter of the relevant valve: resulting clearance should be 0.025-0.060mm/0.0010-

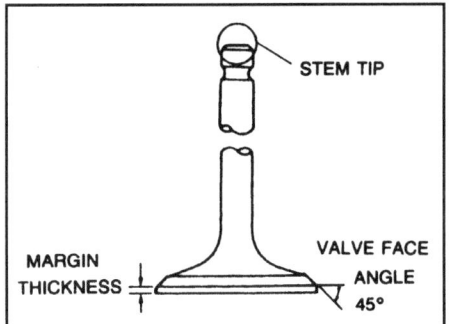

D8/13 CHECK VALVE HEAD AND TIP.

0.0023in (intake) and 0.030-0.065mm/0.0012-0.0025in (exhaust). If you don't have a micrometer, insert the valve (having checked it's in tolerance) into the guide until the valve head is around 6mm/0.25 inch from its seat. With your fingers rock the valve head back and forth: anything more than barely perceptible play means that the guide should be renewed.

15 + Place two small blobs of fine valve grinding paste on opposite sides of the valve face. Lightly lubricate the valve stem and lower the valve onto its seat (the head should be combustion

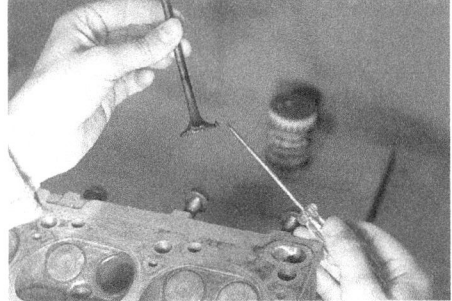

8/15a Apply grinding paste and then grind ...

chamber side up on your bench). Press the rubber suction cup of a valve grinding tool lightly against the valve head and then, by moving the palms of your hands to-and-fro either side of the tool's handle, impart a reciprocating motion to the valve head. After every 5 or 6 back-and-forth movements lift the valve head and turn it through 90 degrees, and repeat this process until the valve head has been turned a full 360 degrees. Lift the valve out and wipe the grinding paste from valve head and seat.

16 Inspect the seat on the back of the

8/16 Unbroken bright ring of correct depth.

valve first, it should be unbroken and free of pitting, should be in the center of the angled face on the back of the valve head and should not be wider than 0.8-1.4mm/0.031-0.055 inch. If the seat is not continuous, repeat the grinding process, only this time use coarse grinding paste first followed by fine. If you still cannot achieve a continuous seat, it indicates some distortion in the valve head or valve seat. Too wide a seat on the valve head or a seat that's off-center indicates the need to recut the corresponding seat in the combustion chamber.

17 Now inspect the seat in the valve port in the combustion chamber. It, too, should be

8/17 Another unbroken bright ring.

unbroken and free of pitting, in the center of the seat area and about the same width as the seat on the valve. If the seat is not continuous, try regrinding with coarse and fine paste as described in the previous step.

18 If you still haven't achieved a continuous seat it's most likely that the valve seat in the combustion chamber needs to be recut. In cross-section the standard seat is actually comprised of three differently angled faces (see diagram) made with different cutting tools in order to achieve a centrally positioned, 45 degree valve seat that's not too wide. We strongly recommend taking the head to a machine shop for seat recutting as it's really easy to make a mistake and end up trashing the head. If, after the port seats have been recut, you still can't get a continuous seat on a valve, throw

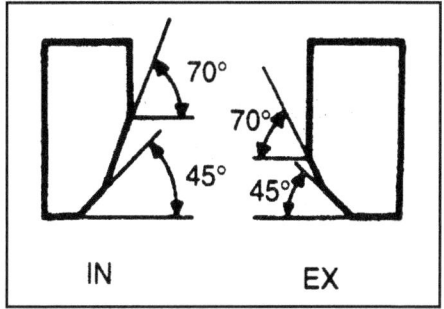

D8/18 VALVE SEAT CUT ANGLES.

the valve away and start again with a new one. **Caution!** All new valves have to be lapped in with grinding paste as previously described.

19 After valve lapping, or seat recutting, check that the valve seats are not now recessed too far into the head. Hold the valve against its seat and then, using the tail of a vernier gauge, measure the

8/19 Measuring valve stem protrusion.

protrusion of the valve stem from the head as shown. Valve stem protrusion of more than 45mm/1.776 inch means buying a replacement cylinder head ...

20 **Caution!** Ensure all traces of grinding paste are removed from valves, valve stems and valve seats once valve seating has been satisfactorily completed.

VALVE SPRINGS CHECKING AND REPAIR

21 Visually inspect the springs, spring seats, spring caps and valve keepers for obvious damage

Mazda Miata, MX-5, Eunos & Roadster

8/22 Check valve spring length.

or wear. These are high stress components so, if in any doubt about serviceability, renew.

22   Using a vernier gauge, measure the free length of each spring. Less than 46.26mm/1.821in (intake and exhaust) means that a new spring is needed. Buy a complete set, even if some of the old springs are in tolerance.

23   Place a set square on a flat surface and then stand each spring alongside the vertical section of the square. Turn the spring until it shows the greatest deviation from vertical whilst the base of the spring is still touching the set square. Maximum

8/23 Check valve spring for distortion.

deviation at the top of the spring must not exceed 1.62mm/0.0638 inch for intake and exhaust valve springs.

CAMSHAFTS AND CAMSHAFT BEARINGS CHECKING AND REPAIR

24   If you have access to V-blocks, use them to support the front and rear bearing journals of a camshaft. Set up a dial gauge to read from the center bearing journal and then rotate the camshaft in the blocks to measure runout. If runout exceeds 0.03mm/0.0012 inch, discard the cam. Repeat the process with the second cam. If you haven't got this measuring equipment, don't worry too much as it's unlikely that a cam will bend in service.

25   Visually inspect the cam bearing journals and lobes for wear. The lobe faces should be blackish in color which shows that the surface hardening is still intact. Bright, shiny areas, wear that can clearly be seen or felt with a fingernail, indicate that the cam should be renewed. Bearing surfaces should be shiny, smooth and free of scratches or gouges. If you want to double-check and have the equipment, use a micrometer to read the maximum height of each cam lobe from base circle to lobe tip taking a reading from each side.

Bearing journals, too, can be measured with a micrometer, taking readings from each side and at two positions around the circumference of each journal. Minimum lobe heights are 43.894mm/1.7281in intake and 44.400mm/1.7480in exhaust. Minimum bearing journal diameter is 25.940mm/1.0213in and out of round maximum is 0.03mm/0.0012 inch.

26   Lubricate the cam bearing journals in the head and rest the two cams in place - they're marked "I" and "E" so you'll know which is which - without fitting the cam followers. Lubricate the bearing caps and temporarily replace them in their correct positions - each cap is marked with a

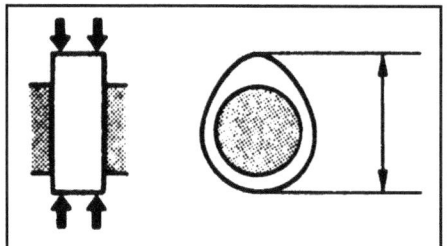

D8/25 CHECK CAM LOBES FOR WEAR.

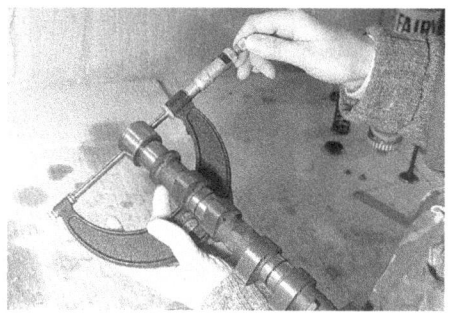

8/25 Check cam journals for wear.

number and an arrow (see rebuild instructions for more detail). Tighten the retaining bolts in three stages to a torque of 11.3-14.2 Nm/115-145kgf cm/100-125lbf in using a sequence which spirals outward from the center of each cam.

27   Measure the lash (endplay) of each cam. You can do this with feeler gauges between the thrust face at the back of each front bearing and the cam, or by mounting a dial gauge at the front of the cambox. Either way, lash (endfloat) should not exceed 0.20mm/0.008 inch: if it does, replace the camshaft. If this doesn't fix the problem you'll need to buy a replacement head too.

8/27 Check camshaft lash (endfloat).

28   You'll need some "Plastigage" to measure the camshaft bearing wear; you can get it and the measuring strip from your Mazda parts shop or a good tool shop. Remove the two intermediate bearing caps from each camshaft. Wipe the journal and bearing cap dry, then lay a strip of Plastigage parallel with the cam across the journal: take care not to squeeze or damage the Plastigage strip. Repeat the process on the other three journals. Install the bearing caps and tighten each to the correct torque. Remove the four intermediate bearing caps again to reveal four strips of squashed Plastigage. Match the width of each strip to a bar on the measuring tool which will give a corresponding clearance measurement. Maximum bearing clearance is 0.15mm/0.006 inch; more than that and a replacement head is needed. Remove the remaining bearing caps using a loosening sequence which spirals in from the ends of each cam. Clean off any residue of Plastigage.

Caution! If you have to fit new camshafts, fit new cam followers too - otherwise rapid wear will result.

CAM FOLLOWERS CHECKING AND REPAIR

29   Inspect the surface upon which the cam lobe bears: it should be shiny but not scratched or gouged. Clearly visible wear means replacement and you should think of renewing the cams at the same time. It's not really possible to check if the hydraulics of the follower are working properly. Therefore, if the engine's done 62,000km/40,000 miles or more, it's probably wise to replace the followers while you have the opportunity.

30   The maximum clearance between any cam follower and its bore in the head is 0.18mm (0.0071in). As most wear will occur in the head,

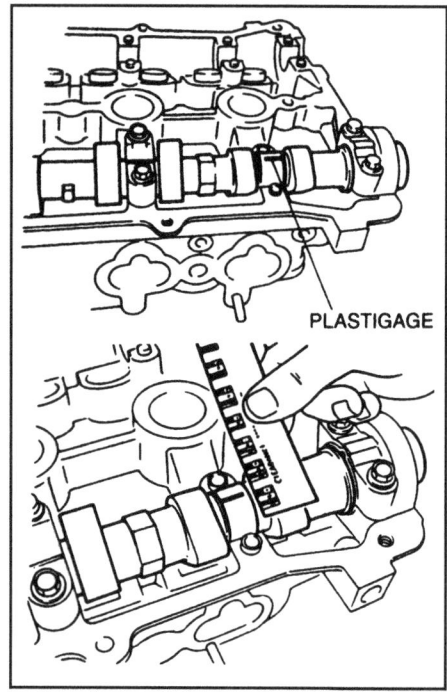

D8/28 USING PLASTIGAGE TO CHECK CAM BEARING WEAR.

3: Engine & clutch

you'll need to buy a replacement head if clearance is excessive.

CYLINDER BLOCK CHECKING AND REPAIR: CORE PLUG RENEWAL

31 Make a visual inspection of the block, looking for obvious damage. If you find any cracks, you should discuss them with a machine shop in case the block is salvageable. Deep scratches in the bores or pronounced wear ridges at the top of the bores will necessitate a re-bore and new pistons.

32 If any of the core (Welch) plugs appear to have been leaking they should be renewed. Drive a small chisel through the old plug and lever it out. Clean up the plug housing thoroughly. Coat the rim of a new plug with gasket cement and place the plug, dished-side out, over its housing. Cover the plug with a block of hardwood and then use a hammer to drive the plug fully and evenly into its housing.

33 Check the cylinder block deck lengthways, crosswise and diagonally (see diagram) using a straightedge and feeler gauges. A gap exceeding 0.15mm/0.006 inch under the straightedge means the deck will need to be reground (milled) by a machine shop. The maximum amount of metal which can be removed to rectify distortion is 0.20mm/0.008 inch. Minimum total block height is 221.5mm/8.720 inch.

34 Take a commonsense attitude to bore wear. If the engine's been burning oil and showing poor compression, or if it's done a high mileage (though wear will depend upon the quality of past maintenance), chances are the bores and piston

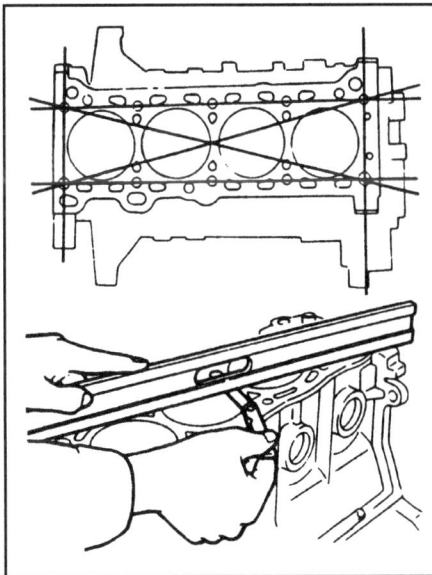

D8/33 CHECK CYLINDER BLOCK DECK FOR DISTORTION.

rings will be well worn. Have your local machine shop rebore the cylinders to the next nearest oversize and supply new pistons and rings to suit. Recommended rebore oversizes go up in increments of 0.25mm/0.010 inch. If the engine's already been rebored, you'll usually be able to find the oversize stamped in the piston crowns. Failing this, measure the bottom of a cylinder bore with an internal micrometer: the standard original bore size is in the range 83.000-83.019mm/3.2678-3.2684 inches.

35 If you're not sure whether the bores are serviceable, bore wear needs to be measured carefully. If you have access to an internal micrometer this is the best and most accurate tool. Measure the diameter of each bore around 25mm/1 inch below the deck and again at the very base of the cylinder where no wear will have occurred. At each of these depths take a reading across the bore in line with the crankshaft centerline and another at 90 degrees to the first to establish ovality. The maximum difference between the worn and unworn sections of the bore is 0.019mm/0.0007 inch. These figures are also the maximum for ovality.

PISTONS: REMOVING CARBON

36 If the piston is still on its con-rod you can clamp the rod in a vise fitted with jaw protectors so that the piston skirt rests on top of the jaws. If you have to grip the piston itself between the vise jaws, wrap it first with cardboard or thick rag and only apply the very minimum pressure needed to pro-

8/38 Clean piston crown and, very carefully, ...

vide a light grip.

37 If the rings are still fitted, wrap adhesive tape around them to minimize contamination with carbon dust. **Caution!** After the removal of carbon is completed the rings and grooves should be brushed liberally with kerosene (paraffin) to ensure that all carbon dust is removed.

38 Mount a small diameter - 25mm/1 inch approx - wire brush in an electric drill. Use the brush to clean all traces of carbon from the piston crown, valve cutouts and the area of the piston above the top ring groove. **Caution!** The pistons are made of a pretty hard aluminum alloy, but the cleaning process must not be allowed to remove any metal.

39 Carbon can be scraped carefully from the ring grooves with a fine-bladed screwdriver, or with a piece of broken piston ring. Proprietary tools designed for this task are also available. **Caution!** Take great care not to gouge or enlarge the grooves.

40 The rings, once removed from the pistons, can be cleaned with fine wire wool.

PISTONS, PISTON RINGS AND PISTON PINS CHECKING AND REPAIR

41 The first thing to say is that if you're having

8/39 ... the piston ring grooves.

the cylinder block rebored you'll have to fit new pistons and rings of appropriate oversize, so there's no point in checking the old ones.

42 Inspect each piston visually. Percussion damage to the crown, cracks or any pieces broken off - no matter how small - will mean discarding the component. Likewise for deep scratches in, or bad burning of, piston sides.

43 Having checked first that bore wear is within tolerance, slide each piston (without rings) into its bore until the crown is 50mm/2in below the deck. The piston should be normally orientated (i.e. skirt cutout over oil jet). Using feeler gauges measure the clearance between the piston and cylinder at various points around the circumference of the piston. If the biggest clearance between piston and bore is more than 0.15mm/0.006 inch the piston must be replaced. If you do need to fit new pistons then, rather than fitting new pistons into a partly worn bore, consider a rebore to the next oversize: it will bring piston and bore tolerances back to as-new standards.

44 **Caution!** Pistons should only be replaced as complete sets. Note: the new pistons will come complete with rings and piston pins.

8/42 Check piston for damage and wear.

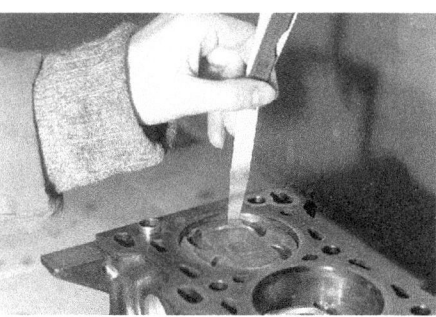

8/43 Check piston to bore clearance.

Mazda Miata, MX-5, Eunos & Roadster

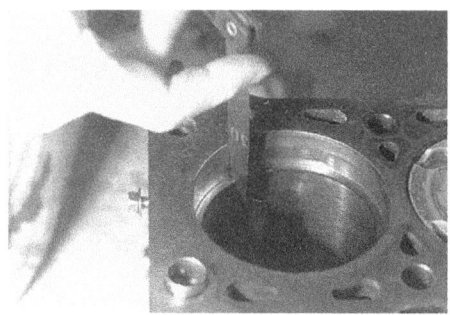

8/45 Check piston ring gaps.

45 　Check a random selection of the piston rings - at least eight - by pushing them, one at a time, into a cylinder bore. Position each ring about 50mm/2in from the deck - you'll find that using an inverted piston to push the ring down the bore will help to keep it square with the deck. Measure the ring gap with feeler gauges: more than 1.0mm/0.039 inch shows that a ring is worn out and that it (and all the other rings) must be renewed. Realistically, if the top and middle rings have gaps exceeding 0.50mm/0.019in it would be unwise to re-use them because their service life will be short.

46 　The piston pin should be a tight fit in the piston when both are cold. If the pin moves freely it, and its piston, should be renewed.

47 　Slide the piston pin into the con-rod bushing until it's central. There should be no perceptible up and down movement of the pin. If you have access to micrometers, measure the diameter of the center of the piston pin at two points 90 degrees apart: the tolerance is 19.987-19.993mm/0.7869-0.7871 inch. Measure the internal diameter of the con-rod bushing which should be in the tolerance range 20.003-20.014 mm/0.7876-0.7879 inch. Calculate the difference between the two measurements you have taken to work out the clearance which should be in the tolerance range of 0.010-0.027mm/0.0004-0.0010 inch. Replace components which are worn beyond tolerance.

CONNECTING RODS CHECKING AND REPAIR

48 　Checking of the piston pin bushing was described in the previous step.

49 　If you suspect that a connecting rod is bent or twisted - which could be caused by a broken or seized piston, water entering the combustion chamber or the camshaft drivebelt breaking and allowing valve to piston contact - you'll have to arrange for a machine shop to make the necessary measurements.

50 　If not done during the engine teardown, temporarily fit each rod, complete with lubricated bearing shells, to its original journal on the crank. Tighten the cap retaining nuts progressively to a torque of 50Nm/5.1kgf m/36lbf ft. Measure the maximum gap between the side of the bearing housing and the flange of the crank web. Maximum connecting rod side clearance is 0.30mm/0.012 inch.

CRANKSHAFT AND CRANKSHAFT BEARINGS CHECKING AND REPAIR

51 　If there were symptoms of crankshaft bearing wear - knocking, rumbling and/or low oil pressure - before the engine was dismantled, all of the crankshaft bearing journals should be reground by a machine shop. Regrinding is undertaken in increments of 0.25mm/0.010 inch, and undersized main and con-rod bearings are available to suit. Normally, the machine shop will decide which undersize to go for and will supply appropriate new bearings. **Caution!** Tell the machine shop that it must preserve the 1.5mm/0.06in radius roll fillets on each side of each journal.

52 　Crankshaft shell bearings are not hugely expensive, therefore, if the engine has covered more than 80.500km/50,000 miles, you would be wise to consider fitting new bearings of the same size. Undersize bearings usually have the size marked on the backs of the shells, whilst standard shells are unmarked. If in doubt, check journal diameters as described later.

53 　Inspect the crankshaft visually. Any scratching of the bearing journals will necessitate a regrind.

54 　If the engine has been subjected to a major breakage like a smashed piston, or has seized at speed, it would be a good idea to have your local machine shop crack test the crank and check it for straightness.

55 　Measure the bearing journals with a micrometer. Take two measurements at 90 degrees to one another on both sides of each journal; in other words, four measurements per journal. Tolerances are as follows:

Standard main	49.938-49.956mm/1.9661-1.9667in
-0.25mm/0.010in	49.704-49.708mm/1.9569-1.9570in
-0.50 mm/0.020 in	49.454-49.458mm/1.9470-1.9471in
-0.75 mm/0.030 in	49.204-49.208mm/1.9372-1.9373in
Standard con-rod	44.940-44.956mm/1.7693-1.7699in
-0.25 mm/0.010 in	44.690-44.706mm/1.7595-1.7600in
-0.50 mm/0.020 in	44.440-44.456mm/1.7497-1.7502in
-0.75 mm/0.030 in	44.190-44.206mm/1.7398-1.7403in

Maximum ovality (all crankshaft journals) 0.05mm/0.0020in

If any of the journals are close to or beyond maximum tolerance in any size range, the crank will have to be reground to the next undersize. If the tolerance for maximum undersize is exceeded, you'll need to replace the crank or talk to your local machine shop about having the journals built up. **Caution!** It's OK to have main and con-rod bearings in different undersizes, but all the bearings in each category should be of the same undersize.

8/47 Check piston pin and con-rod.

56 　+ Place the cylinder block upside-down on your workbench. Fit the main bearing shells into their housings and fit the two thrust washers, cutouts outward, into their recesses in the side of the bearing housing. Lubricate the bearings and then carefully lower the crankshaft into place, making sure the thrust washers don't get knocked out of place. When the crank is properly seated, measure the maximum gap between thrust washer and crank flange with feeler gauges. This only needs to be done on one side of the main bearing, but constant downward pressure must be applied to the crank which must also be pulled or pushed hard up against the thrust washer on the other side of the main bearing. Normal service tolerances are 0.080-0.282mm/0.0032-0.0111 inch and maximum lash (endfloat) is 0.30mm/0.012 inch. If lash is excessive, remove the crank and check the thickness of the thrust washers with a micrometer. Thickness tolerances are as follows for standard and undersized washers:

Standard	2.500-2.550mm/0.0985-0.1003in
-0.25mm/0.010in	2.625-2.675mm/0.1034-0.1053in
-0.50mm/0.020in	2.750-2.800mm/0.1083-0.1102in
-0.75mm/0.030in	2.875-2.925mm/0.1132-0.1151in

8/56a Check crankshaft lash (endfloat).

8/56b You can use a dial gauge instead.

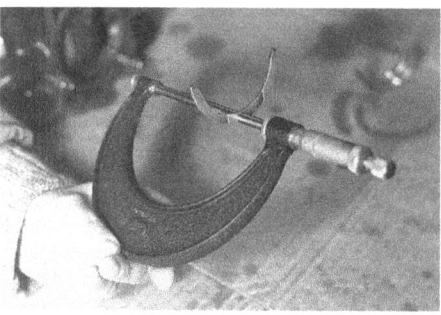

8/56c Measuring thrust washer thickness.

3: Engine & clutch

If fitting new standard or oversized thrust washers will bring the endplay back into normal tolerance, then do that. If not, have the crank thrust faces reground to the next undersize.

57   If you're re-using used bearing shells/thrust washers because they've only done a small mileage and the crank journals are not worn, check them very carefully for scratches, heat blueing or uneven wear - if in any doubt, renew.

58   Use pipe cleaners to ensure that the crankshaft oil drillings are clear and clean. **Caution!** If you've had the crank journals reground, insist the machine shop verifies that the crankshaft

8/57 Check bearing shells and thrust washers.

drillings have been cleaned thoroughly and all swarf removed before accepting delivery.

CAMSHAFT DRIVEBELT, TENSIONER, IDLER AND PULLEYS CHECKING AND REPAIR

59   If the camshaft drivebelt has covered 50,000km/30,000 miles or more, it would sensible to replace it whilst you have the opportunity. Otherwise, check the belt for delamination, cracking and damaged teeth. Also check for contamination by oil or grease - if any of these problems are evident replace the belt. **Caution!** Do not twist, bend or turn the belt inside-out. Do not attempt to clean the belt with any fluids.

60   Check that both tensioner and idler wheels run freely and without noise and that the wheel surfaces are free of serious scratches. Replace if in doubt. **Caution!** Don't clean the wheels with any fluid; use a soft dry cloth only.

61   Measure the free length of the tensioner spring (see diagram). If it exceeds 59.2mm/2.331in, it's tired and should be renewed.

62   Check crankshaft and camshaft pulleys for obvious damage and wear. Replace if the 'teeth' are losing their profile or if there are faults which might damage the belt. **Caution!** Do not clean the

8/58 Clear and clean crankshaft oilways.

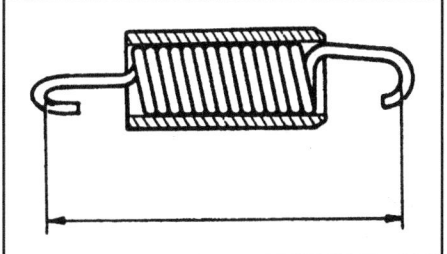
D8/61 CHECK TENSIONER SPRING FREE LENGTH.

pulleys with any fluid; use a soft, dry cloth only.

OIL PUMP CHECKING AND REPAIR

63   Check that the inner face of the rotor cover is flat and unscratched.

64   Using a straightedge placed across the pump body, check the side clearance of both rotors. Maximum permissible is 0.14mm/0.0055 inch.

65   Using feeler gauges, determine the clearance between the outer rotor and chamber walls, as shown. Maximum is 0.20mm/0.0079 inch.

66   Measure the gap between rotor tooth tips, as shown, using feeler gauges. More than 0.20mm/0.0079 inch is too much.

67   **Caution!** If the pump components are worn outside of the tolerances given, replace the whole pump: a weak pump will have a detrimental effect by allowing general engine wear to accelerate.

68   Using a vernier gauge, measure the free length of the oil pressure relief valve spring. It should not be shorter than 45.94mm/1.809in otherwise maximum oil pressure will be lower than it should be.

69   Check that the relief valve plunger moves

8/64 Check pump rotor side clearance.

8/65 Check rotor to wall clearance.

8/66 Check rotor tooth tip clearance.

8/68 Check oil pressure relief valve spring.

8/70 Oil jet components - use new washers.

freely in its bore and that neither the plunger or bore are scratched or otherwise damaged.

OIL JETS CHECKING AND REPAIR

70   Using a screwdriver press the ball valve in the banjo bolt: be sure it springs back freely. Blow through the jet pipe from the jet end to make sure it is clear. Get new copper washers.

FLYWHEEL, PILOT BEARING AND STARTER RING GEAR CHECKING AND REPAIR

71   Check the friction surface of the flywheel for obvious wear or damage. Minor blueing or scratching can be removed with progressively finer grades of emery paper mounted on a flat rubbing block. Deep scratches or a worn area perceptibly below the original surface of the flywheel will have to be machined out by your local machine shop. **Caution!** If you don't rectify such damage clutch wear will be very rapid and smooth engagement impossible.

72   If you suspect the flywheel is distorted, you should have it checked by a local machine shop. Maximum runout is 0.2mm/0.008 inch. Replace or remachine as necessary.

73   Rotate the pilot bearing with a finger whilst

Mazda Miata, MX-5, Eunos & Roadster

simultaneously applying sideways pressure. Noise or stickiness of operation indicate the need for renewal. Replacement would be sensible if the engine has covered a high mileage.

74 Pilot bearing removal. Obtain a piece of solid round bar of exactly the same diameter as the spigot of the transmission input shaft - sorry, we forgot to measure it! Fill the pilot bearing center with grease. Engage the bar in the bearing and then give the bar a sharp blow with a hammer: hydraulic pressure will force the bearing out.

75 Pilot bearing fitting. The new bearing can be gently drifted into place using a suitably-sized socket or tube. Lubricate it with high temperature grease.

76 Check the ring gear teeth for severe wear or damage such as broken or missing teeth. If a new ring gear is needed, remove the old item by sawing partway through it with a hacksaw and then splitting it with a chisel.

77 Heat the new ring gear to a temperature of 250-300 degrees C/480-570 degrees F - a conventional domestic oven/cooker will reach the lower range of these temperatures. When the ring gear has reached the desired temperature, pick it up with tongs or protective hand gear and place it into position on the flywheel as quickly as possible, ensuring that the side with chamfered teeth is towards the engine. If the ring gear is hot enough it may go fully and evenly home with just a few light taps of a hide mallet. Failing this, a soft metal drift and hammer should do the job. Work quickly before the flywheel draws heat from the ring gear.

DRIVEPLATE (AUTO-TRANS CARS) AND STARTER RING GEAR CHECKING AND REPAIR

78 There's not too much to go wrong with a driveplate, but check it visually for obvious damage such as cracking or distortion. Replace if serious faults are evident.

79 Inspect the starter ring gear ☞ 3/8/76-77.

CLUTCH COVER, DISC, RELEASE BEARING AND RELEASE FORK CHECKING AND REPAIR

80 First of all let's say that you're gambling with a relatively short remaining service life if you re-use any of these components after they've covered 40,000km/25,000 miles or more.

81 Check the friction surface of the cover plate for blueing, scratching and cracking. The first two types of damage can often be removed with emery paper wrapped around a flat-faced block, but if cracking is in evidence, trash the cover. Check the fingers of the diaphragm spring: broken, bent, cracked or heavily worn fingers all point (forgive the pun!) to the need for renewal.

82 Check the thickness of lining material on the disc; as a minimum it must be 0.3mm/0.012 inch above the rivet heads - but that's not going to give you much more service. If lining thickness is OK, check for burning, oil contamination, obvious distortion and loose linings, rivets or torsion rubbers. Also check the central hub splines for obvious wear or damage. Any of these faults should be enough to make you dig in your pocket.

83 Release bearing. Grasp the inner race and turn it whilst pushing it inwards as hard as you can. Noise or stickiness indicate the need for a new bearing.

84 Release fork. Check the tips of the two prongs where they bear against the back of the release bearing and the inside of the recess which fits over the pivot head. There should be plenty of metal left and no signs of severe wear. Replace the fork if serious wear is evident. Check the spring clip which grips the back of the pivot pin: apart from the circular section the spring should snap closed.

9. ENGINE REBUILD

☞ First read 1/1, 2.

ENGINE REBUILD GENERAL

1 To ensure maximum life and reliability from a rebuilt engine not only must the work be done with great care and thoroughness, but also in a clean environment with completely clean components and tools. Also, all internal moving components must be thoroughly lubricated with engine oil as they are reassembled/installed.

2 Before the rebuild begins replace any bolts, screws, studs or nuts, the threads of which are in any way damaged. All threads must be clean and torque wrench settings strictly observed.

3 ⚫ Have a complete set of new gaskets and seals ready before work starts, together with silicone based fluid gasket material and thread locking fluid.

4 **Caution!** If a component won't fit, don't force it. Stop, stand back, think about the problem and resolve it properly before proceeding.

5 **Warning!** Take your time, get it right and

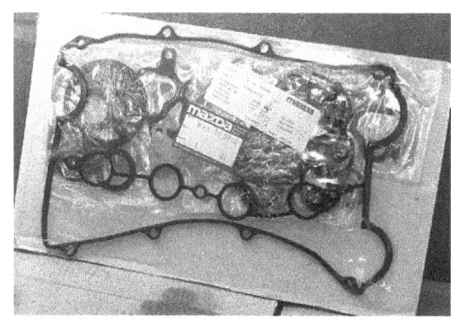

9/3 Engine gasket set.

keep your personal safety and the safety of others in mind at all times.

PISTON RINGS INSTALLATION

6 ⚫ ⊞+ First fit the corrugated oil scraper ring spacer into the lowest of the three piston grooves. **Caution!** It is essential the ring is installed so that the final corrugation is closed side downwards. Fit the thin oil scraper rings one above and one below the corrugated spacer. Before doing this adjust the spacer ring so that the ring gap is above one end of the piston pin. Fit the lower oil rail ring

9/6 Fit piston rings very carefully!

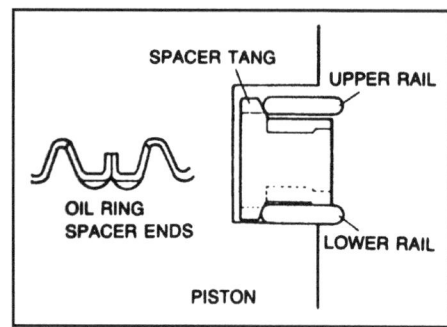

D9/6A CORRECT INSTALLATION OF OIL SCRAPER RINGS.

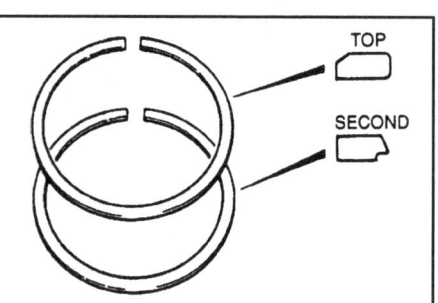

D9/6B PISTON RING PROFILES.

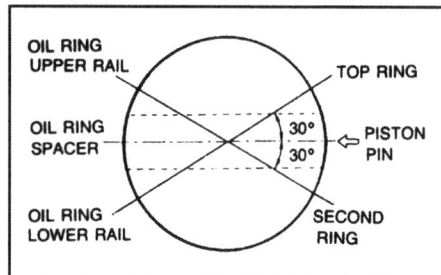

D9/6C CORRECT ORIENTATION OF FITTED RINGS.

first and set its gap 30 degrees anti-clockwise from the corrugated ring gap, then fit the top rail ring and set its gap 30 degrees clockwise of the corrugated ring gap.

7 **Caution!** It's very easy to break the upper piston rings by opening them too much or twisting them too much. Using three old feeler gauge blades, or three strips of hacksaw blade or a purpose-designed tool, very carefully slide the middle (second) piston ring over the piston and into its groove. The top of the ring which must be upwards may be marked "TOP," if not you can identify the

3: Engine & clutch

correct orientation by the ring's profile (see diagram). Set the gap of the middle ring 30 degrees clockwise from one end of the piston pin.

8   The top ring has a chamfer top rear (see diagram) or may even be marked "TOP": it must be installed the correct way up. Set this piston ring so that its gap is 60 degrees anti-clockwise from the middle ring's gap.

9   Repeat this procedure with the other three pistons.

PISTONS AND CONNECTING RODS REBUILD AND INSTALLATION

10   Mount the connecting rod in a vise fitted with jaw protectors; the rod needs to protrude from the jaws by 75mm/3in or so. Make sure you know which side of the rod is the oil jet side and don't forget to apply oil liberally to the connecting rod piston pin bearing, the pin itself and the piston pin bore in the piston.

11   Fit one new spring clip into its groove in the piston pin bore. Make sure you know which way the piston will go on the con-rod so that the cutout in the skirt will be over the oil jet. Heat the piston with a butane torch for around a minute until it's too hot to touch - but don't overdo it. Wrap the piston in rag and quickly fit it over the con-rod, and then push the piston pin home through the piston and con-rod bearing until it contacts the spring clip. Fit the second spring clip to retain the pin. **Caution!** Double-check that both pin retaining clips are seated fully and securely in their grooves and that the con-rod swings freely on the piston pin.

12   If not already in place, fit lengths of rubber or plastic tube over the con-rod studs to prevent damage to crank journal surfaces.

13   Stand the cylinder block on end or on its side. Lubricate the rings, grooves and piston pin/con-rod bearing thoroughly before installing each piston; with your fingers rub oil around the cylinder bore also. **Caution!** Make sure you know to which bore each piston/con-rod assembly belongs.

14   ◻ Guide the rod and piston into the bore until the lowest piston ring is approximately half an inch from the top of the cylinder block. Make sure that the piston and connecting rod assembly is fitted so that the cutout in the piston skirt is over the oil jet (if your engine still has original pistons, you'll probably find that there is a dot on the piston crown indicating the side of the piston which should face toward the front of the engine). You also need to check that the piston ring gaps are still correctly positioned as described earlier. **Caution!** If the crankshaft is in place, great care must be taken to guide the connecting rod studs away from the crankshaft bearing journal as the piston is pushed into the bore. A gouge or bad scratch will necessitate a crankshaft regrind ...

15   ◻ Use an ordinary piston ring compressor to squeeze all of the piston rings fully into their grooves so that the piston can be pushed home into its bore. Don't forget to thoroughly lubricate the inner part of the ring compressor before clamping the piston and rings. **Caution!** Don't try to fit pistons without a ring compressor: the likely result will be a broken ring. Compressors are not expen-

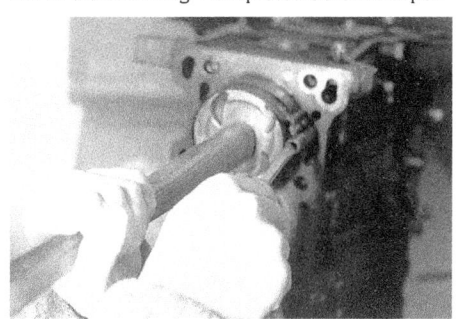
9/15 ... using a piston ring compressor.

sive and are available from the same places that you buy your parts and tools.

16   Repeat the process for the other three pistons.

OIL JETS REBUILD AND INSTALLATION

17   ◻ Assemble each oil jet in the following sequence. Fit a new copper washer to the banjo bolt followed by the oil jet union (jet pointing away from bolt head) and another new copper washer. Screw the banjo bolt loosely into its threaded recess in the cylinder block and move the jet union from side-to-side until its locating pin locks it in place. The banjo bolt can then be tightened to its correct torque of 11.8-17.5Nm/120-180kgf cm/105-156lbf in.

CRANKSHAFT AND BEARING SHELLS INSTALLATION

18   Turn the cylinder block upside-down on your bench. Check that the main bearing seats are scrupulously clean. **Caution!** Even the smallest piece of debris could lift a shell and create a tight spot. Ensure, too, that the bearing shells are equally clean.

19   ◻ Fit the main bearing shell halves in

9/19 Fit crankshaft bearing shells.

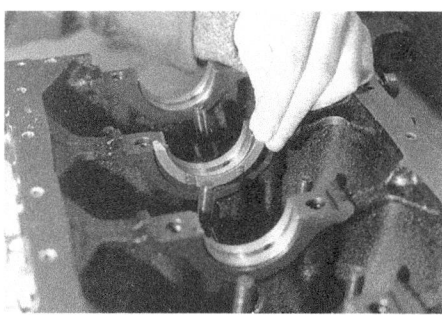
9/20 Fit thrust washers.

9/21 Lubricate generously.

place in the cylinder block and bearing caps, making sure that the tongue in each shell is engaged with the cutout in the seat, and also that each end of the shell is flush with the top of the housing. If you are re-using serviceable shells, make sure they are installed in their original positions.

20   ◻ Fit the two semi-circular thrust washers into the side recesses of the fourth main bearing. The cutaways in the thrust washers should be facing outward, away from the bearing.

21   ◻ Check that all of the crankshaft bearing journals are spotlessly clean and that the oilways are clear. Push all of the pistons to the tops of their

9/14 Slide piston and rod into bore ...

9/17 Fit oil jets using new washers.

9/22 Bolt holes MUST be clean.

Mazda Miata, MX-5, Eunos & Roadster

bores. Lubricate all of the bearings and thrust washers thoroughly before lowering the crankshaft gently into position, taking great care not to knock out the thrust washers sitting each side of the fourth main bearing, also not to scratch journals on the connecting rod studs.

22 Caution! Make sure that the threaded holes for the main bearing cap retaining bolts are clean and completely free of oil or debris. A doubled-over pipe cleaner is a good tool for this job.

23 Lubricate the bearing shells in the main bearing caps thoroughly and then, noting the dot-punched location ID, lower each bearing cap into its correct position and finger-tighten its retaining bolts (which should have clean, dry threads). Remember, the arrow cast into each bearing cap points toward the front of the engine.

24 The final torque for the main bearing cap 14 mm bolts is 54-58Nm/5.5-6.0kgf m/40-43lbf ft. Tighten the bolts in three stages using a sequence which spirals outward from the central cap (see diagram). If the connecting rods are not yet in place, the crankshaft should be free to rotate under hand pressure after the bearing caps have

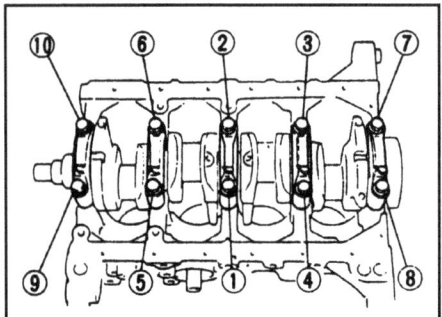

D9/24 MAIN BEARING CAPS TIGHTENING SEQUENCE.

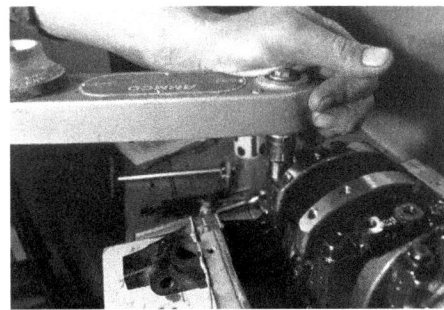

9/24 Apply correct torque to cap bolts.

been torqued. If it won't rotate, remove the caps and check that there is no foreign matter between bearing shell backs and seats. If the problem persists, you'll need to consult the bearing supplier or the machine shop which carried out the regrind.

CONNECTING RODS AND CAPS FITTING TO CRANKSHAFT

25 Make sure that the bearing housings of both the connecting rods and their caps are spotlessly clean. Ensure, too, that the bearing shells are equally clean before fitting them to rods and caps; be sure to engage the shell tabs in the seat cutouts.

26 Lubricate the connecting rod bearing shells thoroughly, then pull the connecting rods onto their crankshaft journals - it's best if all four crank webs are at more or less the same height rather than two being up and two down.

27 You'll have no trouble identifying which bearing cap goes with which connecting rod if, as was recommended, you dot punched their position numbers into the side of the caps and connecting rods during the engine teardown. If not, all may not be lost! On our engine the manufacturer had stamped a diagonal stamp mark across the joint

9/27 Con-rod caps all numbered.

9/28 Torque con-rod cap bolts.

(matching face) of each connecting rod and cap so, by matching the two parts of one diagonal stamp, you can identify which cap goes with which connecting rod.

28 Lubricate the crankshaft con-rod journals liberally and dribble oil into the oilways which should be facing upwards. Fit the caps and tighten the two 14mm nuts retaining each cap in three stages until a final torque of 48-50Nm/4.8-5.1kgf m/35-36lbf ft is reached. Check that the crankshaft is free to rotate once all of the cap nuts have been torqued. You'll find that rotation will be stiff because of the friction between the piston rings and their bores. If the crank won't rotate, remove the caps and check that there is not foreign material between shells and seats. Should the problem persist, consult your bearing shell supplier or the machine shop which re-ground the crank.

CRANKSHAFT REAR COVER: OIL SEAL INSTALLATION

29 Mount the rear cover on top of a vise as shown and, using a blunt chisel or punch, drive the old oil seal through the housing.

30 Lubricate the outer lip of the new oil seal

9/29 Carefully drift out the old seal.

and lightly tap it into position with a nylon or rubber-faced hammer, whilst supporting the cover casting on the vise and turning it a little after each blow so that the seal is driven home evenly. **Caution!** The closed side of the oil seal must face outward from the rear of the engine and must be flush with the outer face of the housing.

CRANKSHAFT REAR COVER INSTALLATION

31 Apply a bead of silicone gasket cement to the area shown. Lubricate the inner lip of the seal and the boss of the flywheel mounting where the seal bears on the crank.

32 Fit the cover to the rear of the cylinder block, feeding the seal carefully over the flywheel boss on the crankshaft end. Fit the four retaining bolts, noting that the two longer bolts must be positioned closest to the oil pan flange. Tighten the cover retaining 10mm bolts to a torque of 7.9-10.7Nm/80-110kgf cm/69-95lbf in. If you don't have a torque wrench capable of reading such small torque levels, use a box end wrench and fingertip pressure only to tighten the bolts.

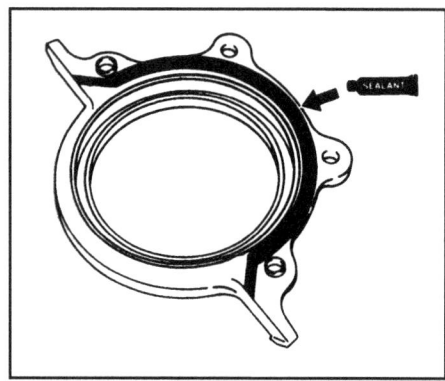

D9/31 APPLY SEALANT AS SHOWN HERE.

9/31 Allow sealant to dry a little.

3: Engine & clutch

9/32 Tighten seal housing bolts.

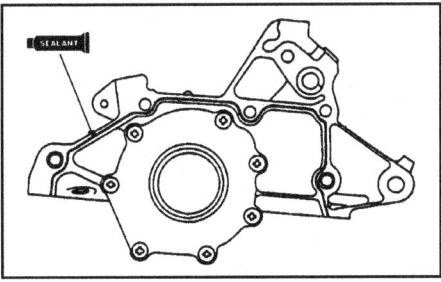

D9/35 APPLY A SMALL BEAD OF SEALANT AS SHOWN HERE.

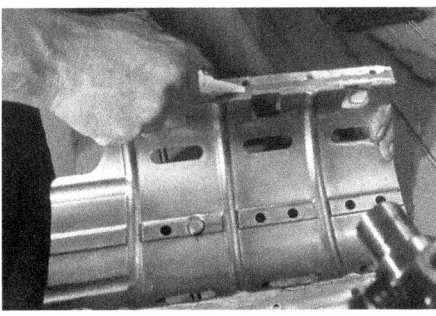

9/39 Apply sealant to the baffle.

OIL PUMP REBUILD AND FITTING NEW OIL SEAL

33   Lubricate the rotors thoroughly, then fit the cover to the rear of the oil pump body (without using any sealing compound). The crosshead screws should be tightened to a torque of 5.9-8.8Nm/60-90kgf cm/53-78lbf in. If you have a hexagonal-shaped crosshead bit from an impact driver you will be able to mount this in a socket and use a torque wrench conventionally. **Caution!** It is important that the crosshead bit you use is a good fit in the screw heads and that constant downward pressure is applied during tightening.

34   Before fitting the oil pump to the crankshaft nose it will be necessary to fit a new oil seal in the pump housing. Turn the pump housing face down on a vise or hard work surface and, using a small diameter chisel or punch from behind, drive out the old seal. Turn the pump body over so that the pump backplate is on your bench. Lubricate the outer lip of the new oil seal and, after positioning it carefully closed side facing outward, drive it home with evenly spaced light blows from a nylon or rubber faced hammer. **Caution!** The face of the seal must be flush with the face of the housing after

9/36 Oil pump fits over crank nose.

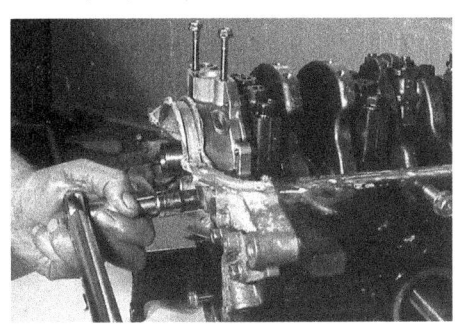

9/37 Torque tighten pump bolts.

with the flats on the crankshaft, and then slide the whole oil pump into position against the front of the cylinder block.

37   The pump body casting is secured to the cylinder block by six 12mm bolts. The longest bolts fit the bolt holes closest to the oil pan flange on each side of the pump body. The shortest bolt fits the single hole closest to the water pump. Tighten the screws by hand and then progressively in a diagonal sequence to a final torque of 19-25Nm/1.9-2.6kgf m/14-18lbf ft.

OIL PAN BAFFLE, OIL PUMP PICKUP PIPE AND OIL PAN INSTALLATION

38   If the baffle flanges were bent during removal, carefully straighten them using a flat surface and a flat-faced hammer.

39   Apply a bead of silicone-based jointing compound along the flanges - cylinder block side - of the baffle. The bead should run down the center of the flange diverting around the inside of each hole. **Caution!** Unless the manufacturer says otherwise, once the sealing compound has been applied, no more than 30 minutes must elapse before the oil pan is fitted to the cylinder block.

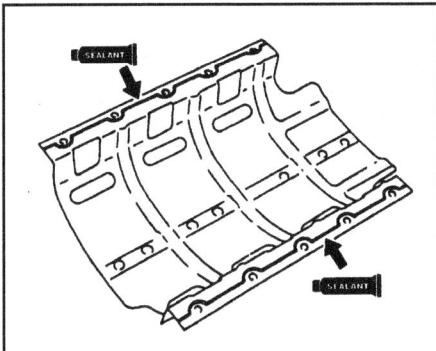

D9/39 SEALANT BEAD SHOULD WEAVE AROUND HOLES AS SHOWN HERE.

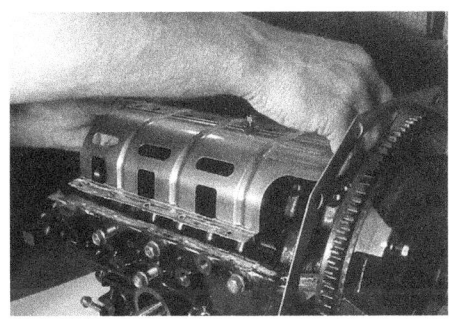

9/40 Install oil pan (sump) baffle.

40   Fit the baffle into position on the inverted cylinder block and line up with the oil pan bolt holes.

41   Fill the oil pump body with engine oil, then place a new gasket on the pickup flange of the pump body - no gasket cement is needed. Position the pickup assembly and fit the two 10 mm bolts and one 10 mm nut that secure it to the pump and baffle. Tighten the bolts and nut to a torque of 7.9-10.7Nm /80-110kgf cm /70-95lbf in. Tightening with a box end wrench (ring spanner) and fingertip pressure is OK.

42   You'll notice that there are grooved bridges over both crank rear seal housing and oil pump body. Starting and ending approx 12mm/ 0.5 inch each side of these bridges, run a continuous bead of sealant over each bridge. Whilst the sealant in the grooves is still tacky, fit the appropriate new rubber seal in each bridge. Make sure that the tab in each seal is located in the notch in the side of the housing.

43   Apply a continuous bead of sealant to

9/34 Drive out the old seal.

installation.

OIL PUMP INSTALLATION

35   Smear the oil pump joint face with silicone gasket compound; only a thin smearing is necessary. **Caution!** Unless the sealant manufacturer says otherwise, you'll need to install the pump within five minutes of applying the sealant.

36   Lubricate the oil seal inner lip and the area of the crankshaft nose that the seal bears upon. Line up the flats on the oil pump central rotor

Mazda Miata, MX-5, Eunos & Roadster

9/42 Apply sealant then fit seal.

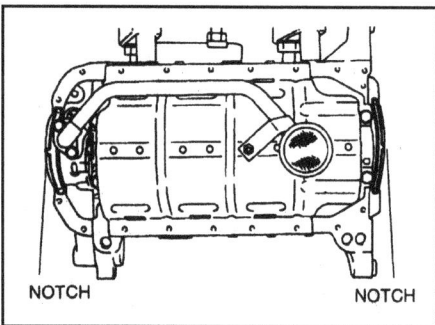

D9/42 MAKE SURE SEALS ARE CORRECTLY LOCATED IN NOTCHES.

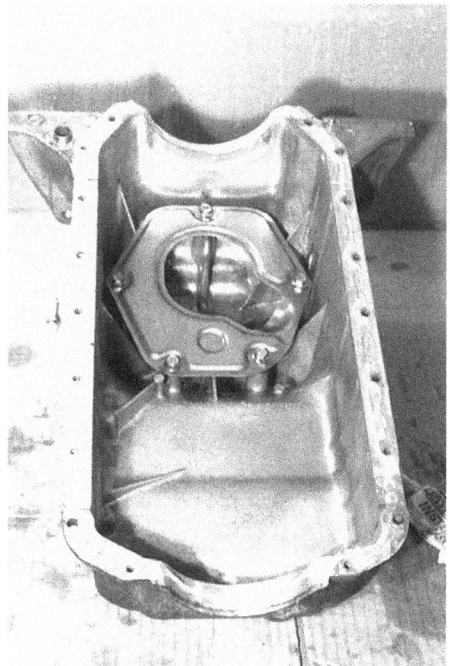

9/43 Apply sealant to the oil pan flange.

the flange of the oil pan. The bead should run along the center of the flange, diverting around the inside of holes as necessary. Fit the oil pan and the eighteen 10 mm bolts that secure it, including the two long bolts adjacent to the flywheel. Tighten the bolts in three stages and in a sequence which spirals outward from the center bolts to a final torque of 7.9-10.7Nm/80-110kgf cm/70-95lbf in.

44   Fit a new copper sealing washer to the oil pan drain plug and tighten the plug securely.

ENGINE BACKPLATE INSTALLATION

45   Turn the engine over so that it is resting on the oil pan base and place a block of wood between the shallow end of the pan and the bench to stabilize the unit.

46   📷 Position the engine backplate so that it locates over the two projecting spigots, and secure it with a single 10mm bolt toward the top left of the plate. Tighten the bolt to 7.9-10.7Nm/80-110kgf cm/70-95lbf in.

FLYWHEEL (DRIVEPLATE - AUTO TRANS) INSTALLATION

47   📷 Check that the threaded bolt holes in the crankshaft rear flange are clear and clean; a doubled-over pipe cleaner is a good tool for this purpose. If old sealer has hardened in the threads, you'll need to use a tap to clear them. The bolt threads, too, need to be clean.

48   📷 Flywheel (manual transmission) installation. Apply thread locking/sealant fluid to the threads of each of the flywheel retaining bolts. Hold the flywheel in position over the rear of the crankshaft and fit the retaining bolts finger-tight.

49   Driveplate (auto transmission) installation. Apply thread locking/sealant fluid to the threads of

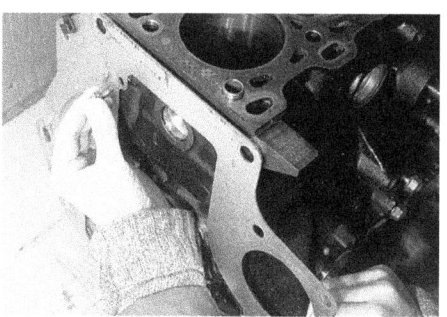

9/46 Backplate secured by one bolt.

9/47 Threaded bolt holes must be clean.

9/48 Apply locking/sealing fluid to bolts.

9/51a Use a new gasket, fit water pump ...

9/51b ... and torque retaining bolts.

each of the flywheel retaining bolts. Fit the adaptor collar to the rear of the crankshaft, followed by the driveplate and its backing plate. Fit bolts finger-tight.

50   Lock the flywheel or driveplate by temporarily fitting a bellhousing bolt and then wedging a screwdriver into the ring gear teeth and against the bolt. Tighten the flywheel or driveplate 19mm retaining bolts progressively, and in a diagonal sequence, to a final torque of 97-102Nm/9.8-10.5kgf m/71-75lbf ft.

WATER PUMP INSTALLATION

51   📷+ Use a new gasket - no gasket cement is necessary. Hold the water pump in position at the front of the cylinder block and retain by fitting the four bolts finger-tight. Tighten the 12mm retaining bolts, in a diagonal sequence, to a final torque of 19-25Nm/1.9-2.6kgf m/14-18lbf ft. Don't forget to fit the rubber seal to the top of the water pump body.

VALVES, SPRINGS AND VALVE STEM OIL SEALS INSTALLATION

52   📷 Fitting new valve stem seals. Note that intake and exhaust valve seals are different: exhaust valve seals have two circular ridges, while intake seals have none, or one (see diagram). Place the cylinder head (combustion chambers downward) on your workbench. Fitting seals is a fiddly job because access is restricted; however, using fingers only, push the new oil seal over the top of the valve guide until the seal seems to be fully seated. Using the depth gauge section of a vernier gauge, check that the shoulder of the seal is 18.3-18.9mm/ 0.721-0.744 inch above the surface of the head. Adjust as necessary, then repeat the process until a new seal has been fitted to every guide.

53   **Caution!** The following procedures as-

3: Engine & clutch

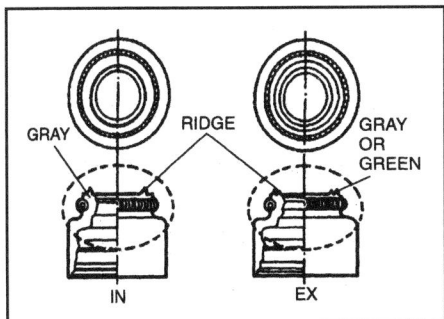

D9/52 INTAKE VALVE STEM SEALS HAVE A SINGLE RIDGE, OR NO RIDGE. EXHAUST SEALS HAVE TWO RIDGES.

sume that the individual valves have been checked and lapped ☞ 3/8. Mount the cylinder head horizontally in a vise (fitted with jaw protectors) in such a way that you have access to a complete row of valves from both sides of the head. Tighten the vise just enough to grip the head.

54 From the combustion chamber side insert the valve, having first thoroughly lubricated its stem. **Caution!** If re-using valves it is essential that they are each returned to their original locations and the seat with which they were lapped. Even new valves must be fitted to the seat with which they were lapped.

55 📷 From the other side of the head, fit the spring seat followed by the spring itself. **Caution!** If you look closely at the spring you'll see that the coils at one end are closer pitched (together): this end of the spring must be closest to the cylinder head. Fit the spring cap.

56 You'll need the spacer constructed earlier and an ordinary valve spring compressor. Make sure the compressor is fitted centrally and securely over both valve head and spacer, then compress the spring until enough of the recess in the valve stem is revealed to fit the keepers.

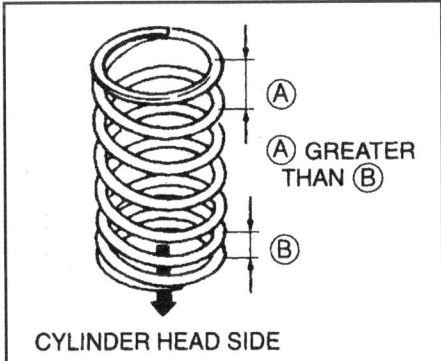

D9/55 VALVE SPRING COILS ARE CLOSER TOGETHER AT THE CYLINDER HEAD END.

57 📷 Now the fun really begins! Stick each keeper in turn to a small screwdriver with a blob of grease, then position the keeper, taper downwards, into the spring cap. Repeat the process with the second keeper, so that both keepers are contained within the spring cap and the heads of the keepers are below the top of the recess in the valve stem. You'll find this much more difficult than it

9/57 Install the valve keepers (collets).

sounds, but patience will be rewarded with success.

58 Gradually release the compressor, making sure that the two keepers slide up the valve stem and then engage positively in the stem recess. Release the compressor completely and remove it. **Warning!** Stay out of the line of fire, whilst giving the valve stem tip three sharp blows with a small hammer to seat the keepers. **Caution!** Check, and double-check, that the keepers are securely and properly seated in the valve stem recess - still keeping out of the line of fire.

59 Repeat the valve fitting process until all valves are in place.

CYLINDER HEAD INSTALLATION

60 📷 Check that all of the threaded bolt holes in the top of the cylinder block are clean to their full depth; a doubled-over pipe cleaner's a good tool for this. Turn the crankshaft, via the flywheel, until all of the pistons are approximately halfway down their bores. Pour a little engine oil into each cylinder and spread it around the rim of the pistons and over the cylinder walls with your fingers.

9/60 Bolt holes MUST be clean.

9/61 New cylinder head gasket in place.

9/62 Locate cylinder head over dowels.

61 📷 Position a new cylinder head gasket over the dowels on the deck of the cylinder block. Make sure the gasket is the right way up so that the oilway on the right of the engine is left open. No gasket cement is needed.

62 📷 Lower the cylinder head into position until it positively locates over the two protruding dowels. Lightly oil their threads and head shoulders, then replace the ten bolts which secure the head and screw them in finger-tight.

63 📷 Using a 12mm socket, short extension and torque wrench, tighten the cylinder head

9/63 Torque head bolts in correct sequence.

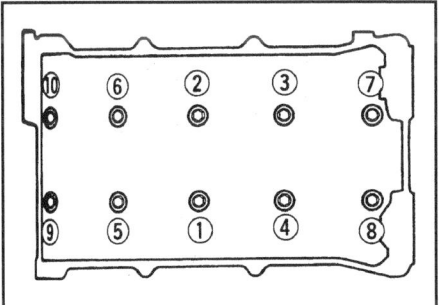

D9/63 CYLINDER HEAD BOLT TIGHTENING SEQUENCE.

bolts to a final torque of 76-81Nm/7.7-8.3kgf m/ 56-60lbf ft. Tighten the bolts in three stages and in a sequence which spirals outward from the two central bolts (see diagram).

THERMOSTAT HOUSING INSTALLATION

64 Fit a new rubber sealing ring into the groove in the flange of the thermostat housing: no sealant is necessary.

65 📷 Hold the housing in position against

3:37

Mazda Miata, MX-5, Eunos & Roadster

9/65 Tighten thermostat housing bolts.

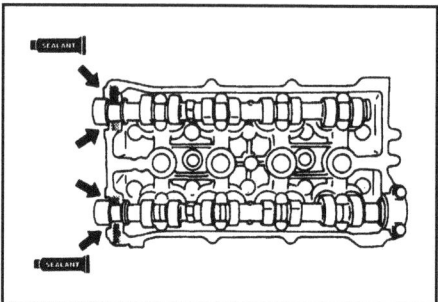

D9/72 APPLY SEALANT IN SHADED AREAS.

9/76 Carefully tap new seals into their housings.

the front of the cylinder head and replace the two retaining bolts finger-tight. Access to the bolts is limited, so use a socket with a small diameter drive or a box end wrench. Tighten the 12mm bolts to a torque of 19-25Nm/1.9-2.6kgf m/14-18lbf ft.

CYLINDER HEAD SEAL PLATE INSTALLATION
66   Fit a new rubber seal into the section of the seal plate which fits around the thermostat housing. Locate the seal plate at the front of the cylinder head, making sure it's properly positioned astride the thermostat housing and over the water pump body, and that the bolt holes line up.
67   Fit the six 10mm seal plate retaining bolts and tighten them to 7.9-10.7Nm/80-110kgf cm/70-95.4lbf in.

CAM FOLLOWERS INSTALLATION
68   Generously lubricate the valve springs and rub oil around the bores in which the cam followers fit. **Caution!** If you're re-using cam followers it is essential that they are returned to the housing from which they were originally taken.
69   Slide each cam follower, open side downwards, into its bore and make sure it moves freely.

9/67 Seal plate fixed by six bolts.

CAMSHAFTS INSTALLATION
70   Check that the cap bolt holes in the head are completely free of debris and fluid. Thoroughly lubricate the camshaft bearings in the head and the tops of the cam followers, ensuring that none of the oil runs into the cleaned bolt holes.
71   Gently lay each camshaft into its bearings, taking care not to damage the bearings with the sharp edges of the cam lobes. Arrange each cam so that the spigot on its nose is as high as possible. Note: the exhaust cam is the longer of the two because it carries the drive for the camshaft position

sensor and it fits on the left.
72   Apply a very thin smear of silicone sealant at the cambox sealing flange to seal the joint with the front bearing caps/seal carriers (see diagram). **Caution!** Take care not to get any sealant on the cam journals. Allow the sealant to harden for around five minutes.
73   Lubricate all of the camshaft bearing caps and fit them into position. The caps must be fitted in their original positions and be correctly orientated. Each cap is embossed with an arrow which must point toward the front of the engine, and stamped with the letter "I" (intake) or "E" (exhaust) in combination with a number. Therefore, for example, cap "E/3" is the third cap from the front of the exhaust camshaft. These markings can be quite faint, in which case you should have dot punched the caps to indicate their correct positions.
74   Fit the cap bolts and tighten them finger-tight for the moment.
75   Tighten the camshaft bearing cap bolts in three stages to a final torque of 11.3-14.2Nm/115-145kgf cm/100-125lbf in. **Caution!** These bolts must be tightened in stages and in a sequence which spirals outward from the central cap of each camshaft (see diagram). Be especially careful to tighten the caps evenly, particularly where you find the caps are initially prevented from engaging with their locating dowels because of the need for the cam lobes to partially force open some of the valves.

CAMSHAFT OIL SEALS INSTALLATION
76   Lightly lubricate the inner lip and outer circumference of a new oil seal. Slide the seal over the nose of the camshaft and then, with a very light flat-faced hammer, tap the seal fully into its housing, making sure that the blows are applied evenly

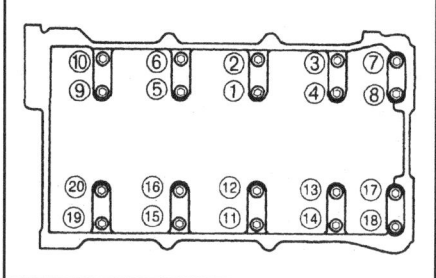

D9/75 CAMSHAFT BEARING CAP BOLT TIGHTENING SEQUENCE.

around the circumference so that the seal is driven home square. The face of the seal must be flush with the front of its housing when finally in position. Make sure you keep the face of the hammer square to the seal so that neither the seal or alloy housing are damaged. You may need to use a flat-ended drift just to tap the lower part of the seal (where the seal plate limits access) into place. Repeat the process for the second camshaft seal.

CAMSHAFT PULLEYS INSTALLATION
77   If necessary, and using a 24mm crescent wrench (open-ended spanner) on the hex-shaped section, rotate each cam until the spigot on the pulley boss is almost vertically above the bolt hole. You'll find each cam will 'rest' in this position.
78   Refit both camshaft pulleys using the marks you made earlier to identify exhaust and intake cam pulleys, and which of the three slots the spigot on the camshaft engages with. If you didn't mark the pulleys as recommended, install them so that the manufacturer's "I" mark of the inlet cam is a few degrees clockwise of vertical, with the "E" mark on the same pulley being a few degrees clockwise of the "E" mark and line on the head seal

9/78 Align paint mark with spigot.

plate. The exhaust cam pulley will have a manufacturer's "E" mark maybe one or two degrees anti-clockwise of vertical, with the "I" mark on the same pulley one or two degrees anti-clockwise of the "I" mark and line on the head sealing plate.
79   Put a dab of thread locking fluid on each camshaft pulley retaining bolt, fit its washer and then screw it home finger-tight. Use a wrench on the hexagonal section of the camshaft (between caps two and three) to lock it, while each 14mm pulley bolt is tightened to a torque of 50-60Nm/5-6.2kgf m/37-44lbf ft. **Caution!** Do not allow the

3: Engine & clutch

9/79 Torque pulley retaining bolt.

crescent wrench used to lock the cams to wedge against the sides of the cambox - it's easily damaged.

CAMSHAFT DRIVEBELT IDLER AND TENSIONER WHEELS, AND TENSIONER SPRING INSTALLATION

80   If the tensioner wheel pivot pin is rusty, it should be cleaned off with a strip of emery paper (but don't overdo it). Place a blob of copper-based grease on the tensioner pulley pivot pin. Also spread a thin smear of the same grease on the alloy boss on which the tensioner pulley bracket slides.

9/80 Lightly lubricate pulley pivot pin.

9/82 Tensioner spring correctly fitted.

81   Place the tensioner wheel and bracket in position and screw in the 14mm retaining bolt, but leave it loose enough for the tensioner wheel to move back-and-forth.

82   Hold the tensioner spring so that the longer eye is at the wheel end and open downwards. Clip the spring into the recess in the tensioner wheel bracket and, using needle-nosed pliers, stretch it until the other end can be clipped over the anchor pin. Ensure both ends of the spring are securely located in their respective cutout and groove.

83   Pull the tensioner wheel outward, against the spring tension, as far as it will go and then tighten the 14mm center bolt to lock it in this position until the drivebelt is fitted.

84   Fit the idler wheel to the left-hand side of the engine and tighten its 14mm retaining bolt to 38-51Nm/3.8-5.3kgf m/28-38lbf ft.

CRANKSHAFT INNER (CAM DRIVEBELT) PULLEY INSTALLATION

85   Temporarily fit the 21mm-headed crankshaft center bolt, and, using a socket and T-bar to apply leverage, rotate the crankshaft until the keyway in its nose is facing upward. A sharp tap on the T-bar in the reverse direction will slacken the bolt once more without moving the crankshaft. Remove the bolt. **Caution!** Take care when turning the crank in case the valve heads come into contact with the pistons; (although this couldn't be made to happen with our engine, it's a possibility with modified engines).

86   Rub a smear of oil over the crankshaft nose and in the keyway. Fit the cam drivebelt pulley over the nose of the crankshaft - flanged side toward the rear - and rotate it until the cutout in the pulley aligns with the cutout in the crankshaft.

87   Hold the locking key so that the chamfered end points toward the oil pump body and the chamfer (taper) is toward the crankshaft. Push the key into its slot with your fingers.

88   Refit the crankshaft pulley lock bolt temporarily but don't tighten it to full torque.

CAMSHAFT DRIVEBELT INSTALLATION AND VALVE TIMING

89   + Before fitting the camshaft drivebelt, ensure that the notch in the crankshaft drive pulley is aligned with the pointer on the face of the oil pump, and that the camshaft pulleys are

9/87 Insert key (chamfer inward and toward crank).

9/89a Notch aligned with pointer = TDC.

in the position previously described with the "I" on the inlet pulley almost vertical and the "E" on the exhaust pulley almost vertical (see diagram).

90   If necessary, rotate the crankshaft (if they're fitted, removing the sparkplugs will make this easier) using the 21mm pulley locking bolt until the notch in the flange at the back of the crankshaft inner pulley aligns with the triangular pointer cast into the oil pump body. This represents TDC (Top Dead Centre).

91   Begin fitting the drivebelt by first sliding it half on to the crankshaft pulley, threading it up past the idler wheel on the exhaust side of the engine,

9/89b Pulley positions (see diagram, too).

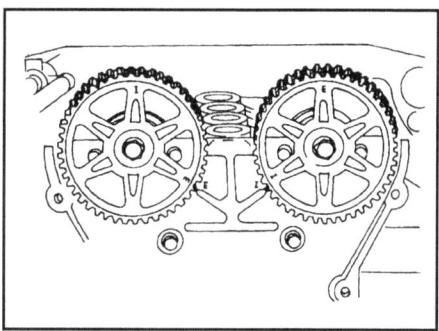

D9/89 DIAGRAM ILLUSTRATES MORE CLEARLY THE RELATIONSHIP OF TIMING MARKS ON SEAL PLATE AND PULLEYS.

and then halfway onto the exhaust camshaft pulley. **Caution!** It's important that there is no slack on this, the 'pulling' side, of the camshaft drive system. Keeping the belt taut between the crank pulley and the exhaust cam pulley, pull the belt onto the intake cam pulley until it's about halfway on. Feed the belt around the tensioner wheel and then push it fully home onto the three pulleys. Don't release the tensioner wheel lock bolt yet.

92   The marked section of each pulley flange adjacent to the letter "I" or "E" should be in alignment with the center of the pointer embossed in the seal plate behind the camshaft pulleys and bearing the same ID letter. On our project engine the exhaust cam pulley lined up OK, but we had to turn the intake cam pulley a little with a 14mm spanner and move the belt one notch.

93   Frankly, it's hard to tell with Mazda's system whether or not you've got everything lined up exactly as it should be - which is why we recommended adding additional reference marks before removing the original drivebelt. If you added those extra marks, carry out the procedure outlined

Mazda Miata, MX-5, Eunos & Roadster

9/93 Dot on pulley coincides with straightedge.

so far and then place a straightedge over the centers of the crank and exhaust cam pulley retaining bolts. Check that with the drivebelt taut between these pulleys, your marks line up with the straightedge. When satisfied, move the straightedge to cover the centers of the crank and intake cam pulleys to make sure the marks on that side also line up. If they don't, without moving the other pulleys, or losing the tension of the belt between the crank and exhaust cam pulleys, reposition the intake pulley, tooth-by-tooth, until you are satisfied all is in alignment. Double-check that the crank pulley is still aligned with the TDC marker and that the "I" of the intake cam and "E" of the exhaust cam are still more or less vertical.

94   If you think you've got it right, using a socket on the crankshaft nose bolt, rotate the crankshaft through four complete turns until the TDC notch in the pulley rear flange once again aligns with the indicator in the oil pump body. Check that both camshaft drive pulleys still register correct alignment. If the alignment is not right,

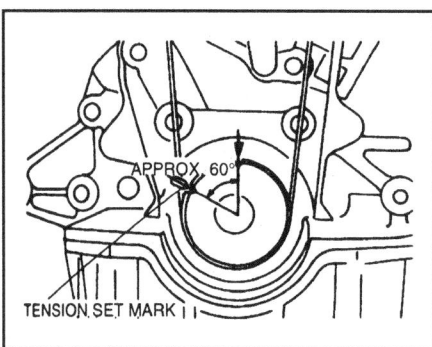

D9/95 NOTCH ALIGNED WITH 60 DEGREE MARKER AFTER ALMOST TWO TURNS OF CRANK (SEE TEXT).

repeat the valve timing procedure until you're satisfied that all is correct.

95   Turn the crankshaft 1 and 5/6ths turns (660 degrees) clockwise (looking at the crankshaft nose), at which point the cutout in the rear flange of the crankshaft pulley will be aligned with the belt tension setting marker (see diagram), which is 60 degrees anti-clockwise of the TDC pointer.

96   Slacken the camshaft belt tensioner wheel locking bolt until the tensioner springs forward and takes up the belt's slack. Tighten the tensioner locking bolt to a torque of 38-51Nm/3.8-5.3kgf m/28-38lbf ft.

97   Check that the cam drivebelt is correctly tensioned by placing a straightedge on the top of the cam belt where it crosses between the two cam pulleys and then, using the T-bar of a socket set, press the cam drivebelt down between the two pulleys (see photo) and measure how far the cam belt can be deflected from the straightedge. With a pressure of 10kg or 22lb applied, the cam belt deflection should be 9-11.5mm/0.36-0.45 inch. If necessary, repeat the tensioning procedure.

98   If fitted, temporarily remove the 21mm crankshaft pulley lock bolt. Slide the camshaft

9/97 Checking drivebelt tension.

9/98 Guide plate and lock bolt installed.

drivebelt guide plate over the nose of the crankshaft, engage it with the key protruding from the camshaft drivebelt pulley and then reinstall the crankshaft pulley lock bolt. Tension the bolt to 157-166Nm/16-17kgf m/116-122lbf ft.

CAMSHAFT DRIVEBELT COVERS, WATER PUMP PULLEY AND CRANKSHAFT PULLEY INSTALLATION

99   Start by fitting the lowest cover first. Slide the section of the cover that covers the cam drivebelt jockey wheel into place between the jockey wheel and the power steering pump mounting bracket. You will then find that the rest of the cover can be swung around the boss of the water pump and into position. Engage the protecting spigots of the cover into the bolt holes of the water pump body.

100   Before fixing the lower cover in position, slide the center cover over the water pump center boss and engage it with the bottom cover, then fit the four 10mm headed retaining bolts that secure both covers and tighten them with a box end wrench using fingertip pressure only. Note that the bolt which fits closest to the water pump central boss is longer than the other three.

101   Fit the top section of the cover in place, flexing it just a little to clear the thermostat housing body. Note the cover is held by four 10mm bolts and that both bolts on the left-hand side also secure brackets. See photo.

102   Fit the cankshaft pulley over the crankshaft nose and engage it with the spigot in the cam belt guide plate (**Caution!** If fitted, the crankshaft position sensor rotor at the rear of the pulley is easily damaged). Fit the retaining plate and then the four 10mm bolts and torque them to 13-17Nm/125-175kgf cm/109-151lbf in. If necessary, prevent the crankshaft from rotating by using a screwdriver wedged in the starter ring gear. Note that the pulley

9/101 Bolts at top left secure brackets too.

3: Engine & clutch

is a tight fit over the crankshaft nose, and therefore needs to be pulled on evenly by the four screws.

103   Fitting the water pump pulley. Place the water pump pulley on the flange of the water pump, noting that the recessed side of the pulley should face toward the engine. Put a drop of thread lock on each of the three retaining bolts and then tighten them to a torque of 7.9-10.7Nm/80-110kgf cm/70-95lbf in - about fingertip pressure tight - using a box end spanner. You can lock the pulley to tighten the bolts by wrapping the drivebelt around the pulley and gripping the belt firmly in one hand.

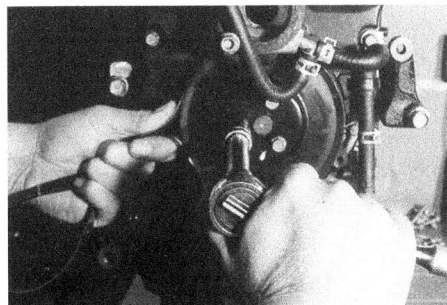

9/103 Hold pulley with drivebelt.

CAMBOX COVER INSTALLATION

104   Apply a bead of silicone sealant to the 'corners' in the cambox sealing flange created by the camshaft seal and camshaft position sensor housings (see photo). Allow the sealant to harden for around five minutes.

105   Fit a new seal into the groove on the underside of the cambox cover. This is a complex seal which also encompasses sealing for the sparkplug access tubes.

106   Douse all of the camshaft lobes with oil and then lower the cambox cover into place.

9/104 Apply sealant in arrowed positions.

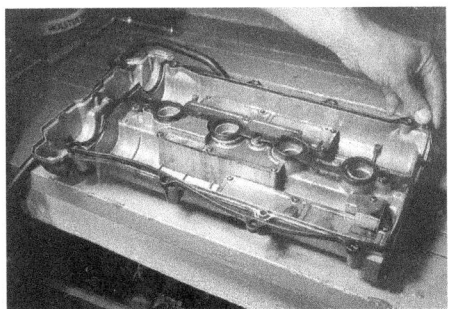

9/105 Fit new seal to cambox cover.

9/106 Lower cambox cover into place.

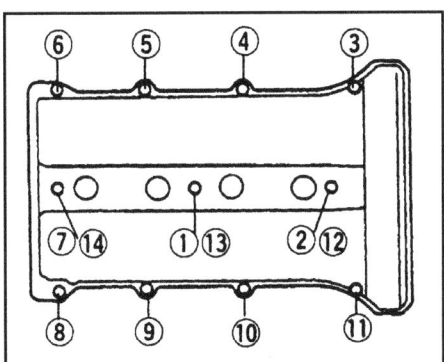

D9/107 CAMBOX COVER BOLT TIGHTENING SEQUENCE.

sure the front of the cambox cover engages properly with the top of the cam drivebelt cover on the front of the cylinder head.

107   Install the cambox cover's eleven 10mm bolts, noting that two of the front ones secure brackets. Tighten the bolts in a spiral sequence (see diagram) and in five or six steps.

108   Tighten the eleven 10 mm dome-headed bolts to a torque of 7Nm/70kgf cm /55lbf in. If you don't have a torque wrench that reads this low, you'll find that moderate finger pressure against a wrench is sufficient and will compress the rubber seal enough to seal the cambox.

THERMOSTAT AND THERMOSTAT HOUSING COVER INSTALLATION

109   Fit the thermostat into the recess in its housing so that the two valves are on a diagonal line between the cover fixings. Note that the small brass valve should be higher.

110   Fit a new gasket to the housing, noting that if the gasket has a bent tab device it should be

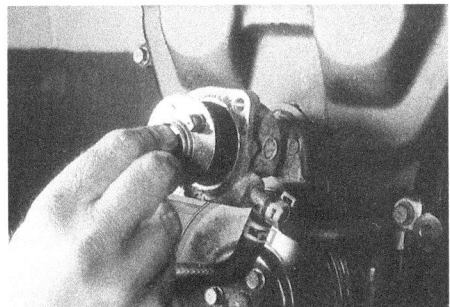

9/109 Install thermostat (see text).

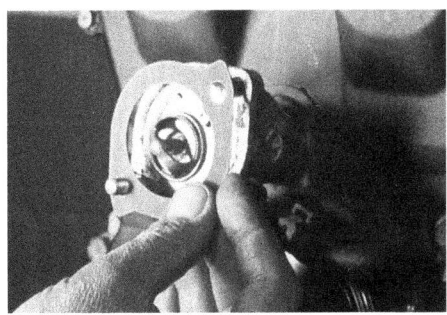

9/110 Fit a new thermostat housing gasket.

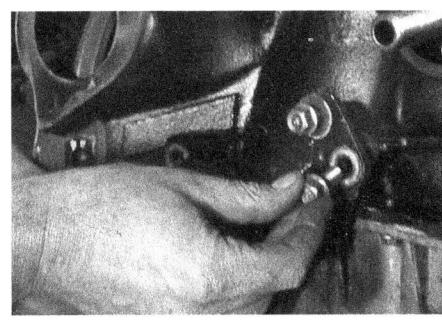

9/111 Install engine mounting bracket.

at the top and pointing toward the thermostat cover. No gasket cement should be necessary if both sealing flanges have been thoroughly cleaned. Fit the thermostat housing cover and tighten the two 12mm fixings to a torque of 22Nm/2.3kgf m/17lbf ft.

ENGINE MOUNTING BRACKET (RIGHT-HAND) INSTALLATION

111   The bracket is secured by three 14mm bolts which are of two different lengths. Looking at the bracket, the bolt on the left and the upper bolt on the right are both short. Tighten the bolts to a torque of 37-53Nm/3.7-5.5kgf m/27-39lbf ft.

OIL PRESSURE GAUGE SENDER UNIT INSTALLATION

112   The oil pressure gauge sender unit screws into a threaded drilling on the right-hand side of the cylinder block immediately adjacent to a core plug and just slightly above, and to the left of, the oil filter boss.

113   Apply silicone sealant to the threads of the sender unit, but take care to ensure the final 1.5mm/0,06in of thread is not coated (see diagram).

114   Using your fingers screw the sensor

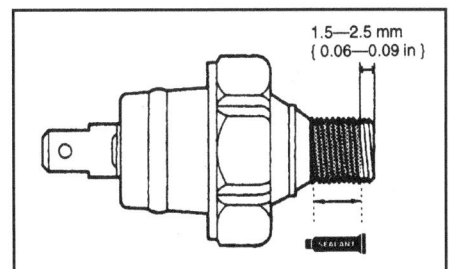

D9/113 APPLY SILICONE SEALANT TO OIL PRESSURE SENDER THREAD, EXCEPT AT END.

3:41

Mazda Miata, MX-5, Eunos & Roadster

9/114 Install the oil pressure sender unit.

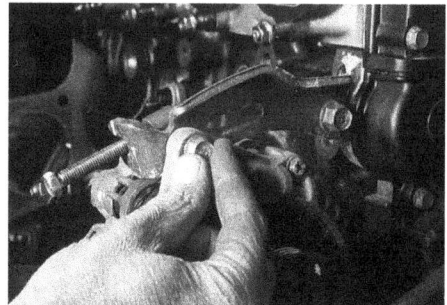

9/117 Install lock bolt.

9/122a Install oil cooler unit ...

body into the cylinder block. Do the final tightening with a 22mm crescent wrench (open-ended spanner) bearing on the hexagonal section of the sensor just above the threaded stem. **Caution!** If applicable, do not try to tighten the sensor by using the hexagonal section just below the electrical connector blade.

ALTERNATOR INSTALLATION

115 The alternator bracket is fixed to a boss protruding alongside the cam belt cover, and is secured by a single 14mm bolt: tighten the bolt to

9/118 Install alternator drivebelt.

9/122b ... and tighten retaining nut.

the adjusting strap and screw it into the adjuster screw's block. Leave everything a little loose for the moment.

118 Push the alternator toward the cylinder block and fit the drivebelt over the crankshaft, water pump and alternator pulleys.

119 Tighten the 12mm adjuster bolt until there's about 12mm/0.5 inch of deflection when strong thumb pressure is applied to the drivebelt midway between water pump and alternator pulleys.

120 Tighten the alternator pivot bolt nut to 38-51Nm/3.8-5.3kgf m/28-38Ibf ft. Tighten the lockbolt which passes through the support strap to 19-25Nm/1.9-2.6kgf m/14-18Ibf ft.

OIL COOLER AND OIL FILTER INSTALLATION

121 Fit a new sealing ring to the back of the oil cooler unit.

122 + Slide the oil cooler unit over the hollow stud protruding from the centre of the oil filter boss: note the correct orientation of the two small bore hoses (see photo). Secure the oil cooler with its 30mm, brass-colored nut. Torque the nut to 30-39Nm/3-4kgf m/22-28Ibf ft.

123 Take the new oil filter and smear engine oil around the sealing ring in its face. Screw the filter

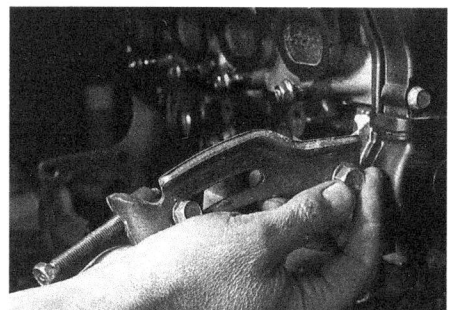

9/115 Install alternator bracket.

9/116 Install alternator pivot bolt.

38-51Nm/3.8-5.3kgf m/28-38Ibf ft.

116 Slide the alternator mounting lugs over the projecting bosses of the cylinder block and oil pump. It may be quite a tight fit and you may need to work the alternator to-and-fro until it slides fully into position. Once the pivot pin holes in the mounting and boss line up, smear the 14mm pivot bolt lightly with grease and push it home from the rear of the alternator. Finger-tighten the bolt 14mm retaining nut for the time being.

117 Lift the alternator upward and pass the single 12mm lockbolt through its boss and through

9/121 Install new oil cooler sealing ring.

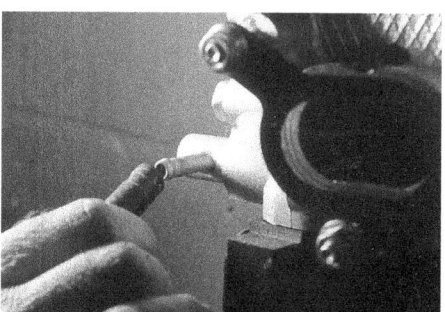

9/124 Connect oil cooler hose to c/head stub.

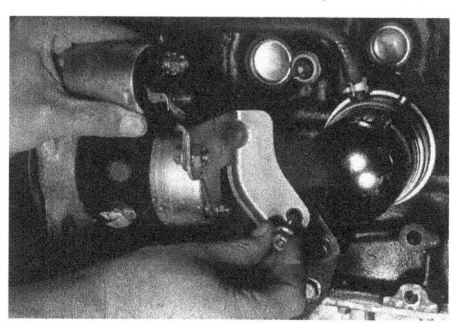

9/125 Fit bolt through s/motor rear bracket.

fully home by hand only.

124 Reconnect the hose from the oil cooler to the stub at the rear of the cylinder head and retain with its spring clamp.

STARTER MOTOR INSTALLATION

125 Fit bolt through s/motor rear bracket. Slide the nose of the starter motor through the hole in the backplate until the face of the starter motor body closes right up to the backplate: the hole in the starter motor bracket should be in alignment with the bolt hole in the engine mounting

3: Engine & clutch

9/126 Install a new gasket then install ...

9/127 ... the heater outlet cover.

9/130 Wires (l to r) connect to cylinders 3, 2, 1, 4.

9/133 Disc MUST be centered on pilot bearing.

bracket. Fit the 14mm retaining bolt through the starter motor rear bracket and engine mounting bracket and tighten to a torque of 38-51Nm/3.8-5.3kgf m/28-38lbf ft.

HEATER OUTLET COVER INSTALLATION

126   📷 Fit a new gasket over the stud protruding from the water outlet in the rear of the cylinder head - no gasket cement is needed.

127   📷 Fit the cover in place, screw in the one retaining bolt and fit the nut on the projecting stud. Tighten both 12mm nut and bolt to 19-25Nm/1.9-2.6kgf m/14-18lbf ft.

IGNITION COILS AND SPARKPLUG WIRES INSTALLATION

128   Note: If you intend to reinstall the engine and transmission as a single unit, consider leaving the fitting of the coil unit until after the engine is back in place, otherwise you'll find that the coil unit can hit the engine compartment firewall/bulkhead, because of the acute angle taken by the engine/transmission assembly during installation.

129   📷 Fit the coil assembly in position on the back of the cylinder head, and replace the two 12mm headed bolts which hold the coil bracket to

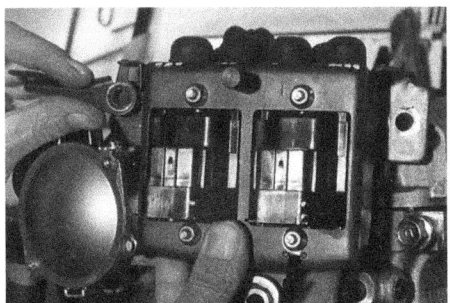

9/129 Don't forget bracket at top left.

the top rear of the cambox cover (note that the upper left bolt also secures a bracket. There is a further 12mm bolt to secure the base of the coil bracket and this, too, needs to be installed. Tighten the bolts to a torque of 19-25Nm/1.9-2.6kgf m/14-18lbf ft.

130   📷 Refit the HT leads to their individual sparkplugs and position the individual leads in the clips in the cam cover valley. Viewed from the rear (see photo) the coil towers - left to right - connect to sparkplugs as follows: 3, 2, 1, 4.

CLUTCH COVER AND DISC INSTALLATION

131   📷+ Place the disc on the friction surface of the cover with the protruding side of the disc facing the diaphragm. Hold both together by inserting a finger from the back of the coverplate.

132   Push the clutch assembly against the flywheel face and locate it in position over the pins projecting from the flywheel. Install the six 14mm cover retaining bolts and finger-tighten.

133   📷 The next bit can be tricky! It's important that the splined center hub of the disc is centered in relation to the pilot (spigot) bearing so that the transmission input shaft slides through the

9/131a Correct orientation of clutch disc.

9/131b Fit cover and disc to flywheel.

former into the latter - otherwise installing the transmission will be difficult. Whilst the cover retaining bolts are only finger-tight, you'll still be able to move the disc, so now's the time to get it right. You can buy or hire a universal mandrel designed for clutch centering, then simply select sleeves suitable to fit the pilot bearing and clutch hub: move the disc around until the mandrel slides into place easily. If you don't have a mandrel, align the disc by eye as we did. Using one eye only, ensure that the disc hub and pilot bearing are concentric with the ring formed by the diaphragm spring fingers.

134   📷 When you're satisfied that the disc is centered, tighten the 14mm cover retaining bolts in a diagonal sequence, and in a minimum of three stages, to a torque of 18-26Nm/1.9-2.7kgf m/14-19lbf ft. To lock the flywheel, temporarily install a bellhousing bolt, then use a screwdriver wedged against the bolt and into the ring gear teeth.

ENGINE MOUNTING BRACKET (LEFT-HAND) INSTALLATION

135   These brackets are handed so there can be no confusion as to which side of the engine they

9/134 Torque clutch cover bolts.

fit. The bracket is retained by three 14mm bolts which should be tightened to a torque 37-53Nm/3.7-5.3kgf m/27-39lbf ft. Note: engine installation may be easier if fitting of this bracket is left until the engine is suspended in place.

POWER STEERING PUMP BRACKET INSTALLATION

136   The power steering pump bracket is fixed to the left-hand side of the cylinder block by three 14mm bolts, which should be tightened to a torque of 38-51Nm/3.8-5.3kgf m/28-38lbf ft. If necessary,

Mazda Miata, MX-5, Eunos & Roadster

once the three bracket securing bolts have been torqued, the pivot pin spacer can be driven back into its correct position in the bracket. Oil the section of the spacer which will slide into the bracket. Fit the pivot bolt through the front eye of the mounting, screw its retaining nut on backwards so that the washer surface is facing the spacer, and then screw the nut fully up the threaded section until it jams against the unthreaded portion of the bolt.

137 ◘ The bolt can now be used as a drift to push the spacer back into its housing in the bracket. Hit the head of the bolt with a nylon or copper-

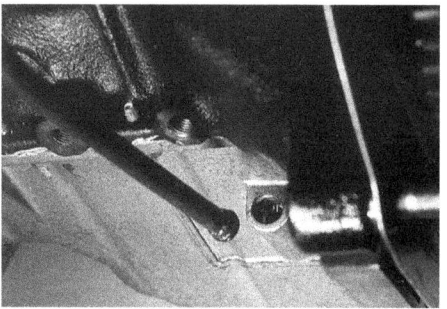
9/139 Push dipstick tube into oil pan boss.

9/143 Camshaft position sensor drive dogs.

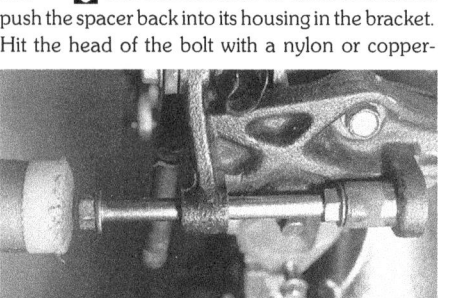
9/137 Install spacer in original position.

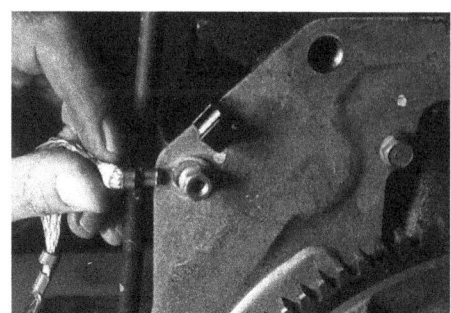
9/140 Don't forget ground strap.

9/145 Camshaft position sensor lock bolt.

faced hammer, and drift the spacer home slowly until the position mark made before removal aligns once more with the bracket.

COOLANT INLET CASTING INSTALLATION

138 ◘ Hold a new gasket over the water inlet casting flange and then pass the two 12mm bolts through the holes in the flange to hold the gasket in position. Fit the casting to the water pump inlet and tighten the retaining bolts to a torque of 19-25Nm/1.9-2.6kgf m/14-18lbf ft. No gasket cement should be necessary if the water pump and inlet pipe

9/138 Install inlet casting.

flanges are clean and free of all old gasket material. For the moment, leave the metal heater return pipe bracket loose on the appropriate manifold stud because it cannot be fixed until the manifold is in place.

DIPSTICK TUBE INSTALLATION

139 ◘ Fit a new rubber seal ring over the end of the dipstick tube and then smear it with engine oil. Gently push the tube into its recess in the oil pan (sump) until you feel the seal slide into position, and the tube support bracket stud aligns with, and

passes through, its hole in the engine backplate.
140 ◘ Fit the (cleaned) eye of the engine ground (earth) strap over the stud and tighten the 10mm retaining nut 7.9-10.7Nm/80-110kgf cm/70-95.4lbf in. Fit the dipstick in its tube.

ENGINE LIFTING EYES INSTALLATION

141 ◘ Fit the engine lifting eye with its integral bracket to the rear of the cylinder head on the right-hand side of the engine. The eye should be vertical and the two tangs in its bottom edge should face inward toward the cylinder head. Tighten the

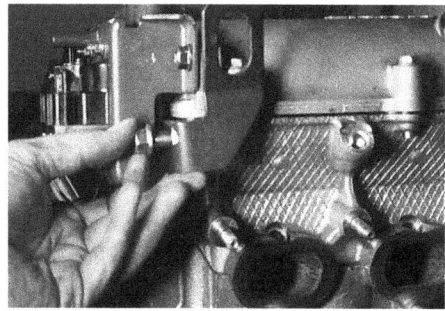
9/141 Install engine lifting eye.

retaining 14mm bolt to a torque of 38-51Nm/3.8-5.3kgf m/28-38lbf ft.
142 Fit the engine lifting eye to the front left-hand side of the cylinder head. Note that the tangs at the base of the bracket should face inward, toward the cylinder head, and that the retaining 14mm bolt should be torqued to 38-51Nm/3.8-5.3kgf m/28-38lbf ft.

CAMSHAFT POSITION SENSOR INSTALLATION

143 ◘ You'll find that the drive dogs on the

spindle of the camshaft angle sensor are shaped so that it will only fit into its recess when it has the correct relationship with the camshaft and cannot be fitted 180 degrees out.
144 Fit a new rubber O-ring seal into the groove in the sensor boss and lubricate the seal and the drive dogs with a little engine oil. Set the drive dogs to match the slots in the cam and then slide the angle sensor into position: if it won't go home with a little to-and-fro twisting, pull it out, rotate the drive spindle 180 degrees and try again. Once the drive dogs engage the rear of the camshaft, push the angle sensor body fully home against the rear of the cylinder head and loosely install the retaining bolt.
145 ◘ If you marked the relationship of the camshaft angle sensor body to the cylinder head, realign the marks and tighten the 12mm lock bolt to a torque of 19-25Nm/1.9-2.6kgf m/14-18lbf ft.
146 If you didn't mark the position of the sensor relative to the head before removal, you'll need to follow the ignition timing adjustment procedure ☞ 5.

MANIFOLDS INSTALLATION SPECIAL NOTE

147 Because we wanted photos of installing the intake and exhaust manifolds with the engine in the car, we installed the engine without the manifolds. If you wish to install the intake and exhaust manifolds prior to engine installation ☞ 3/11/31-33 and 41-46.
148 You'll find that there are some advantages to installing the engine without the manifolds, particularly in terms of engine mounting access from above and the overall weight/bulkiness of the engine unit. On the other hand, it's undoubtedly easier to fit the intake manifold with the engine on a bench or stand.

3: Engine & clutch

10. TRANSMISSION (GEARBOX) - INSTALLATION (ENGINE OUT OF CAR)

☞ First read 1/1, 2.

1 Manual transmission only. Spread a thin smear of copper-based lubricant on the nose and splines of the transmission input shaft - don't overdo it!

2 Manual transmission only. Bring the engine and transmission unit together, making sure that the transmission input shaft enters the center of the clutch, and that the bellhousing is correctly lined up with the engine backplate. If the clutch disc

10/2 Bring engine and transmission together.

has been well centered, the transmission bellhousing should go fully home against the engine backplate with no more than a little joggling around. Life will be more difficult if the clutch disc has not been well centered and, in extreme cases, you'll have to withdraw the transmission and re-center the friction disc before attempting again to make the transmission fit. Once the transmission bellhousing slides fully home, make sure it engages on the hollow spigots projecting from the rear of the cylinder block.

3 Auto transmission only. Make sure the torque converter is fully engaged with the oil pump behind it. Place a straightedge across the face of the bellhousing and measure the depth to the rim of the torque convertor (see diagram), which should be 22.5mm/0.89in. If the depth is not correct, press the convertor inward while rotating it slowly until you feel it move and engage with the pump with a 'clunk.' Check the measurement again. **Caution!** Once correctly engaged with the pump, make sure the torque convertor does not slide forward subsequently.

4 Automatic transmission only. Bring the

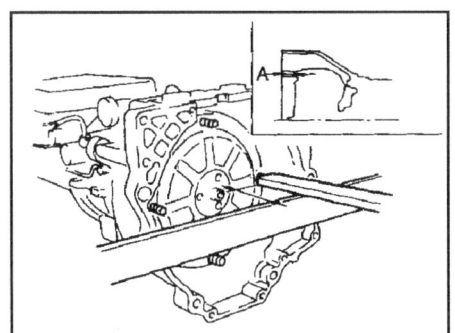
D10/3 CORRECT DEPTH (SEE TEXT) INDICATES TORQUE CONVERTOR PROPERLY ENGAGED.

engine and transmission unit together, making sure that the bellhousing is correctly lined up with the engine backplate, and that if the torque convertor has threaded studs they are lined up with the holes in the driveplate. Once the transmission bellhousing slides fully home, make sure it engages on the hollow spigots projecting from the rear of the cylinder block. Note that the driveplate fixings need to be fitted when the engine's in the car; this is because it's not a good idea to tilt the auto transmission sideways.

5 Fit the two topmost bellhousing bolts which are 17mm (x 60mm) and screw them into place finger-tight. This will be enough to stop the transmission coming away from the back of the engine.

6 With the help of an assistant, tilt the whole engine/transmission unit a little to one side and then the other, in order to allow the fitting of the two lowermost 17mm (x 60mm) bolts which, again, should be screwed in finger-tight at this stage.

7 Position the exhaust pipe support bracket over the two bolt holes on the left-hand side of the bellhousing. Secure the bracket, with flange facing rearward, with two 17mm bolts, the upper of which is longer (70mm), although there seems no good reason for this. Screw the bolts

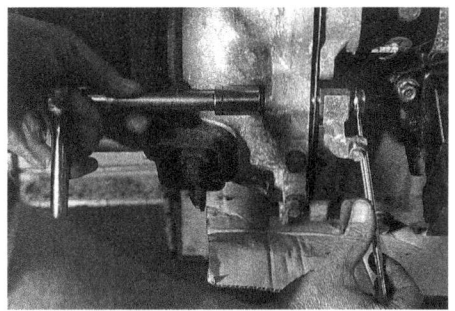
10/7 Install clutch pipe support bracket.

home finger-tight. Fit the 17mm nut and bolt which secures the clutch slave cylinder pipe bracket (if fitted) on the right-hand side. Note: the remaining fasteners in the starter motor area will be fitted later.

8 Tighten all of the 17mm bellhousing bolts to 64-89Nm/6.5-9.1kgf m/48-65lbf ft.

11. ENGINE AND TRANSMISSION - INSTALLATION AS A UNIT

☞ First read 1/1, 2.

Throughout this section you'll find that the colors of electrical connectors, hose markings, etc., are mentioned in an effort to make component identification as easy as possible. However, you should bear in mind it's possible that the colors of these components and markings may vary.

PREPARATION

1 **Caution!** Check that the engine bay is clear and that all pipes, wires and cables are tied back out of the way, so that the engine and transmission unit will not become entangled as it passes through the engine compartment. This particularly applies to the clutch flexible hydraulic pipe (right-hand drive cars with manual transmission) which runs across the top of the bellhousing and shares a clip with the main wiring harness. Tie this bracket high up on the right of the compartment. As with engine removal, the car will need to be raised and securely supported high enough above the ground to give good access to the underside. ☞ 1/3.

2 Spread old towels over the nose of the car and the fender (wing) tops: this will help protect the paintwork from damage.

3 You'll need at least one assistant to help you install the engine and transmission units as an assembly, as well as a small mobile engine crane of the type that can be hired from the tool and plant hire companies you find in every medium-sized town. **Warning!** Sorry, we weren't able to weigh them, but we believe the engine and transmission together weigh up to 180kg (400lb) so the rope and crane you use should be capable of lifting twice this weight as a safety margin. Also, the lifting hook of the crane's boom should be capable of reaching a height of around 1830mm (6ft) above the ground.

4 Tie several strands of very strong nylon rope tightly between the two lifting eyes positioned on each side of the cylinder head; one toward the front of the engine and one toward the back. It's important to keep the rope as tight as possible; you'll be surprised how much the rope will stretch once the crane takes the strain. Engage the crane's hook with the rope sling and lift the engine/transmission unit far enough from the ground to clear the front edge of the engine compartment opening. Line the crane and engine up in front of the car on the car's centerline.

5 Lubricate the driveshaft (propshaft) nose.

ENGINE/TRANSMISSION INSTALLATION

6 With an assistant holding the transmission tailshaft extension to stop the engine/transmission unit swaying, gently roll the crane forward until the tailshaft end is approximately over the center of the engine compartment. Now, the transmission end of the unit needs to be pushed downward to achieve the steepest angle possible, as the engine/transmission is pushed further back into the compartment and simultaneously lowered. **Caution!** Take great care not to crush or snag any components, pipework, etc.

7 Once the rear of the cylinder head gets close to the firewall/bulkhead - put an old towel or

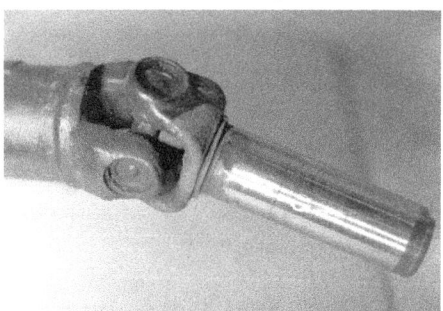
11/5 Lubricate driveshaft nose.

3:45

Mazda Miata, MX-5, Eunos & Roadster

similar between the two - begin to level up the engine/transmission unit. **Caution!** If the coil and camshaft angle sensor units are fitted, take great care not to bang them against the firewall. To relieve this latter problem and to allow the engine to be moved further back, it's helpful to lift the transmission extension on a wheeled jack so that the whole engine/transmission unit takes on a more level stance. Of course, it's necessary to engage the driveshaft (if fitted) with the transmission tailshaft as the engine/transmission unit nears its fitted position.

8   When the engine/transmission unit is

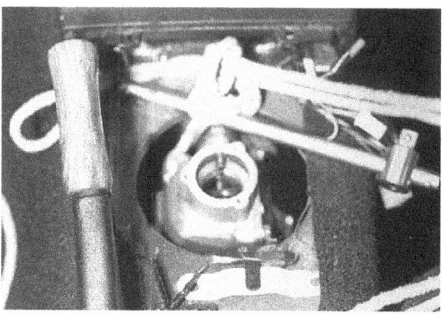
11/10a Rope sling for transmission.

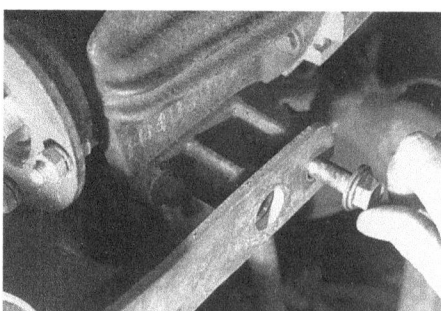
11/13 Fit PPF through bolts.

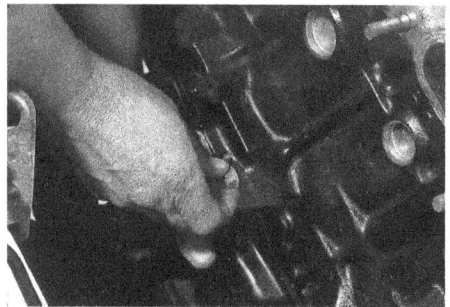
11/8 You may need to remove left-hand mount.

11/10b Remake transmission's wiring connections.

11/14 Install transmission bracket.

almost in final position it can be carefully maneuvered until the studs protruding from the engine mountings pass through the hole and slot in the subframe. Note: you may find it necessary, as we did, to remove the left-hand engine mounting bracket from the engine and fasten the mounting to the subframe independently of the engine. This allowed us to maneuver the engine sufficiently to engage the stud of the right-hand mounting in its slot, at which point the retaining nut and washer were immediately screwed into place. Then, the engine was twisted and lowered until the mounting bracket on the left-hand side aligned once more with the bolt holes in the side of the engine. The three bolts were fitted and tightened to a torque of 37-53Nm/3.7-5.5kgf m/27-39lbf ft.

9   As the engine reached its final location, we also found it helpful (manual transmission cars only) to tie the transmission tailshaft extension to a crossbar bridging the gearshift lever hole in the transmission tunnel so that the transmission end of the unit was held as high as possible, but was still free to move backwards and forwards a little. You can, of course, use a wheeled jack to support the transmission as it moves backwards. Note: if you do leave both engine mountings in place on the engine during installation, you'll need to push the studs the last 13mm (half inch), or so, toward their holes with a long screwdriver or similar, but you're going to find it a tricky task. Taking the mounting bracket off will save a lot of sweat and swearing ...

10   Once the engine is sitting safely on its mountings, the crane can be released and withdrawn. Temporarily lower the jack or rope sling supporting the transmission unit. Above the transmission case you'll see that several wires sprout from the main harness (four connectors man. trans./five connectors auto trans.); these are the connectors for the sensors and switches mounted in the transmission outer casing. You'll see that they have different types of connector so there can be no confusion over which connections are for which switch or sensor. On manual transmission cars, because the harness is still loose, it's possible to pull the two wires with connectors over the top of the transmission so that they can be seen between the transmission and the left-hand side of the transmission tunnel, making reconnecting the back-up (reverse) light switch much easier. Note that these connectors need to click home. Now remake the connections to the neutral indicator switch, noting that it doesn't matter which wires you connect to each other: this is also true for the back-up light switch. The neutral indicator switch connectors have locking tabs which you need to hear click to indicate that the connection is properly made.

11   From beneath the car put the PPF in place by sliding it forward onto its mounting on the right side of the transmission, then pushing it up around the side of the differential unit until it slides onto its mounting. Note: you may have to lift the driveshaft flange end of the differential slightly to get the PPF to slide into engagement. The end of the PPF frame with round drillings is the differential end.

12   With the PPF roughly positioned, install the two 17mm-headed bolts that pass through the lower flange of the PPF, up through the transmission casing and then screw into the top flange of the PPF. For the moment, these bolts should be left finger-tight.

13   Move to the rear end of the PPF and install the 17mm through-bolts that clamp the PPF to the side of the differential casing. Fit the bolt without a collar first, followed by the bolt with the collar. It's suggested that you spray the shanks of both bolts with WD40 or similar silicone-based lubricant as they seem prone to corrosion. You may need to lift the nose of the differential casing a little to align the holes in the differential casing and the PPF. Tighten the two bolts snugly but not fully at this stage.

14   Move once again to the forward end of the PPF and install the support bracket between the PPF and the tailhousing of the transmission. If there's a rope supporting the transmission and it's in the way, you should remove it before installing the bracket. Hold the bracket in place above the lower flange of the PPF and finger-tighten the 17mm retaining bolt. Insert the two 14mm bolts that secure the bracket to the transmission extension housing and, once again, tighten them finger-tight. You may need to lift the tail of the transmission slightly to make the bracket align with the threaded holes in the transmission casing. Tighten the two 17mm PPF to transmission side bolts to a torque of 104-123Nm/10.6-12.6kgf m/77-91lbf ft.

15   Next, tighten the PPF to differential 17mm side bolts to the same torque. Make sure the collar on the forward bolt is properly engaged in the recess in the PPF.

16   Move to the transmission tailshaft housing support bracket and tighten the 17mm bolts to the same torque as the other 17mm bolts. Then tighten the bracket's 14mm bolts to a final torque of 37-53Nm/3.7-55kgf m/27-39lbf ft.

17   Use a straightedge to bridge the 'chassis' box section longerons, measure the distance between the straightedge and the base of the PPF (see diagram). The gap should be in the middle of these tolerance ranges: 61-71mm/2.41-2.79in for manual transmission cars and 51.5-61.5mm/2.02-2.41in for auto transmission cars. If the gap is not correct, slacken the bolts securing the PPF to the transmission casing and the bolts securing the tailshaft housing support bracket and, as appropriate, lift or pull downward the transmission to get the correct gap before retightening the fixings.

3: Engine & clutch

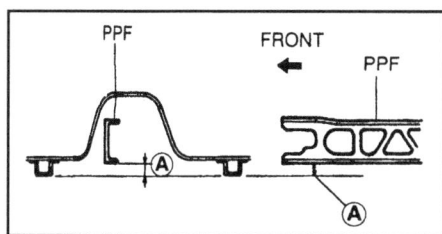

D11/17 HOW TO MEASURE PPF HEIGHT (SEE TEXT).

Check the gap again.

18   Auto transmission cars only. Using the access opening in the bottom of the bellhousing, fit the nuts or bolts, as applicable, which secure the driveplate to the lugs of the torque convertor, rotating the torque convertor and driveplate for access. Note that if you are re-using the original driveplate and torque convertor, you should ensure that the marks you made on dismantling are aligned. Lock the driveplate with a screwdriver and then, in a diagonal sequence, tighten the four bolts or nuts to 35-49Nm/3.5-5kgf m/26-36lbf ft. Install the access opening cover and secure with two bolts.

19   Reattach the engine ground (earth) strap to the bodywork and tighten its 10mm retaining screw. Note that the eye of the earth strap has a tang which locates in a hole in the bodywork.

20   If not already in place, fit a new gasket to the flange and then refit the the aluminium coolant inlet housing to the left-hand side of the engine. Tighten the two 12mm bolts to a torque of 19-25Nm/1.9-2.6kgf m/14-18lbf ft.

21   Re-attach the small bore hose from the thermostat housing to the stub on the coolant inlet housing and secure with a clamp. Ensure the small hose is clipped into the bracket on the timing cover.

22   If fitted, release the air conditioning system compressor from its ties and fix it to its mounting bracket, tightening the bolts to 15-21Nm/1.5-2.2kgf m/11-15lbf ft.

23   If fitted, untie the power steering pump and slide it between the bosses of each mounting bracket and spacer, so that the lightly lubricated pivot bolt can be passed through one of the holes in the pump's pulley and slid through both bracket and pump body. Screw the retaining nut onto the end of the bolt, but leave finger-tight for the moment.

24   Attach the adjustment strap to the pump mounting bracket using a 14mm bolt. Leave finger-tight.

11/23 Install p/s pump pivot bolt.

11/24 Install p/s pump adjustment strap.

25   Pass the 12mm lock bolt through the back of the adjustment bracket, through the strap and through the threaded block, and fix with its 12mm nut, tightened finger-tight for the moment.

26   Pass the 12mm adjuster bolt through the adjustment bracket and screw it into the thread block, but don't screw it right through the block at this point.

27   Push the power steering pump body as close to the cylinder block as possible, and, whilst doing so, fit the drivebelt over its and the crankshaft's pulleys (air conditioner pulley, too, if fitted).

11/25 Install p/s pump adjuster lock bolt.

11/26 Install p/s pump adjuster bolt.

11/27 Install p/s pump drivebelt.

28   Note that cars with air conditioning, but without power steering, will have an adjustable idler pulley mounted on a bracket where the power steering pump would otherwise be.

29   Then, using the adjuster bolt, set the belt tension until there is about 12.5mm/0.5in of deflection at the mid-point between the two pulleys on the longest run. When the correct tension is achieved, tighten the pump's 14mm pivot bolt and nut and the 14mm strap bolt. Also tighten the 12mm nut and bolt on the adjustment strap.

30   Fit the connector hose between the water

11/29 Set belt tension via adjuster bolt.

outlet casting on the cylinder block and the radiator bottom hose rigid pipe fixed to the inner fender (wing). Secure with clamps.

31   If applicable, release the heater metal return pipe bracket from the manifold stud.

32   Having ensured the seating area is completely clean, fit a new gasket over the exhaust manifold studs of the cylinder head.

33   + Install the exhaust manifold over the studs, install the heater pipe bracket and then fit the nine 14mm manifold retaining nuts. Tighten the nuts in a progressive manner, working in a repeating

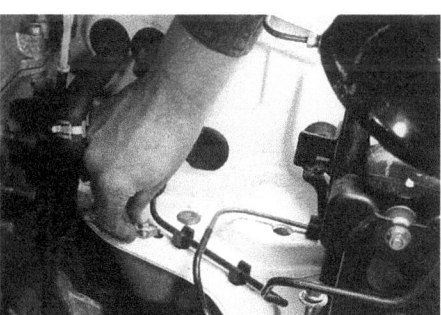

11/19 Re-attach engine ground strap.

11/20 Install coolant inlet housing.

Mazda Miata, MX-5, Eunos & Roadster

11/32 Install a new exhaust manifold gasket.

11/33a Install manifold, plus pipe bracket.

11/33b Tighten manifold nuts progressively.

11/34 Connect heater hoses to firewall stubs.

11/36 Reconnect radiator top hose.

11/37 Fit live feed wire to starter motor.

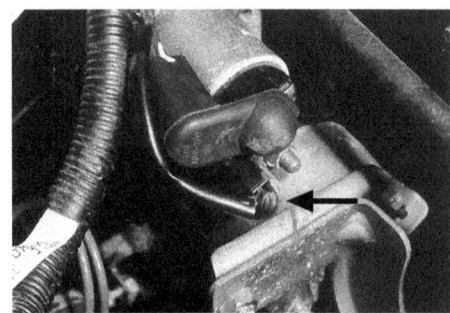

11/38 Attach starter motor solenoid connector.

11/39 Connect oil pressure sensor and alternator.

11/40 Install harness support bracket.

11/41 Install new intake manifold gasket.

spiral from the centre nut to the outsides: the correct torque is 39-46Nm/3.9-4.7kgf m/29-33lbf ft.

34   📷 Fit the two heater hoses to the stubs protruding through the engine bulkhead (the hose from the water outlet at the back of the head goes to the left-hand stub). Secure with spring clamps.

35   If necessary, install the radiator complete with fan or fans ☞ 6.

36   📷 At front of engine, reconnect the top hose to the radiator and secure with its spring clamp.

37   📷 On the right-hand side of the engine, fit the live feed wire eye to the starter solenoid and secure with its 12mm nut. **Caution!** Don't forget to replace the rubber cover over the connection.

38   📷 Fit the electrical connector to the starter motor solenoid.

39   📷 Fit the electrical connector to the oil pressure sensor. Insert the grey plug into its recess in the alternator body so that it is fully home and locks into place. Fit the wire's eye to the alternator terminal and secure with its 12mm nut. **Caution!** Don't forget to replace the rubber cover over the connection.

40   📷 Fit the wiring harness support/ground strap bracket which is secured by a single 17mm bolt. Tighten the bolt to 64-89Nm/6.5-9.1kgf m/48-65lbf ft.

41   📷 Having cleaned the gasket surfaces of both the cylinder head and the intake manifold, fit a new gasket over the studs protruding from the head.

42   Next, slide the manifold over the studs, ensuring you don't trap any wires or hoses between the manifold and the block.

43   Now the nightmare begins! The manifold is retained by nine 12mm nuts. Getting the five upper nuts onto their studs is relatively easy, so do this and screw them up finger-tight. From above the engine, the studs under the manifold are invisible, but there are four of them and they are positioned roughly at mid-points between the upper studs, which will give you an idea of where they are. The studs nearest the rear of the engine can be reached pretty easily with fingers; however, the last two are more difficult. We found that using a quarter inch drive socket set with a 6 inch extension, and the nuts glued into the socket with gasket cement, allowed us to start the nuts on their studs, although, even then, this was only achieved with the help of one of those small mirrors on a flexible shaft that you can buy in tool shops, and someone lighting the stud locations from beneath the engine.

44   Once all the nuts are in place, tighten them to 19-25Nm/1.9-2.6kgf m/14-18lbf ft starting in the centre and working outward in a spiral pattern in progressive stages.

45   📷 Feed the shaped rigid EGR pipe (which connects the intake manifold to the exhaust manifold) around the back of the cylinder head, noting that the union end has to pass around the outside of the dipstick tube. This is quite fiddly

3: Engine & clutch

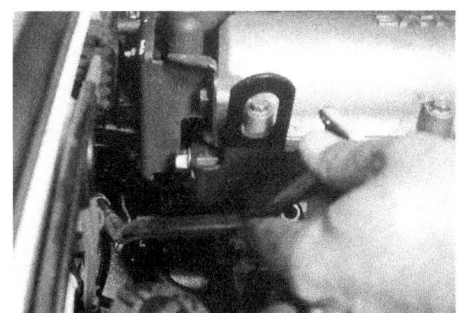
11/45 Feed EGR pipe behind head.

11/46 Tighten nuts securing EGR pipe flange.

because the bracket which supports the mid-point of the pipe has to be located on the heater outlet casting at the back of the engine.

46   Don't forget to use a new gasket at the intake manifold end of the EGR pipe. Once everything's in place, tighten the 12mm nut securing the bracket to the heater outlet, followed by the two 10mm nuts securing the pipe to the inlet manifold and the 22mm union nut at the exhaust manifold end. Note that the union nut needs to be tightened with a crescent wrench.

47   Locate four new sealing/insulator rings into the individual fuel injector recesses in the head. They snap into position very positively.

48   Push the four individual injectors into their seats in the head, making sure that they are fully engaged and that their electrical connections are uppermost. Also ensure that each injector has an O-ring and grommet at the fuel rail end.

49   Slide the two fuel hoses of the fuel rail down through the gaps between the intake runners of cylinders 1, 2 and 3, and maneuver the rail into position so that it engages with all four injectors.

50   Fit the fuel injector rail locating collars into their head recesses and be very careful not to knock them out of their seats during subsequent

11/50 Install fuel rail locating collars.

procedures: we dislodged one and it immediately took refuge within the engine mounting bracket, which we had to remove to retrieve the collar ... Push the injector rail firmly onto the individual injectors, ensuring that the O-rings are fully engaged in the rail recesses. This can be a fiddly procedure because, if the rail moves about too much, the individual injector sealing/insulating washers can disengage from the head, stopping the injector rail fixing brackets from engaging properly with their collars. Wriggle everything around until it snaps home. **Warning!** Don't try using the rail retaining bolts to force everything into correct position: it is the correct alignment of the rail and injectors relative to the head which ensures all the high pressure seals work correctly.

51   Replace the three 12mm bolts securing the rail to the cylinder head and tighten them to 7.9-10.7Nm/80-110kgf cm/69-95.4lbf in of torque.

52   Fix the wiring harness bracket to the right-hand side of the bellhousing with a 10mm bolt.

53   Fix the wiring harness to the PPF frame by pushing the studs of all the white plastic clips through the holes in the PPF.

54   Reconnect the speedometer drive to

11/51 Tighten bolts securing fuel rail.

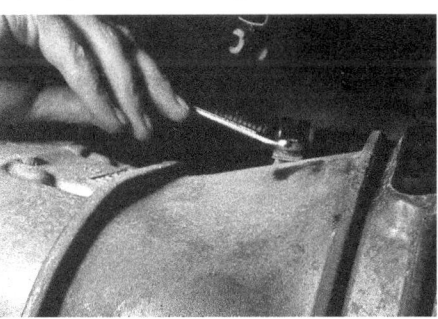
11/52 Harness bracket secured by one bolt.

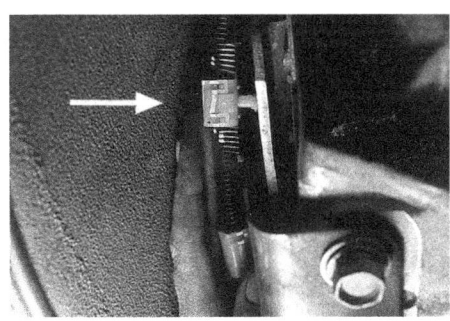
11/53 Push harness clip studs through PPF.

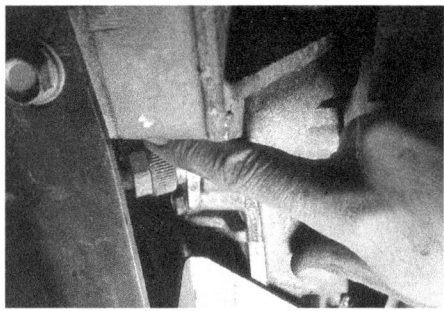
11/54 Connect speedo drive cable.

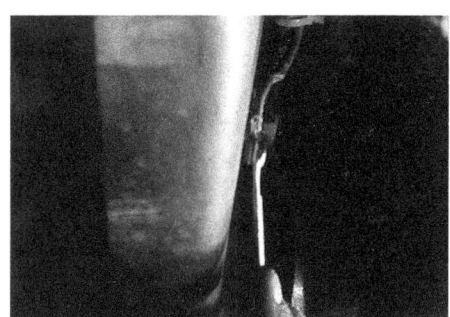
11/55 Ground strap secured by single bolt.

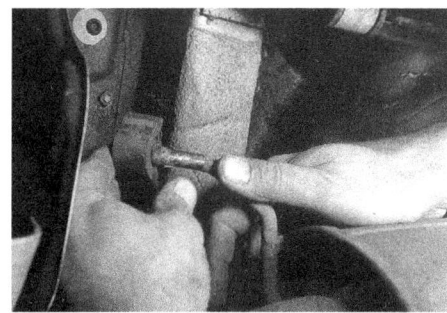
11/56 Attach rear exhaust box to its hangers.

the transmission; you may have to rotate the cable a little to get it to engage properly. Tighten the knurled nut securing the drive with vise grip pliers.

55   Fix the rear ground (earth) connection to the PPF and secure with its 10mm screw, having first ensured that the fixing area of the PPF and the electrical connector eye are clean so that good contact is made.

56   Slide the complete exhaust system under the car until it is on the floor approximately in the right position for fitting. Fit a new gasket over the studs of the exhaust manifold flange. Lift the front downpipe flange up through the gap between the transmission and the front suspension subframe while an assistant twists the system at the rear of the car to get the alignment right. Once the downpipe flange is aligned with the three studs, push it over the studs as your assistant lifts the rear end of the system to its normal height. When the studs pass through the flange, immediately get at least one nut screwed on part-way, then, moving to the rear of the car, attach the rear exhaust box to its hangers so that the system is supported front and rear. Reattach the exhaust system to all of its rubber hangers: you'll find that lubricating the support

Mazda Miata, MX-5, Eunos & Roadster

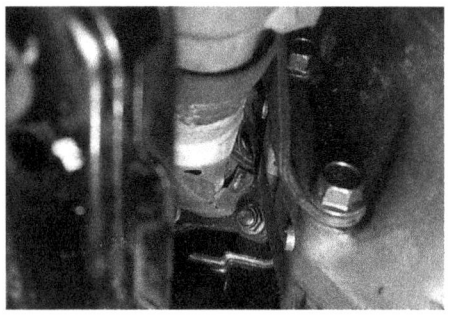

11/57 Access to manifold flange limited.

pins with silicone spray (e.g. WD40) will help.

57   Fit any remaining nuts to the manifold flange (you may have to feed them on with a socket). Next - and this sounds much easier than it actually is - using a combination of socket, extensions and a universal joint, tighten the three exhaust manifold 14mm flange nuts to 38-51Nm/3.8-5.3kgf m/28-38lbf ft.

58   Reinstall the 12mm bolt which secures the downpipe support clamp to the bellhousing bracket and tighten to 19-25Nm/1.9-2.6kgf m/14-18lbf ft. The bolt is best accessed through the space

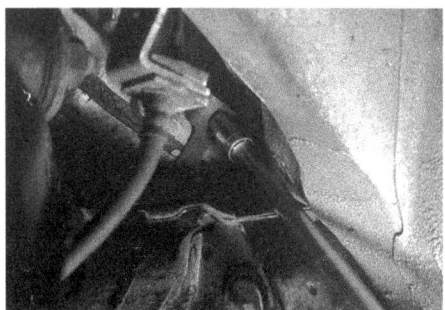

11/58 Fix downpipe clamp to support bracket.

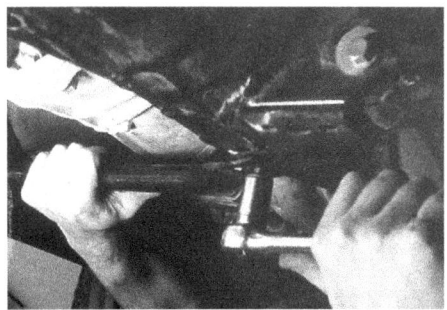

11/59 Install front 'performance rod.'

11/60 Install rear 'performance rod.'

between the subframe and the left-hand inner fender (wing).

59   If applicable, reattach the front subframe cross brace ('performance bar') and secure with its two 17mm bolts, tightened to 63-93Nm/6.4-9.5kgf m/47-68lbf ft. Note the two dots which help ensure the bar is reinstalled exactly as it originally was.

60   On top of the rear right-hand side of the rear brace bar ('performance bar') assembly there is a hook, so start by hooking this over the suspension subframe in the vicinity of the bolt hole. The latter makes fitting the frame easier because one corner is held, which means you can move to the other side of the frame and screw in a couple of the 17mm securing bolts. Altogether the frame is held by six bolts, all of which should be fitted and tightened to 55-80Nm/5.6-8.2kgf m/41-59lbf ft.

61   Fit a new sealing washer and apply a copper-based, heat-resistant grease to the threads of the heated oxygen sensor, then pass it and its 'pigtail' wire down behind the dipstick tube and the EGR tube. Give the sensor several twists anti-clockwise (twisting the wire as you do so to compensate for the wire twists that will occur as it's screwed into the exhaust downpipe). Thread the sensor into the exhaust downpipe and tighten to 30-49Nm/3-5kgf m/22-36lbf ft using a 22mm open-sided socket designed for the purpose. For those using a crescent wrench (open-ended spanner) instead of a socket, for further information on how to tighten fasteners by feel ☞ 1/2/52-55. (If your car is a later model fitted with a second heated oxygen sensor in the exhaust system behind the catalytic convertor, now would be a good time to refit it using the same procedure.)

62   Fit the wiring from the heated oxygen sensor into the clip on the backplate periphery, just behind the dipstick tube.

63   Connect the black connector to the terminal on the water temperature gauge sender mounted in the heater outlet housing at the rear of the cylinder head.

64   Take the black connector block (heated oxygen sensor) and press its retaining pin into the bracket just above the camshaft position sensor.

65   Next, take the two grey connector blocks (which you previously marked), and connect them to the two coils.

66   The green connector has to be connected to the engine coolant temperature sensor in the heater outlet housing at the back of the cylinder head: this is extremely fiddly.

67   Fix the grey connector with a bracket to the right-hand engine lifting eye mounting using the eye's 14mm bolt.

68   Connect the four grey connectors to the individual fuel injectors, ensuring they lock home securely.

69   Fit the small ground (earth) wire to the bracket at the rear of the intake manifold.

70   Plug the PCV pipe's non-return valve into the grommet in the the right-hand side of the cam cover.

71   Reconnect the small bore hose from the pressure regulator on the fuel rail to the pressure

11/67 Fix harness connector to lifting eye.

11/69 Attach ground wire to manifold.

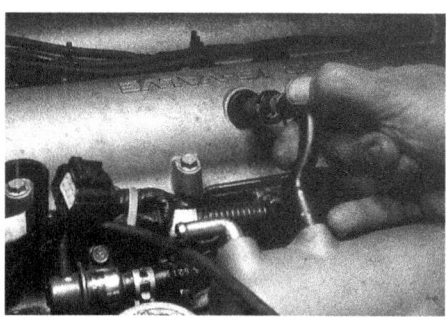

11/70 Plug PCV valve into grommet.

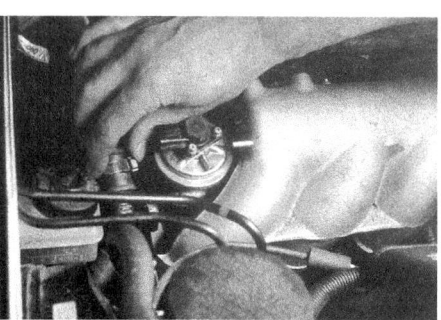

11/73 Fix wiring harness to bracket.

regulator control solenoid towards the front of the intake manifold.

72   If it is tied to one side, release the main wiring harness for the right-hand side of the engine.

73   First, fix the harness to the bracket at the rear of the intake manifold using the plastic tie.

74   Join the female black connector to the fuel injector harness connector of the same colour. Make sure it clicks home securely.

75   Fit the black connector to the EGR valve at the rear of the manifold, ensuring that it clicks home securely.

3: Engine & clutch

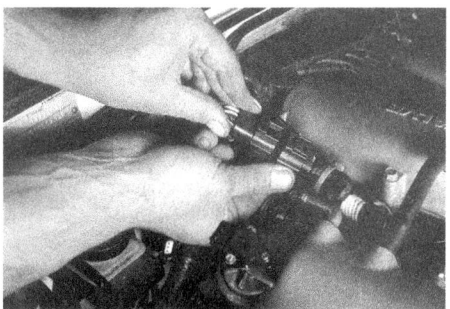

11/74 Remake fuel injector harness connection.

11/78 Fit connector to camshaft position sensor.

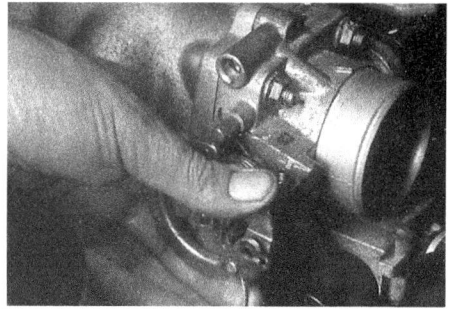

11/81 Twist throttle quadrant, fit nipple and cable.

11/75 Fit connector to EGR valve.

11/79 Make fuel line connections and clamp securely.

quadrant to release cable tension, push the throttle cable stop/adjuster back into the slot in the manifold bracket and, if necessary, tighten the nut at the back of the bracket.

82   Refit the vacuum hose from the servo unit to the stub on the manifold and secure with its spring clamp.

83   Refit the small bore hose from the purge valve to the stub at the front of the manifold.

84   Release the secondary harness for the right-hand side of the engine from its temporary ties.

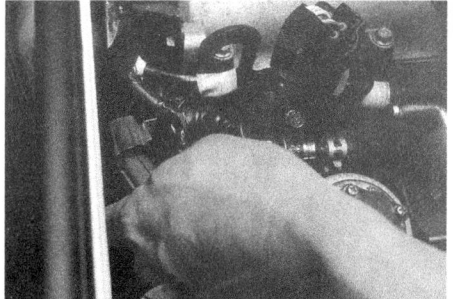

11/76 Connector at right of coil bracket.

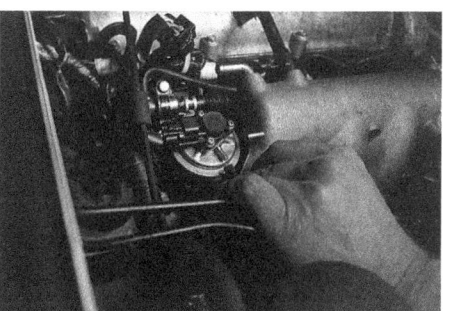

11/80a Connect hose to EGR valve.

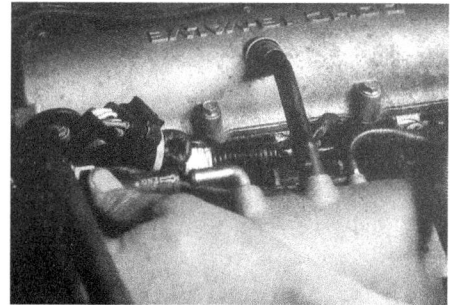

11/82 Connect servo hose to manifold stub.

11/77 Remake oxygen sensor connection.

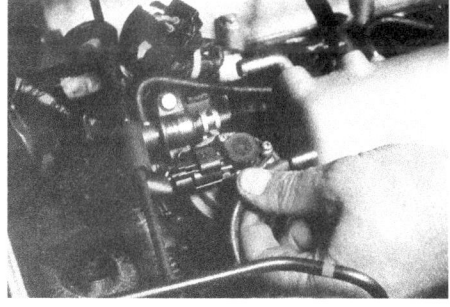

11/80b Fit EGR solenoid hose to manifold stub.

11/83 Connect purge valve hose to manifold stub.

76   Fit the grey connector to the connector block on the right-hand side of the coil bracket.

77   Fit the black (oxygen sensor) connector to the male connector mounted on a bracket at the camshaft position sensor.

78   Fit the grey connector to the camshaft position sensor.

79   Refit the two flexible fuel lines protruding from beneath the inlet manifold to the rigid pipes on the right-hand inner fender. Note that the flexible hose nearest the front of the engine attaches to the rearmost rigid pipe. Make sure you

work the flexible pipes right down to the second collar on the rigid pipes, and then retain with spring clamps.

80   Reconnect the small bore flexible hose with red dashes to the EGR valve at the rear of the manifold, and the flexible hose with blue dashes to the stub at the rear of the intake manifold plenum chamber.

81   Twist the throttle quadrant clockwise and insert the nipple of the throttle cable into the nipple slot, then feed the cable around the circumference of the quadrant. While twisting the

11/85 Fit bracket and ground eye over stud.

Mazda Miata, MX-5, Eunos & Roadster

85   📷 Fit the wiring harness support bracket and ground (earth) strap eye over the stud on the bracket at front right of the engine and secure with its 10mm nut.

86   📷 Fit the green connector block to the black idle air control valve solenoid on the underside of the throttle body.

87   📷 Fit the black connector to the throttle position sensor unit on the inside of the throttle body.

88   📷 Fit the black connector to the fuel pressure regulator control solenoid in the valley of the intake manifold; it should click home securely.

11/86 Fit connector to IAC valve solenoid.

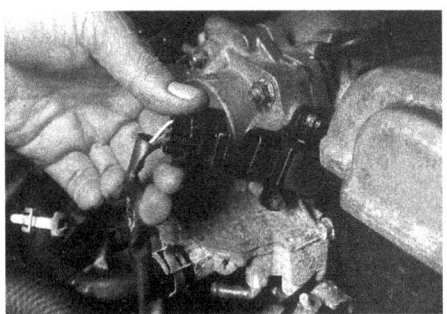
11/87 Fit connector to TPS unit.

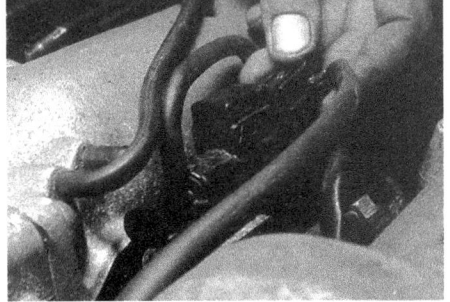
11/88 Connect fuel pressure control solenoid.

11/89 Fit connector to sensor on p/s pump.

If your car is fitted with a crankshaft position sensor, remake its wiring harness connection.

89   📷 If applicable, fit the connector to the sensor in the top of the power steering pump: make sure it's wiring is secured in the bracket at top left of the timing cover.

90   Refit the heatshield over the exhaust manifold and secure with seven 10mm bolts and three 10mm nuts tightened to 7.9-10.7Nm/80-110kgf cm/70-95Ibf in.

91   If not already done, refit the radiator bottom hose to the radiator stub and the stub of the rigid pipe secured to the left-hand inner fender (wing). Secure with hose clamps.

92   📷 Refit the lower air filter housing, noting that the projecting boss on its underside needs to engage with the bracket on the left-hand chassis rail, while simultaneously the stud just at the front of the front suspension turret needs to be engaged, too.

93   Secure the lower air filter box with two 12mm bolts and one 12mm nut (note that, where fitted, the headlamp dimmer heat sink also utilises the stud in front of the suspension turret: the other end of the dimmer unit is secured by a 10mm bolt).

94   📷 Fit a new air filter element.

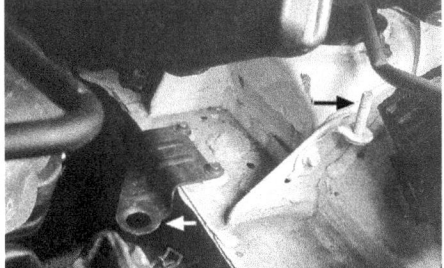
11/92 Air filter body locating bracket and stud.

11/94 Install air filter element.

95   Refit the air filter cover and secure with four 10mm bolts.

96   Fit the air intake to the air filter; it's secured by a clamp with a 10mm bolt at the air filter end and a 10mm bolt at the inner wing end.

97   Connect the two small bore water hoses to their stubs beneath the throttle body/BACs valve. Secure with hose clamps.

98   📷 Refit the rigid air tube which connects the air filter to the throttle body. It's secured by clamps with 8mm bolts at both ends. Connect the bypass hose from beneath the throttle body to the stub on the rigid air tube and secure with its spring clamp. Reconnect the small bore air hose from the cambox cover to the stub on the rigid air intake.

99   📷 On the left-hand side of the engine compartment, reconnect the black connector to the MAF sensor of the air filter unit.

100   📷 Manual transmission cars. Place a dab of molybdenum disulfide or copper-based grease on the ball end of the clutch release (slave) cylinder pushrod. Engage the pushrod in the clutch actuating arm of the bellhousing, and then secure the clutch release cylinder to the bellhousing with two 10mm

11/95 Install air filter cover and MAF unit.

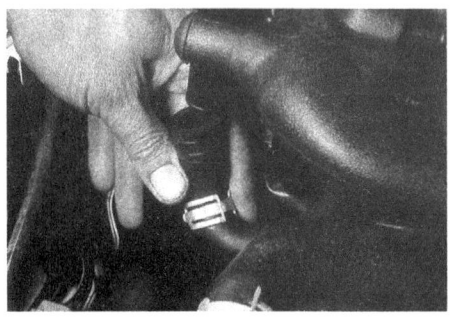
11/98 Don't forget bypass hose.

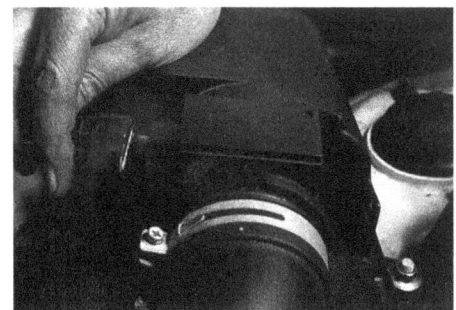
11/99 Fit connector to MAF sensor.

11/100 Release cylinder and pipe bracket fixings.

3:52

3: Engine & clutch

bolts. Tighten the bolts to 16-22Nm/1.6-2.3kgf m/12-16lbf ft. Above the release cylinder is a bracket which holds a coil of rigid hydraulic pipe. This bracket should be secured with its 10mm bolt tightened to 16-22Nm/1.6-2.3kgf m/12-16lbf ft. You can get access to the pipe bracket bolt and the upper release cylinder bolt via the space between the suspension subframe and the inner fender, but will need to tighten the lower slave cylinder bolt with a box end wrench (ring spanner) from beneath the engine (or you could use a universal joint on a socket with extensions).

101   From beneath the car, fit the two 12mm bolts through the bellhousing and into the starter motor flange. Note that the innermost of these two bolts also carries a support bracket for the clutch release cylinder's hydraulic pipe connection (manual trans. cars), whilst the other carries a wiring harness bracket. Manipulating these bolts into position is difficult - but not impossible! Both can be tightened to 38-51Nm/3.8-5.3kgf m/28-38lbf ft with a 12mm socket in conjunction with a universal joint and extensions.

102   Refit the inlet manifold support strut by maneuvering it into position from beneath and then inserting the top two 14mm screws and

11/103 Engine mount from beneath car.

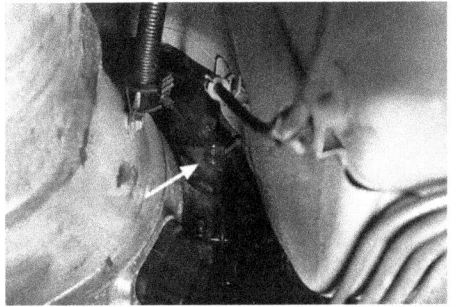
11/101 One of the bolts carries a bracket.

11/102 Manifold support strut top bolt fixings.

tightening them finger-tight, followed by insertion of the lower 14mm bolt. The lower bolt can be tightened with a 14mm socket and universal joint and extension bar, whilst the top two simply require a socket and extension bar. Tighten the bolts to 38-51Nm/3.8-5.3kgf m/28-38lbf ft.

103   From beneath the car, fit washers and nuts to the engine mounting studs and tighten the 14mm nuts to a torque of 57-78Nm/5.8-8kgf m/42-57lbf ft.

104   Fit a new sealing ring to the 19mm oil pan (sump) drain plug and tighten the plug to 30-

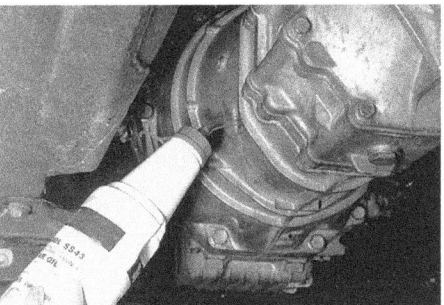
11/105 Fill with oil until level with filler hole.

41Nm/3-4.2kgf m/22-30lbf ft.

105   Manual transmission. Fit a new sealing ring to the 24mm transmission (gearbox) drain plug and tighten the plug to 40-58Nm/4-6kgf m/29-43lbf ft. Using a 16mm socket, remove the filler plug (halfway up the left-hand side of the transmission case) and add 2 litres/2.1US quarts/1.8Imp quarts of the approved gear oil. Assuming the car is level, allow any excess oil to drain out of the filler hole before refitting the filler plug. Note that a thin smear of silicone sealant or a wrapping of plumber's thread tape should be applied to the plug threads before it is refitted and tightened.

106   Auto transmission. For the moment, if applicable, check that the oil pan retaining bolts have been retightened.

107   Check that the radiator drain plug is tight.

108   **Caution!** Using a torch or inspection light, double-check that all of the electrical and hose connections visible from beneath the car have been made and are secure. Check that all nuts and bolts have been correctly fitted and tightened. Ensure all loose wiring and hoses are properly secured to prevent contact with moving or hot components.

109   Engage the centre rear of the engine undertray with the tongue which projects forward from the suspension subframe. Replace the 10mm bolts retaining the undertray in the wheelarches where there are three fixings on each side. You'll also have to replace the 10mm nut that holds the stay (or stays) to the lower part of the front fender/wing (or fenders/wings). Note that on some right-hand drive cars the windscreen washer reservoir is mounted forward of the left-hand wheelarch, in which case one of the undertray fixings will be a deeply recessed 10mm nut near the reservoir body. Replace the two 10mm bolts at the rear of the undertray and three at the front.

110   Replace the front wheels.

111   Installing the hood/bonnet stay. The gold colored end of the stay with the longer leg fits in the hinge clip. The clip is located high on the left chassis rail, just behind the headlight assembly. Make sure the nylon clip is open and pass the leg of the stay through the circular section of the clip and metal bracket, then close the latch over the vertical section of the stay. Lay the stay across the front of the engine compartment and fix the free end into its clip.

112   With the help of an assistant carefully position the hood so that its rear corners are

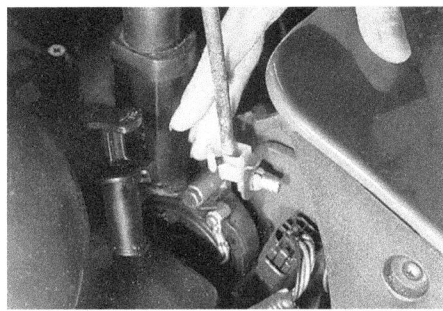
11/111 Install the hood (bonnet) stay.

wedged into the gap on each side of the car between the windshield lower rail and the fender/wing: rest the rear corners on rag or cardboard to protect the paintwork. Quickly lift the hinges and push them over the protruding studs on the underside of the hood, and then tighten the two 14 mm nuts on each side finger-tight. Prop the hood open with its stay. If there are positional marks on the hinges, manipulate the hood/hinge relationship until the marks re-align and then tighten the 14mm nuts to 22Nm/2.2kgf m/17lbf ft. Repeat the process with the second hinge. If the hinges do not have positional marks, you'll have to slide the hood backwards and forwards in the hinges until you are able to close the hood and obtain even gaps all the way around; then tighten the retaining nuts.

113   Reconnect the windshield washer pipe to the pipework union stub on the underside of the bonnet.

114   If the engine is completely 'dry' (has been rebuilt), add 4 liters/4.2US quarts/3.5Imp quarts of fresh engine oil. If the engine has simply been drained of oil and fitted with a new filter, it will require 3.8 liters/4US quarts/3.3Imp quarts, and if it has been drained but has not had a new filter fitted, it will require 3.6 litres/3.8US quarts/3.2Imp

3:53

Mazda Miata, MX-5, Eunos & Roadster

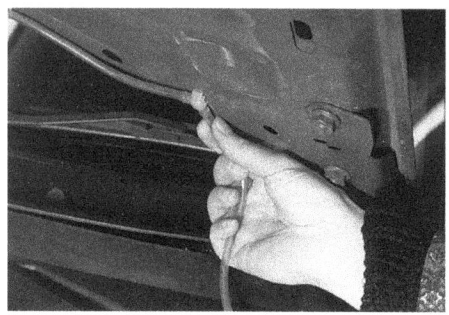

11/113 Reconnect windshield washer pipe.

quarts of fresh oil. The oil should be poured slowly into the oil filler on top of the cambox. Do not overfill. If the engine is not dry, check oil level and top-up accordingly.

115 Automatic transmission cars. If appropriate, refill the transmission unit with ATF☞ 2. If the ATF level just requires checking and topping-up, wait until after a short test run☞ 2.

116 Double-check that all water hoses have been reconnected and properly clamped, then refill the cooling system with coolant☞ 6. **Caution!** Don't forget to replace and tighten radiator and reservoir caps.

117 **Caution!** Check all around the engine for hose and electrical connections which have not been remade. Remember that accessories like cruise control devices and aftermarket security devices could have electrical connections and hose connections which have not been mentioned in the foregoing text. Check that all nuts and bolts have been correctly installed and tightened. Ensure all loose wiring and hoses are properly secured to prevent contact with moving or hot components.

118 If applicable, fit and tighten the fuel filler cap.

119 Manual transmission cars (auto transmission skip to☞ 3/11/129). From inside the car, carefully pour 80-95cc/4.9-5.8cu in of the specified transmission oil into the open shiftlever turret of the transmission. Spread a little of the same lubricant over the shiftlever ball and the nylon cap at the end of the lever.

120 Apply a thin smear of gasket sealant to both sides of a new gasket, then lay the gasket on top of the shiftlever turret.

121 📷 Holding it approximately in neutral position, carefully lower the gearshift lever assembly into position, making sure the cutout in the seating ball engages with the peg in the seat. You may need

11/121 Lower shift lever into turret.

to move the lever around just a little to make sure it engages with the shift rods in the transmission, at which point its flange will contact the top of the transmission turret.

122 📷 Refit and tighten the three 10mm bolts which secure the shiftlever to the transmission turret.

123 📷 If it was completely removed, refit the rubber boot (gaiter) over the shiftlever. Push the boot baseplate down against the transmission tunnel and, if applicable, position the bracket over the two rearmost boltholes. Replace and tighten the four 10mm bolts which secure the shiftlever boot base to the transmission tunnel.

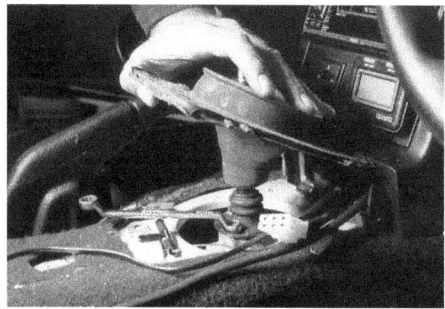

11/122 Tighten shift lever securing bolts.

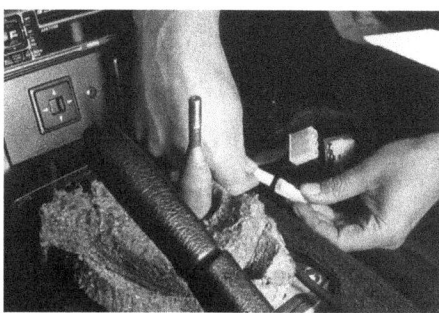

11/123 Tighten boot baseplate securing bolts.

11/124 Don't forget shaped soundproofing wads.

124 📷 Refit the two shaped wads of soundproofing material to the shiftlever base.

125 Reconnect the two white connector blocks of the console (ashtray light and the power windows, if applicable). Both connectors have locking tabs which will click home.

126 Engage the cutouts in the rear of the between-seats console over the trunk (boot) and fuel filler release levers and fit the console in place on the transmission tunnel. Make sure no wiring is protuding from beneath the edges of the console.

127 Replace and tighten the crosshead (Philips) screws which secure the console: there are two in the storage compartment; one in the space beneath the ashtray and one each side at the front end.

128 Screw the shiftlever knob onto the shiftlever, making sure the shift pattern embossed in the top is correctly orientated. Refit the ashtray.

129 Ensure the ignition is switched to off. From inside the trunk, reconnect the ground (earth) cable to the battery's negative (-) terminal and tighten the clamp nut with a 10mm socket on an extension to restore the car's electrical power. **Warning!** The extension bar will cross the battery's positive (+) terminal to reach the negative terminal clamp, so make absolutely sure the positive terminal is fully insulated otherwise a dangerous dead short can occur. Note: it's possible that if your car is fitted with an audible security alarm system, it will sound off as the battery is reconnected - check the system manufacturer's instructions.

130 Repressurise the fuel system ☞ 5/13.

131 If you want to check that everything works before the car is lowered to the ground and easy access is lost, now's the time to do it ☞ 3/11/133. Note: because the car is rigidly supported on a hard surface, it has lost the sound and vibration deadening properties of rubber mounts, suspension and tires; in other words it will sound terrible because every small mechanical knock and whir is magnified: you've been warned!

132 Carefully lower the car to the ground ☞ 1/3.

133 Start up time! **Warning!** If you haven't done so, check the following - drain and filler plugs tight; engine and transmission oil levels; brake and, if applicable, clutch master cylinder fluid levels; coolant level, hose connections, radiator and reservoir caps tight; fuel level; fuel filler cap tight and fuel pipe connections good; sparkplugs fitted; all wiring reconnected; drivebelts correctly tensioned.

134 Ensure that the gearshift lever is in the neutral position; 'N' or 'P' for cars with automatic transmission. Have a car or garage-type fire extinguisher handy.

135 Start the engine in the usual way. It may not fire as quickly as usual, but should start within 15 seconds of continuous cranking. When the engine first starts after a rebuild, there will be a considerable amount of mechanical noise until oil under pressure circulates fully. It's also quite normal for new gaskets, sealant and the paint on new components to create burning smells. **Caution!** If no oil pressure is registered within 15 seconds of start-up, stop the engine, investigate and rectify the problem; likewise if oil, water or fuel leaks become evident. **Caution!** Do not rev the engine but allow it to idle until normal operating temperature is registered on the temperature gauge.

136 If the starter does not operate, check its wiring and terminals carefully. If it still doesn't work ☞ 7.

137 If the starter operates but the engine fails to start, and there is no obvious reason (like an empty gas tank), run through all of the steps detailed in the engine installation procedure to double-check that all work has been completed. If, before the engine

3: Engine & clutch

was removed, you temporarily disconnected the fuel circuit opening relay, check that you really did reconnect it properly! Should the engine still fail to start, check ignition timing and, if that doesn't solve the problem, valve timing (via camshaft drivebelt) by referring to the appropriate parts of this book.

138   In the trunk, check that breather pipes are properly connected to the battery, that terminal insulators are in place and that the battery is correctly clamped. Install the battery cover moulding and secure by pushing the retaining nuts (or nut) over the stud or studs and then clipping the cover to the row of stud fasteners on the trunk floor. Install the spare wheel and secure with its collar and wing-nutted bolt.

139   Reset the clock!

140   Road test the car to ensure performance is normal and, for the first week or so, check fluid levels often.

141   **Caution!** If the engine has been rebuilt, don't use the car's full performance right away, instead gradually increase your use of potential performance over 3-5000km/2-3000 miles. Avoid laboring the engine, sustained high revs and constant speed running. After 1000km/600 miles, replace the engine oil and oil filter, re-torque the exhaust and intake manifold retaining bolts/nuts after slackening them half a turn first.

142   Note: in some markets the car will be fitted with a security coded radio. If your car has such a radio, after battery disconnection you'll need to re-enter your personal security number before the radio will work. Consult the radio manufacturer's handbook.

12. ENGINE - INSTALLATION (WITHOUT TRANSMISSION)

☞ First read 1/1, 2.

Throughout this section you'll find that the colors of electrical connectors, hose markings, etc., are mentioned in an effort to make component identification as easy as possible. However, you should bear in mind it's possible that the colors of these components and markings may vary.

PREPARATION

1   You'll need an assistant to help you install the engine, as well as a small mobile engine crane of the type that can be hired from the tool and plant hire companies you find in every medium-sized town. **Warning!** Sorry, we weren't able to weigh it, but we believe the engine weighs around 136kg/300lb so the rope and crane you use should be capable of lifting twice this weight as a safety margin. Also, the lifting hook of the crane's boom should be capable of reaching a height of around 1830mm (6ft) above the ground.

2   Tie several strands of very strong nylon rope tightly between the two lifting eyes positioned on each side of the cylinder head; one toward the front of the engine and one toward the back. It's important to keep the rope as tight as possible; you'll be surprised how much the rope will stretch once the crane takes the strain.

3   **Caution!** Check that the engine bay is clear and that all pipes, wires and cables are tied back out of the way so that the engine will not become entangled as it is moved into position within the engine compartment. This particularly applies to the clutch flexible hydraulic pipe on right-hand drive cars which runs across the top of the bellhousing and shares a clip with the main wiring harness. Tie this bracket high up on the right of the compartment.

4   As with engine removal, the car will need to be safely supported high enough above the ground to give good, safe access to the underside, and you'll find it much easier if the raised car is level ☞ 1/3.

ENGINE INSTALLATION

5   Place a jack beneath the transmission bellhousing and lift the transmission as high as possible without it, or the components above it, coming into contact with the floorpan.

6   Manual transmission cars only. Rub a thin smear of copper-based lubricant on the nose and splines of the transmission input shaft - don't overdo it!

7   Auto transmission cars only. Make sure the torque converter is fully engaged with the oil pump behind it. Place a straightedge across the face of the bellhousing and measure the depth to the rim of the torque convertor (see diagram), which should be 22.5mm/0.89in. If the depth is not correct, press the convertor inward while rotating it slowly until you feel it move and engage with the pump with a 'clunk.' Check the measurement again. **Caution!** Once correctly engaged with the pump, make sure the torque convertor does not subsequently slide forward.

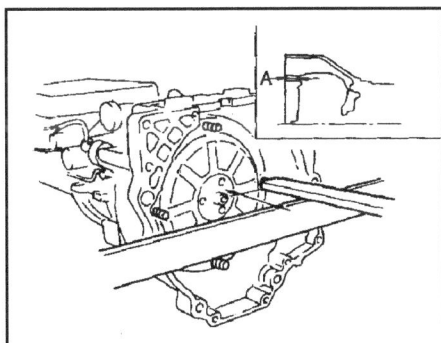

D12/7 CORRECT DEPTH (SEE TEXT) INDICATES TORQUE CONVERTOR PROPERLY ENGAGED.

8   Spread old towels over the nose of the car and the fender (wing) tops: this will help to protect the paintwork from damage.

9   Engage the crane's hook with the rope sling and lift the engine far enough from the ground to clear the front edge of the engine compartment opening. Line the crane and engine up in front of the car on the car's centreline. With an assistant holding the engine to stop it swaying, gently roll the crane forward until the unit is approximately over the center of the engine compartment. Gently lower the engine until it is approximately level with the transmission, then tilt the engine just a little so that its longitudinal axis is roughly the same as the transmission's. Move the engine toward the transmission, adjusting its height simultaneously, until the transmission input shaft is about to enter the clutch cover (manual transmission cars). Adjust the vertical and lateral position of the engine so that the input shaft is centered on the clutch (manual transmission cars).

10   **Caution!** Once the rear of the cylinder head gets close to the firewall/bulkhead, put an old towel or similar between the two as a cushion and, if the coil unit and camshaft angle sensor units are fitted, take great care not to bang them against the firewall.

11   Manual transmission cars. Bring the engine and transmission unit together, making sure that the transmission input shaft enters the center of the clutch, and that the bellhousing is correctly lined up with the engine backplate. If the clutch disc has been well centered, the transmission bellhousing should go fully home against the engine backplate with no more than a little joggling around. Life will be more difficult if the clutch disc has not been well centered, and, in extreme cases, you'll have to withdraw the engine, slacken the clutch cover and re-center the disc before attempting again to make the connection. As the engine backplate goes fully home against the transmission bellhousing, make sure that the hollow spigots projecting from the rear of the cylinder block engage with their locating holes in the bellhousing.

12   Automatic transmission cars. Bring the engine and transmission unit together, making sure that the transmission is correctly lined up with the engine backplate. As the engine backplate goes fully home against the transmission bellhousing, ensure that the hollow spigots projecting from the rear of the cylinder block engage with their locating holes in the bellhousing.

13   From beneath the car quickly fit the two lowermost 17mm (x60mm) bellhousing bolts. Screw the bolts in just enough to prevent any movement between the engine backplate and transmission bellhousing.

14   Lower and remove the jack that was supporting the bellhousing.

15   The threaded studs of both engine mountings should now be directly above their fixing hole and slot in the subframe. Lower the engine gently until you can maneuver the left-hand mounting stud through its hole, after which the stud of the right-hand mounting can be fed through its slot in the subframe. Note: you may find it necessary, as we did, to remove the left-hand engine mounting bracket from the engine and fasten the mounting to the subframe independently of the engine. This allowed us to maneuver the engine sufficiently to engage the stud of the right-hand mounting in its slot, at which point the retaining nut and washer were immediately fitted. Then, the engine was twisted and lowered until the mounting bracket on the left-hand side aligned once more with the bolt holes in the side of the engine. The three bolts were fitted and tightened to a torque of 37-53Nm/3.7-5.5kgf m/27-39lbf ft.

3:55

Mazda Miata, MX-5, Eunos & Roadster

16 Once the engine is sitting safely on its mountings, the crane can be released and withdrawn.

17 Fit the two topmost bellhousing bolts which are 17mm (x60mm) and screw them into place finger-tight. Note: you'll need 14mm and 17mm sockets, universal joint and extensions of around 450mm (18in) to reach some of the bellhousing fasteners.

18 Position the exhaust pipe support bracket over the two bolt holes on the left-hand side of the bellhousing. Secure the bracket, with flange facing rearward, with two 17mm bolts, the upper of which is longer (70mm), although there seems no good reason for this. Screw the bolts home finger-tight. Fit the 17mm nut and bolt which secure the clutch slave cylinder pipe bracket (if fitted) on the right-hand side. Note: the remaining fasteners in the starter motor area will be fitted later.

19 Automatic transmission cars. Fit and finger-tighten the 17mm (x 60mm) bolt at lower right of the bellhousing.

20 Tighten the bellhousing's 17mm fasteners to 64-89Nm/6.5-9.1kgf m/48-65lbf ft. Note: access to these fasteners is not easy so you'll need an appropriate socket attached to a universal joint, which is, in turn, attached to extensions of around 350mm (14in) and then a ratchet handle. A couple of these bolts also have nuts and the nut or bolt head on the engine side which can be locked with a wrench/spanner via the opening in the inner wheelwell.

21 From within the engine compartment release the wires, brackets, etc., for the bellhousing area which were tied out of harm's way.

22 Automatic transmission cars. Using the access opening in the bottom of the bellhousing, screw the bolts which secure the driveplate to the lugs in the torque convertor into place, rotating the torque convertor as necessary to get the correct alignments. Lock the driveplate with a screwdriver and then, in a diagonal sequence, tighten the four bolts to 35-49Nm/3.5-5kgf m/26-36lbf ft. Install the access opening cover and secure with two bolts.

23 ☞ 3/11/19-51, 56-59, 61-104, 107-118, 129-141.

13. CAMSHAFT DRIVEBELT (TIMING BELT) - REPLACEMENT (ENGINE IN CAR)

☞ First read 1/1, 2.

1 It's best if the car's on level ground. Apply the parking brake and, if the ground is not level, use wheel chocks, too.

2 Isolate the electrical system by disconnecting the battery negative (-) terminal after first having disarmed the audio unit's security system. **Warning!** When loosening the negative (-) terminal, take great care not to short the tool you are using across the positive (+) terminal (for more information ☞ 7).

3 Open the hood (bonnet) and support with its stay. Protect the paintwork around the engine compartment with thick cloth - old towels are ideal.

4 Drain the engine coolant from the radiator ☞ 6. Collect the coolant in a clean container as, if in good condition, it can be re-used. Note that if you don't intend to remove the radiator, it's only necessary to drain sufficient coolant to bring the level below the thermostat housing.

5 Release their clamps and detach all hose connections to the thermostat housing.

6 Remove the radiator complete with fan or fans ☞ 6 (not absolutely necessary, but will give the best access to the front of the engine).

7 Remove the power steering pump/air conditioning compressor (if fitted) drivebelt followed by the alternator drivebelt ☞ 2. If the drivebelts are in good condition they can be re-used.

8 Using a 10mm socket, and gripping the pulley with the drivebelt as shown in the photograph, slacken and remove the three bolts securing the water pump pulley to the pump spindle boss.

9 Unscrew the four 10mm bolts that secure the crankshaft pulley to the crankshaft nose. Rock the pulley gently side-to-side to work it off the boss on the crankshaft nose.

10 Unscrew the 21mm crankshaft pulley bolt. Manual transmission cars can be put in first gear and have their roadwheels chocked to 'lock' the crankshaft. The bolt will have to be jarred loose on auto transmission cars. Once the bolt is removed, the camshaft belt guide plate can be pulled forward over the square key in the crankshaft nose.

11 Pull each of the sparkplug wire (HT lead) connectors from its sparkplug bore using your fingers only: start at the front of the engine and work backwards. As each sparkplug connector is released, free its cable from the clips in the valley of the cambox. Leave all four connectors lying on top of the cambox for the moment.

12 Disconnect the two wiring harness connectors at the rear of the coil unit. Part of the wiring harness is held by a metal support at the base of the coil bracket; you can bend this open with your fingers to release the wiring.

13 The coil bracket is secured to the cylinder head by three 12mm bolts; one each side at the top of the bracket and one in the middle at the base of the bracket. The upper bolts are visible, but you'll have to feel your way (perhaps with the aid of a mirror) to the lower bolt. Once the bolts are removed, the coil unit can be lifted away complete with sparkplug wires.

14 Remove the four sparkplugs using a sparkplug socket with a cushioned interior to prevent insulator damage.

15 Pull the PCV valve from the right-hand side of the cambox cover.

16 Unscrew and remove the thirteen 10mm chrome dome-headed bolts which hold the cambox cover to the cylinder head. Unscrew the bolts progressively in a diagonal sequence until they are all loose enough to unscrew with your fingers. Note: a short (75mm/3 inch) extension is also needed. There are four cambox cover bolts down each side of the cambox; three in the center valley and two at the front. Note that the two front bolts, which also secure the vent hose clips, are shorter than the others. Once the bolts have been removed the cambox cover can be lifted clear of the cylinder head.

17 Undo and remove the four 10mm bolts securing the upper section of the timing cover. Pull the cover forward slightly at the top, and then lift away from the lower section.

18 There are four 10mm bolts retaining the middle and lower drivebelt covers. One of these is adjacent to the water pump center boss and is longer than the other three. Once the bolts retaining the drivebelt covers have been removed, the covers can be withdrawn, the lower one having to be maneuvered around the power steering pump bracket if that is still in place.

19 **Caution!** Mazda has provided various markings to assist in making sure that the two camshafts and crankshaft are correctly positioned relative to each other when fitting a camshaft drivebelt, and thus, critical valve timing is preserved. Frankly, we found the manufacturer's markings hard to use and open to error. Therefore, while we do describe use of the manufacturer's markings, we strongly recommend you use the following backup procedure before removing the existing camshaft drivebelt.

20 Temporarily replace the crankshaft nose bolt, then, using a 21mm socket on the bolt, rotate the crankshaft clockwise (viewed from the front) until the cutout in the rear flange of the crankshaft drivebelt pulley is vertical and aligns with the arrow-shaped boss in the oil pump body. Simultaneously, the letter "E" on the exhaust (left-hand) cam pulley and the letter "I" on the intake cam pulley should both be more-or-less vertical. Note: this coincidence of relative positions will occur only once in every two revolutions of the crankshaft because the cams turn at half crankshaft speed.

21 When all is correctly positioned, use a straightedge running from the center of the crankshaft pulley and across the center of each camshaft pulley in turn, to make alignment marks with a scriber or indelible pen at the two points where the straightedge crosses the rim of each camshaft pulley - don't allow the pulleys to move at all until all alignment marks have been made. Identify the exhaust cam pulley with the letter "E" written in indelible ink.

22 If the camshaft drivebelt is to be re-used - a false economy unless the belt has been in place for less than 50,000km/30,000 miles and is completely damage-free - mark the outward edge of the belt with a white dot (typist's correction fluid is good for this) so that the belt can be reinstalled to run in the same direction.

23 Slacken the central locking bolt on the tensioner jockey wheel and pull the wheel backwards as far as possible to relieve the tension on the drivebelt. While holding the wheel back, retighten the central screw. The drivebelt will now be loose

24 **Caution!** Avoid rotating the crankshaft whilst the drivebelt is loose or removed. If you must turn the crankshaft, do it very slowly and carefully, stopping at the least sign of contact between valve heads and pistons - which could result in bent valve stems. In fact, our engine showed no signs of such

3: Engine & clutch

contact when we checked by turning the crank with the cams in various different positions, but it's possible tolerances will vary from engine to engine, particularly if high-performance camshafts are fitted.

25   The camshaft drivebelt can now be slid off the three pulleys.

26   ☞ 3/8/59-62. **Caution!** These checks are important: don't be tempted to skip them.

27   **Caution!** If the new (where applicable) camshaft drivebelt is marked with a direction arrow, it's important to make sure it's fitted correctly. When looking at the front of the engine, the camshaft drivebelt runs in a clockwise direction.

28   ☞ 3/9/89-108. You can skip the bit about dousing the camshafts with oil, unless they have been removed or have had the lubricant wiped from them.

29   Reconnect the small hose between the intake manifold and the cambox PCV valve.

30   Fit the coil unit and tighten its three 12mm retaining bolts to a torque of 19-25Nm/1.9-2.6kgf m/14-18lbf ft.

31   Remake the wiring harness connections at the back of the coil unit, making sure the connectors are fully home. Secure the wiring harness in the clip behind the coil unit.

32   Refit the sparkplugs, then, using fingers only, reconnect the wire connectors to the sparkplugs, starting with the plug nearest the coil and working forwards. Push the wires into their clips in the cambox valley.

33   Fit and tension the alternator drivebelt and, if fitted, power steering pump/air-conditioning compressor drivebel t☞ 2.

34   Install the radiator complete with fan or fans ☞ 6.

35   Refit the two small hoses and the radiator top hose to the thermostat housing and secure with clamps. Note: a little silicone-based lubricant sprayed onto the radiator and thermostat housing stubs will make fitting the hoses easier.

36   Refill the radiator/reservoir with coolant ☞ 6. Check for leaks.

37   Remake the battery connection. **Warning!** When tightening the negative (-) terminal, take great care not to short the tool you are using across the positive (+) terminal (for more information ☞ 7).

38   Start the engine and allow it to warm up to normal operating temperature at idle speed, checking for leaks as it does so.

14. CAMS & FOLLOWERS - REMOVAL & INSTALLATION (ENGINE IN CAR)

☞ First read 1/1, 2.

1   ☞ 3/13/1-25. This will take you to the point where the camshaft drivebelt has been removed.

2   There is a hex-shaped section on each of the two camshafts between bearings two and three (counting from the front of the engine). Use a 24mm crescent wrench to hold each cam in a locked position (**Caution!** Do not wedge the wrench against the side of the cambox - it's a fragile casting

14/3 Mark pulley and spigot.

which could easily be broken) while the 14mm bolt retaining each drive pulley is slackened and removed, together with the large washer (don't remove the pulleys yet).

3   ⚠ Note that each drive pulley is located on a spigot which can engage with any of three slots. To ensure correct orientation on rebuild, place a paint mark across the top of the spigot and onto the adjoining area of the pulley (see photo). Also mark the pulley with an "I" (intake) or "E" (exhaust) as appropriate. Each drive pulley can now be pulled forward off its locating spigot.

4   The camshaft angle sensor is driven from the rear of the exhaust camshaft, so it's located at the rear of the cambox/cylinder head on the left-hand side. Release its spring clip and pull the harness connector from the camshaft angle sensor unit. Mark the relative position of the angle sensor body and the cambox, using an indelible pen or blob of paint. Then unscrew and remove the single 12mm bolt with the elongated head from the adjustment slot. Once the bolt is removed, the angle sensor can be pulled backwards until it is clear of its housing in the cambox/cylinder head. **Warning!** It may come free suddenly.

5   Camshaft and followers removal ☞ 3/7/63-66.

6   Checking components ☞ 3/8/24-30. **Caution!** These checks are important: don't be tempted to skip them.

7   Note that if you're fitting new camshafts, it's always advisable to fit new cam-followers at the same time (unless the existing followers have been in use for a negligible mileage). This advice is particularly important if you're fitting high performance camshafts. New cams and old followers, or vice-versa, are likely to produce rapid wear and loss of performance.

8   ☞ 3/9/68-79.
9   ☞ 5/29a.
10   ☞ 3/13/27-38.

15. CYLINDER HEAD - REMOVAL AND INSTALLATION (ENGINE IN CAR)

☞ First read 1/1, 2.

CYLINDER HEAD REMOVAL

1   Relieve fuel system pressure ☞ 5/13.
2   Remove air filter body ☞ 3/4/19-38, 47, 49-55.

3   Remove the camshaft drivebelt (ignoring duplicated instructions) ☞ 3/13/1-25.

4   Release the heater intake hose from its stub (the one closest to the centre of the car) on the firewall after loosening the clamp.

5   Release the small bore hoses from the oil cooler from their connections at the heater outlet casting at the rear of the head, and the BAC valve beneath the throttle body.

6   Release the electrical connectors of the engine coolant temperature sensor, and the temperature gauge sender unit on the heater outlet casting at the rear of the head.

7   Release the heated oxygen sensor 'pigtail' wire from its clip on the engine backplate. If the unit's wiring connector is still fixed to the bracket above the camshaft position sensor, free it by depressing the spring tabs which secure it. Tie the oxygen sensor's wiring out of harm's way.

8   If applicable, with a 10mm socket, release the bolt securing the ground/earth wire connection to the engine lifting bracket at the rear of the cambox cover on the right-hand side.

9   Using a 10mm socket, remove the fixings that secure the exhaust manifold heatshield to the manifold; there are six bolts and three nuts. Lift away the heatshield.

10   To gain best access to the exhaust manifold flange nuts it will be necessary to raise the front or left-hand side of the car and support securely ☞ 1/3.

11   From beneath the car you can just about see three 14mm nuts which hold the exhaust downpipe to the exhaust manifold. To get at and undo these nuts you need to put together extensions of at least 360mm (14in) and a universal joint. The combination should be socket, universal joint, extension or extensions, then the T-bar or ratchet handle. Two of the nuts can be accessed from the gap between the transmission and subframe, whilst the third nut can be reached from the gap above the subframe in the left-hand front wheelwell. It would be advisable to spray these three nuts and their studs with penetrating oil and allow it to soak in for half-an-hour, or so, before attempting to remove the nuts. Once the nuts have been removed the car can be lowered to the ground.

12   If you are removing the head to replace the head gasket, the exhaust and intake manifolds can be left attached to the head when it is removed. If you intend to leave the manifolds in place, skip to ☞ 3/15/15.

13   Remove the exhaust manifold. Using a crescent wrench (open-ended spanner), unscrew the 22mm union nut securing the EGR pipe to the exhaust manifold. Using a 14mm socket and extension, unscrew the nine exhaust manifold retaining nuts (the threaded studs will normally be corroded which can make it very difficult to get the nuts off without damaging them - penetrating oil may help). Lift away manifold and gasket.

14   Remove the intake manifold ☞ 3/7/2-7.

15   (Applicable only if exhaust manifold left in place.) Looking through the branches of the exhaust manifold, you will see that the small bore rigid heater return pipe is fixed to the exhaust

Mazda Miata, MX-5, Eunos & Roadster

manifold flange by a single 14mm nut. Remove the nut using a 125mm/5 inch extension and release the bracket.

16   Double-check for any missed wiring/hose connections and then remove the cylinder head ☞ 3/7/67-68.

CYLINDER HEAD CHECKING

17   ☞ 3/8/1-9.

18   Also inspect the piston tops for damage and the bores for serious scratching. If damage is evident, it might be as well to dismantle the engine further to rectify it.

19   If you wish to remove carbon from the piston tops, bring each piston in turn to the top of its bore. Pack the gap between the piston and bore with grease and then scrape off the carbon with a brass or aluminum scraper. When you've finished, use a plastic or wooden spatula to scrape the contaminated grease from around the piston. **Caution!** Take great care not to allow debris to fall into oilways or waterways.

CYLINDER HEAD INSTALLATION

20   Clean the gasket surfaces of the head and cylinder block thoroughly, taking great care not to contaminate oilways and waterways with debris.

21   Install the cylinder head ☞ 3/9/60-63.

22   (Applicable only if exhaust manifold already installed on head.) Looking through the branches of the exhaust manifold, you'll see that the small bore rigid heater return pipe is fixed to the exhaust manifold flange by a single 14mm nut. Place the bracket over the manifold stud and, using a 125mm/ 5 inch extension and socket, tighten the nut to 39-46Nm/3.9-4.7kgf m/29-33lbf ft.

23   Fit the exhaust manifold (if applicable). Before installing the manifold, clean its and the engine gasket surfaces thoroughly. Always use a new gasket. Slide the manifold over the studs and then slide the water pipe bracket over the relevant stud before replacing the manifold securing nuts. Using a 14mm socket, tighten the nuts progressively (working in a spiral outward from the centre) to a torque of 39-46Nm (3.8-4.7kgf m, 29-33lbf ft).

24   Install the intake manifold (if applicable) ☞ 3/11/41-46.

25   Using a new gasket, reconnect the exhaust downpipe. You'll find the only way to tighten the manifold flange nuts is with the same tools you used during removal - a 14mm socket attached to a universal joint attached to an extension of at least 360mm (14in), and then a ratchet or T-bar. Both of the lower nuts can be tightened from beneath the car; the top nut is most easily accessible via the left-hand front inner wheelarch. Torque the three nuts to 38-51Nm (3.8-5.3kgf m, 28-38lbf ft).

26   When you fit the manifold heatshield, use copper grease on the retaining bolt and stud threads to prevent the fixings from 'freezing' (seizing). Tighten the six bolts and three nuts (all 10mm) to 7.9-10.7Nm/80-110kgf cm/70-95lbf in.

27   Refit the inlet manifold support strut by maneuvering it into position from beneath and then inserting the top two 14mm screws and tightening them finger-tight, followed by insertion of the lower 14mm bolt. The lower bolt can be tightened with a 14mm socket and universal joint and extension bar, whilst the top two simply require a socket and extension bar. Tighten the bolts to 38-51Nm/3.8-5.3kgf m/28-38lbf ft.

28   If applicable, fit and tighten the 10mm bolt securing the ground/earth wire connection to the engine lifting bracket at the rear of the cambox cover on the right-hand side.

29   Secure the heated oxygen sensor unit's wiring to the clip on the engine backplate and then reattach the electrical connector block to the bracket over the camshaft position sensor.

30   Reattach the electrical connectors of the engine coolant temperature sensor, and the temperature gauge sender unit on the heater outlet casting at the rear of the head.

31   Reattach the small bore hoses from the oil cooler to the stub on the heater outlet casting at the rear of the head, and to the BAC valve beneath the throttle body.

32   Reattach the heater intake hose to its stub (the one closest to the centre of the car) on the firewall and secure with the clamp.

33   Install the camshaft drivebelt (ignoring duplicated instructions) ☞ 3/9/89-108.

34   Remake electrical and hose connections and refit the air filter body (ignoring duplicated and inapplicable instructions) ☞ 3/11/65-99.

35   Fit and tension the alternator drivebelt and, if fitted, power steering pump/air-conditioning compressor drivebelt ☞ 2.

36   Install the radiator complete with fan or fans ☞ 6.

37   Refit the two small hoses and the radiator top hose to the thermostat housing and secure with clamps. Note: a little silicone-based lubricant sprayed onto the radiator and thermostat housing stubs will make fitting the hoses easier.

38   Refill the radiator/reservoir with coolant ☞ 6. Check for leaks.

39   **Caution!** Double-check that all electrical and hose connections have been remade and are properly secured. Make sure wiring harnesses are fixed safely away from moving/hot components. Check that all fixings have been correctly tightened. Remake the battery connection. **Warning!** When tightening the negative (-) terminal take great care not to short the tool you are using across the positive (+) terminal (for more information ☞ 7).

40   Repressurise fuel system ☞ 5/13.

41   Start the engine and allow it to warm up to normal operating temperature at idle speed, checking for leaks as it does so.

16. CRANKSHAFT FRONT OIL SEAL - REPLACEMENT (ENGINE IN CAR)

☞ First read 1/1, 2.

1   You will find it helpful to raise the front of the car and support it securely: this will improve access to the seal area ☞ 1/3.

2   Remove the engine undertray ☞ 3/4/15.

3   Remove the camshaft drivebelt ☞ 3/13/1-25.

4   Using your fingers or, if necessary, pliers, remove the square key protruding from the crankshaft nose. Find some small screws which will fit into the threaded holes in the face of the camshaft drivebelt (timing belt) pulley. The screws we found were approximately 3mm in diameter. Once the screws are in place, use a pair of vise grip (mole grip) pliers to grasp them and to pull the pulley forward off the crankshaft nose.

5   You will now be able to see the oil seal, which is located in the oil pump body and surrounds the nose of the crankshaft.

6   ◘ The oil seal's 'skeleton' is a thin metal pressing which is easy to buckle. Using a small chisel or an old screwdriver and fairly gentle hammer blows, force the sides of the seal away from its housing at one or more points until the seal is sufficiently buckled to be able to lever it free of the housing. Alternatively, you can drive the tip of the tool right through the front of the seal and, once the seal is impaled, lever it out of the housing. Use a small piece of wood or plastic at the lever's fulcrum point to prevent damage to the oil pump body. **Caution!** Be careful not to hammer your screwdriver or chisel blade against the machined surface of the crankshaft where the oil seal lip bears, or against

16/6 Remove old seal very carefully (see text).

16/8 Drift new seal into its housing.

the seal's seat in the oil pump body.

7   Lubricate the outer circumference and inner lip of a new oil seal and position it in the entry to the oil seal housing with your fingers. The seal must have its closed side facing outwards.

8   ◘ Using a soft-faced hammer and a socket, or a piece of metal tubing of close to the same outer diameter as the seal, gently drift the seal fully home into its housing. The seal's outer diameter is 50.5mm/1.99in. If you don't have an appropriate piece of tubing or socket, you can drift the seal into its housing with direct but light blows from a very

3: Engine & clutch

small hammer. If you use this method, make sure you tap the seal home squarely and that you keep the hammer face flat against the seal, otherwise damage will result. The seal is properly installed when its face is flush with the lip of its housing in the oil pump. **Caution!** The seal face must not be recessed by more than 1mm/0.04in into the seal housing.

9   Check components ☞ 3/8/59-62. **Caution!** These checks are important: don't be tempted to skip them.

10   Rub a smear of oil over the crankshaft nose and in the keyway. Fit the cam drivebelt pulley over the nose of the crankshaft - flanged side toward the rear - and rotate it until the cutout in the pulley aligns with the cutout in the crankshaft.

11   ☞ Hold the locking key so that the chamfered end points toward the oil pump body and the chamfer is toward the crankshaft. Push the key into its slot with your fingers.

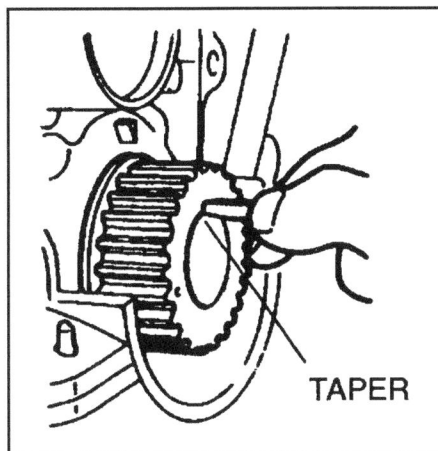

D16/11 INSTALL KEY WITH TAPER INWARD AND FACING CRANKSHAFT.

12   Install the camshaft drivebelt ☞ 3/13/27-35.

13   Engage the centre rear of the engine undertray with the tongue which projects forward from the suspension subframe. Replace the 10mm bolts retaining the undertray in the wheelarches where there are three fixings on each side. You'll also have to replace the 10mm nut that holds the stay (or stays) to the lower part of the front fender/wing (or fenders/wings). Note that on some right-hand drive cars the windscreen washer reservoir is mounted forward of the left-hand wheelarch, in which case one of the undertray fixings will be a deeply recessed 10mm nut near the reservoir body. Replace the two 10mm bolts at the rear of the undertray and three at the front.

14   Lower the car to the ground ☞ 1/3.

15   Refill the radiator/reservoir with coolant ☞ 6. Check for leaks.

16   Remake the battery connection. **Warning!** When tightening the negative (-) terminal take great care not to short the tool you are using across the positive (+) terminal (for more information ☞ 7).

17   Start the engine and allow it to warm up to normal operating temperature at idle speed, checking for leaks as it does so.

17. CRANKSHAFT REAR OIL SEAL - REPLACEMENT (ENGINE IN CAR)

☞ First read 1/1, 2.

1   The first task is to remove the transmission unit (gearbox). Manual ☞ 4/1, 2/Auto ☞ 4/1, 3.

2   Manual transmission cars only. Remove the clutch cover plate and clutch disc ☞ 3/7/31-34. **Warning!** Failure to undo all of the bolts progressively could easily result in the one or two bolts left under tension suddenly shearing, and the cover plate flying off the flywheel. When the cover plate bolts have been removed, lift away the cover plate and clutch disc together.

3   Flywheel (manual transmission cars) removal. Jar the bolts loose, then lock the flywheel as described in the previous step, then undo and remove the six 19mm bolts holding the flywheel to the crankshaft flange. Note: the bolts should be loosened half a turn each initially, in a diagonal sequence. **Caution!** It's a good idea to make sure that the same relationship between crankshaft and flywheel position is kept on reassembly to maintain balance. Mark the top of the flywheel and mark the top of the crankshaft (once the flywheel has been removed) using indelible ink so that the flywheel can be installed in exactly the same position. Once the bolts have been removed the flywheel can be lifted away - it's heavy!

4   Driveplate (auto transmission cars) removal. The procedure is the same as the flywheel removal procedure in the previous step, except that the driveplate will be lighter, there will be a backing plate between the bolt heads and the face of the driveplate and an adaptor between the crank and driveplate.

5   The oil seal's 'skeleton' is a thin metal pressing which is easy to buckle. Using a small chisel or an old screwdriver and fairly gentle hammer blows, force the sides of the seal away from its housing at one or more points until the seal is sufficiently buckled to be able to lever it free of the housing. Alternatively, you can drive the tip of the tool right through the front of the seal and, once the seal is impaled, lever it out of the housing. Use a small piece of wood or plastic at the lever's fulcrum point to prevent damage to the oil pump body. **Caution!** Be careful not to hammer your screwdriver or chisel blade against the machined surface of the crankshaft where the oil seal lip bears, or against the seal's seat in the oil pump body.

6   Lubricate the outer circumference and inner lip of a new oil seal and position it in the oil seal housing with your fingers, noting that the closed side of the seal must face outward.

7   Drift the seal into its housing with direct but light blows from a small hammer, making sure that the seal is driven home evenly. If you use this method, make sure you keep the hammer face flat against the seal, otherwise damage will result. The seal is properly installed when its face is flush with the lip of its housing in the oil pump. **Caution!** The seal face must not be recessed by more than 1mm/0.04in into the seal housing.

8   Inspect flywheel or driveplate and clutch components: ☞ 3/8/78-84. **Caution!** Don't be tempted to skip these checks: they're important.

9   Check that the threaded bolt holes in the crankshaft rear flange are clear and clean: a doubled-over pipe cleaner is a good tool for this purpose.

10   Flywheel (manual transmission) installation. Apply thread locking fluid to the threads of each of the flywheel retaining bolts. Using the marks made earlier for correct alignment, hold the flywheel in position over the rear of the crankshaft and fit the retaining bolts finger-tight.

11   Driveplate (auto transmission) installation. Apply thread locking fluid to the threads of each of the flywheel retaining bolts. Fit the adaptor collar to the rear of the crankshaft, followed by the driveplate and its backing plate. Fit the retaining bolts finger-tight.

12   Lock the flywheel or driveplate by temporarily fitting a bellhousing bolt and then wedging a screwdriver into the ring gear teeth and against the bolt. Tighten the flywheel or driveplate retaining bolts progressively, and in a diagonal sequence, to a final torque of 97-102Nm/9.8-10.5kgf m/71-75.9lbf ft.

13   Fit the clutch disc and cover plate (manual transmission cars) ☞ 3/9/131-134.

14   Fit the transmission. Manual ☞ 4/8. Auto ☞ 4/9.

18. CAMSHAFT OIL SEAL - REPLACEMENT (ENGINE IN CAR)

☞ First read 1/1, 2.

1   Remove camshaft drivebelt (timing belt) and camshaft pulleys ☞ 3/14/1-3.

2   The camshaft oil seals are now in plain view.

3   The oil seal's 'skeleton' is a thin metal pressing which is easy to buckle. Using a small chisel or an old screwdriver and fairly gentle hammer blows, force the sides of the seal away from its housing at one or more points until the seal is sufficiently buckled to be able to lever it free of the housing. Alternatively, you can drive the tip of the tool right through the front of the seal and, once the seal is impaled, lever it out of the housing. Use a small piece of wood or plastic at the lever's fulcrum point to prevent damage to the cylinder head. **Caution!** Be careful not to hammer your screwdriver or chisel blade against the machined surface of the camshaft where the oil seal lip bears, or against the seal's seat in the cylinder head.

7   Lubricate the outer circumference and inner lip of a new oil seal and position it in the entry to the oil seal housing with your fingers. The seal must have its closed side facing outwards.

8   Using a very light flat-faced hammer, tap the seal fully into its housing, making sure that the blows are applied evenly around the circumference so that the seal is driven home square. The face of the seal must be flush with the front of its housing when finally in position. Make sure you

3:59

Mazda Miata, MX-5, Eunos & Roadster

keep the face of the hammer square to the seal so that neither the seal nor alloy housing are damaged. You may need to use a flat-ended drift just to tap the lower part of the seal (where the seal plate limits access) into place. Repeat the process for the second camshaft seal.
9   Install the camshaft pulleys ☞ 3/9/77-79.
10   Install the camshaft drivebel t☞ 3/13/27-38.

19. STARTER RING GEAR - REPLACEMENT (ENGINE IN CAR)

☞ First read 1/1, 2.
1   The first task is to remove the transmission and flywheel/driveplate ☞ 3/17/1-4.
2   For information on how to replace the ring gear and about inspecting flywheel or driveplate and clutch components: ☞ 3/8/71-84. **Caution!** Don't skip these checks: they're important.
3   Fit the flywheel and clutch/driveplate and transmission ☞ 3/17/9-14.

20. ENGINE MOUNTINGS - REPLACEMENT (ENGINE IN CAR)

☞ First read 1/1, 2.
1   You'll need enough room beneath the car to access the undersides of the engine mountings. Raise the front of the car and support securely ☞ 1/3.
2   Centre a jack beneath the oil pan/sump, place a piece of protective wooden packing on its pad and raise the pad until it just contacts the underside of the pan. Raise the pad a further 6-7mm/quarter inch to take the weight from the engine mountings. **Caution!** Don't jack the engine any higher.
3   Each of the mounting brackets is held to the cylinder block by three 14 mm bolts, which are a little inaccessible but otherwise not too difficult to undo: you'll find a short extension will help. Note that one of the bolts on the right-hand mounting also passes through the starter motor mounting.
4   From beneath the car, undo and remove the 12mm nuts and spring washers which secure the engine mountings to the subframe: you'll need a 125mm/5 inch extension to reach up inside the turrets.
5   You should now be able to withdraw the mounting brackets, complete with mountings and mounting covers, from the sides of the engine: the right-hand bracket will need to be worked out from beneath the starter mounting bracket. The mounting covers should fall off.
6   ▢+ Place the engine mounting in a vise and, using a 14mm socket with a 125mm/5 inch extension, undo the nut that holds the mounting to its bracket.
7   Fit the new mounting in the vise, noting that there is a square boss on the back of the mounting which should engage with the square recess in the mounting bracket. Tighten the retaining nut to a torque of 57-78Nm/5.8-8kgf m/42-57lbf ft. Repeat the process for the second mounting.
8   Fit the outer covers, noting that the two large drain holes should be at the bottom when the mountings are in place. Hold the outer cover in place whilst lowering the threaded stud of each mounting through its hole or slot in the subframe. When both mountings are resting in place, fit securing washers and nut finger-tight from beneath the car.
9   You should now be able to fit the mounting brackets to the cylinder block sides, remembering that the right-hand one has to be pushed under the starter bracket. The bracket is secured by three 14mm bolts which are of two different lengths. Looking at the bracket, the bolt on the left and the upper bolt on the right are both short. Note: you may have to manipulate the engine height a little using the jack, to achieve bracket alignment with the bolt holes in the cylinder block. Tighten the 14mm bolts which retain the brackets to a torque of 37-53Nm/3.7-5.5kgf m/27-39lbf ft.
10   Lower and remove the jack supporting the engine.
11   From beneath the car tighten the mounting nuts to a torque of 57-78Nm/5.8-8kgf m/42-57lbf.
12   That's it; lower the car to the ground.

21. CLUTCH & RELEASE BEARING - REMOVAL & INSTALLATION (ENGINE IN CAR)

☞ First read 1/1, 2.
1   The first task is to remove the transmission and the clutch ☞ 3/17/1-2.
2   ▢ ▣ Release its rubber boot, then pull the clutch release fork outwards, which will simultaneously release it from its pivot and the back of the release bearing. The release bearing

20/6a Remove mounting from bracket.

20/6b Engine mounting components.

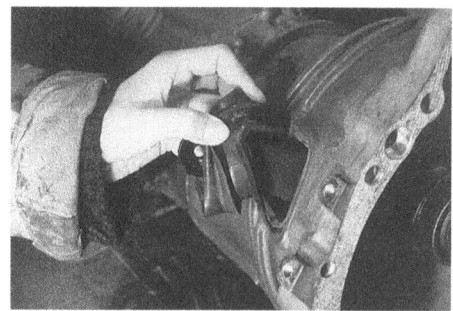
21/2 Remove release fork's rubber boot.

21/6 Pull out the release fork.

can now be pulled forward off the transmission input shaft sleeve. The release fork can be pulled inward through the square hole in the side of the bellhousing.
3   Pull the release bearing off over the nose of the input shaft.
4   Inspect the flywheel and clutch components ☞ 3/8/78-84. **Caution!** Don't skip these checks: they're important.
5   Smear high melting point copper or molybdenum grease thinly over the sleeve of the transmission input shaft, and spread a little of the same in the pivot socket on the back of the clutch release fork and the two pads which bear upon the release bearing.
6   ▢ Pull the release fork tail out through the square hole in the side of the bellhousing. Take the release bearing and place it on the input shaft sleeve with arms facing towards the back of the transmission.
7   Now the tricky bit is to push the arm against its pivot ball so that the retaining clip springs open and locks around the back of the ball whilst, simultaneously, the arm fork tips engage with the arms on the back of the release bearing. In fact, it's easier than it sounds!
8   Fit the clutch to the flywheel ☞ 3/9/131-134.
9   Fit the transmission. Manual ☞ 4/8. Auto ☞ 4/9.

22. CLUTCH MASTER CYLINDER - REMOVAL AND INSTALLATION

☞ First read 1/1, 2.

REMOVAL

1   **Caution!** Clutch hydraulic fluid - which is

3: Engine & clutch

D21/0 MAJOR COMPONENTS OF CLUTCH AND OPERATING SYSTEM.
1 Clutch pedal. 2 Clutch master cylinder. 3 Clutch release (slave) cylinder. 4 Clutch release bearing (thrust washer/release collar). 5 Clutch release fork (lever). 6 Clutch cover (pressure plate). 7 Clutch disc (driven disc). 8 Pilot (spigot) bearing. 9 Flywheel.

9   Remove the polyethylene sheet from beneath the reservoir cap, then bleed the hydraulic system ☞ 3/26.
10 Check clutch pedal height and free play adjustments ☞ 3/28.

23. CLUTCH MASTER CYLINDER - OVERHAUL

☞ First read 1/1, 2.
1   **Caution!** It is our advice that you replace a faulty master cylinder with a new or exchange unit. However, if you wish to rebuild the master cylinder yourself, or you're fitting new seals to a serviceable unit as part of a maintenance program, then the procedure is as follows -

DISMANTLING AND CHECKING
2   **Caution!** You must not rebuild the master cylinder using the old seals so, before you start, check that the overhaul kit you've purchased contains a new cup-shaped main seal, piston seal, reservoir seal and snap ring (circlip).
3   Remove the master cylinder ☞ 3/22. Unscrew the reservoir cap, remove the protective cover beneath and the cap sealing ring. Tip the fluid contents of the cylinder into an old oil container ready for safe disposal.
4   Mount the cylinder in a vise fitted with jaw protectors so that the mounting flange faces upward.
5   Using snap ring/circlip pliers, whilst simultaneously pushing the piston down the bore with a screwdriver, release and withdraw the snap ring (circlip) from the cylinder bore. Gently withdraw the screwdriver and, if the piston emerges from the bore, pull it out.
6   Remove the cylinder from the vise and try shaking out the bore's contents. If this doesn't work you'll have to apply compressed air to the pipe terminal on the side of the cylinder, having first installed the reservoir cap and wrapped the whole thing in rag to catch the parts as they are expelled. **Warning!** Point the open end of the cylinder away from yourself and others when applying compressed air.
7   Pull the plastic reservoir body from the cylinder body.
8   Discard the old seals and snap ring; you'll need to lever the piston seal off with a screwdriver, taking great care not to damage the piston.
9   Using methylated spirit only, clean every component that is to be re-used until it is spotless.
10 Inspect the cylinder bore for damage in the form of scratching or corrosion. If such damage is evident, scrap the cylinder. Check, too, that the spring is not corroded and that the piston is undamaged: again, damage dictates renewal.

REBUILD
11 **Caution!** Work on a totally clean surface - newspaper is ideal.
12 Pour a little fresh brake fluid into the cylinder bore and rub it around the bore with your fingers. Lubricate the new cup seal with hydraulic

the same as brake fluid - is an extremely effective paint stripper so, whenever disconnecting hydraulic pipes or removing hydraulic components, make sure you have placed rags to catch and absorb spillages. Wipe off any spillages on paintwork immediately.
2   The master cylinder is mounted on the engine side of the firewall/bulkhead immediately in front of the clutch pedal position.
3   Unscrew the cylinder's reservoir cap and stretch a piece of thin polyethylene (one skin of a plastic bag or food wrap) across the open reservoir before replacing the cap. This simple procedure will stop the cylinder leaking fluid when its union is undone.
4   Unscrew the 10mm union nut which fixes the rigid hydraulic pipe to the side of the cylinder; when it's completely unscrewed, gently pull the rigid pipe out of the cylinder. Plug, cap or tape wrap the open end of the pipe to reduce fluid spillage.
5   The mounting flange of the master cylinder is fixed to the firewall/bulkhead by two 12mm nuts. We believe that on most cars these nuts will be on the engine side of the firewall but, on our left-hand drive car, one of the nuts was on the driver's side of the firewall. Undo and remove the nut, or nuts, on the engine side of the firewall using a socket and short extension. If there's a retaining nut inside the car, you'll find that access is made easier by removing the large plastic access cover beneath the steering wheel; it's held by two medium crosshead screws. Even so, you'll have to almost stand on your head to reach up to the offending nut: you might even consider removing the seat ...
6   The master cylinder can now be removed. Note: there's an insulating gasket against the cylinder's mounting flange: if it's damaged, replace it.

INSTALLATION
7   Place a dab of white brake grease on the tip of the pushrod - which should be protruding from the firewall. As you fit the cylinder into position, re-engage the pushrod from the pedal. Tighten the two 12mm retaining nuts to a torque of 19-25Nm/1.9-2.6kgf m/14-18lbf ft. If you had to remove the cover beneath the steering wheel, install it and secure with its two crosshead screws. **Warning!** Make sure the cover is properly installed: you don't want it to drop down on your feet when you're driving.
8   Remove the plug or cap - leaving absolutely no blockage or debris behind in the pipe - and then fit the pipe union into its recess in the side of the cylinder. **Caution!** It's very easy to cross-thread these unions, so screw the union nut home with your fingers (not possible if cross-threaded) whilst holding the pipe square to the cylinder body. Finally, tighten the union using the pull of two fingers at the end of an ordinary wrench (spanner).

3:61

Mazda Miata, MX-5, Eunos & Roadster

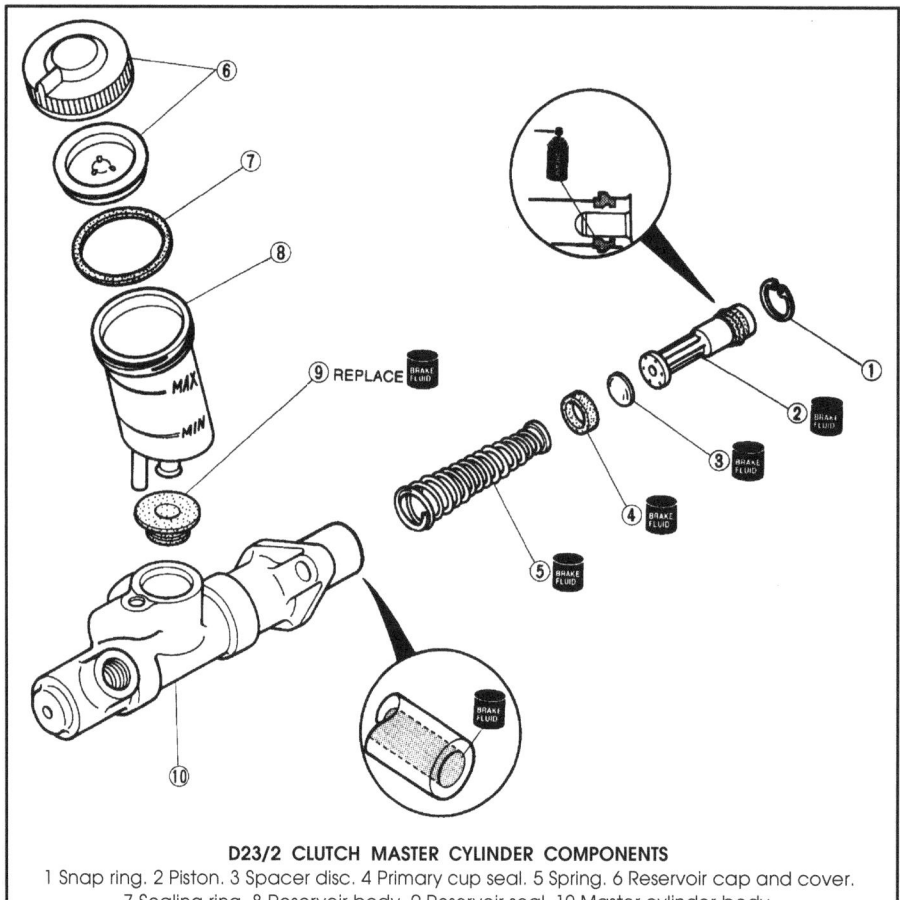

D23/2 CLUTCH MASTER CYLINDER COMPONENTS
1 Snap ring. 2 Piston. 3 Spacer disc. 4 Primary cup seal. 5 Spring. 6 Reservoir cap and cover.
7 Sealing ring. 8 Reservoir body. 9 Reservoir seal. 10 Master cylinder body.

the pipe union nut from the cylinder's body. Once the nut is completely free, pull the pipe from the union and then plug, cap or tape over the pipe end to prevent the ingress of dirt.
6   Free the clutch release cylinder from its mounting by removing the two 12mm retaining bolts. Access to these bolts is difficult, but the lower bolt can be reached from beneath with a wrench, while the upper bolt can be undone with a socket mounted on a 350mm/14 inch extension inserted through the gap above the subframe in the right-hand front inner wheelarch.

INSTALLATION
7   Place a dab of copper-based or molybdenum grease on the pushrod seat in the clutch release lever. Position the release cylinder on its mounting bosses whilst simultaneously engaging the pushrod with the release fork.
8   Fit and tighten the 12mm bolts which retain the cylinder. Tighten to a torque of 16-22Nm/1.6-2.3kgf m/12-16lbf ft.
9   Remove the plug or cap - leaving absolutely no blockage or debris behind in the pipe - and then fit the pipe union into its recess in the side of the cylinder. **Caution!** It's very easy to cross-thread these unions so screw the union nut home with your fingers (not possible if cross-threaded), whilst holding the pipe square. Finally, tighten the union using the pull of two fingers at the end of an ordinary wrench.
10   Remove the polyethylene sheet from beneath the reservoir cap, then bleed the hydraulic system ☞ 3/26.

25. CLUTCH RELEASE (SLAVE) CYLINDER - OVERHAUL

☞ First read 1/1, 2.
1   **Caution!** It is our advice that you replace a faulty clutch release cylinder with a new or exchange unit. However, if you wish to rebuild the cylinder yourself, or you're fitting new seals to a serviceable unit as part of a maintenance program, then the procedure is as follows -

DISMANTLING AND CHECKING
2   **Caution!** You must not rebuild the cylinder using the old seal so, before you start, make sure you have a new piston seal available. The kit should also contain a new pushrod boot and a cover for the bleed valve.
3   Remove the cylinder from the bellhousing ☞ 3/24.
4   Pull the pushrod from its boot and then pull the boot off of the cylinder. Discard the boot. Shake the piston from the cylinder bore, taking care not to drop it on the ground. If it won't come out, apply compressed air to the pipe terminal, having first wrapped the cylinder in rag to catch the ejected parts. **Warning!** Point the open end of the cylinder away from yourself and others when applying compressed air.
5   Using a small screwdriver, and taking great care not to scratch the piston, lever the old piston

fluid and then fit its open side over the cap at the small end of the spring. Whilst holding the cylinder closed end upwards, feed the larger diameter end of the spring into the bore and then push the spring and seal together as far into the bore as they will go. **Caution!** It's important that the spring pad stays seated in the seal cup during this process, and that the cup does not get turned inside out as it enters the bore.
13   Using your fingers only, fit a new seal into the groove at the pushrod end of the piston: the chamfered side of the protruding seal lip should face the pushrod end of the piston.
14   Rub brake fluid all over the piston and the spacer disc. Place the spacer disc on the thrust pad of the piston (opposite end to pushrod recess) and, whilst holding the cylinder closed end upwards, push the spacer and piston into the bore.
15   Mount the cylinder in the vise as before and, whilst pushing the piston down into the bore with a screwdriver, fit a new snap ring into the groove at the pushrod end of the cylinder bore. Keep the piston pushed down into the bore and, using a cotton bud, apply a smear of white brake grease around the bore just below the snap ring. Release the piston and place a dab of the same lubricant into the pushrod recess of the piston.
16   After lubricating it with brake fluid, fit a new reservoir seal into the top of the cylinder body and then push the reservoir into the seal until it is firmly home. Temporarily install the reservoir's cap seal, cover and cap. Tape over the cylinder's outlet to prevent the ingress of dirt until it's installed.
17   Install the master cylinder ☞ 3/22.

24. CLUTCH RELEASE (SLAVE) CYLINDER - REMOVAL AND INSTALLATION

☞ First read 1/1, 2.
REMOVAL
1   **Caution!** Clutch hydraulic fluid - which is the same as brake fluid - is an extremely effective paint stripper so, whenever disconnecting hydraulic pipes or removing hydraulic components, make sure you have placed rags to catch and absorb spillages. Wipe off any spillages from paintwork immediately.
2   Remove the cap from the clutch master cylinder, stretch a thin piece of polyethylene sheet over the reservoir top and then fit and tighten the cap. This will prevent the leakage of fluid when the release cylinder is removed.
3   You'll need good, safe access to the underside of the car in the vicinity of the bellhousing. Raise the right-hand side of the car and support securely ☞ 1/3.
4   You'll find the release cylinder bolted to the lower right-hand side of the bellhousing.
5   Using a 10mm wrench (spanner), unscrew

3: Engine & clutch

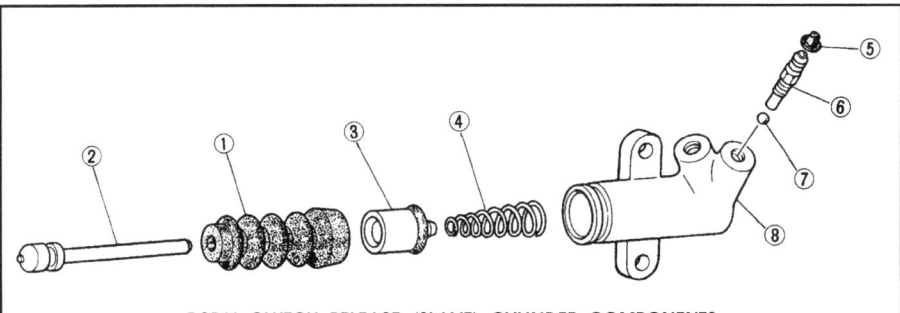

D25/4 CLUTCH RELEASE (SLAVE) CYLINDER COMPONENTS.
1 Boot. 2 Pushrod. 3 Piston and seal. 4 Spring. 5 Bleed valve cap. 6 Bleed valve. 7 Steel ball.
8 Cylinder body.

seal off and discard it.
6   Using an 8mm wrench (spanner), unscrew and remove the bleed valve from the cylinder. Note: beneath the valve there's a steel ball which you should now tip out into your hand.
7   Using methylated spirit only, clean every component that is to be re-used until it is spotless.
8   Inspect the cylinder bore for damage in the form of scratching or corrosion. If such damage is evident, scrap the cylinder. Check, too, that the spring is not corroded and that the piston is undamaged: again, damage dictates renewal.

REBUILD
9   **Caution!** Work on a totally clean surface - newspaper is ideal.
10   Lubricate the seal and the piston with brake fluid and then, using your fingers only, fit the new seal to the piston. **Caution!** The chamfered side of the seal should face the pushrod end of the cylinder.
11   Pour a little fresh brake fluid into the cylinder bore and rub it around the bore with your fingers. Once more lubricate the piston and seal assembly with brake fluid, and then engage the small end of the spring with the boss at the seal end of the piston. Spring first, feed the piston and spring assembly into the cylinder bore.
12   Smear white brake grease into the pushrod recess of the piston and around the exposed end of the bore. Fit the pushrod boot over the end of the cylinder until it engages with its groove, and then slide the pushrod into the boot, ball end outward.
13   Drop the steel ball into the bleed valve's threaded bore and then install the bleed valve, which can be left finger-tight until it is bled.
14   Install the cylinder on the side of the bellhousing ☞ 3/24.

26. CLUTCH HYDRAULIC SYSTEM - BLEEDING

☞ First read 1/1, 2.
1   If air bubbles are trapped in the hydraulic system you may well find that you need to pump the clutch pedal to make the clutch work at all, or the pedal action may have a 'soft' feel to it. This is because air is much more compressible than brake fluid (which is the hydraulic fluid used by your car's clutch system), and therefore a reduced amount of movement is transmitted to the clutch release fork. These same symptoms can be created by aged brake fluid which has absorbed water vapor from the atmosphere.
2   **Caution!** Brake fluid is an extremely effective paint stripper so, whenever working on an hydraulic system, make sure you have placed rags to catch and absorb spillages. Wipe off any spillages from paintwork immediately.
3   The clutch release cylinder is bolted to the lower right-hand side of the bellhousing and, to bleed the hydraulic system, constant access to the cylinder's bleed valve is required. Therefore, raise the right-hand side of the car and support securely ☞ 1/3. Note: do not raise the car any higher than is necessary for comfortable access because, if the car is too far from level, bleeding will not be as effective.
4   Gather together a good supply of fresh, high quality brake fluid, a 500mm/20 inch length of bleed tubing (any flexible tubing that will fit tightly over the ball-shaped end of the bleed valve), a 8mm wrench (spanner), a clear plastic bottle or jar that will hold around a half liter/one pint of fluid - oh, and three beers. Three beers? Yep, one for yourself and one for each of the two assistants you're going to need for about ten minutes.
5   Remove the cap and cover from the master cylinder reservoir, and make one assistant responsible for keeping the fluid level topped up above the "Min" level **at all times** during the bleeding process, starting now.
6   Your other assistant gets to sit comfortably behind the wheel and pump the clutch pedal when required.
7   Unless you're a real smooth talker, you get the dirty job! Pour brake fluid into the clear container until it reaches a depth of around 50mm/2in. Take this, the wrench/spanner and the bleed tube with you beneath the car. Fit the wrench on the bleed valve and check that it's closed (tight). Leave the wrench in place whilst pushing one end of the bleed tube firmly onto the bleed valve head. Immerse the other end of the tube in the brake fluid in the clear container and note that the tube end **must stay immersed through the whole process**, otherwise air will be sucked into the system.
8   Get your friend in the driving seat to pump the pedal slowly 4-5 times. Let the pedal rise and then, on your instruction, your pal should begin to depress the pedal at a speed that will take 2-3 seconds before the pedal hits the floor. At the start of the stroke, open the bleed valve around half a turn: you'll immediately see bubbles and fluid shooting out the end of the bleed tube. As soon as the stroke is complete, close the bleed valve (your friend should keep the pedal against the floor until you've closed the valve and shouted "OK"). Let the pedal return to its normal height.
9   Repeat the process detailed in step 8 until the fluid emerging from the bleed tube is completely free of bubbles. Then close the bleed valve, remove the bleed tube and fit the protective cover over the bleed valve. **Caution!** Do not re-use brake fluid bled from the system; instead dispose of it safely, as you would old engine oil.
10   Lower the car to the ground, top up the master cylinder to the "Max" mark, fit the reservoir cover and cap. You've finished, so you can all drink your beers!

27. CLUTCH HYDRAULIC LINES/HOSES - REPLACEMENT

☞ First read 1/1, 2.
1   The hydraulic line system for the clutch is comprised of rigid and flexible pipes joined together by bracket-mounted unions. The pipework connects the master and release (slave) cylinders. Whether your car is left or right-hand drive, it seems that the pipework is identical between the union mounted on the firewall at the left-hand side of the engine compartment and the release cylinder - which means that, on right-hand drive cars, the pipework doubles back on itself!
2   **Warning!** Clutch hydraulic fluid must not be swallowed nor allowed to enter the bloodstream: seek medical aid if this happens. **Caution!** Clutch hydraulic fluid - which is the same as brake fluid - is an extremely effective paint stripper so, whenever disconnecting hydraulic pipes or removing hydraulic components, make sure you have placed rags to catch and absorb spillages. Wipe any spillages from paintwork immediately.
3   **Caution!** If you're renewing rigid hydraulic pipes, we advise you to buy preformed replacements. However, if you do intend to bend straight replacement piping to fit ☞ 9/3.
4   Before you disconnect any pipework stretch a piece of thin polyethylene sheet across the top of the master cylinder reservoir, then fit and tighten the cap: this will minimize fluid loss when pipes are separated.
5   The only piece of clutch pipework that's easy to replace is the rigid section between the master cylinder and the union at the left-hand rear firewall. Unscrew the pipe's 10mm union at the master cylinder, then, using pliers, pull the spring locking clip from the union bracket at the other end of the pipe. Push the union through the bracket sufficiently to allow access to the 17mm hex on the flexible pipe. Lock the flexible pipe's collar with a

3:63

Mazda Miata, MX-5, Eunos & Roadster

17mm wrench (spanner) whilst undoing the 10mm union nut with another. Pull the pipe from its firewall clips.

6 The problem with the remaining bits of pipework is the access to the second union above the starter motor on the bellhousing. If you're extremely dexterous, or have some fancy tools, it's possible you can separate the union in order to replace the length of flexible pipe which crosses the firewall behind the engine. However, for mere mortals we recommend removing the rigid (union to release cylinder) and flexible pipes together and then separating the two. The procedure is detailed in the following steps 7 to 10.

7 The clutch release/release cylinder and associated piping is bolted to the right-hand side of the bellhousing and, to gain access to the right-hand side of the car, will have to be raised and supported securely ☞ 1/3.

8 From beneath the car, reach up to the pipe union bracket on the right and, using pliers, pull the locking spring clip from the bracket. Push the union upward sufficiently to allow the rigid pipe to be pulled through the slot in the bracket. You might just have enough room now to undo the union with 10mm and 12mm wrenches; if not carry on to the next step.

9 You'll see that the coiled section of the rigid pipe is fixed to the bellhousing by a bracket. Remove the 17mm nut from the transmission side of the bellhousing and then withdraw the bracket securing bolt from the engine side.

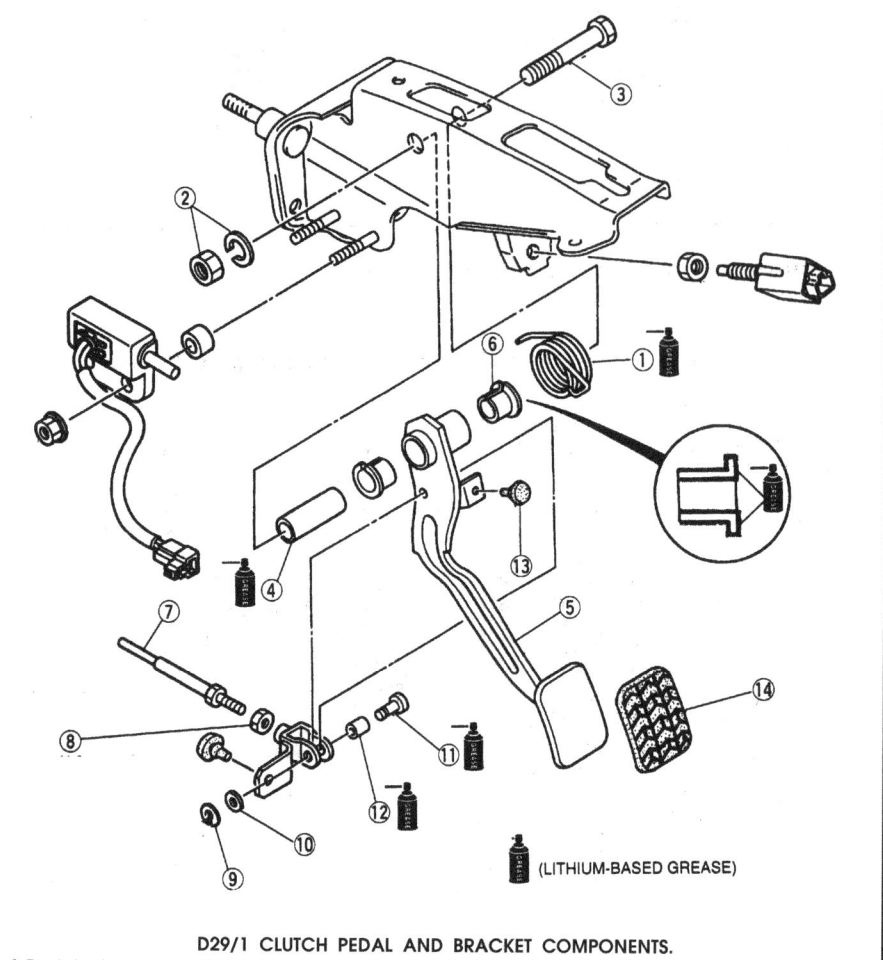

D29/1 CLUTCH PEDAL AND BRACKET COMPONENTS.
1 Pedal return spring. 2 Nut and lockwasher. 3 Bolt. 4 Spacer. 5 Clutch pedal. 6 Bush. 7 Pushrod. 8 Nut. 9 Clip. 10 Wave washer. 11 Pin. 12 Spacer. 13 Stop. 14 Pedal pad.

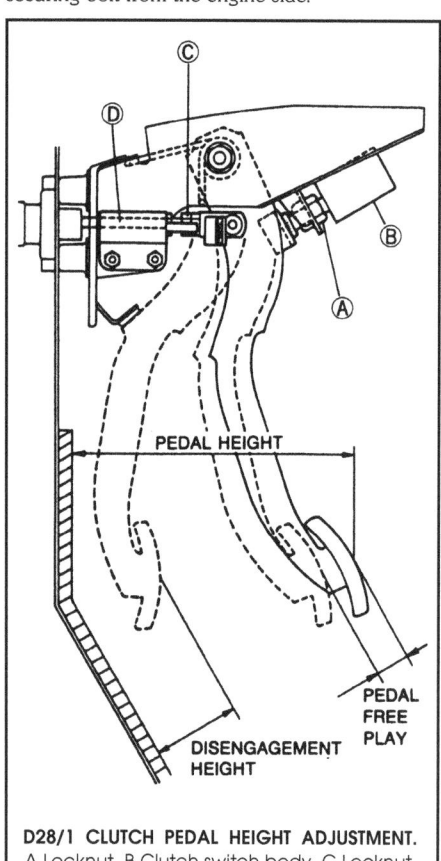

D28/1 CLUTCH PEDAL HEIGHT ADJUSTMENT.
A Locknut. B Clutch switch body. C Locknut. D Pushrod.

10 Unscrew the 10mm union nut on the release cylinder to free the pipe or pipes, which can now be removed from the car.

11 Renew the section or sections of piping as necessary, noting that the pipe unions should not be tightened with more pressure than the pull of two fingers at the end of an ordinary wrench/spanner. Install the lower rigid pipe and the flexible hose first, making sure they are safely secured in their brackets. Retighten the pipe bracket bellhousing bolt to a torque of 80Nm/8kgf m/60 lbf ft.

12 Fit the top section of rigid piping, making sure it is firmly secured in the firewall spring clips.

13 **Caution!** Union bracket spring clips must be installed so that the bowed side faces away from the bracket; also make sure the spring clips are fully home.

14 **Caution!** When connecting unions to master or release cylinders, screw the union nuts home with your fingers before final tightening: this simple precaution will prevent cross-threading.

15 Remove the polyethylene sheet from the master cylinder reservoir and bleed air from the hydraulic system ☞ 3/26. Lower the car to the ground ☞ 1/3.

28. CLUTCH PEDAL HEIGHT AND FREE PLAY - CHECKING AND ADJUSTMENT

☞ First read 1/1, 2.

PEDAL HEIGHT

1 With the pedal in its normal position, measure the distance between the center of the pedal's footpad and the carpet surface on the vertical firewall/bulkhead behind the pedal. The correct height is 175 to 185mm/6.9 to 7.25in.

2 The height of the pedal is dictated by the threaded stop of the electrical switch, which senses when the clutch is engaged and is mounted in the top of the pedal box.

3 Access to the clutch pedal box area is easier if the plastic cover beneath the steering wheel is removed: it's retained by two medium-sized crosshead screws. By standing on your head in the driver's footwell, and generally adopting a position that would make a contortionist proud, you'll be able to reach the switch. If you've got real problems with access, you might think about removing the seat to make things easier.

4 Release the switch's 16mm locknut and then screw the 21mm switch body backwards or

3: Engine & clutch

forwards until the correct pedal height is achieved. Retighten the locknut and check pedal free play (lash).

PEDAL FREE PLAY (LASH)

5   The amount of free play is the distance between the pedal footpad's highest position and the position at which clutch resistance is first felt when the pedal is pressed by hand. This measurement should be between 5 and 13mm/0.2 and 0.5 inch.

6   If you need to adjust the lash, take up the contortionist's position again, slacken the 12mm locknut on the clutch cylinder pushrod and then, using a 10mm wrench (spanner), rotate the pushrod clockwise or anti-clockwise until the desired free play is achieved.

7   Now ensure that the pedal's disengagement height is correct. At the point at which the clutch disengages, measure the distance between the center of the pedal's footpad and the carpet of the sloping section of the firewall behind the pedal. The dimension should be 68mm/2.68in minimum: if necessary, readjust the length of the pushrod.

When you're satisfied with both free play and disengagement height, retighten the pushrod locknut.

8   If you had to remove the cover beneath the steering wheel, fit it and secure with its two crosshead screws. **Warning!** Make sure the cover is properly installed: you don't want it to drop down on your feet when you're driving.

29. CLUTCH PEDAL REMOVAL AND INSTALLATION

☞ First read 1/1, 2.

1   It's likely you want to remove the clutch pedal because the pivot bushings are worn, or the pedal return spring has broken; therefore, it's only necessary to withdraw the pedal's pivot pin having first released its 12mm nut and spring washer. Of course, this is easier said than done because of the pivot pin's position high up behind the dash panel. Access to the clutch pedal box area is easier if the plastic cover beneath the steering wheel is removed: it's retained by two medium-sized crosshead screws. By standing on your head in the driver's footwell, and generally adopting a position that would make a contortionist proud, you'll be able to reach the pivot pin. If you've got real problems with access, you might think about removing the seat to make things easier.

2   Once the pin is withdrawn, it should be possible to remove the pedal, complete with pushrod. Fit well-greased new bushings inside and a new spring outside the pedal pivot tube and then slide the pedal and pushrod back into position.

3   Fit the pivot bolt and secure with its nut. Using needle-nosed pliers, a screwdriver and infinite patience, lock the tang end of the return spring in place and hook the hooked end of the spring behind the pedal so that tension is restored. When you've successfully located the spring, tighten the pivot bolt locknut to a torque of 20-34Nm/2-3.5kgf m/15-25lbf ft.

4   If you had to remove the cover beneath the steering wheel, fit it and secure with its two crosshead screws. **Warning!** Make sure the cover is properly fitted: you don't want it to drop down on your feet when you're driving.

Notes

4

Transmission (gearbox) & driveline

1. TRANSMISSION (GEARBOX) - PREPARATION FOR REMOVAL

☞ First read 1/1, 2.

1   The transmission unit, whether manual or automatic, can be removed by itself or in unit with the engine. If removal of the engine would allow you to do some beneficial work on that unit, too, it's worth considering removal of both components together for the small amount of extra work it will entail ☞ 3/4.

2   To remove and install the transmission unit you'll need easy access to much of the car's underside. If you have access to, or can hire, a garage pit or whole vehicle hoist, go for it - your life will then be much easier. Otherwise, as a sensible minimum, you're going to need four strong jack stands (axle stands) and a hard and level surface as your workplace ☞ 1/3.

3   **Caution!** If your car has a faulty automatic transmission unit, have the problem professionally diagnosed before the transmission is removed.

4   📷 **Warning!** The transmission unit is a heavy and large item; you'll need occasional assistance ... unless your name's Schwarzenegger.

5   After removal, and before any dismantling

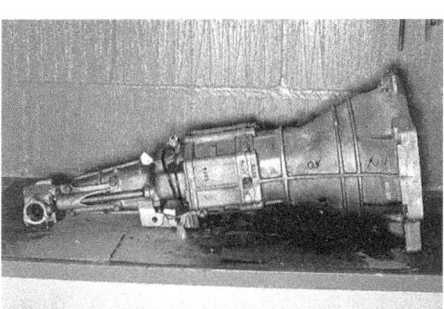

1/4 Transmission ready for work to begin.

begins, the outside of the transmission unit will need to be thoroughly cleaned. Make sure you've got solvents (proprietary brands or kerosene/paraffin), brushes, scrapers, rags and old newsprint ready. **Warning!** Do not use gasoline/petrol as a cleaning solvent.

6   Specific tool requirements are described in the text.

7   Read through the whole procedure before starting the job.

2. TRANSMISSION (GEARBOX), MANUAL - REMOVAL

☞ First read 1/1, 2.

1   Isolate the battery ☞ 7/2.

2   Raise and support the whole car securely and at a height sufficient to give easy access to the underside ☞ 1/3. (**Warning!** Do not venture beneath the car unless it is safely supported and completely stable.)

3   📷 From inside the car unscrew the knob from the gearshift lever.

4   📷+ Lift the ashtray from the center con-

2/3 Unscrew gearshift knob.

2/4a Lift out ashtray.

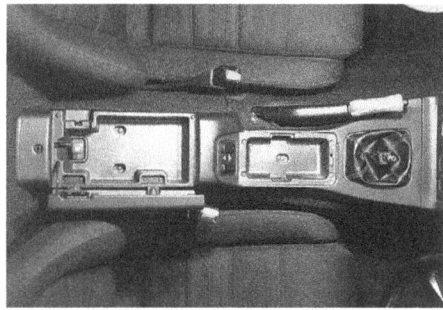

2/4b Remove retaining screws ...

2/4c ... and lift away console.

sole: it's held by spring clips. Lift the lid of the storage compartment. All of the crosshead screws retaining the transmission tunnel console are now exposed; two in the storage compartment, one beneath the ashtray and one on each side of the moulding adjacent to the shift lever. Once the five screws are removed, spring the front side pieces of the console outwards slightly, then lift the console enough to move it forward and off of the fuel filler flap and trunk release levers. **Caution!** Do not attempt to remove the console completely before disconnecting the wiring. For transmission removal,

4:1

Mazda Miata, MX-5, Eunos & Roadster

2/6 Remove boot unit retaining bolts.

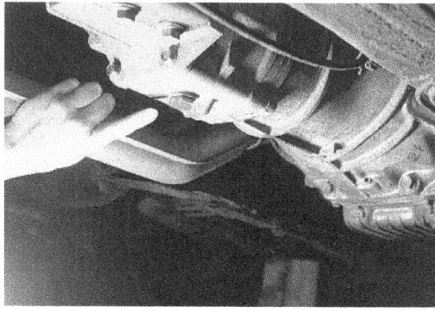

2/10a Remove transmission drain plug ...

it's sufficient to leave the wiring in place and lay the plastic console alongside the tunnel.

5   Remove the shaped sound deadening material from around the shift lever boot (gaiter) base.

6   ◘ Remove the four 10mm bolts which secure the gearshift lever's rubber boot to the transmission tunnel.

7   ◘+ Once the lever boot is released from the tunnel, it can be lifted high enough to give access to the three 10mm bolts fixing the shift lever base pivot to the transmission turret. Once the

2/7a Remove three bolts ...

2.10b ... and drain oil completely.

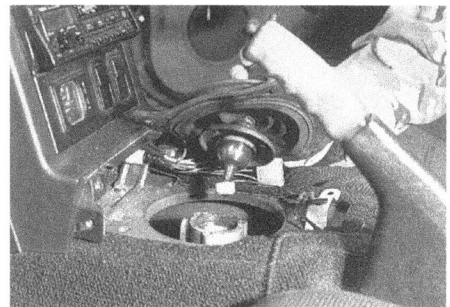

2.7b ... and lift the shift lever from the turret.

three bolts are removed, the whole shift lever assembly, complete with boot, can be lifted away. **Caution!** The lever assembly may drip oil, so have a rag ready to wipe the lever before oil is dripped onto upholstery or carpets.

8   Remove the engine undertray ☞ 3/4/14-15.

9   Unscrew and remove the two 17mm bolts securing the front 'performance' bar which bridges the front subframe beneath the engine.

10   ◘+ Next you'll need a bowl or a drainer can capable of holding at least 3 liters/6 pints of

fluid. Place the bowl directly beneath the transmission drain plug and undo the plug with a 24mm socket. It's best to do the final unscrewing by hand so the plug can be held in place until the last moment, then quickly removed so that oil doesn't spray everywhere. Note: the drain plug is magnetic so it'll collect any metal fragments in the transmission lubricant. If the plug has never been removed and cleaned, it's quite normal for there to be a small amount of deposited fine metal debris, but if there are any large pieces of swarf it is possible that one of the transmission components is damaged and wearing rapidly. Once the oil has drained, the plug can be installed finger-tight to stop residual oil dripping to the ground. Discard the oil you have drained by taking it to a local oil disposal/recycling point. Do not attempt to re-use the oil.

11   Remove the complete exhaust system ☞ 5/38/7-12.

12   ◘+ The next job is to remove the driveshaft (propshaft). However, before undoing the four nuts and bolts holding the driveshaft flange to the differential flange, use a blob of white paint to mark the relative positions of both flanges. Alternatively, a small groove can be filed across the joint for the same purpose. It is important to mark the

relative position of the two components because the driveshaft may be out of balance in another position. Using a diagonal sequence, slacken in turn each of the 14mm nuts and bolts a little before removing them completely. You may need to apply the parking brake to lock the driveshaft.

13   ◘ Once the four nuts and bolts have been released, separate the driveshaft and differential flanges by pushing the shaft forward further into the transmission; then lower the axle end of the shaft before withdrawing the shaft's nose from the tail of the transmission. Note: some oil will drip from the transmission once the driveshaft is

2/12a Mark propshaft flange ...

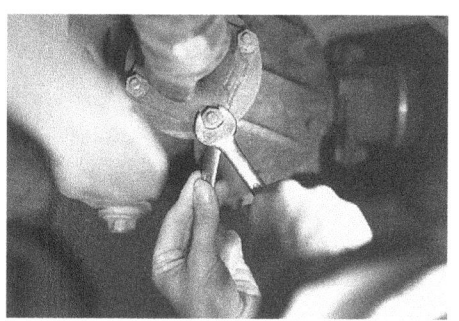

2/12b ... & remove retaining nuts & bolts.

removed; place a plastic bag over the end of the transmission tail and secure with a rubber band.

14   Once the driveshaft has been removed completely, replace the bolts, locking washers and nuts finger-tight in the differential flange for safe-keeping.

15   ◘+ Free the clutch release cylinder from its mounting on the bellhousing by removing the two 12mm retaining bolts. Access to these bolts is difficult but the lower bolt can be reached with a wrench from beneath the car, and the upper bolt with a socket mounted on a 360mm (14 inch) extension via the gap above the subframe accessible

2/13 Slide shaft forward.

4: Transmission (gearbox) & driveline

in the right-hand front wheelarch. The cylinder can be left to hang loose or tied back out of harm's way. **Caution!** Remember not to press the clutch pedal until the cylinder is once again bolted in position.

16   The speedometer drive cable needs to be removed from the rear end of the transmission casing. Simply unscrew the large knurled nut with your fingers - you may need to use pliers just to get it started. Once the nut is fully loosened the speedometer cable can be withdrawn from the transmission and tied to the brake pipes running alongside the chassis member.

17   Release the wiring harness from the side of the PPF (the Power Plant Frame running from transmission to diff housing) by squeezing the retaining ears of each plastic clip with your fingers or pliers and then, whilst the ears are squeezed together, pulling the clip free of the frame. Some of these clips are very fiddly but with care they can all be removed without breaking them. Don't forget to release the ground wire held by a 10mm bolt toward the rear end of the PPF and the harness clip on the side of the bellhousing which is held by a 10mm screw. There is some more wiring above the transmission; however, this cannot be disconnected until a little later.

18   + Remove the support bracket between the PPF and the transmission tail casting by first unscrewing the 17mm headed bolt holding the bracket to the PPF, followed by the two 14mm headed bolts holding the bracket to the transmission. Remove the bracket and install the bolts finger-tight in their original positions for safekeeping.

19   Place a jack beneath the transmission, just ahead of the front end of the PPF. Raise the jack until the rear of the transmission is supported and very slightly lifted: this will relieve the strain on the PPF.

20   At the front of the PPF two bolts secure the PPF to the transmission. Note the holes in the PPF are elongated; therefore, it's a good idea to mark the relative position of the PPF and the transmission casing with a dab of paint to ensure perfect reassembly when the time comes. Unscrew and remove the two 17mm bolts (they're 198mm/8in long!).

21   Using a 17mm socket, unscrew and remove the rearmost long bolt securing the PPF to the differential casing. The second bolt (nearest front of car) is the so-called 'reamer bolt' because it is a precise fit in its shaped housing and this

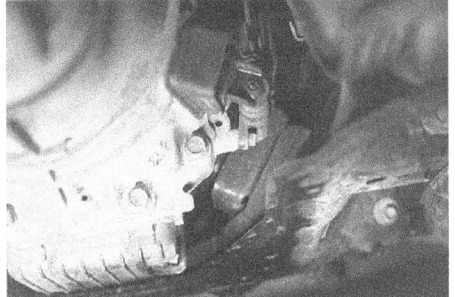
2/15a Remove release cylinder bolts ...

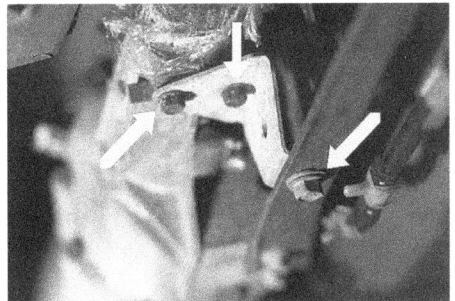
2/18a Release these bolts ...

2/20 Remove front PPF bolts.

ensures that the PPF is correctly aligned. Mark the bolt collar position relative to the PPF with a dab of paint to ensure everything goes back together exactly as it was on reassembly, then undo and remove the second 17mm bolt. Note that even on our two-year-old, 14,500km/9000 mile car, the two bolts at the rear of the PPF were heavily corroded and therefore may be difficult to remove on older cars: use plenty of penetrating oil.

22   Using a chisel or pry bar (jemmy) in the cutouts, lever the reamer bolt collar out of the PPF.

2/15b ... one accessible thru wheel well.

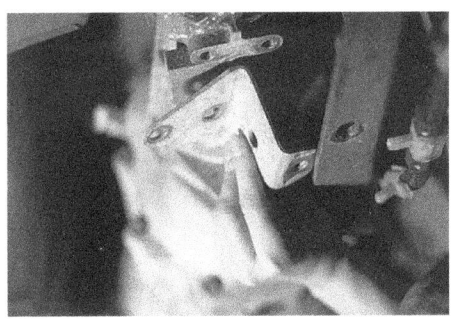
2/18b ... and remove bracket.

2/21 Remove rear PPF bolts.

23   Once the collar is removed the rear of the PPF can be moved sideways until clear of the differential casing and then pulled backward, freeing it from the transmission casing, after which the PPF can be removed from the car (you may need to adjust the jack supporting the transmission to allow this). **Caution!** Do not remove the upper spacers from the rear of the PPF: if they are removed, the PPF will have to be replaced as vehicle handling will be severely impaired.

24   The next task is to remove the bolts and nuts around the periphery of the bellhousing.

2/16 Disconnect speedo cable.

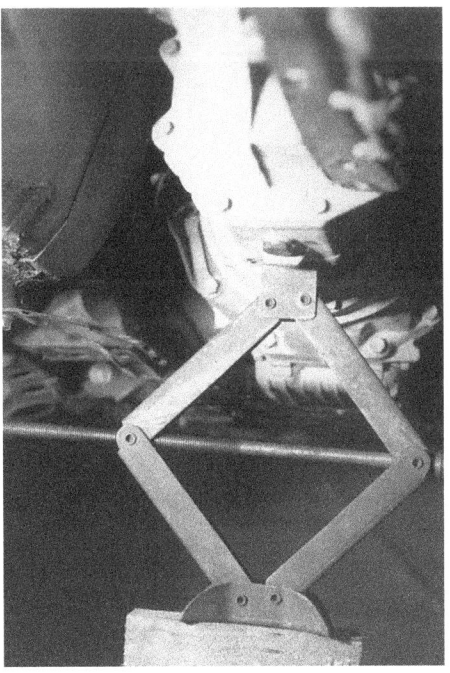
2/19 Lift rear of transmission unit.

Mazda Miata, MX-5, Eunos & Roadster

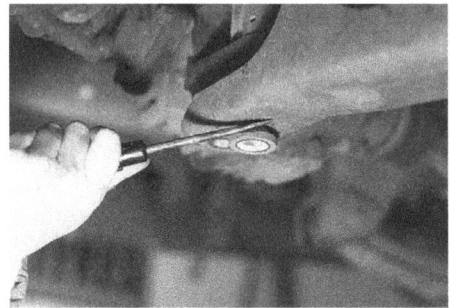

2/22 Lever out collar.

However, the jack supporting the transmission will probably be in the way, so here's a method which will allow its temporary removal. Place a T-bar or crowbar over the empty gearshift lever hole inside of the car, then thread a piece of rope down around the transmission tailhousing and back up through the hole and tie it to the supporting bar. Ensure the rope used is strong enough to support the weight of the transmission. Once the rope is in place and tight, the jack can be removed to allow removal of the bellhousing bolts.

25   Removal of bellhousing bolts and nuts.

2/24 Place sling around transmission.

Note: you'll need 14mm and 17mm sockets, a universal joint and extension(s) of at least 450mm (18 inches) to reach these fixings, which are also very tight!

26   Start by removing the nut and bolt holding the starter motor. Both nut and bolt are 14mm (smaller than most of the bellhousing bolts) and are situated about halfway up the right-hand side of the bellhousing. The head of the lower bolt holding the starter motor will have to be held by a second person, and can be accessed via the space above the front subframe in the right-hand front wheelarch. Once a helper is holding the bolt head, the nut can be released from the transmission side. There are no nuts for the other two 14mm bolts, one of which secures the top of the starter motor: these bolts can be unscrewed and removed from the transmission side. Note: both of these bolts also secure brackets fixing wiring and hydraulic pipe. Once free, tie these brackets and their wiring/pipework to one side away from the bellhousing.

27   You are now left with seven 17mm headed bolts and one 17mm nut and bolt holding the transmission bellhousing to the engine. Using a diagonal sequence, first of all loosen each of these bolts by half a turn. Then remove all of the bolts

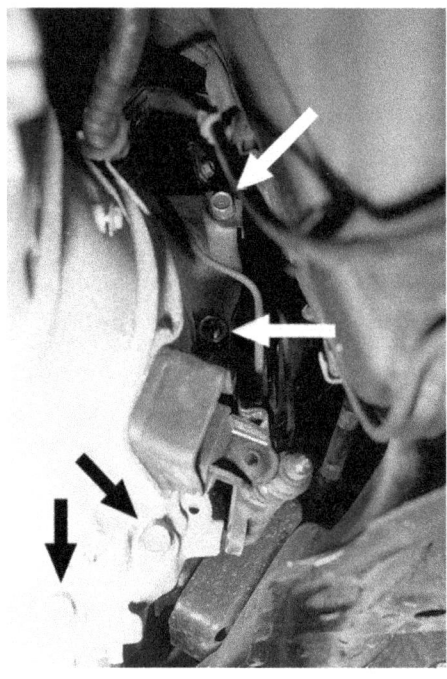

2/26 Location of some of the bellhousing bolts.

except two, one top and one bottom, which should be left in place but loosened by half a turn.

28   Release the sling around the tailhousing of the transmission (if applicable) after placing the jack back under the transmission. Lower the transmission as far as it will go and then jack it up again just 13mm/half- an-inch so that the engine mountings are not strained.

29   There should now be enough space above the lowered transmission to disconnect the wiring to the neutral and reverse switches.

30   The whole wiring harness can now be

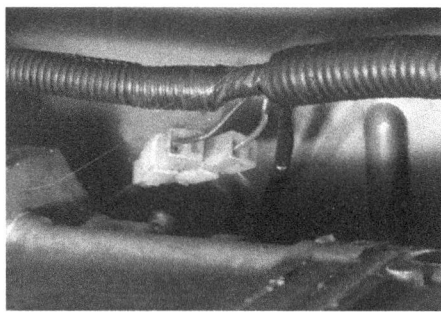

2/29 Disconnect transmission wiring.

pulled to one side and tied to the brake pipes alongside the chassis rail out of harm's way.

31   Carefully undo and remove the last two bellhousing bolts.

32   Using a wooden packing piece, place a jack under the rear end of the engine oil pan/sump adjacent to the bellhousing and jack upwards until the weight of the transmission is just released from the existing jack. **Caution!** Don't jack the engine any higher than this. The jack which was used to support the transmission should now be removed.

33   With the help of a strong assistant, or by

2/32 Clutch accessible if attention required.

supporting the weight of the transmission on a wheeled jack, pull the transmission backward whilst supporting the weight of the unit - which we think is around 46kg/100lb. **Warning!** If you and your assistant are doing this job without a wheeled jack, neither of you should position yourselves directly beneath the transmission in case it drops. Once the input shaft is clear of the clutch, the whole transmission unit can be lowered to the ground and then removed from beneath the car. Note: there will probably be a considerable amount of oil left in the transmission gearshift lever turret, so tip the unit onto its side and drain that oil into a suitable container.

3. TRANSMISSION (GEARBOX), AUTOMATIC - REMOVAL

☞ First read 1/1, 2.

1   Isolate the battery ☞ 7/2. Raise and support the whole car securely and at a height sufficient to give easy access to the underside ☞ 1/3. **(Warning!** Do not venture beneath the car unless it is safely supported and completely stable.)

2   Take a look at the diagram; it will help clarify all of the following steps. Disconnect the shift mechanism (**1**) from the right-hand side of the unit.

3   Remove the engine undertray (**2**) ☞ 3/4/14-15.

4   Unscrew and remove the two 17mm bolts securing the front 'performance bar' which bridges the front subframe beneath the engine (**3**).

5   Remove the complete exhaust system (**4**) ☞ 5/38/7-12.

6   Drain the automatic transmission fluid (ATF). You'll need a bowl or tray larger than the transmission's oil pan/sump and capable of holding 7 liters/6.2 Imp. quarts/7.4 US quarts. Slacken the oil pan bolts until their heads are protruding by around 6mm/a quarter inch and then gently pull one end of the pan away from the transmission unit; this will allow the fluid to drain. When draining is complete nip up the bolts and wipe ATF from the pan's exterior.

7   The next job is to remove the driveshaft (**5**) ☞ 4/2/12-14.

8   Unscrew the large knurled nut holding the speedo drive cable (**6**) to the transmission casing and then withdraw the cable. Tie the cable end to the brake pipes alongside the chassis rail.

9   Remove the single bolt securing the rigid

4: Transmission (gearbox) & driveline

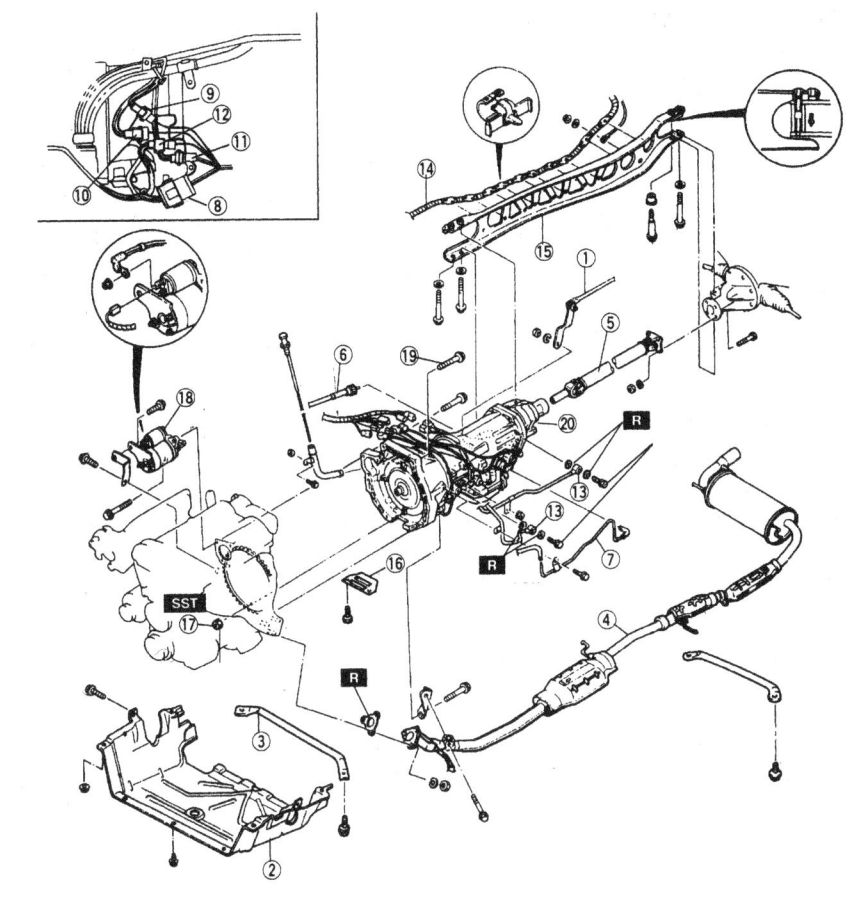

D3/2 AUTOMATIC TRANSMISSION REMOVAL SEQUENCE
1 Shift rod. 2 Engine undertray. 3 'Performance rod' brace. 4 Exhaust system (except manifold). 5 Driveshaft (propshaft). 6 Speedometer cable. 7 Vacuum pipe/hose. 8 Range switch connector. 9 Input/turbine speed sensor connection. 10 Solenoid connector. 11 ATF temperature sensor. 12 Clutch solenoid connector. 13 Oil cooler pipes. 14 Wiring harness. 15 PPF (power plant frame). 16 Access cover. 17 Torque convertor nuts or bolts (as applicable). 18 Starter motor. 19 Bellhousing bolts. 20 Auto transmission unit. R = Replace.

D3/6 DRAINING ATF.

section of the small bore vacuum pipe (**7**) to the left-hand side of the casing. Pull the rubber section of the pipe from its union stub.

10 Also on the left of the unit you'll see the oil cooler feed and return pipes (**13**). Both are secured to the transmission casing and bellhousing by clips and then at their unions by banjo bolts. Remove the bolts securing the clips and the banjo bolts, then tie the loose pipes out of harm's way.

11 Detach the wiring harness (**14**) and remove PPF (**15**) ☞ 4/2/17-23.

12 At the front of the unit on the right-hand side you'll see the transmission dipstick tube. Remove the dipstick, unscrew the nut and bolt securing the tube's support bracket and then pull the tube from the transmission case.

13 Remove the cover (**16**) of the access hole in the bottom of the bellhousing. With a blob of paint or an indelible marker, mark the relative positions of the driveplate and torque convertor so that they can be reattached in the same positions on reassembly.

14 Reach up into the bellhousing and unscrew and remove the four nuts or bolts (**17**), as applicable, fixing the torque convertor to the driveplate. You can lock the driveplate by jamming a large screwdriver into the starter ring gear teeth and simultaneously wedging it against the side of the access hole.

15 Release bellhousing bolts and nuts ☞ 4/2/25-27.

16 Lower the transmission as far as it will go until the jack pad just comes free and then jack it back up just 13mm/half-an-inch so that the engine mountings are not too strained.

17 There should now be sufficient room above the transmission to reach and separate the five electrical connector blocks (**8**, **9**, **10**, **11**, **12**). **Caution!** Before disconnecting, check the color coding of the wires each side of each connector: if necessary, tag wires so you know what goes with what on refit. The wiring harness can now be pulled to the side and tied to the brake pipes out of harm's way.

18 Carefully undo and remove the last two bellhousing bolts.

19 Using a wooden packing piece, place a jack under the rear end of the engine oil pan/sump adjacent to the bellhousing and jack upwards until the weight of the transmission is just released from the existing jack. **Caution!** Don't jack the sump any higher than this. The jack which was used to support the transmission should now be removed (unless it's a wheeled jack).

20 With the help of a strong assistant, or by supporting the weight of the transmission on a wheeled jack, pull the transmission backward whilst supporting the weight of the unit - which we think is around 70kg (155lb). **Warning!** If you and your assistant are doing this job without a wheeled jack, neither of you should position yourselves directly beneath the transmission in case it drops. Once the spigots in the bellhousing joint face are clear, the whole transmission unit can be lowered to the ground and then removed from beneath the car. **Caution!** It is essential that the automatic transmission unit is kept the right way up at all times, otherwise sediment and debris from the oil pan (which will still contain fluid) can be dislodged and allowed to contaminate fine drillings and valves.

4. TRANSMISSION (GEARBOX), MANUAL - DISMANTLING & REBUILD GENERAL

☞ First read 1/1, 2.

1 ☐ Read the text on teardown and rebuild before you start the job so that you have a good idea of what's involved ☞ 4/5, 6, 7.

2 Most of the work can be undertaken with ordinary tools, but there are a few tasks requiring

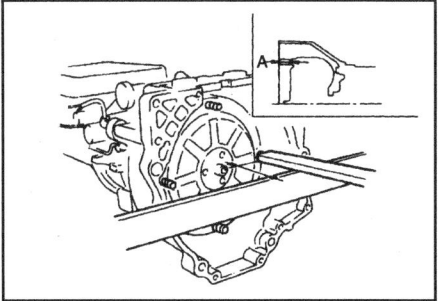

D4/1 CHECK THAT TORQUE CONVERTOR PROPERLY ENGAGED WITH OIL PUMP
'A' = 22.5mm/0.89in.

Mazda Miata, MX-5, Eunos & Roadster

some inventiveness to get round the lack of Mazda's special tools: our solutions are described but maybe you can do better?

3   It's recommended that the dismantling is carried out on top of several thicknesses of newsprint: you'll be amazed at how much oil there is to soak up.

4   As dismantling proceeds, clean all components in batches using proprietary oil/grease remover or kerosene/paraffin, and making sure all components are thoroughly dried afterwards. **Warning!** Do not use gasoline/petrol for cleaning purposes. **Caution!** Don't immerse bearings in cleaning fluid: they should simply be wiped with a cloth.

5   Immediately after cleaning, it's a good idea to slide components removed from transmission shafts on to lengths of metal tube or wire. This system removes any confusion about the order in which parts should be reassembled and their correct orientation. You'll need three tubes or wires representing the transmission's three shafts.

6   Have a supply of small transparent bags for the storage of groups of small components and don't forget to label the bags. A marker pen with indelible ink will prove very useful.

4/5 Keep shaft components together.

7   Don't throw away any old components, including gaskets and seals, until you have the correct replacements. It's surprising how often an old component is a useful pattern or source of reference.

8   For the rebuild you'll need a strong workbench and a vise fitted with jaw protectors.

9   To ensure maximum life and reliability from a rebuilt transmission, not only must the work be done with great care and thoroughness, but also in a clean environment and with completely clean tools and components. Also all internal moving components must be thoroughly lubricated with transmission oil as they are reassembled/installed.

10   Before the rebuild begins replace any bolts, screws, studs or nuts, the threads or heads of which are in any way damaged. All threads must be clean and torque wrench settings strictly observed.

11   Have a complete set of new gaskets and seals ready before work starts, together with silicone-based fluid gasket cement. Also buy ahead of time the new components and tools that you know you'll need.

12   If a component won't fit, don't force it. Stop, stand back, think about the problem and resolve it properly before proceeding.

13   Take your time, get it right and keep your personal safety and the safety of others in mind at all times.

5. TRANSMISSION (GEARBOX), MANUAL - TEARDOWN

☞   First read 1/1, 2.

1   + Start by removing the rubber boot around the clutch operating arm: squeeze the base of the boot to release it from the bellhousing casting.

2   + With two pairs of pliers pull the two spring tags protruding from the clutch release fork

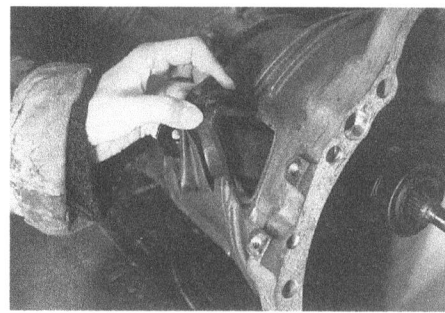

5/1 Remove rubber boot.

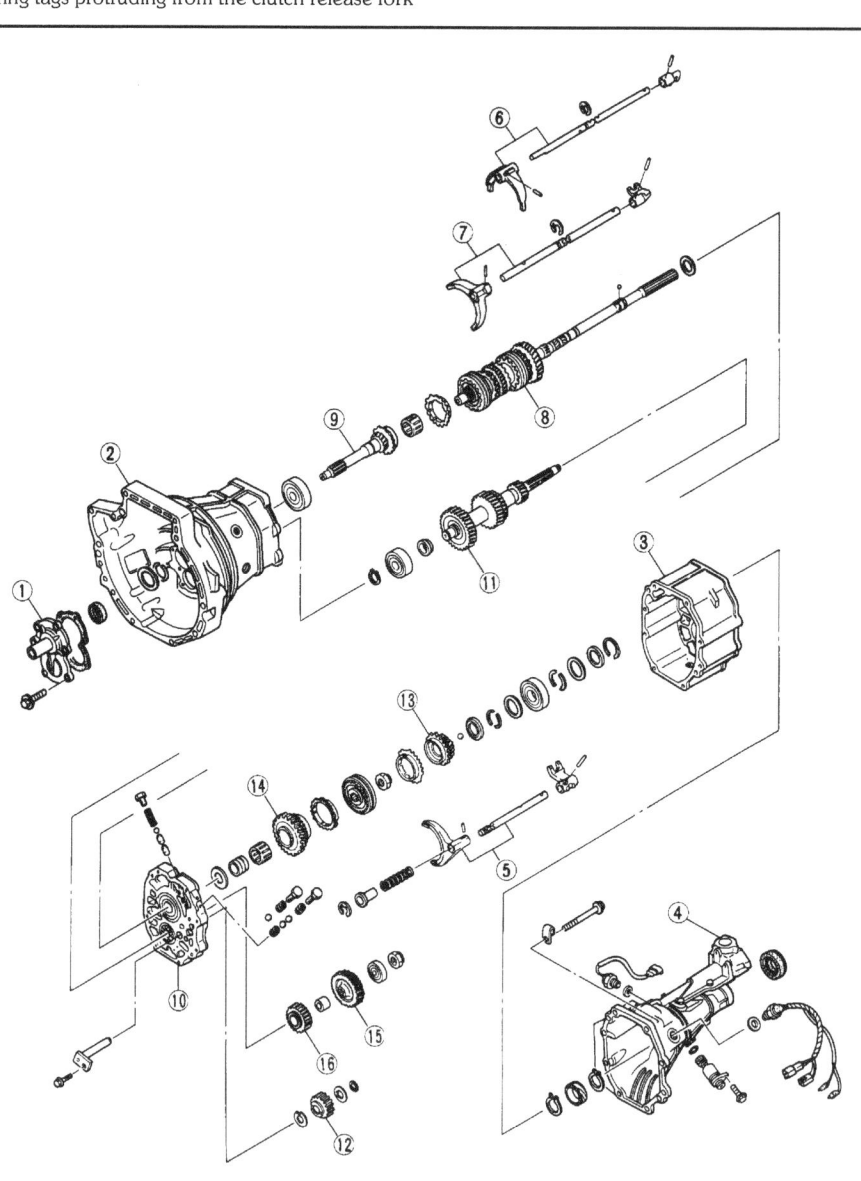

D5/1A EXPLODED VIEW OF MANUAL TRANSMISSION (GEARBOX)
1 Front cover. 2 Bellhousing and front casing. 3 Main casing. 4 Extension housing and tailshaft casing. 5 Shift fork and rod: 5th/reverse. 6 Shift fork and rod: 1st/2nd. 7 Shift fork and rod: 3rd/4th. 8 Mainshaft/ tailshaft and gear cluster. 9 Input shaft. 10 Central bearing carrier. 11 Countershaft. 12 Reverse idler. 13 5th gear. 14 Reverse gear. 15 Countershaft 5th gear. 16 Countershaft reverse gear.

4: Transmission (gearbox) & driveline

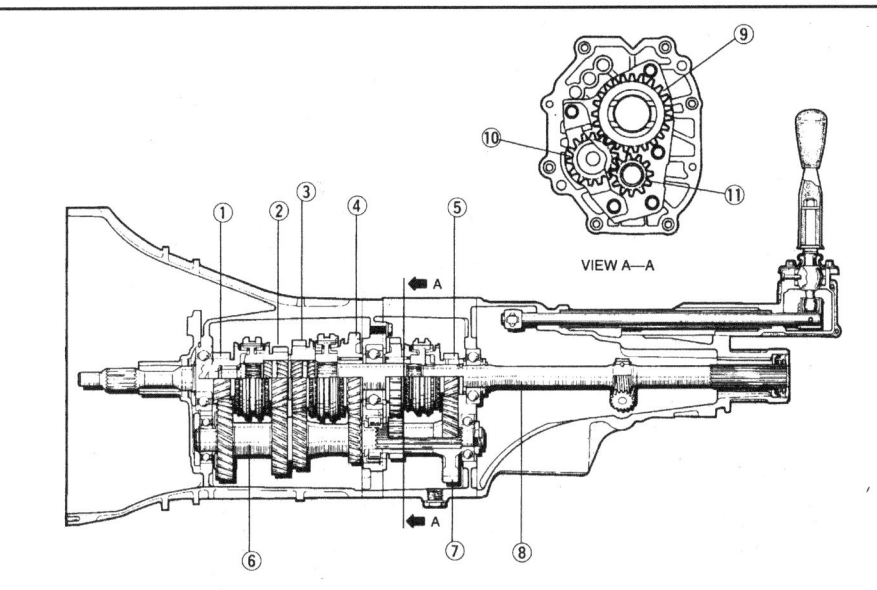

D5/1B RELATIONSHIP OF MANUAL TRANSMISSION (GEARBOX) INTERNAL COMPONENTS
1 4th gear. 2 3rd gear. 3 2nd gear. 4 1st gear. 5 5th gear. 6 Countershaft. 7 Countershaft 5th gear. 8 Mainshaft and tailshaft. 9 Reverse gear. 10 Reverse idler gear. 11 Countershaft reverse gear.

pletely and then pulling the front cover from the transmission casting. **Warning!** The cover may come free suddenly, as the gasket's adhesion breaks. **Caution!** Don't use a sharp tool between the bellhousing and cover in order to lever it free. Draw the front cover forward carefully on the input shaft as you don't want to damage the rubber oil seal it contains on the input shaft splines. Behind the front cover and on top of the input shaft bearing there is a spacer washer. This, too, should be removed and kept with the housing.

5   Remove the snap ring/circlip from the input shaft in front of the bearing. This is a fiddly

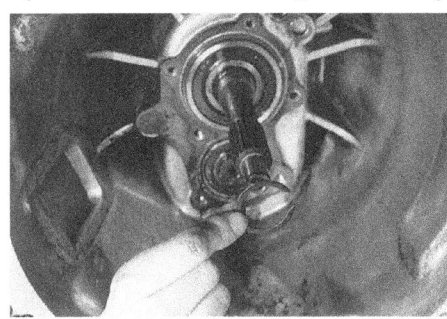

5/5 Remove input shaft snap ring (circlip).

task and is probably best accomplished by springing the clip with a pair of expanding snap ring pliers and working a small, thin-bladed screwdriver between the snap ring and bearing face until the snap ring is fully free of its groove in the input shaft, and can be drawn forward and off the shaft. You'll probably find this easier if one person uses the snap ring pliers and another fits the screwdriver blade behind the snap ring.

6   Speedometer drive gear removal. The speedometer drive gear is retained in the transmission tail casing by a single 10mm bolt.

5/2a Release spring clips ...

5/3 Remove release bearing.

5/6a Undo retaining bolt ...

5/2b ... and pull out fork.

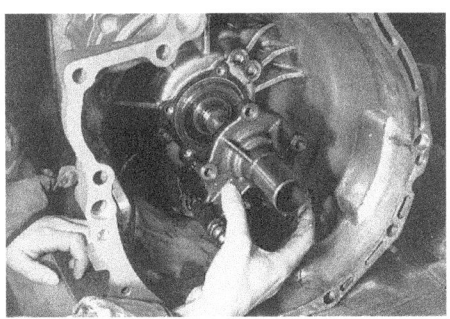

5/4a Unscrew bolts ...

outwards, the arm can then be pulled off of its pivot pin and out of the release bearing. Once clear of the bearing and pivot pin, the arm should be withdrawn from inside the bellhousing.

3   The clutch release bearing can now be pulled off the transmission input shaft.

4   The transmission front cover, which incorporates input shaft sleeve and release fork pivot, is fixed by six 12mm bolts, and you'll need a 250mm/10 inch extension with the socket to reach them. Slacken each of these by half a turn, in a diagonal sequence, before unscrewing them com-

5/4b ... and withdraw cover.

5/6b ... & withdraw speedo drive gear.

Mazda Miata, MX-5, Eunos & Roadster

Undo and remove the bolt and withdraw the speedometer drive gear. **Warning!** The gear will come away suddenly as it's a tight fit in its housing.

7 📷+ Unscrew and remove the neutral switch from the top of the transmission tail casing. You'll need a 24mm crescent wrench/spanner.

8 📷 Unscrew and remove the back up/reversing light switch from the left-hand side of the transmission tail casing, again using a 24mm crescent wrench.

9 📷+ Transmission tailshaft/extension casing removal. The tailshaft casing is held to the central part of the transmission by a ring of eight

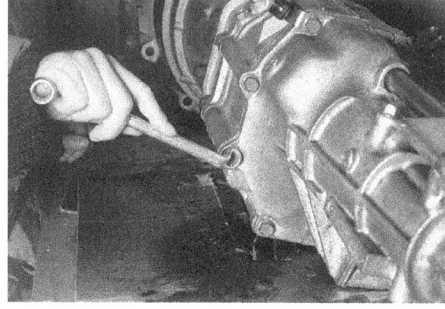
5/9a Slacken tailshaft casing bolts ...

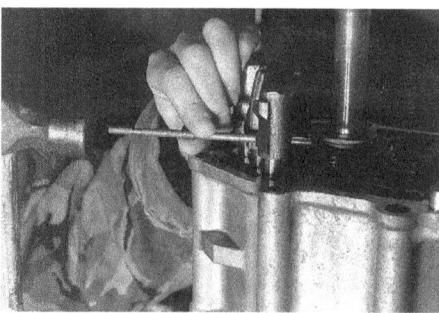
5/11a Drift out roll pins ...

5/7a Unscrew and ...

5/9b ... including these two.

5/11b ... and remove shift rod arms.

5.7b ... remove neutral switch.

the two offending bolts are loose, there's no longer sufficient room to withdraw the socket from the PPF bracket casting! Note that both of the top bolts also have wire clips under their heads.

10 📷+ Once the through bolts have been removed, pull the extension housing backwards to free it from the main transmission casing. As soon as the joint is broken, turn the extension housing clockwise, looking from the rear, which will allow the whole unit to be drawn off of the transmission tailshaft. **Caution!** Pull the unit over the tailshaft carefully so the rubber oil seal doesn't get damaged.

11 📷+ Stand the transmission unit on its nose and remove the three shift rod arms. Each arm is held in place by a single roll pin, which can be pushed out with a 4mm drift and a light hammer. Get someone else to hold the roll pin as it emerges otherwise it might drop into the transmission. Once the roll pin is out, the shift rod arm can be removed. Repeat the process for the other two arms.

12 Once the three arms are off, lift away the main casing. **Warning!** It may come free suddenly.

13 📷+ The next step is to pull the bellhousing/front casing off. Create a simple puller, like the

5/8 Remove backup (reversing) light switch.

5/10a Remove tailshaft casing bolts ...

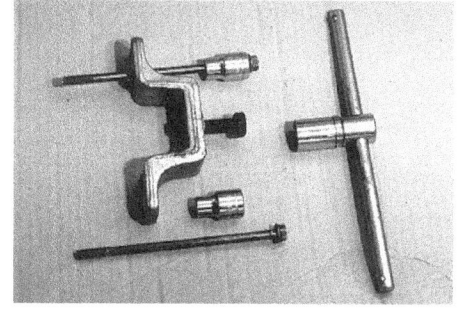
5/13a Components of puller used to ...

12mm bolts. These should be loosened progressively in a diagonal sequence and then removed completely. Two of the bolts are accessible to a socket and extension via holes in the PPF mounting on the right-hand side of the transmission. You'll need an extension of at least 570m/5 inches to reach these bolts, although you could get to them with a box end spanner. Note: if you do use a socket set through the PPF mounting casting, you need to put the socket on the bolt first and then feed the extension through. Don't try to undo the bolts completely with a socket as you'll find that, once

5/10b ... and withdraw casing.

5/13b ... pull bellhousing off.

4: Transmission (gearbox) & driveline

5/14 The naked transmission!

5/16a Remove detents but ...

5/20a Withdraw 5th/rev shift rod ...

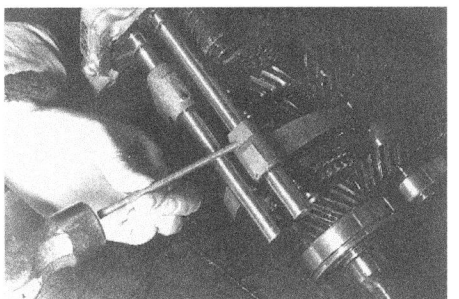

5/15 Drift out shift fork roll pin.

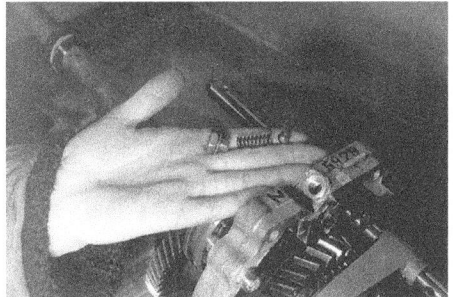

5/16b ... watch out for flying balls!

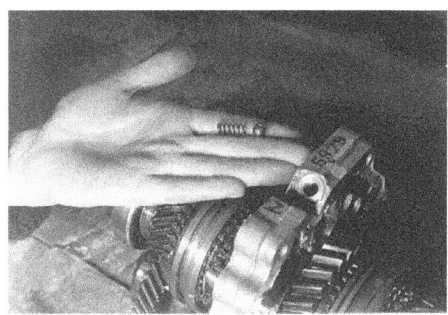

5/20b ... releasing this detent.

one we show, using a proprietary brake drum/hub puller, a couple of sockets and two of the transmission through bolts which were removed earlier. Fit the puller, as shown, and tighten the two long bolts to take up any slack. Screw the center bolt inward, which will pull the casing over the countershaft bearing and the input shaft through its bearing. Once it's free, lift the bellhousing/gearbox front casing away to reveal a large part of the gear train.

14 　If you want to see how the transmission works now's a good time to experiment. Bear in mind that drive comes into the transmission via the single gearwheel on the input shaft and is transmitted to the countershaft. Now try moving a clutch hub sleeve backwards or forwards until it locks with the adjacent gear; turn the input shaft and watch what happens. Play around, try reverse, and very quickly, despite its apparent complexity, you'll see what a simple mechanism the transmission really is.

15 　Back to work! Each of the three shift forks is locked to its shift rod by a roll pin: drive the pins out with a 4mm drift and light hammer whilst, where possible, supporting the shift fork.

16 　+ Around the central bearing carrier of the transmission there are three detents operating on the three shift rods. Each detent is held in place by a 14mm bolt, which should be unscrewed and removed, then the spring and ball collected from each detent. Note: the spring on the shortest shaft is lighter and the bolt does not have a copper washer, unlike the other two bolts. The long shift rod with the central fork selects first and second gears, the other long shift rod third and fourth and, of course, the short shift rod fifth and reverse.

17 　Remove the snap ring from the first/second shift rod. With some difficulty, it can be pushed off with two screwdrivers.

18 　The first/second shift rod can now be pulled

5/17 Remove 1st/2nd shift rod snap ring.

through the shift fork and through the transmission bearing carrier casting.

19 　Remove the snap ring from the third/fourth shift rod, then withdraw the rod from the bearing carrier casting and the shift fork in the same way as for the first/second shift rod. The shift forks can now be lifted from the clutch hubs.

20 　+ The fifth/reverse shift rod can then be pulled forward through the shift fork and transmission bearing carrier, complete with collar and spring. Note: as the rod is withdrawn from the bearing carrier casting, a second detent ball and spring will pop out.

5/19 Withdraw 3rd/4th shift rod.

21 　If you look at the transmission's bearing carrier casting, the three shift rod bores lie side-by-side, and you'll see that there are elongated detents in a bore between the two outer rods and the inner rod. These detents can be pushed out through the bore vacated by the first/second shift rod detent.

22 　+ Speedo drive gear removal from output shaft. Using a pair of snap ring pliers on the snap ring nearest the end of the output shaft, open the snap ring and slide it out of its groove, over the splines and off the shaft. Do the same with the nylon drive gear itself. There is a ball-bearing in a

5/22a Remove snap ring and ...

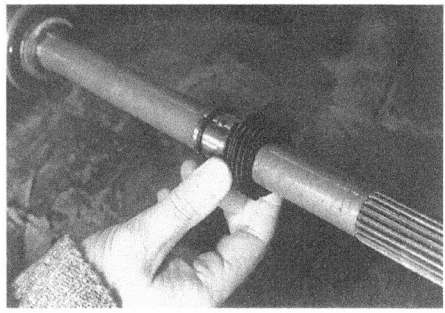

5/22b ... withdraw speedo gear.

Mazda Miata, MX-5, Eunos & Roadster

recess in the output shaft which locks the speedo driven gear in position: remove the ball-bearing and keep it together with the gear and its snap rings. Remove the second snap ring in the same way as the first.

23 ◘+ Using snap ring pliers and a screwdriver, open the mainshaft bearing retaining snap ring and slide it out of its groove, and then along and off of the end of the mainshaft. The snap ring should be followed by the thick spacing washer and the thin ring which retains the two C-shaped sections of the selective C-washer.

24 ◘ Now the mainshaft bearing needs to be

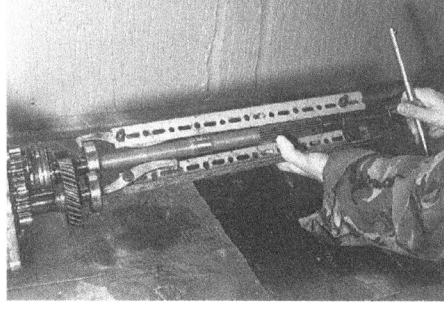
5/25a Use puller to free bearing ...

5/27a Release locknut locking tab ...

5/23a Remove snap ring, spacer and ring ...

5/25b ... then slide bearing off mainshaft.

5/27b ... and remove nut.

5/23b ... followed by C-washers.

moved, pull off the washer which retains the two C-washer segments, which will then fall clear of the mainshaft. Next, pull off the thick washer which abuts the fifth gearwheel and remove the single ball-bearing which locks the washer on the shaft. **Caution!** Keep ball-bearing, C-washers, C-washer locking ring and the thick spacing washer together as a set: they need to go back in exactly the same position and must not be confused with similar components removed earlier from the mainshaft. It's a good idea to put all of these components in a small plastic bag, seal it and then write an identifi-

5/27c Lock countershaft.

pulled off, which is a bit of a problem as the bearing's so far down the shaft. We made a puller for this job by dismantling our ordinary two-pronged puller and then reassembling it with two lengths of slotted shelving framework between the puller's yoke and arms. Okay, it looks pretty rough but it does work ... perfectly!

25 ◘+ Using a long reach bearing puller, pull the mainshaft bearing off its seat and then off the mainshaft. Wipe the bearing clean and mark its identity and orientation on the outer race with an indelible pen.

26 ◘ With the mainshaft rear bearing re-

5/26 C-washers, retainer, spacer and ball.

cation on the outside.

27 ◘+ Note: the four photos relating to the next two steps wrongly show the mainshaft rear bearing still in place - we all have bad days! Using a screwdriver, lever the dimple in the countershaft/layshaft locknut's rim out of the groove in the shaft. Then use a 32mm socket to unscrew and remove the nut. The countershaft can be locked by clamping the fifth gearwheel in vise jaws, but do ensure you have protectors mounted in the vise jaws otherwise the hardened gear teeth could be chipped. You can actually lock the countershaft by moving

the two synchromesh hubs shown towards each other to engage first and reverse gears simultaneously. **Warning!** The nut is very tight and will give very suddenly, so be careful.

28 ◘ After removing the locknut from the countershaft, the countershaft bearing should be removed using a puller. However, it's difficult to get a proprietary puller to do this job because there is little space to get the hooked legs of the puller between the rear face of the bearing and the fifth gearwheel. Instead, it is recommended that, as shown, you use a conventional proprietary puller to release the fifth gearwheel and countershaft

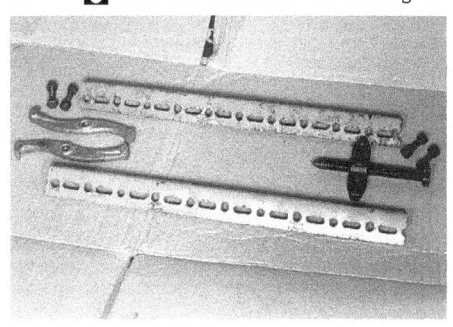
5/24 Homemade mainshaft bearing puller.

5/28 Using puller to free 5th gearwheel.

4: Transmission (gearbox) & driveline

5/29 Pull spacer from countershaft.

5/30a Withdraw 5th gear pinion ...

5/30b ... followed by synchro ring.

5/31 Release locknut's locking tab.

5/32 Unscrew locknut (see text) & slide off ...

5/33 ... hub, synchro ring, rev pinion & cage.

5/34 Remove inner race & selective washer.

5/35 Pull off countershaft reverse pinion.

5/36a Release snap ring and remove ...

5/36b ... tabbed washer and gear pinion.

bearing simultaneously. Wipe the bearing clean and mark its identity and orientation on the outer race with an indelible pen.

29　　Pull the countershaft fifth gear from the splines on the countershaft. Note: the forward side of the gear is marked with a white spot; however, if no such orientation mark is present, use an indelible pen to mark the gear pinion for correct reassembly. The spacer between the fifth gear and the countershaft reverse gear can now be pulled free of the countershaft.

30　　Pull the fifth gear pinion along the mainshaft until it can be removed. Next, pull off the fifth gear synchro ring.

31　　Release the locking tab of the large mainshaft locknut from the cutout in the shaft using a screwdriver as shown. Slide first and reverse clutch hubs towards the transmission center casting to simultaneously engage both gears and therefore lock the mainshaft.

32　　Undo the mainshaft locknut with a 41mm tube wrench slid down the mainshaft and over the nut: a pipe wrench on the exterior of the tube wrench should then release the nut. If, like us, you cannot obtain such a large tube wrench, a cold chisel and light blows from a hammer can be used to rotate the nut until it is slack enough to turn by hand. The idea, of course, is to get the chisel just behind one of the nut corners and then to drive the nut around by holding the chisel at an oblique angle.

33　　Once loose the locknut can be undone with fingers and pulled off of the transmission mainshaft, followed by the clutch hub which should be slid off of its locking splines on the mainshaft. **Caution!** Take care not to pull the clutch hub's sleeve too far out of position, otherwise you could have springs and keys flying everywhere ... Remove the second synchro ring, followed by the reverse gear pinion, together with its roller bearing cage.

34　　Remove the inner race of the reverse gear pinion, followed by the thick selective washer.

35　　The countershaft reverse gear can now be pulled off of the splined section of the countershaft (it was only left in place to enable the mainshaft to be locked).

36　　Remove the snap ring on the end of the reverse idler shaft, followed by the tabbed washer and then the gear pinion itself (noting that, in the case of our transmission, there is a white spot on the side of the pinion facing the rear of the transmission) and, finally, the thrust washer from the bearing plate side of the pinion.

37　　Undo and remove the five 12mm bolts holding the bearing retaining plate to the central bearing carrier. Note that the five bolts all have spring washers.

38　　With the bolts removed the bearing retaining plate can be pulled over the main and countershafts.

39　　Take the weight of the countershaft

4:11

Mazda Miata, MX-5, Eunos & Roadster

5/38 Remove bearing retainer.

gear cluster and, with the aid of a screwdriver but without using any real force, lever out the center race of the countershaft bearing. If this proves difficult, leave the race in place for the moment.

40 📷 Once the inner race is removed you may find that the countershaft can be disengaged from the input shaft and mainshaft gears to allow its removal. If not, don't worry.

41 With an assistant taking the weight of the gear clusters so that they're not straining the bearings, grasp the bearing carrier firmly and use a copper or nylon-faced hammer to tap the counter-

5/39 Lever out bearing center race.

5/40 If possible, remove countershaft.

shaft and mainshaft back through their bearings. You'll find that the countershaft does not need to be tapped back very far (particularly if you were successful in removing the bearing center race) before it can be removed. **Caution!** Make sure that both shafts move back through the bearing carrier by more or less the same amount, otherwise the gears on the two shafts will foul each other and damage may result. As soon as it is free enough, remove the countershaft from the central bearing housing.

42 📷 Once the countershaft is removed the

input shaft can be pulled forward to disengage it from the transmission mainshaft. **Caution!** Take care not to drop the synchro ring attached to the main drive gear pinion. Make sure, too, that the bearing in the tail of the input shaft doesn't fall out and become damaged.

43 📷+ With your assistant holding the gear cluster to take the strain from the bearing, continue to tap the mainshaft through its bearing in the central carrier. As soon as the bearing boss clears the bearing's inner race, the shaft becomes very loose and can be withdrawn completely. Note that on the back of the bearing there is a large spacer,

5/42 Remove input shaft.

which is selective.

44 📷 The first gear pinion, together with its needle bearing cage and inner race, can be slid along the mainshaft and removed from the splined end. Remove the synchro ring from the back of the first/second gear clutch hub and slide it off of the tail of the mainshaft.

45 📷 Turning to the front of the mainshaft you'll see that there is a snap ring retaining the clutch hub for third and fourth gears. Using snap ring pliers, open and remove the snap ring.

46 Wrap the first and second gear clutch hub

5/43a Withdraw mainshaft from carrier ...

5/43b ... then selective spacer.

5/44 Remove 1st gear pinion & bearing.

5/45 Remove snap ring.

in a rag and pull its outer sleeve forward and off, dislodged springs and keys will be caught within the rag. Collect together the pieces and store them in a safe place.

47 📷+ You'll now find that you can use an ordinary proprietary puller to pull the clutch hub, synchro ring and third gear pinion off the mainshaft together.

48 📷+ Using inverted jaw protectors, mount the transmission mainshaft in a vise so that the shoulders of the second gear pinion assembly are supported by the vise but the mainshaft is free.

5/47a Use puller to remove ...

5/47b ... clutch hub & 3rd gear pinion.

4: Transmission (gearbox) & driveline

5/48a Drive mainshaft thru 2nd gear pinion ...

5/48b ... and withdraw these components.

5/49 Drift out countershaft bearing.

that which has a retaining snap ring/circlip. Using a length of metal piping (or a socket of a diameter great enough to bear evenly on the outer race of the bearing), and a soft-faced hammer, drive the bearing gently through the carrier until it is removable. If the bearing is a very tight fit in the bearing carrier you can apply a little heat to the aluminum casting using a butane torch: this will have the effect of expanding the aluminum slightly and should make the bearing easier to remove. **Caution!** If you use heat on the plate don't play it on the plastic side pieces of the mainshaft bearing. Note that there may be a spacing shim behind the snap ring/circlip.

50   Removal of the mainshaft bearing from the bearing carrier is a similar procedure to that described for the countershaft bearing, except that access to the outer race of the bearing is via two cutouts. Therefore, the bearing should be driven out by using a brass or copper drift against the outer race, and alternating from cutout to cutout with every other blow so that the bearing remains square in its bore as it moves through the bearing housing. **Note.** There is likely to be a shim between the bearing and its seat.

51   The input shaft bearing can be removed

5/50 Drift out mainshaft bearing.

from the bellhousing casting using the techniques just described. The bearing should be driven outward from the transmission side.

52   If you wish to remove the reverse idler gearshaft from the center casting, first remove its single fixing bolt. Position the center casting over inverted vise jaw protectors and then, using a nylon or copper-faced hammer, drift the shaft out of the casting.

53   From this point to the end of this section, the text describes the teardown of the extension housing and, therefore, need only be followed if you wish to service components in the extension.

54   From the rear of the shift turret, remove the 19mm bolt, washer, spring and steel ball. Keep the components together in a bag.

55   From the underside of the shift turret, undo and remove the two 10mm securing bolts and then remove the spring cap, gasket, spring and plunger of the shift lock. Keep the small parts together in a bag.

56   In the turret side cover plate, angled downwards, is a 21mm bolt which should be removed, followed by washer, spring and plunger. Again, keep the components together.

57   Unscrew and remove the four bolts secur-

ing the turret side cover plate. Remove the plate.

58   Angle the control lever cup advantageously and then, using a 4mm metal drift and light hammer blows, drive the roll pin far enough through the cup to release the shift rod. Pull the shift rod out from inside the extension casing. Withdraw the cup from the turret and mount it in a vise to drive the pin out completely.

59   Lift the nylon ball seat bearing, and the wave washer beneath, from the turret top.

60   Unscrew and remove the four 12mm bolts which secure the turret to the extension body. Lift away the turret, pulling it backwards at the same time to free the shift rod cover tube.

61   Remove the oil supply rail from within the extension housing after releasing the single 10mm bolt securing its bracket.

6. TRANSMISSION (GEARBOX), MANUAL - COMPONENTS CHECKING & REPAIR

☞ First read 1/1, 2.

1   After thorough cleaning it's essential that all transmission components are checked thoroughly for damage or excessive wear. The following steps cover standard areas of wear and common faults, but be on the lookout for the unexpected, too, and, if in the slightest doubt about any component, replace it for the sake of your own peace of mind.

2   Take a commonsense attitude to new parts. If your car's done over 100,000km/60,000 miles, chances are the wearable bits in the transmission are showing their age, even if, technically they're not worn out. It's not worth putting such components back into a rebuilt transmission. For a really good rebuild to restore the car's original slick gearshift and quietness, replace bearings, synchro rings, clutch hubs, shift forks and detent springs

3   **Caution!** All roll pins, snap rings, locknuts and gaskets must be replaced.

MAINSHAFT GEAR PINIONS

4   Inspect the individual teeth, which should be unchipped, uncracked and have nice, squarish edges to the tooth tips. Heavy wear of gear pinions would have manifested itself as gear whine when the transmission was in use, and should now show up as unevenness in tooth shape and bright patches of obvious wear.

5   On one side of each pinion is the conical boss upon which the synchro ring affects its

6/4-5 Check pinion, synchro boss & teeth (dogs).

Mazda Miata, MX-5, Eunos & Roadster

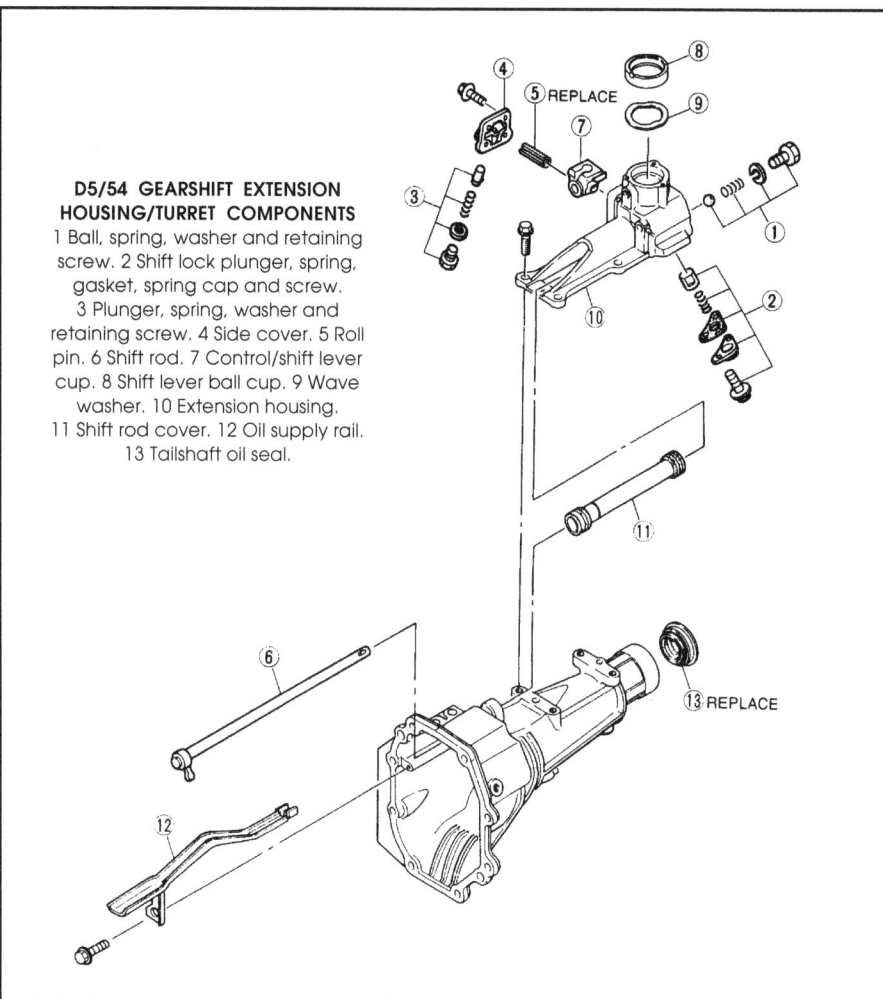

D5/54 GEARSHIFT EXTENSION HOUSING/TURRET COMPONENTS
1 Ball, spring, washer and retaining screw. 2 Shift lock plunger, spring, gasket, spring cap and screw. 3 Plunger, spring, washer and retaining screw. 4 Side cover. 5 Roll pin. 6 Shift rod. 7 Control/shift lever cup. 8 Shift lever ball cup. 9 Wave washer. 10 Extension housing. 11 Shift rod cover. 12 Oil supply rail. 13 Tailshaft oil seal.

braking action, and ring of teeth or dogs with which the clutch hub sleeve locks when the gear is selected. There is unlikely to be any wear on the boss as the synchro ring is made of softer material; however, it's possible the dogs will be worn or damaged: check each one carefully.

6 Place each of the mainshaft gears in its normal position on the mainshaft and, using feeler gauges, check that the clearance between gear and shaft does not exceed 0.15mm/0.006in.

MAINSHAFT

7 Check for obvious damage to splines, gear and bearing seats. If you have the facilities, check that the shaft's runout does not exceed 0.03mm/0.0012 in.

INPUT SHAFT AND COUNTERSHAFT

8 Check for obvious damage to splines, gear and bearing seats. Check condition of gear teeth as described in step 1.

CLUTCH/SELECTOR HUBS & FORKS

9 Check that the outer sleeve of the clutch hub moves freely and defaults to central position. Pull the hub apart, having wrapped it in rag to catch the bits, and inspect the inner hub's inner and outer splines, the sleeve's inner splines and the keys for obvious damage or wear.

10 Fit the relevant shift fork into the sleeve's outer groove. Push the fork finger to one side of the groove and then, using feeler gauges, measure the gap between the finger's thrust pad and the wall of the groove on the other side of the same finger. Ideal clearance is between 0.2 and 0.3mm/0.008 and 0.012in and will mean a very long serviceable life ahead. Maximum permissible clearance is 0.5mm/0.020in, but such a clearance will result in lower quality gearshift and short service life.

SYNCHRO RINGS

11 Check the teeth (or dogs) around the periphery of each ring for wear or obvious damage:

6/9 Check clutch hub including inner splines.

6/11 Check synchro rings.

the teeth should have good, squarish edges. The conical center of each ring should be covered with uniformly crisp but tiny oil retaining grooves: if these have disappeared, severe wear is indicated.

12 Place each synchro ring on the relevant gear's boss, making sure it is evenly seated. Using a feeler gauge, measure the gap between the back of the synchro ring and the flank of the gear. Standard clearance is 1.5mm/0.059in and minimum clearance is 0.8mm/0.031in: the latter will mean a short service life and poorer quality gearchanges.

BEARINGS

13 Rotate each bearing with your fingers. Any noisiness or stickiness indicates the need for replacement.

14 The surface of built-in oil seals, where applicable, should be undamaged.

15 The races should not be corroded, cracked or chipped.

SPRINGS

16 + Serviceable free length of springs is as follows (shorter means replacement): fifth and re-

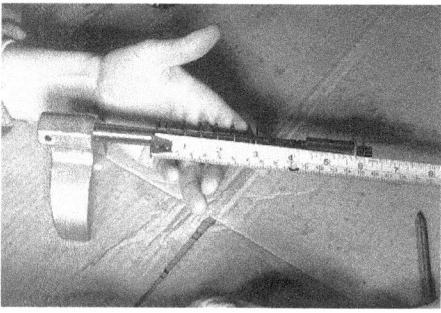

6/16a Check rod and ...

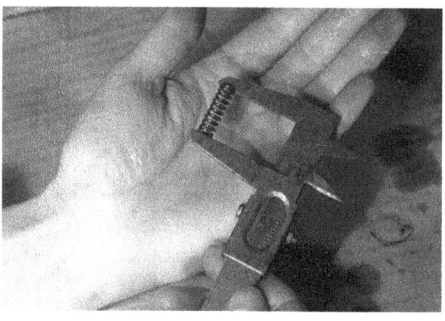

6/16b ... detent springs.

4: Transmission (gearbox) & driveline

verse shift rod spring, 75mm/2.953in; short detent springs (x2), 17.0mm/0.669in; long detent springs (x2), 22.5mm/0.886in.

CASINGS

17   Inspect visually for obvious damage. Check joint faces and remove light scratches with fine emery paper.

7. TRANSMISSION (GEARBOX), MANUAL - REBUILD

☞ First read 1/1, 2.

1   Note: as it's likely the transmission is being rebuilt with a number of new components, it's also more than likely that some tolerances will have to be adjusted with shims and selective washers as the rebuild proceeds. Unfortunately, it's not possible to predict what thicknesses of shims will be required before the rebuild starts; therefore, you should expect to have to stop the rebuild at least twice whilst you obtain suitable replacement shims. Transmission rebuilding is a job best done at a relaxed pace over a few evenings. Don't be tempted to cut corners; you'll end up with a noisy, notchy, short-life transmission unit.

2   Lubricate all components with fresh transmission oil as they are installed and keep tools, components and workplace clean at all times. If you have the slightest doubt about the serviceability of a component, replace it; you'll be glad you did, even if it hurts your pocketbook for a while ...☞ 4/4.

3   Fit the bearings to the transmission bearing carrier, remembering to install any shims that were originally fitted. Drive each bearing into place with either a tube or socket large enough to bear against the outer race, or by placing a block of hardwood over the whole bearing face and then hammering on that. **Caution!** Whichever method you choose, drive each bearing home squarely.

4   ◨ Check by how much the bearing face stands proud of the bearing carrier by placing a straightedge across the bearing face, and then measuring the gap between the straightedge and bearing carrier (or bearing if it's sunk in its housing) with a feeler gauge. You should do this for both countershaft and mainshaft bearings. Note that the bearing face can be flush with the bearing housing or proud by up to 0.1mm (0.004 inches) but no more. If the bearing is protruding from the carrier too much you will need to remove it as previously

7/4 Check bearing protrusion.

described, and then fit an appropriately thinner shim behind the bearing in place of the original so that it seats further into the bearing carrier. If the bearing face was found to be below the face of the housing, then a thicker packing washer is needed. Replacement shims are available in sizes of 0.1mm (0.004 inches), 0.15mm (0.006 inches) and 0.3mm (0.012 inches). When correct bearing fit has been achieved, carry on with transmission assembly.

5   ◨ Fit the bearing carrier bearing retaining plate in place and refit, finger-tight, the five bolts and spring washers which hold the plate to the carrier. **Caution!** If the spring washers have be-

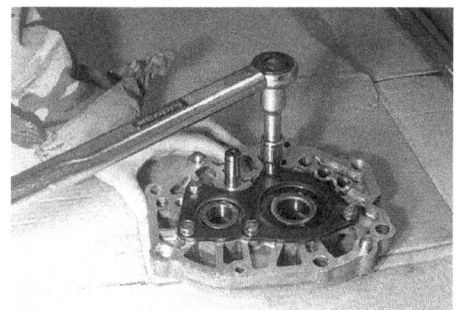

7/5 Torque tighten retainer plate bolts.

come flattened they must be replaced. Using a diagonal sequence, tighten the five bolts to a torque of 22 Nm/2.2 kgf m/17lbf ft.

6   If the reverse idler gearshaft is being installed, after pressing the shaft into position, its retaining bolt should be tightened to 12 Nm/120 kgf cm/100 lbf in.

7   Reassemble the reverse idler gear components by first fitting the thrust washer on the gearshaft, followed by the idler pinion (white spot toward rear of transmission), after having lubricated the gearshaft. Next, fit the spacer washer with its center tang in the shaft's groove and, finally, fit a new snap ring to the groove at the end of the shaft, making sure the snap ring is fully seated.

8   ◨ Using a feeler gauge check that the free play between the spacer washer and snap ring does not exceed 0.1mm (0.004 inches). If the clearance is greater than the maximum allowed, remove the snap ring and substitute a new spacer washer of a thickness appropriate to give the desired clearance. Replacement washers are available in sizes of 2.6mm (0.102 inches) /2.8mm (0.110 inches) and 3.0mm (0.118 inches). When the correct clearance has been achieved, transmission reassembly can continue.

7/8 Check lash (freeplay).

9   ◨ Mount the mainshaft in a vise so that the splined tail section is upward. **Caution!** You must use soft jaw protectors to ensure that the shaft is not damaged. Lubricate the whole of the mainshaft and then fit the second gear pinion, sliding it down the shaft until it meets the flange which separates it from third gear on the nose of the shaft. The pinion should be fitted so that the selector dogs are toward the rear of the transmission.

10   ◨ Next, fit the second gear synchro ring so that the cutouts face toward the rear end of the transmission.

11   If you've managed to get your clutch/

7/9 Fit 2nd gear pinion.

7/10 Fit 2nd gear synchro ring.

selector hub mixed up, you will find it useful to know that the largest hub (approximately 97mm/ 3.8 inches diameter) is the first/second hub, the second largest (90mm/3.54 inches diameter) is the hub for third and fourth gears and finally the smallest hub (84mm/3.3 inches diameter) is for fifth and reverse.

12   Fit the first/second clutch hub over the splines at the end of the mainshaft and slide it down the shaft into position. Note that the chamfered side of the hub's splined section should face toward the front of the transmission. Also, if you've dismantled the hub, ensure that the hub sleeve is fitted so that the side with the slight extension faces toward the rear of the transmission. Lastly, make sure the synchro keys on the clutch hub are lined up with the cutouts in the already positioned synchro ring before the clutch hub is pushed fully home onto its splines.

13   ◨ Ideally, a length of metal piping of at least 560mm/22 inches in length and 35mm/1.37 inches internal diameter, should be used to drift the hub fully onto its splines. Alternatively, you can temporarily remove the shaft from the vise and then, using the inverted jaw protectors as a seat for the clutch hub, tap the nose of the shaft until the

4:15

Mazda Miata, MX-5, Eunos & Roadster

7/13 Drive mainshaft into position.

hub is fully home on its splines. **Caution!** Don't forget to align the synchro keys and the cutouts in the synchro ring. Drive the hub home until there is no perceptible backward and forward play in the second gear pinion. Leave the mainshaft sitting on the clutch hub for the next procedure.

14   Having lubricated its seating, slide the third gear pinion over the nose of the mainshaft with the selector dogs facing toward the front of the transmission. Fit the synchro ring over the conical boss on the pinion with its cutouts facing toward the front of the transmission.

15   In our case, the third/fourth clutch hub had come apart during transmission dismantling and needed to be reassembled. A clutch hub is comprised of the central splined hub, an outer sliding sleeve, three keys and two synchro key retaining springs.

16   📷 Slide the central hub into the outer sliding sleeve. Then slide the three keys - which look like tiny cars in profile - into the hub slots with their 'roofs' facing outward. Leave each key protruding slightly into the recess in the central hub.

17   📷 Take one of the key retaining springs and fit its angled end into the hole in the side of the center hub's recess, then push the spring into position so that it holds each of the three keys in place. Note that the spring will only press against all three keys, which it must do, when it's fitted a certain way round. Carefully turn the hub assembly around and fit the spring on the other side, once again ensuring that it contacts all three keys when in the fully seated position.

18   Double-check on each side of the hub that each spring is in contact with all three keys, and that the spring lies against the recessed part of each key so that neither the keys nor the spring can fall out.

19   📷+ Fit the third/fourth clutch hub over

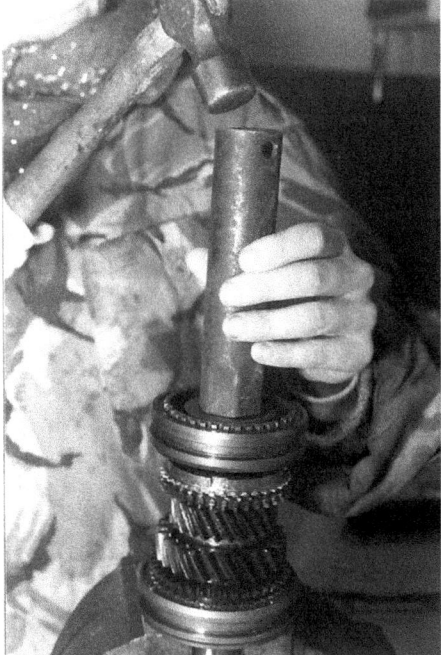

7/19a Drift 3rd/4th clutch hub into place ...

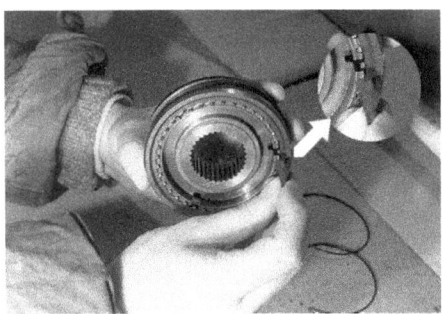

7/16 Correct fitting of keys ...

7/17 ... and springs.

7/19b ... until snap ring groove is exposed.

the nose of the mainshaft, ensuring that the chamfered side of the splined center faces toward the rear of the transmission. Make sure the splined section of the mainshaft is well lubricated. Engage the splines of the hub and then, using a length of metal piping, or a tube wrench of suitable diameter to bear on the central part of the clutch hub, drive the hub fully home on its splines. **Caution!** Make sure that the cutouts in the synchro ring align with the keys in the clutch hub, otherwise both could be damaged and neither will work properly. The tube wrench or metal pipe used as a drift needs to have an internal diameter of 35mm/1.37 inches to clear the boss of the mainshaft. You can tell when the hub is fully home as the snap ring groove in the mainshaft boss will be fully exposed.

20   Spring the snap ring into place, making sure that it is firmly and completely seated in its groove.

21   Turn the mainshaft assembly over in the vise and clamp the forward end of the mainshaft between jaw protectors.

22   📷 Slide the second synchro ring for the first/second clutch hub over the shaft and into position with the ring cutouts engaged with the keys in the clutch hub.

7/22 Align ring cutouts with keys.

23   Slide the inner race for the first gear bearings down the mainshaft and into position against the hub of the clutch.

24   📷+ Slide the bearing cage for the first gear pinion over the central race, having lubricated it thoroughly. Fit the first gear pinion with its selector dogs facing toward the front of the transmission, having first oiled the synchro ring which is already in position. Put the spacing washer over the mainshaft until it is in position against the rearward facing side of the first gear pinion. The whole assembly should now look like this.

25   📷 Fit the selective washer over the splined section of the countershaft so that it is pushed right up against the gear pinion. Remove the mainshaft assembly from the vise and lay it on your bench.

26   📷 If the front bearing is not fitted to the countershaft, now's the best time to do it. Mount the countershaft in a vise fitted with jaw protectors and then, using a metal tube or tube wrench of appropriate size to bear against the bearing's inner race, drift the bearing squarely, and fully, home. Fit a new snap ring, making sure it's fully seated in its groove.

27   📷 Place a block of wood on your workbench. Stand the nose of the mainshaft on the

4: Transmission (gearbox) & driveline

7/24a Fit bearing cage ...

7/24b ... lubricate ...

7/24c ... and fit 1st gear pinion.

7/25 Fit selective washer to countershaft.

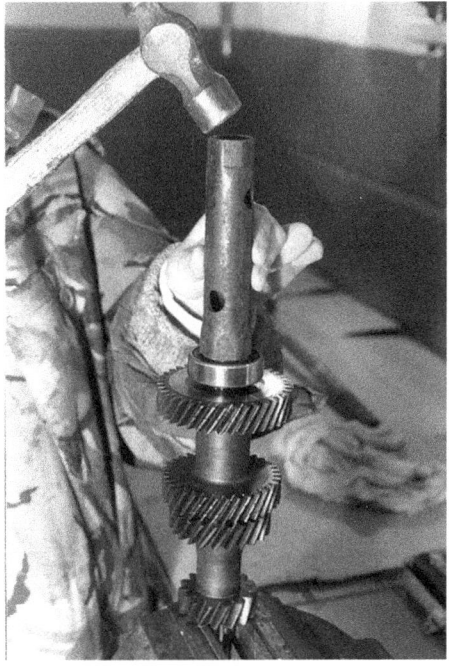

7/26 Drift bearing into place.

7/27 Drift bearing carrier onto shaft.

7/28a Grease bearing recess ...

7/28b ... and slide input shaft into position.

7/28c This is how it should look.

block of wood. Slide the transmission bearing carrier down the mainshaft (with the reverse idler pinion facing the rear of the transmission) until resistance is felt. Using a nylon-faced hammer, tap alternately on each side of the bearing retaining plate until the bearing carrier is fully home against the back of the first gear pinion.

28   ☐+ Pick up the transmission input shaft and place a dab of molybdenum disulfide grease into the base of the bearing recess at the back end of the shaft. Grease the bearing cage with the same grease and fit it in place in the end of the shaft.

Lubricate the conical boss behind the selector dogs of the primary drive gear and then position the synchro ring. Slide the input shaft over the boss on the front end of the mainshaft, making sure that the cutouts in the synchro ring are engaged with the keys in the third/fourth clutch hub. The mainshaft and countershaft assemblies should now look like this.

29   ☐ Install the countershaft. The fact that the countershaft's bearing is missing its inner race allows the countershaft to be introduced at such an angle it can be meshed with all of the gears on the input and mainshaft. You might find that you have

7/29 Fit countershaft.

to tap the mainshaft back through its central bearing slightly just to give clearance past the selector dogs of third gear: we were just able to do it without having to knock back the mainshaft. **Caution!** If you do have to tap the mainshaft back through its bearing, don't forget to return it to the correct position as soon as the countershaft is in place.

30 Mount the whole gear assembly in a vise with the face of the large pinion on the countershaft sitting on jaw protectors. From the rear of the center casting slide the countershaft bearing inner race down over the splined section (with collar towards rear of transmission) and, if neces-

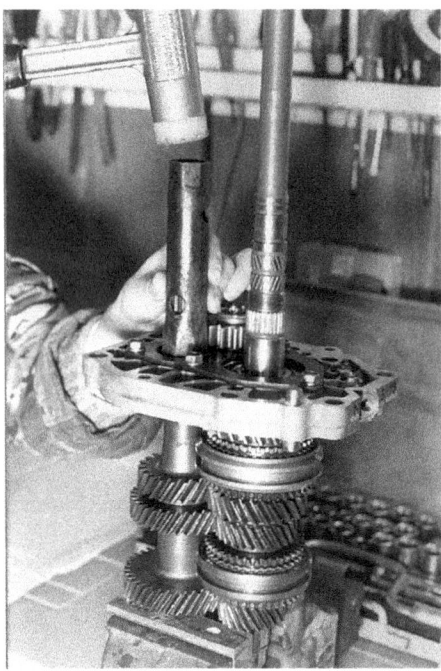

7/30 Gently drift in inner race.

sary, using a tube wrench or metal pipe of appropriate dimensions to drift the inner race gently home.

31 Lubricate the splines of the countershaft and slide the countershaft reverse gear pinion down over the splines, collar side toward the front of the transmission, until it engages with the idler pinion teeth and finally goes home against the inner race of the center bearing.

32 Fit the large selective washer over the mainshaft and let it drop onto the face of the mainshaft center bearing. Fit the inner race of the reverse gear pinion bearing onto the mainshaft. Drop it down until it abuts the washer.

33 Note: don't forget to keep lubricating the mainshaft and individual components as they are fitted.

34 Fit the reverse gear pinion bearing cage over the inner race, having lubricated it well.

35 Fit the mainshaft reverse gear pinion with the selector dogs facing toward the rear of the transmission. You'll need to engage the teeth of the pinion with the reverse idler pinion before it will go fully home against the large washer.

36 Next, fit the reverse synchro ring with the cutouts facing toward the rear of the transmission.

The ring seats over the conical boss on the back of the gear pinion.

37 Slide the first and reverse clutch hub down the mainshaft, making sure that the side with the central boss is toward the front of the transmission (this is also the side with the slight chamfer to the splined center section). Slide the clutch hub down the mainshaft until it engages with the shaft splines. Rotate the synchro ring until its cutouts align with the keys in the clutch hub.

38 The clutch hub now has to be driven fully onto the splined section of the mainshaft. Ideally, you'll have a piece of hollow metal pipe

7/37 Fit 1st/reverse clutch hub.

7/38 Drift clutch hub into place.

that's 432mm/17 inches long and has an internal diameter of 35mm/1.37 inches. However, if you don't have such a piece of metal piping you'll find that a shorter tube wrench will do almost as well, but don't forget to tap evenly around the top of the tube wrench, or pipe, so that the clutch hub does not tilt and jam.

39 Slide a new 41mm locknut down the mainshaft, collar toward the rear of the transmission, and finger-tighten it on the threaded section of the shaft until it contacts the inner hub of the clutch hub. It's going to be tricky to tighten this nut unless you have access to Mazda's special tool, which amounts to an elongated socket, but which does allow controlled tightening of the nut to 128-235 Nm, 13-24 kgf m or 94-174lbf ft. This really is pretty tight, so if you're using a 41mm tube wrench and pipe wrench - which is the second favored method after the official special tool - you'll need to tighten the nut as much as you can without applying additional leverage to the wrench. When we rebuilt our transmission we were working in a small community near to a fairly large town where we tried tool specialists and even agricultural suppliers for a 41mm tube wrench, but no-one had such a tool in stock. You may well find the same problem.

Therefore, we had to resort to a chisel to tighten the nut. The technique for tightening a nut with a chisel is to set the chisel point behind one of the corners of the nut and then to drive that corner forward or, in other words, around. Continue this process until the nut will not move any further using moderate blows from a 1lb hammer.

40 Using the corner of the chisel or a center punch, push a section of the nut's collar into the cutout in the mainshaft to lock the nut in place.

41 Fit the first reverse clutch hub synchro ring, cutouts toward the front of the transmission, ensuring that the three cutouts are aligned with the

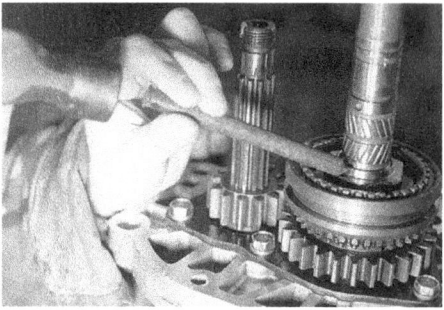

7/40 Stake the locknut.

7/43 Fit ball and selective washer.

three keys in the clutch hub.

42 Slide the fifth gear pinion down over the mainshaft, selector dogs toward the front of the transmission, until it sits snugly in the synchro ring of the clutch hub.

43 Carefully push the ball-bearing into its recess just behind the fifth gear pinion. Then slide the thick selective washer with central cutout down the shaft and engage the cutout with the ball-bearing to prevent the washer from rotating. Position the two halves of the C-washer on top of the washer you have just installed so that they are seated in the groove in the shaft. Then slide the large retaining ring down the shaft and over the outside of the C-washer halves to keep them together.

44 + Using a feeler gauge measure the space between the C-washers and the selective washer behind. This represents fifth gear lash/endfloat. The clearance should be in the range 0.1 - 0.3mm (0.00 - 0.012 inches) and, if not, then a replacement selective washer should be obtained of appropriate size to correct the discrepancy. Selective washers are available in four sizes: 6.2mm (0.244 inches), 6.4mm (0.252 inches), 6.5mm (0.256 inches) and 6.6mm (0.260 inches).

4: Transmission (gearbox) & driveline

7/44a Check gear lash (endfloat).

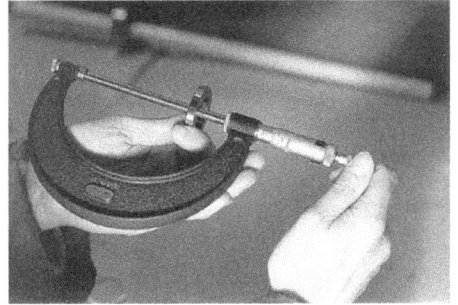

7/44b Measuring selective washer.

45   Slide the spacer down the countershaft until it sits on the reverse pinion.
46   Slide the countershaft fifth gear into position, protruding boss toward the front of the transmission.
47   Fit the mainshaft rear bearing by sliding it down over the shaft until it will go no further. The bearing will need to be driven the rest of the way home against the C-washers using the piece of metal piping previously used, or an appropriate tube wrench.
48   Fit the two C-washers into the slot behind the mainshaft rear bearing, followed by their retaining ring.
49   Using a feeler gauge check that there is no lash/endfloat between the inner race of the mainshaft rear bearing and the C-washers. There should be no play at all, but up to 0.1mm (0.004 inches) is permissible. If there is a discrepancy this should be corrected by fitting C-washers of different thicknesses. Replacement washers are available in thicknesses of 2.9mm (0.114 inches), 3.0mm (0.118 inches), 3.1mm (0.122 inches) and 3.2mm (0.126 inches).
50   Fit the large spacing washer over the mainshaft and against the C-washers. Fit a new snap

7/49a Check lash (endfloat).

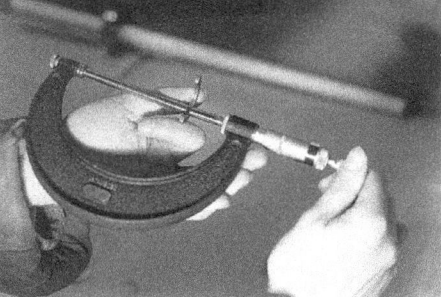

7/49b Measuring thickness of C-washer.

ring into the groove behind the washer and make sure it's fully seated and secure.
51   Fit the countershaft rear bearing in place and drive it home against the fifth gear pinion using a 20mm socket and a nylon or copper-faced hammer.
52   Lock the countershaft by engaging first and reverse gears simultaneously (shift their respective clutch hub sleeves toward the center bearing carrier plate).
53   With your fingers screw a new 32mm locknut onto the end of the countershaft, then torque the nut to 170 Nm/1.7 kgf m/125ft lbs.
54   Using a center punch or small chisel, peen the locking ring of the countershaft locknut into the groove in the shaft.
55   Disengage first and reverse gears by moving both synchro rings back to a central position, thus setting the transmission in neutral.
56   Reassembling detents. Remove the whole gear cluster assembly from the vise and place on your workbench so that the countershaft is at the bottom and the mainshaft on top. Looking at the rear side of the center casting you'll see the three holes through which the shift rods slide. The

7/51 Drift countershaft bearing home.

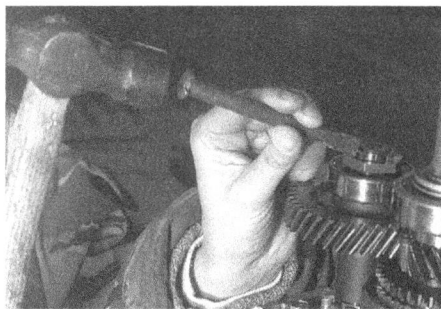

7/54 Stake locknut.

7/56 Ready to refit detents.

7/57 Drop spring & ball into detent bore.

lowest hole carries the shift rod for reverse and fifth gear, the middle hole the shift rod for third and fourth gear and the top hole the shift rod for first and second. Using blocks of wood, support the bearing plate and transmission input shaft so that the detent bores for shift rods reverse/five and three/four are vertical in both planes.
57   Take the spring for the lower part of the fifth/reverse detent (you have two long and two short springs; both short springs are used in the fifth/reverse detent bore). Drop the spring into the top of the detent bore and, if necessary, guide it into position below the shift rod bore. The spring should be followed by the round detent ball. With a little luck you should end up with the ball sitting on top of the spring. If not, using fingers or screwdrivers, manipulate the ball until it is sitting on top of the spring.
58   Lubricate the fifth/reverse gear shift rod (it's the shortest rod with a spring and spring collar butting against a snap ring at one end). Using a screwdriver inserted from the rear side of the center casting, press down the ball in the shift rod bore whilst inserting the nose of the rod from the other side of the casting until the screwdriver is displaced and the rod itself is holding the ball and

4:19

Mazda Miata, MX-5, Eunos & Roadster

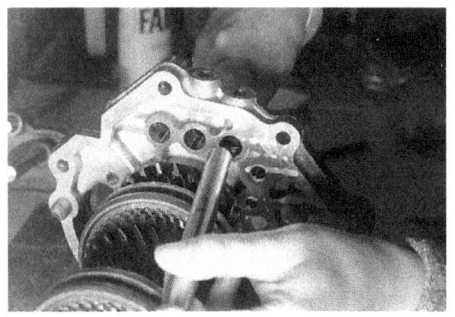
7/58 Hold down detent & fit shift rod.

7/60 Drive in new roll pin.

7/66 Fit 1st/2nd shift rod.

7/59 Feed shift rod thru fork.

7/62 Drop in detent 'ball'.

7/67 Fit detent ball, spring and bolt.

spring in place. For the moment the fifth/reverse shift rod should only protrude about half an inch through the rear side of the center casting.

59 Position the fifth/reverse shift fork on the fifth/reverse clutch hub. Then feed the shift rod through the fork until the roll pin holes align. Note that the side of the shaft with three detent notches should be facing away from the gear train. Note that the protruding side of the fork boss should point toward the rear of the transmission.

60 Drive a new roll pin, seam facing forward, into position to lock the fork to the shift rod. Use a light hammer to drive the pin home, whilst holding a heavier hammer against the other side of the yoke to absorb the hammer blows.

61 Rotate the bearing carrier plate until the bore for the first/second detent is vertical in both planes.

62 Take one of the elongated detent balls and drop it into the top of the first/second detent bore: hopefully, it will drop right the way down through to sit on top of the fifth/reverse shift rod. If it doesn't, you'll need to manipulate it into position with your fingers.

63 Push the third/fourth shift rod into its bore from the rear side of the bearing carrier, making sure that the end with a flattened section is toward the front of the transmission. Hold the third/fourth shift fork in position on its clutch hub so that the rod can also be pushed through the fork's mounting boss.

64 Make sure that the three detent notches in the third/fourth shift rod face away from the mainshaft gear train. Line up the roll pin drilling in both fork and shift rod, then drive a new roll pin home, seam facing forward, as previously described.

65 Drop the second elongated detent ball into the detent bore for the first/second shift rod. With luck, it should drop right the way through to

7/63 Fit 3rd/4th shift rod.

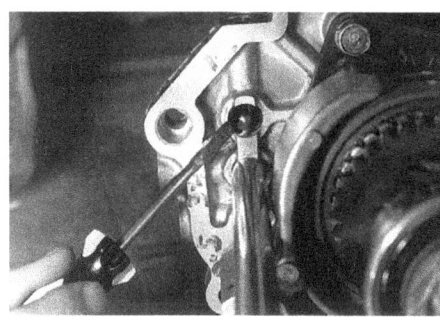
7/65 Drop in detent 'ball'.

bear against the newly installed third/fourth shift rod. If necessary, you can manipulate the ball with fingers or a screwdriver until it drops into place. **Caution!** Don't forget to lubricate the detent bores and detent balls during assembly.

66 Insert the first/second shift rod from the rear of the bearing plate, whilst holding the first/second fork in position on its clutch hub so that the shaft also passes through the fork. Set the three detent grooves so that they face away from the third/fourth shift rod and then align the roll pin bore in the shift fork and rod, before driving the pin home as described previously. **Caution!** It's important that the slot in the pin faces toward the front or rear of the transmission and not toward the side.

67 Rotate the bearing carrier so that the bore for the fifth/reverse shift rod detent is vertical in both planes. Put a drop of oil into the detent bore, followed by a round detent ball, the second short spring and, finally, the retaining bolt, to which I suggest you apply a little thread locking fluid for the sake of security. Tighten the retaining bolt to a torque of 22 Nm/2.2 kgf m/17lbf ft.

68 Repeat this procedure using the remaining balls and two long springs for the detent bores of the third/fourth shift rod and the first/second shift rod. Note that the retaining bolts for these two detents both have copper washers, whilst that for the fifth/reverse detent does not. Again, it's suggested you put a little thread lock on the retaining bolt threads for the sake of security. Torque wrench settings are the same as before. Fit the snap rings/circlips to the shift rods for first/second and third/fourth gears. Make sure that the new clips are firmly and securely seated in their grooves.

69 Set all of the clutch hub sleeves in their central 'relaxed' position so that no gears are engaged. Using feeler gauges measure the gaps

7/68 Fit new snap rings.

4: Transmission (gearbox) & driveline

7/69 Measuring fork clearance.

between the shift fork thrust pads and the sides of the clutch sleeves; make and record this measurement both sides of the same shift fork tip (only measure one tip for each fork) and for each of the three shift forks.

70 It is important that the clutch hub sleeves run centrally on the shift fork tips. The measurements you have just recorded should show that the hub sleeves are centered on the fork tips, or are, at least, within 0.3mm/0.012in of being so. If the hubs are not central enough the very bad news is that you'll have to dismantle the mainshaft again to reset the whole shaft, and therefore the clutch hub sleeves, further forward or backward as appropriate.

71 The mainshaft's longitudinal position is adjusted by the selective spacers to be found on each side of the shaft's center casting bearing. The total thickness of the two spacers must be between 5.9 and 6mm/0.2323-0.2362in. Individual spacer washers are available in the following thicknesses: 2.2mm/0.0866in; 2.7mm/0.1063in; 3.0mm/0.1181in; 3.2mm/0.1260in; 3.7mm/0.1457in.

72 Whoa, don't panic! It's not as complex as it sounds. Here's how. Say the measurements you took showed that the whole mainshaft was too far forward by 0.3mm/0.012in (the gap on the side of the shift fork tip is bigger, by 0.3mm/0.012in, on the side that faces the front of the transmission), then the required adjustment is a thinner spacer in front of the center casting bearing to move the mainshaft back by 0.3mm/0.012in. Comprendez vous? Tres bon!

73 Record the adjustment required and then teardown the gearshafts, as you've done before, until you've got the mainshaft out of the center casting. Measure the individual thickness of the existing spacers, making sure you know which spacer came from which position. To make it easy in our example we'll say that we found both existing spacers to be 3.0mm/0.1181in thick. To move the mainshaft backwards through the bearing we need a forward spacer 0.3mm/0.012in thinner, i.e., a new spacer that's 2.7mm/0.1063in thick. Remember that the total thickness of both spacers must be between 5.9-6.0mm/0.2323-0.2362in, therefore, the second new washer that's appropriate from the range available is of 3.2mm/0.1260in thickness. This time, when you've reassembled the transmission, you should find the shift fork fingers slap bang in the middle of the clutch hub sleeve grooves.

74 Stand the whole gear cluster assembly on its nose in an open vise with the front face of the countershaft first gear resting on jaw protectors.

75 Spread a thin, but continuous, bead of silicone sealant around the flange of the bearing carrier and allow it to dry for around five minutes. Rub oil over the three shift rods, the rims of the countershaft and mainshaft rear bearings, and also liberally oil the whole gear train. Lower the transmission main casing into position, carefully feeding it over the three shift rods and making sure that the mainshaft and countershaft bearings are aligned with their housings in the back end of the casting.

76 Fit the three shift rod end arms in the arrangement shown in the photograph. As when fitting the shift forks, use a large hammer to absorb the blows when driving roll pins home. Make sure that the roll pin openings face toward the front of the transmission. Fit the shift rod end with the shortest pawl first and the one with the longest pawl last. **Caution!** Be careful not to drop the roll pins into the transmission center housing.

77 Stretch a rag over the transmission center housing so that you cannot drop components into the casing, then fit a new snap ring into the groove of the mainshaft nearest the center

7/75 Fit main casing.

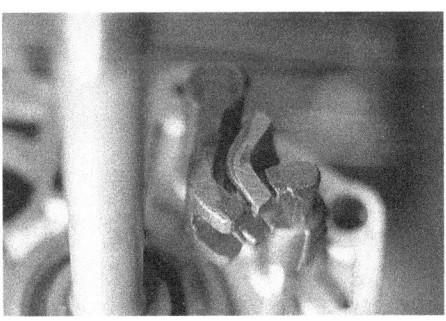

7/76 Correct arrangement of shift rod arms.

7/77 Fit locking ball and speedo drive.

casing. Make sure the snap ring is securely located in its groove. Fit the small ball-bearing into the recess in the mainshaft; this bearing will lock the speedometer drive gear in position and prevent it rotating. Slide the speedometer drive gear over the mainshaft and align one of its internal grooves with the ball-bearing so that the speedometer drive gear can be pushed fully home against the snap ring that has already been fitted. Fit the second new snap ring to retain the speedometer drive gear, ensuring the snap ring is securely seated in its groove.

78 Steps 80 to 88 describe the rebuild of the transmission extension housing, and only apply if the unit is disassembled.

79 Fit the oil rail inside the extension housing and fix with the single 10mm bracket bolt. Tighten the bolt with a wrench using finger pressure only.

80 Lubricate the rubber seals of the shift rod tube with oil and then push the end of the tube with the forward mark into position in the extension housing.

81 Spread silicone sealant over the turret mounting pads on top of the extension and then fit the turret in place, taking care to engage it with the free end of the shift rod cover tube. Fit the turret's four 12mm retaining bolts and tighten the bolts to

7/81 Torque tighten turret bolts.

a torque of 22 Nm/2.2 kgf m/17lbf ft.

82 From inside the extension housing, slide the lubricated shift rod back into position and simultaneously engage it with the shift cup in the turret. Check that the shift finger of the rod is pointing downward and then align the roll pin hole in the cup with that in the rod. Drive a new roll pin home, making sure that its seam faces the front of the transmission.

83 Spread a thin, but continuous, smear of silicone sealant around the side flange of the shift turret. Four 10mm bolts retain the cover plate on the side of the turret and these, too, should each be

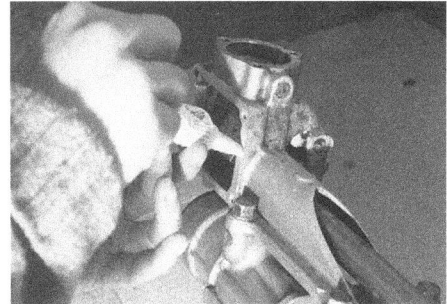

7/83 Apply silicone sealant.

4:21

smeared with silicone sealant before they are fitted. Once the bolts are in place and finger-tight, tighten them fully using just a box end wrench and finger pressure. Note that the cover should be fitted with the angled threaded bore facing downwards.

84 + Oil them first, then slide the thrust pin and spring up into the bore in the side of the turret cover - the domed part of the thrust pin first. Fit and tighten the 21mm retaining bolt by wrench and finger pressure only. Do not overtighten.

85 Turn the extension housing upside down and, from the base of the shift turret, insert the spring-loaded locking plunger, dome end first,

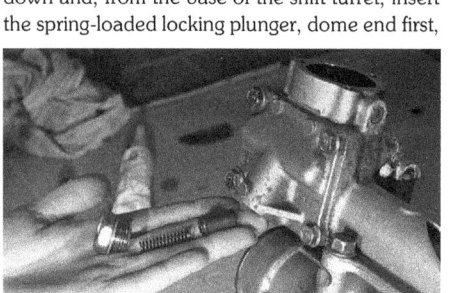
7/84a Fit thrust pin and spring ...

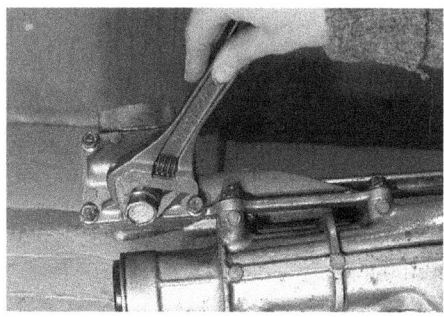
7/84b ... then retaining bolt.

making absolutely sure that the side with three flats faces toward the detent bore; in other words, toward the back of the transmission. Oil the plunger before installing it. With the plunger in position, insert the spring into its center followed by the thrust cap which, of course, should be sealed with a new gasket. Tighten the two 10mm bolts securing the thrust cap using a wrench and finger pressure only.

86 Oil the spring and ball for the shift lock detent and then insert the ball, followed by the spring, into the detent bore at the rear of the shift turret. Smear the whole threaded area of the

7/85 Locking plunger components.

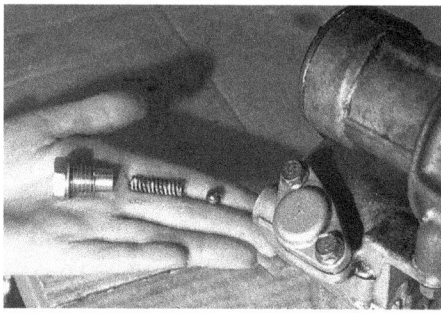
7/86 Shift lock detent components.

7/88 Apply silicone sealant.

retaining hollow bolt with silicone sealant. Engage the protruding spring end with the hollow center of the bolt and screw the 19mm bolt home. Tighten with a wrench and finger pressure only. Do not overtighten.

87 Fit the wave washer, followed by the nylon ball seat, into the top of the turret.

88 Spread a thin, but continuous, bead of silicone sealant around the rear flange of the transmission main casing and allow it to dry for around five minutes.

89 Using a screwdriver or your fingers, move the shift cup in the transmission extension housing to the reverse position. In other words, looking from the rear of the transmission it will be laid over as far as possible to the left and pushed as far as possible forward. Hold it in this position and then lower the extension gently into position and twist it slightly to the right. As the gap between the center housing and extension housing closes to about 13mm/half an inch, you should be able to see the extension housing shift engage with the shift arms on the end of the shift rods; as soon as that happens, twist the extension casing to the left and lower it into final position. Before going further, check that the shift is working by temporarily installing the gearshift lever and gently selecting gears. You may need to lift the assembly out of the vise to do this so that the gear train is free to rotate a little.

90 + If the input shaft front bearing was removed from the bellhousing, now is the time to refit it, or fit a new bearing. First, fit a new snap ring into the groove in the outer race of the bearing, making sure the snap ring is securely seated in the groove. Lubricate the outer race of the bearing and position it over its housing in the bellhousing casting (from the open bellhousing end). Using a 200mm/8 inch length of hardwood timber of

7/90a Fit new snap ring ...

7/90b ... position bearing ...

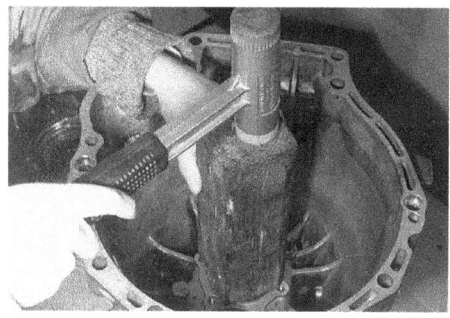
7/90c ... then drift home.

75x75mm/3x3 inches or more square, or a piece of metal pipe with an outside diameter matching the bearing's outer race, drift the bearing home until the snap ring contacts the bellhousing casting. Remember to tap the wood block or drift in a circular pattern so that the bearing is driven home evenly.

91 Using a vernier depth gauge, or a straight-edge and feeler gauges, measure the height of the bearing face above the face of its housing and make a note of the measurement as 'B'. Then, using the same tools, measure the depth of the second recess (almost same diameter as the input shaft bearing) in the rear of the input shaft cover and note this measurement as 'A'. The input shaft cover serves as a bearing retainer which should secure the input shaft bearing with virtually no lash/endfloat. Measurement 'B' can be between 0 and 0.1mm/0 and 0.004in smaller than measurement 'A': it must not be larger. Adjustment shims, which fit between the bearing's front face and the back of the cover, are available in three sizes: 0.10mm/0.004in; 0.15mm/0.006in; 0.30mm/0.012in.

92 Place the bellhousing casting clutch end down on your bench, then spread a thin but continuous bead of silicone sealant around the rear

4: Transmission (gearbox) & driveline

flange of the transmission bellhousing casting.

93 ⚙ Lubricate the forward ends of the shift rods and also liberally oil the whole gear train. Gently lower the transmission assembly into the bellhousing until the joint flanges meet. Be careful to ensure that the shift rods have lined up with their supporting bores in the back of the bellhousing, and also that the input shaft is lined up with its bearing and the countershaft bearing with its housing. Once you are confident all is correctly lined up, you can use a rubber or nylon-faced hammer around the forward flange of the extension housing to tap the whole assembly together.

7/93 Fit transmission assembly to bellhousing.

94 Once the gap between the bellhousing casting rear flange and the front flange of the central bearing carrier is no more than 6-7mm/a quarter inch apart, you can insert the transmission casing through bolts and, in a diagonal sequence, gradually tighten them to evenly close and seal all of the transmission joints. Note: before inserting the bolts, a bead of sealant should be put under the head of each and remember that the two uppermost bolts retain wiring clips. Final torque for the 12mm through bolts is 20 Nm/2.0 kgf m/15lbf ft.

95 ⚙ Input shaft front cover oil seal replacement (if required). Mount the input shaft cover in a

7/95 Buckle old seal ...

vise, clamping the input shaft sleeve between jaw protectors. Using gentle blows, drive a screwdriver blade between the outer rim of the seal and the casting.

96 ⚙ You'll then find you can lever the buckled seal out of its seat. Lubricate the outer rim of the new seal.

97 ⚙ Place the seal over its housing and, using very gentle taps from a rubber or nylon-faced hammer against the outer rim of the seal only, gently tap it home into its housing.

98 ⚙ Transmission rebuild continued. Place a new gasket in position on the front housing flange

7/96 ... and lever out.

7/97 Tap new seal into position.

7/98 Fit a new gasket.

inside the bellhousing, having first smeared the back of the gasket with oil to make it stick in place. Smear the flange of the housing with oil, and also lubricate the inner lip of the oil seal and the area of the input shaft the seal lip bears upon. If bearing shims are required (see step 82), fit them into the rear of the housing.

99 ⚙ Slide the housing into position inside the bellhousing casting and tighten its six retaining bolts finger-tight. It's recommended you put a smear of silicone sealant around the threads of each of the bolts before inserting them. Tighten the

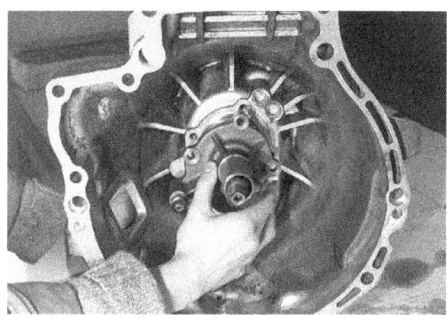
7/99 Slide housing into position.

bolts to a torque of 22/2.2 kgf m/17lbf ft. Don't forget to tighten in a diagonal sequence.

100 ⚙+ Smear high melting point, copper-based or organic molybdenum grease on the input shaft sleeve and on the clutch release fork pivot. Put another blob in the socket on the back of the release fork and more on the tips of the release arm's fork fingers.

101 ⚙ Pass the release fork tail out through the square hole in the side of the bellhousing. Take the clutch release bearing and place it on the input shaft sleeve with its arms facing toward the back of

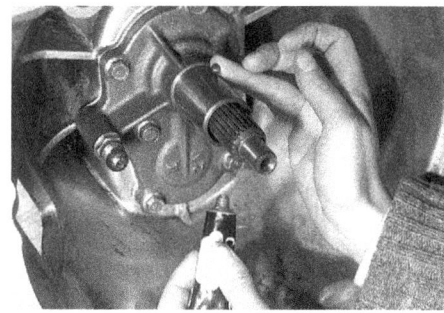
7/100a Grease input shaft sleeve ...

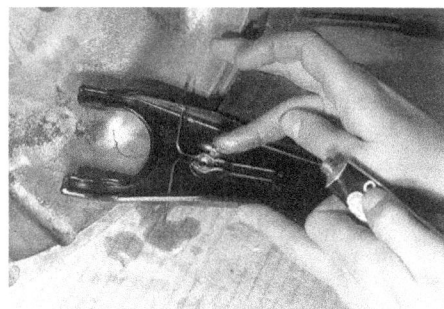
7/100b ... and release fork pivot socket.

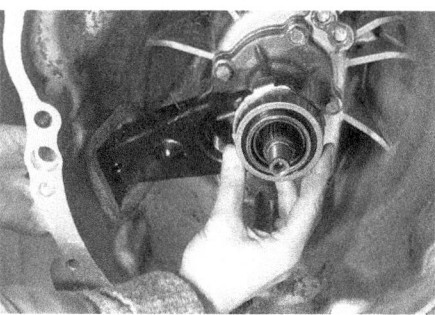
7/101 Fit release bearing and fork.

4:23

Mazda Miata, MX-5, Eunos & Roadster

the transmission. Note that the fork tips of the release fork must engage with these arms once the whole assembly is in place. Now the tricky bit is to push the arm against its pivot so that the spring opens and retains the arm, whilst at the same time the fork tips of the arm engage with the extensions on the back of the thrust washer. It's easier than it sounds!

102   Replace the rubber boot around the protruding part of the clutch release arm, making sure its lip is engaged with the bellhousing casting.

103   Fit the backup/reverse light switch to the left-hand side of the transmission rear extension. This is the switch with red cables and enscapulation around the top. Tighten the 24mm hexagonal section of the switch using an crescent wrench and finger pressure only. Do not overtighten. Don't forget the copper sealing ring which should be replaced every time the switch is removed.

104   Fit the neutral sensor switch at the top right of the extension casing. Once again, don't forget a new sealing washer, and tighten the switch's 24mm hexagonal section by hand pressure only.

105   Turn the transmission onto its left-hand side and on the right-hand side of the transmission extension casing you'll see an opening for the speedometer driven gear. Lubricate the gearwheel thoroughly and gently slide the driven gear assembly down into its housing. When the driven gear is fully home in its housing, fit the 10mm bolt which retains it and tighten with a wrench using finger pressure only.

106   That concludes the transmission rebuild. If it's the first one you've ever done, you should celebrate!

8. TRANSMISSION (GEARBOX), MANUAL - INSTALLATION

☞ First read 1/1, 2.

1   Spread a thin smear of copper-based lubricant on the nose and splines of the transmission input shaft - don't overdo it!

2   Using protective packing on the jack's pad, jack the front of the engine 50mm/2 inches, which will have the effect of tilting the rear of the engine slightly downwards. **Caution!** Don't jack so far that the camshaft angle sensor or coil unit contact the firewall, and check that hoses and wiring harnesses are not getting stretched.

3   With the help of a strong assistant or, better still, by supporting the weight of the transmission on a wheeled jack, bring the engine and transmission unit together. Make sure that the transmission input shaft enters the center of the clutch cover and that the bellhousing is correctly lined up with the engine backplate. If the clutch disc is well centered, the transmission bellhousing should go fully home against the engine backplate with no more than a little joggling around. Life will be a little more difficult if the clutch disc isn't well centered and, in extreme cases, you'll have to withdraw the transmission, slacken the clutch cover, re-center the disc and retighten the cover bolts before attempting again to make the transmission fit.

Once the transmission bellhousing slides fully home, make sure it engages on the hollow spigots projecting from the rear of the cylinder block.

4   Fit the two topmost bellhousing bolts, which are 17mm (x60mm), and screw them into place finger-tight which, for the moment, will be enough to stop the transmission coming away from the back of the engine again. Fit the two lowermost 17mm (x60mm) bolts which, again, should be screwed in finger-tight at this stage.

5   At this point you may find it helpful to support the transmission on a sling or jack after removing the jack at the front of the engine.

6   Position the exhaust pipe support bracket over the two bolt holes on the left-hand side of the bellhousing. Secure the bracket, flange facing rearward, with two 17mm bolts, the upper of which is longer at 70mm although there seems no good reason for this. Screw the bolts home finger-tight. Note: the four remaining fasteners in the starter motor area will be fitted later.

7   Tighten all of the 17mm bellhousing bolts to 64-89Nm/6.5-9.1kgf m/48-65lbf ft.

8   Temporarily, lower the jack or rope sling supporting the transmission unit. Above the transmission case you'll see that several wires sprout from the main harness (four connectors); these are the connectors for the sensors and switches mounted in the transmission outer casing. You'll see that they have different types of connector so there can be no confusion over which connections are for which switch or sensor. Because the harness is still loose, it's possible to pull the two wires with connectors over the top of the transmission so that they can be seen between the transmission and the left-hand side of the transmission tunnel, making reconnecting the backup (reverse) light switch much easier. Note that these connectors need to click home. Now remake the connections to the neutral indicator switch, noting that it doesn't matter which wires you connect to each other: this is also true for the backup light switch. The neutral indicator switch connectors have locking tabs which you need to hear click to indicate that the connection is properly made.

9   Place a dab of molybdenum disulfide or copper-based grease on the ball end of the clutch release (slave) cylinder pushrod. Engage the pushrod in the clutch actuating arm of the bellhousing, and then secure the clutch release cylinder to the bellhousing with two 10mm bolts. Tighten the bolts to 16-22Nm/1.6-2.3kgf m/12-16lbf ft. Above the release cylinder is a bracket which holds a coil of rigid hydraulic pipe. This bracket should be secured with its 10mm bolt tightened to 16-22Nm/1.6-2.3kgf m/12-16lbf ft. You can get access to the pipe bracket bolt and the upper release cylinder bolt via the space between the suspension subframe and the inner fender, but will need to tighten the lower slave cylinder bolt with a box end wrench (ring spanner) from beneath the engine (or you could use a universal joint on a socket with extensions).

10   From beneath the car, fit the two 12mm bolts through the bellhousing and into the starter motor flange. Note that the innermost of these two

bolts also carries a support bracket for the clutch release cylinder's hydraulic pipe connection (manual trans cars), whilst the other carries a wiring harness bracket. Manipulating these bolts into position is difficult - but not impossible! Both can be tightened to 38-51Nm/3.8-5.3kgf m/28-38lbf ft with a 12mm socket in conjunction with a universal joint and extensions.

11   Install the PPF☞ 3/11/11-17 & 52-55.
12   Install driveshaft (propshaft)☞ 4/10/7-8.
13   Install the exhaust system☞ 5/38/18-27.
14   If applicable, re-attach the front subframe cross brace ('performance bar') and secure with its two 17mm bolts, tightened to 63-93Nm/6.4-9.5kgf m/47-68lbf ft. Note the two dots which help to ensure the bar is reinstalled exactly as it originally was.
15   On top of the rear right-hand side of the rear brace bar ('performance bar') assembly there is a hook, so start by hooking this over the suspension subframe in the vicinity of the bolt hole. The latter makes fitting the frame easier because one corner is held which means you can move to the other side of the frame and screw in a couple of the 17mm securing bolts. Altogether the frame is held by six bolts, all of which should be fitted and tightened to 55-80Nm/5.6-8.2kgf m/41-59lbf ft.
16   Refill the transmission with appropriate oil☞ 2/8.
17   Install the engine undertray and refit front wheels☞ 3/11/108-110.
18   Install gear shift lever and console; restore electrical power☞ 3/11/119-129.
19   Carefully lower the car to the ground☞ 1/3.

9. TRANSMISSION (GEARBOX), AUTOMATIC - INSTALLATION

☞ First read 1/1, 2.

1   ☐ Make sure the torque converter is fully engaged with the oil pump behind it. Place a straightedge across the face of the bellhousing and measure the depth to the rim of the torque convertor (see diagram), which should be 22.5mm/0.89in. If the depth is not correct, press the convertor inward while rotating it slowly until you feel it move and engage with the pump with a 'clunk.' Check the

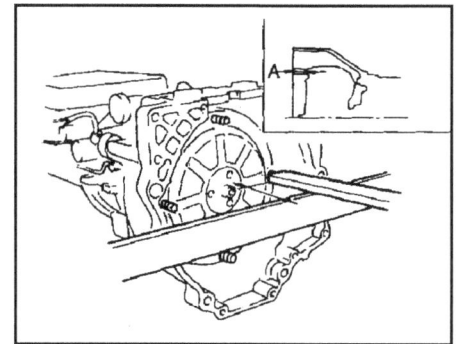

D9/1 CHECK THAT TORQUE CONVERTER IS PROPERLY ENGAGED WITH OIL PUMP.
'A' = 22.5mm/0.89in.

4: Transmission (gearbox) & driveline

measurement again. **Caution!** Once correctly engaged with the pump, make sure the torque convertor does not slide forward subsequently.

2   Using protective packing on the jack's pad, jack the front of the engine 50mm/2 inches, which will have the effect of tilting the rear of the engine slightly downwards. **Caution!** Don't jack so far that the camshaft angle sensor or coil unit contact the firewall, and check that hoses and wiring harnesses are not getting stretched.

3   Supporting the weight of the transmission on a wheeled jack, bring the engine and transmission unit together. If the torque convertor carries threaded studs, rotate it to ensure the studs are lined up with the holes in the driveplate. Note that if you are re-using the original driveplate and torque convertor, you should make sure the marks you made on dismantling are aligned. Make sure that the transmission bellhousing is correctly lined up with the engine backplate so that it engages on the hollow spigots projecting from the rear of the cylinder block.

4   Fit the two topmost bellhousing bolts which are 17mm (x60mm) and screw them into place finger-tight which, for the moment, will be enough to stop the transmission coming away from the back of the engine again. Fit the two lowermost 17mm (x60mm) bolts which, again, should be screwed in finger-tight at this stage.

5   At this point you can remove the jack at the front of the engine.

6   Position the exhaust pipe support bracket over the two bolt holes on the left-hand side of the bellhousing. Secure the bracket, flange facing rearward, with two 17mm bolts, the upper of which is longer at 70mm although there seems no good reason for this. Screw the bolts home finger-tight. Note: the four remaining fasteners in the starter motor area will be fitted later.

7   Tighten all of the 17mm bellhousing bolts to 64-89Nm/6.5-9.1kgf m/48-65lbf ft.

8   Temporarily lower the jack supporting the transmission unit. Above the transmission case you'll see that several wires sprout from the main harness (five connectors); these are the connectors for the sensors and switches of the auto transmission. You'll see that they have different types of connector so there can be no confusion over which connections are for which switch or sensor. Note that these connectors need to click home.

9   From beneath the car, fit the two 12mm bolts through the bellhousing and into the starter motor flange. Note that the innermost of these two bolts also carries a support bracket for the clutch release cylinder's hydraulic pipe connection (manual trans cars), whilst the other carries a wiring harness bracket. Manipulating these bolts into position is difficult - but not impossible! Both can be tightened to 38-51Nm/3.8-5.3kgf m/28-38lbf ft with a 12mm socket in conjunction with a universal joint and extensions.

10   Using the access opening in the bottom of the bellhousing, fit the nuts or bolts, as applicable, which secure the driveplate to the lugs of the torque convertor, rotating the torque convertor and driveplate as necessary for access. Lock the driveplate with a screwdriver and then, in a diagonal sequence, tighten the four bolts to 35-49Nm/3.5-5kgf m/26-36lbf ft. Install the access opening cover and secure with two bolts.

11   Install the PPF☞ 3/11/11-17 & 52-55.
12   Install driveshaft (propshaft)☞ 4/10/7-8.
13   Fit a new O-ring to the base of the transmission dipstick tube and smear it with ATF. Push the base of the tube into position in the transmission unit, and then fit the bolt and nut which secure the tube's bracket. Tighten to a torque of 7.9-10.7Nm/80-110kgf cm/70-95.4lbf ft.

14   On the left of the transmission, reconnect the two oil cooler pipes by installing their banjo bolts complete with new, ATF-lubricated sealing washers. Fit the bolts fixing the pipe's support brackets to the side of the transmission and bellhousing, and tighten to a torque of 7.9-10.7Nm/80-110kgf cm/70-95.4lbf ft. The banjo bolts should be tightened to a torque of 24-35Nm/2.4-3.6kgf m/17-26lbf ft.

15   Also on the left is the vacuum pipe. Push the rubber end of the pipe over the union stub in the transmission case and secure the rigid section of pipe by installing its clip bolt and tightening it to a torque of 7.9-10.7Nm/80-110kgf cm/70-95.4lbf ft.

16   Reconnect the selector lever to the shaft in the transmission casing and secure with nut and washer; tighten the nut with a wrench and finger pressure only.

17   Install the exhaust system☞ 5/38/18-27.
18   Install engine undertray and refit front wheels☞ 3/11/108-110.
19   If applicable, re-attach the front subframe cross brace ('performance bar') and secure with its two 17mm bolts, tightened to 63-93Nm/6.4-9.5kgf m/47-68lbf ft. Note the two dots which help to ensure the bar is reinstalled exactly as it originally was.

20   On top of the rear right-hand side of the rear brace bar ('performance bar') assembly there is a hook, so start by hooking this over the suspension subframe in the vicinity of the bolt hole. The latter makes fitting the frame easier because one corner is held which means you can move to the other side of the frame and screw in a couple of the 17mm securing bolts. Altogether the frame is held by six bolts, all of which should be fitted and tightened to 55-80Nm/5.6-8.2kgf m/41-59lbf ft.

21   If applicable, check that the transmission's oil pan bolts have been retightened.
22   Carefully lower the car to the ground☞ 1/3.
23   Reconnect the battery☞ 3/11/129.
Refill the transmission with appropriate ATF to the correct level☞ 2/9.

10. DRIVESHAFT (PROPSHAFT) - REMOVAL, CHECKING, REPAIR & INSTALLATION

☞ First read 1/1, 2.

REMOVAL

1   Raise, and securely support, the rear of the car high enough to give good access to the underside as far forward as the transmission unit☞ 1/3. If you raise the rear of the car as opposed to the left-hand side, you can avoid having to drain or partially drain the transmission oil/ATF.

2   Remove the rear section of the exhaust system☞ 5/38.
3   ◘ Remove driveshaft (propshaft)☞ 4/2/12-14.

CHECKING AND REPAIR

4   Clean the driveshaft with oil solvent or kerosene/paraffin and wipe dry before making a

10/3 Driveshaft flange & diff. (exhaust removed).

visual inspection. **Warning!** Do not use gasoline/petrol for cleaning purposes. **Caution!** Do not immerse the universal joints in solvent. The propshaft is not a serviceable item so any significant fault will necessitate replacement.

5   If you suspect the driveshaft is bent, take it to a machine shop and have it check the runout. Alternatively, if you have two large V-blocks, a long flat surface and a dial gauge, you can easily check the runout yourself. Maximum runout is 0.4mm/0.016in.

6   Mount the shaft in a vise, but don't squeeze it too tightly. One at a time, grasp the drive flange at one end of the shaft and then the sliding sleeve at the other and try to twist them backwards and forwards. If you feel a significant amount of lash/freeplay, then the bad news is it's time to replace the shaft as the UJs cannot be repaired.

INSTALLATION

7   Rub engine oil over the section of the driveshaft that enters the transmission tailhousing and engages with the transmission mainshaft splines. This ensures that the transmission tailshaft oil seal is well lubricated.

8   Slide the front end of the driveshaft into the tail end of the transmission unit: you may have to rotate the shaft just a little to allow the splines to engage. Then, lift up the rear end of the propshaft and engage its flange with the differential drive flange, lining up the marks you made when the propshaft was removed. Install the four 14mm bolts, spring washers (**Warning!** If the spring washers show any signs of having become flattened, they must be renewed) and nuts (nuts toward the front of the car) and tighten to a torque of 50-58Nm/5-6kgf m/37-43lbf ft. Note: you can apply the parking brake (handbrake) if the rear wheels are off the ground in order to stop the driveshaft rotating

Mazda Miata, MX-5, Eunos & Roadster

when you torque the nuts.
9   Fit the exhaust system rear section☞ 5/38.
10   Lower the car to the ground☞ 1/3.

11. TRANSMISSION (GEARBOX) REAR OIL SEAL - REPLACEMENT

☞ First read 1/1, 2.
1   Remove the driveshaft☞ 4/10/1-3.
2   📷 Using a small chisel engaged with the flange of the oil seal (see photo), and a light

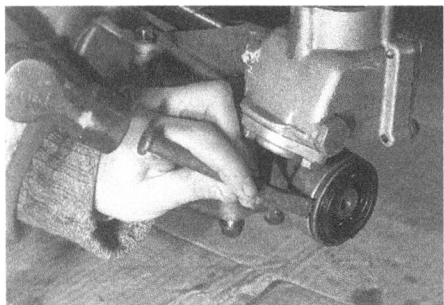

11/2 Drive old seal out.

11/3 Drift new seal in.

hammer, drive the oil seal out of the housing. Don't forget to work from side-to-side so that the seal comes out evenly.
3   📷 Spread oil (ATF for auto. trans.) around the outer periphery of the new seal and around the inner lip. Position the new seal in the tailhousing, spring side inward. When you are satisfied that it is square to its housing, use a length of metal tubing with a diameter to match the rim of the seal, or a block of wood, and a hammer to drive it evenly home into the transmission tailshaft housing.
4   Install the driveshaft☞ 4/10/7-10.

12. PPF (POWER PLANT FRAME) - REMOVAL & INSTALLATION

☞ First read 1/1, 2.

REMOVAL
1   You'll need good access to much of the car's underside to carry out this work, so raise the whole car to a suitable height and support securely☞ 1/3.
2   Remove the PPF☞ 4/2/16-23.
3   **Warning!** The PPF makes a fundamental contribution to your car's good handling but is, unfortunately, not a component that can be repaired. If the PPF is bent, cracked or seriously corroded, it should be replaced. Take the old PPF to a scrap metal dealer: that much alloy has to have some value.

INSTALLATION
4   PPF installation☞ 3/11/11-17, 52-55.
5   Check that nothing has been missed, then lower the car to the ground☞ 1/3.

13. DRIVEAXLES - REMOVAL, CHECKING, REPAIR & INSTALLATION

☞ First read 1/1, 2.

REMOVAL
1   Remove the hubcap from the appropriate wheel. Use a narrow chisel or an old screwdriver to release the staking of the hub locknut from the groove in the driveaxle (driveshaft/halfshaft).
2   With the parking brake and footbrake applied, loosen and then remove the 29mm hub locknut: it'll be real tight, so you may need to use a heavy-duty socket and drive and extend the socket's T-bar with a length of hollow steel pipe. **Warning!** The locknut's likely to release suddenly: be ready!
3   Slacken the lugnuts (wheelnuts) of the appropriate wheel or wheels, and then jack the rear of the car high enough to give easy access to the differential unit and driveaxles and support safely☞ 1/3.
4   Unscrew and remove the lugnuts, then lift away the road wheel to expose the hub and brake disc.
5   Using an indelible marker pen or paint, mark the relative positions of the driveaxle inner CV unit and the differential.
6   Behind the brake caliper, low down, you'll see the head of the caliper's lower mounting pin: if applicable, prise the cover off with your fingers or pliers. Unscrew and remove the pin using a 10mm box end wrench or socket.
7   📷 Swivel the caliper body upward thru 90 degrees and then slide the caliper off of its top mounting pin. Tie the caliper out of harm's way and so that the brake hose is not strained. **Caution!** Don't press the car's brake pedal until the caliper is back in place over the disc.
8   📷 Unscrew and remove the 14mm nut of

13/7a Remove cover and ...

13/7b ... unscrew and remove pin.

13/8 Tie caliper out of harm's way.

13/10 Remove nut and swivel pin.

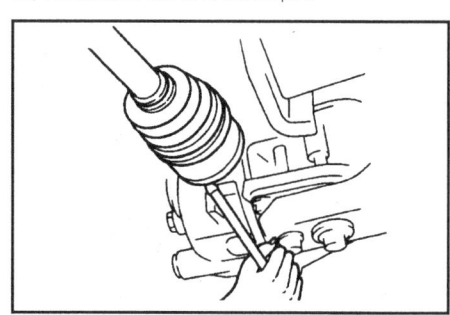

D13/10 GENTLY LEVER DRIVEAXLES OUT OF DIFFERENTIAL HOUSING.

swivel pin connecting the lower wishbone to the hub upright: withdraw the pin.
9   Swing the hub carrier outward sufficiently to allow the driveaxle to be withdrawn. Note: if the driveaxle sticks in the hub, install the old locknut so that its top is flush with the end of the driveaxle. Gently tap the nut and shaft end with a nylon-faced hammer, while supporting the carrier, until the shaft begins to slide through the hub bearings. Remove the nut and withdraw the shaft from the hub.
10   📷 At the differential end of the shaft,

4: Transmission (gearbox) & driveline

insert a large, flat blade screwdriver, or the blade of a small prybar (crowbar), between the differential casing and the shaft's CV joint (see diagram). Apply sufficient force to dislodge the shaft from the differential and be prepared for a little oil spillage as it does so. **Caution!** Take great care not to damage the differential casing or driveaxle.

CHECKING & REPAIR

11 Check the rubber boots (gaiters) at both ends of the shaft for cracks and holes. Don't attempt to repair such damage; instead, replace the whole boot. Check that the boot retaining straps are tight and in good condition.

12 If the shaft itself has sustained obvious damage it should be replaced.

INSTALLATION

13 Mazda recommends that a new clip (spring ring) is fitted to the differential end of the driveaxle on installation. After fitting the new clip, check that its fitted diameter is not excessive (see diagram): fit another clip if the diameter is not in tolerance.

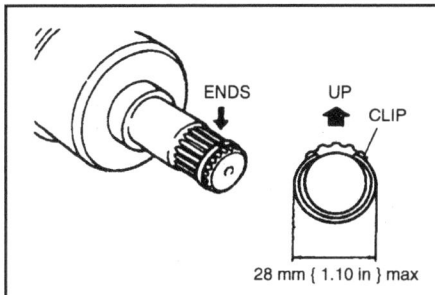

D13/13 MEASURE SPRING CLIP DIAMETER.

14 Carefully line up the alignment marks made before removal, then push the splined section of the shaft into the differential until the spring clip is felt to engage. **Caution!** As you feed the clip through the seal, ensure the sharp ends of the clip don't damage the seal lip.

15 Feed the splines of the other end of the shaft through the hub having first smeared a little copper or molybdenum-based grease over the splines. Push the upright backward until the shaft protrudes through the wheel side of the hub.

16 Smear copper-based grease over the shaft of the wishbone to hub upright swivel bolt and, having lined up the upright and wishbone, push the bolt home. Install and tighten the bolt's 14mm retaining nut to a torque of 63-74Nm/6.4-7.6kgf m/47-54lbf ft.

17 Smear a little copper-based grease over the top caliper swivel pin and then slide the caliper body over the pin. Swing the caliper body downwards until the disc is once more properly sandwiched between the pads. Smear a little copper-based grease on its shank and then fit the lower caliper mounting pin and tighten it to a torque of 34-39Nm/3.5-4kgf m/25-29lbf ft. If applicable, install the pin's plastic cover.

18 Apply the parking brake and then screw a new hub locknut into position, but only to hand pressure tightness at this stage.

19 Check and, if necessary, top up the differential unit's oil ☞ 2/10.

20 Lower the car to the ground ☞ 1/3. Tighten the lugnuts (wheelnuts).

21 Have someone apply the footbrake (the parking brake should be applied, too) whilst you tighten the hub locknut to a torque of 216-294Nm/22-30kgf m/160-216lbf ft. Phew! Using a blunt punch or chisel, stake the locknut flange ring into the groove in the shaft. **Warning!** The staking should be at least 1mm/0.04in deep for security. Fit the hubcap.

14. DRIVEAXLE - DISMANTLING, REBUILD & NEW BOOTS

☞ First read 1/1, 2.

1 Each driveaxle has two constant velocity joints; one at each end. Unfortunately, the CV joint at the wheel end is not repairable so there seems little point in describing the dismantling and overhaul of the CV joint at the other end of the shaft, as both joints will wear at approximately the same rate. If either of the CV joints is worn and has become noisy in service, fit a completely new or exchange reconditioned driveaxle.

2 New original-type boots (gaiters) cannot be fitted without dismantling the differential end CV joint. However, for this kind of situation, aftermarket manufacturers usually offer replacement boots which can be split and refastened once in position. **Caution!** CV joints and boots should be filled with the special grease supplied with the boot kit. New boot retaining bands should be fitted with the folded tongue facing away from the direction of normal rotation.

15. DIFFERENTIAL UNIT AND CARRIER - REMOVAL & INSTALLATION

☞ First read 1/1, 2.

REMOVAL

1 Slacken the lugnuts (wheelnuts) of the two rear wheels, jack the car high enough to give easy access to the whole of the underside and support securely ☞ 1/3. If you have access to a workshop pit or a vehicle hoist, this will make the task much easier.

2 Unscrew and remove the lugnuts, then lift away each rear road wheel to expose the hub and brake disc.

3 Remove the rear section of the exhaust system ☞ 5/38.

4 ☞ 4/2/12-14. Note: there is no need to withdraw the front of the propshaft from the gearbox tailhousing, which would cause oil to leak.

5 At this point the official Mazda procedure is to remove the whole of the PPF frame; however it seems to the writer that it would probably be sufficient simply to release the differential end of the frame and then, when the time comes, to slide the diff. unit out of the frame. Unfortunately, this is a piece of supposition which cannot be verified. If you want to remove the whole PPF ☞ 4/2/16-23, otherwise just follow the appropriate steps of the same section to release the diff end of the PPF. **Caution!** Once the PPF is released, support the transmission on a jack to prevent the camshaft position sensor and coil unit being crushed against the firewall (bulkhead).

6 Have a container of at least 1 liter/2 pint capacity in place beneath, and then unscrew and remove the differential's 24mm filler plug and 24mm drain plug. Unscrew the last few threads of the drain plug with your fingers, holding the plug in position until it's completely unthreaded, and then withdrawing it suddenly to minimize oil seepage. Allow the oil to drain and then install the plugs finger-tight.

7 Using an indelible marker pen or paint, mark the relative positions of the driveaxle inner CV units and the differential casing of both driveaxles (halfshafts/driveshafts).

8 Behind the brake caliper, low down, you'll see the head of the caliper's lower mounting pin: if applicable, prise the cover off with your fingers or pliers. Unscrew and remove the pin using a 10mm boxend wrench or socket.

9 Swivel the caliper body upward thru 90 degrees and then slide the caliper off of its top mounting pin. Tie the caliper out of harm's way and so that the brake hose is not strained. **Caution!** Don't press the car's brake pedal until the caliper is back in place over the disc.

10 Unscrew and remove the 14mm nut of the swivel pin connecting each lower wishbone to the hub upright, and withdraw the pin. At the differential end of the driveaxle, insert a large, flat blade screwdriver, or the blade of a small prybar (crowbar), between the differential casing and the shaft's CV joint. Apply sufficient force to dislodge each shaft from the differential. **Caution!** Take great care not to damage the differential casing or driveaxle.

11 Support the weight of the differential unit on a wheeled jack, and then unscrew and remove the single 17mm nut and two 12mm nuts from each of its carrier mountings. Lower the differential unit and wheel it out from beneath the car. Note: if the PPF is still in place, it will be necessary to lower the diff. sufficiently to allow it to be disengaged from the PPF before the differential unit can be withdrawn (the transmission unit will need to be supported whilst the differential unit is out of the car).

INSTALLATION

12 Support the differential unit on a wheeled jack and raise into position until the carrier mountings engage with the three studs on each side. Note: if the PPF is still in place, engage the differential casing with the PPF before raising fully.

13 Fit the three nuts securing each mounting. Tighten the central 17mm nut of each mounting to 84-98Nm/8.5-10kgf m/62-72lb ft, and the two outer 12mm nuts to 18-26Nm/1.8-2.7kgf m/14-19lbf ft.

14 Mazda recommends that new clips (spring rings) are fitted to the differential ends of the

Mazda Miata, MX-5, Eunos & Roadster

driveaxles on installation. After fitting the new clip to each shaft, check that its fitted diameter is not greater than 28mm/1.10in: fit another clip if the diameter is not in tolerance.

15   Carefully line up the alignment marks made before removal, then push the splined section of each shaft into the differential until the spring clip is felt to engage. **Caution!** As you feed the clip through the seal, ensure the sharp ends of the clip don't damage the seal lip.

16   Smear copper-based grease over the shaft of the wishbone to hub upright swivel bolt and, having lined up the upright and wishbone, push the bolt home. Install and tighten the bolt's 14mm retaining nut to a torque of 63-74Nm/6.4-7.6kgf m/47-54lbf ft.

17   Smear a little copper-based grease over the top caliper swivel pin, and then slide the caliper body over the pin. Swing the caliper body downwards until the disc is once more properly sandwiched between the pads. Smear a little copper-based grease on its shank, and then fit the lower caliper mounting pin and tighten to a torque of 34-39Nm/3.5-4kgf m/25-29lbf ft. If applicable, install the pin's plastic cover.

18   Install the PPF☞ 3/11/11-17, 52-55. If only the rear end of the PPF was disengaged, follow the relevant parts of the same text.

19   Lift up the rear end of the propshaft and align its flange with the mating marks on the differential flange. Install the four 14mm bolts, spring washers (**Warning!** If the spring washers show any signs of having become flattened, they must be renewed) and nuts (nuts toward the front of the car) and tighten to a torque of 50-58Nm/5-6kgf m/37-43lbf ft. Note: you can apply the parking brake (handbrake) if the rear wheels are off the ground in order to stop the driveshaft rotating when you torque the nuts.

20   Install the rear section of the exhaust system 5/38/18-27.

21   Replenish the differential unit with the specified oil☞ 2/10. **Caution!** Remember to use new sealing washers and to tighten both drain and filler plugs.

22   Fit the roadwheels and lower the car to the ground☞ 1/3. **Warning!** Don't forget to tighten the roadwheel lugnuts.

16. DIFFERENTIAL SIDE (DRIVEAXLE) OIL SEALS - REPLACEMENT

First read 1/1, 2.

1   Remove the appropriate rear driveaxle (halfshaft/driveshaft) and check its condition☞ 4/13/1-13.

2   The oil seal's 'skeleton' is a thin metal pressing which is easy to buckle. Using a small chisel or an old screwdriver and fairly gentle hammer blows, force the sides of the seal away from its housing at one or more points until the seal is sufficiently buckled to be able to lever it free of the housing. Alternatively, you can drive the tip of the tool right through the front of the seal and, once the seal is impaled, lever it out (using a small piece of wood or plastic at the lever's fulcrum point to prevent damage to the oil pump body). **Caution!** Be careful not to hammer your screwdriver or chisel blade against the machined surface of the seal's seat in the differential housing.

3   Lubricate the outer circumference and inner lip of a new oil seal, and position it in the oil seal housing with your fingers, noting that the closed side of the seal must face outward.

4   Drift the seal into its housing with direct but light blows from a small hammer, making sure that the seal is driven home evenly. If you use this method, make sure you keep the hammer face flat against the seal, otherwise damage will result. The seal is properly installed when its face is flush with the lip of its housing.

5   Install the driveaxle☞ 4/13/14-22.

17. DIFFERENTIAL NOSE (PINION) OIL SEAL - REPLACEMENT

☞ First read 1/1, 2.

1   Jack the car high enough to give easy access to the front of the differential and support securely☞ 1/3. If you have access to a workshop pit or a vehicle hoist, this will make the task much easier.

2   Remove the rear section of the exhaust system☞ 5/38/7-12.

3   Partially remove the propshaft☞ 4/2/12-13 (but note that there is no need to pull the front of the shaft out of the transmission, which would result in some oil leakage).

4   Apply the parking brake - you may need an assistant to operate the footbrake at the same time - and then unscrew and remove the large nut (sorry, forgot to record its size ...) and washer retaining the differential pinion flange. **Warning!** The nut will be tight, and will probably loosen suddenly: be prepared.

5   Using an ordinary proprietary two- or three-legged puller, pull the pinion flange off the pinion shaft.

6   Drive a thin chisel or screwdriver through the face of the oil seal and then lever it out of its housing. Note: there may be some oil loss if the car is not level.

7   Smear the periphery of the new seal with oil and then position it squarely over its housing. Use a piece of metal tube of the same outer diameter as the seal to drift it squarely home until the seal's face is flush with the housing. If you don't have an appropriate piece of tube, use a nylon-faced hammer to tap around the face of the seal until it's fully home: take care to keep the face of the hammer square to the face of the seal.

8   Smear the seal area and internal splines of the pinion flange with oil, do the same to the lip of the seal and then push the flange home onto the pinion shaft. Fit the washer and a new nut. Apply the parking brake and then tighten the nut to a torque of 118-176/12-18kgf m/87-130lbf ft.

9   ☞ 4/10/7-9.

10   If there was any loss of oil when the seal was removed, check the differential oil level and top up as necessary   2/10.

11   Lower the car to the ground☞ 1/3.

18. DIFFERENTIAL UNIT CARRIER MOUNTINGS - REPLACEMENT

☞ First read 1/1, 2.

1   You will need to replace these rubber/metal composite mountings if the rubber section has broken away from the metal or has become over-compliant through age and/or high mileage.

2   Remove the differential unit☞ 4/15/1-11.

3   You will need to find a machine shop with a press capable of pushing the new mountings into place with a pressure of 19,600N/2000kgf/4400lbf, so you might as well have the same shop remove the old mountings. Note that the voids in the new mountings must face front and rear of the car.

4   Install the differential unit☞ 4/15/12-22.

19. DIFFERENTIAL UNIT - TEARDOWN AND REBUILD

☞   First read 1/1, 2.

1   We hope you won't think we've taken the soft option, but we strongly advise you not to attempt a differential teardown and rebuild. A number of specialist tools are required and the whole unit must be reassembled with precise regard to adjustments and tolerances if it is to work efficiently and quietly.

2   Unless some manufacturing fault comes to light, which would almost certainly happen within the warranty period, the differential should last the life of the car. However, if your car's differential does require attention, or you want to have a limited slip differential (LSD) fitted or different ratio gears, then remove the differential carrier (complete with diff.) and take it to your Mazda dealer or engineering shop for the work to be done.

20 TRANSMISSION (GEARBOX), AUTOMATIC - TROUBLESHOOTING

1   If you suspect there is something wrong with the automatic gearbox on your car, carry out the following checks.

2   Is the ATF level correct?☞ 2/9.

3   Is the ATF clean? If the ATF is dirty change the fluid completely☞ 2/9.

4   Does the ATF look (it should be a clean red colour) or smell (sniff some new ATF to make the comparison) unusual? If it looks wrong or smells wrong, there's a strong chance of an internal problem with the transmission; however, it's worth refilling with fresh ATF to see whether it makes a difference☞ 2/9.

5   Is the engine idle speed correctly set?☞ 2/7.

6   Are all the connections between the wiring harness and the transmission unit (between underside of transmission tunnel and top of the

4: Transmission (gearbox) & driveline

transmission unit) clean and secure?
7   Is the shift lever linkage undamaged and are all the links secure/unworn?
8   If the fault persists after the foregoing checks, you'll have to take the car to a Mazda dealer or auto transmission specialist to have the fault diagnosed. Realistically, this electronically-controlled unit is so sophisticated that, without a truckload of specialist tools, you're unlikely to find the specific fault – which could still be as simple as a faulty solenoid or a maladjusted band.
9   You are strongly advised to have any suspected fault diagnosed before removing the automatic transmission unit.

Notes

5

Engine management, fuel & exhaust systems

1. INTRODUCTION

1   This chapter covers fuel, air, exhaust, and emissions control systems, along with the car's central computer and related sensing and regulating sub-systems. These systems and devices interrelate to such an extent that there is little point in dealing with them in isolation; to check one you invariably need to deal with another to some degree. Various acronyms are used colloqially to describe the central processor which automatically controls so many aspects of the modern car's functionality: PCM (Powertrain Control Module), ECM (Engine Control Module), ECU (Engine Control Unit) and even EMS (Engine Management System). To avoid confusion, and to reflect the fact that these processors have gone beyond engine control alone, we'll try to be consistent and use the term "PCM" within these covers.

2   Viewed overall, the central processor, its sensors and their inter-relationships amount to an extremely complicated system, and this makes methodical diagnosis of a suspected fault essential. It's very easy to jump to the wrong conclusion and waste a lot of time checking the wrong area, especially if the simplest and most likely causes are not investigated first. At worst, you could actually introduce further problems, making diagnosis even more difficult.

3   It is important to have a clear grasp of the various components and sub-systems which make up the engine management system. Some of these are quite simple, and their function obvious, others less so, but they all affect each other to some degree. Section 2 of this chapter describes individual components and the various related systems.

4   Are you in the United States? If so, you should be aware that many emissions control system components are subject to a Federally-mandated extended warranty. Your Mazda dealer will be able to advise you which components are covered by this legislation.

2. PCM SYSTEM - COMPONENT SUMMARY

1   There follows a summary of the primary engine management system components. We suggest that you spend a little time getting familiar with what each component and sub-system does and the terminology. You can also refer to this section as a glossary of terms if you encounter something unfamiliar in later sections.

2   Automotive terminology varies widely. We have deliberately kept closely to Mazda's choice of names and abbreviations in this respect - we figured that it would be helpful if you spoke the same language as your Mazda dealer in these matters.

Air cleaner (ACL)

3   This, as you might expect, filters the incoming air to remove dust particles which would otherwise enter the engine and cause premature wear. As long as the air cleaner element is clean and

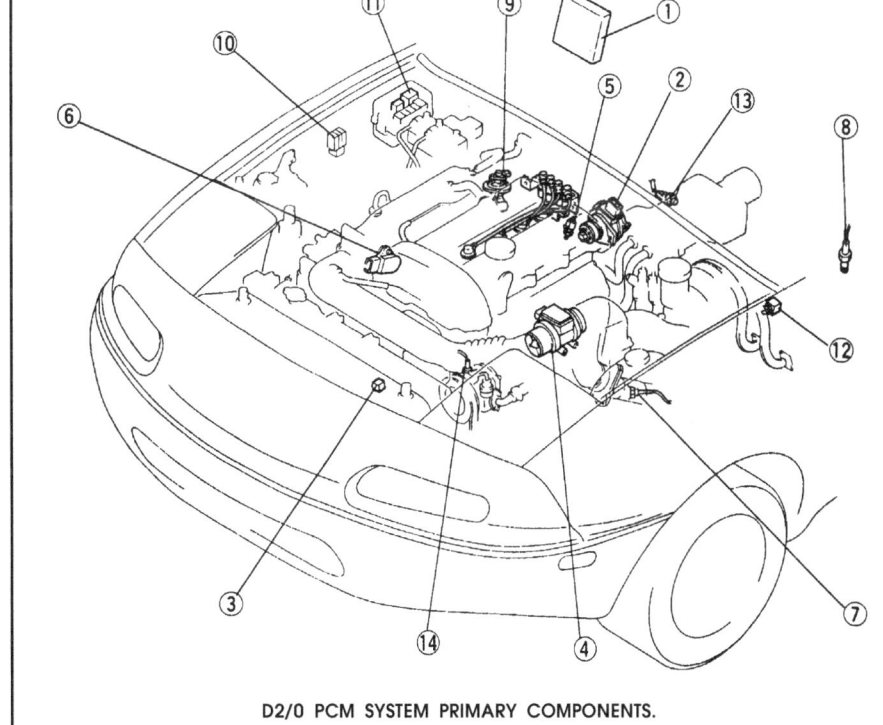

D2/0 PCM SYSTEM PRIMARY COMPONENTS.
1 PCM (computer) unit location for LHD cars; located in passenger footwell RHD cars.
2 Camshaft position sensor. 3 Crankshaft position sensor. 4 Mass airflow sensor. 5 Coolant temperature sensor. 6 Throttle position sensor. 7 Heated oxygen sensor (front). 8 Heated oxygen sensor (rear). 9 EGR valve position sensor. 10 EGR boost sensor. 11 Main relay. 12 Clutch switch.
13 Neutral switch. 14 Power steering pressure switch.

Mazda Miata, MX-5, Eunos & Roadster

uncontaminated by oil or water, it will function correctly. If damaged or clogged with dirt it will adversely affect the fuel/air mixture and make normal engine operation impossible.

Air valve (BAC valve)
4   The air valve is housed beneath the throttle body on the intake manifold and makes a cold engine idle at increased rpm to speed the warm-up process. From a cold start the valve varies the amount of intake air allowed to bypass the throttle butterfly at idle in response to engine temperature (measured by thermowax). It is automatic in operation, responding directly to engine temperature, and functioning independently of the rest of the engine management system. The idle air control (IAC) valve is built into the BAC valve.

Camshaft position sensor (CMP)
5   This device (often referred to as a "crank angle sensor") is driven by the exhaust camshaft (which runs at half crankshaft speed) and tells the PCM when the piston in cylinder No.1 is at top dead center (TDC) once every two *crankshaft* revolutions (ie: on the firing stroke), it also sends a separate signal every 180 degrees of *crankshaft* revolution. The PCM utilizes this information to calculate the ignition and fuel injection timing.

Catalytic converter
6   Most vehicles sold around the world are catalytic converter equipped. The catalytic converter helps reduce harmful emissions of hydrocarbons, carbon monoxide and nitrous oxide in the exhaust gases. The 'cat' brings about high temperature reactions in the exhaust gases, converting the more toxic elements into relatively harmless gases. The catalytic convertor is of the "three-way" type as it reduces HC, CO and NOx emissions.

Charcoal canister
7   Part of the EVAP system. The charcoal canister acts as a holding vessel for unburned hydrocarbons in the form of fuel vapor (the charcoal absorbs the vapor) from the fuel tank. When combustion conditions are appropriate, this vapor is drawn into the intake system of the engine and burnt normally to purge it.

Clutch switch
8   This is a simple switch which allows the PCM to detect whether or not the clutch is engaged. The switch is off when the clutch is not in use.

Coolant temperature sensor
9   A thermister (resistance varies with temperature) located at the rear of the engine above the bellhousing; it measures coolant temperature and sends signal back to PCM.

Crankshaft position sensor (CKP)
10   This device (fitted to 1996 and later cars), which is mounted in the block near the crankshaft pulley, reads changes in crankshaft rotational speed. Reads crankshaft angle (in relation to 360 degrees of revolution).

Data link connector (DLC)
11   A multi-pin connector providing access for external systems diagnosis/service checks on the PCM system. (You will find this in the engine compartment on the left side. It is clearly marked **DIAGNOSIS** on the cover, and the pin positions are shown on a label inside the cover.)

Exhaust gas recirculation (EGR) system
12   If the emission levels of oxides of nitrogen are close to becoming excessive, cooling combustion temperature will lower the level. Such a reduction of combustion temperature can be achieved by recirculating a small amount of exhaust gas through the intake system, and this is what the EGR system does under the control of the PCM. The EGR system comprises an EGR valve with a valve position sensor, EGR boost sensor which is sensitive to atmospheric pressure (1996 and later models), EGR vent solenoid and the EGR vacuum solenoid.

Fuel pump relay (FPR)
13   This device controls the operation of the fuel delivery sub-system, shutting off the electrical supply to the fuel pump when the engine is switched off. Some cars feature a relay which controls fuel pump speed, and this would be referred to as "fuel pump relay (speed)."

Fuel filter
14   Removes small particles from the fuel pumped from the fuel tank to prevent damage or obstruction of the injectors.

Fuel pump
15   Maintains pressure in the fuel system while the engine is running. The submerged electric pump supplies fuel via low and high pressure filters and the fuel delivery line to the injector rail, from there unused fuel is returned to the tank through a pressure regulator and the fuel return line.

Fuel vapor valve
16   Fuel vapor is vented from the fuel tank to the charcoal canister via this valve in the top of the tank. A simple shut-off valve is incorporated which prevents fuel running from the fuel tank into the charcoal canister in the event that the vehicle is inverted in an accident.

Heated oxygen sensor
17   Located in the exhaust downpipe, once it reaches 600 degrees F (315 C) this sensor detects the amount of oxygen in the exhaust gases and relays this information to the PCM, which then adjusts fuel mixture as appropriate: this is a constant process. To monitor the performance of the 'cat,' 1996 and later cars for some markets have a second sensor located in the exhaust system after the catalytic converter.

Idle air control (IAC) valve
18   Part of the air valve (BAC), this device allows an amount of intake air to bypass the throttle butterfly at idle regardless of engine temperature. It is controlled by the PCM.

Ignition coil
19   There are two ignition coils mounted at the rear of the cylinder head. Each coil has two high tension towers and is connected via high tension wires to two sparkplugs which are fired simultaneously. The PCM controls the timing of ignition pulses.

Ignition control module
20   Installed in ignition coil assembly. Receives spark signal from PCM and initiates generation of high voltage pulse in coil. Detects high voltage pulse and sends signal to PCM.

Ignition switch
21   Applies power to the engine management system and electrical system when turned on. Also sends 'engine cranking' signal to the PCM while turned to the **START** position.

Injector
22   A precision device for atomizing and injecting fuel under high pressure into the intake port. Each injector opens and closes in response to electronic control signals from the PCM, passing a controlled amount of fuel to its cylinder.

Intake air temperature (IAT) sensor
23   Housed inside the mass airflow sensor, this device measures ambient air temperature and relays the information back to the PCM.

Main relay
24   Controls current to the main sub-assemblies of the engine management system (injectors, PCM, etc.). It is located in the fuse block in the engine compartment.

Malfunction indicator lamp
25   Light on dashboard which remains illuminated after ignition if the PCM detects a fault in its systems. Warning lamp can be cancelled after rectification of problem by disconnecting battery negative cable and pressing brake pedal for 20 seconds.

Mass airflow sensor (MAF)
26   This device measures the volume of air flowing through the intake system by the cooling effect it has on a hot wire. This information is then fed to the PCM which adjusts fuel injector mode accordingly.

Neutral switch
27   Detects when transmission is in neutral and sends the information to PCM.

On board diagnostic (OBD) system
28   A system whereby the PCM evaluates the performance of its various sensors and systems and reports the nature and likely location of faults by a system of codes. The original system used on early 1995 and earlier models reported the nature of some faults by various flashing sequences of the

5: Engine management, fuel, ignition & exhaust systems

dashboard "Check" (engine symbol) light but, unfortunately, SSTs (special service tools) are needed to interrogate the OBD II system fitted to late 1995 and later models.

Positive crankcase ventilation (PCV) valve
29 This emissions-related valve, mounted in the camshaft cover, controls evacuation of blowby gases from the engine and feeds them into the intake system for combustion.

Power steering pressure (PSP) switch
30 Detects operation of power steering (where fitted) and relays operational information back to PCM.

Powertrain control module (PCM)
31 This is a dedicated computer. The brain of the engine management system, the PCM, reads a constant stream of information from the various sensors throughout the engine management and other systems, and applies this information to pre-programmed data to produce appropriate control signals, which are fed back to the relevant parts of the engine management and other systems. In addition, it provides self diagnostic (OBD) information and can be interrogated by the appropriate external service tools.

Pressure regulator
32 Located in the fuel rail this device maintains optimum fuel pressure at the injectors by imposing a controlled resistance to fuel flow in the return line to the tank.

Pressure regulator control (PRC) solenoid valve
33 This device monitors manifold vacuum and controls the operation of the pressure regulator so that fuel pressure is kept within desirable confines for the operating conditions prevailing. To prevent the percolation of fuel when a hot engine (coolant temperature 90 degrees C/194 F or higher) is restarted in a hot climate (70 degrees C/158 F or higher) and allowed to idle, the PCM operates the PRC valve solenoid for 150 seconds. During this time, manifold vacuum (applied via the pressure regulator) is shut off, allowing fuel pressure to rise to 284kPa (2.9kgf/cm2, 41psi).

Purge solenoid valve
34 Allows accumulated fuel vapor to feed from the charcoal canister to the engine under control of the PCM.

Resonance chamber
35 Part of the rigid air hose which connects the air filter to the intake manifold. Smooths out pulses in the intake air and improves mid-range torque.

Stoplight switch
36 Apart from its obvious function, sends signal back to PCM to indicate braking (deceleration).

Throttle body
37 This is where you come in! The throttle body provides the driver's means of regulating engine speed (with a little help from the PCM) by controlling intake air volume. Also has sensors for throttle butterfly angle and the idle air control (IAC) valve and feeds this data back to PCM.

Throttle sensor
38 Senses by how much the throttle butterfly (which is controlled by the accelerator pedal) is open and feeds this information to the PCM which modifies the amount of fuel injected in line with the driver's requirement (eg: hard acceleration, constant speed, slowing down, etc).

Two port check valve (three port check valve, automatic transmission models)
39 Controls air pressure in fuel tank.

3. PCM SYSTEM - OVERVIEW

1 In this section we'll look at how the

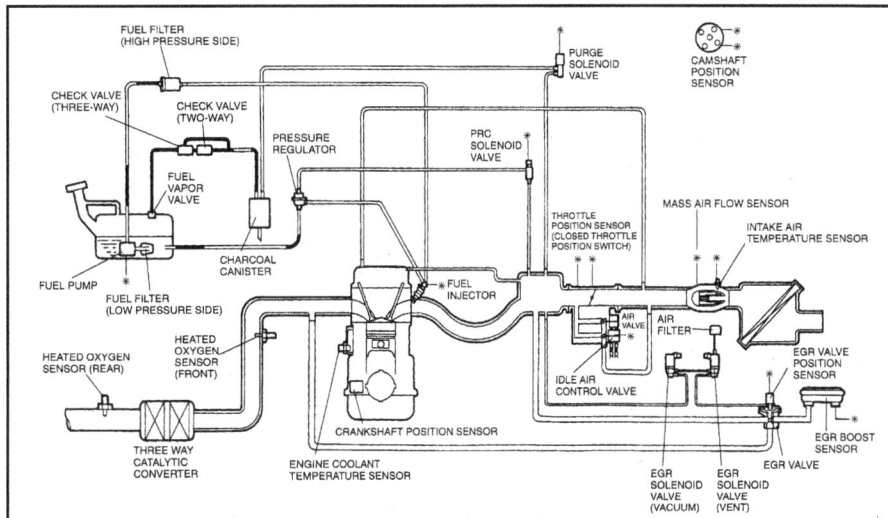

D3/1 OVERVIEW OF THE FUEL AND EMISSION CONTROL SYSTEMS.
Note that this illustration is presented like a wiring diagram and shows the inter-relationship of components: it does not indicate their true locations in the car (eg: the EGR valve is mounted on the intake manifold, not close to the mass airflow sensor, which is mounted on the opposite side of the engine compartment). * = electrical signal (not all are shown).

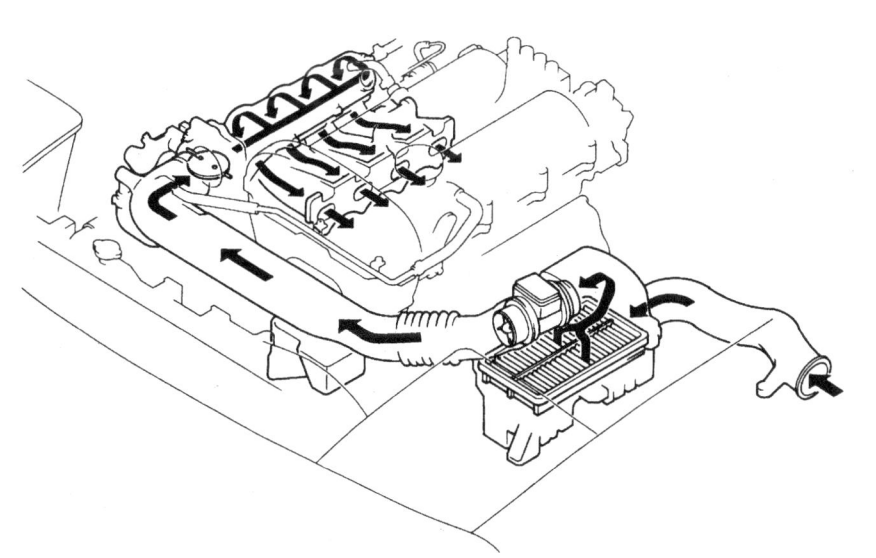

D3/5 AIR INTAKE SYSTEM.
For correct operation the system should be 'sealed.' This means that air at ambient pressure should not be able to enter the system at any point other than the open air intake: this factor is particularly critical after the throttle butterfly (valve) in the throttle body, which is here shown fully open.

system operates and how each component fits into the overall scheme of things.

Fuel system

2   The fuel system is pressurised by a submersed, electrically-powered pump housed in the fuel tank. The pump draws fuel through a low-pressure intake filter to remove any contaminants which might damage the pump. The outgoing fuel passes through a remote external high pressure filter which removes fine contaminants that could obstruct the injectors.

3   Fuel flows along the fuel feed line to the injector rail. A pressure regulator maintains a constant fuel pressure in the rail and allows excess fuel to return to the fuel tank. This fuel cycle is continuous.

4   The individual fuel injectors (one for each cylinder) are controlled by the PCM, which regulates the amount of fuel supplied by each one in response to varying engine/driver demands. Fuel volume is controlled by the length of time the injector is allowed to remain open.

Air intake system

5   The air intake system cleans and controls the incoming air being sucked in by the engine. Air is admitted via a resonance chamber and air filter. It then passes through the mass airflow sensor, the rigid airhose (incorporating a second resonance chamber) across the front of the engine, the throttle body (where the engine speed is regulated by a butterfly valve connected to the accelerator pedal), the intake manifold, the individual cylinder ports and then the open intake valve into the combustion chamber.

6   Unlike older cars with a choke device (automatic or manual), in which the intake butterfly (valve) is held slightly open at idle, the throttle body butterfly is closed at idle on these cars. Therefore, an automatic idle speed control system allows a controlled amount of intake air to bypass the throttle body butterfly and ensures smoothness at idle speed at all engine temperatures. This system comprises an idle air control (IAC) valve and the air valve (BAC). The PCM-controlled IAC valve regulates the volume of bypass air throughout the engine temperature range, and for cold starts is supplemented by the temperature sensitive air valve, which operates automatically from temperatures below 40 degrees C (104 F) until the engine reaches its normal working temperature.

Emission control system

7   **Positive crankcase ventilation (PCV) system.** Utilizes intake manifold vacuum to suck blowby gases (which contain unburned fuel and oil vapor) past a one-way valve into the intake system, where they are drawn into the engine, burnt and expelled through the exhaust.

8   **Exhaust gas recirculation (EGR) system** To keep NOx emissions to acceptable levels, it is necessary to introduce a small amount of exhaust gas to the intake side of the system and thereby reduce combustion temperatures. The introduction of exhaust gases to the incoming charge is confined to normal running when the engine is under light or moderate load, acceleration and warm-up. EGR operation is stopped at idle, during deceleration, at high speed and when the engine is under heavy load. To meet these operational requirements, the amount of contolling vacuum applied to the EGR valve (which regulates the amount of recirculated exhaust gas going to the intake manifold) is controlled, via the PCM, by two EGR solenoid valves: one can vent the control system to close the EGR valve, the other can subject the EGR to manifold vacuum and therefore open it. For 1996 and later models, additional control data is supplied by a boost valve which measures atmospheric pressure.

9   **Evaporative emission control (EVAP) system.** Utilizes a charcoal canister to contain fuel vapor given off by the fuel in the fuel tank. Fuel vapor passes through the fuel vapor valve (which also prevents fuel spillage should the vehicle overturn in an accident). From here it is passed through a two-port (three-port, automatic transmission models) check valve to the charcoal canister in the engine compartment, where the vapor is held in temporary storage.

10   The PCM monitors the engine operating conditions and, when it judges conditions to be appropriate to do so, opens the purge solenoid valve to allow the accumulated fuel vapor to be fed back into the engine and burnt normally. Purging will only take place after the engine has warmed up and the PCM can sense that the vehicle is being driven in gear, with the throttle above idle speed and when the oxygen sensor detects normal oxygen levels.

11   **Dechoke control system** is fitted to allow the engine to be cleared after accidental flooding with fuel. The PCM monitors the camshaft position sensor, engine coolant temperature sensor and throttle position sensors, and will prevent injection of fuel if the accelerator pedal is fully depressed while operating the starter of a cold engine.

12   **Catalytic converter.** Part of the exhaust system, its function is to reduce emissions of unburned hydrocarbons, carbon monoxide and nitrous oxide. The 'cat' is fitted in-line between the

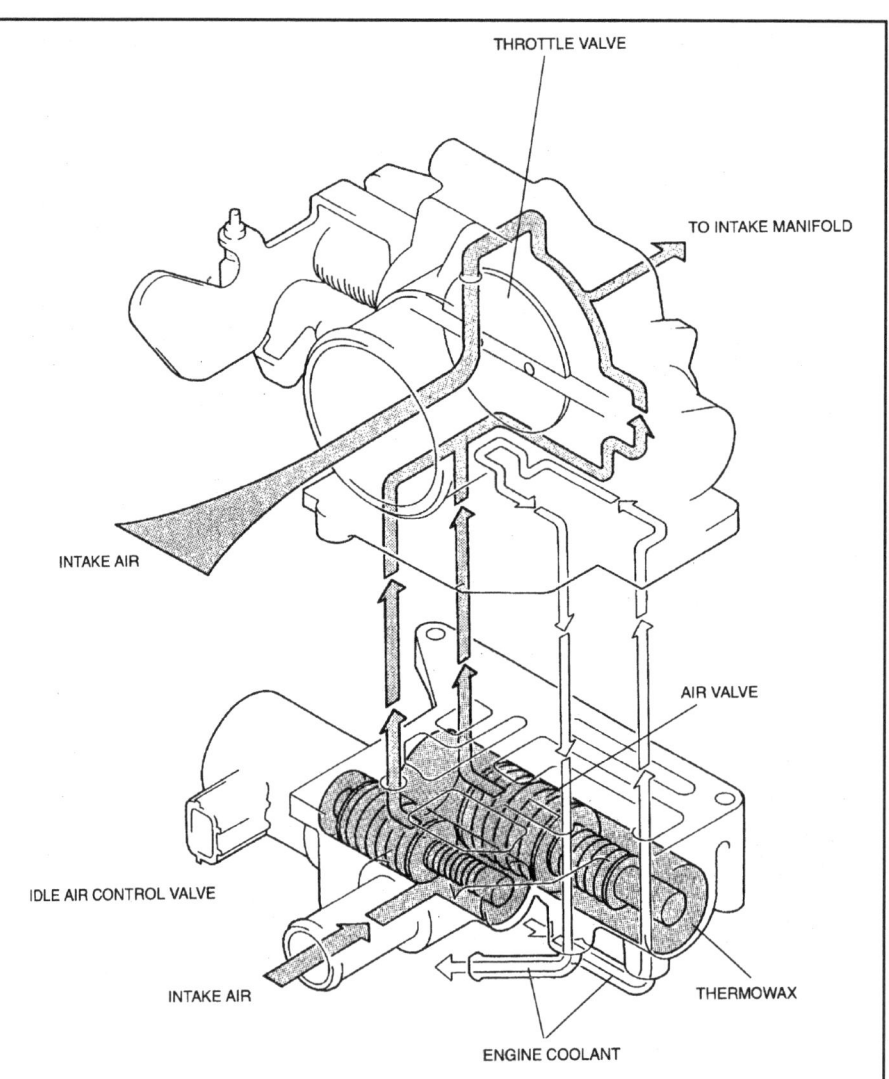

D3/6 OVERVIEW OF THE IDLE AIR CONTROL SYTEMS, THE THERMOSTATIC IDLE AIR VALVE AND THE IDLE AIR CONTROL VALVE.

5: Engine management, fuel, ignition & exhaust systems

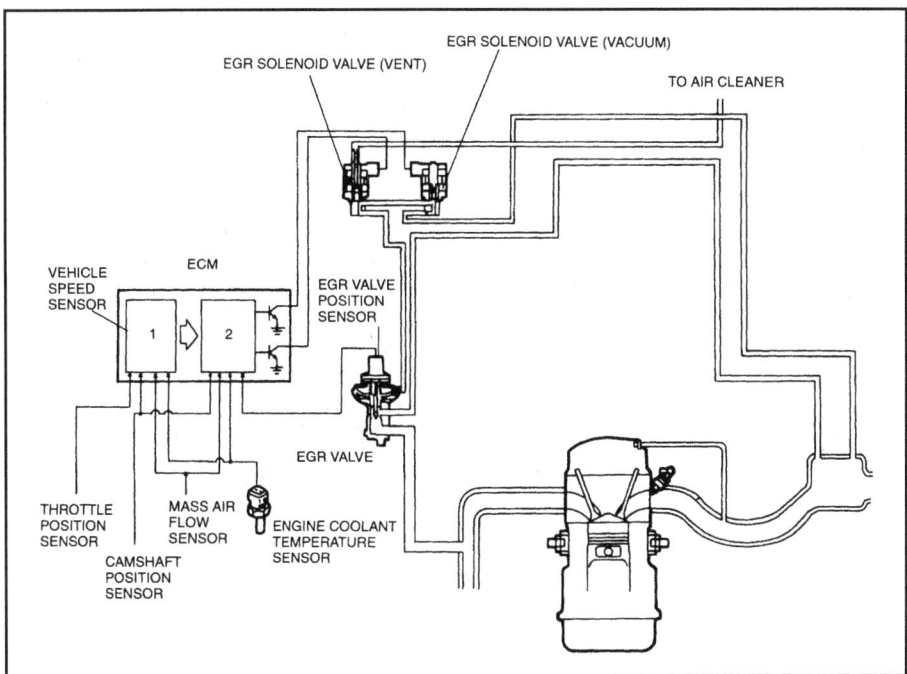

D3/8 OVERVIEW OF THE EXHAUST GAS RECIRCULATION (EGR) SYSTEM.

exhaust manifold and the main muffler/silencer.

13   **Ignition**. The PCM reads the engine operating condition and uses this data to determine the exact point of ignition for each cylinder for optimum efficiency. Once triggered by the PCM, each coil generates a high voltage which fires two sparkplugs simultaneously.

14   **Power train control module (PCM)**. Also known as the ECU or ECM. The main control element in the engine management system - the car's brain. Tucked safely away inside the cockpit, it constantly monitors engine operating conditions through the battery of sensors previously described. It uses a basic pre-programmed set of instructions ('maps') overlaid by the varying conditions it reads from the rest of the vehicle to control engine operation

4. POWERTRAIN CONTROL SYSTEM - TROUBLESHOOTING TIPS

1   DONT PANIC! It's too easy to assume that, because the PCM and its associated components and wiring make a complex system, the slightest stumble from the engine is bound to be caused by the failure of some mysterious little part deep inside the PCM: this is not so.

2   The fact is that the PCM and the components to which it is linked are designed to last the life of the car without replacement, and are therefore unlikely to give trouble.

3   What this means is that if the engine stops, it's most likely that you're out of fuel; if it misfires, that the sparkplug wires or sparkplugs are shot or wet; and, if it fails to start, that the battery is flat or the auto transmission's in **D**. Keep it simple: eliminate the most likely problems with a logical process before hunting for extremely obscure and unlikely faults.

4   The "Troubleshooting" chapter will point you in the right direction; meantime those with earlier cars just got lucky and are off to a head start with fault diagnosis -

FAULT CODES

5   The PCM of 1994 and early 1995 models using the original OBD (on board diagnosis) rather than the OBD II system, will report the general nature of a fault by a sequence of flashes of the dashboard mounted 'Check' light. Whenever you turn the ignition key to the **ON** position (this applies to later models, too), the 'Check' light illuminates to indicate that its bulb is working. Once the engine is started it will go out if the PCM has detected no faults in the system. If the light stays on when the engine is started, the PCM is telling you that a fault exists in the PCM circuitry, componentry

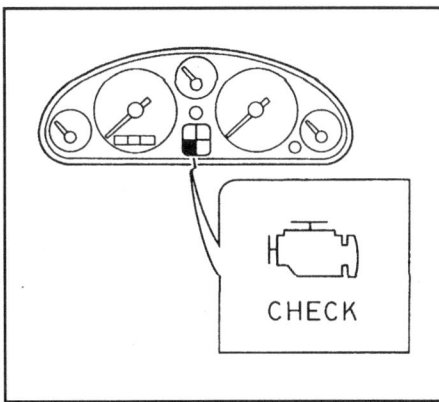

D4/5 THE DASHBOARD MOUNTED ENGINE 'CHECK' LIGHT.

controlled by/reporting to the PCM or within the PCM itself.

6   For models with the original OBD system, after getting the engine to normal operating temperature, determine the nature of the fault as follows. Switch off the engine. Switch off all accessories (eg: air conditioning, lights, radio, etc.) and put the transmission in neutral. Do not press the accelerator or clutch pedals during the test.

7   Open the data link connector on the left-hand inner fender (wing) and, with a piece of stiff copper wire, or a paperclip, bridge terminals **TEN** (test engine) and **GND** (ground). Turn the ignition switch to **ON** (do not start the engine).

8   If the PCM has stored a fault code the check light will give a series of flashes separated by 4 second pauses. A short flash indicates a single digit, so 3 short flashes repeating every 4 seconds would indicate **fault code 3**. A long flash equates to 10, so 2 long flashes and 3 short flashes repeating every 4 seconds would indicate **fault code 23**. Got it? If you get more than one type of flashing sequence every four seconds, multiple faults are being reported. Take your time to determine the fault codes; the light sequence will continue until you turn the ignition off.

9   Note that once a fault has been rectified, the fault code can be cleared from the PCM (and therefore the check light) by disconnecting the battery negative cable and pressing the brake pedal for at least 20 seconds.

10   The check light system reports just 16 codes, though there are many more which can be picked up by SSTs (Special Service Tools). The codes are as follows -

Code 01: A problem with the ignition system or associated circuitry.
Code 03 and **04**: A problem with the camshaft position sensor or associated circuitry.
Code 08: A problem with the MAF (mass airflow) sensor or associated circuitry.
Code 09: A problem with the engine coolant temperature sensor or associated circuitry.
Code 10: A problem with the air temperature sensor (within MAF unit) or associated circuitry.
Code 12: A problem with the throttle position sensor or associated circuitry.
Code 14: A problem with the barometric pressure sensor (located within PCM) or associated circuitry.
Code 15 and **17**: A problem with the heated oxygen sensor or associated circuitry.
Code 16: A problem with the EGR valve position sensor, associated circuitry or hoses.
Code 25: A problem with the PRC solenoid valve, associated circuitry or hoses.
Code 26: A problem with the purge solenoid valve, associated circuitry or hoses.
Code 28: A problem with the EGR solenoid valve (vacuum), associated circuitry or hoses.
Code 29: A problem with the EGR solenoid valve (vent), associated circuitry or hoses.
Code 34: A problem with the idle air control valve, associated circuitry or hoses.

Mazda Miata, MX-5, Eunos & Roadster

5. ENGINE COMPRESSION CHECK

☞ 1/1,2.

1   If the engine is worn the loss of compression will affect the operation of the engine management system, and can produce a number of faults which might otherwise be attributed to it. Eliminate engine wear as a problem by carrying out a compression check, using a proprietary compression gauge. Check that the battery is fully charged and in good condition, and that the engine is at normal operating temperature.

2   📷 Disconnect the ignition coil connector to disable the ignition system, then remove all the sparkplugs. Fit the compression gauge to cylinder No.1, hold down the accelerator pedal and crank the engine until the maximum pressure reading stabilizes. Note the reading and then repeat the check on the remaining cylinders.

3   1.6 litre: the normal compression pressure in a new engine is 1324kPa (13.5kg/cm2, 192psi) at 300rpm. On a used engine, a pressure above 932kPa (9.5kg/cm2, 135psi) is acceptable, with less than 196kPa (2.0 kg/cm2, 28psi) difference between cylinders.

1.8 litre: the normal compression pressure in a new engine is 1255kPa (12.8kg/cm2, 182psi) at 300rpm. On a used engine, a pressure above 883kPa (9.0kg/cm2, 128psi) is acceptable, with less than 196kPa (2.0kg/cm2, 28psi) difference between cylinders.

4   If you find one cylinder reading low, add a small quantity of oil through the sparkplug hole and repeat the check. If the reading improves, piston ring or bore wear is indicated. If the reading is unchanged, suspect a cylinder head or valve problem. Either way, you should investigate and remedy the fault before investigating the PCM system further.

5   You should note that though a compression check is useful for identifying a number of mechanical faults without having to dismantle the engine, it does not provide an exhaustive test of engine condition. If you are convinced that you have mechanical problems, consider getting a dyno check carried out. This will provide more information than a simple compression check, and will probably either identify the fault or set your mind at rest about general engine condition.

6. AIR INTAKE SYSTEM CHECKS

☞ 1/1, 2.

1   If you suspect a fault in the intake system, it is well worth carrying out a simple preliminary check before serious investigation is undertaken. First, make sure that the air filter element is clean and serviceable - a dirty or contaminated element will adversely affect performance and fuel efficiency. Note that the element cannot be cleaned, even with compressed air. If it is dirty, damaged or contaminated with oil or water, fit a new one ☞ 2.

2   It's also important there are no air leaks in the intake system. If there are, you will find it impossible to get the engine to run smoothly and predictably, because misleading data will be fed to the PCM from its sensors. Check the integrity of the airways and joints between air filter body and intake manifold, check the plethora of small hoses/pipes connected to intake airways and manifold (eg: PCV valve connections/hose). Check the hose clips for security. Check injector seals. Listen for air leaks at the intake manifold gasket. **Warning!** Beware of moving/hot components. Repair/renew as necessary.

3   You might find it helpful to spray WD40 on a suspected leak while the engine is running. If a leak is present, the lubricant will be drawn into the intake system and burnt as it passes into the engine,

5/2 Cylinder compression test.

the resulting exhaust smoke helping to confirm the leak. This method can often locate obscure leaks in areas like the manifold to head joint and injector seals. This test is only relevant to the part of the intake system between throttle butterfly (valve) and cylinder head. **Caution!** Don't spray WD40 onto other parts of the intake system as it could contaminate the air cleaner.

4   If you have a suitable vacuum gauge it is a useful exercise to measure intake manifold vacuum. Conduct this test after the car has been used so that the engine is thoroughly warm. Connect the vacuum gauge to the stub on the throttle body (see illustration) and, with the engine idling, the gauge should record 18inHg (60kPa/450mmHG) of vacuum. A higher reading is ok, but a lower reading indicates air leaks between the throttle valve and the cylinder head, too slow idle or piston ring/valve wear or damage.

7. THROTTLE BODY - REMOVAL, INSPECTION & INSTALLATION

☞ 1/1, 2.

Isolate the electrical system by disconnecting the battery negative (-) terminal after first having disarmed the audio unit's security system. **Warning!** When loosening the negative (-) terminal take great care not to short the tool you are using across the positive (+) terminal (for more information ☞ 7).

REMOVAL

1   Clean the external surfaces of the throttle body to prevent contamination.

2   The next task is to partially drain the cooling system until the coolant level is below the base of the throttle body ☞ 6.

3   📷+ Disconnect the small bore cambox

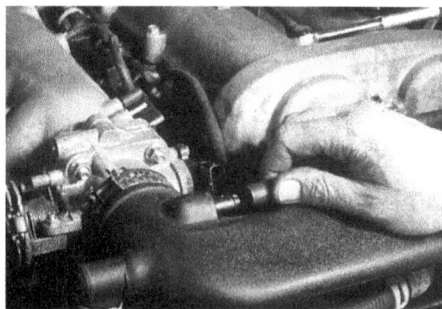

7/3a Release cambox ventilation hose ...

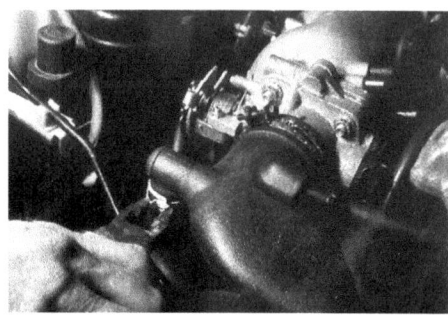

7/3b ... followed by bypass hose ...

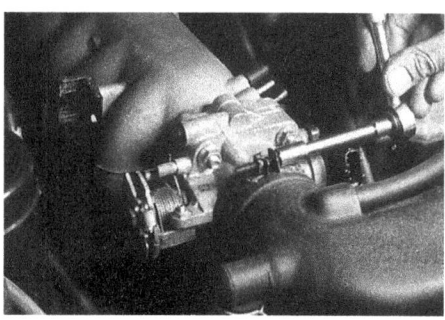

7/3c ... undo throttle body clamp ...

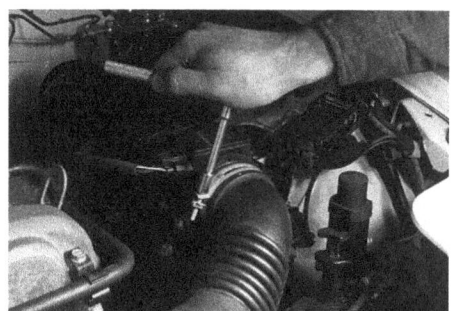

7/3d ... MAF clamp ...

7/3e ... then remove rigid air hose.

5: Engine management, fuel, ignition & exhaust systems

ventilation hose from the rigid air hose, followed by the air bypass hose (from rigid air hose to air valve). Loosen the clamps (clips) securing the rigid plastic intake hose to the nose of the throttle body and the MAF unit. The rigid hose can then be removed.

4 ◘ Disconnect the two small bore water hoses which connect to the air valve (BAC) beneath the throttle body.

5 ◘+ Twist the throttle body quadrant and release the accelerator cable from the pulley when it is slack enough. Disconnect the IAC valve and throttle position sensor electrical connectors. Using a 12mm socket, remove the two bolts and two nuts

7/4 Disconnect BAC valve water hoses.

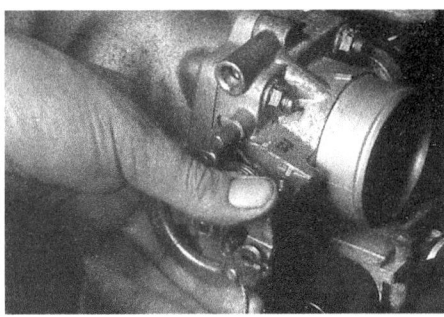
7/5a Release accelerator cable.

7/5b IAC valve wiring connector.

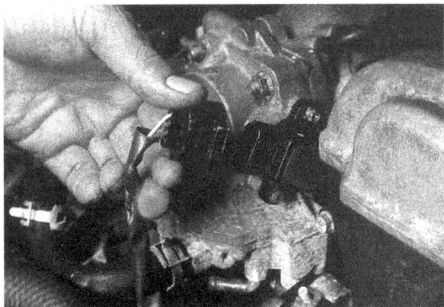
7/5c TPS wiring connector.

which secure the throttle body to the intake manifold and pull the unit clear.

INSPECTION

6 Check that the throttle butterfly valve is fully closed. Turn the throttle pulley and check that the valve moves smoothly and easily to the fully open position. There should be no tight spots. If found, these could indicate that the throttle body has become distorted. Check for lash in the throttle spindle bushings: excessive clearance here will allow air leakage which will upset the air fuel mixture and cause erratic running.

7 Repair possibilities are limited; the official remedy to any malfunction of the throttle body is replacement and, generally speaking, this is the only practical course of action. You may find a specialist machine shop which could undertake limited mechanical repair work, but this is unlikely to prove cost effective.

8 If the throttle body bore and butterfly are coated with carbon they can be cleaned with a soft brush (a toothbrush is ideal) and proprietary carburettor cleaner. **Caution!** The cleaner must be suitable for use with oxygen sensors and catalytic convertors. Note that the throttle butterfly valve and throttle body bore are coated with a thin sealing compound: this **must not** be removed.

INSTALLATION

9 Clean the gasket faces of the throttle body and intake manifold and fit a new gasket over the studs on the manifold mounting face. Position the throttle body and fit the two retaining nuts and bolts finger-tight. Tighten the bolts evenly and progressively to 19-25Nm (1.9-2.6kgf m, 14-19lbf ft).

10 Reconnect the throttle cable and check that it operates smoothly. Set the throttle cable lash to 1-3mm (0.039-0.118in) using the adjuster at the end of the outer cable. Fit the IAC valve and throttle position sensor wiring connectors and the small bore water hoses. Install the rigid air hose and bypass air hose. Fill the cooling system with ethylene glycol based coolant to the bottom of the radiator filler neck ☞ 6. Don't fit the radiator filler cap yet.

11 Start the engine and check for correct throttle operation, then let the engine idle until the radiator top hose gets hot. This procedure will allow the water level to stabilize and any air in the cooling system to work its way out. If necessary, top up the radiator and the coolant reservoir, and then fit the radiator cap. Leave the engine running for a while to allow the system to reach normal operating pressure, then check the water hose connections at the IAC valve for leaks.

8. ACCELERATOR CABLE & PEDAL - ADJUSTMENT & CABLE REPLACEMENT

☞ 1/1, 2.

Isolate the electrical system by disconnecting the battery negative (-) terminal after having first disarmed the audio unit's security system.

1 The accelerator cable is normally a durable component of little or no interest to anyone.

Until it breaks, that is. Cables always like to break at night, miles from home, and usually when it's raining; they never break right outside your local Mazda dealership on a sunny afternoon when you have a couple of hours to kill. It is well worth giving it a quick visual check from time-to-time. Watch for signs of fraying of the inner cable strands where it exits the outer cable and on the throttle quadrant; this is the first warning of impending failure. The broken strands can also catch in the inner cable causing the accelerator to stick. Depending on circumstances, this can be inconvenient, scary or downright dangerous. The rule here is if the inner cable is frayed or kinked, fit a new one before it lets you down.

2 Wally, our technical adviser, says that it is a good idea to keep a spare cable in the car - they're small enough to stow in the trunk. Maybe so, but we disagree. We reckon it is much better to fit the new cable as soon as you note signs of fraying on the old one, because it rates highly on our list of difficult jobs and, believe us, you won't ever want to attempt this on the roadside. We recommend that before attempting this feat, you become proficient in yoga. This will both improve your physical flexibility and your ability to remain comfortably upside down for long periods - you will need to be accomplished in both these respects. It will also impart the inner calmness you will find essential during the later stages of the removal operation ...

3 ◘+ First, the easy part. Start work under the hood by turning the throttle valve pulley quadrant and unhooking the cable inner once there's enough slack. Next, back off the cable adjuster locknut and free the cable adjuster from the bracket on the intake manifold. The bracket has a keyhole slot in it, and a sharp tug will allow the rubber grommet to be pulled clear. Follow the

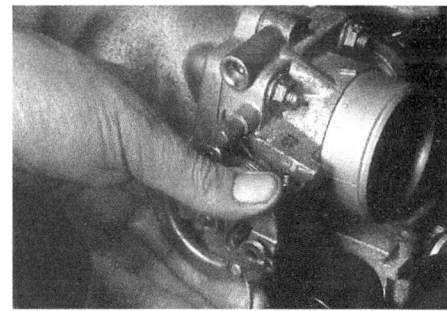
8/3a Release accelerator cable.

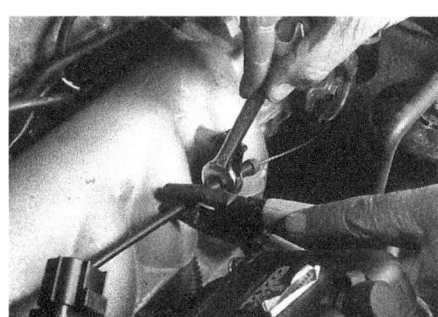
8/3b Slacken cable adjuster nuts.

Mazda Miata, MX-5, Eunos & Roadster

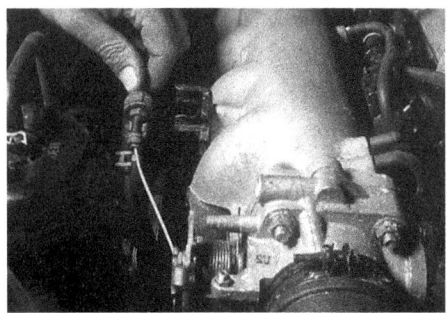

8/3c Release outer cable from stop bracket.

cable back to the firewall and release any cable ties or support blocks. Most of the cable ties used on these cars have small release tabs on the buckle, and if you lift or press these with a finger nail (depending on the type fitted) it can be slid apart and re-used later. You may encounter non-releasing cable ties; these will have to be cut off with wire cutters or a craft knife and a new one fitted during installation. Support blocks are retained in their brackets by small tabs which should be squeezed together to release them.

4   Moving inside the car, remove the two screws which retain the access cover below the steering wheel, and unclip and remove the cover. Grab the accelerator pedal pad, then feel with one hand up the pedal until you reach the lever end. When you get to the cable, work back along it to the firewall where you'll find a plastic cable stop recessed in the sound insulation and clipped firmly into the firewall. This is the part which is going to cause you BIG TROUBLE.

5   To have any chance of seeing what you are doing here, you will need to assume the Veloce Accelerator Cable Removal Position™, an advanced yoga-like position not recommended for

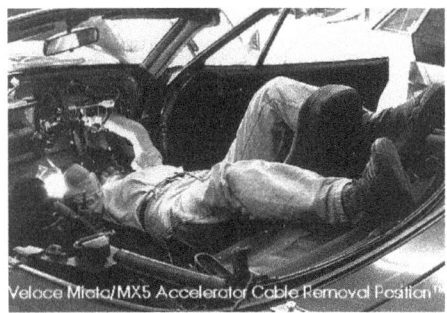

8/5 Know a good chiropractor?

couch potatoes. **Warning!** If you suffer from claustrophobia, we recommend that you do not attempt this operation (actually, don't even read the rest of this section). You will also need an assistant who you can trust to pass tools to you without laughing or making provocative remarks. (Better still, read through the following procedure, then get your assistant to do the work while *you* pass the tools and give instructions.) If you know a good chiropractor, invite him or her round before you start. Sit on the driver's seat facing backwards (yes, really) and maneuver your head under the steering wheel and into the aperture below the steering column. Place your feet either side of the seat back, resting them on the rear deck. With your head somewhere near the pedals (and using a flashlight or inspection lamp) you should be able to locate the cable stop in the firewall.

6   Around the back of the pedal lever you will feel two small tabs; these lock the cable in the lever end and can be released by squeezing them until the plastic clip pops free. Pull the clip clear of the pedal lever end and disengage it from the slot. Similar tabs lock the cable stop in the firewall; all you need do is squeeze them together and push the

8/6 Release cable from back of lever.

stop and cable through the firewall and withdraw it from under the hood. The problem here is that you need to compress four fairly stiff tabs simultaneously in a confined space. We tried different combinations of fingers and every pair of pliers we had, but to no avail.

7   You can improve access a little by moving the sound insulation away from the firewall and removing the accelerator pedal. The sound insulation is held in place by large flanged plastic retainers, which can be unscrewed from their studs as required - you can probably do this by hand unless they are unusually tight. The pedal pivot is secured by one of those tiny clips which, when dislodged with a screwdriver, travel at near warp speed to the nearest inaccessible recess, where they defy all attempts at recapture. Try to hold some rag around the clip as it is levered off the pivot (better still, purchase one or two new ones before starting the job). Note the relative positions of the pedal spring and its fitting direction, then slide the pedal out of its mounting. The spring will come off the pedal as it is removed, so fit it back on the pivot and place both parts to one side. You can now peel back the sound insulation to get a clearer view of the cable stop. Access may be further improved by detaching any relay(s) which are obstructing your view of the stop. If you can now depress the tabs enough by hand to push the stop back through the firewall, great. Wally couldn't, so we devised the Veloce Cable Stop Removal Method™ as follows.

8   Get your assistant to pass you two 16mm crescent wrenches. On each side of the stop there are two tabs, with a solid section at the center. What you need to do is push the crescent wrenches over the pairs of tabs so that they are held compressed, allowing you to push the stop into the firewall. Yep! it really does work. Once the tabs have passed through the firewall, have your assist-

8/8 How to compress cable stop tags.

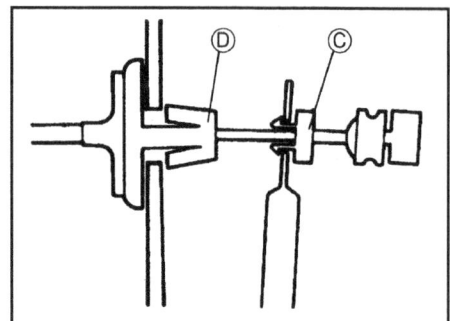

D8/8 ACCELERATOR CABLE (PEDAL END). Both the outer cable stop (D) and the inner cable stop (C) are retained by sprung tabs.

ant check that the cable is free by pulling it through from the engine compartment. You can now attempt to escape from under the dashboard - don't rush this. We suggest that you then sit quietly until you feel normal again; and don't worry, installation is easy by comparison.

9   Thread the new cable into position, securing the cable outer in the firewall by clicking the stop into position. Climb under the dashboard,

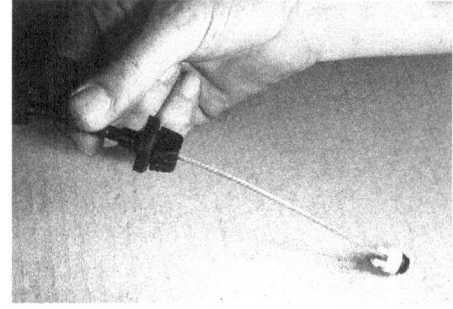

8/9 The cable stop and clip devices.

taking with you the pedal and pedal spring and the securing clip. When reassembling the pedal, lubricate the pin with molybdenum grease, because you don't ever want it to wear out and need changing. Fit the retaining clip carefully, making sure that it is fully seated in its groove. Check that the return spring is correctly positioned and that the pedal moves smoothly before reconnecting the cable. Hook the cable end over the pedal lever and click its stop into place. Working under the hood, fit the cable clips and connect the cable at the throttle body end. Set the adjuster nuts so that you have 1-

5: Engine management, fuel, ignition & exhaust systems

3mm (0.039-0.118in) lash in the cable inner (see photo). Finally, have someone floor the accelerator pedal and check that the throttle valve reaches the fully open position. If you need to, you can set the pedal travel by moving the stop bolt just above the pivot pin.

10 That's about it. Wally said that as soon as he's out of traction he's going to learn how to do this job by feel alone and make a fortune fitting accelerator cables. Meanwhile, next time you're at your Mazda dealer, just casually mention that you changed the accelerator cable, and see the *awe* on their faces.

9. INTAKE MANIFOLD - REMOVAL, CHECKING & INSTALLATION

☞ 1/1, 2. ☞ 5/13.

Isolate the electrical system by disconnecting the battery negative (-) terminal after first having disarmed the audio unit's security system.

Warning! Before commencing removal of the intake manifold it is essential to release fuel system pressure ☞ 5/13. Even if the engine has not been run for a while, high pressure remains in the system until this procedure has been undertaken. Note also that the cooling system must be drained, or partially drained, before the intake manifold water hose connections are disturbed.

REMOVAL

1 ☞ Remove the throttle body complete with air valve ☞ 5/7. Disconnect all hose connections to the manifold and attached components, including those from servo unit, PCV valve, purge solenoid valve, EGR valve and PRC solenoid valve. Detach the accelerator cable from the manifold ☞ 5/8. Detach the electrical connectors to all manifold mounted devices.

2 ☞+ Mark one of the rigid fuel lines and its flexible connecting hose using PVC tape/a paint mark to act as a guide during installation. Using a rag to catch any residual fuel spray, disconnect

9/1 Detach all hoses from manifold, including servo.

both fuel hoses and plug the open ends of the pipes to exclude dirt and to prevent fuel weeping out.

3 Release the electrical connector block at

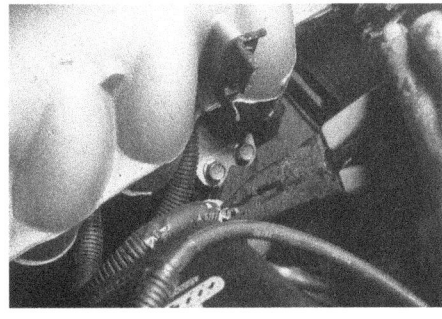
9/2a Release fuel hose clamp (clip).

9/2b Detach hose from rigid pipe. Plug pipe.

each individual injector. This is done by squeezing inwards the tag at the top of the connector block, after which the connector block can be pulled away from the side of the injector body.

4 Release the injector loom connector block from its mounting bracket at the rear end of the intake manifold. Squeeze the lugs on the retaining pin with pliers, and then the connector block can be freed from the bracket. Release the injector system wiring ground strap from the manifold by unscrewing the 10mm nut which secures it.

5 There is a small vacuum hose running between the pressure regulator valve on the fuel rail and a stub on the manifold. This hose should be disconnected simply by pulling it from either of its unions: there are no spring clips.

6 The fuel rail is fixed to the cylinder head by three 12mm bolts. Withdraw the bolts leaving the fuel rail free for removal. **Caution!** There are locating collars between the rail and its two mountings, which will be dislodged as the fuel rail is moved and could easily be lost or damaged. Note: if you don't want to disturb the fuel rail and injectors, they can be left in place and it will still be possible to remove the intake manifold. Pull the rail assembly away from the manifold to release the injectors from their bores, and then move the whole thing towards the rear of the engine and manipulate it up between the cambox and intake manifold plenum chamber. At the same time, push the fuel hoses up through the gaps between the individual intake manifolds and pull the injector wiring loom clear as necessary. **Caution!** As the injectors clear the manifold, their individual insulators will come away with them; be careful not to lose these if you don't have replacements.

7 ☞ Unscrew and remove the two 10mm nuts securing the EGR tube (from the exhaust manifold) to the rear of the intake manifold. Undo

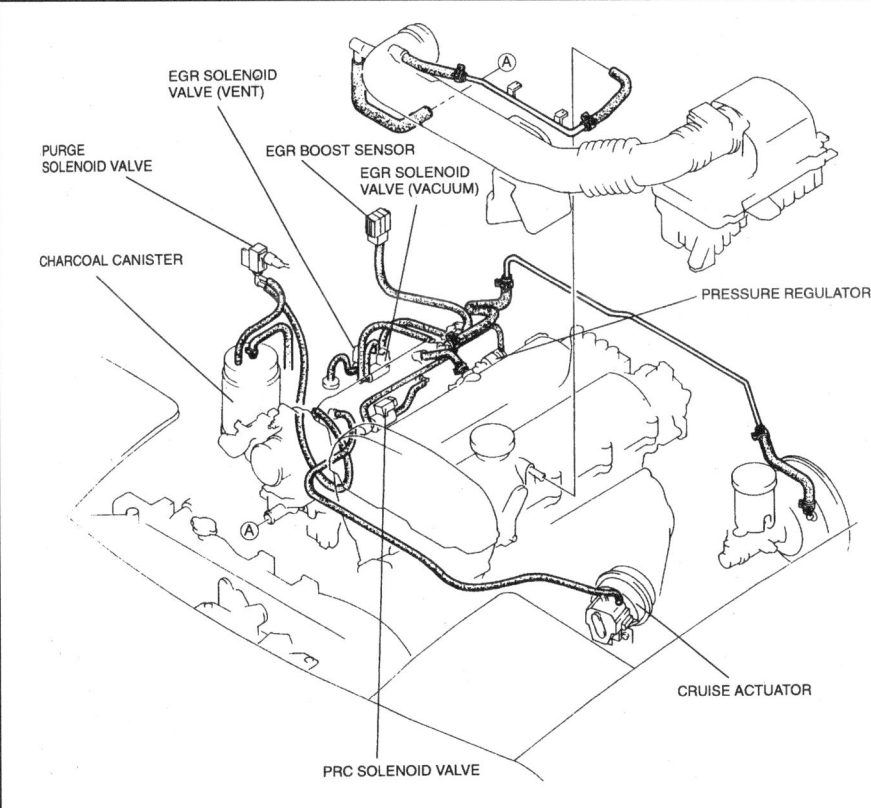

D9/1 VACUUM HOSE ROUTING.
It is essential that all these hoses are maintained in good condition and that connections do not leak, otherwise poor performance, and even engine damage, could result. Note that the "cruise actuator" is part of the cruise control system, if fitted. EGR system boost sensors are fitted to 1996 and later models.

Mazda Miata, MX-5, Eunos & Roadster

9/7 Release EGR pipe from the intake manifold.

9/8 These bolts fix manifold to bracket.

the single 12mm nut securing the pipe bracket to the rear of the engine.

8 Undo and remove the two 17mm bolts holding the manifold to the aluminum support bracket. Now, using a 12mm socket on a 250mm (9.5in) extension, you'll be able to reach most of the nine individual nuts retaining the manifold (once you have maneuvered the socket between the individual intake trunks until you find a gap large enough for it to pass through). If you use a smaller drive socket system it will need to be of extremely good quality because these bolts are tight. The nuts and bolts should be loosened in a diagonal sequence and, once the bolts and nuts have been removed, the manifold can be slid off the studs left protruding from the cylinder head. If the gasket stays fixed to the head, or manifold face, peel it off. **Caution!** Don't damage the cylinder head by trying to free/scrape off the old gasket with a sharp tool, and don't try to re-use the gasket - it's a false economy.

CHECKING

9 Clean the manifold using a proprietary aerosol carburettor cleaner (**Caution!** The cleaner should be suitable for cars equipped with oxygen sensors and catalytic convertors). Once clean, check the manifold carefully for signs of cracking or other damage. Any cracks will allow air leakage into the manifold and will make it impossible to get the engine to run normally.

10 Check the gasket faces using a straight-edge placed across each one at various angles. Again, if the gasket face is warped it will be impossible to get the manifold to seal correctly. You should also consider why the warping has occurred; it may have been due to an isolated case of overheating, but be sure to check that the engine is not running hot due to the fuel/air mixture ratio being incorrect. (Remember that once the air leak has occurred, the mixture will be weak anyway, until the fault is corrected, compounding the problem.)

11 If you discover damage, the easiest option is to fit a new manifold. If you want to keep costs down, consult a reputable engineering shop, which will be able to advise whether any cracks can be repaired by welding, and whether warped gasket faces can safely be machined flat again. Don't be tempted to re-use a manifold which you know is damaged; if you do you will never get the engine to run correctly, and could risk further engine damage due to the weakened mixture.

INSTALLATION

12   Having cleaned the gasket surfaces of both the cylinder head and the intake manifold, fit a new gasket over the studs protruding from the head. Next, slide the manifold over the studs, ensuring you don't trap any wires or hoses between the manifold and the block.

13 Now the nightmare begins! The manifold is retained by nine 12mm nuts. Getting the five upper nuts onto their studs is relatively easy, so do this and screw them up finger-tight. From above

9/12 Use a new intake manifold gasket.

the engine, the studs under the manifold are invisible, but there are four of them and they are positioned roughly at mid-points between the upper studs, which will give you an idea of where they are. The studs nearest the rear of the engine can be reached pretty easily with fingers; however, the last two are more difficult. We found that using a quarter inch drive socket set with a 6 inch extension, and the nuts glued into the socket with gasket cement, allowed us to start the nuts on their studs, although even then this was only achieved with the help of one of those small mirrors on a flexible shaft that you can buy in tool shops, and someone lighting the stud locations from beneath the engine.

14 Once all the nuts are in place, tighten them evenly in a pattern which spirals outwards from the central nut to a torque of 19-25Nm (1.9-2.6kgf m/14-18lbf ft).

15 Locate four new sealing/insulator rings into the individual fuel injector recesses in the head. They snap into position very positively.

16 Push the four individual injectors into their seats in the head, making sure that they are fully engaged and their electrical connections are uppermost. Also ensure that each injector has an O-ring and grommet at the fuel rail end.

17 Slide the two fuel hoses of the fuel rail down through the gaps between the intake runners of cylinders 1, 2 and 3, and maneuver the rail into position so that it engages with all four injectors.

18 Fit the fuel injector rail locating collars into their head recesses and be very careful not to knock them out of their seats during subsequent procedures: we dislodged one and it immediately took refuge within the engine mounting bracket, which we had to remove to retrieve it ... Push the injector rail firmly onto the individual injectors, ensuring that the O-rings are fully engaged in the rail recesses. This can be a fiddly procedure because, if the rail moves about too much, the individual injector sealing/insulating washers can disengage from the head, stopping the injector rail fixing brackets from engaging properly with their collars. Wriggle everything around until it snaps home. **Warning!** Don't try using the rail retaining bolts to force everything into correct position: it is the correct alignment of the rail and injectors relative to the head which ensures that all the high pressure seals work correctly.

19 Replace the three 12mm bolts securing the rail to the cylinder head and tighten them to 7.9-10.7Nm/80-110kgf cm/69-95.4lbf in of torque.

20 Reconnect fuel hoses, all wiring connectors, the ground (earth) strap, the EGR system pipe (with new gasket) and all vacuum hoses. Fit the throttle body complete with air valve using new gaskets 5/7. Install the accelerator cable bracket, tightening the retaining bolts to 7.9-10.7Nm (80-110kgf cm/69-95lbf in).

21 Reconnect the throttle cable and check that it operates smoothly. Set the throttle cable lash to 1-3mm (0.039-0.118in) using the adjuster at the end of the outer cable. Install the resonance chamber and bypass hose and secure with hose clips. Fit and tighten the radiator drain plug, then fill the cooling system 6, leave the radiator cap off for the moment.

22 The next job is to prime the fuel system. Locate the diagnosis connector which is mounted on the left-hand inner wing near the suspension turret. Open the connector cover and identify terminals **F/P** and **GND** as shown on the chart inside the connector cover. Make up a short jumper wire from a piece of insulated electrical wire with the ends bared. Connect together the two terminals and switch on the ignition for around ten seconds to allow the system to pressurize. Turn the ignition switch off, remove the jumper wire and close the connector cover. Check that there have been no fuel leaks.

23 Start the engine and check for correct throttle operation, and for indications of air leakage anywhere around the manifold (indicated by unusual hissing or whistling noises), and investigate and repair as required.

24 Let the engine idle until the radiator top hose gets hot. This will allow the water level to stabilize and any air in the cooling system to work out. If necessary, top up the radiator and the coolant reservoir, and then fit the radiator cap. Leave the engine running for a while to allow the

5: Engine management, fuel, ignition & exhaust systems

system to reach normal operating pressure, then check the air valve water hose connections for leaks.

10. AIR INTAKE CONTROL (IAC) VALVE - CHECKING

☞ 1/1, 2.

Isolate the electrical system by disconnecting the battery negative (-) terminal, after first having disarmed the audio unit's security system.

1   The IAC valve is a component part of the air (BAC) valve located under the throttle body of the intake manifold.

2   The ambient temperature around the BAC valve needs to be around 68 degrees F (20 degrees C) to undertake this test: if necessary, you could run the engine for a short time to warm the BAC valve area. Release the electrical connector from the IAC valve, then, using a multimeter, measure the resistance between the valve's two terminals. The reading should be between 10.7 and 12.3 ohms. If the reading is not within tolerance the BAC valve (which incorporates the IAC valve) will have to be replaced.

11. AIR (BAC) VALVE - REMOVAL, CHECKING & INSTALLATION

☞ 1/1, 2.

Isolate the electrical system by disconnecting the battery negative (-) terminal, after first having disarmed the audio unit's security system.

REMOVAL

1   Before you can remove the air valve it will be necessary to partially drain the cooling system to below the level of the valve ☞ 6.

2   ◙ The air valve is located beneath the throttle body of the intake manifold. Disconnect the water hoses from the air valve stubs, using a rag to catch any residual coolant. Disconnect the bypass hose from the BAC valve. Detach the electrical connector from the IAC valve.

3   The air valve itself is fixed to the throttle body by four crosshead (Phillips) screws. The four screws should be loosened slightly in a diagonal sequence before they are fully unscrewed.

CHECKING

4   You can check the operation of the air valve as follows. Clean the valve and place it in a

11/2 BAC & IAC valve securing screws.

plastic bag, then put it in a domestic freezer for an hour, or so, to cool it to 0°C (32°F). Remove the valve from the bag and make a mark on the internal shaft using an indelible marker. Then, using a hot air gun or warm water circulated through the valve's waterway, warm the valve body, which should cause the valve to operate. If the BAC valve does not operate it will have to be replaced.

INSTALLATION

5   Fit the air valve using a new rubber seal. Tighten the securing screws evenly and in a diagonal sequence. Reconnect and secure the water hoses and the bypass hose. Re-attach the electrical connector to the IAC valve. Refill the cooling system and check for leaks ☞ 6.

12 FUEL SYSTEM - DESCRIPTION

The fuel system provides fuel storage in the fuel tank at the rear of the car. The system delivers pressurised fuel to the fuel injectors via a pump, two filters, rigid and flexible fuel pipes and the fuel rail. Fuel pressure is maintained by a regulator under the control of manifold vacuum and the PCM. With the fuel filler cap in place, the fuel system is sealed apart from controlled entry of air to the fuel tank as it empties (otherwise a vacuum would form). Fuel vapor is stored in a charcoal canister until such time as it can be burnt by the engine without creating excess emissions. The latter system is really a component of the emission control system rather than the fuel system.

13. FUEL SYSTEM - SAFETY, DEPRESSURIZING & REPRESSURIZING

☞ 1/1, 2.

1   **Warning!** Before undertaking any work which necessitates disconnecting any part of the fuel system, read through this section - it contains information on safety precautions which must be adopted before work commences, plus general information on working procedures.

2   **Warning!** Whenever the fuel system is disconnected, fuel vapor will be present. Be aware of the potential fire hazard. Have available a fire extinguisher of the type approved for automotive fires. Make sure that the working area is well ventilated - working in a poorly ventilated building will increase the risk of a dangerous build-up of fuel vapor. Ensure that there are no naked flames, glowing elements or electrical sparks in the vicinity (including the pilot flames/ignitors of gas appliances). Observe a no smoking policy when working with fuel systems. We do not recommend that you carry out fuel system work with the vehicle over an access pit - fuel vapor is heavier than air and will collect in the access pit, where it will persist for some time, presenting a significant fire hazard. Whenever possible, work with the car's battery disconnected (☞ 7/2).

3   **Warning!** Before commencing work which requires disconnection of the fuel hoses or related parts it is essential to release fuel system pressure. Even if the engine has not been run for a while, high pressure remains in the system until the following procedure has been undertaken.

RELEASING FUEL SYSTEM PRESSURE

4   ◙ Working inside the car, remove the two screws which secure the access cover beneath the steering column. Unclip and remove the cover to gain access to the fuel pump relay.

The exact appearance of the fuel pump relay may vary, but on our project car the outer connector is bright yellow, and it is plugged into a

13/4 Fuel pump relay location (typical rhd).

white inner connector on a black-bodied unit (see photo). The colours of the relay's four wires are white/red, blue/red, light green and white/red. If in doubt, it is relatively easy to confirm the identity of the fuel pump relay as follows. Start the engine and then disconnect the wiring connector from what you think is the opening relay. If you have unplugged the fuel pump relay, the fuel pump will cut off and the engine will stall.

Once the engine has stalled, the fuel system is depressurized. Turn off the ignition switch and plug the relay back into the connector, then refit the inspection cover.

DISCONNECTING FUEL LINES

5   **Warning!** Release fuel system pressure ☞ 5/13/4. Isolate the electrical system by disconnecting the battery negative (-) terminal, after first having disarmed the audio unit's security system. ☞ 7.

6   **Warning!** When disconnecting any fuel line, cover the joint with a rag to catch fuel spray as separation occurs. Once a fuel line is disconnected, plug the open end to prevent dirt getting into the

Mazda Miata, MX-5, Eunos & Roadster

fuel system. Golf tees work fine for this or, if you don't play golf, try using small bolts of appropriate diameter. **Warning!** If you need to connect a fuel pressure gauge to the system to measure fuel pressure, **always** secure the connections with suitable hose clamps (clips) or they may fail under system pressure - this applies equally to plugged hose ends when they are under fuel system pressure. **Warning!** Main fuel line hoses must be pushed onto their stubs by at least 25mm (1in) and their clamps (clips) fitted securely to ensure a good seal.

PRIMING FUEL SYSTEM

7   After work on the fuel system is complete, it is preferable to prime the fuel system to avoid excessive engine cranking - remember that the battery is small by normal automotive standards, and has little reserve capacity. Ensure that all residual fuel vapor has dispersed, then reconnect the battery negative (-) terminal ☞ 7/2. Open the data link connector (marked **DIAGNOSIS** and mounted on the left inner wing near the suspension turret). Refer to the table inside the cover, and connect pins **F/P** (fuel pump) and **GND** (ground) using a short insulated jumper wire.

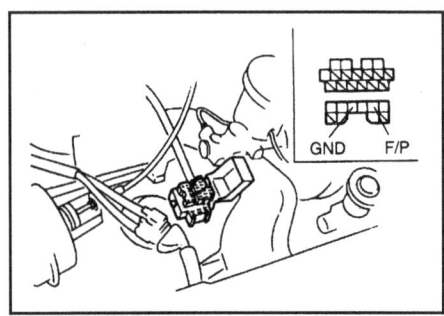

D13/7 DATA LINK CONNECTOR LOCATION (ALL MODELS).
Ground (GND) and fuel pump (F/P) terminals.

8   Turn on the ignition switch for about ten seconds, during which time the fuel pump will be running, and check for fuel leaks around any connection which has been disturbed. Turn the ignition switch off, disconnect the jumper wire and close the data link connector unit's cover.

14. FUEL SYSTEM - CHECKING

☞ 1/1, 2 & 5/13.

1   If the engine fails to start and you suspect that fuel is not reaching the injectors, you can perform a quick check to see if the pump is operating. You first need to bypass the fuel pump relay so that the pump will operate as soon as the ignition switch is turned on. Open the data link connector (marked **DIAGNOSIS** and mounted on the left inner wing near the suspension turret). Refer to the table inside the cover, and connect pins **F/P** (fuel pump) and **GND** (ground) using a short insulated jumper wire.

2   Turn the ignition switch to **ON** and then remove the fuel filler cap. Listen carefully at the fuel filler opening to hear if the pump is running. You'll need somewhere quiet for this. If you can hear the high-pitched whine from the pump, try starting the engine. If it now starts normally, you'll need to check the circuit opening relay.

FUEL PUMP RELAY CHECKING

3   Remove the two screws which secure the access cover around the lower section of the steering column. Unclip and remove the cover to gain access to the relay.

4   The exact appearance (see photo 13/4) of the fuel pump relay may vary, but on our project car the outer connector is bright yellow, and it is plugged into a white inner connector on a black-bodied relay unit. The colours of the relay's four wires are white/red, blue/red, light green and white/red. Unplug the relay harness connector and remove the single 10mm headed bolt which retains the relay unit to its bracket, then take the relay to the workbench for checking. You'll need a 12 volt battery, some insulated jumper leads with miniature clip probes, and a multimeter.

5   Refer to the accompanying diagram for

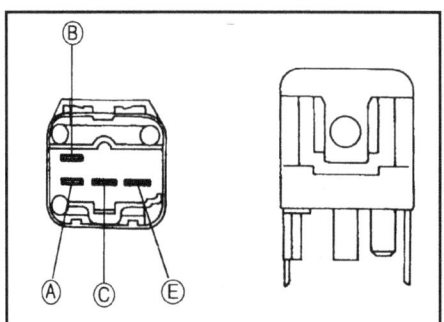

D14/5 FUEL PUMP RELAY CHECKING. WHEN BATTERY VOLTAGE IS APPLIED TO TERMINAL A AND TERMINAL B IS GROUNDED, THERE SHOULD BE CONTINUITY BETWEEN TERMINALS C AND E.

terminal identification. Using jumper leads, apply battery voltage as shown. If you don't get the right results, fit a new relay.

6   Install the relay and the access cover.

FUEL PUMP CHECKING

7   (D13/7) Open the data link connector cover and connect terminals **GND** and **F/P** using an insulated jumper wire (this allows the fuel pump to run as soon as the ignition switch is turned on by bypassing the circuit opening relay). Turn the ignition to **ON** and then remove the fuel filler cap. Listen carefully at the fuel filler opening to see if the pump is running. You will need somewhere quiet for this. If you can hear the high-pitched whine which indicates that the pump is running, suspect the opening relay (see above). If the pump does not run, check for battery voltage at the pump electrical connector as follows.

8   Temporarily switch off the ignition but leave the jumper in the data link connector. Working inside the car, carefully lever out the black plastic clips which secure the carpet to the rear deck. We found that the best technique for this was to use two flat-bladed screwdrivers to lift each clip. Don't be tempted to pull on the carpet to release the clips

14.8 Covers removed to give access.

- it will just pull off over the clip heads. You need to remove sufficient clips to allow the carpet to be rolled back clear of the access cover above the fuel tank. You'll find that there are three bright metal access covers. Ignore the long cover at the front edge of the deck - we are interested in the larger of the two remaining covers. Remove the 10mm screws which retain the cover and remove it. Locate and separate the fuel pump wiring connector. Connect the positive (+) probe of a voltmeter to the white/red wire's harness side terminal and the negative (-) probe to ground (earth). Turn the ignition switch to **ON**. If 12 volts is shown, you know that battery voltage is reaching the pump. If no voltage is shown, check the EFI 30amp fuse; if that's OK, check the wiring connections between fuse and fuel pump connector. Next, using an ohmmeter, check for continuity between the pump connectors harness side black wire terminal and ground (earth) using an ohmmeter. If continuity is shown (virtually no resistance), the pump circuit is fine, which means that you will have to replace the fuel pump. If not, check and repair the ground (earth) circuit

FUEL PRESSURE CHECKING

9   To carry out these checks, you'll need a fuel pressure gauge which can be Tee'd into the fuel delivery line with the joints securely clamped. You'll also need to be able to blank off the gauge outlet securely. The easiest access point for gauge connection is alongside the intake manifold.

FUEL PRESSURE HOLD CHECKING

10   Start by depressurizing the fuel system ☞ 5/13. Once pressure has been released, disconnect the battery negative (-) terminal (☞ 7). Working inside the engine compartment, identify the fuel delivery hose which connects to the front of the injector rail. Have some rag handy to catch any residual fuel leakage as the delivery line is pulled off. Disconnect the fuel hose and fit the fuel pressure gauge to the open hose end and a plug to the gauge outlet. **Warning!** Use hose clamps to secure all hose connections. Reconnect the battery negative (-) terminal after any fuel spillage has been mopped up and fuel vapor cleared. Moving to the data link connector, open the cover and fit an insulated jumper wire between terminals **F/P** and **GND**. Turn the ignition switch on for ten seconds to allow the fuel system to pressurize, then switch off and remove the jumper wire. You now need to

5: Engine management, fuel, ignition & exhaust systems

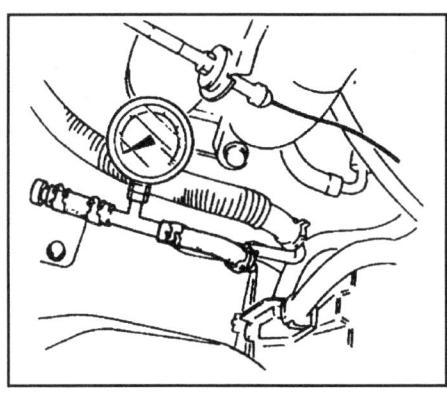

D14/10 MAXIMUM FUEL PRESSURE AND PRESSURE HOLD ARE MEASURED WITH A PRESSURE GAUGE CONNECTED TO THE FUEL FEED LINE AND WITH THE GAUGE OUTLET SIDE PLUGGED. ENSURE ALL CONNECTIONS ARE SECURELY CLAMPED.

wait for five minutes, after which a residual pressure reading of at least 147kPa (1.5kg/cm2, 21psi) should be shown on the gauge. If the hold pressure is below specification, check that there are no fuel system leaks. If no leaks are found between the pump outlet at the top of the tank and the gauge connection point (including the fuel filter and its joints), there is excessive back-leakage through the pump, indicating the need for pump replacement. Go to the next check.

FUEL MAXIMUM PRESSURE CHECKING

11   (D13/7) With the pressure gauge fitted as described for the hold pressure check, refit the jumper wire between terminals **F/P** and **GND** of the data link connector: switch the ignition to **ON** until a maximum pressure reading is shown on the gauge. This should be 481-589kPa (4.6-6.0kg/cm2, 64-85psi). Remove the jumper wire and go to the next check.

Fuel line pressure checking

12   After the hold and maximum pressure checks are completed disconnect the battery (7). Wrap some rag around the pressure gauge

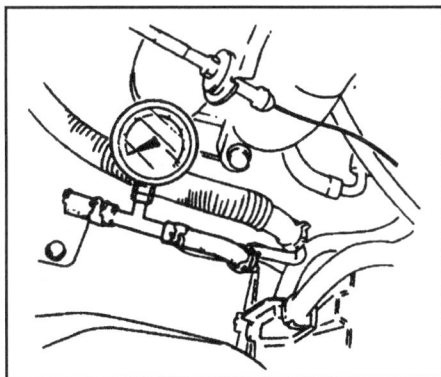

D14/12 FUEL LINE PRESSURE IS MEASURED WITH A PRESSURE GAUGE IN SERIES WITH THE FUEL LINE AS SHOWN HERE, AND WITH THE ENGINE RUNNING. ENSURE ALL CONNECTIONS ARE SECURELY CLAMPED.

connections to catch any fuel spray (there will be high residual pressure and it will not be possible to depressurise the system by the normal method), then connect the gauge in series in the fuel supply line (see illustration), again, using secure clamps. Reconnect the battery (7) when leaked fuel has been mopped up and fuel vapor has dispersed. Start the engine and run it at idle speed. The pressure recorded should be 216-264kPa (2.2-2.7kgf/cm2, 32-38psi) for 1994 to 1996 models, 197-245kPa (2-2.5kgf/cm2, 29-35psi) for 1997 and later models.

13   While the engine is idling, disconnect the vacuum hose from the fuel pressure regulator: fuel pressure should rise to around 284kPa (2.9kgf/cm2, 41psi) for all models.

14   If the line pressure readings are below the lower figures specified, a new pump should be fitted, after first checking for restrictions in the fuel feed line and its filters. If pressure is above the suggested range, test the function of the PRC valve and/or renew the pressure regulator, also check for restrictions in the fuel return line. If the fuel pressure does not rise to the indicated level when the vacuum hose is disconnected from the regulator, replace the regulator.

15   After the pressure checks are completed, carry out the normal system pressure release procedure 5/13. Disconnect the battery (7). Wrap some rag around the pressure gauge connections to catch any fuel spray (there will be high residual pressure), then disconnect the gauge. Reconnect the fuel pipe/s. **Warning!** Main fuel line hoses must be pushed onto their stubs by at least 25mm (1in) and their clamps (clips) fitted securely to ensure a good seal. Reconnect the battery (7) after all fuel spillage has been mopped up and vapor cleared. Prime the system as previously described 5/13.

Pressure regulator control (PRC) valve checking

16   If the fuel pressure checks cast doubt on the function of the PRC valve, check it *in situ* as follows. Disconnect the valve's vacuum hoses at the pressure regulator and the manifold. Release the valve's electrical connector.

17   Blow through the valve from port A (see illustration) and verify that air flows from port B. Apply battery voltage to one of the valve's terminals and ground the other, then repeat the blow test. This time air should exit from the air filter rather than port B. If the PRC valve does not perform as described, replace it.

14/16 Release electrical connector from PRC valve.

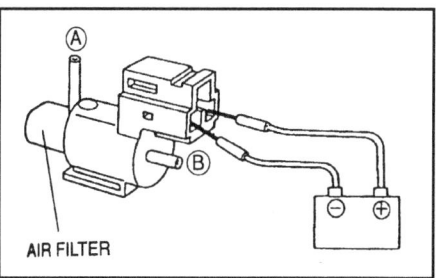

D14/17 PRC SOLENOID VALVE CHECK (see text).

INJECTOR OPERATION CHECKING

18   Have an assistant crank the engine while you listen to each injector in turn. If you don't have the luxury of a purpose-made stethoscope, use a long screwdriver with the tip held against the injector body and listen at the handle end. You should be able to hear a succession of clicks as the injector discharges. (Remember not to depress the accelerator pedal during this check - if the engine is cold the dechoke system will disable the injectors.) If the injectors appear to operate normally but the problem persists, you may have a low fuel system pressure problem - check the pressure regulator.

19   If the injectors seem inoperative or intermittent, disconnect the battery negative

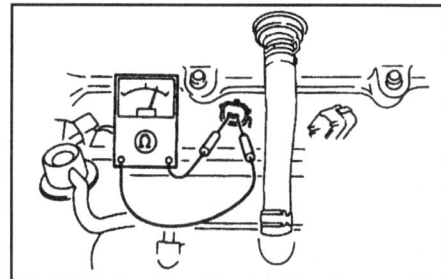

D14/19 FUEL INJECTOR RESISTANCE CHECK.

terminal and then remove the electrical connector from each injector after pressing its release tag. You'll see that the injector side of the connector has two terminals; using an ohmmeter, measure the resistance between the two terminals (see illustration) which should be 12-16ohms. If an injector is out of the specified range, fit a new one.

Fault not located?

20   If the checks detailed in this section fail to isolate the problem, the fault is likely to lie with the PCM. Have a full diagnostic test carried out by a Mazda dealer, or you could waste money replacing expensive components that are fine.

15. FUEL TANK - REMOVAL, CHECKING & INSTALLATION

 1/1, 2 & 5/13.

1   This operation is complicated, even if you have access to a 2-post vehicle lift and a transmission jack. Without this equipment we would advise you to consider having the work done profession-

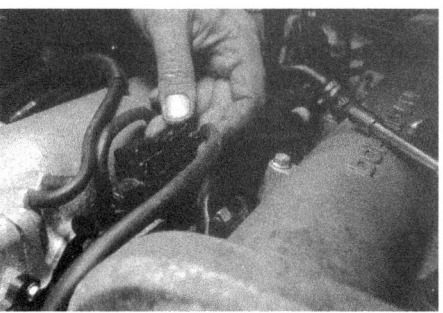

Mazda Miata, MX-5, Eunos & Roadster

ally. We're not saying that you can't do it at home, but it will entail a lot of work. Read through the procedure first, and then decide for yourself if you want to attempt it. You will have to remove the rear subframe assembly to obtain clearance for fuel tank removal, so if there is anything else requiring attention in this area, this would be a good time to do it.

PREPARATION

2   Before you start work, note that it will be necessary to drain the tank before you remove it. It follows that it would be advantageous to run the tank low before you start this procedure.

Warning! If you want to syphon the tank via its filler, do not be tempted to create a syphon effect by mouth - liquid fuel and heavy fuel fumes are extremely damaging to the lungs and the damage will be permanent (if you live ...).

Warning! Have a fire extinguisher to hand, and make sure that you take all sensible precautions to avoid every potential fire risk - there will inevitably be some fuel spillage and fuel vapor around.

The first task is to get the car raised high enough for access to the underside ☞ 1/3. Once you're satisfied that the car is raised sufficiently to give reasonable access, and that it is secure on its

15/3 Install fuel filter cover.

jack stands (axle stands), you must depressurize the fuel system ☞ 5/13. Having done this, disconnect the battery negative (-) terminal to isolate the electrical system ☞ 7/2.

DRAINING THE FUEL TANK

3   📷 Moving under the car, locate the plastic cover which conceals the fuel filter. This is on the right side of the car at the rear of the floorpan, and is held onto the body by cunningly designed plastic clips. At first sight, you might be forgiven for thinking that they are crosshead screws seated in cup washers. On closer examination, however, they turn out to be two-piece plastic fasteners, which are more complicated to deal with than you might think: for more advice ☞ 1/2 (*Wrestling with two-piece plastic panel fasteners.*)

4   Back to the job in hand. Remove all the fasteners which hold the filter cover in place. Lift the cover away to reveal the filter and fuel hose connections. The next step is to drain the fuel from the tank, and this is best done by disconnecting the fuel delivery hose at the filter as described below.

5   📷 Draining the fuel tank via the filter connection point is pretty easy because the fuel will siphon out of the tank once you've disconnected the delivery pipe. Find a clean, sealable container suitable for gasoline and place it under the car. If the tank is full, you will need something with a capacity of at least 48 liters (12.7 US gallons/10.5 Imp. gallons). A funnel would be useful here, too. The next stage can be messy and it's easy to get your arm soaked in fuel. **Warning!** Wear rubber gloves and coveralls to keep the fuel off your skin: wear safety glasses to protect your eyes. Try to disconnect the pipe quickly to minimize the mess. As an alternative method, you'll find a drain plug on the underside of the tank: clean off the underbody sealant before you attempt removal of the plug. If the plug seems abnormally tight, we recommend that you drain the tank as described below - you could easily tear the plug out of the tank base if you apply too much pressure, and that will mean fitting a new tank.

6   📷 Using pliers, grip the ends of the fuel delivery pipe clip and slide it up the pipe and clear of the stub on the filter. The stub is quite long - move the clip away by at least an inch or so, or it will still grip the stub. Using a screwdriver, push the hose off the stub (don't try pulling it off or it will just grip the stub tighter). The fuel system hoses are a tight fit on the metal pipes - they have to be because

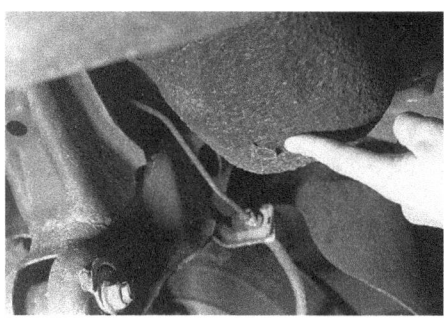

15/5 Fuel tank drain plug.

15/6 Make sure hoses are secure.

of the high fuel pressure they contain. If the hose won't yield to gentle screwdriver pressure, try fitting a pair of pliers loosely around the metal pipe and using the sides of the jaws to apply pressure to the hose end. Don't grip the pipe with the pliers, just let it slide over the pipe.

7   As the hose comes away, quickly position the end in the container or funnel and allow gravity to do the rest (remember to release the fuel filler cap so that the air can enter the tank as the fuel runs out). Once the tank has drained completely, remove the drain container, fit its cap and store it safely away from any source of fire, in a well-ventilated area. **Warning!** Fuel must be stored in a sealed container designed for the purpose. Plug the open end of the fuel hose with a golf tee or similar to prevent dirt entering the fuel system. We suggest that you check your service schedule for the car and see whether it is about due for a new fuel filter - if so, this is a great time to fit one - remember that if you don't do it now, you will have to endure the arm-soaked-in-gasoline procedure all over again when the time comes! **Warning!** If you did get fuel on your skin or clothes, get cleaned up as quickly as possible.

REMOVING THE EXHAUST SYSTEM

8   You need to drop the exhaust system clear of the underside of the car to get access to the PPF and propshaft (actually, you may be able to get by if you just remove the main muffler, but access is much better with the whole system out of the way, and it takes little extra time to do) ☞ 5/38.

REMOVING THE POWER PLANT FRAME (PPF)

9   The next step is to remove the Power Plant Frame (PPF). Unless you have access to SST 49 0259 440, which prevents oil leakage from the transmission housing when the propshaft coupling is detached, you will need to drain the oil from the transmission ☞ 2.

10   Start by disconnecting and removing the propshaft. Before undoing the four nuts and bolts holding the shaft flange to the differential flange, use a blob of white paint to mark the relative positions of both flanges.

11   The bolts have 12mm heads, while the nuts are 14mm, so you'll need a combination of two wrenches to release each nut and bolt. Using a diagonal sequence, slacken in turn each of the nuts and bolts a little before removing them completely. You may need to apply the parking brake to lock the propshaft while each nut and bolt is freed, turning the shaft and reapplying the brake to gain access to all four fasteners.

12   Once the four nuts and bolts have been released, separate the driveshaft and differential flanges by pushing the shaft forward further onto the transmission tailshaft, and then lowering the axle end of the shaft before withdrawing the shaft's nose from the tail of the transmission. Note: some residual oil will drip from the transmission end once the propshaft is removed; place a plastic bag over the end of the transmission tail and secure with an elastic band to contain the drips and prevent dirt getting into the transmission bearings.

13   Once the driveshaft has been removed completely, replace the bolts, locking washers and nuts finger-tight in the differential flange for safekeeping.

14   📷+ Release the wiring loom from the side of the PPF by squeezing the retaining ears of each plastic clip with your fingers or pliers and then, while the ears are squeezed together, pulling the clip free of the frame. Some of these clips are very fiddly but with care they can all be removed without breaking them. Don't forget to release the ground wire held by a 10mm bolt toward the rear

5: Engine management, fuel, ignition & exhaust systems

15/14a Release wiring from PPF clips ...

15/14b ... don't forget ground terminal.

end of the PPF, and the loom clip on the side of the bellhousing, which is held by a 10mm screw.

15 Remove the support bracket between the PPF and the transmission tail casting by first unscrewing the 17mm headed bolt between the PPF and the bracket, followed by the two 14mm headed bolts holding the bracket to the transmission. Remove the bracket and fit the bolts finger-tight in their appropriate places for safekeeping.

16 Place a jack beneath the transmission, just ahead of the front end of the PPF. Raise the jack until the rear of the transmission is supported and very slightly lifted: this will relieve the strain on the PPF.

17 At the very front of the PPF there are two 17mm headed bolts which pass upward, right through the transmission casing, and screw into the top of the PPF. Slacken and remove both of these bolts, which are 198mm (8in) long!

18 At the rear end of the PPF there are two more long bolts, this time passing through the differential casting. Slacken and remove both bolts with a 17mm socket wrench. You will notice that the forward bolt has a shoulder. Note: before removal of the long bolts and collar holding the PPF to the diff, it's a good idea to soak the whole area with penetrating oil as the collared bolt is a tight fit in the spacer and its shaped bore in the diff: even on our low mileage car, the forward bolt was pretty well corroded in place.

19 When the bolts have been removed the collar in the forward bolt position also has to be removed. If you look carefully at the shoulders of the collar you will see a couple of cutouts. Initially, tap a chisel or an old screwdriver into these recesses until the collar begins to move away from the PPF. Once movement has started you can lever the collar out with a screwdriver, moving from side-to-side and working it out gradually.

20 Once the collar is removed the rear of the PPF can be moved sideways until clear of the differential casing, and then pulled backward, freeing it from the transmission casing, after which the PPF can be removed from the car.

REAR SUBFRAME REMOVAL

21 If you lie under the rear of the car, you can see the fuel tank mounted above the rear subframe assembly. The tank is wedge-shaped, and during removal must be moved forward and then rotated around the front edge of the subframe. As you will see, there is not enough room to do this with the subframe bolted in position; you have to lower it enough to permit the tank to be removed. In theory, you don't have to remove the subframe completely, but doing so confers some advantages. Firstly, you get unrestricted access to the tank and, secondly, you can check over the subframe and the normally-hidden areas of the bodyshell, so you have a great opportunity for inspection and rustproofing. The extra work required to detach the subframe completely, rather than just lowering it, is worth the extra time taken on this job if you need to check or repair these areas.

22 What we will be doing here is supporting the rear subframe as an assembly on a normal wheeled hydraulic jack, and lowering it from under the car. As well as the jack, you will need a couple of assistants, one on each side of the subframe, to steady and support it as it is lowered and to help maneuver it out. The first step is to remove the rear wheels and place them to one side. If you just want to lower the subframe enough to get the tank out, proceed as described below. If you want to remove the subframe so you can check over the subframe components and body underside, skip down to paragraph 26.

23 From under the car, locate the brake pipe distribution block on the subframe. Remove the two nuts which secure the block to the subframe, but leave the brake lines connected. Next to the distribution block you will see the battery cables and other wiring running though a square-section guide. Disconnect this from the subframe by pulling it out carefully.

24 Position a wheeled hydraulic jack below the differential housing, making sure that the finned area sits squarely in the jack pad. Raise the jack slightly to take the weight of the subframe assembly. Working from each side of the car through the wheelarch, slacken and remove the subframe fasteners. On each side there are two 19mm headed nuts at the front and rear mounting points, with a single 19mm headed bolt between the two (it's possible that the center bolt is not fitted on all vehicles). You will need a fairly long socket extension to reach them, the center bolt being accessed through the gap in the upper wishbone. As you remove the fasteners, note that the subframe will come free, and you should have an assistant at each side to steady it and prevent it from toppling off the jack.

25 Slowly lower the jack, with your assistants guiding it downwards on each side. As it moves down, keep a close eye on the wiring, brake lines, fuel lines and parking brake cables - these are easily strained if they get caught up as the crossmember descends. Get the assembly as low as you can without risking damage to the above connections, then support the ends of the assembly by positioning strong crates or pieces of lumber under the lower wishbones. Make sure that it sits securely and is in no danger of toppling off the supports. Note that because the suspension is still connecting the subframe and body, it should be pretty stable, but try not to place undue stress on the suspension parts.

26 If you want to get the subframe out completely to allow a detailed inspection as discussed above, there are a few additional steps to follow. From inside the car, back off the parking brake adjuster to allow plenty of slack in the cable. You can turn the hexagonal adjuster with a screwdriver; you'll find the adjuster at the side of the parking brake lever. At the wheel end of the parking brake cable, slacken the cable locknut and disengage the cable adjuster from its bracket. You can now free the cable inner from the operating lever and disengage the cable assembly. Repeat this procedure on the remaining wheel.

27 Working below the car, disconnect the brake pipe which runs from the front of the car at its union with the distributor block. Free the pipe end, and plug the distributor block thread and cap the pipe end to keep dirt out of the hydraulic system. Disconnect the square-section guide which carries the battery cables and wiring along the crossmember and lodge them clear of the working area. On each side of the car, remove the suspension unit lower mounting bolt from the lower wishbone, passing a 17mm socket through the access hole (when you remove the subframe the suspension units will be left hanging from their top mountings, reducing the weight and overall height of the subframe assembly).

28 Position a wheeled hydraulic jack below the differential housing, making sure that the finned area sits squarely in the jack pad. Raise the jack slightly to take the weight of the subframe assembly. Working from each side of the car through the wheelarch, slacken and remove the subframe fasteners. On each side there are two 19mm headed nuts at the front and rear mounting points, with a single 19mm headed bolt between the two. (The center bolt may not be fitted on all cars). You will need a fairly long socket extension to reach them, the center bolt being accessed through the gap in the upper wishbone. As you remove the fasteners,

Mazda Miata, MX-5, Eunos & Roadster

15/31a Remove cover ...

15/31b ... to reveal pipe connections.

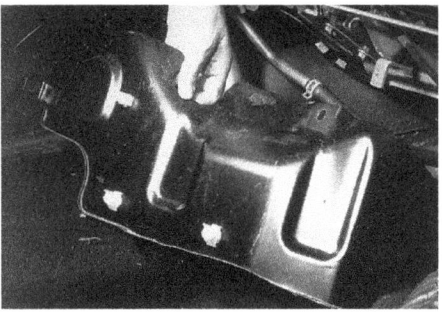

15/31c This cover in the trunk (boot) ...

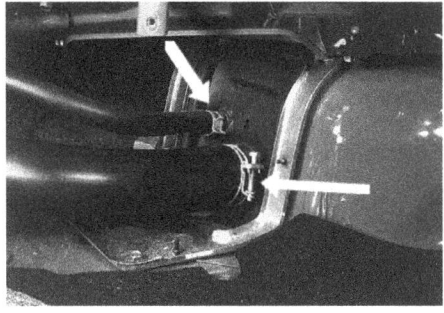

15/31d ... also gives access.

note that the subframe will come free, and you should have an assistant at each side to steady it and prevent it from toppling off the jack.

29   Slowly lower the jack, with your assistants guiding it downwards on each side. As it moves down, keep a close eye on the wiring, brake lines, fuel lines and parking brake cables - these are easily strained if they get caught up as the crossmember descends. Note that if your car is wired differently to ours, or if aftermarket wiring has been added in the vicinity of the subframe, you may need to disconnect or re-route it.

30   Once the subframe has been lowered enough to clear the body, it can be removed from the rear of the car. Wheel it out on the jack, with your assistants steadying each end. You will need to arrange some kind of support for the subframe by positioning strong crates or pieces of lumber under the lower wishbones. Make sure that it sits securely and is in no danger of toppling off the supports.

TANK REMOVAL

31   ◘+ With the subframe removed or lowered sufficiently for access, you can at last begin to remove the fuel tank. Start by lifting the rear deck carpet and removing all of the inspection covers above the tank (for more information ☞ 5/14). At the back of the deck, removal of the smallest of the three covers will reveal the fuel filler and vent pipes connected to tank stubs. Free the vent pipe by squeezing together with pliers the tabs on the retaining clip and sliding the clip back along the pipe. The pipe can then be worked off its stub. The filler pipe can be removed in the same way, except that it is secured by a screw-type clip. If you have difficulty reaching the hose connections, note that you can also reach them from inside the trunk after you have removed the access cover forward of the tool recess. Note that this is the access point for the filler and vent hose upper connection points, should you need to replace them. There is a rubber closing seal around the stubs, and it and its metal surround should be removed after releasing the 10mm headed nuts and bolts which retain them. Note that if there is still some fuel in the tank, now is the time to remove it. We recommend one of those hand pumps sold in auto parts stores. Once you have started the flow of fuel from the tank filler opening into a sealable container suitable for gasoline, it should continue to siphon out as long as the container is below tank level.

32   ◘ Working through the larger aperture above the tank, disconnect the fuel gauge sender/fuel pump wiring connector and lodge the connector clear of the tank. (It's a good idea to pull the wiring out of the tank recess and tape it to the body so that it won't accidentally get trapped under the tank during installation.) Grasp the fuel delivery and return hose clips with pliers and slide them away from their stubs, then push the hoses off using the flat blade of a screwdriver, having first marked one of the hose ends and its stub with paint or typist's correcting fluid as a guide during installation. Plug the hose ends with golf tees or similar, and cap the stub ends to exclude dirt from the fuel

15/32 Remove wiring and hoses.

system. The vent hose can similarly be disconnected and taped up outside the access aperture.

33   Moving back under the car, you can now remove the four fixing bolts, making a note of the plates and rubber gaskets fitted either side of the tank flange. Since these are all that now hold the tank, be ready to support it as the fasteners are released. The tank can now be lowered and removed, maneuvering it round the subframe if this is still below the car.

INSPECTION AND REPAIR

34   Examine the tank for corrosion or damage and assess the best course of action. If the damage or corrosion is serious, a new tank should be fitted and, in view of the work needed to remove and install a tank, we would be inclined to fit a new one whatever the problem, just to make sure that you won't need to repeat the procedure in the near future. Minor damage may be repaired, but this **must** be entrusted to a professional welder. **Warning!** Fuel tanks are notoriously dangerous to repair by welding and it is essential that they are steam cleaned first to remove any residual fuel vapor. (We know a guy who is very relaxed about welding fuel tanks. "No problem", he says, "You just put the torch to the tank filler and let the vapor burn away". He's an odd-looking guy, with no eyebrows or eyelashes.)

35   Whatever you choose to do, you'll first have to teardown the tank. Remove the crosshead screws which secure the fuel pump flange to the tank. Carefully free the flange and its seal from the top of the tank. The seal is pegged into the pump flange, but may be stuck to the tank; if so, work a screwdriver around the edge of the seal to free it.

36   Carefully remove the pump and fuel gauge sender as an assembly, noting that you will have to maneuver the assembly as it is lifted out so the fuel gauge sender float comes free of the tank. Don't bend the float arm, or the fuel gauge readings will be affected. Once you have removed the assembly, cover the hole in the tank with clean cloth to exclude dirt and minimize the escape of fuel vapor.

37   Next, remove the fuel vapor valve from the tank by removing the four crosshead screws which secure the valve to the tank. Release the single 10mm headed bolt which retains the two-way check valve (three-way check valve, automatic transmission models) and lift away the two components, leaving them connected together by the vent hose. If you intend to re-use the tank, make sure that it is clean inside, with no sediment lying around to block up the pump.

38   Install the removed components on the repaired or new tank, noting that the bolt securing the two-way check valve (three-way check valve, automatic transmission models) should be tightened to 3.9-5.9Nm (40-60kgf cm/34-52lbf in).

39   When you fit the pump/sender assembly, be careful not to bend the float arm or you will get incorrect gauge readings. The fuel pump/fuel gauge sender flange screws have a torque range of 7.8-11Nm (80-110kgf cm/69-95 lbf in) and the fuel vapor valve screws should be tightened down to 1.1-1.6Nm (11-17kgf cm/9.5-14.8lbf in).

5: Engine management, fuel, ignition & exhaust systems

INSTALLATION

40　Fit the tank in the car, securing it with the bolts and retainer plates, noting that the bolts should be tightened to 22-30Nm (2.1-3.1kgf m/16-22lbf ft). Remember to check during installation that any wiring or hoses have not become trapped under the tank. Reconnect the fuel pump and vent hoses, installing the securing clips where fitted, and ensuring that the hoses are pushed onto the stubs by at least 25mm (1in). Install the closing seal and its surround at the rear of the tank, tightening the fasteners to 7.8-11Nm (80-110kgf cm/69-95lbf in). Reconnect the fuel filler and vent hoses. Fit the hose retaining clips, making sure that they are secure. Reconnect the fuel pump/sender wiring connector. Leave the access panels and deck carpet removed at this stage. Push the filler hose onto its stub by at least 35mm (1.4in), main line fuel hoses by at least 25mm (1in) and vent hoses by at least 20mm (0.8in) and fit their clamps (clips) securely to ensure a good seal

41　Working under the car, install the (preferably new) fuel filter and reconnect the hoses, securing them with their spring clips. **Warning!** Main fuel line hoses must be pushed onto their stubs by at least 25mm (1in) and their clamps (clips) fitted securely to ensure a good seal. It is a good idea to check all the disturbed connections at this stage. Fill the fuel tank, then temporarily reconnect the battery ☞ 7/2. Prime the fuel system (for details ☞ 5/13) which will show that the pump is operating correctly. Next, check all fuel line connection points for leaks - if necessary, depressurize the system and remake connections, or fit new hoses if leaks are found. Check the fuel filler hose for leaks, and check that the fuel gauge operates normally (check the wiring connections at the fuel tank flange if there is no response from the gauge). When you are satisfied that all is well, disconnect the battery negative (-) lead (☞ 7/2) and resume reassembly. Start by installing the rear deck inspection covers, and then fit the deck carpet.

42　Reposition the rear subframe and carefully jack it back into position, checking that nothing gets trapped or strained as it is raised. Install the subframe mounting bolts and nuts, tightening them evenly to 93-117Nm (9.5-11.9kgf m/69-86lbf ft). Where they were removed, make sure that you guide the bottoms of the suspension units into their recesses in the lower wishbone. Fit the suspension unit lower mounting bolts and tighten them to 73-93Nm (7.4-9.5kgf m/54-69lbf ft).

43　If the brake hydraulic system was disconnected, then bleed and secure the pipe unions, then bleed the hydraulic system at each rear caliper ☞ 9/2. Otherwise, fit the distributor block, tightening the mounting nuts to 13-22Nm (1.3-2.2kgf m/9.4-16lbf ft) Reposition the fuel filter cover and secure it with its two-piece plastic fasteners. Fit the wiring harness/battery cable guide to the subframe. Fit the brake cables, if removed, and secure their locknuts. Check and adjust the parking brake ☞ 9/20. Check that any accessory wires disconnected during removal are reconnected properly.

PPF INSTALLATION

44　From beneath the car put the PPF in place by sliding it forward onto its mounting on the right side of the transmission, then pushing it up around the side of the differential unit until it slides onto its mounting. Note: you may have to lift the propshaft flange end of the differential slightly to get the PPF to slide into engagement. The end of the PPF with round drillings is the differential end.

45　With the PPF roughly positioned, install the two 17mm-headed bolts that pass through the lower flange of the PPF, up through the transmission casing and then screw into the top flange of the PPF. For the moment, these bolts should be left finger-tight.

46　Move to the rear end of the PPF and install the 17mm through bolts that clamp the PPF to the side of the differential casing. Fit the bolt without a collar first, followed by the bolt with the collar. It's suggested that you spray the shanks of both bolts with WD40 or a similar silicone-based lubricant as they seem prone to corrosion. You may need to lift the nose of the diff casing a little to align the holes in the diff casing and the PPF. Tighten the two bolts snugly but not fully at this stage.

47　Move once again to the forward end of the PPF and install the transmission extension housing support bracket between the PPF and the tailhousing of the transmission. If you've used a rope or a jack to support the transmission, and it's in the way, you should remove it before installing the bracket. Hold the bracket in place above the lower flange of the PPF and finger-tighten the 17mm retaining bolt. Insert the two 14mm bolts that secure the bracket to the transmission tailshaft and, once again, tighten them finger-tight. You may need to lift the tail of the transmission slightly to make the bracket align with the threaded holes in the transmission casing. Tighten the two 17mm PPF to transmission side bolts to a torque of 115Nm (11.5kgf m/85lbf ft).

48　Next, tighten the PPF to differential 17mm side bolts to the same torque. Make sure the collar on the forward bolt is properly engaged in the recess in the PPF.

49　Move to the tailshaft support bracket and tighten the 17mm bolts to the same torque as the other 17mm bolts. Then tighten the bracket's 14mm bolts to a final torque of 45Nm/4.5kgf m/35lbf ft.

WIRING LOOM FITTING TO PPF

50　Start to secure the loom by fixing its support bracket to the side of the transmission with the short, sheet metal screw provided.

51　Work your way along the PPF, pushing each loom retaining clip into place as you go. Note that the first clip, at the engine end, is at the top of the PPF and the second clip about halfway down the side of the frame. The following clips run along the frame about two thirds of the way down on the right-hand side, while the last two clips, at the axle end of the PPF, are at the top.

52　Toward the rear end of the PPF there is a ground (earth) wire sprouting from the loom which should be re-secured to the PPF by tightening its 10mm retaining bolt. Note: before fastening the ground (earth) strap, clean the eye and the contact area of the PPF with abrasive paper. Smear both with petroleum jelly (Vaseline) and then replace and tighten the screw.

PROPSHAFT INSTALLATION

53　Rub engine oil over the section of the propshaft that enters the transmission tailhousing and engages with the transmission mainshaft splines. This ensures that the transmission tailshaft oil seal is well lubricated.

54　Slide the front end of the propshaft into the tail end of the transmission unit: you may have to rotate the propshaft just a little to allow the splines to engage. Then, lift up the rear end of the propshaft and engage its flange with the differential drive flange, lining up the marks you made when the propshaft was removed. Fit the four bolts and nuts (nuts toward the front of the car) and tighten to a torque of 29Nm (2.9kgf m/21lbf ft). **Warning!** If the spring washers show any signs of having become flattened, they should be replaced. Note: you'll need to apply the parking brake in order to stop the propshaft rotating when you try to torque the nuts.

TRANSMISSION OIL

55　Now's a good time to refill the transmission with oil if it has been emptied. Manual transmission: first check that the 24mm drain plug is tight, then remove the filler plug halfway up the left-hand side of the transmission case. Add 2 liters (0.43 Imp gal/0.52 US gal) of the approved gear oil and then replace and tighten the filler plug. If the transmission oil was not emptied, check oil level and top-up as necessary ☞ 2/8 or 9. On automatic transmission cars, remember to check the transmission fluid level after installation is complete ☞ 2/9.

EXHAUST SYSTEM - INSTALLATION AS A ONE-PIECE ASSEMBLY

56　The following procedure deals with fitting the complete exhaust system as opposed to fitting a new system in parts. It is assumed that the whole exhaust, from manifold (header) flange to rear tailpipe, is in one piece and is exactly as it was when removed. It would, of course, be a false economy to refit a broken or corroded system. If you removed only part of the system in the course of this procedure, refer to the appropriate paragraphs of the installation sequence.

57　Slide the exhaust system along the ground until it is in approximately the correct position beneath the car. Note that the heatshields on top of various sections of the exhaust system should be in good condition and, where so marked, be correctly orientated.

58　Lubricate the studs on the exhaust manifold with copper-based grease. Slide a - preferably new - metal gasket over the studs, noting that no sealing compound is necessary if both mating faces are clean.

59　Have an assistant support the rear end

Mazda Miata, MX-5, Eunos & Roadster

of the system, while, from beneath the car, you begin to maneuver it into position. You'll find that you'll have to twist the system to one side a little in order to work the exhaust pipe flange past the bellhousing bracket, but once past the bracket it will comfortably slide up roughly into position.

60   When the flange at the front of the exhaust system engages with the three manifold studs, quickly spin on any one of the three nuts by a few turns and just leave it at that for the moment. Note: each of the three retaining nuts has a spring washer, which should be replaced if it has become flattened.

61   Your assistant should now lift the rear exhaust box and fix it to the underside of the car by pushing the eyes of the rubber supports over pegs and hangers: this process is made so much easier by spraying the rubber supports with silicone-based lubricant, that it can then be done without tools.

62   Moving back to the front of the system, it should now be easy to push the exhaust system flange fully home against the manifold flange. Note: the three manifold flange nuts and washers are very difficult to get into place. I spent quite a lot of time cursing and trying to get one of the two lower nuts to nip the threads when, in fact, the easiest nut to place - and it can be without its washer initially - is the top nut. What you need here is an assistant who will reach through the gap between the front subframe and chassis from the left-hand front wheelarch to fit the nut to the top stud. Once you have a nut in place it becomes comparatively easy to fit the others.

63   You'll find the only way to tighten the manifold flange nuts is with a 14mm socket attached to a universal joint attached to an extension of at least 360mm (14in), and then a ratchet or T-bar. Both of the lower nuts can be tightened from beneath the car; the top nut is most easily accessible via the left-hand front inner wheelarch. Torque the three nuts to 38Nm (3.8kgf m/30lbf ft).

64   Once the manifold flange nuts have been tightened, work your way back along the exhaust system fitting all of the rubber hangers. As mentioned before, a quick spray with silicone fluid will make this job so easy you can just push each rubber hanger over its pin with your fingers.

65   When all of the hangers are in place, come back to the front of the system and, after lubricating it with copper-based grease, insert the 12mm bolt that fixes the exhaust pipe clamp to the bracket on the side of the bellhousing. The bolt can be inserted and tightened through the gap between the subframe and chassis rail in the left-hand front wheelarch. Torque the bolt to 24Nm (2.4kgf m/17lbf ft).

66   Fit the rear brace bar, noting that the rear right hand corner has a clip which attaches over its bracket. Secure the bar with six 17mm bolts tightened to 55-80Nm (5.6-8.2kgf m/41-59lbf ft).

67   That's about it. Mazda recommends that the rear suspension adjustment is checked and reset as required (☞ 7). We suggest that you get the alignment checked by a tire specialist, but there should be no reason why these settings would have been altered as a result of the procedures described above.

16. FUEL PUMP/FUEL GAUGE SENDER - REMOVAL & INSTALLATION

☞ 1/1, 2 & 5/13.

1   The fuel injection system is powered by a high-pressure electric fuel pump housed in the fuel tank. It is, in practice, a sealed-for-life unit, so the only reason you will need to remove it is for replacement, or for access to the low-pressure filter in the event of fuel contamination.

2   You should depressurize the fuel system (☞ 5/13) before starting work, and also remove the fuel filler cap to prevent any pressure build-up in the tank. **Warning!** Have a fire extinguisher to hand, and make sure that you take sensible precautions to avoid any potential fire risk - the fuel tank will be open to atmosphere once the pump is removed, and there will inevitably be a lot of fuel vapor around. Disconnect the battery negative (-) terminal ☞ 7/2.

3   Working inside the car, carefully lever out the black plastic clips which secure the carpet to

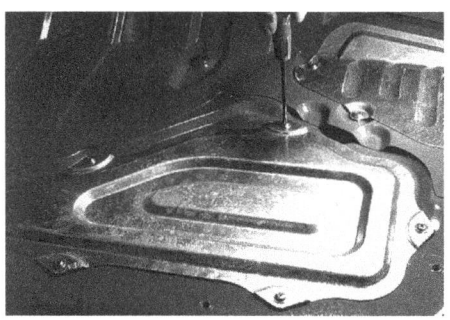

16/3 Remove this access cover.

16/4 Unplug wiring connector.

the rear deck. We found that the best technique for this was to use two flat-bladed screwdrivers or cranked needle-nosed pliers to lift the clips. Don't be tempted to pull the carpet to free the clips - it will just pull off over the clip heads. You need to remove sufficient clips to allow the carpet to be rolled back clear of the access cover above the fuel tank. You'll find that there are three bright metal access covers. Ignore the long cover at the front edge of the deck - we're interested in the larger of the two remaining covers. Remove the 10mm screws which retain the cover and lift it away.

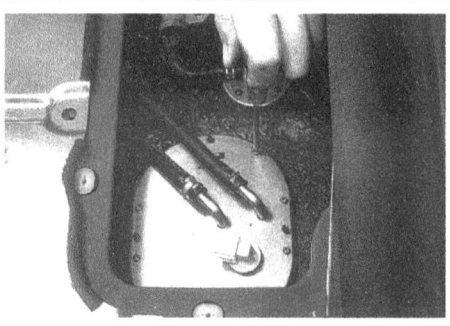

16/5 Remove hoses and then screws.

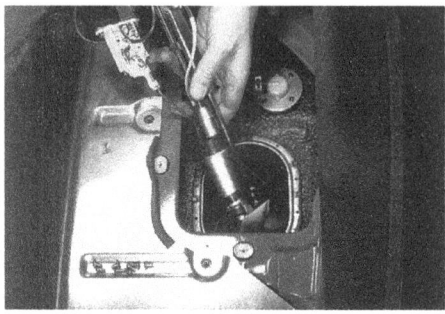

16/6 Lift out pump/sender unit.

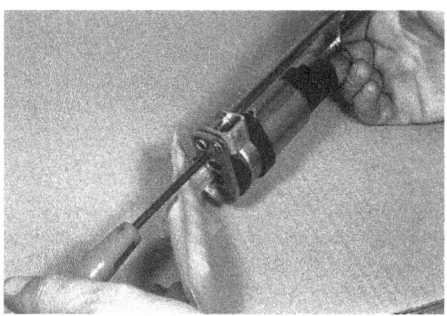

16/7a Remove screw ...

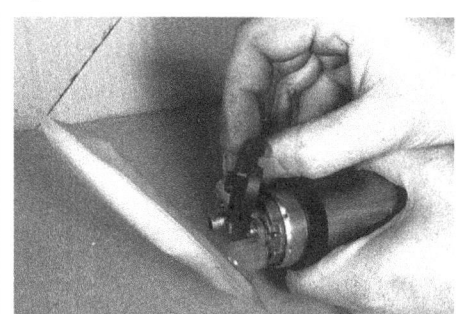

16/7b ... pull plate away ...

4   You now have access to the top of the fuel tank, and the fuel pump mounting plate, the fuel hoses and the associated check valve and vapor valve will be visible. Mark one of the fuel pipes and its stub with paint as a guide to correct reassembly, then release the hose clips with pliers and push the hoses off their stubs. Have some rag handy to catch any residual fuel; try not to let any fuel spills run down the outside of the tank or into the car - especially the trunk. Disconnect the fuel pump wiring connector.

5   Remove the crosshead screws which

5: Engine management, fuel, ignition & exhaust systems

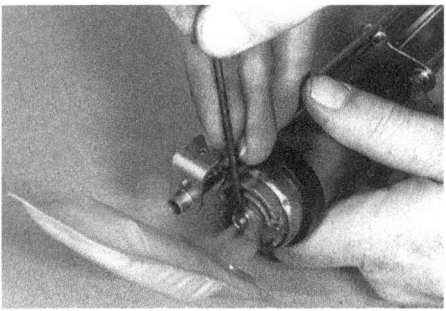

16/7c ... release spring clip ...

16.7d ... and remove filter.

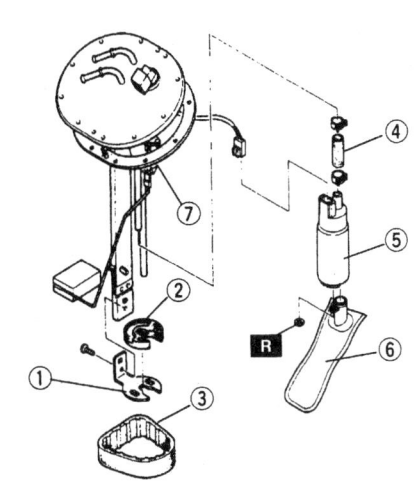

D16/8 FUEL PUMP/FUEL GAUGE SENDER UNIT (1997 AND LATER CARS).
1 Baseplate. 2 Rubber seat (mount). 3 Pump retaining band. 4 Fuel hose connector. 5 Fuel pump. 6 Fuel filter (low pressure side). 7 Fuel gauge sender unit.

secure the fuel pump mounting plate to the tank top. Carefully free the plate and its seal from the top of the tank. The seal is pegged into the pump flange, but may be stuck to the tank; if so, work a screwdriver around the edge of the seal to free it.

6　　Carefully remove the pump and fuel gauge sender as an assembly, noting that you will have to maneuver the assembly as it is lifted so that the fuel gauge sender float comes out of the tank without damage. Don't bend the float arm, or the fuel gauge readings will be affected. Once you have removed the assembly, cover the opening in the tank with a heavy clean cloth to exclude dirt and to minimize the escape of fuel vapor.

7　　+ Moving to a clean workbench, commence dismantling by removing the single screw which holds the metal baseplate to the pump support. The plate and the rubber seat (mount) can now be lifted away. The low pressure filter takes the form of a nylon gauze strainer and is held in place by a tiny spring clip. Be warned, this is another of those parts which will attempt escape at high velocity when you try to remove it, so place some rag in front of it to impede its flight as you pry it loose. Carefully work it off the peg with a small, flat-bladed screwdriver, moving it a little at a time to avoid damage.

8　　Unplug the pump wiring connector from the top of the fuel pump. The connector will be a particularly tight fit - we assume that this is intentional on the part of the manufacturer, and that it is meant to minimize the risk of the wiring coming unplugged in service and the consequent risk of an electrical spark in the fuel tank (Boom!). Now remove the serrated rubber band which supports the pump body on the side of the pickup pipe - note how this locates around the pump and pickup pipe as a guide during installation. For models up to 1996, you can now disengage the

16/8 Unplug wiring connector.

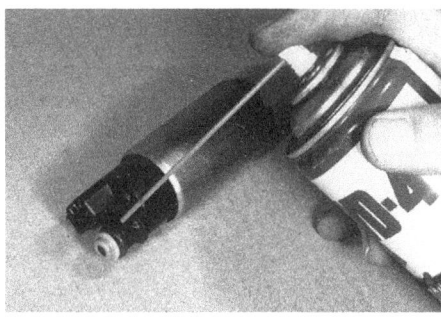

16/9a Lubricate O-ring ...

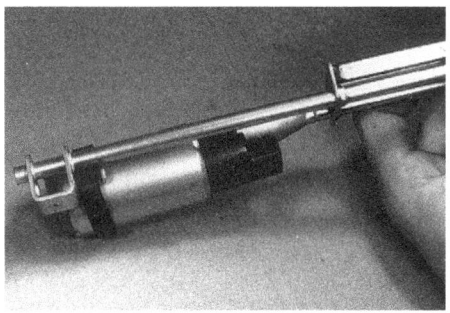

16/9b ... and fit pump to socket.

pump from its seating by pulling it down until it comes free of the socket. For 1997 and later models, release the hose clamp (clip) closest to the pump body and slide the clamp up the hose. The pump can then be pulled free of the hose connection.

9　　+ Whether or not you intend to fit a new pump, for 1996 models and earlier, you must use a new O-ring seal during pump installation, or leakage may occur. Apply a little oil to the O-ring to lubricate it during pump installation, and be sure to check that the pump seats securely and squarely. For 1997 and later models, for the moment simply push the pump outlet stub into the hose until the hose contacts the pump body (don't clamp it yet), taking great care not to apply sideways force to the stub on the pump body. All models: fit the serrated band around the pump body and hook it over the bracket.

10　　Clean the low pressure filter and then check it very carefully for holes or splits - if you find any, fit a new filter to avoid the risk of damage to the pump. Fit the filter and carefully push the retaining clip fully home to secure it.

11　　Place the pump seating in position, then fit the retaining plate and screw. We recommend that you apply a drop of non-permanent thread-locking compound to the screw threads. Pull down on the pump body to make sure it seats correctly on its seat, with the retaining band arranged to keep it pulled against the seat. For 1997 and later models, slide the hoe clamp into its

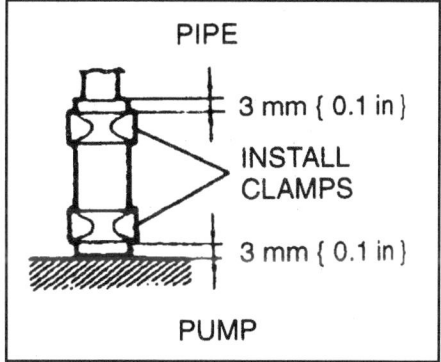

D16/11 CORRECT INSTALLATION OF FUEL HOSE CONNECTOR AND CLAMPS (1997 AND LATER CARS).

correct position (see illustration). Once assembled, it's a good idea to check that the pump is sealed correctly by blowing compressed air down the delivery pipe and making sure that it doesn't leak at the pump to pickup pipe joint. Plug in the pump wiring connector, ensuring that it snaps into place securely.

12　　Check that the new pump mounting plate seal is correctly positioned and that its locating pegs are pushed though the holes in the flange. Maneuver the pump and fuel gauge sender back into the tank, again taking care not to bend the float arm. Fit the mounting screws, pulling them down evenly. Reconnect the fuel hoses and the external wiring connector. **Warning!** Main fuel line hoses must be pushed onto their stubs by at least 25mm (1in) and

Mazda Miata, MX-5, Eunos & Roadster

their clamps (clips) fitted securely to ensure a good seal.

13 It makes sense to check that everything works at this stage, before fitting the rear deck components. If there's no fuel vapor around, reconnect the battery negative (-) terminal (☞ 7/2), then go through the fuel system priming routine ☞ 5/13. While the jumper is in place during priming, you should hear a whine from the pump, indicating normal operation. Listen at the fuel filler opening with the filler cap removed. Assuming that all is well, fit the access panel and screws, then roll back the carpet and fit the retaining clips.

17. FUEL PUMP RELAY - REMOVAL & INSTALLATION

☞ 1/1, 2.

1 The fuel pump relay is housed behind the access panel which covers the lower section of the steering column inside the car. Remove the two crosshead (Phillips) screws securing the panel, pull the bottom of the panel toward the seat to release the invisible clips at the top; lift the panel away.

2 The exact appearance of the fuel pump relay may vary, but on our project car the outer connector is bright yellow, and is plugged into a white inner connector on a grey-bodied unit. The colors of the relay's four wires are white/red, blue/red, light green and white.

3 If in doubt, it is relatively easy to confirm the identity of the fuel pump relay as follows. Start the engine and then disconnect the wiring connector from what you think is the opening relay. If you have unplugged the fuel pump relay, the fuel pump will cut off and the engine will stall.

4 If you need to fit a new relay, be sure to obtain it through a Mazda dealer, and let him know the vehicle's engine and chassis numbers to be sure of getting the correct part.

18. FUEL PRESSURE REGULATOR - REMOVAL & INSTALLATION

☞ 1/1, 2 & 5/13.

1 The fuel pressure regulator is held by two bolts to the rearmost (firewall) end of the injector rail. If the fuel system checks described elsewhere have indicated that replacement is required, first depressurize the fuel system ☞ 5/

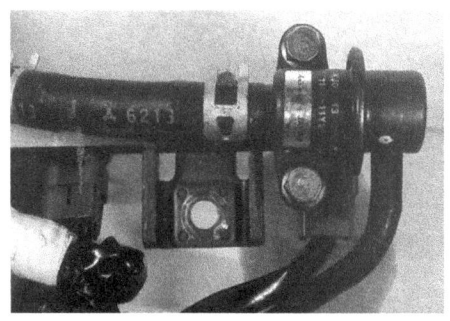

18/1 Typical fuel regulator unit.

13. Disconnect the battery negative (-) terminal ☞ 7/2.

2 Using a flat-bladed screwdriver, push off the small vacuum hose. Release the return hose clip, then push the hose off the stub, using a rag to catch any residual fuel. Plug the hose with a golf tee, or similar, to prevent dirt entering the fuel system.

3 Remove the two screws and pull the regulator from the fuel rail.

4 Whether you are refitting the original regulator or a replacement, use a new O-ring to seal its connection with the injector rail. Fit the fuel return hose to its stub, securing it by sliding the hose clip back into position. **Warning!** Main fuel line hoses must be pushed onto their stubs by at least 25mm (1in) and their clamps (clips) fitted securely to ensure a good seal. Fit the vacuum hose.

5 Pressurise the fuel system ☞ 5/13. While the system is priming, check that there are no signs of leakage at the return pipe to regulator joint. Once you've checked and primed the system, remove the jumper wire from the diagnosis connector and close its cover. Fit the fuel filler cap, and check that the engine starts and runs normally.

19. FUEL INJECTORS & RAIL - REMOVAL, LEAK TESTING & INSTALLATION

☞ 1/1, 2 & 5/13.

1 Before starting work on the injector components, depressurize the fuel system (☞ 5/13), then disconnect the battery negative (-) terminal to isolate the electrical system ☞ 7/2.

2 If you want to remove the complete rail assembly (and you'll have to if you want to do leak tests) ☞ 9/2-7. Then skip to step 5.

3 If you simply want to remove and install injectors, then remove the PCV hose between cambox and intake manifold and any other vacuum hose which restricts access. Release the main electrical connector to the injector wiring, followed by the individual injector electrical connectors. All of these connectors have tang locks which can be released with pressure from a small screwdriver. Once all connectors are released, together with cable ties (if fitted), the injector wiring loom can be moved out of the way.

4 Release the three 12mm bolts securing the injector rail to the cylinder head, and pull the

19/3a Disconnect PCV hose.

19/3b Release injector wiring main connector.

rail away from the head sufficiently to free the individual injectors (take care not to lose the rail location collars which will be dislodged by this procedure).

5 The injectors can be checked for leakage as follows. Assemble the injectors on the injector rail, remembering to fit the grommet as the injector is installed. Secure the injectors in position using lengths of wire to hold them firmly against the rail (see photo). Temporarily reconnect the fuel hoses. Connect the battery negative (-) terminal (☞ 7/2), then prime the fuel system ☞ 5/13. While the system is priming, hold the injector rail

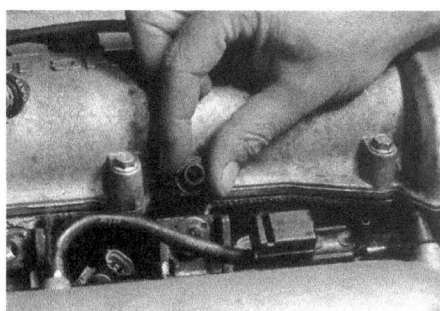

19/4 Don't lose these collars.

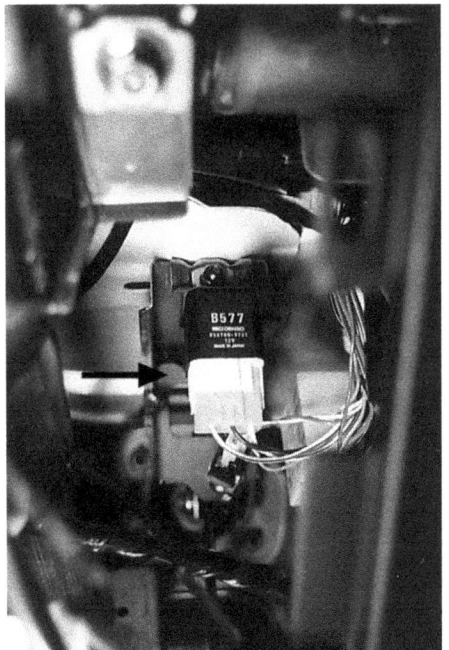

17/2 Our project car's fuel circuit opening relay.

5: Engine management, fuel, ignition & exhaust systems

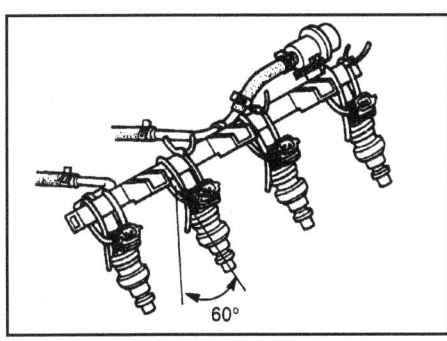

D19/5 FUEL INJECTOR LEAK TEST.
Each injector is securely wired to the fuel rail and tilted to an angle of approximately 60 degrees.

with the injector pointing downwards at about 60°. There should be no obvious sign of leakage from any injector, though a single drop leaking after one minute is considered acceptable. If one or more injectors is leaking, replacement will be required, and it is good practice to replace them as a set.

6   After completing the leak check, depressurize the fuel system again, and then turn off the ignition switch and disconnect the battery negative

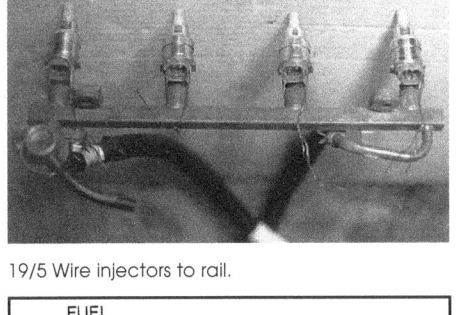

19/5 Wire injectors to rail.

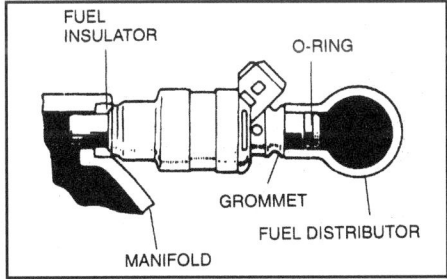

D19/7 CORRECTLY INSTALLED FUEL INJECTOR.
Note that "fuel distributor" is another name for the fuel rail (which actually has a square cross-section).

(-) terminal. A little fuel may leak out when you disconnect the fuel hoses - prepare for this by wrapping the hose end in rag as it is pushed off its stub. **Warning!** Wear overalls, rubber gloves and protective glasses to fend off any fuel spray.

7   Each injector is sealed to the injector rail by an O-ring seal fitted in a groove at the top of the injector. The O-ring should be replaced each time it is disturbed, using a small amount of oil to lubricate it during installation. Do not omit to fit the grommet which seals the base of the injector top

(these should be replaced if they've seen a good amount of use). Make sure that the injector enters its bore squarely, or the injector or its O-ring may be damaged. You will also need a set of insulators to seal the injectors where they enter the injection ports.

8   During installation, make sure the fuel rail locating collars are in place (see photo), tighten the injector rail bolts to 19-25Nm (1.9-2.6kgfm/14-18lbfft). Reconnect the injector wiring, the fuel hoses and the PCV and vacuum hoses. **Warning!** Main fuel line hoses must be pushed onto their stubs by at least 25mm (1in) and their

19/8a Rail location collars in place.

19/8b Rail located on collars, ready for bolts.

19/8c Tighten rail bolts to correct torque.

clamps (clips) fitted securely to ensure a good seal. Prime the fuel system (☞ 5/13) and check for leaks. If all is well, remove the jumper wire from the diagnosis connector, start the engine and check that it runs normally.

20. FUEL FILTER - REMOVAL & INSTALLATION

☞ 1/1, 2 & 5/13.

1   This section deals with the removal and installation of the high pressure fuel filter. For information relating to the low pressure filter attached to the fuel pump ☞ 5/16.

2   The main reason for removing the fuel filter is as part of the normal servicing schedule. The job is not in itself too difficult but the location of the filter, on the underside of the car, means that an inspection pit is needed or the car will have to be safely supported to gain access ☞ 1/3. Although there is relatively little pressurised fuel on the tank side of the filter, release fuel system line pressure ☞ 5/13. Disconnect the battery negative (-) terminal to isolate the electrical system ☞ 7/2.

3   Moving under the car, locate the plastic cover at the rear of the floorpan which conceals the fuel filter. This is on the right side of the car, and is held onto the body by cunningly designed plastic clips. At first sight, you might be forgiven for thinking that they are crosshead (Phillips) screws seated in cup washers. On closer examination, however, they turn out to be two-piece fasteners and they can be difficult to to remove if you take the wrong approach ☞ 1/2 (*Wrestling with two-piece plastic panel fasteners*).

4   Back to the job in hand. The rear suspension brace bar can be left in place. Remove

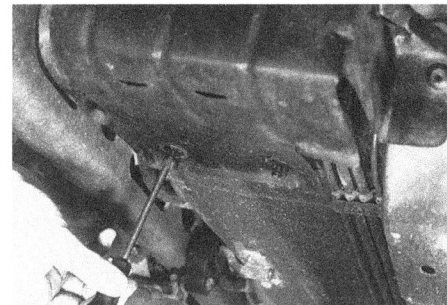

20/3 Remove fuel filter cover.

all the clips which hold the filter cover in place. Lift the cover away to reveal the filter and fuel hose connections.

5   **Warning!** Before you attempt to disconnect the hoses, be aware that even with the fuel system depressurized, fuel will flow fast from the tank side hose once it's disconnected. You should leave the fuel filler cap in place. Arm yourself with something to plug the open hose ends as soon as they are pulled off - golf tees worked well for us. Wear overalls and rubber gloves to keep the gasoline off your skin. Wear safety glasses to keep gasoline splashes out of your eyes. Have everything ready so that once the hoses are disconnected they can be plugged quickly, keeping spillage to a minimum.

6   Using pliers, grip the tangs of the hose clamps (clips) and slide them along the hoses and clear of the stubs on the filter. Using a screwdriver, push the tank side hose off the stub (don't try pulling it off or it will just grip the stub tighter) on the filter. The fuel system hoses are a tight fit on the metal pipes - they have to be because of the high fuel pressure they contain. If the hose won't yield to gentle screwdriver pressure, try fitting a pair of pliers loosely around the metal pipe and using the sides of the jaws to apply pressure to the hose end.

Mazda Miata, MX-5, Eunos & Roadster

Don't grip the pipe with the pliers, just let the jaws slide along the pipe). As the hose comes away, quickly fit a golf tee (or other suitable plug) to plug the end and prevent the tank contents siphoning out.

7   Repeat the procedure to free the injector side hose from the filter. There will only be a little residual fuel in the line, but plug it anyway to keep out any dirt. The filter unit is held by a bracket, which is, in turn, bolted to the body. Remove the two 10mm bolts which retain the bracket to the body and lift away the filter with its bracket attached.

8   ☐+ The new filter comes complete with a mounting bracket. Fit the filter and tighten the two 10mm mounting bolts to 7.9-10.7Nm (80-110kgf cm/69-95.4lbf in). Fit the outlet hose (injector side) first, followed by the inlet hose (tank side), securing both by sliding the clips back into position. **Warning!** Main fuel line hoses must be pushed onto their stubs by at least 25mm (1in) and their clamps (clips) fitted securely to ensure a good seal.

9   When any fuel spills have been mopped up, and fuel vapor cleared, reconnect the battery (☞ 7/2) and repressurize the fuel system (☞ 5/13) and check the hose connections for leaks.

20/8a Reconnect hoses & clip securely ...

20/8b ... before securing new filter.

When all is well, fit the filter cover, securing it with those pesky plastic clips, then lower the vehicle to the ground.

21. EMISSIONS CONTROL SYSTEM - INTRODUCTION

1   Emissions control-related systems and components are fitted to the car to minimize its negative impact on the environment we all share. In most parts of the world, fully operational emissions control systems are a legal requirement; even if this is not the case, we all have a moral responsibility to ensure that the system on our car is working correctly. Note that if certain emissions-related sub-systems are not working, or working inefficiently, the fuel economy and performance of the engine will be adversely affected. Diagram 3/1 gives an overview of the emissions control system.

22. PCV VALVE - CHECKING & REPLACEMENT

☞ 1/1, 2.

1   The PCV (Positive Crankcase Ventilation) valve is a passive device, operating under manifold vacuum to draw crankcase gases from the cambox and allowing them to be drawn into the intake system, where they pass into the engine and are burnt. While the engine is switched off, the valve remains closed, trapping the gases in the engine. At idle, the valve opens slightly, drawing a small amount of crankcase gas back into the intake system. As engine speed increases, the valve opens wider to admit a greater volume of crankcase gases. The system also features a second hose from the exhaust side cambox to the air filter side of the intake system to allow circulation of air through the camboxes.

2   To perform a quick check of the PCV

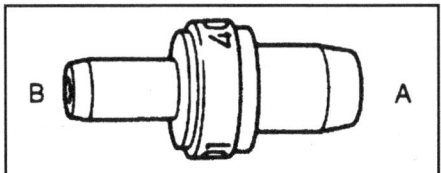
D22/3 PCV VALVE CHECK.
Air should flow from A to B, but not from B to A.

22/3 Pull PCV valve from cambox.

valve's operation, disconnect it from the cambox cover by pulling it out of its rubber seat, leaving the vacuum hose in place. Start the engine and allow it to idle. If you now place a finger over the open end of the valve you should be able to feel the vacuum.

3   ☐ ☐ Disconnect the valve from the hose, after releasing the retaining clip, and wipe it clean. The valve has stubs of unequal size; if you blow through the valve from the larger (cambox side) stub, air should pass easily through the valve. If you now blow from the other end, air should not pass through the valve. If the valve is either completely blocked, or if it passes air both way, it should be replaced.

4   Detach the PCV valve hose from the intake manifold and blow through the hose to make sure there are no blockages. Replace the hose if necessary.

5   When installing the PCV valve, note that it can only be fitted in one direction. Fit the valve to the vacuum hose and secure it with its hose clip, then fit the remaining end into the cambox cover.

6   ☐ Detach the PCV system vent hose from the rigid intake hose near the throttle body and

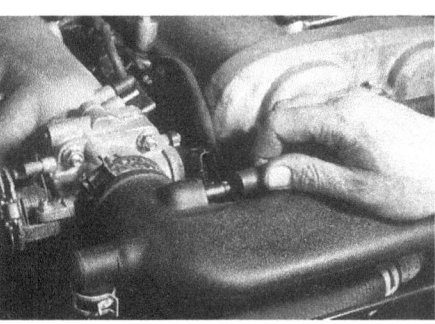
22/6 Detach PCV ventilation hose.

from the exhaust side cambox. Blow through the hose to make sure there are no blockages. Replace the hose if necessary.

23. EVAP/EGR SYSTEMS - COMPONENT CHECKING & REPLACEMENT

☞ 1/1, 2 & 5/13.

1   The EVAP (Evaporative Emission Control) system prevents the release of unburned hydrocarbons in the form of fuel vapor to the atmosphere. For many years, the fuel systems on motor vehicles incorporated uncontrolled atmospheric vents to allow the release of pressure and to prevent vacuum forming within the fuel tank and carburettor as fuel moved from one point to another, and expanded or contracted in response to temperature. Along with other manufacturers, Mazda employs a system which prevents the venting of fuel vapor to the atmosphere, and so reduces this aspect of atmospheric pollution.

2   One of the main problems is releasing the fuel vapor which is created in the fuel tank while the vehicle is parked. This is accomplished by routing the vapor from the tank to a charcoal canister under the hood. The canister acts as a temporary store for the vapor. When the engine is started, the PCM assesses operating conditions, and when certain criteria is met, allows the vapor to be purged by drawing it into the engine, where it is burnt along with the normal combustion mixture. The purge process is controlled by the PCM through a purge control valve. The PCM reads operating conditions from its various sensors, and uses this data to determine the rate at which purging takes place. This ensures that the process does not itself cause undue pollution by upsetting the combustion mixture.

5: Engine management, fuel, ignition & exhaust systems

3   In this section we look at the various EVAP system components, starting at the fuel tank and working forwards. The fuel vapor valve, the two-way check valve (three-way check valve, automatic transmission models), the charcoal canister and associated pipework all require attention at appropriate service intervals, or when faults develop.

FUEL VAPOR VALVE

4   Disconnect the battery negative (-) terminal to isolate the electrical system ☞ 7/2. Remove the fuel filler cap to prevent pressure build-up in the tank. **Warning!** Have a fire extinguisher to hand, and make sure that you take sensible precautions to avoid any potential fire risk - there will inevitably be a lot of fuel vapor around.

5   Working inside the car, carefully lever out the black plastic clips which secure the carpet to the rear deck. We found that the best technique for this was to use two flat-bladed screwdrivers or a pair of cranked needle-nosed pliers to lift the clips. Don't be tempted to pull up on the carpet - it will just pull off over the clip heads. You need to remove sufficient clips to allow the carpet to be rolled back clear of the access cover above the fuel tank. You'll find that there are three bright metal access covers. Ignore the long cover at the front edge of the deck - we are interested in the larger of the two remaining covers. Remove the 10mm screws which retain the cover and lift it away.

6   You now have access to the top of the fuel tank, and the fuel pump mounting plate, the fuel hoses and the associated check valve and vapor valve will be visible. Have some rag handy to catch any residual fuel; try not to let any fuel spills run down the outside of the tank or into the car, especially the trunk; it'll smell for weeks afterwards.

7   📷 The fuel vapor valve's purpose is to allow vapor to pass through it, but to shut off this

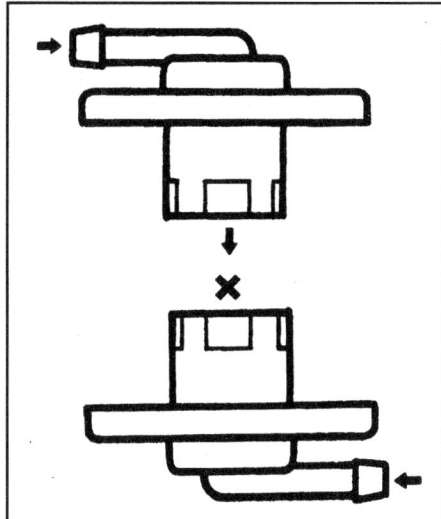

D23/8 FUEL VAPOR VALVE CHECK.
Blow through the valve from the hose stub. When the valve is the correct way up, air should flow freely. When the valve's inverted it should not be possible to blow through it.

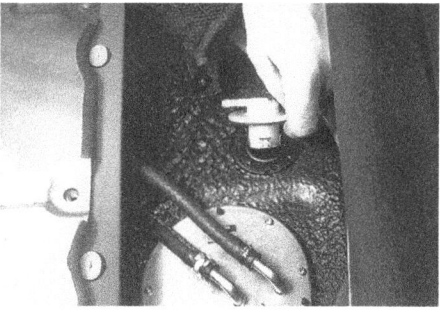

23/10 Refit vapor valve.

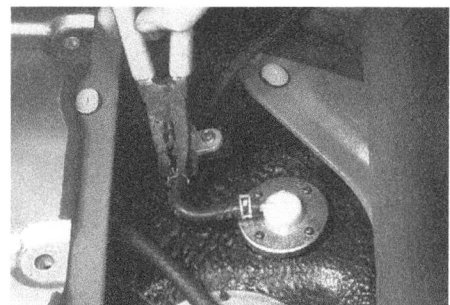

23/11a Release hose and then ...

23/11b ... unscrew check valve's bolt.

outlet in the event that the car is inverted in an accident. You can check that this is the case after removing the valve from the tank by disconnecting the hose (held by a spring clip) and then removing the screws which secure the valve to the tank.

8   🖼 With the valve removed, hold it in its normal position (pipe stub at the top) and blow through the stub. Air should pass with little resistance. Now turn the valve over so that the stub is at the bottom and repeat the check. The valve should be closed, obstructing the flow of air.

9   📷 If the valve does not work as described,

the official remedy is to fit a new one. We found that the valve is both simple to dismantle and in construction, so if it is not working, you may as well check to see if the problem can be fixed before fitting a new one. Unclip the metal cover from the end of the valve body and tip out the spring and valve plunger. Check for dirt in the conical tip of the plunger and its seat in the body - if the valve was not sealing this could well be the cause. Make sure that the plunger slides freely in the body, and that there are no obvious signs of damage at the sealing point. If the problem is dirt, cleaning the valve components will probably cure the fault. If damage

is discovered, replace the valve. If you are intending to re-use the valve after cleaning, reassemble carefully, making sure that the end cover is clipped into place over the body.

10   📷 Fit the valve to the tank and secure it with its four retaining screws. Do not fit the access panel yet - you need to check the operation of the two-way check valve as described below.

TWO-WAY CHECK VALVE (THREE-WAY CHECK VALVE, AUTO TRANS MODELS)

11   📷+ The check valve is accessed through

the fuel pump access panel, the removal of which is described ☞ 5/23.4-5. Disconnect the pipes after sliding back the retaining clips, then remove the single 10mm bolt which retains the valve.

12   📷 🖼+ The official checking procedure for the two-way valve is to apply a specified vacuum from a vacuum pump at the valve stubs (see illustration). If you apply approx -2kPa (-15mm Hg, -0.59in Hg) at stub A, air should flow through the valve. Applying -5.9kPa (-44mm Hg, -1.73in Hg) at stub B should produce the same result. On cars fitted with automatic transmission, a three-way check valve is used. Referring to the illustration,

23/7 Remove vapor valve's screws.   23/9 Components of the vapor valve.

23/12 Two-way check valve.

Mazda Miata, MX-5, Eunos & Roadster

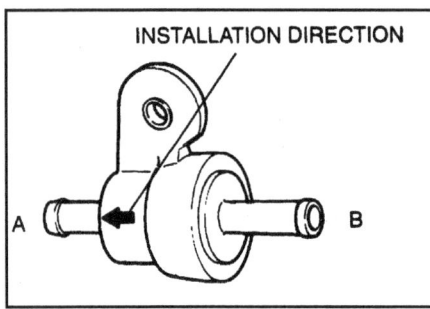

D23/12A CHECK VALVE (TWO-WAY) CHECK.
(See text.)

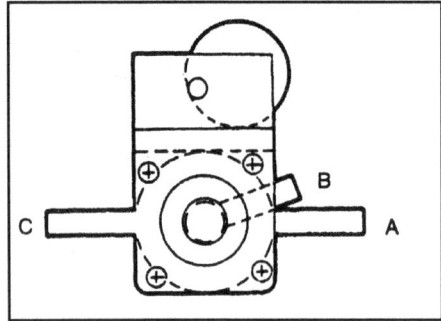

D23/12B CHECK VALVE (THREE-WAY) CHECK.
(See text.)

apply vacuum to ports A and B in turn. Air should flow when approximately -4.9kPa (-37mm Hg, -1.5in Hg) is applied to port A, and when -9.3kPa (-70mm Hg, -2.8in Hg) is applied to port B. Not having a vacuum pump handy, we translated this into blowing through the valve and noting that there was a greater resistance in one direction than the other. Not precise, but a fair indication of function. If the valve is either completely blocked, or shows no resistance, replace it.

13 After fitting the valve (tighten the single bolt to 3.9-5.9Nm (40-60 Kgf cm/34-52lbf in), make a final check of the various hose connections and hose condition, then fit the access cover and rear deck carpet.

EVAP SYSTEM HOSES

14 Make a visual check of the EVAP system hoses running from the check valve, along the underside of the car, and up to the charcoal canister, purge control valve and intake system. Replace the hose(s) if damaged or if they appear aged.

CHARCOAL CANISTER

15 Working under the hood, locate the charcoal canister on the right-hand inner fender (wing), near the coolant reservoir. Disconnect the vent and smaller vacuum hose from the canister top, then pull the canister up and clear of its mounting bracket. Disconnect the remaining hose and remove the canister for inspection.

16 Check the canister body for damage and signs of leakage. Check also for indications of corrosion on the metal end plate. If found, a new canister must be fitted - repair is not practical. Check that the hoses are in good condition. Fit the canister, noting that the lower hose should be fitted

23/15 Location of charcoal cannister.

before the canister is installed in its bracket. Once in position, connect the remaining vent hose and the vacuum hose.

PURGE SOLENOID VALVE

17 The solenoid valve is operated by the PCM and controls the venting of the charcoal canister. It is located close to the canister on the right side inner fender (wing), and is connected to the canister and manifold by small bore hoses.

18 With both hoses and the wiring connector disconnected, remove the single mounting bolt and lift the valve away for inspection. Check that, with no power applied, the valve does not allow air to flow in either direction.

19 With the unit on the bench, connect a

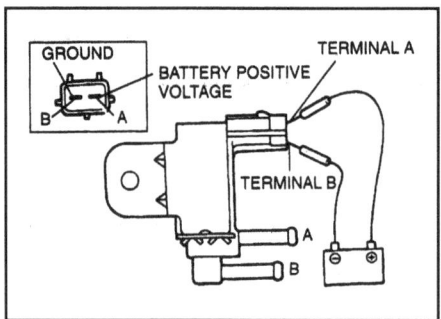

D23/19 PURGE SOLENOID VALVE CHECK.
When battery voltage is applied to terminal A and terminal B is grounded, air should flow between hose stubs A and B.

12 volt supply to the wiring terminals, the positive (+) lead to the terminal pin nearest the end of the valve unit, negative (-) to the remaining terminal (see diagram). The valve should produce an audible click, and air should now flow through it. It is not possible to repair the valve - if it doesn't work as described, fit a new one.

EGR VALVE

20 The EGR valve is located at the end of the intake manifold, near the firewall (bulkhead). The valve controls the recirculation of a controlled amount of exhaust gas through the intake system.

21 Start the engine and let it idle. Detach the vacuum hose from the valve (see photo) and attach the hose from a vacuum pump in its place. Apply approximately -10kPa (-80mmHg, -3inHg) of vacuum and check that this causes the engine to run roughly, or even stall. If this effect does not occur, replace the EGR valve using a new gasket.

23/21a EGR valve vacuum hose connection.

23/21b EGR valve secured by two bolts.

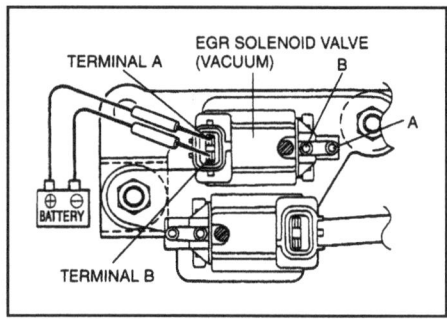

D23/24 EGR SOLENOID VALVE (VACUUM) CHECK.
(See text.)

EGR SOLENOID VALVES

22 The pair of solenoid valves control whether the EGR valve is subject to manifold vacuum (open) or atmosphere (closed). The solenoids are linked to the EGR valve by a single vacuum hose and are located in the engine compartment on the right-hand inner fender (wing).

23 Disconnect the hoses and electrical connectors from the two valves, and then remove the valve assembly to a workbench.

5: Engine management, fuel, ignition & exhaust systems

24 🔧 Apply battery voltage to terminal A of the vacuum solenoid and ground terminal B (see diagram). Blow into port A: air should flow from port B. Without battery voltage applied there should be no airflow. If the valve does not perform correctly, replace it.

25 🔧 Apply battery voltage to terminal A of the vent solenoid and ground terminal B (see diagram). Blow into port A: air should flow from port B, but not from C. Without battery voltage applied air should flow from both port B and C when you blow into port A. If the valve does not perform correctly, replace it.

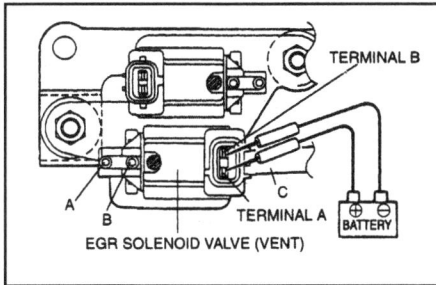

D23/25 EGR SOLENOID VALVE (VENT) CHECK.
(See text.)

EGR BOOST SENSOR

26 Fitted to 1996 and later models, the EGR boost sensor is mounted in the engine compartment on the right-hand inner fender (wing), and has a single hose connection and an electrical connection. This unit supplies a variable output voltage to the PCM, depending on the air pressure or vacuum levels it senses. At neutral pressure, for instance, it sends a 3.6-4.4 volt signal. The unit does not operate at battery voltage and therefore it needs to be tested using special service tools. If you suspect the boost sensor is faulty, for the price of a beer you can replace it temporarily with an identical unit from a friend's car; if this fixes the running problem you know you can buy a new sensor without wasting your money.

EGR VALVE POSITION SENSOR

27 🔧 This electrical unit is mounted on top of the EGR valve. Release the electrical connector from the sensor. Using an ohmmeter, measure the electrical resistance between terminals A and B (see illustration) on the sensor side of the connector. The reading should be 2.7k-ohms: if the reading is not correct, replace the EGR valve.

D23/27 EGR POSITION SENSOR CHECK.
(See text.)

24. DECHOKE CONTROL SYSTEM - DESCRIPTION

☞ 1/1, 2.

1 These cars feature a dechoke control system designed to allow a flooded engine to be cleared. If a cold engine is inadvertently flooded with gasoline while attempting to start it, depress the accelerator fully. This locks out the injection system, allowing the excess fuel to be cleared quickly (hopefully, before you flatten the battery). Note that the system only works with a cold engine.

2 There are no general checks of this subsystem, but, given the marginal battery capacity, we thought you might like to be reminded of its existence, should you get the engine gassed up one morning ...

25. IGNITION SYSTEM - INTRODUCTION

1 The ignition system function is controlled by the PCM in response to a number of sensor signals, the control level includes the distribution (there is no distributor) and timing (in relation to number 1 cylinder TDC) of high voltage pulses to the sparkplugs. The PCM sends low voltage pulses to each of the two coil assemblies in turn. These pulses cause a high voltage field to be induced in the coil winding which travels to two sparkplugs simultaneously via high tension plug wires. At the sparkplugs the high voltage pulse is grounded to the cylinder head after jumping the gap between the sparkplug electrodes (thus creating the spark which fires the fuel air mixture in the combustion chambers). The PCM also reads data from the coils, which provides it with information on engine speed, which is also relayed to the car's electronic tachometer.

2 There are few regular maintenance tasks to be performed on modern electronic ignition systems. Apart from periodic checking and adjustment of the ignition timing, maintenance is confined to fitting new sparkplugs at the prescribed service interval, making sure that wiring connections are kept clean and dry, and periodically replacing the high tension ignition wires (HT leads) between the coils and sparkplugs.

3 It is worth noting that these cars are very sensitive to any deterioration in the performance of the high tension ignition wires, probably because the ignition voltage is high and the wires are not only in close proximity to one another, but also to the metal cambox cover, giving plenty of scope for 'leakage.' If you get a misfiring problem, or the engine doesn't seem to be running as 'cleanly' as usual, try a new set of wires before investigating further. At the same time, dry/clean the sparkplug wells and spray in some water repellant, such as WD40. It is recommended that the high tension wires are replaced every 20,000 miles (32,000km) or more frequently.

26. IGNITION TIMING - CHECKING & ADJUSTING

☞ 1/1, 2.

1 To carry out this check, you'll need a 12 volt stroboscopic timing light ("Strobe") of the sort that has crocodile clip connectors and an inductive sensor which clips on the outside of a high tension ignition wire. You should also check the timing marks on the lower (crankshaft) pulley and the nearby scale. Clean the marks and, if necessary, use typist's correction fluid/white paint to make them more visible. Note that each mark equates to two degrees of crankshaft rotation. The test should be conducted at normal operating temperature, so run the engine for a while before starting the test, or do it after a run. Switch off the engine.

2 Open the data link connector cover and bridge the **TEN** (test engine) and **GND** (ground) terminals with a piece of stiff copper wire. Terminal positions are marked inside the cover.

3 There is a purpose-supplied 12 volt power source in the engine compartment in the form of a blue connector block with a single brass male terminal; it's located just behind the left-hand headlamp. Clip the power lead of your timing light to this terminal, and clip the ground cable to any bare metal item on the engine block. Clip the timing light inductor clip to the ignition wire feeding the sparkplug nearest the radiator (number one cylinder). **Warning!** Ensure all timing light leads are tied back well away from the fans and moving pulleys. **Warning!** Make sure you are not wearing loose clothing that could get caught in moving parts (no, we're not suggesting you work in the buff - but wearing a tie would be a very bad idea ...).

4 🔧 Start the engine, and, if necessary, adjust the idle speed (☞ 2) to the specified 800-900rpm (manual transmission) or 750-850rpm

26/4a Timing marks 'frozen' by strobe light.

26/4b Cam position sensor lock bolt (from rear).

5:25

Mazda Miata, MX-5, Eunos & Roadster

26/4c Flat box-end wrench is best tool.

(auto transmission). Aim the light at the timing marks near the crankshaft pulley at the front of the engine. The mark on the pulley should appear frozen against the scale at 10 degrees btdc (plus or minus 1 degree). If adjustment is needed, slacken the camshaft position sensor 12mm lock bolt (see photo) just enough to allow the sensor body to be rotated. Note this lock bolt has a tall head to make it more accessible, but it is still not easy to access: a flat, box-end wrench (ring spanner) is the best tool for the job. Rotate the sensor body gently (anti-clockwise = advance) until the timing is correct, then tighten the lock bolt securely.

5   Recheck the timing setting, then gradually increase engine speed and confirm that the ignition timing mark advances in relation to the scale. If it fails to do so, you'll need to check the ignition system. Finally, disconnect the timing light, remove the jumper wire and close the data link connector cover.

6   Note that if you had to adjust the ignition timing, it will almost certainly have had an effect on idling speed, which should be checked and reset as necessary.

27A. IGNITION SYSTEM CHECKS

☞ 1/1, 2.

Warning! High voltages are present in the ignition system, and shocks from the sparkplugs or plug leads can be dangerous. During any check with the ignition on, handle the plugs, leads and terminal caps with insulated pliers only.

SELF-DIAGNOSIS (OBD SYSTEM) CHECKS

1   The Miata/MX5 has provision for self-diagnosis, assuming that you have the required SSTs (Special Service Tools). We have assumed that this type of equipment is going to be confined to Mazda dealers, and suggest that if you have an ignition fault, you could save a lot of time and effort by getting your Mazda dealer to run the self-diagnosis sequence for you. This should pinpoint the cause of the problem very quickly.

2   If you want to use the Mazda dealer only as a last resort, you can follow the checking sequence outlined in this section - it will not take long. We're inclined to be philosophical about this situation. We figure that if you know you have a fault, it is cost effective to get it checked out by your dealer (you can still fix it yourself), rather than waste a lot of time trying to figure it out at home. (Wally, our technical adviser, often complains that technical sophistication is bad news for the enthusiast owner, but we bet he complained when coil ignition replaced hot tubes.) We digress ...

SPARKPLUGS

3   📷+ 🖼 Welcome back all you non-SST owners! If you suspect an ignition problem, start by checking for a spark at the plugs. Remove one plug lead by pulling off the terminal cap and unscrew and remove the plug. Fit the plug back into its

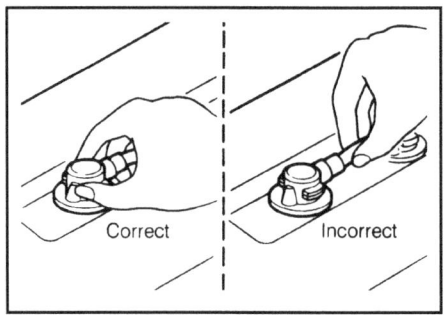

D27A/3 HOW TO REMOVE PLUG CAPS.

27A/3a Pull off terminal cap ...

27A/3b ... and unscrew sparkplug.

terminal cap after removal.

4   🖼 Using insulated pliers, hold the plug so that the plug body is 5-10mm (0.2-0.4in) from the cambox cover - the plug terminals should be visible and not grounded (earthed). **Warning!** Ignition systems generate high voltages which can be dangerous if mishandled - be sure that your insulated pliers are undamaged and dry before use. Have an assistant crank the engine while you observe the plug. A strong, blue spark should jump across from the plug to the cambox cover if all is well.

5   If the spark is absent or a weak, yellowish

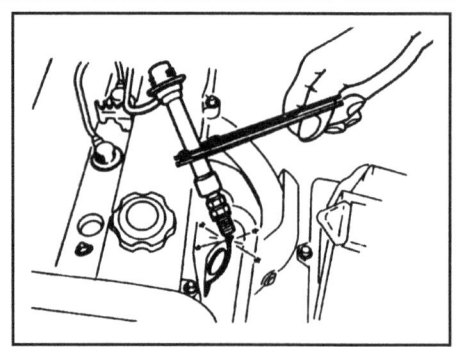

D27A/4 TESTING SPARKPLUG.

color, try a new plug and repeat the check. If you now have a strong spark, you can assume that the original plug is faulty. Don't assume that the plug is serviceable just because it looks OK; plugs can look fine, and even spark convincingly at atmospheric pressure, but once under combustion pressures can fail or operate intermittently. Plugs are relatively cheap - our advice is to fit new ones whenever you suspect a fault. That way you can be reasonably certain that you have eliminated one common source of trouble. Repeat the check on the remaining plugs, noting that it is preferable to replace the plugs as a set.

6   📷+ Check the electrode gap with feeler gauges or a plug electrode gauge before you fit the new (or used) plugs - this should be set to 1.0-1.1mm (0.040-0.043in). If you need to adjust the gap, we recommend that you use a commercially available plug gapping tool. Set the gap by bending the outer, ground electrode only - if you put pressure on the center electrode you'll almost certainly damage the porcelain insulator nose. Fit the new plugs using an anti-seize compound on the threads and tighten them to 15-32Nm (1.5-2.3kgf

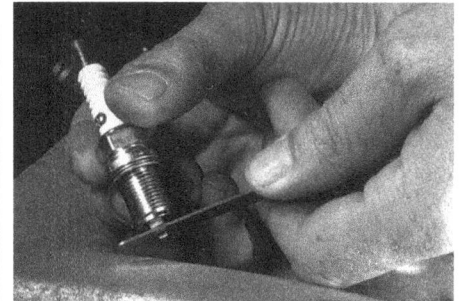

27A/6a Measure and adjust plug gap ...

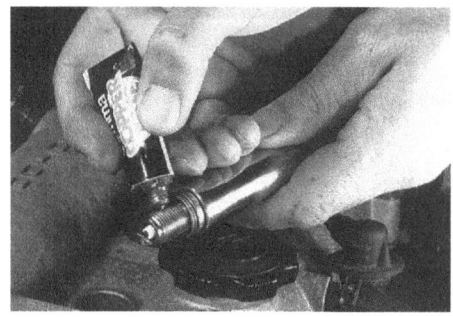

27A/6b ... copper-based grease on threads ...

5: Engine management, fuel, ignition & exhaust systems

27A/6c ... torque tighten.

m, 11-17lbf ft) and see whether this has resolved the problem.

7   Note that if you find a strong spark on two plugs, and a weak or non-existent spark on the remaining two, this points to a coil failure. The car utilizes a 'spare spark' ignition system. There are two double-ended coils, each coil sparking two plugs simultaneously. This means that the plugs each spark twice during an engine cycle, one of the sparks being wasted, or 'spare' during the exhaust phase. It follows that if you discover a fault on two plugs you are likely to find that they share the same, defective, coil. Cylinders 1 and 4 share a coil, as do 2 and 3.

SPARKPLUG LEADS

8   + Next check the plug wire resistances using an ohmmeter. Disconnect and remove each lead in turn and check the resistance between the terminals at each end. The correct resistance figure is 16k ohm per meter (3 feet) - you'll have to measure the length of the lead to calculate the appropriate value; for example a 45mm lead should

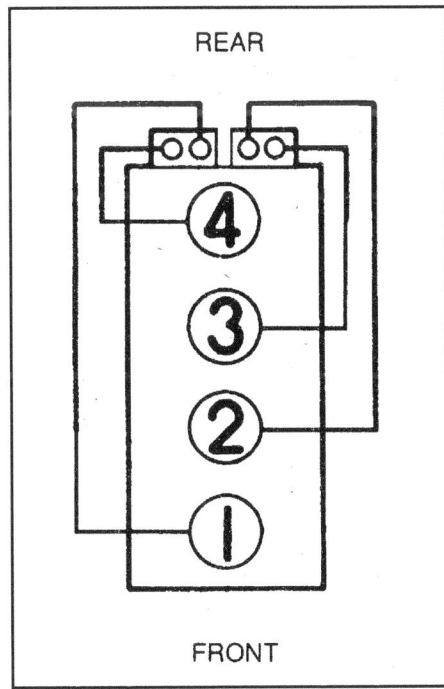

D27A/8A CORRECT SPARKPLUG WIRE (HT LEAD) CONNECTIONS.

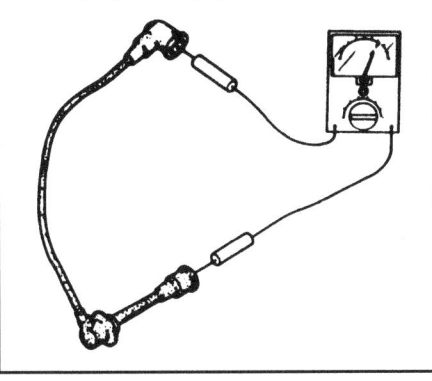

D27A/8B CHECKING HT LEAD RESISTANCE.

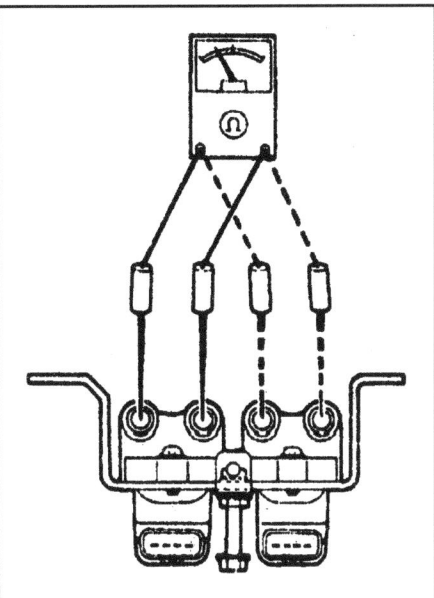

27A/11 COIL SECONDARY COIL WINDING RESISTANCE CHECK.
(See text.)

read 7.2k ohm. You can expect a little variation from the recommended figure, but if the resistance is very high, assume that the lead needs replacement. Note that if one plug wire (HT lead) has failed, the others are likely to follow suit; replace them as a set.

It's worth noting that these cars are very sensitive to any deterioration in the performance of the high tension ignition wires, probably because the ignition voltage is high and the wires are not only in close proximity to one another, but also to the metal cambox cover, giving plenty of scope for 'leakage' to ground and cross-firing. If you get a misfiring problem, or the engine doesn't seem to be running as 'cleanly' as usual, try a new set of wires before investigating further. At the same time, dry/clean the sparkplug wells and spray in some water repellant, such as WD40. We recommended that the high tension wires are replaced every 20,000 miles (32,000km) or more frequently.

IGNITION COILS

9   The following tests are conducted with the ignition off. Check the coils for obvious physical damage, especially if the engine has recently been removed from the engine compartment. Also check for tracking marks made by high voltage leaks: this can occur if the coil bodies are damp, dirty or cracked.

10   Remove the ignition wire connectors from the towers on the top of each coil.

11   Using an ohmmeter, measure the electrical resistance between the terminals in the two towers of each coil. The correct resistance figure is 8.7-12.9k ohms at approximately 20 degrees C (68F). If the resistance is not correct, replace the faulty coil.

12   Check that the electrical connectors behind the coils are clean, dry and fully engaged.

27B. IGNITION COILS - REMOVAL & INSTALLATION

☞ 1/1, 2.

1   The twin ignition coils are mounted in a bracket attached to the rear of the cylinder head on the intake side. Disconnect the battery negative terminal to isolate the electrical system ☞ 7/2. Space is very limited, so you might want to remove the camshaft position sensor to give yourself slightly better access.

2   Disconnect the ignition leads from the coil towers. Disconnect the two wiring harness connectors at the rear of the coil unit (see photo). Part of the wiring harness is held by a metal support at the base of the coil bracket (see photo), you can bend this open with your fingers to release the wiring.

3   The coil bracket is secured to the cylinder head by three 12mm bolts, one each side at the top of the bracket and one in the middle

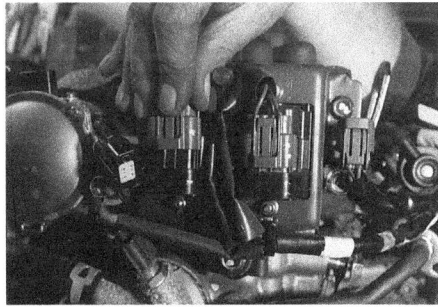

27B/2 Release connectors behind coils.

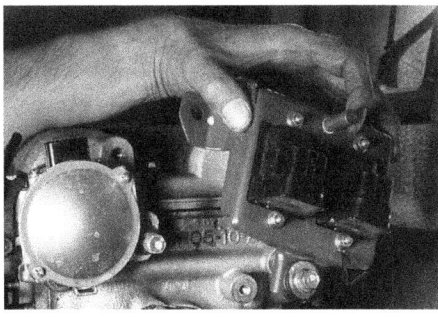

27B/3 Lift coil bracket from rear of head.

5:27

Mazda Miata, MX-5, Eunos & Roadster

below the bracket. The upper bolts are visible, but you'll have to feel your way (perhaps with the aid of a mirror) to the lower bolt. Once the bolts are removed, the coil unit can be lifted away.

4   Note that each individual coil is secured to the bracket by two 8mm nuts and bolts.

5   When refitting the coil bracket note that the top right-hand bolt secures a secondary bracket. Tighten the bracket bolts to 19-25Nm (1.9-2.6kgf m, 14-18lbf ft). Remake all electrical connections to the coils, including the high tension ignition wires. Make sure that the insulated clip at the base of the bracket has been reshaped to support the wiring harness. Reconnect the battery.

28. PCM (POWERTRAIN CONTROL MODULE)

☞ 1/1, 2.

1   The Powertrain Control Module (PCM) can be regarded as the 'brain' of the car. As we have described earlier in the chapter, the PCM is a dedicated microcomputer. It reads data from a range of sensors around the vehicle, and uses this information to control the engine function and

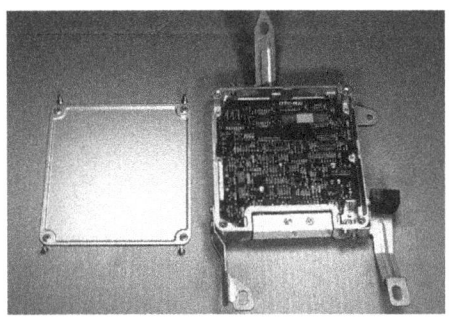

28/1 Inside a typical PCM.

some other systems.

2   In practical terms there is very little you can do with the PCM unit without a battery of special service tools, and that's just to point you in the direction of what to look for.

3   We reckon that the best course of action if you suspect an PCM fault is to take the car into a Mazda dealer for the diagnostic work to be carried out. This may offend the real enthusiasts out there, but it is the only really cost effective option - at home you are forced to work on a trial-and-error basis, and with a modern engine management system you could be doing that forever! The dealer may go through the full check sequence, though it is common practice in the automotive trade simply to substitute a new (or known good) PCM to localize the problem. That way, the operator can quickly say "Yep!- the PCM's burned out" - or not, as the case may be - without a laborious and complex diagnostic procedure to follow.

4   There is another option for the enthusiast owner. If you know another owner *really* well, you may be able to persuade him or her to let you borrow their identical PCM to see whether it eradicates the problem, but be warned, if your PCM was damaged by a fault in an external component and that fault remains unresolved, it could do the same to the substitute PCM, and so you could end up buying two new ones ...

5   So what approach should you take with PCM problems - is it really 'take it to your dealer' time? Well, maybe ... Before you do, there are two basic rules to note. First, there is a good chance that the fault is in a related sensor, solenoid or whatever, not the PCM itself. So if you've got a fault, check what you can first. Go back over the outline at the beginning of the chapter, and, taking a common sense approach, try to figure out which sensors, valves, systems or other components could be responsible, and check them out. Secondly, the fate of supposedly dead PCMs in the automotive trade is interesting - across most manufacturers that operate a service exchange deal with their dealers, *less than 20% of the returned ECUs prove to have a fault when tested.* Strange, but true - but how can this be?

6   What seems to happen is that the car comes in with a fault, the dealer tries a fresh PCM and Hey Presto! the fault is cured. The mysterious recovery of over 80% of returned units is actually easily explained. When the technician unplugs the suspect unit and plugs in a new one, he or she disturbs the multi-pin connectors. If there was a problem with corrosion or a loose contact on the terminal pins, this action cleans them, so the substituted unit works normally. The technician, reasonably enough, assumes that the old PCM is no good. Of course, unless this is a warranty return, guess who ends up paying the bill for the new PCM ...? We suggest that before you take the car to a dealer, you simply disconnect and reconnect the

28.8a Remove cover panel (rhd cars) ...

28/8b ... to expose PCM (rhd cars).

PCM connectors to see whether this cures your problem.

7   For some markets the PCM is located on the bulkhead behind the right-hand seat (see illustration) and can be accessed by sliding the seat forward and then lifting the trim, which is fixed by Velcro and plastic studs.

8   For other markets the PCM is buried deep in the passenger footwell and can be accessed

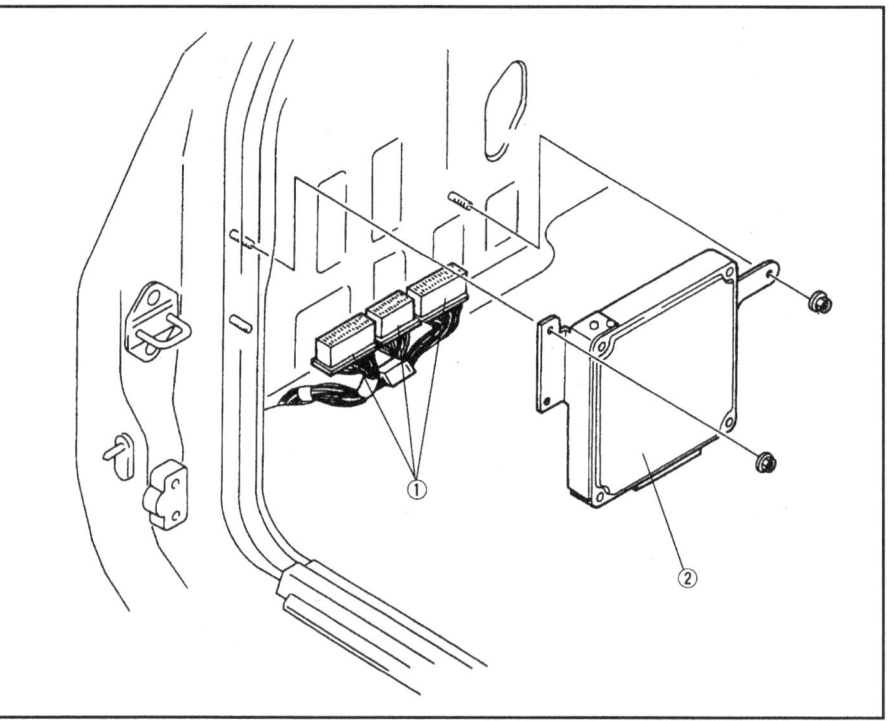

D28/7 LOCATION AND FIXING OF PCM (LATER LEFT-HAND DRIVE CARS).
Note that for 1994/5 models there are two connector blocks.

5: Engine management, fuel, ignition & exhaust systems

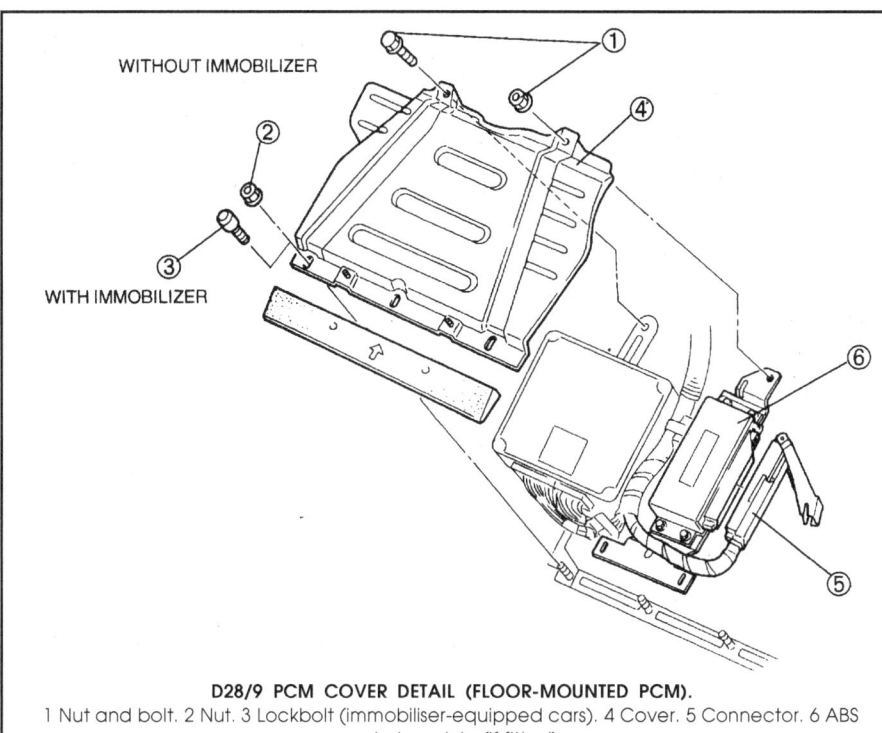

D28/9 PCM COVER DETAIL (FLOOR-MOUNTED PCM).
1 Nut and bolt. 2 Nut. 3 Lockbolt (immobiliser-equipped cars). 4 Cover. 5 Connector. 6 ABS control module (if fitted).

as follows. Lift the carpet on the passenger side of the car to reveal the PCM access panel. To get the carpet up, you will have to unscrew the screws holding the kick panel on the top of the door sill. Lift the inner edge of the panel and unhook the carpet edge retainers from underneath, then pull the carpet back.

9 Remove the 10mm bolts and nuts which secure the PCM cover panel. Note that on some cars fitted with immobilisers, the cover panel will be secured by lockbolts. Mazda's official removal procedure for these bolts is to chisel a groove into their heads and then use an impact driver or pliers to remove them. We feel such percussive violence close to the delicate electronics of the PCM (and ABS control module in some markets) is not a good idea, and urge you to take your car to the dealer for removal and installation of this cover so that they have the responsibility for any damage. Of course, if you know the PCM is going to be junked it doesn't matter if it is further damaged by the cover removal procedure.

10 With the battery negative (-) terminal disconnected to isolate the electrical system, disconnect the PCM wiring connectors. Check all terminals for signs of corrosion. **Caution!** Do not attempt to clean the gold-plated terminal pins, but by all means use a switch cleaning lubricant on them. Reconnect the wiring and check whether the fault has disappeared. If so, great - you just saved yourself a significant parts bill. If not, at least you will know that the fault really could be with the PCM.

11 When installing the PCM cover of immobiliser-equipped cars, the new lockbolts have temporary heads which shear off leaving a blank head when the correct torque is reached.

29A. CAMSHAFT POSITION SENSOR - REMOVAL, CHECKING & INSTALLATION

☞ 1/1, 2.

1 The camshaft position sensor (on earlier models, this device used to be called the "crank angle sensor" until a second device with the same name was added to the system) is located at the back of the cambox cover on the exhaust side. Note that the sensor can be adjusted to set the ignition timing - so apply a paint mark between the adjustment slot and the lock bolt washer (see photo) so you can refit the sensor without affecting the timing.

2 Disconnect the battery negative (-) terminal to isolate the electrical system ☞ 7/2. Disconnect the camshaft position sensor's wiring connector from the top of the unit, then release the single 12mm lock bolt which retains the sensor. You'll find that a flat, box-end wrench (ring spanner) is the best tool for this job as access is very limited. Pull the sensor toward the firewall and, when it comes free, lift it away.

3 Without SST (Special Service Tools) it is

29A/1 Apply a blob of paint as a reference.

not possible to check the sensor for more than obvious damage or wear. With the right SSTs a dealer or specialist can check that the unit sends four 5 volt (SGT signal) pulses and one 5 volt (SGC signal) pulse during every revolution of its spindle. The unit cannot be repaired, so must be replaced if faulty.

4 When installing the sensor, note that the drive dogs on the sensor are shaped to match the slots in the rear of the camshaft, which means

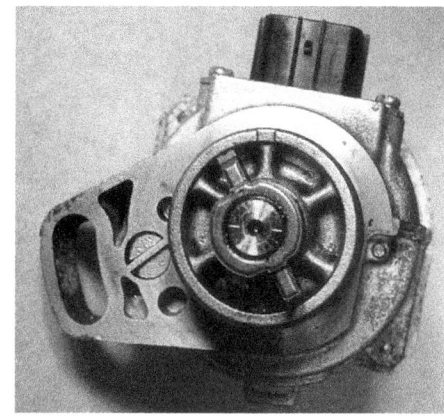

29A/4 Sensor drive dogs differently shaped.

that the sensor can only be fitted correctly, not 180° out.

5 Fit a new rubber oil seal into the groove in the sensor boss and lubricate the seal and the drive dogs with a little engine oil. Set the drive dogs to match the slots in the cam and then slide the angle sensor into position: if it won't go home with a little to-and-fro twisting, pull it out and rotate the drive spindle 180° and try again. Once the drive dogs engage the rear of the camshaft, push the angle sensor body fully home against the rear of the cylinder head and loosely fit the retaining bolt.

6 If, as advised, you marked the relationship of the camshaft position sensor body with the cylinder head, realign your marks and tighten the 12mm lock bolt to a torque of 22Nm (2.2kgf m/ 17lbf ft). Connect the harness wiring connector to the top of the sensor and reconnect the battery.

7 If you didn't mark the setting of the camshaft position sensor, or if you are fitting a new unit, set it temporarily in mid-position and then follow the ignition timing adjustment procedure ☞ 5/26.

29B. CRANKSHAFT POSITION SENSOR - CHECKING, ADJUSTMENT, REMOVAL & INSTALLATION

☞ 1/1, 2.

1 The crankshaft position sensor (used on 1996 and later models) is mounted alongside the crankshaft pulley on the left-hand side of the engine. You may find that it is easier to access the sensor via the flap in the engine undertray.

2 Disconnect the battery negative (-) terminal to isolate the electrical system ☞ 7/2. To check the unit, disconnect its connector plug from the wiring harness. On the sensor side of the

Mazda Miata, MX-5, Eunos & Roadster

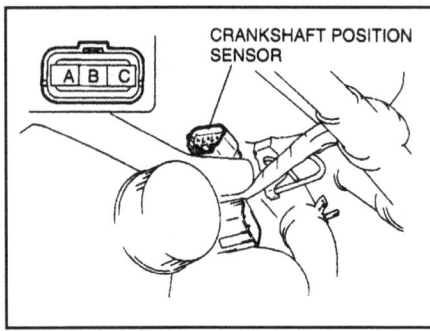

D29B/2 CRANKSHAFT POSITION SENSOR RESISTANCE CHECK.
(See text.) Note this drawing is not model specific.

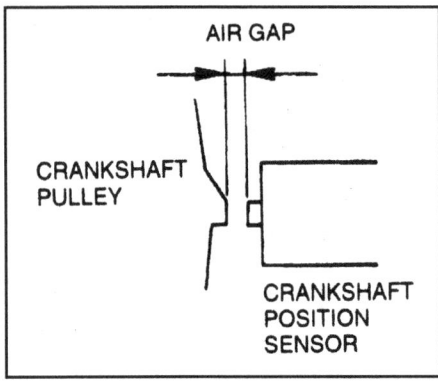

D29B/3 CRANKSHAFT POSITION SENSOR AIR GAP CHECK.

connector, measure the resistance between terminals **A** and **B** (see diagram). The resistance should be in the range 500 to 600 ohms at approximately 20 degrees C (68F). If the readings are faulty, replace the sensor.

3   Using feeler gauges, measure the air gap between the 'pip' on the rim of the crankshaft pulley and the sensor's nose (see diagram): it should be 0.5-1.5mm (0.020-0.059in).

4   If necessary the air gap can be adjusted by loosening bolt **A** (see diagram) and moving the bracket until the correct clearance is achieved. Tighten bolt **A**. To remove the unit undo bolt **B** (see diagram) to release the sensor from its mounting bracket. Install the unit in the bracket, replace bolt **B**. Both bolts should be tightened to a torque of 7.9-10.7Nm (80-110kgf cm, 69.5-95.4lbf in).

5   If necessary, close the flap in the engine

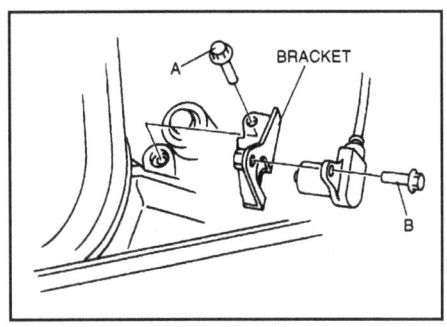

D29B/4 CRANKSHAFT POSITION SENSOR FIXING DETAIL.

undertray. Reconnect the unit's wiring harness connector and reconnect the battery.

30. MASS AIRFLOW (MAF) SENSOR - REMOVAL, CHECKING & INSTALLATION

☞ 1/1, 2.
1   Disconnect the battery negative (-) terminal to isolate the electrical system ☞ 7/2.
2   + The mass airflow sensor is mounted on the top of the air cleaner assembly on the left-hand inner fender (wing), and can be removed

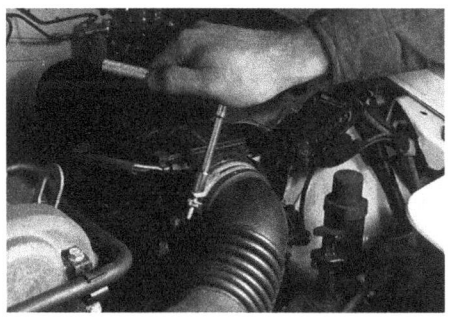

30/2a Release the MAF/air hose clamp (clip).

30/2b Release the harness connector.

after the rigid air trunking has been detached. The trunking is secured to the nose of the MAF sensor by a clamp (clip) and can be pulled away after this has been slackened. Unplug the harness wiring connector. Remove the four 10mm bolts which retain the sensor and remove it.

3   The MAF sensor unit contains the 'hot wire' mechanism used to sense the volume of airflow through the intake system. The unit can only be checked for obvious damage without access to the SSTs (Special Service Tools) that would

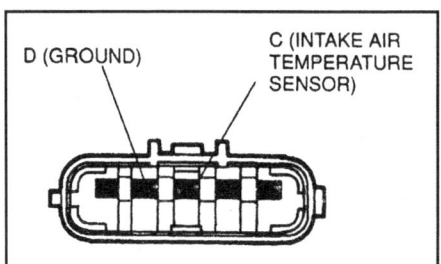

D30/4 AIR INTAKE TEMPERATURE SENSOR CHECK.
(See text.)

allow its function to be tested. If the MAF sensor is faulty it must be replaced.

4   The MAF sensor unit incorporates an intake air temperature sensor, the function of which can be checked with an ohmmeter. Measure the resistance between terminals **C** and **D** of the MAF side of the unit's electrical connector (see diagram). The resistance should be 2.21-2.69k ohms at approximately 20 degrees C (68F).

5   When installing the MAF sensor tighten the 10mm retaining bolts to 7.9-10.7Nm (80-110kgf cm/69-95lbf in). Fit the intake air trunking and tighten the securing clamp (clip). Reconnect the harness connector and reconnect the battery.

31. ENGINE COOLANT TEMPERATURE SENSOR - REMOVAL, CHECKING & INSTALLATION

☞ 1/1, 2.
1   The sensor unit, which is a thermistor, is mounted in the heater outlet casting at the back of the engine above the bellhousing (see photo). Access is eased by removal of the camshaft position sensor and, if necessary, the coil unit.
2   Disconnect the battery negative (-) terminal

31/1 Location of coolant temperature sensor.

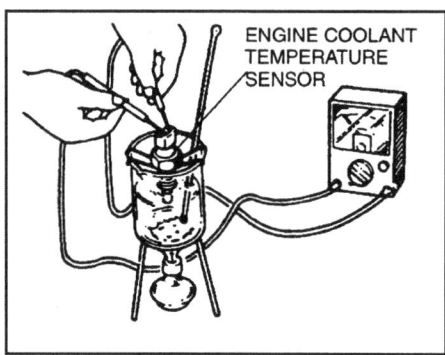

D31/4 ENGINE COOLANT TEMPERATURE SENSOR CHECK.

to isolate the electrical system ☞ 7/2. Partly drain the cooling system to below the level of the sensor ☞ 6.
3   Disconnect the sensor wiring harness connector and unscrew the sensor.
4   To check the sensor, you need to suspend it so that it is immersed up to its body threads (but no higher) in water which can be heated. Place a thermometer in the water and connect an ohmmeter across the two terminals in

5: Engine management, fuel, ignition & exhaust systems

the top of the sensor to measure changing electrical resistance.

5   To start with, heat or cool (with ice cubes) the water until a temperature of 20 degrees C (68F) is reached, at which point the resistance reading should be 2.21-2.69k ohms. Now heat the water to 80 degrees C (176F), when the resistance reading should be 0.287-0.349k ohms.

6   If the sensor is outside specification, fit a new one. You should remember that the sensor provides the engine temperature readings on which the PCM bases numerous control decisions. This sensor may not look very important, but if it is malfunctioning it will affect the way the engine runs to a significant degree: if you're the least uncertain about its condition, and running faults indicate that the sensor may be the problem, we suggest that you fit a new one to eliminate all doubt.

7   When installing the sensor, whether the old one or a new one, fit a new sealing washer. Tighten the sensor to 25-29Nm (2.5-3.0kgf m/18-22lbf ft) and connect the wiring connector. If removed, fit the camshaft position sensor and coil unit. Reconnect the battery. Top-up the coolant ☞ 6.

32. TPS UNIT - CHECKING, ADJUSTMENT, REMOVAL & INSTALLATION

☞ 1/1, 2.

CHECKING

1   The throttle position sensor feeds information about the position of the throttle body butterfly valve back to the PCM. It is mounted on the side of the throttle body and presents no access problems. To check the operation of the throttle sensor you'll need a set of feeler gauges and a continuity sensor (either a test lamp or a multimeter set to one of the resistance ranges). Note that the following test only checks that the TPS is correctly set and operating correctly at that setting. In fact, the TPS tells the PCM exactly how far open the throttle valve is through its whole range of movement by sending a varying voltage signal between 0.1-1.1 volts (fully closed) and 3.0-4.6 volts (fully open). SSTs (Special Service Tools) are required to test full function.

2   Remove the rigid air hose from the front of the engine. It is secured by clamps to the throttle body and MAF sensor. Don't forget to release the bypass hose from its throttle body connection and the cambox ventilation hose from the rigid air hose.

3    Disconnect the battery negative (-) terminal to isolate the electrical system ☞ 7/2. Disconnect the sensor wiring harness connector. Inside the sensor side of the connector are four terminals (see diagram).

4   Check that the throttle valve (butterfly) is fully closed (if it is not, there is insufficient slack in the accelerator cable or the throttle adjusting screw [TAS] has been tampered with and incorrectly set).

5   Check that there is continuity between terminals **A** and **B**. If there is no continuity, adjust the TPS unit as detailed later in this section before proceeding with the checks.

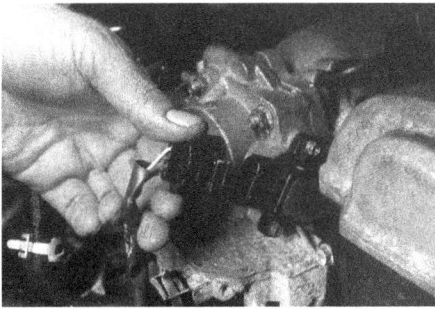

32/3 Throttle position sensor connector.

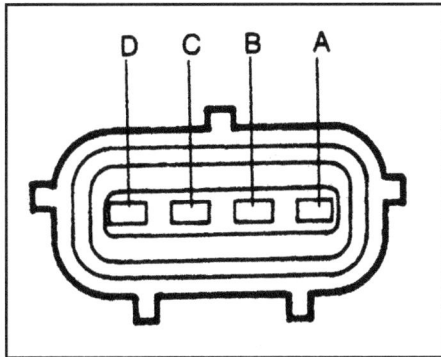

D32/3 THROTTLE POSITION SENSOR (TPS) CHECK.

6   Insert an 0.4mm (0.016in) feeler gauge between the throttle adjusting screw and the stop lever of the throttle quadrant. The continuity between terminals **A** and **B** should now be broken. If there is continuity, adjust the throttle position sensor.

ADJUSTMENT

7    Slacken the throttle sensor mounting crosshead (Phillips) screws just enough to allow the unit to be rotated with your fingers. Using feeler gauges between the throttle adjusting screw and the stop lever of the throttle quadrant, slowly turn the sensor back and forth until a position is found which gives continuity at 0.3mm (0.012in) and no continuity at 0.4mm (0.016in). The simplest way to do this would be to use a 3.5mm (0.014in) gauge, turn the sensor fully anti-clockwise (looking at it from the engine side) and then slowly turn it clockwise until continuity is lost. Hold the sensor in that position and tighten the screws. Repeat the test. **Do not try to adjust the throttle adjusting screw** which is factory set and 'locked' with paint.

32/7 Elongated slots allow adjustment of TPS.

8   If all is correct, reconnect the sensor's harness connector, fit the rigid air hose and reconnect the battery.

9   If the TPS unit cannot be made to give the correct test results, replace it with a new unit.

REMOVAL AND INSTALLATION

10   Disconnect the battery negative (-) terminal to isolate the electrical system ☞ 7/2. The sensor can be removed by unplugging the wiring connector and removing the two mounting screws.

11   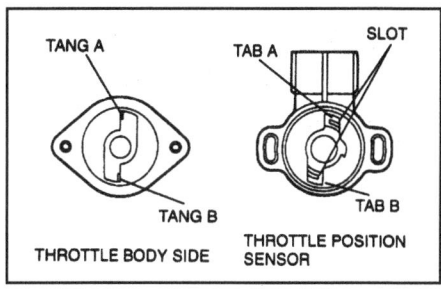 Note that the throttle valve spindle has two arms with tangs (see diagram). When fitting the sensor, make sure that tang **A** on the throttle body aligns with tab **A** of the sensor: the tangs of the throttle body should engage with the tabs of the sensor on the sides without slots. Once it is correctly engaged, rotate the sensor so that screw holes in the throttle body align with the adjuster slots in the sensor. Replace the screws and then carry out the adjustment procedure previously described. Reconnect the battery.

D32/11 CORRECT ENGAGEMENT OF TPS WITH THROTTLE BODY.
(See text.)

33. HEATED OXYGEN SENSOR - CHECKING, REMOVAL & REPLACEMENT

☞ 1/1, 2.

1   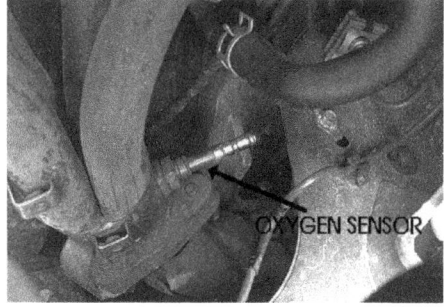 The heated oxygen sensor (mounted in the exhaust downpipe just below the manifold flange) responds to the proportion of oxygen in the exhaust gases, feeding information back to the PCM in the form of a varying voltage. This information is used to make constant adjustment to the richness of the fuel mixture so that it is always close to the low emissions ideal of 14.7:1 (air to fuel). 1996 and later models feature a second heated oxygen sensor in the exhaust pipe aft of the catalytic convertor.

33/1 Heated oxygen sensor location.

Mazda Miata, MX-5, Eunos & Roadster

Checking

2   Note the following checking procedure applies only to models with a single heated oxygen sensor. For 1996 and later models fitted with two sensors, Mazda recommends the function of the sensors (as read at the PCM) be checked using SSTs (Special Service Tools). We can't state it categorically, but believe that the two individual oxygen sensors of 1996 and later models could be checked in the manner described here, though we don't know what the wiring/connector arrangement for the rearmost sensor is because our project car was not so equipped.

3   The sensor is tested in position, with the engine at normal operating temperature - the latter is important. Release the sensor's connector from the wiring harness connector at the rear of the cambox on the exhaust cam side.

4   Using a voltmeter capable of reading low voltages - the sensor produces only about 1 volt maximum - connect the voltmeter positive (+) probe to terminal **A** (see diagram) of the sensor connector (sensor side) and ground the negative probe. Start the engine and run it at about 3000rpm until the meter shows a reading of about 0.55 volts. Suddenly open and close the throttle several times

33/3 Heated oxygen sensor connector.

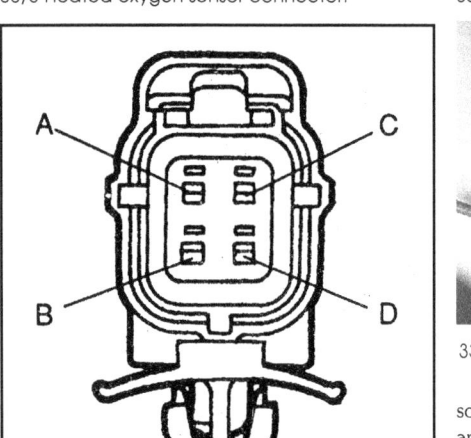

D33/4-5 CHECKING HEATED OXYGEN SENSOR CONNECTOR.

and check that, when the engine speed is rising, a reading of 0.5-1.0 volts is shown. As the engine speed falls, the reading should drop to between 0 and 0.5 volts. At idle 1.0 volt or less should register.

If the readings shown are outside this range, fit a new sensor.

5   Using an ohmmeter, measure the resistance between terminals C and D of the sensor (sensor side) connector. The correct resistance is 13 ohms at approximately 20 degrees C (68F). Replace the sensor if it fails this test.

REMOVAL AND INSTALLATION

6   Removal is usually easier if the manifold is hot. **Warning!** Wear protective gloves and shield your arms: access is difficult and the manifold will be very hot.

7   Disconnect the battery negative (-) terminal to isolate the electrical system ☞ 7/2. The sensor's wiring is very tight and, to create slack, it's necessary to remove the black connector block at the rear of the left-hand cambox cover from its bracket. This is done using needle-nosed pliers to squeeze together the retaining tabs beneath the bracket and lifting the socket. Once that's done, the wires can be pulled downwards through their brackets to create slack at the sensor unit.

8   Working behind the rear edge of the exhaust manifold heatshield, and using a 22mm crescent wrench (unless you have a purpose-built

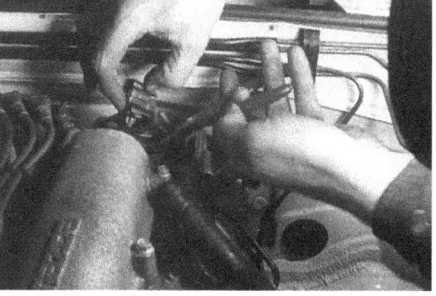

33/7 Release sensor connector from bracket.

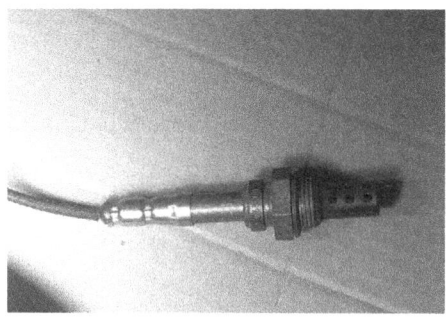

33/8 The heated oxygen sensor unit.

socket with a slotted side), unscrew the exhaust gas analyser unit from the exhaust pipe boss. Be careful not to strain the unit's 'pigtail' wires as you turn it out. Remove the sensor and its sealing washer. Once removed, treat the sensor gently and do not allow it to become contaminated with dirt or fluids.

9   When installing the sensor, use a new sealing washer and apply copper-based heat-resistant grease to its threads. The correct torque is 30-49Nm (3-5kgf m/22-36lbf ft). For those using a wrench instead of a socket, information on how to tighten fasteners by feel ☞ 1/2/52-55.

10   Reconnect the sensor to the wiring harness and reconnect the battery.

34. POWER STEERING PRESSURE SWITCH - CHECKING, REMOVAL & INSTALLATION

☞ 1/1, 2.

1   This section applies only to those vehicles with power steering! The power steering pressure switch feeds information back to the PCM to indicate whether the steering is being turned.

Checking

2   The power steering pressure switch is a simple on-off device, and can be checked using a continuity tester or a multimeter set to a resistance range. Disconnect the pressure switch wire, and connect the meter or tester between the switch terminal and ground (earth). **Warning!** Beware of hot and moving components. Have an assistant start the engine and, while it is running, turn and release the steering wheel a number of times. When the wheel is turned, the tester or meter should show continuity; while at rest no continuity should be indicated. Replace the switch if faulty.

34/2 Power steering pressure switch connector.

REMOVAL AND INSTALLATION

3   Disconnect the battery negative (-) terminal to isolate the electrical system ☞ 7/2. With the switch wire disconnected, unscrew the switch and remove it and its sealing washer(s) - note the position and order of the washers as they are removed. If the switch is faulty, fit a new one - you cannot repair this component. Fit the new switch, making sure that the sealing washers are in the right positions, and torque it to 25-29Nm (2.5-3kgf m, 19-21lbf ft). Reconnect the battery.

35. MAIN (FUEL INJECTION) RELAY - CHECKING & REPLACEMENT

☞ 1/1, 2.

1   + This relay is housed in the fuse block in the engine compartment on the right-hand inner fender (wing). Its position (**FUEL INJ**) is marked on the fusebox cover.

2   The first check is to listen to the relay and make sure it clicks when the ignition switch is turned to **ON** - a simple check, but often a good indicator as to whether the unit is serviceable.

5: Engine management, fuel, ignition & exhaust systems

35/1a Fuel injection relay location marked.

35/1b The fuel injection relay (typical).

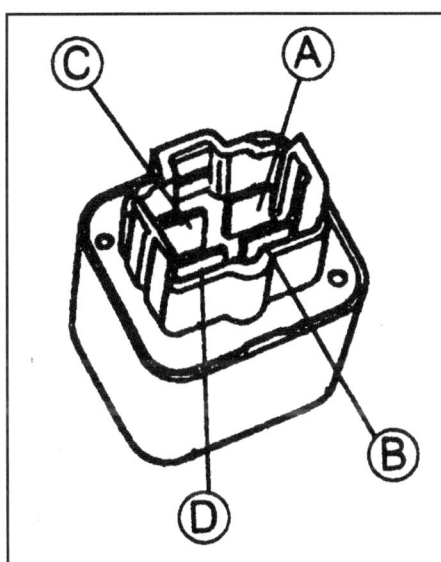

D35/3 MAIN (FUEL INJECTION) RELAY CHECKING.
(See text.)

3   The next stage is to unplug the relay for bench tests. For these you will need a continuity tester or a multimeter set to a resistance range, plus a 12 volt battery and a pair of jumper leads. Refer to the accompanying line drawing for details of the relay terminal positions.

4   Using the jumper leads apply battery voltage to terminal **A** of the relay while grounding terminal **B**. Connect the continuity tester or multimeter between relay terminals **C** and **D**, which should show continuity. With the battery disconnected, no continuity should be shown. If the relay does not perform as specified, fit a new one, seating it firmly in its recess in the fuse box.

36. CLUTCH SWITCH - CHECKING, REMOVAL & INSTALLATION

☞ 1/1, 2.

1   This section relates to manual transmission cars only. The clutch switch is used by the PCM to determine whether or not the clutch is engaged.

2   Disconnect the battery negative (-) terminal to isolate the electrical system ☞ 7/2. From inside the car remove the access panel under the steering column (two screws, then unclip it), unplug the clutch switch wire and connect a continuity tester,

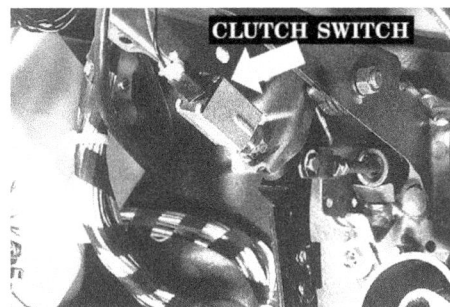

36/1 Location of clutch switch.

or a multimeter set to the resistance range, across the switch terminals (you may need to adopt something close to the Veloce MX-5 Accelerator Cable Removal Position™ ☞ 5/8). Check that continuity is shown when the pedal is depressed, and that no continuity exists when the pedal is released. If not as specified, fit a new switch. Reconnect the battery.

Removal & installation

3   Disconnect the battery and access the switch as previously described. To remove the switch, unplug the wiring connector, then back off the 16mm locknut on the switch body side of the mounting bracket and unscrew the 21mm switch body. After the new switch has been fitted (or old one refitted), check the clutch pedal height adjustment. Measure the distance between the rearmost edge of the pedal horizontally back to the carpet on the firewall. If this is outside the range 175-185mm (6.89-7.28in), unplug the switch wiring connector, back off the locknut and adjust the switch position until it's within specification. Tighten the locknut and reconnect the switch wiring.

4   Now check the clutch pedal lash (free play). Move the pedal with your hand until resistance is just felt. There should be 0.6-3.1mm (0.02-0.12in) lash measured at the pedal end. If incorrect, locate the 12mm locknut on the pushrod, and back it off a turn. Now rotate the pushrod by hand until the correct lash is obtained and secure the locknut.

5   Mazda instructs that, after setting the pedal height, you must adjust the pedal lash, which seems fine by us. But then, Mazda says that after you adjust the pedal lash you need to check the pedal height. Of course, when you've done that you need to ... yep, you guessed it! Our technical adviser, Wally, spent three days locked in a continuous cycle of adjustment until someone heard groaning noises coming from the garage. He was discovered babbling and locked into the Veloce MX-5 Accelerator Cable Removal Position™ - he had to be winched out of the car with an engine crane. After months of therapy - and even though he can now stand up unaided - he won't open that access panel ... Don't be fooled like poor Wally, do the job just once. Refit the access panel and reconnect the battery.

37. NEUTRAL SWITCH - CHECKING, REMOVAL & INSTALLATION

☞ 1/1, 2.

1   This section relates to manual transmission cars only. The neutral switch is used by the PCM to determine when neutral is selected. To check the operation of the switch you will need to raise the car and support it safely ☞ 1/3. You'll also need an assistant to operate the gearshift while you make the test. Disconnect the battery negative (-) terminal to isolate the electrical system ☞ 7/2.

2   With the car raised and securely supported on jack stands, climb underneath armed

37/2 Neutral switch connectors.

37/3a Neutral switch location (trans removed).

with an ohmmeter (a continuity checker will do the job, too). High up on the right-hand side of the gearbox, you'll see two connectors (see photos), which you should disconnect.

3   Connect the tester probes to the switch terminal wires (doesn't matter which way round) and check that continuity is shown when neutral is selected, and that no continuity is shown when a gear is selected. If not as specified, fit a new switch. The switch, which is simply screwed into place, is located near the top of the transmission casing just forward of the tail extension. Note that

Mazda Miata, MX-5, Eunos & Roadster

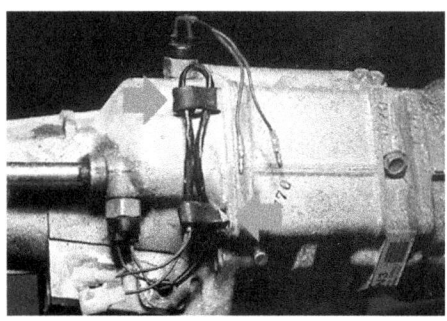

37/3b Excess wire length held by straps.

the switch's excess pigtail wiring is held by two thin metal straps at the top of the gearbox (see photo): you can't see these straps from beneath, but you can reach up and open them with your fingers to release the wiring.

4 When the switch is installed, tighten it securely (if you can measure the torque it should be 25-29Nm/2.5-3kgf m/19-21lbf ft). Secure excess wire in a loop retained by the straps above the gearbox. Reconnect the switch wires to the harness and reconnect the battery. Lower the car to the ground.

38. EXHAUST SYSTEM - CHECKING & SYSTEM/ COMPONENT REMOVAL & REPLACEMENT

☞ 1/1, 2.

1 The exhaust system comprises four main parts: the exhaust manifold, the downpipe, the catalytic converter and the main muffler/silencer. In addition, there are a number of related minor parts - heatshields, brackets and gaskets, for example, which form the rest of the system.

2 Inspection or dismantling of the exhaust system requires access to the underside of the car. This is easiest if a vehicle lift is available, but, if not, the car can be raised by jacks and supported securely on jackstands (axle stands) ☞ 1/3. You should leave enough room at the rear of the car so that the exhaust system can be slid out from underneath. If you're working in your garage, drive the car in front first, or you may not have room to pull the exhaust system out from underneath. **Warning!** The catalytic converter gets extremely hot in service, and, even though it is covered by a heatshield, will cause severe burns if touched. It also retains heat longer than other parts of the system. Wait until the system is stone cold before starting work.

3 Inspection of the system is pretty straightforward, but take care not to forget its top surface, nearest the bodywork. Holes will be immediately evident, but check carefully for smaller cracks, especially near the various joints. Sooty marks on the vehicle underside indicate leaks - due either to failure or incorrect assembly. If you know you have a leak somewhere but can't track it down, get an assistant to run the engine at idle and partially block off the muffler outlet with a rag. The increased pressure in the system should show up any leak. You should also check for impact damage along

the system (eg: from grounding the exhaust on a rock) because the resulting restriction can have an adverse effect on engine performance.

4 Exhaust system repair products are available. These take the form of pastes and bandages which harden when heated. We feel that these products have their place in emergencies, but don't regard them as permanent (whatever the packaging says to the contrary). That said, if the system is nearly worn out, you may be able to postpone the expense of replacing it by judicious use of these products. Check whether such repairs are legal in your area. In our experience, repair by welding falls into the same category; fine for a while, but normally another hole or split will appear soon. Given the proximity of the fuel tank and pipes, and the risk of damage to the electrical system and electronics (arc welders can easily zap your PCM), you must remove the system before attempting this type of repair.

5 It is unusual to have to remove the exhaust system in its entirety; the manifold section normally lasts the life of the car and is, in any case, removed from the engine compartment rather than from beneath the car. So, in this section, we'll deal with the rest of the system, from the downpipe back to the main muffler, all of which is removed from under the car.

6 We recommend that you remove the whole of this assembly in one piece because it's easier, but there are other good reasons, too. Firstly, once you have removed the assembly, you'll find it much easier to work on cleaning and separating the individual parts than would be the case if you were under the car. Secondly, even if you are only replacing a single component in the system, you should dismantle everything first, then reassemble loosely (with the new section in place), leaving final tightening until it is all back on the car. This ensures that the system is not under stress, which might lead to premature failure of joints, or put undue strain on the hangers. There are instances, however, where you will want to remove only the rear section of the system, from the catalytic converter back, to gain access to other components or assemblies. If this is the case, you will not need to separate the system at the (rather inaccessible) downpipe to manifold (header) joint. Instead, start the dismantling process by separating the system at the back of the catalytic converter.

7 Disconnect the battery negative (-) terminal to isolate the electrical system ☞ 7/2. Arm yourself with overalls, safety glasses, a wire brush, penetrating oil and the appropriate tools. Position yourself under the car, get as comfortable as you can (an old cushion will save you a lot of neckache) and get busy with the brush, removing dirt and loose rust around the joints and brackets. Once you've got them fairly clean, soak the nuts in penetrating fluid and leave to soak for as long as possible - overnight would be great, but a half hour or so will probably work.

8 Unscrew the two 17mm bolts securing the brace bar which runs across the car beneath the gearbox and remove the bar. Moving to the back of the car, release the six 17mm which secure the rear brace bar to the underframe and remove the brace bar assembly.

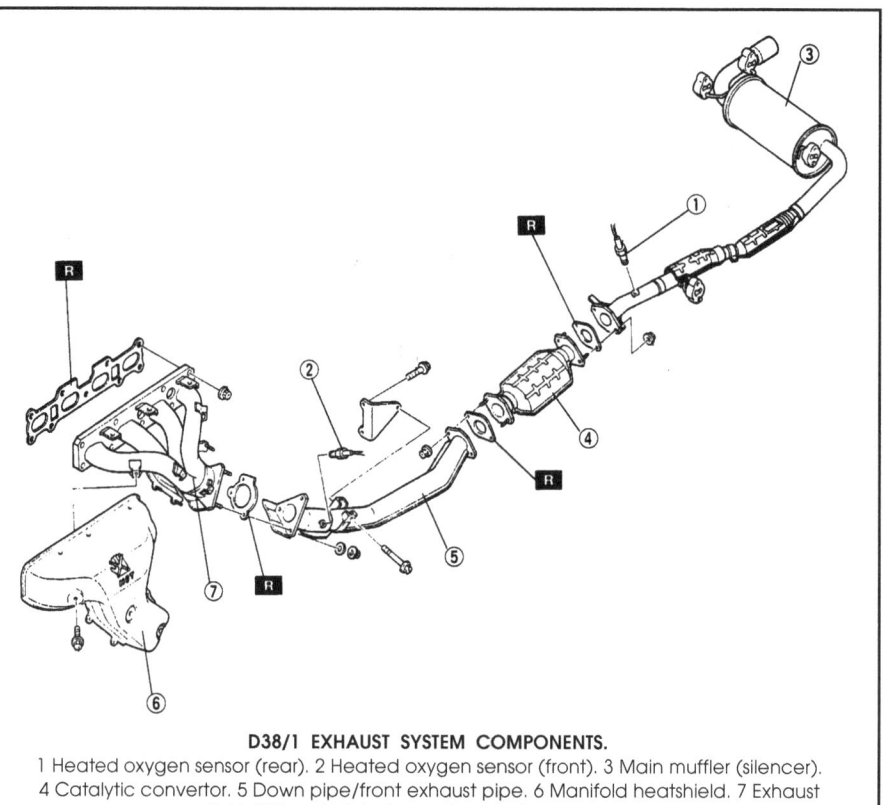

D38/1 EXHAUST SYSTEM COMPONENTS.
1 Heated oxygen sensor (rear). 2 Heated oxygen sensor (front). 3 Main muffler (silencer). 4 Catalytic convertor. 5 Down pipe/front exhaust pipe. 6 Manifold heatshield. 7 Exhaust manifold. "R" gaskets to be replaced whenever disturbed.

5: Engine management, fuel, ignition & exhaust systems

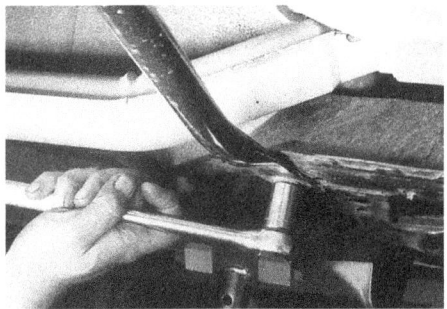
38/8a Release front underframe brace.

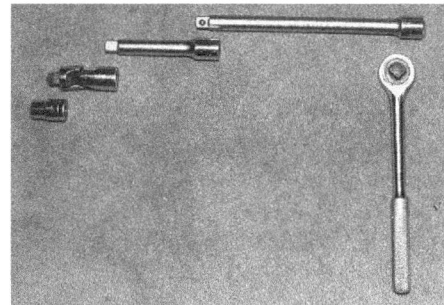
38/10a The tools you'll need.

38/11c ... and this one ...

38/8b Rear brace held by 3 bolts per side: one ...

38/10b Access from wheelwell.

38/11d ... and these by levering ...

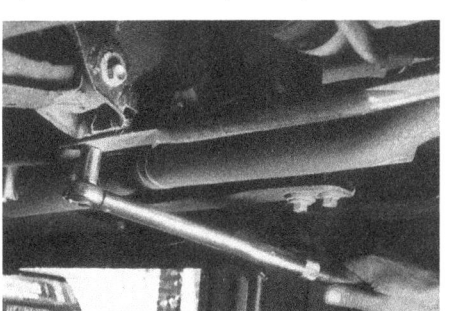
38/8c ... two ...

38/11e ... rubber supports over pins.

38/8d ... three. Lift brace away.

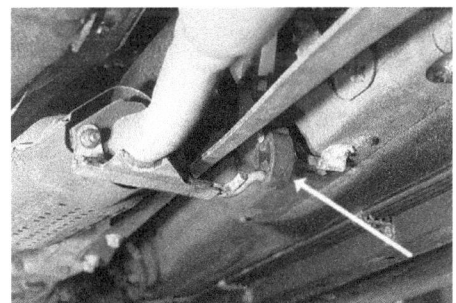
38/11a Release this support ...

38/11b ... and this one ...

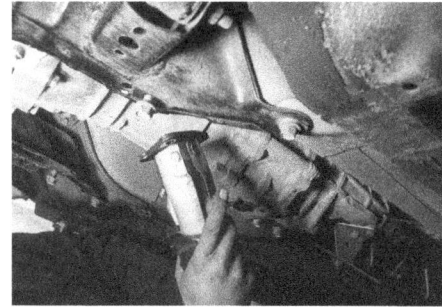
38/12 Feed downpipe down through gap.

9   If your car has a heated oxygen sensor in the exhaust pipe after the catalytic convertor, release it's wiring connector and then unscrew the sensor ☞ 5/33.7-8. **Caution!** Once removed, treat the sensor carefully and do not allow it to become contaminated by dirt or fluids.

10   ▢+ From beneath the car you can just about see three 14mm nuts which hold the exhaust downpipe to the exhaust manifold. To get at and undo these nuts you need to put together extensions of at least 360mm (14in) and a universal joint. The combination should be socket, universal joint, extension or extensions, then the T-bar or ratchet handle. Two of the nuts can be accessed from the gap between the transmission and subframe, while the third nut can be reached from the gap above the subframe in the left-hand front wheelarch.

11   ▢+ Next, release the exhaust downpipe bracket attached to the bellhousing. There is a captive nut on the bellhousing bracket and the pinch-bolt can be undone through the gap above the front subframe in the front left-hand wheelarch. The bolt has a 12mm head. Despite penetrating oil, our bolt still sheared! Working backward from the bellhousing, there are five rubber supports for the exhaust system. With the use of a screwdriver the rubber can be stretched over either the body or exhaust system hanger pin. The technique is to push the blade of the screwdriver through the hole in the rubber mounting alongside the hanger pin - from the back of the pin, of course - and, once the blade tip is past the mushroomed end of the hanger pin, use the screwdriver like a tire lever to lever the rubber mounting over the head of the pin.

12   ▢ The complete exhaust system can now be lowered toward the ground and the downpipe manipulated through the gap between

5:35

Mazda Miata, MX-5, Eunos & Roadster

the subframe and bellhousing. The writer managed this single-handed: two people would make it a whole lot easier. If you are working alone, you may find it helps to prop the front of the system on a cardboard carton while you free the remainder.

13 Once the system is out from the underside of the car, you will find it much easier to work on. Clean off any remaining dirt and rust, and apply penetrating oil as required. Separate the catalytic converter from the downpipe and main muffler, releasing the two nuts which secure each flange.

14 Inspect each part for damage or deterioration. You will have to assess whether the system parts are serviceable, or in imminent danger of blowing - bearing in mind that if they do so a week after you fit the system, you'll be doing this all over again. External rusting tends to take place along seams and welded joints, and even where plating or metal spraying has kept the system generally intact, it is at these points that corrosion shows up first. Less easy to spot is corrosion from the inside of the system. All exhaust systems have low spots where moisture condenses when the system cools down, and this moisture, combined with acidic gases, produces the corrosive effects which eventually eat through the metal. With a screwdriver probe any areas which look to be on the verge of perforation to check this.

15 The catalytic converter, in particular, leads a stressful existence. It is subject to extremes of temperature, alternately heating up and cooling each time you use the car. Climate and the type of journeys undertaken will affect the life of the system, but 2-3 years' life should be considered about average. Note that the heatshield around the catalytic converter seems to be one of the first things to burn through, and indicates that the converter body will be doing the same thing fairly soon. In some areas it is illegal to use the vehicle in this condition - it is easy to start a fire by parking on tall grass which can ignite under the car with expensive consequences. Check your local laws for details, but in general, fit a new converter rather than run this sort of risk.

16 Non-original replacement parts are generally inadvisable - they usually don't last as long as the originals, may not fit well, and may affect engine performance noticeably. Aftermarket performance systems are a different matter: those from reputable suppliers should be as good, or better, than the original, and the price will undoubtedly reflect this. If you use them, note any installation advice supplied, and check whether you need to modify any other parts of the car to suit.

17 When fitting the system, assemble it loosely using new gaskets at each joint. Check the hanger rubbers, replacing any that are damaged or aged. Slide the system under the car and prop the front end on the carton (you did keep it, didn't you?).

18 ◘+ Slide the exhaust system along the ground until it is in approximately the correct position beneath the car, and, if working alone, prop it in position on the carton you used during removal. Note that the heatshields on top of various sections of the exhaust system should, where

38/18a Check 'Cat' underbody heatshield

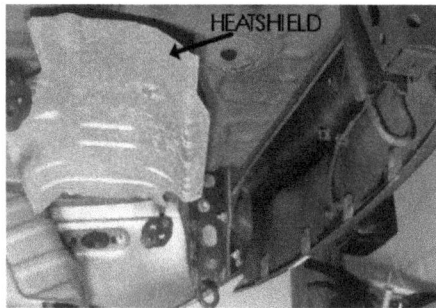

38/18b Check muffler underbody heatshield.

so marked, be correctly orientated. Where there are body heatshields fitted, check them for corrosion and security before you install the system.

19 Lubricate the studs on the exhaust manifold with copper-based grease. Slide a new metal gasket over the studs, noting that no sealing compound is necessary if both mating faces are as clean as they should be.

20 Have an assistant support the rear end of the system, while from beneath the car you begin to maneuver it into position. You'll find that you'll have to twist the system to one side a little in order to work the exhaust pipe flange past the bellhousing bracket, but once past the bracket it will comfortably slide up roughly into position.

21 When the flange at the front of the exhaust system engages with the three manifold studs, quickly spin on any one of the three nuts by a few turns and just leave it at that for the moment. Note: each of the three retaining nuts has a spring washer, which should be replaced if it has become flattened.

22 Your assistant should now lift the rear muffler and fix it to the underside of the car by pushing the eyes of the rubber supports over pegs and hangers: this process is made so much easier by spraying the rubber supports with silicone-based lubricant that it can then be done without tools.

23 Moving back to the front of the system, it should now be easy to push the exhaust system flange fully home against the manifold flange. The three manifold flange nuts and washers are very difficult to get into place. I spent quite a lot of time cursing and trying to get one of the two lower nuts to nip the threads when, in fact, the easiest nut to place - and it can be without its washer initially - is the top nut. What you need here is an assistant who

will reach through the gap between the front subframe and chassis from the left-hand front wheelarch to fit the nut to the top stud. Once you have a nut in place it becomes comparatively easy to fit the others (then, if necessary, you can take off the first nut and refit it with its washer).

24 You'll find the only way to tighten the manifold flange nuts is with the same tools you used during removal - a 14mm socket attached to a universal joint attached to an extension of at least 360mm (14in), and then a ratchet or T-bar. Both of the lower nuts can be tightened from beneath the car; the top nut is most easily accessible via the left-hand front inner wheelarch. Torque the three nuts to 38-51Nm (3.8-5.3kgf m, 28-38lbf ft).

25 Once the manifold flange nuts have been tightened, work your way back along the exhaust system, fitting all of the rubber hangers. As mentioned before, a quick spray with silicone fluid will make this job so easy you can just push each rubber hanger over its pin with your fingers.

26 When all of the hangers are in place, come back to the front of the system and, after lubricating it with copper-based grease, insert the 12mm bolt that fixes the exhaust pipe clamp to the bracket on the side of the bellhousing. The bolt can be inserted and tightened through the gap between the subframe and chassis rail in the left-hand front wheelarch. Torque the bolt to 19-25Nm (1.9-2.6kgf m, 14-18lbf ft).

27 Install the rear oxygen sensor (if applicable), making sure you apply anti-seize compound to its threads and use a new sealing washer. Torque the sensor to 30-49Nm (3.0-5.0kgf m, 22-36lbf ft) and then reconnect it to the wiring harness. Install the two underframe braces and tighten their 17mm retaining bolts to 63-93Nm (6.4-9.5kgf m, 47-68lbf ft). Lower the car to the ground and reconnect the battery.

39 EXHAUST MANIFOLD REMOVAL AND INSTALLATION

EXHAUST MANIFOLD REMOVAL

1 If you need to remove the exhaust header/manifold assembly, most of the work is done from the engine compartment.

2 Disconnect the battery negative (-) terminal to isolate the electrical system ☞ 7/2. You will first need to detach the front downpipe at the flange joint as described earlier in this section ☞ 5/38.2, 7-11. Do not allow this to strain the oxygen sensor wiring: disconnect if necessary.

3 ◘+ Working inside the engine compartment, detach the rigid air hose from the airflow meter and throttle body stubs and remove it - the hose is secured by a worm-drive clamp (clip) at each end. Don't forget to release the cambox ventilation hose and bypass hose to the throttle body.

4 ◘ Press the locking tang and release the wiring connector from the side of the mass airflow sensor.

5 ◘+ Using a 10mm socket, remove the

5: Engine management, fuel, ignition & exhaust systems

bolts securing the air intake tube to the left-hand front wing. Using a 10mm socket, slacken the clamp holding the air intake hose to the air filter body. Pull the hose off the stub on the filter body and remove the intake assembly.

6   📷 Using a screwdriver, release the cable tie securing the wiring loom to the air filter cover. Place the loom out of harm's way on the inner wing.

7   📷+ Using a 10mm socket, remove the four bolts securing the air filter cover/MAF unit. Lift the cover off and lift the air filter element out of the air filter body.

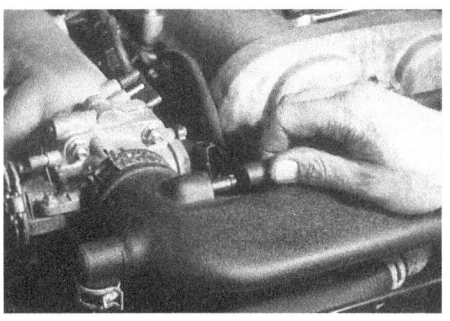
39/3a Release cambox ventilation hose ...

39/7b ... and then lift away cover/MAF unit.

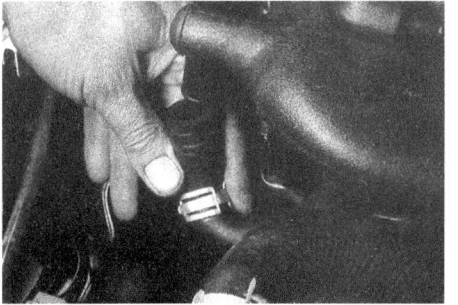
39/3b ... followed by the bypass hose ...

39/5a Release securing bolt & clamp ...

39/7c Lift out paper air filter.

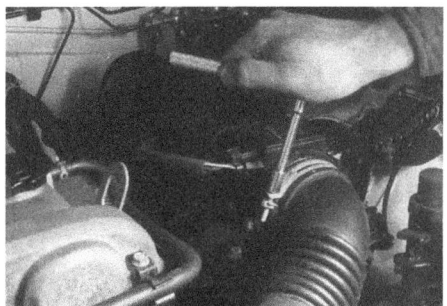
39/3c ... release clamps at MAF and throttle body ...

39/5b ... then lift air intake tube away.

39/8 Release headlight dimmer (if fitted).

8   📷 Remove the 10mm bolt securing the headlight dimmer unit to the left-hand inner fender (this unit is not fitted for all countries).

9   📷+ Next, using a 12mm socket, remove the two bolts and one nut securing the air filter lower body to the left-hand inner wing. Lift out the air filter lower body.

39/3d ... lift rigid hose away.

39/6 Release wiring clip.

39/4 Release MAF unit electrical connector.

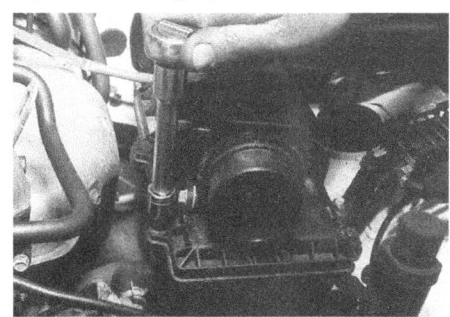
39/7a Remove securing bolts ...

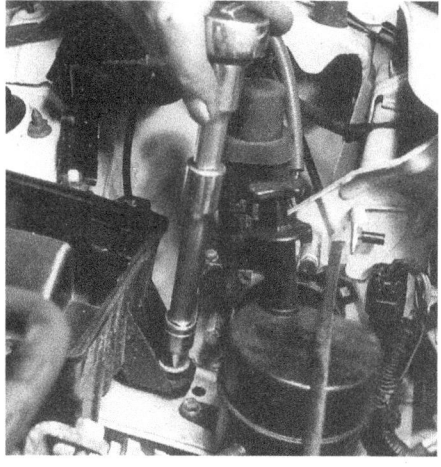
39/9a Unscrew securing bolts and nut ...

5:37

Mazda Miata, MX-5, Eunos & Roadster

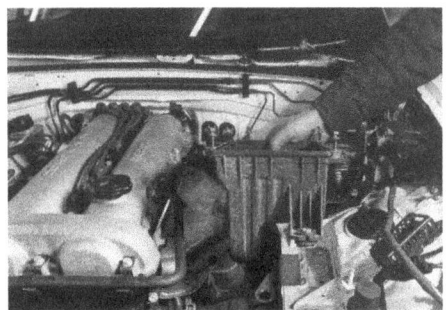

39/9b ... and lift out air filter lower body.

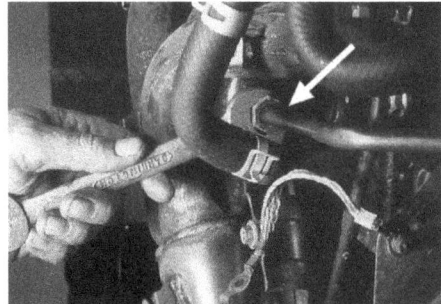

39/11 Release EGR pipe union.

39/14b ... and torque retaining nuts.

39/10a Unscrew securing bolts & nuts ...

39/13 Fit a new exhaust manifold gasket.

39/10b ... and lift away heatshield.

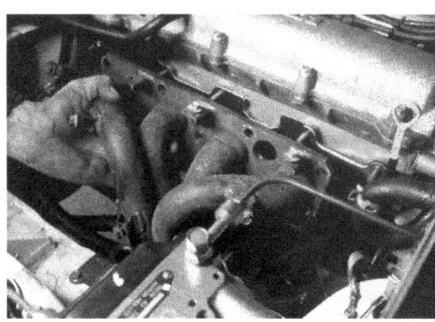

39/14a Slide manifold over studs ...

10   ○+ Using a 10mm socket, remove the fixings that secure the exhaust manifold heatshield to the manifold; there are six bolts and three nuts. Lift away the heatshield.

11   ○ Using an open-ended spanner, unscrew the 22mm union nut securing the solid pipe of the EGR system that runs from the exhaust manifold to the intake manifold/plenum.

12   Using a 14mm socket and extension, unscrew the nine exhaust manifold retaining nuts. Note: if possible it's a good idea to soak the studs protruding through the nuts with penetrating oil as many hours before doing this job as you can. The threaded studs will normally be corroded and this can make it very difficult to get the nuts off without damaging them: we had to buy several new nuts. Lift away the manifold and remove the old gasket.

EXHAUST MANIFOLD INSTALLATION

13   ○ Before installing the manifold, clean its and the engine gasket surfaces thoroughly. Always use a new gasket.

14   ○+ Slide the manifold over the studs and then slide the water pipe bracket over the relevant stud before replacing the manifold securing nuts. Using a 14mm socket, tighten the nuts progressively (working in a spiral outward from the centre) to a torque of 39-46Nm (3.8-4.7kgf m, 29-33lbf ft). Reconnect the EGR pipe union to the manifold and tighten securely.

15   When you fit the manifold heatshield, use copper grease on the retaining bolt threads to prevent them from seizing in the manifold brackets.

16   Using a new gasket, reconnect the exhaust downpipe. You'll find the only way to tighten the manifold flange nuts is with the same tools you used during removal - a 14mm socket attached to a universal joint attached to an extension of at least 360mm (14in), and then a ratchet or T-bar. Both of the lower nuts can be tightened from beneath the car; the top nut is most easily accessible via the left-hand front inner wheelarch. Torque the three nuts to 38-51Nm (3.8-5.3kgf m, 28-38lbf ft).

17   After lubricating it with copper-based grease, insert the 12mm bolt that fixes the exhaust pipe clamp to the bracket on the side of the bellhousing. The bolt can be inserted and tightened through the gap between the subframe and chassis rail in the left-hand front wheelarch. Torque the bolt to 19-25Nm (1.9-2.6kgf m, 14-18lbf ft). Lower the car to the ground.

18   If it was disconnected, reconnect the heated oxygen sensor wiring.

19   Install the lower body of the air filter housing, noting that the projecting boss in its underside needs to engage with the bracket while, simultaneously, the stud at the front of the suspension turret is engaged (if applicable, the headlight dimmer unit also uses this stud). Secure the air filter housing with two 12mm bolts and a single 12mm nut, all torqued to 19-25Nm (1.9-2.6kgf m, 14-18lbf ft).

20   Install the air filter element. Install the air intake tube which is secured by a clamp with a 10mm bolt at the filter end and a 10mm bolt at the body end, which should be torqued to 7.9-10-7Nm (80-110kgf cm, 69.5-95.4lbf in). Install the air filter cover/MAF unit and tighten its four 10mm securing bolts securely. Remake the MAF unit's electrical connection. Fix the wiring loom to the clip at the rear of the air filter body.

21   Install the rigid air hose between the throttle body and the MAF unit, not forgetting to remake the cambox ventilation and throttle body bypass hose connections. Secure the hose clamps.

22   Reconnect the battery.

Visit Veloce on the Web - www.veloce.co.uk

6

Cooling, heating and air conditioning systems

1. INTRODUCTION

☞ These cars use a conventional cooling system in which the water-based coolant is circulated around the engine by a small centrifugal pump driven by a belt from the crankshaft. Engine heat is transferred to the coolant, which is constantly circulated through the radiator. Air passing though the radiator matrix reduces coolant temperature before it circulates once again through the engine. Hot air is sucked from the engine compartment by the airstream created by the moving car. An electric cooling fan switches on at a predetermined coolant temperature to draw air through the radiator matrix. This ensures adequate cooling in very hot temperatures, or when in slow-moving traffic.

During cold weather, the interior of the car is heated by a system like the engine cooling system running in reverse: hot coolant from the engine is diverted through the heater matrix below the dashboard, and air is passed through the matrix to extract heat to warm the passenger compartment. The heater control allows the occupants to control a combination of recirculated and fresh air, and to boost the incoming airflow with an electric fan.

An optional air conditioning system is available. This works pretty much like a domestic refrigerator. An engine-driven compressor circulates refrigerant through the condenser - effectively another radiator - mounted in the nose of the car. The condenser, backed up by an electric fan, is designed to dump unwanted heat into the passing airstream. Refrigerant is piped to the cooling unit (evaporator) mounted under the dashboard. Hot air from the car's interior is passed through the evaporator, the refrigerant absorbing the air's heat and thus reducing its temperature. The warmed refrigerant evaporates into a gas which is pumped back to the condenser, where it cools and liquefies: the cycle is then repeated.

2. ENGINE COOLANT - TOPPING-UP & CHANGING

☞ 1/1, 2 & 6/1.

Warning! If the engine has been run within the last hour or so, the engine coolant will be hot and under pressure. Removing the radiator cap or coolant reservoir cap can result in the coolant suddenly boiling as pressure is released, resulting in scalding steam being ejected. Always allow the engine to cool before removing either cap. Wear eye protection, gloves and overalls for safety. Place rag over the radiator cap, then turn the cap slowly counterclockwise until it reaches the first stop position.

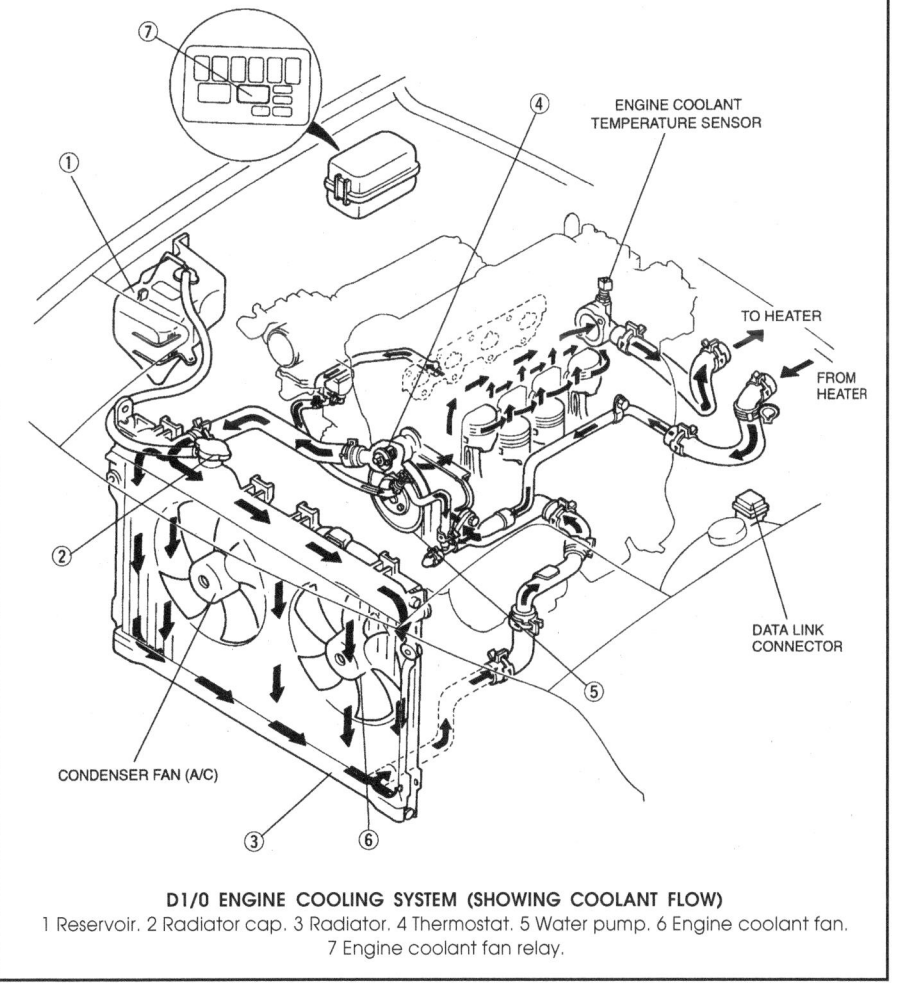

D1/0 ENGINE COOLING SYSTEM (SHOWING COOLANT FLOW)
1 Reservoir. 2 Radiator cap. 3 Radiator. 4 Thermostat. 5 Water pump. 6 Engine coolant fan.
7 Engine coolant fan relay.

Mazda Miata, MX-5, Eunos & Roadster

2/2 Topping-up radiator.

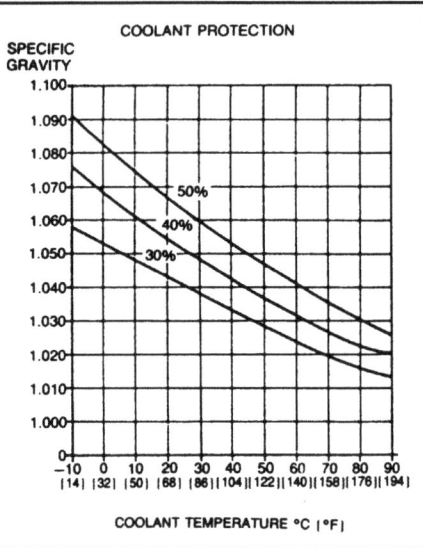

D2/5 COOLANT PROTECTION GRAPH.

2/9a Radiator drain plug.

2/9b Let coolant drain into receptacle.

Wait until pressure has vented before removing the cap completely.

Warning! Antifreeze is very toxic and yet its sweet smell can be attractive to children and animals: mop up spills quickly, and keep containers tightly sealed out of the reach of youngsters. Antifreeze can cause skin damage and will damage paintwork, too.

1   The engine coolant level should be checked regularly and topped up as required - we suggest that you give the level a quick visual check on a weekly basis. The check should be carried out on fairly level ground and with the engine cold, to avoid any risk of scalding (see warning above).

2   Check that the radiator coolant level is just below the filler neck, and that the coolant level in the reservoir is between the **FULL** and **LOW** level marks. Add only pre-mixed coolant to adjust the levels as necessary.

MIXING ENGINE COOLANT

3   It is important to use coolant made up in the correct proportions from distilled or demineralized water and ethylene glycol-based antifreeze. Never use water direct from the faucet (tap) or you risk corrosion and scale deposits in the cooling system. Never use alcohol or methanol-based antifreeze.

4   To check the existing coolant mixture you will need a thermometer and a coolant hydrometer. The specific gravity of the coolant mixture varies according to ambient temperature and the water/antifreeze ratio. The recommended proportions for frost protection at various air temperatures are as follows -

Protection down to (degrees)	Water /Antifreeze (%)	Specific gravity at 20C/68F
- 16C/3F	65/35	1.054
- 26C/-15F	55/45	1.066
- 40C/-40F	45/55	1.078

5   Note the point made above about how ambient temperature will affect the specific gravity of the coolant. The accompanying graph illustrates this relationship.

6   Having checked the specific gravity required for operation in your temperature zone, mix the appropriate proportions of antifreeze and distilled/demineralized water in a clean container. Store the mixture in a sealed plastic drum or similar for use when topping up the cooling system.

TOPPING UP THE COOLING SYSTEM

7   Before adding fresh coolant, check the general condition of the existing coolant. Look for signs of scale build-up around the filler neck, and also for signs of oil contamination. If the coolant is dirty or contaminated, you should drain the system, flush it out, and then add fresh coolant. Note that if oil contamination is present, this may indicate a failed seal or gasket in the engine, especially if there has been a significant coolant loss recently. If, for example, the head gasket blows between a cooling system passage and a combustion chamber, combustion pressure may well force coolant out of the system and cause oil contamination of the remainder. Always investigate and monitor such incidents closely - you could avoid expensive repair bills if you act quickly.

CHANGING THE COOLANT

8   The engine coolant should be changed at the specified intervals, or more frequently if there have been signs of contamination or deterioration of the existing coolant (see above). This task should be undertaken with the engine cold. The cooling system capacity is 6.0 liters (6.3 US qt/5.3 Imp qt), so you'll need a container of sufficient size to hold this amount of liquid comfortably.

9   Remove the radiator filler cap. Position the drain container below the radiator drain plug (there's an access opening in the engine undertray). Loosen the drain plug using a screwdriver and allow the coolant to drain.

10   Place a hose in the radiator filler neck and allow the system to flush through for a while, until the emerging water is completely clear, then allow the system to drain completely. While this is taking place, remove, empty, wash out and refit the coolant reservoir. Tighten the radiator drain plug and tighten it securely.

11   Slowly add fresh coolant to the radiator - no faster than 1 liter (1.1 US qt/0.9 Imp qt) per minute - until the level is just below the filler neck. Run the engine at idle for a while with the radiator cap removed. When the top radiator hose feels hot to the touch, top up the coolant to bring the level back to just below the filler neck. Switch off the engine, fit the radiator cap and top up the coolant reservoir to between the **FULL** and **LOW** marks.

3. COOLING SYSTEM - CHECKING

☞ 1/1, 2 & 6/1.

Warning! If the engine has been run within the last hour or so, the engine coolant will be hot and under pressure. Removing the radiator cap or coolant reservoir cap can result in the coolant suddenly boiling as pressure is released, resulting in scalding steam being ejected. Always allow the engine to cool before removing either cap. Wear eye protection, gloves and overalls for safety. Place rag over the radiator cap, then turn the cap slowly counter-clockwise until it reaches the first stop position. Wait until pressure has vented before removing the cap completely.

Warning! Antifreeze is very toxic and yet its sweet smell can be attractive to children and animals: mop up spills quickly, and keep containers tightly sealed out of the reach of youngsters. Antifreeze can cause skin damage and will damage paintwork, too.

1   Visually check the cooling system components for signs of leakage or deterioration. System leaks are sometimes obvious, with dried coolant streaks indicating the source of the problem. Sometimes, though, the fault is less easily located. Tiny pinhole leaks from the radiator matrix are often hard to spot. These can be due to deteriora-

6: Cooling, heating & air conditioning systems

tion of the matrix due to corrosion, or from physical damage such as stone impacts or crash damage.

2   Other causes of leakage from the system include wear or damage of the radiator pressure cap (or dirt caught under the sealing washer). Problems of this type mean that cooling system pressure cannot be maintained, and at normal atmospheric pressure there will be coolant loss due to boiling of the coolant. Finally, do not forget the problem of head gasket failure mentioned previously - this can cause mysterious losses of coolant, sometimes without oil contamination of the remainder.

3   If you have a problem of this type, the easiest and best solution is to have the cooling system pressure tested to highlight the source of the trouble. Many garages and gas stations will perform this type of check at little cost. If you think the radiator cap is at fault, as they are not too expensive, try a new one to eliminate this possibility.

4. COOLING SYSTEM - HOSE REPLACEMENT

☞ 1/1, 2 & 6/1.

Warning! If the engine has been run within the last hour or so, the engine coolant will be hot and under pressure. Removing the radiator cap or coolant reservoir cap can result in the coolant suddenly boiling as pressure is released, resulting in scalding steam being ejected. Always allow the engine to cool before removing either cap. Wear eye protection, gloves and overalls for safety. Place rag over the radiator cap, then turn the cap slowly counter-clockwise until it reaches the first stop position. Wait until pressure has vented before removing the cap completely.

Warning! Antifreeze is very toxic and yet its sweet smell can be attractive to children and animals: mop up spills quickly, and keep containers tightly sealed out of the reach of youngsters. Antifreeze can cause skin damage and will damage paintwork, too.

1   The main hoses associated with the cooling system are the large bore top and bottom hoses connecting the engine to the radiator. There are additional smaller bore hoses which relate to the heater and engine management system, and these, too, can leak - all are described in the course of this section. Hoses deteriorate due to natural ageing and the effects of heat. Before they get so bad that they burst or leak, they should be replaced.

2   Start by draining the cooling system. Each hose is secured by a steel clip at each end. These are freed by grasping the tangs on the clip and squeezing them together with a pair of pliers. The clip can then be slid along the hose until it is free of the stub. The hose can then be worked off the stub, using a flat-bladed screwdriver to push it off, rather than attempting to pull the hose (this has the effect of tightening the hose on the stub and rarely succeeds in shifting it). If the hose has been in place for some time it may well be stuck: you can help free it by working a small electrical screwdriver between the stub and the hose, where access permits. As a last resort, make sure you have the correct replacement hose ready to fit, then cut off the old one by slitting it lengthways with a craft knife - take care not to cut into the stub. Clean the stub before fitting the new hose.

TOP HOSE REMOVAL

3   ◘+The top hose connects the thermostat housing to the top stub of the radiator, and is the easier of the two main hoses to reach.

BOTTOM HOSE REMOVAL

4   The bottom hose connection consists of two short hose sections with a metal pipe between them. These are less easy to reach, being partially hidden below the exhaust manifold and, where fitted, the power steering pump. You may just about be able to remove and fit this assembly from the top of the engine bay, but most likely you'll need access from below.

5   ◘+The car will need to be jacked up and supported on safety stands (☞ 1/3). You can access the bottom hose via a flap in the undertray, but, for easiest access, remove the engine undertray completely (☞ 3/4/14-15).

6   ◘+Free the hose ends at radiator stub,

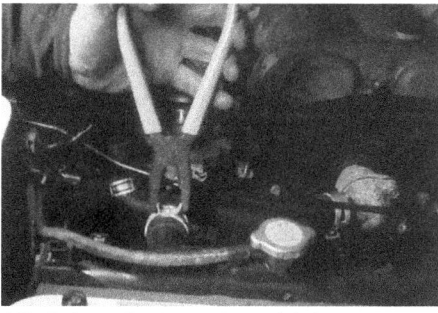
4/3a Release the hose clamp (clip) ...

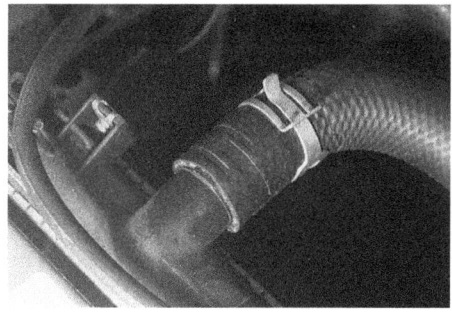
4/3b ... move the clamp along the hose ...

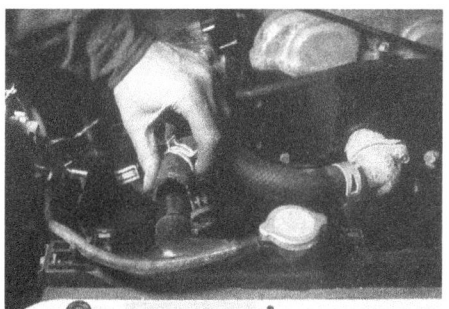
4/3c ... and push hose off stub.

4/5a Single bolt secures panel ...

4/5b ... giving access to the bottom hose.

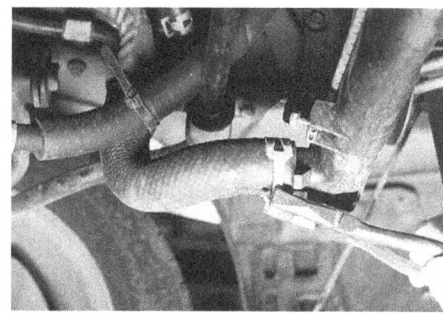
4/6a Release bottom hose at radiator stub ...

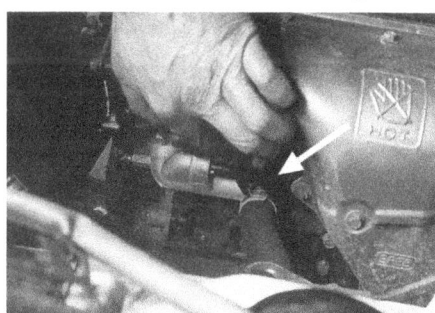
4/6b ... release bottom hose clamp at engine ...

4/6c ... and at metal connecting pipe.

Mazda Miata, MX-5, Eunos & Roadster

metal pipe stubs and at the block end. On cars with power steering, there may be a plastic cable tie holding the p/s pump hose to the bottom hose - free this by pulling back on the locking tab with your fingernail.

COOLANT INLET CASTING AND HOSE CONNECTIONS

7   At the front left-hand side of the block there is a casting, through which engine coolant is passed from the bottom hose into the engine cooling system passages. It is not easy to reach this - it will be partially covered by the power steering and/or air conditioning pumps, but you should not normally need to disturb this component between engine overhauls.

8   Connected to an elbow at the front of the casting is a small hose which runs up to a Tee piece at the thermostat housing. If you need to replace this hose, free it after releasing the retaining clips as described above.

HEATER HOSE CONNECTIONS

9   A metal pipe runs back from the coolant inlet casting, the back end being secured on one of the exhaust manifold studs. This is the heater return pipe, the hose connection to which can be accessed at the back of the engine compartment. The other end of the hose connects to the heater outlet stub at the firewall (bulkhead). The heater hoses are easy to reach at the firewall end, and are secured by the usual clips.

10   The heater inlet hose is connected from the outlet cover on the back of the block to the heater inlet stub at the firewall. Access to the engine end of this hose will require removal of the ignition coil assembly. The outlet cover itself is retained by one 12mm bolt and one 12mm nut, should removal be required. The cover also carries the water thermosensor.

INTAKE MANIFOLD HOSE CONNECTIONS

11   The final secondary hoses are those associated with the intake manifold. These small bore hoses are retained by the usual clips and are generally pretty accessible.

AFTER FITTING NEW HOSES

12   After fitting new hose(s), refill the cooling system (☞ 6/2) then fit the filler cap and run the engine to allow the system to pressurize. Check carefully for leaks.

5. RADIATOR - REMOVAL & INSTALLATION

☞ 1/1, 2 & 6/1.

1   Start by raising the front of the car sufficiently to permit safe access below the engine compartment. You need enough room to work underneath when disconnecting the radiator bottom hose ☞ 1/3.

Isolate the electrical system by disconnecting the battery negative (-) terminal, after first having disarmed the audio unit's security system. **Warning!** When loosening the negative (-) terminal, take great care not to short the tool you are using across the positive (+) terminal (for more information ☞ 7).

2   Moving to the underside of the car, the next job is to remove the engine's plastic undertray (☞ 3). Drain the radiator as previously described. Release the air bypass hose and the small bore

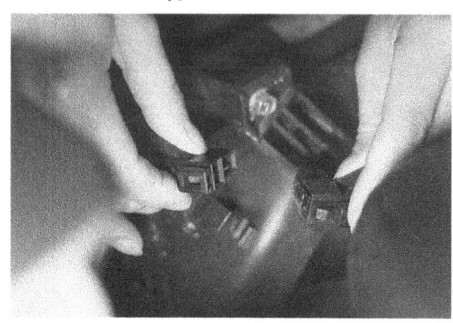

5/3 Release fan electrical connector.

hose from the left-hand cam cover from their stubs on the rigid air hose. Loosen the clips securing the rigid air hose to throttle body and air filter housing and lift it away.

3   Release the electrical wire from the clip in the fan housing by pulling back the catch on the side of the clip, and thereby releasing the wire

4/8 Release clamp (clip).

4/9 Release heater hose clamps at firewall.

4/10 Bolt and nut secure heater outlet casting.

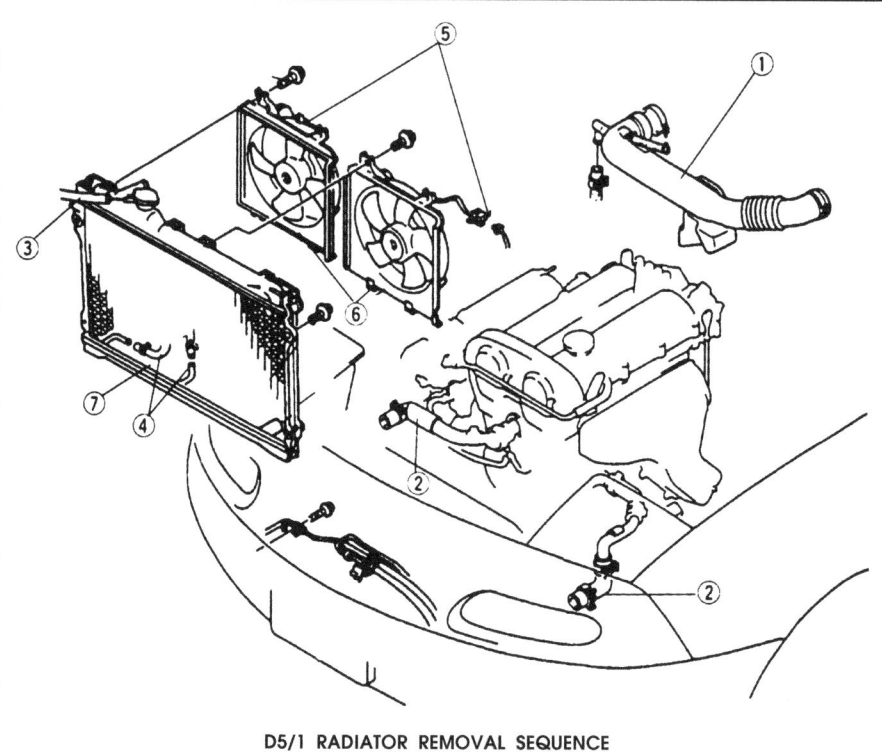

D5/1 RADIATOR REMOVAL SEQUENCE
1 Remove rigid air hose. 2 Disconnect top & bottom hoses. 3 Disconnect reservoir hose.
4 Disconnect oil cooler hoses (auto trans cars). 5 Release electrical connectors to engine coolant fan & (a/c cars) condenser unit fan. Remove radiator.

6: Cooling, heating & air conditioning systems

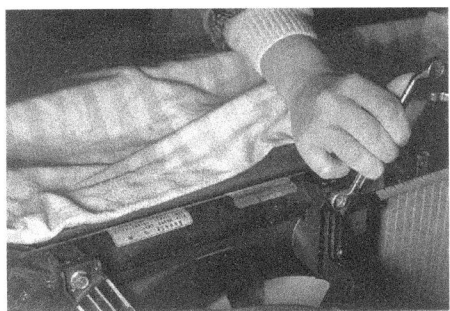

5/4a Unscrew fan fixings ...

5/4b ... and lift fan away from radiator.

retainer. The electrical connector block can now be separated by pushing the outer catch inwards and pulling the two halves apart. If your car has air conditioning, you'll need to repeat this process on the second fan.

4 ☐+ Removal of the electric fan (or fans) from the radiator is optional: if you're removing the rad for better access to the camshaft drivebelt area, the fan/s can be left in place. Each electric fan housing is fixed to the radiator body by four 10mm bolts, threaded into spring clips. Note: you may find, as we did, that the bottom retaining bolts and their clips are considerably corroded. If this is the case, a soaking with penetrating oil some time before the bolts are removed will help. Once the two top bolts have been removed and the two bottom bolts loosened, the cooling fan assembly can be lifted away from the car.

5 Remove the radiator top hose by squeezing the ears of each spring clip with pliers, and moving the clips back until they stop clamping the stubs. The hose can then be worked off of both the radiator stub and the thermostat housing stub.

6 Note: you may find that coolant hoses are difficult to release from metal stubs and pipes - we did, even though our project car was less than two years old. The problem is caused by a combination of very tight-fitting hoses and metal corrosion. Generally, it's better to push the hoses off than to pull them. Often, working a screwdriver into and around the joint - taking care not to gouge either hose or union stub - helps; simultaneously squirting a silicone-based water repellent lubricant such as WD40 will help greatly, too. If the hose simply refuses to budge, with a craft knife carefully slit it lengthways along the union joint, taking care not to gouge the union stub. This method means, of course, that you'll have to buy a new hose. Release the overflow pipe from its union just beneath the radiator filler cap.

7 Next, remove the bottom hose after releasing, if applicable, the plastic tie holding the power steering pump hose against the radiator hose. To release the tie, pull back the locking tab with a fingernail and then slide the tail of the tie through the clip. The bottom hose can be removed after releasing both of its spring clips and working the hose off of its unions. Easier said than done, but persevere and the hose will come free.

8 If the car has auto transmission, release the two small bore hoses from the oil cooler at the bottom of the radiator. You may have to remove a single 10mm bolt securing a pipe clip. ATF will drip from these hoses, so tie them up as high as possible and temporarily block their ends with golf tees or similar.

9 ☐ Remove the two 12mm headed bolts towards the top and on each side of the radiator. The radiator can then be lifted upward out of its bottom brackets and removed from the car. Store in a safe place.

10 Once the radiator has been removed, check it carefully for signs of damage. Bent fins on the radiator matrix can be carefully straightened using a small screwdriver, but take care not to

5/9 Lift radiator out of bottom brackets.

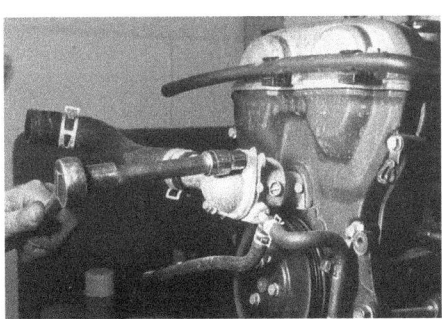

6/3 Bolt and nut secure thermostat cover.

6/4 Pull thermostat from housing.

overdo this or you will probably end up causing a leak. Remove bugs, leaves and dirt by brushing them off the matrix or, better still, with a high-pressure air hose. If you have a lot of problems with stones or debris getting in through the air intake at the front of the car, you may want to consider fitting one of the aftermarket grilles available for these cars.

11 If you discover serious corrosion or damage, you have two options; repair or replacement. Radiator repairs are specialist work, and there are agencies for specialist companies in most towns. The best course of action is to check the price of a new radiator, then take the damaged one to a repair specialist for assessment: have it repaired if it proves economic to do so.

12 When installing the radiator, make sure that all hose connections are secure (you might consider fitting new hoses while you have easy access). Refill the cooling system and then run the engine for a while to check for leaks. Check ATF level in auto transmission cars.

6. THERMOSTAT - REMOVAL, TESTING & INSTALLATION

☞ 1/1, 2 & 6/1.

1 The thermostat senses water temperature and opens and closes in response to changes. At low temperatures, the valve remains closed, and water is shut off from the radiator. This causes the engine to reach operating temperature quickly, reducing engine wear. As normal temperatures are reached, the thermostat valve opens to permit water circulation through the radiator. Note that most thermostats fail in the open position - an abnormally long warm-up period often signifies this. The engine management system will compensate for a slow warm-up by prolonging the rich mixture phase, and you may not notice any problem. If your heater seems to take forever to start working, and your fuel consumption seems abnormal, check out the thermostat. **Caution!** If the temperature gauge reads high, but the top hose feels barely warm, it's likely the thermostat is stuck in the closed position: fit a new thermostat quickly, otherwise engine damage will result.

2 Isolate the electrical system by disconnecting the battery negative (-) terminal, after first having disarmed the audio unit's security system, if applicable. **Warning!** When loosening the negative (-) terminal, take great care not to short the tool you are using across the positive (+) terminal (for more information ☞ 7). Drain the engine coolant.

3 ☐ Undo and remove the 12mm bolt and nut holding the thermostat cover to the thermostat housing. Once they have been removed the cover can be pulled away from the housing, but be careful as it will come away suddenly once the gasket releases: also be prepared for some coolant spillage.

4 ☐ **Caution!** Do not use a sharp instrument to lever the cover from the housing. With the cover removed the thermostat can be lifted from its housing.

Mazda Miata, MX-5, Eunos & Roadster

5   Check the thermostat visually - if it is obviously damaged or leaking, fit a new one.

6   You can check the thermostat's operation by heating it in water. Suspend the unit in the water, together with a thermometer, so that they are clear of the sides of the container, and start heating the water. At 86.5-89.5°C (188-193°F) the main valve should start to open, and should be fully open (8mm/0.31in lift) at 100°C (212°F). The smaller valve should start to open at 83.5-86.5°C (183-187 F) and be fully open (1.5mm/0.06in lift) at 100°C (212°F). If in any doubt, fit a new thermostat.

7   When installing the thermostat, check that the gasket faces of the housing and cover are clean, using a solvent cleaner or a blunt scraper to remove any residual gasket material. The thermostat is fitted into the housing so that spring side is inward and the smaller valve is uppermost. Fit the cover using a new gasket, noting that the gasket tab must face the top of the cover. Tighten the cover bolt and nut to 19-25 Nm (1.9-2.6 kgf m/14-18 lbf ft). Fill the cooling system and then run the engine to check for leaks.

7. WATER PUMP - REMOVAL & INSTALLATION

☞ 1/1, 2 & 6/1.

1   The water pump is unlikely to be a source of problems unless the cooling system has become badly contaminated with scale, or the pump bearings have been damaged by wear or by water leaking past the shaft seal. Should this occur, you will probably find that the coolant level drops significantly. You can check this by leaving a sheet of cardboard under the engine bay when the car is parked overnight. Residual pressure in the cooling system will mean that the pump will continue to leak, and signs of leakage below the front of the engine will help confirm the fault. This check will also pinpoint the leak if it is from another source, such as a damaged hose.

2    Access to the water pump is by no means easy. It's mounted on the front of the engine block, just below the cylinder head joint. You'll need to follow the procedure for camshaft drivebelt renewal (☞ 3/13) because the belt needs to be removed to give the necessary access. The accompanying illustration summarises the procedure.

3   Once you have access, disconnect the water inlet pipe from the side of the water pump, leaving it attached to its hoses and the rigid small bore bypass pipe. Tie it clear of the pump.

4   The water pump can now be removed after releasing the four 12mm mounting bolts. The pump may well be stuck in place - use a hide mallet, or a block of wood and a hammer to jar it free. **Caution!** On no account lever the pump body as you'll damage the gasket faces or pump body.

5   If the pump is worn or damaged, you'll have to fit a new one. In common with most manufacturers, Mazda specifically advises that the pump should not be dismantled.

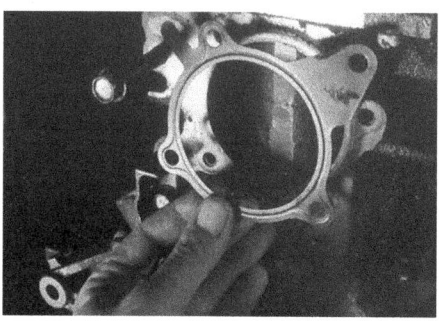
7/6a Fit a new water pump gasket.

7/6b Torque water pump mounting bolts.

6   📷+ Clean the gasket face of the cylinder block and make sure there's no debris in the threaded holes. When installing the pump, use a new mounting gasket, and tighten the mounting bolts evenly to 19-25 Nm (1.9-2.6 kgf m/14-18 lbf ft). Use a new gasket on the water inlet pipe, tightening its mounting bolts to the same torque figure as the pump body. Fit the various components removed to gain access to the pump (☞ 3/13): the accompanying illustration gives an overview.

7   After refilling the cooling system, reconnect the battery negative (-) lead and run the engine. Check carefully for leaks after the cooling system has warmed up and become pressurized. Check, and, if necessary, top up, the cooling system.

8. RADIATOR FAN/S - TESTING, REMOVAL & INSTALLATION

☞ 1/1, 2 & 6/1.

1   In normal circumstances, the car's motion creates sufficient airflow through the radiator for engine temperature to be kept within the optimum range (below 97°C (206 F). However, in high ambient temperatures, and especially in heavy traffic, the natural airflow has to be supplemented by an electrically operated fan. This fan is mounted immediately to the rear of the radiator. The fan is controlled - via the ECM (engine control module)/PCM (powertrain control module) - by a coolant temperature sensing thermister located immediately above the bellhousing at the back of the engine. Cars with air conditioning will have a second fan to augment the airflow through the system's

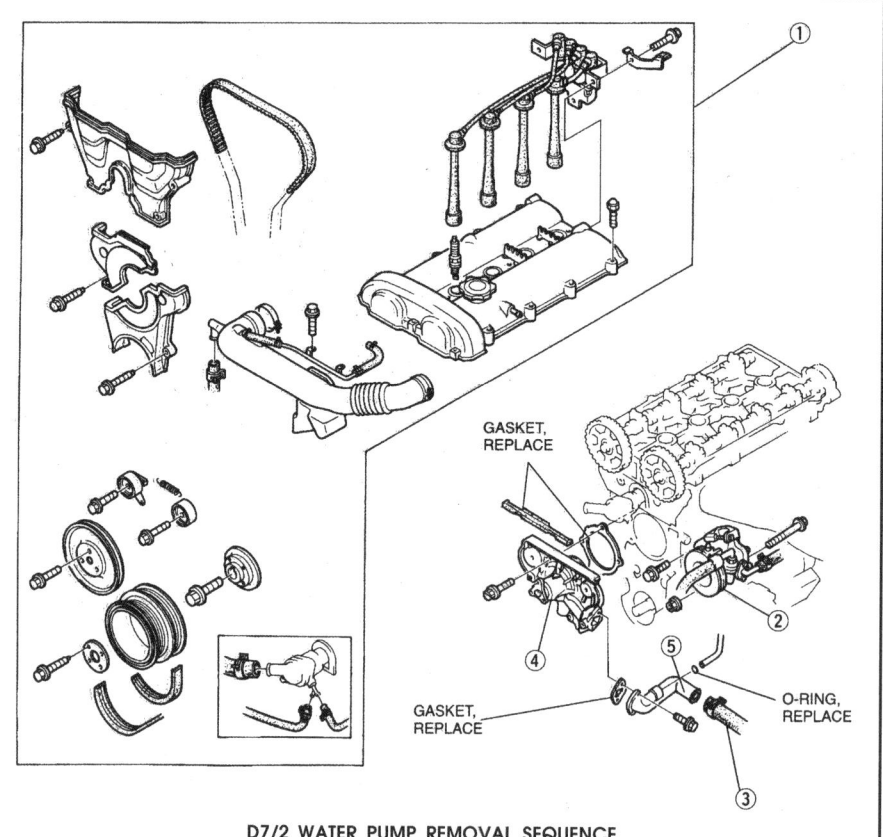

D7/2 WATER PUMP REMOVAL SEQUENCE
1 Remove all these items, including the timing belt. 2 Power steering pump (if fitted).
3 Water inlet casting. 4 Water pump.

6: Cooling, heating & air conditioning systems

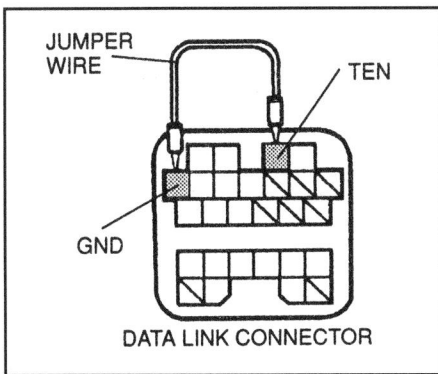

D8/2 BRIDGE TERMINALS GND (GROUND) AND TEN (TEST ENGINE) OF THE DATA LINK CONNECTOR ON THE LEFT-HAND INNER FENDER (WING).

condenser. This fan will run when coolant temperature exceeds 108°C (226°F).

2   If you suspect a fan is not operating when it should, it can be checked as follows. **Warning!** The fan operates during this test - keep hands and loose clothing well away from the fan area during the test. Open the diagnostic cover and locate terminals **GND** and **TEN**. Connect these terminals with an insulated jumper wire (see diagram). Turn the ignition **ON** (but don't start the engine) and check that both fans operate when the accelerator pedal is depressed. If the fans run with the jumper in place, the fault is most likely to be in the relevant relay or, perhaps, the temperature sensor. If the fans don't operate, turn the ignition switch off and check the wiring connections, then repeat the test. If a fan is still inoperative, check its motor. If the problem is that a fan runs continually, it is likely that the coolant temperature sensor has failed and the system has gone into safety default mode.

CHECKING COOLANT TEMPERATURE SENSOR

3   Remove the radiator cap (*see precautions* ☞ 6/2). Hold a thermometer in the radiator so that the bulb is just below the water level. Start the engine and allow it to run so that the coolant warms up. The fan should cut in when the temperature reaches approximately 97°C (206°F). If the fan does not run, check the sensor as follows.

4   Once the engine has cooled, drain

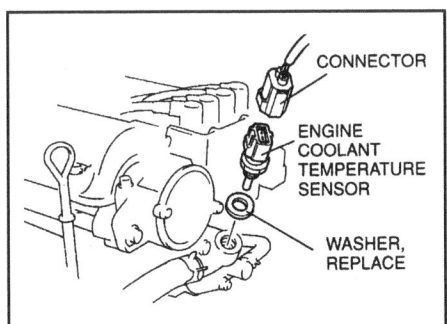

D8/4A ENGINE COOLANT TEMPERATURE SENSOR LOCATION.

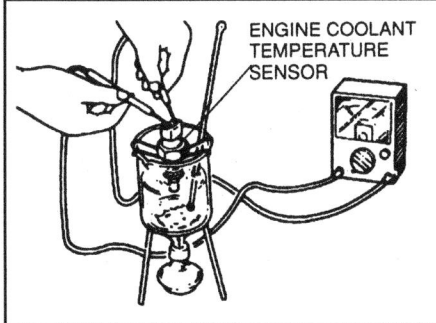

D8/4B ENGINE COOLANT TEMPERATURE SENSOR CHECKING.

about half the coolant from the engine (save it as it can be used again). Remove the ignition coil assembly (☞ 5), disconnect the coolant temperature sensor's electrical connector and then unscrew and remove the sensor. Suspend the sensor and a thermometer in a pan of water (keep the switch terminals dry). Connect an ohmmeter across the sensor terminals, then begin heating the water. At 20°C (68°F) the resistance should be between 2200 and 2690 ohms, while at 80°C (176°F) it should have decreased to between 287 and 349 ohms. If the sensor fails to work as specified, fit a new one using a new sealing washer. Tighten the sensor to 25-29Nm (2.5-3.0kgf m/19-21 lbf ft). Refill the cooling system and check for leaks.

FAN MOTOR TESTING

5   Disconnect and remove the vehicle battery (☞ 7) and check that it is fully charged (or use a spare car battery for this check). Disconnect the fan motor electrical connector. Connect the battery and an ammeter as shown in the accompanying illustration. The fan should operate smoothly and relatively quietly. The cooling fan should draw

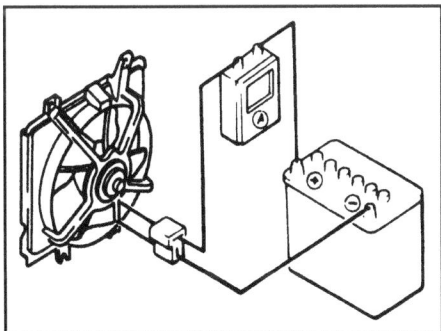

D9/5 TESTING THE FAN MOTOR.

5.9-6.5 amps (manual trans cars) and 6.7-7.37 amps (auto trans cars). **Warning!** Take care not to short the two battery wires.

FAN MOTOR REMOVAL AND INSTALLATION

6   Isolate the electrical system by disconnecting the battery negative (-) terminal after first having disarmed the audio unit's security system, if applicable. **Warning!** When loosening the negative (-) terminal, take great care not to short the tool you are using across the positive (+) terminal (for more information ☞ 7). Release the electrical wire from the clip in the fan housing by pulling back the catch on the side of the clip, and thereby releasing the wire retainer. The electrical connector block can now be separated by pushing the outer catch inwards and pulling the two halves apart.

7   The fan housing is fixed to the radiator body by four 10mm bolts threaded into spring clips. Note: you may find, as we did, that the bottom retaining bolts and their clips are considerably corroded. If this is the case, a soaking with penetrating oil some time before the bolts are removed will help. Once the two top bolts have been removed and the two bottom bolts loosened, the cooling fan assembly can be lifted away from the car.

8   With the assembly removed, unscrew the central nut which secures the fan unit to the motor shaft. Pull the fan off the shaft, then unscrew and remove the three motor mounting bolts to free the motor from the cowling. When installing the motor, tighten the mounting bolts to 4.0-4.9 Nm (40-50 Kgf cm/35-43 lbf in). Fit the fan to the motor spindle, tightening the retaining nut to 1.5-2.4 Nm (15-25 kgf cm/14-21 lbf in). Fit the cowling to the radiator, tightening the mounting bolts to 7.9-10.7 Nm (80-110 kgf cm/70-95 lbf in).

FAN RELAY TESTING

9   Another possible cause of a cooling or condenser fan failing to operate normally is that the

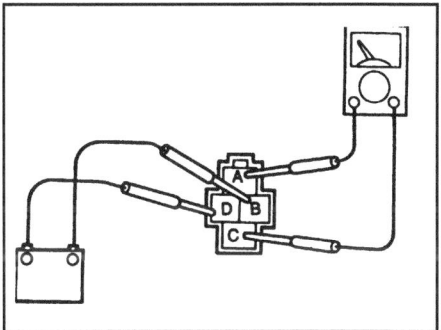

D8/9 COOLANT FAN RELAY CHECKING.

relevant fan relay has failed. These relays are housed in the fusebox on the right side of the engine compartment, their individual locations being shown on the fusebox cover.

10   Cooling fan relay: apply battery voltage

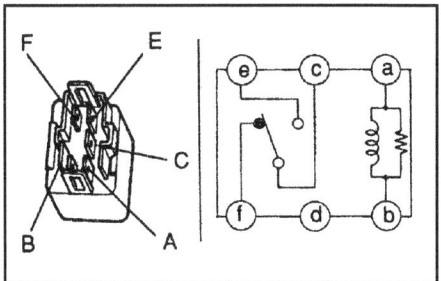

D8/10 CONDENSER FAN RELAY (A/C CARS) CHECKING.

Mazda Miata, MX-5, Eunos & Roadster

across terminals **D** and **B** and check continuity between terminals **A** and **C** (see illustration). With battery voltage applied as described, you should get a continuity reading (and you should hear a click as the relay operates). Condenser fan relay: apply battery voltage across terminals **A** and **D** and check for continuity across terminals **C** and **E**. With battery voltage applied as described, you should get a continuity reading (and you should hear a click as the relay operates). If the results obtained do not correspond with those described, fit a new relay.

9. HEATING & VENTILATION SYSTEM - HOW IT WORKS

☞ 1/1, 2 & 6/1.

1   The car interior is heated by hot coolant diverted through a heater matrix from the main cooling system. A slider on the heater control panel regulates the matrix temperature by controlling the flow of hot coolant through it. A second slider regulates the proportions of fresh and recirculated air passing over the matrix by varying the position of a flap inside the heater unit. A third slider control selects how the air is distributed inside the vehicle, again, using flap valves in the heater unit.

2   Connected by trunking to the heater unit, an electrically operated blower unit forces air through the matrix and into the passenger compartment according to the control settings. The blower motor has three operating positions, selected by a rotary switch on the control panel. A resistor assembly within the blower unit is used to control motor speed according to the switch setting.

3   The entire heating and ventilation system is mounted inside the car, behind the dash panel. The coolant system connections are accessible from the engine compartment, but removal of the heater unit will first require removal of the entire dashboard. The blower motor is easily accessible after the glovebox has been removed, and it is possible to remove the heater control panel after releasing the operating cables, again, requiring removal of the glovebox, plus the steering column access cover. Unusually, the blower unit of pre-1996 models was protected by a resettable circuit breaker housed in the internal fusebox, below the dash panel. 1996 and later models are protected by a fuse in the same location.

10. BLOWER UNIT - CHECKING

☞ 1/1, 2 & 6/1.

If the blower does not operate, or does not operate at different speeds when they are selected, carry out the following checks -

CHECKING THE CIRCUIT BREAKER OR FUSE

1   If the blower unit fails to operate, the first thing to check is the circuit breaker (to 1995) or fuse (1996 and later), both rated at 30 amps. This will be found in the fusebox below the dash panel.

10/2 Circuit breaker location in fusebox.

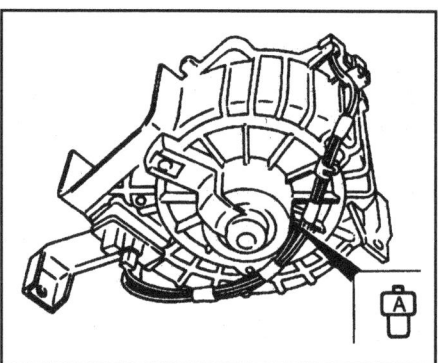

D10/3 HEATER BLOWER MOTOR CHECKING.

On left-hand drive cars, the fusebox is mounted above the dead pedal on the left side of the car. In the case of right-hand drive cars, it is mounted above the accelerator pedal. In both cases, you can get to the fuses without any dismantling, but the location makes access awkward. First, remove the two screws which secure the access panel below the steering column, then unclip the panel. You'll need to slide the driver's seat right back and lie across it with your head in the footwell to be able to see the fusebox, and you will find that a flashlight will prove useful here.

2   Open the fusebox cover and locate the circuit breaker or fuse (positions are marked on the fusebox cover). For pre-1996 cars, check whether the red button of the circuit breaker has popped out, indicating that a fault has occurred and that the circuit breaker is open. If it has, try pressing it in (**Caution!** Don't hold it in). It is possible that a momentary fault triggered the circuit breaker, and depressing the button may restore operation. If, however, the button pops straight back out when you switch on the ignition and the blower switch you'll need to investigate and repair the fault before it can be reset. An intermittent fault may mean that the breaker can be reset, but that it will pop out again when the fault next shows up. For 1996 and later cars, replace the burnt fuse with a new one and make the same tests.

CHECKING THE BLOWER MOTOR VOLTAGE

3   Remove the two sheet metal screws which secure the glovebox hinges to the hinge bar. Open the glovebox and lift it out of the dashboard. With the glovebox out of the way you have good access to the blower unit. Looking at the underside of the unit, locate the motor wiring connector

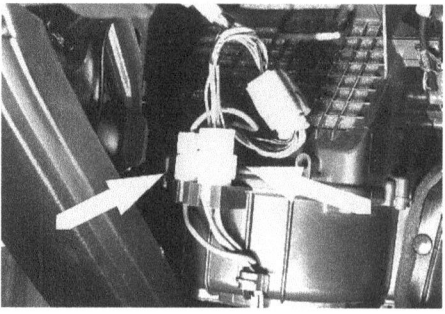

10/4 Blower wiring connectors.

which is close to the circular end of the motor body. Unplug the connector and identify terminal **A** (see illustration). Using a voltmeter or multimeter, connect the meter negative (-) probe to ground and measure the voltage at terminal **A** of the wiring connector with the ignition **ON** and the blower switch at position **4** (maximum). You should read approximately 12 volts. If there's no voltage, there is a break in the wiring between the connector and the blower motor switch, or the switch itself is faulty. If there are 12 volts but the blower doesn't run, renew the blower motor. If the circuit breaker operates or the fuse blows, there is a short in the wiring between the fusebox and the blower motor: check the wiring, connectors and switch for damage/moisture and repair as necessary.

CHECKING THE BLOWER RESISTOR

4   If the blower does not operate at four different speeds, locate the two wiring connectors (one single pin and one four pin); they are clipped to the side of the blower casing. Separate the connectors and, using a multimeter, check for continuity between terminal **B** and each of the other three terminals on the motor side of the connector block. If there is a lack of continuity, the resistor is at fault and should be replaced. If all's ok here, the blower switch itself must be at fault.

11. BLOWER UNIT - RESISTOR REMOVAL & INSTALLATION

☞ 1/1, 2 & 6/1.

1   If you need to replace the resistor block, it is secured to the underside of the blower casing by two sheet metal screws. Once these have been removed and the connectors slid out of their clips on the casing, the resistor unit can be lifted

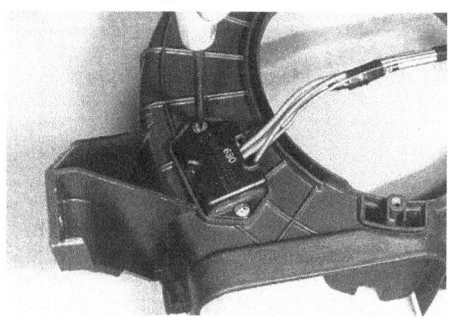

11/1a Unscrew the two retaining screws ...

6: Cooling, heating & air conditioning systems

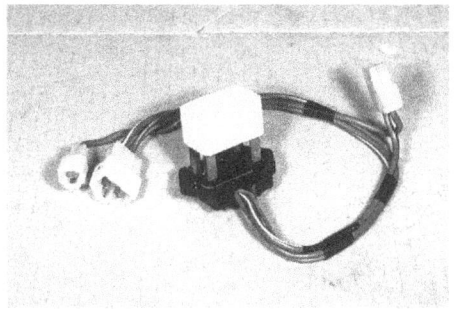

11/1b ... and lift the blower resistor from casing.

away. Fit the new unit to the underside of the casing, securing it with its screws, then fit the connectors to their clips and reconnect the wiring. Check that the blower system works normally before fitting the glovebox.

12. BLOWER MOTOR - REMOVAL & INSTALLATION

☞ 1/1, 2 & 6/1.

1   If the motor is inoperative, you will have to fit a new one; it is not possible to dismantle or repair it. Remove the two sheet metal screws which secure the glovebox hinges to the hinge bar. Open the glovebox and lift it out of the dashboard. With the glovebox out of the way you have good access to the blower unit. Unplug the single motor wiring connector from the underside of the motor casing, then remove the three sheet metal screws which retain the blower motor unit to the bottom of the blower casing. The motor and its integral fan can now be lifted away.

2   Fit the new motor to the underside of the blower casing - noting that it only fits in one position - and tighten the retaining screws evenly. Reconnect the motor wiring and check that the blower works on all settings before installing the glovebox.

13. BLOWER UNIT - REMOVAL & INSTALLATION

☞ 1/1, 2 & 6/1.

1   Given the easy access to the blower motor and resistor block, it is hard to imagine any real need to remove the complete unit, other than for general access to the area around the unit. Apart from the blower motor and resistor block covered in the preceding sections, the blower unit consists of the main casing and a flap valve arrangement used to select either fresh air or recirculated air or a mixture of the two. This is operated from the control unit at the center of the dash panel.

2   To remove the unit, first detach the glovebox by removing the two sheet metal screws which secure the hinges to the hinge bar. The glovebox can then be lifted out of the dash panel, leaving a large access aperture.

3   ◘+ Working in the footwell area, trace the control cable back to the spring clip which anchors the cable outer to the unit. Pop this out of

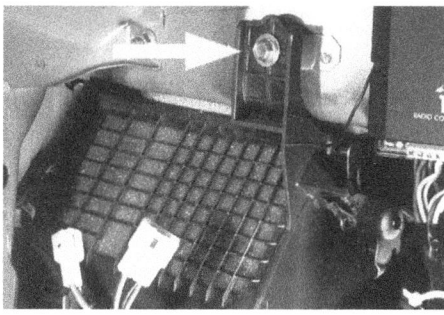

13/3a Blower unit upper mounting.

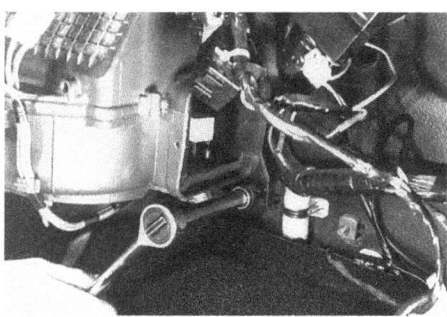

13/3b One of blower unit lower mountings.

13/3c Lift out blower unit.

the clip, then unhook the wire loop from the operating lever. Disconnect the two wiring connectors from the side of the unit (there is no need to disconnect the wiring which runs down to the blower motor). The unit can be removed from the car after releasing the two 10mm nuts and single 10mm bolt which secure it to its mounting points below the dash panel. On standard cars, note that the trunking linking the blower unit to the heater unit should be disconnected after withdrawing the plastic pin which anchors it. On air conditioned cars, the A/C cooling unit fits in place of the trunking, the join between it and the blower unit being secured by an over-center clip band. Flip the tab of the clip to free the connection.

4   There is little that you can do with the unit once removed, but it's worth checking the operation of the flap valve arrangement. If you operate this by hand you'll see how the mechanism has a cam arrangement, which seals the flap firmly at each end of its travel. This relies on the foam layer on each side of the flap, the resilience of which allows the cam system to obtain a good seal. We can envisage that ageing of the foam might lead to deterioration of the seal - you may be able to recondition the flap by purchasing some thin foam

sheeting from a hardware store and sticking it to each side of the flap, once the remains of the old foam have been cleaned off. Check with the foam supplier that the adhesive used is suitable for use on plastic materials. Note that a similar foam seal is fitted around the aperture at the top of the casing which connects to the fresh air inlet. The flap can be removed from the unit after releasing the single screw which retains the operating link.

5   When installing the unit, tighten the fasteners evenly to avoid distorting the plastic housing. Reconnect the operating cable, noting that the lever on the control panel should be set to fresh air rather than recirculated air before the cable is connected. Check that, after the cable has been connected, the mechanism moves fully between the fresh and recirculated air positions when the control lever is operated. Reconnect the wiring connectors and check blower operation on all settings. Check that the trunking/air conditioning cooling unit joint is secure, then install the glovebox.

14. HEATER UNIT - REMOVAL, INSPECTION AND INSTALLATION

☞ 1/1, 2 & 6/1.

REMOVAL

1   The heater unit is installed below the dashboard at the center of the car, access for its removal requiring removal of the dashboard assembly; a complicated procedure not to be undertaken lightly. We know of no workarounds here. Access to the operating cables, one on each side of the unit, is possible through the glovebox aperture and by removing the access cover below the steering column.

2   Drain the cooling system (☞ 6/2). You now need to remove the dashboard from the car. As mentioned above, this is a time-consuming and complex procedure - be sure that you leave adequate time for the job. If you know that you need to fit a new unit, you should have this ready to be fitted, or the car will have to remain off the road until you obtain a new one. Removal and installation procedure for the dashboard ☞ 10.

3   Once the dashboard has been removed, the heater unit is relatively easy to deal with. From the engine compartment, locate the two hose connections to the heater stubs which project through the firewall. Using pliers, squeeze the ears of the hose clips and slide them along the hoses, clear of the stubs. Use a screwdriver blade to push each hose off its stub, marking one stub and hose to ensure that they are refitted correctly. Allow any residual coolant to drain out of the stubs.

4   ◘+ Inside the car, the heater control cables will have been detached during removal of the dash panel. Remove the trunking (non-air con cars) by pulling out the small pin which retains it. On air conditioned models, release the heater to cooling unit by flipping the tab of the over-center clip which secures the joint between the two. Remove the two 10mm nuts at the top rear of the heater unit and the single 10mm nut at the lower

Mazda Miata, MX-5, Eunos & Roadster

14/4a One of heater unit top mountings.

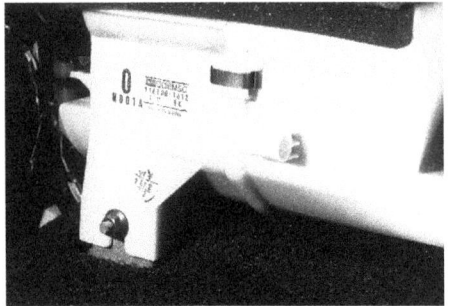

14/4b Heater unit lower mounting.

> **Oh no! The heater's leaking ...**
> *If you ever have the misfortune of having the heater matrix spring a leak on you while driving, you can minimize damage if you act quickly. First, pull off the road so that you can work on the car in safety. As quickly as you can, open the hood and wrap thick rag over the radiator cap, then turn it counter-clockwise to the first stop to release cooling system pressure - this will slow the leak to a trickle and you can then work more calmly. It is a good idea to allow the cooling system to cool down for a while - take this time to mop up inside the car as best you can. When the system is cool enough to handle safely, use pliers to slide back the clips which secure the hoses to the heater stubs at the firewall. Work the pipes off the stubs with a screwdriver blade. If you have something in the car that you can push into the open ends of the hoses (maybe a couple of large bolts or rods), do so, then refit the clips to secure and close the hose ends. Otherwise, trace the hoses back to where they connect to the water thermosensor housing on the back of the engine, and to the return pipe which runs forward below the exhaust manifold. You now need to connect the two pipe ends together. Use the pipe from the thermosensor housing, bending it round to connect to the return pipe end, having first removed its hose. Don't worry too much about kinking the hose - the object is to take the heater out of the cooling system but to maintain circulation for engine cooling.*
> *Once you've done this, try to find water to top up the cooling system (use the water in the screen washer reservoir if you need to, or even mineral water), then refit the radiator cap and run the engine to check for leaks. If all is well, you can continue your journey - the car can be used like this until you can get a new matrix fitted.*

front. The unit is now free to be removed, but, before pulling the stubs back through the firewall, try to tip the unit back a little to empty remaining coolant. We also suggest that you put some rag over the carpet - there will be some coolant spillage and this may contain sediment that could cause staining.

DISMANTLING AND INSPECTION

5   The heater unit is handed depending on whether the car is left- or right-hand drive. On left-hand drive models, the heater matrix is fitted from the left, while on right-hand drive cars it fits from the right. The various linkages are handed accordingly. The linkages and the various flap valves in the unit are great fun to play around with - it's worth doing so before you start any dismantling so that you form a picture of how they operate - this could help during assembly.

6   You need to remove the linkages from each side of the unit before the heater matrix can be removed. The arrangement is shown in the line drawing accompanying this section - study this carefully before you start to avoid confusion later! Remove the linkages and put them to one side, preferably marked left and right side for identification.

7   Separate the casing halves after prying off the spring clips which secure the join. Place some rag over the clips as you lever them off to prevent their escape. With the unit on its side, separate the casing halves, trying to leave the flap valves in position in the lower half. Release the heater matrix pipe clamps and lift the matrix out of the casing.

8   The heater matrix is the vital component in the unit, and should be closely scrutinized. Accumulated debris on the outside of the matrix can be removed by washing or blowing it through with compressed air. Check carefully for signs of leakage. We would recommend that even a slight leak is good cause for fitting a new unit. Remember how long it took you to get at the heater unit, and ask yourself whether you want to go through the procedure again. No? - nor us. Also consider the hassle if the heater suddenly sprang a major leak in service, and the damage to the car's interior that might be caused.

9   Connect a garden hose to one of the matrix stubs and run water through it. This will probably expel some sediment, but the important thing to check is that the water flows freely. If the matrix is restricted, it is probably partially blocked - poor heater function would suggest this. If so, the best option is to fit a new matrix.

10   We suggest that you do not disturb the operating linkage without good cause. There is provision for coarse adjustment on some of the link rods - these have threaded ends held in plastic clips - but this is intended for the initial set-up of the flap interconnection during assembly of the unit, not later adjustment. If you do need to disturb the linkages, we suggest that you place the assembly on a sheet of paper and trace around it as an assembly template. In the case of adjustable link rods, mark their position with paint or typist's correcting fluid before you remove them, and exactly duplicate this setting during reassembly.

11   The flap valves can be left in the casing unless you need to remove them for some reason. If you do, make a sketch of their positions and mark the visible end of each one to assist you during

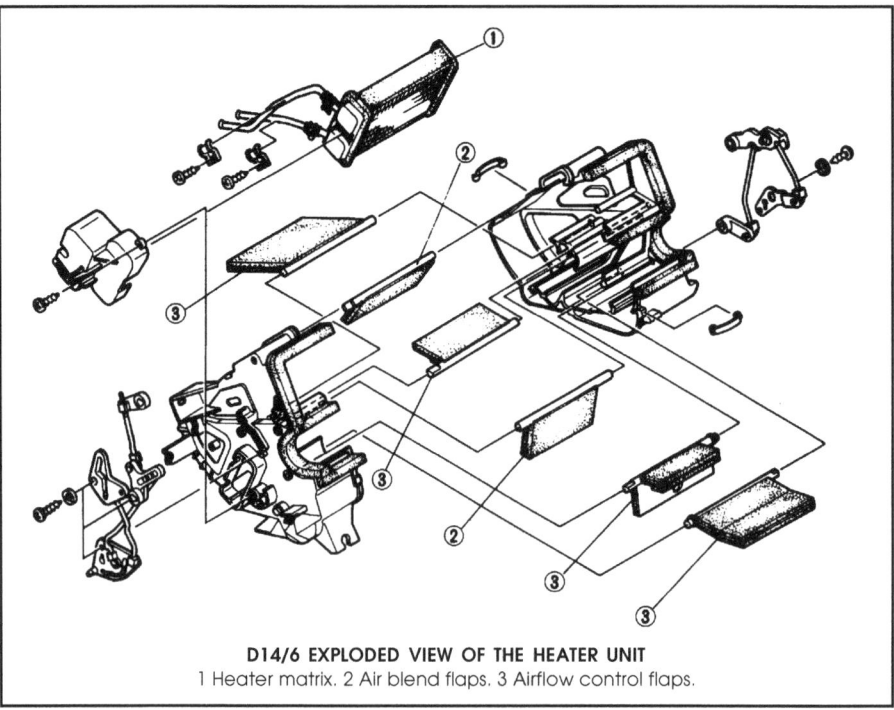

D14/6 EXPLODED VIEW OF THE HEATER UNIT
1 Heater matrix. 2 Air blend flaps. 3 Airflow control flaps.

6: Cooling, heating & air conditioning systems

assembly. If possible, remove just one flap at a time to avoid confusion. The flaps and casing should not normally require attention, but if the foam covering on the flaps has begun to break up, the selection of the various vent outlets will be a little imprecise. You could consider fitting new foam - try a hardware store for thin foam sheeting and a suitable adhesive.

REASSEMBLY AND INSTALLATION

12   Fit any of the vent flaps removed, checking that they are fitted in their correct relative positions and move freely. Install the heater matrix and fit the pipe securing clips. Close the two halves of the housing, guiding the vent flaps into position before securing the two halves with the spring clips. Fit the operating linkages at each end of the unit, checking that the vent flaps locate correctly and that, when assembly is complete, the mechanism operates normally.

13   When installing the unit in the car, feed the heater stubs through the firewall and locate the lugs over the mounting studs. Tighten the fixing nuts securely, but do not overtighten. Reconnect the trunking or cooling unit connection (depending on the equipment fitted to your car). Reconnect the heater pipes to the stubs in the engine compartment and fit the securing clips.

14   Reinstall the dashboard (☞ 10). When connecting the heater unit cables, you'll find it helpful to move the control unit sliders to the positions which allow easiest reconnection.

15. HEATER/AIR CON CONTROL ASSEMBLY - REMOVAL, INSPECTION & INSTALLATION

☞ 1/1, 2 & 6/1.

1   Isolate the electrical system by disconnecting the battery negative (-) terminal, after first having disarmed the audio unit's security system, if applicable. **Warning!** When loosening the negative (-) terminal, take great care not to short the tool you are using across the positive (+) terminal (for more information ☞ 7). To gain access to the heater/air conditioning control assembly it's necessary to remove the console between the seats, and also the center console ☞ 10.

2   With the centre console out of the way, you'll find that the heater control unit is retained by four sheet metal screws. Once these have been removed, the control unit will be loose in the center console recess, located over pegs in the plastic moulding. Pull the unit toward you, feeding the control cables through from under the dashboard as you do so - they are quite stiff and will tend to snag. Once you can reach behind the unit, locate and unplug the wiring connector/s and lift away.

INSPECTION

3   ◨+ If cable replacement was your objective in removing the control unit, you can go ahead and do it at this stage. Each cable is secured to the control unit by a clamp, the inner wire being attached by either a circular eye or a simple stepped end to its lever. The knobs on the lever ends just pull off the levers, and the levers themselves are

15/3a Two cables at top of control unit ...

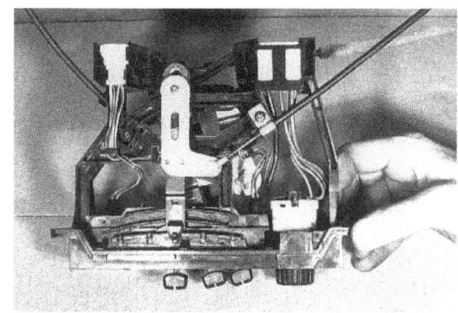

15/3b ... and one underneath.

retained by screws and guide blocks. Our photographs, plus the exploded view of the unit, will help you identify how it all fits together, but it is quite complex. We suggest that you study how the lever system operates before dismantling anything - the levers use a neat arrangement which makes the ends slide across their travel instead of moving through a small arc as you would expect, and this makes for a little extra complication. We further recommend that you deal with one lever assembly and cable at a time to avoid any confusion.

4   ◨+ To remove the blower switch, pull off

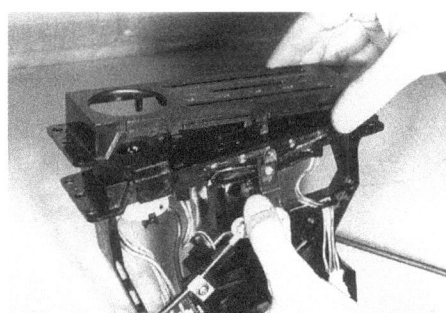

15/4a Unclip the front panel ...

15/4b ... peel off the thin facia plate ...

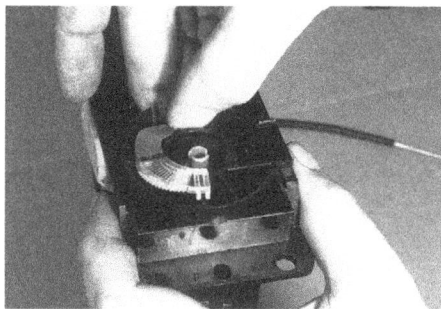

15/5 ... lift out light guide prism ...

the lever and switch knobs and unclip the front panel from the unit. Carefully peel away the thin facia plate - this has a self-adhesive backing.

5   ◨ Underneath you'll find an interesting piece of clear plastic with tiny prisms on the front surface. This is a light guide carrying illumination from a nearby light to the back of the switch surround - the prisms ensure even lighting.

6   ◨+ Lift the light guide out to reveal the two screws which secure the switch. Remove the screws to free the switch, unclipping the wiring connector from the back of the control assembly.

15/6a ... unscrew two securing screws ...

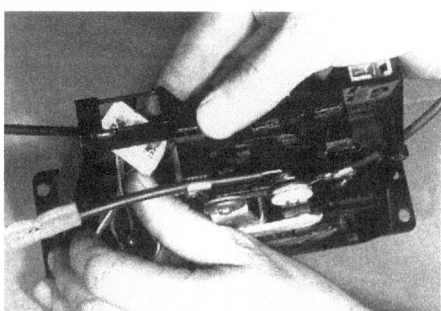

15/6b ... and release the wiring connector.

7   Finally, whatever else you do while the unit is out, we recommend that you check all the bulbs and replace any that are burned out - there would be a lot of work to be done all over again if you missed this opportunity and noticed the problem later.

CHECKING THE BLOWER & AIR CONDITIONING SWITCH

8   The operation of the blower/air conditioning switch can be checked after the heater control assembly has been removed as described above.

Mazda Miata, MX-5, Eunos & Roadster

Position		Terminal							
		a	b	c	d	e	f	g	h
Blower switch	OFF								
	First	O					O		
	Second		O					O—O	
	Third				O			O—O	
	Fourth			O				O—O	
A/C switch	OFF								
	ON	O—►|—O		O—►|—O			O		

O—O : Indicates continuity
O—►|—O : Indicates diode

D15/9 CHECKING BLOWER & AIR CONDITIONING SWITCH.

15/9 Testing blower and a/c switch.

9 📷 🔧 Use a continuity checker or a multimeter set to a resistance range to check for continuity at the various switch positions. These are shown in the accompanying diagram and table. Note that, in the case of the air conditioning switch (where fitted), there are diodes fitted between the terminal pairs. This means that continuity should be shown in one direction, with no continuity if the test probes are reversed.

INSTALLATION

10 Check that the control unit is reassembled correctly and that the control sliders and cables operate normally. Fit the light guide in the front of the unit, then clip the front panel into place and fit the slider and switch knobs. Install the control unit in the center console, connecting the wiring connectors and feeding the control cables into position. The cables cannot easily be connected incorrectly; the longest cable runs to the blower unit (recirculating or fresh air control), while the remaining two have different ends and fit either side of the heater unit.

11 Before you connect the cables, you should set up the control sliders as follows: set the top slider (temperature blend control) to the maximum heat position (fully to the right). The center slider (recirculated or fresh air control) should be set fully to the right. Set the bottom slider (airflow mode control) fully to the left. After reconnecting the cables, check that the control levers move smoothly and fully through their complete range. Once you are satisfied the controls operate normally, secure the unit with the four sheet metal screws (where fitted).

12 You can now install the center console front panel, remembering to reconnect the wiring to the stereo (don't forget the antenna cable), the clock, the hazard light/headlight lifter switches and any other accessories installed in the panel. Make sure that you route the wiring correctly, and that it does not become trapped as the panel is fitted. We strongly suggest that, before finally securing the panel, you check the operation of all electrical switches and accessories. Only when you are sure that these are operating correctly should you fit the two retaining screws through the eyeball sockets, and the two lower screws securing the panel to the transmission tunnel bracket.

13 Pop the vents back into their sockets (note how easily they install - you might assume that they are not fitted correctly, but just try pulling them out again). Fit the steering column access panel and the glovebox. Install the rear console, remembering to reconnect the ashtray light wire and, where fitted, the window winder switch connector.

16. AIR CONDITIONING SYSTEM - CHECKING

☞ 1/1, 2 & 6/1.

Warning! Skin contact with refrigerant contained in the air conditioning system could result in frostbite.
Warning! Combustion or heating of refrigerant will produce toxic gas.
Warning! Discharge to the atmosphere of refrigerant is **ILLEGAL** in most countries, and immoral in all.
Warning! Under no circumstances attempt disconnection of any part of the air conditioning system unless it has been professionally discharged and you have been told it is safe to do so. (See 'Precautions').
Caution! For 1995 models and up, the refrigerant used in the air conditioning system was changed to R-134a, which is said to be more environmentally-friendly. Earlier models used R-12 refrigerant. The two types of refrigerant, and the oils used with them, are non-compatible.

1 🔧 As mentioned at the start of this chapter, air conditioning is offered as an option on these cars. The system, where fitted, integrates with the standard heating and ventilation system; the compressor mounts on the left side of the engine and is connected by pipes and hoses to the cooling unit and condenser (radiator), which is secured to the front of the cooling system radiator. An additional electric fan is fitted to improve the airflow through the double radiators, and is switched via the ECM/PCM.

2 Inside the car, the pipework to and from the condenser passes through the firewall (bulkhead) and into the cooling unit (evaporator), which is mounted under the dashboard, on the passenger side of the car. This unit simply replaces the plastic ducting used on non-air conditioned cars, and connects directly between the heater and blower units.

PRECAUTIONS

3 Almost any mechanical work on the air conditioning system requires that the refrigerant is

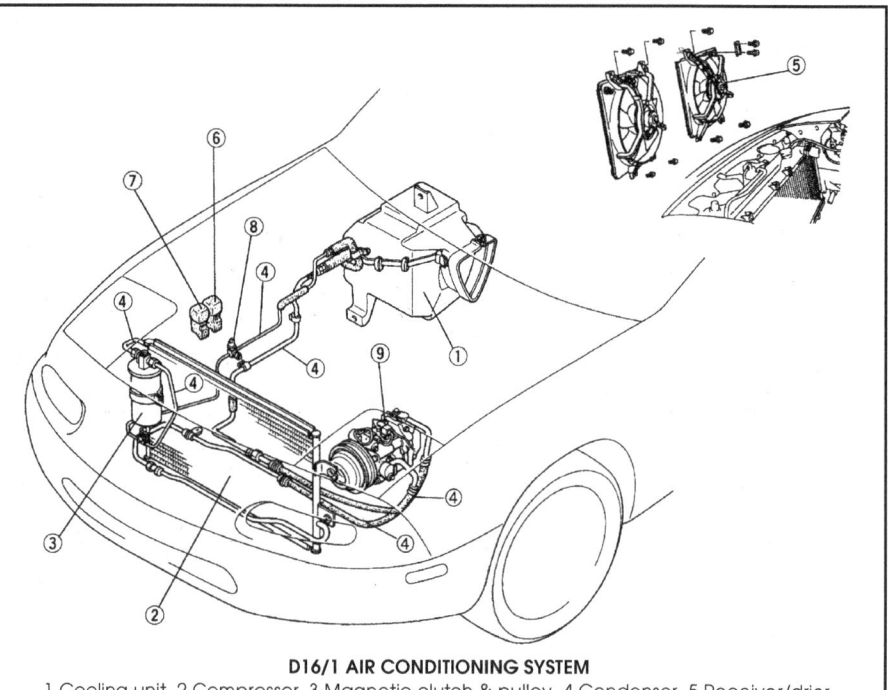

D16/1 AIR CONDITIONING SYSTEM
1 Cooling unit. 2 Compressor. 3 Magnetic clutch & pulley. 4 Condenser. 5 Receiver/drier.
6 A/C relay. 7 Condenser fan relay. 8 Refrigerant pressure switch. 9 A/C compressor.

6: Cooling, heating & air conditioning systems

first discharged into a commercial recovery unit, and that the system is later recharged and its operation tested professionally. Although R-134a refrigerant recharging kits are available for non-professional use, we do not recommend them because of the safety/environmental implications. Under no circumstances should the system be vented to the atmosphere.

4   You should also be aware of the risk of personal injury posed by contact with the refrigerant; any contact with the skin will result in localized frostbite, and suitable protective clothing must be worn at all times. Also, contact between the refrigerant and flame/heat will produce an extremely toxic gas. Given the high cost of the equipment required to handle the refrigerant, and the attendant health and safety risks, we consider that all such work should be carried out professionally, either by a suitably equipped Mazda dealer, or by a qualified air conditioning specialist.

5   We regret that we are unable to cover mechanical procedures in greater depth, but feel that personal safety and environmental considerations preclude this. This section covers preliminary checks of peripheral equipment only.

VISUAL CHECK OF REFRIGERANT CHARGE

6   A quick check of the refrigerant charge can be made by opening the hood and observing the sight glass which is located on top of the receiver/drier unit, and visible through the circular access hole in the panel in front of the radiator.

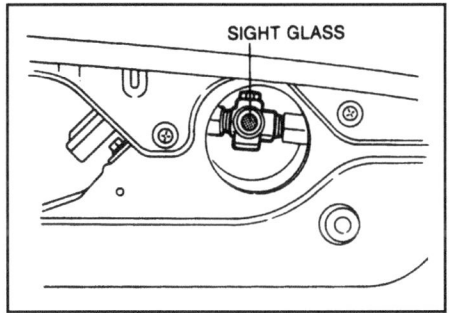

D16/6 LOCATION OF A/C SIGHT GLASS IN FRONT PANEL OF ENGINE COMPARTMENT.

7   Start the engine, and run it at a fast idle for a few minutes. Meanwhile, the air conditioning should be run at maximum cooling with the doors open or the top down. Check the refrigerant visible in the sight glass: if the charge is correct, no bubbles/foam should be seen. Bubbles in the refrigerant usually indicate insufficient charge, though they may be present if the ambient air temperature is extremely high.

8   Immediately the air conditioning is turned off, the refrigerant in the sight glass should foam, then become clear. If there is no foaming, the refrigerant charge is excessive. If you find indications that the refrigerant charge is incorrect, have the system checked professionally and recharged as required.

CHECKING THERMOSWITCH OPERATION

9   The thermoswitch monitors the temperature of the evaporator in the cooling unit, the switch contacts being open below 0°C (32°F) and closed above this temperature. To check the operation of the switch, remove the glovebox by unscrewing the two sheet metal screws which retain it to the hinge bar. Lift away the glovebox to reveal the cooling unit mounted between the blower and heater units. Release the over-centre clip on the seal between the cooling unit and the heater and slide the seal to the heater side. Insert a thermometer through the gap between the cooling unit and the heater.

10   Start the engine and allow it to idle for a few minutes, with the air conditioning switch turned off and the blower set to maximum. After a few minutes, turn off the blower switch and stop the engine. Locate and disconnect the thermoswitch wiring connector at the heater side of the cooling unit. Connect a continuity tester or a multimeter set to a resistance range to the switch terminals (see illustration). A continuity reading should be indicated. If the engine is now run again with the air conditioning switched on, the thermoswitch contacts should open as the cooling unit reaches 0°C (32°F). If the results are not as indicated, have the cooling unit removed and the thermoswitch checked further and replaced if required.

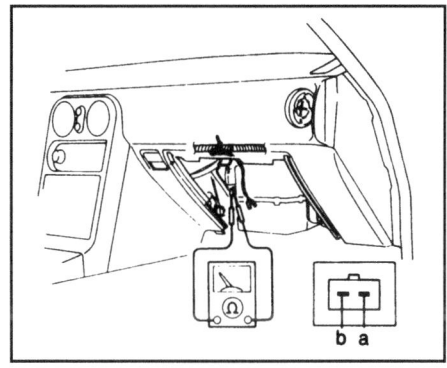

D16/10 CHECKING THERMOSWITCH AT CONNECTOR.

CHECKING SYSTEM FITTINGS AND REFRIGERANT LINES

11   Check the cooling system components and refrigerant lines, paying particular attention to any sign of staining around any of the pipe or hose unions. If staining is noted, a leak is indicated, and the car should be taken to a Mazda dealer or air conditioning specialist for testing with a gas leak tester. If necessary, have the system discharged, the faulty joint, union or line replaced/repaired, and the system recharged and tested.

CHECKING THE CONDENSER COOLING FAN

12   See 6/8.

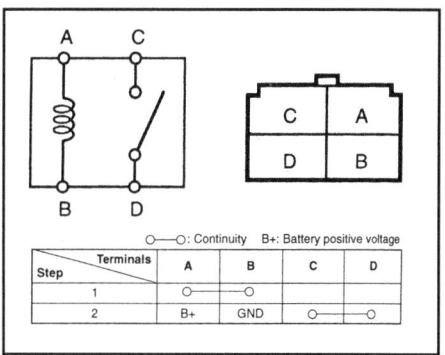

D16/14 AIR CONDITIONING SYSTEM RELAY CHECKING.
GND = ground (earth).

CHECKING THE AIR CONDITIONING RELAY

13   If the air conditioning system refuses to operate, it is possible that the air conditioning relay is faulty.

14   Unplug the relay (see illustration D16/1 for location) and, using a multimeter, carry out the continuity checks detailed in the accompanying illustration. If continuity is not as specified, the relay must be replaced.

MAGNETIC CLUTCH CHECKS

15   The air conditioning compressor operation is controlled by a magnetic clutch, which is switched on under certain operating conditions: the air conditioning and blower switches must be turned on and the engine must be running. This information is sensed by the ECM/PCM, which establishes a ground circuit to the air conditioning relay. The relay operates, applying battery voltage to the magnetic clutch. The clutch is then locked up and the system operates.

16   If the magnetic clutch appears to be inoperative, check the following items in sequence:

- Check the **WIPER (20A)** fuse housed in the fusebox inside the car.
- Check the **AD FAN (20A)** fuse housed in the fusebox in the engine compartment.

If either of the fuses has burned out, check the wiring for shorts and repair as necessary before fitting a new fuse.

17   Check the air conditioning system relay as previously described.

18   If the fuses check out OK, open the hood and disconnect the single pin wire connector of the a/c compressor. Apply 12 volts to the terminal on the compressor side of the connector and ground (earth) to the compressor body. The magnetic clutch should operate; if it doesn't, it needs to be replaced.

19   If you are unable to diagnose and correct the fault using the above sequence, you'll have to have the system checked by a Mazda dealer, who will be able to perform a refrigerant pressure switch test and fit a new switch if necessary.

6:13

Notes

7

Electrical system

1. INTRODUCTION

For a little car, Mazda's roadster sure has a big electrical system! When we set about producing this book, we decided against the conventional approach of putting every electrical subsystem and component together in one chapter: it would have been a huge and complicated part of the book and confusing to try to work from. In this chapter, then, we look at the purely electrical items like the charging and starting systems, plus lighting and signalling. If you've just turned to this chapter with an electrical problem and you don't find it described here, refer to the chapter of the book which seems most relevant.

On these cars, electrical subsystems interconnect to a large degree, many having the PCM (powertrain control module) in common. For example, you may have turned to this chapter to try to work out why the air conditioning condenser fan won't run. Mostly, this will be covered in chapter 6, but it just might be refusing to run because of a PCM problem, which you'll find covered in chapter 5. We're sorry about this, but it's down to the inter-relationship of components and systems which are so much a feature of modern cars.

2. ELECTRICAL SYSTEM - PROCEDURES, PRECAUTIONS & JUMP STARTING

1   Before you tackle work on the electrical system, you should read through this section which will give you some useful advice and some important information that could save you damaging components or assemblies - or yourself. Remember that the car depends on the PCM to function - if this unit, or any subsidiary electronic unit, is damaged by bad testing procedures, you could immobilize the car and land yourself with a major repair bill. **Note**: throughout this chapter the terms 'V_B' or '$B+$' mean battery voltage, and 'V_0' means zero voltage.

ISOLATING & RECONNECTING BATTERY

2   **Caution!** You should always isolate the battery from the electrical system before commencing work on the car, unless the particular task requires that the electrical system remains live. This practice avoids any risk of damage to electronic components, or to your test equipment.

3   **Caution!** Note that many modern audio systems are security coded - if the power supply to the unit is interrupted, and you don't have the security code number, the unit won't operate when the supply is restored. Check the audio unit manufacturer's instructions. **Caution!** Many cars are fitted with intruder alarms designed to go off if the electrical supply is terminated. Usually, the manufacturers of such systems provide a key or code to allow the alarm to be disabled: check the manufacturer's instructions.

4   **Caution!** Some work on the car's fuel system will require the fuel sytem to be depressurised; this procedure requires a live electrical system so, if applicable, depressurise the fuel system before disconnecting the battery.

2/5 Disconnect battery negative (-) terminal.

5   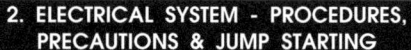 Open the trunk (boot). Undo the 13mm plastic nut holding the battery cover to the bodyshell near the rear lamp lens: this can usually be done with your fingers. Lift the battery cover off the poppers along its base and remove it. Using a 10mm crescent or box-end wrench, slacken the battery negative (-) terminal clamp fixing, and pull the clamp off the terminal post. If you decide to use a socket for this, be very careful that the extension bar does not short against the positive (+) terminal (normally protected by a plastic cover). You don't need to remove the remaining wire. **Warning!** Once disconnected, make sure the negative terminal clamp cannot swing back onto its terminal post.

6   When reconnecting the battery, apply a little petroleum jelly (Vaseline) to the battery post before refitting the negative (-) terminal clamp and tightening it securely. Note that the battery cover retaining nut is designed to be pushed on.

ELECTRICAL TEST EQUIPMENT

7   Work on the electrical system will require a few pieces of equipment in addition to normal hand tools - we're not getting into oscilloscope territory here, just basic additions to your toolkit, which you may well have already.

8   You will need a simple test lamp arrangement which you can make up yourself using easily obtained materials. The basic requirement is for a 12 volt bulb rated at between 1.4 and 3.4 watts (don't exceed this value or you could damage electronic circuits). Connect to it two test leads. Ideally, get a bulb in a bulbholder, like an accessory warning lamp from an auto part store - this will prevent the bulb getting damaged in use and make connection of the leads easier. If you want to make a professional job of it, buy a couple of probe leads (the finer the probes, the better) from an electronics hobby shop, and attach these to the test lamp. As an alternative, most auto parts stores will sell you a ready-made tester - these are often in the form of a screwdriver-shaped tester with a built-in lamp, and a single test lead and probe.

9   Many of the tests need either an ohmmeter or a voltmeter. We recommend an inexpensive multimeter, of the sort which will allow you to do volt, ohm and current (amps) checks and, maybe, has a continuity checker in the form of a buzzer. This last feature is great - you can check for continuity without having to look at the meter; indispensable in awkward or confined spaces. We

7:1

Mazda Miata, MX-5, Eunos & Roadster

got by with the standard probes supplied with our meter, but finer probe ends would be useful for getting in the back of the wiring connectors - some of these have very small terminal pins and you risk damage if the probes are too big. Again, pick these up at electronic hobby stores. **Caution!** Never do resistance or continuity checks while the car's battery is connected. If you make a mistake, you can zap your meter.

10 You'll need one or two jumper wires. These are simple insulated wires with either probe or miniature clip ends which allow you to make temporary connections during testing. You can improvise these with odd lengths of electrical wire, but we reckon it's worth buying proper jumper wires, again, from an electronics hobby shop.

WIRING CONNECTORS

11 You will find many types of these. Most are superficially similar, with varying numbers of pins. They differ in design and pin configuration to prevent you from making incorrect wiring connections. You should always tag both sides of a connector when disconnecting more than one section of wiring, or you will end up wasting a lot of time when you come to remake the connections later.

12 Most connectors have a latching arrangement which stops them from coming apart in service. In most cases, they also have some sort of

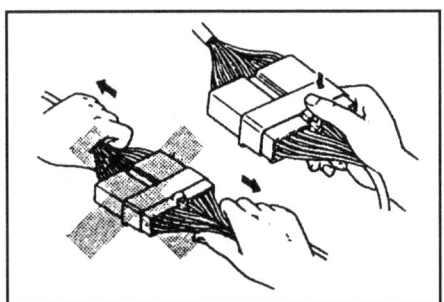

D2/12 DON'T PULL WIRING TO SEPARATE CONNECTOR!

key built in, so they can only be assembled one way. To separate the connector halves, find the latch tab and either depress or lift it (depending on the design), then grasp the connector halves and pull them apart. **Caution!** Never pull the wiring when doing this, or you may damage the wiring or connector pins. When closing connectors, make sure you hear them click shut, indicating that they are properly latched.

13 Some electrical tests are made with the connector unplugged (for example, switch continuity checks), while others require the connector to be plugged together. This dictates how and where you use the meter probes. **Caution!** In general, you should insert the probes from the *back* of the connector wherever possible - this minimizes the risk of damaging the terminals. An exception to this rule is waterproof connectors - where these are used the joint between connector and wire is sealed so you cannot access the back, and tests have to be made from the front of the connector.

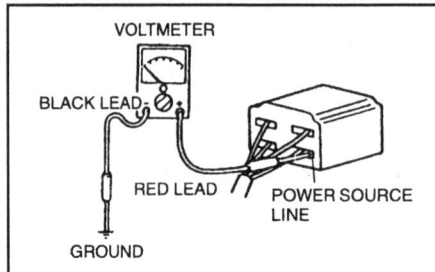

D2/13 INSERT PROBE ON WIRING SIDE OF CONNECTOR.

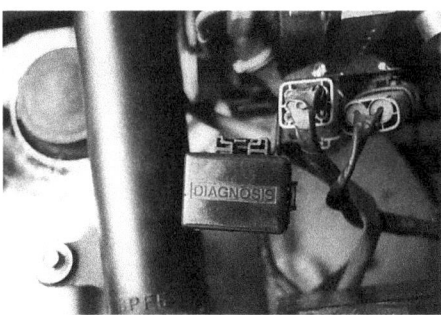

2/14a The data link connector unit.

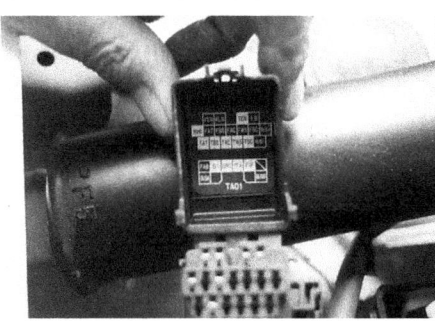

2/14b Data link terminal identification.

2/14c Data link terminals.

14 A special case is the data link connector, which you will encounter many times when working on various electrical systems on the car. This unit will be found under the hood (bonnet) on the left-hand inner fender (wing). It has a hinged cover, clearly marked "**DIAGNOSIS**," and inside the lid is a diagram (see photo) showing the terminal identification. The primary use of this connector is to hook up Special Service Tools (SSTs) for self-diagnosis procedures. You can, however, get by with a simple jumper wire in many cases - we will indicate in the text where it is possible and describe

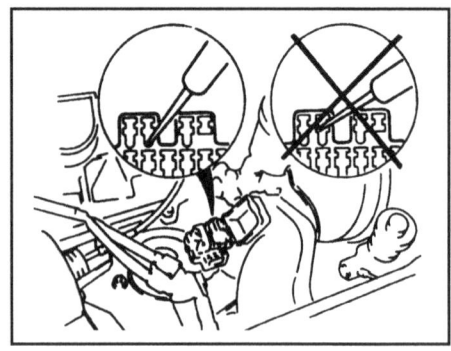

D2/14 HOW TO INSERT JUMPER WIRE.

the terminals to be jumped. **Caution!** To avoid damage to the diagnosis connector terminals (which might make subsequent SST connection impossible), you should always fit jumpers into the service hole of the terminal, not into the main terminal hole - see the accompanying illustration for guidance.

15 When checking connectors, always make a point of pulling *gently* on each wire to ensure that it is secure in the connector body. Each terminal pin or socket is latched into the connector's plastic body by a small tab: you'll need to depress this if you want to remove a terminal pin or socket for replacement or checking. The accompanying diagram shows how to release the two types of terminals: we use a set of jeweler's screwdrivers to reach and release the locking tabs.

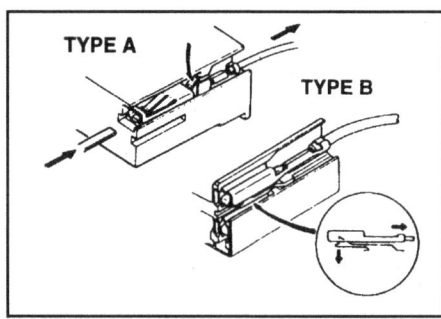

D2/15 PULL INDIVIDUAL WIRES GENTLY TO CHECK SECURITY.

WIRING AND COLOR CODING

16 The Mazda's wiring is color coded and abbreviations are used to describe each of the individual colors used. We have stuck to Mazda's abbreviations throughout this book, so that there should be no confusion on this point (see diagram). Where more than one color is indicated, for example LB/Y, the main wire color is shown first (light blue) and the second, or tracer, color is shown after the slash (yellow). Physical tracing of individual wire is next to impossible on a modular harness system of this complexity (some of the main harness sections we encountered must have held a hundred or more individual wires, all tightly bound into a harness, but spurring off here and there). You can check continuity between each end of a wire within a section of harness, but you can't be certain of its route through several harnesses. If you come across

7: Electrical system

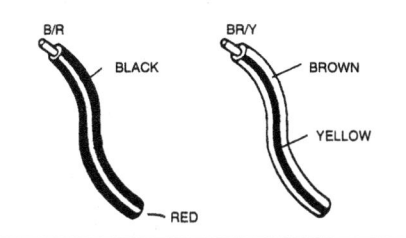

D2/15 WIRE COLOR CODES & TWO EXAMPLES.

a broken wire, your only alternative to fitting a new harness section is to cut off each end of the wire in question, and to add a new wire of the same specification to bypass the damaged one.

17   In fairness, modern wiring (or rather its connections) is of such high quality that you would be unlucky to experience problems in the life of the car. In most cases - unless physical damage to a harness or wire is evident - continuity faults will be found at the wire ends - usually at the connector terminal - or will turn out to be a component failure. If you do find an internally broken or intermittent wire, try to trace the route of that part of the harness, and, with electrical insulation tape, tape a new bypass wire of the same size and, preferably, the same color as the original to the outside of the harness.

18   If you need to add wiring to the car, try to do it intelligently. When fitting accessory items, it is tempting to do the minimum of dismantling to gain access, and this invariably means that later access to some part of the car will be difficult because of straggling wires. Try to use connectors of the type already used on the car, so that panels or assemblies can still be removed for servicing. Be aware that if you patch into existing wiring using Scotchloks or similar 'Piggy Back' type connectors, you may be imposing too much load on that circuit or fuse. Patching in like this is just about unavoidable, but be intelligent about it. For example, if you were foolish enough to hook into the instrument panel lighting circuit to run the rear window demister on your new hardtop, you'll be drawing power through a 10A fuse, so don't be surprised when it blows.

19   📷+ If you need to cut an accessory wire in the course of removing other components, you should reconnect it in a way that allows for subsequent dismantling. We prefer to use screw-type connectors. Cut the wire and bare the ends using an insulation stripping tool. After twisting the bared ends of the wires, fit them into the connector and tighten the screws to secure them.

FUSES AND RELAYS

20   The electrical circuits are protected by fuses (or, in the case of the heater blower motor

pre-1996, a circuit breaker). Note that if a fuse burns out, you should always investigate the fault and repair it before fitting a new fuse. For more information see section 3 of this chapter, and individual details in subsequent sections of this, and other, chapters.

21   In addition to the fuses, there are numerous relays around the car. Some of these are operated by the PCM (ECU), allowing it to handle higher currents than it would otherwise be capable of doing. Others simply react to switch operation, doing the actual switching work while imposing no significant load on the switch contacts. Diagram

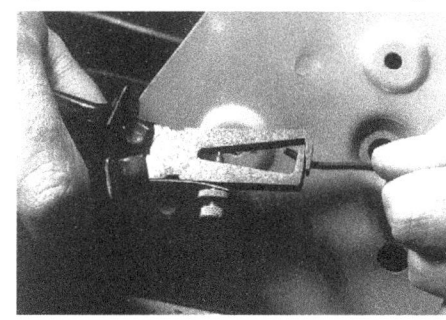

2/19 Bare end of wire ...

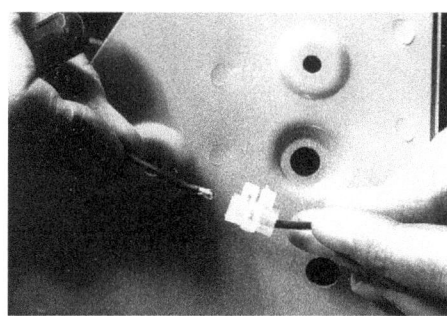

2/19b ... insert into connector ...

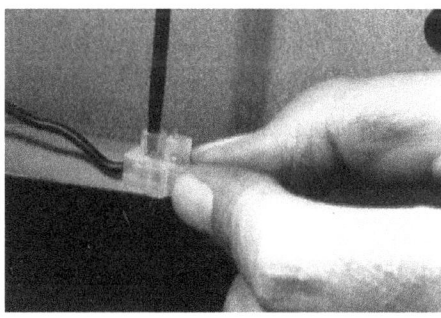

2/19c ... and tighten retaining screw.

2/22 Engine compartment power point.

D3/9 shows the usual locations of major relays.

POWER POINT

22   📷 In the engine compartment will be found (usually just behind the left-hand headlamp) a blue plastic connector with a single terminal. This terminal supplies power at battery voltage for externally powered test equipment, and is protected by the 20A **WIPER** fuse in the fuse block 1.

BOOSTER (JUMP) STARTING

23   If you have starting problems, try eliminating the battery as the cause of the fault by using a spare battery hooked up with jump wires. Open the trunk, and remove the battery cover to get access to the terminal posts. If you are jumping from a battery installed in another vehicle, position it so that the battery is within reach of the jump leads, but make sure that the two vehicles don't touch each other. (This is a precaution in case the other vehicle uses a positive (+) ground electrical system - you can accidentally weld cars together this way, and at the very least will certainly cause damage to one or other of the vehicles' electrical systems.)

24   Connect the red jump wire between the positive (+) terminal posts of both batteries, then carefully connect the black jump wire between the two negative (-) terminals. Be very careful not to ground any of the wire clamps while you're doing this - access around the Mazda's battery is severely restricted. If the car now starts normally, you know that the problem lies with the battery. It may just need charging (☞ 7/5), but if the problem occurs repeatedly, you should check the charging system

---

BUYING BOOSTER (JUMP) CABLES
If you need to buy a set of booster cables (jump leads), it's worth buying the best you can afford. Cheap cables have poor quality clamps, and the cable used usually has several thick strands of aluminum wire. We've used these in the past and they're not really worth having - You'll spend as much time repairing these cables as you do using them. The cables fracture easily, which means that they present a high resistance when you try to jump start with them - the poor quality clamps exacerbate the problem. You can tell if the cables are conducting the starting current well. If they get hot, you're wasting energy heating the cables, instead of using it to turn the starter motor.

Good quality cables are easy to spot - they have heavy, well-made clamps, and the cables are flexible instead of stiff like the aluminum leads. If you look at where the cables attach to the clamps, you'll see a thick bunch of fine copper strands. The more strands and the thicker the bunch, the better the quality. Note also that access above the battery terminal posts on these cars is restricted - try to find cables with short clamps which will fit under the bodywork without risk of shorting.

Mazda Miata, MX-5, Eunos & Roadster

(☞ 7/6).

25 If you succeed in getting the car started, leave the wires connected for a couple of minutes while the engine is running - this will allow the tired battery to charge a little. Turn off the ignition switch, then carefully remove the jump leads, starting with both red ends, or positive (+) wire, then the black, or negative (-) wire. **Caution!** Be very careful not to ground any of the clamps while you do this.

26 The foregoing procedure will usually get you moving if you are stuck on the roadside with a discharged battery, but note that if the charging system is not working correctly, the effect will be limited. Try to get the car home using minimal electrical power. Once the engine is running, it requires minimal electrical power, but the lights, wipers and other electrical systems will soon drain the battery again if the charging system is down. You may get by during daylight, but you won't get far at night like this.

27 Whenever you've had to jump start your car, charge the battery as soon as possible, and monitor its condition regularly for a while. If the battery goes flat repeatedly, check that the charging system is functioning normally (☞ 7/6). If this is OK, the problem lies with a tired battery (check and replace if required), or it indicates that you may be exceeding the capacity of the charging system in some way. A good example is the rear window defroster circuit. This uses a lot of power, and, if left on continuously, would soon flatten the battery - this is why it has a timer circuit. You can impose similar loads on the system without realizing it. If you do a lot of stop/start driving, or spend a lot of your journey in heavy, slow-moving traffic, the normal drain of the lights and wipers, plus the heater blower and stereo, may be just too much for the system to keep up with.

3. FUSES & RELAYS - LOCATION, REMOVAL & REPLACEMENT

☞ 1/1, 2 & 7/2.

1 Most of the electrical subsystems are protected by their own fuse. All cars have at least two fuseboxes. One is mounted in the engine compartment, on the right-hand inner fender (Mazda call this the **"Main Fuse Block"**). It has a lid carrying a label which identifies the positions of the fuses - the exact arrangement varies according to where the car was sold and what electrical options are fitted, though the position of the **MAIN** 80 amp fuse is always the same (see diagram). The block also contains a fuse puller for standard type fuses and, depending on market, may contain some spare fuses.

2 A second fusebox will be found in the passenger compartment and can be reached after removing the access panel beneath the steering column (the panel is secured by two crosshead screws, and is clipped into the dash panel). Mazda call this **"Fuse Block No.1"** - note that in addition to various fuses it also houses a resettable circuit breaker (pre-1996 models only), which protects the heater blower circuit. The block's cover contains a fuse puller and a spare fuse.

3 Many cars have another small fuse box in the trunk, near the base of the radio antenna (**"Fuse Block No.2"**). This contains fuses for the

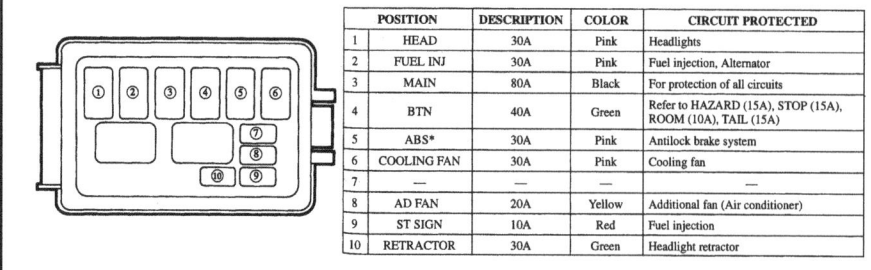

POSITION	DESCRIPTION	FUSE RATING	COLOR	CIRCUIT PROTECTED
1	HEAD	30A	Pink	Headlights
2	FUEL INJ	30A	Pink	Fuel injection, Alternator
3	MAIN	80A	Black	For protection of all circuits
4	BTN	40A	Green	Refer to HAZARD (15A), STOP (15A), ROOM (10A), TAIL (15A)
5	ABS*	30A	Pink	Antilock brake system
6	COOLING FAN	30A	Pink	Cooling fan
7	—	—	—	—
8	AD FAN	20A	Yellow	Additional fan (Air conditioner)
9	ST SIGN	10A	Red	Fuel injection
10	RETRACTOR	30A	Green	Headlight retractor

D3/1A TYPICAL "MAIN FUSE BLOCK" ARRANGEMENT (NORTH AMERICA).
Consult the "Owner's Manual" (handbook) that came with your car for precise arrangement.

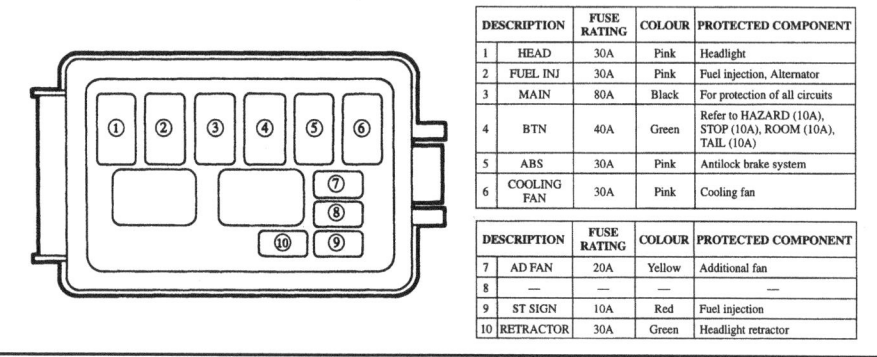

DESCRIPTION	FUSE RATING	COLOUR	PROTECTED COMPONENT
1 HEAD	30A	Pink	Headlight
2 FUEL INJ	30A	Pink	Fuel injection, Alternator
3 MAIN	80A	Black	For protection of all circuits
4 BTN	40A	Green	Refer to HAZARD (10A), STOP (10A), ROOM (10A), TAIL (10A)
5 ABS	30A	Pink	Antilock brake system
6 COOLING FAN	30A	Pink	Cooling fan

DESCRIPTION	FUSE RATING	COLOUR	PROTECTED COMPONENT
7 AD FAN	20A	Yellow	Additional fan
8 —	—	—	—
9 ST SIGN	10A	Red	Fuel injection
10 RETRACTOR	30A	Green	Headlight retractor

D3/1B TYPICAL "MAIN FUSE BLOCK" ARRANGEMENT (RIGHT-HAND DRIVE CARS).
Consult the "Owner's Manual" (handbook) that came with your car for precise arrangement.

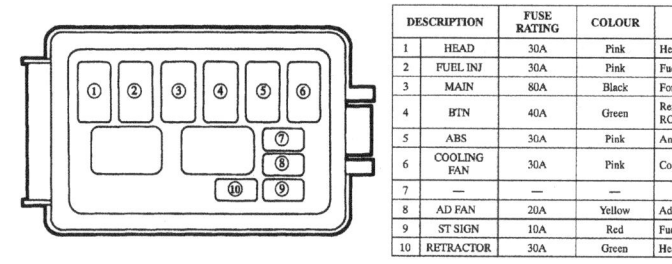

DESCRIPTION	FUSE RATING	COLOUR	PROTECTED COMPONENT
1 HEAD	30A	Pink	Headlight
2 FUEL INJ	30A	Pink	Fuel injection, Alternator
3 MAIN	80A	Black	For protection of all circuits
4 BTN	40A	Green	Refer to HAZARD (10A), STOP (10A), ROOM (10A), TAIL (10A)
5 ABS	30A	Pink	Antilock brake system
6 COOLING FAN	30A	Pink	Cooling fan
7 —	—	—	—
8 AD FAN	20A	Yellow	Additional fan
9 ST SIGN	10A	Red	Fuel injection
10 RETRACTOR	30A	Green	Headlight retractor

D3/1C TYPICAL "MAIN FUSE BLOCK" ARRANGEMENT (LEFT-HAND DRIVE CARS).
Consult the "Owner's Manual" (handbook) that came with your car for precise arrangement.

3/1a Lid (typical) identifies fuse positions/ratings.

3/1b Main Fuse Block layout (typical).

3/2a Blower circuit breaker or fuse.

7: Electrical system

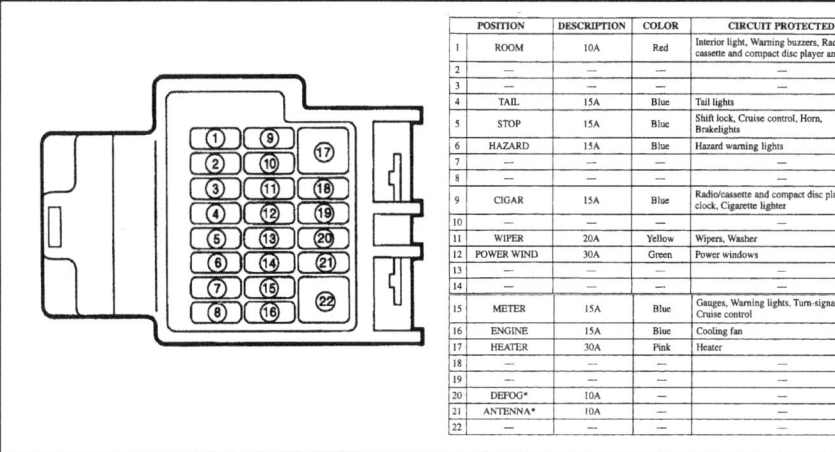

POSITION	DESCRIPTION	COLOR	CIRCUIT PROTECTED
1	ROOM	10A	Red	Interior light, Warning buzzers, Radio/cassette and compact disc player and clock
2	—	—	—	
3	—	—	—	
4	TAIL	15A	Blue	Tail lights
5	STOP	15A	Blue	Shift lock, Cruise control, Horn, Brakelights
6	HAZARD	15A	Blue	Hazard warning lights
7	—	—	—	
8	—	—	—	
9	CIGAR	15A	Blue	Radio/cassette and compact disc player and clock, Cigarette lighter
10	—	—	—	
11	WIPER	20A	Yellow	Wipers, Washer
12	POWER WIND	30A	Green	Power windows
13	—	—	—	
14	—	—	—	
15	METER	15A	Blue	Gauges, Warning lights, Turn-signal lights, Cruise control
16	ENGINE	15A	Blue	Cooling fan
17	HEATER	30A	Pink	Heater
18	—	—	—	
19	—	—	—	
20	DEFOG*	10A	—	
21	ANTENNA*	10A	—	
22	—	—	—	

D3/2A TYPICAL "FUSE BLOCK NO.1" ARRANGEMENT (NORTH AMERICA).
Consult the "Owner's Manual" (handbook) that came with your car for precise arrangement.

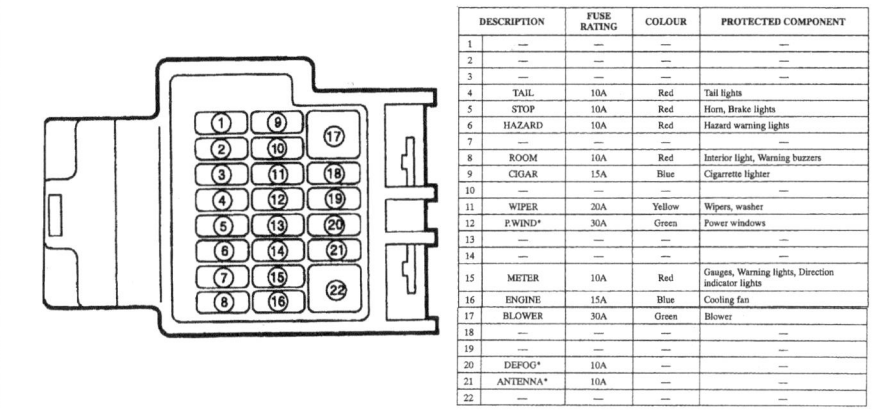

	DESCRIPTION	FUSE RATING	COLOUR	PROTECTED COMPONENT
1	—	—	—	
2	—	—	—	
3	—	—	—	
4	TAIL	10A	Red	Tail lights
5	STOP	10A	Red	Horn, Brake lights
6	HAZARD	10A	Red	Hazard warning lights
7	—	—	—	
8	ROOM	10A	Red	Interior light, Warning buzzers
9	CIGAR	15A	Blue	Cigarette lighter
10	—	—	—	
11	WIPER	20A	Yellow	Wipers, washer
12	P.WIND*	30A	Green	Power windows
13	—	—	—	
14	—	—	—	
15	METER	10A	Red	Gauges, Warning lights, Direction indicator lights
16	ENGINE	15A	Blue	Cooling fan
17	BLOWER	30A	Green	Blower
18	—	—	—	
19	—	—	—	
20	DEFOG*	10A	—	
21	ANTENNA*	10A	—	
22	—	—	—	

D3/2B TYPICAL "FUSE BLOCK NO.1" ARRANGEMENT (RIGHT-HAND DRIVE CARS).
Consult the "Owner's Manual" (handbook) that came with your car for precise arrangement.

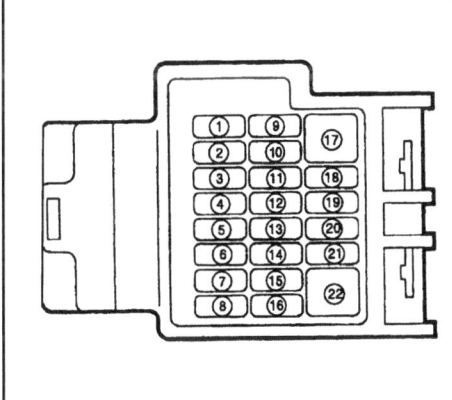

	DESCRIPTION	FUSE RATING	COLOUR	PROTECTED COMPONENT
1	ROOM	10A	Red	Interior light, Warning buzzers
2	—	—	—	
3	—	—	—	
4	TAIL	10A	Red	Tail lights
5	STOP	10A	Red	Horn, Brake lights
6	HAZARD	10A	Red	Hazard warning lights
7	—	—	—	
8	R.FOG*	10A	Red	Rearfog lamp, Headlight levelling
9	CIGAR	15A	Blue	Cigarette lighter
10	H/CLEAN*	20A	Yellow	Headlight cleaner
11	WIPER	20A	Yellow	Wipers, washer
12	P.WIND*	30A	Green	Power windows
13	—	—	—	
14	—	—	—	
15	METER	10A	Red	Gauges, Warning lights, Direction indicator lights
16	ENGINE	15A	Blue	Cooling fan
17	BLOWER	30A	Green	Blower
18	—	—	—	
19	—	—	—	
20	DEFOG*	10A	—	
21	ANTENNA*	10A	—	
22	—	—	—	

D3/2C TYPICAL "FUSE BLOCK NO.1" ARRANGEMENT (LEFT-HAND DRIVE CARS).
Consult the "Owner's Manual" (handbook) that came with your car for precise arrangement.

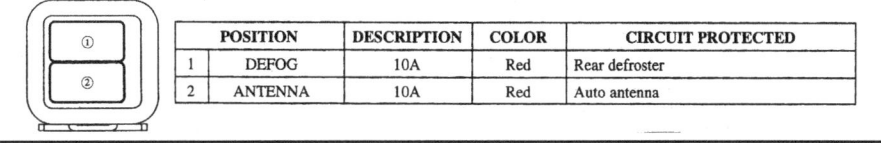

POSITION	DESCRIPTION	COLOR	CIRCUIT PROTECTED
1	DEFOG	10A	Red	Rear defroster
2	ANTENNA	10A	Red	Auto antenna

D3/3 TYPICAL "FUSE BLOCK NO.2" ARRANGMENT (ALL MARKETS), IF FITTED.
"DEFOG" = defroster (rear window). "ANTENNA" = radio aerial (electric extend/retract).

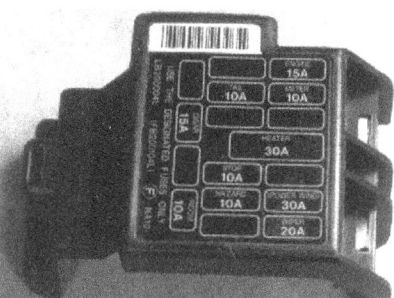

3/2b Lid (typical) identifies fuse positions.

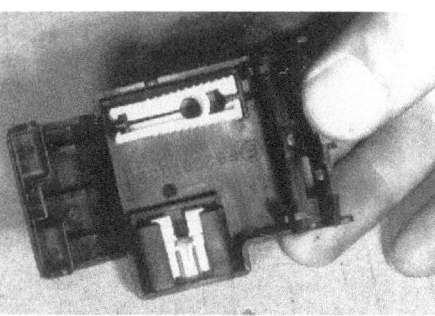

3/6a Spare fuse & fuse gripping tool in lid.

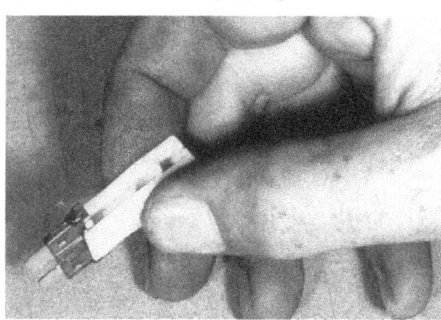

3/6b Fuse gripping tool in action.

power antenna and rear window defroster (where these are fitted). We believe that for some models these latter fuses will be found in Fuse Block No. 1.

4 If a fuse burns out in service, the usual cause will be a short circuit (where the component or circuit power supply is being fed directly to ground/earth), or an overload, for example, where the loading on a fused circuit exceeds the rated capacity of the fuse. We suggest that you obtain a selection of fuses and stow them safely, along with a selection of spare bulbs and a flashlight.

5 You'll find details of the individual circuits/components protected by individual fuses in the 'Owner's Manual' (handbook) that came with your car (or available through Mazda dealerships by quoting the VIN number of your car). Those with Eunos or Sportster models originally sold in the Japanese domestic market will need to get a translation of the relevant section of the original handbook. Fuse ratings are always marked on the individual fuses, though someone could have fitted a wrong fuse in the past, so check the rating with the fusebox cover and/or the correct official "Owner's Manual" (handbook).

6 ◨+ The fusebox mounted under the dash panel (Fuse Block No.1) has a puller tool clipped

Mazda Miata, MX-5, Eunos & Roadster

into its lid, together with a single spare fuse. This device allows you to grip and remove or install the flat type fuses - they can be hard to grasp with the fingers because they are fitted closely together. If a fuse has burned out as the result of an overload, remove the damaged fuse with the puller and install a new fuse of the same rating. If the new fuse fails as soon as the circuit which it protects is used, you'll have to trace and rectify the fault before normal operation is restored; refer to the appropriate section of this, and other chapters for details on testing individual circuits and their components.

7   The 30A circuit breaker (pre-'96) used to protect the heater blower circuit is a special case. If this is overloaded, it breaks the circuit, the small red button at the center of the fuse block popping out to show that this has occurred. Try resetting the breaker by pressing the button in, then run the blower to see if it now operates normally. If the button pops out again, you should refer to chapter 6 for information on checking this circuit and relevant components.

RELAYS

8   There are numerous relays around the car. In the main, these perform the actual switching of circuits in response to low current 'instructions' from manual switches or the PCM (ECU). The majority of the relays are of two types: normally open (NO) or normally closed (NC). The NO relays leave the circuit broken unless power is applied to them, while the NC type maintains the circuit until power is applied. In addition, there are specialist relays, such as the turn signal/hazard warning relay, that do more than just switch something on or off - in this case the relay flashes the turn signal lights in response to the turn signal switch setting or hazard switch setting.

9   📷+ The relays will be found in a number of main locations. All cars have the EGI and Cooling Fan relays housed in the main fuse block in the engine compartment. In addition,

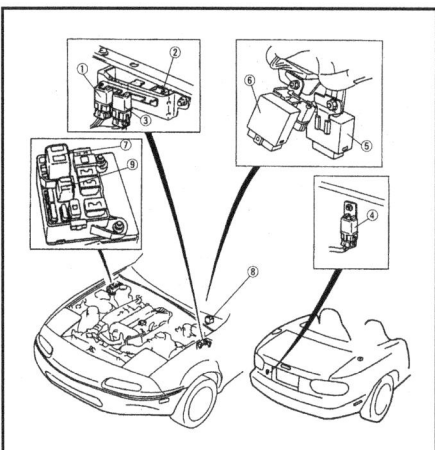

D3/9 RELAY LOCATIONS (TYPICAL)
1 Headlight. 2 TNS (tail, number/license & sidelight). 3 Horn. 4 Rear windoe defog/defrost. 5 Headlight retractors. 6 Flasher unit. 7 Fuel injection. 8 Fuel pump (circuit opening). 9 Coolant fan.

3/9a Relays protected by a latched cover.

3/9b Relay bracket secured by two fixings.

3/9c Typical panel of relays.

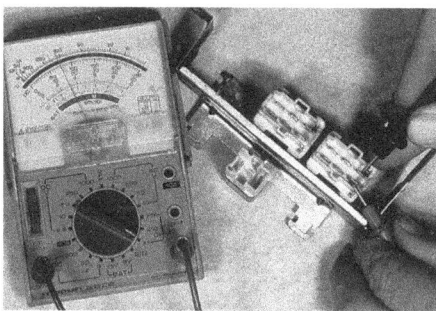

3/10 Testing relay with multimeter (typical).

there's a bank of relays mounted above the left-hand inner fender (wing) in the engine compartment and, on later models, a couple of relays in the vicinity of the charcoal canister on the right-hand inner fender. The relays found here depend on the country in which the car was sold. Further individual relays will be found under the dash panel. Again, the exact arrangement depends on the country in which the vehicle was originally sold. Refer to the accompanying illustrations for details.

10   📷 Further details on the location and testing of individual relays will be found in the various sections of this chapter, and in other chapters where relevant: most of the data on relays associated with the PCM, for example, will be found in chapter 5. Note that when dealing with relays, always isolate the battery (☞ 7/2) before removal and handle carefully - dropping a relay on a hard surface can damage it.

4. CHARGING SYSTEM - GENERAL

☞ 1/1, 2 & 7/2.

1   The charging system comprises the alternator and rectifier, the regulator, the battery and the associated wiring.

2   When dealing with charging system problems, it should be noted that the condition of the battery is of great significance. These cars are fitted with an original battery which is tiny by normal automotive standards. It was developed specifically for the car - so specifically, in fact, that you can't even purchase an identical replacement unit from Mazda or other sources (if you need to fit a new battery, you will have to obtain an equivalent unit, and install it using a special kit from Mazda or the battery manufacturer - more on this later).

3   The battery, though technically advanced and commendably compact and lightweight, has a limited capacity when compared with more conventional units. This means that it is very easy to wind up with a flat battery should you accidentally overload the system. If the car is difficult to start, for example, you'll find that you won't be able to crank the engine for long before the battery gives up on you. Equally, if the charging system is performing inadequately, the normal electrical demands on the system may exceed the charge rate, so any fall-off in charging performance will have to be investigated and rectified promptly.

4   We recommend that you keep a set of jump wires (leads) in the trunk (you can stow these in the recess which runs forward from the right side of the trunk). These can get you out of trouble if you're ever stuck with a flat battery, and if you have automatic transmission on your car, you should consider them essential - you can't push-start an auto.

5. BATTERY - REMOVAL, CHECKING, CHARGING & INSTALLATION

☞ 1/1, 2 & 7/2.

Warning! Although the battery is semi-sealed and maintenance-free, note that the battery electrolyte is extremely corrosive. Take care not to drop or damage the battery casing. Take care to avoid eye or skin contact during handling (use disposable plastic/rubber gloves and eye protection). If electrolyte splashes onto the skin, wash immediately with copious amounts of water and get medical assistance if burning is noted. If splashes enter the eyes, wash immediately with copious amounts of water and then get immediate medical assistance. Contact between electrolyte and clothing will quickly cause damage - wash immediately in water to

7: Electrical system

minimize damage. The hydrogen gas given off by a battery is inflammable and can be explosive if very concentrated.

1   In the author's experience, the original batteries supplied with these cars generally last around three years in normal use. If you have a battery problem, you'll need to remove the battery from the car for checking. However, before you start, if your car is fitted with a sophisticated intruder alarm that activates as the battery's disconnected, use the key, or code, to disable the alarm. If the car has a security coded audio unit, make sure you know the code because you'll have to enter it when the battery is reconnected otherwise the audio unit will not work.

REMOVAL & CLEANING

2   First, remove the spare wheel after releasing the wing nut which secures it. Undo the 30mm plastic nut holding the battery cover to the bodyshell near the rear lamp lens: this can usually be done with your fingers. Lift the battery cover off the poppers along its base and remove it from the trunk. Use a 10mm wrench or socket to loosen the negative (-) terminal clamp. **Warning/Caution!** Take great care not to short the tool against the

5/2 Remove cover & disconnect wire clamps.

positive (+) terminal (which should be fully covered by a plastic protector). Lift the negative terminal clamp from its post and tie it back out of harm's way. Lift the protector, then loosen and remove the positive terminal clamp.

3   If your battery fixing arrangement features a tall metal end bracket, release it after releasing the two 10mm bolts which secure it. Loosen the single 10mm clamp nut until the hook of the threaded rod can be released from the base bracket. Lift the clamp away. **Warning/Caution!** Take great care not to short the two battery terminals with the clamp as it is removed.

4   Pull off the two vent hoses from the battery vent manifold. Lift the battery out of the trunk and place it on the bench for examination and charging.

5   The original type battery is of a semi-sealed design, this being dictated by its location in the trunk where any loss of electrolyte or excessive gas into the trunk would cause problems. Even so, be wary of signs of leakage: if found, it may be that the battery casing has been damaged, in which case a new battery must be fitted. If electrolyte has leaked into the trunk, you must remove and neutralize any traces, or serious corrosion will

5/4a Pull off vent hoses ...

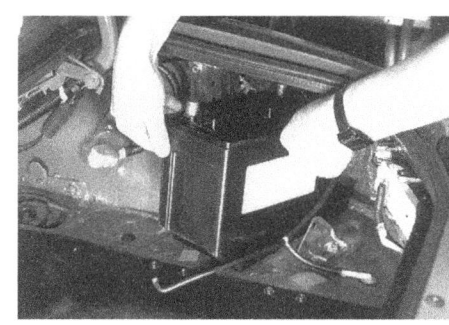
5/4b ... & lift battery from trunk (boot).

result. With luck, any leakage will be confined in the plastic tray which the battery sits in.

6   You will need to wash the affected area with an alkaline solution to neutralize the acidic electrolyte. Make up a solution of warm water to which a couple of tablespoons of sodium bicarbonate/baking soda have been added and dissolved. You can get sodium bicarbonate from pharmacies and general stores, where it is sold as a raising agent for home baking. The solution will fizz as it contacts the electrolyte. **Warning!** Don't breathe the fumes produced, and wear eye and skin protection

5/5 Battery tray is important.

5/8 Testing the battery.

throughout the operation.

7   If the battery is undamaged, wipe over its casing with a rag or paper wipe dampened with the sodium bicarbonate solution. This will clean the casing and neutralise any acid residue. The terminal posts can be cleaned using abrasive paper or a small wire brush (or you can buy special cleaning tools from auto parts stores). Once clean, coat the terminals with petroleum jelly or battery terminal grease to prevent corrosion - don't use regular grease for this.

BATTERY VOLTAGE CHECK

8   You can check battery condition by using a voltmeter (or a multimeter set on the volts range). Connect the meter negative (-) probe to the battery negative terminal, and the positive (+) probe to the battery positive terminal.

9   A reading of 12.4 volts or more shows that the battery is in good condition.

10   If you get a reading of below 12.4 volts, go through the normal recharging procedure. If the battery voltage remains below 12 volts after recharging, you need to fit a new battery. If, after charging, the battery voltage is above 12.4 volts, but you still experience repeated battery discharge, check the charging system ☞ 7/6.

BATTERY CHARGING

Warning! Excessively high charging rates could explode the battery due to overheating and gas build-up. Any form of charging releases hydrogen from the battery. This is a potentially explosive gas - keep well away from any potential source of ignition, and make sure the charging area is well ventilated. When handling the battery, take care to avoid short circuits - they can be dramatic and dangerous. Mazda recommends that during recharging the battery be stood in a tray of water with the water level at half the battery's height.

11   The standard S46A24L(S) battery fitted to these cars when new should normally be recharged at 3A or less. This slow (trickle) charging procedure is always preferable where time allows. **Caution!** If you need to fast charge the battery, never exceed 20A and not for more than 30 minutes, and be aware that repeated fast charging shortens battery life. If the battery becomes hot to the touch during charging, discontinue charging and allow it to cool down, or reduce the charge rate.

12   Depending on how discharged the battery is, trickle charging at 2-3 amps could take 12 to 16 hours to restore it fully. It is always preferable to use a current-controlled charger, so if you intend to buy a charger try to get one of these units if you can. A current-controlled charger allows you to set the charge rate. Cheaper, voltage-controlled units find their own charging current - the current starts out high, then slowly falls back to zero as the battery reaches full charge. With this type of charger it is harder to gauge how long you need to perform the charging operation and there is a real possibility of battery damage.

13   Noting the precautions outlined earlier, check that the battery terminals are clean, then

Mazda Miata, MX-5, Eunos & Roadster

connect the charger clamps to the battery terminal posts, negative (-) to negative, and positive (+) to positive. Switch on the charger at the selected rate and charge for the prescribed amount of time. On cheaper units watch the charger meter to ensure it does not charge the battery at over 3 amps for more than half an hour before falling below 3 amps and then to zero. Disconnect the charger and check the battery voltage. Resume charging for a while if required.

14 If you are unable to get the battery up to 12 volts, this indicates that it's at or near the end of its useful life.

BATTERY INSTALLATION

15 With the battery clean and fully charged, place it in its tray in the trunk, remembering to install the vent hoses. Reassemble and secure the clamp (do not overtighten it). Install the end bracket (if applicable), then connect the battery leads, positive (+) wire clamp and protector first, negative (-) wire clamp last. Take care not to short the battery terminals with the wrench or battery clamp during installation. Install the battery cover, followed by the spare wheel.

INSTALLING A NEW BATTERY

16 Any purpose-designed replacement battery you purchase is likely to require some modification to securing brackets/clamps and to the battery cover. The battery will come with instructions and, maybe, a fitting kit. **Warning/Caution!** Do not try to fit anything but a sealed battery in place of the original type.

6. CHARGING SYSTEM - TROUBLESHOOTING

☞ 1/1, 2 & 7/2.

1 In the event of charging system problems, run through the following troubleshooting procedure.
2 *Check 1.* Is battery voltage above 12.4V?

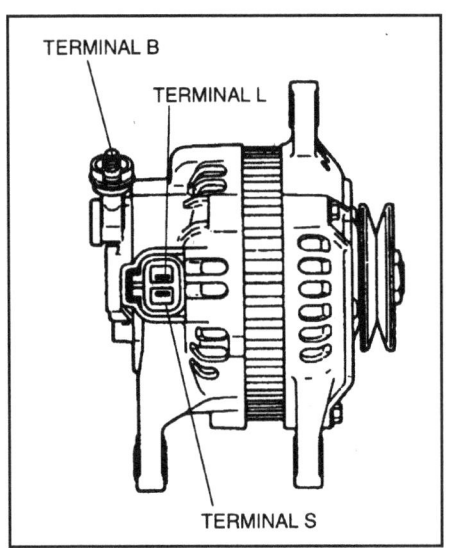

D7/1 ALTERNATOR TERMINALS.

Yes, go to check 2. No, check battery ☞ 7/5.
3 *Check 2.* Switch ignition to ON, then check that voltage is readable at each alternator terminal. Yes, go to check 3. No, check wiring harness and alternator wiring connections.

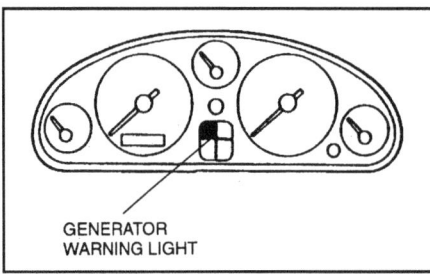

D7/3 LOCATION OF GENERATOR WARNING LIGHT.

4 *Check 3.* Start engine and check that alternator charge warning light goes out. Yes, go to check 4. No, check alternator ☞ 7/7.
5 *Check 4.* Is alternator drivebelt tension correct? Yes, go to check 4. No, replace or retension drivebelt ☞ 2/4.
6 *Check 5.* Check level of dark current. If OK, charging system normal. If too high, check for source of current leakage ☞ 7/7.

7. ALTERNATOR - CHECKING

☞ 1/1, 2 & 7/2.

CHECKING THE TERMINAL VOLTAGES

1 ☞ You need to check the alternator terminal (see diagram) voltages with the unit installed and with its wiring connected normally. Access is restricted, but you should just about be able to get in there with a meter probe. Connect the meter negative (-) probe to a convenient ground, then check each of the three alternator terminals in turn, using the positive (+) probe. You need to make the checks three times; initially, with the ignition switch **OFF**, then with the switch **ON** and, finally, with the switch **ON** and the engine at idle. **Warning!** Be very careful to keep your hands/fingers, loose clothing and the meter's wires away from the moving drivebelts. Readings should be as follows -

	Ignition OFF	Ignition ON	Ignition ON+Idle
Terminal *B*	c.12V	c.12V	12V+
Terminal *L*	zeroV	c1V	12V+
Terminal *S*	c.12V	c.12V	12V+

2 If the readings you get are incorrect, check the wiring connections between the alternator, battery, regulator and ignition switch. If these appear loose, damaged or corroded, repair or replace them as required, then check the terminal voltages again.

CHECKING ALTERNATOR OPERATION

3 ☞ Start the engine and check whether the alternator (generator) charge warning light on the instrument panel (see diagram) goes off. The alternator has a self-diagnosis function which means

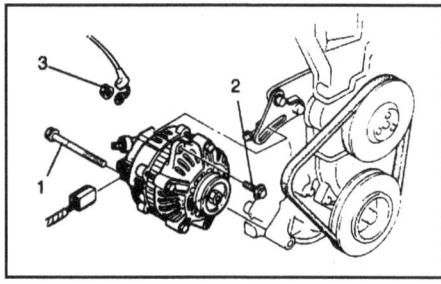

D8/3 ALTERNATOR MOUNTING DETAILS.
1 Swivel bolt. 2 Adjuster lockbolt. 3 10mm live terminal nut.

that the light stays on if:

a) The switch circuit is open.
b) There is no output voltage.
c) The field circuit is open.
d) The battery circuit is open, or
e) The output voltage is too high.

If you find that the warning light stays on, it indicates one of the above conditions - you will either have to fit a new or reconditioned unit, or remove, test and repair the existing alternator (☞ 7/8). Before you do anything else, check drivebelt condition and adjust tension - fit a new belt if the existing one is worn/contaminated (☞ 2/4) - then check whether this has resolved the problem.

CHECKING THE DARK CURRENT

4 This has nothing to do with mystical practices or Star Wars - it refers instead to the current flow still taking place when everything that can be has been switched off. While the car is parked, a small current still flows to systems like the PCM, clock, intruder alarm, audio unit, etc. In normal circumstances, the current drawn is very small, the maximum allowable figure being 20mA. You can check the level of dark current by disconnecting the battery negative (-) terminal clamp and then taking a reading between the negative terminal clamp and the negative battery post.

5 If the current exceeds that mentioned above, you'll need to track down the cause of the excess leakage - a formidable task with an electrical system of this complexity. The best bet is to start by disconnecting each of the car's fuses in turn, checking the current drawn while each one is removed. If you find that the reading drops to normal when one of the fuses is out, you can then concentrate on checking the circuits which it protects. Areas to check are courtesy/trunk light switches, audio unit left switched on with the volume down, damp wiring connections, damaged wiring (though you would normally expect this to have burned out the fuse), and, finally, shorted or damaged electrical components, such as a sticking relay, or possibly an alternator or related charging system fault.

8. ALTERNATOR - REMOVAL, OVERHAUL & INSTALLATION

☞ 1/1, 2 & 7/2.

7: Electrical system

1   If you need to work on the alternator, the first step is to remove it from the car. It is awkwardly located on the right-hand side of the engine, partially covered by the intake manifold. Start by disconnecting the battery negative (-) terminal ☞ 7/2. The following procedure assumes you'll work from above the engine; however, an alternative method would be to remove the engine undertray and work from beneath.

2   To improve access, you'll need to do a little preliminary dismantling. Remove the rigid air hose connecting the air cleaner to the throttle body at the front of the manifold, don't forget to release the small bore throttle bypass hose and the small bore cambox vent hoses. Full details ☞ 3/4/34. You may also find it worthwhile to remove the engine undertray ☞ 3/4/14-15.

3   Refer to the accompanying diagram and disconnect the alternator wiring. The heavy live cable attached to the threaded terminal is retained by a 10mm nut and is accessible once you pull back the protective covering, the remaining two wires share a single plug-in connector. If you intend to dismantle the alternator after removal, we suggest that you slacken the pulley center 22mm nut at this stage. With luck, there will be enough friction in the drivebelt to allow you to do this, but if it won't come free, don't worry - we'll deal with it later.

4   Slacken the alternator pivot bolt, the adustment strap inner bolt and the adjuster lockbolt. Turn the adjusting screw anti-clockwise to slacken the drivebelt until there's enough slack to allow drivebelt removal. Unscrew and remove the pivot bolt and strap bolt, and lift away the alternator. From here on, you have several choices: overhaul the unit yourself (as far as is practical); buy a reconditioned (probably exchange) unit from your local auto-electrical specialist, or buy a new unit.

8/4a Slacken pivot bolt ...

8/4b ... followed by adjustment strap bolt ...

8/4c ... followed by lockbolt. Turn adjuster bolt ...

8/4d ... anti-clockwise to release belt tension.

8/4e Unscrew & remove pivot bolt ...

5   Frankly, we would go for a new or reconditioned unit every time, given the awkward access to the alternator, and the limited scope for home repairs. If you fit a new unit, or one which has been professionally overhauled, you can expect long and troublefree service. Superficially, dismantling and rebuild of the alternator looks easy, but in reality you can get into real difficulties here. We left Wally, our Technical Adviser, to overhaul our project car's alternator ...

DISMANTLING

6   First thing to do is remove the 22mm pulley nut - if you managed to slacken it while it was still in the car you can skip this paragraph. You need to hold the pulley somehow while the nut is removed. You may be able to do this using a vise fitted with soft jaws, but be very careful that you don't crush and distort the pulley. A better way is to wrap an old drivebelt around the pulley and clamp that in your vise, keeping it as tight as you can. This will grip the pulley evenly and you can unscrew and remove the nut and its spring washer.

7   With the pulley nut and spring washer removed, the pulley comes off in two halves, followed by a spacer. Next, remove the four 8mm

8/4f ... and lift away alternator.

8/6 Remove pulley nut.

8/7 Unscrew & remove thru bolts.

8/8 The dismantled alternator.

through bolts which hold the unit together. Carefully lift away the end cover (pulley end), leaving the rotor sitting in the remaining casing half - push on the rotor shaft end to separate the two halves. Inside the (pulley end) casing is the main rotor bearing, held in place by a square retainer plate. The plate can be removed after unscrewing the four crosshead screws which secure it, and the old bearing drifted out of the casing using a socket of around 15mm.

8   Wally's next move was to pull the rotor out of the remaining casing half - as he did so the

Mazda Miata, MX-5, Eunos & Roadster

rotor shaft moved clear of the brushes, which popped out under spring pressure. Wally failed to find a way to remove the stator assembly or the brush holder/rectifier unit without causing damage - this means big problems later. As far as we can tell, the stator can be pulled out of the casing, and the brush holder and rectifier assembly released after removing the retaining screws. However, Wally couldn't get ours apart, and, discretion being the better part of valor, he decided to quit before he did any damage.

9   At this point poor Wally's problems were just beginning ... To get the rotor back into the casing, the brushes have to be held back against spring pressure while the rotor is fitted. Unfortunately, the back of the casing is blind - there is no apparent method of doing this. In the end, Wally drilled a small access hole in the end of the casing center, and used a length of welding wire to hold the brushes back while he slid the rotor back into position.

10   What we think should happen is that the stator windings should be pulled out of the casing, and the brush plate and rectifier assembly released by removing the external retaining screw as they are withdrawn. We have to confess that we never really resolved this problem - if you have had more success with an alternator teardown than Wally did, we would like to hear how you did it.

INSPECTION

11   The first thing to do is assess the overall condition of the alternator. If something catastrophic has happened, and the rotor and/or stator are obviously trashed, further work would be academic - it's time to say 'Hi!' to your Mazda dealer or auto electrical specialist.

12   Check the rotor windings for signs of damage. If they appear burned or the shiny coating is beginning to break up, you will need to get the stator rewound - again, check local auto-electrical specialists for price and availability, and compare this with the cost of a new Mazda part. Even if the windings look OK, check for shorting with a resistance check. At 20 degrees C (68F) you should find a resistance of 3.5-4.5 ohms (measured between the two slip rings). Next, check for grounding of the windings by checking the resistance between each slip ring and the steel core of the rotor. No continuity should exist. If the windings are outside the specified range or shorted to ground, you should fit a new or reconditioned rotor.

13   Now turn your attention to the stator windings. Again, these must be undamaged, and there should be continuity between the stator leads. There must be no continuity between the stator leads and the metal core. If the stator does not meet these criteria, fit a new one.

14   Inspect the brushes for wear. If they have worn down to or near the wear limit indicated by the rectangular surround of the Mitsubishi logo (8mm/032in overall length), you should fit new ones. We would suggest that it might be worth fitting new brushes as a precaution anyway, unless the existing ones are almost unworn.

15   You are supposed to check the brush

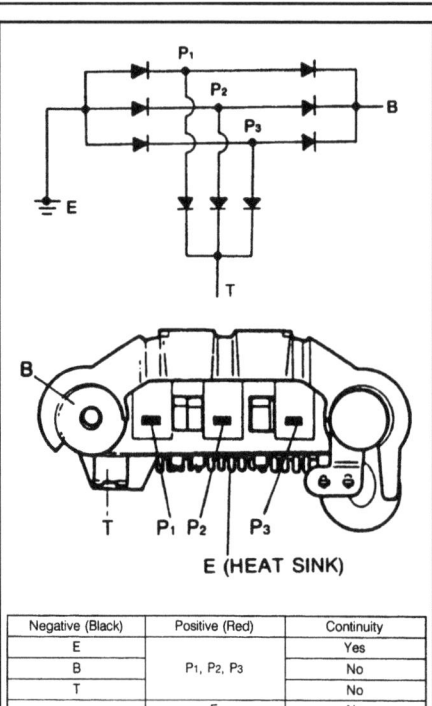

Negative (Black)	Positive (Red)	Continuity
E	P1, P2, P3	Yes
B		No
T		No
P1, P2, P3	E	No
	B	Yes
	T	Yes

D8/16 ALTERNATOR RECTIFIER - TESTING DIODES.

spring pressure at this stage. With the brush projecting from the holder by 2mm, the standard reading should be 3.2-4.3N/0.32-0.44kgf/0.71-0.96lbf), and the service limit is 1.6-2.3N/0.16-0.24kgf/0.36-0.52lbf). If you have some way of determining this, then check it by all means. We suggest that it might be good policy to fit new springs along with the brushes.

16   Finally, check the rectifier assembly, referring to the accompanying drawing. Note that in this test you are checking for continuity of the rectifier diodes. For each pair of terminals, check for continuity, then reverse the meter leads and repeat the test. You should read continuity in one direction only. If in any of the checks you find continuity both ways, or no continuity either way, the diode has burned out and the rectifier should be replaced.

REBUILD

17   Fit the brush holder and rectifier unit assembly over the end of the rotor, checking that the brushes fit correctly over the slip rings - use a small screwdriver to lift the brushes over the slip rings as the rotor is slid home. Install the assembly into the casing, tightening the external screw which retains the brush holder and rectifier to 5.9-9.8 N (60.0-100.0 kgf cm/52-87 lbf in). Fit the other casing half and install the long through bolts, tightening them to 2.6-6.4 N (30.0-65.0 Kgf cm/26-56 lbf in).

18   Fit the spacer, the alternator pulley, spring washer and 22 mm nut. Hold the pulley using an old drive belt while the nut is tightened to 59-98 N (6.0-10.0 kgf cm/26-56 lbf ft). Check that the pulley can be turned smoothly and easily before installing the rebuilt unit.

INSTALLATION

19   Install the alternator in the car, fitting the fixing bolts finger-tight at this stage. Install the drivebelt. Set the adjuster bolt to give the correct amount of freeplay in the drivebelt. Tighten the lockbolt, adjustment strap bolt and pivot bolt. Full details, if required, ☞ 3/9/115-119.

20   Reconnect the live wire eye to the threaded stud of the terminal, making sure the securing nut is covered by its protective boot. Push in the two-pin connector until it locks in place.

21   Install the rigid air pipe between air filter and throttle body, not forgetting the two small bore hoses attached to it. Full details, if required, ☞ 3/11/98. If applicable, replace the engine undertray ☞ 3/11/108-110.

9. STARTER SYSTEM - DESCRIPTION & TROUBLESHOOTING

☞ 1/1, 2 & 7/2.

1   The starter motor/magnetic switch (solenoid) assembly is mounted on the bellhousing/engine backplate on the right-hand side of the engine. A heavy live wire runs from the battery positive terminal to the **B** (battery) terminal on the magnetic switch (see diagram). The magnetic switch contacts are normally open, but when the ignition switch is turned to the **START** position, current is applied to the **S** (switch) terminal of the unit.

2   In the case of cars with manual transmission, for some markets an interlock switch is fitted. This device ensures that the starter circuit is not completed and therefore the engine cannot be started, unless the clutch pedal is depressed. Where automatic transmission is fitted, the transmission range switch prevents starting unless the shift lever is in the **PARK** or **NEUTRAL** position.

3   When the circuit is made, the magnetic switch (solenoid) pulls the starter pinion into engagement with the starter ring on the engine flywheel, closes the heavy electrical contacts which allow current to flow through the starter motor, and the engine is cranked. As soon as the ignition key is released, it springs back to the **IDLE** position and power is disconnected to the magnetic switch. This, in turn, cuts power to the motor and pulls the starter pinion out of engagement with the flywheel.

INITIAL CHECKS

4   If you experienced starting problems, always check the battery before you do anything else (☞ 7/5). If the problem persists with a fully charged battery, proceed as follows.

5   Have an assistant operate the ignition switch. You should hear a click from the starter magnetic switch (solenoid) indicating that it is operating. If the solenoid operates, but the starter doesn't, you'll need to remove the starter motor for further checks ☞ 7/10. If no click is heard, proceed as follows.

6   Connect a voltmeter with the positive (+)

7: Electrical system

probe to the magnetic switch **S** terminal and the negative (-) probe to ground (earth). Have your assistant operate the ignition switch once more, and check that you read battery voltage (approx 12V). If battery voltage is shown, remove the starter motor to check it and the magnetic switch ☞ 7/10. If no voltage is shown ☞ 7/9/7 (manual transmission with interlock), ☞ 7/9/8-11 (auto tranmission), ☞ 7/9/12 (manual transmission without interlock).

INTERLOCK SWITCH - CHECKING (MANUAL TRANS)

7   Working in the footwell on the driver's side, check for battery voltage between the starter side of the starter interlock switch and ground when the starter is operated. The switch is attached to the left side of the clutch pedal support and should not be confused with the centrally mounted clutch switch. If battery voltage is present, check the wiring and connections between the interlock switch and the starter magnetic switch, and repair or replace as necessary. If no voltage is read, check for battery voltage on the ignition switch side of the interlock switch. If the switch has failed, fit a new one, otherwise trace back and repair the wiring between the ignition and interlock switches.

RANGE SWITCH CHECKING & ADJUSTMENT (AUTO TRANS)

8   The range switch on auto transmission models provides an interlock with the starter system, which ensures that the engine may only be started while **P** (Park) or **N** (Neutral) is selected. In addition, the inhibitor switch also operates the backup (reversing) lights so, if you've noticed that the backup lights operate in anything other than reverse gear, you have a good indication that there is a range switch problem. The range switch is adjustable - if you find that sometimes the starter fails to work, try moving the shifter back and forth slightly. If you find that you can get the starter working this way, you should check the range switch adjustment.

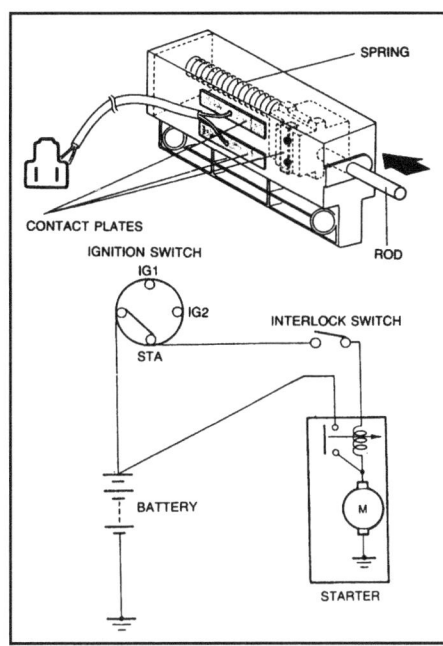

D9/7 STARTER INTERLOCK LAYOUT AND ELECTRICAL SYSTEM.

9   To check the range switch you'll need to jack the vehicle and place it securely on safety stands so that you can work in complete safety underneath ☞ 1/3. Isolate the battery ☞ 7/2.

10   The range switch is located on the right-hand side of the transmission casing, around the shift shaft boss. Trace the wiring from the switch to its connector. Unplug the connector and, using a multimeter, check for continuity between the terminals on the range switch side of the connector. The diagram shows what you should find at each selector position. If the readings are faulty, try adjusting the switch first, and, if necessary, replace it.

11   Range switch adjustment. Set the shift lever to the **N** (neutral position. Beneath the car, remove its securing nut then pull the selector lever off the selector spindle (see diagram), being very careful not to rotate the spindle at all in the process.

12   Remove the single screw on the switch

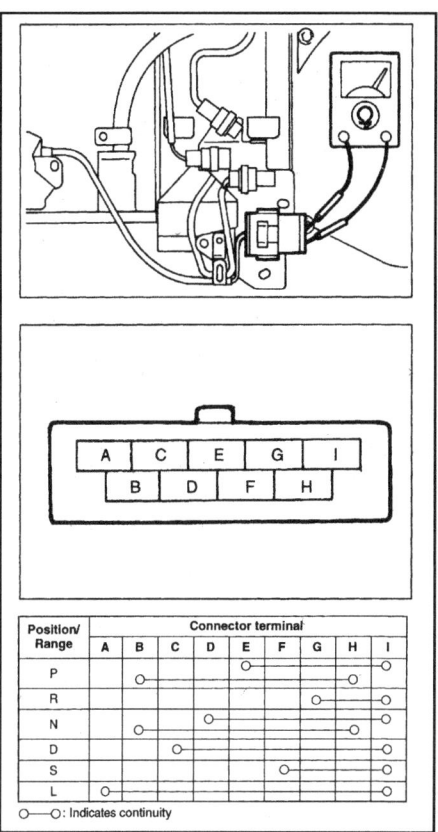

D9/10 TRANSMISSION (AUTO) RANGE SWITCH ELECTRICAL CHECKS.

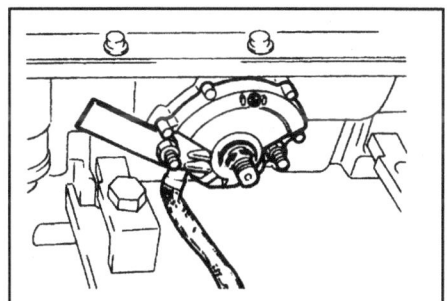

D9/11 TRANSMISSION (AUTO) RANGE SWITCH WITH SELECTOR LEVER REMOVED.

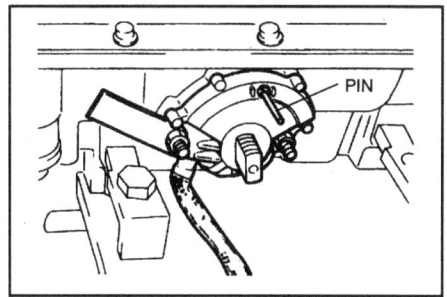

D9/12 TRANSMISSION (AUTO) RANGE SWITCH WITH ALIGNMENT CHECK PIN IN PLACE.

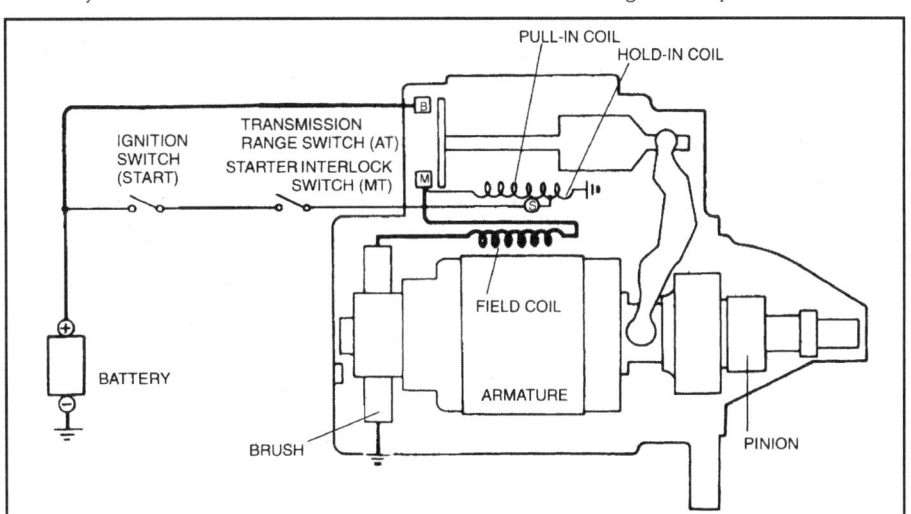

D9/1 STARTER MOTOR COMPONENT LAYOUT & ELECTRICAL SYSTEM.
"AT" = automatic transmission, "MT" = manual transmission.

Mazda Miata, MX-5, Eunos & Roadster

body. Slacken the nut securing the range switch, and rotate the switch slowly back and forth about the spindle until the screw hole is aligned with the small aperture inside the switch - you may need a flashlight to see this. Use a 2mm/0.079in diameter pin to ensure that the holes are truly in alignment (see diagram), and then retighten the switch securing screws.

13   Withdraw the pin and install the original screw in its place. Place the selector lever over the spindle and secure with its nut tightened to a torque of 45-63Nm/4.5-6.5kgf m/33-47lbf ft.

14   If the above checks have not resolved the starter fault, check the wiring and connections between the battery, starter motor and ignition switch. If no fault can be found, you will have to remove the starter for testing.

10. STARTER MOTOR - REMOVAL, OVERHAUL & INSTALLATION

☞ 1/1, 2 & 7/2.

REMOVAL

1   Isolate the battery ☞ 7/2. You'll find access is pretty restricted - the motor is masked by the intake manifold. Working through the engine compartment, disconnect the starter wiring - one pull-off connector and, under a plastic cover, a 12mm nut. Free the starter motor support bracket by removing the single 14mm bolt which fixes it to the engine block (remove the bracket from the motor once you've got the assembly out of the car).

2   Working under the car (☞ 1/3), remove the two upper mounting bolts and the single lower bolt and nut which secure the motor to the bellhousing. The motor can now be pulled forward until it disengages from the ring gear, and maneuvered out of the engine compartment.

TESTING

3   Clamp the motor in the vise using soft jaws. Do not overtighten the vise - just enough to hold the motor firmly in place. Using a spare battery (or remove the battery from the car), check motor operation as follows. Connect a set of jump (booster) wires, battery positive (+) to the **S** terminal on the motor, and the battery negative (-) terminal grounded to the motor body - this should operate the magnetic switch. You should hear a click as the solenoid operates. If the magnetic switch fails to operate, it should be checked as described later in this section.

4   With the battery connected as described above, measure with feeler gauges the gap between the outer face of the starter pinion and its stop. The correct gap is 0.5-2.0mm (0.02-0.08in). If you need to adjust the gap setting, this can be done by installing or removing shims between the magnetic switch (solenoid) and the motor casing, the adjustment requiring removal of the magnetic switch as described later.

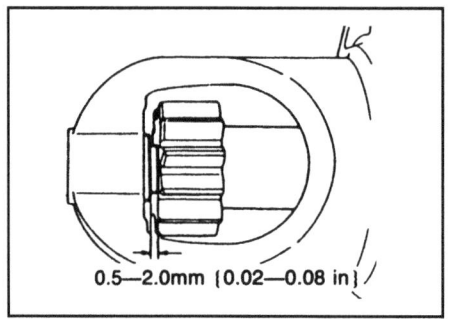

D10/4 CHECKING PINION GAP.

5   Check the pinion return by disconnecting the motor wire from the magnetic switch **M** terminal, and applying the positive jump wire to the terminal (not the disconnected wire) and grounding the body. Pull the pinion out using a screwdriver and check that it holds in this position. Now disconnect the battery and check that the pinion returns to its normal position.

6   To check the motor no-load operation you will need an ammeter capable of reading up to around 100A, a dc voltmeter, a small switch, some electrical wire, a set of jump (booster) wires and a fully charged car battery. You need to make up the test rig shown in the accompanying drawing. Use the jump leads between the battery and the motor, connecting the circuit through the ammeter (**A**) and connecting the voltmeter (**V**) between terminal **B** and ground. Use the wire to connect the switch between terminals **B** and **S** of the magnetic switch.

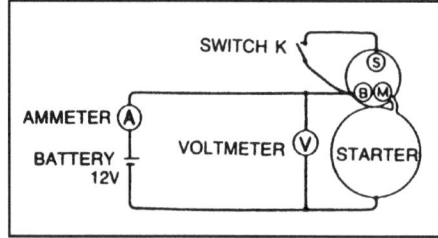

D10/6 NO-LOAD TEST.

7   When the switch is operated, the motor should run, drawing a current of 60A or less, and showing 11.5 volts on the voltmeter. The motor speed should be around 6600rpm or more - largely academic since it is next to impossible to check this at home, but you should get the impression that it runs smoothly and quite fast. If the operation of the motor seems sluggish, or if the current drawn is unusually high or low, the motor needs attention.

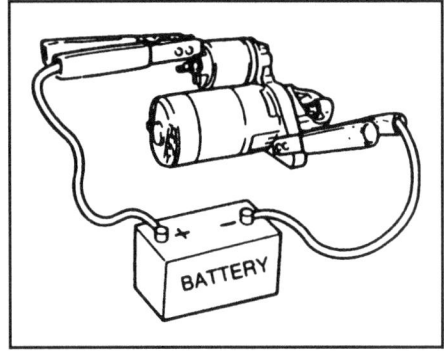

D10/3 TESTING STARTER MOTOR.

OVERHAUL

8   Before you start dismantling the motor for further testing and repairs, give some thought to the best way to approach this. If the motor is generally worn out or obviously burnt out, you might want to consider getting a new or reconditioned motor, or purchasing a used motor from a wrecker (scrapyard). This could save you a lot of time and work, and may be more cost effective than attempting repair of a damaged motor yourself. Remember that if you need to get the motor rewound, or the armature needs machining, you'll end up getting this work done by an auto electrical specialist anyway, in which case you may as well take the complete, assembled motor in for repair.

9   Note also that if the starter pinion teeth are worn, it is likely that similar wear of the starter ring gear has probably taken place. Using a flashlight and a small mirror, you may just be able to check this. If the ring gear is worn, fitting a replacement means removing the engine or transmission - you may want to leave this task until it gets to be a real problem.

10   Remove the nut which secures the braided copper cable to the lower terminal on the magnetic switch (solenoid). Lift off the cable terminal

10/10a Remove switch body ...

10/10b ... detach switch core from nylon lever.

10/10c Component parts of switch.

7:12

7: Electrical system

and refit the nut on the terminal. Remove the two magnetic switch retaining crosshead screws and lift away the switch body. The switch core will remain attached to the forked end of the drive pinion lever - lift it away and tip up the switch body to displace the core return spring.

11   ⬛ If the motor support bracket is still attached to the motor body, remove it. Below the bracket, what appears to be two projecting studs with 8mm nuts are, in fact, the motor through bolts. Unscrew and remove these, then lift away the motor front cover and drive pinion lever, disengaging it from the pinion groove. The pinion lever can

10/11 Remove thru bolts & front cover.

be removed from the front cover after displacing the metal plate and seal which cover the pivot.

12   Remove the two retaining screws from the motor end cover and remove the cover, noting that the brush plate assembly should be left in position on the armature if possible. Note also that there are loose shim washers on the brush end of the armature - retain these and fit them in the order they were removed during assembly. Disengage the brush plate assembly from the armature and remove the armature from the motor yoke.

13   Use a multimeter or continuity checker to test for insulation between the commutator segments and the core and spindle of the armature. If you find continuity at any point, fit a new armature, or see whether you can get the old one reconditioned.

14   ⬛ Examine the commutator for wear or damage. Light discoloration and minor damage can be corrected by cleaning the commutator with fine sandpaper. Wrap the paper round the commutator and turn the armature until a bright, smooth finish is restored. In cases of more severe damage, have the armature set up in a lathe and remove the minimum amount of metal possible to restore the surface of the commutator segments. Note that if

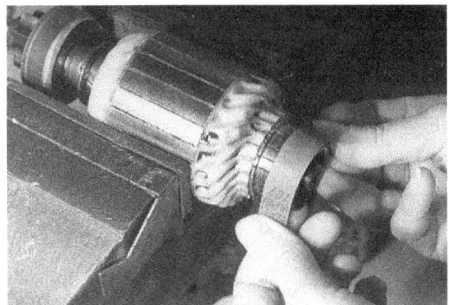

10/14 Cleaning the commutator.

the repair work would result in the commutator diameter being reduced to 30.8mm (1.21in) or less, the armature should be scrapped and a new one fitted.

15   Check that the commutator runout is within limits. Set the armature up on V-blocks or between lathe centers, and use a dial gauge to measure commutator runout. The service tolerance is 0.03mm (0.001in) or less. Again, minor damage can be corrected by machining the commutator in a lathe, but more severe damage will mean a new armature.

16   ⬛+ After working on the commutator,

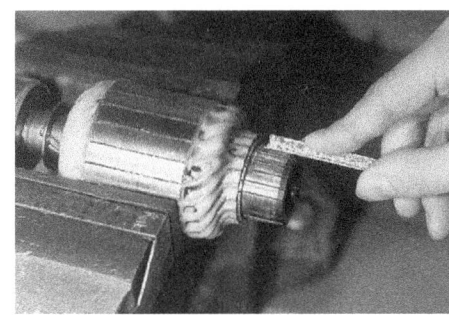

10/16a Undercutting commutator insulators ...

10/16b ... use switch cleaner to clear debris.

check the depth of the grooves between each segment. If these are less than 0.2mm (0.008in), you will need to recut them. You can make up your own recutting tool from a section of used hacksaw blade. Find the end where the teeth point back towards you as you hold the blade - this will be the cutting end, so wrap some tape around the other end to form a handle. Now grind the sides of the blade flat until it is a good fit in the commutator grooves. Undercut the grooves by drawing the tool along each one until you achieve the specified undercut of 0.5-0.8mm (0.020-0.031in), then repeat the process on the remaining grooves. Use a little fine sandpaper to remove any burring that results, then clean the commutator with switch cleaner.

17   Moving to the motor body, check for continuity between the brushes and the yoke (field coil) terminals. If the circuit is broken you will need to fit a new or reconditioned unit. Don't attempt removal of the yoke assembly from the motor casing - it needs to be installed using a jig to ensure correct alignment and centering. Similarly, if either field coil is loose, get a new or reconditioned yoke assembly. Check the insulation between the yoke and the motor body - if you find continuity, the yoke assembly will have to be reconditioned or

replaced.

18   The magnetic switch (solenoid) can be checked for continuity between terminals **S** (switch terminal) and **M** (motor terminal). If there is a break in continuity, fit a new switch. Next check that there is insulation between the **S** terminal and the switch body. If insulation has broken down, fit a new switch.

19   Check the brush holder assembly for shorting between each brush and the holder plate. If continuity is indicated, fit a new brush holder assembly.

20   Measure each brush for wear. If worn to or beyond the limit (bottom of the box surrounding the Mitsubishi logo), fit new brushes. The standard new brush length is 17mm (0.67in) and the wear limit is 11.5mm (0.46in). Given the inaccessibility of the motor, we would suggest fitting new brushes, irrespective of condition, and this should always be done if the commutator has been skimmed.

21   ⬛ Fit the armature through the motor yoke and reposition the brush holder assembly over the commutator, lifting each brush into place with a small screwdriver. Apply a little grease to the bearing, fit any shims found on dismantling and install the motor end cover, fitting the two small

10/21 Position brush holder over commutator.

screws to secure the brush holder.

22   Install the front cover, ensuring that the drive pinion lever engages correctly and that the metal plate and seal over its pivot have been installed. Fit the motor through bolts and tighten them to 3.9-7.1Nm/39-72kgf cm/34-62lbf in.

23   Install the magnetic switch core, hooking it over the lever fork. Fit the core return spring into the switch body and fit the assembly over the core end. Fit the two switch securing screws, tightening them to 4.1-7.5Nm/42-77kgf cm/36-67lbf in. Reconnect the braided copper cable to the lower switch terminal.

INSTALLATION

24   When installing the starter motor assembly, tighten the bellhousing mounting bolts and nut evenly to 38-5Nm/3.8-5.3kgf m/28-38lbf ft. The bolt holding the bracket halves together should be tightened to 16-22Nm/1.6-2.3kgf m/12-16lbf ft), and the bracket mounting bolt to 38-5Nm/3.8-5.3kgf m/28-38lbf ft.

25   Reconnect the motor wiring, securing the heavy battery wire by tightening the retaining nut to 9.9-10.7Nm/100-120kgf cm/87-95lbf in. Temporarily reconnect the battery and check that

Mazda Miata, MX-5, Eunos & Roadster

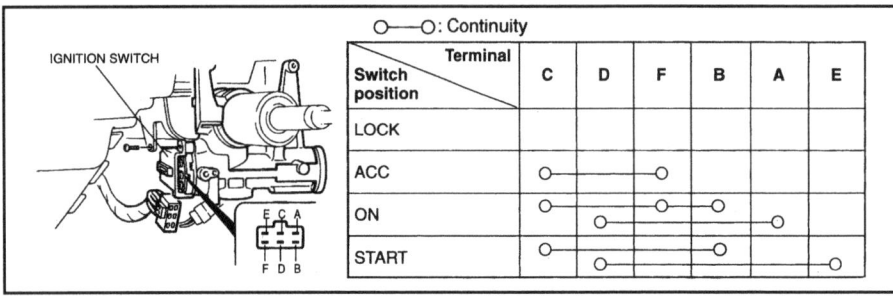

D11A/4 IGNITION SWITCH: CHECKING CONTINUITY.

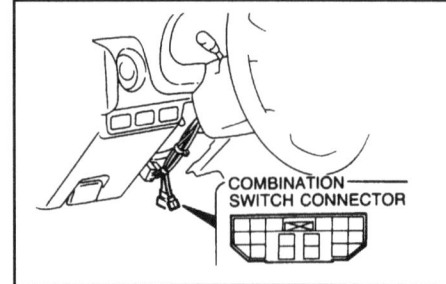

D12/1 COMBO SWITCH: CONNECTOR LOCATION.

the motor works normally before lowering the car to the ground.

11A. IGNITION SWITCH - T/SHOOTING, REMOVAL & INSTALLATION

☞ 1/1, 2 & 7/2.

1 **Warning!** It is essential that the airbag system has been disabled by isolating the battery ☞ 7/2 **and waiting at least 5 minutes** for the system's built-in capacitance to release its charge.

2 The ignition switch/steering lock unit is housed in a two-piece housing which covers the area of the steering column between the dash panel and back of the steering wheel.

3 Once the four retaining screws (one is deeply recessed) have been removed, gently pull the housing halves apart and manipulate the top half over the stalks. The two halves clip together, and care should be taken when separating them not to break off the small guide pins around the edge of the joint.

4 ☐ Unplug the wiring connector on the left-hand side of the switch/lock unit. Using a continuity tester or a multimeter, check the switch continuity at the various key positions (see diagram). If the switch does not operate as specified in the table, or if some of the switch settings are intermittent, fit a new switch.

5 The switch can be removed from the end of the steering lock assembly after removing the single retaining screw. Install the new switch, secure with its single screw and connect it to the wiring harness.

6 Install the two halves of the switch housing and secure with four screws. Note that the non-

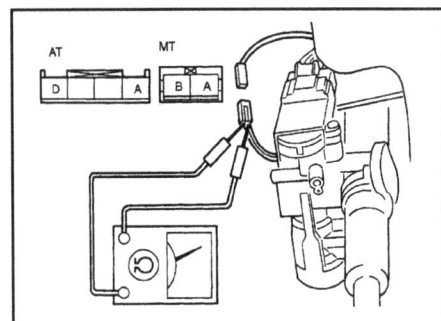

D11B/2 KEY (IGNITION) REMINDER SWITCH CHECKING.
See text. "MT" = manual trans, "AT" = auto trans.

recessed screw at the back is actually a set screw which screws into the metal steering lock body: replace this screw first to correctly locate the housing.

7 Reconnect the battery ☞ 7/2. **Warning!** Before using the car, turn the ignition key to the **ON** position and confirm that the **AIRBAG** warning light on the dash panel illuminates for around 4 to 8 seconds and then goes out (thus indicating that the airbag system is functional).

11B. KEY (IGNITION) REMINDER SWITCH - TROUBLESHOOTING

☞ 1/1, 2 & 7/2.

1 ☞ 7/11a/1-3.

2 ☐ Unplug the key reminder switch's harness connector and check terminal continuity on the switch side of the connector (see diagram). There should be continuity between terminals **B** and **A** (**D** and **A** - auto trans) when the ignition key is inserted, no continuity when the key is removed. If the switch is faulty - and you can't live without the key reminder warning - you'll need to replace the steering lock, which is a job for your Mazda dealer because of various security features.

3 ☞ 7/11a/6-7.

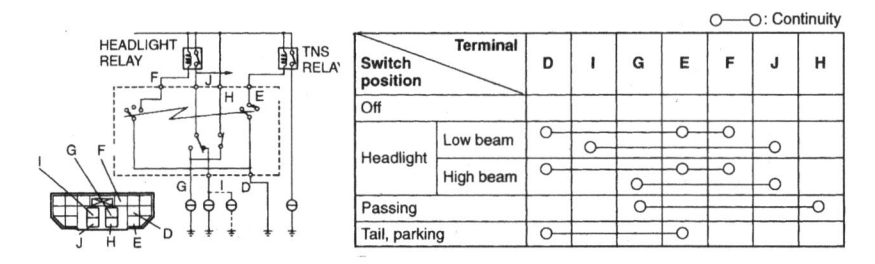

D12/2A COMBINATION SWITCH: CHECKING HEADLIGHT SWITCHING.

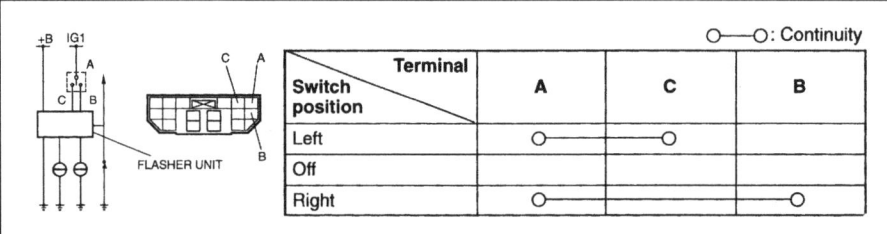

D12/2B COMBINATION SWITCH: CHECKING TURN SIGNAL (INDICATOR) SWITCHING.

12. COMBINATION SWITCH - T/SHOOTING, REMOVAL & INSTALLATION

☞ 1/1, 2 & 7/2.

Warning! For **all** of the following procedures it is essential that the airbag system has been disabled ☞ 7/44.

CHECKING

1 ☐ Combination switch operation can be checked without dismantling the steering column. Remove the inspection panel beneath the column. Unplug the combination switch connector from its harness connector (see diagram), and proceed as follows.

2 ☐+ Refer to the accompanying diagrams and check for continuity at the switch positions and connector terminals (switch side) indicated. If continuity is not as shown, the normal course of action is to fit a new combination switch. Before you do so, it's worth removing the old switch and spraying the switch contacts with a silicone-based switch cleaner/lubricant to see if this improves switch operation.

REMOVAL

3 If you need to remove the switch, you

7: Electrical system

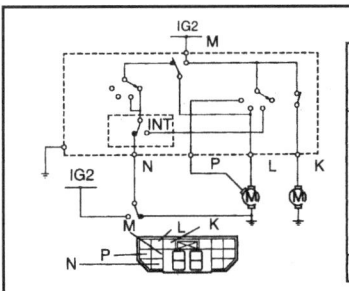

D12/2C COMBINATION SWITCH: CHECKING WINDSHIELD WIPER & WASHER SWITCHING.

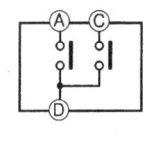 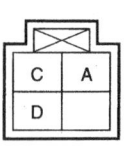

D12/2D COMBINATION SWITCH: CHECKING CRUISE CONTROL SWITCHING (IF APPLICABLE).

must first remove the airbag and steering wheel - having set the front wheels to the straight ahead position - ☞ 8/11.

4 📷 Remove the three crosshead screws

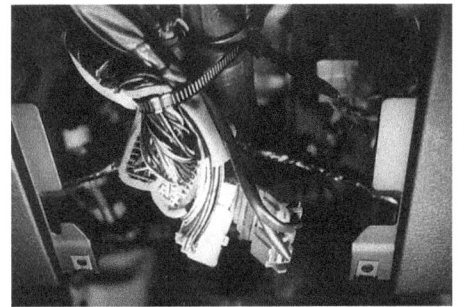

12/4 Combination switch connectors & tie.

securing the combination switch, release all of its electrical connections and any cable ties and remove the switch from the column. **Warning!** If it is to be re-used, handle the switch unit very carefully, as damage to the clockspring could cause unexpected airbag deployment after re-installation.

INSTALLATION

5 Install the combination switch and secure with three retaining screws. Remake the switch's electrical connections to the wiring harness. Install the switch covers.

6 📷 **Warning!** It is essential that the airbag 'clockspring' is correctly adjusted before the steering wheel is installed: proceed as follows (see diagram). Turn the clockspring clockwise as far as it will go, then rotate it 2.75 turns in the opposite direction: the arrows on the clockspring and switch body should now be in, or very close to, alignment. Align the two arrows.

7 Install the steering wheel and airbag unit ☞ 8/11.

8 Reconnect the battery ☞ 7/2 and re-arm the airbag system ☞ 7/44.

13. H/LIGHT RETRACT & HAZ. WARN. SWITCH - REMOVAL, T/SHOOTING & INSTALLATION

☞ 1/1, 2 & 7/2.

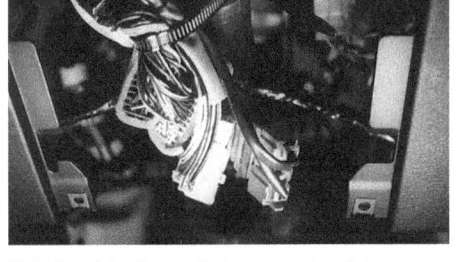

13/1 Switch is secured by screws.

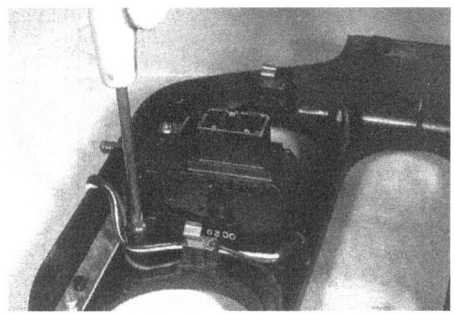

D12/6 'CLOCKSPRING' ADJUSTMENT.
Step 1: turn clockspring clockwise as far as it will go.
Step 2: turn anti-clockwise 2.75 turns.
Step 3: align pointers.

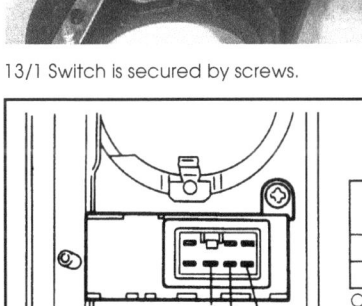

Switch	Terminal		
	b	d	f
Off	○――――――――○		
On		○――――○	

○―○: Indicates continuity

D13/2A CHECKING HEADLIGHT RETRACTOR SWITCH.

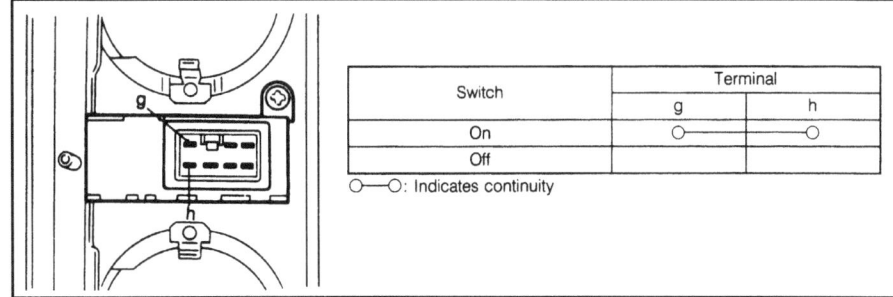

Switch	Terminal	
	g	h
On	○――――○	
Off		

○―○: Indicates continuity

D13/2B CHECKING HAZARD WARNING SWITCH.

Mazda Miata, MX-5, Eunos & Roadster

1   ☐ Isolate the battery 7/2. This switch assembly is located centrally in the dash panel, between the eyeball vents. Access to the switch requires removal of the center section of the dash panel ☞ 10/3. With the dash panel center section removed, unplug the wiring connector.

2   ☐+ Using a continuity tester or multimeter, check the operation of the switches, referring to the accompanying illustration for details of terminal identification and continuity. If not as specified, you'll have to install a new switch; it's not possible to dismantle or repair the switch.

3   Fit the new switch and secure it with its screws, Move the dash panel center section into position and fit the switch's wiring connector. At this stage, temporarily reconnect the battery and check switch operation before finally installing the dash panel center section and eyeball vents ☞ 10/3.

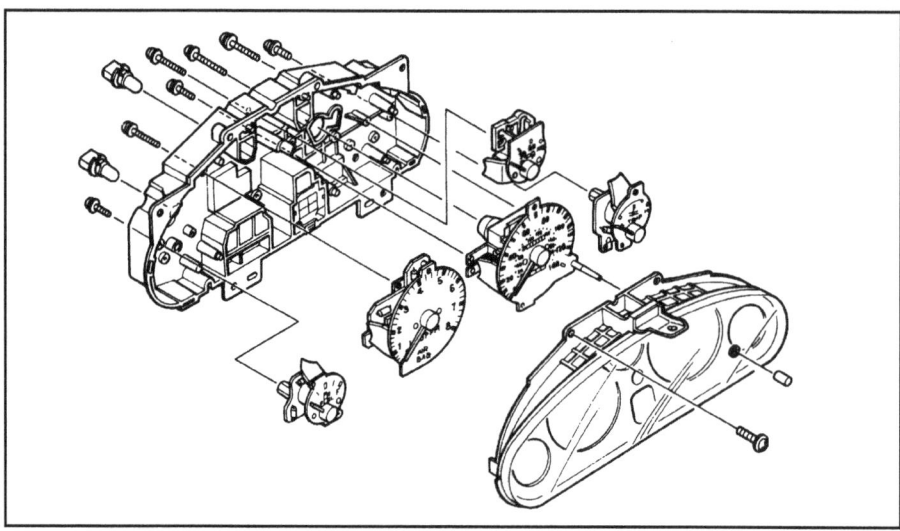

D14/4 INSTRUMENT PANEL AND INSTRUMENT DETAIL.

14. INSTRUMENT PANEL - REMOVAL, COMPONENT T/SHOOTING & INSTALLATION

☞ 1/1, 2 & 7/2.

1   **Warning!** For **all** of the following procedures it is essential that the airbag system has been disabled by isolating the battery ☞ 7/2 **and waiting at least 5 minutes** for the system's built-in capacitance to release its charge.

REMOVAL

2   On the underside of the column switch housing, remove the four crosshead (Philips) screws and pull the housing halves apart. The two halves clip together, and care should be taken when separating them not to break off the small guide pins (where applicable).

3   ☐+ Remove the two sheet metal screws which retain the instrument panel hood (bezel/shroud). These are fitted at the front lower edge of the hood and pass upwards to secure it to the dash panel. Once you've released the screws, the housing can be pulled back until it disengages from the dash panel. The rear of the housing is held to the dash panel by three metal clips and located by a long plastic pin.

14/4a The instrument panel is held by 4 screws.

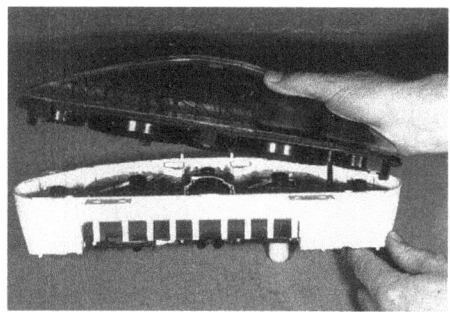

14/5a Unclip lens from front of panel.

14/3a Remove two sheet metal screws ...

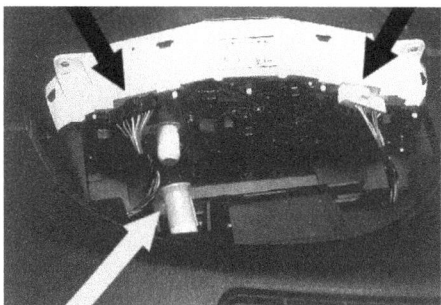

14/4b Release speedo cable and connectors.

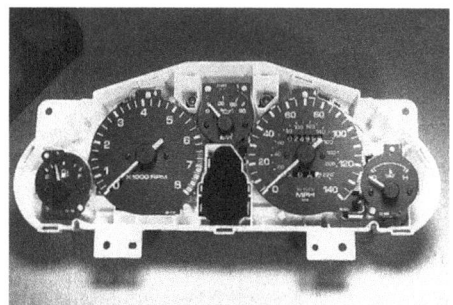

14/5b Individual instruments now accessible.

14/3b ... then disengage the instrument hood.

14/4c Carefully lift the panel away.

14/5c Printed circuit and bulb holders.

7: Electrical system

4   [icons]+ You now have clear access to the four screws which secure the instrument panel. Remove the screws and pull the panel towards you. As it moves away from the dash, unplug the instrument panel connectors - there are two of these, one at top left and one at top right - each is secured by a locking tab. The panel can now be pulled back further, but is still held by the speedometer drive cable. This is secured on the back of the instrument panel by (you guessed it) a locking tab. Press this in and pull the cable off the back of the speedometer, then lift the instrument panel away.

5   [icon]+ Individual gauges are screwed to the

14/6 Twist bulb holder to remove.

panel from the back, and can be removed after you've unclipped the lens from the front of the instrument panel. - see the accompanying diagram (D14/4) for details.

BULB REPLACEMENT

6   [icon] With the instrument panel removed, you have access to the back for bulb replacement. We suggest that you check all the bulbs while the unit is out of the car - you may have one or more burned-out bulbs which you haven't noticed. The bulb holders are removed by twisting them coun-

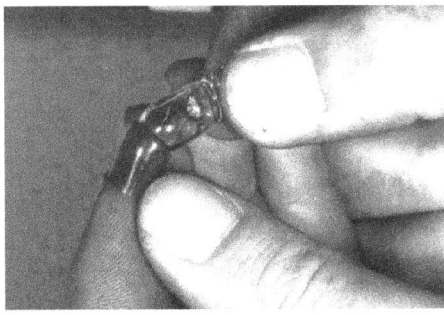

14/7 Some of the bulbs wear tiny condoms!

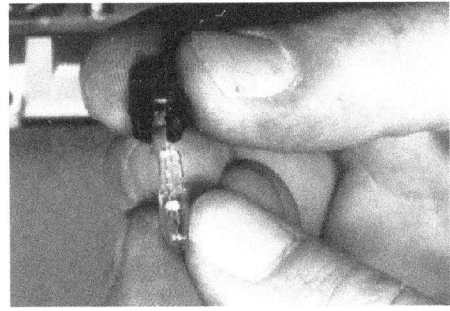

14/8 Capless bulbs are a push fit in holders.

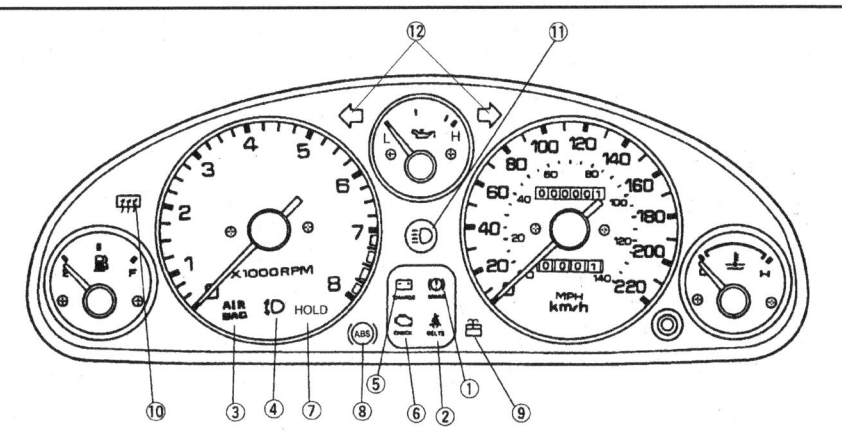

D14/9 TYPICAL ARRANGEMENT OF INSTRUMENT PANEL WARNING & INDICATOR LIGHTS.
Note that not all models will have all of these warning lights and that symbols vary: consult the owner's manual (handbook) that came with your car.
1 Brake system warning. 2 Seatbelt warning. 3 Airbag warning. 4 Headlight retractor indicator.
5 Generator (alternator) warning. 6 Malfunction indicator light (MIL)/"CHECK" warning.
7 "HOLD" warning (auto trans). 8 ABS (anti-lock brake system) warning. 9 Windshield washer fluid level warning. 10 Rear window defogger (defroster) warning. 11 Headlight high beam warning.
12 Turn signal (indicator) lights.

ter-clockwise - they can then be removed, together with the bulb. Note that most of the holders are black, but there are several green ones - these contain the illumination bulbs which are themselves colored.

7   [icon] The illumination bulbs are covered by what looks like tiny green rubbers/condoms (Wally, our Technical Adviser, assures us that this is because they practice safe illumination - and who are we to argue?). We don't know if the bulbs come this way if you buy them from a Mazda dealer, but we do know that you can roll the plastic sheaths off the bulbs and refit them easily enough, so if your replacement bulb is clear, remember to transfer the colored sheath before you fit it.

8   [icon] The bulbs are of the capless type, and are a push-fit in the holders. When you remove or fit them, make sure that the fine wire contacts do not get pushed out of alignment, or the bulb will not work. Note when purchasing replacement bulbs that there are two different physical sizes and various wattages. All are 12 volt and rated at 1.4W or 3.4W (except the airbag warning lamp, which is rated at 2W).

9   [icon] The exact arrangement of warning and illumination lamps varies according to the country in which the car was sold - on most models you'll find at least one unoccupied warning lamp recess on the back of the panel, and the bulbs have different functions, depending on market. We suggest that you remove bulb holders individually, noting where on the panel each was fitted to avoid confusion later (if you are unsure about whether a bulb was fitted to a particular hole in the panel, look for indentations in the soft copper tracks around the hole - the unused holes will be unmarked).

SPEEDOMETER

10   If you suspect that the speedometer has failed, it's worth noting that if the speedometer is not reading, but the odometer and trip meters continue to work, the instrument head can be considered to be at fault (drive is obviously reaching the unit but it has broken internally). The speedometer can be checked by inserting a small screwdriver in the back of the drive connection and spinning it with the fingers - if the needle moves, you can be fairly confident that the instrument is intact and that the fault lies in the drive cable.

11   [icon] If the cable appears to be broken, you will need to raise the car onto safety stands ([icon] 1/3) so that you can reach the lower connection at the transmission. This can then be detached by holding the hexagon end with a crescent wrench and unscrewing the knurled retaining ring with pliers.

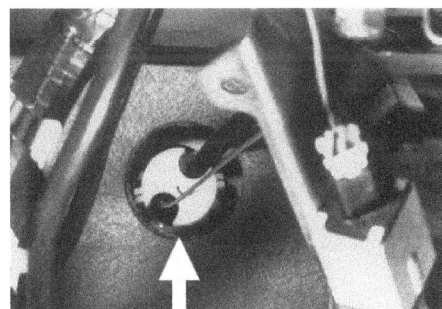

14/11 Speedo cable holder in firewall.

To allow the upper end of the cable to pass through the firewall, you need to push out the large plastic cup through which the cable passes.

12   Once you have removed the cable, any break is likely to be immediately obvious - they normally break at either end. If the cable is unbroken, check that it turns smoothly and without undue resistance. If it jerks badly when it is turned, this usually indicates that the cable is kinked and that it should be replaced - a wavering speedometer needle often indicates this problem. When installing the cable, remember to snap the plastic

Mazda Miata, MX-5, Eunos & Roadster

cup at the upper end back into its hole in the firewall.

13   The instrument head is held in the panel moulding by two screws, located either side of the projecting drive connection. If you are uncertain about its condition, you can, in theory, get the unit checked on a speedometer tester by your Mazda dealer, though normally they usually work fine, or not at all. The instrument head is installed by placing it in the panel recess and tightening the securing screws evenly.

TACHOMETER

14   You can check tachometer faults using a test tachometer hooked up to the instrument panel connectors. Alternatively, if you know another owner, ask whether you can swap instrument panels to check whether the fault lies in the tachometer or its wiring. If the test (or substitute) tachometer reads engine speed normally, you'll know that the fault lies in the wiring to the instrument or in the PCM (ECM).

ENGINE TEMPERATURE SENDER UNIT & GAUGE

15   The water temperature gauge operation can be checked without removing the instrument panel. With the engine cold, disconnect the wiring from the temperature gauge sender on the side of the heater outlet casting at the rear of the cylinder head. Connect the positive probe of an ohmmeter to the sensor terminal, and the negative probe to ground (earth). The meter should indicate a resistance of around 183 ohms. Start the engine and note the reading as the engine warms up. You are unlikely to reach the maximum engine temperature, but this should be 18-20 ohms.

16   Alternatively, you can remove the sender and heat its threaded area to 50°C (112°F) and measure the resistance between the central terminal and the sender body, which should be in the range 189-260 ohms. Use sealer on the unit's threads when installing it.

17   If the sender seems to be performing correctly, but the gauge does not, check the sensor wiring (black/blue) between the sensor connector and the **2L** terminal at the instrument panel connector. Continuity indicates that the wire is intact. If required, repair the wire or bypass it using a new wire of the same size and, preferably, color, taped to the harness.

18   If it looks like the gauge is faulty, you can get this checked on an SST by your Mazda dealer - take in the instrument panel assembly for this check. Alternatively, you could simply substitute a known good gauge to check whether your car's has failed.

FUEL GAUGE SENDER & FUEL GAUGE

19   As with the temperature gauge, much of the fuel gauge testing can take place without removing the instrument panel. The full procedure starts with tests on the sender unit. Remove the combined fuel pump/fuel gauge sender unit ☞ 5/16.

20   With the sender unit well away from the

14/19 Remove this access panel.

open fuel tank, measure the varying resistance it creates as the float is raised and lowered. Use an ohmmeter or a multimeter set to an appropriate resistance range (0-120 ohms), positive probe to the yellow wire terminal of the sender connector, and ground the negative (-) probe.

21   With the float at full droop (empty tank), you should get a reading of around 110 ohms. As the sender is moved to its highest position (full tank), the reading should fall to 3 ohms, with a reading of around 32.5 ohms at the mid point.

22   You can expect the meter needle to fluctuate through the test, as the sender wiper contact moves across the variable resistance (rheostat) windings - don't interpret this as a fault unless the reading stays at infinity for a significant part of the range, denoting broken or corroded rheostat windings. If you read infinite resistance or no resistance throughout the test, the sender can be considered inoperative.

23   If you have diagnosed a sender fault, you should install a new unit. However, before you rush out to buy a new unit to replace an intermittent one, we suggest that you try spraying switch cleaner into the sender unit and then working the float arm through its travel a few times. Hook up the ohmmeter as described earlier and recheck the resistance reading as you move the arm. With a little luck, you may have cleaned the contact surfaces enough to restore normal operation.

24   If the sender checks out OK, test continuity of the wire from the sender unit to the instrument panel (yellow wire on the fuel pump/sender connector to terminal **1A** (yellow wire) at the instrument panel connector. Continuity indicates that the wire is intact, infinite resistance indicates a break in the wire, and continuity between the wire and ground indicates a short. If required, repair the wire or bypass it using a new wire of the same size and, preferably, color, taped to the harness.

25   If you have got this far in the sequence, it looks like the gauge itself may be the problem. You can get this checked out by your Mazda dealer by taking in the instrument panel assembly - the check requires an SST. Alternatively, you could simply substitute a known good gauge to check whether your car's has failed.

OIL PRESSURE GAUGE

26   The oil pressure gauge operation can be checked without removing the instrument panel. With the engine stopped, disconnect the wiring

14/27 Removing oil pressure sensor.

from the oil pressure sender (located below the intake manifold, near the oil filter). Check that there is continuity between the unit's terminal and ground (earth).

27   Start the engine and check that continuity is lost within a few seconds as the oil pressure builds.

28   Check back along the sensor wiring (yellow/red) between the sensor connector and the **2B** terminal at the instrument panel connector. A reading of continuity indicates that the wire is intact, infinite resistance indicates a break in the wire, and continuity between the wire and ground indicates a short. If required, repair the wire or bypass it using a new wire of the same size and, preferably, color, taped to the harness.

29   If it looks like the gauge is broken, you can get this checked on an SST by your Mazda dealer - take in the instrument panel assembly for this check. Alternatively, you could simply substitute a known good gauge to check whether your car's has failed.

GENERAL CHECKS

30   Before installing the instrument panel, check that the flexible printed circuit on the back of the unit is in good condition. There is no obvious reason why this should ever get damaged, but if the circuit gets bent sufficiently, the tracks may become broken. Check for corrosion on the copper tracks where bulb holders and the two wiring connectors contact them. You can use switch cleaner to ensure a good contact and prevent damage from corrosion. If the tracks are already corroded, this can be removed with careful use of a pencil eraser to restore a clean polished finish, which can then be protected with switch cleaner/lubricant. If the corrosion is bad, or if the printed circuit is damaged, fit a new one.

INSTALLATION

31   Check that all bulb holders are secure and that the instruments have been fitted correctly. Position the unit over the steering column and reconnect the speedometer drive cable and the two wiring connectors. Place the unit against the dash panel and fit the four retaining screws, tightening them evenly. Clip the hood in place, then secure with two screws. Fit the steering column (combination) switch housing.

32   Reconnect the battery ☞ 7/2. Check the operation of the gauges, warning lamps and instrument illumination.

7: Electrical system

15. WARNING LAMPS, SWITCHES & SENSORS - LOCATION & TROUBLESHOOTING

☞ 1/1, 2 & 7/2.

1   The various warning lamps are housed in the instrument panel - for details on removal, bulb replacement and installation ☞ 7/14. If you have a single inoperative warning lamp the chances are that the bulb has burned out - always check this first. If all warning lamps are inoperative, this suggests that the main associated fuse (**METER 15A**) has burned out. If a warning lamp stays on all the time, it is either doing its job of warning you of a fault, or the warning lamp circuit concerned has a fault. Individual circuit checks are described below.

BRAKE WARNING CIRCUIT

2   If the brake warning lamp comes on, you should stop the car immediately and check the brake fluid level. If this is below the **MIN** level on the reservoir, check the cause of the level drop (badly worn brake pads or a hydraulic leak ☞ 9. **Warning!** This is a potentially dangerous situation - do not drive the car until you have checked the hydraulic system and pads.

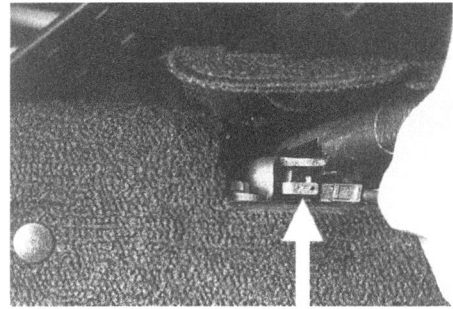

15/3 Parking brake switch from above.

3   ◨ If there is no fault in the brake system, check the operation of the parking brake switch - you can just about get to this on the side of the parking brake lever. If you find access difficult, remove the single screw holding the brake lever cover in place, and remove it by pulling the two halves apart - you will need to pull back the carpet around the lever base - this is held by a velcro pad.

4   Check for continuity between the switch terminal and ground. With the lever fully released, you should read zero continuity. There should be continuity when the lever is raised by one notch. If the readings are not as described, either adjust the switch or fit a new one.

5   If the parking brake circuit and brake system check out OK, this leaves the brake fluid level sensor in the master cylinder as prime suspect.

HAZARD WARNING INDICATOR LIGHT CIRCUIT (NOT FITTED ON ALL MODELS)

6   If the hazard warning light circuit operates normally, but the indicator light in the instrument panel does not come on, it is pretty certain that the bulb has burned out. Check and replace the bulb as necessary. If the fault persists, check the wiring from the indicator light to the hazard warning/turn signal relay. For some reason, Mazda does not detail this connection on its circuit diagrams, but we're pretty sure that the indicator light is connected by an orange wire to the flasher unit.

"HOLD" CIRCUIT (AUTO TRANSMISSION MODELS)

7   Check the bulb located in the back of the tachometer gauge if the "HOLD" warning light fails to operate, and replace it if it is burned out. If the problem remains unresolved after replacing the bulb, check the wiring between the instrument panel **1J** terminal (blue/black wire) to the switch at the side of the shifter base. The switch can be accessed after the between seats console has been removed ☞ 10/2.

8   ◨ Disconnect the harness wiring connector. Take a voltage reading at the A terminal (see diagram) of the switch side connector. You should read c.12 volts when the shift lever switch is released, and no voltage when it's depressed. If the readings are faulty, check that there is continuity between terminals **A** and **B** when the switch is depressed: if not, the shift knob (which includes the switch) will need to be replaced.

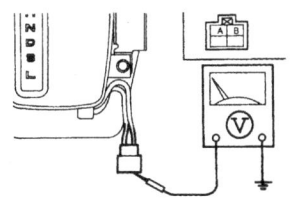

Position	Connector terminal	
	A	B
Normal (V)	B+	0
Depressed (V)	0	0

B+: Battery positive voltage
(V): Voltage

D15/8 "HOLD" SWITCH (AUTO TRANS) CHECKING.
See text.

SEATBELT WARNING CIRCUIT (WHERE FITTED)

9   ◨ Locate the warning (timer and buzzer) unit after removing the access panel under the steering column. The unit will be found amongst a group of relays mounted under the dash panel. If the unit operates as normal, of course, you can track it down by operating the buzzer, otherwise, refer to the accompanying diagram for location details.

10   If the light remains on for more than six seconds after the ignition switch is turned on, check the unit as follows. Unplug the wiring connector

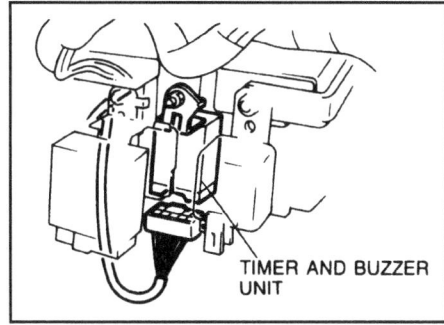

D15/9 LOCATION OF SEATBELT WARNING (TIMER & BUZZER) UNIT.

from the unit and turn the ignition switch to **ON**. If the instrument panel warning light comes on, check

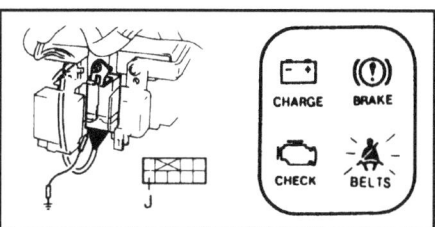

D15/11 GROUND TERMINAL 'J.'

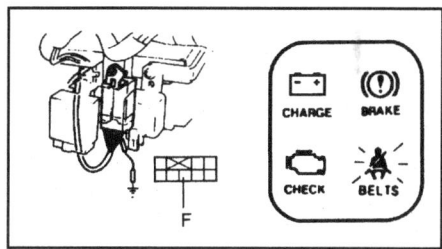

D15/12 GROUND TERMINAL 'F.'

the wiring between the unit and the warning lamp (blue/green wire to terminal **1B** on the instrument panel wiring connector). If the light does not come on, you need to fit a new timer and buzzer unit.

11   ◨ If the light fails to operate when the ignition switch is turned to **ON**, ground terminal **J** of the warning unit connector (which should be connected to the harness). Check that the light comes on when you turn the ignition switch to **ON**. If the light comes on, check the ground wire from the unit to the chassis, and repair or replace it as required. If the light does not illuminate, move on to step 12.

12   ◨ Ground terminal **F** of the connector and switch the ignition to **ON**. If the seat belt warning light illuminates, check the ground wire from the unit to the chassis. If the light does not illuminate, move on to step 13.

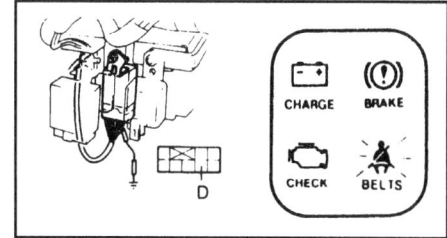

D15/13 GROUND TERMINAL 'D.'

7:19

Mazda Miata, MX-5, Eunos & Roadster

13 Next, ground terminal **D** of the connector and switch the ignition to **ON**. If the warning light comes on when the ignition is switched on, you will have to fit a new timer and buzzer unit. If the light does not come on, check the warning light bulb, and check the wiring between the unit and the instrument panel connector.

14 + Finally, you should check the seat belt buckle switch connectors for continuity and the buckle switch for correct operation (see diagrams). With the buckle fastened, you should read no continuity, unfastened - continuity. Repair the wiring harness or replace the buckle switch as necessary.

WINDSHIELD WASHER FLUID LEVEL SENSOR CIRCUIT (WHERE FITTED)

15 The washer level indicator light should come on when the level in the washer reservoir falls below **MIN**. If you have a fault, first check the bulb and replace it if it is burned out.

16 If the fault remains, disconnect the washer reservoir level sensor connector from the harness (washer reservoir location varies with market), and drain the reservoir. Check for continuity between terminals **A** and **B** of the reservoir side connector (see diagram) as the reservoir is refilled. While the washer fluid level is below **MIN** you should read continuity and above **MIN** no continuity: replace the sensor if necessary.

17 If the sensor and bulb are OK, check the continuity of the blue wire between the sensor to terminal **1L** of the instrument panel connector.

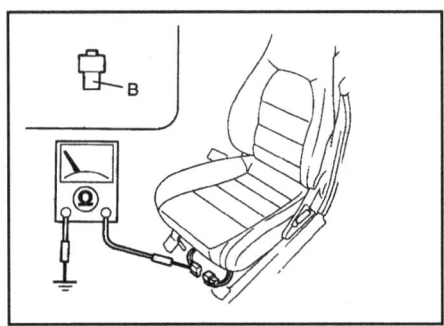

D15/14A CHECKING SEATBELT BUCKLE SWITCH CONNECTOR.

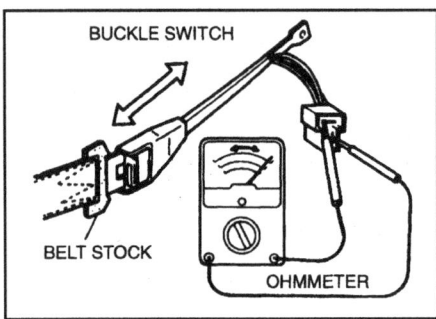

D15/14B CHECKING SEATBELT BUCKLE SWITCH & CONNECTOR.

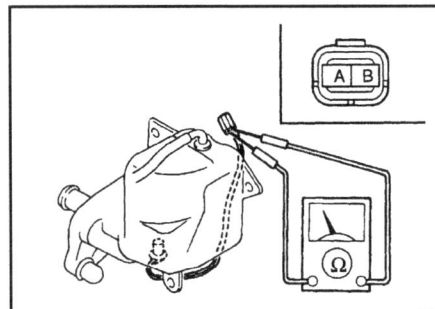

D15/16 CHECKING WINDSHIELD WASHER FLUID LEVEL SENSOR.

16. LIGHTING SYSTEM - INITIAL TROUBLESHOOTING

☞ 1/1, 2 & 7/2.

1 These cars come equipped with the normal range of lights. Specific details of the lighting arrangments and specification vary according to the country in which the car was sold, but, on the whole, the lighting system is pretty much as you'd find on any modern car. For the most part, initial troubleshooting of the lighting system is as you would expect - checking for burned out bulbs and testing switches, relays and wiring.

2 The use of pop-up headlights introduces a little electromechanical complexity; each headlight has its own motor arrangement controlled from the column lighting switch, a separate center panel switch and, if a problem arises, manually at the light itself.

3 When you are trying to track down a fault with any of the lighting circuits, give the nature of the fault some thought first. About the most common cause of problems will be a burned out bulb; if one headlight is not working on high beam, you can be pretty safe in assuming that the bulb has burned out a filament. If, on the other hand, the entire headlight circuit is down, you should be looking at the circuit in general, starting with the fuse which protects it, because it would be more than unlikely that all of the related bulbs would have burned out simultaneously.

4 If a headlight appears dim, the most likely cause is a poor ground (earth) circuit: check wiring and connectors for bad connections and/or dampness.

5 In the following sections we will be looking at diagnosing faults and circuit and component checks. Where more detailed testing or dismantling procedures are involved, references to other sections of this chapter will be found in the text.

17. HEADLIGHT CIRCUIT - TROUBLESHOOTING

☞ 1/1, 2 & 7/2.

Step 1

1 If the headlights fail to illuminate, start by checking the **HEAD 30A** fuse housed in the main fuse block in the engine compartment on the left-hand inner fender (wing). If the fuse has burned out it may be due to a brief overload, caused by a bulb burning out, for example, or it could be more serious. If the new fuse burns out immediately the lights are switched on, you'll need to investigate the headlight system wiring and connectors for faults. If the fuse was found to be undamaged ☞ Step 2.

Step 2

2 Locate the headlight relay which is mounted along with other relays on a bracket at the left side of the engine compartment (see diagram D7/3/9). The following voltage checks should be made with the relay connected to the wiring harness

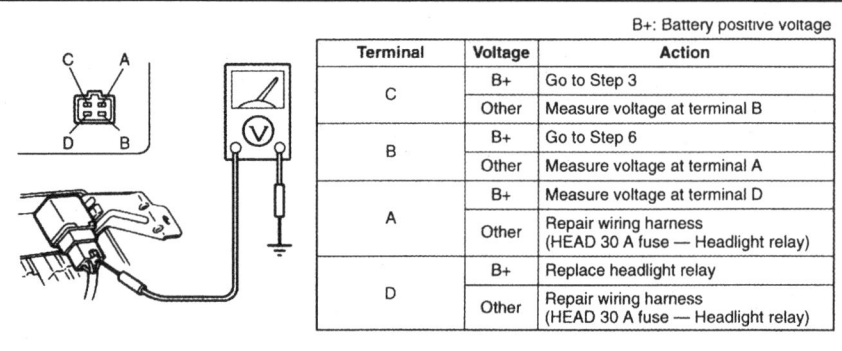

		B+: Battery positive voltage
Terminal	Voltage	Action
C	B+	Go to Step 3
	Other	Measure voltage at terminal B
B	B+	Go to Step 6
	Other	Measure voltage at terminal A
A	B+	Measure voltage at terminal D
	Other	Repair wiring harness (HEAD 30 A fuse — Headlight relay)
D	B+	Replace headlight relay
	Other	Repair wiring harness (HEAD 30 A fuse — Headlight relay)

D17/2 CHECKING HEADLIGHT RELAY.

			B+: Battery positive voltage
Terminal	Switch position	Voltage	Action
J	—	B+	Measure voltage at terminal I
		Other	Repair wiring harness (Headlight relay — Combination switch)
I	Low beam	B+	Measure voltage at terminal G
		Other	Replace combination switch
G	High beam	B+	Go to Step 4
		Other	Replace combination switch

D17/3 CHECKING HEADLIGHT TERMINALS OF COMBINATION SWITCH (1).

7: Electrical system

and with the headlights switched on. Insert the voltmeter positive (+) probe through the back of the wiring connector to the terminal to be checked, and ground the meter negative (-) probe. Note the reading found at each terminal and proceed as advised (see diagram).

Step 3

3   Access the combination switch connector ☞ 7/12 (**Caution!** The battery needs to remain connected, so take great care when working around the steering column not to cause the airbag to deploy). Using the meter positive (+) probe through the back of the wiring connector (don't separate the connector halves), and the meter negative (-) probe connected to ground, check the voltages at the terminals. Note the readings shown and follow the instructions given (see diagram). Leave the access panel off for now - you may need to make further tests at the connector.

Step 4

4   Check the headlight bulbs ☞ 7/27. If the bulbs have burned out, replace them. If the bulbs are OK, leave the bulb connectors off and move to Step 5.

Step 5

5   With the headlight bulb wiring connectors detached from the bulb terminals, check the voltages at the terminals. Note the readings found and follow the instructions given (see diagram).

Step 6

6   Moving back to the combination switch connector under the dash panel, carry out the following voltage checks. Insert the meter positive (+) probe through the back of the wiring connector (don't separate the connector halves), and the meter negative (-) probe connected to ground. Check the voltages at the terminals and follow the instructions given (see diagram).

18. HEADLIGHT RAISE/RETRACT SYSTEM - TROUBLESHOOTING

☞ 1/1, 2 & 7/2.

HEADLIGHT RETRACTORS INOPERATIVE ON BOTH SIDES

1   Start by isolating the exact nature of the fault by operating the headlight and retractor (center panel) switches separately. If the retractor system operates normally when the headlight switch is turned on ☞ Step 5; if not, try operating the center panel retractor switch. If the headlight retractor system operates ☞ Step 4; otherwise ☞ Step 1.

Step 1

2   Check the **RETRACTOR 30A** and **HEAD 30A** fuses in the main fuse block in the engine compartment on the left- hand inner fender (wing). If you find a burned out fuse, fit a new fuse of the correct rating and check whether the system operates normally. If the fuse fails again, you need to check the associated wiring for faults and repair as necessary. If the fuses prove to be undamaged, move to Step 2.

Step 2

3   If the headlights are fully or part way up, isolate the battery ☞ 7/2. Retract the headlights fully using the manual control, which will be found on the top of each retractor motor after pulling off the dust boot: turn the control knob clockwise until the headlight is fully down.

4   Disconnect the harness wiring connector at each motor. Reconnect the battery ☞ 7/2.

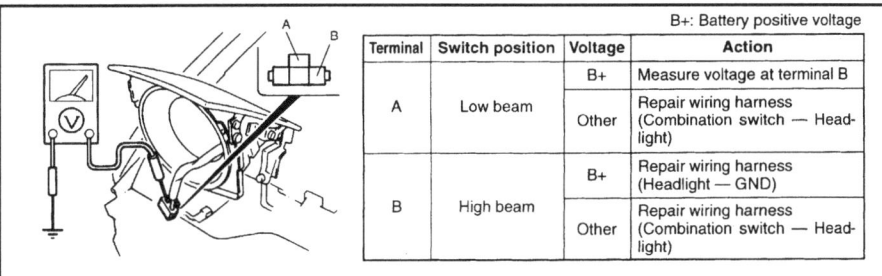

Terminal	Switch position	Voltage	Action
A	Low beam	B+	Measure voltage at terminal B
A	Low beam	Other	Repair wiring harness (Combination switch — Headlight)
B	High beam	B+	Repair wiring harness (Headlight — GND)
B	High beam	Other	Repair wiring harness (Combination switch — Headlight)

B+: Battery positive voltage

D17/5 CHECKING HEADLIGHT BULB CONNECTOR.

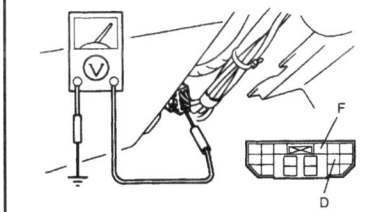

Terminal	Voltage	Action
F	B+	Measure voltage at terminal D
F	Other	Repair wiring harness (Headlight relay — Combination switch)
D	B+	Repair wiring harness (Combination switch — GND)
D	Other	Replace combination switch

B+: Battery positive voltage

D17/6 CHECKING HEADLIGHT TERMINALS OF COMBINATION SWITCH (2).

Terminal	Voltage	Action
A	B+	Measure voltage at terminal B
A	Other	Go to Step 5
B	B+	Measure voltage at terminal D
B	Other	Repair wiring harness (Headlight relay — Retractable headlight relay)
D	B+	Repair wiring harness (Retractable headlight relay — GND)
D	Other	Measure voltage at terminal G
G	B+	Repair wiring harness (Retractable headlight relay — Retractable headlight actuator)
G	Other	Replace retractable headlight relay

B+: Battery positive voltage

D18/7 CHECKING HEADLIGHT RETRACTOR RELAY.

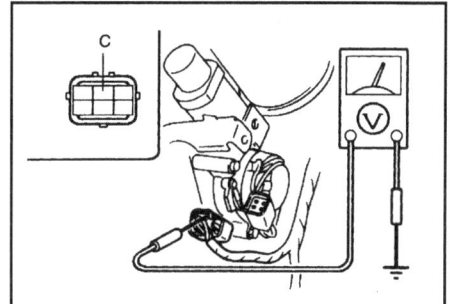

D18/4 CHECKING HEADLIGHT RETRACTOR CONNECTOR.

Connect a voltmeter positive (+) probe to the **C** terminal (red/yellow wire) on the harness side of the connector (see diagram). Turn on the headlight and retractor switches and check for battery voltage at. If you read battery voltage ☞ Step 3, if you read zero volts ☞ Step 4.

Step 3

5   With the retractor motor wiring connectors still unplugged, check for continuity between the ground (black wire) terminal and a body ground (earth) point. If there's continuity, you'll need to check the retractor motor ☞ 7/23. If no continuity is shown, check and repair or replace the black ground wire as necessary. Reconnect the motor wiring harness connectors.

Step 4

6   The retractor relay is located under the dash panel close to the flasher unit (see diagram D7/3/9) and is accessible once the cover beneath the steering column is removed.

7   Connect the meter negative (-) probe to ground, and then, with the positive (+) probe, check the terminal voltages (retractor switch should

7:21

Mazda Miata, MX-5, Eunos & Roadster

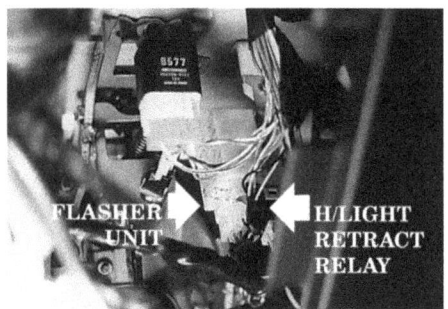

18/6 Flasher & h/lamp retract relays (rhd).

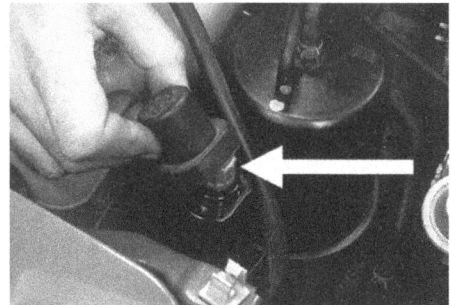

18/11 Manual headlight lifter/retractor.

be off, headlight switch on. Note the readings and follow the instructions (see diagram).

Step 5
8   Check the terminal voltages at the retractor switch in the center panel. Note that this check will require considerable preparatory dismantling ☞ 10/3.
9   Using the voltmeter positive (+) probe through the back of the wiring connector, with the negative (-) probe connected to ground, check the terminal voltages and follow the instructions (see diagram).

HEADLIGHT RETRACTORS INOPERATIVE ON ONE SIDE ONLY

10   In the event that one of the headlights refuses to pop up or retract, or is stuck part way, the usual cause will be something caught in the mechanism. The location of the headlights makes them prone to picking up twigs or small stones flung up by other traffic, and in cold climates, ice can build

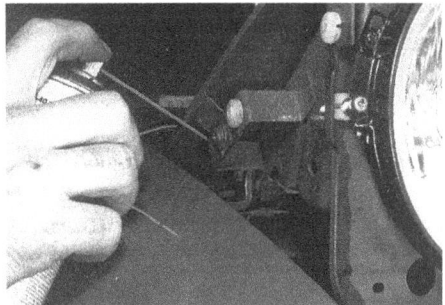

18/10 Lubricate headlight hinges often.

up and prevent the system operating normally. Regular lubrication of the hinges with WD40 or similar will help prevent this.
11   If a headlamp fails to raise or retract while you are driving, stop the car and turn the ignition switch off, then remove the **RETRACTOR 30A** fuse from the main fuse block in the engine compartment. Pull off the protective cap, and then use the manual knob (see photo) on top of the motor to raise or lower the headlight so that the obstruction (if there is one) can be removed, reinstall the fuse and check the operation of the system. If there's still a problem ☞ 7/18/3-5.

19. HEADLIGHT DIM-DIP SYSTEM (IF FITTED) - TROUBLESHOOTING

☞ 1/1, 2 & 7/2.
1   Cars produced for some markets (including the UK) are equipped with a headlight dim-dip system. This is designed to prevent the car being driven at night with parking lights only. If the parking lights are left on, and the car is subsequently driven away, the dim-dip system automatically turns on the headlight low beams at reduced power.
2   If you experience problems with the dim-dip system, check that the retractor system is operational by turning the headlight switch on. If the retractor motors fail to operate, the fault lies in this area ☞ 7/18.
3   If the headlights function normally, the terminal voltages at the dim-dip relay need to be checked. The relay is located on the relay bank in the engine compartment on the left of the car.

Terminal	Retractor switch position	Voltage	Action
C	Any	B+	Measure voltage at terminals B and D
		Other	Repair wiring harness (RETRACTOR 30 A fuse — Retractor switch)
B	OFF	B+	Repair wiring harness (Retractor switch — Retractable headlight actuator)
		Other	Replace retractor switch
D	ON	B+	Repair wiring harness (Retractor switch — Retractable headlight actuator)
		Other	Replace retractor switch

B+: Battery positive voltage

D18/9 CHECKING HEADLIGHT RETRACTOR SWITCH.

Removing the air intake hose and lifting the data link connector from its bracket will improve access to the relay bank and allow easier removal of the plastic cover over the relays. The relay is positioned at the rear of the outer bank. To gain access for testing, remove the relay bank from the body (10mm bolts) and turn it so that the meter probes can be inserted from the back of the wiring connector.
4   Refer to the accompanying diagram, and check the various terminal voltages according to the table. Note that the ignition switch must be turned to **ON** for this test, and the headlight switch

19/3 Relay bank on inner fender.

should be turned to the first position. If the terminal voltages check out as specified in the table, trace the white wire back from the relay to the dim-dip resistor (on bridge between air cleaner body and inner wing). Disconnect the wiring connector and check for resistance between the two resistor terminals. This should be around 1 ohm - if the resistance found is significantly different to this, fit a new resistor.

20. HEADLIGHT PASSING LIGHT (FLASHER) SYSTEM - TROUBLESHOOTING

☞ 1/1, 2 & 7/2.
1   If you experience problems with the passing light (headlight flasher) system, raise the headlights and check whether the high beams illuminate when the passing switch is operated. If not, for details of headlight circuit checks ☞ 7/16-18.
2   It appears that cars for some markets (ie Austria) have separate bulbs for the passing lights. We have never seen one of these cars, and Mazda doesn't mention where the bulbs might be located, but we guess you will know if you own such a car. If you do, check - and, if necessary - replace the passing light bulb(s).

21. HEADLIGHT BEAM - ADJUSTMENT

☞ 1/1, 2 & 7/2.
1   Before attempting adjustment of the headlight beams, be aware that most countries have strict legislation regarding headlight settings. We suggest that you have this setting carried out professionally using a commercial headlight alignment system. In an emergency, such as after installing a new headlight, or after impact damage has affected

7: Electrical system

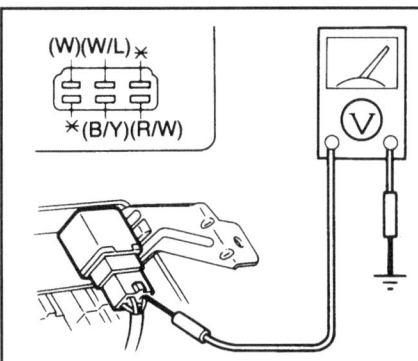

Wire	Voltage	Action
(B/Y)	12V	Next, check wire (W/L)
	0V	Repair wire (B/Y) (METER 10A fuse—Dim-dip relay)
(W/L)	12V	Next, check wire (W)
	0V	Repair wire (W/L) (Headlight switch—Dim-dip relay)
(W)	12V	Go to Step 3
	0V	Check dim-dip relay. If dim-dip relay is OK, repair wire (R/W) (Dim-dip relay—Headlight)

D19/4 DIM-DIP RELAY (IF FITTED): TESTING.

headlight aim, proceed as described below, and have the setting verified at the earliest opportunity.

2 Carry out this check at dusk or early evening, having first insured that all tire pressures are correct. Check that the unladen vehicle is standing on a flat, level surface, about 10 meters/ 10 yards from a flat wall or a garage door. Measure the height from the ground to the center of the headlight lens, and mark a horizontal line on the wall at this height.

23/1b ... and lever off link.

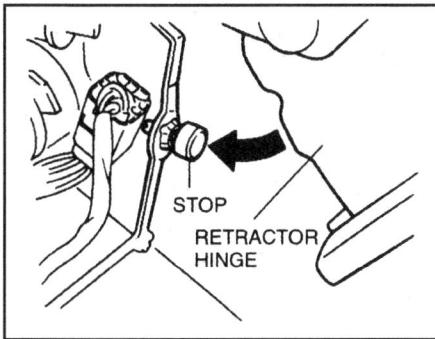

D22/2 HEADLIGHT DECK HEIGHT ADJUSTER STOP.

surrounding bodywork (close the hood while making this check). If necessary, adjust the headlight cover stop until the headlight is aligned correctly, then reconnect the retractor link.

23. HEADLIGHT RETRACTOR MOTOR - T/SHOOTING, REMOVAL & INSTALLATION

☞ 1/1, 2 & 7/2.

CHECKING OPERATION

1 ◻+ If you think there's a fault on one of the headlight retractor motors, it can be checked as follows. Retract the headlights fully, then isolate battery ☞ 7/2. Open the hood and locate and unplug the motor wiring connector from the harness. Using a screwdriver blade, push off the retractor link from the motor arm.

2 ◻ Check motor operation by connecting an external 12 volt battery as follows (see diagram). Connect the battery negative (-) lead to the motor

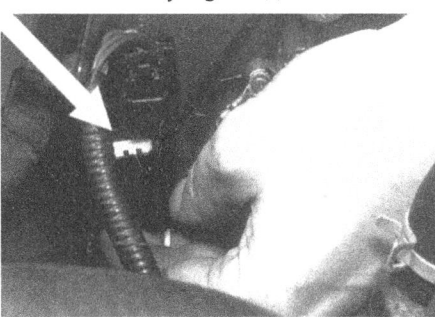

23/1a Unplug retractor wiring connector ...

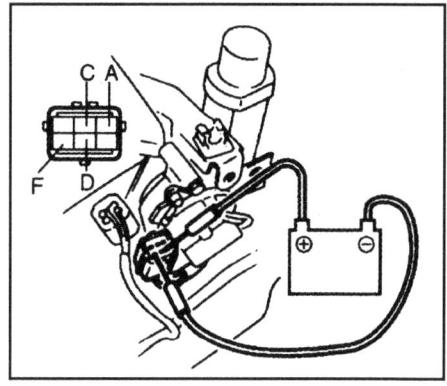

D23/2 HEADLIGHT RETRACTOR MOTOR: CHECKING OPERATION.

connector A terminal, then touch the battery positive (+) lead to the C terminal. The motor should run and lift the headlamp. Now move the battery positive (+) lead to the D terminal. The motor should run and retract the headlight. If the motor fails to operate, it should be replaced or repaired.

REMOVAL

3 ◻+ With the battery and wiring connec-

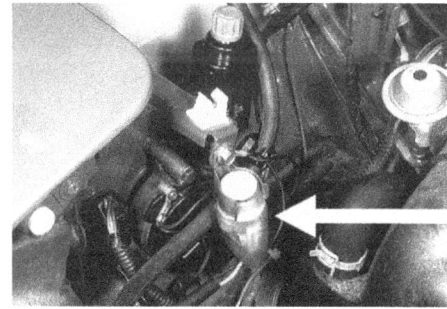

23/3a Remove foglight relay (if fitted) ...

23/3b ... disconnect wiring ...

21/3 Horizontal adjustment screw.

3 ◻ Turn the light switch on and set the lights at high beam. Check that the brightest spots on the wall coincide with the line made earlier, and that the beam centers are the same distance apart as the headlights. If you need to make adjustments, turn the screw under the headlight to adjust it in a vertical plane, and the screw at the 9 o'clock position (see photo) to move the light horizontally.

22. HEADLAMP DECK HEIGHT - ADJUSTMENT

1 If the headlight covers have been pushed down below hood (bonnet) deck level, try opening the hood and gently lifting the front edges of the headlight covers until you achieve the desired height.

2 ◻ If the covers keep falling below or lifting above the hood deck height, there is a more permanent form of adjustment. Open the hood, and locate the retractor motor arm where it connects to the retractor link. Pull off the link from its operating pin (the plastic cup will pop off if it is levered gently away with a screwdriver blade). Check that the headlight cover is flush with the

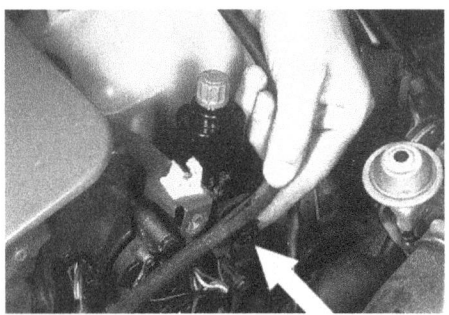

23/3c ... and move hoses.

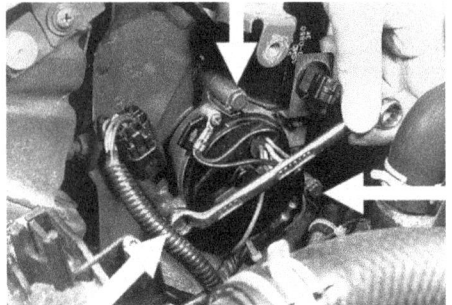

23/4 Remove motor securing bolts.

tors disconnected, and the retractor link still off the motor arm as described above, you can remove the motor. First, remove any fittings obstructing motor removal. On our project car, we had to unclip the fog lamp relay from its bracket, remove the bracket and free the ground wires; the radiator to reservoir hose was disconnected from its bracket on the side of the motor. On the left side, the power steering reservoir (where fitted) will need to be released and moved to one side for access. Depending on options and accessories fitted to your car, you may need to detach or move other items to get access to the motor.

4   Once you have sufficient working access, remove the three 10mm bolts which secure the motor to its mounting, and maneuver it clear of the headlight area. We found that we could not remove all three bolts fully due to space restrictions - in fact they are intended to remain in position in the motor body holes, and have plastic washers to prevent them from dropping out as the motor is removed.

CHECKING CONDITION

5   In theory, if the motor fails to run during the check described earlier, it should be discarded and a new unit fitted. This is certainly the easiest solution, but we thought that we would check out the alternatives. We found that it is perfectly possible to dismantle and reassemble the motor. While you cannot get replacement parts for the motors from Mazda, you might be able to find suitable brushes at an auto-electrical specialist, which could also carry out any repair work to the windings and commutator. It is also quite possible that the fault is due to dirt or oxidation, in which case a good clean may get the motor working again. So, if the motor is otherwise scrap, why not give it a try? Finally, remember that you might be able to obtain a serviceable motor from a wrecker's yard (scrapyard) at a considerable saving on the cost of a new unit.

6   + The first area to check is the contacts and switch rotor under the circular end cover. Remove the two securing screws and lift the cover off, noting that one of the screws carries a ground wire tag. Under the cover you will find three small spring contacts which run on copper tracks on the rotor. Check the contacts and the tracks for corrosion and oxidation. You can clean these after removing the grease with a solvent-moistened rag. We found that a pencil eraser will restore the surface without causing scoring. To make sure that

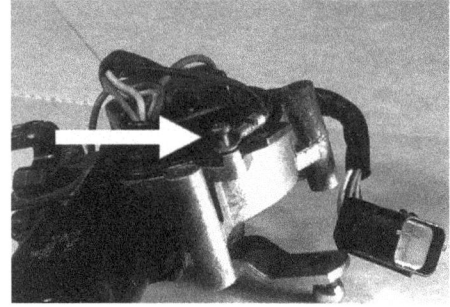

23/6a Remove securing screws and ...

23/6b ... lift cover off.

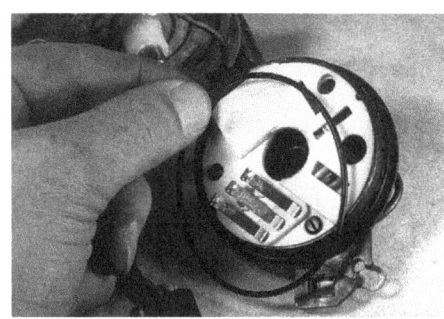

23/6c Note sealing ring.

the contacts are pressing firmly on the rotor, bend them outwards slightly. When everything looks clean and shiny, apply some silicone grease to the rotor. Check, and if necessary replace, the O-ring on the cover, then refit it and check whether the motor now operates normally.

7   The motor itself can be dismantled after pulling off the manual operating knob at the end of the motor armature, and removing the two crosshead screws holding the motor body to the gearbox. As you pull the motor body away, the armature will probably come with it, pulling out from the brush assembly. Remove the armature from the body (it will be held by the pull of the permanent magnets in the body), noting the shims on the outer end of the armature spindle - keep these safe and in the correct order. There is also a tiny bearing ball fitted to the inner end of the spindle - retrieve this and keep it safe.

8   Use a multimeter or continuity checker to test for insulation between the commutator segments and the core and spindle of the armature. If you find continuity at any point, you will need to fit a new motor (it is unlikely to be worth attempting to get the armature rewound).

9   Examine the commutator for wear or damage. Light discoloration and minor damage can be corrected by cleaning the commutator with fine sandpaper. Wrap the paper round the commutator and turn the armature until a bright, smooth finish is restored. In cases of more severe damage, have the armature set up in a lathe and remove the minimum amount of metal possible to restore the surface of the commutator segments. There are no specified service limits for the commutator, but if repair work would result in its diameter being reduced by an appreciable amount, the motor should be scrapped and a new one fitted.

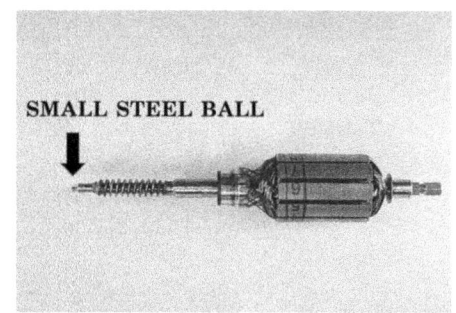

23/9 Armature: check the commutator carefully.

10   Check that the commutator runout is acceptable. Set the armature up on V-blocks or between lathe centers, and use a dial gauge (DTI) to measure commutator runout. Again, we have no service limits for this, but if the runout is greater than about 0.03mm (0.001in), either correct this by skimming in a lathe, or scrap the motor and fit a new one.

11   After working on the commutator, clean out the grooves between each segment. You can make up your own cleaning/recutting tool from a section of used hacksaw blade. Find the end where the teeth point back towards you as you hold the blade - this will be the cutting end, so wrap some tape around the other end to form a handle. Now grind the sides of the blade flat until it is a good fit in the commutator grooves. Undercut the grooves by drawing the tool along each one until you achieve a small undercut, then repeat the process on the remaining grooves. Use a little fine sandpaper to remove any burring that results.

12   If the brushes are worn down appreciably, you might like to try an auto-electrical specialist, which can probably supply something suitable as a replacement. You may not get an exact fit, so check this and, if necessary, file the brushes to fit the

7: Electrical system

holder, then solder them into the brush plate (or you could get the supplier to do this for you).

13   ◨+ When you assemble the motor, you'll need to hold the brushes back in their holders while you fit the armature. We used the plastic sleeve that protects the ends of new sparkplugs. Slit the sleeve lengthways and slip it into the center of the brush holder to retain the brushes. Put a small dab of grease in the hole on the inner end of the armature and stick the bearing ball in place. Slide the armature into position, removing the sleeve once the brushes are in place over the commutator. Fit the shims to the armature outer end.

23/13a Using a sleeve to hold back brushes.

23/13b Slide the armature into place.

14   When you fit the motor body, be aware that the magnets inside it will try to pull the armature out of the gearbox. You can prevent this by applying pressure on the operating arm so that the armature resists pulling out - you will need to experiment to find the correct amount of pressure to apply - it needs to be just less than that required to turn the armature.

15   ◨ Fit the body over the armature and install the retaining screws, tightening them evenly. Fit the manual knob over the armature end. There is an adjuster screw and locknut at the commutator end of the motor unit - this permits adjustment for

23/15 Adjusting armature endfloat/lash.

armature lash, the screw bearing on the steel ball in the end of the armature. If movement seems excessive, slacken the locknut and turn the screw inwards until it just contacts the ball. Back it off slightly to give just perceptible movement and secure the locknut. Now repeat the check described in paragraph 2. If the motor now runs as it should, you've just saved the cost of a new one.

INSTALLATION

16   Before installing the new or rebuilt motor, check that the mounting bolts are held in place by their plastic washers - there is not enough room to fit them through the mounting holes later. We recommend that you use copper/silicone-based grease on the threads - they are exposed to water and road dirt in use, and ours had begun to corrode badly.

17   Position the motor and tighten the three 10mm mounting bolts evenly. Snap the connecting link back onto the motor arm and reconnect the wiring connector. It is a good idea to temporarily reconnect the car's battery and check motor operation at this stage. Finally, reconnect and install any components removed to give access to the motor.

24. HEADLIGHT UNIT - REMOVAL, INSTALLATION & BULB REPLACEMENT

☞ 1/1, 2 & 7/2.

1   Bulb replacement is carried out after removing the headlight unit from its housing.

2   ◨+ Start by opening the hood (bonnet) and raising the headlights by operating the retractor switch. Remove the two screws on each side of the assembly and lift away the plastic headlight surround. Slacken the three small crosshead screws which secure the headlight retaining ring, if

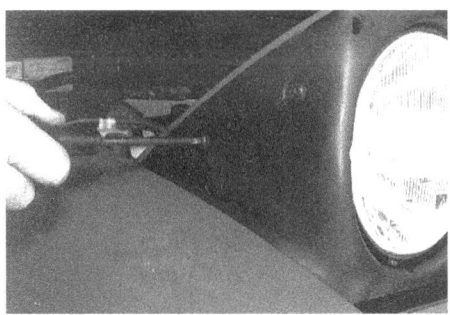
24/2a Remove the headlight surround ...

24/2b ... & remove three retaining screws ...

24/2c ... use penetrating oil if screws corroded.

necessary using a little WD40, or similar, to deal with corroded threads. (Note: do not disturb the headlight adjustment screws - you need to slacken the three black-finished screws spaced equally around the unit.) Turn the unit so that the screws pass through the enlarged slots of the retaining ring, and lift it out of its mounting.

3   ◨ Unplug the headlight wiring connector and lift the headlight unit away from the car.

4   ◨+ Models with separate bulbs only. Pull off the dust boot from the back of the bulb. Disengage the wire clip which retains the bulb and

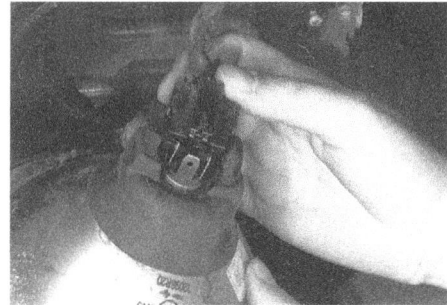
24/3 Unplug wiring connector ...

24/4a ... pull off boot ...

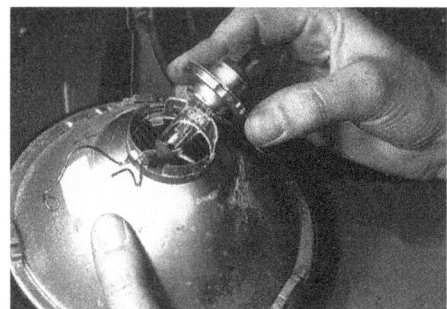
24/4b ... release clip & remove bulb.

Mazda Miata, MX-5, Eunos & Roadster

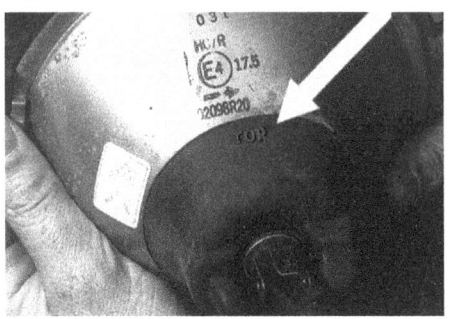

24/4c Make sure boot is right way up.

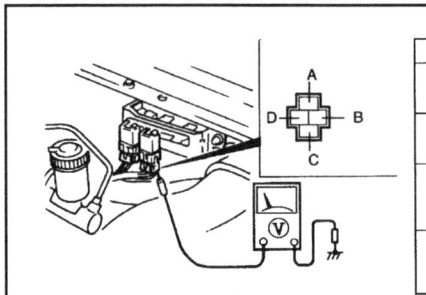

D25/4 PARKING LIGHT CIRCUIT: CHECKING TNS RELAY.
For some markets the fuse will be marked "TAIL 10A."

Terminal	Voltage	Action
C	B+	Go to Step 3
C	Other	Measure voltage at terminal D
D	B+	Go to Step 4
D	Other	Measure voltage at terminal A
A	B+	Measure voltage at terminal B
A	Other	Repair wiring harness (TAIL 15 A fuse — TNS relay)
B	B+	Replace TNS relay
B	Other	Repair wiring harness (TAIL 15 A fuse — TNS relay)

B+: Battery positive voltage

remove it from the headlight unit. **Warning!** The quartz halogen bulb gets extremely hot in use - take care to allow it time to cool down before handling. **Caution!** Never touch the bulb envelope with the fingers or skin acids may etch into it, causing it to shatter when it gets hot - handle the bulb only by its metal parts. Install the new bulb in the headlight (it will only fit in the correct position) and secure with the retaining clip. Fit the dust boot, noting that the **TOP** mark must be positioned uppermost.

5   Fit the wiring connector and the retaining ring, then reposition the headlight unit,

24/5 Headlight cover retained by two screws.

checking that the screw heads fit through the enlarged holes. Turn the retaining ring to lock it in place, then tighten the securing screws.

25. PARKING LIGHT (SIDELIGHT) CIRCUIT - TROUBLESHOOTING

PARKING FRONT & REAR, SIDE MARKER (IF APPLICABLE) AND LICENSE (NUMBER) PLATE LIGHTS.

☞ 1/1, 2 & 7/2.

1   In the event of problems with the above circuit/lights, follow each step in the checking sequence to identify the cause of the problem.

Step 1

2   Remove the access panel below the steering column and open the lid of the fusebox (Fuse Block No.1) below the dash panel. Remove the **TAIL 15A/TAIL 10A** fuse using the removal tool and check whether it is burned out. If it is, fit a new fuse and recheck operation. If the new fuse burns out, check the associated wiring for damage and shorts to ground, repairing or replacing damaged wires as necessary.

3   Remove the **BTN 40A** fuse from the main fuse block in the engine compartment and check its condition, fitting a new fuse if required. If the new fuse burns out, check the associated wiring for damage and shorts to ground, repairing or replacing damaged wires as necessary.

Step 2

4   With the headlight switch turned to its first position (parking/side lights), measure the terminal voltages of the TNS relay which is mounted on the relay bank on the left-hand side of the engine compartment (probably blue/green, white/blue & red/black wires). Refer to the accompanying drawing and table for details of terminal locations, the voltage reading expected and the check sequence.

Step 3

5   Check the condition of the bulb(s) in the affected lights, referring to the bulb replacement procedures described elsewhere in this chapter. If a burned out bulb is found, fit a new one of the correct rating and check operation of the system. If no burned out bulbs are discovered, check the wiring - particularly black ground wires - connected to the affected unit for continuity, repairing or replacing damaged wires as necessary; check connectors for dampness/damage.

Step 4

6   Access the combination switch connector ☞ 7/12. Unplug the switch from the wiring harness and then check continuity between connector terminals on the switch side (see diagram). If not as specified, fit a new combination switch.

26. DAYTIME RUNNING LIGHTS CIRCUIT - TROUBLESHOOTING

☞ 1/1, 2 & 7/2.

1   Cars for some markets (eg Canada) are equipped with daytime running lights (DRL) which should operate whenever the vehicle is driven (even when the headlight switch is turned off) unless the turn signals or hazard warning lights are on, or the parking brake applied. System operation can be checked as follows.

DRLS DO NOT ILLUMINATE (TURN SIGNAL LIGHTS OK)

2   **Warning!** Before going further, place wood blocks or chocks front and rear of the wheels to prevent the car from moving. Start the engine and allow it to idle, then release the parking brake. The running lights should illuminate. Note that if the turn signal switch is operated, the lights on that side should flash, while the remaining lights stay on constantly. Operating the hazard lights should override the running lights.

3   If the system does not work as described above, and the turn signal and hazard warning light systems are functioning normally, follow the check sequence described next.

Step 1

4   Remove the access panel below the steering wheel to gain access to the DRL control module, which can be identified by wire colors (probably L, W/B, L/Y, R, B, G/W, G/B, G/Y, G/O wires).

5   With the ignition switch turned to **ON** and the wiring connected to the DRL unit, measure the terminal voltages, referring to the accompanying drawing and table for terminal identification, expected voltage readings and suggested action.

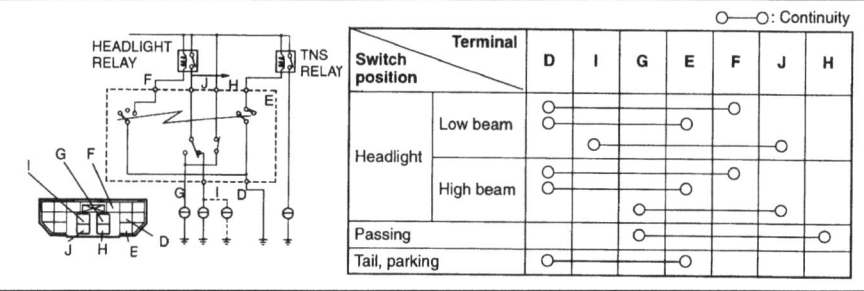

D25/6 PARKING LIGHT CIRCUIT: CHECKING COMBINATION SWITCH.

7: Electrical system

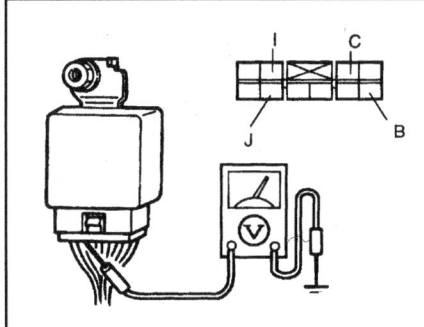

Terminal	Connection	Test condition	Regular voltage		Action
J	WIPER 20 A fuse	Constant	B+	OK	Measure voltage at terminal I
				NG	Repair wiring harness (WIPER 20 A fuse— DRL control module)
I	GND	Constant	Yes	OK	Measure voltage at terminal B and C
				NG	Repair wiring harness (DRL control module — GND)
B	Parking brake switch	Parking brake released	B+	OK	Go to step 2
				NG	Replace the DRL control module
C	Headlight switch	Headlight switch off	0	OK	Go to step 3
				NG	Replace the DRL control module

D26/5 DRL CIRCUIT: CHECKING CONTROL MODULE.

Use the meter positive (+) probe through the back of the wiring connector, and ground (earth) the negative (-) probe.

Step 2

6   Remove the single screw which secures the two halves of the parking brake lever plastic cover. Separate and remove the cover halves to gain access to the parking brake switch. Using a continuity tester or multimeter, check for continuity between the switch terminal and ground (see diagram). With the lever fully released, there should be no continuity, while continuity should be

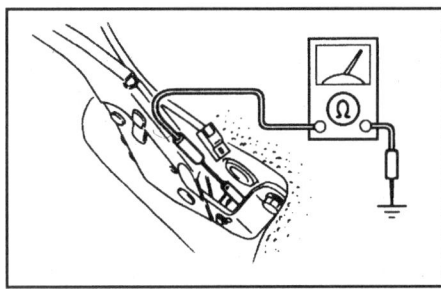

D26/6 DRL CIRCUIT: CHECKING PARKING BRAKE SWITCH.

indicated if the lever is pulled up one notch or more.

7   If the continuity check produces the specified result, check the wiring from the parking brake switch to the DRL unit (probably red wire) and repair or rewire as necessary. If the expected test result is not obtained, adjust or replace the parking brake switch.

Step 3

8   Access the combination switch connector ☞ 7/12. Unplug the switch from the wiring harness and then check continuity between connector terminals on the switch side (see diagram). If not as specified, fit a new combination switch. If the combination switch is operating

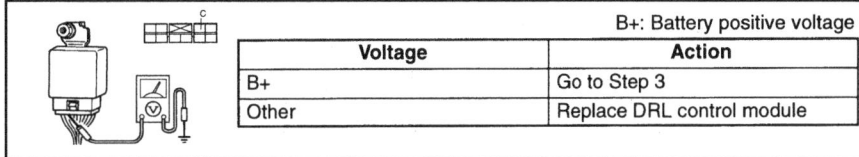

	Voltage	Action
	B+	Go to Step 3
	Other	Replace DRL control module

D26/11 DRL CIRCUIT: CHECKING CONTROL MODULE.

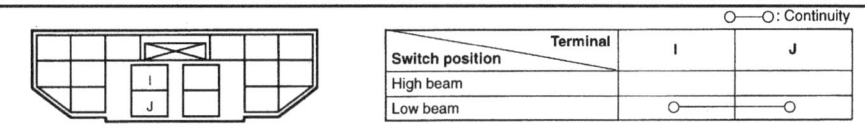

Switch position	Terminal	I	J
High beam			
Low beam		O——O	

D26/12 DRL CIRCUIT: CHECKING COMBINATION SWITCH.
Fuse will be marked "STOP 10A" on some models.

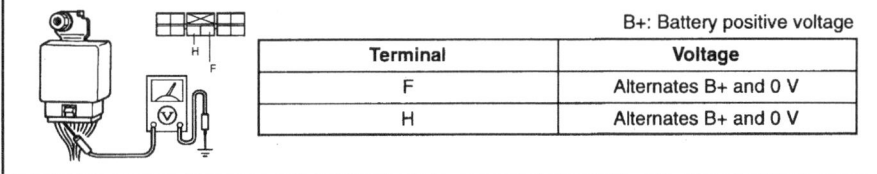

Terminal	Voltage
F	Alternates B+ and 0 V
H	Alternates B+ and 0 V

D26/13 DRL CIRCUIT: CHECKING CONTROL MODULE.

correctly, check and repair the wiring harness.

DRLS FAIL TO CANCEL

9   If the DRL system operates but does not cancel when it should, first check which switch setting is faulty as follows. **Warning!** Before going further, place wood blocks or chocks front and rear of the wheels to prevent the car from moving. Start the engine and allow it to idle, then release the parking brake. The running lights should illuminate.

Step 1

10   If the DRL system does not cancel when the headlight switch is turned on ☞ Step 2. If the system does not cancel when the turn signal or hazard warning switch is turned on ☞ Step 4. If the DRL system fails to cancel when the parking

brake is applied ☞ Step 5.

Step 2

11   Remove the access panel below the steering wheel to gain access to the DRL control module which can be identified by wire colors (probably L, W/B, L/Y, R, B, G/W, G/B, G/Y, G/O wires). With the ignition turned to **ON** and headlight switch at its first position, check the voltage at terminal **C** (see diagram) of the DRL control module.

Step 3

12   Access the combination switch connector ☞ 7/12. Unplug the switch from the wiring harness and then check continuity between connector terminals on the switch side (see diagram). If not as specified, fit a new combination switch. If the combination switch is operating correctly, check and repair the wiring harness.

Step 4

13   With the ignition switch in the **ON** position and the turn signal (indicator) switch on, check the voltage at terminals **H & F** (see diagram)

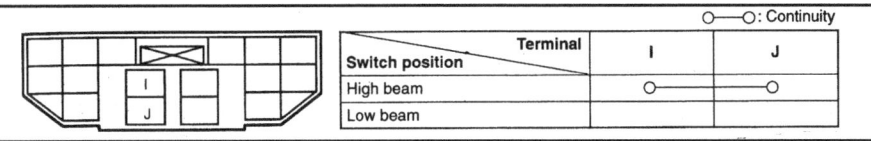

Switch position	Terminal	I	J
High beam		O——O	
Low beam			

D26/8 DRL CIRCUIT: CHECKING COMBINATION SWITCH.

Mazda Miata, MX-5, Eunos & Roadster

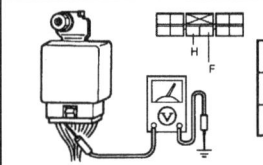

Terminal	B+: Battery positive voltage
	Voltage
F	Alternates B+ and 0 V
H	Alternates B+ and 0 V

D26/14 DRL CIRCUIT: CHECKING CONTROL MODULE.

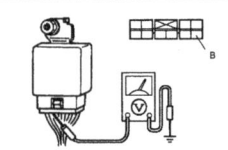

	B+: Battery positive voltage	
Voltage		Action
B+		Go to Step 6
Other		Replace DRL control module

D27/2 STOP LIGHT CIRCUIT: CHECKING SWITCH.

of the DRL control module.

Step 5

14 With the ignition turned to **ON**, pull the parking brake on by more than one notch; check the voltage at terminals **B** (see diagram) of the DRL control module.

Step 6

15 ☞ 7/26/6-7.

27. STOP (BRAKE) LIGHT CIRCUIT - TROUBLESHOOTING

☞ 1/1, 2 & 7/2.

ALL STOP LIGHTS FAIL TO ILLUMINATE
Step 1

1 If the stop lights are completely inoperative, the first thing to check is the fuse. This is the **STOP 15A** or **STOP 10A** fuse housed in Fuse Block No.1 under the dash panel - you'll need to remove the access cover beneath the steering column to reach the fuse. If the fuse has burned out, fit a new one and check the operation of the stop lights. If the fuse burns out again, check through the associated wiring and repair any short discovered; also check connectors.

Step 2

2 ☞ ☐ If the fuse checked out OK and the fault persists, turn on the ignition switch and check the voltages on the stop light switch as follows (see

27/2 Location of stop light switch.

diagram). Connect the meter negative (-) probe to ground, then introduce the positive (+) probe through the back of the wiring connector to each terminal in turn.

			B+: Battery positive voltage
Inspection condition	Terminal	Voltage	Action
Constant	A	B+	Measure voltage at terminal B
		Other	Repair wiring harness (STOP 15 A fuse — Brake switch)
Brake pedal depressed	B	B+	Go to Step 3
		Other	Inspect brake switch

D27/2 BRAKE LIGHT CIRCUIT: CHECKING SWITCH.

	B+: Battery positive voltage
Voltage	Action
B+	Repair wiring harness (Brake light — GND)
Other	Repair wiring harness (Brake switch — Brake light)

D27/4 STOP LIGHT CIRCUIT: CHECKING LIGHT UNIT CONNECTORS.

Step 3

3 If the switch is working normally, check the condition of the stop light bulbs. If they are burned out, fit new ones and check the operation of the stop light system again. If the bulbs are intact ☞ Step 4.

Step 4

4 ☐ If the fault remains, the problem lies in the wiring to the rear light units. Unplug the connectors to the stop lights in both combination light units and, if applicable, the high level stop light. With the ignition switch to **ON** and the brake pedal depressed, check the voltage readings on the harness side of the connectors (see diagram). Also check ground (earth) wire terminals (black wires) for continuity to the car's body.

ONE STOP LIGHT FAILS TO ILLUMINATE

5 If only one stop light is affected, the most likely cause is a burned out bulb, and you should always check this first. If this does not rectify the problem ☞ 7/27/4.

28. TURN SIGNAL & HAZARD WARNING CIRCUIT - TROUBLESHOOTING

☞ 1/1, 2 & 7/2.

1 Where the turn signal warning lamp on the instrument panel flashes rapidly, this almost invariably means a burned out bulb in one of the turn signal lights, or an open circuit in the associated wiring - always check this before moving to the check sequence described below.

TURN SIGNAL & HAZARD WARNING LIGHTS FAIL TO ILLUMINATE
Step 1

2 Check the **HAZARD 15A** or **HAZARD 10A** and the **METER 15A** or **Meter 10A** fuse in the Fuse Block No.1 under the dash panel, removing the access panel to do so. If the fuse has burned out, fit a new one, having first checked the wiring for shorts or damage.

Step 2

3 ☐ ☞ Locate (see diagram D7/3/9) the flasher unit under the dash panel after removing the access panel beneath the steering column. Without unplugging the unit's connector, check the voltage at terminal **H** (see diagram).

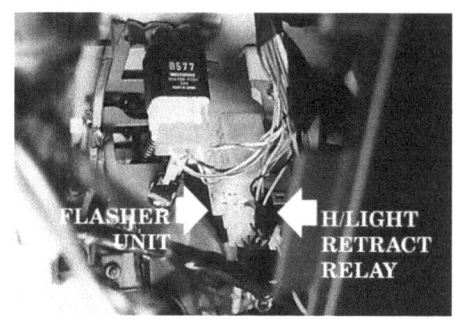

28/3 Location of flasher unit (rhd cars).

7: Electrical system

Step 3

4   📖 Unplug the flasher unit connector. Use a continuity tester or ohmmeter to check for continuity between terminal **A** and body ground (see diagram). Plug the connector together again.

Step 4

5   📖 Access the combination switch connector ☞ 7/12. Without unplugging the connector, with the ignition **ON** and the turn signal switch on (either direction), check voltage at terminals **C** & **B** (see diagram).

Step 5

6   📖 With the ignition **ON** set the turn signal switch to right turn. Without unplugging the flasher unit's connector, check the voltage at terminal **F** (see diagram).

Step 6

7   📖 With the ignition **ON** set the turn signal switch to left turn. Without unplugging the flasher unit's connector, check the voltage at terminal **E** (see diagram).

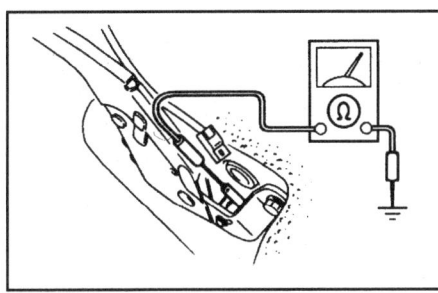

D28/6 TURN & HAZARD LIGHT CIRCUIT: CHECKING FLASHER UNIT.

Step 7

8   📖 Check continuity of the hazard warning/retractor switch ground terminal (black wire) and body ground (see diagram). Note that this check will require considerable preparatory dismantling ☞ 10/3.

Step 8

9   📖 Check continuity of the hazard warning switch **G** & **H** terminals (see diagram). If correct ☞ Step 9, if incorrect replace retractor/hazard switch.

Step 9

10   📖 Unplug the harness connector from the flasher unit. Operate the hazard warning switch. Check for continuity between terminal **C** of the harness side connector and body ground (see diagram).

Step 10

11   📖 Reconnect the flasher unit harness connector and turn the ignition switch to **ON**. Set the turn signal switch to the turn right position. Measure the voltage at terminal **G** of the connector (see diagram).

Step 11

12   📖 Reconnect the flasher unit harness connector and turn the ignition switch to **ON**. Set the turn signal switch to the turn left position. Measure the voltage at terminal **D** of the connector (see diagram).

Step 12

13   📖 Disconnect the turn signal light connectors at front and rear of the car. Turn the ignition switch to **ON** and set the turn signal switch to turn right and turn left, as appropriate, as you

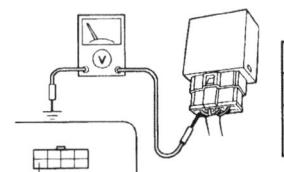

Voltage	Action
B+	Go to Step 3
Other	Repair wiring harness (HAZARD 15 A fuse — Flasher unit)

B+: Battery positive voltage

D28/3 TURN & HAZARD LIGHT CIRCUIT: CHECKING FLASHER UNIT.

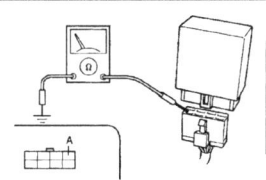

Continuity	Action
Yes	Reconnect connector and go to Step 4
No	Repairing wiring harness (Flasher unit — GND)

D28/4 TURN & HAZARD LIGHT CIRCUIT: CHECKING FLASHER UNIT.

Terminal	Voltage	Action
C	B+	Measure voltage at terminal B
	Other	Inspect combination switch
B	B+	Go to Step 5
	Other	Inspect combination switch

B+: Battery positive voltage

D28/5 TURN & HAZARD LIGHT CIRCUIT: CHECKING COMBINATION SWITCH.

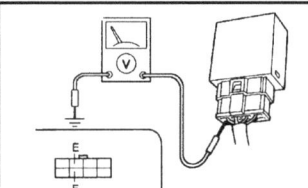

Voltage	Action
B+	Turn ignition switch to LOCK and go to Step 7
Other	Repair wiring harness (Combination switch — Flasher unit)

B+: Battery positive voltage

D28/7 TURN & HAZARD LIGHT CIRCUIT: CHECKING FLASHER UNIT.

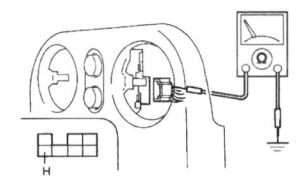

Continuity	Action
Yes	Go to Step 8
No	Repair wiring harness (Hazard warning switch — GND)

D28/8 TURN & HAZARD LIGHT CIRCUIT: CHECKING HAZARD SWITCH.

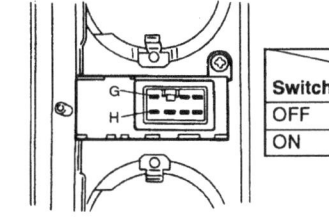

Switch position \ Terminal	G	H
OFF		
ON	O	O

O—O: Continuity

D28/9 TURN & HAZARD LIGHT CIRCUIT: CHECKING HAZARD SWITCH.

Mazda Miata, MX-5, Eunos & Roadster

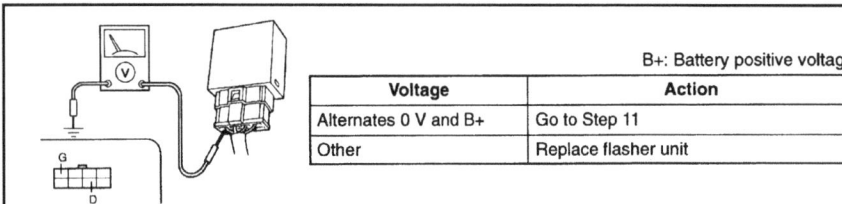

D28/10 TURN & HAZARD LIGHT CIRCUIT: CHECKING FLASHER UNIT.

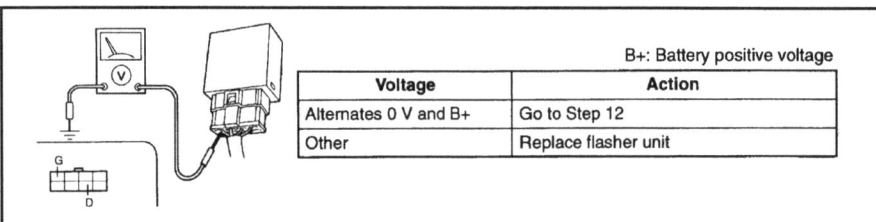

D28/11 TURN & HAZARD LIGHT CIRCUIT: CHECKING FLASHER UNIT.

D28/12 TURN & HAZARD LIGHT CIRCUIT: CHECKING FLASHER UNIT.

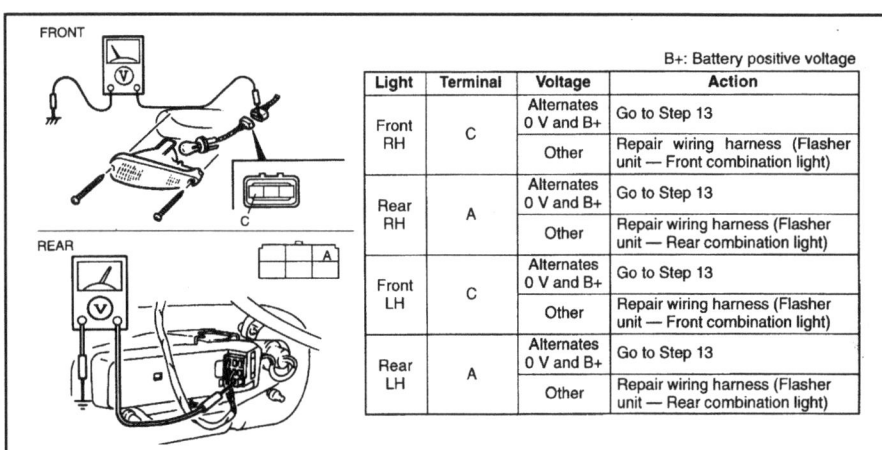

D28/13 TURN & HAZARD LIGHT CIRCUIT: CHECKING LIGHT UNIT CONNECTORS.
Fuse will be marked "HAZARD 10A" on some models.

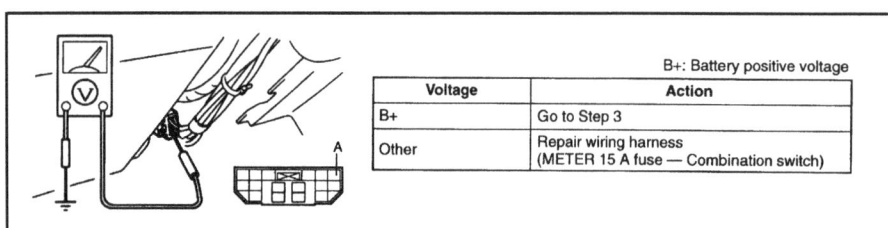

D28/16 TURN SIGNAL LIGHT CIRCUIT: CHECKING COMBINATION SWITCH.
Fuse will be marked "METER 10A" on some models.

check connector terminal voltages on both sides of the cars (see diagram). If you have to check and repair wiring, pay special attention to ground circuit continuity.

Step 13
14   Remove and check the bulbs and check the condition of the bulb holders. Replace any bulbs that have broken filaments.

TURN SIGNAL LIGHTS FAIL TO ILLUMINATE (HAZARD WARNING OK)

Step 1
15   Check **METER 15A** or **METER 10A** fuse in Fuse Block No.1.

Step 2
16   🔲 Access the combination switch connector ☞ 7/12. Without unplugging the connector and with the ignition **ON** check the voltage at terminal **A** (see diagram).

Step 3
17   🔲 With the ignition **ON** set the turn signal switch to right or left turn. Without unplugging the combination switch connector check the voltage at terminals **C** & **B** (see diagram).

Step 4
18   🔲 With the ignition **ON** set the turn signal switch to right turn. Measure the voltage at terminal **F** of the flasher unit (see diagram).

Step 5
19   🔲 With the ignition **ON** set the turn signal switch to left turn. Measure the voltage at terminal **E** of the flasher unit (see diagram).

HAZARD WARNING LIGHTS FAIL TO ILLUMINATE (TURN SIGNAL OK)

Step 1
20   🔲 Check continuity of the hazard warning/retractor switch ground terminal (black wire) and body ground (see diagram). Note that this check will require considerable preparatory dismantling ☞ 10/3.

Step 2
21   🔲 Check continuity of the hazard warning switch **G** & **H** terminals (see diagram). If correct ☞ Step 3, if incorrect replace retractor/hazard switch.

Step 3
22   ☞ 7/28/10.

29. BACKUP (REVERSING) LIGHT CIRCUIT - TROUBLESHOOTING

☞ 1/1, 2 & 7/2.

1   If you have problems with the backup/reversing lights, always check bulb condition before you do anything else. If one light only has failed, you know that the system is operating normally, but that the non-functioning bulb has either burned out, or the light's wiring is damaged. If both lights are inoperative, check the **METER 15A** or **METER 10A** fuse in Fuse Block No.1. Fit a new fuse if necessary, and check whether the lights operate normally. If the fuse burns out again, check for a short in the wiring.

7:30

7: Electrical system

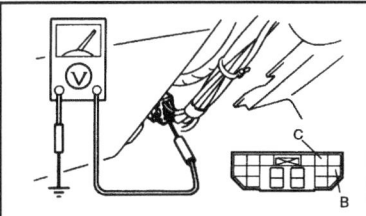

Terminal	Voltage	Action
C	B+	Go to Step 4
C	Other	Inspect combination switch (Refer to page T-12)
B	B+	Go to Step 5
B	Other	Inspect combination switch (Refer to page T-12)

B+: Battery positive voltage

D28/17 TURN SIGNAL LIGHT CIRCUIT: CHECKING COMBINATION SWITCH.

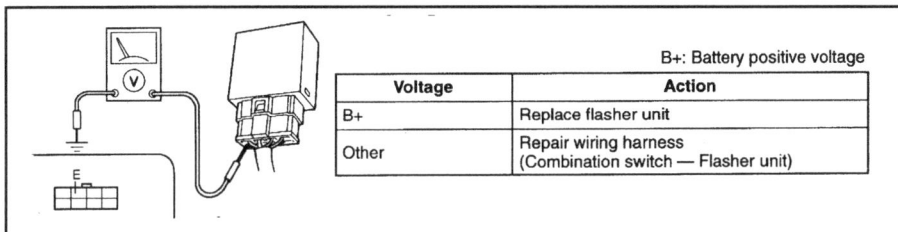

Voltage	Action
B+	Replace flasher unit
Other	Repair wiring harness (Combination switch — Flasher unit)

B+: Battery positive voltage

D28/18 TURN SIGNAL LIGHT CIRCUIT: CHECKING FLASHER UNIT.

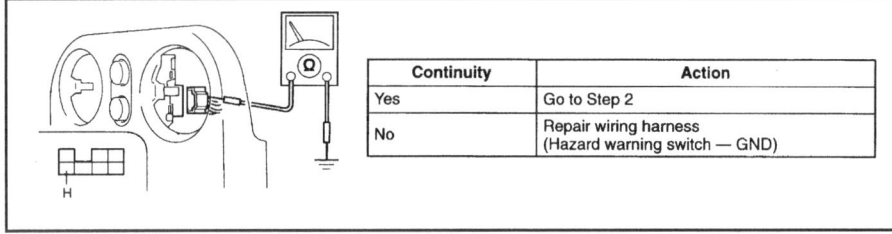

Voltage	Action
B+	Replace flasher unit
Other	Repair wiring harness (Combination switch — Flasher unit)

B+: Battery positive voltage

D28/19 TURN SIGNAL LIGHT CIRCUIT: CHECKING FLASHER UNIT.

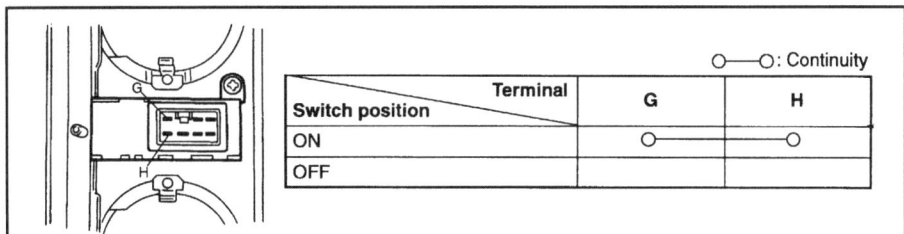

Continuity	Action
Yes	Go to Step 2
No	Repair wiring harness (Hazard warning switch — GND)

D28/20 HAZARD LIGHT CIRCUIT: CHECKING SWITCH.

Switch position \ Terminal	G	H
ON	O——O	
OFF		

O——O: Continuity

D28/21 HAZARD LIGHT CIRCUIT: CHECKING SWITCH.

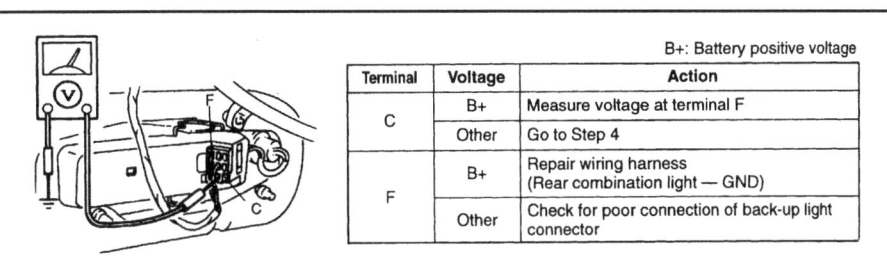

Terminal	Voltage	Action
C	B+	Measure voltage at terminal F
C	Other	Go to Step 4
F	B+	Repair wiring harness (Rear combination light — GND)
F	Other	Check for poor connection of back-up light connector

B+: Battery positive voltage

D29/2 BACKUP LIGHT CIRCUIT: CHECKING COMBINATION LIGHT CONNECTOR.

2 If the bulbs and fuse are intact, check for battery voltage at the rear light combination unit connectors which should not be unplugged (see diagram). With the ignition switch turned to **ON** and reverse selected, you should read battery voltage at the **C** terminal (probably red/green wire). If not, try grounding the black wire terminal to a sound body ground point - if the light then works, you need to check and repair the ground wiring/connection.

3 If you still read zero volts at the **C** terminal, you'll need to check the switch operation. On manual transmission cars, the switch is located

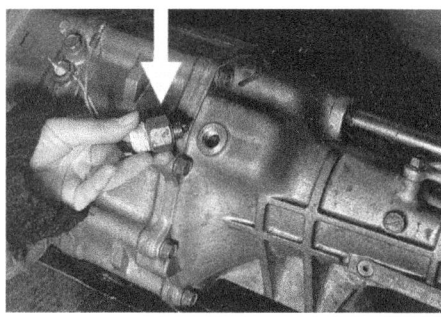

29/3 Reversing light switch (man. trans. cars).

on the tail extension of the transmission, just to the left of the centerline (see photo). If there is not continuity between the two terminals when reverse is selected (and zero continuity in all other positions), fit a new switch. If the switch checks out OK, check the wiring connections between the **METER** fuse and the switch, and then between the switch and the light units.

4 On automatic transmission cars, the backup (reversing) lights are operated by the transmission range switch, and this may require adjustment. Check that, with the ignition switch turned to **ON**, the lights do not flash on at some point as the shift lever is moved through its travel. If so, the need for adjustment is indicated ☞ 7/9/8-13. If the problem is not one of adjustment, unplug the range switch connector and check terminals **G** & **I** (on the switch side) for continuity with reverse selected (see diagram). In this situation, the switch should show continuity and no continuity in all other selector positions: replace the switch if it gives faulty readings.

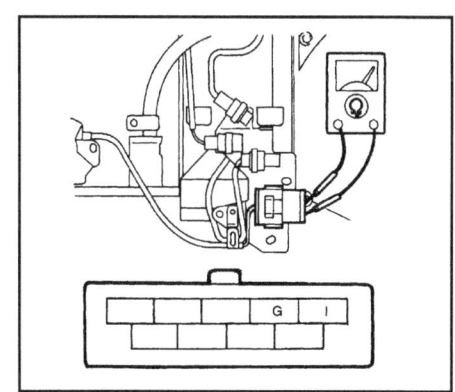

D29/4 BACKUP LIGHT CIRCUIT: CHECKING RANGE SWITCH (AUTO TRANS).

Mazda Miata, MX-5, Eunos & Roadster

30. TAIL LIGHT UNIT - BULB & LENS REPLACEMENT

☞ 1/1, 2 & 7/2.

BRAKE, TURN SIGNAL (INDICATOR), PARKING (SIDE) & BACKUP (REVERSING) LIGHTS

1   ◻+ The tail and brake light bulbs can be removed after their shared bulb holder assembly has been unclipped from inside the trunk: if fitted, the bulb of the high mount brake light can be pulled out after its holder is twisted out of the light unit in the trunk lid. The turn signal bulb holder is fitted separately and can be removed by turning it counter-clockwise. Check that any replacement bulbs are of the correct voltage and wattage, noting that the wattage details vary according to the country in which the car was originally sold. The bulbs (except the capless bulb for the high mount brake light) are standard bayonet fitting - press them lightly into their holders, then turn them counter-clockwise to release them.

2   ◻+ In the event of damage to the light unit lens, the light unit can be removed from the car after detaching the bulb holder assembly as de-

30/1a Unclip bulb holder from rear of light ...

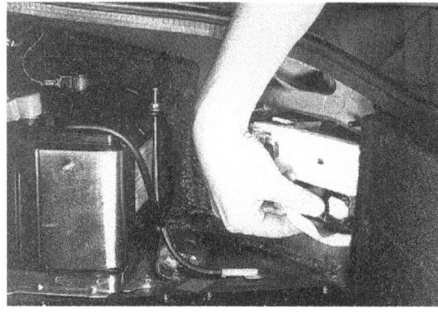
30/2a Free wire clips & remove bulb holder ...

30/2b ... remove nuts from four mounting studs ...

30/2c ... remove light unit ...

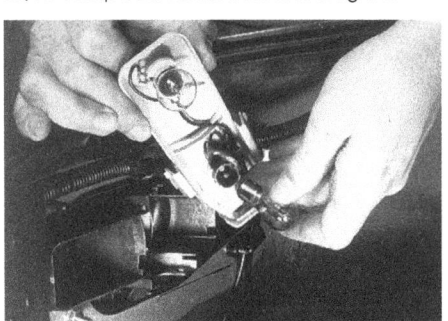
30/1b ... and remove tail/brake light bulbs.

30/2d ... and foam seal.

30/1c Turn signal bulb holder twists out.

scribed above. Where fitted, unclip and remove wiring clips from the projecting end of the mounting studs, then unscrew the four 10mm nuts to allow the unit to be removed from the car. Take care not to damage the foam seal, which can be carefully peeled off the back of the unit.

3   It is possible to fit a new lens once any remaining fragments of the old lens have been removed. The lens is bonded to the light unit with a hot-melt adhesive, and this can be softened by careful use of a hot air gun (the whole assembly is made of plastic, so don't overdo the heating).

4   If the old lens is more or less intact, insert a wood rod (or a small hammer handle) through one of the light apertures and use this to push the lens away from the unit. Where only fragments of lens remain, pick these off the unit with a screwdriver blade. When removing the lens, try to leave the hot-melt adhesive in place if you can - it can then be re-used to hold the new lens - just soften the adhesive with the hot air gun and press the new lens into place, making sure it beds firmly around the outer edge.

5   If you were unable to re-use the hot-melt adhesive, remove all traces of it from the unit, then apply a bead of suitable waterproof adhesive to retain the new lens. We have found that, on similar jobs, a clear, silicone-rubber gasket compound is just about unbeatable; it sticks the new lens securely in position, stays resilient, and is totally waterproof. If you use this type of sealant, apply a thin bead all the way round the unit sealing face and let it stand for about 5 minutes. Press the lens onto the sealant, and then leave it to harden for a while - preferably overnight.

6   Before fitting the unit back into the car, you should check that the lens seal is watertight by partially immersing the unit in water. Install the foam gasket, then install the unit into its recess and fit the retaining nuts, tightening them evenly to avoid stressing the plastic unit. Fit any wiring guide clips by pressing them over the projecting thread ends, then clip the bulb holder back into place.

31. FRONT COMBINATION LIGHT UNIT - BULB REPLACEMENT

☞ 1/1, 2 & 7/2.

TURN SIGNAL (INDICATOR) & PARKING (SIDE) LIGHTS

1   Access to the front combination light bulb or bulbs (depending on market) requires removal of the light unit. Remove the two screws which retain the light unit to the body and lift it away. Release the bulb holders by twisting them counter-clockwise.

2   ◻+ If two bulbs are fitted, the smaller of the two is of the capless type and can be removed from its holder by pulling. The larger turn signal or combination bulb can be removed by depressing it slightly and turning it counter-clockwise.

3   When fitting new bulbs, make sure that you use replacements of the correct rating. When

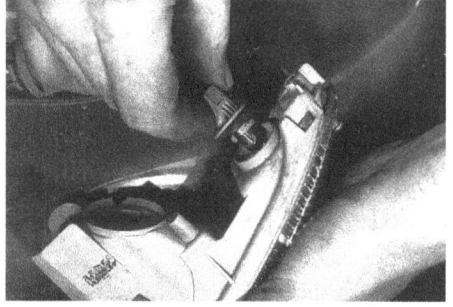
31/2a Twist out bulb holder and ...

7: Electrical system

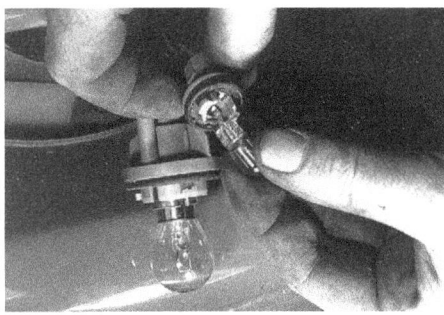

31/2b ... pull out capless parking (side) light bulb.

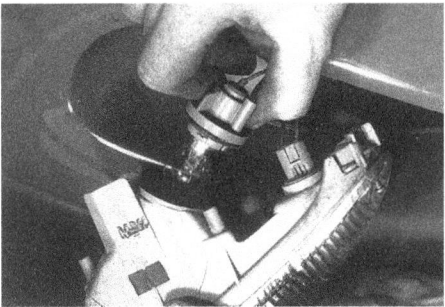

31/2c Twist out bulb holder and ...

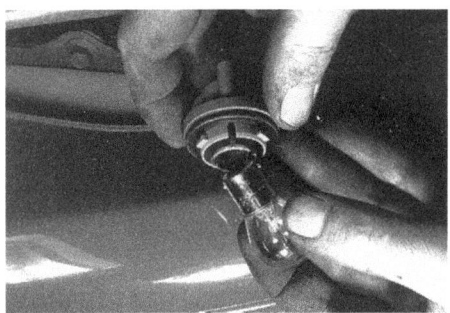

31/2d ... twist out larger turn signal bulb.

installing the unit, fit the retaining screws and tighten them evenly. Do not overtighten.

32. SIDE MARKER LIGHTS (WHERE FITTED) - BULB REPLACEMENT

☞ 1/1, 2 & 7/2.

1   📷 Access to the side marker (front & rear) light bulbs requires removal of the two screws which retain the light unit to the body. Release the bulb holder by twisting it counter-clockwise.

2   The bulb is of the capless type and can be removed from its holder by pulling. When fitting new bulbs, make sure that you use replacements of the correct rating. When installing the unit, fit the retaining screws and tighten them evenly - do not overtighten.

3   Note that cars sold in some markets have reflectors in place of illuminating side marker lights.

33. TURN SIGNAL SIDE REPEATER LIGHTS (WHERE FITTED) - BULB REPLACEMENT

☞ 1/1, 2 & 7/2.

1   📷+ Access to the side repeater light bulb requires removal of the light unit. Using a screwdriver covered with tape to prevent paint damage, and with a piece of card between the blade and the car body, from the back edge gently pry out the unit. Release the bulb holder by twisting it counter-clockwise.

2   The bulb is of the capless type and can be removed from its holder by pulling it gently. When fitting new bulbs, make sure that you use a replacement of the correct rating. When installing the unit, check that it snaps back securely into its recess.

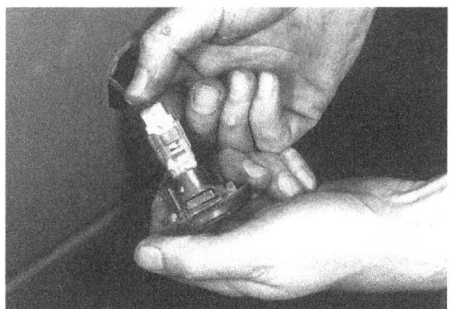

33/1a Pry light unit from body ...

33/1b ... to access bulb.

34. LICENSE PLATE LIGHT - BULB REPLACEMENT

☞ 1/1, 2 & 7/2.

1   📷 If the license plate is lit from above, access to the bulb requires removal of the two screws which pass through the lens and light unit and secure it to the bodywork of the car. Lift away the lens and lower the unit so that the bulb can be accessed. The bulb is of the capless type and can be removed from its holder by pulling it gently. When installing the unit, check that it is positioned correctly,

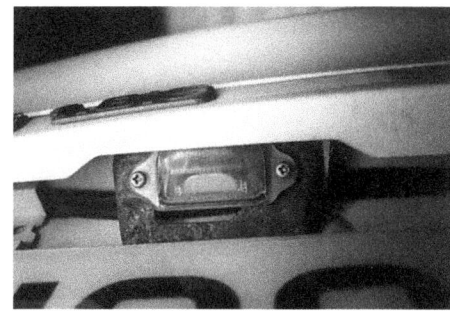

34/1 Remove screws to access bulb.

then fit the two screws to secure the unit and lens, taking care not to overtighten.

2   If the license plate is lit from the side, the bulb holder can be twisted out from inside the trunk (boot). Press the bulb into the holder and twist it counter-clockwise to remove it.

3   When fitting new bulbs, make sure that you use replacements of the correct rating.

35. FOGLIGHT, REAR (WHERE FITTED) - BULB REPLACEMENT

☞ 1/1, 2 & 7/2.

1   📷 Remove the two screws which secure the lens to the light unit. Lift away the lens so that the bulb can be reached. The bulb can be removed from its holder by pushing it inwards slightly, then turning it counter-clockwise.

2   When fitting a new bulb, make sure that you use a replacement of the correct rating. When installing the lens, check that it is positioned correctly, then fit the two screws to secure the lens to the light unit, taking care not to overtighten.

35/1 Bulb accessible after lens removed.

36. DRIVING/FOGLIGHTS, FRONT (WHERE FITTED) - BULB REPLACEMENT

☞ 1/1, 2 & 7/2.

1   📷+ The driving/fog lights (if fitted) are mounted inside the air intake at the nose of the car. To access to the bulbs, remove the two screws which retain the outer lens assembly and lift the lens away. Remove the two screws which secure the light unit, lift it out slightly and disconnect the wiring. Release the bulb by disengaging the wire clip which retains it in the back of the reflector.

32/1 Side marker lens/reflector held by screws.

Mazda Miata, MX-5, Eunos & Roadster

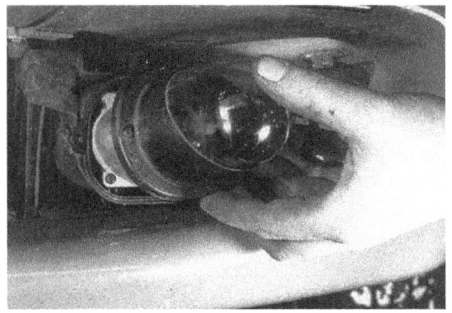

36/1a Remove outer lens ...

36/1b ...lift out light unit & disconnect wiring.

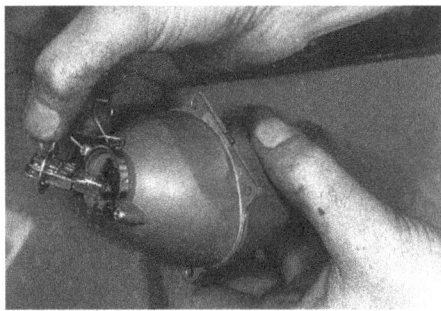

36/2a Align new bulb in its holder ...

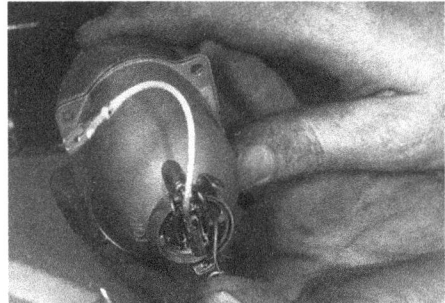

36/2b ... & secure with wire clip.

2   ◻+ Fit the new bulb, turning it to align it in the holder. Fit the retaining clip, then reconnect the wires to the unit. Install the unit in its casing and tighten the retaining screws evenly. Fit the outer lens assembly.

37. INTERIOR LIGHTS - TROUBLESHOOTING & BULB REPLACEMENT

☞ 1/1, 2 & 7/2.
1   ◻+ 1996 and earlier cars have one or two

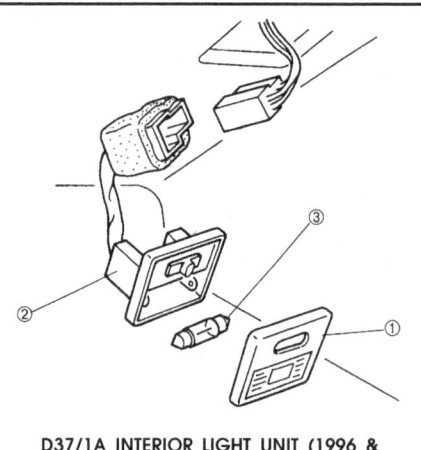

D37/1A INTERIOR LIGHT UNIT (1996 & EARLIER).
1 Lens. 2 Light unit. 3 Bulb.

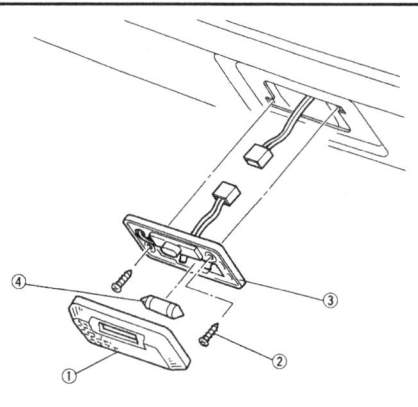

D37/1B INTERIOR LIGHT UNIT (1997 & LATER).
1 Lens. 2 Retaining screw. 3 Light unit. 4 Bulb.

interior lights mounted on the dashboard to illuminate the seat/footwell area. Later cars have an interior light mounted in the top rail of the windscreen.

2   Interior lighting is controlled by a three position switch, allowing it to be turned off completely, turned on manually, or operated automatically by the door switches.

3   If the light (or one of the lights) is not working, the most likely cause is a burned out bulb. Check this by removing the light unit lens, using a small screwdriver to carefully pry it off. Remove the bulb and, if it is burned out, replace with a new bulb of the correct rating.

4   If both lights are inoperative in any switch position, check the **ROOM 10A** fuse, replacing if burned out. If the new fuse burns out, check the wiring between the fuse, lights and door switches, repairing or rewiring any faulty section.

5   ◻ ◻ If the operation of a door switch is suspect, remove the switch from the car after unscrewing its mounting screw. Disconnect the switch from its wire, and check for continuity between the switch terminal and mounting plate. Continuity should exist while the switch is released, with no continuity shown while it is depressed (see

37/5 Wiring of door switch (trim removed).

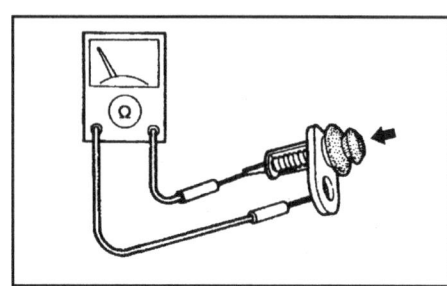

D37/5 INTERIOR LIGHT CIRCUIT: CHECKING DOOR SWITCH.

diagram). If not as described, fit a new switch.

ASHTRAY LIGHT

6   ◻+ There is a further minor interior light in the form of the ashtray light in the rear (between seats) console. If this is not working, check first that it is not simply obscured by cigarette ash - it is right in line for this to happen. If you need to fit a new bulb, you will have to remove the center console ☞ 10/2. The bulb holder is secured to the underside of the console by a single screw and a locating peg.

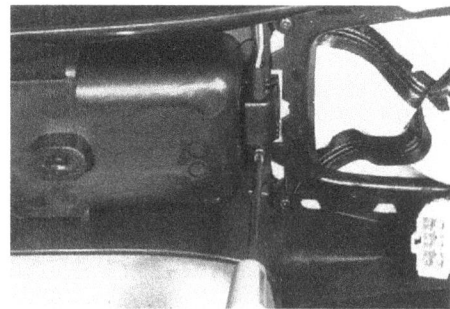

37/6a Ashtray light unit is secured by a screw.

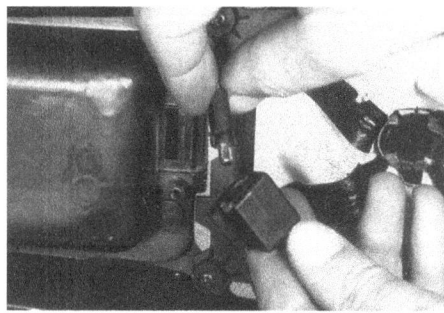

37/6b Pull out bulb holder & remove bulb.

7: Electrical system

38. TRUNK (BOOT) LIGHT - TROUBLESHOOTING & BULB REPLACEMENT

1   Some models feature a trunk light operated by a switch built into the trunk lock. To replace the bulb simply pull the existing bulb from the bulbholder and replace with a new bulb of the correct wattage.

2   If the trunk light fails to illuminate and the bulb is known to be good, check and, if necessary replace the **ROOM 10A** fuse in Fuse Block No.1.

3   ⌻ If the light still does not work, unplug the electrical connector from the trunk lock and

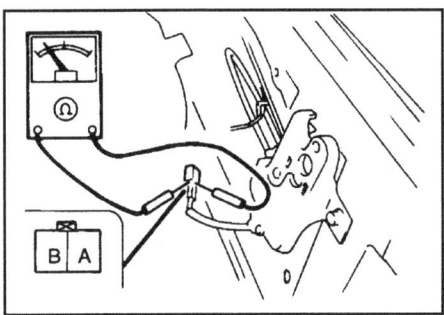

D38/3 TRUNK LIGHT: CHECKING SWITCH.

check for continuity between the two terminals (switch side) with the trunk lid latched and open (see diagram). There should be continuity when the trunk lid is open and none when it is closed. If the switch is faulty, you'll need to replace the trunk lock.

4   If the fault still persists, check and repair the wiring between the fuse, light and switch.

39. PANEL LIGHT CONTROL SWITCH (WHERE FITTED) - TESTING

☞ 1/1, 2 & 7/2.

1   ⌻ The panel lighting intensity can be regulated using this rotary switch, on models so equipped. To check its operation, pop the switch

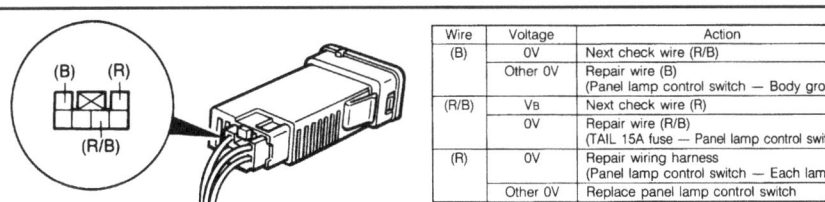

D39/1 PANEL LIGHT CONTROL SWITCH: CHECKING.

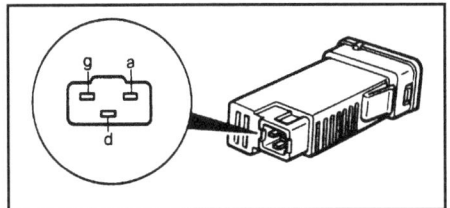

D39/2 PANEL LIGHT CONTROL SWITCH: TERMINAL IDENTIFICATION.

control out of the dash panel (use a screwdriver blade to gently pry it out). Turn the headlight switch on, and set the panel light control switch to its **MAX** position, then use a voltmeter to check the terminal voltages as shown in the accompanying illustration and table.

2   ⌻ Next, disconnect the panel light control switch, and connect the positive (+) battery voltage to terminal **d** of the switch and ground (earth) terminal **g**. Connect the voltmeter positive (+) probe to the switch terminal **a**, and ground the negative (-) probe.

3   Check the voltage reading on the meter. With the switch at **MIN**, approx. zero volts should be shown, increasing to around 10 volts at the **MAX** position. If the readings are faulty, fit a new switch unit.

40. HORN CIRCUIT - TROUBLESHOOTING & HORN REPLACEMENT

☞ 1/1, 2 & 7/2.

BOTH HORNS FAIL TO WORK -
Step 1

1   Check the condition of the **STOP 10A** or **STOP 15A** fuse in Fuse Block No.1. If it has burned out, fit a new fuse and check horn operation. If the fuse burns out immediately, check the horn wiring for shorts, repairing or rewiring as necessary.

Step 2

2   ⌻ 📷 Disconnect the wiring connectors from the horn units. Apply battery positive (+) voltage to the horn terminal, and ground the horn body. If the horn sounds, move to step 3. If not, fit a new horn. The horn units are each retained by a single mounting bolt in the nose of the car: note that access is improved if the closing panel above them is removed.

Step 3

3   Remove the airbag module from the steering wheel ☞ 7/44 & 7/46. **Warning!** The airbag module contains an explosive charge which deploys the bag when triggered electrically. Note that triggering can take place even if the car's battery is disconnected, unless the current retained by the electrical system's capacitance is allowed to discharge.

4   ⌻ With the airbag module removed, check for continuity between the horn switch connector and the steering column. If the horn switch is

40/2 Location of horns (radiator removed).

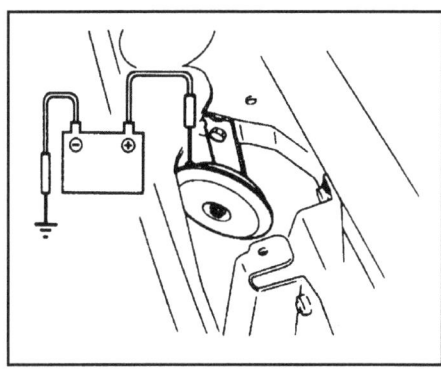

D40/2 HORN CIRCUIT: CHECKING HORN.

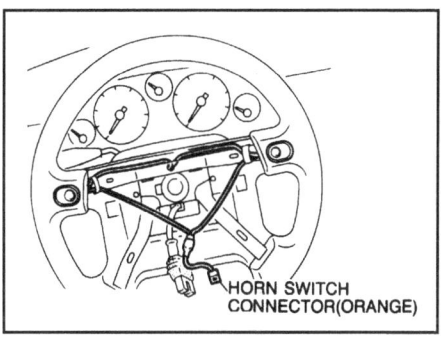

D40/4 HORN SWITCH CONNECTOR.

pressed there should be continuity, but none when it is released. If the switch does not work as described, the horn switches will have to be replaced as an assembly with the steering wheel. If the switches check out okay, move to step 4.

Step 4

5   ⌻ Check continuity of the horn switch connector as shown in the accompanying drawing. If there is no continuity, you'll need to fit a new combination switch assembly. If continuity is shown, check and repair the wire between the horn relay and the clock spring connector.

Step 5

6   ⌻ Temporarily reconnect the battery. Remove the access panel below the steering column and trace the horn to horn relay wire (probably green/orange). Ground the wire from its connector terminal (see diagram) and note if the horn sounds. If it does, repair the wiring between the combination switch and horn relay. If it does not sound go to Step 6.

7:35

Mazda Miata, MX-5, Eunos & Roadster

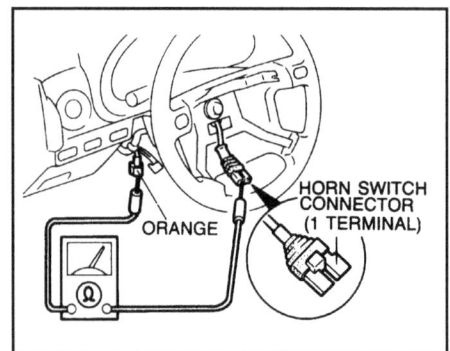

D40/5 HORN SWITCH CIRCUIT: CONTINUITY CHECK.

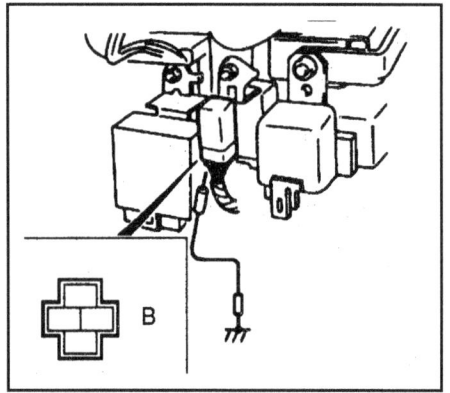

D40/6 HORN SWITCH CIRCUIT: WIRING CHECK.

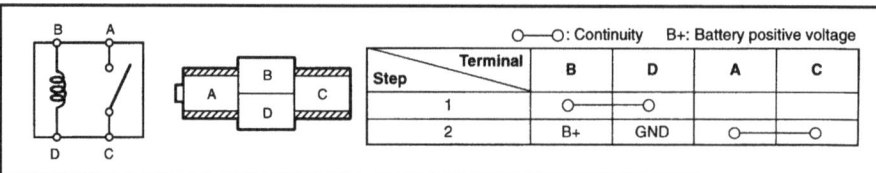

D41/3 REAR WINDOW DEFOGGER CIRCUIT: CHECKING RELAY OPERATION.

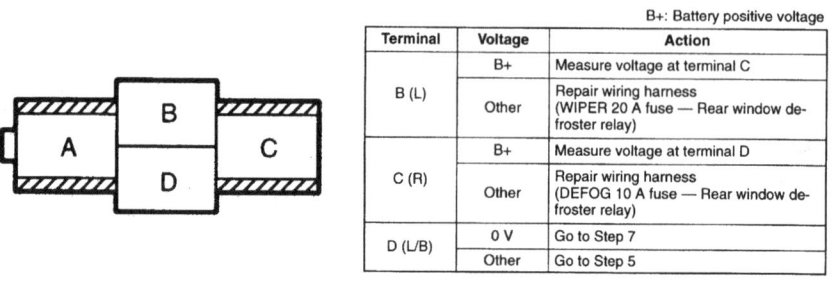

D41/4 REAR WINDOW DEFOGGER CIRCUIT: CHECKING RELAY VOLTAGES.

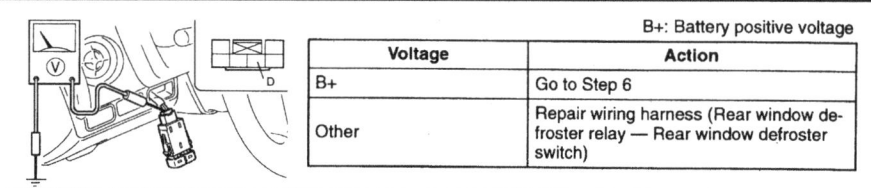

D41/5 REAR WINDOW DEFOGGER CIRCUIT: CHECKING WIRING TO SWITCH.

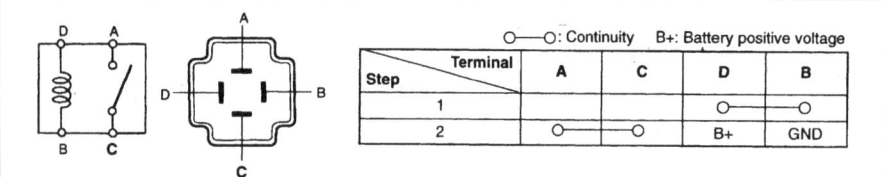

D40/7 HORN SWITCH CIRCUIT: RELAY CHECK.

Step 6

7   Remove the horn relay and apply battery positive (+) voltage to the terminals and check for continuity (see diagram). If the relay is faulty, replace it.

ONE HORN FAILS TO WORK -
8   ☞ 7/40/2.

41. REAR WINDOW DEFOGGER (WHERE FITTED) - TROUBLESHOOTING & REPAIR

☞ 1/1, 2 & 7/2.

The rear window defogger (defroster) is available as part of the factory hardtop option. If the defogger fails to operate, or operate properly, use the following procedures to locate the fault.

Step 1

1   Check the **DEFOG 10A** fuse in Fuse Block No.2 (trunk, near the antenna mounting) or, some models, in Fuse Block No.1. If the fuse has burned out, fit a new one of the correct rating and check defogger operation. If the new fuse burns out, check the wiring and connectors between fuseboxes and defogger and repair any faulty section. If the fuses are OK, move to next step.

Step 2

2   Check the **WIPER 20A** fuse in the Main Fuse Block in the engine compartment. If the fuse has burned out, fit a new one of the correct rating and check defogger operation. If the new fuse burns out, check the wiring and connectors between fuseboxes and defogger and repair any faulty section. If the fuses are OK, move to next step.

Step 3

3   Remove the defroster relay from its mounting in the trunk (you may need to remove the battery cover and spare wheel for better access), and check for continuity between terminals A & C when battery voltage is applied to terminal B and terminal D is grounded (see diagram). If the readings are incorrect, replace the relay.

Step 4

4   Turn on the ignition and defogger switches. With the defroster relay connected to its wiring, measure the terminal voltages as indicated in the accompanying diagram.

Step 5

5   Remove the access panel beneath the steering column. Reach behind the dashpanel and press in the retaining tabs of the defogger switch. Withdraw the switch (still connected to the harness) from the front of the dashpanel. Turn the switch off and measure the voltage at terminal D (see diagram). If you read battery voltage go to the next step, otherwise check wiring and connectors between switch and defogger.

Step 6

6   Remove the harness connector from the defogger switch and check for continuity between the terminals as shown in the diagram. If not as indicated, replace the switch, otherwise check the ground wiring of the switch.

Step 7

7   Measure the voltage at the rear window defroster element connector terminals as shown in the diagram.

CHECKING THE DEFOGGER ELEMENT
8   With the ignition and defroster switches turned on, check with a voltmeter the voltage at the

7:36

7: Electrical system

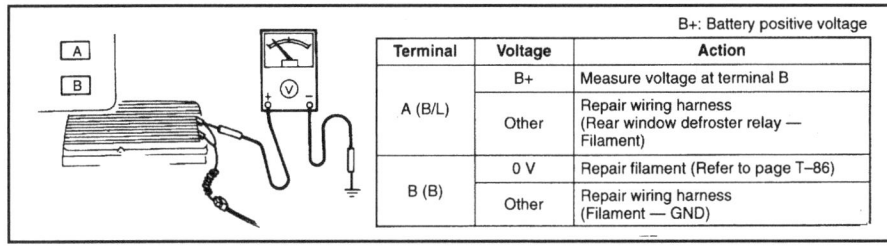

D41/7 REAR WINDOW DEFOGGER CIRCUIT: CHECKING WIRING TO DEFOGGER.

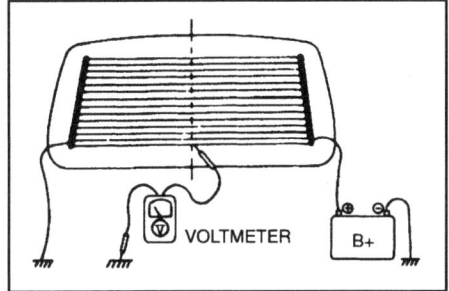

D41/6 REAR WINDOW DEFOGGER CIRCUIT: CHECKING SWITCH.

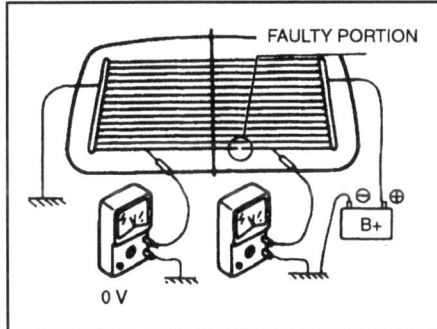

D41/8 REAR WINDOW DEFOGGER CIRCUIT: CHECKING DEFOGGER ELEMENTS.

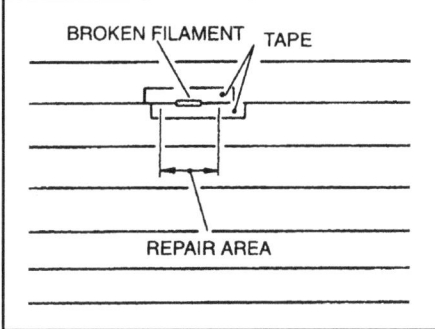

D41/12 REAR WINDOW DEFOGGER CIRCUIT: REPAIRING DEFOGGER FILAMENT.

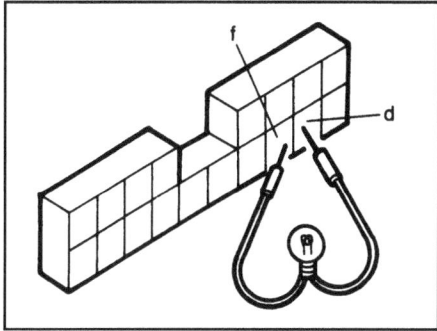

D42/2 TEST LIGHT ACROSS CRUISE CONTROL CONNECTOR TERMINALS.

center of each filament of the defogger element (grid). Connect the meter negative (-) probe to ground, then touch the positive (+) probe to the center of each filament in turn.

9 Normally, you should expect a reading of around 6 volts at the filament center. If the voltage reading is significantly higher than this, a short circuit is indicated. If the reading is lower or zero (a more common fault), the filament may be broken.

10 Examine the faulty filament closely, looking for signs of a break. You can confirm this by checking the voltage on each side of the suspected break - there will be a marked difference if there is a true break.

D41/10 REAR WINDOW DEFOGGER CIRCUIT: LOCATING BREAK IN DEFOGGER FILAMENT.

REPAIRING THE DEFROSTER ELEMENT

11 If you discover a break in one of the defroster filaments, it is possible to repair it using a special conductive paint containing silver. You can get this through your Mazda dealer or from most auto parts stores or electronic hobby shops.

12 Clean the area to be repaired with paint thinner or ethyl alcohol to remove any grease or dirt. Carefully mask the glass on each side of the filament, then apply the paint across the break, overlapping the 'good' filament by about 12mm/ 0.5in each side. Leave the paint to dry for at least 24 hours before using the defogger. If you're in a hurry, you can accelerate the drying process by using a hot air gun or hairdryer to heat the area to around 60 degrees C (140F), in which case it will be safe to use the defroster after 30 minutes, or so. **Caution!** Don't localize the heat too much, especially in cold weather.

42. CRUISE CONTROL SYSTEM - SELF-DIAGNOSIS FUNCTION

☞ 1/1, 2 & 7/2.

1 The cruise control unit incorporates a self-diagnosis facility which can greatly reduce the time needed to pinpoint a system fault. If you experience problems with the cruise control system, you can either get your Mazda dealer to check the system for you, or you can attempt diagnosis yourself. No exotic tools are needed for this, but you need to understand how to read the self-diagnosis data. To perform the self-diagnosis procedure, you'll need a 12 volt, 1.4W test lamp connected to two fine probes. Don't use a bulb with a higher wattage than this, or you'll risk damage to the cruise control unit.

2 Locate the cruise control unit, which you'll find behind the kick panel in the passenger side footwell. Connect the test light to the cruise control unit connector terminals **f** and **d** (see diagram), noting that the probes should be pushed gently through until they contact the terminals. (There is no terminal on the wiring connector side of the **d** terminal - you need to push the probe through until it contacts the terminal in the cruise control unit.)

3 When the self-diagnosis procedure is initiated, any fault will be indicated by the test light flashing, the number of flashes, their duration and the gap between flashes denoting a fault code number - a little like morse code.

4 Number codes are indicated by groups of flashes separated by 4 second gaps. A single short flash (0.4 secs) equals 1 and a single long flash (1.2 seconds) equals 10. Therefore 4 short flashes repeating at 4 second intervals equals 1+1+1+1 (code 4), while 2 long flashes - a gap of 1.6 seconds - and two short flashes repeating very 4 seconds equals 10+10+1+1 (code 22). Got it?

5 Okay, that's the theory - let's give it a try. Connect up the test light and then turn the ignition switch to **ON**. Turn the cruise control system on by pressing the **MAIN** switch. Now press and hold the **RESUME/ACCEL** control for at least three seconds. The test light should come on for 3 seconds then go out for 2 seconds, indicating that the cruise control self-diagnosis procedure has been initiated.

6 If there is a fault present, the test light will begin transmitting it in the code sequence we described above. Watch the test light and note the sequence of flashes, and then determine from this the code being sent by the unit. The code sequence will repeat after a four second gap, so don't worry if you don't get it first time around.

7 Note that if there is more than one fault in the cruise control system only the fault with the highest priority will be indicated, so when you have fixed that fault you should repeat the diagnostic/

Mazda Miata, MX-5, Eunos & Roadster

repair sequence until no further faults are reported.

8   The fault codes, their meanings and the area(s) you need to check are as follows -

Code 01 - *Indicates defective wiring between the actuator and the cruise control unit, or between the cruise control unit and the brake switch (check and repair the wiring). It could also indicate a defective actuator (check and replace as necessary), or a defective stoplight switch (check and replace as necessary).*

Code 05 - *Indicates STOP fuse burned out (replace) or a wiring fault between the cruise control unit and the fuse (check and repair).*

Code 07 - *Indicates a fault in the brake switch (check).*

Code 11 - *Indicates defective cruise control switch (check and replace as necessary).*

Code 15 - *Indicates defective cruise control module (check and replace if required).*

9   A further set of checks relates to the cruise control switches and sensors, and requires exactly the same test set-up as the last test. Start by setting the cruise control main switch (dashboard mounted) to **OFF** to reset the cruise control system, then initiate the next test sequence by turning the ignition switch to **ON**. Simultaneously turn the cruise control main switch to **ON** and the stalk switch to **RESUME/ACCEL**. In these tests, we will be operating each of the cruise control switches in turn and looking for a specific code displayed by the test light. If the code is flashed correctly, the switch concerned is operating normally. If the light fails to flash, the relevant switch requires attention. On automatic transmission cars, move the shift lever to **D** and on manual transmission cars select any gear before starting these tests.

10   Press the **SET/COAST** switch. The test light should send the code 21. If it fails to do so, check the cruise control switch and replace it as required ☞ 7/12.

11   Press the **RESUME/ACCEL** switch. The test light should send the code 22. If it fails to do so, check the cruise control switch and replace it as required ☞ 7/12.

12   Press the brake pedal. The test light should send the code 31. If it fails to do so, check the brake light switch and replace as required ☞ 7/27.

13   On automatic transmission cars, set the shift lever to **P** or **N**. The code 35 should be indicated. If this is not the case, check, adjust or replace the transmission range switch ☞ 7/9.

14   On manual transmission cars, depress the clutch pedal or move the shift lever to neutral. Code 35 should be shown. If not, check the clutch switch for continuity and replace it if defective.

15   Finally, drive the car at more than 25mph (40kph) and check that code 37 is displayed. If it is not, the speed sensor (incorporated in speedometer) should be checked: if it is working normally, check for faults in the wiring to the cruise control system.

16   After you have completed this diagnosis check, note that the cruise control system will be inoperative until the procedure is cancelled. This can be done by turning the main switch to **OFF** so that the indicator light goes out.

43. CRUISE CONTROL SYSTEM - TROUBLESHOOTING

☞ 1/1, 2 & 7/2.

1   In this section we will be running through the full troubleshooting sequence for the cruise control system. Before starting the sequence, check that the **METER** fuse (10 or 15 amp, depending on market) which protects the system is OK. Also check the **STOP** fuse (10 or 15 amp, depending on market). If either has burned out, fit a new fuse of the correct rating and see if the system now operates normally. If the fuse burns out again, check the associated wiring for shorts.

Step 1

2   Turn the ignition switch to **ON** and the cruise control main switch to **ON** and verify that the indicator light comes on. If the light comes on, skip to Step 3, otherwise, move to Step 2.

Step 2

3   ☞ + Remove the access panel beneath the steering column, reach up behind the dashboard and press in the tabs (see diagram) securing the cruise control main switch; pull the switch out of the

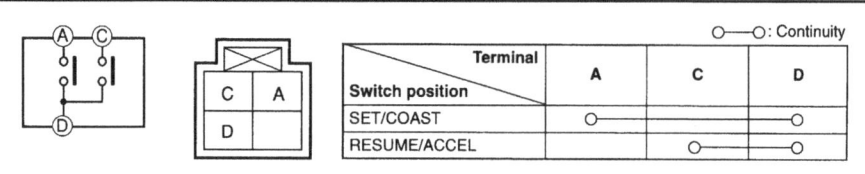

D43/3A CRUISE CONTROL MAIN SWITCH REMOVAL.

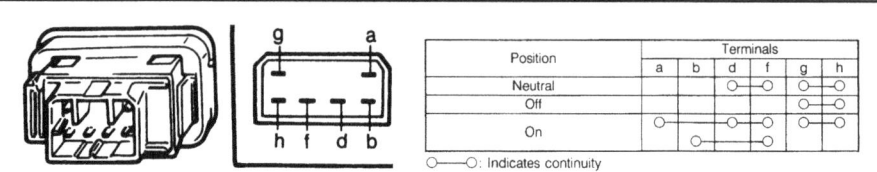

D43/3B TESTING CRUISE CONTROL SWITCH: CHECKING CONTINUITY.

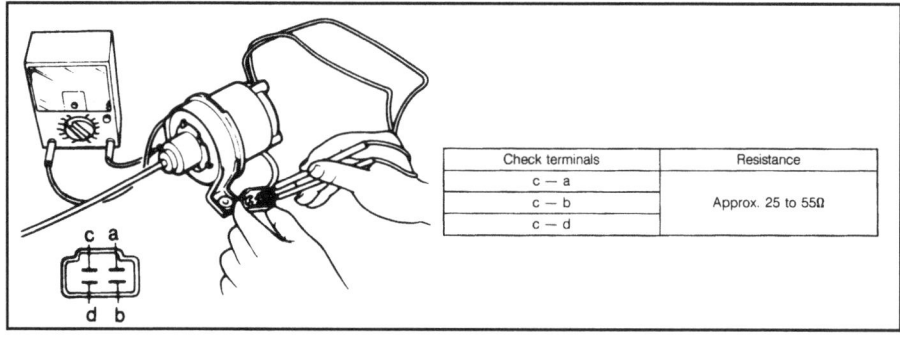

D43/6 CRUISE CONTROL ACTUATOR: CHECKING SOLENOID TERMINAL RESISTANCES.

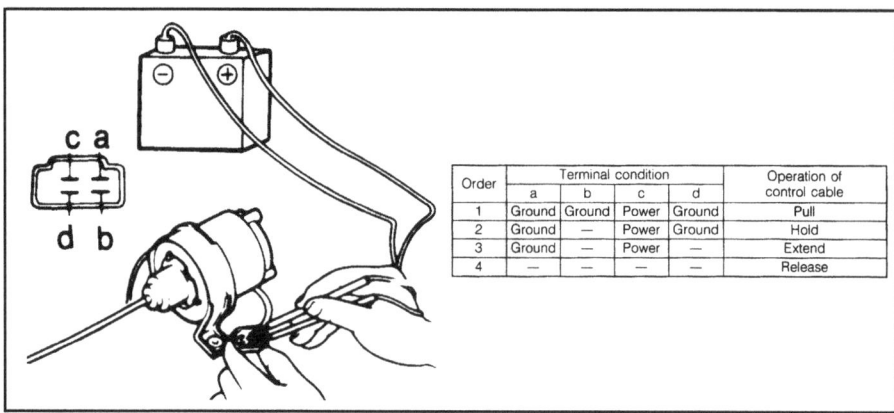

D43/8 CRUISE CONTROL ACTUATOR: CHECKING AFFECT OF BATTERY VOLTAGE ON TERMINALS.

7: Electrical system

dashboard and unplug the wiring connector. Using a continuity tester or multimeter, check continuity across the switch terminals as shown in the diagram. If the switch is not working as specified, fit a new one. If the switch is OK, check and repair as necessary the wiring between the switch, the **METER** fuse and the switch ground connection. Plug the switch back into the harness.

Step 3

4 + Locate the cruise control unit which is adjacent to Fuse Block No. 1 (see diagram). Unscrew the bolts retaining the unit and, leaving the wiring

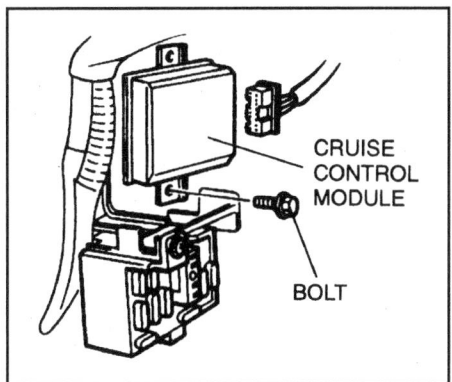

D43/4A CRUISE CONTROL MODULE LOCATION.

harness connector plugged in, pull the unit out to give better access to the connector terminals. Use a multimeter to check the terminal voltages as indicated in the accompanying diagram.

5 Terminal **A** (probably G/Y) - Actuator: Ignition switch **ON**. With the cruise control main switch **OFF**, zero volts should be read. With the switch **ON**, you should read 9 volts. If the readings are other than these, check the actuator as follows.

6   Working in the engine compartment, trace and separate the actuator wiring connector. Use an ohmmeter or multimeter to check the actuator solenoid resistances according to the accompanying diagram and table.

7 If the resistances are not as shown, fit a new actuator. If the resistances check out okay, disconnect the actuator cable at the accelerator pedal, start the engine and allow it to idle.

8   Apply battery voltage to the terminals indicated in the accompanying diagram and table, and check that the actuator responds as indicated. If it does not work as shown, fit a new actuator.

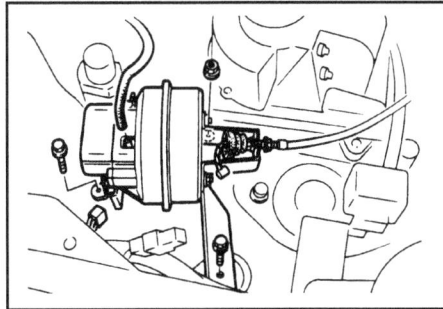

D43/8 CRUISE CONTROL ACTUATOR REMOVAL.

9 Disconnect the cable from the actuator and pry off the vacuum hose. Remove the two bolts and single nut which retain the actuator assembly and lift it away. When installing the new unit, adjust the cable freeplay to 1-3mm/0.04-0.12in and check that the vacuum hose is reconnected.

10 Terminal **B** (probably G/B) - Actuator: Ignition switch **ON**. With the cruise control main switch **OFF**, zero volts should be read. With the switch **ON**, you should read 9 volts. If the readings are other than these, check the actuator as previously described.

11 Terminal **C** (probably G/O) - Actuator: Ignition switch **ON**. With the cruise control main switch **OFF**, zero volts should be read. With the switch **ON**, you should read 9 volts. If the readings

B+: Battery positive voltage

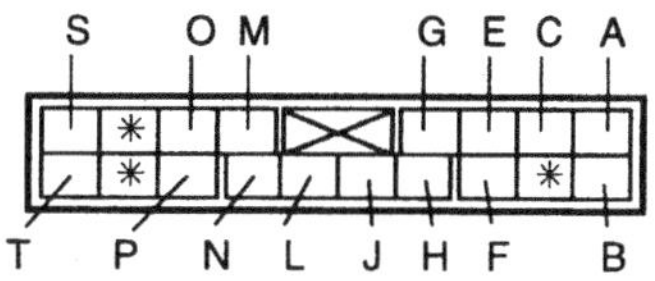

Terminal		Signal	Connection	Test condition	Voltage	Inspection area
A		Cruise actuator on signal	Cruise actuator (vent 1)	Ignition switch at ON		
				Cruise control main switch on	9 V	• METER 15 A fuse • Cruise control main switch • Cruise actuator
				Other	0 V	
B		Cruise actuator on signal	Cruise actuator (vac)	Ignition switch at ON		
				Cruise control main switch on	9 V	• METER 15 A fuse • Cruise control main switch • Brake switch • Cruise actuator
				Other	0 V	
C		Cruise actuator on signal	Cruise actuator (vent 2)	Ignition switch at ON		
				Cruise control main switch on	9 V	• METER 15 A fuse • Cruise control main switch • Brake switch • Cruise actuator
				Other	0 V	
E		Cruise control main switch on/off signal	Cruise control main switch (N.C)	Ignition switch at ON	Other	B+	• METER 15 A fuse • Cruise control main switch
				Cruise control main switch off side pushed	0 V	
F		Cruise control main switch on/off signal	Cruise control main switch (N.O)	Ignition switch at ON	Cruise control main switch off side pushed	0 V	• METER 15 A fuse • Cruise control main switch
				Other	B+	
G		O/D off signal	TCM	Ignition switch at ON	B+	TCM
H		Brake on signal	Brake switch	Ignition switch at ON and cruise control main switch on	Release brake pedal	9 V	• METER 15 A fuse • Cruise control main switch • Brake switch
				Depress brake pedal	B+	
J	AT	Selector lever position signal	Transmission range switch	Ignition switch at ON	N or P range	0 V	Transmission range switch
				Other	B+	
	MT	Clutch switch on signal	Clutch switch	Ignition switch at ON	Depress clutch pedal	0 V	Clutch switch
				Other	B+	
L		Cruise control switch on signal	Cruise control switch	Ignition switch at ON and cruise control main switch on	SET/COAST switch pushed	0 V	• METER 15 A fuse • Cruise control main switch • Clock spring • Cruise control switch
M		Brake on signal	Brake switch	Depress brake pedal	B+	• STOP 15 A fuse • Brake switch
				Other	0 V	
N		Cruise control switch on signal	Cruise control switch	Ignition switch at ON and cruise control main switch on	RESUME/ACCEL switch pushed	0 V	• METER 15 A fuse • Cruise control main switch • Clock spring • Cruise control switch
O		Cruise actuator on signal	Cruise actuator	Ignition switch ON and cruise control main switch on	Depress brake pedal	0 V	• METER 15 A fuse • Cruise control main switch
				Release brake pedal	9 V	
P		Vehicle speed sensor on signal	Vehicle speed sensor	Rear tires rotating	Alternates 0 V and 5 V	• Vehicle speed sensor • Instrument cluster
S		+B	STOP 20 A fuse	Constant	B+	STOP 15 A fuse
T		GND	GND	Check for continuity to ground	Yes	GND

D43/4B CRUISE CONTROL MODULE: CHECKING.

7:39

Mazda Miata, MX-5, Eunos & Roadster

are other than these, check the actuator as previously described.

12 Terminal **E** (probably R) - **Main switch:** Ignition switch **ON**. With the cruise control main switch **OFF**, zero volts should be read. With the switch **ON**, you should read 12 volts. If the readings are other than these, check the (probably R) wire between the cruise control unit and main switch and repair or rewire as necessary.

13 Terminal **F** (probably Y/B) - **Main switch:** Ignition switch **ON**. With the cruise control main switch **OFF**, zero volts should be read. With the switch **ON**, you should read 12 volts. If the readings are other than these, check the (probably Y/B) wire between the cruise control unit and main switch and repair or rewire as necessary.

14 Terminal **G** (probably LG/B) - **TCM (auto trans cars):** With the ignition switch **OFF**, zero volts should be read. With the ignition switch **ON**, you should read 12 volts. If the readings are other than these, check the TCM (Transmission Control Module) by substituting a new one, or have the unit checked out by a Mazda dealer.

15 Terminal **H** (probably Y) - **Brake switch:** Ignition switch **ON**, cruise control main switch **ON**. With the brake pedal depressed, zero volts should be read. With the pedal released, you should read 9 volts. If the readings are other than these, check the switch for continuity after disconnecting the switch wiring (see diagram). If not as described, fit a new switch.

16 Terminal **J** (probably B/L) - **Range switch (auto trans cars):** Ignition switch **ON**. With **N** or **P** selected, zero volts should be read. In any other shifter position, you should read 5 volts. If the readings are other than these, check the transmission range switch ☞ 7/9.

17 Terminal **J** (probably BR/W) - **Clutch switch (manual transmission cars):** Ignition switch **ON**. With the clutch pedal depressed, zero volts should be read. With the pedal released, you should read 12 volts. If the readings are other than these, check the switch for continuity after disconnecting the switch wiring (see diagram). If not as described, fit a new switch.

18 Terminal **L** (probably R/L) - **Cruise control switch (SET and COAST switches):** Ignition switch **ON**. With the main switch **ON**, 12 volts should be read. Leave the main switch **ON**, and then turn on the **SET** switch. The reading should drop back to zero volts. If not as described, check the cruise control combination switch via its wiring connector ☞ 7/12. If the switch is defective, replace it. If the switch checks out OK, check for wiring damage or shorts between the switch and the cruise control unit.

19 Terminal **M** (probably G) - **Brake switch:** ☞ 7/15.

20 Terminal **N** (probably R/W) - **Cruise control switch (RESUME and ACCEL switches):** Ignition switch **ON**. With the main switch **ON**, 12 volts should be read. Leave the main switch **ON**, and then turn on the **RESUME** switch. The reading should drop back to zero volts. If not as described, check the cruise control combination switch via its wiring connector ☞ 7/12. If the switch is defective, replace it. If it checks out OK, check for wiring damage or shorts between the switch and the cruise control unit.

21 Terminal **O** (probably P) - **Actuator:** Ignition switch **ON**. With the cruise control main switch **OFF**, zero volts should be read. With the switch **ON**, you should read 9 volts. If the readings are other than these, check the actuator as described above.

22 Terminal **P** (probably G/R) - **Speed sensor:** Ignition switch **ON**. If you have access to a rolling road, check that while the rear wheels are turning, the voltage reading alternates between zero and 5 volts (or drive the car slowly and have an assistant check the voltage readings for you).

23 If the results are not as indicated, remove the instrument panel ☞ 7/14. Connect a continuity tester or multimeter between terminals **2f** and **2d** of the instrument panel (see diagram). Using a small screwdriver, turn the speedometer drive and verify that continuity is indicated four times during each revolution of the shaft. If not, you will have to fit a new sensor. We are not certain about this, but it would appear that the sensor is

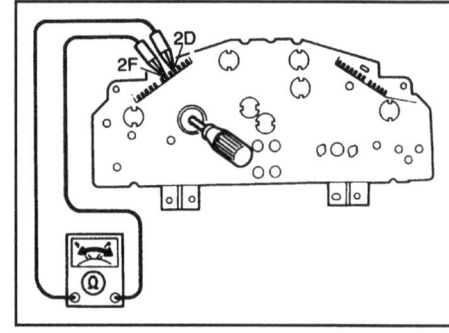

D43/23 TESTING THE SPEEDO SPEED SENSOR.

supplied as part of the speedometer assembly - check this with your local Mazda dealer.

24 Terminal **S** (probably W/G) - **Battery:** Check for battery voltage (12 volts) between the (probably W/G) wire terminal and ground. If not as described, check the (probably W/G) wire to the **STOP** fuse (10 or 15 amp depending on market) and repair or rewire as necessary.

25 Terminal **T** (probably B) - **Ground:** Check for continuity between this terminal and a good body ground connection. If continuity is not shown, repair or rewire to restore the ground connection.

44. AIRBAG SYSTEM - WORKING PROCEDURES, DISARMING & RE-ARMING

☞ 1/1, 2 & 7/2.

DESCRIPTION

1 On models equipped with SRS (Supplementary Restraint System), an airbag module mounted on the steering wheel provides the driver with additional crash protection. Some models also feature a passenger airbag mounted in the top of the dashboard which offers similar protection to the passenger. In the event of a sufficiently forceful impact, an electrical signal from the SAS (Sophisticated Airbag Sensor) module is sent to the airbag module via a dedicated wiring harness (and the clockspring on the driver's side). The signal causes the generation of nitrogen gas which temporarily inflates the airbags in micro seconds. (The 'clockspring' is a spring device which, despite the movements of the steering wheel, ensures a constant electrical connection between the SAS unit and the steering wheel airbag module.) The SAS unit monitors the airbag system and warns the driver of malfunctions through a warning light in the instrument panel. On some models, if the warning light fails, a buzzer will sound 5 times in 5 cycles if a fault is present.

2 Because your personal safety may depend upon the correct and safe functioning of this sophisticated system, we recommend referring all suspected problems to your Mazda dealer. We also recommend that you do no more than remove and install the airbag modules in the course of other work.

WORKING PROCEDURES

3 **Warning!** Airbags inflate explosively with

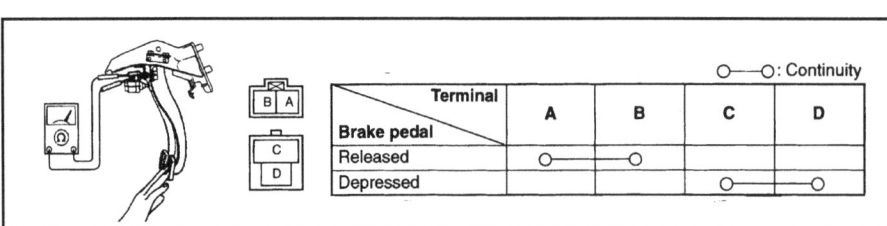

D43/15 BRAKE SWITCH: CHECKING.

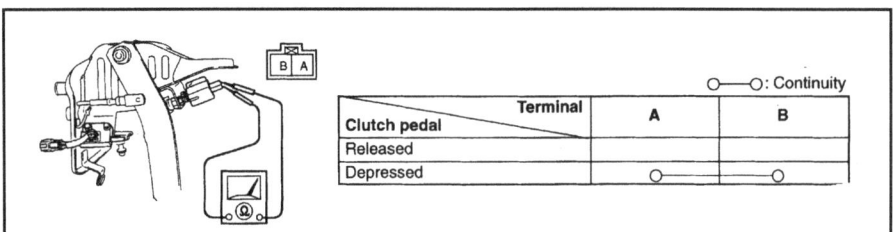

D43/17 CLUTCH SWITCH: CHECKING.

7: Electrical system

great force and generate considerable heat: they are potentially dangerous if triggered accidentally. **Do not attempt to disturb, remove or even work in the vicinity of airbags, airbag system wiring or the SAS unit until the battery is disconnected and the airbag system disarmed.**

4   **Warning! Under no circumstances** attempt to dismantle an airbag module or the SAS unit. If a fault is diagnosed, replace the component as an assembly.

5   **Warning! Under no circumstances** attempt to repair damaged airbag system wiring. If a damaged wire or terminal is discovered, replace the affected harness section.

6   **Warning! Under no circumstances** attempt to diagnose faults on the airbag module using an ohmmeter or multimeter or a live wire. These could generate enough current to trigger the explosive charge.

7   **Warning!** When handling a live airbag module, do so with the trim side (deployment side) away from you to minimize injury in the event of accidental deployment. Always store/place the module with the trim side facing upward - this will prevent the module being thrown into the air if accidentally deployed.

8   **Warning!** If you have reason to handle a deployed airbag module, be aware that it contains sodium hydroxide deposits. This substance is a residue produced by the gas-generating combustion process and is caustic. Always wear appropriate clothing (gloves, coveralls and safety glasses) when handling a deployed airbag, and place the airbag in a sealed plastic bag as soon as possible.

9   **Warning!** Do not pour water on a deployed airbag - even if it is hot - a gas will be produced which could make breathing difficult.

10   **Warning!** When disposing of a deployed airbag, do so in a responsible manner. Seek advice from your local authority about the best way to deal safely with this task, or ask your Mazda dealer to arrange disposal for you.

11   **Warning!** Handle airbag modules very, very carefully: improper handling could cause an airbag to deploy suddenly, which might cause you serious injury.

12   **Warning!** Do not attempt to disturb (or install) the SAS unit (behind the heater, under the dashboard) unless the airbag system has been disabled and the SAS unit disconnected from the electrical harness.

13   **Warning!** Whenever the airbag system has been worked on, check that the instrument panel warning light indicates that the system is functioning normally. The light should come on for around six seconds each time the ignition is switched on, and then go out. If the light fails to go out or flashes, there is a problem with the system. If the light does not come on, check for a burned out fuse, wiring damage or a burned out warning light bulb.

14   **Warning!** Check that the horn operates correctly after disturbing the airbag module.

DISARMING/RE-ARMING AIRBAG SYSTEM

15   Turn the front wheels to the straight ahead

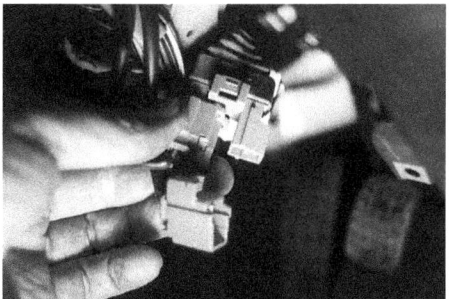

44/18 Airbag & clockspring connectors.

position and then remove the ignition key to operate the steering lock.

16   Isolate the battery 7/2.

17   **Warning!** Wait 5 minutes for the airbag electrical system capacitance to discharge before proceeding further.

18   ☐ ☞ Remove the access panel below the steering column (glovebox on the passenger side) for access (see diagrams), then disconnect the airbag module and clockspring wiring connectors. Note that, where applicable, the orange connector must be released first, followed by the blue connector.

19   Install all airbag system components carefully and remake airbag system wiring connections (blue first, then orange, where applicable). Reconnect the battery ☞ 7/2. **Warning!** At arm's length, from outside the car, turn the ignition switch to **ON**: do not sit inside the car to carry out this procedure. **Warning!** Ensure the airbag system is operating correctly by observing the instrument panel lamp which should not stay illuminated for more than 8 seconds. If the light stays on or flashes ☞ 7/45.

45. AIRBAG SYSTEM - TROUBLESHOOTING

☞ 1/1, 2 & 7/2 & 7/44.
Warning! *Before* **attempting any work on the airbag system, read** ☞ 7/44.

1   Turn the ignition switch to ON and observe the airbag warning light in the instrument panel.

AIRBAG WARNING LAMP DOES NOT ILLUMINATE

2   Check **METER** and **ENGINE** fuses in Fuse Block No.1 (depending on market, they'll be rated at 10 or 15 amps). Replace any burned fuses with new fuses of the correct rating. If the new fuses blow, check the appropriate wiring harnesses for damage, open or short circuits and poor connections.

3   If the warning light still fails to light, check the bulb and replace as necessary ☞ 7/14.

AIRBAG WARNING LAMP STAYS ON

4   This indicates a problem with the SAS unit or its wiring harness connector. Check the connection; if the fault remains, consult your Mazda dealer as quickly as possible.

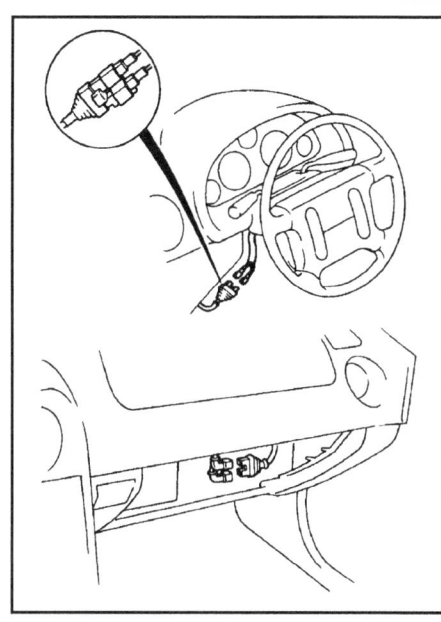

D44/18 AIRBAG MODULES: DISCONNECTING FROM WIRING HARNESS.

AIRBAG WARNING LIGHT FLASHES

5   A sequence of 3 short flashes repeating: code 3. This code indicates a problem with the battery (low voltage), faulty wiring between battery, **ENGINE** fuse and SAS unit or/and faulty wiring between battery, **METER** fuse and SAS unit. Check wiring and connectors. If the fault remains, consult your Mazda dealer as quickly as possible.

6   A sequence of 6 short flashes repeating: code 6. This code indicates a fault in the clockspring or/and a fault in the wiring between the clockspring and the SAS unit. Check that the clockspring is correctly adjusted and that all relevant connectors are securely connected. If the fault remains, consult your Mazda dealer as quickly as possible.

7   A sequence of 7 short flashes repeating: code 7. Indicates a fault in the wiring between the SAS unit and the passenger side airbag. Check that all relevant connectors are securely connected. If the fault remains, consult your Mazda dealer as quickly as possible.

8   **Warning!** Airbag system faults are reported one at a time in order of priority. If you repair a fault, always check that the warning light then indicates that all is well with the system: there may be more than one problem. If a fault remains that you cannot fix, consult your Mazda dealer as quickly as possible.

46. AIRBAG MODULE (DRIVER'S) - REMOVAL & INSTALLATION

☞ 1/1, 2 & 7/2 & 7/44.

REMOVAL

1   **Warning!** Read working procedures and disarm the airbag system and disconnect the airbag wiring behind the steering column access panel (☞ 7/44) *before* starting work on removing the airbag module.

Mazda Miata, MX-5, Eunos & Roadster

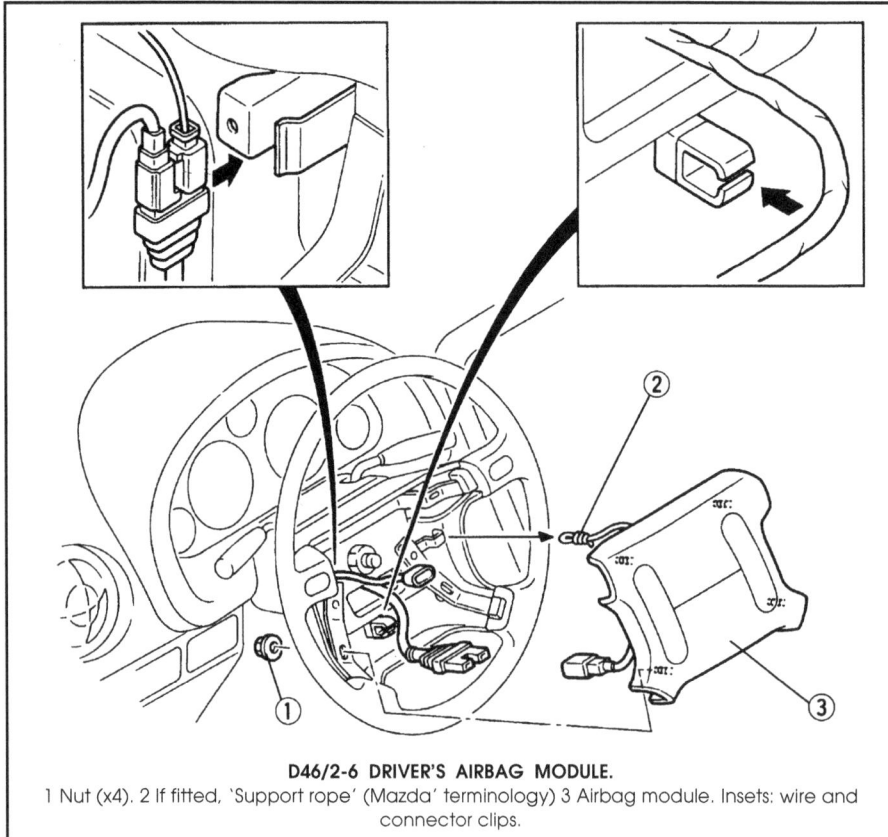

D46/2-6 DRIVER'S AIRBAG MODULE.
1 Nut (x4). 2 If fitted, 'Support rope' (Mazda' terminology) 3 Airbag module. Insets: wire and connector clips.

2 📷 🔲 One of two types of airbag module retention may be employed.

1) If there is a rubber grommet in each side of the steering wheel boss, pull out the grommets and remove the 10mm bolt on each side (see photo), then go to step 3.

2) If there are no grommets in the side of the steering wheel boss, remove the combination switch covers behind the steering wheel (two parts, retained by four screws) and then remove the four nuts securing the airbag module (see diagram).

3 📷+ Gently lift the module away from the steering wheel sufficiently to allow the release of the support 'rope' (if applicable) and to give enough room to free the module's electrical connector from its clip (see photo). Without straining the wires, first release the orange connector then the blue connector. Remove the airbag module from the car (**Warning!** See disposal, handling & storage instructions ☞ 7/44).

INSTALLATION

4 📷 Hold the module close enough to the steering wheel to plug in the electrical connectors (blue first), and to hook the loop of the support

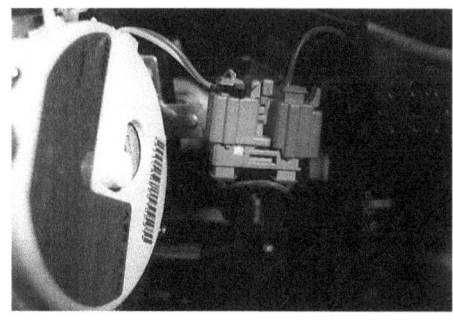

46/4 Airbag connection correctly made.

'rope' (Mazda's terminology) over the metal hook on the right of the steering wheel boss. Make sure wires and connectors are fixed into their retaining clips (see diagram D46/2-6), then carefully seat the airbag module.

5 🔲 Fit the two securing bolts or four securing nuts and tighten them progressively in the order shown (see diagram) to 4-5.8Nm/40-60kgf cm/35-52lbf in). As applicable, refit the combination switch

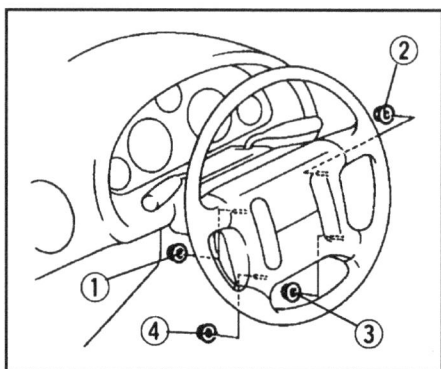

D46/5 AIRBAG MODULE INSTALLATION.
Tighten retaining nuts progressively and in this order.

covers (set screw first) or the two steering wheel hub grommets.

6 Reconnect the lower airbag/clockspring electrical connectors and install the access panel beneath the steering column.

7 Re-arm the airbag system ☞ 7/44/19.

47. AIRBAG MODULE (PASSENGER'S) - REMOVAL & INSTALLATION

☞ 1/1, 2 & 7/2 & 7/44.

46/2 Bolts (one each side) retain airbag module.

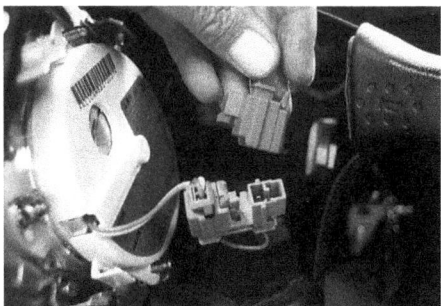

46/3b Release airbag module connectors.

46/3a Airbag connector held by clip.

46/3c Rear of typical airbag module.

7: Electrical system

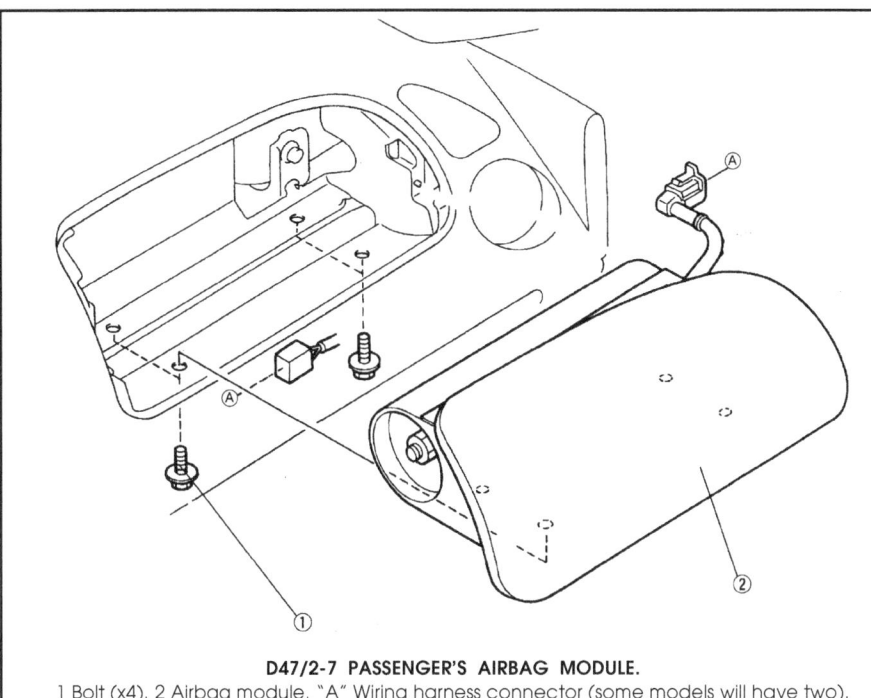

D47/2-7 PASSENGER'S AIRBAG MODULE.
1 Bolt (x4). 2 Airbag module. "A" Wiring harness connector (some models will have two).

REMOVAL

1   **Warning!** Read working procedures and disarm the airbag system *before* starting work on removing the airbag module ☞ 7/44.

2   ⬚ Remove the screws securing the hinge of the glove compartment and lift the glove compartment out of the dashboard. Disconnect the now exposed airbag module electrical connector or connectors (see diagram).

3   Via the glove compartment (glovebox) opening, remove the four bolts securing the airbag module (see diagram).

4   Gently lift the airbag module away from the dashboard and remove from the car (**Warning!** See disposal, handling & storage instructions ☞ 7/44).

INSTALLATION

5   Carefully seat the airbag module in its recess in the dashboard, taking care to ensure the unit's wiring is correctly routed.

6   Fit the four securing bolts and tighten them progressively to 4-7.8Nm/40-80kgf cm/35-69lbf in).

7   Reconnect the airbag module to the wiring harness (there may be one or two connectors, depending on model). Install the glove compartment.

8   Re-arm the airbag system ☞ 7/44/19.

48. WINDSHIELD WIPER & WASHER SYSTEM - TROUBLESHOOTING

☞ 1/1, 2 & 7/2.

Wipers inoperative

1   The wiper motor has a built-in circuit breaker to protect it against overload, so, if the wipers don't work, turn them off for 5 minutes then try again. If the wipers still don't work, check the **WIPER 20A** fuse in Fuse Block No.1. If it has blown, try fitting a new fuse and see whether the wiper now operates normally. If the fuse burns out again, check the wiper system wiring for shorts, open circuits and bad connections: repair or rewire as necessary.

2   Remove the access panel below the steering column. Turn the ignition switch to **ON** and check for battery voltage at terminal **M** (blue wire) of the combination switch wiring connector. If no voltage is shown, check and repair the wiring and connections between the **WIPER 20A** fuse and the combination switch connector.

3   Next (ignition still **ON**), check for battery voltage at combination switch terminal **P** (blue/red wire) with the wiper switch set to **Hi** and terminal **L** (blue/white wire) with the wiper switch set to **Lo**. If battery voltage is not indicated, check the wiring/connectors between wiper motor and switch connector, and check windshield wiper/washer (combination) switch ☞ 7/12.

4   If the fault persists check the wiper motor ☞ 7/49.

Wipers do not park correctly.

5   Turn the ignition to **ON**. Check for battery voltage at the blue wire of the wiper motor wiring connector in the engine compartment. If zero volts is indicated, check and repair the blue wire between the motor and **WIPER 20** fuse. If battery voltage is read, check the wiper motor ☞ 7/49.

Intermittent function inoperative.

6   From inside the car, remove the steering column access panel. Check for continuity between the black wire terminal and a good body ground (earth) connection. If no continuity is found, repair or rewire the motor ground connection. If you read continuity, check the wiper (combination) switch ☞ 7/12.

One-touch function inoperative - all cars.

7   Check the wiper (combination) switch ☞ 7/12.

Wipers will not switch off.

8   Check the wiper (combination) switch ☞ 7/12.

Windshield washer will not switch off.

9   Check the wiper (combination) switch ☞ 7/12.

Windshield washers not working (wipers OK).

10   📷 If motor can be heard running, check reservoir water level - top up as required. Check for blocked washer jet - clear using a pin or fine wire. You can release the jet from the hood by squeezing together the locking tabs on the underside if removal is necessary. Washer fluid could be frozen.

11   Remove the access panel below the steering column. Turn the ignition switch to **ON**. Check

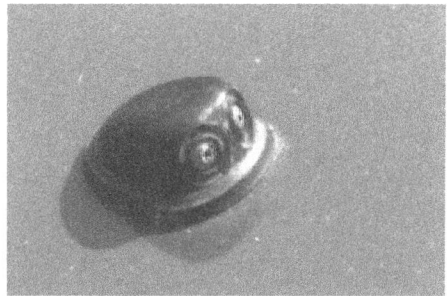

48/10 Clear jet nozzles with a pin or thin wire.

for battery voltage at the blue/orange wire of the combination switch wiring connector while pressing the washer switch. If no voltage is shown, check the washer (combination) switch operation ☞ 7/12.

12   Ignition switch **ON**. Check for battery voltage at terminal **A** (without ABS) or terminal **B** (with ABS) at the washer motor connector (see diagram D51/2 for terminal location) while pressing the washer switch. If zero volts are indicated, check and repair the wiring/connectors between the switch and motor.

13   Disconnect the washer motor wiring connector and check the harness side of the connector for continuity between the **B** terminal (without ABS) or the **A** terminal (with ABS) and a good body ground connection. If no continuity is found, repair or rewire the motor ground connection. If continuity is shown, check the washer motor ☞ 7/51.

49. WIPER MOTOR - T/SHOOTING, REMOVAL, O/HAUL & INSTALLATION

☞ 1/1, 2 & 7/2.

Mazda Miata, MX-5, Eunos & Roadster

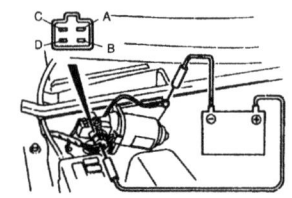

Terminal	Operation speed
C	Low
A	High

D49/1 WIPER MOTOR: CHECKING OPERATION.

TROUBLESHOOTING

1   You can check the windshield wiper motor operation by disconnecting it from the wiring harness and then applying positive (+) battery voltage (you can use a fly lead from the power source in the engine compartment) to terminals C and A of the motor side connector (see diagram).

2   When battery voltage is applied to terminal C the wipers should operate at low speed, and at high speed when applied to terminal A.

3   If the motor does not run, check for continuity between its casing and a good body ground connection. If continuity is not present, repair the wiring between the motor and ground.

4   If the motor still does not work, the official solution is to fit a new motor. We, of course, decided to take ours apart - you probably won't be able to get parts from a Mazda dealer, but you may be able to fix the fault by cleaning the commutator or fitting new brushes. Wally, our Technical Adviser, asks us to point out that the photographs show our right-hand drive project car - on left-hand drive cars everything is reversed, but otherwise similar. Wally says to hold the book in front of a mirror if you are working on a LHD model ...

REMOVAL

5   Isolate the battery ☞ 7/2.

6   + Start by disconnecting the motor's wiring harness connector.

7   On the passenger side there is a plastic cover that covers the blower air intake which is retained by a row of four black crosshead screws along the lower edge of the windshield, a single small silver screw near the fender, and a couple of clips into the firewall (these fixing arrangements may differ a little, model to model).

8   Disconnect the linkage from the motor crank arm to the wiper mechanism. This is reached from behind the panel carrying the motor; you can free the link by levering it gently away with a screwdriver blade - the plastic socket will pop off the pin end on the motor arm.

9   Depending on the country in which the car was originally sold, and on options fitted, you may need to remove other components to allow space for the wiper motor to be removed. On LHD cars, for example, you'll need to release the two securing nuts and move the fuse block from its mounting (without disconnecting wires).

10   Release the three mounting bolts (one may be fitted from the back of the firewall) and lift the motor away, feeding the crank arm through the hole in the firewall.

OVERHAUL

11   Remove the three screws which retain the gearbox end cover and lift it away. Inside, you will find the plastic gear in which are embedded contact tracks. On the cover are three spring contacts which operate on the tracks. The spring contacts transfer power to the motor brushes, their position deciding whether the motor is under power or not. Note that if these contacts are not working correctly, the motor may not run, or the parking function may be inoperative.

12   If you have dismantled the motor because of such problems, you can clean the contacts and tracks after removing the grease with a solvent-moistened rag. We found that a pencil eraser will restore the surface without causing scoring. To make sure that the contacts are pressing firmly on the rotor, bend them outwards slightly. Install the cover and reconnect the wiring, then check if the motor operates normally.

13   The motor itself can be dismantled after removing the two crosshead screws holding the motor body to the gearbox. As you pull the motor body away, the armature will probably come with it, pulling out from the brush assembly. Remove the armature from the body (it will be held by the pull of the permanent magnets in the body) noting the bearing ball fitted to the end of the

49/6a Unplug motor's wiring connector ...

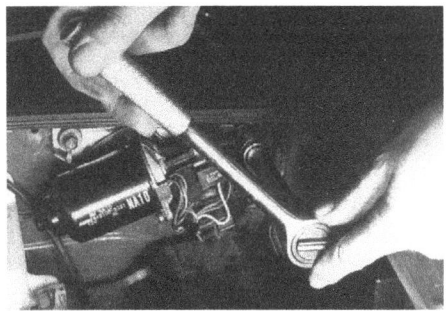

49/6b ... and undo mounting bolts.

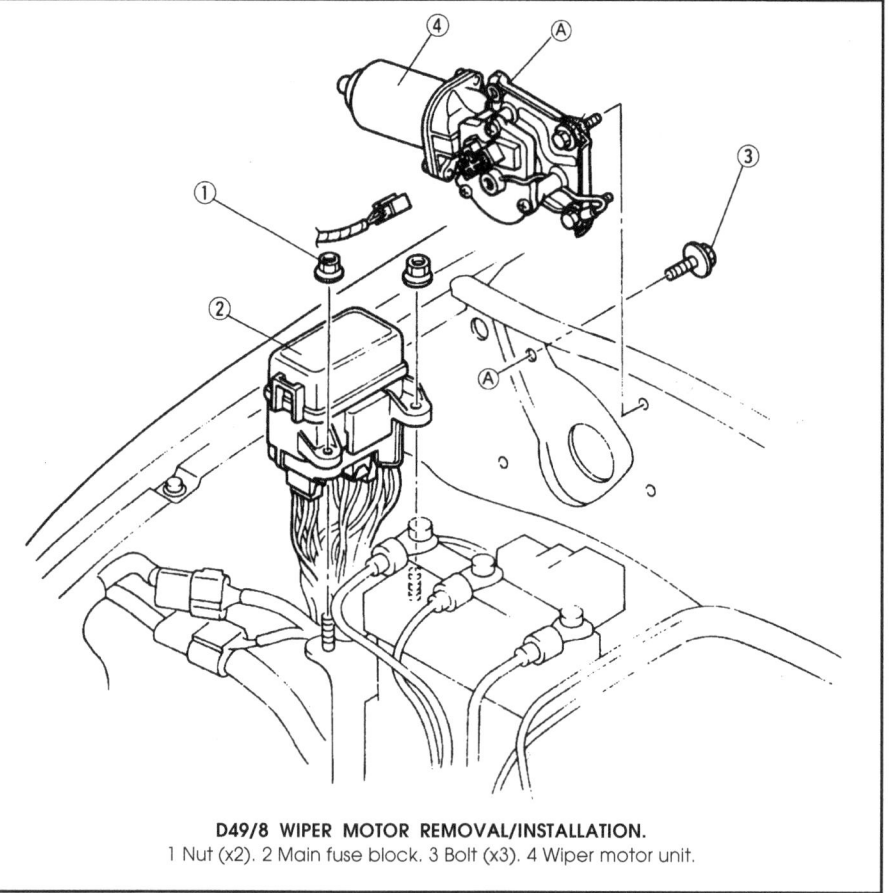

D49/8 WIPER MOTOR REMOVAL/INSTALLATION.
1 Nut (x2). 2 Main fuse block. 3 Bolt (x3). 4 Wiper motor unit.

7: Electrical system

spindle - retrieve this and keep it safe.

14 Use a multimeter or continuity checker to test for insulation between the commutator segments and the core and spindle of the armature. If you find continuity at any point, you will need to fit a new motor (it is unlikely to be worth attempting to get the armature rewound).

15 Examine the commutator for wear or damage. Light discoloration and minor damage can be corrected by cleaning the commutator with fine sandpaper. Wrap the paper round the commutator and turn the armature until a bright, smooth finish is restored. In cases of more severe damage, have

49/13 Major components of wiper motor.

the armature set up in a lathe and remove the minimum amount of metal possible to restore the surface of the commutator segments. There are no specified service limits for the commutator, but if the repair work would result in its diameter being reduced by an appreciable amount, the motor should be scrapped and a new one fitted.

16 Check that the commutator runout is acceptable. Set the armature up on V-blocks or between lathe centers, and use a dial gauge (DTI) to measure commutator runout. Again, we have no service limits for this, but if the runout is greater than about 0.03mm/0.001in, either correct this by skimming in a lathe, or scrap the motor and fit a new one.

17 After working on the commutator, clean out the grooves between each segment. You can make up your own cleaning/recutting tool from a section of used hacksaw blade. Find the end where the teeth point back towards you as you hold the blade - this will be the cutting end, so wrap some tape around the other end to form a handle. Now grind the sides of the blade flat until it is a good fit in the commutator grooves. Undercut the grooves by drawing the tool along each one until you achieve a small undercut, then repeat the process on the remaining grooves. Use a little fine sandpaper to remove any burring that results.

18 If the brushes are worn down appreciably, you might like to try an auto-electrical specialist, which can probably supply something suitable as a replacement. You may not get an exact fit, so check this and, if necessary, file the brushes to fit the holder, then solder them into the brush plate (or you could get the supplier to do this for you). Note that the brush plate may carry an internal fuse (see diagram). We have no information about this fuse, but if it has blown it is presumably as a result of a dead short in the motor, or because the motor has been stalled by some obstruction in the mechanism. We suggest that you try an auto-electrical specialist for advice in the event that the fuse needs replacing.

19 When you assemble the motor, you'll need to pull the brushes back in their holders while you fit the armature in place. If you leave the ends of the brush springs unhooked while you fit the armature, this is relatively easy to do - but don't omit to hook the spring ends into place afterwards. It's helpful to leave the brush baseplate loose until the armature has been fed into position, after which the two securing screws should be fitted. Put a small dab of grease in the hole on the end of the

49/19a Leave brush springs unhooked ...

49/19b ... feed armature into place ...

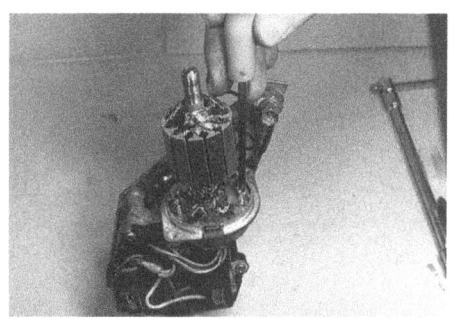

49/19c ... and tighten brushplate screws.

armature and stick the bearing ball in place.

20 When you fit the motor body, be aware that the magnets inside it will try to pull the armature out of the gearbox. You can prevent this by applying pressure on the operating arm so that the armature resists pulling out - you will need to experiment to find the correct amount of pressure to apply - it needs to be just less than that required to turn the armature.

21 Fit the body over the armature and install the retaining screws, tightening them evenly.

49/22a Torque tighten three fixing bolts.

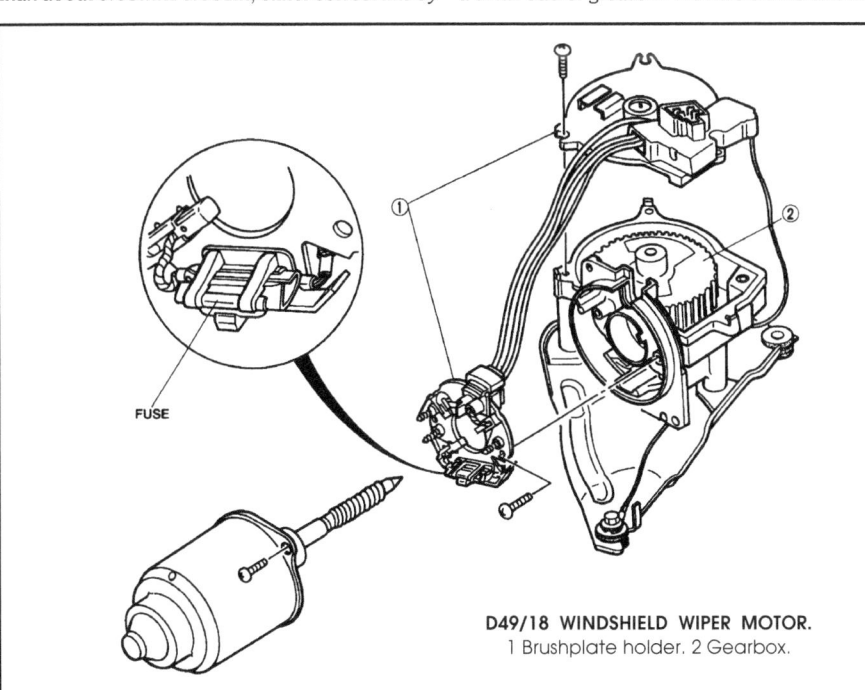

D49/18 WINDSHIELD WIPER MOTOR.
1 Brushplate holder. 2 Gearbox.

Mazda Miata, MX-5, Eunos & Roadster

49/22b Operating arm in correct park position.

50/1c ... pull arm from spindle.

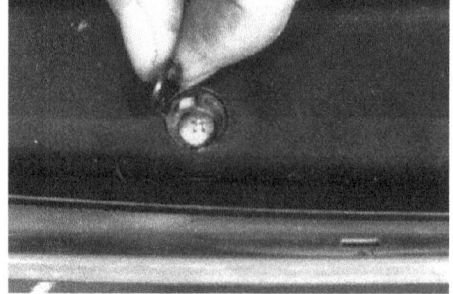

50/4b Screws accessible once caps removed.

INSTALLATION

22   📷+ Install the motor on the firewall and fit the three retaining bolts, tightening them evenly to 7-9Nm/70-100kgf cm/61-86lbf in). If the motor has been dismantled, it is likely that the operating arm will be in the wrong position for reconnection. To remedy this, reconnect the wiring connector, reconnect the battery and turn the ignition to **ON** - if the arm position is wrong, the motor should run until the right position is achieved and then park as shown in the accompanying photograph (Note: RHD shown). Install the wiper mechanism connecting link by snapping it over the head of the motor crank arm pin.

23   Fit any components removed to make access easier during removal, then check the operation of the wipers under all switch positions.

50. WIPER MECHANISM - REMOVAL, INSTALLATION & ADJUSTMENT

☞ 1/1, 2 & 7/2.

1   📷+ To release the wiper arms from their spindles, pry out the plastic plugs from the lower

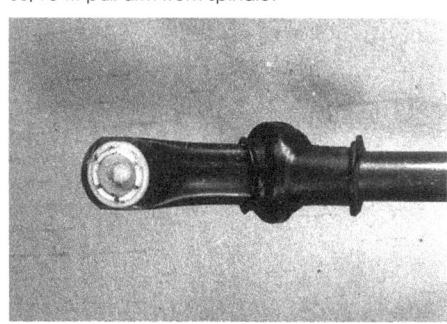

50/2 Nylon cup of wiper link arm.

end of the arm, then remove the flanged nut which secures the arm to the spindle. Note the position of the wiper blade in relation to the screen (this is usually obvious unless the screen is unusually clean. The arm can now be pulled off - you may need to twist it a little to get it free.

2   📷 If you need to remove the linkage, start by removing the arms as described above, then disconnect the link from the motor end by levering it off with a screwdriver blade - the cup-shaped link is snapped in place over the round head on the motor arm. The remaining link connections can be removed in the same way.

3   The wiper gearboxes are each retained by two bolts fitted from above, and can be removed once the bolts have been released and the connecting links detached. Alternatively, you can remove the links and gearboxes as an assembly. The problem here is that the gearbox mounting bolts are covered by what Mazda describes as the 'cowl grille' - the windshield lower trim panel. This is held in place by crosshead screws, but the screw heads are covered by plastic caps which are incredibly difficult to remove.

4   📷+ The caps have small tangs which

locate and latch them into the panel. To remove them, you need to introduce a curved tool under the edge of the panel to depress the tangs so that the caps pop out - you can't lever them out from above. We made up a tool with a piece of mild steel (see photograph, which shows the tool and the removed panel) - you may be able to modify an old screwdriver to do the same job. Pass the tool under the lip of the panel and feel around with the end until you locate the tang. Now push fairly hard, keeping your hand over the cap to prevent it flying off at high speed (Wally managed to lose two of our car's caps during removal ...).

5   📷+ With the caps removed, you can unscrew the panel retaining screws and lift the panel away to reveal the wiper gearbox mounting bolts. On the passenger side there is a plastic cover which covers the blower air intake. There is no specific need to remove this, but, if you wish to do so, it is retained by a row of four black crosshead screws along the lower edge of the windshield, a single small silver screw near the fender, and a couple of clips into the firewall. Remove the bolts and withdraw the gearboxes and linkage - the rods can be freed by prying the ends off the gearbox

50/5a Unscrew panel retaining screws.

50/1a Carefully pry off plastic cover ...

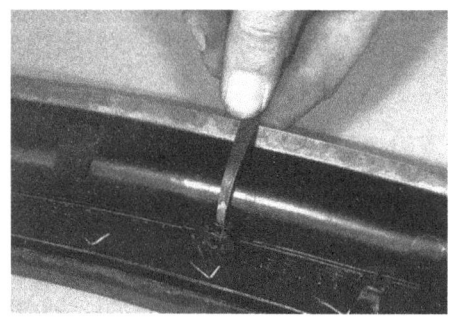

50/1b ... unscrew & remove flanged nut ...

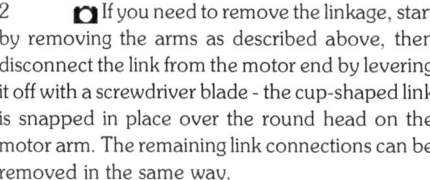

50/4a Cap removal tool demo (trim panel out).

50/5b ... and lift panel away ...

7:46

7: Electrical system

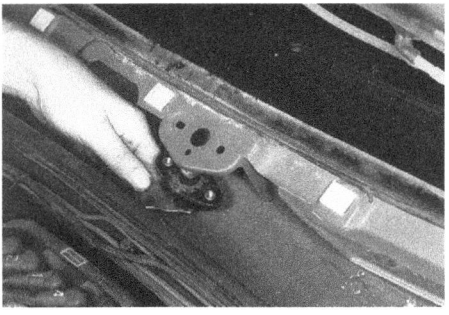

50/5c ... remove bolts securing link gearboxes.

50/5d This panel covers blower intake.

50/6 Wiper with airfoil goes on drivers side.

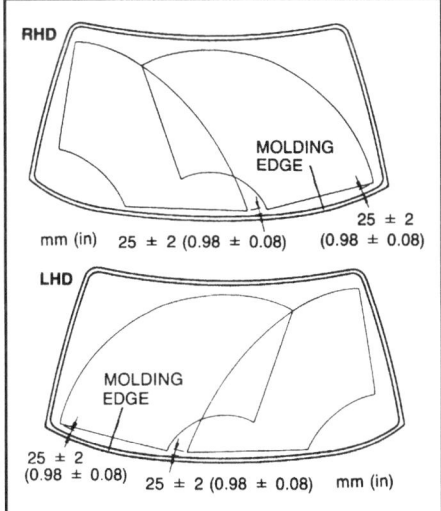

D50/6 WINDSCREEN WIPER ADJUSTMENT DIAGRAM.

crank pins.

6   ☐ ⚙ When installing the gearboxes, tighten the mounting bolts to 7-9Nm/70-100kgf cm/61-86lbf in). Fit the cowl grille (trim panel), snapping the screw caps back in place after the screws have been tightened. Snap the connecting links back into place, where these were removed. Fit the wiper arms (the one with the tiny airfoil fits on the driver's side) and tighten the flange nuts provisionally. Check the arm height setting, comparing it with the accompanying drawing. After making any necessary adjustment to the arm position, tighten the flanged nuts down to 16-19Nm/1.6-2kgf m/12-14lbf ft) and fit the plastic caps.

51. WINDSHIELD WASHER PUMP MOTOR - TESTING & REPLACEMENT

☞ 1/1, 2 & 7/2.

1   ☐ The washer pump motor (and reservoir tank) design and location vary somewhat according to specification and options fitted, though the most common arrangment is to find the reservoir on the right-hand inner fender (non-ABS models), and in the forward part of the left-hand front wheel well (ABS models). The washer motor snaps into a recess on the reservoir (its stub being sealed by a grommet), and can be removed by pulling it away and unplugging its wiring connector.

2   ⚙ Check the pump motor operation by unplugging its harness connector, and then connecting terminal **B** of the motor side connector to the positive (+) side of an external battery and terminal **A** to ground (-) (see diagram) - if the motor runs, it's OK, if it doesn't, fit a new one. We suggest that you take your dead pump unit along when purchasing a new one to make sure that you get one of the same design.

52. HEADLIGHT WASHER SYSTEM (IF FITTED) - TROUBLESHOOTING

☞ 1/1, 2 & 7/2.

1   ⚙ If the pump runs but no water emerges from the jets, check that the washer jets are clear: use a pin or fine wire to clear any obstruction.

2   Check the **H/CLEAN 20A** fuse in Fuse Block No.1. If it has blown, try fitting a new fuse and see whether the headlight washer system now

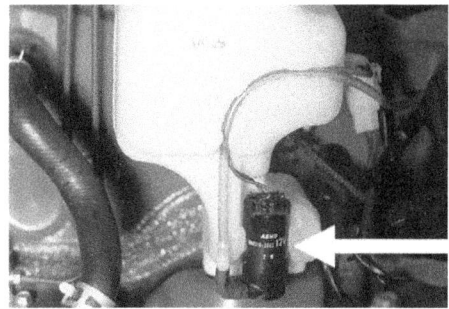

51/1 Washer system pump/motor (location varies).

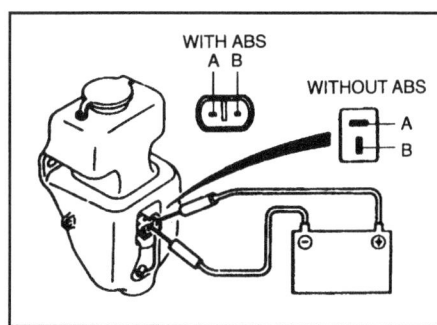

D51/2 WASHER MOTOR: CHECKING OPERATION.

operates normally. If the fuse burns out again, check the washer system wiring for shorts, open circuits and bad connections: repair or rewire as necessary.

3   At the relay bank on the left side of the engine compartment, locate the headlight cleaner relay. Check for battery voltage on the red/yellow wire with the headlight retractor switch on. If no voltage is found, check and repair the wiring between the relay and the switch.

4   Turn the ignition switch on to the **ACC** position, and check for battery voltage at the green wire at the relay connector. If zero volts is shown, check the green wire to the fuse and repair or rewire as necessary.

5   ⚙ If you have not located the fault at this point, check the relay continuity, referring to the accompanying diagram for details.

6   ⚙ Next, check for continuity between terminals **c** and **d** as shown in the accompanying

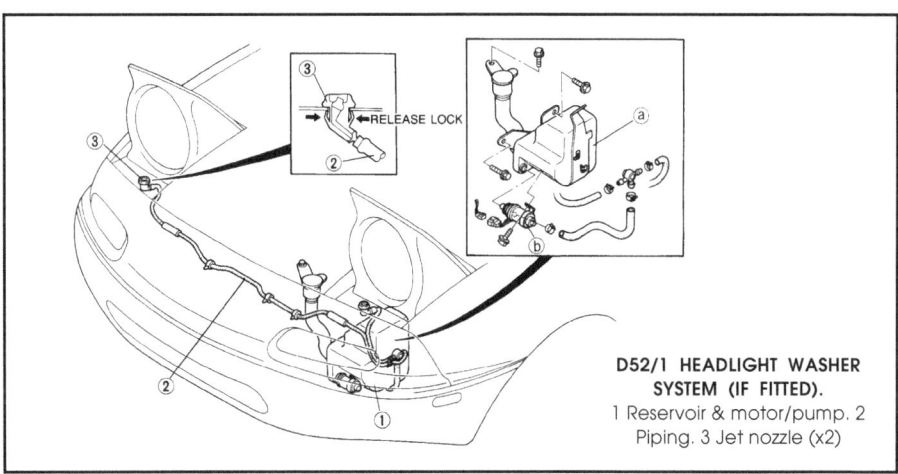

D52/1 HEADLIGHT WASHER SYSTEM (IF FITTED).
1 Reservoir & motor/pump. 2 Piping. 3 Jet nozzle (x2)

Mazda Miata, MX-5, Eunos & Roadster

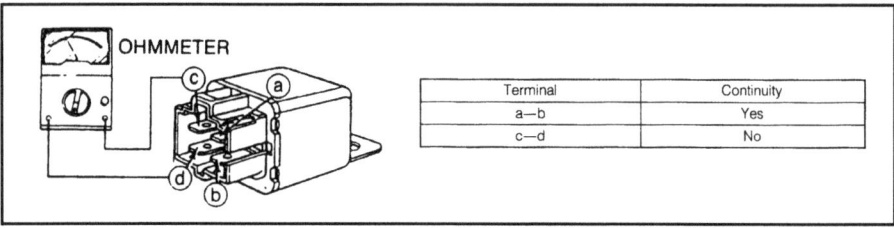

D52/5 HEADLIGHT WASHER RELAY: CHECKING CONTINUITY (1).

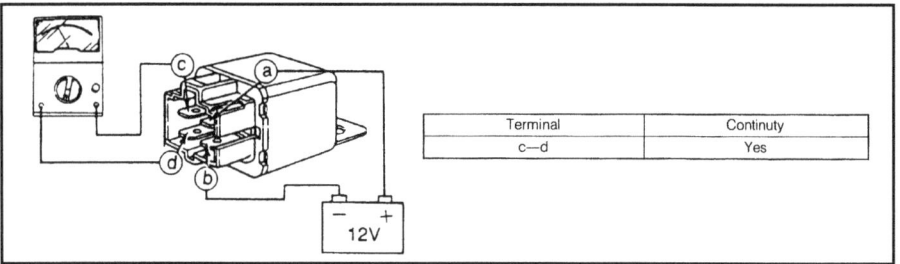

D52/6 HEADLIGHT WASHER RELAY: CHECKING CONTINUITY (2).

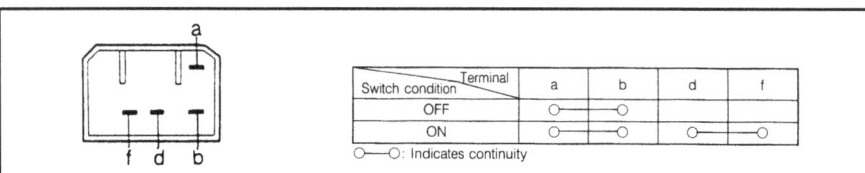

D52/8 HEADLIGHT WASHER SWITCH: CHECKING TERMINAL CONTINUITY.

53/4a Unplug wiring connector ...

53/4b ... and push lighter body thru dashpanel ...

53/4c ... depress locking tabs & push out sleeve.

53/4d Component parts of the cigarette lighter.

diagram and table, while applying 12 volts to terminals **a** and **b**. If the above checks do not give the expected results, fit a new relay.

7 Check for battery voltage on the yellow/black terminal of the headlight cleaner switch. If battery voltage is not present, check the wiring/connectors between the switch and the relay.

8 Referring to the accompanying diagram and table, check the headlight cleaner switch continuity. If not as shown, replace the switch.

9 Check continuity between the headlight cleaner switch connector black wire terminal and a good body ground connection. If no continuity is found, repair or replace the ground wire.

10 With the retractor and headlight switches on, check for battery voltage at the yellow/white terminal of the headlight cleaner motor. If battery voltage is not present, check the wiring/connections between the motor and the relay.

11 Check continuity between the headlight cleaner motor connector black wire terminal and a good body ground connection. If no continuity is found, repair or replace the ground wire.

12 Disconnect the motor wiring connector. Referring to the accompanying diagram for terminal positions, apply 12 volts (+) to the motor **a** terminal and ground (-) the **b** terminal. If the motor fails to operate, fit a new one.

53. CIGARETTE LIGHTER - REMOVAL & INSTALLATION

☞ 1/1, 2 & 7/2.

1 The cigarette lighter is mounted in the dash panel. If it stops working, check the **CIGAR 15A** fuse in Fuse Block No.1, fitting a new one if it has blown. Check what is inside the lighter body - kids love to stuff things in there, and if what they stuffed into yours was metal foil from a candy bar, you may've found what blew the fuse. Poke around with a screwdriver to dislodge the crud and then suck it out with a vacuum cleaner. If the heating coil has burned out, this is pretty easy to replace - pull out the old one, push in the new one. Done.

2 If you haven't solved the problem at this stage, either quit smoking or keep a Zippo in the glovebox (you can probably get a really nice one with the Miata/MX-5/Sportster logo on it). Even those cheap, plastic disposables aren't so bad compared with fitting a new lighter body in the dash panel.

3 OK, so you *really need* to have the dash-mounted lighter working - well, don't say we didn't warn you. Before you go any further, remove the access panel under the steering column (two screws and unclip it). Feel behind the dash panel and see if you can reach the lighter unit. See - we told you! We reckoned that if we had six-inch long fingers with about three extra knuckle joints we could have done it. ET could probably reach it easily, but then he could light a cigarette with his finger, anyway ...

4 You might try prying out the interior light above the cigarette lighter as another, limited, means of access. The aperture is too small to get your hand in (though if you can find the kid who put the aluminum foil into the lighter and burned it out, his hand might fit). You need to wiggle the lighter body around and push it out of the dash panel. As the lighter body comes out of the recess, disconnect the wiring connector and remove it. If you need to remove the plastic surround and metal cup, reach behind and squeeze the ears of the plastic surround and push it out, then remove the cup.

5 Clean everything up before you install the new body. Fit the metal cup and plastic surround. Clip the wiring connector in place on the lighter body and slide it home. Now check that it works.

6 How did we get those shots of the inside of the dash panel? Easy. We took the dash panel out - nothing's too much trouble for our readers!

7: Electrical system

54. AUDIO SYSTEM - GENERAL & TROUBLESHOOTING

☞ 1/1, 2 & 7/2.

1 Beyond saying that audio systems are usually fused via **CIGAR**, **ROOM** & **BTN** fuses, there's not very much we can say about the practical aspects of audio system repair, because such a plethora of different systems - both original equipment (but by different manufacturers) and aftermarket - will be found fitted to these cars.

2 Whatever make of audio equipment is fitted to your car, its manufacturer will have supplied a handbook detailing system operation, specification, troubleshooting and any relevant security aspects, such as dedicated number codes. If you do not have such a handbook, you can probably contact the equipment manufacturer (perhaps even on the web) to get the information you need. Failing this, any car audio specialist should be able to help.

3 Given the wide variety of installation options, we felt it would be pointless to attempt to offer specific coverage. Instead, we do give some general advice which we hope will be helpful.

AUDIO UNIT REMOVAL & INSTALLATION

4 Make sure you have the audio unit security code (if applicable), then disconnect the battery ☞ 7/2.

5 ▣ The audio unit will be mounted in the center panel of the dashpanel. Generally, the unit will be held in a metal cage, the securing screws of which will be accessible once the center panel is removed ☞ 10/3. Release the screws and withdraw the audio unit cage sufficiently to disconnect it from harness and antenna (aerial) wiring.

6 ▣ Some units will be removable while the center panel is still in place: such units will usually have small trim panels on each side of their fascias which can be gently levered off and which cover 'service holes.' The correct special tools need to be slid into the 'service holes' on each side of the audio unit to release the retaining latches and allow the unit's withdrawal and disconnection (see diagram).

7 Install the audio unit after remaking its electrical connections to wiring harness, speaker wires and antenna wire. If applicable, replace the cage securing screws followed by the center panel ☞ 10/3.

8 Reconnect the battery ☞ 7/2 and, if applicable, enter the audio unit's security code.

SECURITY

9 Depending on your neighborhood, we feel that you would be crazy not to have a good quality alarm system, particularly where the usual convertible top is fitted. The car is very vulnerable to break-ins, even with the roof up: you don't even need to get past the door lock to get to the car's interior if you have a knife. Though most car audio systems have a security code feature, they still get stolen, even if the thief has to abandon them when he's unable to get the unit to work.

10 Audio unit security usually comes in the form of a removable faceplate allied to a security code known only to the rightful owner. Generally, the security code has to be re-entered whenever the audio unit has been isolated from the car's electrical system (including when the battery has been disconnected). Make sure you keep a record of the security code somewhere away from the car. Do try to remember to take the faceplate with you whenever you leave the car because, if the faceplate's in place, the audio unit's worth stealing and it will generally be ripped out to save time: this will mean plenty of damage to the center panel and wiring. This is said with conviction because it happened to our project car, unfortunately with the 'bonus' of a deliberately smashed side window ...

11 Fix prominent window stickers on the car underlining the fact that the audio unit is security coded and that an alarm is fitted (even if this is untrue) - this may be enough to deter the casual thief.

AUDIO SYSTEM TROUBLESHOOTING

12 Problems can be divided into three main groups; unit problems, speaker problems and antenna problems. The first thing to do if you have problems with your stereo system is to determine which part of the system is to blame. The checklist below will give you a good start with this:

Nothing works

• Check **CIGAR**, **ROOM** & **BTN** fuses. There may also be a fuse in the live feed to the audio unit.

• Check that the unit is turned on, and that power is available to it - turn the ignition switch to **ACC**.

• Check if the anti-theft system has been activated. If *"CODE"* or a similar message is displayed, you need to enter the security code for your unit. Refer to the manufacturer's literature for details of this procedure.

• If you see a message like *"Err"* (error) displayed, you'll need to get the unit reset or exchanged by the supplier.

• If the unit shows nothing on the display, you'll need to remove it and check the wiring connections at the back, the associated wiring and the fuse. It is also possible that an internal battery or capacitor has failed.

System works on one stereo channel only

• Check the position of the balance control - it may have been accidentally knocked to the fully left or fully right position.

• Check the speaker wiring, working from the connector on the back of the unit to the individual speaker(s). Reconnect, repair or replace as necessary.

• Check the speaker(s). The resistance across the speaker terminals should be 4 ohms - if significantly outside this, you'll need to install new speaker(s).

System won't play cassette tapes

• Check the unit control settings and try playing a known good tape.

• Check for dirt or oxide buildup in the tape player mechanism. Use a good quality head cleaner tape and see if problem is resolved.

• Try playing a tape with the volume turned right back. Listen for the sound of the tape running in the player unit; if no sound is heard, the drivebelt may have broken. (Consult Mazda dealer or car audio specialist.)

• If tape will not load into the unit, replace the unit or have it repaired or serviced.

Radio inoperative (cassette tape player OK)

• If the radio is completely inoperative, or there are bad static or interference problems, check the antenna and antenna connections, working along the antenna lead from the audio unit antenna socket to the antenna itself.

• Check for continuity between the antenna and a body ground; no continuity should be shown, and if the antenna is grounded, a new one should be installed.

• Check that the antenna base is securely grounded. If no continuity is shown, or

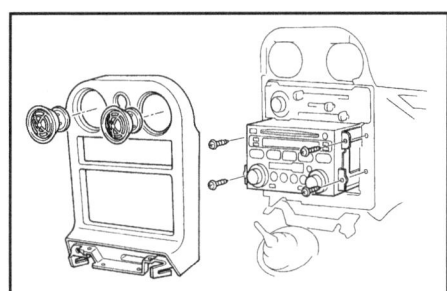

D54/5 AUDIO UNIT REMOVE/INSTALL (1).

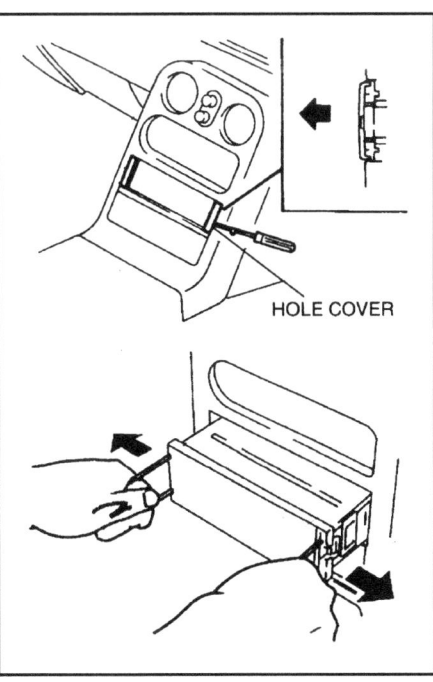

D54/6 AUDIO UNIT REMOVE/INSTALL (2).

Mazda Miata, MX-5, Eunos & Roadster

there is intermittent or poor contact, check for corrosion. Clean the contact area and protect from further corrosion with petroleum jelly (Vaseline) before tightening the antenna mounting.
• If you are unable to resolve the fault, have the unit checked by a Mazda dealer or car audio specialist.

CD player inoperative - disc will not load
• Try another disc - if the original disc was dirty or damaged, the unit will reject it.
• Check the remaining audio system - if this is OK, have the CD player section checked and repaired by a Mazda dealer or car audio specialist.

CD skips during play
• This is usually caused by driving over a rough road surface.
• If skipping occurs on a particular disc only, it may be dirty or damaged.
• If skipping occurs randomly, or while the car is stationary, have the unit checked professionally (may be a tracking fault).

55. ANTENNA (MANUAL) - REMOVAL & INSTALLATION

1   The standard (original equipment) manual antenna (aerial) fitment is mounted in the right-hand rear fender and trunk.
2   To remove the antenna from the car, first unscrew and remove the antenna mast from the base unit, then unscrew the chrome retainer ring using a wide blade screwdriver or snap ring (circlip) pliers.
3   Unplug the antenna lead in the trunk, then remove the single 10mm nut at the base bracket and lift the assembly away. Note the installation sequence of the chrome retainer, the rubber spacer and the ground plate on the underside of the body.
4   When installing the antenna, check that the mounting points (particularly where the raised tabs of the ground plate contact the body) are clean and corrosion-free to ensure a good ground contact. Install the ground plate with the tabs upward (they're supposed to dig into the body to make good contact). Use petroleum jelly (Vaseline) to prevent subsequent corrosion problems. Don't tighten the chromed mounting nut until the antenna is fixed to its bottom bracket. Check that the plug from the antenna is firmly inserted into its jack.

56. ANTENNA (POWER) - REMOVAL & INSTALLATION

1   The power antenna (aerial) is fitted

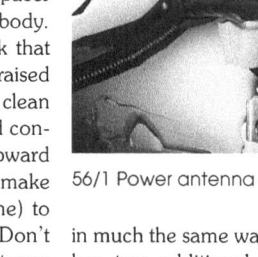

56/1 Power antenna (aerial) installation.

in much the same way as the manual version, but has two additional wiring connections and is protected by the **ANTENNA 10A** or **AERIAL 10A** fuse, which may be in Fuse Box No.2 in the trunk (boot), or Fuse Block No.1 behind the access panel on the driver's side of the dashboard. The unit comprises the antenna, the motor and associated gearbox and drive rack and the relay unit. When connected to a compatible audio unit, the antenna raises automatically when the audio unit is turned

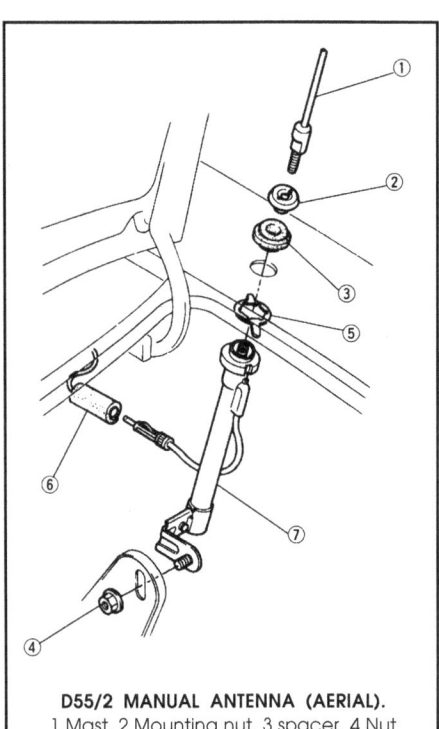

D55/2 MANUAL ANTENNA (AERIAL).
1 Mast. 2 Mounting nut. 3 spacer. 4 Nut (10mm). 5 Ground (earth) plate. 6 Wiring jack. 7 Antenna body.

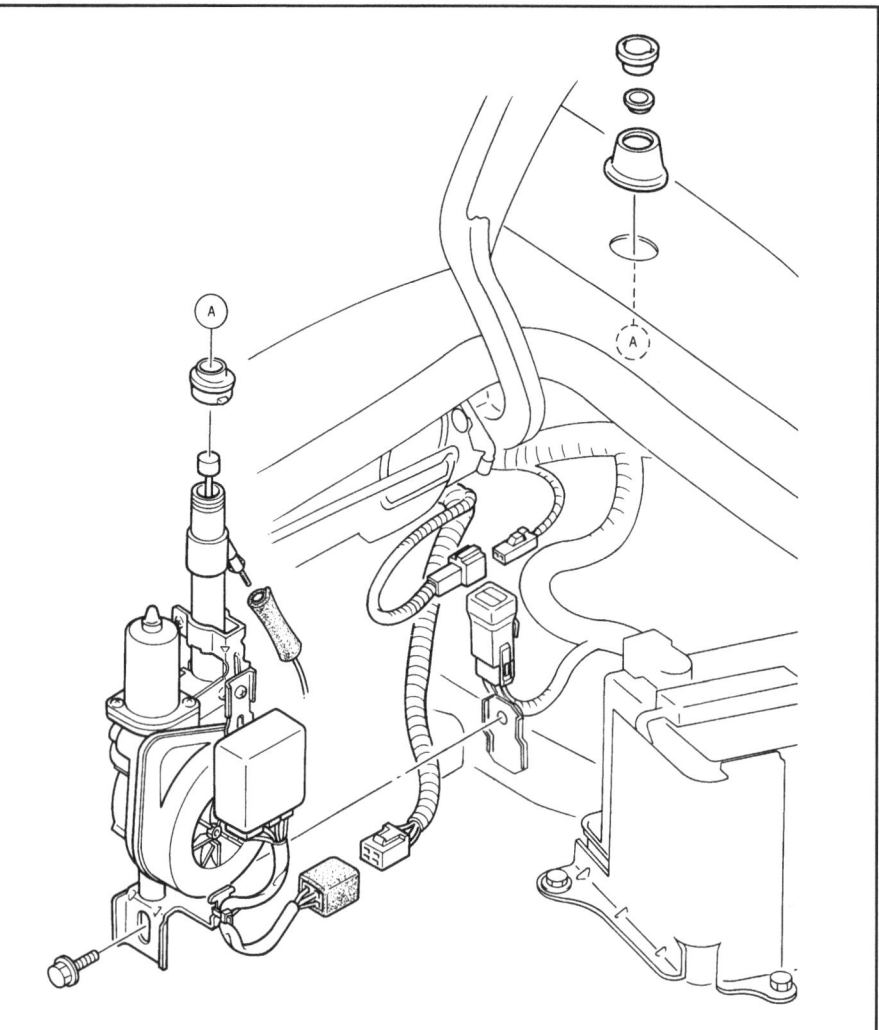

D56/1 POWER ANTENNA (AERIAL).

7: Electrical system

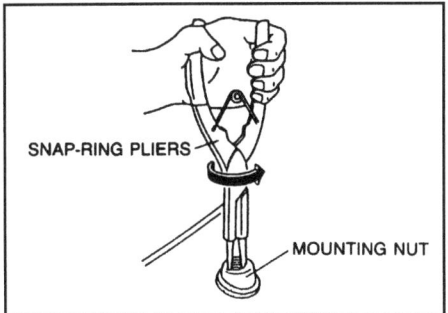

D56/2 ANTENNA MOUNTING NUT CAN BE UNSCREWED WITH SNAP RING PLIERS.

on, and retracts when it is turned off.

2   The mounting nut on the top of the unit has slots either side of the antenna mast end, and, with the mast retracted, can be unscrewed using snap ring (circlip) pliers. With the ignition switch turned to the **ON** or **ACC**, turn the radio on and the antenna mast will be pushed out of the unit body and can be removed.

3   If there have been problems with antenna system operation, check the end of the plastic rack for damage; there should be a smooth taper on the end of the rack end (opposite side to the teeth). If the rack end or its teeth are damaged or broken, you'll have to fit a new mast.

4   To install the mast, make sure the radio is switched off and, as the rack is retracted into the unit, guide the mast into position. Fit the mounting nut, then operate the radio switch to check that the antenna extends and retracts normally.

5   If the antenna seems mechanically sound, but does not operate normally, either the motor unit or the relay may have failed. These are best checked by substitution. If you have a Miata-MX5 owning friend with a power antenna, try swapping motor units and relays to identify the faulty part, or have your Mazda dealer track this down for you.

57. ALARMS & IMMOBILISERS - GENERAL

1   We're afraid that there is not a lot of

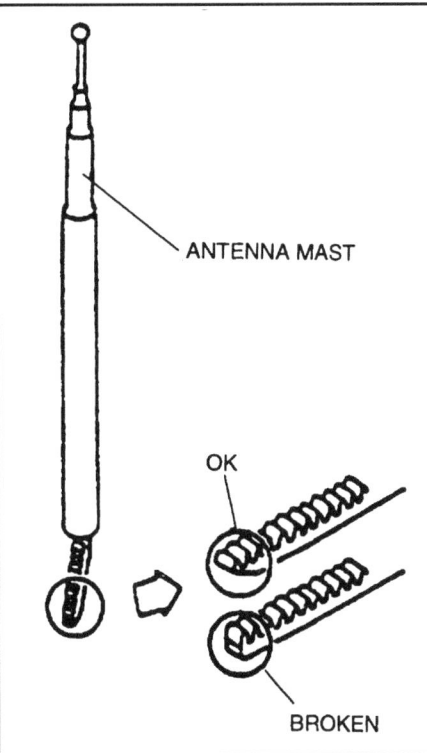

D56/3 POWER ANTENNA MAST RACK.
Check end of rack and teeth for damage.

practical help we can give in relation to these devices, as there's a huge number of products which work in various diffrent ways and have their own unique wiring and, sometimes, connections to other of the car's systems.

2   The majority of these security systems will have been fitted by the dealer when the car was new, and relevant literature will have been included with the 'Owner's Manual' (handbook) and service book. Hopefully, this information will still be with the car, even if you are not the original owner. Otherwise, you'll have to find a brand name somewhere and try to contact the manufacturer. Your first port of call should be your usual Mazda dealer, which will probably be able to identify the security device if it was approved by Mazda for dealer fitment.

3   **Warning!** Don't mess with immobiliser systems. When activated, some will allow you to drive the car for a short distance before immobilising the car, locking you in and sounding a very high decibel alarm! "Beam me up, Scotty ...".

4   A word of advice. If the security device on your car is activated/de-activated by a small electrical device on your keyring, open the device to find what size and type of battery it uses. Always keep a spare new battery (you can get keyring battery holders) to save you the embarrassment of not being able to de-activate your car's alarm in a busy car park because the original battery has faded.

58. WIRING DIAGRAMS - GENERAL

1   We have not included a set of wiring diagrams because we feel it is a pointless exercise. The first problem is that Mazda's hugely popular roadster is truly a 'world car', which has featured an enormous number of wiring variations depending on market, specification and model year (meaning that there are almost enough wiring diagrams to fill a book ...). The second - and more important - problem is that the car's wiring system is modular and comprises up to 22 separate harnesses. This means that, although you can trace a wire by color from one end of a single harness to the other, you can't do this through multiple harnesses as the wire color may change at one or more connections.

2   Instead of incorporating wiring diagrams, what we've done is define the troubleshooting of individual electrical components/circuits very closely, telling you exactly how to check out the relevant switch, connector, relay, light, motor, wire harnesses and fuses to identify and repair a fault.

Notes

8

Suspension & steering

1. INTRODUCTION

☞+ Renowned for their excellent and responsive handling, these cars are equipped with fully independent suspension front and rear. The suspension at all four wheels is of the double wishbone (A-arm) type, with the wishbones carried on rubber-bushed pivots supported by subframes. The suspension units are the "coil over" type, which means that the shock absorbers (dampers) are co-axial with externally mounted coil springs.

The lower wishbone pivot points (front and rear suspension) are adjustable using eccentrics, thus permitting adjustment of both caster and camber angles. This system provides servicing adjustment, as well as allowing for the application of non-standard geometries for competition purposes.

Body roll is controlled by front and rear stabilizer (anti-roll) bars.

Steering is by a rack and pinion system which is usually power-assisted.

2. WHEEL ALIGNMENT - GENERAL

☞ 1/1, 2.

1   Mazda has built in comprehensive adjustment facilities for the suspension and steering geometry. This does not mean that you need to adjust the suspension on a regular basis - the adjustment facility is there primarily to allow the correct standard alignment settings to be restored

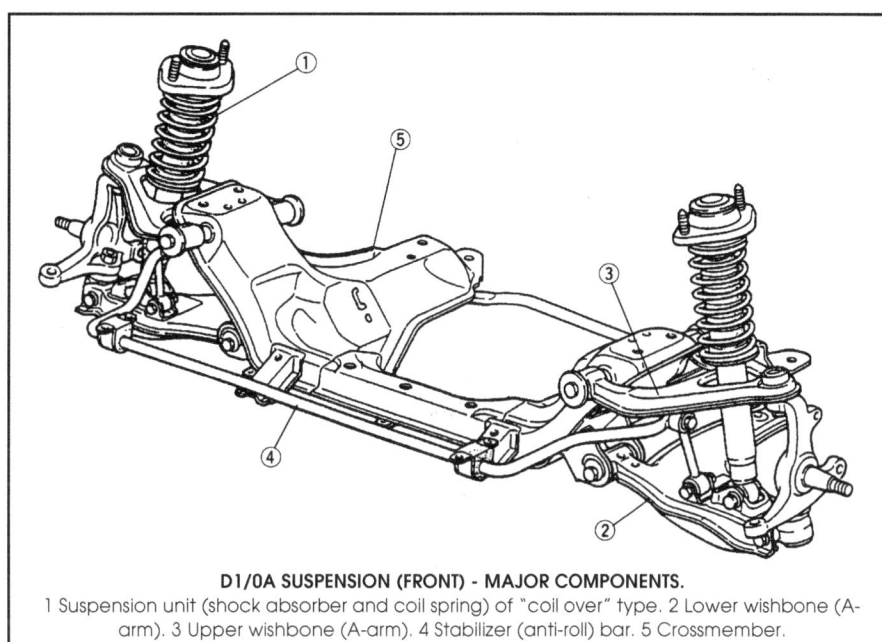

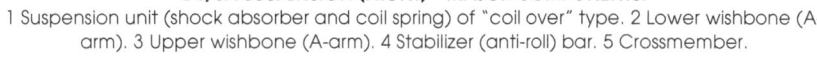

D1/0A SUSPENSION (FRONT) - MAJOR COMPONENTS.
1 Suspension unit (shock absorber and coil spring) of "coil over" type. 2 Lower wishbone (A-arm). 3 Upper wishbone (A-arm). 4 Stabilizer (anti-roll) bar. 5 Crossmember.

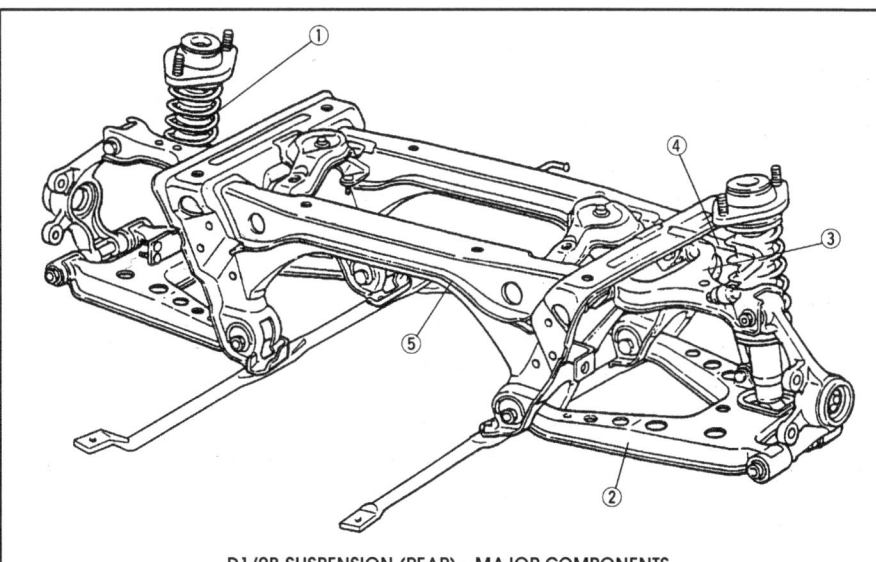

D1/0B SUSPENSION (REAR) - MAJOR COMPONENTS.
1 Suspension unit (shock absorber and coil spring) of "coil over" type. 2 Lower wishbone (A-arm). 3 Upper wishbone (A-arm). 4 Stabilizer (anti-roll) bar. 5 Crossmember.

Mazda Miata, MX-5, Eunos & Roadster

after new suspension parts have been installed, or as wear occurs. Mazda put in a lot of work developing and optimizing the car's suspension geometry, and, for road use, departure from the standard settings will normally cause more problems than it solves. It may be, however, that you need to apply different settings if you intend to use the car in competition, where ride comfort can be ignored in favor of optimum handling. Also, installation of non-standard suspension parts may call for revised suspension geometry - if this is necessary, then consult the supplier or manufacturer of the parts for detailed set up instructions.

2   There are four elements to the adjustability of the steering and suspension -

Steering angle (maximum): Each front wheel pivots on the two balljoints of the stub axle's upright section to provide steering. "Maximum steering angle" describes the maximum amount of inward and outward turn of each wheel expressed as an angle (with the straight ahead position being 0 degrees). Mazda's setting is 37 degrees 23 minutes (plus/minus 2 degrees) inward turn and 32 degrees 32 minutes (plus/minus 2 degrees) outward turn. In practice, you need not concern yourself about this setting because if the toe-in has been correctly set (with the steering wheel on centre in the straight ahead position), maximum steering angle will automatically be correct.

Toe-in: "Toe-in" describes the asymetry between two wheels on the same axle plane which

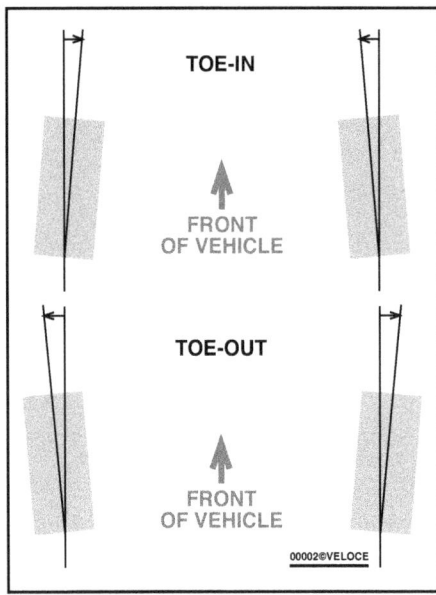

D2/2A SIMPLE ILLUSTRATION OF "TOE-IN" (TRACKING).

are pigeon-toed, intentionally angled toward each other: in other words, the distance between the two tyre walls (at hub height) ahead of the axle is shorter than the distance behind the axle ("toe-out" is the opposite of toe-in). The purpose behind this deliberate asymetry is that there will be some compliance at every joint in the steering/suspension system. However, when the car is moving forwards, the steering/suspension joints are under compression and any compliance is taken up: toe-in compensates for this small movement and allows the wheels on the same axle to run parallel to each other when the car is in forward motion and being steered in a straight line. See diagram.

Caster: Just like the wheels on a shop-

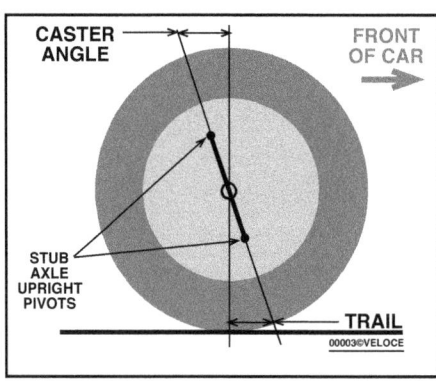

D2/2B SIMPLE ILLUSTRATION OF "CASTER."

ping kart (trolley), the wheels of a car use caster to make them prefer pointing straight ahead to being turned. To achieve this effect, the contact patch of the wheel needs to trail the axis about which the wheel pivots. This all sounds horribly complex, but here's a case of "a picture's worth a thousand words" as the accompanying diagram shows how simple caster really is. Caster is measured in degrees: the measurement being the amount that the wheel's pivot axis is inclined from vertical. See diagram.

Camber: If the tops of the wheels on one axle are closer to each other than the bottoms, the wheels have negative camber; if the bottoms are closer the wheels have positive camber. Camber compensates for body roll and suspension movement when driving through a curve (cornering), and keeps each wheel as close to vertical as possible for maximum tyre grip. Camber is measured in degrees: the measurement representing the amount by which a wheel is inclined from vertical. See diagram.

3   When checking wheel alignment (steering and suspension geometry), it's assumed that the tires are in serviceable condition and correctly inflated, that the wheel bearings are serviceable and that the steering and suspension joints are unworn. Alignment should be checked on smooth, level ground. Note that the fuel tank should be full, the engine coolant and oil levels should be normal, and the spare wheel, jack and tools should be in their normal positions in the trunk. There should be no luggage or occupants in the car.

4   In addition to normal hand tools, you'll need gauges to check wheel alignment. It's possible to check and adjust toe-in using a simple beam-type tracking gauge or drive-over type gauges of the type sold by most automotive tool stores. Camber gauges are also readily available from automotive tools stores and will work on any car.

5   Checking and adjusting caster and camber angles is a little complex. The adjustment procedure itself is not too difficult, but since adjustable

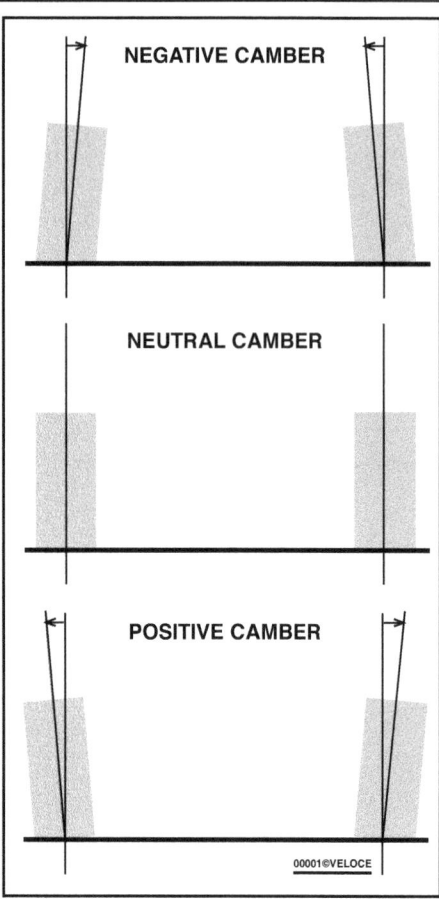

D2/2C SIMPLE ILLUSTRATION OF "CAMBER."

suspension of this type is relatively rare on road cars, you may find suitable equipment for measuring caster difficult to source. Given that you'll only rarely need to check and adjust these settings, if you do need to disturb the suspension settings you can record/mark the current settings/relative positions during dismantling, and simply return components to the same positions during installation. This method will be accurate enough to allow you to drive the car - at a sensible speed - to the nearest tire specialist or Mazda dealer to have the steering/suspension settings checked. We detail the adjustment procedure below for the benefit of owners with access to the necessary equipment, and who are familiar with its use.

6   Before starting the geometry checks, always bounce the car on its suspension a few times to check suspension efficiency and settle the car in its normal position. When you push down on each corner of the car, it should bounce back up and settle quickly - excessive bouncing indicates wear in the shock absorber units, and this should be investigated and rectified before proceeding.

7   You now need to measure and note down the exact distance between the fender rim and the center of each wheel. The difference in height on each side of the car (front and rear) must not exceed 10mm/0.39in. The rear of the car should sit slightly higher than the front by 18mm/0.71in (10-30mm/0.39-1.18in difference is acceptable). If you find a serious discrepancy during

8: Suspension & steering

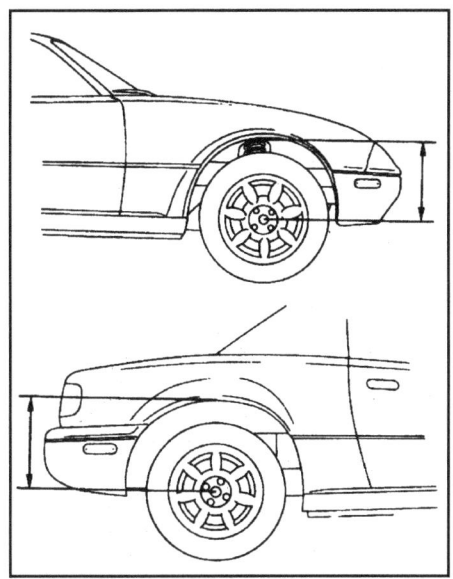

D2/7 CHECK HEIGHT BETWEEN WHEEL CENTRE AND FENDER RIM (WHEELARCH) FRONT & REAR.

this check, you should suspect the coil springs, which may have sagged through normal wear. Note also that wear in the suspension pivots can cause height irregularities. Finally, it's very possible that a previous owner has changed the car's ride height deliberately.

8   Before you start work on caster or camber angle checks and adjustments, we strongly recommend that you first spray thread releasing fluid or WD40 onto the suspension cam bolts, so that subsequent adjustment is made easier. There are two of these to each wheel, at the lower wishbones, where they attach to the subframe. Similarly, if you need to adjust toe-in, clean and lubricate the ball joint threads. You can just about get to the required areas without jacking the car (**Warning!** Take care not to get the lubricating fluid on the brake parts.)

9   Lastly, these cars have great handling. This is because they have an extremely well designed suspension and steering system which is finely engineered and assembled with small tolerances. If you want to keep your car's handling sharp, don't ignore tired bushes, ball joints, springs or dampers: they will all have an adverse affect on handling and your fun ...

3. WHEEL ALIGNMENT - CHECKING & ADJUSTMENT

☞ 1/1, 2.

TOE-IN (FRONT WHEELS) - ADJUSTMENT

1   ☞ 8/2. Note that if you are going to check camber and caster too, those checks and adjustments should be made before toe-in.

2   Check the toe-in (tracking) adjustment whenever caster or camber has been adjusted, or if unusual tire wear characteristics indicate that the tracking is set incorrectly.

3   Unless you are using drive over gauges, raise the front of the car so that the front wheels are just clear of the ground, supporting the body by placing stands below the front jacking points (☞ 1/3).

4   Use a proprietary tracking gauge to check the toe-in, following the manufacturer's instructions, or use the following method. First, mark the tread area centerline of each tire by turning the wheel by hand while marking a line with chalk. Support the chalk by holding it against a block placed in front of the tire so that you get an even, unbroken line around the tire. Now measure the distance between the two lines at the front and rear

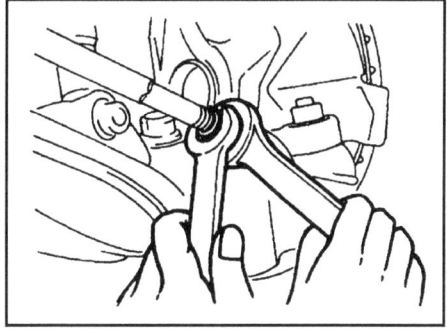

D3/6 RELEASE LOCKNUT THEN TURN TIE ROD TO ADJUST TOE-IN.

of the tires, ensuring that the measurement is made at the same height (axle height) front and rear of the tires.

5   Mazda's official toe-in figure is 3mm (plus or minus 4mm)/0.12in (plus/minus 0.15in) or, if your tracking gauge reads in degrees, 18 minutes (plus/minus 24 minutes). As the tolerance is greater than the nominal setting, this means that even a tiny amount of toe-out is acceptable. However, we recommend you set the tracking to give 1.6mm/0.062in/9 minutes of toe-in. If the measurement obtained is outside these limits, adjust the tracking as follows.

6   Release the clip which secures the rack's dust boot (if installed) to each tie rod end so that the tie rod is free to turn without twisting the boot. If necessary, wire brush the tie rod threads and then apply some releasing fluid or WD40 to the threads at the outer ends of the tie rods and slacken the 17mm locknuts. Using a 20mm crescent wrench (open-ended spanner), turn the left and right tie rods by the same amount, until the prescribed toe-in is achieved. Note that both tie rods have right-hand threads, and so they must be turned in opposite directions when making this adjustment. Each full revolution of a tie rod alters the toe-in by about 7mm (0.28in).

7   Once the setting is correct, tighten the locknuts securely. (Mazda specifies a torque wrench setting of 35-39Nm/3.5-4.0Kgf m/26-28lbf ft). Check that the steering rack boots are not twisted and then tighten the retaining clips.

CASTER ANGLE (FRONT WHEELS) - ADJUSTMENT

8   Set up the caster angle guage, following the maker's instructions, and check the caster angle. Mazda's specified setting varies with the height between wheel centre and fender rim (see diagram D2/7) -

Fender rim height	Caster setting
328-337mm/12.9-13.3in	5 deg. 16 min.
338-347mm/13.3-13.7in	5 deg. 02 min.
348-357mm/13.7-14.1in	4 deg. 49 min.
358-367mm/14.1-14.4in	4 deg. 35 min.
368-377mm/14.4-14.8in	4 deg. 21 min.
Tolerance	1 deg.
Max. difference side to side	1 deg. 30 min.

9   Refer to the accompanying diagram and table for details of cam movement and effect. Slacken the cam bolt 17mm locknuts just enough to permit the bolts to be turned - too much slack will introduce error here. Turn the front and/or the rear 17 mm cam bolts in the direction indicated to obtain the correct setting. Leave the locknuts loose until you have checked the camber angle. Note:

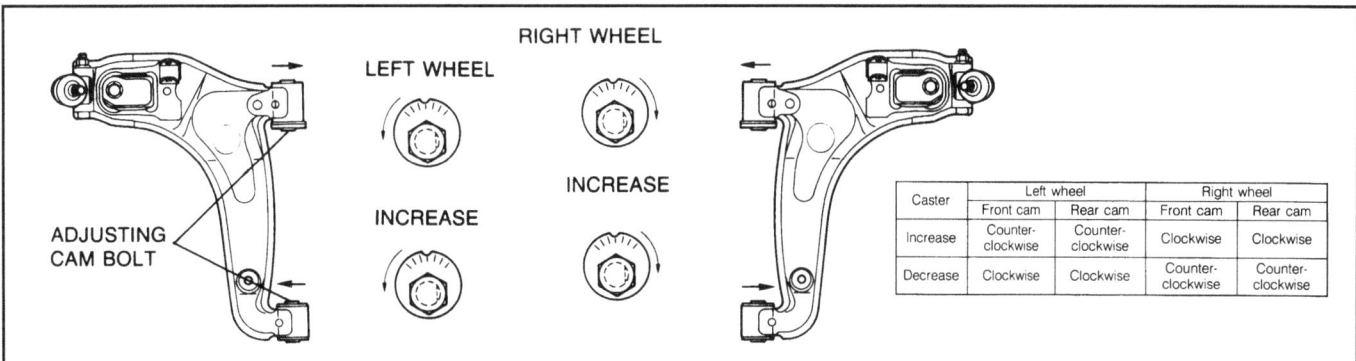

D3/9 FRONT WHEEL CASTER ADJUSTMENT.

Mazda Miata, MX-5, Eunos & Roadster

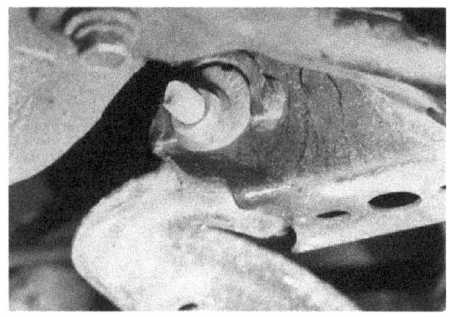

3/9 Wishbone pivot adjustment cam.

one graduation on the cam alters the caster angle by about 22 minutes. Check and adjust camber and toe-in.

CAMBER ANGLE (FRONT WHEELS) - ADJUSTMENT

10 Check and adjust caster angle before making this check/adjustment.

11 Set up the camber angle gauge, following the maker's instructions, and check the camber angle. Mazda's specified setting varies with the height between wheel centre and fender rim (see diagram D2/7) -

Fender rim height setting	Camber
328-337mm/12.9-13.3in	-0 deg. 20 min.
338-347mm/13.3-13.7in	0 deg. 03 min.
348-357mm/13.7-14.1in	0 deg. 24 min.
358-367mm/14.1-14.4in	0 deg. 44 min.
368-377mm/14.4-14.8in	1 deg. 02 min.

Tolerance 1 deg.
Max. difference side to side 1 deg. 30 min.

12 Refer to the accompanying diagram and table for details of cam movement and effect. With the 17mm cam bolt locknuts slackened just enough to permit the 17mm bolts to be turned (too much slack will introduce error), adjust the camber angle as follows. Turn the front and rear cam bolts by equal amounts in opposite directions to obtain the correct setting. Note: one graduation on the front cam alters the camber angle by about 25 minutes. Moving the rear cam by one graduation alters the camber angle by only about 2 minutes.

13 If you are unable to make the camber angle adjustment within the range provided by the cams, go back to the caster angle adjustment sequence and reposition the cams to give enough range for the camber adjustment sequence. After you have adjusted the caster and camber angles, tighten the cam bolt locknuts to 94-112Nm/9.5-11.5kgf m/69-83lbf ft. Finally, check the toe-in - any adjustment of caster or camber angle will have had some affect on this setting.

TOE-IN (REAR WHEELS) ADJUSTMENT

14 ☞ 8/2.

15 Set up the toe-in (tracking) gauge, following its maker's instructions, and check the rear wheel toe-in. The specified setting is 3mm/0.12in/18 degrees (plus or minus 4mm/0.15in/24 minutes). As the tolerance is greater than the nominal setting, this means that even a tiny amount of toe-out is acceptable. However, we recommend you set the tracking to give 1.6mm/0.062in/9 degrees of toe-in. If the measurement obtained is outside these limits, adjust the tracking as follows.

16 Refer to the accompanying diagram and table for details of cam movement and effect. Slacken the 17mm cam bolt locknuts just enough to permit the bolts to be turned (too much slack will introduce error). Turn the front and/or the rear 17mm cam bolts in the direction indicated to obtain the correct setting. Leave the locknuts loose until you have also checked the camber angle. Note: one graduation on the cam alters toe-in by about 2.8mm (0.11in).

CAMBER ANGLE (REAR WHEELS) ADJUSTMENT

17 Check and adjust toe-in before camber.

18 Refer to the accompanying diagram and table for details of cam movement and effect. With the 17mm cam bolt locknuts slackened just enough to permit the bolts to be turned (too much slack will introduce error), adjust the camber angle as follows. Turn the front and rear 17mm cam bolts by an equal amount in opposite directions to obtain the correct setting. Note: one graduation on the front cam alters the camber angle by about 15 minutes. Moving the rear cam by one graduation alters the camber angle by only about 6 minutes.

19 If you are unable to make the camber angle adjustment within the range provided by the cams, go back to the rear wheel toe-in adjustment sequence and reposition the cams to give enough range for the camber adjustment sequence. After you have adjusted the toe-in and camber angle, tighten the cam bolt locknuts to 73-95Nm/7.4-9.7kgf m/54-70lbf ft).

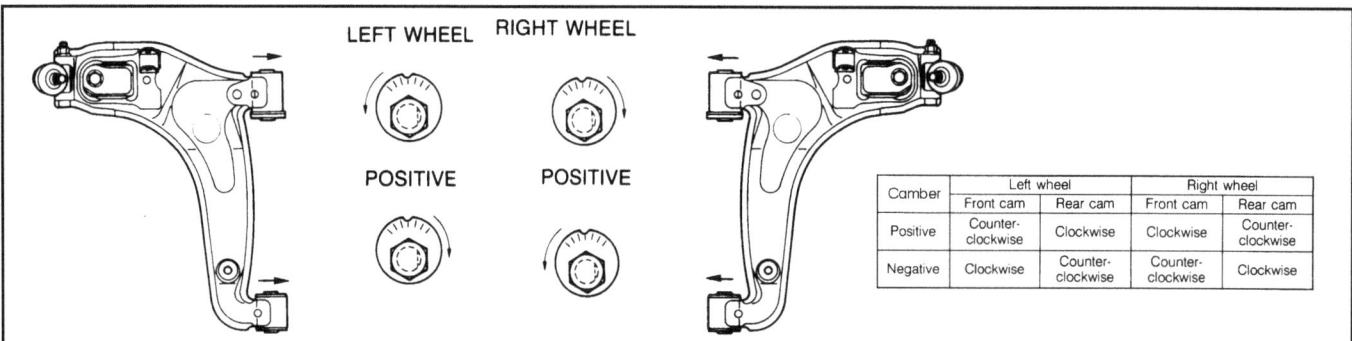

D3/12 FRONT WHEEL CAMBER ADJUSTMENT.

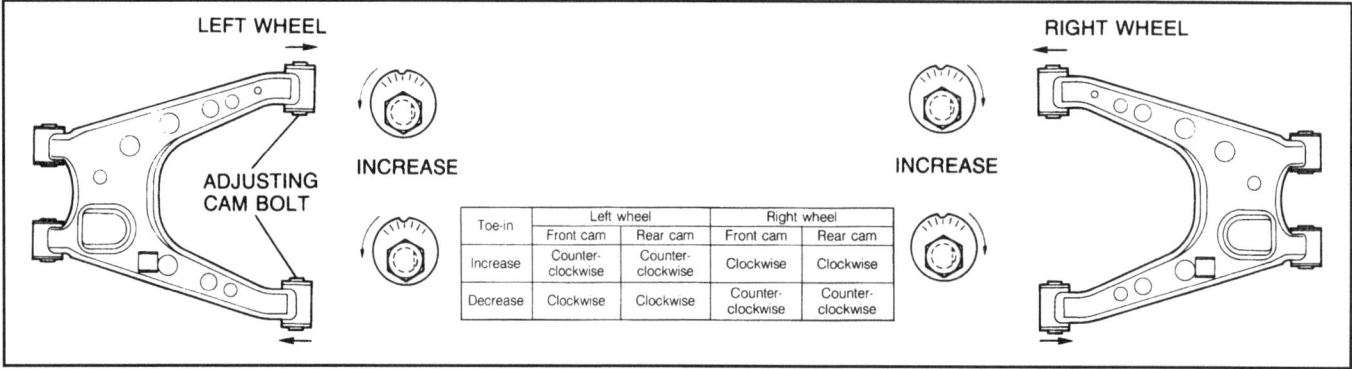

D3/16 REAR WHEEL TOE-IN ADJUSTMENT.

8: Suspension & steering

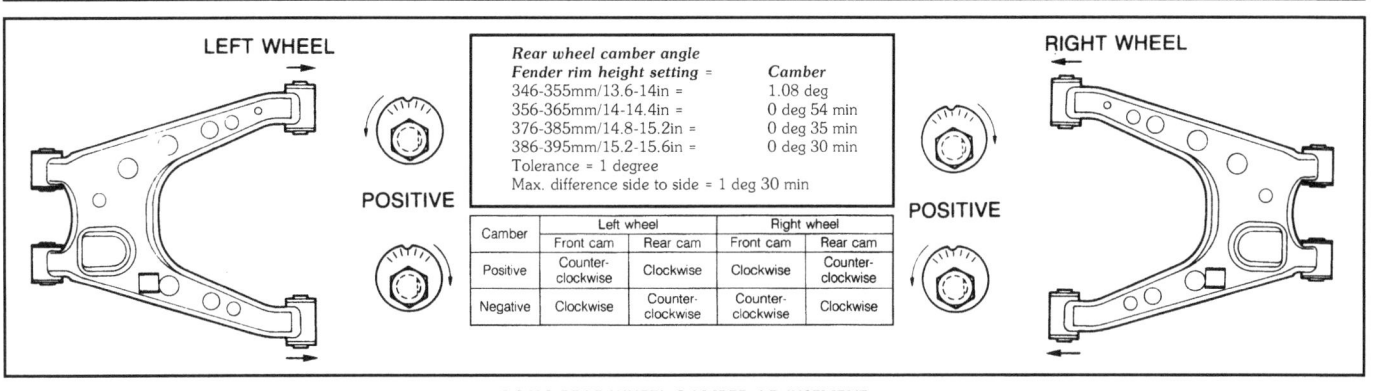

D3/18 REAR WHEEL CAMBER ADJUSTMENT.

4. SHOCK ABSORBER & SPRING (FRONT) - REMOVAL, O/HAUL & INSTALLATION

☞ 1/1, 2.

REMOVAL

1   Position the vehicle on a smooth, level surface and apply the parking brake. Place chocks back and front of the rear tires. Remove the front hub caps, and loosen the lugnuts (wheelnuts) by around one turn. Raise the front of the car and support on jackstands (☞ 1/3). Unscrew the lugnuts (wheelnuts) and remove the wheel.

2   ▣ Locate the end of the stabilizer bar (anti-roll bar) and remove the 14mm nut, bolt and spring washer which secure it to the link rod. As the bolt is removed, the stabilizer bar may move slightly, but it's not under a great deal of pressure.

3   You now have to separate the hub carrier (upright) upper arm ball joint. Start by straightening and withdrawing the cotter pin (split pin) which secures the ball joint's castellated nut. Keep the cotter pin as a pattern (you'll need to install a new one of the correct size during reassembly). Remove the 21mm ball joint nut, then, using a proprietary ball joint separator, release the ball joint pin from its tapered hole in the hub carrier.

4   ▣ There is very little space around the ball joint - we tried a couple of proprietary separators and found it impossible to get them in position. Eventually, we used a wedge-type separator, driving the forked taper of the tool between the upper wishbone and hub carrier. This works, but it's easy to damage the ball joint dust boot. Note that Mazda recommends the dust boot is replaced each time disassembly takes place, in which case damage to the old boot will not be a problem.

5   If all else fails, try screwing the nut onto the threads (upside down and positioning the nut so it is flush with the pin end to protect the threads). Now tap the pin end sharply with a hammer to shock the tapered joint apart, remove the nut, and separate the joint. Again, access is difficult, and you must take great care not to damage the pin end - if you do you will have to replace the upper wishbone and ball joint as an assembly.

6   ▣ Working inside the engine compartment, locate the two 14mm nuts on either side of the suspension top mount dust cap. Remove the two nuts to free the upper end of the suspension unit. **Warning!** Do not remove the large central nut which is covered by the dust cap - if you do, the strut unit will separate under considerable pressure from the suspension spring, and become firmly wedged in place - you could also suffer injury as the whole thing flies apart ...

7   ▣+ Moving back to the underside of the fender, mark the position (using typist's correction fluid or paint) of the lower wishbone pivot bolts in relation to the crossmember: this will provide useful guidance during installation. If you fail to do this, you'll have to set up the suspension from scratch, which takes a lot of time and can only be done using the correct tools. Remove the suspension unit lower mounting bolt, nut and spring washer. Slacken the lower wishbone pivot bolts so that the wishbone can be pushed down slightly, then disengage the upper end of the suspension unit, thread it out of the upper wishbone and remove it to the

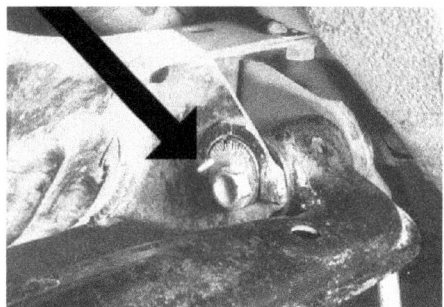

4/7a Mark position of bolt cams before removal.

4/2 Undo the stabilizer bar link.

4/6 The strut top is secured by two nuts.

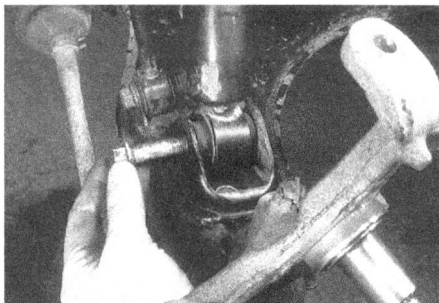

4/7b Withdraw strut lower mounting bolt.

4/4 Release the top ball joint.

4/7c Pull strut thru top wishbone.

Mazda Miata, MX-5, Eunos & Roadster

workbench. **Caution!** Do not push down too far on the lower wishbone or you may strain the brake hose.

DISMANTLING

8 Clamp the suspension unit in a vise, using soft jaws to protect the paint finish on the spring. Lever off the cap and then unscrew the 17mm center nut by a couple of turns (**Warning!** On no account remove it at this stage). Using a suspension spring compressor (which you can easily hire), compress the suspension spring until it can be turned freely on the shock absorber. **Warning!**

4/8 Compress the suspension spring.

Take care when assembling the spring compressor: follow the maker's instructions, and be sure that it is seated securely before compressing the spring.

9 + With the spring safely compressed, unscrew and remove the center nut, lift away the upper mounting plate, then remove the spring and compressor tool. If the spring is to be re-installed, leave it in the compressor. Pull off the dust boot to reveal the shock absorber body.

CHECKING

10 Before cleaning the shock absorber,

4/9a Remove centre nut & mounting plate ...

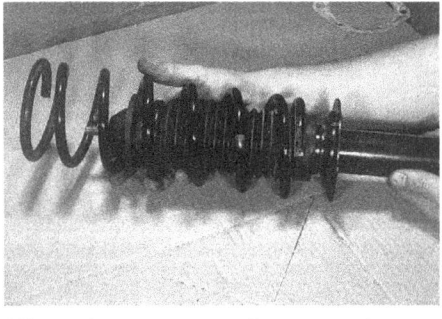

4/9b ... release compressor & remove spring.

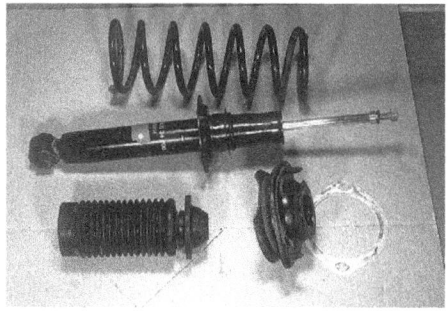

4/10 Suspension strut components.

check carefully for signs of oil leakage. A very light misting of oil on the shock absorber body around the damper rod seal is normal and acceptable - the units work hard in service, and a tiny amount of oil vapor is almost certain to escape. There should not be an appreciable amount of leakage, however, and if you can see that oil has been running down the shock absorber body, it's time to install a new set.

11 If there is no sign of leakage, clean the shock absorber, then check its operation. The unit is filled with gas at low pressure. When compressed by hand, you should be able to feel the damping effect, and when released the unit should move smoothly back to the extended position. If the action of the unit is abnormally stiff or noisy, or if it fails to extend to its normal position, the need for replacement is indicated.

12 If it is to be re-used, clean off the spring (while it is still in the compressor) and check it for obvious damage such as a broken coil. If a coil spring does break, it's usually close to the seat: the part that has broken off may be small - and missing - so check carefully. Always replace springs in axle pairs.

13 When new shock absorber units are to be installed, note that they should be replaced as axle pairs, not individually, or you may suffer suspension imbalance as a result.

14 + Assemble the spring compressor and compress the spring sufficiently for it to be fitted to the shock absorber. Install the dust boot over the shock absorber, making sure that it installs over the locating collar correctly (see diagram). Install the compressed spring over the shock absorber, followed by the top mounting plate. Install the spring washer and nut to the end of the damper rod and tighten by hand (**Warning!** Make sure it is well engaged with the thread.

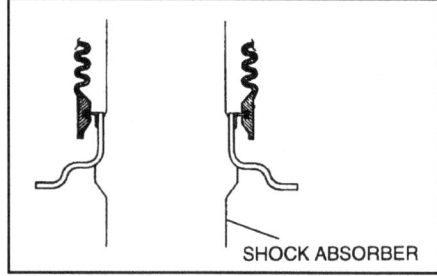

D4/14 CORRECTLY FITTED SHOCK ABSORBER BOOT.

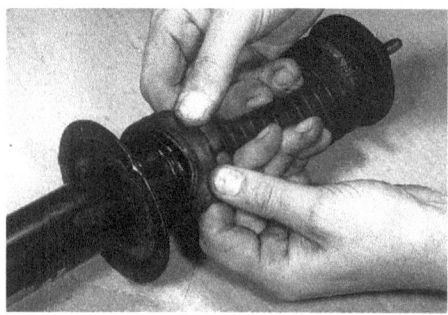

4/14a Refit shock absorber dust boot ...

4/14b ... recompress spring (carefully!) ...

4/14c ...fit mounting plate & centre nut.

15 Set the bottom eye of the shock absorber in the same plane as the two top mount bolts

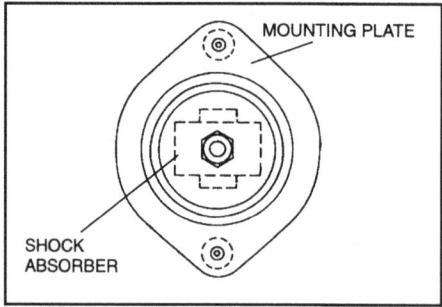

D4/15 CORRECT RELATIONSHIP BETWEEN SUSPENSION UNIT MOUNTING PLATE AND LOWER EYE.

(see diagram), then gradually release the spring compressor, all the time checking that the two ends of the spring engage properly with their seats. The compressor can be removed once the shock absorber is under spring tension. Clamp the top mounting plate in a vise and tighten the damper rod nut to 31-46Nm/3.2-4.7kgf m/23-34bf ft. Finally,

8: Suspension & steering

clamp the unit upside down by the top plate in a vise (use soft jaws). If necessary, install a screwdriver or smooth metal bar through the shock absorber eye, and adjust the unit so that its lower eye and upper mounting plate studs still lie on the same axis.

INSTALLATION

16 Before commencing installation, check the suspension ball joint dust boot for deterioration or damage. If replacement is required, you will have to remove the upper wishbone to do the job, so now is a good time to get on with it (☞ 8/6).

17 ◻ Install the plastic gasket over the top of the suspension unit. Position the suspension unit, passing the lower end through the hole in the upper wishbone. You'll need to push the wishbone down slightly so that the unit can be maneuvered into place. (**Caution!** Don't overdo it - you could strain the brake hose.) Install the suspension unit lower mounting bolt (head towards the rear of the car) and install the spring washer and nut finger-tight at this stage. Position the suspension unit top mounting and install the two retaining nuts from inside the engine compartment. If you have difficulty positioning the unit, the small scissor jack supplied with the car can be used to raise the assembly a little.

18 ◻ Re-align the link rod and stabilizer (anti-roll) bar, again using the car's jack if you need to, then install the mounting bolt (head faces outwards). Install the spring washer and nut finger-tight. Next, position the upper ball joint pin in its tapered hole in the hub carrier. Place a block of wood over the top of the ball joint and tap it reasonably hard to seat the taper. This will allow the nut to be installed and tightened. (If the ball joint turns during tightening, tap it once more and try again.) Torque the nut to 42-60Nm/4.2-6.2kgf m/31-44lbf ft (noting that the hole through the pin end must align with a gap in the castellations). Install a new cotter pin (split pin) to secure the nut, bending the ends over to secure the pin. Install the roadwheel and finger-tighten the lugnuts.

19 Jack the front of the car (☞ 1/3) so that the jackstands (axle stands) can be removed, then lower it so that its weight is taken on the suspension and bounce the corner of the car a few times to settle the suspension (this ensures that the suspension components are in the normal positions before final tightening). You'll need access to all the fasteners which were slackened during removal, so we suggest that you use fabricated steel ramps under the front wheels to obtain working clearance.

20 Check carefully the position of the lower wishbone pivot bolts, setting each to the alignment marks made during dismantling. Tighten the pivot bolt nuts to 84-102Nm/8.5-10.5/kgf m/62-75lbf ft.

21 ◻ Tighten the suspension unit bottom mounting bolt nut to 73-93Nm/7.4-9.5kgf m/54-68lbf ft, and the upper mounting nuts to 30-36Nm/3.0-3.7kgf m/22-26lbf ft. Install the plastic cap over the suspension unit upper mounting plate center. Finally, tighten the lugnuts (specified torque is 89-117Nm/9.0-12.0kgf m/66-86lbf ft). That's about it. If you made sure that the lower wishbone pivot bolts were installed in *exactly* the same positions as they were before removal, the suspension geometry should be unchanged. Note, however, that Mazda recommends the settings should be checked (☞ 8/3) after this work.

5. WISHBONE, LOWER FRONT - REMOVAL, O/HAUL & INSTALLATION

☞ 1/1, 2.

REMOVAL

1 Position the vehicle on a smooth, level surface and apply the parking brake. Place chocks back and front of the rear tires. Remove the front hub caps, and loosen the lugnuts (wheelnuts) by around one turn. Raise the front of the car and position jackstands (axlestands) under the jacking points at the front of each sill (☞ 1/3). Unscrew the lugnuts and remove the wheel.

2 Locate the end of the stabilizer bar (anti-roll bar) and remove the 14mm nut, bolt and spring washer which secure it to the link rod. As the bolt is removed, the stabilizer bar may move slightly, but it's not under a great deal of pressure. Next, you should remove the suspension unit lower mounting 17mm nut, bolt and spring washer. Push out the bolt to free the lower end of the suspension unit.

3 You now have to separate the hub carrier (upright) lower ball joint. Start by straightening and withdrawing the cotter pin (split pin) which locks the ball joint castellated nut. Keep the used pin as a pattern - you'll need to install a new one of the same size during assembly. Remove the ball joint 21mm nut, then, using a proprietary ball joint separator, release the ball joint pin from its tapered hole in the knuckle.

4 ◻+ Access around the ball joint is restricted - we tried a couple of proprietary separators and found it impossible to get them in position. You can cheat a little here, but only if you know that you don't need to replace the ball joint - leave the ball joint attached to the hub carrier and, instead, remove the single 17mm bolt which secures the rear of the ball joint casting to the wishbone. You can just get to this, through the cutout in the top surface of the wishbone, with the suspension unit pushed back a little. Next, remove the outer 17mm pivot bolt which installs horizontally through the two components. Once the bolts are removed, you can swing the knuckle and hub clear of the wishbone with the ball joint undisturbed.

5 If you have used the alternative method just described, you can leave the steering and suspension lower ball joints attached to the knuckle (unless they specifically require attention). If you need to detach the lower ball joint from the steering knuckle, you may now have enough room to use a wedge-type separator, driving the forked taper of the tool between the lower wishbone and the steering knuckle. This will work, given the right tool, but you have to take care not to damage the

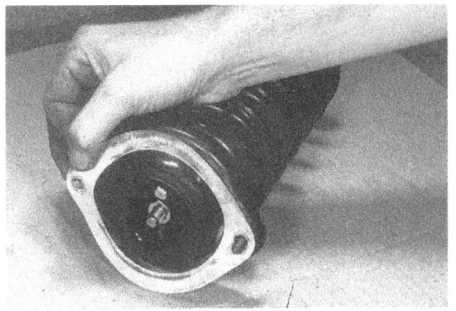
4/17 Don't forget plastic gasket.

4/21 Refit dust cover if it was removed.

5/4a This bolt and ...

5/4b ... this one secure ball joint casting.

4/18 Lock nut with new cotter (split) pin.

Mazda Miata, MX-5, Eunos & Roadster

ball joint or its dust boot. (Of course, if the joint is worn out, it won't matter if you wreck it during removal).

6 If all else fails, try screwing the upside down nut onto the threads and positioning it so it is flush with the pin end to protect the threads. Now tap the pin end sharply with a hammer to shock the tapered joint apart, remove the nut, and separate the joint. Again, access is difficult - you may need to use a drift to reach the pin end. If you need to remove the steering ball joint from the knuckle, a similar technique can be employed but, normally, this too can be left attached to the steering knuckle.

7 Mark, using typist's correction fluid or paint, the position of the lower wishbone pivot bolts in relation to the crossmember: these marks will be useful during installation. If you fail to do this, you will have to set up the suspension from scratch, which takes a lot of time. Once you've marked the position of both bolts, remove the nuts and tap out and remove the pivot bolts. Pull the wishbone clear of the crossmember, and install the bolts in their respective positions in the crossmember for safe keeping.

CHECKING AND OVERHAUL

8 Clean off the wishbone, and check for damage. **Warning!** If you find signs of cracking, rusting or impact damage, install a new wishbone - repairs are inadvisable on suspension components.

9 If the wishbone is serviceable, you should install new mounting bushes before installing it. You can press the old bushes out using a socket, but you will need something to press them into. Place a large socket on the other side of the bush, clamp the assembly in a vise, and jack the bush out by tightening the vise.

10 We made up our own support block from a 50mm/2in long (approx) section of scaffold tube - any thick-walled steel tubing with an internal bore of a little over 40mm will do fine. You need to make sure that the lip at the end of the bush will install into the support block. One way to do this is to cut a notch out of the wall of the block. The lip can be guided in by turning the block and feeding it in with a small screwdriver. You should make sure that it is not trapped by the block, especially during installation, or the lip will tear off.

11 Once you are sure that everything is positioned correctly, start clamping the vise to force the bush out into the support block. Note that the bush is a very tight fit - use some rubber lubricant or WD40 to ease removal, working it under the lips

5/11 Push out wishbone bush.

at the edges of the bush. Even with lubricant, you'll have to exert a lot of pressure to get the bush moving. We used a sturdy old 4.5 inch engineer's vise - it worked, but we grew concerned about its health during the removal process. If you have doubts about your vise's ability to withstand this sort of pressure, it may be worth getting a local engineering shop to press out the old bushes and install the new ones for you.

12 Installing the new bushes is done using the support block and socket in much the same way. We employed a socket into which had been fitted a short bolt, the bolt acting as a pilot to

5/12a Removed bush & 'special' tool.

5/12b Lubricate bush as it's pushed into place.

hold the socket square and prevent any risk of it slipping out under pressure. This time the support block is needed only to allow the bush to protrude a little during fitting before the natural resilience of the rubber lets it settle back square in the bore. Use rubber lubricant or a little soapy water to ease fitting, and make sure that the bush is positioned centrally in its bore.

13 Turning our attention to the hub carrier (upright) lower ball joint, the official procedure is to remove the old dust boot, re-grease and install a new one as part of any overhaul. The boot has a metal rim which is a tight fit on the ball joint. To remove it, you have to chisel it off, taking great care not to chisel the joint while you are doing so (see diagram). This effectively destroys the boot, so have a new one ready before you start chiselling. Once the boot has been removed, clean off the old grease and apply some fresh, lithium-based general purpose grease to the joint in the area covered by the dust boot.

14 It will be helpful if you can borrow Mazda special service tool SSTH028 301, which is a dust boot installer. This tool is essentially a short tube with a double diameter lip at the end. The seal installs into the tool and is then pressed onto the

ball joint. If you don't happen to have the tool, you will need to use a socket or a suitably sized piece of tubing to press the dust boot onto the joint, but it's easy to damage the boot without the special tool.

15 You should now check the ball joint condition by measuring the torque required to turn the ball joint pin. You can use the appropriate SST (49 0180 510B) and the Mazda approved pull scale, or improvise this check. The specified rotational torque is 0.5-1.4Nm/5-15kgf cm/4.4-13lbf in and the pull scale reading using the SST should be 4.9-14.7N/ 0.5-1.5kg/1.1-3.3lb.

16 We feel that you can do without the SST. If you can easily turn the ball joint pin with your bare fingers, it's too loose. On the other hand, if you attach vise grip pliers to the pin (not too tightly, and use something to protect the threads), and can't make it rotate by pushing the pliers with the side of your index finger (at a distance of 50mm/2in from the pin centre), it's too tight. Replace the ball joint if in any doubt.

17 Oops, nearly forgot! Mazda says that before you do the above torque test you must shake the ball joint five times ... (yes, seriously!) We have a number of theories about why this should be done; our best guess is that it is to ward off evil spirits. We don't know what fate might befall you if you accidentally shake the joint more than five times ...

INSTALLATION

18 The assembled wishbone can now be installed, remembering that the pivot bolts are fitted so that the two bolt heads face each other across the gap in the wishbone. Install the eccentric washers and nuts, finger-tight only at this stage. If the ball joint is still attached to the hub carrier (upright), slide it back into the end of the wishbone, tightening the vertical mounting bolt to 73-93Nm/ 7.4-9.5kgf m/54-68lbf ft. The horizontal mounting bolt is fitted with the head facing forward, and should be tightened to the same torque figure.

19 If you separated the lower ball joint from the steering knuckle, clean its taper and reposition the pin end through the tapered hole in the knuckle. Place a block of wood below the head of the ball joint, then give it several sharp upward blows to seat it in the knuckle. You should now be able to install the castellated nut, tightening it to the lower

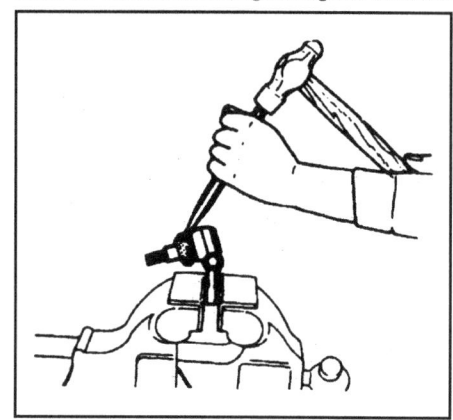

D5/13 REMOVING BALL JOINT BOOT.

8: Suspension & steering

end of its torque range of 57-77Nm/5.8-7.9kgf m/42-57lbf ft. If the pin turns, reseat it and continue tightening. Check to see if any pair of gaps between castellations align with the hole in the ball joint pin - if necessary, tighten the nut a little more until a new cotter pin (split pin) can be fitted. Bend over the ends of the pin to secure the nut, trimming off any excess with wire cutters.

20 If you separated the steering ball joint from the steering knuckle during the teardown, check that the ball joint taper is clean, then install it to the steering knuckle, tapping it sharply into position so that the pin is gripped in the tapered hole. Install the

5/18a Slide wishbone into place ...

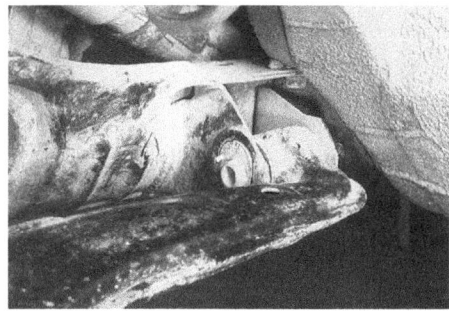
5/18b ... position cams correctly.

5/18c Secure ball joint casting (if removed).

castellated nut, then tighten it to the lower end of the 30-44Nm/3.0-4.5kgf m/22-32lbf ft torque range. If the pin turns during tightening, tap it again to seat the taper and try again. Check whether the hole through the pin aligns with a pair of gaps between castellations and tighten further if required until it does line up. Install a new cotter (split) pin and bend the ends over to secure the nut.

21 Install the suspension unit lower mounting bolt (head towards the rear of the car) and install the spring washer and nut finger-tight at this stage. If you have difficulty positioning the unit, the small scissor jack supplied with the car can be used to raise the assembly as required. Re-align the link rod and stabilizer (anti-roll) bar, again using the car's jack if you need to, then install the mounting bolt (with the head facing outwards). Install the spring washer and nut finger-tight.

22 Jack the front of the car (☞ 1/3) so that the safety stands can be removed, then lower it so that its weight is taken on the suspension. Bounce the suspension a few times. This ensures that the suspension components are in their normal positions before final tightening. You will need access to the fasteners which were slackened during removal, so we suggest the use of steel ramps under the front wheels to achieve this.

23 Check carefully the position of the lower wishbone pivot bolts, referring to the alignment marks made during dismantling. Turn the bolts until the marks are correctly aligned, then tighten the pivot nuts to 94-112Nm/9.5-11.5kgf m/69-83lbf ft.

24 Tighten the suspension unit bottom mounting bolt nut to 73-93Nm/7.4-9.5kgf m/54-68lbf ft. Finally, tighten the lugnuts (wheelnuts) to specified torque of 89-117Nm/9.0-12.0kgf m/66-86lbf ft. That's about it. If you made sure that the lower wishbone pivot bolts were fitted in *exactly* the same positions as they were before removal, the suspension geometry should be unchanged. Note, however, that Mazda recommends the settings should be checked (☞ 8/3).

6. WISHBONE, UPPER FRONT - REMOVAL, O/HAUL & INSTALLATION

☞ 1/1, 2.

REMOVAL

1 Position the vehicle on a smooth, level surface and apply the parking brake. Place chocks either side of the rear tires. Remove the front hub cap/s, and loosen the lugnuts (wheelnuts) by around one turn. Raise the front of the car and position jackstands (axlestands) under the jacking points at the front of each sill (☞ 1/3). Unscrew the lugnuts and remove the wheels.

2 Moving to the underside of the car, the next job is to remove the undertray from beneath the front of the engine - access to the upper wishbone pivot bolts is restricted, and you will need to get the undertray clear to improve access. Remove the 10mm bolts retaining the engine undertray, starting in the wheelarches where there are three fixings on each side. You'll also have to remove the 10mm nut that holds the stay (or stays) to the lower part of the front wing (or wings). Note that on some right-hand drive cars the windscreen washer reservoir is mounted forward of the left-hand wheelarch, in which case one of the undertray fixings will be a deeply recessed 10mm nut near the reservoir body. Remove the two 10mm bolts at the rear of the undertray and three at the front; then lift the undertray out from beneath the car (photos ☞ 3/4/15).

3 ☞ See diagram. Remove the suspension unit lower mounting 17mm nut, bolt and spring washer. Push out the bolt to free the lower end of the suspension unit.

4 You now have to separate the hub carrier (upright) upper ball joint. Start by straightening and withdrawing the cotter pin (split pin) which secures the ball joint castellated nut. Keep the old pin as a pattern - you'll need to install a new one of the same size during reassembly. Remove the ball joint 21mm nut, then, using a proprietary ball joint separator, release the ball joint pin from its tapered hole in the knuckle.

5 Access around the ball joint is restricted - we tried a couple of proprietary separators and found it impossible to get them in position. Eventually we used a wedge-type separator, driving the forked taper of the tool between the upper wishbone and knuckle. This works, but you have to take care not to damage the ball joint or its dust boot.

6 If all else fails, try screwing the nut onto the threads upside down and positioning the nut so it is flush with the pin end to protect the threads. Now tap the pin end sharply with a hammer to shock the tapered joint apart, remove the nut, and separate the joint. Again, access is difficult, and you must take great care not to damage the pin end - if you do you'll have to replace the upper wishbone and ball joint assembly ...

7 Slacken and remove the pivot bolt 21mm nut and its spring washer. You can now withdraw the pivot bolt towards the front of the car, noting that if it has become corroded, it will help to apply some releasing fluid or WD40, leaving it to soak in for a while before attempting removal. Once you've pulled the pivot bolt free, the wishbone can be maneuvered off the suspension unit and withdrawn.

CHECKING AND OVERHAUL

8 Clean off the wishbone, and check for damage. **Warning!** If you find signs of cracking, rusting or impact damage, install a new wishbone - repairs are inadvisable on suspension components. Check the pivot bolt bore through the crossmember end, sliding the bolt into position and checking for freeplay. If this is excessive, try fitting a new pivot bolt. In extreme cases, the bore through the crossmember may be worn, in which case you'll have to consider fitting a new crossmember.

9 You should now check the ball joint condition by measuring the torque required to turn the ball joint pin. You can use the appropriate SST (49 0180 510B) and the Mazda approved pull scale, or improvise this check. The specified rotational torque is 0.4-1.7Nm/4-18kgf cm/3.5-15.6lbf in and the pull scale reading using the SST should be 4.0-17.6N/0.4-1.8kg/0.9-3.9lb.

10 We feel that you can do without the SST. If you can easily turn the ball joint pin with your bare fingers, it's too loose. On the other hand, if you attach vise grip pliers to the pin (not too tightly, and use something to protect the threads), and can't make it rotate by pushing the pliers with the side of your index finger (at a distance of 50mm/2in from the pin centre), it's too tight. Replace the ball joint if in any doubt.

11 As with the lower ball joint, Mazda says that before you do the above torque test you must

Mazda Miata, MX-5, Eunos & Roadster

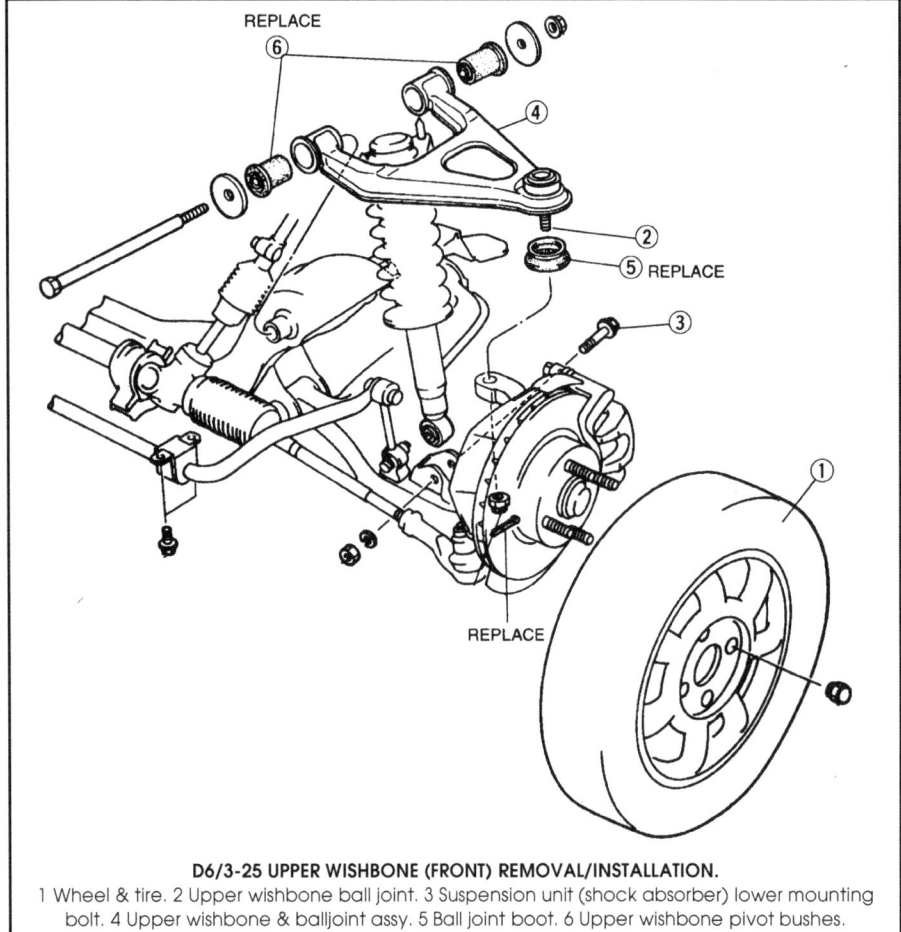

D6/3-25 UPPER WISHBONE (FRONT) REMOVAL/INSTALLATION.
1 Wheel & tire. 2 Upper wishbone ball joint. 3 Suspension unit (shock absorber) lower mounting bolt. 4 Upper wishbone & balljoint assy. 5 Ball joint boot. 6 Upper wishbone pivot bushes.

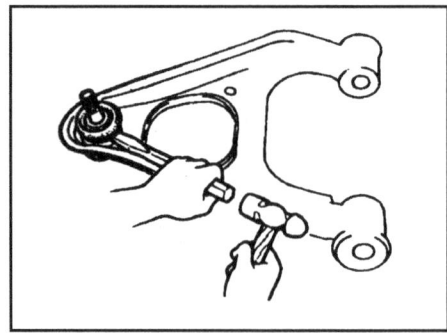

D6/15 REMOVING BALL JOINT BOOT.

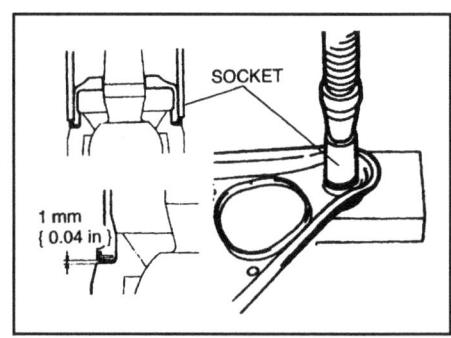

D6/16 INSTALLING NEW BALL JOINT BOOT WITH 30MM SOCKET.

shake the ball joint five times. (This is driving us nuts, why should it be shaken *five* times? - what happens if you shake it four times, or six ... We still haven't figured out a sane explanation for this; Wally scoffed at our suggestion about warding off evil spirits - he says that maybe it compensates for gravitational anomalies ...)

12 If the ball joint's worn out (we warned you not to shake it six times ...), the good news is that you get a free ball joint with every upper wishbone purchased; the bad news is that the upper ball joint is an integral part of the wishbone so, if the ball joint's worn out, don't waste any more time on the wishbone.

13 If the wishbone (and the ball joint) is serviceable, you should install new mounting bushes before fitting it. You can press the old bushes out using a socket, but you'll need something to press them into. Place a large socket on the other side of the bush, clamp the assembly in a vise, and jack the bush out by tightening the vise. It's possible to fabricate your own support block ☞ 8/5/10.

14 The procedure for removing and installing the bushes is exactly the same as that described for the lower wishbone (☞ 8/5/9-12), except the bushes are slightly different, having a head which fits to the outside of the wishbone. Press the old bushes out from between the wishbone mounting bores, and install the new ones from the outer edges of the bores.

15 Before fitting the wishbone, note that it is official procedure to remove the old dust boot, re-grease the joint and install a new boot as part of any overhaul. The boot has a metal rim which is a tight fit on the ball joint. To remove it, you have to chisel it off, taking great care not to damage the joint while you are doing so (see diagram). This effectively destroys the boot, so have a new one ready before you start. Once the boot has been removed, clean off the old grease and apply some fresh, lithium-based general purpose grease to the joint in the area covered by the dust boot.

16 To install the new dust boot you'll need to use a 30mm socket to press it onto the ball joint (see diagram). Take care that you press the boot onto the joint squarely and evenly, or you will damage the metal rim of the boot, making installation impossible. Do not use excessive force - the boot should be pressed into place until it just contacts the seat on the joint. After installation, check that there is no more than 1mm (0.04 in) clearance between the boot and the joint seat.

17 OK, we're ready to install the wishbone. Thread it over the suspension strut and fit it back into position; then slide in the pivot bolt. We suggest that you coat the bolt in molybdenum grease before you install it. Install the spring washer and nut, tightening lightly at this stage.

18 Position the suspension upper ball joint pin in its tapered hole in the hub carrier (upright). Place a block of wood over the top of the ball joint and tap it reasonably hard to seat the taper. This will allow the nut to be fitted and tightened. (If the ball joint turns during tightening, tap it once more and try again.) Get the nut as close as you can to the lower end of the specified torque range of 42-60Nm/4.2-6.2kgf m/31-44lbf ft, noting that the hole through the pin end must align with gaps between the nut castellations. Tighten a little more as required to make the holes line up, then install a new cotter pin (split pin), bending the ends over to secure the nut.

19 Install the suspension unit lower mounting bolt (head towards the rear of the car) and install the spring washer and nut finger-tight at this stage. If you have difficulty positioning the unit, the small scissor jack supplied with the car can be used to raise the assembly as required. Install the roadwheel and tighten the lugnuts.

20 You can now install the plastic undertray. You'll need to get to the pivot bolt and nut heads to tighten them in a while, but this is just about possible with the undertray in place. Engage the centre rear of the engine undertray with the tongue which projects forward from the suspension subframe. Replace the 10mm bolts retaining the undertray in the wheelarches where there are three fixings on each side. You'll also have to replace the 10mm nut that holds the stay (or stays) to the lower part of the front fender/wing (or fenders/wings). Note that on some right-hand drive cars the windscreen washer reservoir is mounted forward of the left-hand wheelarch, in which case one of the

8: Suspension & steering

undertray fixings will be a deeply recessed 10mm nut near the reservoir body. Replace the two 10mm bolts at the rear of the undertray and three at the front.

21 Jack the front of the car so that the safety stands can be removed, lowering it so that its weight is taken on the suspension. Bounce the suspension several times. This ensures that the suspension components are in their normal positions before final tightening. You will need access to the fasteners which were slackened during removal, so we suggest the use of steel ramps under the front wheels to achieve this.

22 Tighten the suspension unit bottom mounting bolt nut to 73-93Nm/7.4-9.5 kgf m/54-68lbf ft. Tighten the upper wishbone pivot bolt to 118-137Nm/12.0-14.0kgf m/87-101lbf ft. Finally, tighten the lugnuts (wheelnuts) to specified torque: 89-117Nm/9.0-12.0kgf m/66-86lbf ft. Note that Mazda recommends the suspension alignment settings should be checked (☞ 8/3).

7. STABILIZER BAR (FRONT) - REMOVAL, CHECKING & INSTALLATION

☞ 1/1, 2.

REMOVAL

1 Position the vehicle on a smooth, level surface and apply the parking brake. Place chocks either side of the rear tires. Remove the front hub caps, and loosen the lugnuts (wheelnuts) by around one turn. Raise the front of the car and position jackstands (axlestands) under the jacking points at the front of each sill (☞ 1/3). Unscrew the lugnuts and remove the wheels.

2 Moving to the underside of the car, the next job is to remove the undertray from beneath the front of the engine - access to the upper wishbone pivot bolts is restricted, and you will need to get the undertray clear to improve access. Remove the 10mm bolts retaining the engine undertray, starting in the wheelarches where there are three fixings on each side. You'll also have to remove the 10mm nut that holds the stay (or stays) to the lower part of the front wing (or wings). Note that on some right-hand drive cars the windscreen washer reservoir is mounted forward of the left-hand wheelarch, in which case one of the undertray fixings will be a deeply recessed 10mm nut near the reservoir body. Remove the two 10mm bolts at the rear of the undertray and three at the front; then lift the undertray out from beneath the car (photos ☞ 3/4/15).

3 See diagram. Locate the two support brackets which retain the stabilizer bar to the underside. Remove the two 12mm bolts which secure each bracket and remove the brackets, for now leaving the rubber support blocks in place on the stabilizer bar. Remove the bolt, nut and spring washer which secures each of the two stabilizer bar control links to the lower wishbones, and remove the stabilizer bar and links from the vehicle. The links can be removed from the stabilizer bar ends by releasing the 14mm nut, bolt and spring washer which retains them. Before removing the rubber support blocks from the stabilizer bar, check that the alignment marks which indicate the correct position of the blocks are clearly visible - if not, mark the bar with paint or typist's correction fluid to use as a guide during installation.

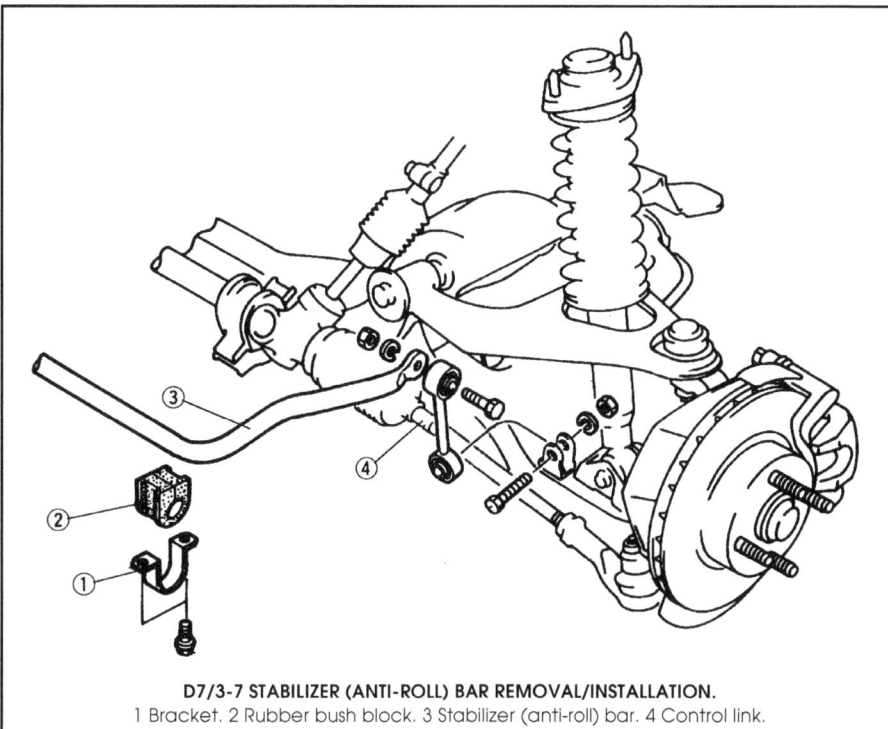

D7/3-7 STABILIZER (ANTI-ROLL) BAR REMOVAL/INSTALLATION.
1 Bracket. 2 Rubber bush block. 3 Stabilizer (anti-roll) bar. 4 Control link.

CHECKING

4 The stabilizer bar is unlikely to require replacement unless accident damaged, or a high performance unit is being installed. If the stabilizer bar has been bent or twisted, or is badly corroded, it should be replaced. Check the stabilizer bar control links for signs of similar damage, and check the condition of the rubber bushes at each end. If these are obviously worn or deteriorated, install new links. Check the stabilizer bar support blocks for wear or deterioration, replacing them if obviously worn or damaged (wear in the blocks can produce mysterious clanks, rattles and squeaks from the suspension).

INSTALLATION

5 Position the rubber support blocks on the stabilizer bar, making sure that they line up with the alignment marks you made during removal. Install the control links to the ends of the stabilizer bar, bolt heads outwards, leaving the nuts loose for now. Reposition the assembly under the car, installing the control link to lower wishbone bolts, nuts and spring washers with the bolt heads facing the front of the car. Tighten the nuts finger-tight only at this stage.

6 Jack the front of the car (☞ 1/3) so that the jackstands can be removed, then lower it so that its weight is taken on the suspension. Bounce the suspension several times. This ensures that the suspension components are in the normal running positions before final tightening. You'll need access to the fasteners which were slackened during removal, and also room to install the undertray, so we suggest the use of steel ramps under the front wheels to achieve this.

7 Tighten the control link nuts to 37-53Nm/3.7-5.5kgf m/27-39lbf ft. Reposition the stabilizer bar brackets over the rubber support blocks, ensuring that these have not moved on the stabilizer bar (check the alignment marks). Install and tighten the mounting bolts to 18-26Nm/1.6-2.7 kgf m/14-19lbf ft.

8 You can now install the plastic undertray. You'll need to get to the pivot bolt and nut heads to tighten them in a while, but this is just about possible with the undertray in place. Engage the centre rear of the engine undertray with the tongue which projects forward from the suspension subframe. Replace the 10mm bolts retaining the undertray in the wheelarches where there are three fixings on each side. You'll also have to replace the 10mm nut that holds the stay (or stays) to the lower part of the front fender/wing (or fenders/wings). Note that on some right-hand drive cars the windscreen washer reservoir is mounted forward of the left-hand wheelarch, in which case one of the undertray fixings will be a deeply recessed 10mm nut near the reservoir body. Replace the two 10mm bolts at the rear of the undertray and three at the front.

8. CROSSMEMBER (FRONT) - REMOVAL & INSTALLATION

1 The front suspension attaches to a fabricated steel subframe, or crossmember, attached to

the car's bodyshell. The subframe also provides engine mounting points and, in theory, it's possble to remove the engine, transmission, suspension and steering as one big assembly.

2 In reality, such a procedure would be pretty much impossible outside of a full commercial workshop. You would need a vehicle lift at the very least, and sufficient space overhead to lift the car clear of this major assembly. It is also doubtful if carrying out this procedure successfully would convey any particular advantage to the home mechanic; it is really just a convenient way of putting cars together on an assembly line.

3 If you need to remove the crossmember and the attached steering/suspension parts, note that you'll first need to jack the car well clear of the ground and support it on jackstands (axlestands). You'll also need an engine crane or hoist which will reach over the top of the engine bay so that the weight of the engine and transmission can be supported while the crossmember is detached and removed.

4 Our considered advice here is don't bother - on balance, it is probably best not to attempt removal of this assembly. We looked into this on our project car, and in the end could see lots of problems and few reasons for wanting to remove the crossmember. The only time we envisage this being a realistic proposition would be in the context of a full structural restoration; a little beyond the scope of this book.

5 The suspension and steering parts can be removed/replaced/worked on without removing the crossmember, as can the engine and transmission. If the crossmember itself requires attention, it is likely to be as a result of serious impact damage, in which case professional help will be needed anyway (if your car's crossmember is bent, we wouldn't care to think about how the body looks!). You'll need to get the car checked out on a body jig, either by a Mazda dealer or a reputable body shop.

6 Similarly, if rusting is the reason for removal, we suggest that you get the car checked out professionally. In reality, we suspect that the rest of the car will have been eaten away to nothing long before rust gets to be a problem in this area.

7 For those absolutely determined to carry out this work, the accompanying diagram shows the removal and installation procedure in a numerical sequence.

9. STEERING (MANUAL) - DESCRIPTION

These cars are all equipped with rack and pinion steering. Depending on which option was chosen when the car was ordered, this will be manually-operated or speed-sensitive power-assisted; the latter being described and covered in detail later in this chapter.

Turning motion from the steering wheel is transmitted down a collapsible steering column to an intermediate shaft. The shaft has universal joints at each end, allowing an indirect line between the column and steering rack.

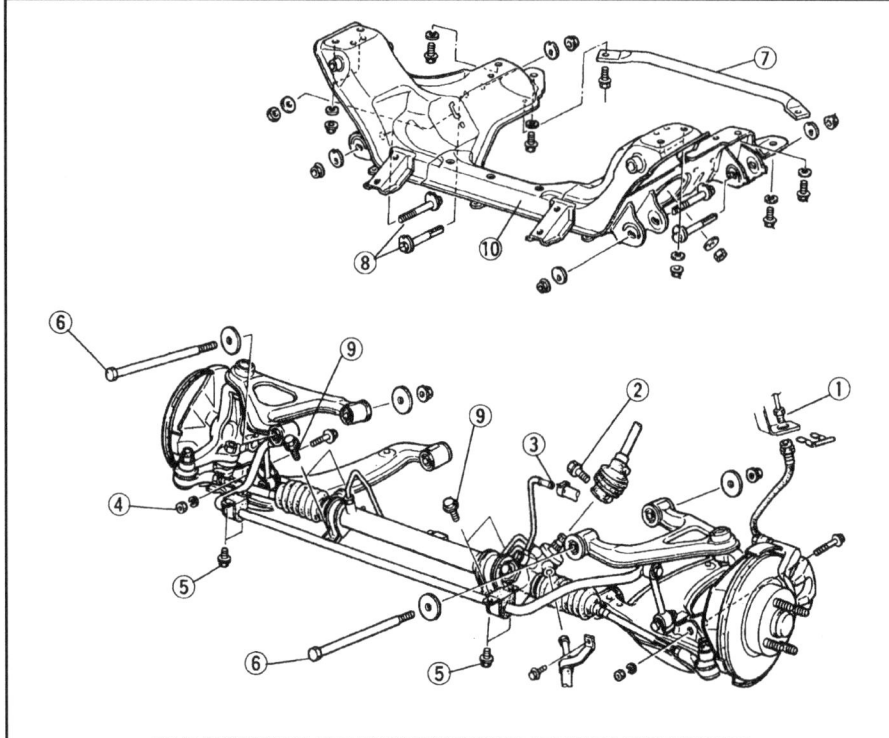

D8/7 SUSPENSION CROSSMEMBER (FRONT) REMOVAL/INSTALLATION.
1 Brake pipe union. 2 Steering shaft clamp bolt. 3 Power steering pipe. 4 Suspension unit (shock absorber) bolt. 5 Stabilizer bar bracket bolt. 6 Upper wishbone pivot bolt. 7 "Performance rod" (brace bar). 8 Lower wishbone pivot/cam bolts. 9 Rack & pinion bracket bolt. 10 Crossmember.

Inside the rack, the intermediate shaft turns a small pinion, which, in turn, drives the rack from side-to-side as the steering is operated. Motion from the rack ends is conveyed by articulated tie-rods terminating in steering ball joints attached to the hub carriers (uprights/steering knuckles). The effective length of the tie-rod is adjustable to permit the correct amount of front wheel toe-in to be set.

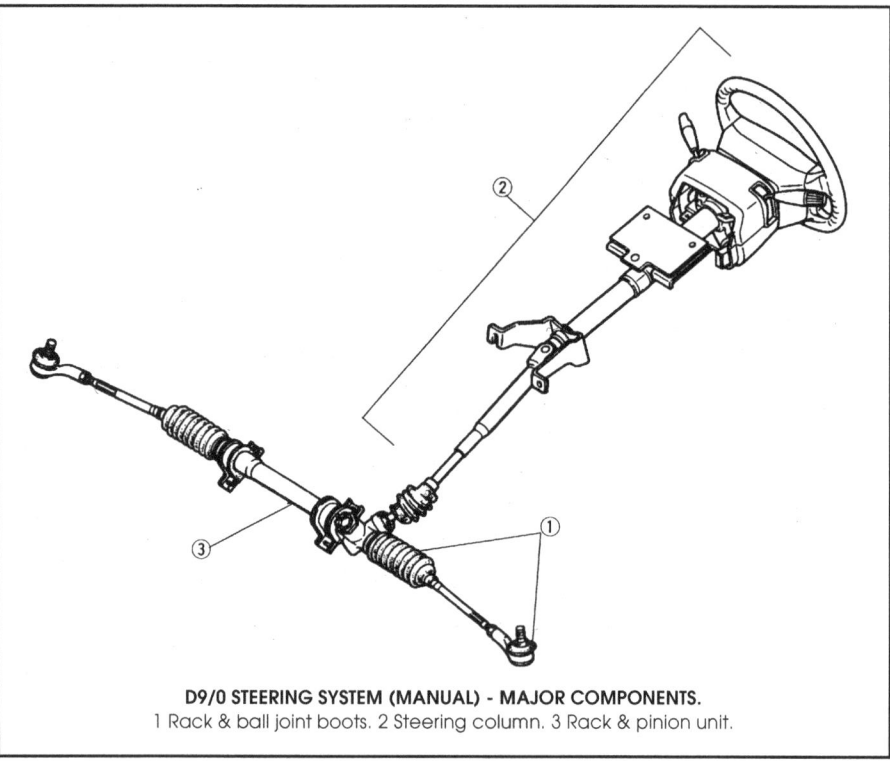

D9/0 STEERING SYSTEM (MANUAL) - MAJOR COMPONENTS.
1 Rack & ball joint boots. 2 Steering column. 3 Rack & pinion unit.

8: Suspension & steering

10. STEERING (MANUAL) - CHECKING

☞ 1/1, 2.

1   Preliminary checks on the steering can be carried out without a teardown. Sit in the driver's seat with the front wheel in the straight ahead position, and gently turn the wheel to and fro to gauge the amount of free play before any slack in the steering mechanism is taken up. You can gauge this better by leaning out of the car and noting when the road wheel just begins to move. Maximum acceptable free play at the steering wheel rim is 30mm/1.18in. Excessive play normally indicates wear in the steering ball joints, steering column universal joints (less likely), or the rack mechanism. Other possible causes are loose steering column clamps or rack mountings.

2   Try pulling/pushing the steering wheel left and right, then up and down, at right angles to the steering column. Pull the steering wheel towards you and push it away from you. There should be no play felt in any of these planes. If there is, check for wear in the steering column and joints and check the security of the steering wheel; also check the clamps at the upper and lower ends of the intermediate shaft.

3   The final check requires the car to raised so that the front wheels are clear of the ground. Position the vehicle on a smooth, level surface and apply the parking brake. Place chocks front and back of the rear tires. Raise the front of the car and position jackstands (axlestands) under the jacking points at the front of each sill (☞ 1/3). Turn the steering from lock-to-lock at least five times to settle the steering components. While doing so, note any unusually slack or tight spots which might indicate wear or damage in the intermediate shaft joints or rack mechanism, possibly as a result of impact damage. If noted, these faults should be investigated and rectified.

4   If the steering is abnormally stiff with the wheels clear of the ground, the rack may be at fault, or the steering ball joints may be badly worn, frozen (seized) or damaged. Hook a pull scale (spring balance) to the outer edge of one of the steering wheel spokes and check the effort needed to turn the wheel during one complete revolution. This should be in the range 5-29.4N/0.5-3.0kg/1.1-6.6lb, so a fair amount of latitude is available, but if it is outside these limits a problem is indicated.

5   Lastly, be aware that incorrect toe-in, camber and caster settings, and tyre pressures (not just at the front of the car) can have a profound affect on steering 'feel.' None of these things will make the steering feel sloppy, but they can create a pull to one side, vagueness and loss of directional stability.

11. STEERING WHEEL & COLUMN - REMOVAL, CHECKING & INSTALLATION

☞ 1/1, 2 & 7/2, 44.

REMOVAL

1   See accompanying diagram.
2   Before starting work, note that the steering wheel may not need to be removed. If you simply need to remove the column assembly, remove the airbag module for safety (see following comments), but leave the wheel attached to the steering column. Note that you'll have to remove the steering wheel to allow the combination (steering column) switch to be removed from the column.

3   **Warning!** On all cars, start by disconnecting the battery ☞ 7/2 and disarming the airbag system and then disconnecting the airbag/clockspring wiring connectors behind the steering column access panel ☞ 7/44.

4   The airbag module can now be removed from the steering wheel ☞ 7/46.

5   ◐+ Non-airbag equipped cars. Remove the access panel below the steering column. If steering wheel removal is required, remove the moulded safety cover at the center of the steering wheel: on our project car, a Momo wheel was installed, and the cover simply clipped over the spokes of the steering wheel. If a central horn switch is fitted, pry it out with a small screwdriver and disconnect the switch wire.

6   ◐+ ☞ All models. If the steering wheel is to be removed, check that the road wheels are positioned straight ahead and that the steering wheel spokes are level. Although not strictly essential, we marked the relationship of the steering wheel and column with a dab of paint to avoid any problems with alignment during reassembly (irrelevant if both the steering wheel and the column are removed). Slacken and remove the central 21mm Nyloc nut which retains the steering wheel. You'll now need a puller to draw the wheel off the steering column splines. The exact design of the puller is dependent on the type of steering wheel fitted - you'll need to find something which can be attached securely to the wheel, with a center bolt that can be used to apply pressure against the end of the column. You may find it helpful to release the

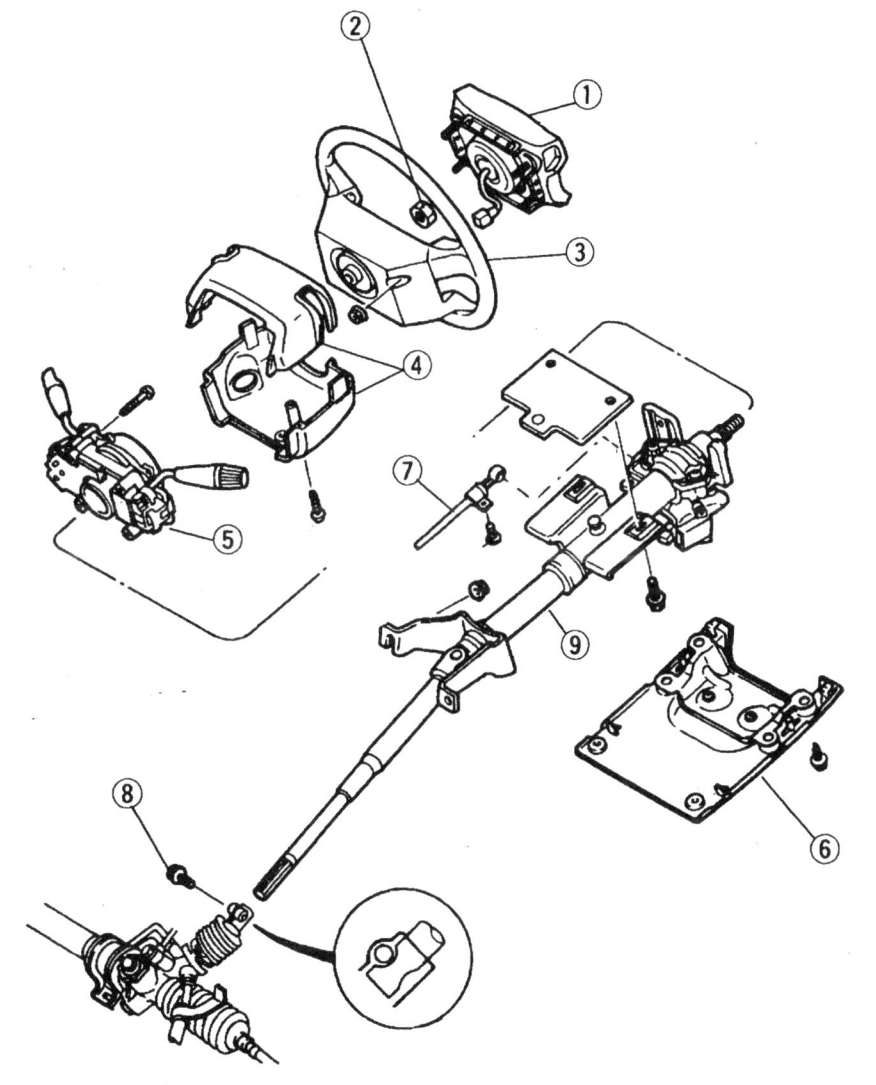

D11/1-25 STEERING COLUMN - REMOVAL/INSTALLATION.
1 Air bag module (if fitted). 2 S/wheel retaining nut. 3 Steering wheel. 4 Combination (column) switch housing. 5 Combination (column) switch. 6 Access panel. 7 Key interlock cable (auto trans). 8 Clamp bolt. 9 Steering column (shaft).

Mazda Miata, MX-5, Eunos & Roadster

11/5a Non-airbag cars. Remove horn button ...

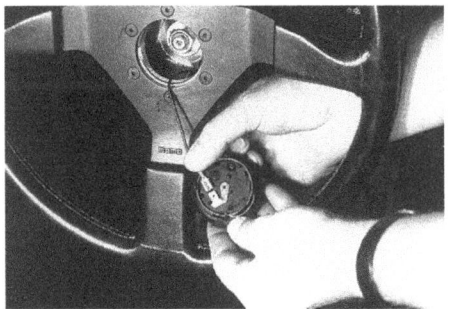

11/5b ... or central cover. Disconnect horn wire.

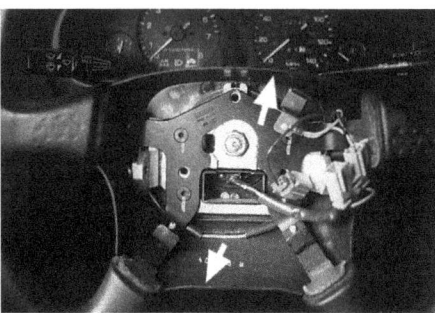

11/6c Trim (arrowed) can be released.

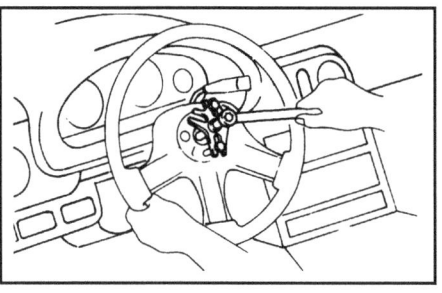

D11/6 USING PULLER TO REMOVE STEERING WHEEL.

plastic trim behind the wheel hub (see photo) to allow better access to the metal hub of the steering wheel. **Caution!** Under no circumstances should you try shocking the wheel free by striking the end of the column - you can easily collapse the column by doing this.

7   Wally, our Technical Adviser, encountered problems in removing the Momo steering wheel without damage using the method described by Mazda. He tried using a puller lodged below the aluminum spokes, but when the center bolt was tightened, the pressure crushed the pressed steel

11/6a Remove s/wheel nut (non-airbag models).

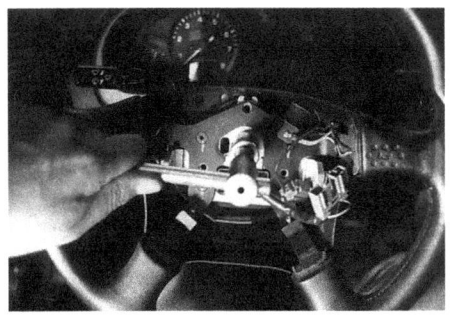

11/6b Remove s/wheel nut (airbag models).

retainer ring which locates the horn switch. In the end, we removed the countersunk socket screws which retain the wheel to the wheel boss, removed the horn switch retainer ring, fitted the wheel again, and then used the puller to draw it off the column. Depending on the arrangement you find on your car, you may need to adopt a similar method to avoid damage.

8   If not already removed, free the two halves of the switch housing which are secured by four crosshead (Philips) screws, one of which is deeply recessed. You'll need to maneuvre the top part over the stalks.

9   Remove the three crosshead screws securing the combination switch, release all of its electrical connections and remove the switch from the column. **Warning!** If it is to be re-used, handle the switch unit very carefully as damage to the clockspring could cause unexpected airbag deployment after re-installation.

10   📷 Unplug the ignition switch wiring, and, on automatic transmission cars, free the ignition switch interlock cable. Working below the dash panel, locate and separate the two halves of the cover (if installed) which protects the lower end of the column. The two cover halves snap together and can be separated by pulling them apart.

11   📷 In the footwell at the base of the column you'll find the clamp bolt which secures the intermediate shaft coupling to the steering column. Slacken and remove the clamp 12mm bolt, then remove the two 10mm nuts (arrowed in the photograph), which secure the steering column lower mounting bracket to the firewall, to free the lower end of the column.

12   📷 Moving to the upper end of the column, slacken and remove the two 12mm bolts which secure the column upper bracket to the underside of the dash panel. The column assembly can now be pulled back into the car until the intermediate shaft coupling splines drop free, then lifted out. Take care not to snag the wiring as you remove the unit.

CHECKING

13   📷+ Do not attempt to remove the steering lock unit from the column unless it needs to be replaced. If removal is necessary, you'll have to release the shear-head security bolts which retain it. Either center punch and drill the heads of the bolts, and then use a stud extractor to unscrew the bolt shanks, or chisel a slot in the heads and

11/10 Separate two halves of lower cover.

11/11 Release lower mounting clamp.

unscrew them with a screwdriver. Note that you will need to obtain a pair of replacement shear-head bolts during installation. Install the lock in position and tighten the bolts evenly until the heads shear off. **Important note**: some models will be fitted with an immobiliser system which uses a coil and pre-amplifier in the steering lock to sense whether the correct key is being used and to send a code signal to the immobiliser unit and ECM. If your vehicle is fitted with such a system, you'll need to discuss the installation of a new steering lock with your Mazda dealer, as it will be necessary to input appropriate codes to the new unit.

11/12 Release upper bracket.

8: Suspension & steering

14   Examine the column assembly for signs of wear or damage. If the column bearing is worn, or if it feels stiff or uneven when turned, you should install a new column assembly - it is not considered repairable by Mazda. Check the overall length of the column inner shaft. If outside the range 577.8-579.8mm/22.75-22.82in, it is possible that impact damage sometime in the past may have partially collapsed the column. Again, install a new one. If wear or damage to the splines at either end of the shaft is noted, replacement is again the only option. If wear is noted, you should also check the intermediate shaft splines for wear and replace,

11/14 Check clamp splines for wear/damage.

11/18a Non-airbag cars. Fit spring, followed by ...

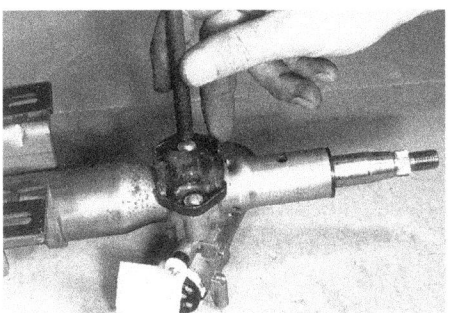

11/13a Centre punch lock bolt and then ...

11/18b ... turn signal sleeve/cam - pins outward.

11/13b ... drill, prior to using a stud extractor.

too, where necessary.

INSTALLATION

15   Position the column assembly, guiding the splined end into engagement with the intermediate shaft coupling. Install the column lower bracket nuts and tighten to 18-26Nm/1.8-2.5kgf m/13-20lbf ft, then install the upper mounting bolts, tightening them to 16-22Nm/1.6-2.3kgf m/12-17lbf ft. Install the column/intermediate shaft clamp bolt and tighten it to 18-26Nm/1.8-2.7kgf m/14-19lbf ft. If applicable, fit together the two halves of the lower column cover.

16   Reconnect the ignition switch wiring, and, on automatic transmission cars, install the interlock cable, tightening the clamp bolt to 4.3-6.1Nm/43-

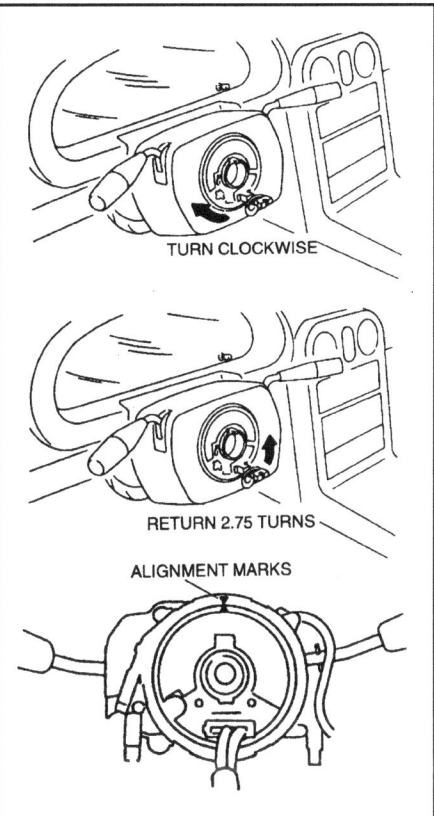

D11/17 AIRBAG CLOCKSPRING ADJUSTMENT.
Turn clockspring fully clockwise against its stop. Rotate the unit 2.75 turns anti-clockwise. Align clockspring and outer housing marks.

63kgf cm/38-54lbf in. Remake the switch's electrical connections to the wiring harness. Install the switch covers.

17   Airbag equipped cars. **Warning!** It is essential that the airbag 'clockspring' is correctly adjusted before the steering wheel is installed; proceed as follows (see diagram). Turn the clockspring clockwise as far as it will go, then rotate it 2.75 turns in the opposite direction: the arrows on the clockspring and switch body should now be in, or very close to, alignment. Align the two arrows.

18   Non-airbag equipped cars. Install the spring and turn signal cancelling sleeve.

19   Install the two halves of the combination switch housing and secure with three screws.

20   Before installing the steering wheel, it

helps to apply a little anti seize or copper grease to the splines to make subsequent removal easier. Check that the roadwheels are in the straight ahead position, and that the steering wheel spokes are level before installing the steering wheel boss over its splines. (Where the wheel was removed without disturbing the column assembly, check the alignment marks made during removal). Where applicable, check that the pins on the turn signal cancelling sleeve locate in the holes on the back of the steering wheel boss.

21   Install the steering wheel and secure

11/20a Apply anti-seize grease to splines.

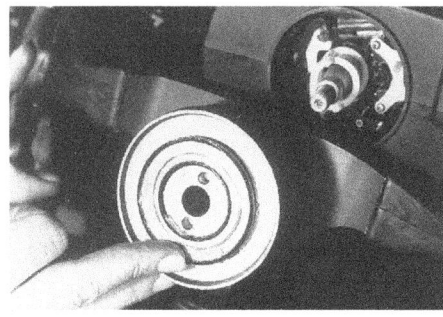

11/20b Lubricate horn ring tracks.

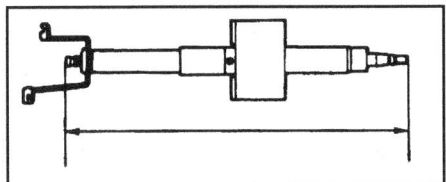

D11/14 STEERING COLUMN: CHECKING LENGTH.

Mazda Miata, MX-5, Eunos & Roadster

11/21a Align correctly & refit steering wheel.

11/21b Torque tighten retaining nut.

with a new 21mm Nyloc nut tightened to 40-49Nm/4.0-5.0kgf m/29-36lbf ft.

22   If applicable, install the two parts of the combination switch cover behind the steering wheel. Note that the rear fixing which is not recessed is a set screw which threads into the steering lock body: fit this screw first to align the housing correctly.

23   Airbag equipped cars. Install the airbag module and reconnect the orange and blue airbag/clockspring electrical connectors to the single wiring harness connector behind the steering column access panel ☞ 7/46.

24   Non-airbag cars. Reconnect and install the central horn switch (where installed). Install the steering wheel safety cover, clipping it in position or securing it with screws, according to the type installed.

25   Install the access panel beneath the steering column.

26   Airbag equipped cars. Reconnect the battery and re-arm the airbag system. **Warning!** Follow correct procedure ☞ 7/2 & 7/44.

27   Non-airbag cars. Reconnect the battery.

12. TIE ROD BALL JOINT & RACK DUST BOOT - REMOVAL & INSTALLATION

☞ 1/1, 2.

1   Position the car on a smooth, level surface and apply the parking brake. Place chocks either side of the rear tires. Remove the front hub cap/s, and loosen the lugnuts (wheelnuts) by around one turn. Raise the front of the car and position jackstands (axlestands) under the jacking points at the front of each sill (☞ 1/3). Unscrew the lugnuts and remove the wheel/s.

2   Straighten and remove the cotter pin (split pin) which locks the tie rod ball joint 17mm castellated nut. You'll find this easier if you use a wire brush, followed by releasing fluid to help deal with any build-up of rust and dirt around the nut/cotter pin. You'll need to install a new cotter pin during assembly, but keep the old one as a pattern. Slacken and remove the ball joint nut.

3   Using a proprietary ball joint separator, free the ball joint from its tapered hole in the hub carrier (upright/steering knuckle). You may find, as we did, that many proprietary separators will not fit easily in the gap between the joint and the knuckle. Instead, you may be able to separate the joint using a wedge-type separator driven between the two parts, but you have to be careful to avoid damage to the ball joint if you intend to reuse it - the dust boot will almost certainly get damaged, but in theory you should replace this anyway. Another removal method involves screwing the upside down castellated nut back onto the pin end until it is flush with the end of the pin - this protects the pin threads from damage. Using a hammer, strike the pin end sharply to jar the taper free. We found that this method worked fine on our project car. Unscrew the nut and separate the joint.

4   Clean off the tie rod to remove all traces of road dirt and rust. Make a reference mark (using paint or typist's correction fluid) across the tie rod locknut and the tie rod threads to use as a guide during installation. Hold the tie rod with a 12mm wrench and slacken the 17mm ball joint locknut by a half turn, then, still holding the tie rod with a 12mm wrench, unscrew the ball joint (20mm) from its end. If you're removing the rack end dust boot/gaiter, you'll also need to remove the ball joint locknut from the tie rod.

5   If you're replacing the steering rack dust boot (gaiter), release the clips which secure the dust boot to the steering rack and the tie rod, and slide the boot and clips off the tie rod. Clean up the exposed rack ball joint and apply lithium-based grease to it, then slide a new dust boot (with new clamps installed) along the tie rod and into position.

12/3 Invert nut and tap sharply to break joint.

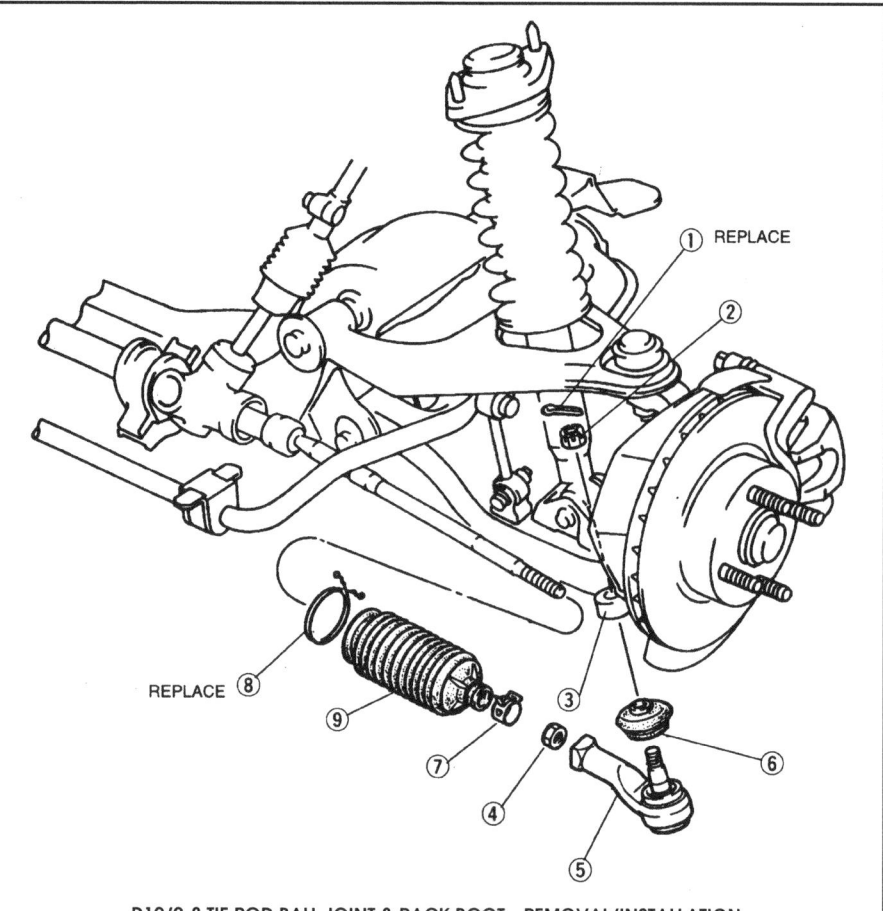

D12/2-8 TIE ROD BALL JOINT & RACK BOOT - REMOVAL/INSTALLATION.
1 Cotter (split) pin. 2 Castellated nut. 3 Hub carrier (upright/steering knuckle). 4 Ball joint locknut. 5 Tie rod ball joint. 6 Ball joint boot. 7 & 8 Boot clamps (clips). 9 Rack dust boot.

8: Suspension & steering

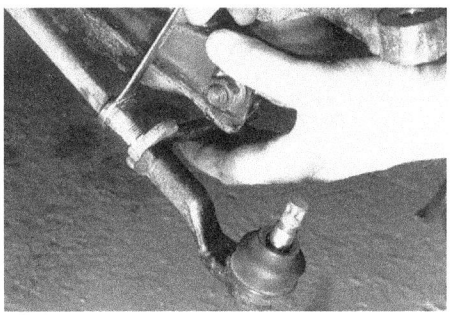

12/4 Hold tie rod & slacken locknut.

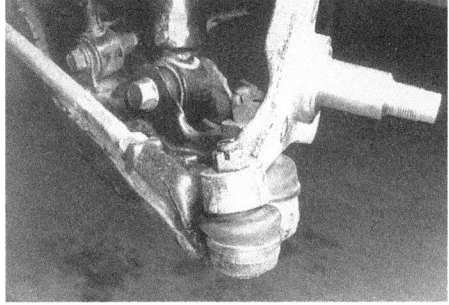

12/8 Tighten ball joint nut & fit cotter/split pin.

Tighten the boot retaining clamp at the rack end.
6   If the tie rod end ball joint is obviously unserviceable, it should be discarded and a new one installed. However, if you wish to replace the ball joint boot, first remove the old one by clamping the ball joint in a vise and carefully chiselling off the boot - it has a metal retaining ring which will be a tight install on the joint rim. Take great care not to damage the joint during boot removal. Clean off any remaining grease around the area normally covered by the boot, then repack the joint using a general purpose lithium-based grease. To install the new boot, you will need SST49 1243 785 to press it into place. This tool is essentially a short tube with a double diameter lip at the end. The seal installs into the tool and is then pressed onto the ball joint. If you can't get hold of the special service tool, you can use a socket or an appropriately sized piece of tubing to press the dust boot onto the joint. It can be done, but it is easy to damage the boot without the tool, so take care.
7   Screw the tie rod ball joint locknut onto the tie rod (if removed) followed by the new or overhauled steering ball joint. Align the marks made during removal and lock the ball joint in position by tightening the locknut to 35-39Nm/3.5-4.0kgf m/ 26-28lbf ft) while holding the tie rod with a 12mm wrench.
8   Check that the ball joint taper is clean, then install it to the steering knuckle, tapping it sharply into position so that the pin is gripped in the tapered hole. Install the castellated nut, then tighten it to the lower end of the 30-44Nm/3.0-4.5kgf m/ 22-32lbf ft torque range. If the pin turns during tightening, tap it again to seat the taper and try again. Check whether the hole through the pin aligns with a pair of gaps between castellations, and tighten further if required until this does line up. Install a new cotter (split) pin and bend the ends over to lock the nut.
9   **Caution!** Once you've completed assembly, you MUST check and adjust the toe-in ☞ 8/3. Once toe-in is correctly set, tighten the clamp securing the boot to the tie rod.

13. STEERING (MANUAL) RACK - REMOVAL, O/HAUL & INSTALLATION

☞ 1/1, 2.

REMOVAL

1   Position the vehicle on a smooth, level surface and apply the parking brake. Set the steering to straight ahead and then withdraw the ignition key to lock the steering. Place chocks either side of the rear tires. Remove the front hub caps, and loosen the lugnuts (wheelnuts) by around one turn. Raise the front of the car and position jackstands (axlestands) under the jacking points at the front of each sill (☞ 1/3). Unscrew the lugnuts and remove the wheels.
2   Moving to the underside of the car, the next job is to remove the undertray from beneath the front of the engine - access to the upper wishbone pivot bolts is restricted, and you will need to get the undertray clear to improve access. Remove the 10mm bolts retaining the engine undertray, starting in the wheelarches where there are three fixings on each side. You'll also have to remove the 10mm nut that holds the stay (or stays) to the lower part of the front wing (or wings). Note that on some right-hand drive cars the windscreen washer reservoir is mounted forward of the left-hand wheelarch, in which case one of the undertray fixings will be a deeply recessed 10mm nut near the reservoir body. Remove the two 10mm bolts at the rear of the undertray and three at the front; then lift the undertray out from beneath the car (photos ☞ 3/4/15).
3   The next task is to free the steering ball joints from the hub carriers (uprights/steering

13/4 Pinch bolt at base of steering column.

knuckles) ☞ 8/12 - you can leave them attached to the tie rods at this stage.
4   Working from underneath the car, or via the engine compartment, locate the 12mm pinch bolt at the base of the steering column intermediate shaft where it installs inside the flexible coupling to the steering rack. There is a reference groove in the intermediate shaft end. Check that a corresponding paint mark is visible on the rack side of the flexible joint, and make a new one if it is not easily visible. Slacken and remove the pinch bolt (note that the shaft end is notched - you can't disconnect the shaft until the bolt is fully withdrawn). **Warning!** On models with airbags if the steering wheel is moved after the intermediate shaft to steering rack joint has been separated, you must check and reset the clock spring ☞ 7/12/6.
5   Remove the four rack mounting 14mm bolts, leaving the rack mounting clamps attached to the rack at this stage. The rack assembly can now be lifted and moved forward to disengage it from the intermediate shaft. Once clear, pull the rack assembly out from the driver's side.

OVERHAUL

6   It's possible to dismantle and repair the steering rack, but a number of special tools are required and it's a complex procedure. We don't

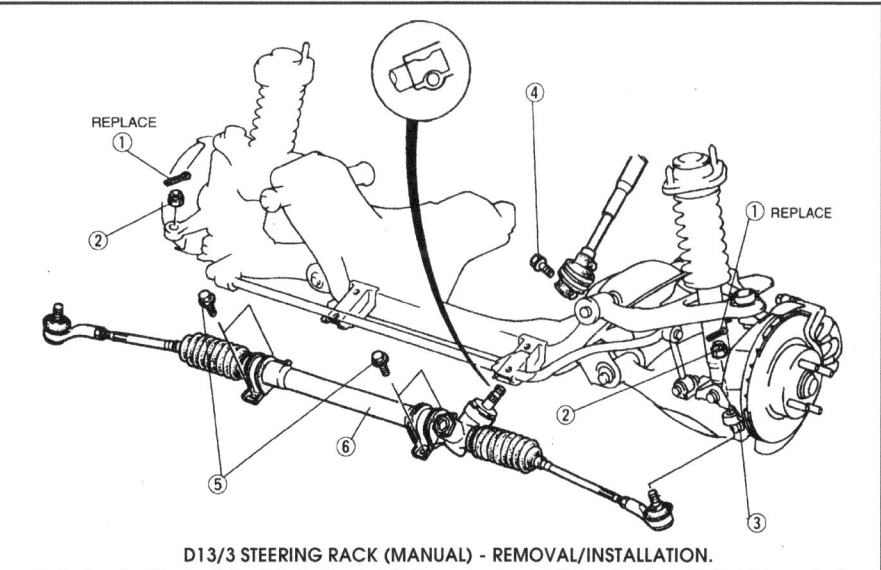

D13/3 STEERING RACK (MANUAL) - REMOVAL/INSTALLATION.
1 Cotter (split) pin. 2 Castellated nut. 3 Hub carrier (upright/steering knuckle). 4 Clamp bolt.
5 Rack clamp bolts. 6 Rack & pinion steering unit.

8:17

Mazda Miata, MX-5, Eunos & Roadster

usually avoid describing tasks just because they're difficult but, in this case, we seriously doubt that a rack rebuild is a cost effective do-it-yourself proposition when so many specialists offer reconditioned exchange units off the shelf. Our advice - and even Wally agrees! - is to buy an exchange unit from a reputable company.

INSTALLATION

7   When installing the rack assembly, lift it into position and check that the steering ball joints will align with their holes in the steering arms of the hub carriers. If necessary, turn the pinion until they are correctly positioned, and then check that the reference marks on the intermediate shaft and pinion splines coincide. Engage the pinion with the steering column clamp.

8   If necessary install the rubber mountings and clamps over the rack body. Install the mounting bolts, tightening them evenly and progressively to 47-58Nm/4.7-6.0kgf m/34-43lbf ft.

9   Tighten the steering column clamp bolt to 18-26Nm/1.8-2.7kgf m/14-19lbf ft.

10   Check that the ball joint tapers are clean, then install each ball joint to its hub carrier, tapping it sharply into position so that the pin is gripped in the tapered hole. Install the castellated nut, then tighten it to the lower end of the 30-44Nm/3.0-4.5 kgf m/22-3lbf ft) torque range. If the pin turns during tightening, tap it again to seat the taper and try again. Check whether the hole through the pin aligns with a pair of gaps between castellations, and tighten further if required until it does line up. Install a new cotter (split) pin and bend the ends over to secure the nut.

11   You can now install the plastic undertray. Engage the centre rear of the engine undertray with the tongue which projects forward from the suspension subframe. Replace the 10mm bolts retaining the undertray in the wheelarches where there are three fixings on each side. You'll also have to replace the 10mm nut that holds the stay (or stays) to the lower part of the front fender/wing (or fenders/wings). Note that on some right-hand drive cars the windscreen washer reservoir is mounted forward of the left-hand wheelarch, in which case one of the undertray fixings will be a deeply recessed 10mm nut near the reservoir body. Replace the two 10mm bolts at the rear of the undertray and three at the front.

12   Once you've completed assembly, check and adjust the toe-in ☞ 8/2, 3.

14. STEERING (POWER) - DESCRIPTION

On cars equipped with the power steering option, the rack and pinion steering system is supplemented by hydraulic pressure generated by the power steering pump. The engine-driven pump circulates ATF (automatic transmission fluid) under pressure to the rack assembly, the effect of the power assistance rising in response to engine speed, giving much of the feel of a manual system without the physical effort.

The adoption of power steering allows the gear ratio of the rack to be changed, and on power steering cars, 2.8 turns of the steering wheel moves the road wheels from lock-to-lock, rather than the 3.36 turns required on manual steering models.

Working on the power steering system is broadly similar to dealing with the manual steering system, with the obvious additional considerations of the power steering pump and associated hydraulic lines.

15. STEERING (POWER) - FLUID LEVEL CHECK & AIR BLEEDING

☞ 1/1, 2.

1   Fluid level in the power steering fluid reservoir should be checked periodically according to the maintenance schedule, and whenever abnormal steering operation is suspected. Note that low fluid level or air in the hydraulic system can result in excessive steering effort being required, or abnormal noise from the steering system. Pull out the combined filler plug and dipstick and check that the fluid level lies between the high and low marks. If you need to add fluid, use only **ATF Dexron®II** or **M-III**.

2   To bleed air from the hydraulic system, jack the front of the car so the wheels are just clear of the ground, and support the car on jackstands (axlestands) placed under the front jacking points (☞ 1/3).

3   With the engine off, turn the steering fully to the left and then back to the right several times, and check whether the fluid level drops in the power steering fluid reservoir. If it does, top up the fluid in the reservoir and repeat this procedure until the level remains stable.

4   Next, start the engine and allow it to idle. Turn the steering wheel fully to the left and then back to the right several times, and check whether

15/1 Power steering reservoir dipstick.

the fluid level in the power steering fluid reservoir drops or becomes foamy. If it does, top up the fluid in the reservoir as necessary, then repeat the procedure until the level remains stable, indicating that any air has been expelled.

16. STEERING (POWER) - CHECKING FOR LEAKS

☞ 1/1, 2.

1   In the event of power steering problems, it is a good idea to check the system for hydraulic fluid leakage at the points arrowed in the accompanying drawing. Note that, in the case of rhd models, there will be slight differences in the pipe routing - see the photographs accompanying this chapter for details. Start by jacking the front of the car so the wheels are just clear of the ground, supporting it on jackstands (axlestands) placed under the front jacking points (☞ 1/3).

2   Start the engine and let it idle. Turn the steering from lock to lock a few times, then hold it at full lock in each direction to place the system under pressure. **Caution!** Do not keep the steering fully turned for more than 5 seconds or damage

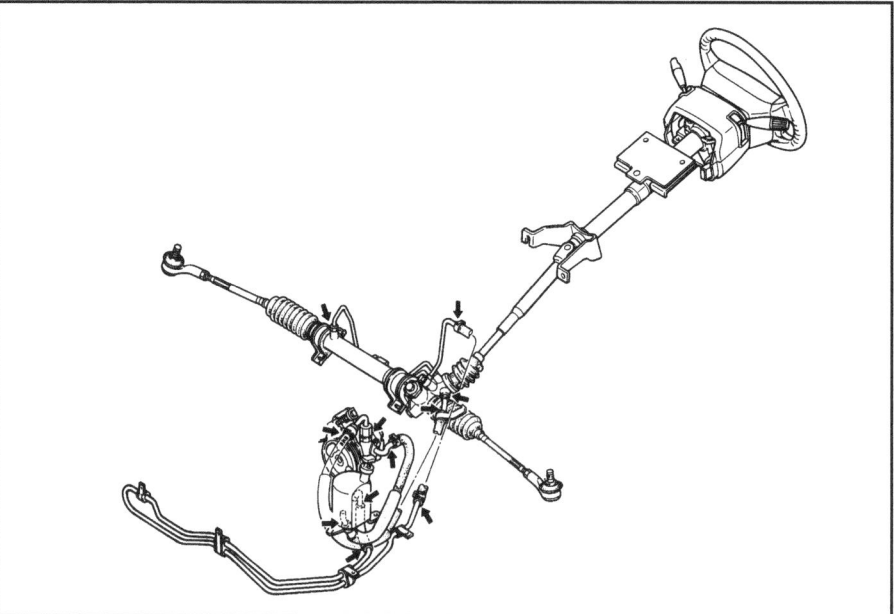

D16/1 POINTS (ARROWED) IN THE POWER STEERING HYDRAULIC SYSTEM WHERE LEAKAGE IS MOST LIKELY TO OCCUR.

8: Suspension & steering

may result. Check for signs of leakage as shown in the drawing. If leakage is found, check and tighten the affected union, or replace worn or damaged hoses as required.

17. STEERING (POWER) - PRESSURE CHECK

☞ 1/1, 2.

1 ☑+ To perform this test, you will need a thermometer and the SSTs shown in the accompanying illustration. These are unlikely to be available to most owners, and we would suggest that you get the check done by your Mazda dealer, who should have the necessary equipment. The pressure test rig should be connected at the power steering pump as indicated in the drawing, noting that the power steering pump hose connections should first be marked to ensure correct reconnection after the test is completed. Assemble the SSTs, tightening the hydraulic connections to 40-49Nm/4.0-5.0kgf m/29-36lbf ft.

2 Start by jacking the front of the car so the wheels are just clear of the ground, and supporting it on jackstands (axlestands) placed under the front jacking points (☞ 1/3).

3 Open the test rig valve fully. Start the engine and let it idle. Bleed any air from the system ☞ 8/15. Place the thermometer in the power steering fluid reservoir, then hold the steering at full lock in each direction until the fluid temperature rises to 50-60 degrees C (122-140 F). **Caution!** Do not keep the steering fully turned for more than 5 seconds or damage may result.

4 Next, close the test rig valve fully and raise engine speed to 1000-1500rpm and note the pressure reading on the gauge. **Caution!** Do not keep the valve closed for more than 5 seconds or the fluid temperature may become excessive, damaging the pump. The specified pressure is 7601-8339kPa/77.5-85.0kg cm2/1103-1208psi. If pressure is low, try adjusting the pump drivebelt tension. If this fails to improve the pressure reading, a new pump should be installed.

5 Open the test rig valve fully, increase engine speed to 1000-1500rpm and turn the steering wheel, holding it at full lock in each direction while noting the system pressure reading. **Caution!** Do not keep the steering fully turned for more than 5 seconds or damage may result. The specified

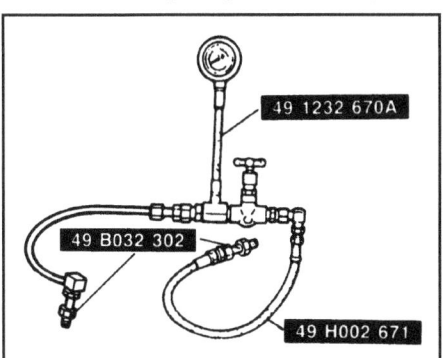

D17/1A ASSEMBLE PRESSURE GAUGE AS SHOWN.

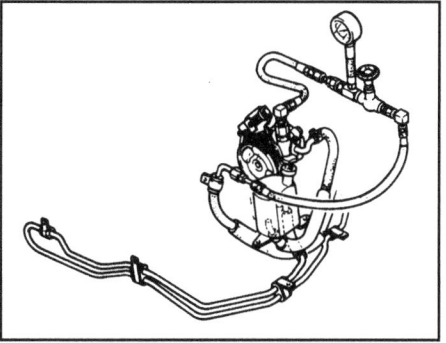

D17/1B CONNECT TO POWER STEERING SYSTEM AS SHOWN.

pressure is 7601-8339kPa/77.5-85.0kgf cm2/1103-1208psi. If the pump pressure is OK, but the system pressure reading is low, wear or damage in the steering rack assembly is indicated.

6 After completing the checks described above, turn the ignition switch to **OFF** and disconnect the test rig. Reconnect the pressure hose to pump union, ensuring it is correctly aligned using the marks made during removal. Tighten the union nut to 32-47Nm/3.2-4.8kgf m/24-34lbf ft. Bleed the air from the power steering system ☞ 8/15.

18. STEERING (POWER) - CHECKING

☞ 1/1, 2.

1 Preliminary checks on the steering can be carried out without a teardown. Sit in the driver's seat with the front wheel in the straight ahead position, and gently turn the wheel to and fro to gauge the amount of free play before any slack in the steering mechanism is taken up. You can gauge this better by leaning out of the car and noting when the road wheel just begins to move. Maximum acceptable free play at the steering wheel rim is 30mm/1.18in. Excessive play normally indicates wear in the steering ball joints, steering column universal joints (less likely), or the rack mechanism. Other possible causes are loose steering column clamps or rack mountings.

2 Try pulling/pushing the steering wheel left and right, then up and down, at right angles to the steering column. Pull the steering wheel towards you and push it away from you. There should be no play felt in any of these planes. If there is, check for wear in the steering column and joints and check the security of the steering wheel; also check the clamps at the upper and lower ends of the intermediate shaft.

3 The next check requires the car to be raised and supported on jack stands (axlestands) so that the front wheels are clear of the ground (☞ 1/3). With the engine running, turn the steering wheel from lock-to-lock until the fluid temperature in the reservoir reaches 50-60 degrees C (122-140 F) - you can check this using a thermometer inserted into the reservoir. While turning the steering wheel, note any unusually slack or tight spots which might indicate wear or damage in the intermediate shaft joints or the rack mechanism, possibly

as a result of impact damage. If noted, these faults should be investigated and rectified.

4 If the steering is abnormally stiff with the wheels clear of the ground, the rack mechanism may be at fault, or the steering ball joints may be badly worn or damaged. With the power steering fluid at the specified temperature and the engine idling, hook a pull scale (spring balance) to the outer edge of one of the steering wheel spokes and check the effort needed to turn the wheel from left to right. This should be in the range 24-35N/2.4-3.6kg/5.3-7.9lb. If the effort required is outside these limits, a problem is indicated. Check the fluid level in the reservoir and bleed any air from the system ☞ 8/15. Check also for fluid leakage (☞ 8/16) and check the system pressure (☞ 8/17).

19. STEERING (POWER) RACK - REMOVAL, O/HAUL & INSTALLATION

☞ 1/1, 2.

REMOVAL

1 Position the vehicle on a smooth, level surface and apply the parking brake. Set the steering to straight ahead and then withdraw the ignition key to lock the steering. Place chocks either side of the rear tires. Remove the front hub caps, and loosen the lugnuts (wheelnuts) by around one turn. Raise the front of the car and position jackstands (axlestands) under the jacking points at the front of each sill (☞ 1/3). Unscrew the lugnuts and remove the wheels.

2 ☑ Moving to the underside of the car, the next job is to remove the undertray from beneath the front of the engine - access to the upper wishbone pivot bolts is restricted, and you will need to get the undertray clear to improve access. Remove the 10mm bolts retaining the engine undertray, starting in the wheelarches where there are three fixings on each side. You'll also have to remove the 10mm nut that holds the stay (or stays) to the lower part of the front wing (or wings). Note that on some right-hand drive cars the windscreen washer reservoir is mounted forward of the left-hand wheelarch, in which case one of the undertray fixings will be a deeply recessed 10mm nut near the reservoir body. Remove the two 10mm bolts at the rear of the undertray and three at the front; then lift the undertray out from beneath the car (photos ☞ 3/4/15).

3 ☑ The next task is to free the steering ball joints from the steering knuckles (☞ 8/12) - you

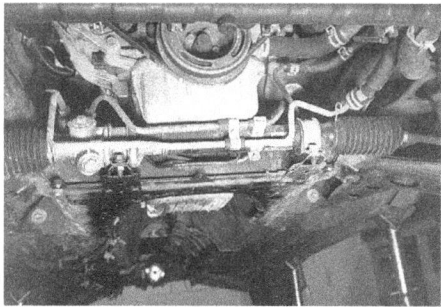

19/2 Rack layout or rhd car with p/steering.

Mazda Miata, MX-5, Eunos & Roadster

can leave them attached to the tie rods at this stage but note that, before you release the ball joints, the 'wheels' should be turned to the straight ahead position, and all subsequent work should be carried out without moving the steering wheel if possible. **Warning!** On models with airbags, if the wheel is moved after the intermediate shaft to steering rack joint has been separated, you MUST reset the clockspring connector ☞ 7/50/12.

4   Working from underneath the car, or via the engine compartment, locate the 12mm pinch bolt at the base of the steering column intermediate shaft where it installs inside the flexible coupling to the steering rack. There is a reference groove in the intermediate shaft end. Check that a corresponding paint mark is visible on the rack side of the flexible joint, and make a new one if it is not easily visible. Slacken and remove the pinch bolt (note that the shaft end is notched - you can't disconnect the shaft until the bolt is fully withdrawn). **Warning!** On models with airbags, if the steering wheel is moved after the intermediate shaft to steering rack joint has been separated, you must check and reset the clockspring ☞ 7/12/6.

5   ◪ Mark the positions of the pressure pipe and return hose where they connect to the rack assembly - these will act as a positional guide during installation. The pressure pipe is also retained by a bracket to the car body on the left side of the rack - release this by removing the single 12mm retaining bolt.

6   ◪ On rhd cars, there are two large bore metal pipes which pick up the pump hose connections on the left side of the car, conveying the hydraulic fluid to the right side of the unit. The feed and return pipes are bracketed together, with a clamp retaining the assembly to the center of the rack - this should be freed to allow the pipes to be disengaged from the rack.

7   Using a small container to catch any ATF

19/5 Pressure pipe & return hose (rhd).

19/6 Release these clamps (rhd).

which spills as the pipe unions are disconnected, free the connections (17 & 12mm) at the rack end, and tie the pipes clear of the working area, having plugged the open ends to keep dirt out of the hydraulic system.

8   Remove the four rack mounting 14mm bolts, leaving the rack mounting clamps attached to the rack at this stage. The rack assembly can now be lifted and moved forward to disengage it from the intermediate shaft. Once clear, pull the rack assembly out from the driver's side.

OVERHAUL

9   It is possible to dismantle and repair the rack, but a number of special tools are required and it's a complex procedure. We don't usually avoid describing tasks just because they're difficult but, in this case, we seriously doubt that a rack rebuild is a cost effective do-it-yourself proposition when so many specialists offer reconditioned exchange units off-the-shelf. Our advice - and even Wally agrees! - is to buy an exchange unit from a reputable company.

INSTALLATION

10   When installing the rack assembly, lift it into position and check that the steering ball joints will align with their holes in the steering arms of the hub carriers. If necessary, turn the pinion until they are correctly positioned, and then check that the reference marks on the intermediate shaft and pinion splines coincide. Engage the pinion with the steering column clamp.

11   Tighten the steering column clamp bolt to 18-26Nm/1.8-2.7kgf m/14-19lbf ft.

12   If necessary, install the rubber mountings and clamps over the rack body. Install the mounting bolts, tightening them evenly and progressively to 47-58Nm/4.7-6.0kgf m/34-43lbf ft.

13   Reconnect the power steering pump pressure and return lines, tightening the pipe unions to 31-47Nm/3.2-4.8kgf m/23-35lbf ft. Install the pressure pipe support bracket to the body, tightening its retaining bolt to 18-26Nm/1.8-2.7kgf m/14-19lbf ft.

14   Check that the ball joint tapers are clean, then install each ball joint to its hub carrier, tapping it sharply into position so that the pin is gripped in the tapered hole. Install the castellated nut, then tighten it to the lower end of the 30-44Nm/3.0-4.5 kgf m/22-3lbf ft torque range. If the pin turns during tightening, tap it again to seat the taper and try again. Check whether the hole through the pin aligns with a pair of gaps between castellations, and tighten further if required until it does line up. Install a new cotter (split) pin and bend the ends over to secure the nut.

15   Once you've completed assembly, check the fluid level in the reservoir and bleed any air from the system ☞ 8/15. Check also for fluid leakage (☞ 8/16) and check the system pressure (☞ 8/17).

16   You can now install the plastic undertray. Engage the centre rear of the engine undertray with the tongue which projects forward from the suspension subframe. Replace the 10mm bolts retaining the undertray in the wheelarches where there are three fixings on each side. You'll also have to replace the 10mm nut that holds the stay (or stays) to the lower part of the front fender/wing (or fenders/wings). Note that on some right-hand drive cars the windscreen washer reservoir is mounted forward of the left-hand wheelarch, in which case one of the undertray fixings will be a deeply recessed 10mm nut near the reservoir body. Replace the two 10mm bolts at the rear of the undertray and three at the front.

17   Check and adjust toe-in ☞ 8/2, 3.

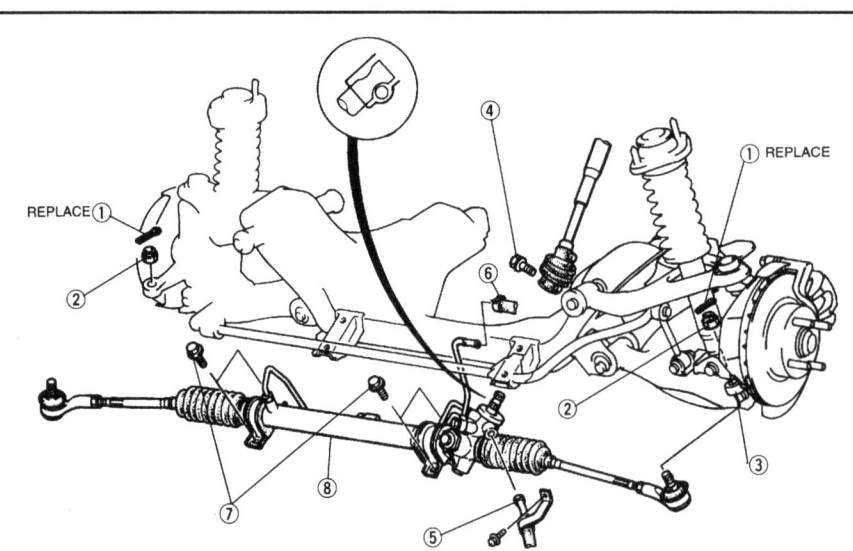

D19/3-14 STEERING RACK (POWER) - REMOVAL/INSTALLATION.
1 Cotter (split) pin. 2 Castellated nut. 3 Hub carrier (upright/steering knuckle). 4 Clamp bolt. 5 Pressure pipe union. 6 Return hose union. 7 Mounting bracket bolts. 8 Rack & pinion steering unit (power).

8: Suspension & steering

20. STEERING (POWER) PUMP - REMOVAL & INSTALLATION

☞ 1/1, 2.

REMOVAL

1   📷 🔧 Slacken the power steering pump mountings (14mm) **A**, **B** and **C** (see diagram D20/5), and back off the belt tension adjuster bolt so that the drivebelt can be lifted off the pump pulley. Note that the pump pulley has holes to permit access to the mounting bolt nut - you may need to turn the engine slightly to align these.

2   Using paint or typist's correction fluid, make a reference mark on the pressure pipe union nut and the adjacent adaptor to act as an alignment guide during installation. Position a rag to catch any oil spills, then slacken the pressure pipe 22mm union nut. Free the pipe support bracket by removing its single mounting bolt, and lodge the pipe clear of the pump, having covered the open end of the pipe to keep dirt out.

3   Disconnect the pressure switch wiring connector from the top of the pump. Squeeze together the return hose clip and slide it along the hose until clear of the union stub. Work the hose off the stub and plug the end to keep dirt out, then tie the hose clear of the pump. Remove the mounting bolt nut and the belt tensioner to mounting bracket bolt and lift the pump away.

INSTALLATION

4   When installing the pump, install the mounting fasteners loosely - you'll need to adjust drivebelt tension before they are finally tightened. Install the return hose and secure it by sliding the hose clip back into position. Reconnect the pressure pipe, aligning the marks made during removal. Tighten the union to 32-47Nm/3.2-4.8kgf m/24-34lbf ft, then install the pipe support bracket bolt, tightening it to 18-26Nm/1.8-2.7kgf m/13-19lbf ft. Reconnect the pressure switch wiring connector.

5   🔧 Install the drivebelt over the pulley and check belt tension adjustment. Referring to the

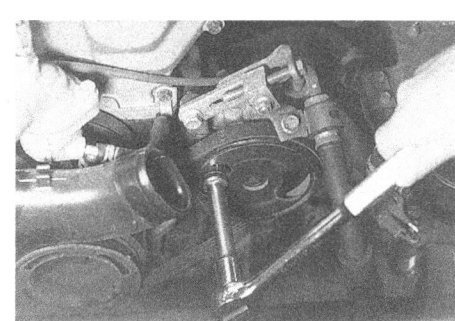

20/1 Access to pivot bolt is thru pulley.

accompanying drawing, turn the adjuster bolt **D** until there's between 9 and 12mm/0.3 and 0.5in of

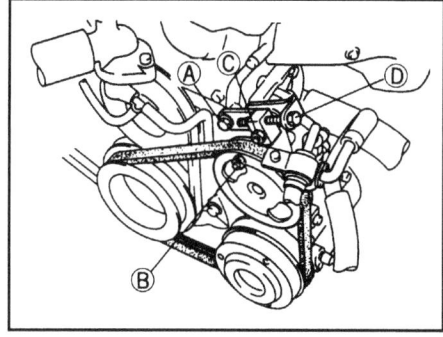

D20/5 POWER STEERING PUMP FIXINGS & ADJUSTMENT (SEE TEXT).

deflection under thumb pressure in the middle of the longest run.

6   Once you have set the belt tension, tighten bolt **A** and nut **B** to 37-53Nm/3.7-5.5kgf m/27-39lbf ft, and the adjuster block nut **C** to 19-25Nm/1.9-2.6kgf m/14-18lbf ft.

7   Check the fluid level in the reservoir and bleed any air from the system ☞ 8/15. Check for fluid leakage (☞ 8/16) and check the system pressure (☞ 8/17).

21. STEERING (POWER) PUMP - DISMANTLING, O/HAUL & REASSEMBLY

☞ 1/1, 2.

DISMANTLING

1   Before starting work on pump disassembly, plug the pressure pipe and return pipe openings to exclude dirt, then clean off the pump with a degreasing solvent. Note that you will require a set of new O-rings during reassembly - these should be obtained before you start. Teardown the pump as described below, laying out the removed parts on clean newspaper.

2   Remove the two 10mm bolts which retain the return hose union to the pump body, and remove the union and its O-ring. Unscrew the pressure switch body (19mm) and remove it and the O-ring, spring and valve body and pin.

3   Unscrew the pressure pipe connector from the pump body and tip out the control valve and spring. Working through the slots in the pump pulley, remove the two bolts which retain the adjuster bracket and lift it away.

4   Release the four 10mm bolts which retain the pump end cover and lift it and its O-ring away. Take care not to lose the small dowel pins from the cover. The cam ring, rotor and blades and the side plate can now be removed for checking.

CHECKING & OVERHAUL

5   Clean the pump components carefully, checking for any signs of dirt or obstructions which may have been impeding its operation. Check the pump body and end cover for signs of wear or cracking - if found, a new pump should be installed.

6   Check the condition of the pump internal components (cam ring, rotor and blades and the side plate) for signs of wear. A bright, polished appearance of the working surfaces is normal and

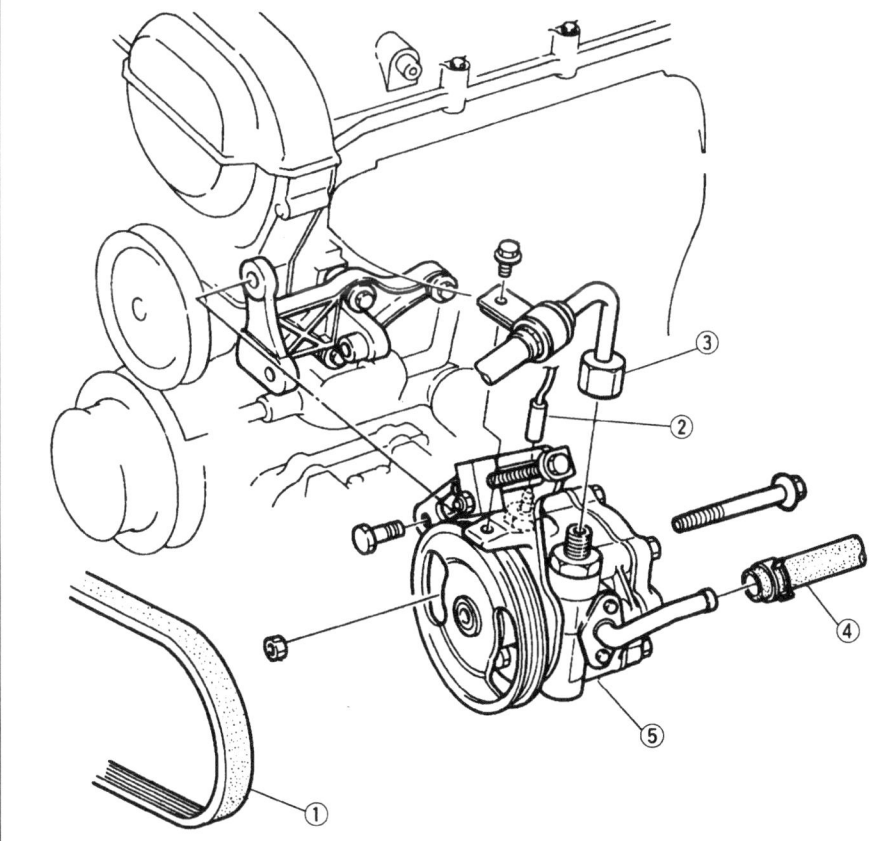

D20/1-5 POWER STEERING PUMP - REMOVAL/INSTALLATION.
1 Drivebelt. 2 Pressure switch electrical connector. 3 Pressure pipe union. 4 Return hose union.
5 Pump unit.

Mazda Miata, MX-5, Eunos & Roadster

to be expected, but signs of more severe wear indicate the need for replacement.

7 Check the fit between the rotor and each blade, which should be a light sliding fit. No specific clearance is given by Mazda, but if the pump pressure was low and there is excessive clearance between these parts, the resulting leakage is likely to have been causing the loss of pressure.

8 Examine the control valve and spring, carefully removing any dirt which may have built up. If the valve is cracked or badly worn, or if the spring is damaged, they should be replaced.

REASSEMBLY

9 Check that the pump components are completely clean, then reassemble the pump as follows, using a little clean ATF to lubricate the moving parts during installation, and installing new O-rings throughout. Clamp the pump body lightly in soft vise jaws with the pulley end downwards. Install the sideplate into pump body, then install the pump rotor, noting that the identification mark must face upwards.

10 Next, install the cam ring with the identification mark facing downwards (into the pump body). Slide each of the rotor blades into position, noting that the rounded edge should face outwards, towards the cam ring surface.

11 Check that the dowel pins are in place in the end cover, then install it on the pump body. Install the cover bolts and tighten them evenly and progressively to 18-21Nm/1.8-2.2kgf m/14-15lbf ft. Remove the pump body from the vise.

12 Install the pump adjuster bracket, securing it with the two mounting bolts installed via the slots in the pulley. Tighten the bolts to 30-39Nm/3-4kgf m/22-28lbf ft.

13 Assemble the control valve, spring and pressure pipe union, remembering to install new O-rings. Tighten the union to 50-68Nm/5-7kgf m/37-50lbf ft. Install the pressure switch components, tightening the switch to 25-29Nm/2.5-3.0kgf m/18-21lbf ft.

14 Finally, install the return hose union, tightening its two mounting bolts to 5.9-9.8Nm/60-100kgf cm/53-86lbf in. After the rebuilt pump is installed, be sure to bleed any air from the system and check the ATF level after doing so ☞ 8/15.

22. SHOCK ABSORBER & SPRING (REAR) - REMOVAL, O/HAUL & INSTALLATION

☞ 1/1, 2

REMOVAL

1 Position the vehicle on a smooth, level surface and apply the parking brake. Place chocks front and back of the front tires. Remove the rear hub cap/s, and loosen the lugnuts (wheelnuts) by around one turn. Raise the rear of the car and position jackstands (axlestands) under the jacking points at the rear of each sill (☞ 1/3). Unscrew the wheel nuts and remove the wheel/s.

2 Position the car's own scissor jack under the lower wishbone, using wood blocks under the jack as required. Raise the jack so that it

22/2a Place car's own jack under wishbone.

22/2b Release stabilizer bar link.

22/2c Withdraw strut lower mounting bolt.

is just contacting the underside of the wishbone. Remove the stabilizer bar control link to wishbone 14mm nut, bolt and spring washer. If the bolt won't pull thru, raise or lower the jack a little until it can be withdrawn easily. Remove the suspension unit lower mounting 17mm bolt, which can be accessed though a hole at the rear of the wishbone. Again, make any necessary height adjustment with the jack to allow the bolt to be withdrawn.

3 Working inside the trunk (boot), remove the suspension unit top mounting 14mm nuts (two per suspension unit), noting that on the left side of the car you will first need to detach the pressed steel cover which conceals the fuel filler pipework. **Warning!** Do not remove the large central nut which is covered by a dust cap - if you do, the unit will separate from the suspension spring under considerable pressure and become firmly wedged in place - you could also suffer injury as it flies apart.

4 Lower the scissor jack to allow the suspension assembly to assume its natural position (it will be under light pressure due to the elasticity of the suspension rubber bushes). You may just about have enough room to pull the unit downward and disengage it - try pushing down a little on the suspension to increase clearance.

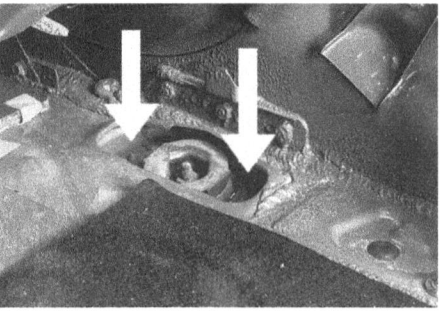

22/3 Suspension strut top mounting nuts.

22/4 Lower jack to release strut.

5 If you need to obtain more clearance, the official procedure is to slacken off the upper wishbone pivot nut and the lower wishbone cam bolt locknuts to allow the suspension to be lowered, but note that this will require the suspension geometry to be checked and adjusted after installation. If you wish to use this method, first mark the position of the cam bolts so that their setting can be restored during installation. Note also that if the wishbone pivots are disturbed, you will need to arrange final tightening of the pivot cam and stabilizer bar fasteners when the car has been lowered onto its wheels. This ensures that the rubber bushes are not under tension. Be aware that this will pose access problems unless you have some ramps or are using full commercial workshop facilities - access is limited when the car is standing on the ground.

6 Our alternative method is to detach the 14mm pivot bolt which connects the upper wishbone to the suspension upright. The lower wishbone and the upright can then be moved sufficiently to allow the suspension unit to be disengaged at its top mounting, then lifted away from the lower wishbone. (Note that our photographs show the suspension upright and brake detached - we removed these for photographic access: in real life they do not need to be disturbed.) This method requires a little more maneuvering when the suspension unit is removed, but will require less work later.

OVERHAUL

7 The rear suspension unit is functionally identical to the front unit, and can be dealt with in exactly the same way (☞ 8/4/10-15).

INSTALLATION

8 Check that the mounting areas and the various bolt threads are clean. Use a wire brush to

8: Suspension & steering

clean the bolt threads and lubricate them with copper or molybdenum grease. Reposition the suspension unit and slide the lower mounting bolt into place. Install the upper mounting nuts finger-tight at this stage.

9   If you used our method to allow suspension unit removal, install the suspension unit to upper wishbone pivot bolt (head towards the rear of the car), spring washer and nut. Reconnect the stabilizer bar control link to lower wishbone bolt. Once everything is loosely assembled, tighten the suspension unit upper mounting nuts to 30-36Nm/3.0-3.7kgf m/22-26lbf ft, and the lower mounting bolt to 73-93Nm/7.4-9.5kgf m/54-68lbf ft. The control link to wishbone pivot bolt nut should be tightened to 37-53Nm/3.7-5.5kgf m/27-39lbf ft. The upper wishbone to suspension upright pivot bolt nut is tightened to 47-66Nm/4.7-6.8kgf m/34-49lbf ft. Because the suspension pivots were not disturbed and the cam bolt adjustment has not been lost, this is about all you need to do using this method, and the car can be lowered to the ground once the wheels have been installed. Once on the ground, tighten the lugnuts to 89-117Nm/9.0-12.0kgf m/66-86lbf ft. Remember to install the pressed steel cover inside the trunk.

10   If you used the Mazda removal method, install the suspension unit, installing the mounting nuts and lower bolt loosely. Reconnect the stabilizer bar control link, again, leaving the bolt and nut finger-tight. You now need to lower the car onto its wheels for final tightening of the suspension-related fasteners, so install the road wheels. If, like us, you don't have a proprietary vehicle lift, access when the car is lowered to the ground will be difficult unless you can lower the rear wheels onto steel ramps.

11   Once the car's resting on its wheels and the suspension has been bounced a few times, position the lower wishbone cam bolts so that the reference marks made during dismantling are aligned, and then tighten the nuts to 73-95Nm/7.4-9.7kgf m/54-70lbf ft. The upper wishbone pivot bolt nuts should be tightened to 47-66Nm/4.7-6.8kgf m/34-49lbf ft. Torque tighten the remaining fasteners to specified torque (☞ 8/22/9).

12   Note that because the suspension geometry was disturbed during this procedure, you should check and adjust the toe-in and camber settings (they should be correct, or very close, if you made the recommended reference marks during the removal process and realigned these during installation) ☞ 8/2, 3.

23. WISHBONE, LOWER REAR - REMOVAL, O/HAUL & INSTALLATION

☞ 1/1, 2.

REMOVAL

1   Position the vehicle on a smooth, level surface and apply the parking brake. Place chocks front and back of the front tires. Remove the rear hub cap/s, and loosen the lugnuts (wheelnuts) by around one turn. Raise the rear of the car and position jackstands (axlestands) under the jacking points at the rear of each sill (☞ 1/3). Unscrew the wheel nuts and remove the wheel/s.

2   Position the car's own scissor jack under the lower wishbone, using wood blocks under the jack as required. Raise the jack so that it is just contacting the underside of the wishbone. Remove the stabilizer bar control link to wishbone 14mm nut, bolt and spring washer. If the bolt won't pull thru, raise or lower the jack a little until it can be withdrawn easily. Remove the suspension unit lower mounting 17mm bolt, which can be accessed though a hole at the rear of the wishbone. Again, make any necessary height adjustment with the jack to allow the bolt to be withdrawn.

3   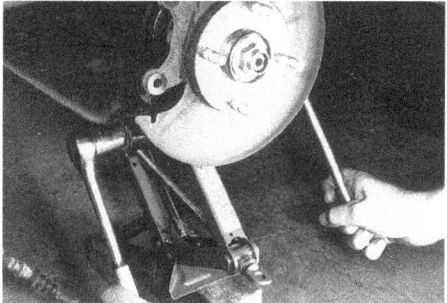 Next, you need to remove the lower wishbone to suspension upright 17mm pivot bolt. We ran into problems here, and it seems highly likely that you will find the same problem on your car. The pivot bore in the suspension upright is partially open at the inner edge, and this means that part of the bolt shank is exposed to all of the road dirt thrown up by the wheels. This, in turn, causes the bolt shank to corrode quite badly, which makes removal of the bolt difficult.

23/3 Slacken & remove lower pivot bolt.

4   Try to remove as much of the corrosion as you can before trying to get the bolt out, and soak it in penetrating fluid. The only thing you can do now is try to drive the bolt out without damaging the thread. Run the nut onto the thread so that it lies flush with the bolt end, then use a hide or rubber hammer to drive it out. The presence of the nut will help stop the threaded end from distorting. Once the nut contacts the wishbone you will have to remove it and use a brass drift to knock the bolt the rest of the way through the wishbone.

5    Using paint or typist's correcting fluid, mark the positions of the cam bolts which secure the wishbone to the crossmember - this will help to maintain suspension geometry during reassembly. Remove the cam bolt 17mm nuts, push out the bolts and lift out the lower wishbone.

23/5 Mark positions of bolt cams.

CHECKING & OVERHAUL

6   Clean the wishbone and check for damage. If you find signs of cracking, rusting or impact damage, don't bother with further work on the wishbone - you'll need to install a new one. **Warning!** Repairs to suspension parts are inadvisable for reasons of safety.

7   If the wishbone is serviceable, you should install new mounting bushes before installing it. The procedure for removing and installing the bushes is essentially the same as described for the front wishbone ☞ 8/5.

INSTALLATION

8   Before starting installation, spend some time cleaning up the lower wishbone to suspension upright pivot bolt, or install a new one. If you plan to re-use the old one, clean off any remaining corrosion with abrasive paper (don't overdo it), and check that it slides through the wishbone and upright bores easily.

9   Position the wishbone against the crossmember and install the cam bolts, noting that the heads should face each other (front bolt head facing rearwards, rear bolt head facing forwards). Install the eccentric washers and nuts, but do not tighten at this stage. Lift the wishbone, guiding the suspension unit lower mounting into its recess and installing the mounting bolt finger-tight.

10    Grease the lower wishbone to suspension upright pivot bolt and slide it through the wishbone and upright, installing the nut finger-tight. We packed the open area of the upright with the thickest, stickiest grease we could find, in the hope that this will prevent further corrosion problems - we suggest you do likewise.

11   If you have difficulty positioning the wishbone while installing the suspension unit or pivot bolts, the small scissor jack supplied with the car can be used to raise the assembly as required. Re-align the link rod and stabilizer (anti-roll) bar, again using the car's jack if you need to, then install the mounting bolt (with the head facing outwards). Install the spring washer and nut finger-tight.

12   You now need to lower the car onto its wheels (☞ 1/3) for final tightening of the suspension-related fasteners, so install the roadwheels. If, like us, you don't have a vehicle lift, access when the car is lowered to the ground will be difficult

23/10 Cover exposed bolt with sticky grease.

Mazda Miata, MX-5, Eunos & Roadster

unless you can lower the rear wheels onto some steel ramps

13   Bounce the rear suspension a few times to settle it. Position the lower wishbone cam bolts so that the reference marks made during the dismantling are aligned, and then tighten the nuts to 73-95Nm/7.4-9.7kgf m/54-70lbf ft. Tighten the suspension unit lower mounting bolt to 73-93Nm/7.4-9.5kgf m/54-68lbf ft. The control link to wishbone pivot bolt nut should be tightened to 37-53Nm/3.7-5.5kgf m/27-39lbf ft, and the lower wishbone to suspension upright pivot bolt nut to 63-74Nm/6.4-7.6kgf m/47-54lbf ft. Tighten the lugnuts to 89-117Nm/9.0-12.0kgf m/66-86lbf ft.

14   Note that because the suspension geometry was disturbed during this procedure, you should check and adjust the toe-in and camber settings (they should be correct, or very close, if you made the recommended reference marks during the removal process and realigned these during installation) ☞ 8/2, 3.

24. WISHBONE, UPPER REAR - REMOVAL, O/HAUL & INSTALLATION

☞ 1/1, 2

REMOVAL

1   Position the vehicle on a smooth, level surface and apply the parking brake. Place chocks front and back of the front tires. Remove the rear hub cap/s, and loosen the lugnuts (wheelnuts) by around one turn. Raise the rear of the car and position jackstands (axlestands) under the jacking points at the rear of each sill (☞ 1/3). Unscrew the wheel nuts and remove the wheel/s.

24/2 Remove upper wishbone pivot bolts.

2   📷 🔧 Position the car's own scissor jack under the lower wishbone, using wood blocks under the jack as required. Raise the jack so that it is just contacting the underside of the wishbone. Remove the upper wishbone to suspension upright 14mm bolt, nut and spring washer. If the bolt seems tight, raise or lower the jack a little until it can be withdrawn easily. Remove the two upper wishbone 14mm pivot bolt nuts and spring washers, then push out and remove the pivot bolts. The wishbone can now be withdrawn from the car.

CHECKING & OVERHAUL

3   The upper wishbone can be overhauled in the same way as described for the lower wishbone ☞ 8/23/6-7. There are only two rubber bushes to be replaced and, again, these can be removed and installed using the technique described for the front wishbone bushes ☞ 8/5, 6.

INSTALLATION

4   When installing the wishbone assembly, lubricate the pivot bolts with molybdenum or copper grease, and install them so that their heads face towards each other. Install the nuts and spring washers finger-tight at this stage. Install the upper wishbone to suspension upright bolt, nut and spring washer, again finger-tight only. Note that the bolt head faces towards the rear of the car.

5   You now need to lower the car (☞ 1/3) onto its wheels for final tightening of the suspension-related fasteners, so install the roadwheels first. If you are not working on a vehicle hoist, the best way of maintaining the necessary access to suspension fixings is to lower the rear wheel onto steel ramps.

6   The car must be resting on its wheels so that the suspension adopts its normal position. Bounce the suspension a few times to settle it, then tighten the upper wishbone pivot bolt nuts and the upper wishbone to suspension upright pivot bolt nut to 47-66Nm/4.7-6.8kgf m/34-49lbf ft. Tighten the lugnuts to 89-117Nm/9.0-12.0kgf m/66-86lbf ft.

7   Note that because the suspension geometry may have been disturbed during this procedure, you should check and adjust the toe-in and camber settings ☞ 8/2, 3.

25. STABILIZER BAR (REAR) - REMOVAL, CHECKING & INSTALLATION

☞ 1/1, 2.

REMOVAL

1   Position the vehicle on a smooth, level surface and apply the parking brake. Place chocks front and back of the front tires. Remove the rear hub cap/s, and loosen the lugnuts (wheelnuts) by around one turn. Raise the rear of the car and

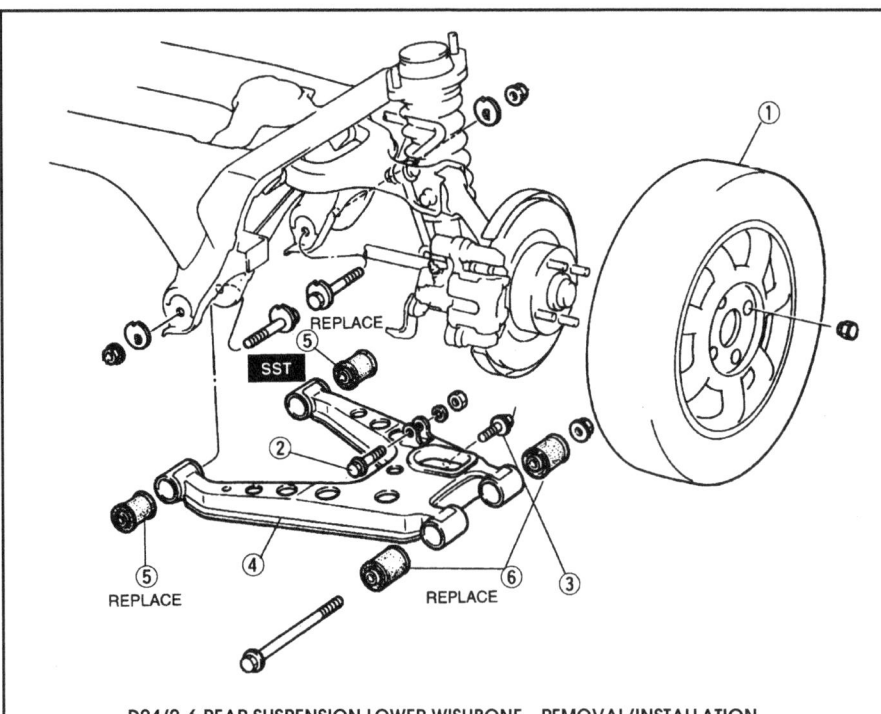

D24/2-6 REAR SUSPENSION LOWER WISHBONE - REMOVAL/INSTALLATION.
1 Wheel. 2 Stabilizer (anti-roll) bar control link bolt. 3 Suspension unit (shock absorber) bolt.
4 Wishbone (A-arm). 5 Pivot bushes (inner). 6 Pivot bushes (outer).

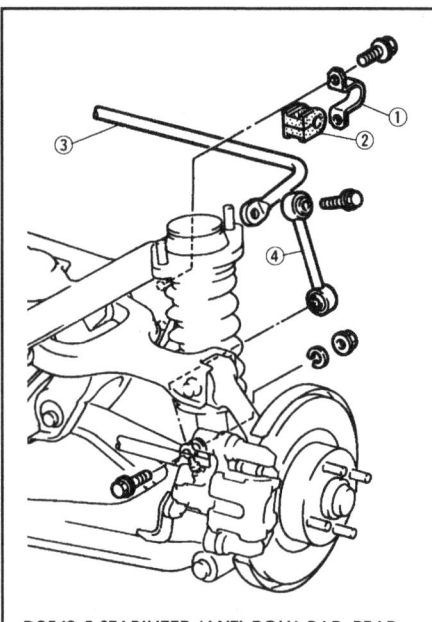

D25/2-5 STABILIZER (ANTI-ROLL) BAR, REAR - REMOVAL/INSTALLATION.
1 Bracket. 2 Bush. 3 Stabilizer (anti-roll) bar.
4 Control link.

8: Suspension & steering

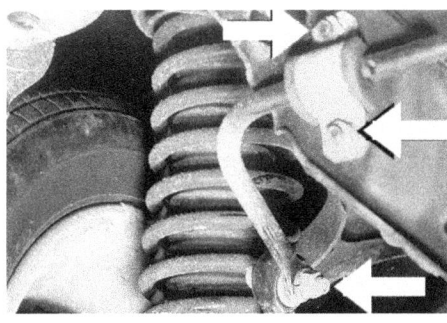

25/2 Stabilizer bar link & mounting nuts.

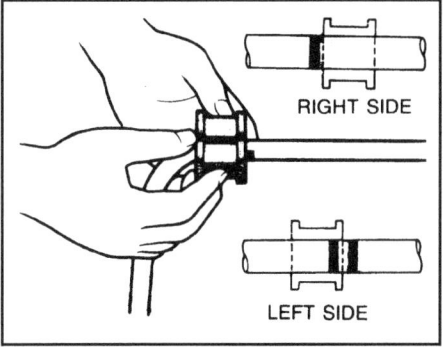

D25/5 ALIGN BUSHES WITH MARKS ON BAR.

position jackstands (axlestands) under the jacking points at the rear of each sill (☞ 1/3). Unscrew the wheel nuts and remove the wheel/s.

2 📷 🔧 Working under the rear of the car, remove the stabilizer bar control link 14mm nuts and bolts. There may be a little tension in the stabilizer bar which could make removal of the bolts difficult. If this is the case, position the car's own scissor jack under the lower wishbone, using wood blocks under the jack as required. Raise the jack so that it is just contacting the underside of the wishbone, then adjust the angle of the suspension so that the control link bolts can be pushed out.

3 The stabilizer bar can now be detached from the crossmember by removing the two brackets and bushes, which are retained by two 14mm bolts.

CHECKING

4 Check the stabilizer bar for signs of damage or corrosion. It is unlikely to require replacement unless it's sustained accident damage or if a high performance unit is being installed. If the stabilizer bar has become bent or twisted, or is badly corroded, it should be replaced. Check the stabilizer bar control links for signs of similar damage, and check the condition of the rubber bushes at each end. If these are obviously worn or deteriorated, install new links. Check the stabilizer bar support blocks for wear or deterioration, replacing them if obviously worn or damaged (wear in the blocks can produce mysterious clanks, rattles and squeaks from the suspension).

INSTALLATION

5 🔧 Position the rubber support blocks on the stabilizer bar, making sure that they line up with the alignment marks (see diagram). Install the control links to the ends of the stabilizer bar, bolt heads outwards, leaving the nuts loose for now. Reposition the assembly under the car, installing the control link to lower wishbone bolts, nuts and spring washers with the bolt heads facing the front of the car. Tighten the nuts finger-tight only at this stage.

6 You now need to lower the car onto its wheels for final tightening of the suspension-related fasteners so, unless the car is on a vehicle hoist, lower the rear wheels onto steel ramps.

7 The car has to be resting on its wheels so that the suspension adopts its normal position. Bounce the suspension a few times to settle it, then tighten the stabilizer bar bracket bolts to 20-28Nm/ 2.0-2.9kgf m/15-20lbf ft. Tighten the control link bolts to 37-53Nm/3.7-5.5kgf m/27-39lbf ft. If the wheels were removed for access, tighten the lugnuts to 89-117Nm/9.0-12.0kgf m/66-86lbf ft.

26. CROSSMEMBER (REAR) - REMOVAL, CHECKING AND INSTALLATION

☞ 1/1, 2.

1 This operation is complicated, even if you have access to a 2-post vehicle lift and a transmission jack. Without this equipment we would advise you to consider having the work done professionally. We're not saying that you can't do it at home, but it will entail a lot of work. The most likely reason for crossmember lowering/removal is to facilitate fuel tank removal/installation, so the whole procedure is covered under that subject heading ☞ 5/ 15 - read through the procedure first, and then decide for yourself if you want to attempt it. **Warning!** If the crossmember needs to be replaced after severe accident damage, we strongly recommend that the job is carried out by a body shop, which has facilities to check and realign any associated body damage.

2 🔧 For those determined to remove the crossmember, the accompanying diagram illustrates the correct sequence (in numerical order) for removal and will also assist with installation.

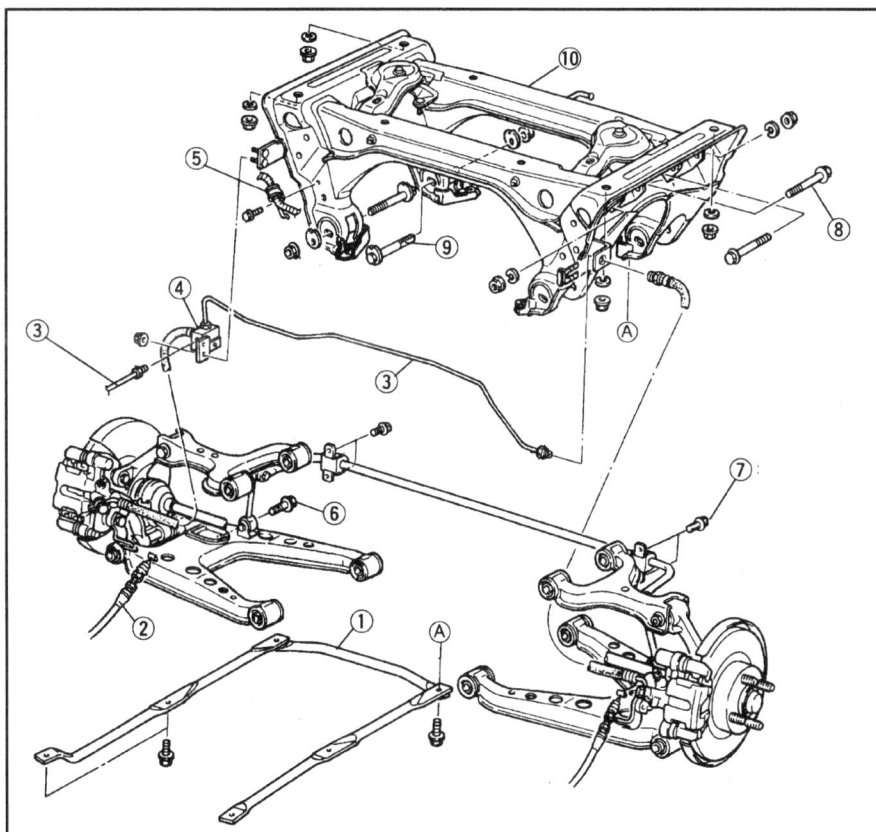

D26/2 CROSSMEMBER, REAR - REMOVAL/INSTALLATION.
See also ☞ 5/15. 1 "Performance rods" (brace bar assembly). 2 Parking (hand) brake cable. 3 Brake pipe. 4 Brake pipe joint. 5 Battery cable bracket. 6 Shock absorber bolt. 7 Stabilizer bar bracket. 8 Upper wishbone bolt. 9 Lower wishbone cam bolts. 10 Crossmember assembly.

Notes

9

Brakes, hubs, wheels & tires

1. BRAKE SYSTEM - INTRODUCTION & ON-VEHICLE CHECKS

These cars use a conventional hydraulic disc brake system, supplemented by a vacuum servo unit (power brake unit), which employs intake manifold vacuum to enhance braking effort. A cable-operated parking (hand) brake is used, acting on the rear wheels.

Some models are fitted with an anti-lock brake system (ABS), which monitors braking and modulates braking effort to reduce the risk of wheels locking and a skid developing. The ABS system is described in the later sections of this chapter, though it should be noted that the scope for owner maintenance and repair of the ABS system is extremely limited.

You can determine quite a lot about the condition of the braking system while driving the car, and you should make a note of any suspected brake problems as they arise. Unusual noises, generally poor brake operation, or pulling to one side, all require further investigation.

When dismantling parts of the hydraulic system, it's good practice to make some provision for covering line (pipe) ends and blocking hydraulic passages to keep dirt out. The line ends can be protected by small plastic caps - suitable caps often come fitted to replacement parts and are normally discarded; we like to keep a few handy in the workshop for jobs like these. We've also used short lengths of plastic tube blanked off with small bolts - not as neat as the caps, but it still keeps out the dirt. The passages in the hydraulic components can be plugged with the same small caps, or you could try golf tees.

Warning! When adding fluid, use only hydraulic fluid conforming to **SAE J1703** or **FMVSS 116, DOT 3** or **DOT 4**. Never use any other type of fluid or oil in the hydraulic system or damage to the seals will result, and there will be a chance of the brakes failing in service.

Warning! Brake friction materials sometimes contain a proportion of asbestos, which is hazardous if inhaled as dust. When working on the brakes, wear protective clothing and a dust mask. Work in a well-ventilated area. Never use compressed air to clean brake parts. Use a commercially available brake cleaner and paper wipes or rags during cleaning, and dispose of the rags or wipes safely after use - do not re-use them.

Warning! There are many aftermarket manufacturers of braking system components, and you'll often find that such components will vary in design from the original equipment components which they replace. All reputable brands will supply fitting instructions with their replacement components, and, where such instructions vary from the directions we give, follow the component manufacturer's instructions rather than ours.

2. BRAKE HYDRAULIC SYSTEM - TOPPING-UP FLUID & BLEEDING

☞ 1/1, 2 & 9/1.

CHECKING AND TOPPING-UP THE FLUID LEVEL

1   The fluid level in the brake master cylinder reservoir should be monitored on a regular basis. In normal circumstances, the level will drop almost imperceptibly as the brake pads wear down, and the hydraulic system compensates for this by repositioning the caliper pistons. A sudden drop in fluid level will require immediate investigation - it indicates a leak somewhere in the system. **Warning!** Although a fluid level warning system is fitted, it should be considered an emergency warning system only - don't wait until the light comes on before

2/2 Topping-up brake master cylinder.

checking the fluid level.

2   📷 Periodic topping-up of the reservoir is normal and acceptable. The fluid level should be maintained between the **MAX** and **MIN** level lines in the reservoir body. If you need to top-up the fluid, first pack some rag around the underside of the reservoir to catch any accidental spills. **Caution!** Hydraulic fluid will damage and discolor painted and plastic parts. If you do spill any fluid, wipe it up immediately, and wash the area with warm water and detergent to prevent damage.

3   **Warning!** When adding fluid, use only hydraulic fluid conforming to **SAE J1703** or **FMVSS 116, DOT 3** or **DOT 4**. Never use any other type of fluid or oil in the hydraulic system or damage to the seals will result, and there will be a chance of the brakes failing in service.

BLEEDING

4   Air bleeding is the procedure used to remove air bubbles from the hydraulic system. If present in the hydraulic system, air will reduce braking efficiency significantly. Unlike hydraulic fluid, air is highly compressible, and much of the braking effort is wasted in compressing the air in the system instead of operating the brakes.

5   It is important to find out how the air got into the system in the first place. If you have recently dismantled any part of the hydraulic system, it may be that minute bubbles in the system have simply joined together to form one or more larger bubbles, and the bleeding process will eliminate them.

6   If the problem is recurrent, air must be entering the system somehow. This problem is often caused by seal failure, usually in the master cylinder. It is not uncommon for a worn master cylinder seal to hold up fine under pressure, but to allow air to be drawn in during the return stroke. If

Mazda Miata, MX-5, Eunos & Roadster

this is the case, bleeding will probably help in the short term, but the problem will soon reappear. The answer is to overhaul the master cylinder.

7   Air can also be introduced as a result of repeated heavy braking which has caused the brake calipers to heat up abnormally. Any water (from atmosphere) in the fluid will boil under the heat generated by heavy braking and will result in vapor bubbles forming in the system. It should be noted that this problem is most likely to occur where the fluid in the system is old. Hydraulic fluid is hygroscopic and gradually absorbs moisture from the air over time, which is why the fluid must be changed at the specified intervals.

8   To carry out the bleeding procedure, you'll need a supply of fresh brake fluid (never use old or used fluid). You'll also need a bleed tube (available from auto parts stores), a glass or plastic (must be transparent) jar and a brake wrench. We strongly recommend that you use an 8mm box-end wrench (ring spanner) to release and tighten the bleed screws. If you try using a crescent wrench, you will probably damage the screw hexagon - it is very small and, invariably, tight. You will also need an assistant during the bleeding procedure.

9   Before you can start work, you'll need to slacken the lugnuts (wheelnuts) by around one turn each, then jack the car and support it on jackstands (axlestands) positioned under the jacking points at each end of the rockers (sills) ☞ 1/3. Remove the lugnuts and lift the wheels away. Remove the dust caps from the bleed screws on the top of each caliper and carefully clean the area around them with a stiff brush. Start the bleeding procedure at the wheel furthest from the master cylinder, and work forwards (i.e.: lhd - r/right, r/left, f/right, f/left; rhd - r/left, r/right, f/left, f/right).

10   ☐ Fit the bleed tube over the ball of the bleed screw and place the free end of the tube into

2/10 Bleeding air from brake hydraulic system.

a jar to which sufficient fluid has been added to submerge the end of the tube. Using the 8mm wrench, slacken the bleed screw very slightly. Install your assistant in the driver's seat. He or she will be operating the brake pedal while you open or close the bleed screw, so it is important you agree on a system of commands so that you each know what the other is doing.

11   The secret to the bleeding operation is to keep the system under pressure whenever the bleed screw is open; you want your assistant to maintain that pressure while you control the bleeding using the bleed screw. Have your assistant apply pressure to the brake pedal, and yell "READY!" when they have done so. Gradually open the bleed screw - your assistant will note that the pedal moves down as the fluid flows out. As soon as the pedal reaches the end of its stroke, your assistant should yell "DOWN!" or something similar to indicate this to you. Close the bleed screw and yell "CLOSED!" to your assistant, who should then release the pedal and reapply pressure (and yell "READY!" again).

12   In this way, you both know exactly what is going on at any given time, and the system remains under constant pressure - air cannot be drawn in accidentally. You should repeat the cycle about 10 times, then pause and top up the reservoir. You will find that after about 20 strokes, any air will have been expelled. You can monitor this by watching for bubbles in the bleed tube. Once all traces of air have gone, you can close the bleed screw, remove the tube, wipe up any fluid spills and fit the dust cap. Move on to the next caliper and repeat the process.

13   When you have bled the air from all four calipers, check brake operation by depressing the pedal. It should feel firm, with no sponginess when pressed. Make a final check of the level of fluid in the reservoir, topping it up to the **MAX** line before fitting the cover and cap. When you've completed the bleeding operation, collect the expelled fluid and dispose of it safely - never tip it down a drain or onto the ground. Your local authority will be able to advise on safe (and legal) disposal procedures.

3. BRAKE SYSTEM HYDRAULIC FLUID - REPLACEMENT

☞ 1/1, 2 & 9/1.

1   The brake hydraulic fluid should be changed at the intervals specified in the service schedule (☞ 2), or whenever you have reason to suspect that the fluid is contaminated or degraded through age. The procedure is essentially similar to the bleeding procedure (☞ 9/2), so set up the car and equipment as described.

2   You need to remove most of the old fluid from the reservoir. This can be done using a suction pump, if you have one. Alternatively, open one of the bleed screws with the bleed tube and jar in position, and pump the brake pedal repeatedly until the level falls to the bottom of the reservoir. Don't keep pumping beyond this point or you'll introduce air to the brake lines.

3   Fill the reservoir with new hydraulic fluid conforming to **SAE J1703** or **FMVSS 116, DOT 3** or **DOT 4**. Starting at the caliper furthest from the master cylinder and working round the car to the nearest, bleed each line in turn until fresh fluid emerges from the bleed tube. There will normally be a slight but definitely perceptible color change as the new fluid begins to flow from the bleed screw. Remember to pause after about 10 pedal strokes and top up the reservoir - if the level falls too low, air will enter the system and you will have to bleed this out. When all four calipers have been bled, check that the pedal feels firm when operated, then install the dust caps and wheels and lower the car to the ground. Make a final check of the level of fluid in the reservoir, topping it up to the **MAX** line before fitting the cover and cap.

4. BRAKE LINES & HOSES - CHECKING & REPLACEMENT

☞ 1/1, 2 & 9/1.

1   The metal brake lines and the flexible brake hoses should be examined at regular intervals as specified in the maintenance schedule (☞ 2), or whenever a leak is suspected.

2   Before you can start work, you'll need to slacken the lugnuts (wheelnuts) by around one turn each, then jack the car and support it on jackstands (axlestandss) positioned under the jacking points at each end of the rockers (sills) ☞ 1/3. You need to raise the car sufficiently to allow clear and safe access underneath. Remove the lugnuts and lift the wheels away.

3   Working back from the master cylinder, check each brake line and union carefully for signs of leaks or damage. In the case of the metal lines, look for percussive damage or corrosion - if found, the line(s) will have to be replaced. Check the flexible hoses to each caliper for signs of deterioration such as abrasion damage, splits, bulges or cracking of the casing material: use a mirror to inspect the back of each hose. If any deterioration is noted, fit a new hose. **Warning!** If a hose needs to be replaced because of abrasion damage, make sure the new hose is correctly mounted to prevent a recurrence of the same, very dangerous, problem.

RIGID LINE REPLACEMENT

4   If you need to fit a new brake line, it is preferable to have the new line ready to install before work starts - that way you can check that the new line will fit exactly, and make any minor adjustments by carefully bending the line (take care not to overdo this or you risk kinking the line and collapsing the walls). Where the official replacement line is unavailable, most garages can make up a suitable line for you, but this normally requires the old line to be removed first so that it can be used as a pattern.

5   Unclip the line from the plastic support clips along its length, then unscrew the 10mm line union at each end to free it. In cases of severe corrosion, it is not uncommon for the line to be frozen (seized) inside the union, in which case it is likely that the line will twist off as the union is unscrewed - this is no real problem if you were intending to fit a new line anyway. As the union is freed, there will be a little fluid leakage. Don't worry too much about this, but use some rag to catch the spills.

6   Position the new line and screw the unions loosely into position with your fingers (this is important to prevent cross threading). Clip the line along its length, checking that it is routed correctly. Finally, tighten the line unions securely, but don't

9: Brakes, hubs, wheels & tires

4/7a Loosen the flare nut ...

4/7b ... then pull out the spring clip.

overtighten. The recommended torque setting for the line unions is 13-22 Nm/1.3-2.2kgf m/9.4-16.0 lbf ft. Bleed the hydraulic system ☞ 9/2.

FLEXIBLE HOSE REPLACEMENT

7   ◻+ When a brake flexible hose is to be replaced, first slacken the 10mm flare nut while the union is still gripped in the body bracket. Using pliers or vise grips, withdraw the retaining spring clip to release the line union from the body bracket. Finish undoing the rigid line's flare nut and then unscrew the hose union 12mm banjo bolt at the caliper end and remove the hose.

8   Install the new hose, using new copper washers at the caliper end. Make sure the banjo union locating peg engages correctly, then tighten the banjo union bolt to 20-29Nm/2.2-3.0kgf m/16.0-22lbf ft. Fit the flexi hose's 'nut' into the recess under the body bracket, and then push the spring clip into place. Connect the rigid line by screwing the flare nut into the flexi hose union - start the thread with your fingers. **Warning!** Be sure that the hose is positioned so that suspension or steering movement will not cause it damage. Bleed air from the system ☞ 9/2.

5. BRAKE PEDAL - REMOVAL, INSTALLATION & ADJUSTMENT

☞ 1/1, 2 & 9/1.

REMOVAL AND INSTALLATION

1   If you need to remove the brake pedal, you'll find it easier if you first detach the access panel under the steering column; remove the two retaining screws and unclip it from the dash panel.

2   🗔 The first thing to do is free the pushrod clevis from the pedal. This pivots on a clevis pin, which is secured by an R-pin (spring clip). Pull out the R-pin and displace the clevis pin to free the pushrod.

3   Remove the pedal pivot bolt 14mm nut and spring washer. The bolt can now be pulled out to free the pedal from its pivot. As you withdraw the pedal, unhook the return spring.

4   Check the pedal pivot bolt, sleeve and bushes, the return spring and the clevis pin for wear or damage, replacing as necessary. Prior to installation, apply copper or molybdenum grease to all moving parts

5   When installing the pedal, tighten the pivot bolt nut to 20-34Nm/2.0-3.5kgf m/14-25lbf ft, and check that the pedal moves smoothly through its travel. Reconnect the pedal return spring, then fit the pushrod, installing the clevis pin to retain it and securing this with the R-pin. Check and adjust the pedal as described below.

ADJUSTMENT

6   🗔 Check the distance between the center of the upper surface of the pedal pad and the carpet on the firewall (see diagram). The specified pedal height setting is 171-181mm/6.73-7.13 in. If adjustment is required, first disconnect the stoplight switch (A) wiring connector, release the switch 17mm locknut and unscrew the switch (21mm)

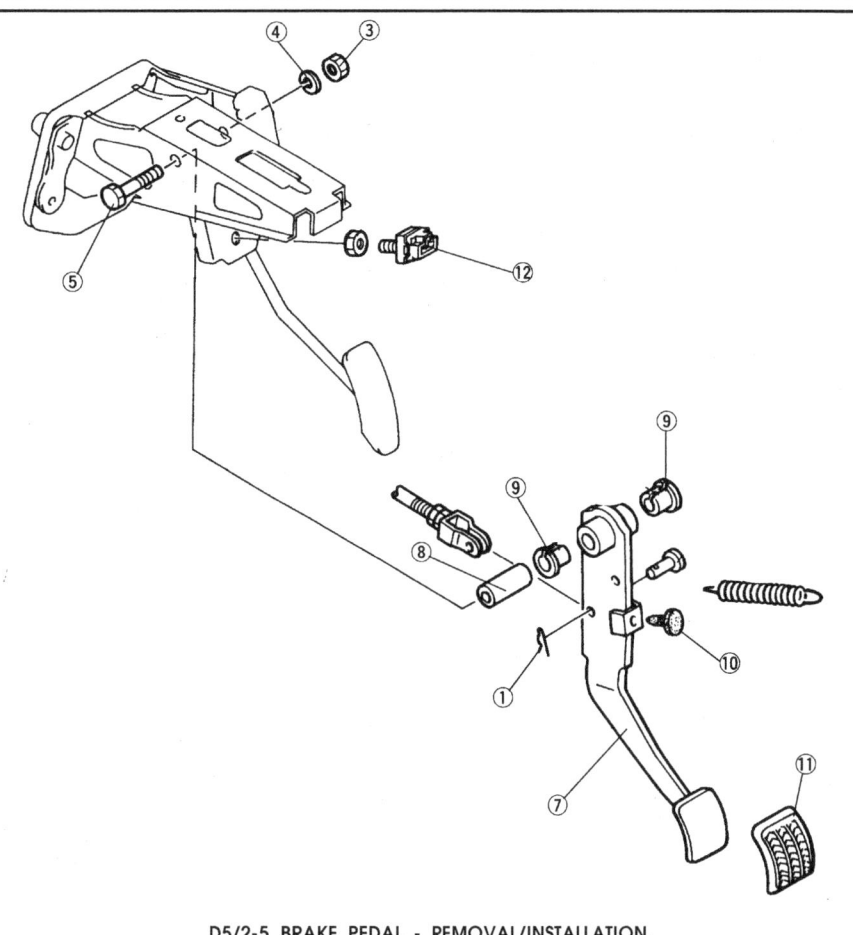

D5/2-5 BRAKE PEDAL - REMOVAL/INSTALLATION.
1 R-clip (spring clip). 2 Clevis pin. 3 Nut. 4 Spring washer. 5 Bolt. 6 Return spring. 7 Brake pedal. 8 Spacer. 9 Bushes. 10 Stop. 11 Pedal pad. 12 Brake (stoplight) switch.

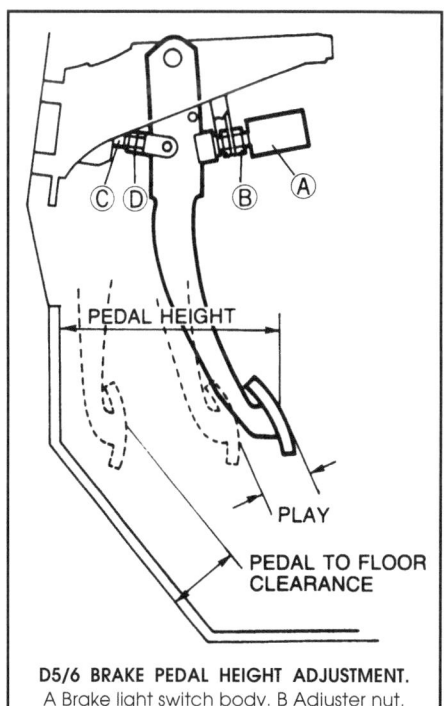

D5/6 BRAKE PEDAL HEIGHT ADJUSTMENT.
A Brake light switch body. B Adjuster nut. C Master cylinder pushrod. D Locknuts.

Mazda Miata, MX-5, Eunos & Roadster

until it is clear of the pedal.

7   Working behind the pedal, slacken the pushrod (C) locknuts (D) and then rotate the pushrod to obtain the prescribed pedal height.

8   Operate the brake pedal a few times to release any residual vacuum in the servo, then depress the pedal by hand until resistance is felt. The distance between the pedal's resting height and the point at which resistance is first felt is the pedal's freeplay. The pedal play should be 4-7mm/0.16-0.28 in. If required, make any necessary correction by adjusting the pushrod (C), then secure locknuts (D).

9   Using its adjustment nut, set the stoplight switch body so that the switch plunger just contacts the pedal: then turn it a further half turn. Secure the locknut and reconnect the wiring connector. Turn on the ignition switch and check that the stoplights are working normally.

10   The pedal to floor clearance can be checked, though this is not an adjustable clearance (assuming the pedal height has been correctly set) - insufficient clearance indicates the presence of air in the hydraulic system. To check this, you need to apply a specified pressure, 589N/60kg/132lb to the pedal. Quite how you do this is another matter. (Wally, our Technical Adviser on this project, suggests that you might use a set of bathroom scales, placing a wood block between the scales and the pedal. We guess it might work, but then again, Wally was in a bar when he suggested this method ...)

11   If you find a way to apply the correct pressure (or just guess at it and press the pedal pretty hard) the pedal to floor clearance, without carpet in place, is 95mm/3.74 in. As we mentioned above, insufficient clearance suggests the presence of air in the hydraulic system. Bleed the system (☞ 9/2) and try the check again.

6. BRAKE MASTER CYLINDER & SERVO - REMOVAL, INSTALLATION & ADJUSTMENT

☞ 1/1, 2 & 9/1.

Unless otherwise stated, the instructions in this section relate to non-ABS cars: if your car is fitted with ABS, study the differing ABS model procedures (near the end of the section) and use those notes in conjunction with the non-ABS text.

1   In addition to your normal hand tools, to carry out this job you will need a supply of rags (in case of hydraulic fluid spills) and a brake wrench (a purpose-made, box-end wrench [ring spanner] with a slot). Some small plastic caps to cover the ends of the brake lines would be useful, too. (These often come on replacement brake parts and are normally discarded - we like to keep a few handy in the workshop for jobs like these.)

2   If you intend to overhaul or replace the master cylinder or servo unit, or both, you'll need to check and adjust the servo unit pushrod to master cylinder clearance during installation. On non-ABS cars, this operation requires a depth gauge tool (SST 49 F043 001) and a hand operated vacuum pump with gauge. If your car has ABS

fitted, you will need the vacuum pump, plus a different depth gauge (SST 49 B043 001). In addition, on ABS models, you will also require a special socket wrench (SST 49 B043 004) and a lock tool (SST 49 B043 003A) **Warning!** If you don't have access to these tools, you'll have to get a Mazda dealer to carry out the work for you. We do not recommend that you proceed without the correct tools - we know of no alternative method of setting up this clearance, and it is important that it is set up correctly. If you are on really good terms with your dealer, you may be able to borrow the tools, otherwise, take the servo unit and master cylinder in for the adjustments to be made.

MASTER CYLINDER REMOVAL

3   ☐ Unplug the master cylinder reservoir level warning switch wiring connector. Disconnect the brake lines at the master cylinder and at the proportioning bypass (brake compensator) valve, using rag to mop up any spills. One of the lines connects to a banjo union bolted to the side of the master cylinder: disconnect this by removing the 14mm union bolt.

4   Note that the bypass valve mounting arrangement varies between cars of different specification. Most have the valve bracketed on the right-hand side of the master cylinder. On our project car, the valve is mounted on the other side of the master cylinder and is positioned in line with it. The basic line connection details are the same, however, as are union sizes at 10mm.

5   If you find that the reservoir is gradually emptying itself now that the lines are off, either plug the outlet hole, or place a small drain container under the master cylinder and allow it to empty.

6   Remove the two 12mm nuts and spring washers which secure the master cylinder and the bypass valve bracket to the vacuum servo unit (power brake unit). Lift away the valve and its bracket, then remove the master cylinder.

VACUUM SERVO (POWER BRAKE) UNIT REMOVAL

7   Remove the master cylinder as described in the preceding steps.

8   ☐ Next, you need to free the pushrod clevis from the pedal. This pivots on a clevis pin, which is secured by an R-pin (spring clip). Pull out the R-pin and displace the clevis pin to free the pushrod. Around the pedal bracket, you'll see the four 12mm nuts which secure the servo unit. Remove these and move back to the

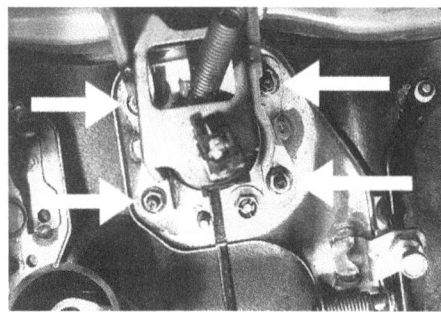

6/8 Four nuts secure the servo unit.

engine compartment.

9   Pull off the vacuum hose at the servo, then remove the servo unit.

VACUUM SERVO (POWER BRAKE) UNIT INSTALLATION

10   Check that the servo unit and firewall gasket surfaces are clean and dry. Fit a new gasket, using a gasket sealant. Have an assistant hold the unit in place while you fit the four retaining nuts and spring washers from inside the car. Tighten these evenly and progressively to 19-25Nm/1.9-2.6 kgf m/14-19lbf ft.

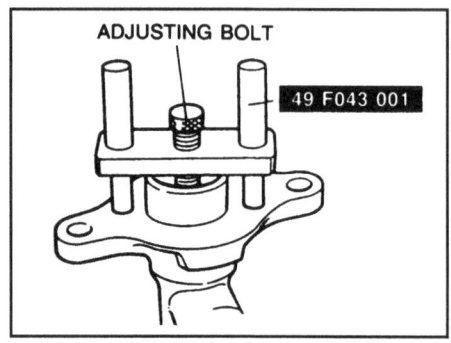

D6/12 TURN ADJUSTMENT BOLT UNTIL IT BOTTOMS IN PISTON.

11   Lubricate the pushrod clevis pin with grease, then install it to retain the pushrod clevis to the pedal end. Fit the R-pin to secure the clevis pin.

12   ☐ Moving back to the engine compartment, you need to check the servo unit pushrod to master cylinder clearance at this point. Place the depth gauge (SST 49 F043 001) over the end of the master cylinder as shown in the diagram, and turn the center screw until it just touches the end of the piston.

13   ☐ Connect the vacuum pump to the stub on the servo unit, and apply 66.7kPa/500mmHg/19.7inHg vacuum to the unit. Turn the depth gauge round and fit it over the end of the servo unit, so that the head of the adjuster screw is immediately above the pushrod end. There should be no clearance between the screw head and pushrod. If there is, or if there is less than zero clearance, slacken the pushrod locknut and adjust the pushrod until zero clearance is obtained. Tighten the locknut to se-

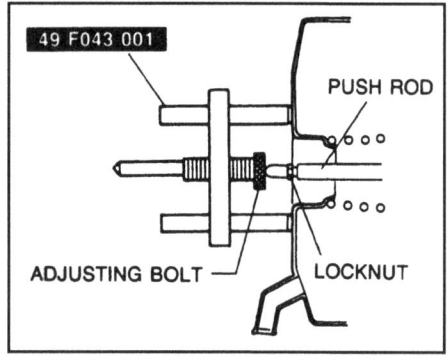

D6/13 MEASURE THE CLEARANCE BETWEEN PUSHROD AND TOOL.

9: Brakes, hubs, wheels & tires

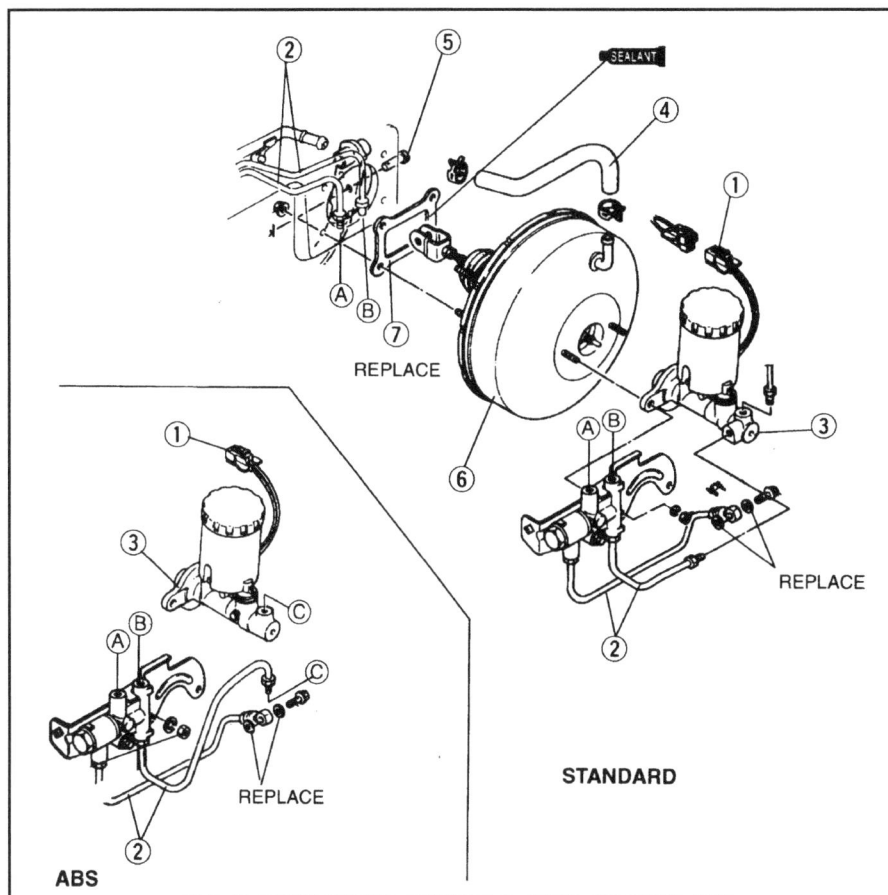

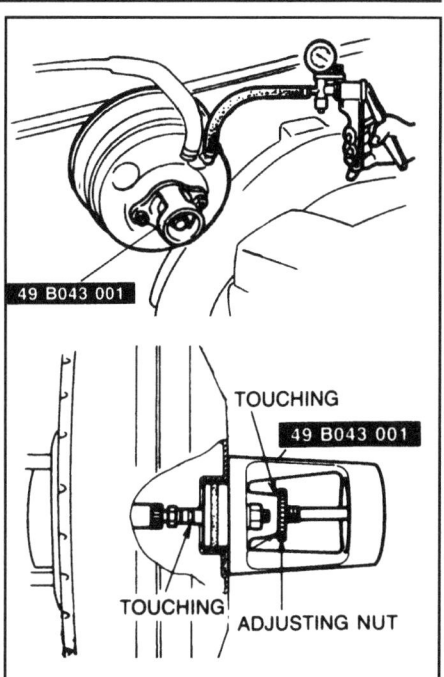

D6/20&21 MOUNT THE TOOL ON THE SERVO BODY AND ADJUST UNTIL GAUGE ROD TOUCHES PUSHROD.

D6/3-19 BRAKE MASTER CYLINDER & SERVO (BOOSTER) UNIT.
1 Connector, fluid level sensor. 2 Brake pipes to proportioning bypass valve. 3 Master cylinder.
4 Vacuum hose with built-in check valve. 5 Clevis pin. 6 Servo (power brake/brake booster) unit.
7 Firewall gasket.

cure the setting. Note that when set as described, this will provide the specified 0.1-0.4mm/0.004-0.016in clearance between the pushrod and master cylinder piston when the servo is installed.

14 After setting the pushrod clearance as described above, reconnect the vacuum hose, noting the fitting direction marking on it (the hose contains a one-way check valve and must be fitted correctly). Secure the hose connections by sliding the hose clips into position over the hose ends.

MASTER CYLINDER INSTALLATION

15 Reposition the master cylinder and the bypass valve bracket assembly, securing them with the two mounting nuts and spring washers. Tighten the nuts to 9.8-16.0Nm/1.0-1.6kgf m/7.2-12.0lbf ft.

16 Reconnect the brake lines, using new copper washers on the single banjo union, and tightening the union bolt to 20-29Nm/2.0-3.0kgf m/14.0-22.0lbf ft. Reconnect the remaining line unions, tightening them to 13-22Nm/1.3-2.2kgf m/9.4-16.0lbf ft. Plug in the fluid warning switch wiring connector. Wipe away any residual fluid spillage around the master cylinder.

17 Fill the reservoir with fresh brake fluid and bleed the system (☞ 9/2), noting that, because air has been introduced near the master cylinder, it may take a while to bleed through. When bleeding is completed, have your assistant press down the brake pedal as hard as possible for a minute or two, and check the disturbed connections for signs of leakage.

SPECIAL NOTES: ABS EQUIPPED CARS

18 In general, the procedure for dealing with the master cylinder and servo unit on cars with ABS fitted is as described previously, with the following exceptions -

19 During master cylinder removal, note that the line connections differ slightly - the master cylinder and servo unit used are similar, but specific to ABS cars.

20 When installing the master cylinder, check the master cylinder to servo unit pushrod clearance as follows. Using SST 49 B043 001, turn the nut fully clockwise to retract the gauge rod. Mount the tool on the servo unit, securing it with the master cylinder mounting nuts, tightening them to 9.8-16Nm/1.0-1.6kgf m/7.2-11.6lbf ft.

21 Connect the vacuum pump to the servo unit vacuum stub and apply 66.7kPa/500mmHg/19.7inHg vacuum to the unit. Turn the gauge nut counter-clockwise until the gauge rod can be felt to be just touching the servo unit pushrod - push the end of the rod gently to confirm

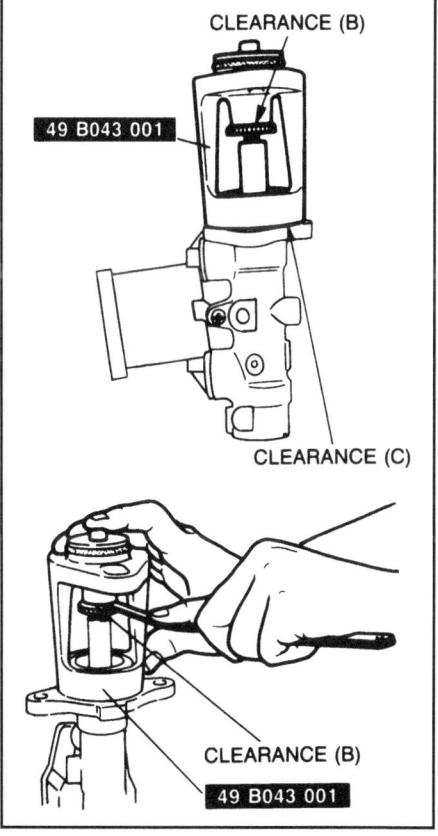

D6/22&23 MOUNT THE TOOL ON THE MASTER CYLINDER TO MEASURE CLEARANCE. ADJUST PUSHROD IF NECESSARY.

Mazda Miata, MX-5, Eunos & Roadster

that it is just seated and no freeplay exists.

22 Remove the gauge from the servo unit, taking care not to move the gauge nut as you do so. Invert the gauge and place it over the end of the master cylinder. Do not press hard on the tool or you will get a misleading reading - the gauge rod should just bottom in the piston end. Refer to the accompanying diagram and check for clearance at (B) between the gauge nut and body, and at (C) between the gauge body and the master cylinder, using feeler gauges.

23 Ideally, there should be zero clearance at either (B) or (C). If you measure any clearance at (B), the servo pushrod is too short; if clearance is found at (C), the pushrod is too long. Either way, you need to adjust it.

24 Assemble the remaining two special

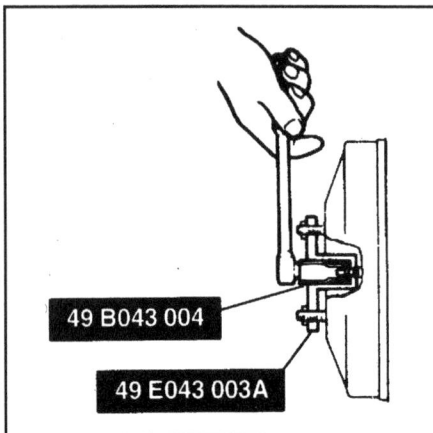

D6/24 FIT TOOLS TO SERVO UNIT AS SHOWN.

tools, the socket wrench (SST 49 B043 004) and lock tool (SST 49 B043 003A) on the servo unit as shown in the diagram.

25 If you read a clearance at (B), turn the socket wrench to lengthen the pushrod by the amount of clearance measured. Note that the pushrod threads will become tight after a certain amount of movement. This is intentional, and prevents the pushrod from loosening. Do not turn the adjuster beyond this point.

26 If clearance was found at (C) in the

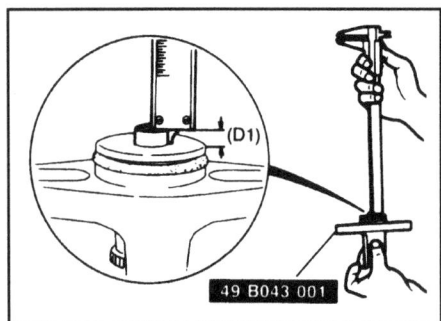

D6/26 USE A VERNIER GAUGE TO MEASURE HEIGHT OF GAUGE ROD (D1).

check, measure the height of the gauge rod at (D1) as shown in the accompanying diagram.

27 Fit the gauge on the master cylinder,

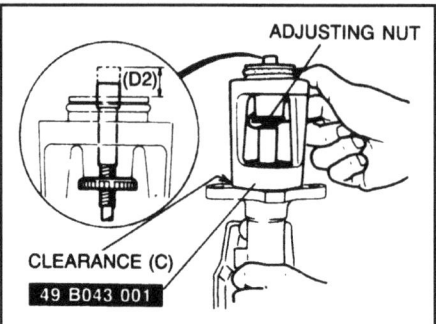

D6/27 MEASURE THE HEIGHT OF GAUGE ROD (D2).

and turn the gauge nut until the rod just contacts the piston end (do not turn it further or you will get an incorrect reading). Measure the resulting changed height of the gauge rod (D2), then subtract (D1) from (D2). The resulting measurement gives the amount by which the servo unit pushrod needs to be shortened. Using the tools as described in paragraphs 24-25 above, adjust the servo pushrod length.

7. BRAKE MASTER CYLINDER - OVERHAUL

 1/1, 2 & 9/1.

The master cylinder and servo unit fitted to non-ABS and ABS equipped cars are similar in construction, with a few detail variations - these are described in the text.

1 If you intend to overhaul either the master cylinder, servo unit or both, you will need to check and adjust the servo unit pushrod to master cylinder clearance during installation. On non-ABS cars, this operation requires a depth gauge tool (SST 49 F043 001), and a hand operated vacuum pump with gauge.

2 If your car has ABS fitted, you will need the vacuum pump, plus a different depth gauge (SST 49 B043 001). In addition, on ABS models, you will also require a special socket wrench (SST 49 B043 004) and a lock tool (SST 49 B043 003A).

3 **Warning!** If you don't have access to the above tools, you'll have to get a Mazda dealer to carry out the work for you. We do not recommend that you proceed without the correct tools - we know of no alternative method of setting up this clearance, and it is important that it is set up correctly. If you are on really good terms with your dealer, you may be able to borrow the tools; otherwise, take the servo unit and master cylinder in for the adjustments to be made.

4 Before starting any dismantling work, check the operation of the fluid level sensor as follows. Connect an ohmmeter or continuity tester to the sensor terminals. With fluid present in the reservoir (above the **MIN** level mark), there should be no continuity indicated. If you now empty the fluid, continuity should be shown. If the sensor does not operate correctly, a new one should be fitted. Note that the above check can be carried out with the master cylinder in place, but you will need some kind of pump or siphon arrangement to drain

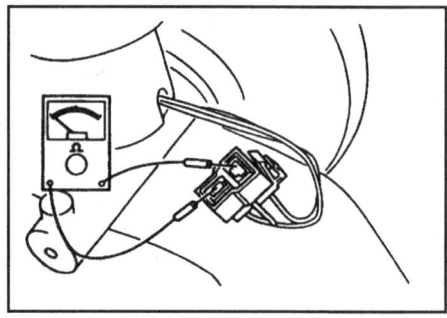

D7/4 BRAKE MASTER CYLINDER FLUID LEVEL SENSOR: CHECKING CONTINUITY AT CONNECTOR.

the fluid from the reservoir. **Warning!** Don't try to start a siphon effect by sucking on the tube.

5 Remove the master cylinder 9/6.

6 With the fluid emptied from the reservoir, remove the single screw which secures the reservoir to the master cylinder, then remove it by pulling it out of the rubber seals in the body. The seals, which should be replaced during assembly, can now be removed from the master cylinder. Pull out and remove the fluid level sensor, then invert the reservoir and tap it on a hard surface to dislodge the filter screen and lower block.

7 On non-ABS cars, remove the small stop screw and its O-ring from the underside of the master cylinder body. On ABS equipped models, the equivalent stop screw is much longer, and is fitted from the side of the cylinder.

8 Remove the snap ring (circlip) from the end of the master cylinder body. On ABS equipped cars, there is a spacing washer behind the snap ring which should also be removed.

9 The primary and secondary piston assemblies should now be displaced by their springs and can be removed. If you have difficulty in removing them, wrap some rag around the master cylinder to catch any fluid spray, then apply compressed air to an outlet drilling to push the piston assembly out of the body. **Caution!** On no account pry or lever the assembly out or damage will result.

10 The overhaul kit you have purchased will contain all of the new components which should be included in the rebuild. However, if the kit is universal or multiple application, it may contain redundant parts as far as your car's master cylinder is concerned - follow the kit manufacturer's instructions.

11 Clean the dismantled parts, which will be re-used using only clean hydraulic fluid or methylated spirit. Never use general purpose degreasing solvents or kerosene to clean brake parts - these can attack and damage the seals, or cause contamination of the hydraulic fluid after reassembly and installation.

12 Check the surface of the cylinder bore, and the outer surfaces of the pistons for wear or damage. They should be clean and smooth, with no signs of scoring or corrosion. Although it is possible to hone damaged bores, our strong recommendation is that brake cylinders with damaged bores should be replaced.

9: Brakes, hubs, wheels & tires

13 When reassembling the master cylinder, have a container with a little fresh hydraulic fluid handy. Use the fluid to lubricate the seals, pistons and cylinder bore as the pistons are installed. Fit the secondary piston into the cylinder bore, pushing it home with a screwdriver against spring pressure (take care not to scratch the cylinder wall or damage the seals during installation).

14 On non-ABS cars, push the secondary piston fully home, then secure it with the stop screw, using a new O-ring. Tighten the stop screw to 1.96-2.45Nm/20-25kgf cm/17.4-21.7lbf in. On ABS equipped cars, the piston must be installed so that the slot in its side aligns with the stop screw hole. Push the piston fully inwards, and secure it with the stop screw, using a new O-ring. Tighten the stop screw to 0.7-1.0Nm/70-100kgf cm/60.8-86.8lbf in. On both types, check that the piston moves normally, and that it is retained by the stop screw.

15 Lubricate and install the primary piston assembly and fit the snap ring (and spacer washer, ABS equipped cars only) to retain it. Lubricate and fit new rubber sealing bushes into the holes in the cylinder, then install the reservoir assembly, fitting the single screw to secure it, tightening it to 0.98-1.47Nm/10-15kgf cm/ 8.7-13.0lbf in. If it was removed, install the fluid level sensor. Fit the master cylinder ☞ 9/6.

8. BRAKE SERVO - CHECKING (IN-SITU)

☞ 1/1, 2 & 9/1.

1 You can make a number of checks on the servo unit without dismantling it. Start by depressing the brake pedal several times to release any residual vacuum. Hold the pedal down while starting the engine. As soon as the engine starts, if the unit is operating correctly, the pedal should move down slightly.

2 Next, run the engine for a minute or two and then stop it. Depress the brake pedal using normal braking force, and note how far down it moves. Release and reapply the brake several times, noting how far it moves each time. If the servo is working normally, the pedal stroke should decrease with successive applications.

3 Finally, start the engine and depress the pedal with normal braking pressure. Hold the pedal in this position and stop the engine. Keep the brake applied for about 30 seconds, during which time the pedal should not move.

4 If any of the above checks indicate abnormal operation, disconnect the servo unit vacuum hose and remove it. The hose contains a one-way check valve - note the arrow mark on the hose which indicates the fitting direction (arrow should point away from the servo unit). Examine the hose for signs of splits or holes. If damaged in any way it should be replaced.

5 The check valve operation can be verified by blowing through the hose. Air should pass only in the direction indicated by the arrow. If the valve allows air to pass in both directions, or if it obstructs flow in both directions, fit a new vacuum hose.

6 Install the vacuum hose, making sure it is pushed fully over the mounting stubs and that it is installed with the arrow in the correct direction. Slide the retaining clips over the hose ends, ensuring that they seat firmly. Repeat the above checks to verify that the unit is now operating correctly.

7 If the above checks failed to resolve a servo fault, you'll need to get the servo checked out by a Mazda dealer. The official method is to use vacuum, hydraulic pressure and pedal depression force gauges to check the operation of the unit in considerable detail.

9. BRAKE PROPORTIONING BYPASS VALVE - CHECKING (IN-SITU)

☞ 1/1, 2 & 9/1.

1 ◼ The brake proportioning bypass valve (let's just call it the bypass valve) has the job of maintaining the correct balance of braking effort between the front and rear wheels. This is important because, as braking effort increases, the car's center of mass transfers forward, so proportionally less effort needs to be applied to the rear brakes. Without this compensation there would be a tendency for the rear wheels to lock and skid under moderate to heavy braking.

9/1 Location of brake proportioning valve (rhd).

2 To check the operation of the bypass valve you need to connect two hydraulic pressure gauges to measure line pressures of the system on the master cylinder and rear brake sides of the bypass valve. These valves rarely give trouble, but if you suspect that the bypass valve is not operating normally, we suggest that you have your Mazda dealer perform a check for you using the appropriate SSTs (special service tools).

10. BRAKE PADS (FRONT) - WEAR CHECK

☞ 1/1, 2 & 9/1.

1 Before you can start this check, you'll need to slacken the front lugnuts (wheelnuts) by one turn each, then jack the front of the car and support it on jackstands (axlestands) positioned under the jacking points at each end of the rockers (sills) ☞ 1/3. You need to raise the car sufficiently to allow you clear and safe access underneath. Remove the lugnuts and lift the wheels away.

2 ◼ There is an inspection hole at the back of each caliper, through which the pad condition can be checked without dismantling. You may find it easier if you first turn the steering so that you can

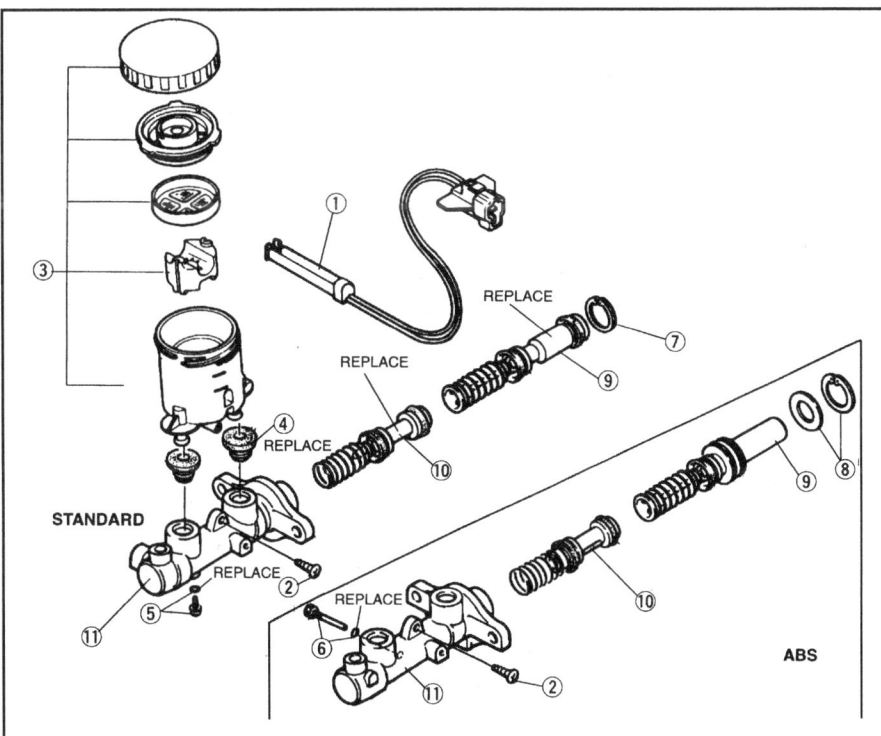

D7/6-15 BRAKE MASTER CYLINDER COMPONENTS.
1 Fluid level sensor connector. 2 Screw. 3 Reservoir. 4 Seals. 5 Stop screw & O-ring. 6 Stop screw & O-ring. 7 Snap ring (circlip). 8 Snap ring (circlip) & spacer. 9 Primary piston. 10 Secondary piston. 11 Master cylinder body.

Mazda Miata, MX-5, Eunos & Roadster

view the back edge of the caliper more easily. On a new pad, the friction material is 9.5mm (0.37in) thick, the service limit being 1.0mm/0.04in. On our project car, the service limit was denoted by the end of the slot in the friction surface (see photo) - this slot may not be present on all pads.

3   **Warning!** It is dangerous to allow the pads to wear beyond the service limit. Not only is there a danger of the disc surface getting damaged by metal-to-metal contact, but the friction material also acts as a heat barrier between the brake disc and the hydraulic system. If this heat barrier is ineffective, you could find that sustained, heavy braking heats the caliper enough to boil the fluid, leading to poor brake performance and even failure.

4   If one or both pads is at or near the service limit, you should replace all four on the 'axle' as a set ☞ 9/11. Note that exaggerated uneven wear of one pad denotes a caliper problem - you should check that the caliper can slide freely on its support pins during the pad replacement operation.

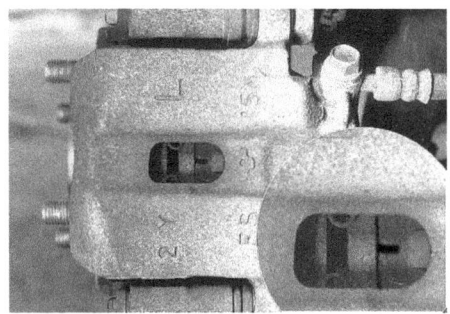

10/2 Disc pad wear check.

11. BRAKE PADS (FRONT) - REMOVAL AND INSTALLATION

☞ 1/1, 2 & 9/1.

Warning! Brake friction materials may contain a proportion of asbestos, which is hazardous if inhaled as dust. When working on the brakes, wear protective clothing and a dust mask. Work in a well-ventilated area. Never use compressed air to clean brake parts. Use a commercially available brake cleaner and paper wipes or rags during cleaning, and dispose of the rags or wipes safely after use - do not re-use them.

Warning! The appearance and design of the pads, springs and clips will vary from manufacturer to manufacturer. All reputable brands of brake pad will come with fitting instructions. If such instructions vary from the directions we give, follow the pad manufacturer's instructions rather than ours.

1   📷 Before starting work, you should have ready a replacement set of four pads, together with the backing shims and anti-rattle clips. These are supplied by Mazda as a set. With the front of the car raised and supported on jackstands (☞ 1/3) and the wheels removed, proceed as follows -

2   📷+ 🖼 Working from the inner face of the caliper, slacken and remove the 12mm caliper lower mounting bolt. This has a long plain shank on which the caliper body slides. Withdraw the bolt, then pivot the caliper upwards and clear of the pads. You can either tie the caliper clear of the pads and mounting bracket, or disengage the caliper from the upper mounting by pulling it inward. If you disengage the caliper, tie or lodge it clear of the working area. **Caution!** Take care not to strain the hydraulic hose. Clean the pivot pin ends and apply high temperature brake grease prior to installation - it is important that the caliper assembly can slide freely on the pins.

3   If you intend to fit new pads, the caliper piston must be pushed back into the body to make room (it will have gradually crept outward to compensate for wear in the old pads), but clean the exposed piston surface (if any) as much as you can before doing this. You may find that thumb pressure will be sufficient to push the piston back. Alternatively, place a tire lever or a similar flat steel strip against the piston end to prevent damage, and

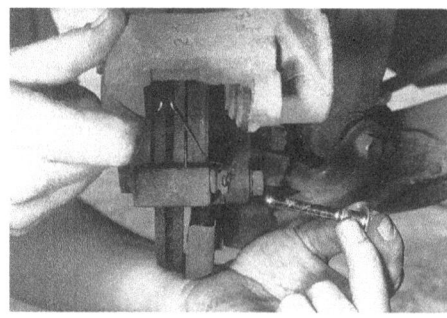

11/2a Remove caliper lower mounting bolt ...

11/2b ... swing caliper up & off.

gently lever the piston back with a screwdriver. Keep an eye on the fluid level in the reservoir while you do this - it may move back above the **MAX** level line, in which case you'll need to remove the excess.

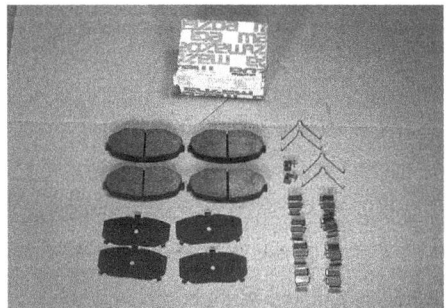

11/1 Components of typical disc pad set.

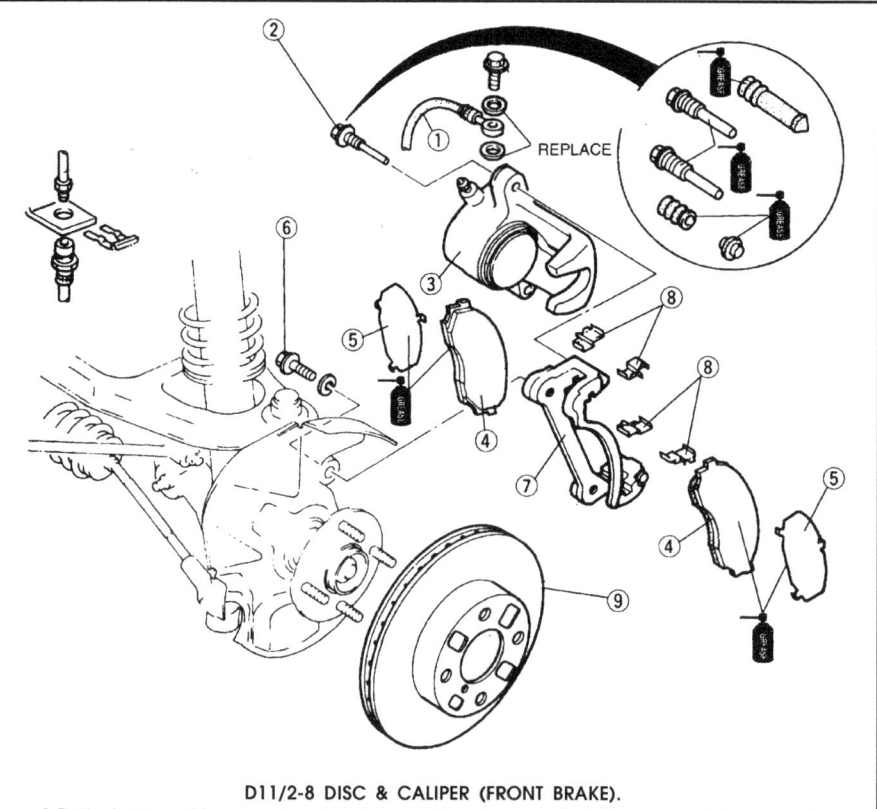

D11/2-8 DISC & CALIPER (FRONT BRAKE).
1 Brake hose and banjo union. 2 Caliper bolt/pin (upper). 3 Caliper body. 4 Brake pads.
5 Backing plates/shims. 6 Caliper bracket bolt. 7 Caliper bracket. 8 Guide plates/clips. 9 Disc (rotor).

9: Brakes, hubs, wheels & tires

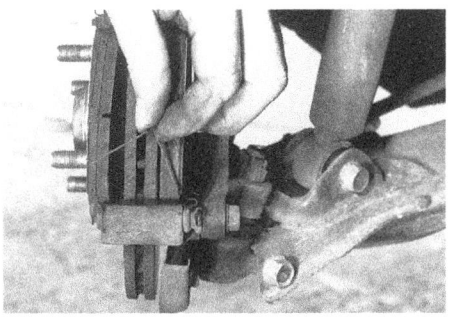
11/4a Remove springs ...

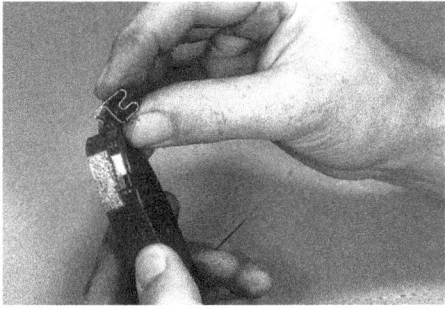
11/5b ... followed by anti-rattle clips ...

11/7b ... apply special grease to backing plates ...

11/4b ... lift out pads with anti-rattle clips.

11/5c ... and shims to caliper body.

11/7c ... fit springs.

4   + Before removing the old pads, take note of the way they and their shims/clips are fitted in the caliper bracket. On our project car, there were two V-shaped springs fitted between the two pads, hooked into holes in the pad backing, and anti-rattle clips attached to the bottom edge of each pad. Mazda does not show the springs or the anti-rattle clips in its literature, though they were certainly supplied with the new pad set - it may be that they are not used on all models, or that they have been introduced as a modification to eliminate brake noise in service. Note also that the condition of the brake discs must be checked before the new pads are installed - see below for details. If the disc condition is acceptable, run a file around the edge of the disc to remove the build-up of scale which will have appeared outside the swept area of the disc.

5   + Fit the backing plates to the new pads, checking that they clip securely over the pad edges. Fit the anti-rattle clips to the bottom lip of each pad. Clip the new anti-rattle shims to the caliper mounting bracket. When installing the pads, apply high melting point brake grease to both sides of the pad backing plates, to the sliding surfaces of the pads and to the contact points of anti-rattle clips and

11/6 If applicable, tighten bracket bolts.

shims. **Warning!** Use the grease sparingly, and never apply any other type of grease which might melt - ruining the new pads and putting you in danger of brake failure.

6   + You don't need to remove the caliper mounting bracket from the hub carrier (upright/steering knuckle) during pad replacement, but if you have disturbed it for any reason, tighten the mounting bolts to 49-69Nm/5.0-7.0kgf m/36-51lbf ft. We recommend that you use a thread locking compound on the mounting bolts for security.

7   + Place the pads in position on the mounting bracket and carefully hook the V-shaped

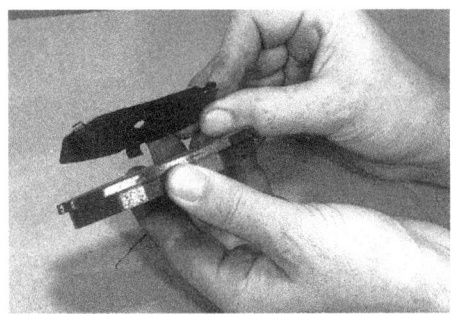
11/5a Fit backing plates to pads ...

11/7a Place pads into the mounting bracket ...

springs (spring shape will vary) into the holes at the pad ends.

8   If the upper swivel pin was disengaged from the caliper bracket, make sure the dust boot is in position and then re-engage the suitably lubricated pin with the bracket. Hold the pads in position, then swivel the caliper body down over the bracket to retain them. Lubricate the lower caliper mounting pin with high temperature brake grease, slide it into position through the caliper and dust boot and tighten it to 78-88Nm/8.0-9.0kgf m/58-65lbf ft.

9   Once the new pads have been fitted on both wheels, operate the brake pedal repeatedly to re-adjust the caliper pistons to the new pads. Fit the road wheels and lower the car to the ground. Road test the car to check brake operation, and remember to use the brakes as gently as possible for the first 100 miles or so to allow the new friction surfaces to bed in properly.

12. BRAKE DISC (FRONT) - CHECKING, REMOVAL & INSTALLATION

☞ 1/1, 2 & 9/1.

Warning! Brake friction materials may contain a proportion of asbestos, which is hazardous if inhaled as dust. When working on the brakes, wear protective clothing and a dust mask. Work in a well-ventilated area. Never use compressed air to clean brake parts. Use a commercially available brake cleaner and paper wipes or rags during cleaning, and dispose of the rags or wipes safely after use - do not re-use them.

1   Before starting this operation, you'll need to remove the front wheels for access. Slacken the front lugnuts (wheelnuts) by around one turn each, then jack the front of the car and support it on

Mazda Miata, MX-5, Eunos & Roadster

jackstands (axlestands) positioned under the jacking points at each end of the rockers (sills) ☞ 1/3. You need to raise the car sufficiently to allow you clear and safe access underneath. Remove the lugnuts and lift the wheels away.

2 Working from the inner face of the caliper, slacken and remove the 10mm caliper lower mounting bolt. Withdraw the bolt, then pivot the caliper upwards and clear of the pads. Disengage the caliper from the upper mounting by pulling it inward, then tie it clear of the working area. **Caution!** Take care not to strain the hydraulic hose.

3 While you don't need to remove the pads from the caliper bracket, you'll find that they will fall out anyway - make a note of their position on the bracket, the arrangement of backing plates (shims) and clips, and also the pad springs, then remove them and place them to one side (☞ 9/14 for more details).

4 Remove the two 14mm bolts which secure the caliper bracket to the hub carrier (upright/steering knuckle), and lift it away. The disc is now free to be lifted off the hub - but leave it in position until you have checked the runout.

5 ▣ Temporarily fit two of the lugnuts (wheelnuts) to secure the disc on the hub. Position

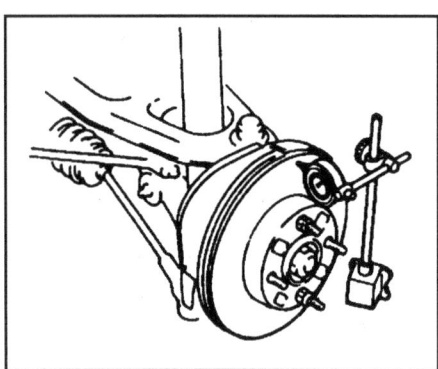

D12/5 CHECKING DISC RUNOUT.

a dial gauge so that the probe touches the outer face of the disc near the outer edge, and zero the gauge. Turn the disc through one revolution and note the runout indicated. 0.05mm/0.002in is the maximum runout - if this figure is exceeded, a new disc must be installed.

6 ▣ Examine the disc visually for signs of wear and serious scoring: the latter usually only occurs when a pad backing plate has come into contact with the disc. A significantly damaged disc surface will rapidly destroy the pads, and the disc

12/6 Measure disc thickness with a micrometer.

should be replaced to avoid this.

7 Check general wear with a micrometer in the area of the disc swept by the pads. The standard thickness of a new disc is 20mm (0.79in). **Warning!** If a disk has worn to less than 18mm (0.71in) it must be replaced (note that discs should be replaced in axle sets to prevent uneven braking). If the disc is serviceable, use a file to remove the scale build-up on the outer edge.

8 Place the disc over the front wheel studs. Install the caliper bracket, tightening the retaining bolts to 49-69Nm/5.0-7.0kgf m/36-51lbf ft. We recommend that you use a thread locking compound on the mounting bolts for security.

9 **Warning!** If new discs have been fitted, you must also install new pads, irrespective of the amount of wear on the old ones - the pad surfaces will have worn to the profile of the old discs and, if refitted, will wear the new discs unevenly and will not make full surface contact. Install the pads, shims, clips and springs, then install the caliper itself ☞ 9/11, 13.

13. BRAKE CALIPER (FRONT) - REMOVAL & INSTALLATION

☞ 1/1, 2 & 9/1.

Warning! Brake friction materials may contain a proportion of asbestos, which is hazardous if inhaled as dust. When working on the brakes, wear protective clothing and a dust mask. Work in a well-ventilated area. Never use compressed air to clean brake parts. Use a commercially available brake cleaner and paper wipes or rags during cleaning, and dispose of the rags or wipes safely after use - do not re-use them.

1 Before starting this operation, you'll need to remove the front wheels for access. Slacken the front lugnuts (wheelnuts) by around one turn each, then jack the front of the car and support it on jackstands (axlestands) positioned under the jacking points at each end of the rockers (sills) ☞ 1/3. You need to raise the car sufficiently to allow you clear and safe access underneath. Remove the lugnuts and lift the wheels away.

2 ▣ Working from the inner face of the caliper, slacken and remove the 12mm caliper lower mounting bolt. This has a long plain shank on which the caliper body slides. Withdraw the bolt, then pivot the caliper upwards and clear of the pads. Next, disengage the caliper from the upper mounting by pulling it inward. **Caution!** Take care

13/2 Remove caliper lower mounting bolt.

not to strain the hydraulic hose.

3 If you intend to dismantle the caliper after removal, you'll need to make a decision about the method of piston removal at this stage (☞ 9/14 for details). If the caliper is not to be dismantled, fit a hose clamp on the caliper hose to prevent fluid leakage, then slacken and remove the hose union bolt to free the hose from the caliper.

4 ▣ When installing the caliper, fit the hose union using new copper sealing washers, making sure that the union locating pin fits into its hole in the caliper body. Fit the union bolt and tighten it provisionally, leaving the hose clamp in place at

13/4 Check pin and tighten banjo union.

13/5 Slide caliper onto upper mounting pin.

this stage.

5 ▣ Assemble the pads, shims and springs on the caliper bracket ☞ 9/11. Apply high melting point brake grease to the upper mounting pin. Make sure its dust boot is in place, then engage the pin with the caliper bracket and pivot the caliper down over the pad assembly. Grease the lower mounting bolt and install it, tightening it to 78-88Nm/8.0-9.0kgf m/58-65lbf ft. Next, tighten the hose union bolt to 22-29Nm/2.2-3.0kgf m/16-22lbf ft and remove the hose clamp.

6 Before the road wheels are installed, bleed the brake system (☞ 9/2), then pump the brake pedal several times to settle the piston and pads in their correct positions.

14. BRAKE CALIPER (FRONT) - OVERHAUL

☞ 1/1, 2 & 9/1.

1 Remove the caliper from the hub carrier (upright/steering knuckle) ☞ 9/13, but don't disconnect the brake hose yet. You need to give some thought at this stage to how you will get the caliper piston out of its bore. If you have a compressed air supply, you can use this to remove

9: Brakes, hubs, wheels & tires

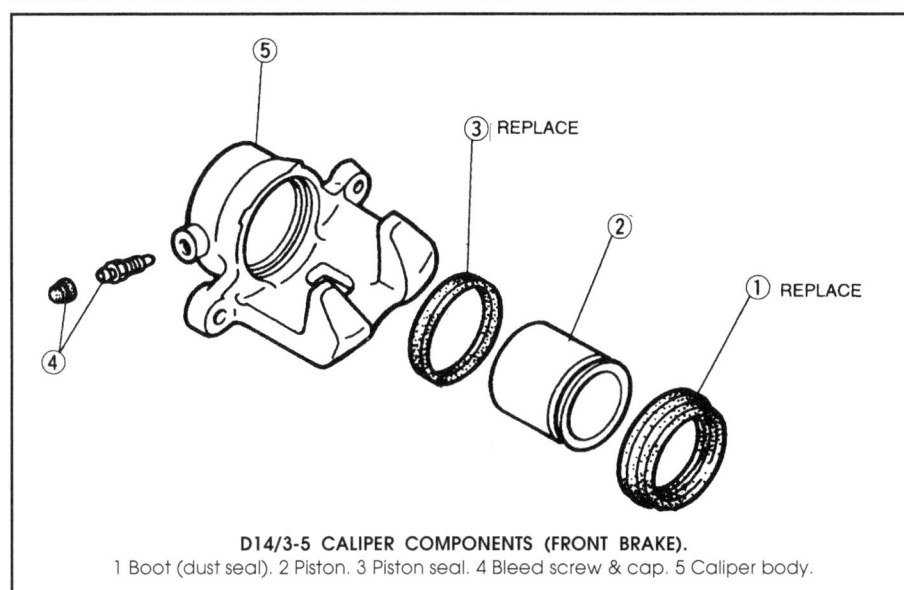

D14/3-5 CALIPER COMPONENTS (FRONT BRAKE).
1 Boot (dust seal). 2 Piston. 3 Piston seal. 4 Bleed screw & cap. 5 Caliper body.

14/5c ... followed by piston.

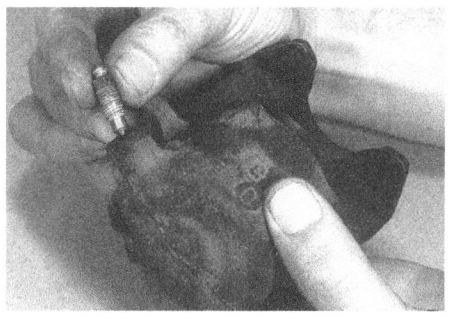

14/5d Fit bleed valve.

the piston after the caliper has been disconnected from the hose. We found it easier to use the hydraulic system to jack the piston out before the hose was disconnected. Place a wood strip across the caliper opening to prevent the piston being pushed out too far, and wrap the caliper in rag to catch any fluid spills.

2 Support the caliper in your hand (**Warning!** Keep your fingers well clear of the caliper opening). Have an assistant pump gently on the brake pedal. With each stroke, the piston will edge out of the caliper. Proceed slowly and, as the dust boot begins to stretch, the piston will pop gently out of its bore and will be retained by the dust boot. Pumping should stop immediately at this point, or you'll risk forcing the boot off, showering you and the caliper with hydraulic fluid. Install a hose clamp on the caliper hose to prevent fluid draining out, then remove the hose union bolts and disconnect the caliper from the hose.

3 Working over a drain tray, lift the edge of the dust boot and tip out the piston, allowing the fluid in the caliper to drain out. Wipe off any excess fluid, then carefully remove the piston seal, using a small screwdriver to work it out of its groove - take care not to scratch the caliper bore while doing this. Put the dust boot and seal to one side - they'll be replaced by new parts during reassembly. Remove the bleed screw, then clean the screw, piston and caliper body in a dish of brake cleaning fluid or methylated spirit. Use compressed air to blow through the caliper passages and the bleed screw drillings.

4 When everything is cleaned up, check the piston and bore surfaces for wear or corrosion damage. If the hydraulic system is kept well maintained, with regular fluid changes, the problem of internal corrosion is unlikely to occur. If neglected, however, the fluid will gradually absorb moisture from the air, and this will allow corrosion to take place. Dirt in the fluid will also cause wear problems. Once the caliper surfaces are damaged and fluid leakage has occurred, you have no choice but to fit a new caliper unit.

5 If the piston and bore are serviceable, fit a new piston seal into its groove in the caliper

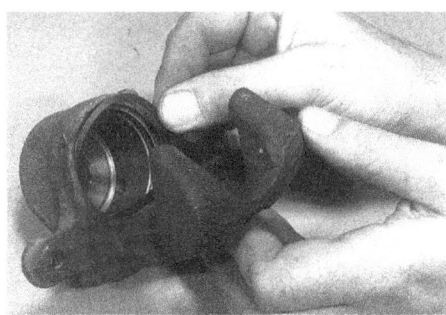

14/5a Fit new piston seal into groove ...

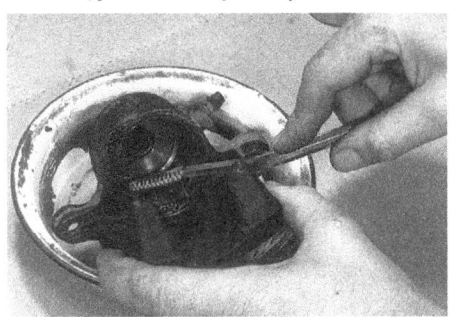

14/3 Clean caliper parts thoroughly.

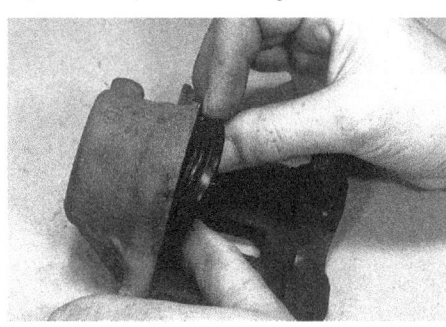

14/5b ... then fit dust seal ...

bore, lubricating it with fresh hydraulic fluid during installation. Lubricate the dust seal with hydraulic fluid and fit it into its groove in the caliper bore. Slide the piston part way into the caliper, working the dust seal over it. As the piston is pushed home, check that the dust seal engages over the piston groove. Install the bleed screw loosely at this stage.

6 Install the caliper (☞ 9/13), noting that you will need to bleed the hydraulic system ☞ 9/2. Get an assistant to press down and hold the brake pedal while you check carefully for signs of leaks at the caliper you've worked on and the hose union.

15. BRAKE PADS (REAR) - WEAR CHECK

☞ 1/1, 2 & 9/1.

1 Before you can start this check, you'll need to slacken the rear wheel lugnuts (wheelnuts) by around one turn each, then jack the rear of the car and support it on jackstands (axlestands) positioned under the jacking points at each end of the rockers (sills) ☞ 1/3. You need to raise the car sufficiently to allow you safe working access around the rear brakes. Remove the lugnuts and lift the wheels away.

2 There is an inspection slot at the back of each caliper, through which the pad condition can be checked without dismantling. On a new pad, the friction material is 8.0mm/0.31in thick, the service limit being 1.0mm/0.04in. On our car, the pads had a slot, the base of which denoted the wear limit - this may not be the case on all replacement pads. The accompanying photograph shows a new pad next to a fairly worn one for comparison purposes.

3 **Warning!** It is dangerous to allow the pads to wear beyond the service limit. Not only is there

Mazda Miata, MX-5, Eunos & Roadster

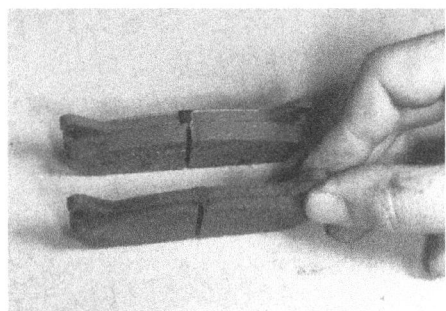

15/2 Comparison of new & part worn pads.

a danger of the disc surface getting damaged by metal-to-metal contact, but the friction material also acts as a heat barrier between the brake disc and the hydraulic system. If this heat barrier is ineffective, you could find that sustained, heavy braking heats the caliper enough to boil the fluid, leading to poor brake performance and even brake failure.

4   If one or both pads is at or near the service limit, you should replace all four on the axle as a set ☞ 9/16. Note that exaggerated, uneven wear of one pad denotes a caliper problem - you should check that the caliper can slide freely on its support pins during the pad replacement operation.

16. BRAKE PADS (REAR) - REMOVAL & INSTALLATION

☞ 1/1, 2 & 9/1.

Warning! Brake friction materials may contain a proportion of asbestos, which is hazardous if inhaled as dust. When working on the brakes, wear protective clothing and a dust mask. Work in a well-ventilated area. Never use compressed air to clean brake parts. Use a commercially available brake cleaner and paper wipes or rags during cleaning, and dispose of the rags or wipes safely after use - do not re-use them.

Warning! The appearance and design of the pads, springs and clips will vary from manufacturer to manufacturer. All reputable brands of brake pad will come with fitting instructions. If such instructions vary from the directions we give, follow the pad manufacturer's instructions rather than ours.

1   Before starting work, you should have ready a replacement set of four pads, together with the backing shims and anti-rattle clips. These are supplied by Mazda as a set. The pad set is shown in the photograph, together with the caliper and

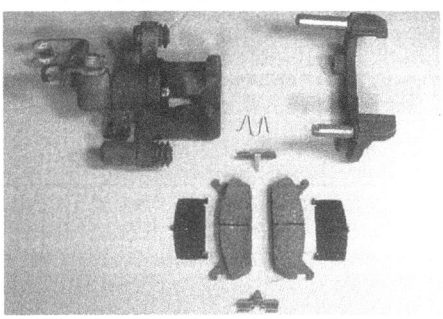

16/1 Typical component parts of brake caliper.

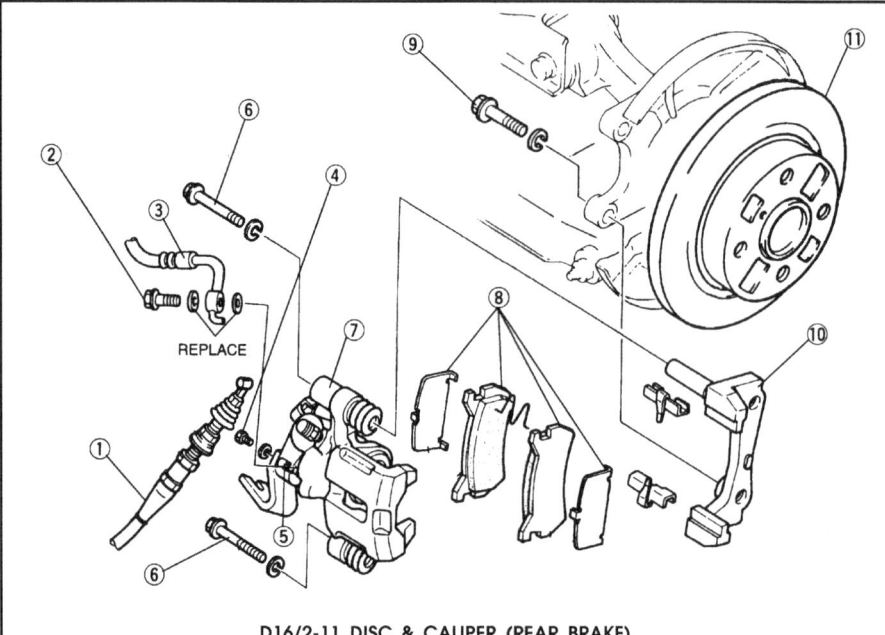

D16/2-11 DISC & CALIPER (REAR BRAKE).
1 Parking brake cable. 2 Banjo bolt. 3 Brake hose. 4 Plug & seal. 5 Retractor/adjuster. 6 Caliper bolts. 7 Caliper body. 8 Brake pads & backing plates/shims. 9 Bracket bolt. 10 Caliper bracket. 11 Brake disc.

mounting bracket. With the car raised and safely supported on jackstands (axlestands) ☞ 1/3, proceed as follows -

2   Remove the filler cap and cover from the brake master cylinder. Working from the inner face of the caliper, remove the 14mm plug bolt and copper washer which cover the piston adjuster screw. Introduce a 4mm or 6mm (as appropriate) Allen key through the adjuster hole, then turn it counter-clockwise to back off the piston - turn the adjuster back until it stops. Keep an eye

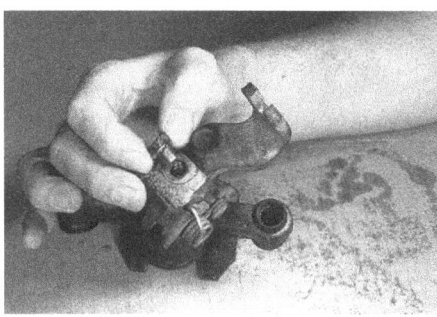

16/2a Remove plug ...

16/2b ... and use Allen key to pull piston back.

on the fluid level in the master cylinder reservoir while you do this - it may move above the **MAX** level line, in which case you'll need to remove any excess. The plug and adjuster screw hole are not easy to see with the caliper installed - our photographs show it removed for clarity.

3   The caliper lower mounting bolt is covered by a black plastic cap, which should be pulled off the bolt head (ours was surprisingly reluctant to come off and had to be twisted quite hard to release its grip on the bolt head). Once the

16/3 Remove cap from lower mounting.

cap is removed, slacken and remove the 10mm caliper lower mounting bolt. This has a long plain shank upon which the caliper body slides.

4   Withdraw the bolt, then pivot the caliper upwards and clear of the pads. You can either tie the caliper clear of the pads and mounting bracket, or disengage the caliper from the upper mounting by pulling it inward. If you disengage the caliper, tie it clear of the working area, taking care not to strain the hydraulic hose. Note that because the parking brake cable is rather stiff, you'll have to wrestle with it a little to find a position it will happily stay in - it

9: Brakes, hubs, wheels & tires

helps to release the parking brake lever, or you could disconnect the parking brake cable to take the pressure off a little.

5 It is a good idea at this stage to clean the plain shanks of the caliper bolts and apply high melting point brake grease ready for installation - it is important that the caliper assembly can slide freely on the pins: if it sticks, uneven pad wear and poor brake operation will result.

6 Before removing the old pads, take note of the way they and their backing shims, clips and springs are fitted in the caliper bracket. On our project car, there was an M-shaped spring fitted between the two pads, hooked into holes in the top edges of the pad backings, and stainless anti-rattle clips attached to the top and bottom of the caliper bracket, on which the pads slide. Each pad had a steel backing shim clipped to it. We assume that all cars will use this, or a similar arrangement.

7 📷 Note also that the condition of the brake discs must be checked before the new pads are installed - see below for details. If the disc condition is acceptable, run a file around the edge of the disc to remove the build-up of rust scale which will have appeared outside the swept area of the disc (it could prevent the new pads

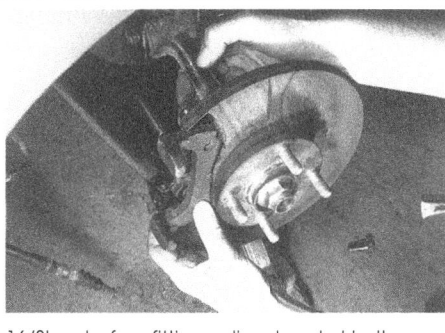
16/8b ... before fitting caliper bracket bolts.

16/10b ... fit springs ...

16/9a Fit anti-rattle shims to caliper bracket ...

16/10c ... slide caliper onto top pin ...

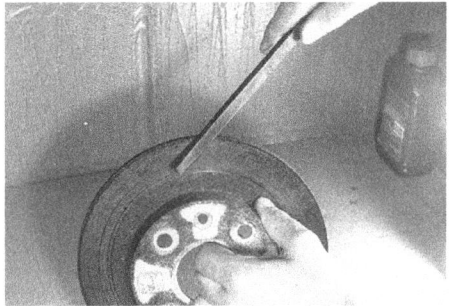
16/7 Removing rust scale from disc edge.

16/9b ... apply copper grease to contact areas.

16/10d ... lower caliper & fit mounting bolt.

seating correctly).

8 📷+ You don't need to remove the caliper mounting bracket from the suspension upright during pad replacement, but if you have disturbed it for any reason, tighten the mounting bolts to 49-66Nm/4.6-6.8kgf m/34-49lbf ft. We recommend that you use a thread locking compound on the mounting bolts for security.

9 📷+ Fit the backing plates to the new pads, checking that they clip securely over the pad edges. Clip the new anti-rattle shims to the top and bottom edges of the caliper mounting bracket. When installing the pads, apply high melting point brake

grease to both sides of the pad backing plates, to the sliding surfaces of the pads and to the contact points of anti-rattle shims/clips. **Warning!** Use the grease sparingly, and never apply any other type of grease which might melt and ruin the new pads, putting you in danger.

10 📷+ Place the pads in position on the mounting bracket and carefully hook the M-shaped spring into the holes at the pad upper ends. Hold the assembly in position, then swivel the caliper body down over the bracket to retain the pads. Fit the lower mounting bolt, then tighten it to 34-39Nm/3.5-4.0kgf m/25-29lbf ft.

11 📷 With the new pads in place, turn the piston adjuster clockwise until the pads just touch the disc surface, then back off the adjuster by $1/3$ turn. Next, operate the brake pedal repeatedly to seat the new pads. Check that the hub can be turned without significant brake drag.

12 You should not confuse brake drag with the inevitable drag from the transmission. If you are unsure, note the amount of effort required to turn the hub with the piston adjuster backed right off, then carry out the adjustment and check if extra drag has been introduced. If necessary, repeat the adjustment operation until satisfactory.

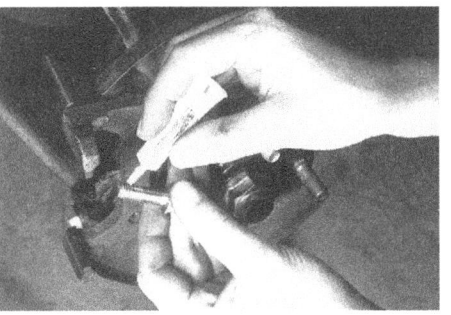
16/8a Apply locking compound ...

16/10a Place pads in position ...

16/11 Adjust piston position.

Mazda Miata, MX-5, Eunos & Roadster

13 Fit the roadwheels and lower the car to the ground (☞ 1/3). Road test the car to check brake operation, and remember to use the brakes as gently as possible for the first 100 miles or so to allow the new friction surfaces to bed in properly.

17. BRAKE DISC (REAR) - CHECKING, REMOVAL & INSTALLATION

☞ 1/1, 2 & 9/1.

Warning! Brake friction materials may contain a proportion of asbestos, which is hazardous if inhaled as dust. When working on the brakes, wear protective clothing and a dust mask. Work in a well ventilated area. Never use compressed air to clean brake parts. Use a commercially available brake cleaner and paper wipes or rags during cleaning, and dispose of the rags or wipes safely after use - do not re-use them.

1 Before starting this operation, you'll need to remove the rear wheels for access. Slacken the rear wheel lugnuts (wheelnuts) by around one turn each, then jack the rear of the car and support it on jackstands (axlestands) positioned under the jacking points at the ends of the rockers (sills) ☞ 1/3. You need to raise the car sufficiently to allow you clear and safe access to the rear brakes. Remove the lugnuts and lift the wheels away.

2 Remove the caliper body from its mounting bracket and tie it clear of the working area ☞ 9/16. While you don't really need to remove the pads from the caliper bracket, you'll find that they will probably fall out anyway - make a note of their position on the bracket, the arrangement of shims, and also the M-shaped pad spring, then remove them and place them to one side. It is not necessary to remove the caliper bracket.

3 Temporarily fit two of the lugnuts

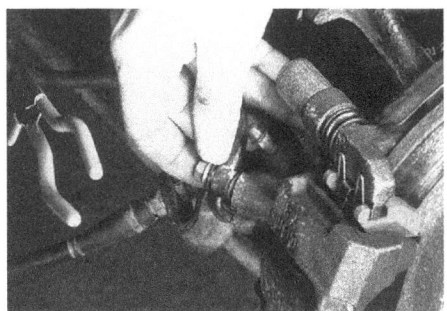

18/2 Remove the hose banjo union bolt.

(wheelnuts) to secure the disc on the hub. Position a dial gauge so that the probe touches the outer face of the disc near the outer edge, and zero the gauge. Turn the disc through one revolution and note the runout indicated. 0.05mm/0.002in is the maximum runout - if this figure is exceeded, a new disc must be installed.

4 Examine the disc visually for signs of wear and serious scoring: the latter usually only occurs when a pad backing plate has come into contact with the disc. A significantly damaged disc surface will rapidly destroy the pads, so the disc should be replaced to avoid this.

5 Check general wear with a micrometer in the area of the disc swept by the pads. The standard thickness of a new disc is 9mm (0.35in). **Warning!** If a disk has worn to less than 8mm (0.31in), it must be replaced (note that discs should be replaced in axle sets to prevent uneven braking). If the disc is serviceable, use a file to remove the scale build-up on the outer edge.

6 When installing the disc, if the caliper bracket was removed for any reason, tighten the retaining bolts to 46-66Nm/4.6-6.8kgf m/34-49lbf ft. Place the disc over the rear wheel studs, then install the pads ☞ 9/16. **Warning!** If new discs have been installed, you must also install new pads, irrespective of the amount of wear on the old ones - the pad surfaces will have worn to the profile of the old discs, and, if refitted, will wear the new discs unevenly and will not make full surface contact.

18. BRAKE CALIPER (REAR) - REMOVAL & INSTALLATION

☞ 1/1, 2 & 9/1.

Warning! Brake friction materials may contain a proportion of asbestos, which is hazardous if inhaled as dust. When working on the brakes, wear protective clothing and a dust mask. Work in a well ventilated area. Never use compressed air to clean brake parts. Use a commercially available brake cleaner and paper wipes or rags during cleaning, and dispose of the rags or wipes safely after use - do not re-use them.

1 Before starting this operation, you'll need to remove the rear wheels for access. Slacken the rear wheel lugnuts (wheelnuts) by around one turn each, then jack the rear of the car and support it on jackstands (axlestands) positioned under the jacking points at the ends of the rockers (sills) ☞ 1/3. You need to raise the car sufficiently to allow you clear and safe access to the rear brakes. Remove the lugnuts and lift the wheels away.

2 ◘ Fit a hose clamp to the caliper hose, then slacken and remove the hose union bolt. Working from the inner face of the caliper, remove the 14mm plug bolt and copper washer which cover the piston adjuster screw. Introduce a 6mm (4mm some models) Allen key through the adjuster hole, then turn it counter-clockwise to back off the piston - turn the adjuster back by one or two turns so that the pads are no longer held close to the disc surface. As the piston moves back, hydraulic fluid will be expelled from the hose union hole - use some rag to catch the fluid spills, and keep the fluid well away from the disc and pads.

3 Check that the parking brake is off, then slacken the cable adjuster locknut at the wheel end by one or two turns so that the cable can be disengaged from the slotted bracket which carries it. Disengage the cable inner from the operating arm and tie it clear of the caliper.

4 The caliper lower mounting bolt is covered by a black plastic cap, which should be pulled off the bolt head (ours was surprisingly reluctant to come off and had to be twisted quite hard to release its grip on the bolt head). Once the cap is removed, slacken and remove the 10mm caliper lower mounting bolt. This has a long plain shank upon which the caliper body slides. Withdraw the bolt, then pivot the caliper upwards and clear of the pads. Disengage the caliper from the upper mounting by pulling it inwards towards the center of the car.

5 It is a good idea at this stage to clean the plain shanks of the caliper bolts and apply high melting point brake grease ready for installation - it is important that the caliper assembly can slide freely on the shanks: if it sticks, uneven pad wear and poor brake performance will result.

6 Unless they are worn, there's no need to remove the pads from the caliper bracket - you can hold them in place with a rubber band or some wire until the caliper is installed. There is no particular need to remove the caliper mounting bracket from the suspension upright during caliper removal.

7 When installing the caliper, it is good practice to apply high melting point brake grease to both sides of the pad backing shims, to the sliding surfaces of the pads and to the anti-rattle shims. **Warning!** Use the grease sparingly, and never apply any other type of grease which might melt - ruining the pads and putting you in danger of brake failure.

8 Place the pads in position on the mounting bracket and carefully hook the M-shaped spring into the holes at the pad upper ends. Hold the assembly in position, then swivel the caliper body down over the bracket to retain them. Fit the lower mounting bolt, then tighten it to 34-39Nm/3.5-4.0kgf m/25-29lbf ft. Reconnect the parking brake cable and tighten the locknuts to 16-23Nm/1.6-2.3kgf m/12-17lbf ft. Fit the brake hose union using new copper sealing washers, checking that the locating pin fits into the hole in the caliper body. Tighten the union bolt to 22-29Nm/2.2-3.0kgf m/16-22lbf ft.

9 Once the caliper is installed, temporarily fit two of the lugnuts (wheelnuts) to hold the disc in place. Turn the piston adjuster clockwise until the pads just touch the disc surface, then back off the adjuster by 1/3 turn. Bleed the brake hydraulic system to remove the air introduced when the system was disconnected ☞ 9/2. Operate the brake pedal repeatedly to seat the pads. Check that the hub can be turned without significant brake drag.

10 You should not confuse brake drag with the inevitable drag from the transmission. If you are unsure, note the amount of effort required to turn the hub with the piston adjuster backed right off, then carry out the adjustment and check if extra drag has been introduced. If necessary, repeat the adjustment operation until satisfactory.

11 Fit the road wheels and lower the car to the ground (☞ 1/3). Road test the car to check brake operation, and remember that if new pads were fitted as part of the overhaul, the brakes should be used as gently as possible for the first 100 miles or so to allow the new friction surfaces to bed in properly.

9: Brakes, hubs, wheels & tires

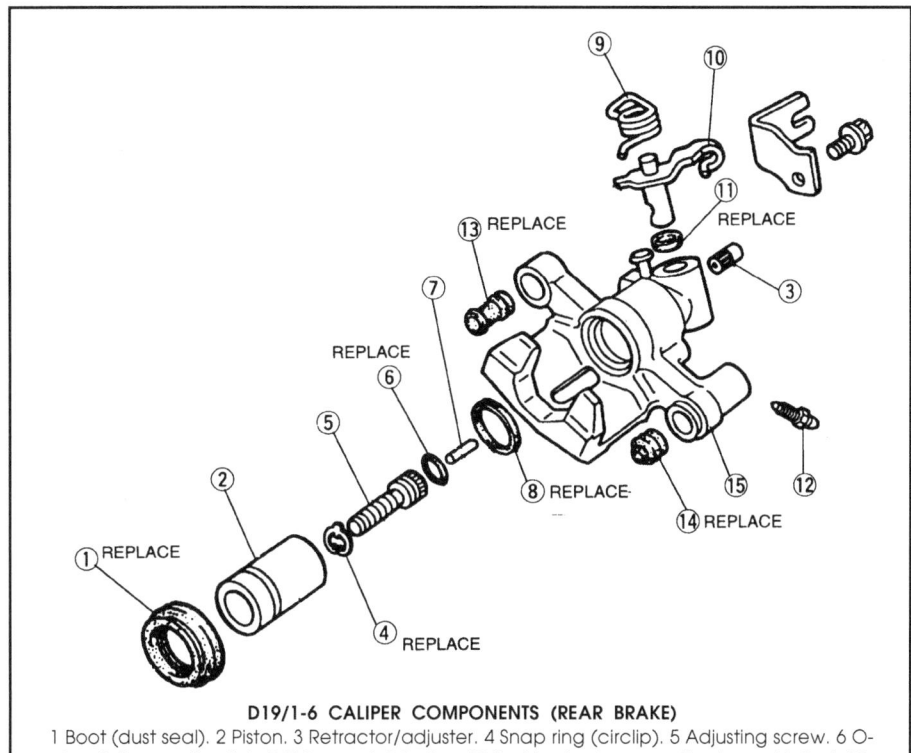

D19/1-6 CALIPER COMPONENTS (REAR BRAKE)
1 Boot (dust seal). 2 Piston. 3 Retractor/adjuster. 4 Snap ring (circlip). 5 Adjusting screw. 6 O-ring. 7 Connecting link. 8 Piston seal. 9 Spring. 10 Parking brake operating lever. 11 Seal. 12 Bleed screw & cap. 13 Boot. 14 Boot. 15 Caliper body.

19/4b At end of the bore is splined adjuster.

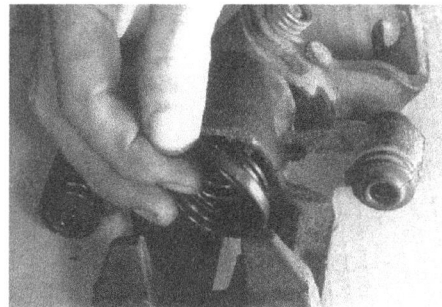

19/5a Fit new seal & dust cover ...

19/5b ... & slide piston into place ...

19. BRAKE CALIPER (REAR) - OVERHAUL

☞ 1/1, 2 & 9/1.

Warning! Brake friction materials may contain a proportion of asbestos, which is hazardous if inhaled as dust. When working on the brakes, wear protective clothing and a dust mask. Work in a well ventilated area. Never use compressed air to clean brake parts. Use a commercially available brake cleaner and paper wipes or rags during cleaning, and dispose of the rags or wipes safely after use - do not re-use them.

1   Start by removing the brake caliper ☞ 9/18. Clean off any road and brake dirt from the outside of the caliper using some methylated spirit or brake cleaner. Remove the 14mm plug bolt from the back of the caliper to gain access to the piston adjuster. Using a 6mm Allen wrench, turn the adjuster screw clockwise until it moves freely. When the piston is free of the adjuster it can be pulled out of the caliper.

2   Working over a drain tray, lift the edge of the dust boot and tip out the piston, allowing the fluid in the caliper to drain out. Wipe off any excess fluid, then carefully remove the piston seal, using a small screwdriver to work it out of its groove - take care not to scratch the caliper bore while doing this. Put the dust boot and seal to one side - they will be replaced by new parts during reassembly. Remove the bleed screw, then clean the screw, piston and caliper body in a dish of methylated spirit or brake cleaning fluid. Use compressed air to blow through the caliper passages and the bleed screw drillings.

3   When everything is clean, check the piston and bore surfaces for wear and/or corrosion. If the hydraulic system is kept well maintained, with regular fluid changes, the problem of internal corrosion is unlikely to occur. If neglected, however, the brake fluid will gradually absorb moisture from the air, and this will allow corrosion to take place. Dirt in the fluid will also cause wear problems. Once the caliper surfaces are damaged and fluid leakage has occurred, you have no choice but to fit a new caliper unit.

4   ◘+ Note that the automatic adjuster mechanism inside the piston is not repairable, and there is little to be gained by removing it, other than access for cleaning being a little easier. If you do remove it, make a careful note of the direction in which it was fitted, and install it in the same position. The adjuster thread can be seen inside the caliper bore - take care not to lose the small plastic adjuster pinion which can fall out of its hole in the caliper if the plug is left out.

5   ◘+ If the piston and bore are serviceable, fit a new piston seal into its groove in the caliper bore, lubricating it with fresh hydraulic fluid during

19/4a Auto adjuster fits inside piston.

installation. Lubricate the dust seal with hydraulic fluid and fit it into its groove in the caliper. Slide the piston into the caliper, working the dust seal lip over the piston.

6   ◘+ You'll need some sort of tool to help work the seal lip around the piston, and we used a modified paperclip to do this (see photo). Push the piston in until the adjuster screw contacts the mechanism, then use the Allen wrench to wind it fully back into the caliper (turn it counter-clockwise). Install the bleed screw loosely at this stage.

7   Install the caliper, setting the piston adjustment as described ☞ 9/18. Bleed the hydraulic

19/6a ... this 'special' tool helps to locate seal ...

9:15

Mazda Miata, MX-5, Eunos & Roadster

19/6b ... and is made from a paper clip!

system (☞ 9/2), then check that when the brake pedal is held down hard for a minute or so, there are no signs of leakage from the caliper you've worked on and its union.

20. PARKING BRAKE - CHECKING & ADJUSTMENT

☞ 1/1, 2 & 9/1.

1 If the parking brake is to work efficiently, it must be adjusted correctly. The adjustment can be checked and set as follows, having first adjusted the rear brake calipers ☞ 9/18.
Press the brake pedal several times and release it. Check that the parking brake stroke is between 7 and 9 notches when the lever is pulled up with a force of 196N/20kg/44lb. Use a spring scale to apply the prescribed force.

2 If adjustment is required, place blocks front and back of the front wheels, then jack the rear of the car and support it on jackstands (axlestands) positioned under the jacking points at the rear end of the rockers (sills) ☞ 1/3. You need to raise the rear of the car sufficiently to allow the rear wheels to rotate freely.

3 ◧+ Remove the plastic cover which is

20/3a Remove securing screw and ...

20/3b ... separate two parts of cover.

20/3c Adjuster is alongside lever base ...

20/3d ... turn with screwdriver or wrench.

fitted around the parking brake lever. This is secured by a single screw; once this is removed the two cover halves can be snapped apart and lifted away from the lever. Using a screwdriver or a socket, turn the hexagonal adjuster clockwise to reduce cable freeplay, setting the adjustment so that the brake is completely off when released, and on by the time the lever has been pulled up by the prescribed 7-9 notches.

4 Check by turning the rear wheels that the brakes do not drag when the parking brake is released. Don't confuse brake drag and transmission drag - remember that when you rotate the rear wheel you are also turning the driveshaft and differential, so some resistance is to be expected. If you find it impossible to eliminate brake drag, check that this is not due to incorrect adjustment of the caliper piston, or to a fault in the main brake system.

5 ◧ Once the parking brake has been adjusted, check that the switch, too, is correctly adjusted. With the ignition switch turned to **ON**, the warning light in the instrument panel should be off when the lever is released, and should come on after the lever is raised by one notch. If necessary,

20/5 Parking brake switch adjustment.

slacken the switch fixing screw and adjust the switch position until the switch operates as described.

6 Refit the handbrake covers. Lower the car to the ground (☞ 1/3).

21. PARKING BRAKE LEVER - REMOVAL, CHECKING & INSTALLATION

☞ 1/1, 2 & 9/1.

1 🛠 Work on level ground and place blocks

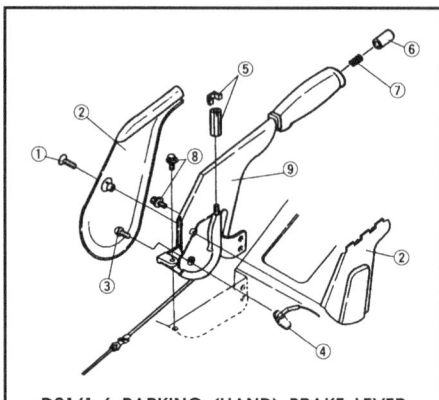

D21/1-6 PARKING (HAND) BRAKE LEVER COMPONENTS.
1 Cover screw. 2 Cover. 3 Bolt. 4 Parking brake switch. 5 Adjusting nut and locking clip. 6 Release button. 7 Spring. 8 Bolts. 9 Brake lever.

front and back of the front wheels, then release the parking brake. Remove the single crosshead screw which passes through the parking brake lever. This secures the two halves of the lever cover, passing through a boss formed inside the larger outer section. The boss in turn fits through a hole in the lever. With the screw removed, pull apart the cover halves, lifting clear the smaller section nearest the transmission tunnel, then disengaging the outer section from the lever and removing it.

2 Slide off the spring clip which 'locks' the cable adjuster, then unscrew and remove the adjuster from the cable end, working between the lever and the transmission tunnel. Disconnect the brake switch wiring connector. Remove the three 12mm bolts which secure the lever bracket to the transmission tunnel and lift it away.

3 Check the mechanism for visible signs of damage such as cracking - if found, fit a new lever assembly. Similarly, if the ratchet mechanism is worn and the brake cannot be operated reliably, install a replacement. A frayed cable will definitely require replacement.

4 Hold the lever assembly roughly in place and feed the cable around the cable quadrant. Secure the cable by turning the adjuster nut onto the cable end by a few turns. You may find it easier at this point to slide on the spring clip which 'locks' the adjuster nut.

5 Install the lever bracket on the transmission tunnel, tightening the mounting bolts to 19-26Nm/1.9-2.6kgf m/14-19lbf ft.

9: Brakes, hubs, wheels & tires

check the brake switch ☞ 9/20. Install the lever covers.

22. PARKING BRAKE CABLE - REMOVAL, CHECKING & INSTALLATION

☞ 1/1, 2 & 9/1.

1   Slacken the rear lugnuts (wheelnuts) by around one turn each. Jack the rear of the car and support it securely on jackstands (axlestands) positioned under the jacking points at the ends of the rockers (sills) ☞ 1/3. You need to raise the car sufficiently to allow working access to the underside of the central floorpan. Remove both rear wheels. Adjust brake caliper pistons ☞ 16/11 & 12.

CHECKING AND CABLE LUBING

2   If a cable is broken, or if there are fraying cable strands or corrosion visible, the faulty cable should be replaced. The compensator link between the front and rear cables should move freely. This component balances the pull from the lever equally between the two main cables, and if it's frozen (seized) by rust or dirt, braking will be out of balance. Inner cables must move freely and without binding in the outer cables.

3   Lubricate cables before re-installing them. Pull back the dust boots at the front end of the cables, and make up temporary funnels by cutting the corners from plastic bags. Push the cables through the bags and secure with electrical tape or a few twists of wire, then hang the cable with the funnel at the top. Pour a little gear oil into the funnel and leave the cable hanging until the oil oozes out the other end of the cable. Remove the funnel and fit the dust boot. As an alternative and faster method, you can use a proprietary cable oiler for this job - if you don't already have one, try your local motocross dealer - they're widely used in dirt bike circles. Coat the exposed section of the front cable with sticky waterproof grease, and similarly lubricate the compensator.

LEVER TO COMPENSATOR CABLE - REPLACEMENT

4   Release all tension from the handbrake cables by removing the adjuster nut at the parking brake lever ☞ 9/21.

5   If the cable between lever and compensator requires replacement, you'll need to remove the heatshield above the catalytic convertor (it's retained by four 10mm bolts) to gain access. (You may think removing the exhaust is worthwhile.)

6   Once the heatshield is out of the way, the clamp securing the cable to the body can be released and the cable seal levered out of the body. Unclip the tension spring from the compensator; the cable nipple can then be released from the compensator and the cable withdrawn.

7   Feed the adjuster end of the new cable into the body and then seat the lip of its seal securely in the floorpan. Secure the cable to the underside of the tunnel with its clamp. Engage the cable nipple with the compensator and install the compensator tension spring. Install the heatshield.

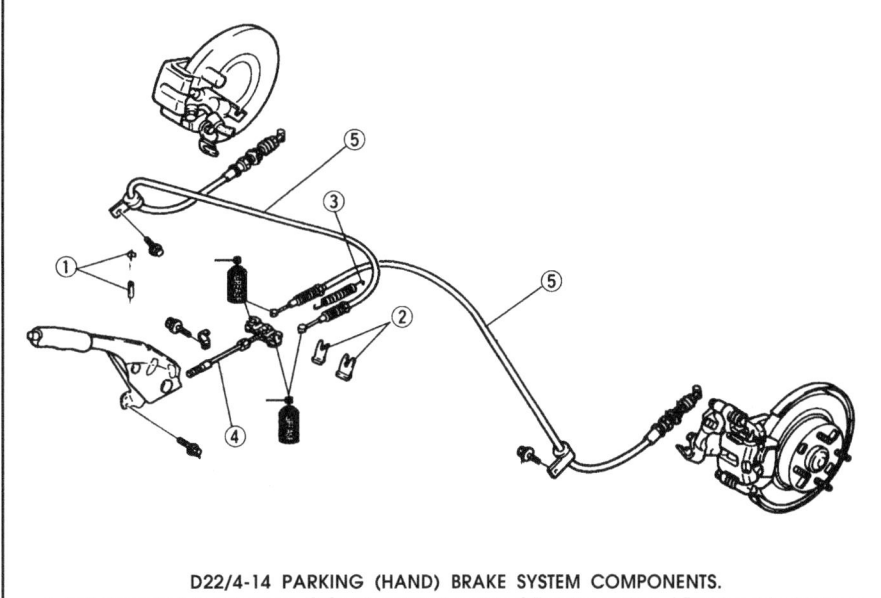

D22/4-14 PARKING (HAND) BRAKE SYSTEM COMPONENTS.
1 Adjuster nut & locking clip. 2 Cable retaining clips. 3 Tension spring. 4 Front cable (lever to compensator). 5 Rear cables (compensator to brake calipers).

8   If there are no more cables to be replaced, reconnect the cable to the handbrake and adjust tension ☞ 9/20 & 21.

COMPENSATOR TO BRAKE CABLES - REPLACEMENT

9   If not already done, release all tension from the handbrake cables by removing the adjuster nut at the parking brake lever ☞ 9/21.

10   At each rear wheel, slacken the 14mm locknuts which secure the cable outers to the caliper brackets. Disengage the cables from the bracket slots, then unhook the cable ends from the operating arms.

11   Release the cable brackets from the underbody.

12   Move to the compensator in the transmission tunnel and pull off the spring clip (see photo) which secures the outer cable to the stop plate. Disengage the cable end from the compensator link. The two main cables can now be threaded out from the underside of the car and removed.

13   When installing the new (or newly-lubed) cables, route them the same way as the originals were installed. Hook the front ends onto the compensator and install the spring clips which secure the cable outers. Secure the cable brackets to the underbody. Reconnect the cables at the brakes, setting the adjuster/locknuts so that the compensator lies at right angles to the front cable. The compensator will take care of small imbalances between the two rear cable adjustments, but it helps if the initial setting is correct. Check parking brake lever adjustment ☞ 9/20.

14   Reconnect the cable to the handbrake and adjust tension ☞ 9/20 & 21.

15   Refit the wheels and lower the car to the ground ☞ 1/3.

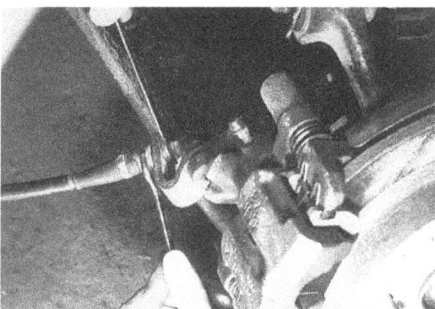
22/10 Free cable from brake caliper bracket.

22/11 Parking brake cable bracket.

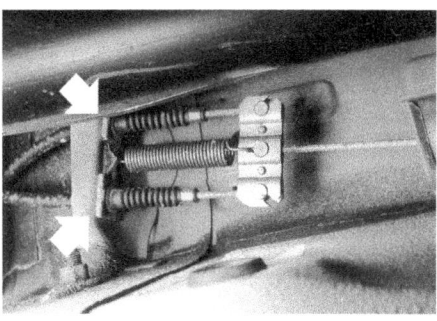
22/12 Cable clips (arrowed) near compensator.

Mazda Miata, MX-5, Eunos & Roadster

23. ABS (ANTI-LOCK BRAKE SYSTEM) - CHECKING

☞ 1/1, 2 & 9/1.

1　📷 The ABS system - fitted as standard on some models and optionally on others - consists of sensors at all four wheels which measure the speed of wheel rotation. The individual wheel sensors are monitored by the ABS control unit, housed next to the PCM (ECU) below a panel in the passenger's footwell or behind the driver's seat. If the system senses that one or more wheels are beginning to

23/1 ABS wheel speed sensor unit.

lock (skid) during braking, the control unit (working through the hydraulic unit mounted close to the firewall at the back of the engine compartment) momentarily reduces hydraulic pressure to the affected brake. This process is repeated as necessary, pulsing the brake on and off, and keeping the wheel turning, which stops a skid from developing. Here, it's important to understand that a locked wheel does not offer as much braking effect as a wheel which still has traction and, if it's a front wheel, all steering effect is lost. In the worst scenario, if all four wheels are locked, you're simply sliding along the road surface on four lifeless blocks of rubber, with no control whatsoever over your speed or direction of travel.

2　In use, the driver will not usually be aware of the system, which is completely automatic, until emergency braking is necessary. When the ABS system begins to operate, a slight pulsation will be felt through the brake pedal, accompanied by slight vibration through the steering wheel and car body. As the speed falls to around 4mph/6kph, you may be aware of the ABS pump motor running for a few seconds as the system self-diagnosis function operates. This is quite normal, and indicates that the system is functioning as intended. If these indicators are not present, and the car skids when braking, it is a reasonable assumption that all is not well with the ABS system.

3　The big problem from the enthusiast owner's perspective is that it's just about impossible to do anything to the ABS system without a lot of expensive equipment. Mazda produces a really neat ABS tester for dealer use. This connects to the ABS control unit, and, when activated, runs the diagnostic procedure, prompting the operator to perform the required tests and indicating, through its LCD panel, the next check in the sequence, with messages informing which component should be checked further. A superb piece of design, but you are helpless without it.

4　Work on the ABS system also requires a number of SSTs (special service tools) to allow the various system components to be removed and installed. We feel that the only realistic way to deal with the ABS system is to have a Mazda dealer carry out the work for you. **Warning!** Without the necessary equipment it would be dangerous to tamper with this system.

24. TIRES - CHECKING

☞ 1/1, 2 & 9/1.

One of the main reasons you bought Mazda's sportster was for its great handling, which is way above average: handling which is down to good design and the quality of the components used in the steering and suspension systems. Fitting tires of inferior quality or the wrong speed rating, or failing to replace tires which are damaged or excessively worn, will compromise the car's handling very significantly. Why reduce a thoroughbred to a carthorse just to save a little money?

1　The relatively small tire contact patches (each about the same area as the sole of a shoe) are the car's only contact with the road. Not only does the car rely *entirely* on these patches for its grip on the road surface, but *all* steering, braking and acceleration forces are also fed through the same patches. Given their importance, it follows that tires must be checked regularly. **Warning!** If you have reason to suspect possible tire damage caused by running over an object in the road, or accidentally curbing the wheels, make a point of checking tires and wheels as soon as possible.

2　Once each week, make a point of checking over each tire. Check the tire generally for wear, splits or other damage, and foreign objects, like stones or nails, embedded in the tire treads. Also check that the tire is correctly inflated. The tire condition and tread wear limit laws vary from one country to another, and you should be aware of and conform with local laws. **Warning!** Modern tires have minimum tread depth indicators built into the tread pattern, and when tire tread wears level with a depth indicator the tire should be replaced.

TREAD WEAR

3　🔲 While checking the tread, take note of how the tread is wearing - this can tell you a lot about potential tire, steering geometry and suspension problems. The accompanying diagram shows exaggerated examples of different types of tire wear.

4　In example (a) **SHOULDER WEAR**, typical effects of under-inflation are shown. If the air pressure in the tire is inadequate, the tread area in contact with the road will be concave in shape, and this type of damage will result. If the tire pressures are correct and have been maintained that way, the problem may just be down to over-enthusiastic cornering. Note also that failure to rotate the tires to even out wear may result in a tire wearing in this

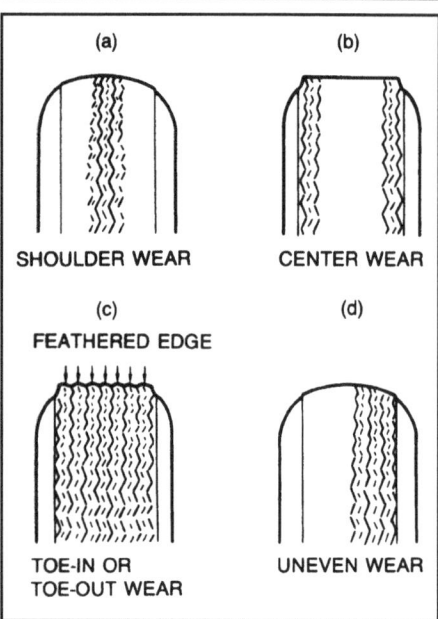

D24/3 EXAMPLES OF TIRE WEAR.

manner.

5　Example (b) **CENTER WEAR** shows the result of over-inflation of the tires. If the pressures are too high, the tread area in contact with the road is convex, and accelerated wear of the center of the tread will result. Again, failure to rotate the tires to even out wear may result in center wear problems.

6　In (c) **FEATHERED EDGE**, the edges of the tire tread blocks have become feathered in one direction. This is caused by the twisting action on the tread that takes place where the toe-in is set incorrectly. As the tread rolls against the road surface, one side is pulled harder against the surface and wears quickly. As the wheel turns further and the tread resumes its normal position, the opposite side is left higher than the worn side, giving the feathered appearance.

7　If, as in (d) **UNEVEN WEAR**, one side of the tread is worn down, you have a suspension geometry problem and should check camber, caster and toe-in, and for wear in ball joints and suspension bushes. If the unevenness shows up as excessive wear at one point on the tire's rotation, check for wheel imbalance or excessive runout on the brake disc. Bear in mind also that a really dramatic panic stop or skid (unless you have ABS) will literally wear miles off the tire at one point only.

TIRE DAMAGE

8　While checking for tread wear, look out for stones, nails or other items embedded in the tire. If found, pry out the object with an old screwdriver or similar tool. Modern tire construction methods give us tires which are pretty resistant to punctures, but if an object has penetrated the tire sufficiently for it to be punctured (you should hear leaking air hissing as the object is pulled out), mark the site of the puncture, then fit the spare and get the damaged tire repaired professionally, or replaced.

9　Examine the tire tread and both sidewalls

9: Brakes, hubs, wheels & tires

(don't forget the inner wall!) for splits, cuts or bulges. Splits or cuts are usually caused by running over road debris - steel strapping from packing cases is a common culprit. Bulges in either the tread or sidewall denote a structural failure of the tire casing, and in extreme cases you may find the casing plies, fine steel strands, sticking out of the tire. If you do find damage of this type, install the temporary spare and drive to a tire specialist to get a new tire fitted.

MATCHING TIRES

10 You'll always get the best and most consistent grip and handling from a matched set of tyres. If you have to replace a tire, always try to match it to the other tire on the same axle - even if it means waiting a couple of days for the supplier to order the required item. The problem of matching is not so critical axle to axle (i.e. one brand/type of tyre on the front axle and another brand/type on the rear axle), but if you do want the best from your car, all four tyres will be identical.

TIRE SIZE & RATINGS

11 On a standard international basis, tires are clearly and boldly marked with a sequence of numbers and letters which define their rim size, aspect ratio and speed rating, amongst other things. As standard, depending on model, these cars have come with 14 or 15 inch rims (6in and 5.5in rim widths, respectively), and with tires rated at **H** (up to 131mph) or (up to 150mph) speed rating, and aspect ratios of **195** or **185** (175 snow tires).

12 **Warning!** It is essential that replacement tires are of the same size and specification (or better) as those originally fitted. If you are in any doubt, consult the 'Owner's Manual' (handbook) that came with your car, or your Mazda dealer, to ascertain the correct tire specification for your model.

25. WHEEL CHANGING (WITH CAR'S TOOLKIT)

☞ 1/1, 2 & 9/1.

WHEEL REMOVAL AND INSTALLATION

1 ☐+ The usual reason for needing to remove and fit a tire is in the event of a flat (puncture). If you think that you may have a punctured tire, pull over as quickly as possible, and try to find a flat area off the road if you can. Inside the trunk (boot) you'll find the temporary spare wheel. Release the wing

25/1a Unscrew bolt & lift spare from trunk.

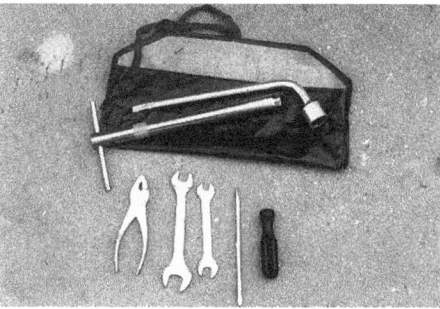

25/1b Typical standard toolkit.

25/1c Remove jack & brace from trunk.

bolt which retains it to the trunk floor, lift the wheel out and remove its cover. Lift the lid of the storage compartment at the left side of the trunk and take out the tool roll and the jack. The jack is retained by another wing bolt. Note the jack's position - it will only go in one way, and it's not too obvious which this is. The jack handle is clipped to the panel at the back of the trunk.

2 ☐ Try to find something to chock the front wheel on the side opposite the puncture, particularly if the car is on a sloping surface. Moving to the punctured tire, use the wrench to slacken

25/2 Use wrench & extension to loosen nuts.

each wheel nut by one turn: if necessary, you can use the tube wrench (box spanner) in the toolkit as an extension to the lugnut wrench to get better leverage.

3 ☐+ Position the jack under the jacking point nearest the punctured tire. The jacking points are reinforced areas at each end of the rockers (sills) - marked by two small cutouts in the base seam - and the jack has a slot in the lifting pad to fit over the reinforced seam. Raise the jack until the tire is clear of the ground, then remove the lugnuts and lift off the punctured wheel. Fit the temporary

25/3a Position jack between cutouts, then ...

25/3b ... raise until wheel clear of ground ...

25/3c ... remove lug nuts & lift off wheel ...

25/3d ... fit spare (see text).

spare wheel and tighten the wheel nuts to nip the wheel, then lower the car to the ground. Tighten the lugnuts as much as you can by *hand* pressure using the lugnut wrench from the toolkit. (As soon as you can, have the lugnut tightness checked: the correct torque is 89-117Nm/9-12kgf m/66-86lbf ft.)

4 ☐ **Warning!** The temporary spare wheel is just that - TEMPORARY, and is for emergency use only. Observe the speed restrictions marked on the spare wheel while it is in place, and get the punctured tire fixed as soon as you can.

Mazda Miata, MX-5, Eunos & Roadster

25/4 Spare in place - **Warning!** See text.

26. TIRES - ROTATION

☞ 1/1, 2 & 9/1.

1   At intervals specified in the maintenance schedule (☞ 2) the wheels should be rotated around the car to even out tire wear. Slacken all lugnuts by around one turn, then jack one side of the car and support it on jackstands (axlestands) positioned under the jacking points at the ends of the rocker (sill) ☞ 1/3. You need to raise the car sufficiently to allow both wheels on one side to be removed.

2   Remove the lugnuts completely. Remove and exchange the front and rear wheels on each side of the car and install the lugnuts. Lower the car to the ground (☞ 1/3) and tighten the lugnuts to 89-117Nm/9-12kgf m/66-86lbf ft.

3   Repeat the process on the other side of the car.

4   Check and adjust tire pressures.

27. TIRE PRESSURES - CHECKING & ADJUSTING

☞ 1/1, 2 & 9/1.

1   Tire pressures need to be maintained regularly, and should be checked when the tires are cold. It is preferable to check these at home, after the car has been standing for some hours. Not only will this mean that the tires are at the right temperature, but you'll also be using the same gauge for checking pressures each time - gas station gauges can vary in accuracy.

2   You can buy pocket pressure gauges at auto parts stores, and if you don't have compressed air in your home garage, you can use a footpump or a small electric compressor to inflate the tires.

3   The specified tire pressure (front and rear) for standard tires is 177kPa/1.8kgf cm2/26psi. The temporary spare tire should be inflated to 412kPa/4.2kgf cm2/60psi.

28. TIRE FITTING & WHEEL BALANCING

☞ 1/1, 2 & 9/1.

TIRE REMOVAL AND FITTING AND TIRE REPAIRS

1   There is no good reason to attempt tire replacement at home - without the right facilities you'll probably damage the wheel rim and it's unlikely that you will get the tire seated correctly.

2   Tire replacement should always be done by a tire specialist using professional tire changing equipment. Always have a new valve installed at the same time. The wheel should be balanced after the new tire has been installed.

3   If you need to get a punctured tire repaired, use a reputable tire specialist. Such a business will be able to advise whether a repair is possible (or legal) in your area, and will be able to fit a new tire if repair is out of the question.

WHEEL BALANCE

4   It is important that the wheels are accurately balanced each time a tire is fitted - any good tire specialist will do this automatically, or at least ask if you require the wheel to be balanced. You should also get wheel balance checked if you notice vibration or shimmying while driving the car. Sudden imbalance may occur after impact damage to the wheel, or if a balance weight has come loose and flown off. The maximum allowable imbalance at the rim edge is 10g/0.35oz.

5   Note that there should be no more than two balance weights fitted to the inner or outer rims of the wheel, and that the combined weight of any balance weights fitted must not exceed 100g/3.5oz. If the wheel won't balance within these limits, the tire should be removed and repositioned on the rim; all wheels and tires have heavy spots, and if the two coincide, the imbalance may be too great to counter with balance weights. Except for models with pressed steel wheels, the weights used must be of the type designed for use on aluminum rims, or the wheel may be damaged when they're fitted. The weights must not protrude more than 3mm/0.12 from the rim edge.

29. WHEELS - CHECKING & MAINTENANCE

☞ 1/1, 2 & 9/1.

1   **Warning!** Accident damage should always be checked professionally - impact with rocks or other debris may damage the wheel, but the true extent of the damage may not be obvious through visual examination. Consult your Mazda dealer, or a wheel and tire specialist for advice. Curbing the wheels can cause damage and distortion. If suspected, jack the car and support it on safety stands (☞ 1/3) so that the wheels can be spun, then check runout at the wheel rim using a dial gauge. If this exceeds 2.0mm/0.079in radially, or 1.5mm/0.059in laterally, the wheel should be replaced.

2   Standard aluminum wheels are tough, but require a degree of care if they are to be kept in good condition. Remove road dirt by washing with warm (not boiling) water. **Caution!** Do not steam clean alloy wheels. Salt, in particular, is bad for aluminum wheels so, if they come into contact with salt water or road salt from winter roads, wash this off as soon as you can to prevent corrosion. Your local auto store (accessory shop) will have a range of products designed for cleaning and maintaining alloy wheels.

3   Standard pressed steel wheels may occasionally require scratches to be painted over to prevent corrosion. If you wish to repaint the wheels completely, your local auto store will stock a range of specialty paints.

30. WHEEL HUBS & BEARINGS - CHECKING & OVERHAUL

☞ 1/1, 2 & 9/1.

FRONT HUB - CHECKING

1   Position the car on a smooth, level surface and apply the parking brake. Place chocks front and back of the rear tires. Loosen the front wheel lugnuts (wheelnuts) by around one turn. Raise the front of the car with a jack positioned at the center of the front crossmember and position jackstands (axlestands) under the jacking points at the front of each rocker (sill) ☞ 1/3. Unscrew the lugnuts and remove the wheel.

2   Remove the brake caliper (☞ 9/13), leaving it connected to the hydraulic hose, and tie it clear of the hub. Be careful not to press the brake pedal while the caliper is removed - it's a good idea to push a wooden wedge into the caliper jaw to prevent the piston moving in this eventuality. Lift away the brake disk.

3   📷 Assemble a dial gauge, using a clamp or magnetic base to mount it on the pressed steel dust cover. Position the gauge pointer so that it just touches the hub surface, and zero the gauge.

4   Move the hub laterally by hand and note the wheel bearing play indicated. If this exceeds the maximum allowable play of 0.05mm/0.002in, action is required. Start by checking and re-torquing the hub nut: it will help to fit the wheel/s and

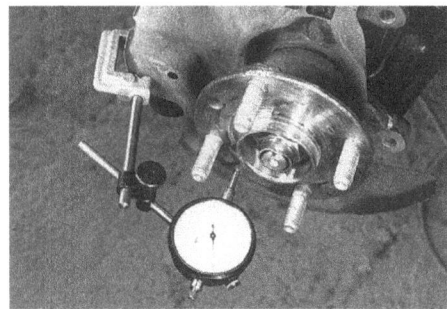

30/3 Testing wheel bearing lash/freeplay.

lower the car to the ground (☞ 1/3) to do this. If the play is still outside specification, you'll have to fit a new hub unit.

FRONT HUB - REMOVAL AND INSTALLATION

5   📷 Position the vehicle on a smooth, level surface and apply the parking brake. Place chocks front and back of the rear tires. Remove the central wheel trim (where fitted), and pry out the metal dust cap which covers the hub nut (with some wheel types, the wheel will have to be removed for access and then refitted). On our project car, the

9:20

9: Brakes, hubs, wheels & tires

30/5 Remove the hub dust cap.

30/10 Withdraw the hub from the stub axle.

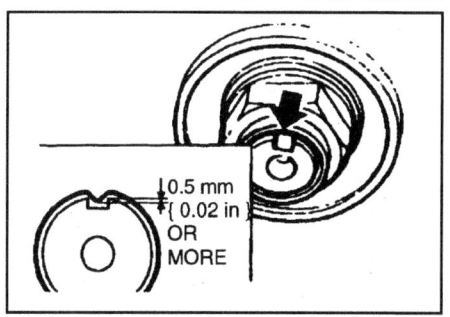

D30/13 STAKE HUB NUT AS SHOWN HERE.

dust cap proved to be surprisingly tight. In the end we used an old wood chisel to remove it - the thin blade was able to work behind the cap flange and allowed us to lever it off - you may need to remove the road wheel to improve access.

6   With the cap out of the way, you can set about slackening the hub nut. This is staked into a groove in the stub axle, and you need to straighten out the staked area so that the nut can be turned. We found that a square-section drift could be used to do this. Be absolutely certain that you relieve the staking fully - you don't want any extra resistance

completely and slide the hub unit off the stub axle. Note that it is not possible to dismantle the hub further - if the bearings are worn, you'll have to buy a new hub unit. On cars equipped with ABS, there is a slotted rotor fitted to the back of the hub. Do not attempt removal of this without good reason - the rotor cannot be re-used if removed. If a new rotor needs to be fitted, note that an SST (special service tool) and a press are needed - have the job carried out by a Mazda dealer.

11   Note also that once the hub has been removed, it is possible to detach the brake disc dust

30/13a Stake the hub nut and ...

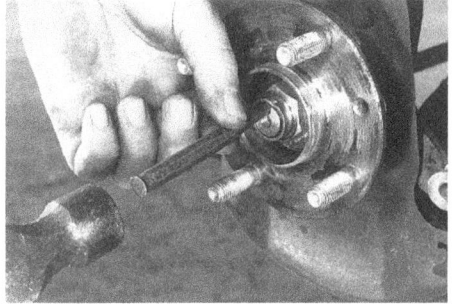

30/6 Use narrow chisel to release staking.

30/11 Backplate is secured by three bolts.

30/13b ... tap the dust cap into place.

when removing the nut.

7   The hub nut will be extremely tight - it is torqued to 167-215Nm/17-22kgf m/123-159lbf ft during assembly. You will need a 29mm socket to fit the nut. This is an unusual size and unlikely to be found in most socket sets - we used a 1 1/8in AF socket which fitted fine.

8   Because the nut is so tight, we found that normal 1/2in drive socket accessories were of little use - our 1/2in drive T-bar simply bent when we tried to shift the nut. We eventually resorted to 3/4in drive equipment, and slid a length of tubing over the T-bar to get extra leverage. This also explains why we are describing the slackening procedure with the road wheel still on the car and firmly on the ground - you need to keep everything as rigid as possible so you can apply sufficient pressure to the nut. Slacken the hub nut by about one turn only at this stage, then loosen the lugnuts by around one turn each.

9   Raise the front of the car with a jack positioned at the center of the front crossmember, and position jackstands (axlestands) under the jacking points at the front of each rocker (sill) ☞ 1/3. Unscrew the lugnuts and remove the wheel.

10   You can now remove the hub nut

cover. This is retained on the steering knuckle by three bolts - if you have reason to remove it, note that the bolts should be tightened to 16-22Nm/1.6-2.3kgf m/12-16lbf ft during installation. We would recommend the use of thread locking compound on these bolts.

12   During installation, fit the hub unit over the stub axle, then secure it using a **new** locknut. Install the brake disc. Install the brake pads and caliper ☞ 9/13. Tighten the hub nut to 167-215Nm/17-22kgf m/123-159lbf ft. Note that it is important to torque this nut to the recommended pressure because it pre-loads the wheel bearings

30/12 Torque tighten the hub nut: phew!

correctly. If necessary, borrow or hire a torque wrench capable of reaching these pressures - many home-use wrenches won't reach the prescribed figure. It will help to fit the wheel and lower the car to the ground ☞ 1/3.

13   Finally, stake the collar section of the hub nut into the stub axle groove, making sure that the staking lies at least 0.5mm/0.02in into the groove. Fit the dust cap, tapping it home with a hide or rubber-faced hammer. Lower the car to the ground (☞ 1/3) and tighten the lugnuts.

REAR HUB - CHECKING

14   Position the vehicle on a smooth, level surface and temporarily apply the parking brake. Place chocks front and back of the front tires, then release the parking brake. Loosen the rear wheel lugnuts by one turn. Raise the back of the car with a jack positioned at the center of the differential casing and position jackstands (axlestands) under the jacking points at the end of each rocker (sill) ☞ 1/3. Unscrew the lugnuts and remove the wheels.

15   Remove the brake caliper (☞ 9/18), leaving it connected to the hydraulic hose, and tie it clear of the hub - the caliper mounting can be left attached to the suspension upright. You may find

Mazda Miata, MX-5, Eunos & Roadster

it difficult to tie the caliper clear with the parking brake cable attached. If so, you can disconnect the cable ☞ 9/22. Be careful not to press the brake pedal while the caliper is removed - it's a good idea to push a wooden wedge into the caliper jaw to prevent the piston moving in this eventuality. Lift away the brake disc.

16 Assemble a dial gauge, using a clamp or magnetic base to mount it on the pressed steel dust cover. Position the gauge pointer so that it just touches the hub surface, and zero the gauge.

17 Move the hub laterally by hand and note the wheel bearing play indicated. If this exceeds the maximum allowable play of 0.05mm/0.002in, action is required. Start by checking and re-torqueing the hub nut: fitting the wheel and lowering the car to the ground will help ☞ 1/3. If the play is still outside specification, you'll have to fit a new hub bearing.

REAR HUB - REMOVAL

18 Position the vehicle on a smooth, level surface and apply the parking brake. Place chocks front and back of the front tires. If applicable, remove the central cover of the rear wheel, then slacken the rear hub nut (with some models the wheel will have to be removed for access). The nut, which secures the outer end of the driveshaft, is staked into a groove in the driveshaft end, and you need to straighten out the staking so that the nut can be unscrewed. We found that a square-section drift could be used to do this. Be absolutely certain that you relieve the staking fully - you don't want extra resistance when removing the nut.

19 The hub nut will be found to be extremely tight - it is torqued to 216-294Nm/22-30kgf m/160-216lbf ft during assembly. You'll need a 29mm socket to fit the nut. This is an unusual size, and unlikely to be found in most socket sets - we used a 1 1/8in AF socket which fitted fine.

20 Because the nut is so tight, we found that normal 1/2in drive socket accessories were of little use - our 1/2in drive T-bar simply bent when we tried to shift the nut. We eventually resorted to 3/4in drive equipment, and slid a length of tubing over the T-bar to get extra leverage. This also explains why we are describing the slackening procedure with the road wheel still on the car and firmly on the ground - you need to keep everything as rigid as possible so you can apply sufficient pressure to the nut to shift it. If acess to the nut is impossible with the wheel in place, have someone operate the footbrake while the parking brake is also applied. Slacken the nut by about one turn only at this stage, then loosen the wheel nuts by one turn each.

21 Raise the rear of the car with a jack positioned under the differential housing, and position jackstands (axlestands) under the jacking points at the rear of each rocker (sill) ☞ 1/3. Unscrew the lugnuts and remove the wheel.

22 📷 Detach the brake caliper from the suspension upright (☞ 9/18), leaving it connected to the brake hose. The caliper should be tied back with a length of wire or string so that it is clear of the working area and no strain is placed on the hose. You'll find that the parking brake cable makes this

30/22 Tie caliper out of harm's way.

30/23 Remove upper pivot bolt.

difficult, and, if necessary, you should disconnect the cable ☞ 9/22.

23 📷 Position the car's own jack under the lower wishbone, using wood blocks under the jack as required. Raise the jack so that it is just contacting the underside of the wishbone. Slacken and remove the upper wishbone to suspension upright 14mm mounting bolt. If the bolt won't slide out easily, raise the jack slightly to release any pressure from the suspension.

24 📷 Remove the hub nut from the end of the driveshaft, then pivot the suspension upright

30/24 Pull hub & backplate off driveshaft.

downwards to allow the driveshaft end to be disengaged. The driveshaft splines can be a tight fit in the hub. To free the splines, fit the hub nut so that it lies flush with the shaft end, then drive the shaft through using a hammer and a drift as you pull the hub toward yourself. Take care to avoid damaging the driveshaft end. On cars fitted with ABS, take care not to damage the ABS rotor which is fitted on the driveshaft outer joint.

25 Next, you need to remove the lower wishbone to suspension upright 17mm pivot bolt. We ran into problems here, and it seems highly likely

that you will encounter the same difficulty on your car. The pivot bore in the suspension upright is partially open at the inner edge, and this means that part of the bolt shank is exposed to all of the road dirt thrown up by the wheels. This, in turn, causes the bolt shank to corrode quite badly, which makes removal of the bolt difficult - the corroded center section will not pass through the suspension upright.

26 Try to remove as much of the corrosion as you can before trying to get the bolt out, and soak it in penetrating fluid. The only thing you can then do is try to drive the bolt out without damaging the thread. Run the nut onto the thread so that it lies flush with the bolt end, then use a brass drift or a hide or rubber-faced hammer to drive it out. The presence of the nut will help stop the threaded end from getting damaged. Once the nut contacts the wishbone, you'll have to remove it and use a brass drift to knock the bolt the rest of the way through the wishbone. Once the bolt has been removed, the suspension upright and hub can be removed to the workbench for further dismantling.

REAR HUB - OVERHAUL

27 Once the suspension upright and hub assembly have been removed from the car, you will need to make a decision about how to proceed from here. To dismantle the assembly further, Mazda recommends a range of SSTs and a press, and you may decide that it is more effective to take the assembly to a Mazda dealer for the new bearing and seal to be fitted. We found that we could just about get by using a selection of sockets in place of the SSTs to drive out the various components.

28 📷 From the back of the upright, pry out and discard the seal - you'll have to fit a new one during installation. Using a suitable socket as a drift, tap out the hub from the upright. You will probably

30/28 Pull the hub from the race.

find that the bearing inner race remains on the hub shaft. To get this off you'll need a suitable bearing puller - you may be able to hire this from a tool hire company. If necessary, start the race moving on the hub using a chisel, then assemble the puller and draw it off.

29 📷 Remove the large snap ring (circlip) which retains the bearing in the suspension upright. Support the upright on wood blocks with the brake disc dust cover downwards - check that the upright is supported by its central boss, not on the dust cover. Using a large socket as a drift, drive out the

9: Brakes, hubs, wheels & tires

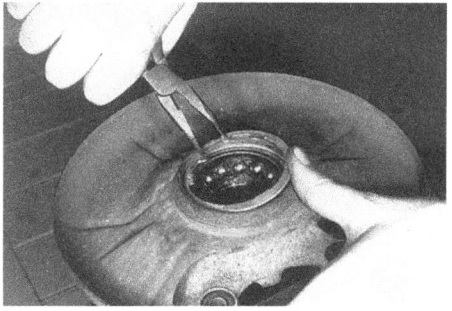

30/29 Remove the large snap ring/circlip.

9/32 Tap the hub into position.

bearing from its bore in the upright. Clean the upright assembly to remove all traces of dirt and grease.

30   The dust cover must not be removed unless it is essential - note that it cannot be re-used once removed. If you need to replace the dust cover, first mark its position in relation to the upright with a paint mark, and make a similar mark in exactly the same position on the new dust cover. Tap off the old cover, then fit the new one, using a section of tubing to drift it into position. Make sure that you align the position marks correctly.

31   Install the new bearing in the upright, using

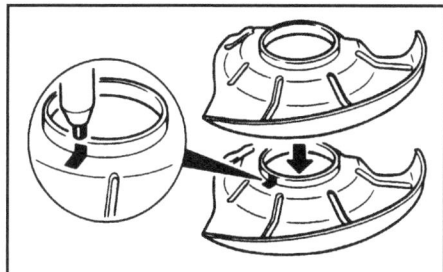

D30/30 MARK THE NEW DUST COVER IN EXACTLY THE SAME PLACE AS THE OLD.

a large socket or tube to drive it into position. It is preferable to press the bearing home if you can - if you have a large vise, use this to wind the bearing into place, taking care to ensure that it enters its bore squarely.

32   Secure the bearing using a new snap ring, then tap the hub into position through the bearing. Carefully tap the new grease seal into its recess at the back of the upright.

REAR HUB - INSTALLATION

33   Before starting installation, spend some time cleaning up the lower wishbone to suspension upright pivot bolt, or fit a new one. If you plan to re-use the old one, clean off any remaining corrosion (don't overdo it) with abrasive paper, and check that it slides through the wishbone and upright bores easily.

34   Grease the lower wishbone to suspension upright pivot bolt, and slide it through the wishbone and upright, fitting the nut finger-tight. We packed the open area of the upright with the thickest, stickiest grease we could find, in the hope that this will prevent further corrosion problems - we suggest you do likewise.

35   Pivot the upright upwards, feeding the driveshaft through the hub as you do so. Fit a new hub nut loosely. Install the upper wishbone to upright pivot bolt and nut, noting that if you have difficulty positioning the wishbone while fitting the suspension unit or pivot bolts, the small scissor jack supplied with the car's toolkit can be used to raise the assembly as required.

36   Tighten the lower wishbone to suspension upright pivot bolt nut to 63-74Nm/6.4-7.6kgf m/47-54lbf ft, and the upper wishbone to suspension upright pivot bolt nut to 47-66Nm/4.7-6.8kgf m/34-49lbf ft.

37   Install the disc and brake caliper (9/18) and, if it was removed, reconnect the parking brake cable 9/22. Fit the road wheel (unless you know the hub nut cannot be accessed with the wheel in place), and lower the car to the ground (1/3), then tighten the lugnuts to 89-117Nm/9.0-12.0kgf m/66-86lbf ft.

38   You now need to torque the hub nut to 216-294Nm/22-30kgf m/160-216lbf ft. Using the socket and accessories used during removal, plus a suitable torque wrench, tighten the nut to the prescribed figure. You may need to borrow or hire a truck-type torque wrench for this - most automotive wrenches do not reach the required pressures. It is important that you torque the nut correctly because this applies the correct bearing pre-load.

39   Once the hub nut is secure, stake the collar into the groove on the driveshaft end using a punch or chisel. The staking should lie at least 0.5mm/0.02in below the shaft diameter (see diagram D30/13). Fit the dust cover.

40   If not already done, fit the road wheels, lower the car to the ground and torque the lugnuts to 89-117Nm/9.0-12.0kgf m/66-86lbf ft.

31. WHEEL STUDS - REMOVAL & INSTALLATION

 1/1, 2 & 9/1.

1   The wheel studs are fitted from the back of the front or rear hub. Removal and installation will require removal of the relevant hub 9/30.

2   The studs are pressed into position in the hub, and should not be removed without good cause - once removed, the studs cannot be re-used.

3   The usual reason for removal is in the event of breakage or thread damage. This sort of damage can be due to over-tightening of the lugnuts (wheelnuts), but is more commonly the result of trying to remove the lugnuts after the stud threads have corroded through neglect.

4   You'll need a press to remove the old or broken stud, and the new stud must also be pressed into position. Unless you have access to a suitable press, you may prefer to entrust this operation to a Mazda dealer or engineering shop.

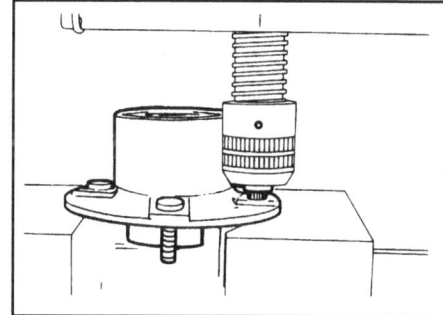

D31/4 PRESS NEW BOLTS INTO HUB FLANGE.

Veloce *SpeedPro* books –

 978-1-903706-59-6
 978-1-903706-75-6
 978-1-903706-76-3
 978-1-903706-99-2
 978-1-845840-21-1
 978-1-787111-68-4

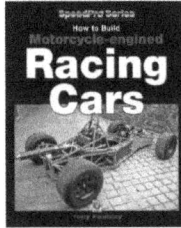 978-1-787111-69-1
 978-1-787111-73-8
 978-1-845841-87-4
 978-1-845842-07-9
 978-1-845842-08-6
 978-1-845842-62-8

 978-1-845842-89-5
 978-1-845842-97-0
 978-1-845843-15-1
 978-1-845843-55-7
 978-1-845844-33-2
 978-1-845844-38-7

 978-1-845844-83-7
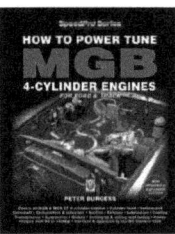 978-1-845846-15-2
 978-1-845848-33-0
 978-1-787111-76-9
 978-1-845848-69-9
 978-1-845849-60-3

 978-1-845840-19-8
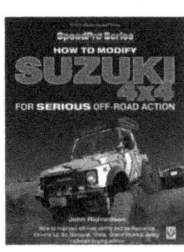 978-1-787110-92-2
 978-1-787110-47-2
 978-1-903706-94-7
 978-1-787110-87-8
 978-1-787110-90-8

 978-1-787110-01-4
 978-1-901295-26-9
 978-1-845841-62-1
 978-1-787110-91-5
 978-1-787110-88-5
 978-1-903706-78-7

10

Interior

1. INTRODUCTION

This chapter relates to the interior details of the car, mainly within the passenger compartment area. It covers most aspects of the interior, but we found that we ran into a problem when it came to the soft top. Is this part of the interior or the body of the car? Eventually, we decided that it, and the hard top, should be covered in chapter 11.

Having made that decision, you may be surprised that we've dealt with the door internal components in this chapter. We figured that, since the door trim was definitely part of the interior, we may as well go on to cover items like the door window and catch assemblies. 'External' aspects of the door will be found in chapter 11.

2. CONSOLE, REAR (BETWEEN SEATS) - REMOVAL & INSTALLATION

☞ 1/1, 2.

REMOVAL
1   Disconnect the battery ☞ 7/2.
2   ◘ Drop the car's soft top to make working inside easier. Start by lifting the ashtray out of its recess in the rear console between the seats.
3   ◘ Manual transmission only. Unscrew the shift lever knob; it can be quite tight.
4   ◘+ Unscrew and remove the crosshead (Philips) screws which secure the rear console: there are two in the storage compartment, one in the space beneath the ashtray and one each side at the front end. Lift the front of the console and pull it forward until it clears the trunk (boot) and fuel filler cap release levers, but note that it's still connected to several wires.
5   ◘+ Disconnect the two white connector blocks which connect the wiring for the ashtray

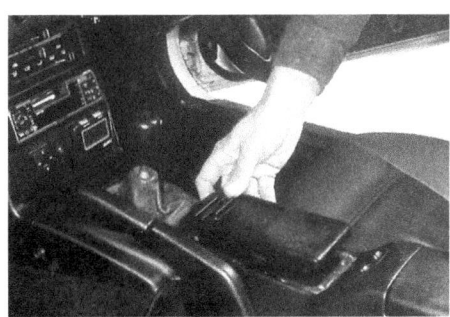
2/2 Lift out ashtray

2/3 Unscrew shiftlever knob, then remove ...

2/4a ... this and two rear compartment screws ...

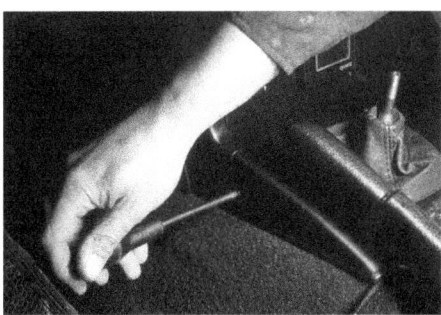
2/4b ... plus a screw at each side.

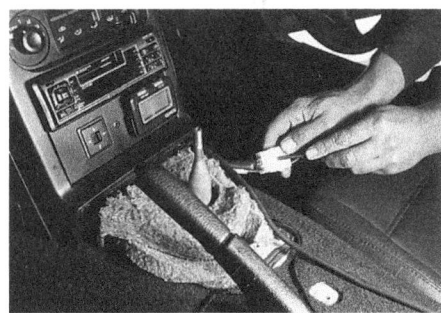
2/5a Release electrical connections ...

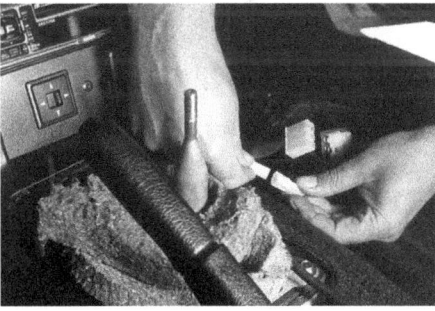
2/5b ... there may be several.

2/6 Two screws secure lock.

Mazda Miata, MX-5, Eunos & Roadster

light and the power windows (if applicable). Both connectors have tabs which need to be pushed down to release them. Remove the console.

6   From the underside of the console you also have access to the storage compartment lock mechanism. This is retained to the underside of the console by two crosshead screws.

INSTALLATION

7   When installing the rear console, remember to reconnect the ashtray light wire and, where fitted, the electric window lifter switch connector. Position the back of the console carefully, ensuring that the fuel filler and trunk release levers pass through the cutouts at the rear. Lower the console over the gearshift lever, guiding the lever through the boot in the case of manual transmission cars.

8   Secure the rear console with the two front screws, the single screw in the ashtray recess, and the two screws through the base of the storage box. Fit the ashtray, and, on manual transmission cars, screw the gearshift knob onto the shift lever.

9   Reconnect the battery ☞ 7/2.

3. DASH CENTER PANEL - REMOVAL & INSTALLATION

☞ 1/1, 2.

1   Before the dash center panel can be removed you will first have to remove the rear console (between seats) ☞ 10/2.

2   Remove the two screws securing the glovebox hinges to the hinge bar and lift the glovebox away. On the driver's side of the car,

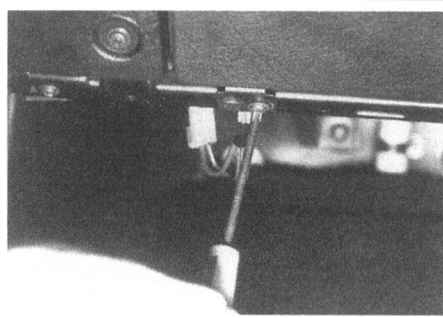

3/2 Remove screws securing hinges.

remove (where fitted) the two screws securing the access panel below the steering column, then unclip and remove the panel. Note that two types of access panel are used (see diagram) - non-US cars have the same type as fitted to Canadian market cars.

3   + Working through the apertures on each side of the dash panel, trace and disconnect the heater control cables. One of the three connects to the blower unit located immediately behind the glovebox, the remaining two connect at each side of the heater control unit which is mounted behind

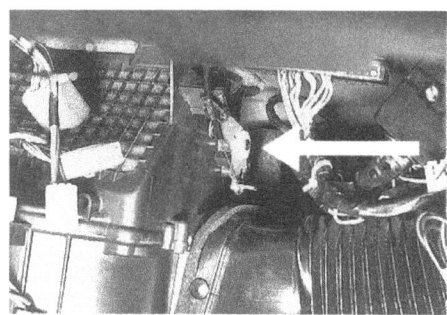

3/3a Blower unit cable connection.

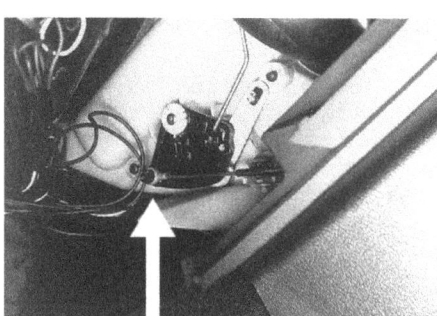

3/3b Heater unit cable connection.

the dash center panel. Unclip each cable outer from its support, and unhook the outer from the operating lever end.

4   To get access to the centre panel fixing screws you need to remove the two eyeball vents (louvers) at the top of the unit. This is no easy task - the vents are secured by two spring clips from the back, and there is no means of external access to them.

5   We suggest that, before starting this operation, you look at the photograph we took of the back of the vent so you can see what you are

3/5 Detail of eyeball vent securing clip.

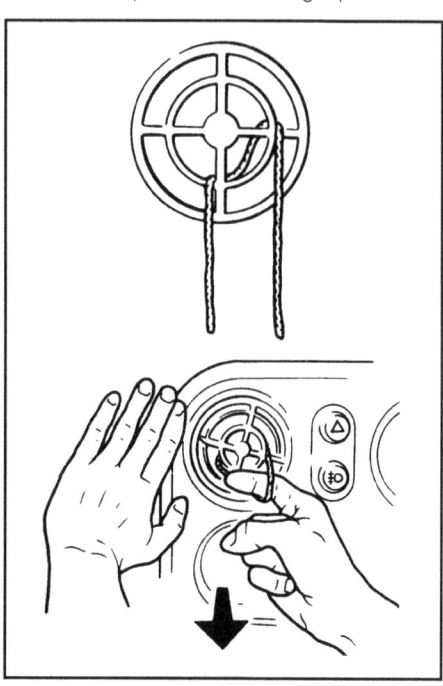

D3/7 THE BEST EYEBALL VENT REMOVAL METHOD.

dealing with. There are two small metal clips, one each side of each vent. Note that you cannot reach the clips to release them while the center panel is in position (and you can't remove the center panel until you've removed the vents ...).

6   When you attempt removal you will probably think, as we did, that the vent will not come out in one piece. You certainly have to apply an undesirable amount of force, and, unless you have much lighter clips than the ones we found on our car, both the panel and the vent assembly will distort (temporarily) quite badly during the removal operation.

7   The best method of removing the vents is pulling them out with a length of cord (see diagram). Feed the cord in through one of the vent slots, then use a piece of wire to hook the end of the cord and pull it back through. Tie the ends of the cord together to form a loop. Once the cord is in place, support the center panel with one hand and pull hard on the cord to pop the vent out of the panel.

8   With the vents removed, remove the two sheet metal screws which pass upwards through the vent recesses to secure the top of the center

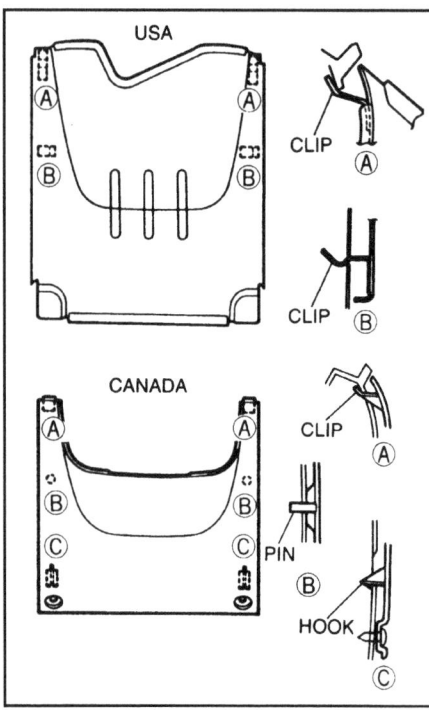

D3/2 STEERING COLUMN ACCESS PANEL FITTING DETAIL.

Note that the majority of non-US cars have the same fixings as Canadian cars.

10: Interior

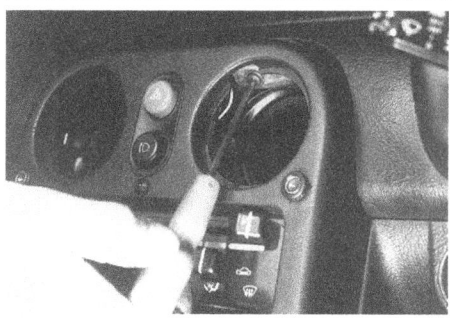

3/8 Remove screw at top of each vent.

panel to the main dash panel assembly.

9 ☐+ At the bottom, there are two further screws securing the panel to a metal support bracket fixed to the transmission tunnel - these should also be removed, leaving the metal bracket in place. The panel can now be pulled away slightly. **Caution!** There will be further wiring to disconnect before it can be removed completely.

10 The wiring connections behind the center panel vary according to the country in which the car was sold, and on what combination of manufacturer's options, and/or aftermarket items

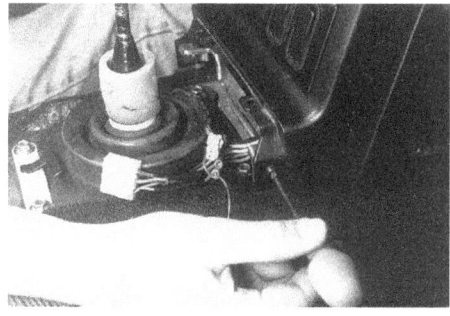

3/9a Remove two screws at unit base ...

3/9b ... and ease console away.

are fitted. The top of the panel carries the eyeball vents and, between them, the switches for the hazard lights and the headlight lifter. Our project car had aftermarket alarm sensors fitted on this part of the panel.

11 The heater control assembly comes next, but, below that, a number of options may be fitted. Our project car had a removable audio unit fitted, and below this was a panel carrying an analog clock and two accessory switch blanks - other options include various audio system types, with or without CD players. The arrangement you find on your car

may differ from ours, and the audio unit may need to be removed before or after the center panel is released, depending on the type of installation. Some audio units are removable for security purposes, in which case the main unit should be unplugged and the wiring connections to the mounting bracket dealt with as the panel is detached.

12 Our best advice here is to move the center panel away from the dashboard carefully, check the wiring connections on the back and disconnect them, noting the position and type of each connector. We suggest that you use colored electrical tape or a permanent marker pen to code the wiring connector halves as they are separated; this will make installation quick and foolproof.

13 Once the center panel wiring has been disconnected, pull the panel gently toward you, feeding the heater control cables through from the access panel and glovebox apertures. Again, depending on accessory items fitted, there may be ground tag connections to be released - our car had two attached to one of the bottom bracket screws. Once all wiring has been freed, the panel can be removed.

14 Finally, whatever else you do while the unit is out, we recommend that you check all the bulbs and replace any that are burned out or beginning to blacken.

INSTALLATION

15 When installing the center panel, position it in front of its mounting point on the dash panel, connecting the wiring connectors and feeding the heater control cables into position. The cables cannot easily be connected incorrectly; the longest cable runs to the blower unit (recirculated/fresh air control), while the remaining two have different ends and fit either side of the heater unit.

16 Before you connect the cables, you should set up the control sliders as follows: set the top slider (temperature blend control) to the maximum heat position (fully to the right); the center slider (recirculated or fresh air control) should be set fully to the right; set the bottom slider (airflow mode control) fully to the left. After reconnecting the cables, check that the control sliders move smoothly and fully through their complete range.

17 You can now install the centre panel, remembering to reconnect the wiring to the audio unit (don't forget the antenna cable), the clock (where fitted), the hazard light/headlight lifter switches, and any other accessories installed in the panel. Make sure that you route the wiring correctly, and that it does not become trapped as the panel is fitted.

18 Before finally securing the panel, check the operation of all electrical switches and accessories: only when you are sure that these are operating correctly should you fit the two retaining screws through the eyeball sockets, and the two lower screws securing the panel to the transmission tunnel bracket. Don't forget to reconnect any ground wires that were disconnected.

19 Before installing the eyeball vents, we suggest spraying a little WD40, or a similar, silicone-based lubricant, on the outer surface of the vent body - this might help a little if the vents need to be removed at a later date. Pop the vents back into their sockets (note how easily they install - you might assume that they are not fitted correctly, but just try pulling them out again!). Install the steering column access panel and the glovebox.

20 Install the rear console ☞ 10/2.

4. DASH PANEL - REMOVAL, CHECKING & INSTALLATION

☞ 1/1, 2. Airbag equipped cars ☞ 7/44.

REMOVAL

General note - Removal of the dash panel is a complex operation, and you should allow plenty of time to complete it - remember that the car will be out of action until it is reinstalled and everything is working correctly again. We spent nearly six hours working on ours, though we were photographing the process, and we spent a lot of time working out the best method of doing things. We would estimate that you should allow around three hours. You should carry out the work under cover, so that you can drop the soft top or remove the hard top for better access. You might also consider removing the seats. The accompanying diagram (D4/1-37) gives an overview of dash panel removal and installation.

1 **Warning!** If your car is fitted with an airbag or airbags, disarm the airbag system ☞ 7/44.

2 Remove the rear (between seats) console and the dash center panel ☞ 10/2, 3.

3 ☐+ Remove the access panel below the steering column - this is secured by two screws near the bottom edge, and can be unclipped once these have been removed.

4 Release all the steering column electrical connections.

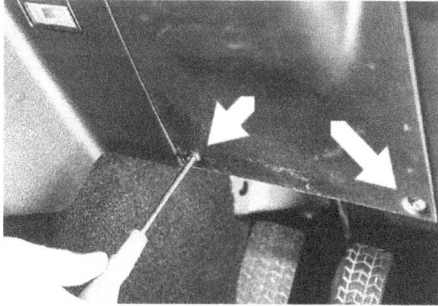

4/3a Remove lower securing screws and ...

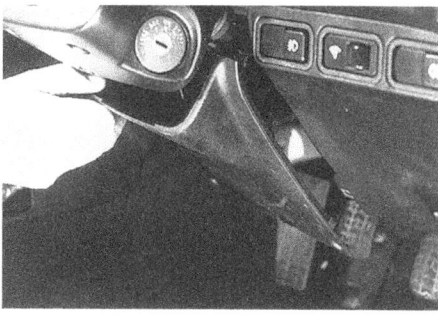

4/3b ... then release panel from clips.

10:3

Mazda Miata, MX-5, Eunos & Roadster

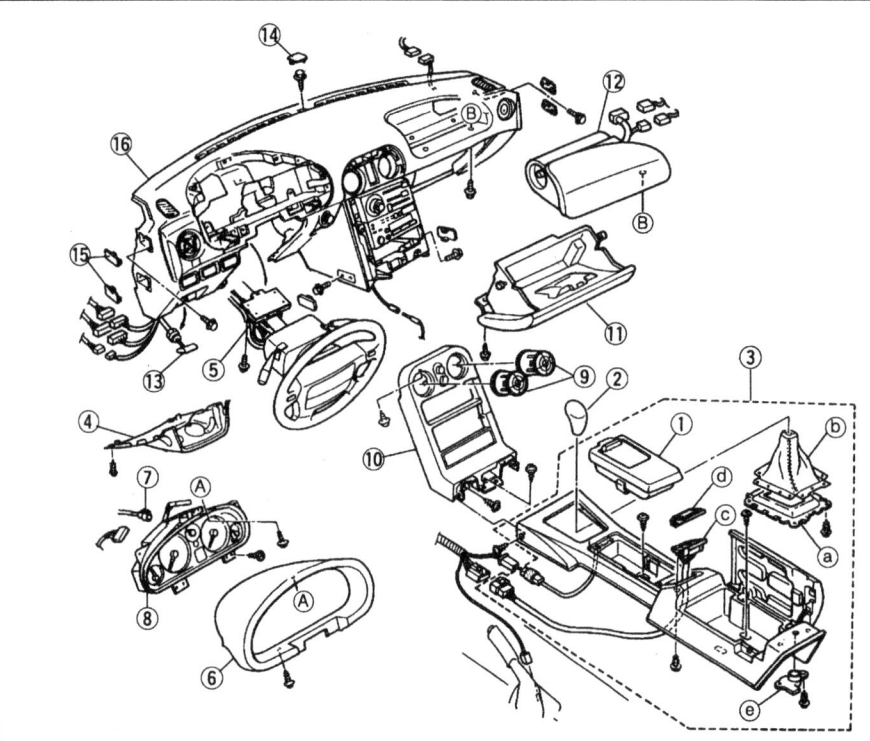

D4/0-37 DASH PANEL (DASHBOARD) REMOVAL & INSTALLATION.
1 Ashtray. 2 Gearshift lever knob (manual transmission). 3 Rear console unit. 4 Steering column cover. 5 Steering column. 6 Instrument hood. 7 Speedo cable. 8 Instrument panel. 9 Eyeball vents (louvers). 10 Dash center panel. 11 Glove compartment. 12 Airbag module. 13 Hood (bonnet) release knob. 14 Fixing bolt cover. 15 Fixing bolt covers. 16 Dash panel.

5   Remove the steering column from the car ☞ 8/11 (note that it is not necessary to remove the steering wheel).

6   Remove the two sheet metal screws which retain the instrument panel hood. These are fitted from the front edge of the hood, and pass upwards to secure it to the dash panel. Once you've released the screws, the hood can be pulled toward you until it disengages from the dash panel. The back of the housing is held by three metal clips on the dash panel (see diagram), and is located by a long plastic pin.

7   With the housing out of the way, you have clear access to the four screws which secure the instrument panel. Remove the screws and pull the panel towards you. As it moves away from the dash, unplug the instrument panel connectors - there are two of these, one at top left and one at top right - each is secured by a locking tab. The panel can now be pulled back further, but is still held by the speedometer drive cable. This is secured on the back of the instrument panel by (you guessed it) a locking tab. Press the locking tab and pull the cable off the back of the speedometer, then lift the instrument panel away from the dashboard.

8   Remove the screws securing the hinge of the glove compartment and lift the glove compartment out of the dashboard. If the car is fitted with a passenger side airbag, disconnect the now exposed airbag module electrical connector or connectors. Remove the passenger side airbag module ☞ 7/47.

9   Free the hood release knob from the lower edge of the dash panel after slackening the locknut which retains it. Move the knob and cable

4/5 Release column top mountings.

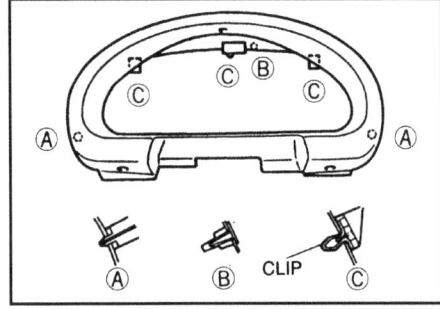

D4/6 INSTRUMENT PANEL HOOD FIXING DETAIL.

4/9 Slacken locknut to free hood (bonnet) release.

clear of the dash panel so that it does not get caught during dash removal.

10   + You now need to pry off the small rectangular access covers which hide the dash panel fasteners. Note that the covers are directional - one end has a deep hook which locates on the edge of the dash panel and a smaller clip at the back edge. The covers should unclip easily, but if they don't pop out when you insert the screwdriver blade they may have been fitted incorrectly - try inserting the blade from the opposite edge to check this. There are two covers near the transmission

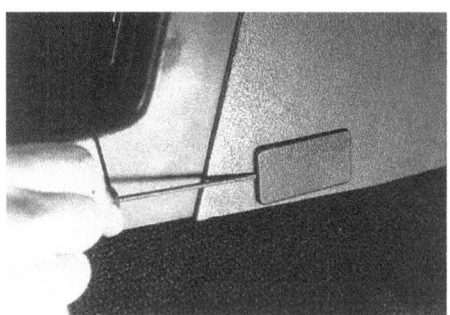

4/10a Pry off screw covers.

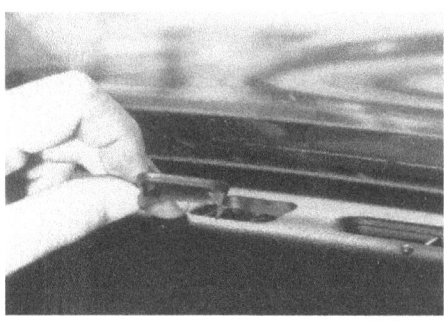

4/10b Pry cover from top centre of dash panel.

tunnel, two right next to each door and a further single cover at the center top of the dash panel, close to the windshield.

11   + The dash panel mounting bolts should be removed at this stage. Start with the 10mm bolts fitted at the top center of the dash panel (one bolt) and on each side of the panel near the door openings (two on each side). Next, remove the four 14mm bolts which retain the center section (two bolts on each side). The dash panel should now be loose.

12   As the dash panel is removed from the car

10: Interior

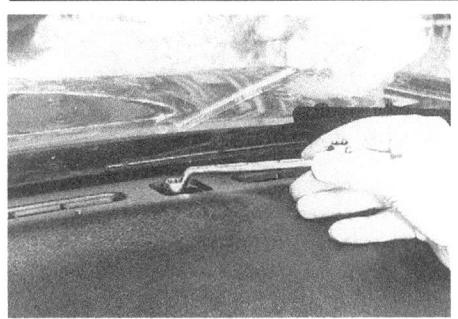
4/11a Unscrew top centre bolt ...

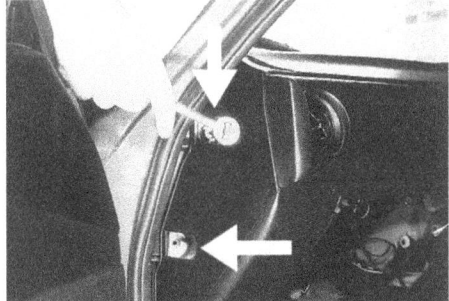
4/11b ... followed by those near doors ...

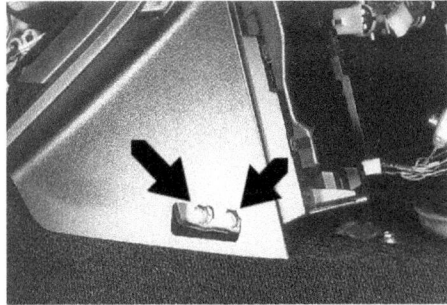
4/11c ... then these each side of trans tunnel.

it will be necessary to disconnect the electrical wiring. This is not as complicated as it seems because the dash panel was obviously pre-wired during manufacture and then simply connected to the electrical system as it was installed. You'll need to check the exact wiring connection details on your particular car, since this varies according to the market and options fitted, plus any accessory items which may have been added.

13 It is not entirely obvious which wiring connectors need to be separated, and which can be left undisturbed. We found that the best method was to gently lift the dash panel and move it out into the car slowly - this way you can see clearly which connectors are impeding removal. It is very useful to have assistance at this stage of the removal sequence - the dash panel assembly is not heavy, but it needs careful manipulation during removal.

14 Don't be too concerned about getting the connectors confused - although many appear similar, they are readily differentiated by the wire colors, number of terminal pins and shape, and are not easily reconnected wrongly. It is useful, but not essential, to mark the connectors with pvc electrical tape or paint dots of different colors - this will speed up installation by making it immediately obvious which connectors go where.

15 On our car, we found that the aftermarket alarm system complicated dash panel removal a little - we had to cut two wires, and these were subsequently reconnected using a terminal strip.

16 You're quite likely to encounter similar minor problems where accessory items have been added to your car, because most will have been installed without removal of the dash panel. If you do need to disconnect accessory wiring, make a written note of the various connections and, where there is a risk of confusion during installation, mark the wires and/or connectors using PVC tape.

17 When you have identified and separated the various wiring connectors, lift the dash panel up and back into the car. Make a final check around the back of the dash for any missed wiring connections, then lift the assembly out of the car, placing it on some soft cloth to protect the surface from scratches until it is needed again.

CHECKING

18 ◻+ With the dash panel removed you have access to various assemblies, like the heater unit and air conditioning unit (where fitted), as well as to the inside of the dash panel itself. The accompanying photographs show a general view of the car interior with the dash panel removed, plus closer shots of the driver's and passenger's sides. These depict a RHD car - LHD versions are similar but with driver's controls and heater blower/air conditioning unit transposed.

19 ◻ The main dash panel molding is carried on a tubular steel fabricated subframe, which both supports the panel and adds to the rigidity of the body. In the event of impact damage severe enough to have damaged the subframe and surrounding bodywork, it is likely that the plastic molding will have sustained damage, too. If this is the case, you'll need to get specialist attention from a body shop, which will have to check the body alignment and install a new dash panel assembly as part of the vehicle repair.

20 Minor components housed inside the dash panel can be removed or replaced as necessary; for example, this is a great time to fit a new cigarette lighter, if required - the lighter is difficult to remove and install while the dash panel is in the car.

21 If you need to remove such items, note carefully how any associated wiring is routed and duplicate the routing when installing the new part - it is preferable to avoid changes in routing because the wiring may become trapped or damaged when the dash panel is installed later. Note also the

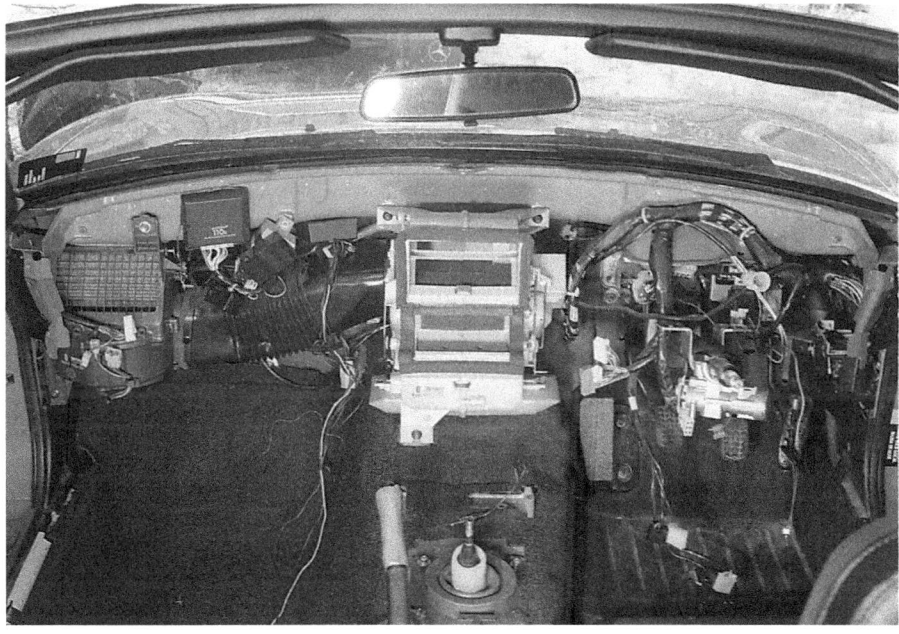
4/18a Components accessible once the dashpanel is removed.

4/18b Rhd right-hand detail and ditto ...

4/18c ... left. (Alarm components non-standard.)

Mazda Miata, MX-5, Eunos & Roadster

4/19 Detail of dash construction which includes a substantial brace bar.

ground (earth) tag connections which will be found at the end of the dash subframe; these should be checked for security, noting that poor ground connections may result in electrical circuits operating intermittently.

22 📷+ Check over the air ducts which are mounted inside the dash panel. These are lightweight ABS moldings which carry air to the defroster slots from the heater unit at the center of the

4/22a Check air duct connections carefully ...

4/22b ... they could be taped for extra security.

under-dash area. The ducts slot together and are held (very loosely) in place by raised pips and ribs. Check that all these sections are correctly engaged. If necessary, you can improve the joints by taping around them with duct tape.

INSTALLATION

23 Before you commence installation, we recommend that you spend a little time preparing the wiring connectors on the main harness side to simplify the process. Again, there will be some variation between cars built for different markets,

but the point of this exercise is to position the connector ends so that they line up with the dash panel connectors when the unit is installed. You may find it easier to lay the dash panel across the seats so that you can check and compare the connector halves side-by-side.

24 With the aid of an assistant, lift the dash panel into position, and start reconnecting the wiring - don't fit any mounting bolts at this stage. Pay careful attention to the routing of each section of wiring so that it is in no danger of it becoming trapped when the dash is fastened in place.

25 📷 Where switches are fitted into the dash panel, pop the switches out of their recesses and feed the related connector through the switch aperture. Connect each switch to the wiring, then snap the switch back into the dash panel.

26 📷 When remaking electrical connections, check each connector for shape, wire colors and terminal positions, and for any identification marks made during removal. Connect each one in turn, ensuring that they latch properly, and check care-

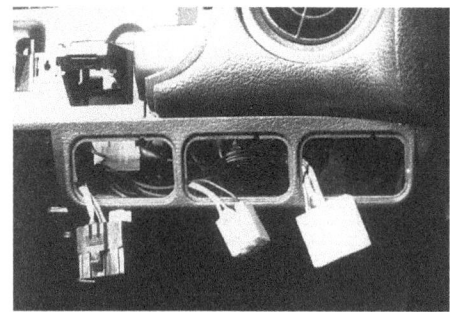

4/25 Pry out switches and unplug connectors.

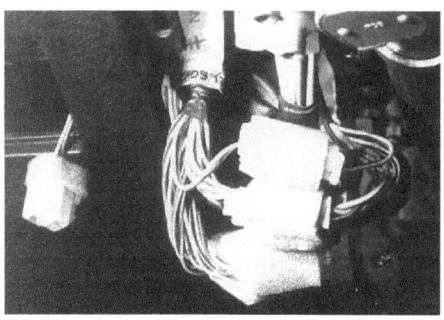

4/26 Some connectors are foam wrapped.

fully behind the dash to make sure that none have been missed. Don't forget to reconnect any accessory wiring which you may have encountered during removal.

27 When you are confident that you have reconnected all the wiring, the dash panel can be fixed in position. Fit the 10mm bolts at the outer edges of the panels, next to the door openings (two on each side of the car), plus the single 10mm bolt at the center of the dash panel, immediately below the windshield. Next, fit the 14mm bolts (two on each side) either side of the dash panel center section. Fit all the bolts finger-tight at first so that minor positional adjustments can be made, then tighten the 10mm bolts to 7.8-11.7Nm/80-120kgf cm/70-104 lbf in) and the 14 mm bolts to 37-53Nm/3.7-5.5kgf m/27-39lbf ft).

28 📷 Clip the plastic covers over the dash panel mounting bolts, taking note of the direction markings; the covers will fit facing either way, but subsequent removal will be made more difficult if positioned incorrectly.

29 Install and reconnect the passenger side airbag (if applicable) ☞ 7/47.

30 Intall the glove compartment and tighten the hinge screws.

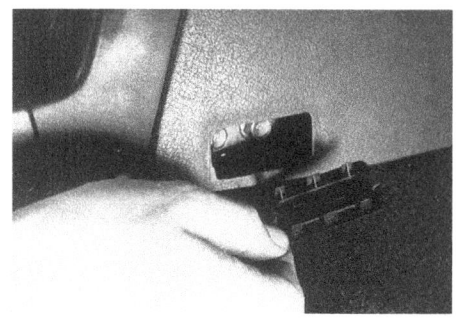

4/28 Screw cover trims clip into place.

31 Fit the hood release control knob, securing it by tightening the locknut firmly.

32 Install the dash center panel assembly (☞ 10/3), noting that the heater control cables must be fed into position and connected as the panel is installed. We suggest that you do not install the eyeball vents (louvers) at this stage; if you need to remove the center panel or the dash panel to correct an installation problem, it'll be easier to do so with the vents removed.

33 Reposition the instrument panel, connecting the speedometer drive cable and the instrument panel wiring connectors as it is fitted. Once connected, fit and tighten the four retaining screws. Fit the instrument panel surround, clipping it in position and securing it with its two retaining screws.

34 Install the steering column (and wheel, if removed) ☞ 8/11. During installation, check the dash panel wiring routing and rearrange this if necessary to prevent wiring getting trapped.

35 Install the rear (between seats) console assembly ☞ 10/2, remembering to reconnect any associated wiring connections (ashtray light, power window switches, etc).

36 If applicable, re-arm the airbag system. **Warning!** Follow the correct procedure ☞ 7/44.

10: Interior

37 Check the operation of the electrical systems controlled from the dash panel. If you find a problem, check and resolve this before proceeding further. Once everything is working correctly, install the steering column access panel. Finally, snap the eyeball vents into place.

5. INTERIOR TRIM - REMOVAL & INSTALLATION

☞ 1/1, 2.

1 In addition to the dash panel, dash center panel and rear console assemblies described in the preceding sections, the remaining metalwork in the car is concealed by plastic trim panels. In some cases these are purely cosmetic coverings, though some also conceal other mechanisms or serve a protective function.

2 Note that the exact fixing methods differ with the age and specification of the car. For useful information on fastener types ☞ 1/2.

FRONT HEADER RAIL TRIM & SUN VISORS (& INTERIOR MIRROR - SOME MODELS)

3 ☐+☒ The front header rail trim covers the top section of windshield surround between the two A-pillars. If the rear view mirror is fixed to the header, first unclip the plastic cover which conceals the mirror mounting (it snaps over the mirror base and is a tight fit), then unscrew the sheet metal screws and remove the mirror. Next, remove the soft top locating cups which are held in place by 6.6mm Torx screws. The cups are adjustable via slotted mounting holes, so temporarily mark their positions relative to the header trim. Now remove the sun visors, each of which is retained by two sheet metal screws. Once these fittings have been detached, lift the header trim at one end until the retaining clip snaps free. Continue working along the trim, noting that the clips are quite tight.

When you have re-installed the trim and external fixings, check that the soft top locating cups are set up correctly (close the top to check), then fully tighten the Torx screws to secure them.

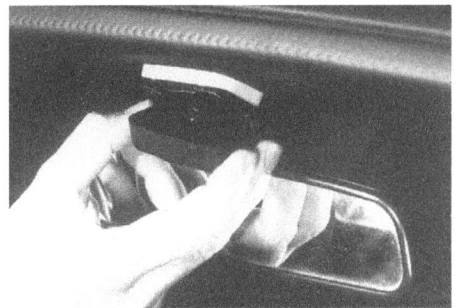
5/3a If applicable, remove mirror mounting trim ...

5/3b ... and unscrew securing screws.

5/3c Sun visors held by 2 screws each.

5/3d Torx screws hold latch cups.

5/3e Lift away header rail trim panel.

D5/3 WINDSCREEN HEADER RAIL TRIM FIXING DETAIL.

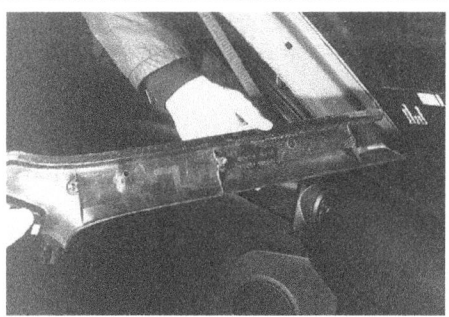
5/4a Unclip A-pillar (post) trim.

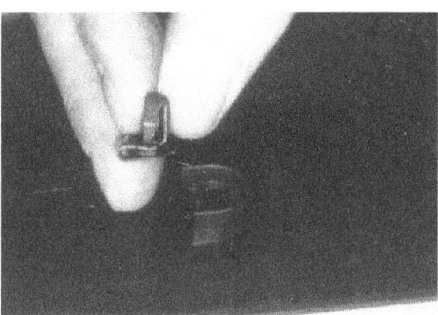
5/4b Clips hook into these cups.

D5/4 A-PILLAR (POST) TRIM FIXING DETAIL.

A-PILLAR TRIM

4 ☐+☒ The A-pillar trim covers the A-pillar (A-post) on each side of the windshield. Before you can remove the individual trim panels, you'll need to pull off the door seal in the vicinity of the relevant trim. Beware of body mastic! Unclip the trim section, working from the top down. Once the clips are free, disengage the locating peg near the top and lift away the lower end of the trim section where it hooks into the A-pillar. Note that the metal clips hook onto the trim section and may drop off as you pull the trim away - check that these are retrieved.

When installing the A-pillar trim, check that it locates correctly around the ends of the header trim, and check that the door seal is snapped back into position correctly.

FRONT SIDE (FOOTWELL) TRIM

5 ☐☒ The front side (footwell) trim is located forward of the door opening on the outer sides of the footwells. The trim section clips into place and is located by small pins. Note also that the back edge of the trim is retained by the door seal, which clips over it and the body seam. The forward top edge is secured by a threaded plastic retainer clip. To remove and install the trim section you'll need to pull away the area of door seal which covers the trim edge.

6 On cars equipped with aftermarket scuff

10:7

Mazda Miata, MX-5, Eunos & Roadster

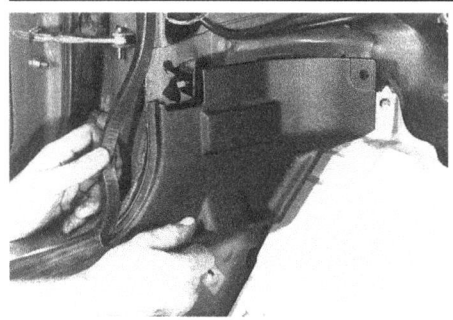

5/5 Pull off door seal to release trim.

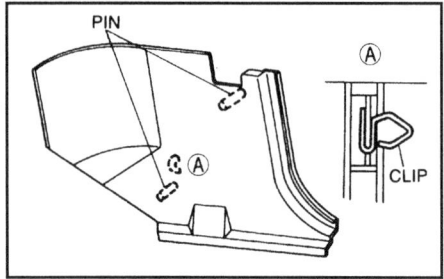

D5/5 FRONT (FOOTWELL) SIDE TRIM FIXING DETAIL.

plates, these may also impede removal; on our project car we needed to free the scuff plate screws to allow the trim section to be removed.

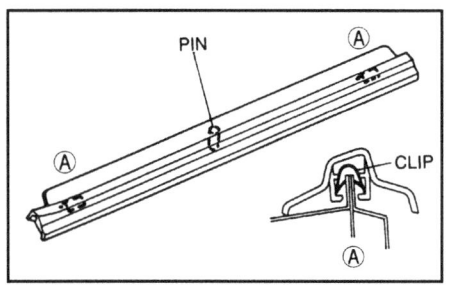

D5/7 SCUFF PLATE (ORIGINAL EQUIPMENT TYPE) FIXING DETAIL.

SCUFF PLATE

7 ▣ The scuff plate is fitted over the raised seam which runs across the bottom of the door openings, protecting the seam and surrounding paintwork from damage by the driver's and passenger's feet. The standard scuff plate is secured by two spring clips and a single locating pin, and may be removed by pulling upwards.

8 Some cars will have been fitted with aftermarket scuff plates which are much wider, and do a better job of protection. On our project car, these were held by sheet metal screws, and the outer edges appeared to have been secured with impact adhesive. (We had no good reason to remove the scuff plates completely, and so decided to avoid risking cosmetic damage by pulling them off.)

QUARTER TRIM

9 The quarter trim panels cover the rear quarters of the car interior, running from the back edge of the door opening around to the package shelf, and providing a housing for the seatbelt mechanisms.

10 ▣ Begin by removing the brace bar ☞ 10/15. Next remove the hard top location stop which is secured by two 6.6mm Torx screws. You should really use a Torx wrench on these screws, though we found it possible to shift them using Allen wrenches - a 5mm Allen wrench is a little slack, while a 6mm wrench may be too tight - you'll have to experiment with your own set to find a snug fit. If the screws on your car prove to be tight, don't risk damaging the screw heads - get the correct

5/10 Hardtop locating pad fixed by Torx screws.

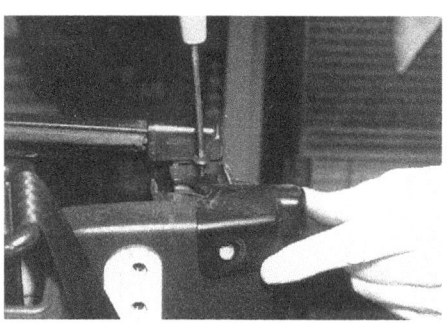

5/11 Remove screw, lift away trim panel.

Torx wrench.

11 ▣ Next, remove the finishing piece at the top corner of the door opening. This is held in place by a single crosshead screw, plus a 10mm headed set screw.

12 ▣+ From the edge of the trim panel just to the rear of the seatbelt top mounting point, unclip and remove the small closing section to provide a gap through which the belt can be passed. You will also need to pull out the clip-in plastic loop through which the belt passes - free this from the trim, leaving it loosely in place around the belt.

5/12a Unclip & remove closing section.

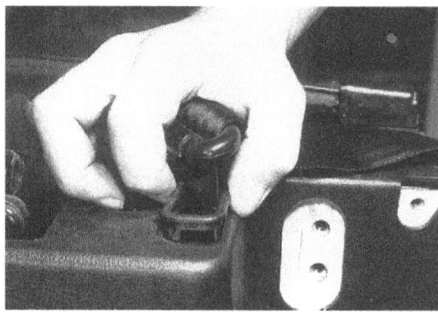

5/12b Release belt aperture trim.

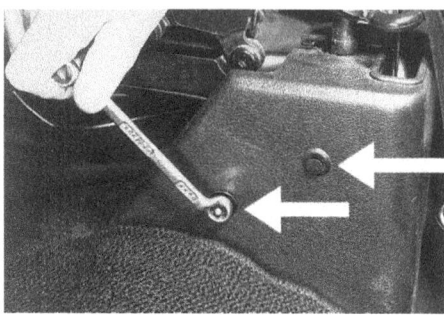

5/13 Remove plastic clip and screw.

13 ▣ On the side of the trim panel, free the single plastic clip, lifting the center section using a small screwdriver, and then lifting the fastener out of its hole. Remove the 10mm set screw adjacent to the clip.

14 ▣ Pull away the door seal where it covers the edge of the trim and the body seam. On our car, which had aftermarket scuff plates, we also needed to release the scuffplate screws - this allows the bottom of the trim to be freed. The rest of the trim edge is tucked under the carpet and comes free easily.

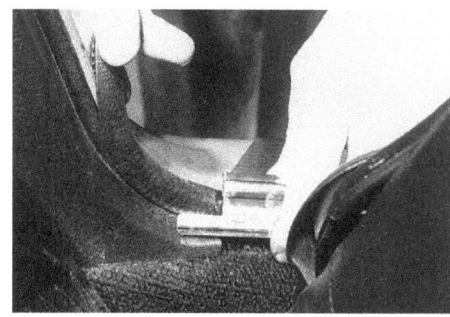

5/14 Pull away door seal to release trim.

5/15 Remove panel feeding s/belt thru slot.

10:8

10: Interior

15 Lift the panel and move it forward, remembering to feed the seatbelt through the slot at the back of the trim.

16 When installing the quarter trim panel, position it in the car, simultaneously feeding the seatbelt through the slot provided, then clip the plastic loop into the panel and install the closing section at the back edge.

17 Fit the plastic clip and set screw on the side of the panel, then fit the finishing piece, securing it with its sheet metal screw and set screw. Check that the edge of the panel is located properly (you may have to lift the carpet a little to cover the edge), and

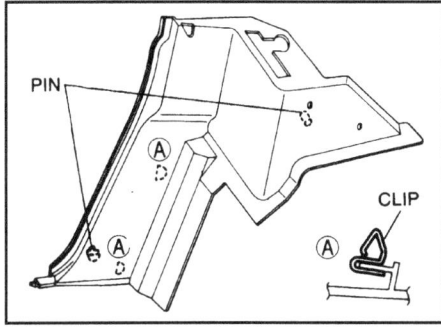

D5/18 QUARTER TRIM FIXING DETAILS.

clip the door seal back in position.

18 If the scuff plate screws were slackened, they should be tightened at this stage. Fit the hardtop location stop and secure it with its two

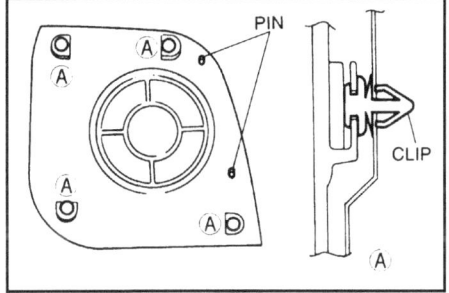

D5/19A SPEAKER TRIM FIXING DETAIL (IF APPLICABLE).

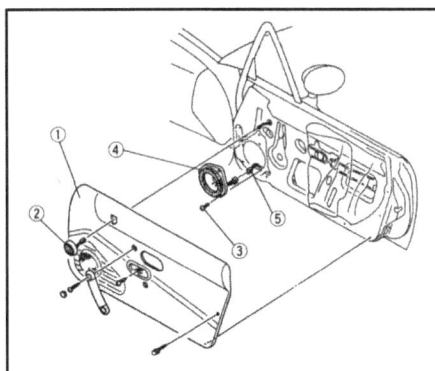

D5/19B ALTERNATIVE SPEAKER ACCESS VIA DOOR TRIM REMOVAL.
1 Door trim. 2 Tweeter speaker. 3 Screw. 4 Woofer speaker. 5 Speaker electrical connection.

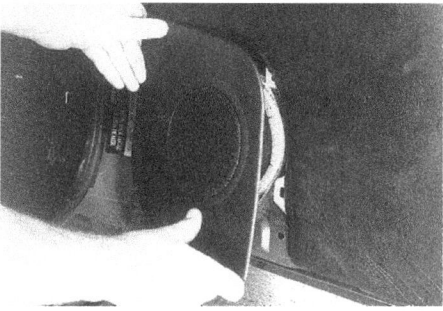

5/19 Unclip speaker cover panel (if applicable).

Torx screws. Finally, install the brace bar and secure with two bolts tightened to 63-93Nm/6.4-9.5kgf m/47-68lbf ft.

DOOR SPEAKER AND GRILLE

19 + On some models the door speakers are covered by a separate trim panel, secured by four plastic clips which push through holes in the door skin (see diagram). The grille can be removed by pulling it away from the door - it helps to get the fingers under the grille near the clip to be freed, working around the grille until all four clips have been displaced. If your car does not have separate trim panels for the speakers, it will be necessary to remove the door trims to access the speakers.

20 + Once the grille has been detached, or the door trim removed, it's possible to remove the speaker after its mounting screws have been removed. As you lift it away, disconnect the speaker's wiring connector. Some models will have a second (tweeter) speaker mounted higher in the door frame.

When installing speakers, always ensure their fixing screws are properly tightened otherwise vibration and sound distortion will occur.

5/20a Speaker is held by screws ...

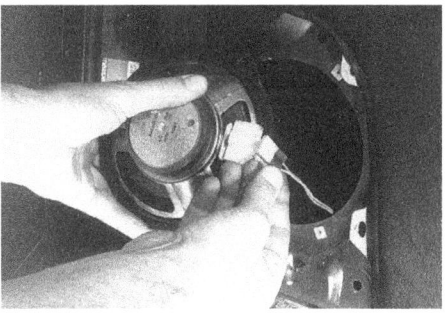

5/20b ... & needs to be unplugged from wiring.

DOOR TRIM

21 The door trim panels need to be

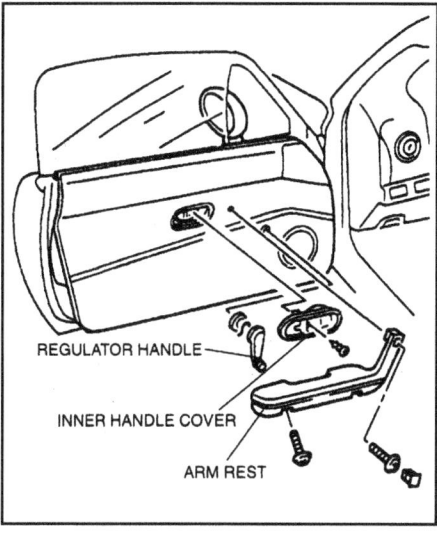

D5/21 TYPICAL DOOR FURNITURE REMOVAL/INSTALLATION.

removed to provide access to the door catch and lock mechanism, mechanical or electric window regulators, power mirror wiring and, where fitted, the central locking solenoid. Door trim style and detail varies from year-to-year and with car specification.

22 Disconnect the battery negative cable to isolate the battery 7/2.

23 On manual window winder cars, start by removing the regulator handle. This is secured on its shaft by a spring clip, and the easiest removal

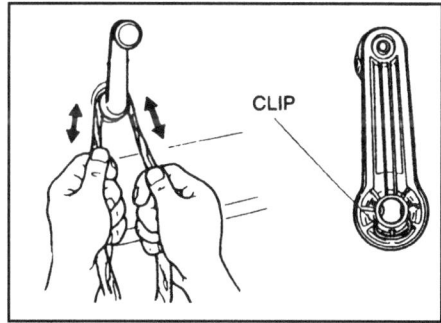

D5/23 WINDOW REGULATOR HANDLE REMOVAL METHOD.

method is to loop a strip of rag around the base of the handle, pulling the loop of rag so that it is forced between the handle and its base (escutcheon).

24 Further pressure on the loop while pulling it back and forth will displace the clip and the handle can then be pulled off.

25 If applicable, remove the separate door speaker trim panel as described earlier. You now need to remove the armrest, which is secured by crosshead screws, the uppermost of which is hidden under a small trim plug. Pry out the plug with a small screwdriver, then remove the three screws and lift the armrest away.

10:9

Mazda Miata, MX-5, Eunos & Roadster

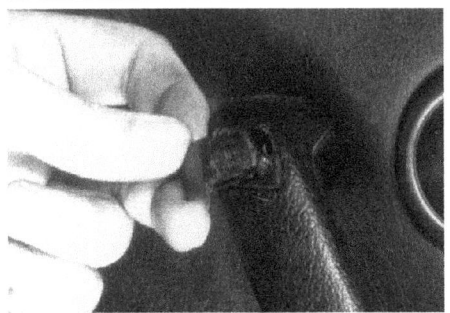

5/25 Pry out screw cover trim.

5/26a Remove securing screw & then ...

5/26b ... slide off handle surround trim.

26 ◘+ Remove the single small crosshead screw which retains the interior door handle surround. Lift the handle about halfway, then maneuver the surround over the handle and remove it.

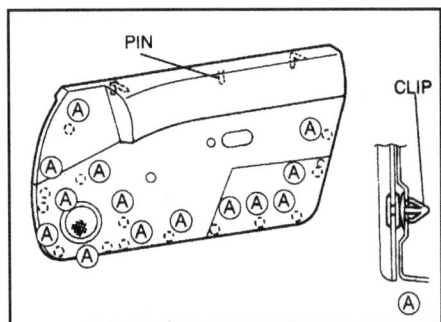

D5/27 TYPICAL DOOR TRIM PANEL FIXING DETAIL.

27 ◘ 🖻 The door trim is now held in place by plastic peg clips around its front, lower and rear edges (see diagram). Work your hand or a thin metal strip between the trim and the door and begin popping the clips out of the door. Once all the clips are free, lift the trim slightly to unhook its top

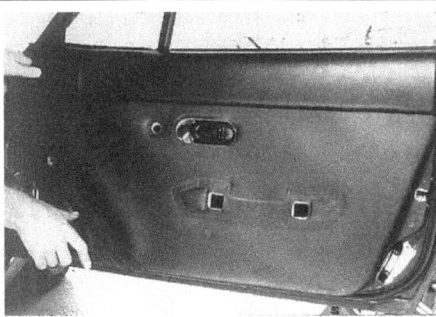

5/27 Once unclipped the door trim lifts off.

edge from the window aperture and remove it.
28 Behind the door trim, you'll find a plastic sheet covering the door apertures; if you need access to the door interior, you will have to remove this. **Caution!** Be careful not to tear it.
29 ◘ Start by removing the interior door handle. This is secured by three crosshead screws; you'll also need to free the ends of the lock and latch rods. The easiest way of doing this is to disconnect the lock rod at the door end and the latch rod at the handle end. The rods are secured by swivel clips. Unclip these from the rod ends and

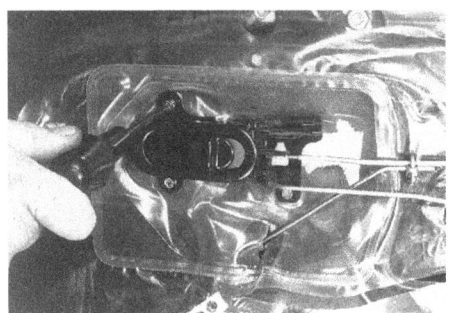

5/29 Unscrew door handle retaining screws.

turn them through 90° until the rod end can be lifted out.
30 Check that nothing else will impede removal (on our car, one of the screw receptor clips had been pushed through the sheet by mistake). Note also that, where aftermarket central locking has been added, you may find, as we did, that the solenoid control rod runs outside of the sheet. If you have to detach the rod - and, like ours, it is clamped to the door locking rod - mark the relationship of the two rods before releasing the clamp.
31 The plastic sheet is held by very sticky black mastic, and you will need somewhere clean to put it when removed. We recommend that you place it face down on a plastic garbage bag for this - it will allow you to re-use the mastic, and the bag can be disposed of.
32 Take care during removal to avoid contact between the mastic and your clothes, or the car upholstery or paintwork. In case of accidental contact, hand cleaner will remove the mastic from your hands, and a proprietary tar remover will get it off paintwork or fabric - refer to the manufacturer's directions when using these products, and always test on a small, unobtrusive area for discoloration effects before using it on the actual stain.

33 If the sheet is torn or holed, you should fit a new one. Either purchase one from your Mazda dealer, or make one up using industrial grade polyethylene sheeting. You can use the old sheet as a template for cutting the new one, but note that the original is shaped to fit the door skin contours, and your home-brewed equivalent may not fit quite as well. Use proprietary automotive mastic to stick the new sheet in place, after removing the old mastic with Stoddard solvent (white spirit).
34 ◘ When fitting the plastic sheet, position it carefully along the top edge and check that it lines

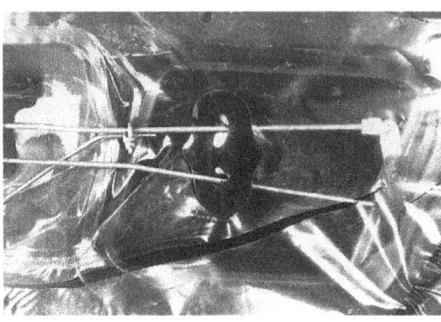

5/34 Don't forget foam sealing pad.

up across the door skin - it will be obvious if this is not the case. Pass the door latch and lock rods through the sheet, positioning the foam sealing pad over the holes in the sheet. If you needed to disconnect the central locking control rod, now is the time to reconnect it, passing it through the plastic sheet and aligning the marks made during removal, before securing the clamp. Press the sheet down onto the mastic in key areas, such as where screws pass through the sheet into the door, before smoothing the sheet down evenly across the door.
35 Hook the door trim on along its top edge, then pivot it down against the door skin. Press around the rear, lower and front edges until the pins have all snapped home. Position the speaker grille and press this home until the four pins have locked in place.

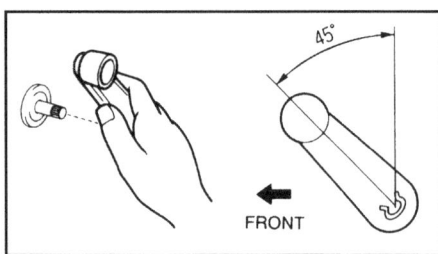

D5/36 CORRECT REGULATOR HANDLE POSITION (GLASS RAISED).

36 🖻 On cars with manual window regulators, install the handle, positioning it 45 degrees off vertical and facing forwards when the glass is fully raised. Check that the window raises and lowers normally.
37 Lift the interior door handle slightly and slide the surround into position. Release the handle

10: Interior

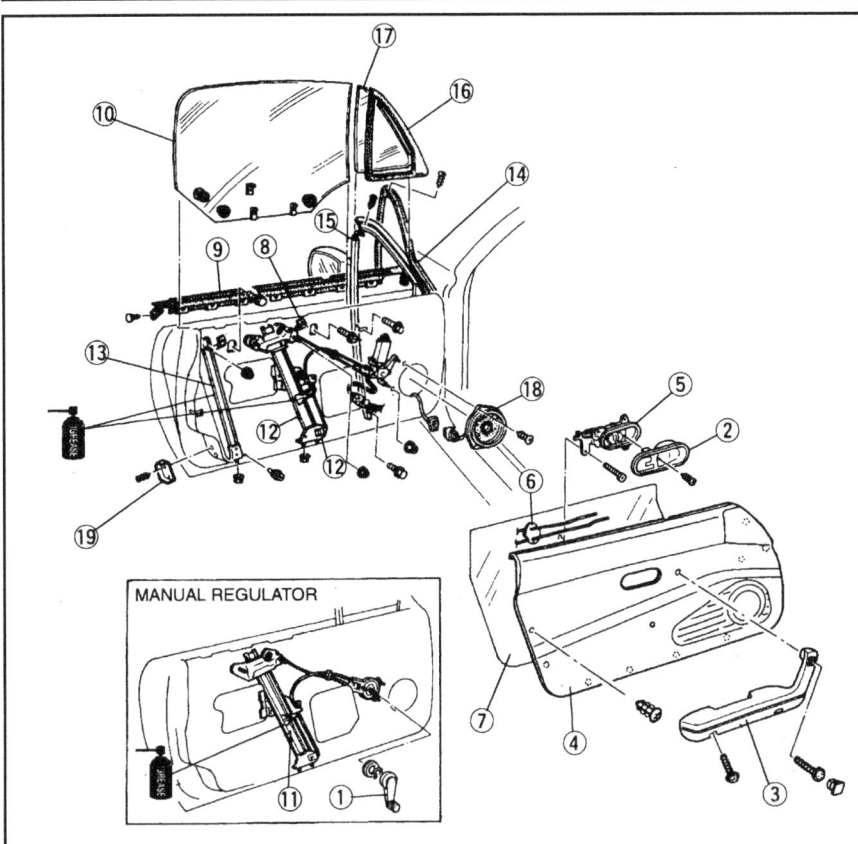

D6/1-17 WINDOW LIFT/REGULATOR COMPONENTS & ACCESS.
1 Regulator handle. 2 Door handle trim plate. 3 Armrest. 4 Door trim panel. 5 Door handle. 6 Actuator rods sealing pad. 7 Sealing sheet. 8 Glass stopper (upper). 9 Door glass. 11 Regulator (manual). 12 Regulator (power window). 13 Glass guide channel. 14 Weatherstrip. 15 Division channel. 16 Quarter glass (light) weatherstrip. 17 Quarter glass. 18 Speaker. 19 Dovetail.

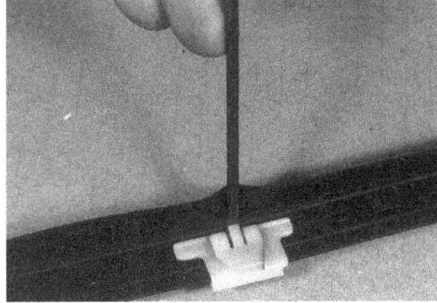

6/3a Tab release demo (molding removed).

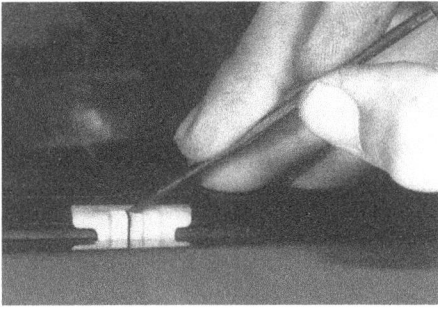

6/3b Lift molding & release each clip.

and fit the single screw which locates the surround.

38 Fit the armrest, tightening the crosshead screws evenly, and remembering to fit the trim plug which conceals the upper screw head.

39 Reconnect the battery (☞ 7/2) and check the operation of the electric windows, power mirrors and central locking systems, where these are fitted.

6. DOOR GLASS & LIFTER MECHANISM - REMOVAL & INSTALLATION

☞ 1/1, 2.

REMOVAL

1 Wind down the door glass to about 190mm (7.5in) from the fully open position - this will roughly position the glass ready for removal, but further adjustment may be needed later. Isolate the battery ☞ 7/2. Remove the door trim and plastic sheet ☞ 10/5.

2 You now need to remove the front beltline molding - the weather seal which fits around the glass at the top of the door. Pry out the plastic pins at the front and back ends of the molding where it wraps around the ends of the door, using a screwdriver blade to lever them out. Next, prepare a small screwdriver by wrapping some PVC tape around the shaft.

3 Using the protected screwdriver (and taking great care to minimize the risk of paint damage in such a conspicuous area), carefully lift the edge of the beltline molding seal lip on the outside of the door. If you peer underneath the lip, you should be able to make out one or more of the retaining clips. At the center of each one is a locking tab, which you need to depress with the screwdriver blade. Gently depress the tab and the clip will pop out of the door recess. Repeat this procedure on the remaining clips and lift the molding away. Our photographs show the method of depressing the central tabs with the molding removed and during removal.

4 To minimize the amount of final adjust-

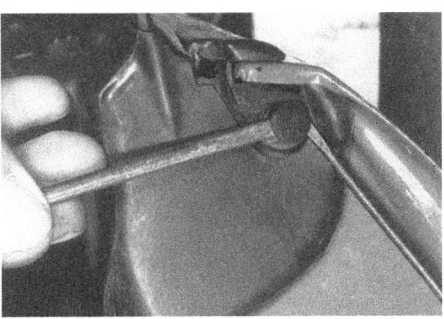

6/2 Pry out molding securing pins.

ment required after reinstallation of the glass, mark the position of all bolt heads in relation to the door inner skin, and the nuts on the underside of the door. You can use paint for this, or as we did, typist's correcting fluid (it's easily visible and dries fast). Mark around the edge of the bolt head or nut so that its position can be duplicated during installation.

5 Remove the two glass stops which are retained by a single bolt each, either side of the regulator mechanism. The bolts can be reached through oval access holes near the top of the door skin - you identify the two bolts concerned by peering down through the top of the door - you will see where the two stops are. Hold each stop in turn, remove the fixing bolt, and lift the stop out of the door.

6 Check the position of the glass in relation to the door. The glass is secured to the regulator mechanism by three crosshead screws, two of which can be reached through the large aperture nearest the back edge of the door, and there is an oval hole for access to the third screw at the front of the regulator mechanism. If you need to reposition the glass so that the front screw aligns with the access hole, on manual window cars, fit the handle

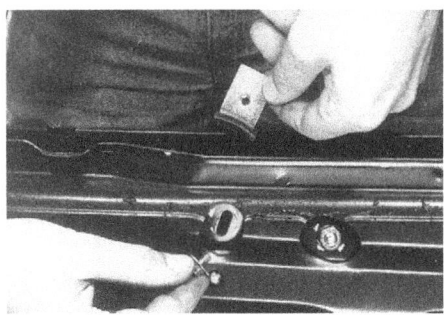

6/5 Remove glass stops.

10:11

Mazda Miata, MX-5, Eunos & Roadster

and move the glass up or down until this screw is visible through the access hole. On cars with power windows, temporarily reconnect the battery and use the power window switch to position the glass as described.

7 ◻ Have an assistant remove the three screws while you support the glass. Once the screws have been removed, lift the glass clear of the regulator mechanism and out of the door cavity. Place the glass safely out of harm's way on some soft cloth until it is needed again.

8 ◻ =The rear glass guide can now be removed if required, again having made sure that

6/7 These three screws support the glass.

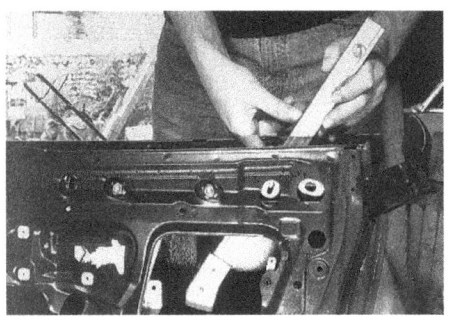
6/8 Slide out rear glass guide.

its fasteners are marked for position beforehand. Once the upper and lower fixing nuts have been removed, the guide can be lifted out through the top of the door.

9 ◻+ The regulator mechanism is similar on both manual and power window versions, and is removed as an assembly with the regulator gearbox or motor assembly. Remove the three 10mm flanged nuts which retain the gearbox/motor assembly to the door inner skin. Note that the mounting points differ between manual and power models, but this does not affect removal (manual winder mounting holes arrowed on

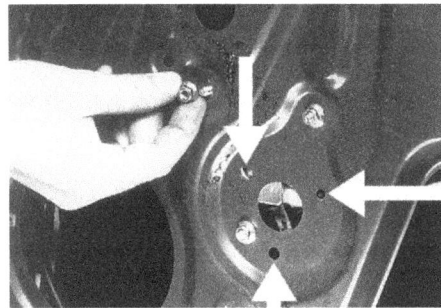
6/9a Three nuts hold motor (arrows: see text).

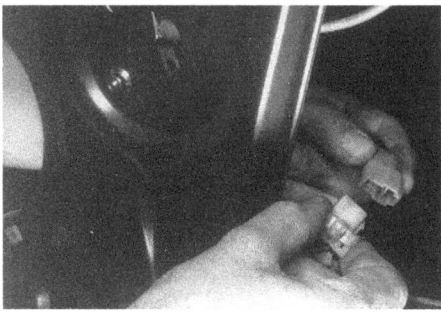
6/9b Unplug power lift motor wiring.

photograph). On power window cars, disconnect the motor wiring connector.

10 ◻+ Feel along the cables inside the door skin and locate the cable guide clips - these push through holes in the door skin and should be displaced after noting their relative positions. The regulator mechanism can now be freed by releasing the two nuts at the top (accessible through holes in the door skin), and two further nuts on the lower edge of the door. Raise the mechanism slightly, then feed it down through the center aperture in the door skin, followed by the

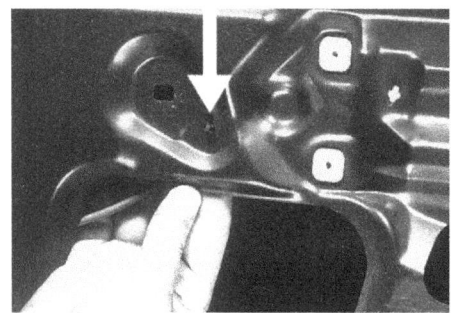
6/10a Feel for the cable clips.

6/10b Release regulator securing nuts ...

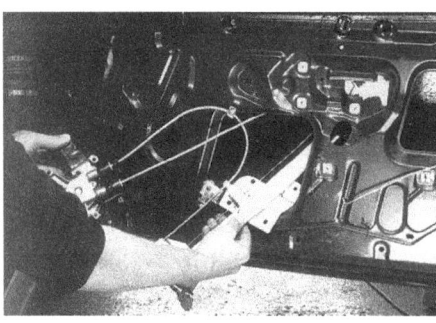
6/10c ... then pull regulator from door.

regulator gearbox/motor assembly.

INSTALLATION

11 During installation, you should fit the removed regulator components and the window glass, making reference to the positioning marks made around the fasteners during removal. This will mean that the assembly is set up more or less exactly as it was prior to removal, but note that you may need to carry out final adjustment of the glass (☞ 10/9). Start by installing the rear glass guide (if it was removed), and provisionally tighten the

6/12a Secure regulator loosely in position.

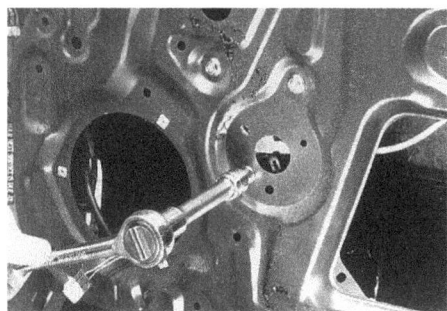
6/12b Secure motor or manual lift.

mounting bolts, noting the positioning marks made during removal.

12 ◻+ Feed the regulator mechanism, together with the gearbox/motor assembly attached on its cables, through the center door aperture. Position the regulator studs through the mounting holes in the door and provisionally tighten the four mounting nuts, observing the position marks made during removal. Fit the gearbox/motor assembly and tighten the three mounting nuts to 8.9-12.7Nm/ 90-130kgf cm/79-112lbf in). Clip the cable guide clips into their holes in the door skin.

13 If you have simply removed and installed the regulator assembly, it will be correctly positioned for installation of the window glass. If, however, the mechanism has been dismantled or moved, you will need to check that the front mounting point in the mechanism is correctly aligned with the access hole in the door skin - if this is not the case you will be unable to fit the fixing screw. This procedure was described earlier (☞ 10/6/6), and should be repeated if necessary.

14 ◻ Lower the window glass through the aperture at the top of the door, engaging the glass guide posts in their channels. Align the fixing holes with the regulator mechanism, then fit and tighten

10: Interior

6/14 Slide glass guides into channels.

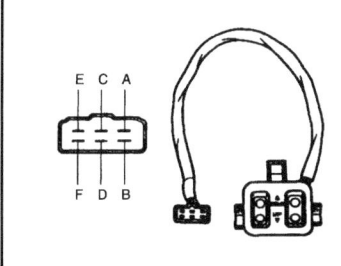

D7/5 POWER WINDOW SWITCH CONTINUITY TESTING.

	Terminal	Driver side				Passenger side			
Switch position		A	B	C	D	A	B	E	F
UP		O——————————O				O——————————O			
			O——O				O——O		
OFF			O——O——O					O——O——O	
DOWN		O——————————O				O——————————O			
			O——O					O——O	

O——O: Continuity

evenly the three fixing screws. It is advisable to have some help at this stage, though you can just about get by unaided.

15 Fit the glass upper stops through the top of the door, securing them with their mounting bolts in the position indicated by the marks you made during removal. Do this carefully, because the stop positions have a significant affect on the fit of the glass against the soft top or hard top weatherstrip.

16 Check the glass adjustment ☞ 10/9. The amount of work this will entail is dependent on whether you made reference marks during dismantling, and whether new parts have been installed. If you have simply removed and installed the existing parts using reference marks during the dismantling operation, you should only need to check the adjustment because there should be no need to set the adjustment from scratch.

17 Once you have carried out the adjustment check, fully tighten the regulator, stop and guide fasteners to 22-27Nm/2.2-2.8kgf m/16-20lbf ft. Install the door trim components ☞ 10/5.

7. WINDOW LIFT SYSTEM (POWER) - CHECKING & OVERHAUL

☞ 1/1, 2.

1 The power window lift system is an option which will be found on most of these cars. In essence, this is a motorized version of the manual regulator arrangement, differing only in the use of an electric motor system to raise and lower the door window glass. The motors are controlled from two switches housed in the rear (between seats) console.

2 In the event of problems with the power window system, the likely cause is either an electrical problem or failure of the regulator mechanism cables - these convey movement between the motor unit and the regulator mechanism. The nature of the fault is likely to be self-evident; if a cable has broken, you will still hear the motor running when the switch is operated, but the glass will not move. (The glass may well have dropped open if the closing cable has broken.) If both windows are inoperative, check the **POWER WIND (30A) or P.WIND (30A)** fuse in the fusebox inside the car. If this has burned out, check the wiring for a short circuit and repair as necessary, then fit a new fuse.

3 If you suspect a cable fault, or if the problem is confined to one side only, start checking inside the affected door after isolating the battery ☞ 7/2 and removing the door trim ☞ 10/5. If you discover a broken cable, you'll need to remove the glass, followed by the regulator mechanism and motor as an assembly ☞ 10/6. Skip to the 'Regulator overhaul and cable replacement' heading.

4 In the case of electrical problems, check the operation of the motor unit as follows. Disconnect the motor wiring connector, and connect a spare car battery to the motor terminals: battery positive (+) to terminal **A** and battery negative (-) to terminal **B**. The motor should operate. Now reverse the battery connections and verify that the motor runs the other way. If the motor does not run, or works intermittently, you'll need to fit a new unit.

5 If the motor checks out okay, trace the wiring back to the switch panel in the rear (between seats) console unit - you'll need to remove the console ☞ 10/2. Disconnect the switch wiring and check switch continuity as shown in the accompanying diagram and table. If the switch is faulty, fit a new unit.

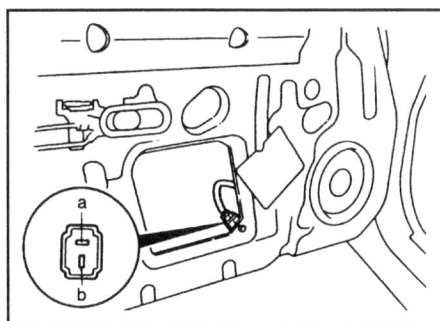

D7/4 POWER LIFT MOTOR TERMINAL IDENTIFICATION.

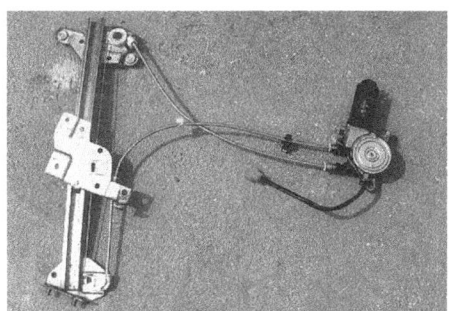

7/6a Both sides of regulator and motor ...

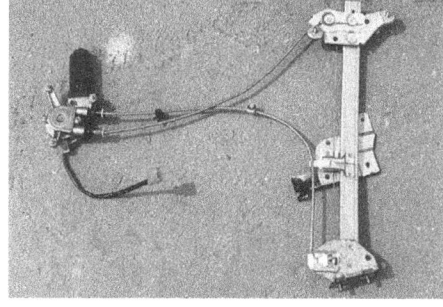

7/6b ... note cable runs & crossover.

REGULATOR OVERHAUL AND CABLE REPLACEMENT

6 With the motor unit and regulator removed as an assembly (☞ 10/6), start dismantling the unit on the bench. Before you start work, lay out the assembly and note how it all fits together. In particular, note how the cables cross over each other - this looks like it might be wrong, but is in fact intentional. The accompanying photographs depict the mechanism from a right-hand door, viewed from both sides, for reference purposes.

7 The lower cable from the motor unit (the **UP** cable) runs to the top of the regulator to a stop. From here the inner cable runs around a pulley and down to the sliding glass bracket. The motor upper cable (the **DOWN** cable) runs to the combined stop and guide block at the bottom of the regulator, the inner cable then connecting to the glass bracket. Note also that you need to have the glass bracket positioned roughly midway along its travel - we started out with ours at the lower extreme of its travel and discovered that it's impossible to get the cables disconnected because they are covered by the lower end of the guide. Finally, note that the **DOWN** cable is significantly longer than the **UP** cable, and this is a good guide during installation: to make life even easier, mark one cable and its attachment points on the motor and regulator with paint dots or typist's correction fluid.

8 To free the cables, start by unhooking the **UP** cable inner from the pulley at the top of the regulator - there is enough give in the system to allow this. The cable outer sits in a plastic stop which pushes over a metal tab, and can be lifted off.

9 Next, unclip the combined guide and stop from the lower end of the regulator. This has two tabs which retain it, and it can be slid out when

Mazda Miata, MX-5, Eunos & Roadster

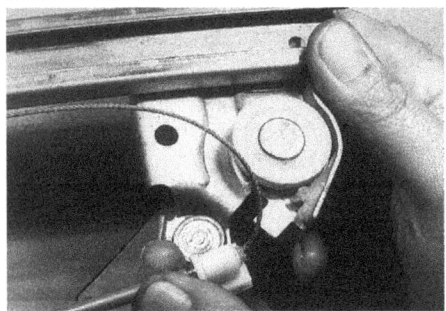

7/8 Pull cable stop from metal tab.

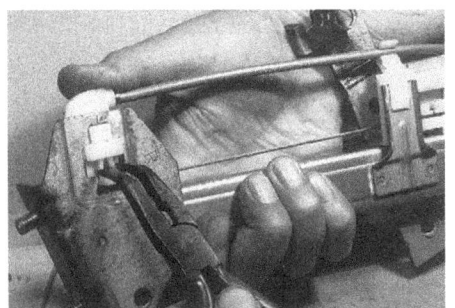

7/9a Squeeze tabs to ...

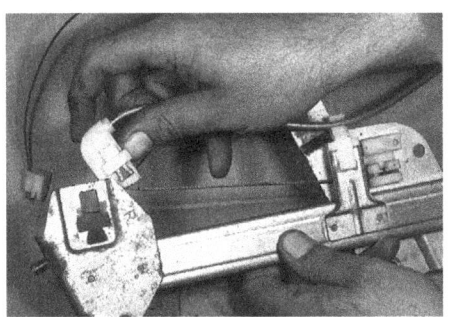

7/9b ... release guide/cable stop block.

7/10 Release both cables from anchor point.

capstan is driven off a square-section shaft from the motor gearbox.

12   Remove the two screws which retain the D-shaped capstan cover and remove it. The capstan will be seen in its recess in the gearbox casting and can be lifted out. Beware! As you lift out the capstan, the inner cable ends will spool off it, so, as it comes away, grasp the cable ends between finger and thumb to prevent this happening. Unwind each cable in turn and unhook its end from the capstan to free it.

13   📷 This is about as far as you will want to go with the teardown - you won't get motor parts,

7/13 Basic motor unit. Replace if faulty.

7/14 Slide cable ends thru ferrules - see text.

and given the relative inaccessibility of the motors, if you have a motor fault, fit a new one. Even if the cables are intact, check them closely. If you see any sign of fraying or other damage, fit a new one to avoid subsequent failure in service.

14   📷 Fit the end of the (longer) **DOWN** cable through the hole in the motor gearbox casting nearest the motor body, and the shorter **UP** cable through the remaining hole.

15   📷+ Attach the cable ends to their holes in the capstan, the **UP** cable end being uppermost and visible when the capstan is installed (the capstan will only fit one way). Note that each cable

7/15a Place cable end in capstan recess ...

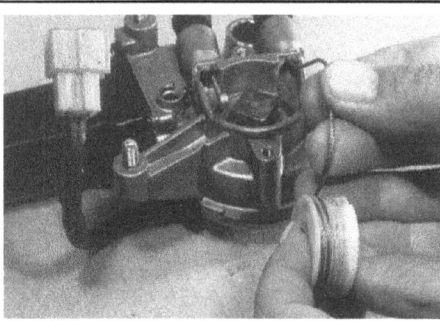

7/15b ... 2.5 turns around capstan ...

7/15c ... repeat with second cable ...

should be wound 2.5 turns around the capstan, the **UP** cable running counter-clockwise and the **DOWN** cable running clockwise. Hold the cables between finger and thumb to prevent them unwinding again.

16   📷+ Grease the capstan and cables thoroughly, then install the capstan assembly in its recess. Fit the capstan cover and secure it with its two screws. The black plastic adjusters provide coarse initial adjustment and probably won't need to be disturbed - on our project car they were very tight in their threads, so take care if you do need to

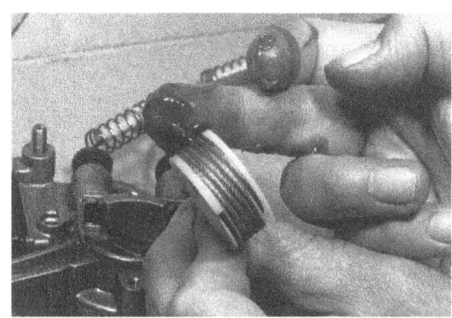

7/16a ... grease cables & capstan then fit ...

7/16b ... capstan & secure with cover.

these have been compressed.

10   📷 The two inner cables will now be relatively slack, and you can unhook them from their shared anchor point on the glass bracket. Lift each cable end and feed it through the slot in the anchor block.

11   Moving to the motor end of the system, you will note that the two cables enter the motor gearbox casting through spring-loaded stops which seat in black plastic adjusters. Inside the gearbox housing, each cable is wound 2.5 times around the capstan before being anchored on one side. The

10: Interior

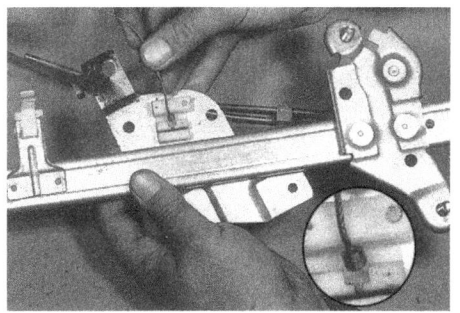

7/17a Hook both cables into anchor.

7/17b Fit stop, run cable around pulley.

reset them.

17 ◐+ Hook both cable ends onto the glass bracket. Feed the **DOWN** cable inner through the slot in the side of its combined stop and guide block, then fit the block into its hole in the base of the regulator, snapping it home until the tabs lock it in position. Connect the **DOWN** cable inner end to the block on the glass bracket. Attach the **UP** cable end to the other side of the block, then fit the upper stop over its locating tab and run the cable around the pulley - the springs at the motor end allow enough movement to facilitate this.

18 Before you install the assembly, we suggest that you temporarily reconnect the battery (☞ 7/2) and motor wiring and check that the mechanism runs smoothly throughout its range. If you do this, take care not to get your fingers in the way - the mechanism is quite powerful and you could get hurt. When you're satisfied that all is well, install the mechanism and motor in the door ☞ 10/6.

8. WINDOW LIFT SYSTEM (MANUAL) - CHECKING & OVERHAUL

☞ 1/1, 2.
1 As we mentioned in the preceding section, there really isn't much difference between the manual and power window systems. On the manual version, the winder motor and gearbox are replaced by a manual equivalent operated by a handle.
2 We should come clean at this point and admit that we have not worked on a manual system. However, the regulator mechanism is identical, and, as far as we can tell, the connection/disconnection details for the cables at the drive end are the same. Refer to coverage of the power lift

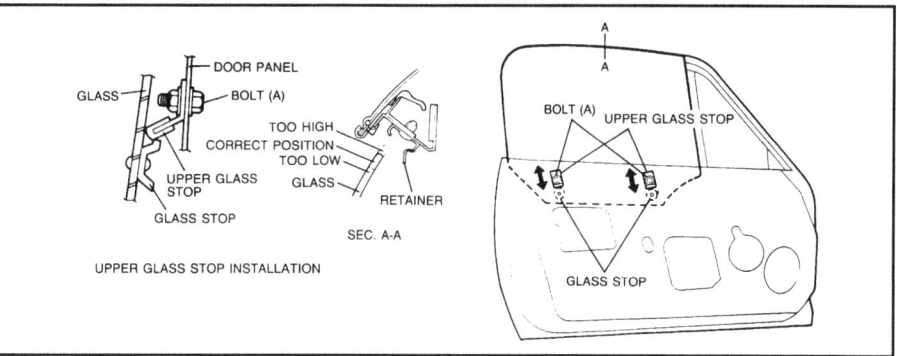

D9/3 DOOR GLASS VERTICAL ADJUSTMENT DETAILS.

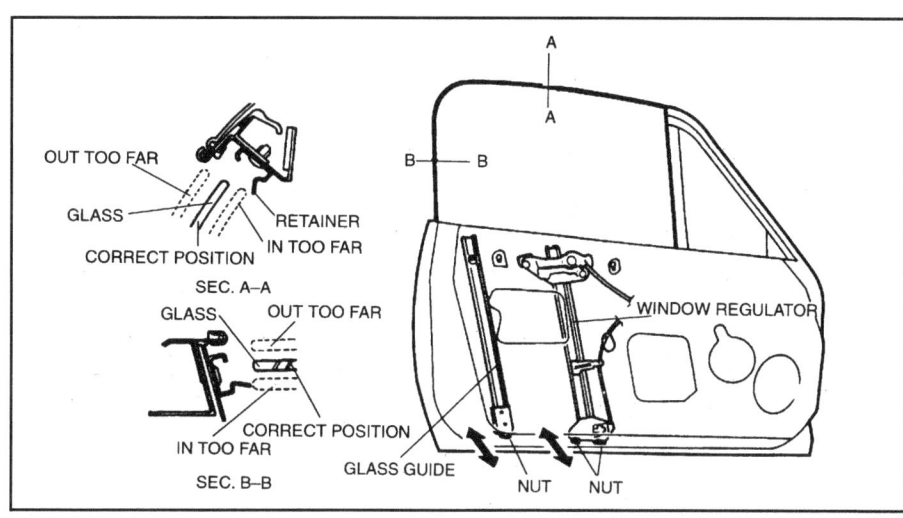

D9/4 DOOR GLASS INWARD/OUTWARD ADJUSTMENT DETAILS.

system (☞ 10/7), making allowances for the absence of the motor and gearbox unit. The accompanying diagram (D6/1-17) illustrates the differences between the two systems.

9. DOOR GLASS ALIGNMENT - CHECKING & ADJUSTMENT

☞ 1/1, 2.
1 Before you attempt to adjust the door window glass, be certain that it *is* the glass which requires adjustment. If you have just dismantled and overhauled the window winder mechanism, or have fitted new parts in the door, then this is quite possible, but bear in mind that other factors can affect the seal between the glass and the hard top or soft top; if the window mechanism has not been disturbed, check the door adjustment (☞ 11/9), the weatherstrip and overall roof alignment on soft top cars (☞ 11/15) and the hardtop alignment/fitting (☞ 11/14). If you're changing from a hardtop to a soft top, or vice versa, it's probable that you'll need to alter the glass adjustment.
2 With the window fully wound up, check the fit of the glass against the weatherseal. This is made of soft foam section and will permit a degree of misalignment, but the edge of the glass should touch evenly all round. If the top edge of the glass

is too high or too low, you need to look at vertical adjustment. If the glass is too far inboard or outboard, you have a inward/outward adjustment problem. It's a good idea to mark the existing position of the glass on the weatherseal before you alter any adjustments. Remove the door trim and associated components ☞ 10/6. Also, familiarize yourself with the glass stop bolt and guide bolt positions. Note that the diagrams which accompany this section show glass position relative to the seal retainers, not the seal itself: this is so that correct seal compression is achieved.

HEIGHT ADJUSTMENT

3 ▣ To alter the height of the top of the glass, you need to reposition the two stops which limit its upward travel. Wind the glass down a fraction, slacken the two stop bolts and move the stops to the required position, then tighten the bolts. Now wind the window fully up and check that it is correctly positioned. Repeat the procedure until the glass is aligned correctly. The official adjustment position is to set the glass so that the top edge is positioned 7.4-11.4mm/0.29-0.45in from the outer lip of the weatherseal retainer.

INWARD/OUTWARD ADJUSTMENT

4 ▣ This adjustment is made by slackening the window regulator and glass guide nuts on the

Mazda Miata, MX-5, Eunos & Roadster

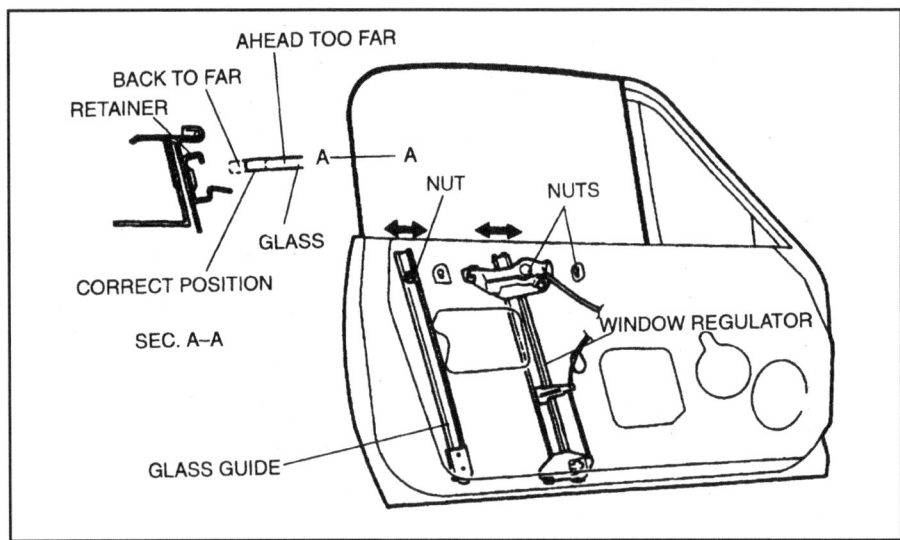

D9/5 DOOR GLASS FORE/AFT ADJUSTMENT DETAILS.

bottom edge of the door (see diagram), and altering the angle of both components. This has the effect of changing the angle of the glass in relation to the weatherstrip. Position the guides so that the glass touches the weatherstrip evenly around the opening. After adjustment, check that the glass moves smoothly throughout its travel, and that it seals correctly.

FORE/AFT ADJUSTMENT

5   This adjustment controls the angle of the side edges of the glass in relation to the weatherseal. Adjustment is made after slackening the nuts securing the top of the regulator and glass guides (see diagram), and moving them to alter the fore-and-aft angle. Note that this adjustment may affect the vertical and horizontal settings.

ADJUSTMENT CHECKS

6   If you have adjusted the glass, you need to check the following points before final tightening and installation of the door trim and fittings.
• Is the weatherstrip aligned correctly?
• Is the weatherstrip mounted correctly?
Check that -
• The glass contacts both vertical stops simultaneously as it is raised.
• The glass raises and lowers smoothly (with the door closed).
• The glass is correctly positioned when fully closed, in good and even contact with the complete weatherstrip.

10. DOOR LATCH AND LOCK ASSEMBLY - REMOVAL, OVERHAUL & INSTALLATION

☞ 1/1, 2.

REMOVAL

1   Before attempting to work on the door latch or lock assemblies, you need to remove the door trim components (☞ 10/5), and set the window glass to its fully raised position. Once you've done this, isolate the battery ☞ 7/2.

2   With the door trim and the inner plastic sheet removed, you'll be able to see the interior door handle and the control rods which run back to the door latch mechanism inside the door. The

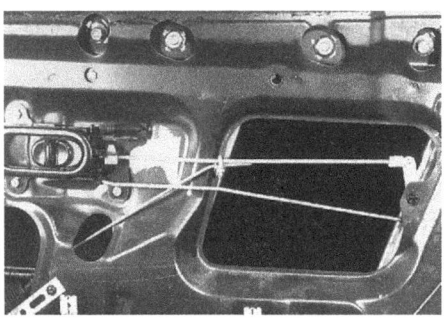

10/2 Control rods (inc. non-std electric lock).

upper rod controls door locking, and runs back to a bellcrank, which, in turn, connects through a curved rod to the door latch mechanism. The lower rod operates the door latch itself and connects directly to the mechanism.

3   Disconnect the upper rod at the bellcrank end, and the lower rod at the interior door handle end. The rod ends are retained by plastic swivel clips - unclip them from the rod and turn through 90 degrees until the rod end can be disengaged. The clips can be left in position.

4   On our project car, aftermarket central locking was fitted, and a third rod was connected from the central locking solenoid to the middle of the upper (locking) rod where it was clamped in position. If you encounter a similar arrangement, mark the relationship between the two rods with an indelible pen or paint marker, then remove the clamp to disengage the extra rod.

5   Remove the three screws which retain the interior door handle assembly to the door inner skin, using a crosshead screwdriver or 8mm nut spinner, and lift the assembly away.

6   The door latch mechanism and the exterior door handle are both removed from inside the door, working through the apertures in the inner skin. It is not easy to see exactly how they are interconnected, and even less easy to disconnect the rods running between them. We found that the best method was to release the fasteners holding each assembly to the door, and to disconnect the rods as they were maneuvered out of the door.

7   Remove the three countersunk screws which secure the latch to the back edge of the door, working from the outside. The latch can now be maneuvered partway out of the door, but is still connected by two rods to the exterior handle and a third to the bellcrank.

10/8a Swivel clip arrowed.

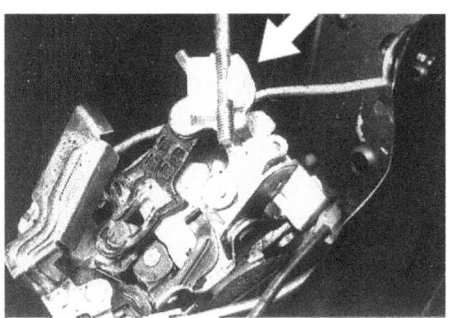

10/8b Adjustable clip arrowed.

10/9 Latch end swivel clip.

8   ☐+ Reach up into the door cavity to the back of the exterior handle and free the end of the thinner of the two rods which run up from the latch. This is secured by another plastic swivel clip. Now disconnect the thicker rod at the latch end. This rod is threaded, and is secured by a plastic clip. Mark the relationship of the rod and the clip with paint before disconnecting it.

9   ☐ Feel inside the door skin and locate the latch end of the bellcrank. This has a similar plastic swivel clip to those described earlier, and should be disconnected at the latch end, leaving the rod

10: Interior

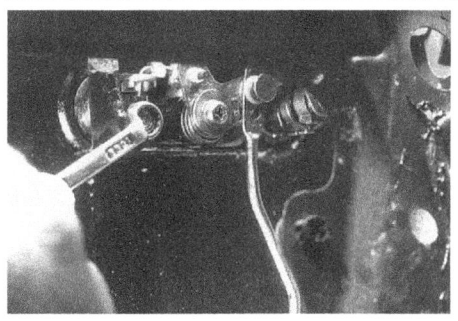
10/10 Handle/lock mechanism fixed by nuts.

attached to the bellcrank. The bellcrank will allow enough movement for this to be achieved. The latch mechanism is now free and can be removed from the door.

10   Working through the door aperture, and through the nearby access hole, remove the two 10mm nuts which fix the exterior handle to the bracket inside the door. The handle can now be displaced and removed, feeding the remaining rod through the door outer skin as you do so.

11   The only part of the mechanism remaining in place is the bellcrank, which will not normally

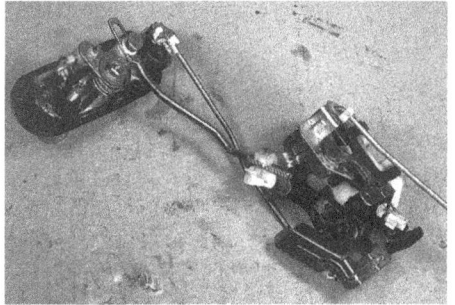
10/12 Control rods temporarily reassembled.

10/13a Release spring clip ...

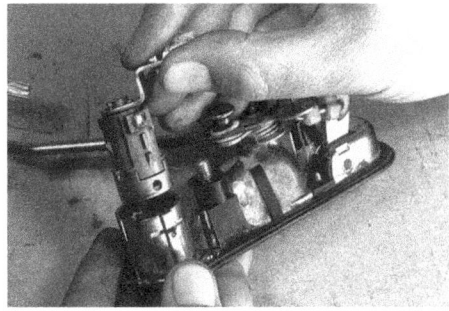
10/13b ... & withdraw lock barrel.

require attention. If you do need to remove it, it's held in place by a plastic mounting, which can be released by squeezing together the locating tabs.

OVERHAUL

12   We suggest at this stage that you temporarily reassemble the connecting rods between the latch and exterior handle so you can see how the mechanism works, which will make installation a little less puzzling. There is little point in attempting further dismantling but, if there is a problem with either assembly, you may be able to figure it out

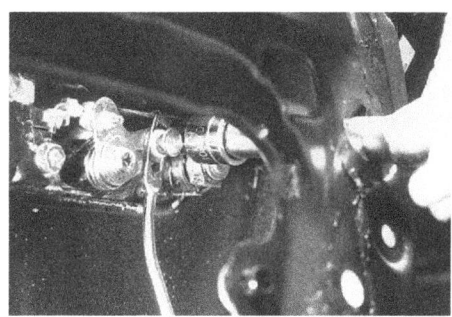
10/14 Torque tighten handle/lock fixing nuts.

and rectify it. It is a good idea to clean the assemblies (try using switch cleaner) and to lubricate the moving parts.

13   The item most likely to fail in the lock mechanism is the lock cylinder, and this can be removed after the wire retainer clip has been released using a small screwdriver blade.

INSTALLATION

14   Install the exterior handle, securing it with its two nuts, which should be tightened to 7.9-10.7Nm/80-110kgf cm/70-95.4lbf in.

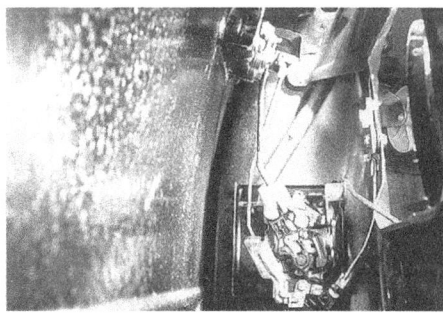
10/17 How it should look.

15   Reassemble the various link rods between the exterior handle and the door latch, remembering to align the paint marks made on the threaded rod end and its retainer. Reconnect the latch to the bellcrank rod.

16   Install the latch assembly, tightening the mounting screws to 4.3-6.1Nm/43-63kgf cm/37-54lbf in.

17   To give you some idea of how it all looks when fitted, we got our Technical Adviser, Wally, to photograph the assembly in the door. It may not be a truly great photograph, but, like Wally

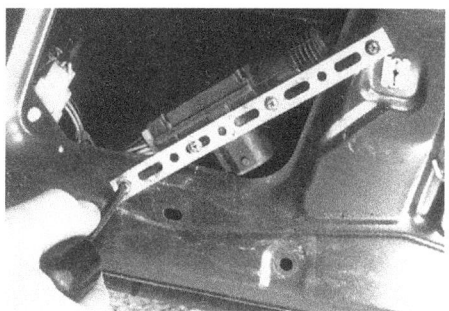
10/19a Electric lock mounted on metal strap.

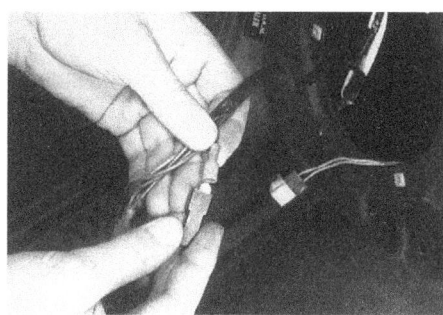
10/19b Connect & route non-std wiring carefully.

said, you try getting your head, floodlights and a 35mm camera inside the door!

18   Install the door trim (☞ 10/5) and reconnect the battery ☞ 7/2.

AFTERMARKET CENTRAL LOCKING

19   Although not strictly a part of this manual, our original project car had a pretty typical add-on central locking system fitted as part of an alarm installation. As we mentioned earlier, this connects to the locking rod from the interior handle, the solenoid being mounted as shown inside the door skin. **Caution!** If you add any electrical item inside the door, make sure that any wiring is well away from the window mechanism: it, or the accessory, may be damaged as the window glass is raised and lowered.

11. SEATS - REMOVAL, CHECKING, OVERHAUL & INSTALLATION

☞ 1/1, 2.

Warning! Take care when working on the seat components - especially in areas where pressed steel parts are normally covered by trim or upholstery. Some of these parts have razor-sharp edges - ask Wally, he still carries the scars.

REMOVAL

1   The seats are retained by four 14mm bolts which pass through the seat runners into the floor of the car. The bolts used are unusual in that the hexagon heads are slightly tapered. **Caution!** It's important that you use a close fitting wrench or socket during removal, or the bolt head will be damaged. We suggest that you use only a hexagon pattern socket or box wrench - a conventional bi-hexagon socket is more likely to slip.

Mazda Miata, MX-5, Eunos & Roadster

2   On cars equipped with the optional headrest speakers and/or any other electrical devices, trace and disconnect the wiring connector/s. Slide the seat right back, and remove the two front mounting bolts. Now slide the seat forward and tip the seat backrest as far forward as you can to improve access to the rear mounting bolts. Remove the bolts and lift the seat out of the car.

CHECKING

3   After inverting the seat, check the security of the seat runners. If they have worked loose, the mounting bolts can be tightened after

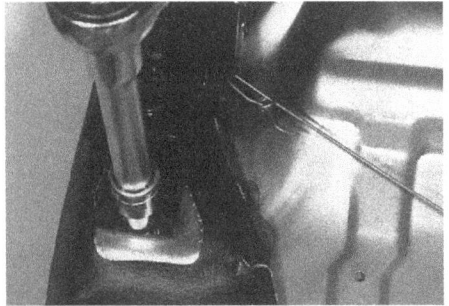

11/3 Check security of seat runners.

positioning the runners so that the bolt heads can be accessed through the access holes provided. Check that the runners move smoothly. If they seem stiff in operation, use aerosol grease to lubricate them, taking care not to get overspray on the upholstery. Check the operation of the recliner mechanism (**Warning!** Watch out - the seat backrest is strongly spring-loaded!)

OVERHAUL

4   To dismantle the seat proceed as follows. Position the runners so that you can reach the

11/5a Remove screw, then side cover.

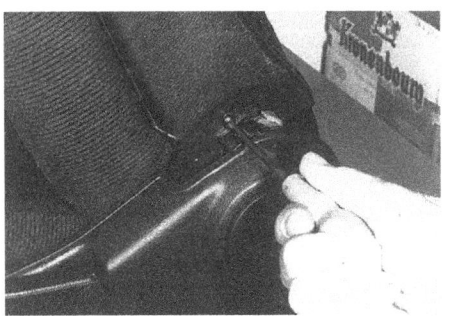

11/5b Remove knuckle retaining bolts.

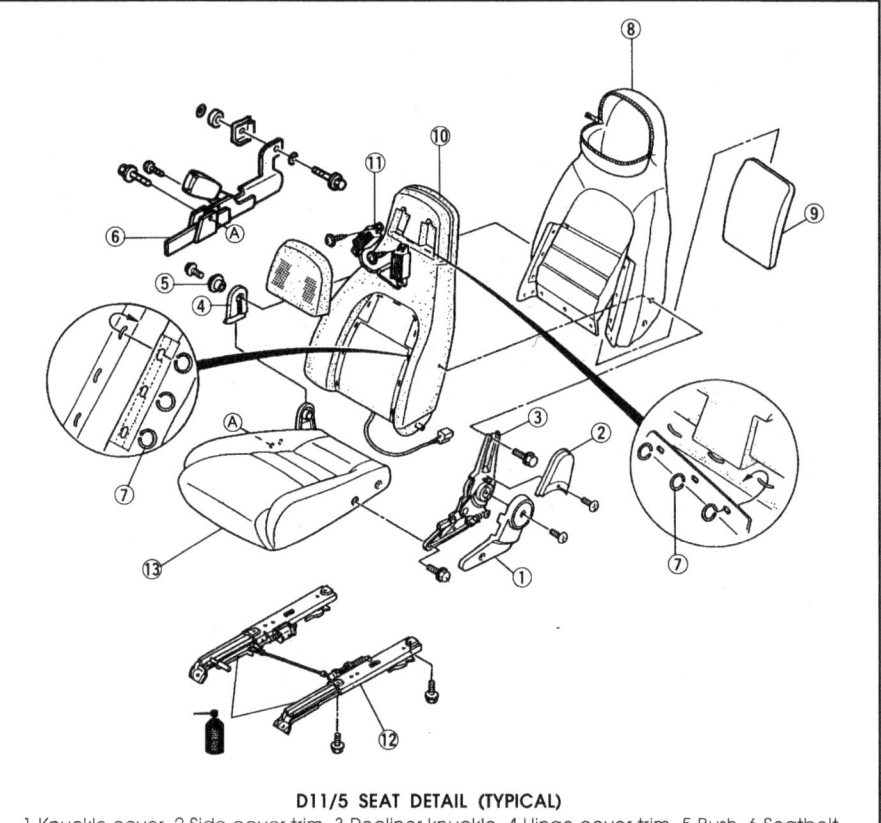

D11/5 SEAT DETAIL (TYPICAL)
1 Knuckle cover. 2 Side cover trim. 3 Recliner knuckle. 4 Hinge cover trim. 5 Bush. 6 Seatbelt anchor unit. 7 Hog ring. 8 Seat backrest trim. 9 Lumbar pad. 10 Seat backrest frame. 11 Headrest speaker (optional). 12 Seat slide. 13 Seat cushion (base).

mounting bolts through the access holes. Remove the runners and adjuster lever as an assembly, noting the arrangement of the link wire which runs between the two latch mechanisms. Apart from cleaning and greasing the runner assemblies, you can do little else to repair them. If they are damaged or distorted, fit new runner assemblies.

5   The accompanying drawing shows how the seat components fit together. You need to detach the knuckle from the outer side of the seat to separate the seat back from the seat cushion. Start by removing the crosshead screw which retains the side cover and lift the cover away. You can now remove the 14mm bolts with ease, but the recliner knuckle cover is a different can of worms altogether ...

6   First, remove the two crosshead screws which secure the plastic cover. In the illus-

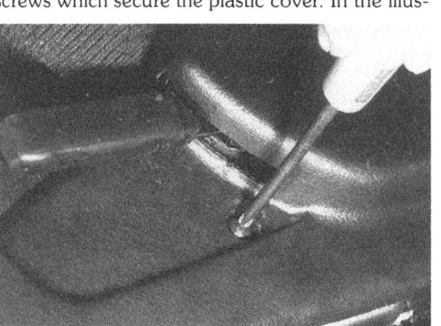

11/6a Remove trim retaining screw.

tration, it looks as if the lower cover will just lift away. It might on your car, in which case, great. On ours, the cover couldn't be maneuvered over the recliner lever. We had to twist and turn the cover so

11/6b Twist cover to give access to bolt ...

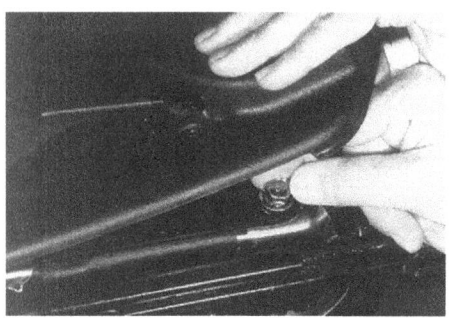

11/6c ... at each end.

10:18

10: Interior

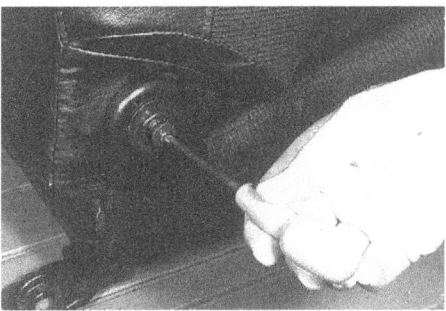

11/7a Remove screw and collar ...

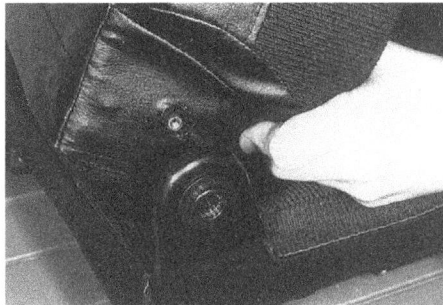

11/7b ... & pry out bush to release seat back.

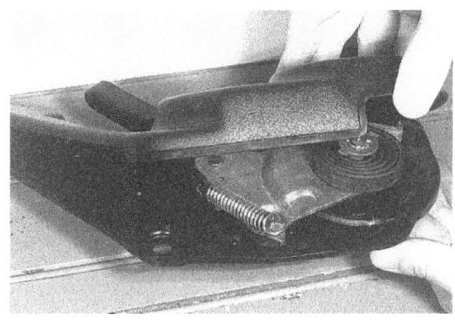

11/7c This is as close as you can get.

that we could get the knuckle unbolted: it is possible, but not easy. Refer to the accompanying photos. Start by turning the cover so that the front bolt can be removed - this is pretty easy to do. The rear bolt, however, requires the cover to be twisted upwards for access. Slacken the bolt with a crescent or box-end wrench, then remove it with your fingers.

7   ◨+ Once you've got the knuckle detached, the inner side of the seat is secured on a short pivot pin. Remove the screw and collar, then pry out the headed bush and slide off the cover, the seat back can be disengaged and removed. Don't even think about trying to take the recliner mecha-

11/8 Open/close hog rings with pliers.

nism apart - you can't, and even if you did, the heavy spring used would be impossible to re-tension. If it's broken, fit a new one.

8   ◨ The seat covers can be removed after releasing the hog rings which retain them. Use pliers to remove the rings, which can be kept and re-used. The top of the seat backrest cover may have a concealed zipper. This can be undone to allow you access to the headrest speaker recesses. The recesses are there on all cars, so you could install your own speakers if you can find suitable units to fit the small recesses. Note also that a removable lumbar support pad is fitted in the seat back.

9   When reassembling the seat, fit the covers, if removed, and secure them with hog rings. Reassemble the inner pivot and cover and fit the securing bolt. You'll need to reverse the wrestling process to fit the knuckle on the outer side of the seat. Tighten the knuckle mounting bolts to 35-55Nm/3.5-5.7kgf m/25-41lbf ft.

INSTALLATION

10   Check that the seat runners are secure on the seat base, and that they lie parallel. Tip the seat backrest fully forward. Lower the seat into the car and fit the rear mounting bolts. Slide the seat fully rearward and recline the seat back. Fit the front mounting bolts. Tighten all four bolts to 39-50Nm/3.9-5.2kgf m/29-37lbf ft. Where fitted, reconnect any wiring to seat components.

12. CARPETS - REMOVAL & INSTALLATION

☞ 1/1, 2.
1   ◨ Before the main carpet section can be removed, you need to remove the following:
   Seats (☞ 10/6)
   Dash panel assembly (☞ 10/4)
   Heater unit (☞ 6/14)
   Package shelf carpet (see following text)

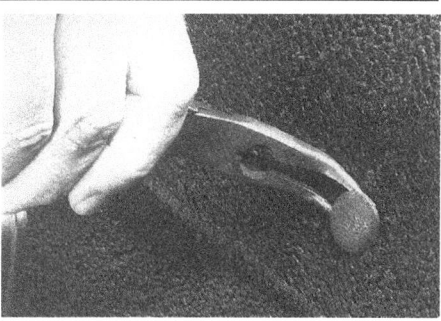

12/2 Clips can be released by cranked pliers.

Front side trim, scuff plates, and quarter trim (☞ 10/5)
Transmission tunnel bracket and driver's footrest.

2   ◨ Start by removing the package shelf carpet. This is secured by a couple of crosshead screws and cup washers, two round plastic stops secured by crosshead screws, plus numerous plastic clips around the edge of the carpet. When removing the clips, use a pair of screwdriver blades or cranked needle-nosed pliers under the head of the pin and lever each one out. Don't be tempted to pull on the carpet - it will just pull off over the head of the pin. Remove the section of carpet which covers the bodywork behind the seat backs, again, by pulling out the plastic pins which secure it.

3   Remove the remaining items listed above. With the interior of the car clear, remove the footrest from the driver's side footwell (two 10mm nuts) and the dash center panel lower mounting bracket (two sheet metal screws). Lift the main carpet away, checking for any missed obstructions as you do so. It's likely that there will be minor variations between models of different years or markets, and further minor dismantling may be needed if interior fixtures/accessories are impeding removal.

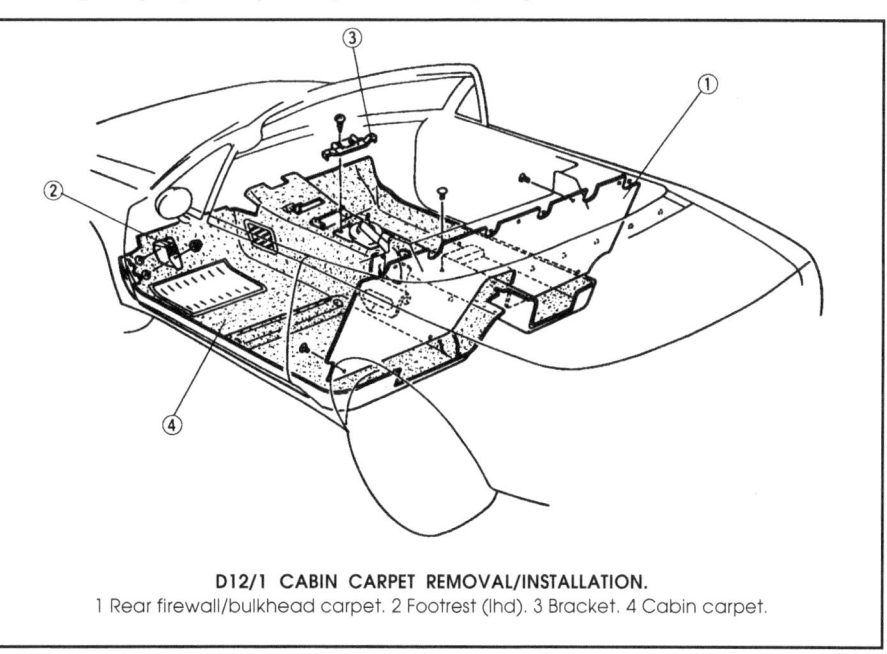

D12/1 CABIN CARPET REMOVAL/INSTALLATION.
1 Rear firewall/bulkhead carpet. 2 Footrest (lhd). 3 Bracket. 4 Cabin carpet.

10:19

Mazda Miata, MX-5, Eunos & Roadster

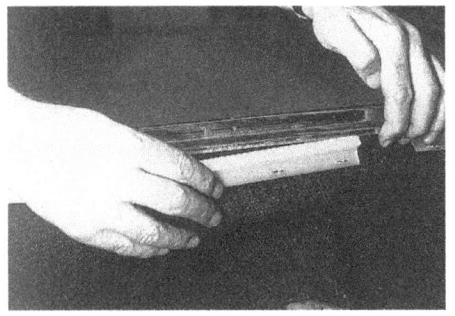
12/4 Slide channel over metal seam.

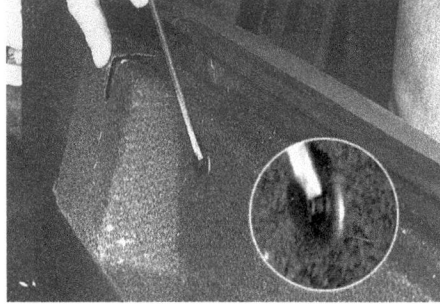
13/3a Use screwdriver to pry up clip center ...

14/2a Remove covering trim ...

4 📷 When installing the carpet, make sure that it sits flat in the car, and that the edges are correctly positioned. At each door opening there is a plastic channel section which hooks over the seam edge - fit this, then secure the carpet at this point with the scuff plates. Once you are satisfied that the carpet is positioned correctly, install the components removed for access, referring to the relevant chapters and sections mentioned above for fitting details and tightening torques.

13/3b ... then pull out clip body.

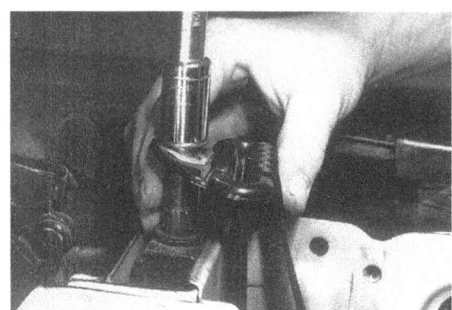
14/2b ... & unscrew top anchor bolt.

13. TRUNK (BOOT) CARPET & TRIM - REMOVAL & INSTALLATION

☞ 1/1, 2.

1 The trunk (boot) carpet can be removed after the spare wheel has been lifted out and the plastic nuts and the snap fasteners which retain the battery cover have been released and the cover removed. When installing the carpet, make sure it aligns correctly around the spare wheel fixing point and battery area, and that the cover section over the tool well on the left side of the car fits properly.

2 📷+ There is a pressed steel access cover concealing the fuel filler and vent hoses. This can be detached after unclipping the jack handle and removing the 10mm bolts which retain it. There is no need to remove the trunk carpet for access.

3 📷+ At the very back of the trunk there is a molded trim cover across the back panel. This is held by plastic clips, and these must be released by lifting the center section of the clip (it looks like a plastic rivet head sitting in a cup washer) with a small screwdriver blade. Once lifted, grasp the whole pin and withdraw it. Repeat this procedure on the remaining clips and lift the trim cover away.

13/2a Remove jack handle from clips & ...

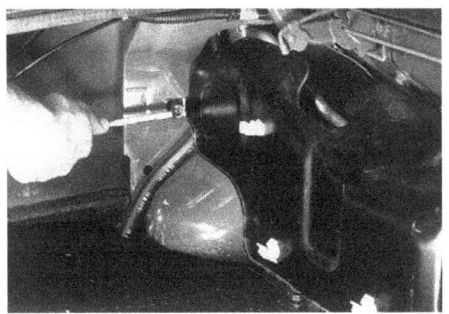
13/2b ... then remove access panel bolts.

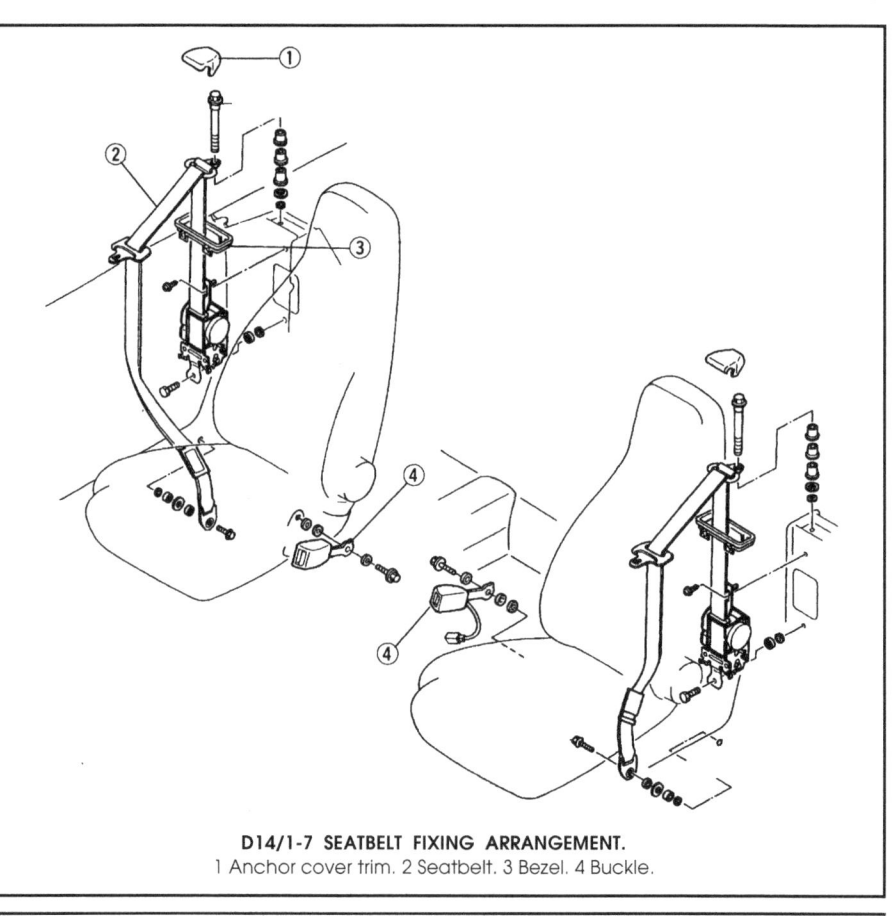

D14/1-7 SEATBELT FIXING ARRANGEMENT.
1 Anchor cover trim. 2 Seatbelt. 3 Bezel. 4 Buckle.

10: Interior

Again, no other parts of the trunk trim affect its removal or installation.

14. SEATBELTS - REMOVAL, CHECKING & INSTALLATION

1   To gain access to the seatbelts you must first remove the brace bar and the relevant rear quarter trim panel ☞ 10/5. On cars so equipped, disconnect the seatbelt wiring connector.

2   Pry off and remove the plastic cover which conceals the head of the upper mounting

14/3d Final anchor bolt is on side of tunnel.

15/1a Lift off trim & unscrew two ...

14/3a Remove the inertia reel's anchor bolt ...

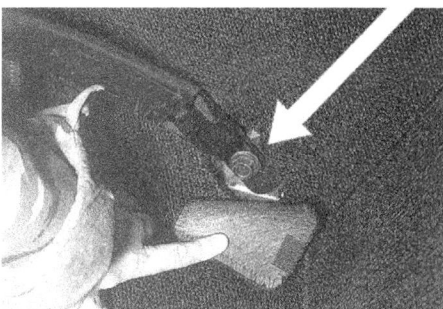
14/4 Buckle section has single anchor bolt.

15/1b ... bolts securing brace bar.

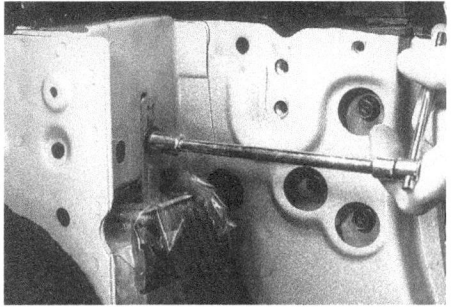
14/3b ... followed by alignment bolt ...

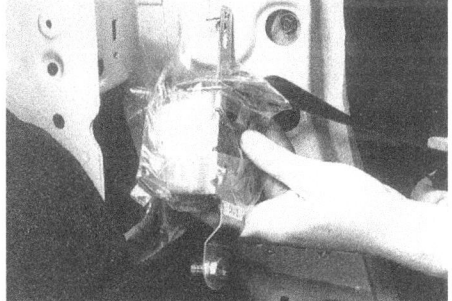
14/3c ... then lift away inertia reel.

bolt. Slacken the bolt using a 17mm socket. There appears to be variation between various years/models of the spacer and washer arrangement used here - make a careful note of the order in which these components are fitted.

3   Remove the 17mm mounting bolt which secures the inertia reel mechanism to the body recess, followed by the smaller 10mm bolt which aligns the mechanism at the top. Free the lower end of the belt by removing the 17mm fixing bolt, again, noting the exact arrangement of the spacers used.

4   If removal is necessary, the buckle section can be freed by unscrewing the 17mm mounting bolt which secures it to the seat bracket. As the buckle is removed, note the exact order of the spacer and washers used.

5   **Warning!** Once removed, the seatbelt mechanism must not be dismantled or interfered with - if there is a fault in the inertia reel mechanism, or if the belt webbing is frayed or cut, a new seatbelt must be installed. Check that the reel mechanism allows the belt to extend smoothly and easily when it is pulled gently with the mechanism held upright. Next, check that the reel mechanism locks if the belt is pulled out quickly or jerked, or when the reel mechanism is inclined at 30 degrees or more from the vertical position. If this is not the case, fit a new belt.

6   **Warning!** Check that the buckle mechanism latches positively and reliably.

7   **Warning!** When installing the belt assembly, fit the spacers and washers in exactly the same order as they were when removed. Tighten all of the 17mm bolts to 39-78Nm/3.9-8.0kgf m/29-57lbf ft. Install the rear quarter trim and brace bar, and connect the seatbelt wiring (where fitted). Check that the belt operates normally.

15. BRACE BAR - REMOVAL & INSTALLATION

REMOVAL

1   Lift the push-fit trim pieces from each end of the brace bar to expose the fixing bolts. Unscrew and remove both bolts and lift the brace bar off.

INSTALLATION

2   Position the brace bar so that the fixing bolt holes are correctly aligned. Install the fixing bolts and tighten to 63-93Nm/6.4-9.5kgf m/47-68lbf ft. Replace the push-fit trim pieces to hide the bolt heads.

Notes

11

Body

1. INTRODUCTION

This chapter relates to the main body assembly and the various external panels which form part of it, plus items like the convertible top and optional hard top. We cover all areas of repair and overhaul appropriate to the enthusiast, which can be dealt with at home using normal tools and equipment - major body repairs on any car require specialist facilities, and, as such, should be left to a Mazda dealer or body shop.

These cars feature a conventional unitary body constructed from welded steel pressings. On the underside of the body, the engine, transmission and front suspension assembly are mounted via a fabricated steel crossmember or subframe. At the back of the car, a second subframe carries the rear axle and suspension components. The two subframes are linked by the PPF ('Power Plant Frame').

The visible parts of the bodyshell comprise various hinged, welded and bolt-on panels; the doors, the hood (bonnet) and trunk (boot) lids, plus the front and rear bumper assemblies. Most of the visible body area is of steel construction, though items like the bumpers are of color-matched plastic. Many aftermarket add-on body parts will be plastic moldings, too.

2. BODY - MAINTENANCE & COSMETIC CARE

WHY MAINTENANCE MATTERS

1   If you intend to keep your car in prime condition, the answer is regular maintenance. This will not just enhance the value of your car, but will bring developing problems to your attention so that you can make repairs *before* it gets very expensive.

2   Body repairs have always posed a problem for the. With just about any other part of the car, you can repair or replace components to keep the car running well. The bodyshell should be regarded as a single, large component to which all the other mechanical assemblies are attached, and it is vital that this component should not be allowed to fall into such disrepair that it needs to be replaced; when a car reaches the point at which the bodyshell has corroded badly, or has sustained serious accident damage, economics usually dictate that it gets scrapped.

3   While you could probably get your Mazda dealer to order a new body for you, the sheer cost and time involved in transferring all the parts across would probably make this option unrealistic. (A little like replacing all the walls in your house - theoretically possible, but almost unworkable in practice.) Next time you pass a wrecker's yard, just consider how and why all those cars got there - chances are that, for most, the entry ticket was down to corrosion or severe damage to the body.

4   The simple key to body maintenance is regular attention. You should wash the bodywork regularly to keep the paint in good condition - this is the first-line defense against corrosion. Washing will remove visible road dirt, and, more importantly, the invisible chemical pollutants which will dull and damage the finish. Of equal importance is regular polishing. This seals the paint and protects it from attack by pollutants. These two operations are especially important on modern cars - the types of paints used now are more environmentally-friendly but, seemingly, less durable than the older style paints were.

WASHING

5   Wash the car using *plenty* of water - a hose or domestic pressure wash is ideal for this. Alternatively, use water from a bucket, but remember to change it regularly before dirt turns it into an abrasive. To avoid any risk of damage to the paint finish, soak the bodywork thoroughly to soften the film of dirt, then gently hose it away using a soft brush or a sponge to agitate the dirt and loosen it. Don't scrub at the paintwork during this stage, or you'll cause tiny scratches to form, dulling the finish.

6   By all means use a detergent additive in moderation - this will help shift the greasy road dirt which builds up where the car is used in areas of high traffic density (in other words, just about everywhere). However, beware of using too much detergent as it will remove body polish as well as the dirt. Whatever method and solution you use for the job, wash the car on an overcast day if possible, or park it in the shade while you work; if the sun is shining on the car and the paintwork heats up, you'll have problems with spotting as the paintwork dries too fast.

7   All external parts of the car should be cleaned in this way, including the plastic body parts, the hard or convertible top and the wheels. Follow up by rinsing *thoroughly* with clean water. When rinsing, check how the water lies on the hood or trunk lid - if it forms small beads, the wax coating is still good, while a continuous film or large sheets of surface water tell you that it's time to polish the car. The paintwork can be dried off using an old (but clean!) towel to prevent marking from the water droplets - some owners may prefer to use a traditional chamois leather; expensive, but effective. You may wish to try out some of the newer, synthetic chamois leathers.

8   In the case of alloy wheels, note that they are lacquer-coated; don't use abrasive cleaners or you'll damage the lacquer film and then rapid corrosion will set in. Never, ever, use a wire brush to clean alloy wheels. If the wheels show signs of peeling lacquer, or damage has resulted from stone chips, have them blasted and relacquered professionally before the alloy surface gets seriously pitted by corrosion. If you encounter stubborn staining or marking of the wheels, you could try one of the specialist products formulated for use on alloy wheels. Check the manufacturer's advice to ensure that it will not damage the protective lacquer coating before use.

9   Don't forget the wheel wells (wheelarches) and the lower edges of the rockers (sills) during regular washes. These areas are easily overlooked, which explains why they are often the first areas to

Mazda Miata, MX-5, Eunos & Roadster

suffer corrosion problems - don't just deal with the easy-to-reach parts. Pay special attention to the lip which lies inside the edge of many panels. These lips give strength and rigidity but, unfortunately, also provide tiny ledges where damp dirt can lodge and build up unnoticed until the paint begins to blister.

10 Inside each wheelwell you'll notice plastic liners attached by 10mm bolts. Be aware that road dirt can get behind these and build up - this can lead to corrosion problems if left too long. It's a good idea to remove the liners once in a while and clean out any build-up of dirt, especially to the rear of the wheels where most dirt and road debris gets thrown by the tires. You can guard against corrosion here (and elsewhere) by applying an underbody coating before the liners are reinstalled.

11 Don't forget that road dirt contains all kinds of pollutants, many of which are corrosive. In temperate areas where the winter roads are salted to clear snow, salt corrosion is a real problem. If you drive your car all year round and live in such an area, during winter you need to wash the bodywork (and underside) often.

POLISHING

12 We recommend that you polish your car at least twice a year, or whenever water stops forming droplets on the hood. Spring and fall are the best times - that way you get protection from summer sun and winter rain and snow. Polishing takes a little time to do, especially if you use a traditional, quality wax. On the other hand, we are talking about Mazda's little roadster here, not a 30 foot RV, so you can afford to lavish attention on the body.

13 The choice of polish is up to you. There are hi-tech, wax-in-30-seconds products, and wax-as-you-wash additives. We've used them, and don't rate them very highly. The way we figure it, if the instant wax products work, why are there still expensive, labor-intensive traditional waxes on sale ... Take our advice and use a traditional, non-abrasive paste or cream body wax - you'll work hard a couple of times a year, but the rest of the time you can rest easy about your paint. If you really don't like wax, use a high quality alternative product.

14 As with washing, waxing should be carried out on a dull day, or under shade, **never** in full sun or while the bodywork is still hot. Be sure to use really soft, clean rag for polishing and buffing the paint. Work on a small area at a time (we like to complete one panel and then move to the next - that way, nothing gets missed). Apply the wax sparingly with a light circular action - if the paint has not been waxed for a long time and the wax soaks in, apply a little more. When it has dried to a white color, use a clean rag to buff to a good finish. Don't skip seams and crevices - they need waxing more than the flat areas. Finally, hand waxing is always preferable to using a power polisher.

VINYL TRIM CLEANERS AND POLISHES

15 These products are great for cleaning items like the convertible top, dash panel, interior trim, various body seals, and the like. They make these parts look like new and offer a degree of protection from sun damage and chemical attack. We have used 'Armor All' and 'Son of a Gun' to good effect. (Those of you who reside in prime convertible top country, where the sun always shines, may prefer to seek out specialized products which may offer better sun protection - the black interior of the car builds up heat in a big way on a sunny day.) This type of cleaner also works well on tire sidewalls.

TAR SPOTS

16 Road tar spotting on your paint can be removed using a proprietary solvent. Always follow the maker's directions, and we further suggest you try out the product on an unobtrusive area first to check for paint discoloration. Note that tar spots are much easier to remove from waxed paintwork than from neglected and faded paint.

COLOR RESTORERS

17 Most of these products are fine abrasives, designed to remove the surface layer of the paint to expose the unoxidised layer below. If you need to use them, do so sparingly, or you could cut through to the primer or bare metal - and the paint finish on these cars is none too thick. That said, if you've just bought a used car with dull paint but at a bargain price, try a color restorer before booking a paint job, you might be pleasantly surprised. You could also try one of the color-impregnated polishes - these are designed to cover minor scratches and blemishes in the paint finish. In either case, follow the maker's directions for use, and with any abrasive restorer or wax, don't rub too hard, especially near panel edges.

3. PAINTWORK - DAMAGE REPAIR

☞ 1/1, 2.

1 Your car is almost certainly going to suffer from at least minor cosmetic damage during its life. One of the most vulnerable areas is the nose of the car: the rounded design with its integrated bumpers looks great, but, unfortunately, is very prone to stone chips. Small stones, flung up by passing traffic, can hardly fail to cause damage if they impact with the front of the car.

2 Like washing and waxing, preventative maintenance beats having to repair paint damage. A popular method of avoiding stone chips on the nose of the car is to fit a front mask or 'bra.' These vinyl covers attach to the nose of the car, usually just forward of the headlight covers, and fend off the worst of the flying debris. We have no personal experience of these devices, but if you can live with the way it makes your car look, then it will probably keep the paint underneath looking good for longer.

3 If you do use a front mask, you might find it worthwhile to remove it regularly to check for dirt and moisture trapped underneath. This problem can also occur with luggage packs which strap directly onto the trunk lid. (We have experienced problems like this with motorcycle tank bags, which are made of similar materials. The airflow tends to blast rain and road dirt underneath where it gets trapped and acts like a cutting compound - beware!)

4 The lower edge of the car is vulnerable to stone chip damage from the car's own wheels. This can be reduced by installing mudguards (mud flaps). These are available as Mazda accessories or through Mazda specialists. We would suggest that you use the correct type in preference to the one-size-fits-all guards sold in most auto parts stores - the fit and appearance will be a lot better. Some models are protected by factory-fitted splash guards (spats) around the back edge of the front and rear wheel wells. These splash guards are color-impregnated to match the rest of the body, and doubtless help protect the bodywork, though it has to be said that they are very vulnerable to damage. If you like the sound of these items, you could try ordering a set through your Mazda dealer.

5 If bodywork/paintwork damage has already occurred, you'll want to do something about it quickly, especially if bare metal is exposed. The best place to buy touch-up paint is from a Mazda dealer - that way you should get a good color match, and you can be certain that the paint will be safe to use on all body parts, steel or plastic. Before you can apply the paint you'll need to rub down the area around the chip or scratch with fine rubbing compound to smooth the edge of the scratch and to remove old body wax. Note that if the car has been waxed with a silicone-based product, you may need to wipe the area with a special solvent to remove silicone residue before the paint will stick. If you think you may have problems here, ask a paint specialist for advice on what to use.

6 Where the damaged area has exposed bare steel, you'll need to apply a primer. Remove any surface corrosion with fine abrasive paper, and apply a rust-inhibiting primer, or use a rust-killing coating, followed by regular primer. Be warned that if you leave traces of rust in the damaged area, it will eventually break through the repair. If the paint damage is deep, use a fine filler paste or stopper to fill the deepest areas before priming and painting. Leave the filler layer just a little lower than the paint surface - if necessary, use fine abrasive paper to rub down any high spots.

7 Using a fine brush, apply a thin coat of paint to the damaged area and allow it to dry. Note that paint supplied in aerosol cans can be sprayed from very close range into the aerosol's cap (or a similar container) to form a small pool of paint which can be applied with a brush, though you'll need to work very quickly. Don't try to use the paint once it gets thick and sticky.

8 Apply coats of paint as often as necessary to bring the level of the new paint slightly higher than the surrounding paint, then leave it to harden fully (around two weeks). You can then use rubbing compound to blend the new paint in with the old, finally sealing the repair by waxing the area.

4. BODY - DAMAGE REPAIR & PAINTING

☞ 1/1, 2.

Please note that the photographs which accompany this section are not of a Miata/MX-5/Eunos; not

11: Body

even for you, Dear Reader, could we bring ourselves to inflict deliberate damage on our project car ... The pictured procedures would, however, apply to any conventional, metal-bodied car, including Mazda's roadster.

1   In this section we're looking at what to do in the event of relatively minor body damage - the sort of thing that happens to everyone's car once in a while in the parking lot (car park) or driveway. If the damage is more severe than paint scraping and minor panel denting, and there is any possibility of hidden structural damage, forget about home repairs and get the car checked out by a Mazda dealer or reputable body shop - don't risk lives by trying to save money.

ASSESSING THE DAMAGE

2   The exact nature of minor impact damage will be dependent on what area of the car is affected. In the case of plastic or composite panels, light impacts may have produced no visible signs of damage, in which case you need carry out no repair work at all, though you should check for underlying damage which may not be outwardly apparent. This is especially important after front-end or rear-end impact, where the bumper may appear unmarked, but underlying deformation of the supporting structure may have occurred. If you are unsure about this, you should seek professional advice. If plastic panels have split or shattered, the best option is to fit new ones. Repairing this type of material is not easy, though some professional body shops may have facilities for such repairs. Once again, seek expert opinion about this.

3   What you do about minor bumps and scrapes depends on the extent of the damage and your ability and facilities. Never forget that while it might be well within your capabilities to fix the damage, you may find that it works out cheaper to get a professional job done if you need to spend heavily on body repair materials and tools.

4   Another thing you need to consider is the potential affect on the car's resale value. Poor quality body repairs are usually pretty obvious under professional scrutiny, and may mean a lower trade-in/selling price. If this would be the result of home repair, you may actually be costing yourself money in the longer term.

5   Before you do anything else, examine the damaged area carefully. You need to assess the true extent of the damage rather than the apparent extent, and that means checking for underlying deformation of any supporting structure. Where you are dealing with a closed section, or a double-skinned area, this may not be easy, but whatever else you do, never just cover up the external damage without making sure that it does not extend to other components. Note that the repair procedures we describe here assume that the damage is superficial, and that the underlying body structure is not affected.

6   The exact method of repair will depend on the type of damage. Shallow scrapes which have not dented the panel by more than about 3mm/^{1}/$_8$in can usually just be prepared, filled and painted, whilst deeper gouges and dents will have to be pulled out first. If the metal has been holed, the gap will have to be bridged with perforated metal mesh or glassfiber matting before you can fill the resulting depression - you need to take this into account when purchasing repair materials.

PULLING OUT A DENT

7   A professional body shop will use equipment and skills unavailable to the home enthusiast to deal with deformed body panels, and in many cases will be able to reshape the damaged panel without needing to apply much filler. The best the amateur can do is try and get the panel as close as possible to the original shape, using whatever tools come to hand. The trick is to avoid pulling the metal out too far - it needs to lie around 3mm/^{1}/$_8$in below the eventual surface level.

8   If you can get behind the damaged area, first try using your hands or a soft pad and lever to push the dent outward. If the dent is on a relatively flat area, you may be lucky and find that it will pop out to its original shape quite easily. On more complicated or heavily curved areas this is less likely, and more work will be required. With this type of dent you'll need to gently hammer out the dent using a tool with the largest/flattest surface area possible, given the access available. Aim to get as close as you can to the original panel shape with the minimum number of blows. Note that the metal will stretch as you work, and you need to minimize this problem. It helps to hold a heavy wood block on the outside of the dent as you strike the inside of the area - this helps ensure that the dent comes out evenly and stretching is minimized.

9   Where access behind the dent is difficult - and in our experience, there is a universal law of physics which dictates that all dents will occur right above a closed box section - you'll need to pull the dent out from the front. Body shops will use a slide hammer to do this. If you have one, you can do the same, otherwise improvise with sheet metal screws. Drill several holes through the panel inside the dent area, and screw the sheet metal screws into them, leaving the screw heads well above the metal surface. You can now grasp the screw heads with a vise grips (mole grips) and pull the dent out. A carpenter's hammer with a claw end for nail removal can also be useful here.

10   + When the dent is as close as you can get it to the original shape, run your hand across it and check for high spots. If you need to, tap these inwards carefully so that no metal area lies above the proposed final surface. Note that this check is

4/10b First give dent enough depth for filler.

important - if you have high spots, you'll never be able to get the repair close to the original contours.

REPAIRING HOLED OR GASHED AREAS

11   If the repair includes a hole, you'll need to deal with this before you start filling. If rust has caused the problem, you must remove all traces or the corrosion will continue and push the filler out of the repaired area. Wire brush or sandpaper the rusted metal until all rust has been removed. You will need to wear gloves, a dust mask and eye protection while doing this. Remove

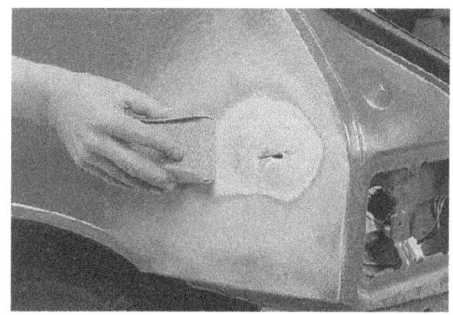

4/11 Remove paint from damaged area.

paint from the damaged area, feathering the surrounding paint edge using fine sandpaper. You will need to provide a key which the filler can grip, so roughen the dent area using a body file, or score the metal with an old screwdriver. Also note that drilling small holes will help. The surface needs to be quite rough to provide a key for the filler paste - using a drill or polisher fitted with a coarse abrasive disc will speed up this process for large areas.

12   Apply a rust removing/neutralising gel or liquid to kill any traces of rust remaining on the metal, and remember to treat the inside of the

4/10a Typical minor dent.

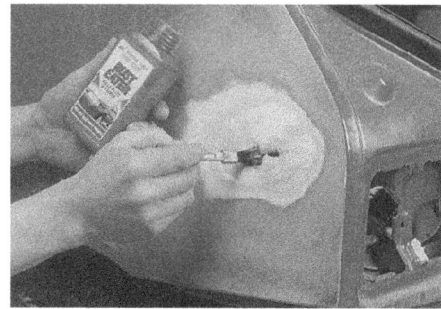

4/12 Treat bare metal & rust with rust killer.

Mazda Miata, MX-5, Eunos & Roadster

panel, too - the paint and any underbody coating will probably have flaked off during the impact. Read the directions on the packaging and take appropriate precautions when handling these products, which are corrosive.

13   To bridge holes or gashes, cut a piece of perforated metal mesh (supplied with most repair kits) to the required shape, and 'glue' this in position with dabs of filler paste. Note also that the quantities of filler and hardener need to be measured accurately - too much or too little hardener may result in the mixture setting too quickly, or not at all. Make sure that the mesh fits the contours of the dent, and that it does not protrude above the bodywork surface. Wait for a while to allow the filler paste to harden and secure the mesh.

14   + Alternatively, some repair kits include glassfiber matting and a liquid resin. These materials are a little trickier to work with, but will permit you to follow intricate contours more faithfully. The matting is cut to shape with scissors, and then the damaged area is coated with resin to which a hardener has been added. Press the matting onto the resin coat, and check that any fibers projecting above the finished surface are removed before the resin sets hard. Use an old paintbrush dipped in

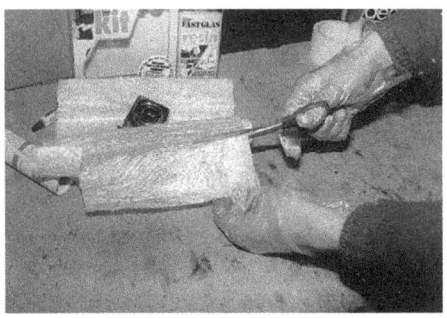
4/14a Cut fiberglass mat to right size & shape.

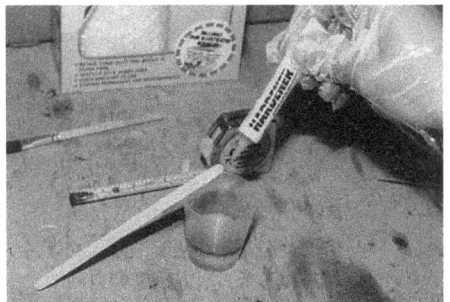
4/14b Mix hardener into resin.

resin to stipple the matting down, and to remove any trapped air bubbles. Depending on the extent of the hole, you may need to build up several layers to complete the repair. You should allow the initial layer to dry hard for an hour or so before adding successive layers - this will give you a firm surface on which to build.

15   **Warning!** Follow the maker's directions when using these products, noting safety instructions and handling precautions. You should wear gloves when working with resins, hardeners and glassfiber, and always ensure adequate ventilation.

Note also that the quantities of resin and hardener need to be measured accurately - too much or too little hardener may result in the resin setting too quickly, or not at all. If using the glassfiber method, leave the repair to harden before moving on to filling.

FILLING

16   By now, the repaired area should begin to look a little more car-shaped; if so, you are ready to apply the filler to reprofile the surface. Following the maker's directions, mix up an

4/16 Mix appropriate amount of filler & hardener.

appropriate amount of filler paste and hardener. Don't be tempted to mix too much at once, it's much better to build up the repair in layers.

17   Use a plastic spreader (normally included in the repair kit) to spread paste over the dented area. As each layer dries hard (usually around 20 minutes), check that you have left no high spots - if you need to, use a body file or a Surform tool to remove these. Try to end up with a smooth surface which conforms as closely as possible to the finished profile and level. Although the filler can be worked with hand tools when it has

4/17 Build filler layer-by-layer.

hardened, it is obviously preferable if you have the minimum amount of sanding to carry out.

SANDING

18   The filled area now needs to be shaped and sanded smooth. You can do this using progressively fine grades of sandpaper, or 'wet-&-dry' paper wrapped round a sanding block. If you need to remove a lot of filler, use a power sander. We suggest that you finish the work by hand, however, because it is very easy to remove too much material with power tools. Whatever method you use to

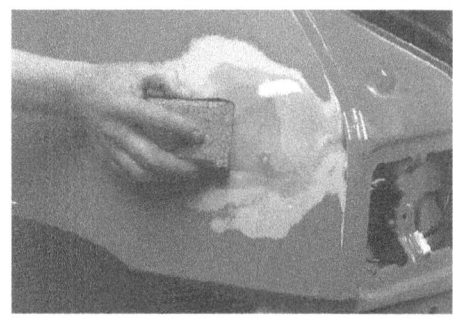
4/18 Abrasive paper creates smooth surface.

remove filler, wear eye protection and a dust mask.
19   The wet-&-dry type abrasive papers allow you to rinse away filler debris, and so last longer than plain sandpaper. Also, by working with a wet surface, any steps or hollows show up well. While the work area is wet, every so often sight along it to check the surface profile. Note that you'll need to ensure the repair is completely dried out before you can apply paint. If you're in a hurry, a hairdrier helps the hardening process.

PAINTING

20   Note that painting operations require a clean environment, comfortable temperatures (around 20 degrees C/68F, or higher) low humidity and no wind, dust or bugs. Spraying paint seems to bring out the suicidal element in the bug population: they come from miles around to hurl themselves at fresh, wet paint, and then crawl around for a while before dying, stuck firmly in your new paint. There is no point trying to remove them if this happens - you'll still need to repair the resulting craters in the paint later. You are likely to get the best results by working in your garage. The work area should be really clean before you start - remove any sources of dust, and damp down the floor with a fine water spray just before spraying commences. **Warning!** Although this sequence assumes the use of spray cans (aerosols), rather than professional-type compressed air spraygun equipment, if you do decide to borrow or hire such equipment, be careful that you get the right type of paint. Seek expert advice on this, and on no account use professional, two-pack paint. Many two-pack paints are isocyanate-based, requiring a full body suit and air-fed mask. Don't try using this type of paint at home - it could kill you if you inhale it. Your paint supplier will need to know the car's paint code details, and you should also explain your facilities and level of experience so that he can advise you on safe usage procedures.

21   Once any necessary repairs have been made and the filled area has dried thoroughly, you can start painting. For this you'll need primer, plus a top coat to match the original paint finish. The paint color of the car is usually identified by a sticker on the underside of the hood (bonnet).

22   Most owners will be using aerosol cans of paint for this job, and these can be obtained through Mazda dealers and automotive accessory stores. You'll also need a can of primer (aerosol spray or brush type), masking tape and some

11: Body

newspaper, plus some very fine abrasive paper and paint cutting compound.

23 Make absolutely sure that the filled area has been rubbed down smooth, and that no holes or low spots are left in the filler surface; don't waste time or paint until you are certain that you've got this right. Check by feel rather than by eye - fingers tend to be more reliable in detecting faults in the surface. The repaired area should be feathered into the surrounding paint, and you should not be able to feel the join between them - if you can, you still have work to do. The surrounding paint must be clean and free from any trace of body wax - you can buy solvents which will remove any wax/silicone from the surface. Note that unless the wax/silicone is removed, the new paint will not adhere properly, and may form pinholes as it pulls away from the wax.

24 Mask off the surrounding area to protect it against overspray. Wherever possible, mask up to a natural boundary line, such as a seam or molding edge. This will make any slight color variation less obvious. In the area to be painted, you should remove any trim, plus items like lights and badges, so that the new paint will cover these areas, too. When complete, the lights, trim, or whatever, can be installed, covering and disguising the new paint edge. Don't try to mask off removable items - it will look terrible because you'll be able to see the edge of the new paint film at these points. Fix sheets of newspaper to the surrounding bodywork to protect them from overspray, securing edges with strips of masking tape.

25 ❍+ Following the directions on the can, brush or spray on the primer coat, making sure that all bare metal is covered. While the primer coat is wet and glossy, sight across the repair, looking for any defects in the surface. The paint's temporary gloss surface will help to identify any rippled or

4/25a Mask off area and apply primer.

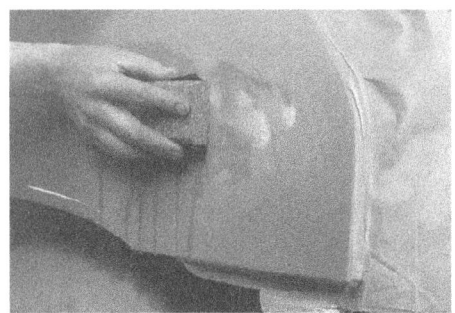
4/25b Sand primer &, if necessary, fill ...

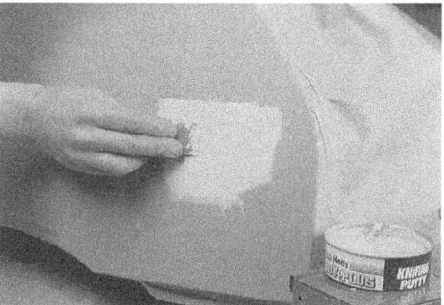
4/25c ... small holes with filler or knifing putty.

sunken areas. If necessary, wait until the primer coat has dried and apply further filler coats or knifing putty to build up such areas, then sand down and repeat the primer coat.

26 Once the primer has been applied satisfactorily, leave it to dry thoroughly for several hours. Then use a very fine wet-&-dry type abrasive paper (around 400 grade or finer) to rub down the primer coat. The paper should be used wet, and rinsed regularly in clean water to remove excess paint from the surface. A small amount of detergent in the water will help here.

27 When the primer surface is completely smooth to the touch, wipe down with a lint-free rag and plenty of clean water, then allow the area to dry. You can speed this up by using a heat gun or fan heater. Immediately before you spray on the top coat, wipe over the surface with a tack rag (available from paint suppliers) to remove any tiny dust specks.

28 ❍ 📷 Agitate the paint can for at least one minute to mix the paint thoroughly. The paint can needs to be held with the nozzle about 8-10 inches from the surface (or the distance given in the instructions on the can). Start moving the can

4/28 Color coat in thin layers.

across the surface, and, as it reaches the edge of the area to be sprayed, depress the nozzle. Keep the can moving slowly and evenly, checking that the nozzle-to-surface distance remains constant. Note that it is easy to find that you are moving the can through an arc. Don't do this or the paint will be applied unevenly, and may sag or run at the center of the arc, where the nozzle gets too close to the body surface.

29 As you reach the far side of the area being sprayed, release the button. Move back to the start point and repeat the process, this time a little lower

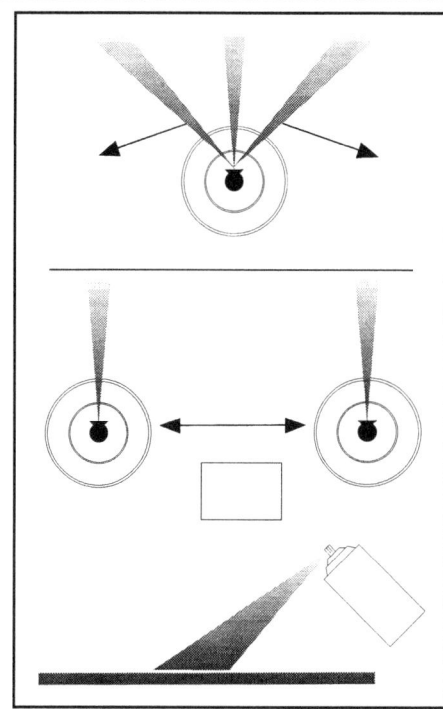

D4/28 SPRAYING TECHNIQUES.
Top: Don't swivel the spraycan. Centre: Do keep the spraycan parallel to the workpiece. Bottom: For horizontal surfaces spray from an angle of 45 degrees, but otherwise use same techniques. (Courtesy Davann).

down so that the bands of paint just overlap. Repeat the sequence until the area is covered.

30 At this stage, the paint film will look semi-transparent. This is correct - don't be tempted to try and apply the paint too thickly or the wet paint film will run or sag. If this happens, you must allow it to dry completely, then rub it down and start over. What you need to do is to apply a thin, even film. Allow this to dry for about 15-20 minutes, then apply a second coat. Continue in this way until the paint coat is even and opaque. Don't worry too much if the finish seems a little rough and has a dull appearance; you can deal with this later using a rubbing compound. Let the new paint dry for an hour or so, then remove the masking.

FINISHING

31 By now you will have got rid of the dent, and the damaged area should be looking a lot better. Your new paint will probably look a little flat and dull because it's difficult to get a good gloss from a spraycan: don't get too despondent about it if this is your first attempt at body repair. Don't be in a hurry to polish the new paint; it needs around two weeks (but follow the maker's instructions) to cure and harden completely. For now, install any trim or other items removed and just use the car as normal until the paint is hard.

32 ❍+ After waiting for an appropriate period, you can set to work with rubbing compound. This is a fine, abrasive paste which will remove any roughness on the paint surface and produce a good gloss finish. Work carefully, taking care not to rub

Mazda Miata, MX-5, Eunos & Roadster

4/32a Rubbing compound smooths paint.

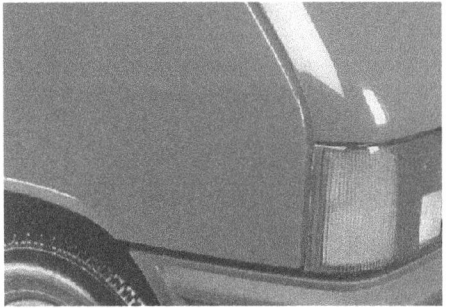

4/32b Magic! Your Mazda's become a Peugeot!

through the new paint. Once you have a smooth, gloss surface, apply a wax coat to seal and protect the new paint. Depending on your care in preparation and the accuracy of the color match, the repair should be pretty well invisible. Remember that some damage remains at the back of the repair, so we suggest that you use a wax-type underbody sealant at the back of the panel to prevent corrosion.

5. HOOD (BONNET) - REMOVAL & INSTALLATION

☞ 1/1, 2.

REMOVAL

1   You'll need an assistant during this operation. Open the engine hood (bonnet) and support with its stay. Protect the paintwork around the engine compartment with thick cloth (old towels are ideal) - this will prevent expensive cosmetic damage if the hood slips during removal or installation.

2   📷 Disconnect the windshield washer jet pipework at the first union by pulling on the pipe and moving it to and fro until the pipe is free. You may find that it helps to push the pipe off its stub

5/2 Disconnect washer pipe at union.

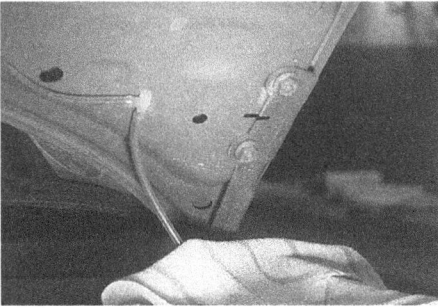

5/3 Mark hinge positions.

using a screwdriver blade.

3   📷 Mark the relative position of the hood and hinge on each side of the car with a marker pen so that the hood can be exactly realigned when refitted. If you are fitting a new hood, you can ignore this step, but alignment will need to be carried out more carefully.

4   With an assistant holding the hood steady, release the two 14mm nuts on each side, and then carefully lift the hood away from the car. Replace the four nuts finger-tight on the projecting studs for safekeeping, and then store the hood safely until it

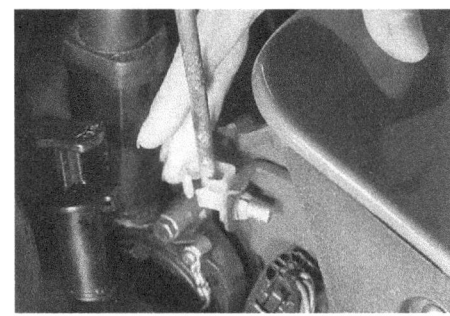

5/5a Clip retains hood support stay.

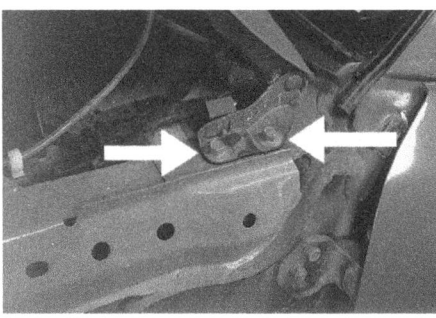

5/5b Hinge removal requires fender off.

is required again.

5   📷+ If required, you can remove the hood support stay by pulling back the outer tag of its nylon swivel clip and levering the clip open with a screwdriver blade. After this, the stay can be pulled out of the clip and removed from the car. Note that if you need to detach the hood hinges from the body, you'll need to remove the front fenders to gain access to the mounting bolts ☞ 11/12.

INSTALLATION

6   The gold colored end of the stay with the longer leg fits in the hinge clip. The clip is located high on the left chassis rail, just behind the headlight assembly. Make sure the nylon clip is open, and pass the leg of the stay through the circular section of the clip and metal bracket, then close the latch over the vertical section of the stay. Lay the stay across the front of the engine compartment and fix the other end into its clip.

7   With the help of an assistant, carefully position the hood so that its rear corners are wedged into the gap on each side of the car between the windshield lower rail and the fender (wing). Quickly lift the hinges and push them over the protruding studs on the underside of the hood, and then tighten the two 14 mm nuts on each side finger-tight. Prop the hood open with its stay.

8   If you made positional marks on the hinges during removal, manipulate the hood/hinge relationship until the marks realign, and then tighten the 14mm nuts to 19-25Nm/1.9-2.6kgf m/14-18lbf ft. Repeat the process with the second hinge. If you are fitting a new hood, there will, of course, be no positional marks, and you'll have to slide the hood

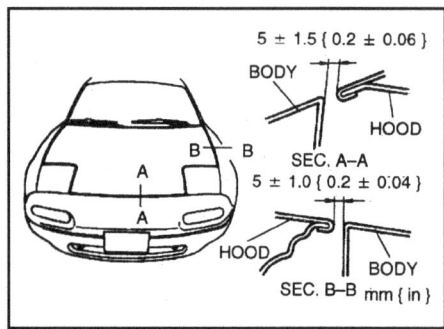

D5/9 HOOD (BONNET) PANEL GAPS.

backwards and forwards in the hinges until you are able to close the hood and obtain even gaps all the way around, then tighten the retaining nuts.

9   📷 The correct clearances around the hood are as follows. On each side, there should be a gap of 3.5-6.5mm/0.14-0.26in. Along the front edge, you should have a clearance of 4-6mm/0.16-0.24in. Make sure that the hood does not contact the surrounding bodywork while closed, or when being opened or shut.

10   **Warning!** After installing the hood, especially if a new hood has been fitted, you should check, and if necessary adjust, the hood latch and safety latch mechanism. Adjust the latch by slackening the mounting bolts and aligning it so that it contacts the striker on the underside of the hood. Tighten the two mounting bolts and single nut to 7.9-10.7Nm/80-110kgf cm/70-95.4lbf in.

11   Reconnect the windshield washer pipe to the pipework union stub on the underside of the hood.

6. TRUNK (BOOT) LID, FITTINGS & REAR PANEL - REMOVAL & INSTALLATION

☞ 1/1, 2.

Warning! The trunk lid is supported on strong

11: Body

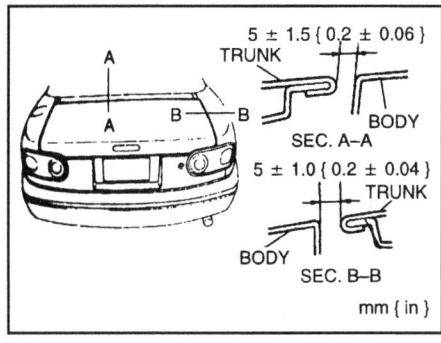

D6/4 TRUNK (BOOT) LID PANEL GAPS.

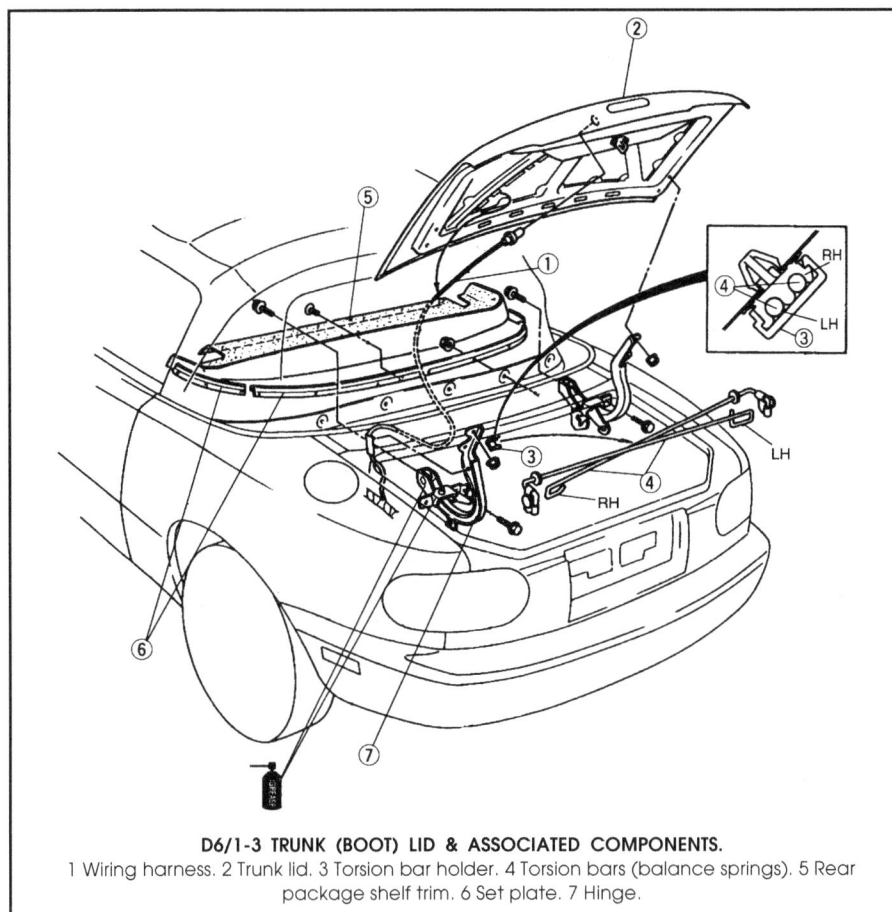

D6/1-3 TRUNK (BOOT) LID & ASSOCIATED COMPONENTS.
1 Wiring harness. 2 Trunk lid. 3 Torsion bar holder. 4 Torsion bars (balance springs). 5 Rear package shelf trim. 6 Set plate. 7 Hinge.

torsion springs (balance springs) fixed between the two hinges. You won't need to disturb these to remove the trunk lid, but you will need to release tension on the springs if the trunk lid hinges are to be removed. Take care when doing this or you could be injured.

TRUNK LID REMOVAL & INSTALLATION

1 Open the trunk lid fully. Mark around the outline of the hinge where it attaches to the trunk lid as a guide during installation. We use typist's correction fluid for this, or you could use paint or a marker pen. On cars so equipped, disconnect the wiring to the hi-mount brake light and/or trunk interior light mounted on the trunk lid.

2 Remove the four 10mm nuts which secure the trunk lid to its hinges. The lid is not especially heavy, but we suggest that you have

6/2 Four nuts fix trunk lid to hinges.

some assistance as the nuts are removed - note that if the lid slips during removal, it will probably damage the paint forward of the trunk opening.

3 When installing the trunk lid, hold it in position against the hinges and install the four retaining nuts loosely. Align the marks made during removal, then provisionally tighten the nuts. If you forgot to mark the hinge positions, or if you are fitting a new or refinished lid, you will need to align the lid in relation to the opening.

4 Lower the lid and check the gap, which should be 3.5-6.5mm/0.15-0.25in at the front edge and 4-6mm/0.16-0.24in at the sides. If necessary, make any minor position adjustments to achieve the correct gaps, then tighten the nuts to 7.9-10.7Nm/80-110kgf cm/70-95.4lbf in. Check that the trunk closes and latches correctly, and, if necessary, check the adjustment of the latch mechanism. Where appropriate, reconnect the hi-mount brake light and/or trunk interior light wiring.

TRUNK LATCH - REMOVAL, INSTALLATION & ADJUSTMENT

5 With the trunk lid raised for access, remove the trunk end trim panel. This is retained by numerous plastic fasteners. To remove them, lift

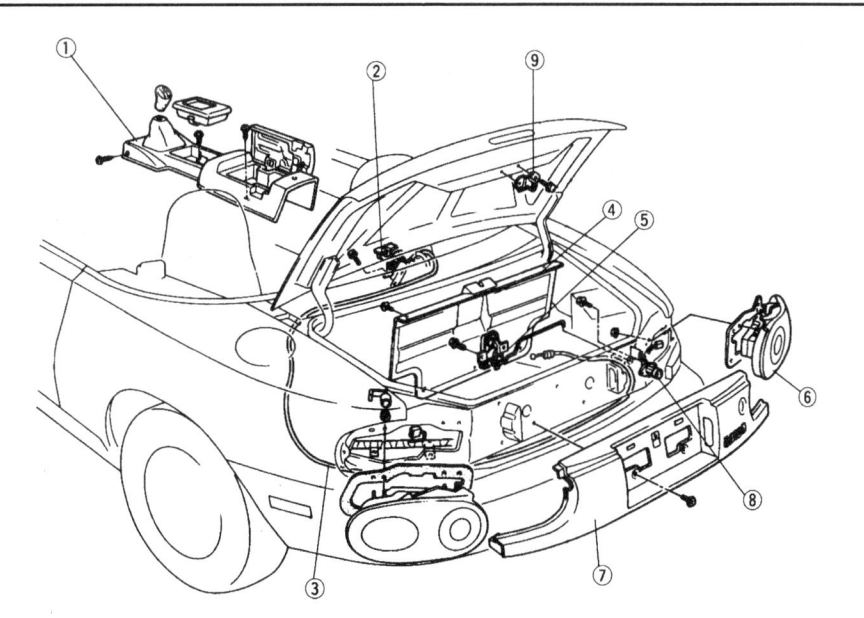

D6/5-18 TRUNK (BOOT) LATCH AND REAR BODY PANEL COMPONENTS.
1 Rear console. 2 Trunk lid release lever. 3 Trunk lid latch cable. 4 Trunk trim panel (rear). 5 Trunk latch unit. 6 Combination light (rear). 7 Rear finisher panel (designs vary). 8 Trunk lid lock cylinder. 9 Trunk lid striker.

Mazda Miata, MX-5, Eunos & Roadster

6/7 Operating rod fixed by clip.

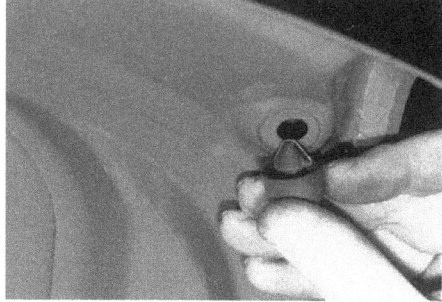

6/9 Trunk lid rubber cushions pull out.

6/13c These screws hidden by license plate.

the center pin with your fingernails or a small screwdriver, then pull the fasteners out to free the panel. For more information on these devices ☞ 1/2.

6   The trunk lid latch mechanism is secured by two 10mm bolts, which also provide adjustment of the latch position. Before removing the bolts, mark around the mechanism with a marker pen or paint, as an alignment guide.

7   ◘ Feel along the operating rod to the lock barrel assembly. Swing the plastic clip away from the rod and unhook the rod end from the barrel

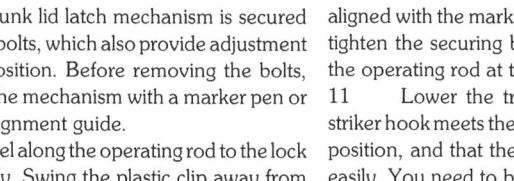

6/8a Release cable stop & nipple.

6/8b Latch striker fixed by two bolts.

lever. Alternatively, you can free the rod from the latch end once the latch is clear of the body.

8   ◘+ Remove the two latch mechanism 10mm fixing bolts, and lift the latch away far enough to slide the release cable out of its stop, then disengage its nipple by turning the cable through the arm slot until it's free. The latch striker hook is fixed to the trunk lid by two 10mm bolts.

9   ◘ To install the latch, engage the release cable nipple with the slotted arm, and then slide the groove of the nylon cable stop nearest the cable ferrule onto the latch bracket (you can use the

other slots to compensate for a stretched cable). If necessary, fix the lock rod to the latch and secure with its plastic clip.

10   With the latch installed in the car and aligned with the marks you made prior to removal, tighten the securing bolts. Reconnect and secure the operating rod at the lock barrel end.

11   Lower the trunk lid and check that the striker hook meets the latch at the correct angle and position, and that the trunk lid closes and latches easily. You need to be able to latch the trunk and release it without requiring excessive effort on the key or release lever. You'll need to work on a trial and error basis to achieve this happy compromise, checking and then repositioning the latch as required.

REAR FINISHER (LICENSE PLATE) PANEL AND TRUNK LOCK BARREL - REMOVAL

12   If you need to remove the lock barrel assembly, note that you'll first need to remove the rear combination light units and the finisher panel from the back of the car. Start by removing the trunk end trim and disconnecting the latch operating rod from the lock barrel unit (☞ 11/6/7).

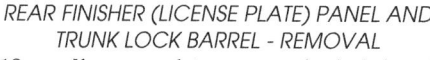

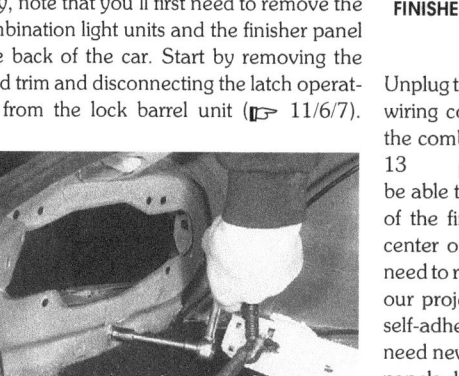

6/13a Release finisher panel nuts ...

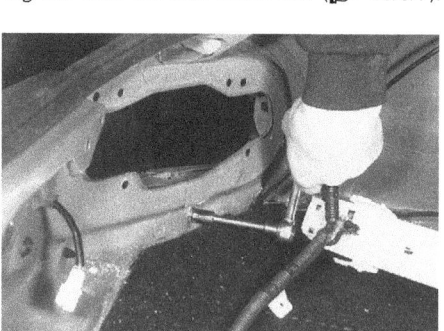

6/13b ... some of which are recessed.

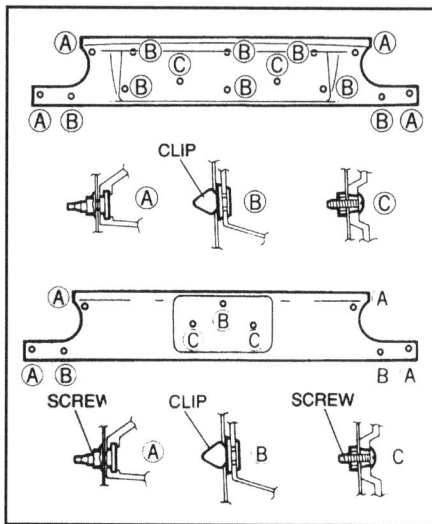

D6/13 DEPENDING ON THE SHAPE OF THE REAR FINISHER (LICENSE PLATE) PANEL, THE FIXINGS DIFFER.

Unplug the combination light and license plate light wiring connectors inside the trunk, then remove the combination lights ☞ 7/37.

13   ◘+☐ With the lights removed, you will be able to access the four 10mm nuts at each end of the finisher panel from inside the trunk. The center of the panel is held by screws and you'll need to remove the license plate to reach these. On our project car the license plate was secured by self-adhesive foam pads - remember that you'll need new pads to re-install. Note that rear finisher panels differ in shape from country to country to accommodate differently sized/shaped license plates, and the clips which locate the panel will vary, too. The diagram illustrates two types of panel and their respective fixing arrangements:

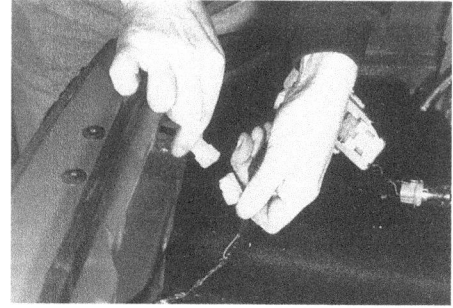

6/14a Disconnect license plate light wiring.

11: Body

6/14b Free accessible clips & pull out panel ...

6/15b ...& then pull out the lock unit.

6/17a Release spring tension at anchor end ...

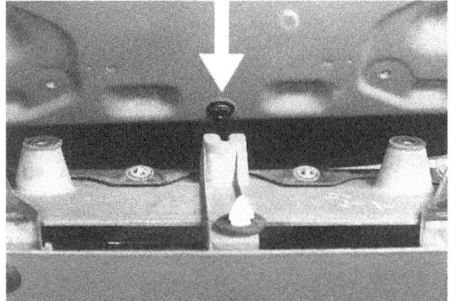
6/14c ... lift panel to free it from this clip.

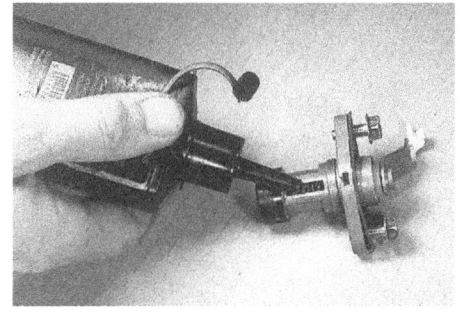
6/15c Lubricate lock before installing.

6/17b ... then disengage from hinge lever.

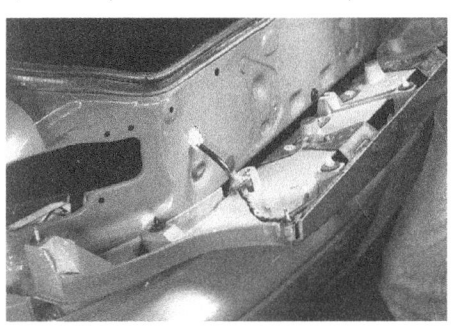
6/14d Free grommet & pull wiring thru.

there may be other variations.

14   📷+ Once the screws have been removed, unclip and remove the finisher. The clips are held in slots on the inner face of the finisher, and push through panel holes. To reduce the risk of damage, squeeze together the clip ends using pliers and working from inside the trunk - the clips will then pull out easily. You'll find that the center clips are hard to reach; they're covered by a welded section inside the trunk. You can depress the clip tangs with a screwdriver blade to help free them. On our project car we found that we could release all but the lower center clip this way - we freed the rest, then unhooked this last clip from the panel by lifting it slightly, leaving the clip attached to the body. Before you lift the panel away, locate and disconnect the license plate light wiring inside the trunk. The lights, plus a short section of harness, need to be fed through the panel hole as the rear finisher panel is removed.

15   📷+ With the trunk end trim and rear finisher panel out of the way, you can detach the lock barrel unit. This is retained by two 10mm fixing bolts which can be unscrewed from inside the trunk. With the bolts removed, maneuver the barrel assembly away from the body. Before reinstalling the lock barrel assembly, or in the event of stiff operation, note that you can lubricate the lock mechanism by applying machine oil through the slot on the underside of the unit.

TRUNK LID BALANCE SPRINGS - REMOVAL, INSTALLATION & ADJUSTMENT

Warning! The trunk lid is supported on strong torsion springs (balance springs) attached between the two hinges. Take care when working on the springs or hinges or you could be injured.

16   📷 Open the trunk lid and arrange some method of supporting it while the springs are re-

leased - Wally (our technical adviser) discovered that if you omit to do this, the trunk lid falls on your head as you release the spring pressure. If you don't have someone like Wally around to support the trunk lid with his head, you can use a length of wood as a prop. Also, note that the retainer at the center of the two springs should be unclipped to free the springs before they are removed at each end.

17   📷+ Wrap the blade of a strong screwdriver with pvc tape to prevent paint damage. Hook the blade through the looped end of the spring and lever upwards to disengage it. Take care

6/18 Use screwdriver to adjust spring tension.

when doing this - the springs are strong; carefully rotate the screwdriver to release pressure in the spring. Once spring tension has been released, disengage and remove it from the fixed end.

18   📷 🖼 When installing the springs, note that you can adjust them to alter the balance, or 'lift,' affect on the trunk lid: useful if the springs have weakened or the extra weight of a rack has been added to the trunk lid. However, before you do adjust the springs, check that the problem is not due to stiffness or lack of lubrication of the hinges. The lift pressure is varied by moving the hooked

6/15a Unscrew 2 fixing bolts ...

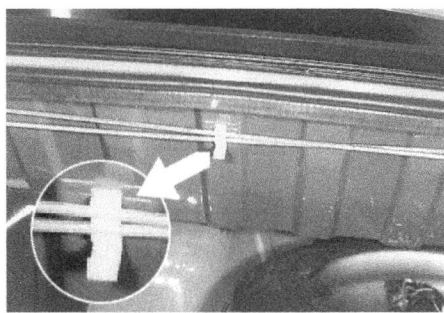
6/16 Central spring retainer/anti-rattle clip.

11:9

Mazda Miata, MX-5, Eunos & Roadster

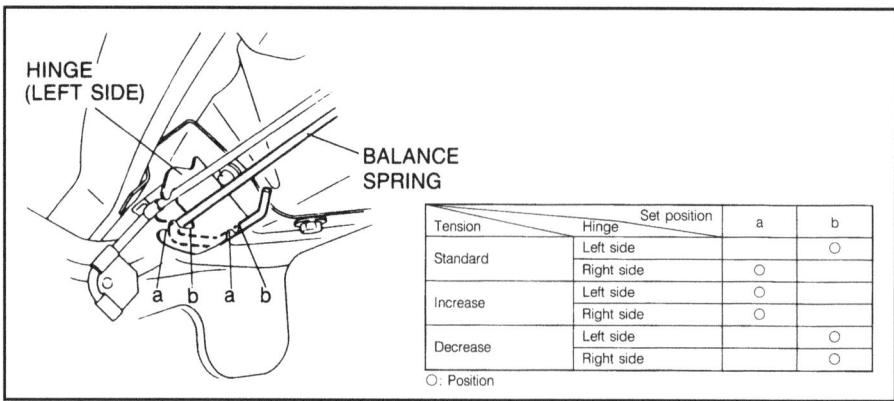

D6/18 SPRING TENSION ADJUSTMENT DETAIL AND TABLE.

end of the spring to one of two positions (see diagram).

TRUNK LID HINGES - REMOVAL & INSTALLATION

19   If you need to remove the trunk lid hinges, first detach the trunk lid and release and remove the balance springs as described earlier. The hinge-to-body fasteners are accessed from inside the car. You'll need to remove the convertible top's set plate to gain access to them. You don't need to remove the top completely for this - just detach the rear edge with the top raised but unfastened, and lift the lower section to get at the bolts and nuts ☞ 11/16.

20   When installing the hinges, fit the mounting bolts and nuts loosely in position at first, then tighten them to 7.9-10.7Nm/80-110kgf cm/70-95.4lbf ft. Install the balance springs and trunk lid. Check, and if required, adjust the balance spring settings and trunk lid position. Check that the lid closes correctly and adjust the latch position if required.

7. FUEL FILLER CABLE & LID - REMOVAL, INSTALLATION & EMERGENCY LID OPENING

☞ 1/1, 2.

1   The fuel filler release lever in the back of the rear console is connected to the filler lid by a cable.

2   In the event of a cable breaking, your first problem is going to be opening the filler lid until you can install a new cable. You can reach the underside of the lid and its catch through the trunk.

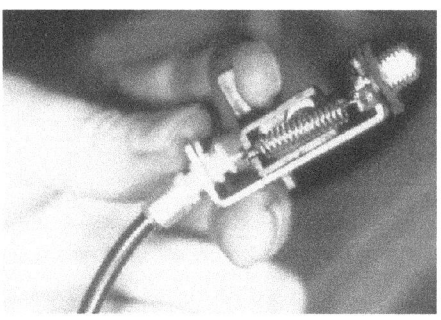

7/3 This trigger manually releases catch.

3   At the catch you'll find a small plastic trigger which allows you to release the filler lid manually. You'll find it easier to use your left hand to reach in and locate the trigger. Once you find it, pull it back to open the lid. Our photograph shows this with the cable and catch removed to show the trigger location.

4   When installing a new cable, start by removing the rear console so that you can reach the

7/5 Release lever fixed by two bolts.

release lever ☞ 10/2.

5   With the console removed, you can reach the lever. Remove the two 10mm mounting bolts and lift the lever assembly so that the cable can be disconnected. To get the old cable out (and the new one in) you'll need to remove the carpet from the package area behind the seats ☞ 10/12.

6   Remove the sheet metal screws which retain the long access panel that runs the width of the package area. You'll be able to see the filler release cable clipped to the body. Unhook the cable from its clips - you should be able to reach these from the access hole and from inside the

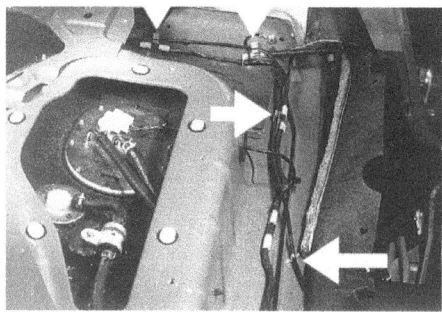

7/6 Cable clips.

trunk, but if you find it difficult to reach the clips, you can remove further access panels in the package area.

7   When working inside the trunk area, you will need to remove the metal panel which conceals the fuel filler and vent hoses - it's secured by 10mm bolts. With the panel detached, you'll be able to reach the remainder of the cable which is clipped in place. With the filler lid open, remove the 14mm nut and washer which retain the catch and withdraw it.

8   + Thread the new cable into place and

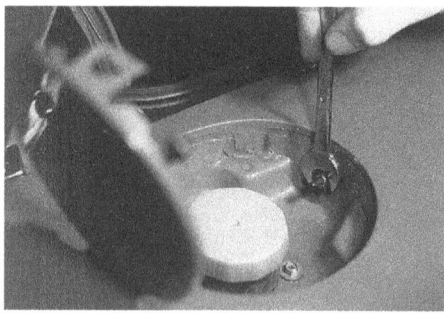

7/7 Catch retained by single nut.

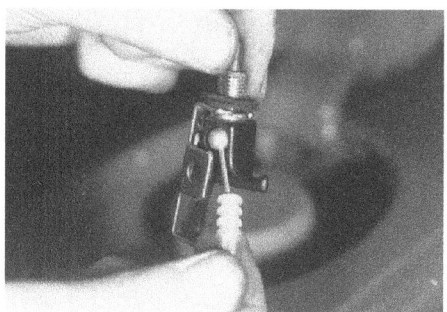

7/8a Fit cable nipple into catch & ...

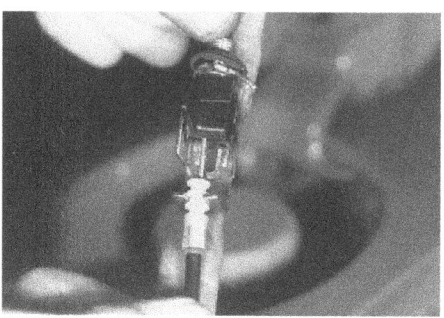

7/8b ... select appropriate groove in cable stop.

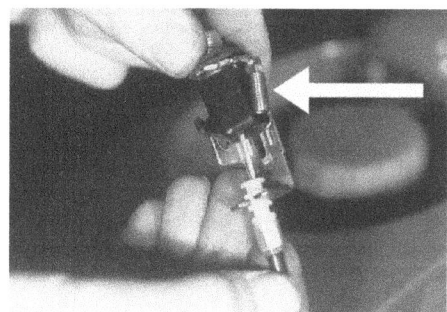

7/8c Make sure return spring is in place.

11: Body

connect it at the operating lever and catch ends. Install the catch and release lever, and check that the mechanism operates normally, then clip the cable in place and install the removed access panels and carpet before fitting the rear console. If you find that you need to adjust the cable at any time, note that at the catch end there are three locating grooves on the cable stop. Select the best groove of the three to adjust the cable length (the center groove is normally used). Check that the small return spring is correctly attached.

9   The filler lid hinge is secured by two screws accessed from inside the filler well. If you need to fit a new lid, check that it fits correctly in the recess. In particular, make sure that it opens and closes without rubbing on the surrounding paintwork. If necessary, you can make minor adjustments by carefully bending the hinge.

8A. DOOR MIRROR - REMOVAL & INSTALLATION

☞ 1/1, 2.

MANUALLY ADJUSTED MIRRORS

1   📷 The door mirrors are secured by screws to the doors. To reach the screws, you'll need to pry up the cover around the mounting. Use a small screwdriver blade wrapped with pvc tape to prevent paint damage. Slide the blade into the recess at the base of the cover and carefully lever it upward until the cover springs free of the base.

2   📷 Turn the base cover slightly until you can get to the mounting screw heads. The cover will not turn far, but will move enough to allow the screws to be removed.

3   When installing the mirror, check that the mounting screws are tight, then snap the cover back into place against the door.

8/1 Spring the cover free & twist ...

8/2 ... to access securing screws.

POWER ADJUSTED MIRRORS

4   Isolate the battery ☞ 7/2.
5   Remove the door trim and plastic waterproof skin ☞ 10/5/21-33.
6   Release the power mirror electrical connections.
7   Removal and installation of the mirror is now as per the manually adjusted type (☞ 11/8/1-3), except that the wiring needs to be withdrawn when the mirror is lifted away from the door and inserted when the mirror is installed.
8   Reconnect the power mirror wiring.
9   Replace the door trim ☞ 10/5/34-39.
10   Reconnect the battery ☞ 7/2.

8B. DOOR MIRROR (POWER) - CHECKING

☞ 1/1, 2.

MIRROR

1   Remove the mirror, or access its wiring connector within the door.
2   Check the mirror side terminals of the wiring connector for continuity (see diagram). If continuity is not as indicated, replace the power mirror.

SWITCH & WIRING

3   Isolate the battery ☞ 7/2. Release the tabs at the rear and carefully pull the switch from its dashpanel mounting, then release the wiring connector. Alternatively, if the switch is mounted in the center panel, remove the center panel (☞ 10/3), then remove the switch and disconnect it from its wiring connector.
4   Check the switch terminal continuity (see diagram). If the continuity at various switch positions is not as indicated, replace the switch. If

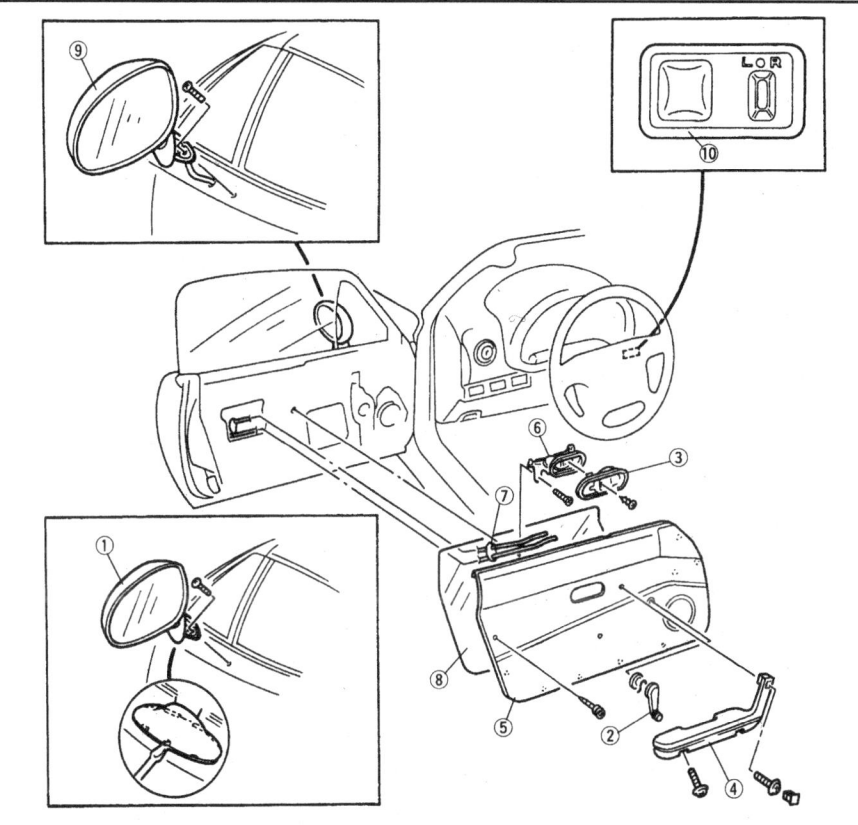

D8A/4-10 DOOR MIRROR - REMOVAL PROCEDURE.
1 Door mirror, manual type (does not require door trim removal). 2 Window lift regulator (if fitted). 3 Inner door handle trim. 4 Armrest. 5 Door trim panel. 6 Inner door handle. 7 Sealing pad. 8 Waterproof plastic membrane. 9 Door mirror, power type. 10 Door mirror adjustment switch (position varies).

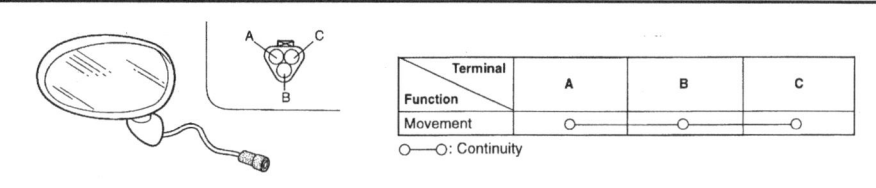

D8B/2 CHECKING FOR CONTINUITY AT POWER MIRROR CONNECTOR.

Mazda Miata, MX-5, Eunos & Roadster

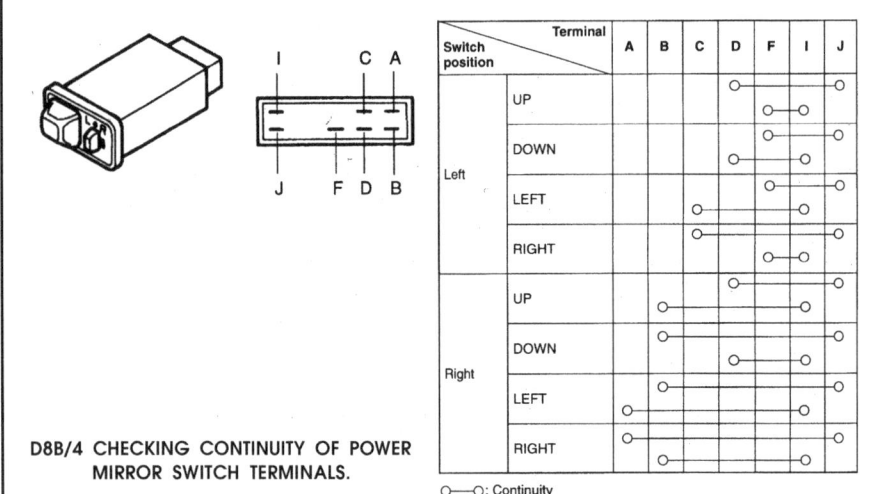

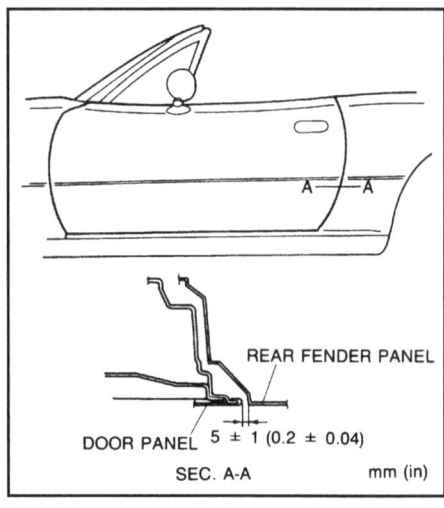

D8B/4 CHECKING CONTINUITY OF POWER MIRROR SWITCH TERMINALS.

D9/8 CORRECT DOOR GAP.

the switch continuity is correct, check the wiring between switch and door mirror.

9. DOOR - REMOVAL, INSTALLATION & ADJUSTMENT

☞ 1/1, 2.
1   Isolate the battery ☞ 7/2.
2   If you need to remove the check strap (door stop) mechanism from the door, first remove the speaker panel (if applicable), door trim panel and the waterproof plastic membrane ☞ 10/5/21-33.
3   Tap out and remove the check strap mechanism pin from its anchor point in the door opening. The hollow pin is tapered, and can be removed by tapping it upward and then pulling it out with pliers. You don't need to remove the mechanism from the door during door removal, but, if you don't, wire the check strap mechanism to prevent it getting pushed back into the door. If you need to remove the check strap mechanism for repair or replacement, remove it by unscrewing the mounting nuts at the door end, and removing the mechanism from inside the door.
4   Pull back the rubber boot from the body end to expose the wiring between door and frame. Separate the wiring connector. Note that where accessory wiring has been added, it may well need to be traced back to the nearest connection point and separated there. The accompanying photograph illustrates the hinge-to-door and hinge-to-body bolts, and the wiring boot. Note that the fender is shown removed for clarity - you don't need to remove the fender to work on the door.
5   With an assistant supporting the weight of the door, slacken and remove the 12mm door hinge bolts and then lift the door away. Place it on some cloth or cardboard to prevent damage to the paint along the lower edge.

6   If you need to remove or repair the internal door components ☞ 10/6-10.
7   When installing the door, tighten the hinge bolts provisionally, reconnect the wiring and wiring boot, and secure the check mechanism.
8   Carefully close the door and check that it aligns normally - look for alignment along the body molding line as a guide. If you need to adjust the door, slacken the hinge bolts just enough to permit movement, then set the door to give a consistent gap of 4-6mm/0.16-0.24in between the back edge of the door and the car body. Tighten the hinge bolts to 22-30Nm/2.2-3.1kgf m/16-22lbf ft.

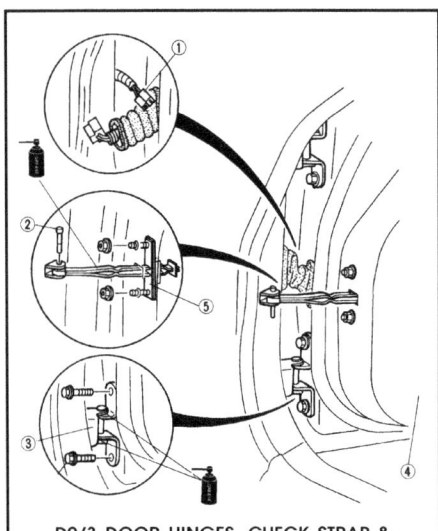

D9/3 DOOR HINGES, CHECK STRAP & WIRING.
1 Wiring connector. 2 Check strap pin.
3 Hinge detail. 4 Door. 5 Check strap detail.

9/3 Tap out check strap tapered pin.

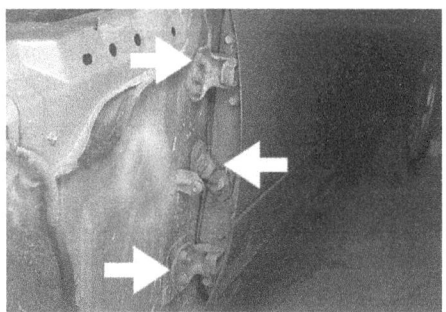

9/4 Hinges & wiring boot (fender removed).

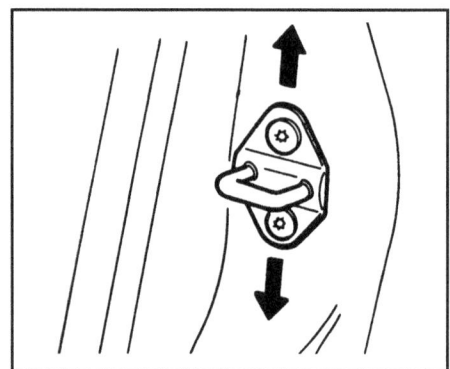

D9/9 DOOR STRIKER ADJUSTMENT.

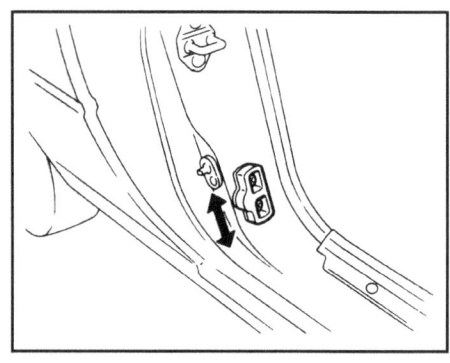

D9/10 DOOR WEDGE ADJUSTMENT.

11: Body

9   If the door striker adjustment is incorrect, loosen the mounting screws and move the striker vertically until the door closes correctly. Tighten the screws to 18-26Nm/1.8-2.7kgf m/14-19lbf ft.

10   Check the adjustment of the door wedge - this locates the door in its closed position. If necessary, slacken the screws and alter the vertical adjustment. Tighten the screws to 4.3-6.1Nm/43-63kgf cm/38-54lbf in).

11   Reconnect the battery ☞ 7/2.

10. BUMPER (REAR) - REMOVAL & INSTALLATION

☞ 1/1, 2.

1   Decide which parts of the assembly you need to remove - this will determine your working method. If you are going to remove the complete bumper assembly, you can leave the finisher panel in place. If you intend to remove just the molded plastic tailpiece, or fascia, as Mazda describes it, you can leave the main bumper structure undisturbed, but note that you'll need to remove the rear finisher panel before you can start work ☞ 11/6.

2   Before you begin work, we suggest that you get the underside of the car and the rear wheel wells pressure-washed to remove accumulated road dirt - this will make the removal procedure much less messy. The first requirement is to raise the back of the car to give access to the fasteners on the underside of the body and bumper. You can raise the car on fabricated steel ramps, or jack the car and support it on jack (axle) stands ☞ 1/3.

3   If fitted, you'll need to detach the rear wheelarch flaps which are designed to prevent mud and grit being thrown over the rear fenders

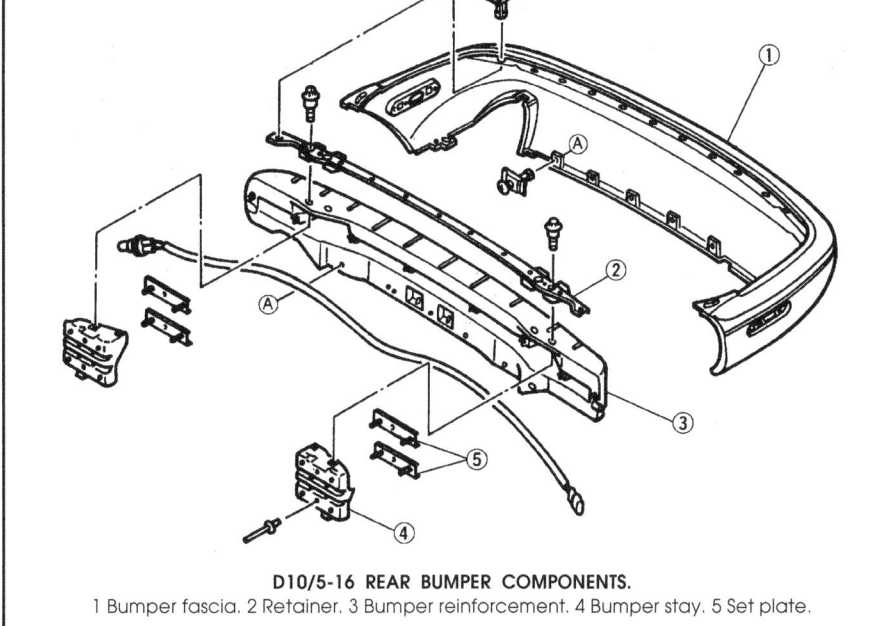

D10/5-16 REAR BUMPER COMPONENTS.
1 Bumper fascia. 2 Retainer. 3 Bumper reinforcement. 4 Bumper stay. 5 Set plate.

and bumper. Owners of cars not fitted with these flaps should skip to paragraph 5.

4   📷+ Each rear flap is in two parts. The short upper section can be removed by pulling off the two flat clips which clamp it to the body seam. The longer lower section is secured by four machine screws with 8mm hexagon heads, screwed into clips attached to the bumper. Three of the screws are fitted horizontally into the leading edge of the bumper, with a fourth fitted from the underside. Remove the screws, lift away the flap and place it to one side.

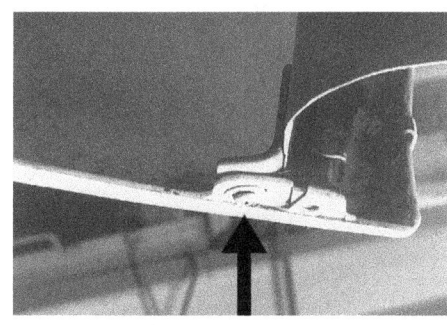

10/5c ... one, fix bumper ends.

5   📷+ On all cars, remove the plastic splash shields. These are fitted in the rear of the wheel well to close the gap between it and the bumper. Each shield is held by three hexagon-headed sheet metal screws. Next, remove the two sheet metal screws which retain each bumper end to the body and wheel well extension - these both fit vertically from below the forward edge of the bumper, one top and bottom at each side of the assembly.

6   📷 On cars with a rear foglight fitted near the lower edge of the bumper, you need to disconnect the wiring at its harness connection inside the

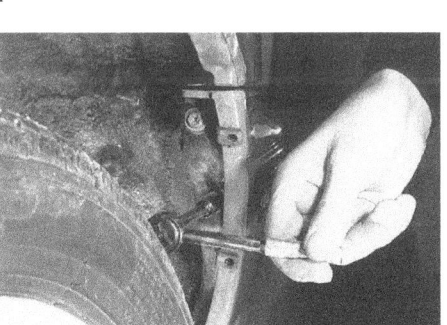

10/4a Upper flap held by clips & ...

10/5a Splash shield held by screws.

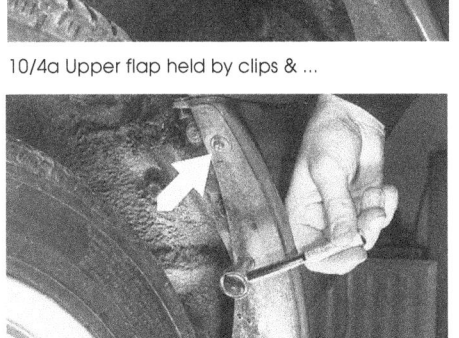

10/4b ... lower flap by screws.

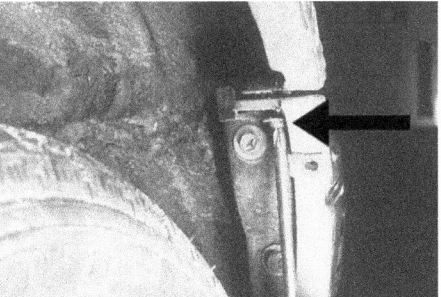

10/5b This screw and this ...

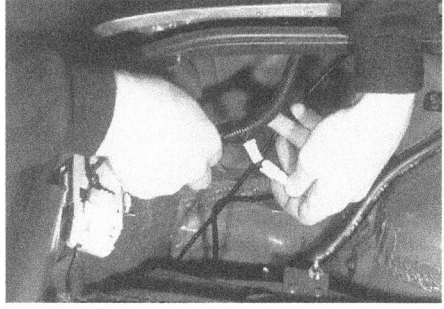

10/6 If applicable, unplug rear foglight wiring.

Mazda Miata, MX-5, Eunos & Roadster

trunk. Separate the connector, and push it and its boot through the panel hole so that it does not impede removal of the bumper. You may need to remove the trunk end trim and open the access panel to the jack recess for access, depending on how the wiring is routed on your car.

7 On cars fitted with bumper mounted illuminating sidemarker lights, trace the wiring to the nearest connector and disconnect. The lights and connecting wiring are removed with the bumper, but you need to separate the connector to the main harness inside the trunk, and feed the connector and boot through the panel hole during removal. You may need to remove the trunk end trim and open the access panel to the jack recess for access, it depends on how the wiring is routed on your car.

8 The bumper assembly should now be retained only by the main mountings. Check that the assembly is free at each end (we think we've described all of the fittings, but you may encounter slight variations for specific markets).

9 ◘+ Working under the back of the car, slacken and remove the eight 14mm nuts which retain the bumper assembly to the reinforced turrets which project downward from the body. Some of these are partly concealed by the exhaust system, and you'll find that removal will be easier if you use a short socket extension. Note that the bumper will come free when you do this, so have some help ready to support it. The assembly is lightweight, but you won't be able to support it and remove the nuts from below at the same time. Pull the assembly back and clear of the body, checking that it or any associated wiring does not get snagged. Place the assembly on some soft cloth to protect it from damage.

10 ◘+ To detach the rear fascia molding from the supporting structure, you need to remove the plastic retainers which fit along the top and

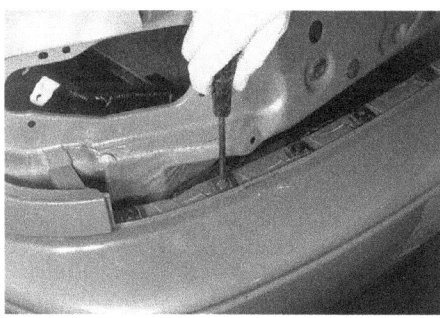

10/10a Release centre screw and ...

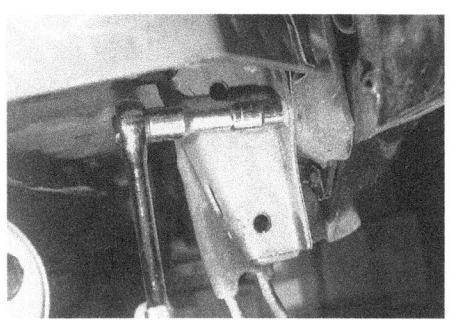

10/9a Remove securing nuts ...

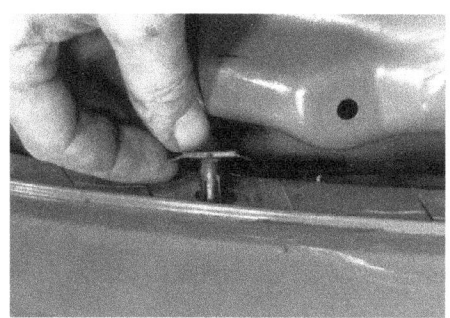

10/10b ... then pull out each retainer ...

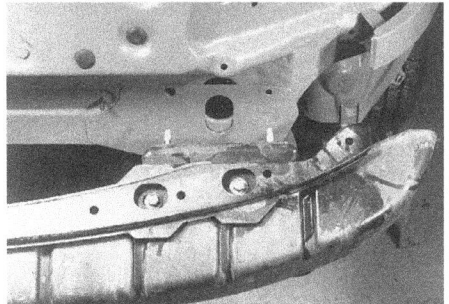

10/9b ... and lift bumper away, making sure ...

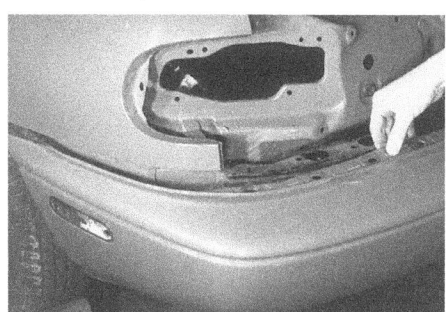

10/10c ... to free the rear fascia molding.

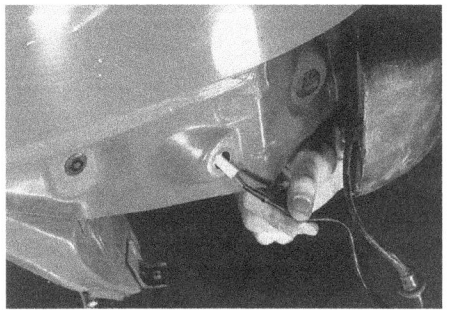

10/9c ... wiring (if applicable) is withdrawn too.

10/11a Two bolts hold retainer strip each side ...

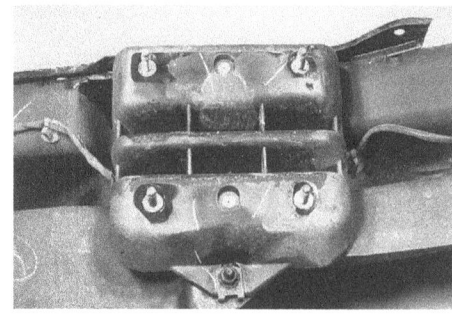

10/11b ... then single nut holds set plate.

bottom edges. Before you do this, detach the sidemarker lights and wiring (where fitted). Unscrew each of the crossheaded (Philips) screws, then pull the rectangular retainers out to free the fascia. If you need to do this without removing the bumper from the car, you can do so after removing the rear finisher panel ☞ 11/6.

11 ◘+ The metal retainer strip can be removed from the top edge of the bumper reinforcement if necessary (two bolts), as can the bumper set plates and stays.

12 The usual reason for removing the bumper is in the aftermath of a rear-end impact, although we know they also get sun-bleached. Just about all of the bumper assembly is made up of molded plastic parts, designed to absorb low-speed impact energies, and to deform under harder impact to prevent damage to the vehicle structure. You'll need to examine the bumper parts closely to check for impact damage - most likely this will not be readily apparent during casual checking. Even where the bumper reinforcement and stays appear to be the right shape, look out for white patches which may indicate stress areas. If you have any doubts, fit new parts.

10/13 Full rearward nudity!

13 ◘ You also need to examine the turrets which support the bumper stays. These are substantial steel fabrications, and we would be surprised if they *ever* got damaged! Even if the turrets themselves are tough, we note that they attach to the regular-gauge steel box-section under the trunk floor. These sections are much lighter in construction, and would bend or deform easily under moderate impact forces, so check these (looking for indications of bending or rippling of the steel) especially carefully. If you think that there might be damage in this area, we recommend that you get

11: Body

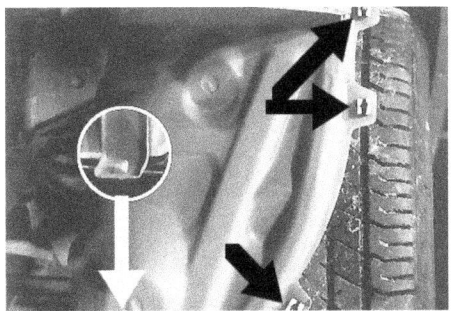

10/14 Check that threaded clips are present.

this checked out by a Mazda dealer or a professional body shop - don't take chances with safety.

14 When assembling the bumper, note that the two bolts which secure the retainer strip to the bumper reinforcement should be tightened to 16-22Nm/1.6-2.3kgf m/12-16lbf ft. Fit the fascia panel over the bumper reinforcement and secure it with the plastic retainers, pushing them into position: they are locked in place by the center screws. We must confess to having trouble with these on our car - screwing them in didn't seem to work too well. We concluded that the 'screws' are simply pressed or tapped into place during initial assembly, and this approach seemed to work better for us during installation. Check that the side marker wiring harness is correctly positioned (where fitted) before installing the bumper. Check also that the various threaded clips are correctly positioned around the edge of the inner wheel well extension.

15 Installing the assembled bumper is quite straightforward, but note that you'll need assistance to hold it in position while you fit and tighten the mounting nuts. Start by positioning the assembly with one person on each side - that way you can make sure that the bumper ends fit correctly around the body, particularly around the wheel wells. Remember, if applicable, to feed rear sidemarker and rear fog lamp wiring through the body holes, and to snap the rubber boot into the hole to seal it. Once the bumper's in place, have your assistant hold it there while you climb underneath and fit the eight mounting nuts. These should be tightened evenly to 16-22Nm/1.6-2.3kgf m/12-16lbf ft.

16 Fit the two sheet metal screws which retain the ends of the bumper at the wheel wells. The top screw is fitted up into the hollow locating peg, while the lower screw fits into the lug at the bottom of the wheelarch extension.

17 Fit the splash shields which close the gap between the bumper and the wheelarch. Each one is secured by three sheet metal screws, threaded into inserted clips on the body.

18 On cars which use them, install the rear flaps. Each lower section is held by four machine screws which thread into body clips. Position the short upper section and retain it with the two spring clips to the body seam. Note that, in addition to the clips, a strip of self-adhesive foam positions these sections. Use commercially-available adhesive foam for this, or alternatively, coat the back of the section with suitable silicone-rubber sealant, position the section, then fit the clips.

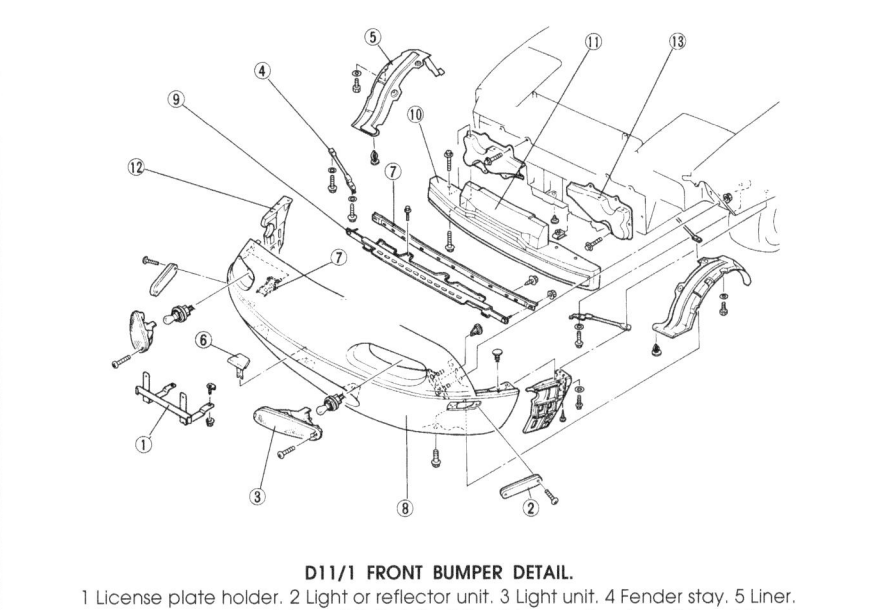

D11/1 FRONT BUMPER DETAIL.
1 License plate holder. 2 Light or reflector unit. 3 Light unit. 4 Fender stay. 5 Liner.
6 Fascia molding grille retainers. 7 Set plate. 8 Front bumper fascia molding. 9 Retainer.
10 Bumper reinforcement. 11 Spacer. 12 Retainer. 13 Bumper mounting bracket.

19 Where appropriate, reconnect the sidemarker light wiring and install the marker lights in the fascia panel. On cars with a bumper-mounted rear fog light, reconnect the wiring in the trunk.

20 Install any removed trim parts and check that all lights work normally.

11. BUMPER (FRONT) - REMOVAL & INSTALLATION

☞ 1/1, 2.

REMOVAL

1 Start by raising the headlights, then isolate the battery ☞ 7/2. Open the hood (bonnet) and support it with its stay.

2 Slacken the front wheel lug nuts by one turn each. Raise the front of the car and support it securely on jack (axle) stands, then remove the lug nuts and lift the wheels away ☞ 1/3.

3 Remove the front license plate holder (if fitted). This will vary in design according to the type and shape of the plate used in each country, but the Mazda support bracket is held by two 10mm nuts under the top edge of the air intake at the nose of the car. Slacken and remove the nuts (after pulling off the protective caps, where fitted) and remove the bracket and plate as an assembly. Note that the projecting studs are attached to plates fitted from above the opening - push these out and remove them, storing them with the plate and nuts.

4 On cars with front sidemarker lights, remove the two screws which secure each light to the bumper fascia, pull out the lights and disconnect the wiring. On cars with plain reflectors at this location, these may be left in position.

5 Remove the front combination lights

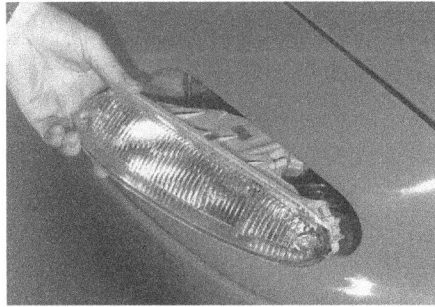

11/5 Remove combination light & unplug wiring.

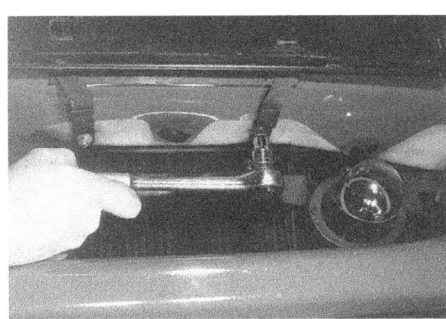

11/3 Bracket held by two nuts.

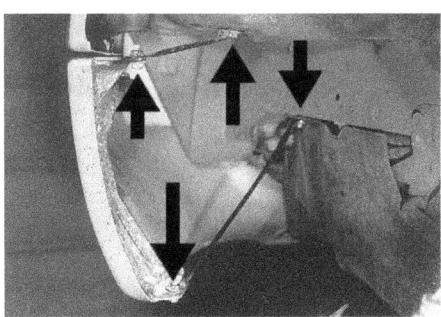

11/6 Stays are bolted at each end.

Mazda Miata, MX-5, Eunos & Roadster

(two crosshead screws) and unplug the bulb holders, which can be left in position. You may wish to remove the bulbs to prevent accidental breakage.

6   Working in each wheel well in turn, remove the stays which locate and support the bumper assembly. These are each retained by a 10mm bolt at each end. You may find that it helps to apply a little releasing fluid to overcome any corrosion on the threads.

7   Next, remove the liners from the wheel wells. These are lightweight plastic moldings secured around the lip of the well by 10mm screws, and to the inner wheelarch panel by two-piece

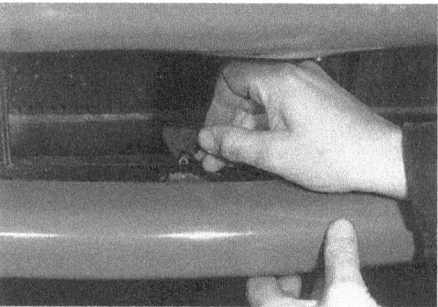
11/9a Three retainers in base of grille & ...

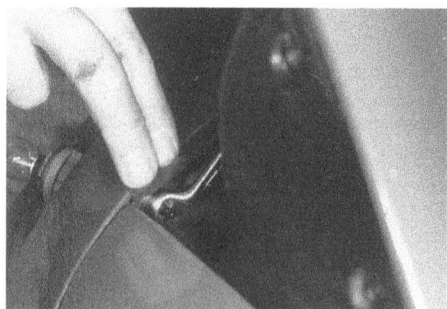
11/10b ... are well hidden.

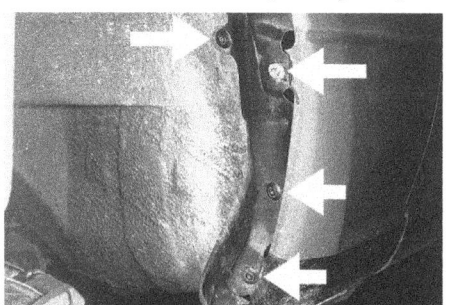
11/7 Liner held by screws & plastic fasteners.

11/9b ... three at the top.

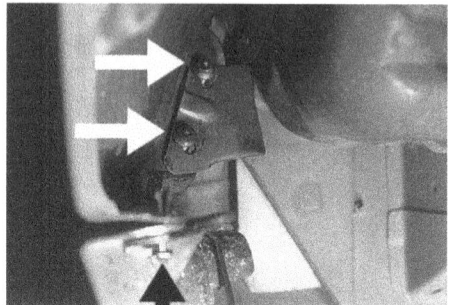
11/11 Fender fixed to supports by two nuts.

plastic fasteners. The fasteners used have plastic crosshead screws at the center which need to be removed before the outer, flanged section can by pried out. You may find, as we did, that you need to lever gently under the flange of the fastener so that it grips the screw threads and the screws can be unscrewed and removed. Check each fastener as you remove it. If it is worn or distorted, fit a new one during installation.

8   + Moving to the air intake, if your car has the optional fog/driving lights fitted, these need to be detached. Each light is mounted on a bracket,

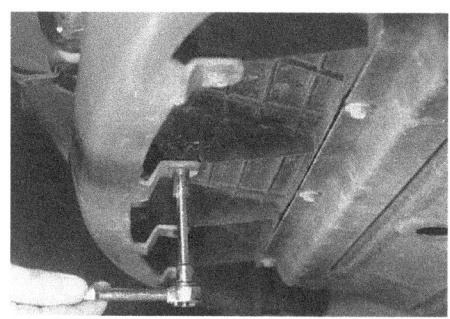
11/9c Four bolts secure base of fascia molding.

held at each end by a 10mm nut. Remove the nuts, pull the light out of the intake and disconnect the wiring, then place it to one side. The mounting studs are loose in the nose, located by flat metal plates reached from above. Push these out and place the studs with the removed lights.

9   + Along the lower edge of the intake are three trapezoidal plastic plates - these form the heads of locating pins which secure the fascia molding. These need to be removed. Note that each one is locked by small tangs on the lower end of the pins - it is preferable to squeeze these tangs together with thin-nosed pliers to facilitate removal.

At the top of the intake, you'll find three plastic crosshead retainers; these should be removed to free the fascia panel from the supporting structure. Finally, remove the four 10mm bolts which secure the lower edge of the fascia to the underside of the car.

10   + Just inside the hood opening, you'll find a steel retainer plate which attaches the bumper assembly to the body. Remove the six 10mm bolts which retain it, plus the single 10mm nut at each end of the retainer - you'll need to lift the rubber plate a little to reach these.

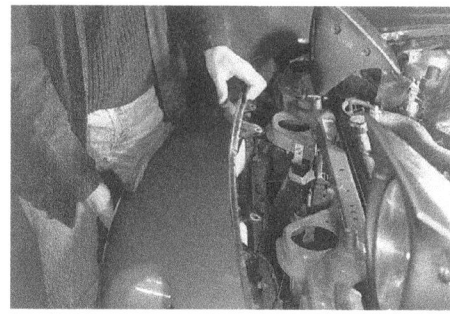
11/12 Lift away the front fascia molding.

11/8a Remove fixing nuts and, if applicable, ...

11/8b ... pull foglights from grille opening.

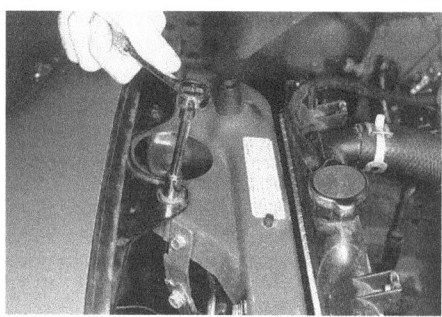
11/10a The retainer plate is held by bolts, two ...

11/14 Bumper reinforcement held by 8 bolts.

11: Body

11 Moving back to the wheel wells, remove the two 10mm nuts which secure the bumper assembly to the outer supports. On our car these had corroded quite badly, so we soaked them in releasing fluid rather than risk breaking the studs during removal. Next, release the sheet metal screw which secures the extreme edge of the bumper on each side of the car.

12 You can now remove the front fascia from the car. Ideally, you should have assistance during this stage to make sure nothing gets snagged as you pull it away. You'll need to guide the outer ends of the fascia away from the support brackets as the unit is removed.

13 If required, the set plate and weather seal can be removed from the fascia. This is in two sections and each is retained by sheet metal screws. Note how the sections overlap at the center, and that each is located over small plastic pegs. The retainers at the outer ends of the fascia can also be removed if required.

14 The bumper reinforcement takes the form of a plastic molding bolted to the two pressed steel brackets at the front of the body. Above the reinforcement is a styrofoam 'spacer' section, which, on our car, was taped in position, and was removed with the reinforcement. Remove the eight shouldered bolts and lift the assembly away.

CHECKING

15 The most usual reason for removing the bumper is in the aftermath of impact damage, although we know they also get sun-bleached. Just about all of the bumper assembly is made up of molded plastic parts, designed to absorb low-speed impact energies, and to deform under harder impact to prevent damage to the vehicle structure. This means that, in some circumstances, little external evidence of the impact will be visible, but you should examine the bumper parts closely to check for telltale signs - most likely this will not be readily apparent during casual checking. Even where the bumper reinforcement appears to be the right shape, look out for white patches, which may indicate stress areas. If you have any doubts, fit new parts.

16 You also need to examine the bumper brackets. These can be unbolted and new ones installed if they have become bent, but check carefully for damage to the underlying bodywork. If this has been damaged or distorted, get professional help with the repair. If you think that there might be damage in any related area, we recommend that you get this checked out by a Mazda dealer or a professional body shop - don't take chances with safety.

INSTALLATION

17 Where they were removed, install the bumper brackets and the bumper reinforcement. Each is secured by bolts which need to be tightened to 16-22Nm/1.6-2.3kgf m/12-16lbf ft.

18 Before installing the fascia assembly, check that the retainers at each end are correctly installed, and that the set plate/weatherstrip sections are in position. In the case of the latter, note that you can't

11/19 Carefully reposition the fascia molding.

easily reach the screws with the fascia installed.

19 Carefully position the fascia assembly, checking that nothing is stopping it from aligning with the surrounding bodywork. Make sure that you don't trap the combination light wiring during installation. Fit the two nuts on each side to the studs projecting through the flange in the front of the wheel well. Tighten the retaining nuts to 7.8-11.7Nm/80-120kgf cm/70-104lbf in.

20 Secure the retainer plate to the body just inside the hood opening, tightening the bolts to 7.8-11.7Nm/80-120kgf cm/70-104lbf in. Fit and

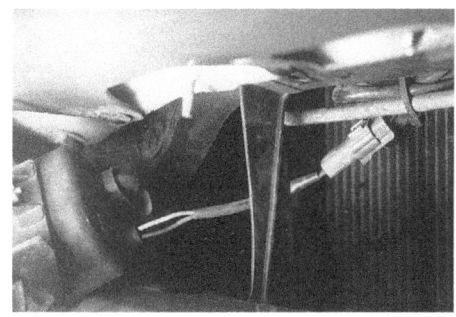
11/21a If applicable, reconnect foglight wires ...

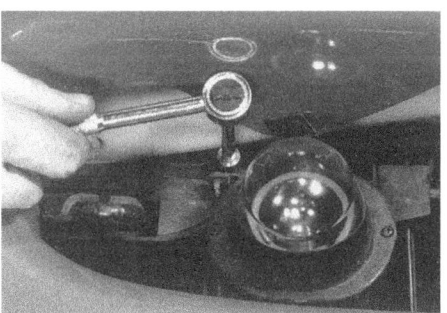
11/21b ... and secure foglights in position.

tighten the nut at each end of the retainer/set plate assembly.

21 Fit the three trapezoidal retainers in the air intake opening, then fit the fog/driving lights (where applicable) and the license plate. Reconnect and install the front combination lights and front sidemarker lights (where fitted).

22 Working in each wheel well in turn, install the inner liners, then fit the stays. Reconnect the battery (7/2) and check that the lights work correctly. Fit the wheels, tightening the lug nuts hand-tight.

23 Jack the car and remove the jack stands, then lower it to the ground and check tighten the lug nuts before fitting the hub caps 1/3.

12. FENDER (WING), FRONT - REMOVAL & INSTALLATION

 1/1, 2.

1 The front fender (wing) is a bolt-on item, which means that minor scrapes and bumps in this area are best dealt with by bolting on a new panel. You'll need to get the new panel painted to match your car, but in most cases you'll get better results this way than attempting to repair and paint the old panel. If you are careful during installation (and have allowed the new paint to harden thoroughly) you can avoid the hassle of masking and spraying the new panel by getting it painted first - this way, even the hidden areas get a coat of paint.

2 Apart from one bolt, you can get at all of the fender fastening points without disturbing other bodywork. The problem of the remaining bolt is that it is hidden under the front bumper fascia, so you will need to remove the front bumper (11/11) before you can remove the damaged fender.

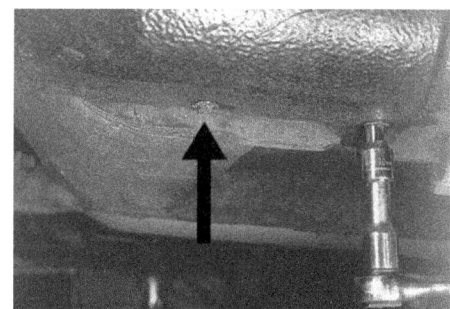
12/3a Two bolts secure lower part of fender.

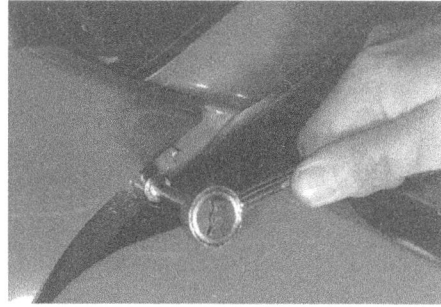
12/3b One bolt concealed in door opening.

12/4a Release bolts along fender top ...

Mazda Miata, MX-5, Eunos & Roadster

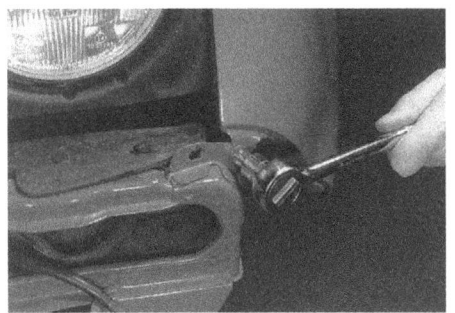

12/4b ... this one at the front ...

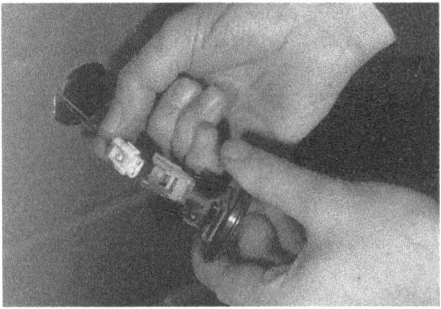

12/4c ...remove and disconnect side repeater ...

12/4d ... leaving just one nut, right at the back ...

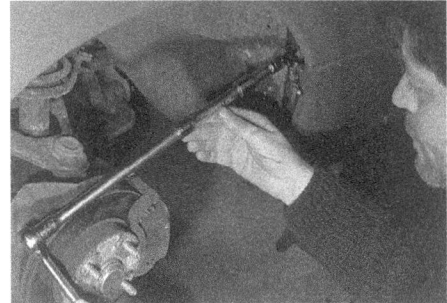

12/4e ... for which you'll need several extensions.

3   ▶+ With the bumper assembly removed, start removing the fender bolts - all have 10mm hexagon heads. There are two at the bottom edge of the fender, just below and forward of the door opening. The next is concealed in the door opening, near the beltline, so you'll need the door part open for access. Use a quarter or three eighths inch drive socket here, to avoid damaging the paint on the door edge.

4   ▶+ Next, remove the five bolts along the top edge of the fender, accessible with the hood raised (the bolt nearest the front of the car is the one

12/5 Lift the fender away.

normally covered by the front bumper). You now need to remove the turn signal side repeater light (if applicable) by popping it out of its hole in the fender and unplugging the wiring connector. Hidden in the recess between the back edge of the fender and the body is the final fixing, a single nut which is normally concealed by the wheelarch liner. You will need several extension bars to allow a socket to reach the nut, which should be slackened by several turns but left attached to its stud.

5   ▶ The remaining fixing points are shared with the bumper, and so will have already been dealt with. Lift the fender away, taking care not to gouge surrounding paint on the sharp edges of the panel.

6   When installing the fender, note that if it is the original panel, you need only align it so that the bolts fit with the unpainted areas at the flanges to ensure a good fit. If it is a new panel, we suggest that you use only an original Mazda part, or you may experience fitting or alignment problems.

7   Fit and tighten loosely all of the fixing bolts, then check the fit against the door and hood. Make any minor adjustments, then tighten the fixing bolts, checking that any shared fixing points with the bumper mountings will align correctly. Finally, install the bumper assembly, checking the fit between it and the new panel.

8   We noted with some surprise that there is a bad potential rust trap area at the bottom of the fender, where it curves under the car.

9   Road dirt (and, of course, any salt used during winter) is flung into the void between the fender and body through gaps between the liner and fender. There is a wedge-shaped cavity formed between the panels near the bottom, and the two panels eventually touch along the lower edge. This means that moisture retaining dirt is trapped between the fender and the body.

10   There is no way to flush this out once it builds up, and it will certainly cause corrosion to take place, given enough time. The problem is compounded because the well below the windshield discharges into this space, and because there is nowhere for the water to go, it soaks into and compacts the dirt between the panels.

11   You could minimize this problem by removing the wheel well liner and the lower fender bolts so that the wing can be bent outward slightly, and the dirt flushed out with a hose or pressure washer. We recommend that, maybe once a year, you clean this area, then apply a wax-based

underbody coating before the fender bolts are tightened and the liner installed. This is a real chore to do, but will be worthwhile if you plan on keeping the car for a while. If Mazda had designed-in a small drainage gap, the problem would not have arisen, but, as things stand, beware of rusting in this area.

13. WINDSHIELD - REMOVAL & INSTALLATION

☞ 1/1, 2.

1   The windshield (and the rear windshield, in the case of cars fitted with hard tops) is located in a recess in the body and sealed in position with a mastic compound, the join area being concealed with trim components. Removal and installation should not be undertaken at home - special tools and sealants will be required, and it is very easy to break the glass if the wrong removal or fitting technique is employed. We suggest that you take the car to a Mazda dealer, or to one of the many companies specializing in vehicle glass - this is the most economic way of dealing with glass replacement.

2   The usual reason for glass replacement is as a result of accident damage or vandalism. Check your insurance before you do anything else - in many instances, your insurance may cover glass damage, though this may not be the case in some countries or states. If you have glass cover, contact one of the approved specialists listed by the insurers.

3   If your car's windshield breaks while driving, pull over as quickly as you can. If your vision is obscured, wind down the door glass so that you can see better. **Warning!** Do not attempt to punch out the damaged screen. This usually results in serious injury to the hand, and you'll be covered in flying glass if you should succeed in breaking through the screen.

4   If your car is fitted with a laminated screen, it will most likely crack from the point of impact, but will remain in one piece and generally unobscured. Toughened glass winshields, on the other hand, tend to shatter into tiny cubes, making vision difficult. If a laminated screen gets chipped, take the car to a windshield specialist as soon as possible, which should be able to fill the chip and make the windshield as good as new - but only if no moisture has entered the lamination. You can also purchase kits at automotive accessory stores which will allow you to make similar repairs yourself.

5   If you have no option but to remove the damaged windshield yourself, cover the hood and the interior of the car with sheets to catch the debris, and wear gloves and eye protection when removing the remaining glass. Be absolutely certain that you have removed all traces of glass from the car interior and from the hood, and take care to avoid glass entering vents. If possible, use an industrial vacuum cleaner to ensure that all glass fragments are removed from the car interior.

6   In some countries and states it may be permissible to fit a temporary plastic windshield until you can get a new one fitted. These are made

11: Body

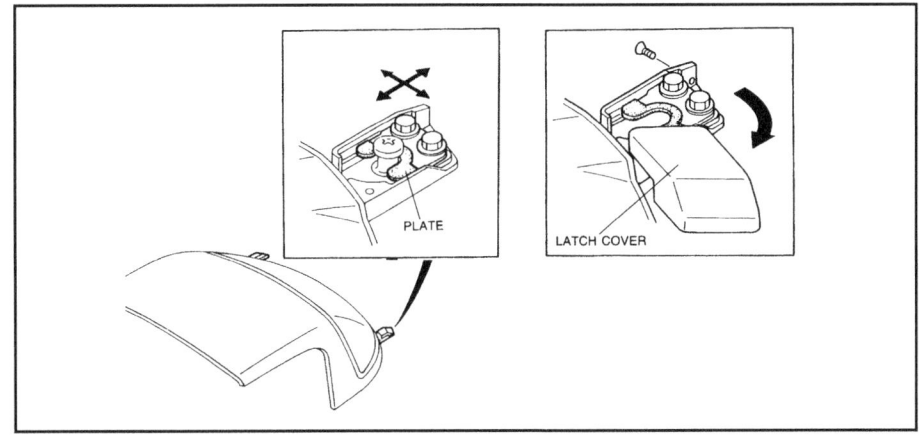

D14/6 HARD TOP LATCH ADJUSTMENT.

the convertible top ☞ 11/15.

5   Specific to the hard top only is the rear deck latch assembly. This secures the back edge of the hard top, and controls its position in relation to the windshield header. If the top is misaligned, remove the small screw which secures the rear deck latch cover plate and hinge it open. Install the top and check its fit with the surrounding panels and the windshield header.

6   If you need to adjust the latch, slacken the mounting plate bolts sufficiently to permit the assembly to move, then adjust its position until a good fit is obtained. Tighten the bolts to 18-26Nm/ 1.8-2.7kgf m/14-19lbf ft, then close the cover and fit the retaining screw. Recheck the adjustment, making sure that the top now latches in the correct position.

15. CONVERTIBLE TOP - REMOVAL, INSTALLATION & ADJUSTMENT

☞ 1/1, 2.

Note: The information in this section applies to original equipment Mazda brand convertible tops only.

REMOVAL

1   The factory convertible top is well designed and manufactured, opens and shuts easily, and keeps out the rain well; it is notable that many more expensive cars are sadly lacking in this respect. If, and when, the time comes for you to remove the top, here's how to do it.

2   Start work inside the car with the top up. We found that it is easier if you remove the seats to give you better access, or at least to adjust them fully forward and tip the seat backs forward. You'll need to remove the carpet which covers the luggage area and the vertical firewall which runs behind the

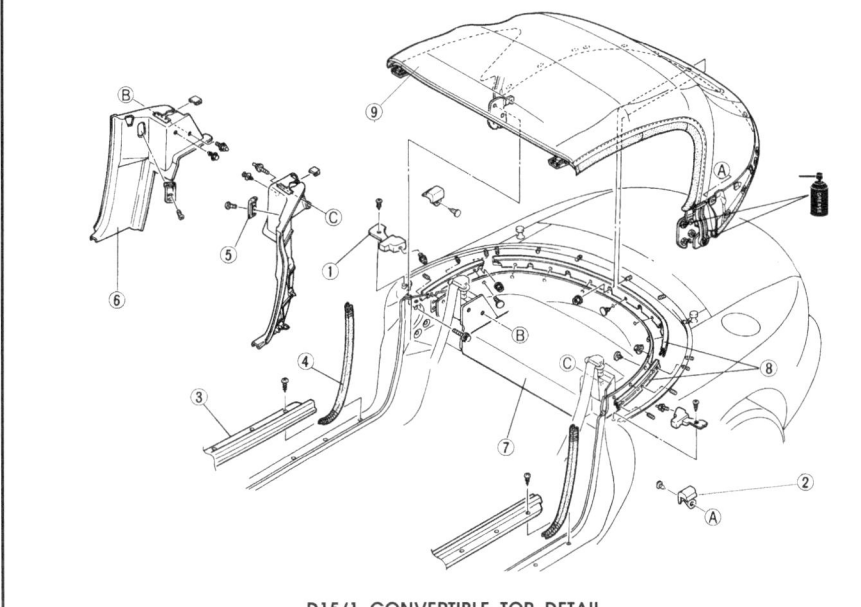

D15/1 CONVERTIBLE TOP DETAIL.
1 Beltline cover trim. 2 Beltline protector. 3 Rocker door sill scuff plate. 4 Door seal. 5 Striker plate. 6 Rear quarter trim panel. 7 Rear package shelf trim. 8 Set plates. 9 Convertible top.

of clear plastic sheeting, and so will soon become scratched in use, especially if the wipers are used; such screens should be regarded as an emergency measure only and a replacement glass windshield must be installed as soon as possible.

14. HARD TOP - INSTALLATION & ADJUSTMENT

☞ 1/1, 2.

1   Mazda offers a removable hard top as an accessory, and it is this standard item that we refer to in this section. Note that there are a number of third-party hard tops available, too: these normally use a similar mounting arrangement to the factory top, but you should refer to the manufacturer's instructions for specific information when dealing with these products.

2   Most owners will wish to use the hard top only through the winter months, and will probably install the soft top during summer. The hard top also offers greater vehicle security in high-risk areas. Installing and removing the hard top should be regarded as a two-person operation - the top is not especially heavy, but it is too cumbersome to maneuver into place alone without risking damage to the top or body.

3   If you have no choice but to remove and fit the top unaided, you should consider purchasing one of the miniature hoists produced for this purpose. These allow you to suspend the top from your garage, drive the car into position, and then lower the top safely into place on the car.

4   After installing the hard top, you should check the various latch adjustments and check the fit of the top in relation to the body and doors. Details of these adjustments and checks will be found in the following text, but the latches and weatherstrips are generally similar to those used on

15/5a Remove the securing nuts, followed ...

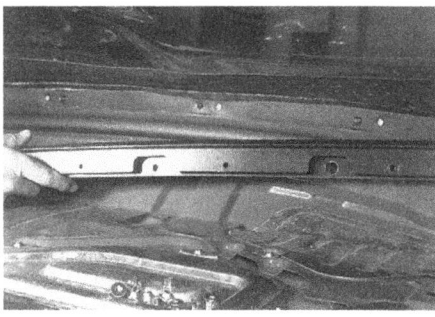

15/5b ... by the set plates themselves.

Mazda Miata, MX-5, Eunos & Roadster

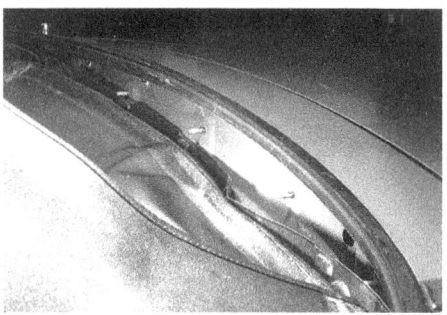
15/5c Carefully pull the soft top from the studs.

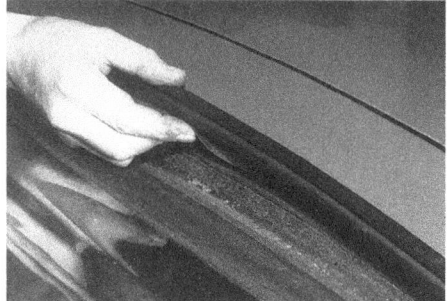
15/9 Make sure rain rail is behind this lip.

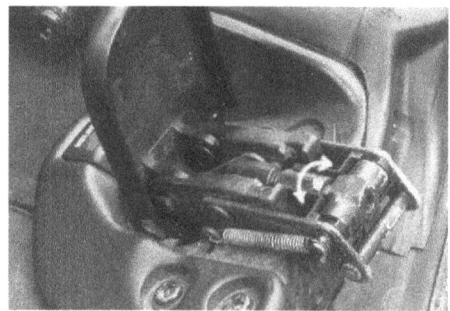
15/12a Soft top latch adjustment.

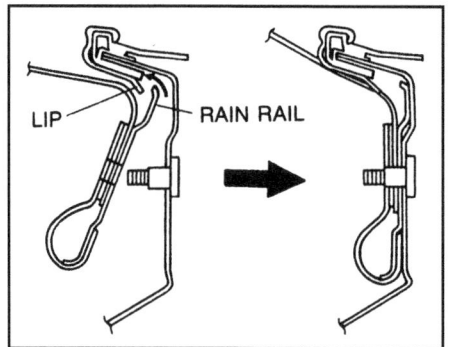
D15/9 CORRECT INSTALLATION OF THE BELTLINE MOLDING.

15/12b We couldn't eradicate all unevenness.

seat. These sections are retained by plastic clips and also by two stops which are retained by screws. For more information ☞ 10/12.

3   Remove the brace bar ☞ 10/15.
4   Remove the two quarter trim panels ☞ 10/5/9-15.
5   ◻+ You now need to free the back edge of the convertible top. This is secured by a three-piece set plate arrangement, each section of which is retained by 10mm nuts. Remove the nuts and pull the set plate sections of the mounting studs. You can now free the back edge of the top by carefully pulling it away from the studs. You need to tip the lower edge of the top away from the body until the lip disengages from the top's rain rail section - do not force this or the top may get damaged.
6   Release the convertible top's front latches,

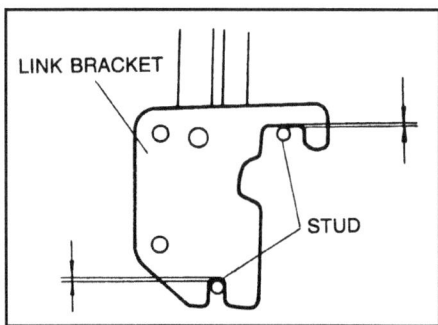
D15/8 THERE SHOULD BE NO CLEARANCE BETWEEN LINK BRACKET & PINS.

but don't fold the top. Unzip the rear window and lay it flat, then carefully fold the top.
7   Have an assistant to help you from this stage onward. Remove the three bolts which secure the main hinge plate (Mazda calls this a 'link bracket') to the body. The top will remain in place, located by pins on each side. Grasp each side of the convertible top, lift it slightly and disengage it from the locating pins. The assembly can now be lifted away from the body.

INSTALLATION

8   ◻ With the help of an assistant, lift the folded top assembly into position, making sure that the link bracket hooks over the locating pins on each side. Check that the extended rain rail molding on each side is positioned correctly - this is brittle and easily damaged if forced into place or mishandled, and if damaged, rain will get into the car. Once it is positioned correctly, fit the retaining bolts and tighten them to 19-25Nm/1.9-2.6kgf m/14-18lbf ft. Note that the link bracket should be resting on the locating pins - there should be no clearance between them.
9   ◻ 🔍 Part-open the top, but do not latch it at the front. Fit the back edge of the top over the row of studs at the back of the luggage area. Note that it is important that the rain rail section hooks under the projecting lip, or rain will leak into the car. We suggest that you check this from the outside - you should be able to run a finger along the rubber lip edge to make sure that it sits over the rain rail. Fit the set plate sections over the studs and tighten the nuts to 7.9-10.7Nm/80-110kgf cm/70-95.4lbf in).
10   Fit the quarter trim panels ☞ 10/5/16-18.
11   Install the brace bar ☞ 10/15.

ADJUSTMENT
Note: These adjustments also apply to the optional hard top.

12   ◻+ The top latch can be adjusted to increase or decrease the clearance between the windshield header and the convertible top or optional hard top. This is achieved by turning the adjuster nut inside the latch assembly, after folding back the protector.
13   🔍 Turning the nut clockwise reduces clearance, while turning it counter-clockwise increases clearance. The specified clearances between the top and the header are as shown in the accompanying diagram. Note that you should lock the

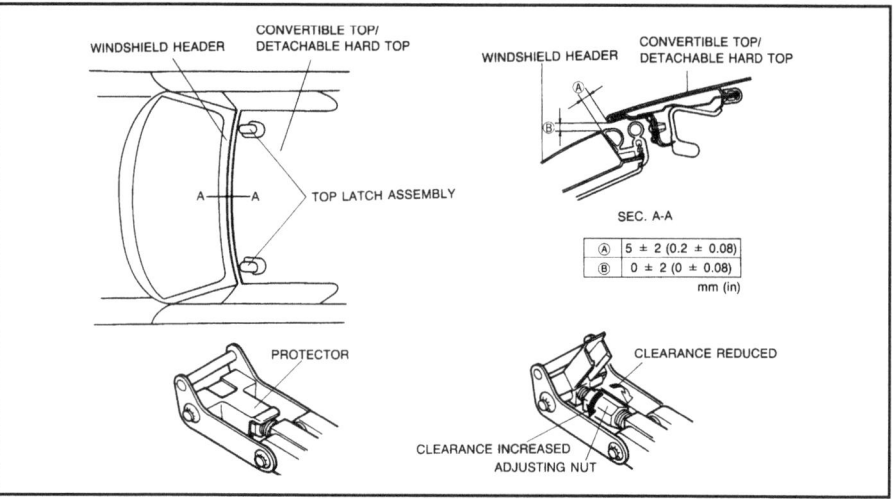
D15/13 CONVERTIBLE TOP TENSION ADJUSTMENT.

11: Body

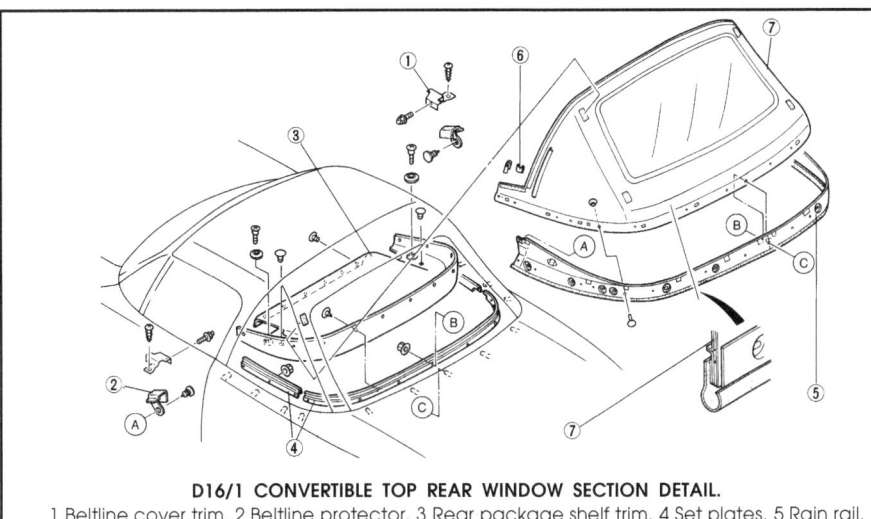

D16/1 CONVERTIBLE TOP REAR WINDOW SECTION DETAIL.
1 Beltline cover trim. 2 Beltline protector. 3 Rear package shelf trim. 4 Set plates. 5 Rain rail.
6 Zipper stop. 7 Rear window section.

adjustment setting afterwards by closing the protector.

14   On cars fitted with hard tops, similar side latches are fitted, and these can be adjusted in the same way as the top latches. Turning the adjuster clockwise will tighten the fit of the latch; conversely, turning it counter-clockwise will loosen the fit. For information on the rear deck latch (hard tops) ☞ 11/14.

16. CONVERTIBLE TOP REAR WINDOW & RAIN RAIL - REMOVAL & INSTALLATION

☞ 1/1, 2.
Note: The information in this section applies to original equipment Mazda brand convertible tops only.

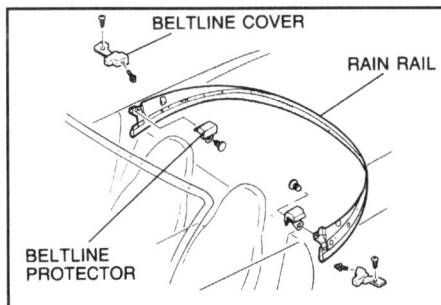

D16/2 BELTLINE COVERS, PROTECTORS & RAIL.

REMOVAL

1   Like just about every other convertible top, the one fitted to these cars employs a flexible plastic rear window. This can be unzipped from the main top fabric, allowing it to be dropped flat without creasing the window material. Care when stowing the top will extend its life considerably, but eventually the window material will become scratched and opaque. When this occurs, the window section can be detached without having to remove the convertible top entirely. The removal

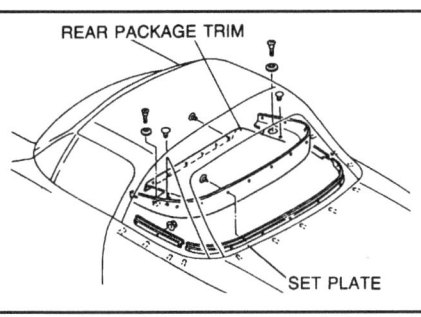

D16/3 REAR PACKAGE SHELF TRIM & SETPLATES.

procedure should be started with the window unzipped and folded flat, and the convertible top lowered fully.

2   Referring to the accompanying drawing, remove the beltline covers. These are each retained by a single sheet metal screw fitted from the top, plus a pip-headed 10mm bolt fitted from the side. Next, release the beltline protectors, which are secured by a plastic pin pushed into the body from the package area. The pin is not easy to spot - it is tucked away in the extreme corner of the soft top well area. The pin also passes through and secures the ends of the rain rail, which needs to be removed a little later in the procedure.

3   Raise the convertible top, but do not

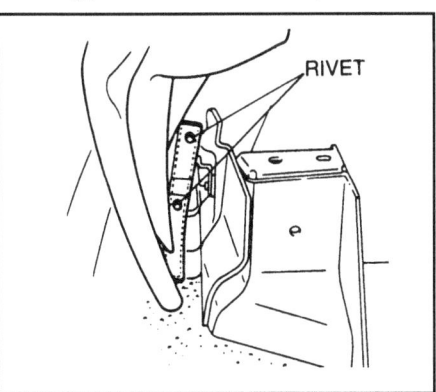

D16/5 DRILL OUT THESE RIVETS.

latch it to the windshield header. Remove the rear package shelf trim (carpet). This is retained by a row of plastic pins around the back edge - these push into the convertible top set plates. There are further pins along the front edge, plus a couple on the flat package area. You also need to remove the

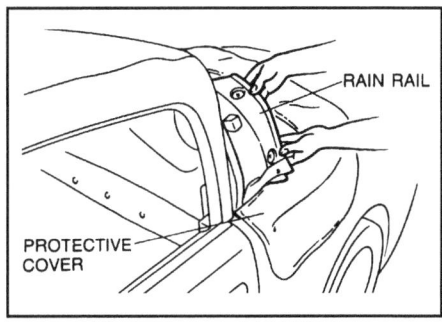

D16/6 REMOVE RAIN RAIL.

two round stops which are retained by crosshead (Philips) screws.

4   Remove the 10mm nuts which retain the convertible top's set plate sections, which, in turn, retain the top along the sides and back. The set plate comes away in three sections.

5   Just next to the seatbelt turrets you'll find the end of the rain rail, riveted to the convertible top link assembly (main hinge). Using a 4mm/

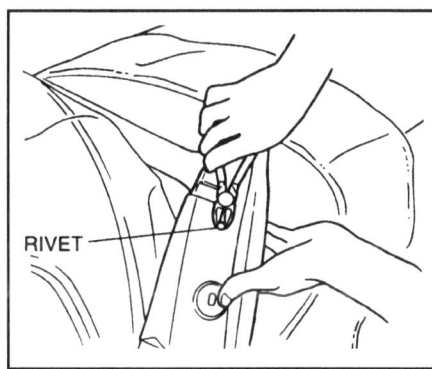

D16/7 REMOVE RIVETS WITH A CUTTER.

0.16in approx. drill, carefully drill out the heads of the two rivets so that the front edge of the rain rail can be detached from the convertible top's mechanism.

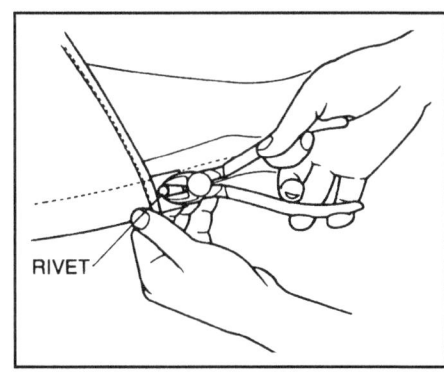

D16/8 REMOVE RIVETS WITH A CUTTER.

Mazda Miata, MX-5, Eunos & Roadster

6   Moving to the outside of the car, lay some old towels or similar around the body opening to form a protective cover. Free the rain rail from the body by pulling it off the mounting studs. Note that the rail is made of thin plastic and is easily torn if mishandled.

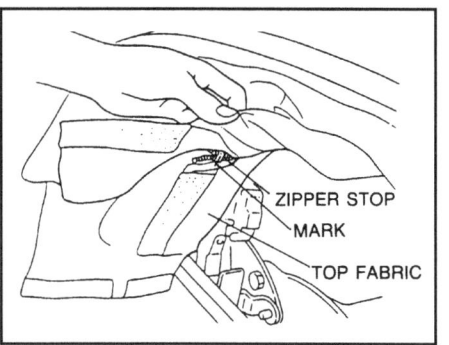

D16/9 REMOVE THE ZIPPER STOPS.

7   Using a pair of sharp side cutters, carefully remove the rivets from the rain rail, taking care not to damage the rail while doing so. Once all the rivets have been cut, remove the rain rail from the top and place it to one side.

8   Using the cutters, remove the rivets from the edge of the rear window section, again,

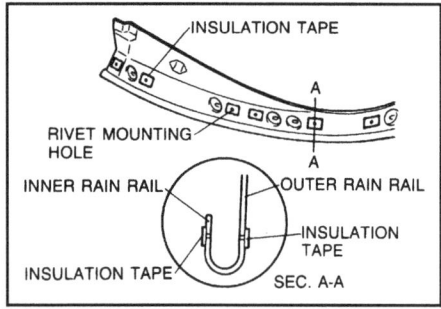

D16/10 COVER RIVET HOLES WITH PVC TAPE.

taking care not to damage the window surround fabric.

9   Locate the ends of the rear window

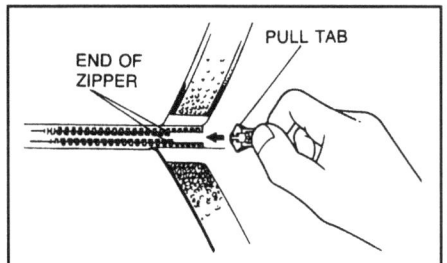

D16/11 ZIP WINDOW INTO PLACE.

zipper. Using paint, mark the position of the zipper stops and the relative positions of each side of the zipper, as a guide during installation. Carefully remove the stops, retrieving them for re-use during installation. The zipper may now be separated completely and the rear window section detached from the convertible top; pull off the pull tab and retain it for use during installation.

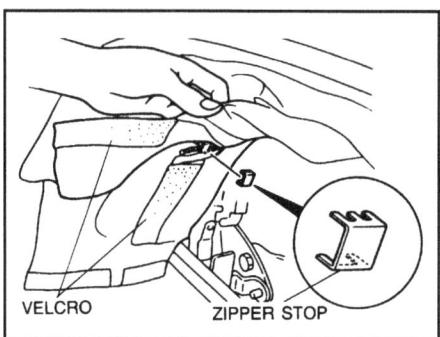

D16/12 INSTALL ZIPPER STOPS.

INSTALLATION

10   Clean and degrease the rain rail using ethyl alcohol, then cover the rivet holes in the rail

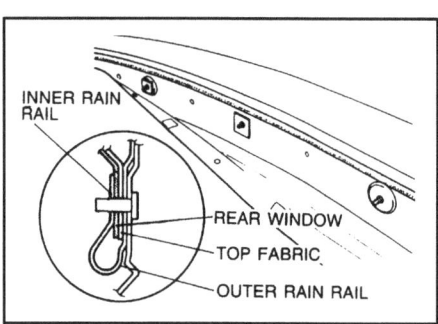

D16/13 FIT SOFT TOP OVER STUDS.

using small pieces of PVC electrical tape. The tape pieces need to be about 20 x 20mm/0.8 x 0.8in.

11   Position the window section in the back of the convertible top. Align the zipper ends, then engage the zipper pull tab over the ends of the zipper and zip the window into the convertible top. Check that the window section is correctly positioned, and that the convertible top is not pulled

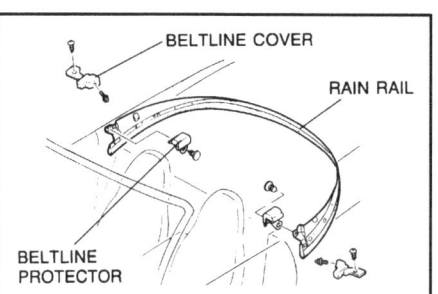

D16/14 FIT BELTLINE COVERS & PROTECTORS.

out of shape. If necessary, remove the pull tab and realign the zipper ends to correct any misalignment.

12   Fit the zipper stops, positioning them as indicated by the paint marks made during removal. Close the join between the top and window sections by pushing together the Velcro pads.

13   Assemble the rain rail, top fabric and window fabric as shown in the accompanying

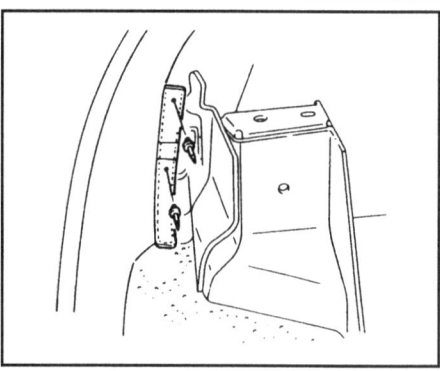

D16/15 RIVET FABRIC TO LINKS.

drawing, positioning the assembly over the body studs. Note the order in which the various elements are fitted, and that the loop of the rain rail encloses the fabric sections. Position the set plates over the studs, working from the left, and fit the nuts finger-tight.

14   Unzip the rear window and lower the convertible top fully. Install the beltline protectors, ensuring that the fixing pins pass through the ends of the rain rail. Install the beltline covers, securing each one with the single sheet metal screw and single pip-headed set screw. Now raise the top, latching it to the windshield header, and zip the window into place.

15   Working inside the car, tighten the set plate nuts, evenly and progressively to a torque of 8.9-11.7Nm/90-120kgf cm/79-104lbf in. Rivet the ends of the rain rail to the link assembly on each side of the car.

16   Install the rear package trim, securing it with its plastic pins and the two round stops. Make a final check of the alignment of the convertible top and rear window section. If any adjustment is needed, realign the zipper.

17. CONVERTIBLE TOP FABRIC - REMOVAL & INSTALLATION

☞ 1/1, 2.
Note: The information in this section applies to original equipment Mazda brand convertible tops only.

1   It is possible to completely dismantle the convertible top to permit a new fabric section to be fitted, or to allow the mechanism to be repaired or replaced. Whether you choose to do so is another

17/3 Lay top upside-down on soft surface.

11: Body

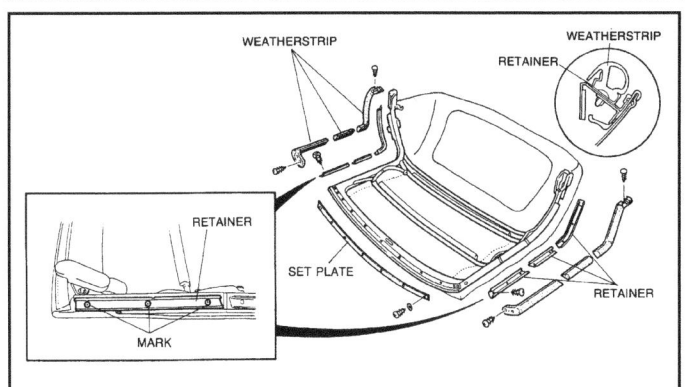

D17/4 CONVERTIBLE TOP DETAIL.

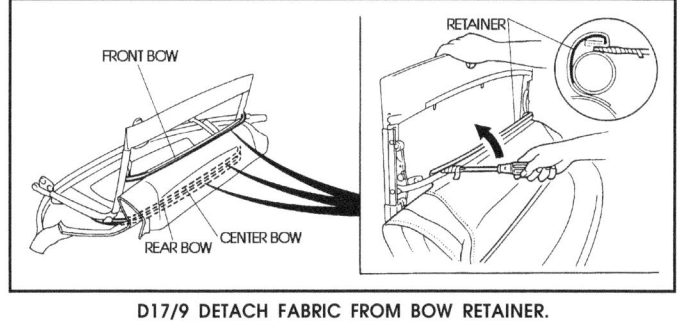

D17/9 DETACH FABRIC FROM BOW RETAINER.

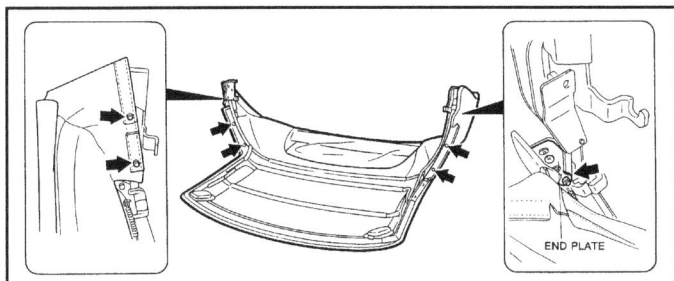

D17/5 REMOVE SCREWS & ENDPLATES FROM LINK ASSEMBLY.

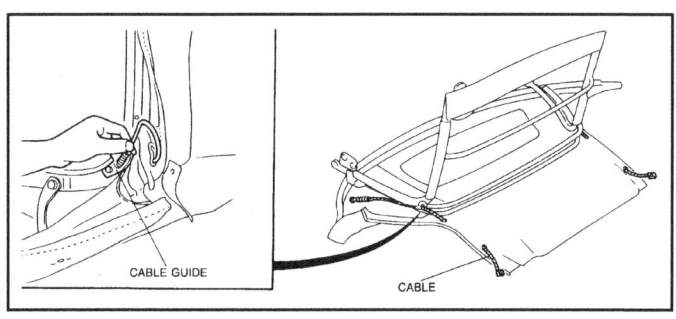

D17/10 REMOVE CABLES FROM GUIDES & FABRIC & CABLES FROM LINKS.

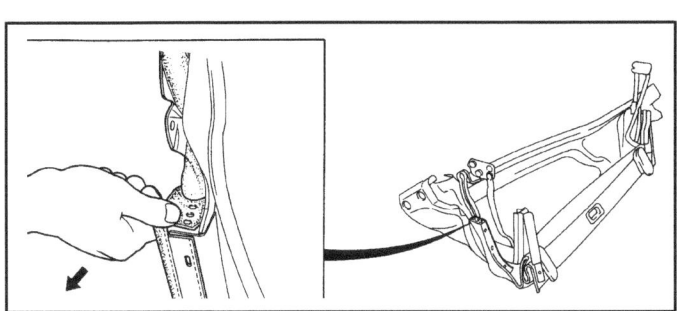

D17/6 DETACH THE FABRIC FROM THE LINK ASSEMBLY.

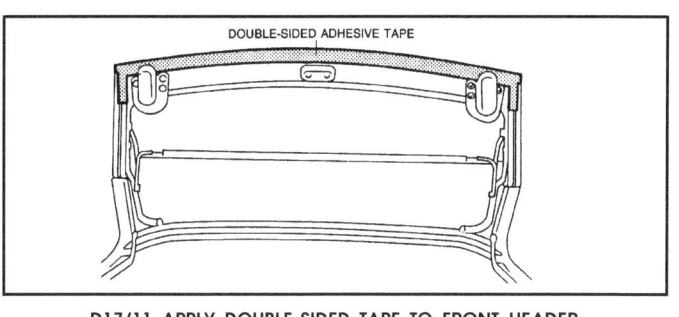

D17/11 APPLY DOUBLE-SIDED TAPE TO FRONT HEADER.

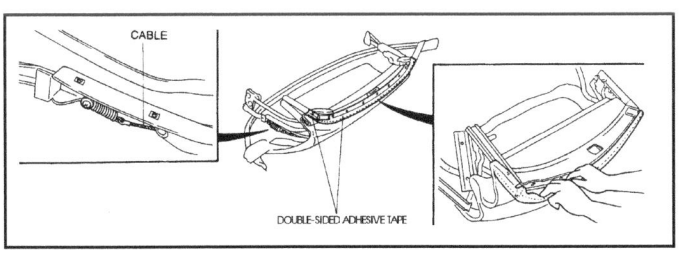

D17/7 REMOVE SCREWS & DISCONNECT CABLES FROM LINKS.

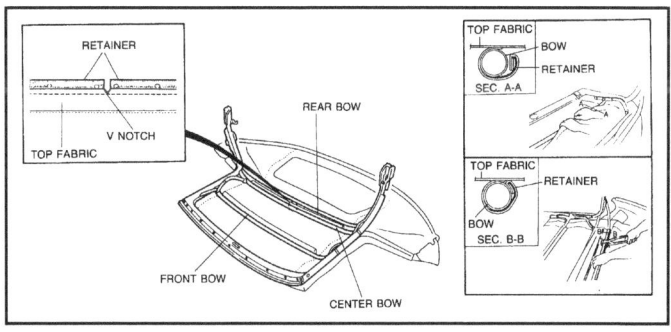

D17/13 FIX FABRIC TO REAR BOW WITH VELCRO.

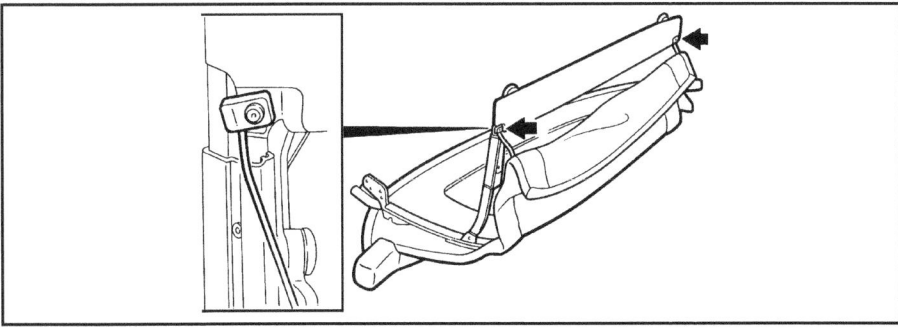

D17/8 DRILL OUT LINK ASSEMBLY RIVETS.

matter - the procedure is complicated, and, without previous experience in this type of work, you could end up with a badly-fitting top.

2   If you do not feel confident about your abilities and facilities, we suggest that you consider removing the top as described above and having a Mazda or trim specialist carry out the necessary repair or overhaul for you - that way it is somebody else's problem if the repaired top does not fit correctly. Either way, start out by removing the complete top ☞ 11/15.

3   📷 Open up the top and lay it upside down on a soft surface. You could do this on a bench

covered in thick cloth, though a grassed area works well enough for this if the weather is good. Before you start, have ready a marker pen, some self-adhesive labels and some tie-on labels, so that each part can be clearly marked - there are a lot of them, and it will get very confusing if you skip this.

4   Remove the weatherstrip sections, the set plate and the weatherstrip retainers, marking each part as it is removed. Note that you should paint-mark the retainers and screws as a position guide during installation

5   Using a 4mm drill, remove the ten rivets which secure the top fabric to the link assembly. Unscrew the screws which secure the end plates to the link assembly and remove them.

6   With the rear window unzipped and the top folded loosely, free the top fabric from the link assembly.

7   Grasp the edge of the top fabric where it attaches to the front header and peel it back - it is secured by double-sided tape. Remove the screws which retain the ends of the top fabric tensioner cable springs and disconnect them from the link assembly.

8   Part unfold the top and position it with the header rail upwards. Using a 4mm drill, drill out the rivets as shown in the drawing to free the front ends of the tensioner cables.

9   Peel back the Velcro at the rear bow. Wrap a screwdriver blade with pvc tape to prevent damage, then carefully bend back the bow retainers to release the fabric from them.

10   Free the tensioner cables from the cable guides, then detach the top fabric and cables from the link assembly. Unthread the cables from the top fabric.

INSTALLATION

11    Check over the link mechanism,

17/11a Lube frame joints with WD40 or similar.

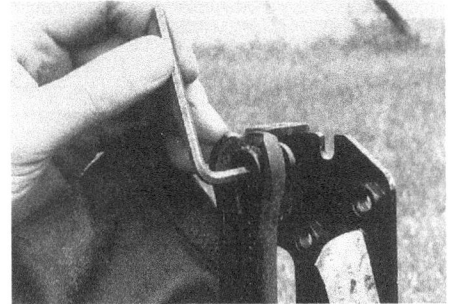

17/11b Tighten any loose joints.

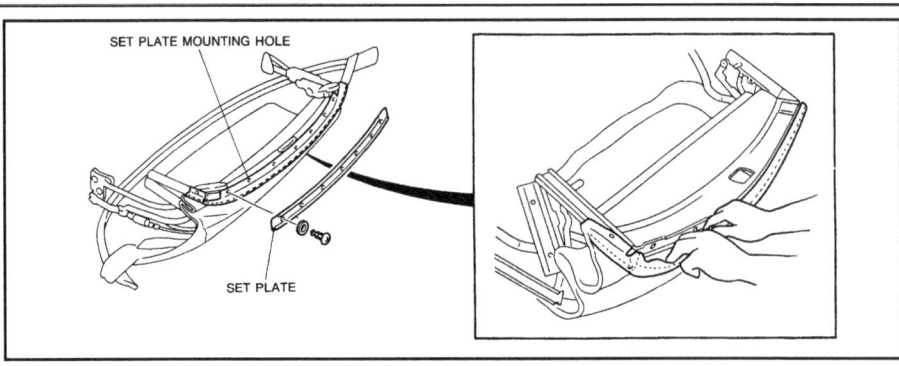

D17/14 FIT THE SET PLATE TO THE LINK ASSEMBLY.

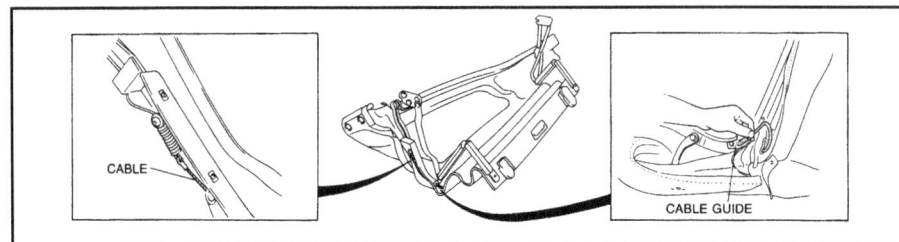

D17/15 PASS CABLES THRU GUIDES & FIT THEM TO LINKS.

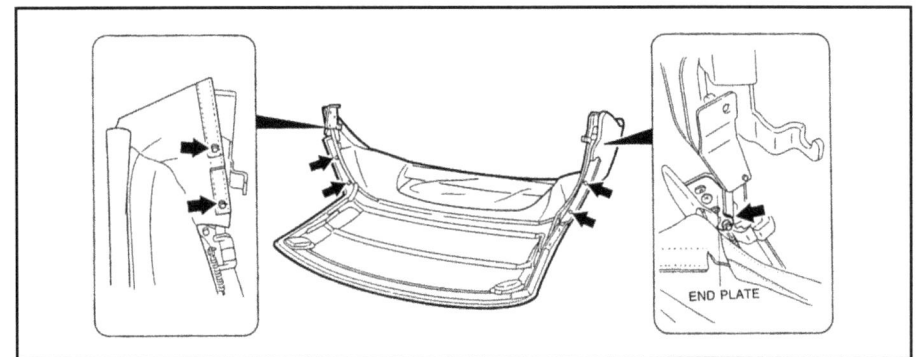

D17/16 FASTEN THE TOP FABRIC TO THE LINKS.

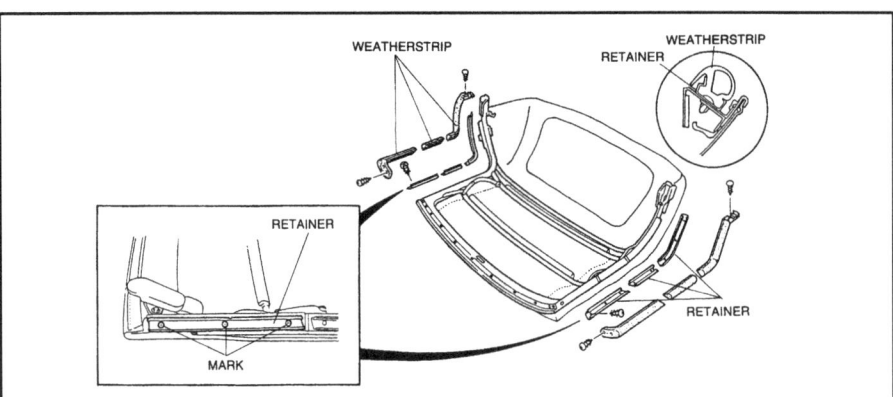

D17/17 FIT WEATHERSTRIP RETAINERS & WEATHERSTRIPS.

lubricating the joints with WD40 or similar, and also tightening any loose joints. Remove all traces of the original double-sided tape from the front header. Degrease the header with ethyl alcohol and allow it to dry, then apply new double-sided tape to the shaded areas as shown in the diagram.

12   Thread the tensioner cables through the top fabric, then lay the top on a soft surface and place the link assembly over it.

13   Cover the jaws of a pair of water pump pliers with pvc tape to prevent damage to the link assembly and top. Starting at the rear bow, align the center of the retainer with the V-notch in the fabric. Hook the end of the top fabric strip over the end of the retainer, then squeeze the retainer shut using the protected pliers. Repeat this procedure

11: Body

on the center and front bows. Secure the top fabric to the rear bow with the Velcro pads.

14 Rivet the front ends of the tensioner cables to the header strip. Turn the assembly over for access, then secure the fabric to the header with the double-sided tape. Take your time with this or the fabric will get puckered during fixing. Pull off a little of the backing paper at a time and don't stretch the fabric. Now position the set plate and secure it with its screws to the header.

15 With the top unfolded halfway, feed the tensioner cables through the cable guides, then secure them at the back by screwing the springs to the link assembly.

16 Fit the top fabric over the end of the link assembly, and align the fabric and end plates with the holes in the link assembly. Secure the plates and fabric with 10 new rivets.

17 Install the weatherstrip retainers, aligning the paint marks made during removal, then fit the weatherstrips in their correct positions in the retainers.

18 Install the convertible top, and check that it operates correctly, that the rear window can be zipped and unzipped normally, and that it aligns correctly, and that the fit between the door glass and weatherstrips is correct.

18. CONVERTIBLE TOP - FABRIC REPAIRS

☞ 1/1, 2.

Note: The information in this section applies to original equipment Mazda brand convertible tops only.

1 If your car's convertible top develops holes or gets torn, it can (within reason) be repaired. You will need some repair sheet (Mazda: NAYIR1 211), adhesive (Mazda: K180 W0 313 or equivalent), and some ethyl alcohol for cleaning the damaged area.

2 If the damage is a small tear, you need to clean around the damaged area with ethyl alcohol on the inside of the top fabric.

3 Now cut a piece of repair sheet slightly larger than the tear, and apply a thick coat of adhesive to both parts (the adhesive should be applied to the *inside* of the top fabric - this is where you will fix the repair sheet material).

4 After the adhesive has been left for a few minutes, press the repair sheet firmly onto the inside of the top fabric. Leave the repair to dry fully before using the car - ideally overnight.

5 If you have a large or jagged hole to deal with, you will need to cut out the damaged part and replace it with a section of repair sheet. This operation is easier if you have an assistant. You will need

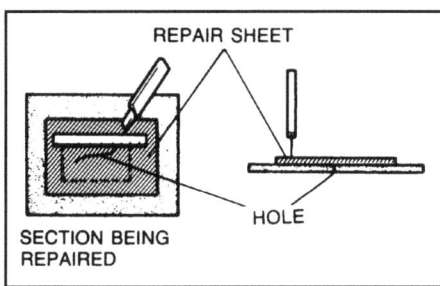

D18/6 CUT THRU REPAIR PATCH & TOP FABRIC.

a piece of lumber to cut against, a craft knife or scalpel and a straightedge.

6 Place a piece of repair sheet on the outside of the top material so that it covers the damaged area. Have your assistant hold the lumber under the area to be cut out, then, using the craft knife and the straightedge, cut through the repair sheet and top fabric together. You should cut out a rectangular area which encloses the damage.

7 The result should be a rectangular hole in the top, and a repair patch which exactly matches this. Do this very carefully, and the repair will be just about invisible when completed. It is worth trying to match the direction of the 'grain' of the top fabric and repair material when cutting the repair section.

8 Cut out another rectangle of the repair sheet material, slightly larger than the hole, to be used as a backing sheet. Degrease the top fabric and repair sheet sections with ethyl alcohol. Apply a thick film of adhesive to the inside of the top material, to the backing sheet, and around the hole edges. Leave the adhesive to start drying for a few

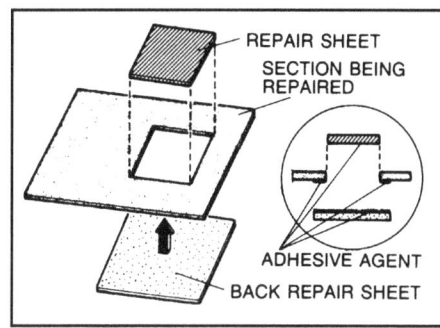

D18/8 BACKING MUST BE BIGGER THAN PATCH.

minutes, then fit the backing sheet from inside the car and press the repair piece into the hole from the outside. Press all parts together firmly, then allow to dry for as long as possible before using the car - preferably overnight.

Notes

12

Rustproofing

1. INTRODUCTION

This chapter describes how to keep the body structure of your car in good shape. The body chapter deals with the visible aspects of the body: here, we consider the hidden areas which impart strength and rigidity to the car.

Like all contemporary cars, Mazda's sportscar is based on a unitary body made up from welded steel panels. This method of construction utilizes the body panels themselves as an intrinsic part of the car's structure. Each panel in isolation is relatively frail, but combined into a unified structure, provides great strength with relatively low weight, a little like an eggshell. Also like an eggshell, the body only maintains its structural integrity whilst it remains intact; once rust gets a hold, or in the event of impact damage deforming the structure, it becomes weakened and, eventually, dangerous.

Repairs to the body structure require skill and experience if they are to be performed safely. It is no good just patching over rust with sheet steel on a car like this, which was designed to be driven hard, placing extra stress on the body, as well as the suspension and steering parts attached to it.

In the following pages, we deal with the best methods of preserving the body structure in safe condition. We also describe how to check the body in the event of a suspected structural fault. We don't tell you how to go about welded repairs, and we recommend that you entrust this type of repair work to a Mazda dealer or professional repair shop.

2. RUSTPROOFING - WHY IT'S A GOOD IDEA

1   The car as supplied new is adequately protected to survive for some years in reasonable conditions, but, like all modern vehicles, it is not exactly over-endowed with paint, especially in the hidden areas not immediately visible.
2   If you intend that the car should survive intact well beyond the manufacturer's corrosion warranty period, you may wish to improve on the corrosion prevention measures already taken by Mazda. In part, the need to do this will depend on where you live; a car used in warm and predominantly dry climates will probably last well without further intervention, but the same car operating close to the sea, or in temperate climates where the roads are salted during winter, will corrode a lot faster.
3   If you intend to trade in your car before it is five years old you might not consider this extra work to be worthwhile: after all, the car is unlikely to start rusting for several years, and you'll derive no benefit from the work. If, on the other hand, you are the owner of an older car, the earlier you carry out this preventative work the better the car will last.
4   A further factor regarding the value of rustproofing concerns second-hand cars exported from the country in which they were originally sold. A good example of this is the flood of Japanese domestic market Miata models being imported to the UK through the so-called "grey market." These cars have less rustproofing than those originally built for the UK market and will therefore benefit greatly from extra rustproofing in the UK's damp winter environment.
5   Always keep in mind that rustproofing is entirely a *preventative* operation - no amount of rustproofing will repair already damaged bodywork.
6   You have options when it comes to rustproofing. In many areas there are specialists who will do this work for you. This is fine if you use an established company which offers guaranteed work; many operate a system where you need to take the car in for checking and maintenance work at regular intervals. If you choose this option, read the small print of the warranty carefully before you sign anything. Remember that you'll be paying for work that is largely impossible to check, and there is a good chance that a small rustproofing operation may have gone out of business well before any problems or failures show up. You should also beware of contacts which obligate you to have additional extensive treatments carried out over a period of years: this can get expensive.
7   You can do the same kind of work yourself, using commercially available rustproofing kits. This has a couple of advantages. Firstly, it is cheaper. Secondly, you know with absolute certainty that the work has been carried out correctly. On the down side, it is a messy job, and requires time and patience to do properly - you may find that you never get around to repeat treatments or checks.

3. RUSTPROOFING PROCEDURE

☞ 1/1, 2.

PREPARATION

1   The first thing to be aware of is that these cars have a complex body structure. In most conventional sedan (saloon) bodies the roof and its supporting pillars form an important part of the structure. With any convertible body design, the absence of an integral roof structure compromises the unitary design, and this has to be compensated for by additional strengthening elsewhere. Between the hidden structural members and the external body panels lie cavities, mostly closed by access panels and trim. This means that, after preliminary cleaning, you will need to dismantle areas of the car to be able to gauge the condition of the body.
2   To conduct a full assessment of the condition of your car, you'll need to clean it thoroughly, and this includes the underbody and areas like the wheel wells (arches). We suggest that you use a pressure-wash facility for this. Note that hot pressure washing or steam cleaning will also tend to remove the existing underbody wax layer. This is not a problem, and could be considered advantageous if you intend to rustproof the car completely, but don't leave the car unprotected after removing this coating. Cold pressure washing should not affect any wax rustproofing materials and can therefore be used safely.
3   Note that if you intend to carry out a full

Mazda Miata, MX-5, Eunos & Roadster

check of the condition of the body, the necessary dismantling work will also provide access for rustproofing, so you may as well carry out any remedial work as part of your check. This being the case, we suggest that you gather together the necessary tools and materials. The main requirement is for a quantity of rustproofing fluid. The best choice here is for one of the wax-based products sold for this purpose. These are widely used by automotive manufacturers, and have largely replaced the earlier bituminous coatings.

4   You should be able to obtain a suitable product through your auto parts store, and in many cases you'll be able to buy a kit containing the fluid, plus application tools. These normally include some sort of hand pump, plus a long-reach probe and nozzles for coating the insides of box sections and body cavities. Check your kit to see if you have enough of the fluid to carry out a full rustproofing job - you may need to buy extra in some cases. Depending on how meticulous you are, and how heavily you apply the product, you'll need 1-2 gallons/5-10 liters of the rustproofer. You'll also need a couple of old paint brushes for spot application of the rustproofing fluid, plus an assortment of bungs and some PVC or duct tape for sealing up any holes made during the procedure. A small flashlight - if possible with a flexible gooseneck head - will also be invaluable for checking inside the box sections and cavities.

5   Once the car is clean and dry, you need to jack it as high as possible and support it on jack (axle) stands to allow clear access to the underbody. **Warning!** On no account get under the car until you are certain that it is supported securely. The road wheels need to be removed for access to the wheel wells. For details of jacking and supporting the car ☞ 1/3.

6   Many of the body cavities are effectively sealed from the outside of the car, but you can usually get to them from the inside. Beneath the carpet and trim panels lie numerous holes and apertures which allow relatively easy access to most of these closed sections. With the interior of the body exposed in this way, you can see how the various body cavities are formed. Using a small flashlight, and perhaps a dentist's mirror, try to assess the condition of the internal surfaces. It is these areas where the manufacturer's protection is at its weakest, and which will benefit most from rustproofing. We recommend that you remove the seats, carpets and interior trim to facilitate this ☞ 10/5 & 10/11.

7   ◻ The external surfaces of the underbody and the wheel wells are easily checked. Wear eye protection to avoid getting dirt in your eyes, and use a wire brush to remove any residual road dirt. You will find that the wheel wells contain splash shields in the form of plastic liners. These are retained by a mixture of sheet metal screws and the ubiquitous plastic fasteners which you'll find throughout the car. Remove the liners so that you can check behind them, and remove any accumulated dirt.

MAIN ROCKER (SILL) SECTIONS

8   The lower body is strengthened by the rocker sections which run between the two wheel wells. These are complex structures which contribute greatly to the longitudinal rigidity of the car, and which are particularly vulnerable to corrosion if left untreated. Moisture inside the sections can cause rusting to start off unseen, and this will only be apparent when it breaks through the external surfaces. Don't confuse this with surface rusting, which may have occurred as the result of stone chips on the outside. If the external paint finish is damaged, you will need to repair the damage before you go any further ☞ 11/3, 4.

9   At the front of the rocker sections, the body panels are overlapped by the rear lower edges of the front fenders (wings). What starts out as a cavity at the back of the wheelarch narrows down until the fender and underlying body panel are in close contact, producing a particularly bad rust trap. Dirt from the front wheels gets past the liners and then builds up in this area. To add to the problem, rain running down from the windshield drains off through this cavity, which, having no intentional outlet, means that the dirt (and any road salt) gets wet and compacted at the lower edge.

10   To clear this area, you'll need to detach the two bolts which retain the rear lower edge of the fender so that it can be pulled away slightly (you don't need to remove the fender entirely - the lower edge will flex enough to allow it to be cleaned out). You can then pressure-wash the area to flush out any dirt and salt. If the lower part of the fender is showing signs of rust penetration, this will almost certainly be caused by dirt and salt trapped in this area. If this is noted, you should detach the fender completely to allow a full check of the underlying body - this will probably have started rusting, too, and measures should be taken to repair any damage ☞ 11/12.

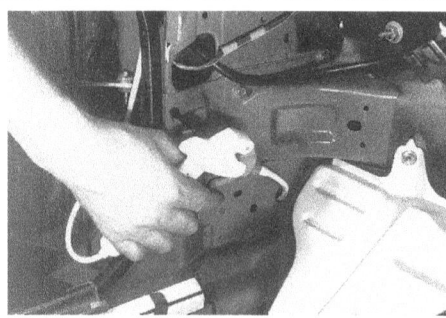

3/11b ... spray head inside rockers (sills).

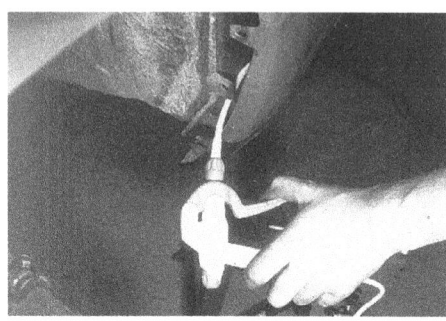

3/12 Clean inside fender & apply rustproofer.

11   ◻+ Working inside the car, locate all suitable injection points through which the rustproofing fluid can be applied. You'll find access holes along the rocker sections and on the sides of the footwell area. If access permits, use a flashlight to check for signs of rust inside the section. Insert the probe into the rocker section, and apply an even coat of wax rustproofing fluid along its length. The best technique is to push the probe as far down the cavity as it will go, and then pump fluid through it as it is withdrawn. When the rustproofing fluid is first applied it is fairly thin, and may drip out from under the car for a while. You might want to place some newspaper under the car to catch the drips. After a while the solvent will evaporate and the coating will dry to a sticky wax finish.

12   ◻ Before you install the wheel well liners, apply a good coat of the wax rustproofing fluid to the areas behind them. Working from the rear wheelarch, you can access the back of the rocker section - coat everything in sight with the fluid. At the front, apply a thick coat to the body and to the inside of the fender, especially where the two come into contact towards the bottom edge. You can spray or brush the fluid onto these areas.

3/7 Remove splash shields to gain access.

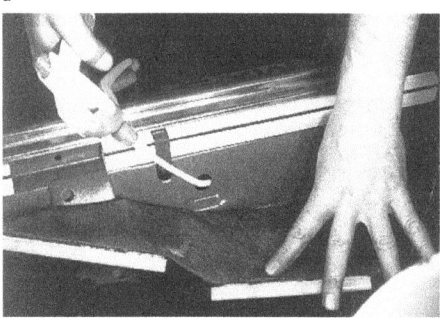

3/11a Use these existing holes to get ...

6/13 Access to longitudinal box members.

12: Rustproofing

LONGITUDINAL BOX SECTIONS

13   Running parallel to the rockers you will find two longitudinal box sections. These are designed to make the floor more rigid, but have little other function. If you look closely, you'll note that they are made from thin gauge sheet steel, and if you ever try to jack the car on these box sections they'll most likely distort considerably. Check that all drain holes are clear, and that there is no build-up of dirt inside the sections (use a high-pressure hose to flush out any dirt, then allow the section to dry out thoroughly). Use the wax-based rustproofing fluid to seal the inside of the box sections and prevent internal rusting. Note that if you have reason to remove the rear trim panel from the back of the car, you have good access to the open ends of these box sections. Again, the probe can be fed into the end of the section and slowly withdrawn as the fluid is applied.

REAR BODY CAVITIES

14   There are a number of complex cavities formed around the back of the car, and in particular behind the outer body panels formed by the rear fenders. You can get to these once the rear quarter trim panels have been removed, and also from the

3/15 Removal of quarter panels gives access.

top if the convertible top is removed ☞ 10/5 & 11/15.

15   With the quarter trim panels out of the way, a large access hole is revealed, and this offers a good access point for rustproofing; in fact, using a flexible probe and a little ingenuity, you can reach just about anywhere from here.

16   If you have also removed the convertible top, you'll have access to a number of holes around the back edge of the package area through which you can feed your rustproofing probe.

17   Note also the two rain drip trays

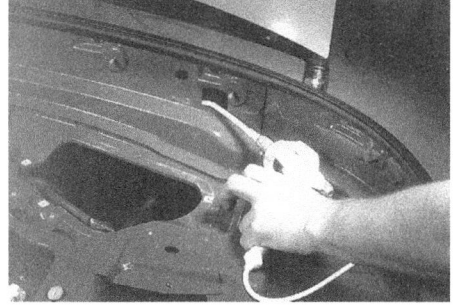

3/16a You need to remove the convertible ...

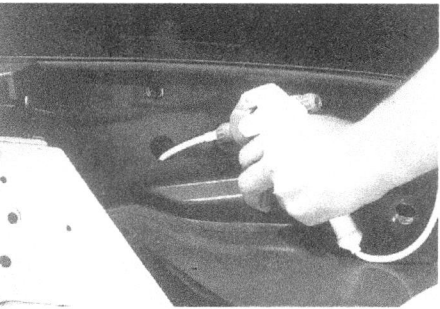

3/16b ... top to reveal these access points.

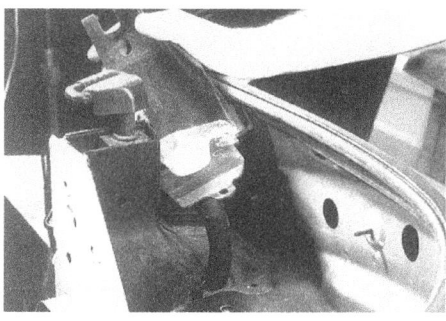

3/17a Pull out drain tube, and then apply ...

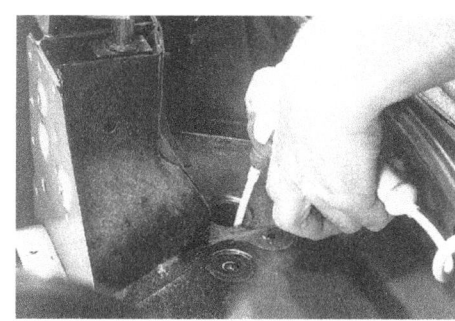

3/17b ... rustproofer thru hole.

3/17c Make sure this drain outlet is not blocked.

located near the convertible top mounting points. These are connected by large-diameter hoses to outlets under the car, and can be withdrawn to give additional rustproofing access points. Working under the car, pull out the large grommet which locates the bottom of each hose, then withdraw the drip tray and hose for access. When you have completed the rustproofing, install the drip trays and hoses, then install the grommets.

18   Additional access to the area above and around the fuel tank can be gained after removing the pressed steel access panels in the

3/18 Removal of covers reveals fuel tank area.

3/19 Trim removal gives access to door interior.

package area. With these removed, you can reach any remaining internal cavities.

DOORS

19   The interiors of the doors should be checked periodically and rustproofed as required. Things to check are that you keep the rustproofing fluid off the glass (ensure that the door glass is wound fully up) and that any drain holes remain unobstructed - check and remove any dirt from inside the door before starting, and check that the waxy rustproofing fluid does not block these

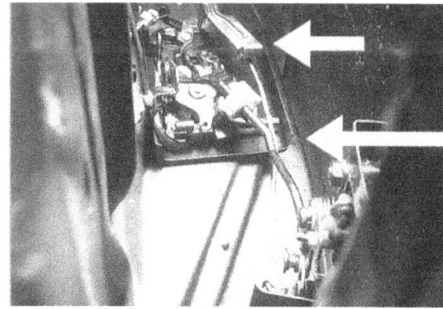

3/20 Make sure fluid runs into all seams.

essential drains. To get access to the door interiors, remove the interior trim panel and the plastic sheet behind it ☞ 10/5.

20   Apply an even coat of rustproofing fluid around the inside of the door. Don't worry about getting this on the door mechanism or wiring - it will help protect and lubricate these areas, too.

OTHER AREAS

21   Apart from the areas for anti-rust treatment already described, apply rustproofing fluid to all other minor closed box sections (eg: hood and

trunk lid reinforcing box sections). In general, these box sections are accessible after preliminary dismantling, as described earlier. If there is no obvious access point available, you can make your own by drilling an access hole, which can then be closed by inserting a suitable plastic or rubber plug. Be careful when doing this - it's easy to accidentally damage wiring or other parts hidden behind a panel. In general, we could find no areas where access through existing holes or cutouts was not possible.

22   Be on the lookout for rustproofing opportunities when doing other jobs on the car. For example, whenever you remove a light unit, take the time to apply some rustproofing fluid to any body areas this exposes - that way you will eventually cover all areas of the car.

23   The pressed steel suspension wishbones and crossmembers are well worth rustproofing. All these components have suitable access holes for the rustproofer spray probe. **Warning!** Take care not to spray rustproofing fluid on brake components, particularly discs and pads.

24   Before installing the removed trim and lowering the car to the ground, apply a film of rustproofing fluid to the whole of the underside of the car and around the wheelwells. When doing this, protect areas like the brakes and exhaust system from accidental overspray by masking with paper or rags.

25   Finally, rustproof minor areas around the car with WD40 or similar silicone-based spray. Items like the headlight surrounds and lids will be protected and lubricated in this way, as will electrical connectors and other small mechanical parts. WD40 does not dry to a thick, waxy consistency, and while this means that it is less permanent, it is useful in more visible areas.

3/22 An opportunity to apply rustproofer.

3/25 Water repellant protects light adjusters.

13

Trouble-shooting

INTRODUCTION

This part of the book is not intended to be an exhaustive guide to troubleshooting. In many respects, that is what much of the rest of the book is about and, like all modern cars, Mazda's sportster is just too complex to summarize all possible problems in a few pages.

What we are attempting to do here is to offer a few helpful pointers in the event of something going wrong on the road, or if you can't get the car started. Inevitably, this advice is going to be pretty generalized, but we hope that it provides a sensible starting point for further investigation.

When you've identified the general area of a suspected fault, we strongly recommend that you refer to the related chapter. Not only will this cover diagnostic checks and procedures in greater detail than is possible here, it also includes important safety and procedural information which you must not overlook.

You'll find that some of the chapters are heavily troubleshooting oriented. In areas like the fuel, ignition, engine management and electrical systems, much of the text is concerned with accurately diagnosing faults. This is a necessary way of presenting this information because of the modular nature of heavily inter-related systems.

One piece of essential advice on the subject of troubleshooting in the event of a roadside breakdown: pull off the road and read through the relevant part of this chapter, then refer to the appropriate part of this book before you even lift the hood. If you know what you are looking for, you're more than halfway to solving the problem, and are likely to save yourself a great deal of time.

It's worth bearing in mind that these cars are unusually sensitive to poorly performing sparkplug wires, sparkplug caps and sparkplugs. If the engine seems below par and the car is more than two years old, treat it to a new set of sparkplug wires, caps and sparkplugs: you may be surprised by the results ... We recommend that sparkplug wires and caps be renewed every 20,000 miles. It's also known that Mazda's sportster is not too happy with some fuel blends: find a brand of fuel that your car seems happy with and stick with it.

ENGINE: WON'T START/STOPS SUDDENLY

ENGINE DOES NOT CRANK WHEN STARTER OPERATED

• Incorrect gear selected and starter system locked out. Make sure that the transmission shift lever is in neutral and the clutch depressed (manual transmission) or in **P**, (automatic transmission), and try again.
• Battery discharged. These cars have a battery of limited physical size and capacity, which is easily discharged if accessory circuits, like the audio system and lights, are used extensively while the engine is not running. Try booster-starting (jump-starting) from a backup battery. If engine now starts normally, remove, test and recharge the car's battery.
• Bad engine ground (earth): check ground strap connections (the ground strap is near the engine oil dipstick).
• If a discharged battery is a recurrent problem, check the charging system - watch for alternator warning light indicating a fault in this component. Frequent, short or low-speed journeys can exceed the charging system's ability to compensate for the heavy drain on the battery made during starting. Also, old and tired batteries have little reserve capacity. If your car's battery is more than about three years old, it may be due for retirement, though some last to a ripe old age.
• If engine will not crank with a fully charged battery, the starter magnetic switch (solenoid) may be damaged or inoperative. Listen for a click from the magnetic switch on the starter motor as the ignition key is turned to the **START** position. No click usually means trouble here.
• Check for broken or damaged wiring connections between the ignition switch, battery and starter motor. If the battery terminals or leads get hot, abnormally high resistance (poor connections) is indicated - check the connections.
• A possible cause of the engine failing to crank on the starter are problems with the interlock switch (manual transmission) or range switch (automatic transmission).
• If everything else checks out, remove and test the starter motor. Sometimes, a starter motor develops a 'dead' commutator segment. If the motor stops in the wrong place, it won't work next time you try it. This can show up as an intermittent (and very annoying) fault. Alternatively, it is possible that teeth are missing (maybe severely worn) on the flywheel ring gear or starter pinion.

The above checks cover the most likely causes of this type of fault. Don't forget, though, that a seriously damaged engine is unlikely to start! If your engine went bang, stopped and now refuses to crank, a major engine fault may have occurred. Get the car trailered to your home or a garage for attention.

ENGINE CRANKS VERY SLOWLY WHEN STARTER OPERATED

• Battery may be partly discharged. Try booster-starting (jump-starting) from a backup battery. If the engine now starts normally, remove, test and recharge the car's battery.
• Check for damaged or corroded wiring connections between the ignition switch, battery and starter motor, paying particular attention to the heavy-duty wire connections at the battery and starter motor. High resistances here may allow other parts of the system to function normally, but won't be able to flow the high current needed for starting. If the wires or terminals get hot when attempting to start the car, a high resistance is indicated. Dismantle, clean and assemble using petroleum jelly (Vaseline) on the connections.
• Bad engine ground (earth): check ground strap connections (the ground strap is near the engine oil dipstick).
• Remove and test the starter motor. If you can, eliminate the motor as a source of trouble by substituting a known good motor. If the starter

Mazda Miata, MX-5, Eunos & Roadster

motor is suspect, get it reconditioned or fit a new one.
• Wrong grade engine oil in very cold conditions.

ENGINE CRANKS NORMALLY, BUT DOES NOT START

• Out of fuel. Check it out, even if the gauge tells you that you have plenty of gas - gauges go wrong sometimes.
• Damp sparkplug leads can allow the ignition spark to ground out instead of sparking at the plug electrodes. Dry the leads carefully, spray with water dispersant (WD40 or similar), and try again.
• Sparkplugs in poor condition.
• Water/dampness in sparkplug wells. Dry the wells carefully, spray with water dispersant (WD40 or similar), and try again.
• Fuel, ignition or control system malfunction. This could be any number of individual faults, and careful, systematic diagnosis is needed. Chapter 5 deals with this in detail. You need to establish that the plugs are sparking and that fuel is reaching the engine.
• Abnormally low engine compression. If the engine is badly worn or damaged, it may not have enough compression to allow normal combustion to take place.
• Exhaust outlet (tailpipe) blocked.
• If you accidentally flood the engine, floor the gas (accelerator) pedal and crank the engine. This shuts off the injector system and allows the flooding to clear.

ENGINE DIFFICULT TO START WHEN COLD

• Out of fuel. Check it out, even if the gauge tells you that you have plenty of gas - gauges go wrong sometimes.
• Damp sparkplug leads can allow the ignition spark to ground out instead of sparking at the plug electrodes. Dry the leads carefully, spray with water dispersant (WD40 or similar), and try again.
• Sparkplugs in poor condition.
• Water/dampness in sparkplug wells. Dry the wells carefully, spray with water dispersant (WD40 or similar), and try again.
• Battery in poor condition.
• Bad engine ground (earth): check ground strap connections (the ground strap is near the engine oil dipstick).
• Summer grade (low RPV) fuel in use producing poor atomization. Change to winter grade fuel if you are operating the car in very cold conditions.
• Fuel, ignition or control system malfunction. This could be any number of individual faults and careful, systematic diagnosis is needed. Chapter 5 deals with this in detail. If the engine management system is getting the wrong information, starting may be difficult or impossible.
• If you accidentally flood the engine, floor the gas (accelerator) pedal and crank the engine. This shuts off the injector system and allows the flooding to clear.

ENGINE DIFFICULT TO START WHEN WARM

• Out of fuel. Check it out, even if the gauge tells you that you have plenty of gas - gauges go wrong sometimes.
• Tired sparkplug wires/sparkplugs, or their caps in poor condition.
• Fuel, ignition or control system malfunction. This could be any number of individual faults and careful and systematic diagnosis is needed. Chapter 5 deals with this in detail.
• Vapor lock in the fuel system due to winter grade (high RPV) fuel. Change to summer grade fuel in warm operating conditions.
• If you accidentally flood the engine, floor the gas pedal and crank the engine. This shuts off the injector system and allows the flooding to clear.

ENGINE: STARTS, BUT DOESN'T RUN NORMALLY

ENGINE IDLE ERRATIC OR ROUGH

• Damaged or tired sparkplug caps or wires. As these components get old, they gradually become less efficient, and can build up high resistances and then leak. These cars are very sensitive to sparkplug wire performance. The easiest way to check for faults in this area is to fit new parts.
• Damp sparkplug leads can allow the ignition spark to ground out instead of sparking at the plug electrodes. Dry the leads carefully, spray with water dispersant (WD40 or similar), and try again.
• Water/dampness in sparkplug wells. Dry the wells carefully, spray with water dispersant (WD40 or similar), and try again.
• Sparkplugs in poor condition. Plugs are cheap and it is worth fitting a new set to see if this resolves the problem. Plugs can malfunction even if they look fine.
• Fuel contaminated with dirt or water. If you've got dirty fuel in the tank, the in-line filter will take care of a certain amount, but will eventually allow water to pass through, or dirt to block the flow of fuel. Refer to chapter 5, and flush out the tank and fit a new filter.
• Fuel, ignition or control system malfunction. This could be any number of individual faults, and careful, systematic diagnosis is needed. Chapter 5 deals with this in detail.
• Malfunctioning or damaged fuel injectors.
• Intake system leak. This will cause erratic fuel/air mixture. Often characterized by squealing or hissing noise around source of leak.
• Incorrect ignition timing. This may be due to misinformation fed to PCM from sensor(s).

ENGINE STALLS

• Out of fuel. Check it out, even if the gauge tells you that you have plenty of gas - gauges go wrong sometimes.
• Fuel contaminated with dirt or water. If you've got dirty fuel in the tank, the in-line filter will take care of a certain amount, but will eventually allow water to pass through, or dirt to block the flow of fuel. Refer to chapter 5, and flush out the tank and fit a new filter.
• Damp sparkplug leads can allow the ignition spark to ground out instead of sparking at the plug electrodes. Dry the leads carefully, spray with water dispersant (WD40 or similar), and try again.
• Water/dampness in sparkplug wells. Dry the wells carefully, spray with water dispersant (WD40 or similar), and try again.
• Damaged or tired sparkplug caps or wires. As these components get old, they gradually become less efficient, and can build up high resistances and then leak. These cars are very sensitive to sparkplug wire performance. The easiest way to check for faults in this area is to fit new parts.
• Fuel, ignition or control system malfunction. This could be any number of individual faults, and careful, systematic diagnosis is needed. Chapter 5 deals with this in detail.
• Idle speed too low. May be due to incorrect signal fed to PCM from power steering or air conditioning systems, or other sensor fault. See chapter 5.

ENGINE HESITATES OR STUMBLES DURING ACCELERATION

• Damp sparkplug leads can allow the ignition spark to ground out instead of sparking at the plug electrodes. Dry the leads carefully, spray with water dispersant (WD40 or similar), and try again.
• Water/dampness in sparkplug wells. Dry the wells carefully, spray with water dispersant (WD40 or similar), and try again.
• Damaged or tired sparkplug caps or wires. As these components get old, they gradually become less efficient, and can build up high resistances and then leak. These cars are very sensitive to sparkplug wire performance. The easiest way to check for faults in this area is to fit new parts.
• Vacuum hose has come adrift from intake manifold, resulting in a weakened fuel mixture.
• Fuel contaminated with dirt or water. If you've got dirty fuel in the tank, the in-line filter will take care of a certain amount, but will eventually allow water to pass through, or dirt to block the flow of fuel. Refer to chapter 5, and flush out the tank and fit a new filter.
• Fuel, ignition or control system malfunction. This could be any number of individual faults, and careful, systematic diagnosis is needed. Chapter 5 deals with this in detail.
• Blocked or dirty fuel injectors. Parts stores sell cleaning chemicals which you can add to fuel, and these will work if the blockage is not too serious. Chapter 5 has more information on injectors.

POWER SURGES/LOSSES WHEN GAS PEDAL HELD STEADY

• Damp sparkplug leads can allow the ignition spark to ground out instead of sparking at the plug electrodes. Dry the leads carefully, spray with water dispersant (WD40 or similar), and try again.
• Water/dampness in sparkplug wells. Dry the wells carefully, spray with water dispersant (WD40 or similar), and try again.
• Damaged or tired sparkplug caps or wires. As these components get old, they gradually become less efficient, and can build up high resistances and then leak. These cars are very sensitive to sparkplug wire performance. The easiest way to check for faults in this area is to fit new parts.
• Clutch slipping. This can allow engine speed to

13: Troubleshooting

rise and fall independent of road speed.
- Vacuum hose has come adrift from intake manifold, resulting in a weakened fuel mixture.
- Fuel, ignition or control system malfunction. This could be any number of individual faults, and careful, systematic diagnosis is needed. Chapter 5 deals with this in detail.

ENGINE LACKS POWER

- Damp sparkplug leads can allow the ignition spark to ground out instead of sparking at the plug electrodes. Dry the leads carefully, spray with water dispersant (WD40 or similar), and try again.
- Water/dampness in sparkplug wells. Dry them carefully, spray with water dispersant (WD40 or similar), and try again.
- Damaged or tired sparkplug caps or wires. As these components get old, they gradually become less efficient, and can build up high resistances and then leak. These cars are very sensitive to sparkplug wire performance. The easiest way to check for faults in this area is to fit new parts.
- Sparkplugs in poor condition. Plugs are cheap and it is worth fitting a new set to see if this resolves the problem. Plugs can malfunction even if they look fine.
- Failure of throttle valve to open fully: check accelerator cable and its adjustment. Make sure nothing is stopping the accelerator pedal from reaching its full travel.
- Poor quality fuel. Try a different brand.
- Incorrect ignition timing, or other ignition system malfunction.
- Brake drag. The drag can make it seem like engine power is down.
- Clutch slip (manual transmission). If engine speed rises as the accelerator pedal is pressed down, but road speed stays the same or drops, your clutch is slipping.
- Transmission problem (automatic transmission). Limp the car home if you can, but get the transmission checked urgently.
- Low tire pressures. The extra drag can make it seem like engine power is down.
- Fuel, ignition or control system malfunction. This could be any number of individual faults, and careful, systematic diagnosis is needed. Chapter 5 deals with this in detail.
- Worn piston rings resulting in low compression pressure: blue smoke will be evident under hard acceleration.
- Worn or damaged valves or valve seats, resulting in low compression pressure. A compression test will reveal this problem.

ENGINE RUNS ROUGHLY DURING DECELERATION (BACKFIRING/POPPING IN EXHAUST)

- Exhaust system fault or damage allowing air leakage.
- Intake system air leak.
- Worn or damaged valves or valve seats. A compression test will reveal this problem.
- Fuel, ignition or control system malfunction. This could be any number of individual faults, and careful, systematic diagnosis is needed. Chapter 5 deals with this in detail.

ABNORMAL FUEL CONSUMPTION

- Changed operating conditions (numerous short journeys, traffic holdups, etc).
- Heavy use of gas pedal to compensate for other factors (dragging brakes, low tire pressures, engine wear).
- Air filter blocked.
- Fuel leakage from tank, lines, filter fuel rail or injectors. **Warning!** Locate and fix urgently.
- Fuel, ignition or control system malfunction. This could be any number of individual faults, and careful, systematic diagnosis is needed. Chapter 5 deals with this in detail.

ENGINE: LOW OIL PRESSURE

- Oil level too low. Check for leaks and fill to correct level.
- Worn crankshaft bearings. Regrind crankshaft and install new bearings.
- Faulty oil pump oil pressure regulator. Replace pump and regulator.
- Faulty oil pressure gauge or sender unit. Check and replace as necessary.

ENGINE: EXCESSIVE OIL CONSUMPTION

- Oil leaking from oil pan joint, front or rear crankshaft seals. Re-seal oil pan joints, replace crankshaft seals as necessary.
- Oil leaking from cambox joint. Install new gasket.
- Oil filter loose or faulty sealing ring. Tighten or replace filter.
- Worn piston rings and cylinder bores allowing oil to enter compustion space and get burned: blue smoke from exhaust under hard acceleration. Fit new pistons, piston rings and have cylinders rebored as necessary.
- Valve stems and/or valve guides worn and/or valve stem oil seals faulty: blue smoke from exhaust, particularly on initial acceleration. Replace components as necessary.

CLUTCH PROBLEMS

CLUTCH DOES NOT RELEASE WHEN PEDAL DEPRESSED

- Pedal offers little or no resistance when pressed -
  Air in hydraulic system: bleed.
  Seal failure in master or release (slave) cylinders: renew seals as necessary.
  Clutch actuating arm or release cylinder pushrod damaged.

CLUTCH SLIPPING

- Clutch disc worn. Fit a new clutch assembly.
- Clutch disc friction material glazed (heat damaged).
- Clutch disc contaminated with oil. Fit a new clutch after rectifying any oil leak.
- Clutch cover diaphragm spring weak or damaged.
- Release (slave) cylinder piston failing to return fully when clutch pedal released.
- Incorrect clutch pedal lash (freeplay) adjustment.

CLUTCH JUDDER

- Worn or damaged clutch cover. Install new cover.
- Worn or damaged clutch disc. Install new disc.
- Friction material loose or broken. Install new disc, reface flywheel and replace clutch cover if necessary.
- Clutch disc contaminated with oil. Fit a new clutch after rectifying any oil leak.
- Flywheel surface damaged. Reface.
- Loose or damaged engine mountings. Replace.

UNUSUAL NOISE

- Grinding noise as gears selected. Air in hydraulic system or faulty seals preventing clutch from releasing fully. Bleed hydraulic system and, if necessary, renew seals.
- Grinding noise as gears selected. Clutch diapragm damaged and preventing clutch from releasing fully. Fit new diaphragm.
- Grinding noise as gears selected. Excessive crankshaft lash (endfloat). Renew crankshaft thrust washers (crank regrind may be necessary).
- Screeching noise during clutch release/engagement. Severe wear of clutch disc friction material allowing metal-to-metal contact. Renew disc and have flywheel refaced.
- Whistling/whirring noise during initial pedal movement. Worn or damaged release bearing. Renew bearing.
- Whistling/whirring noise during clutch operation. Worn or damaged pilot bearing. Replace.

TRANSMISSION (MANUAL) PROBLEMS

GEAR ENGAGEMENT DIFFICULT OR NOISY

- It is well known that the ease of shifting with these gearboxes is better with synthetic oils than mineral oils. If you want the best shifting quality use a synthetic transmission fluid that meets the API Service GL-4 or GL-5 rating. Pre-1994 model year cars had a notoriously stiff change between 1st and 2nd gears, a problem relieved by Mazda's modifications to synchro cone design for later cars.
- Air in clutch hydraulic system. Bleed system to remove air.
- If problem is recurrent after air has been bled from system, check for worn clutch master/release (slave) cylinder seals.
- Incorrect clutch pedal lash (freeplay) adjustment.
- Clutch disc failure.
- Wear or rusting of clutch disc splines causing disc to jam on shaft.
- Clutch cover failure - broken diaphragm spring.
- If pedal travels to floor with little or no resistance, check for complete hydraulic system failure indicated by pool of fluid in vicinity of leak (pipe fracture or total failure of seal).
- If hydraulic system intact, mechanical failure of the clutch, clutch release fork or bearing is indicated.

Mazda Miata, MX-5, Eunos & Roadster

- If the car has been stored for a long period, the clutch disc may have become frozen on the flywheel by rust. You can usually shock the clutch free by towing the car slowly in gear with the clutch pedal depressed.
- Insufficient transmission oil present (transmission will sound noisy and harshness or vibration may be noted).
- Transmission oil degraded or contaminated.
- Worn or damaged transmission synchronizer ring or cone.
- Sticking or worn detents.
- Worn or damaged shift (extension housing) mechanism.
- Excessive axial play on transmission gearshaft(s).
- Worn or damaged bearings in transmission.

TRANSMISSION JUMPS OUT OF GEAR
- Weak or broken detent spring.
- Worn or damaged shift fork.
- Worn clutch hub or sleeve.
- Worn or damaged gears.
- Worn or damaged bearings.
- Excessive gear backlash.
- Worn or damaged shift (extension housing) mechanism - gear not selecting correctly.

UNUSUAL NOISES
- Insufficient transmission oil.
- Oil degraded or contaminated.
- Worn or damaged bearings.
- Worn or damaged gear teeth.
- Excessive gear backlash.

ABNORMAL VIBRATION
- Worn or damaged engine/transmission mountings.
- Incorrectly mounted or loose power plant frame (PPF).
- Worn or damaged bearings.
- Driveshaft (propshaft) bent, unbalanced or UJ damaged/worn.

TRANSMISSION (AUTOMATIC) PROBLEMS

GENERAL
- In the event of a problem with the automatic transmission, your options are limited. In Chapter 4 we describe a number of checks and tests relating to the operation of the transmission, but full diagnosis or repair will require help from an automatic transmission specialist or a Mazda dealer. Have the car trailered to the repairer - don't attempt to tow it or you will almost certainly damage the transmission.

A transmission specialist will need to have the complete car with the transmission in place to be able to locate and identify the fault, so don't think that you can help by removing the transmission.

FINAL DRIVE PROBLEMS

ENGINE RUNS NORMALLY, AND GEARS ENGAGE, BUT CAR DOES NOT MOVE
- Driveshaft splines or UJ or differential unit internal failure. These are not common problems and are most unlikely to occur unless the car has been abused or engine power very substantially increased.

ABNORMAL NOISE OR VIBRATION
- Lack of oil in differential housing.
- Worn or damaged axleshaft joints.
- Loose or damaged driveshaft (propshaft).
- Worn or damaged differential ring gear and/or pinion.
- Worn differential bearings.
- Loose or worn engine/transmission mountings.
- Loose, worn or damaged PPF mountings, or damaged PPF.

COOLING SYSTEM PROBLEMS

OVERHEATING INDICATED &/OR STEAM ESCAPING FROM UNDER HOOD (BONNET)
- Sudden failure of cooling system hose or connection. Pull over and wait until escape of steam subsides, then open the hood carefully and locate source of leak. **Warning!** Allow engine to cool fully before attempting repair or you could suffer serious burns. If damage is to cooling system hose, fit a new hose, top up with fresh coolant, then run the engine to check repair.
- Sudden failure of heater hose or connection. If the leak is in one of the heater hoses, you can take the heater out of the coolant circuit as a get-you-home measure. This procedure is described in Chapter 6.
- Radiator failure. This can be caused by a stone or other debris hitting the radiator core, or by failure due to internal corrosion. Fit a new radiator.
- Radiator cap failure. If the radiator cap has become aged or damaged, it may allow a pressure leak. If this happens, the coolant will boil at a lower temperature and will escape as steam. **Warning!** Wait until the system cools right down, then fit a new cap and check that the problem is resolved.
- Thermostat stuck in closed position. Check and replace as necessary.
- Radiator fan or thermoswitch failure. If the fan system fails to operate at the preset temperature, the coolant may overheat and boil. Check and replace the affected parts as described in Chapter 6.
- Coolant frozen. Although this sounds crazy, if the coolant freezes in the system, you can get local overheating and boiling elsewhere in the system. This will not occur if the correct water/antifreeze mix is used. If coolant has frozen, check very carefully for displaced core (Welch) plugs, hose and radiator damage before using the car.
- General overheating is likely to be caused by lack of sufficient coolant, fan (or operating system) failure, blocked radiator core tubes or internally damaged hoses. See Chapter 6.

COOLANT EJECTED FROM OVERFLOW PIPE/OIL IN COOLANT
- Engine cylinder head gasket 'blown.' Reface block and head faces if necessary; replace head gasket.

TEMPERATURE GAUGE NEEDLE DOES NOT REACH 'NORMAL' SECTOR
- Short journey in extremely cold conditions.
- Thermostat stuck in open position. Check and replace as necessary.
- Temperature gauge or sender unit faulty. Check and replace as necessary.

COOLANT LOSS
- Damaged hoses. Replace as necessary.
- Incorrectly positioned/fastened hose clamps.
- Leaking water pump. Replace water pump.
- Leaking radiator. Replace radiator.
- Leaking heater matrix. Replace heater matrix.
- Overheating engine. See earlier advice in this section.
- Faulty cylinder head gasket. Reface head and block as necessary, replace gasket.

STEERING AND SUSPENSION PROBLEMS

CAR WANDERS OFF LINE
- Wheel alignment incorrect.
- Suspension geometry incorrect (impact damage or incorrect adjustment).
- Incorrect tire pressures.
- Tire/s worn or damaged.
- Different types of tire on same axle.
- Wheel damaged (impact damage).
- Stiff steering balljoints or steering rack.
- Worn hub bearing.
- Weak or broken suspension spring, or worn/damaged shock absorber.
- Lug (wheel) nuts loose.

EXCESSIVE STEERING FREE PLAY
- Worn steering system balljoints.
- Worn steering rack.
- Worn steering column or intermediate shaft joints.
- Steering rack mountings loose or damaged.
- Worn suspension bushes.

STEERING EXCESSIVELY STIFF OR HEAVY (MANUAL STEERING)
- Toe-in setting incorrect.
- Low tire pressures.
- Frozen (seized) steering balljoint.
- Wear or damage in steering rack.
- Worn or frozen (seized) steering column joints.
- Misalignment of steering column or linkages as a result of impact damage.

STEERING EXCESSIVELY STIFF OR HEAVY (POWER STEERING)
(See above, then check the following additional points.)
- Power steering drivebelt slipping/broken.
- Power steering system low on fluid or faulty.
- Power steering hoses/pipes damaged and leaking.

WHEEL (FRONT) WOBBLE OR VIBRATION
- Front wheels and tires out of balance.
- Tire damaged: sidewall bulges or missing tread.

13: Troubleshooting

- Front wheels damaged or distorted.
- Lug (wheel) nuts loose or broken wheel stud.
- Worn or damaged suspension components.
- Front brake disc distorted or damaged.
- ABS system fault.

WHEEL (REAR) WOBBLE OR VIBRATION
- Rear wheels and tires out of balance.
- Tire damaged: sidewall bulges or missing tread.
- Rear wheels damaged or distorted.
- Lug (wheel) nuts loose or broken wheel stud.
- Worn or damaged suspension components.
- Rear brake disc distorted or damaged.
- ABS system fault.
- Driveline joints worn or damaged.

CAR ROLLS EXCESSIVELY OR WALLOWS IN CORNERS
- Wear or damage to suspension components.
- Worn or damaged shock absorbers.
- Weak or broken suspension springs.
- Worn or damaged stabilizer (anti-roll) bar or mounting.

ABNORMAL TIRE WEAR
- Tire pressures incorrect.
- Toe-in settings incorrect.
- Suspension geometry incorrect.
- Worn or damaged shock absorbers.
- Use of vehicle on poor road surfaces.
- Excessively hard driving or braking.

ABNORMAL SMELLS, NOISES OR VIBRATION

FUEL SMELLS IN OR AROUND CAR
- Fuel filler cap not fully tightened.
- Fuel tank filled to overflowing.
- Leaking spare fuel container (if carried in car).
- Damaged or leaking fuel system or evaporative emission system parts.
- Charcoal canister overflow (evaporative emission control system malfunction).
- Fuel, ignition or control system malfunction.

SMELL OF BURNING
- Electrical fault. If suspected, stop immediately and isolate electrical system by disconnecting battery negative (-) terminal. Locate and rectify fault before reconnecting supply.
- Engine overheating. Allow engine to cool down completely, then check coolant level and fan operation.
- Leaking exhaust manifold or system connection (take note of unusual exhaust noise - try blocking end of exhaust pipe and check that pressure builds up quickly. No build-up indicates a system leak)
- Item in contact with exhaust system.
- New exhaust system components (temporary burning smell is normal).
- Oil contamination of catalytic converter. Identify and rectify leak before fitting new converter.
- Brake(s) overheating. May be caused by repeated heavy brake use, in which case stop and allow to cool down. Check pads for glazing. Can also be caused by fault in brake system causing brakes to drag, or by leaving parking brake applied.
- Clutch slipping. Excessive clutch slip will overheat the friction material. Allow to cool, then proceed cautiously to minimize slipping. Repair clutch as soon as you can.
- Automatic transmission fault. Can lead to overheating of transmission oil. Get transmission checked out to avoid possible costly damage.
- Minor fire in trim or upholstery. Can be caused by cigarette dropped inside the car. Stop and extinguish any such problems before the fire takes hold. Note that fire can spread rapidly, especially with soft top down.

SULFUR (SULPHUR) SMELL FROM EXHAUST
- Some sulfur smell is a normal by-product of the catalytic convertor.
- High sulfur fuel in use: change to low sulfur brand.
- Over-rich fuel supply.

UNUSUAL NOISES

PINGING OR KNOCKING SOUND WHEN ENGINE UNDER LOAD
- Incorrect ignition timing.
- Incorrect fuel grade.
- Engine overheating.
- Build-up of carbon deposits in engine.
- Intake air leak.
- Damaged or malfunctioning PCM or related subsystem.

LIGHT TAPPING OR RATTLING NOISE FROM ENGINE
- Excessive valve lash (worn or damaged hydraulic lifter/s, degraded engine oil). Note that some cars are known to suffer from valve lash noise for a short while after starting: this results from a 'stack-up' of production tolerances and is unlikely to be harmful. If in doubt, consult your Mazda dealer.
- Worn valves or valve guides.
- Piston slap (excessive piston/bore clearances).
- Worn or damaged piston pin bearing.
- Loose external components.

RUMBLING OR KNOCKING NOISES FROM ENGINE
- Regular metallic knocking noise (similar to 'diesel knock'): conrod bearing (big end) failure. Usually worse when engine is lightly loaded, and for a few seconds when first started (until some oil pressure is attained).
- Rumbling and vibration: main bearing failure. Usually worse when engine under load. Oil pressure may read low.
- Light or heavy knocking/thumping noises: loose external engine components/broken brackets or engine mounts excessively worn/broken.

SQUEALING OR SCREECHING FROM UNDER HOOD (BONNET)
- Drivebelt slipping (usually when under load; worse in damp or wet weather. Try to note when it happens - if when turning steering wheel, for example, it may be due to added load on power steering pump).

WHISTLING NOISES FROM UNDER HOOD (BONNET)
- Leaking manifold joints. Fit new gaskets/tighten as necessary.
- Hoses detached from intake manifold or intake system.
- Damaged vacuum hoses.

EXHAUST SYSTEM NOISES
- System loose or connection leaking.
- Damaged or rusted exhaust system components.
- Contaminated or obstructed system causing excessive back-pressure.
- Rattling or loose heatshield.
- Damaged or broken mounting or hanger.

DRONING OR RUMBLING FROM WHEEL AREA
- Worn or damaged wheel bearings.
- Worn or damaged differential bearings.
- Differential ring gear/pinion wear or damage.
- Differential bearing wear or damage.

CLUTCH NOISES
- Badly worn clutch disc (metal-to-metal grinding during take-up).
- Worn release bearing (squealing during pedal operation).
- Damaged clutch cover/diaphragm spring (rattles or other noise during pedal operation).

SUSPENSION NOISES
- Worn suspension bushes (knocking or rattling noises on irregular surfaces).
- Loose or worn stabilizer bar (anti-roll bar) mountings/bushes (knocking or rattling noises on irregular surfaces).
- Rusted or frozen (seized) suspension pivots: creaks or groaning as suspension parts move.
- Shock absorber shaft bent.
- Brake pipes rubbing against wheels/tires.
- Oversized tires rubbing bodywork.

BRAKE SYSTEM PROBLEMS

POOR BRAKE PERFORMANCE
- Pads contaminated with water. Allow to dry out.
- Excessive pedal travel/'soft' pedal caused by air/moisture in hydraulic system. Bleed system.
- Hydraulic fluid old or contaminated with moisture. Change fluid.
- Brake pads excessively worn or damaged. Fit new pads.
- Brake pads glazed (heat damaged). Check pads for wear - fit new pads as necessary, or remove glazed surface.
- Brake pads contaminated with oil or grease. Resolve source of leak, then fit new pads.
- Brake pads contaminated with hydraulic fluid. Overhaul or fit new caliper(s), then fit new pads.
- Brake pads of wrong specification fitted (pad

Mazda Miata, MX-5, Eunos & Roadster

material may be too hard). If in doubt, fit genuine Mazda pads.
- Excessively worn brake discs. Replace.
- Master cylinder wear or damage. Overhaul or replace.
- Caliper wear or damage. Overhaul or replace.
- Power brake unit (servo) fault.
- Power brake unit (servo) vacuum hose or check valve fault.
- Deterioration of brake hose(s).
- Malfunctioning bypass valve.
- Malfunctioning ABS system.

BRAKES PULL TO ONE SIDE
- Pad(s) worn, damaged or contaminated on one side.
- Disc surface worn, distorted, damaged or contaminated.
- Sticking calipers.
- Incorrect operation of automatic adjuster mechanism (rear calipers only).
- Caliper damaged or inoperative.
- Damaged or obstructed brake line.
- Incorrect wheel alignment.
- Incorrect tire pressures.

BRAKES DRAGGING
- Insufficient pedal free play.
- Obstructed return port in master cylinder.
- Pad/s jammed or sticking.
- Caliper damaged or piston sticking.
- Brake disc - excessive runout or damage.
- Parking brake applied or out of adjustment.

EXCESSIVE PEDAL MOVEMENT
- Incorrect pedal free play adjustment.
- Air or moisture in hydraulic system.
- Disc distorted or damaged (can result in excessive clearances between pads and disc surfaces).

BRAKE NOISE OR VIBRATION
- Pad/s worn down to backing metal. Check disc for damage. Fit new pads and discs as required.
- Foreign material embedded in pad surface/s. Check pads and discs for damage, Fit new pads and discs as required.
- Loose caliper mounting bolts - check and re-tighten.
- Pad squeal. Apply brake grease to back of pads.

ANTI-LOCK BRAKING SYSTEM (ABS) MALFUNCTION
- Refer to Mazda dealer for diagnosis and rectification.

PARKING BRAKE INEFFECTIVE
- Mechanism out of adjustment.
- Cable broken.
- Cable rusted or jammed with road dirt.

ELECTRICAL PROBLEMS

Note: Chapters 7 and 5 contain much information on the checking of individual components/systems.

BATTERY BECOMES DISCHARGED FREQUENTLY
- Excessive 'dark current' (current flowing from battery when ignition is switched off) load from accessory systems.
- Battery failing internally.
- Battery connections loose or poor.
- Charging system fault (check if warning light is on when engine's idling).
- Alternator drivebelt loose or slipping.
- Fault in accessory system (such as aftermarket alarm or audio unit).

HEADLIGHTS DIM OR INOPERATIVE
- Headlight lenses dirty (this does happen - raise the lights manually to check).
- Blown bulb or fuse.
- Wiring or relay fault.
- Poor ground (earth) connections.
- Loose wiring connection (high resistance).
- Dim-dip system fault (UK cars).

TURN SIGNALS INOPERATIVE ON ONE SIDE ONLY
- Blown bulb.
- Wiring fault.
- Switch fault.

TURN SIGNALS INOPERATIVE ON BOTH SIDES OF CAR
- Fuse burned out.
- Relay fault.
- Switch fault.
- Wiring fault between fuse, switch and relay.

BURNED OUT FUSES OR CIRCUIT BREAKER OPEN
- Wiring of relevant circuit shorted to ground.
- Relay damaged or jammed.
- Incorrect or poor wiring connections.
- Damaged or abraded wire insulation.
- Component (eg: bulb) of too high a wattage fitted in relevant circuit.
- Internal short in motor or other part.
- Water/dampness in switch or connector.
- Motor being forced to work too hard.

Notes

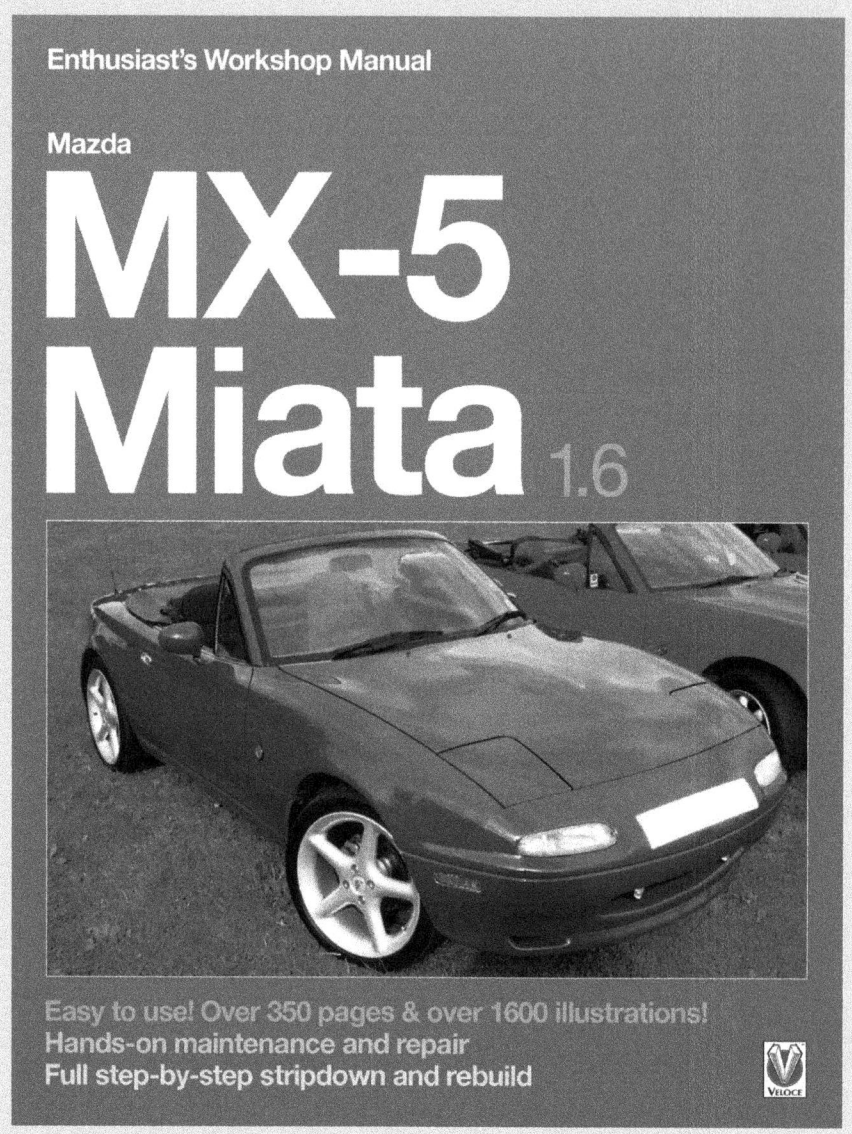

Superbly detailed text with over 1500 photographs, covering every detail of important jobs without resorting to special tools.

ISBN: 978-1-787111-74-5
Paperback • 27x21cm • 368 pages • 1600 pictures

For more information and price details, visit our website at
www.veloce.co.uk • email: info@veloce.co.uk
• Tel: +44(0)1305 260068

Having this book in your pocket is just like having a marque expert by your side. Benefit from the author's years of real ownership experience, learn how to spot a bad car quickly, and how to assess a promising one like a true professional. Get the right car at the right price!

ISBN: 978-1-845842-31-4
Paperback • 19.5x13.9cm • 64 pages • 107 colour pictures

For more information and price details, visit our website at www.veloce.co.uk
• email: info@veloce.co.uk • Tel: +44(0)1305 260068

This is the definitive history of the first generation Mazda MX-5 – also known as the Miata or Eunos Roadster. A fully revised version of an old favourite, now focussing on the original NA series, this book covers all major markets, and includes stunning contemporary photography gathered from all over the world.

ISBN: 978-1-845847-78-4
Hardback • 25x20.7cm • 144 pages • 221 pictures

For more information and price details, visit our website at www.veloce.co.uk
• email: info@veloce.co.uk • Tel: +44(0)1305 260068

New edition of the definitive international history of Mazda's extraordinarily successful Wankel-engined coupés and roadsters, up to the end of production and the introduction of the RX-8. Advice on buying your own RX-7, plus coverage of the RX-7 in motorsport, and production figures. Heavily illustrated in colour.

ISBN: 978-1-787111-33-2
Paperback • 25x20.7cm • 216 pages • 425 colour and b&w pictures

For more information and price details, visit our website at www.veloce.co.uk
• email: info@veloce.co.uk • Tel: +44(0)1305 260068

14 Index

Accelerator cable - see Throttle
Accelerator pedal - see throttle pedal
Aerial - see Antenna
Airbag system 7:40-7:43, 8:13, 8:15, 8:22-8:24, 10:3, 10:4
   Airbag warning light 7:41
   Module (driver's) removal and installation 7:41
   Module (passenger's) removal and installation 7:42
   Troubleshooting 7:41
   Working procedures, disarming and rearming 7:40
Aircleaner (filter) 2:9, 5:1, 5:4, 13:3
   Description 5:1
   Element 5:1, 5:6
   Element replacement 2:9
Air conditioning system 2:2-2:8, 6:1, 6:5, 6:6, 6:9, 6:11-6:13
   Checking 6:12
   Checking system fittings and lines 6:13
   Compressor 6:1, 6:13
   Condenser cooling fan 6:13
      Checking 6:13
   Pulley 3:47
   Refrigerant 1:19, 6:1, 6:13
      Visually checking refrigerant charge 6:13
   Relay - checking 6:13
   Switch 1:19, 6:11, 6:12
   Thermo switch 6:13, 13:4
      Checking 6:13
Air intake control (IAC) valve 5:11
   Checking 5:11
Air intake system 5:4, 5:6, 6:5
   Checking 5:6
Air valve (BAC valve) 1:13, 3:13, 5:2, 5:11
   Description 5:2
   Removal, checking and installation 5:11
Alarms and immobilisers - general 7:51
Alternator 1:14, 3:14, 3:42, 7:6, 7:8-7:10, 13:1, 13:6
   Brushes 7:10
   Checking 7:8
   Drivebelt 2:8, 3:42, 7:8-7:10, 13:6
   Removal, overhaul and installation 7:8
   Rotor 7:10
   Stator 7:10
Anti-lock brake system (ABS) 9:1, 9:4-9:7, 9:18, 9:21, 9:22, 13:5, 13:6
   ABS pump motor 9:18
   Checking 9:18
A-pillars 10:7
A-pillar trim 10:7
Audio system 7:49, 7:50, 10:3, 13:1
   Antenna (manual) 7:49, 7:50
   Antenna (power) 7:49, 7:50
   Removal and installation 7:49
   Security 7:49
   Troubleshooting 7:49
Axleshafts (driveshafts/halfshafts) 1:16
Axle stands 1:5
Back-up (reversing) light 7:30-7:32
   Switch 3:9, 4:4, 4:8, 4:24, 7:31
   Troubleshooting 7:30
Battery 1:13, 2:12, 7:1, 7:3, 7:6-7:8, 7:10-7:12, 13:1, 13:2, 13:6
   Checking charge, specific gravity and electrolyte level 2:12
   Charging 7:6-7:8
   Installation 7:8
   Installing a new battery 7:8
   Isolating and reconnecting 7:1
   Removal 7:7
   Voltage check 2:12, 7:7, 7:8
Bellhousing 4:3-4:9, 4:13, 4:22-4:25
Body - general maintenance 2:16, 11:1
   Color restorers 11:2
   Damage, repair and painting 11:2
   Paintwork - damage repair 11:2
   Polishing 11:2
   Tar spots 11:2
   Vinyl trim cleaners and polishers 11:2
   Washing 11:1
Brace bar 10:21
Brake system 1:6, 1:17, 2:2, 2:3, 2:6, 2:7, 9:1, 13:5
   Bleeding 9:1-9:3, 9:5, 9:15
   Brake warning circuit 7:19, 9:1
   Calipers 1:3, 4:26-4:28, 9:1-9:3, 9:6-16, 9:20 9:23, 13:5, 13:6
      Front - removal and installation 9:10
      Rear - removal and installation 9:14
   Discs 2:5, 9:8-9:10, 9:12-9:14, 9:23, 13:5, 13:6
      Front - checking, removal and installation 9:9
      Rear - checking, removal and installation 9:17
   Flexible brake hoses 2:5, 9:2, 9:3, 13:6
   Fluid 2:2, 2:18, 2:19, 9:1, 9:2, 9:8, 9:11, 9:15
   Fluid replacement 9:2
   Hydraulic system - topping-up and bleeding 9:1
   Lines and hoses - checking and replacement 9:2
   Lights 7:28, 7:32, 7:38
      Troubleshooting 7:28
   Master cylinder 9:1, 9:2, 9:4-9:7, 9:12, 13:6
   Pads 2:2, 2:4, 2:5, 9:1, 9:7-9:14, 13:5, 13:6
      Front (wear check) 9:7
      Rear (wear check) 9:11
   Parking brake (handbrake) 2:2, 2:5, 9:1, 9:13, 9:14, 9:16, 9:17, 9:20-9:22, 13:6
      Removal, checking and installation 9:16
   Pedal 9:1-9:4, 9:7, 9:9, 9:16, 13:5, 13:6
      Removal, installation and adjustment 9:3
   Proportioning bypass (brake compensator) valve 9:4, 9:7, 13:6
      Checking (in situ) 9:7
   Rigid brake lines 9:1-9:3
   Servo unit 9:1, 9:4-9:7, 13:6
      Checking (in situ) 9:7
      Removal, installation and adjustment 9:4
   Parking brake cables 9:16, 9:17, 13:6
   Pipe distribution block 5:15
   Power brake 1:16 1:17, 13:6
      Unit removal and installation 9:4
   Warning circuit - checking 7:19
Breakdowns 1:8
Bumpers 11:13
   Front 11:15-11:17
   Rear 11:13-11:15
Buying new parts 1:7

Camber 1:18, 8:2-8:4, 8:13
   Front wheels - adjustment 8:4
   Rear wheels - adjustment 8:4
Cambox 3:17, 3:41, 3:54, 3:56-3:58, 13:3

Mazda Miata, MX-5, Eunos & Roadster

Camshafts 1:10, 3:20, 3:28, 3:38, 3:57
  Bearing caps 3:20, 3:38
  Bearing journals 3:28
  Bearing oil clearance 1:10
  Bearings 3:28
  Camshafts and followers - removal and installation (engine in car) 3:57
  Camshaft position sensor 1:13, 3:44, 5:2, 5:29
    Description 5:2
    Removal, checking and installation 5:29
  Drivebelt 1:10, 3:1, 3:17, 3:18, 3:31, 3:39, 3:40
    Replacement (engine in car) 3:56-3:59
  Drivebelt tensioner 3:18, 3:31, 3:39
  Endfloat/endplay/lash 1:10, 3:28
  Followers 3:20, 3:28, 3:38, 3:57
  Journal diameter 1:10
  Lobes 3:28
  Lobe height 1:10
  Oil seals 3:38, 3:59, 3:60
    Replacement (engine in car) 3:59
  Pulleys 3:38
  Runout 1:10
Caster 1:18, 8:2-8:4, 8:13
  Front wheels - adjustment 8:3
Center console 6:11
Central locking 10:9, 10:10, 10:16
Charcoal canister 5:2, 5:24, 13:5
  Checking and replacement 5:24
  Description 5:2
Chassis 1:9, 12:1-12:3
Chassis box sections 12:3
Chassis longerons 3:46
Cigarette lighter 7:48
  Removal and installation 7:48
Cleaning components 1:6, 1:7
Cleaning/degreasing solvents 1:7
Clutch 1:14, 2:6, 2:7, 3:16, 3:60, 13:2, 13:3, 13:5
  Clutch and release bearing - removal and installation (engine in car) 3:60
  Cover 3:16, 3:32, 3:43, 13:3
  Disc 3:32, 3:43, 13:3-13:5
  Disc inner diameter 1:14
  Disc minimum thickness 1:14
  Disc outer diameter 1:14
  Disc runout limit 1:14
  Fluid 2:18, 2:19
  Flywheel runout limit 1:14
  Hydraulic lines 3:63, 3:64, 13:3
    Replacement 3:63
  Hydraulic system bleeding 3:63, 13:3
  Installed pressure 1:14
  Operating arm 4:6
  Pedal 3:64, 3:65, 13:3
    Height and freeplay - checking and adjustment 3:64
    Removal and installation 3:65
  Pedal ratio 1:14
  Pedal stroke 1:14
  Release fork 3:32, 3:60, 4:4, 4:16, 4:24
  Release (slave) cylinder 3:62, 4:2, 4:3, 4:24, 4:25, 13:3
    Removal and installation 3:62
    Overhaul 3:62
  Switch 5:33
    Description 5:2
    Removal, checking and installation 5:33

Clutch hub 4:14-4:21
Collets (keepers) 3:21, 3:36-3:37
Combustion chambers 3:26
Compression ratio 1:9
Connecting rods 1:11, 3:25, 3:30, 3:33, 3:34
  Bearings 1:11, 3:34, 13:5
  Caps 3:24, 3:34
Cooling system 1:12, 2:2, 2:4-2:6, 6:1-6:3, 6:6, 6:8, 6:13, 13:4
  After fitting new hoses 6:4
  Bottom hose removal 6:3
  Checking 6:2
  Coolant hoses 6:3, 6:5, 13:4
  Coolant inlet casting and hose connections 3:44, 3:47, 6:4
  Coolant temperature sensor 5:2, 5:30, 5:31, 6:6, 6:7
    Checking 6:7
    Description 5:2
    Removal, checking and installation 5:30
  Cooling unit (evaporator) 6:1, 6:12, 6:13
  Draining 6:2-6:4, 6:7, 6:9
  Hose replacement 6:3
  Temperature gauge 7:18
  Top hose replacement 6:3
Countershaft bearing 4:10-4:13, 4:15, 4:17, 4:19, 4:21
Countershaft (layshaft) 4:10-4:12, 4:14, 4:16 4:19, 4:21
Crankpin diameter 1:11
Crankpin taper and ovality limit 1:11
Crankshaft 1:11, 3:24, 3:30, 3:33, 3:58, 3:59
  Bearing journals 3:30, 3:33, 3:34
  Bearings 3:30, 3:33, 13:3
  Drivebelt 3:17, 3:18, 3:31, 3:56
  Endfloat (lash) 3:24, 3:30
  Front oil seal - replacement (engine in car) 3:58
  Inner pulley 3:19, 3:39
  Main bearing journal diameter 1:11
  Main bearing journal taper and ovality limit 1:11
  Oil seals 3:1, 3:58, 3:59
  Position sensor 5:2, 5:29
    Description 5:2
    Adjustment, removal and installation 5:29
  Pulley 3:12, 3:17, 3:18, 3:31, 3:40, 3:47, 3:56, 5:26, 5:30
  Rear oil seal 3:23, 3:24, 3:34, 3:58
    Replacement (engine in car) 3:59
  Runout 1:11
  Thrust bearings 1:11
Crossmember
  Front 8:5, 8:8, 8:9, 8:11, 8:12, 9:20, 9:21, 11:1, 12:4
    Removal and installation 8:11
  Rear 8:23, 8:25, 12:4
    Removal and installation 8:25
Cruise control system 7:37-7:39
Cylinder block 1:10, 3:29, 3:60, 6:6, 13:3
  Core (Welch) plugs 3:29
Cylinder head 1:9, 1:10, 3:1, 3:20, 3:37, 3:48, 3:49, 3:56-3:58
  Checking 3:58
  Front sealing plate 3:19, 3:38
  Gasket 3:37, 3:57, 6:2, 13:4
  Removal and installation (engine in car) 3:57

Dashboard - see Dash panel
Dash panel 10:2-10:6
Data link connector (DCL) 5:2, 5:25, 7:2, 7:22
  Description 5:2
Daytime running lights (DRL) 7:26-7:28
  Troubleshooting 7:26
De-choke control system 5:4, 5:25
  Description 5:25
Differential 1:16, 3:46, 4:2, 4:3, 4:26-4:28, 5:17, 13:4
  Backlash 1:16
  Carrier mountings - replacement 4:28
  Drain and filler level plugs 2:11, 2:12
  Drive pinion preload 1:16
  Nose (pinion) oil; seal - replacement 4:28
  Oil 1:16
  Oil level checking and changing 2:11
  Oil seals 4:28
  Pinion (nose) oil seal 4:28
  Reduction ratio 1:16
  Removal and installation 4:27
  Ring gear 1:16, 13:4
  Side (driveaxle) oil seals - replacement 4:28
  Teardown and rebuild 4:28
Doors 11:12, 11:13, 12:3
  Door catch/lock 10:9, 10:10, 10:16
  Door speaker/grille 10:9
  Door trim 10:9, 10:10, 10:16
  Glass alignment - checking and adjustment 10:15
  Latch and lock assembly - removal, overhaul and installation 10:16
  Removal, installation and adjustment 11:12
  Door window mechanism 10:9
    Electric 10:9-10:15
      Checking and overhaul 10:15
      Power window motor 10:12-10:15
      Power window regulator 10:12-10:15
    Manual 10:9-10:12
      Checking and overhaul 10:15
      Glass and lifter mechanism 10:11
Door mirrors 11:11
  Manual 11:11
  Power 11:11, 11:12
Drivebelts (external) inspection, replacement and adjustment 2:8
Driveshaft (propshaft) 1:15, 3:45, 4:2, 4:4, 4:25 4:28, 5:17, 13:4
  Maximum runout 1:15
  Removal, checking, repair and installation 4:25
Driveshaft CV joint 4:27
Driveaxles (halfshafts) 4:27
  Rear - checking 2:13
  Removal, checking, repair and installation 4:26
Driveaxle inner CV unit 4:26

EGI relay 7:6
Exhaust gas recirculation (EGR) system
  Description 5:2
  Valves 5:24, 5:25
  Pipe 3:13, 3:48-3:50, 5:9, 5:38
Electrical connections and wire color coding 1:4, 7:2
Electrical system 7:1
  Battery charging system 7:3, 7:4, 7:6, 7:8
  Combination switch 7:14, 7:29, 7:30. 8:14 8:16

14: Index

Troubleshooting, removal and installation 7:14
Fuses 7:3-7:6
Booster (jump) starting 7:3
Power point 7:3
Rectifier 7:6, 7:10
Regulator 7:6, 7:8
Relays 7:3, 7:6
Wiring connectors 7:2
Emissions control system 5:1, 5:4, 5:22
Introduction 5:22
Engine and transmission - installation as a unit 3:45
Engine backplate 3:23, 3:36, 3:55, 3:57-3:59
Engine bore 1:9
Engine compression 1:9
Checking 5:6
Engine control module (ECM) 5:1, 6:6, 6:13, 8:14
Engine control unit (ECU) see PCM
Engine coolant 2:14, 6:1-6:3
Topping-up and changing 2:14, 6:1
Mixing 6:2
Changing 6:2
Engine coolant temperature sensor 1:13, 3:13, 3:50
Engine dipstick 3:16, 3:44, 3:48
Engine dismantling - general advice 3:12
Dismantling 3:13
Engine ground (earth) strap 3:47, 3:54, 3:57, 3:58, 4:3, 5:17, 13:1, 13:2
Engine installation (without transmission) 3:55
Engine management system (EMS) 5:1, 6:5
Engine mountings 3:14, 3:41, 3:43, 3:60, 13:5
Replacement (engine in car) 3:60
Engine oil 1:2, 1:12, 2:2, 2:7
Changing 2:7
Drain plug 2:7, 3:3
Filler cap 2:7
Engine removal methods and preparation 3:1
With transmission 3:1
Without transmission 3:12
Engine stroke 1:9
Engine temperature gauge 7:18
Checking 7:18
Engine temperature sender unit 7:18
Checking 7:18
Engine undertray 3:2, 3:3, 4:2, 4:4, 4:24, 4:25
EVAP system 5:2, 5:4, 5:22, 5:23
Component checking and replacement 5:22
EVAP hoses - checking and replacement 5:24
EVAP solenoid 3:5
Exhaust gas recirculation system (EGR) 5:2, 5:4, 5:5, 5:10, 5:24
Component checking and replacement 5:23
EGR boost sensor - checking and replacement 5:25
EGR solenoid valves - checking and replacement 5:24
EGR valve position sensor - checking and replacement 5:25
Valve - checking and replacement 5:24
Exhaust system 2:3-2:5, 2:7, 2:18, 5:14, 5:17, 5:34-5:36, 12:4, 13:3, 13:5
Catalytic convertor 5:2, 5:4, 5:34-5:36, 13:5
Description 5:2
Checking 2:18

Downpipe 5:34-5:38
Exhaust pipe support bracket 3:45, 3:56, 4:25
Gasket 5:17, 5:34, 5:36, 5:38
Heatshield 5:35, 5:36, 5:38
Manifold 3:15, 3:44, 3:47-3:49, 3:52, 3:55 3:57, 3:58, 5:9, 5:17, 5:18, 5:32, 5:34-5:38, 13:5
Removal and installation 5:36
Removal, checking and installation 5:34
Silencer 5:34, 5:36
Exterior lights 1:18, 2:5, 2:15
Backup (reversing) lights 1:18
Brake/tail 1:18
Fog light, rear (UK) 1:19
Front turn signal/parking (US and Canada) 1:18
Front turn signal (UK) 1:18
Front side marker (US and Canada) 1:18
Bulb replacement 7:33
Headlights 1:18
Hi-mount brakelight 1:18
License plate 1:18
Rear turn signal 1:18
Rear side marker 1:18
Bulb replacement 7:33
Parking lights (UK) 1:19
Side turn signal (UK) 1:18
Eyeball vents 10:2, 10:3, 10:6

Facia - see Dash panel
Fascia - see Dash panel
Fault codes 5:5, 7:37, 7:38
Fender (wing) front 11:17, 11:18
Flywheel 3:16, 3:23, 3:31, 3:32, 3:36, 13:3
Foglights 7:33
Bulb replacement 7:33
Front axle 1:16
Wheel bearing type 1:16
Wheel bearing play 1:16
Front combination light unit - bulb replacement 7:32
Front header rail trim 10:7
Front hub carrier (lower) 8:7, 8:8
Ball joint 8:7, 8:8
Ball joint dust boot 8:8
Front hub carrier (upper) 8:5, 8:7
Ball joint 8:5, 8:7, 8:9
Ball joint boot 8:9
Front side (footwell) trim 10:7, 10:8
Front stabilizer bar (anti-roll) 8:5, 8:7, 8:9, 8:11
Removal, checking and installation 8:11
Front subframe 5:18, 5:35, 5:36
Front subframe cross brace (performance bar) 3:50, 4:2, 4:4, 4:24, 4:25, 5:34
Fuel system 2:3, 2:4, 2:6, 2:7, 5:4, 5:11, 5:12, 13:3, 13:5
Checking 5:12
Fuel 1:13, 5:1
Fuel drain plug 5:14
Fuel filler cable and lid 11:10, 11:11, 13:5
Fuel filler release lever 11:10
Fuel filter 1:13, 5:2, 5:13, 5:14, 5:17, 5:21, 5:22
Description 5:2
Removal and installation 5:21
Fuel gauge 7:18, 13:2
Checking 7:18
Fuel gauge sender 5:16-5:19, 7:18

Removal and installation 5:18
Checking 7:18
Fuel injection system 3:13, 3:14, 5:2, 5:11 -5:13, 5:18, 5:20, 5:21, 5:32, 5:33, 13:2
Fuel injection relay 5:32, 5:33
Line pressure checking
Fuel pressure (see also fuel system depressurising) 1:3, 3:2, 5:11-5:13, 5:17 5:22
Checking 5:12
Hold checking 5:12
Fuel pump regulator 1:13, 3:13, 3:50, 5:13, 5:20
Removal and installation 5:20
Fuel pump 1:13, 5:2, 5:11-5:13, 5:16, 5:18, 5:19, 5:23
Checking 5:12
Description 5:2
Regulator 1:13, 3:13, 3:50, 5:13, 5:20
Removal and installation 5:20
Fuel pump relay (FPR) 5:2, 5:11, 5:12, 5:20
Checking 5:12
Description 5:2
Removal and installation 5:20
Fuel rail 3:14, 3:49, 3:50, 5:9-5:11, 5:20, 5:21, 13:3
Removal, installation and testing 5:20
Fuel system depressuring 3:2, 3:57, 5:11, 5:12, 5:17, 5:18, 5:20-5:22, 7:1
Releasing fuel system pressure 5:11
Disconnecting fuel lines 5:11
Priming fuel systems 5:12
Fuel tank 1:13, 5:11, 5:13-5:19, 5:22, 5:23, 12:3, 13:2, 13:5
Inspection and repair 5:16
Removal, checking and installation 5:13
Fuel vapor 1:3, 5:11, 5:12, 5:19, 5:20, 5:22
Fuel vapor valve 5:2, 5:16, 5:23
Component checking and replacement 5:23
Description 5:2
Maximum pressure checking 5:13

Gas pedal - see throttle pedal
Gas tank - see Fuel tank
Gaskets and seals 1:3, 3:32, 3:37, 3:48, 3:49, 4:6
Gasket cement 1:3
Gear pinions 4:11-4:13, 4:15-4:19
Gudgeon pins - see Piston pins

Handbrake - see Parking brake
Hard top 11:19
Hazard and turn signal (indicator) lights 7:19, 7:28, 7:30, 7:32, 7:33
Flasher unit 7:29, 7:30
Troubleshooting 7:28
Hazard/warning light switch 7:15, 7:16
Headlight washer system 7:47
Motor 7:48
Relay 7:47
Unit removal, installation and bulb replacement 7:25
Reservoir 2:2
Switch 7:48
Troubleshooting 7:47
Headlight retractor system 7:21-7:24
Dimmer diode 3:7

Mazda Miata, MX-5, Eunos & Roadster

Motor 7:21, 7:23, 7:24
    Troubleshooting, removal and installation 7:23
    Relay 7:22
    Retract and hazard warning switch - removal, troubleshooting and installation 7:15
    Switch 7:15, 7:16, 7:47, 7:48
    Troubleshooting 7:21
Headlights 7:20-7:23, 7:25, 7:26, 13:6
    Beam adjustment 7:22
    Circuit troubleshooting 7:20

Deck height adjustment 7:23
Dim-dip system - troubleshooting 7:22
Headlight passing light (flasher) system - troubleshooting 7:22
Headlight relay 7:20-7:22
Heated oxygen sensor 5:2, 5:31, 5:32, 5:35, 5:38
    Description 5:2
    Removal, checking and installation 5:31
Heater and ventilating system 6:1, 6:8-6:13, 10:3
    Blower motor 6:8, 6:9, 7:3
        Removal and installation 6:9
    Blower resistor 6:8
        Removal and installation 6:8
    Blower/air con switch 6:11, 6:13
        Checking 6:11
    Blower unit 6:8, 6:9, 7:6, 10:2, 10:3
        Checking 6:8
        Removal and installation 6:9
    Heater/air con control assy - removal and installation 6:11
    Heater unit - removal and installation 6:9
    Hoses 3:8, 3:48, 3:57, 3:58, 6:4
    How it works 6:8
    Outlet cover 3:43, 3:50
"Hold" circuit (auto trans) 7:19
    Checking 7:19
Hood (bonnet) 11:1, 11:6, 12:3
    Removal and installation 11:6
Horn 2:15, 7:35, 7:36. 8:14
    Checking 2:15
    Troubleshooting and horn replacement 7:35
Hose connections 1:2, 3:54
    Cooling system 1:3, 6:4
    Flexible brake hoses 1:3, 3:4
    Fuel system 1:3
    Heater 6:4
    Intake manifold 6:4
Hoses 2:1
HT leads - see Sparkplug wires
Hydraulic (brake and clutch) fluid 1:3, 2:19, 13:5
    Checking 2:18
Hydraulic jack 1:5

Idle air control (IAC) valve 1:13, 5:2, 5:7, 5:11
    Description 5:2
Idle speed - checking and adjustment 2:10, 2:13
Ignition system 1:14, 2:2, 2:4, 2:7, 5:25, 5:26
    Checks 5:26
    Coils 1:14, 3:16, 3:43, 3:46, 5:2, 5:25, 5:27, 5:28, 6:7
        Checking 5:27
        Description 5:2
        Removal and installation 5:27
    Ignition control module 5:2
        Description 5:2
    Ignition timing 2:13, 5:25, 5:26, 5:29, 13:5
    Ignition timing - checking and adjusting 2:13, 5:25
    Switch 5:2, 7:10, 7:11, 7:14, 13:1
        Description 5:2
        Troubleshooting, removal and installation 7:14
Injectors 1:13
    Checking 5:13
    Description 5:2
Instrument panel 7:16-7:19
    ABS system 1:18
    Air bag 1:18
    Brake 1:18
    Bulb replacement 7:17
    Charge 1:18
    Engine check 1:18
    Headlight retractor 1:18
    High beam warning 1:18
    Illumination 1:18
    Instrument panel lamps 1:18, 7:17, 7:19
    O/D off 1:18
    Rear window defrost 1:18
    Removal, troubleshooting and installation 7:16
    Seatbelts 1:18
    Turn signal 1:18
    Washer low 1:18
Intake air temperature sensor 5:2, 5:30
    Description 5:2
Intake manifold 3:13, 3:44, 3:48-3:51, 5:2, 5:9, 5:11, 6:4, 13:3, 13:5
    Removal, checking and installation 5:9
Interior carpets 10:19, 10:20
Interior lights 1:19
    Air conditioning switch 1:19
    Ashtray 1:19, 3:2, 3:54, 7:34, 10:1, 10:2, 10:5
        Bulb replacement 7:34
    Cruise control switch 1:19
    Hazard switch 1:19
    Heater control panel 1:19
    Interior light 1:19, 7:34
    Panel light 7:35
        Testing 7:35
    Troubleshooting and bulb replacement 7:34 7:35
    Trunk light 1:19, 7:35, 11:7
Interior (rear view) mirror 10:7

Jacking and supporting the car 1:5, 1:6
Jacking points 1:6

Key (ignition) reminder switch - troubleshooting 7:14
King pin inclination (KPI) 1:18

Left hand drive 1:2
License plate lights 7:33
    Bulb replacement 7:33
Lights - checking 2:15

Magnetic clutch (air conditioning compressor) 6:13
    Checking 6:13
Main bearings 1:11, 3:1, 13:5
    Caps 3:24
Main (fuel injection) relay 5:2
    Description 5:2
    Removal, checking and installation 5:32
Maintenance 2:1
Malfunction indicator lamp 5:2
    Description 5:2
Mass Airflow Sensor (MAF) 5:2, 5:30, 5:31, 5:36 5:38
    Description 5:2
    Removal, checking and installation 5:30
Master cylinder (brake) 2:, 2:19, 3:54
    Overhaul 9:6
    Removal, installation and adjustment 9:4
Master cylinder (clutch) 2:2, 2:19, 3:54, 3:60-3:62
    Overhaul 3:61
    Removal and installation 3:60

Neutral light switch 5:2, 5:33
    Description 5:2
    Removal, checking and installation 5:33
Nyloc bolts 1:4, 8:16

Oil cooler 3:14, 3:42
Oil filter 1:12, 2:7, 2:8, 3:14, 3:42, 13:3
    Changing 2:7
Oil pan baffle 3:22, 3:23, 3:35
Oil pan drain plug 3:53, 3:54
Oil pan (sump) 3:22, 3:35, 4:4, 4:5, 13:3
Oil passage relief valve spring 3:31
Oil pickup pipe 3:22, 3:23, 3:35
Oil pressure 1:12
    Oil pressure gauge 7:18, 13:3
        Checking 7:18
    Oil pressure gauge sender unit 3:41, 13:3
    Oil pressure regulator 13:3
    Oil pressure relief valve 3:23
    Oil pressure sensor 3:38
Oil pump 1:12, 3:22, 3:23, 3:31, 3:35, 13:3
Oil pump seal 3:1, 3:35, 3:58
On board diagnostic (OBD) system 5:2, 5:5, 5:26
    Checks 5:26
    Description 5:2
O-rings 1:3
Oil seals 1:3, 3:58

Panel fasteners 1:5
Parking lights (sidelights) 7:26, 7:32
    Troubleshooting 7:26
Petrol tank - see Fuel tank
Pilot bearing 3:31, 3:32, 3:43
Pistons 1:10, 3:1, 3:2, 3:24-3:26, 3:33
    Bore clearance 1:10 1:11
    Diameter 1:10
    Gudgeon/wrist pins 1:10 1:11, 3:25, 3:29, 3:30
    Oil jets 3:25, 3:33
    Pin clips 3:25, 3:33
    Rings 1:10, 1:11, 3:24-3:26, 3:29, 3:30, 3:32, 3:33, 13:3, 13:5
    Ring to groove clearance 1:10 1:11
Plenum chamber 3:13, 3:51, 5:9
Positive crankcase ventilation (PCV) valve 3:56, 5:3, 5:4, 5:9, 5:20-5:22
    Checking and replacement 5:22
    Description 5:3
Power mirrors 10:9, 10:10
Power plant frame (PPF) 3:9, 3:10, 3:46, 3:49, 4:3, 4:8, 4:26-4:28, 5:14, 5:15, 5:17, 11:1, 13:4

14: Index

Removal and installation 4:26
Power steering 8:18-8:22
   Checking 8:19
   Description 8:18
   Drivebelt 2:8, 3:56-3:58, 8:21, 13:4
   Fluid 2:2, 2:5, 2:18, 8:18, 8:20, 8:22, 13:4
      Level checking and bleeding 8:18
   Fluid reservoir 8:18
      Bleeding 8:18
   Pressure (PSP) switch 5:3, 5:32, 8:21
      Checking 8:19
      Description 5:3
      Removal, checking and installation 5:32
   Pump 3:7, 3:8, 3:43, 3:47, 3:52, 3:56, 6:5, 8:18-8:22, 13:5
      Dismantling, overhaul and reassembly 8:21
      Removal and installation 8:21
   Pump pivot pin 3:8
   Pump pulley 3:47
   Rack - removal, overhaul and installation 8:19
Power train control module (PCM - the engine control unit) 1:1, 5:1-5:6, 5:11, 5:13, 5:24, 5:25, 5:28-5:34, 6:6, 6:13, 7:1, 7:3, 7:6, 7:8, 7:18, 9:18, 13:2, 13:5
   Description 5:3
   Overview 5:3, 5:28
   Troubleshooting 5:5
Pressure regulator 5:3
   Description 5:3
Pressure regulator control (PRC) solenoid valve 5:3, 5:5, 5:9, 5:13
   Checking 5:13
   Description 5:3
Purge solenoid valve 1:13, 5:3, 5:24
   Checking and replacement 5:24
   Description 5:3

Quarter trim 10:8, 10:9, 10:21

Radiator 1:12, 3:56-3:58, 6:1-6:4, 13:4
   Cap 2:14, 6:1-6:3, 6:5, 6:7, 13:4
   Cooling fans 6:1, 6:5-6:7, 13:4
      Removal, testing and installation 6:6
   Fan motor 6:7
   Fan relay 6:7, 7:6
      Testing 6:7
   Removal and installation 6:4
Range switch (auto trans) 7:11, 7:12, 13:1
Rear axle 1:16, 2:13, 2:14
   Wheel bearing play 1:16
   Wheel bearing type 1:16
Rear console 10:1, 10:2
Rear finisher (license plate) 11:8, 11:9
   Panel and trunk lock barrel - removal 11:8
Rear stabilizer bar 8:22-8:25
   Bushes 8:25
   Removal, checking and installation 8:24
Rear subframe 5:15-5:17
Rear window defroster unit 7:4, 7:5, 7:36, 7:37
   Troubleshooting and repair 7:36
Rear window zipper 2:2
Resonance chamber 5:3
   Description 5:3
Reverse idler gearshaft 4:11, 4:15
Reversing light switch 3:9, 4:4, 4:8, 4:24, 7:31
Right hand drive 1:2

Rockers (sills) 11:1, 12:2
Rustproofing procedure 12:1-12:4

Safety 1:2
Screws, bolts and nuts 1:4
Screw covers and blanking pieces 1:5
Seatbelt mechanism 10:8, 10:9, 10:21
Seatbelt warning circuit 7:19, 7:20
   Checking 7:19
Seatbelts 2:3, 2:4, 2:7
   Removal, checking and installation 10:21
Seats 10:17-10:19
   Removal, checking, overhaul and installation 10:17
Security alarm 3:54, 7:1, 7:51
Shift (gear) lever 4:1, 4:2, 4:13, 4:24, 4:29, 10:1, 13:1, 13:4
Side marker lights 7:33
Soft (convertible) top 10:1, 11:19-11:25, 12:3
   Rain rail 11:21, 11:22
   Rear window 11:21, 11:22
   Removal and installation 11:19
   Top fabric - removal and installation 11:22
   Top fabric - repairs 11:25
Sparkplugs 1:14, 5:25-5:27, 13:1-13:3
   Checking, cleaning and adjusting 2:9, 5:26
   Firing order 1:14
   Plug gap 1:14, 2:10
   Wires (HT leads) 2:1, 2:9, 3:16, 3:43, 5:25, 5:27, 13:1-13:3
Speedometer 3:39, 3:49, 7:7, 7:17, 7:18
   Cable 3:9, 3:49, 4:3, 7:17, 10:4
   Checking 7:17
   Drive 3:49, 4:7-4:10, 4:21, 7:17
Spring clamps 1:3
Starter interlock switch 7:11, 13:1
Starter motor 1:14, 3:14, 3:42, 3:43, 7:10, 7:12, 7:13, 13:1, 13:2
   Removal, overhaul and installation 7:12
Starter ring gear 3:31, 3:32, 3:60, 7:10, 7:12
   Replacement (engine in car) 3:60
Starter solenoid 7:10-7:13, 13:1
Steering system 1:16, 1:9, 2:2, 2:5-2:7, 2:17, 2:18, 8:1, 8:2, 8:12, 8:13, 13:4
   Ball joints 8:7, 8:12, 8:13, 8:17-8:20, 13:4
   Checking 2:17, 8:13
   Column 1:16, 8:12-8:15, 8:17-8:19, 10:2-10:4
   Description 8:12
   Pinion 8:12
   Rack 8:12, 8:13, 8:17, 8:18, 8:20
   Rack dust boot 8:16, 8:17
   Rack - removal, overhaul and installation 8:17
   Steering angle 8:2
   Universal joints 8:12, 8:13
   Wheel 1:16, 8:13-8:15, 8:19
   Wheel and column - removal, checking and installation 8:13
Stoplight switch 5:3
   Description 5:3
Stub axle 8:2, 9:20, 9:21
Subframe
   Front 8:1, 8:3, 8:11, 8:12, 11:1
   Rear 8:1, 8:3, 8:11, 8:12, 11:1
Sump - see Oil pan
Sun visors 10:7
Suspension 1:9, 1:17, 2:5-2:7, 8:1-8:11, 8:22

8:25, 13:4, 13:5
   Checking 2:17
   Front 1:17, 8:1
      Ball joint dust boots 8:7
      Ball joints 8:3, 8:7, 8:10
      Bushes 8:3, 8:8, 13:4, 13:5
      Cam bolts 8:3, 8:4
      Link rods 8:5, 8:7, 8:9
      Shock absorbers (dampers) 8:1-8:3, 8:5-8:7, 13:4, 13:5
      Springs 8:2, 8:3, 8:5, 8:6
      Strut 8:10
   Rear 1:17, 8:1, 8:22
      Bushes 8:22, 13:4, 13:5
      Removal, overhaul and installation 8:22
      Shock absorbers 8:22, 8:23, 13:4, 13:5
      Springs 8:22
      Uprights 8:22
Swivel pin 4:26, 4:27
Symbols and cross-references 1:1
Synchro rings 4:11-4:18

Tachometer 7:18
   Checking 7:18
Tail lights 7:32
   Bulb and lens replacement 7:32
Technical specifications 1:9-1:18
Temperature gauge sender unit 3:15, 13:4
Thermostat 1:12, 3:16, 3:41, 6:5, 6:6, 13:4
   Housing 3:19, 3:37, 3:41, 3:58, 6:4-6:6
   Removal, testing and installation 6:5
Throttle (accelerator) cable 3:4, 3:5, 5:7, 5:8, 5:10, 5:31
   Adjustment and replacement 5:7
Throttle body 5:6, 5:9, 7:9, 7:10
   Description 5:3
   Removal, inspection and installation 5:6
Throttle position sensor 5:3, 5:7, 5:31
   Description 5:3
Thrust washers 3:30, 3:31, 3:33, 3:34
Tie rods (front) 8:3, 8:12, 8:16, 8:17, 8:20
   Ball joint 8:16, 8:17
   Ball joint and rack dust boot - removal and installation 8:16
Tires 1:9, 1:17, 2:3, 2:5-2:7, 2:15, 2:16, 9:18
   Damage 9:18
   Fitting and wheel balancing 9:20
   Matching 9:19
   Pressures 2:15, 9:18, 9:20, 13:3, 13:4, 13:6
   Removal/fitting 9:20
   Sizes and ratings 9:19
   Tire rotation 2:16, 9:20
   Tread wear 9:18
Toe-in (tracking) 8:2-8:4, 8:12, 8:13, 8:17, 8:20, 8:23, 8:24, 13:4, 13:5
   Front wheels - adjustment 8:4
   Rear wheels - adjustment 8:4
Toe-out 8:2, 8:4
Tools 1:8
Torque converter 3:11, 3:12, 3:45, 3:55, 3:56, 4:5, 4:25
Torque tightening 1:4
Torque wrench 1:4
Towing 1:8
TPS unit - removal, checking and installation 5:31
Transmission (automatic) 1:15, 3:45, 3:53-3:56,

14:11

Mazda Miata, MX-5, Eunos & Roadster

3:59, 4:1, 4:25, 13:3-13:5
Automatic transmission fluid (ATF) 2:2, 2:3, 2:5, 2:7, 4:4, 4:5, 4:28, 5:17, 6:5, 8:18, 8:20, 8:22
ATF capacity 1:15
ATF - checking level and changing 2:11
ATF grade 1:15
ATF oil pan 2:11, 4:4
Driveplate 3:23, 3:31, 3:32, 3:36, 3:56, 3:59, 4:5
Gear ratios 1:15
Installation 4:24
Line pressure at idle 1:15
Line pressure at stall 1:15
Oil cooler 3:8
Removal 4:1
Specified line pressure 1:15
Transmission driveplate 3:12, 4:25
Transmission rear oil seal 4:26
Troubleshooting 4:28
Transmission dipstick 4:5
Transmission input shaft 3:43, 3:45, 3:55, 3:60, 4:4, 4:7, 4:9, 4:13, 4:14, 4:17, 4:22, 4:23
Transmission installation (engine out of car) 3:45
Transmission (manual) 1:14, 2:3, 2:7, 2:10, 2:11, 3:45, 3:52, 3:53-3:56, 3:59, 4:1, 4:5, 4:6, 4:13, 13:3, 13:4
 Component checking and repair 4:13
 Dismantling and rebuild (general) 4:5
 Gear ratios 1:14 1:15
 Installation 4:24
 Mainshaft bearings 4:10, 4:13, 4:15, 4:19, 4:21
 Oil capacity 1:14, 13:4
 Oil drain plug 3:3, 3:54, 4:2, 4:25, 4:27
 Oil filler plug 2:10, 3:54
 Oil grade 1:14, 13:4
 Oil level 2:10, 5:17
  Checking and changing 2:10
 Rebuild 4:15
 Removal 4:1
 Reverse idler gear 1:14, 1:15
 Shift fork and rod 1:14, 1:15, 13:4
 Transmission mainshaft 1:14 1:15, 4:11-4:18, 4:21
 Teardown 4:6
Transmission shift rods 4:9
Transmission tailshaft 4:8, 5:14
Tread (track) 1:9
Troubleshooting
 Abnormal smells, noises or vibration 13:5
 Brake system problems 13:5
 Clutch problems 13:3
 Cooling system problems 13:4
 Electrical problems 13:6
 Engine problems 13:1
 Final drive problems 13:4
 Steering and suspension problems 13:4
 Transmission (manual) problems 13:3
 Unusual noises 13:5
Trunk (boot) 11:6, 11:7, 11:10
 Carpets 10:1910:20
 Hinges 11:10
 Latch 11:7, 11:8
 Latch removal and installation 11:7
 Lid 12:4
 Lid balance springs 11:9, 11:10
 Lid balance springs removal, installation and adjustment 11:9
 Lid removal and installation 11:7
 Lock barrel 11:8, 11:9
 Trim 10:20
Two/three way check valves 5:23, 5:24
 Component checking and replacement 5:23
 Description 5:3
Tyres - see Tires

Valve lapping 3:26, 3:27
Valves 1:9, 3:21, 3:26, 3:27, 3:36, 3:37, 13:3, 13:5
 Clearances 1:9
 Face angle 1:9
 Guides 3:21, 3:22, 3:26, 13:5
  Bore diameter 1:9, 1:10
 Length 1:9
 Projection above head surface 1:9, 1:10
 Seats 1:9, 1:10, 3:26, 3:27, 13:3
 Springs 1:9, 1:10, 3:21, 3:27, 3:28, 3:37, 3:38
 Stem 3:26, 3:27, 3:37
 Stem diameter 1:9 1:10
 Stem to guide clearance 1:9, 1:10
 Timing 1:9, 3:39, 3:56
 Valve stem oil seal 3:21, 3:37
Valve spring compressing tool 3:21
Vehicle Identification Number (VIN) 1:7

Water (coolant) pump 1:12, 3:19, 3:36, 6:6, 13:4
 Drivebelt 3:17, 3:56
 Pulley 3:17, 3:40-3:42, 3:56
 Removal and installation 6:6
Wheel alignment (see also: toe-in/out, camber, caster) 1:18, 8:1-8:4, 13:4, 13:6
 Checking and adjustment 8:3
 Front 1:18, 13:4
 Rear 1:18, 13:4
Wheelbase 1:9
Wheel bearings 2:1, 9:20-9:23
Wheels 1:17, 2:16, 9:19, 9:20
 Balancing 9:20
 Changing (with car's toolkit) 9:19
 Checking and maintenance 9:20
 Hubs and bearings - checking and overhaul 9:20
 Studs - removal and installation 9:23
Wheel wells (arches) 11:1, 11:2, 12:4
Windscreen - see Winshield
Windshield 2:2, 2:5, 11:18, 11:19
 Removal and installation 11:18
Windshield washer system 7:43-7:46
 Checking 2:15
 Hoses 3:2, 3:53, 11:6
 Pump 7:47
 Pump motor 7:47
 Troubleshooting 7:43
 Washer reservoir 2:2, 2:5, 2:15, 7:20
Windshield fluid level sensor 7:20
Wipers
 Arms 7:46, 7:47
 Checking 2:15
 Mechanism - removal, installation and adjustment 7:46
 Wiper (combination) switch 7:43
 Wiper blades 2:2, 2:5, 2:15
 Wiper gearboxes 7:46
 Wiper motor 7:43-7:46
Wire connectors 1:5
Wiring diagrams 7:51
Wiring harness 1:4
Wishbones (front) 4:27, 8:1, 12:4
 Lower 4:26, 4:27, 8:3, 8:5, 8:7, 8:8
  Pivot bolt 8:5, 8:7-8:9
  Removal, overhaul and installation 8:7
 Upper 8:5, 8:7, 8:9, 8:10
  Hub carrier ball joint 8:9, 8:10
  Hub carrier boot 8:9, 8:10
  Hub carrier bushes 8:10
  Pivot bolt 8:9-8:11, 8:19
  Removal, overhaul and installation 8:9
Wishbones (rear) 8:24, 9:22, 9:23, 12:4
 Lower 8:22-8:25, 9:22
  Cam bolts 8:22, 8:23
  Pivots 8:22
  Removal, overhaul and installation 8:23
  Wishbone pivot bolts 8:23-8:25, 9:22, 9:23
 Mounting bushes 8:23
 Upper 8:22, 8:24, 9:23
  Bushes 8:24
  Pivot bolts 8:24, 9:23
  Removal, overhaul and installation 8:24
Working procedures 1:2

Visit Veloce on the Web - www.veloce.co.uk